Apocryphal and Esoteric Sources in the Development of Christianity and Judaism

Texts and Studies
in Eastern Christianity

Chief Editor

Ken Parry (*Macquarie University*)

Editorial Board

Alessandro Bausi (*University of Hamburg*) – Monica Blanchard
(*Catholic University of America*) – Malcolm Choat (*Macquarie University*)
Peter Galadza (*Saint Paul University*) – Victor Ghica (*MF Norwegian School
of Theology, Religion and Society*) – Emma Loosley (*University of Exeter*)
Basil Lourié (*St Petersburg*) – John McGuckin (*Columbia
University*) – Stephen Rapp (*Sam Houston State University*)
Dietmar W. Winkler (*University of Salzburg*)

VOLUME 21

Texts and Studies in Eastern Christianity is intended to advance the field of Eastern Christian Studies by publishing translations of ancient texts, individual monographs, thematic collections, and translations into English of significant volumes in modern languages. It will cover the Eastern Orthodox, Oriental Orthodox and Eastern Catholic traditions from the early through to the contemporary period. The series will make a valuable contribution to the study of Eastern Christianity by publishing research by scholars from a variety of disciplines and backgrounds. The different traditions that make up the world of Eastern Christianity have not always received the attention they deserve, so this series will provide a platform for deepening our knowledge of them as well as bringing them to a wider audience. The need for such a series has been felt for sometime by the scholarly community in view of the increasing interest in the Christian East.

The titles published in this series are listed at *brill.com/tsec*

The fourth day of Creation in Ms *Yerevan* 7634 (the four Gospels); illumination by Deacon Aṙakel from village Dıvanĵ, Erzurum (formerly Karin), 1601. Inscription underneath the miniature: 'Creation of the fourth day: He made the sun and the moon'
COURTESY OF THE NATIONAL INSTITUTE OF ANCIENT MANUSCRIPTS OF ARMENIA (*MATENADARAN*), YEREVAN

Apocryphal and Esoteric Sources in the Development of Christianity and Judaism

The Eastern Mediterranean, the Near East, and Beyond

Edited by

Igor Dorfmann-Lazarev

BRILL

LEIDEN | BOSTON

The logo for the TSEC series is based on a 14th century tombstone of the Church of the East from Quanzhou, South China, courtesy of the Quanzhou Museum of Overseas Communications History.

Library of Congress Cataloging-in-Publication Data

Names: Dorfmann-Lazarev, Igor, editor.
Title: Apocryphal and esoteric sources in the development of Christianity and
    Judaism : the Eastern Mediterranean, the Near East, and beyond / edited by
    Igor Dorfmann-Lazarev.
Description: Leiden ; Boston : Brill, [2021] | Series: Texts and studies in Eastern
    Christianity, 2213-0039 ; volume 21 | Includes bibliographical references and
    index. | In English, French, and Ger
Identifiers: LCCN 2021006678 (print) | LCCN 202100 (ebook) | ISBN 9789004445932
    (hardback) | ISBN 9789004445925 (ebook)
Subjects: LCSH: 0 Judaism–History–Talmudic period, 10-
Classification: LCC BS1700 .A69 2021 (print) | LCC BS1700 (ebook) |
    DDC 229/.06–dc23
LC record available at https://lccn.loc.gov/2021006678
LC ebook record available at https://lccn.loc.gov/2021006679

Typeface for the Latin, Greek, and Cyrillic scripts: "Brill". See and download: brill.com/brill-typeface.

ISSN 2213-0039
ISBN 978-90-04-44593-2 (hardback)
ISBN 978-90-04-44592-5 (e-book)

Copyright 2021 by Igor Dorfmann-Lazarev. Published by Koninklijke Brill NV, Leiden, The Netherlands.
Koninklijke Brill NV incorporates the imprints Brill, Brill Nijhoff, Brill Hotei, Brill Schöningh, Brill Fink, Brill mentis, Vandenhoeck & Ruprecht, Böhlau Verlag and V&R Unipress.
Koninklijke Brill NV reserves the right to protect this publication against unauthorized use. Requests for re-use and/or translations must be addressed to Koninklijke Brill NV via brill.com or copyright.com.

This book is printed on acid-free paper and produced in a sustainable manner.

Contents

Preface XI
List of Figures and Tables XII
Notes on Contributors XVII

Introduction 1

PART 1
Esoteric Writing and Esoteric Cults in the Biblical Religions

1   The Exoteric Appearances of Jewish Esotericism   29
    Ithamar Gruenwald

2   The *Gospel of Peter* between the Synoptics, Second Century, and Late
    Antique 'Apostolic Memoirs'   43
    Tobias Nicklas

3   All Mysteries Revealed? On the Interplay between Hiding and Revealing
    and the Dangers of Heavenly Journeys according to the *Ascension of
    Isaiah*   70
    Joseph Verheyden

4   Early Christianity and the Pagan Mysteries: Esoteric Knowledge?   88
    Jan N. Bremmer

5   The Medieval Dualist *Nachleben* of Early Jewish and Christian Esoteric
    Traditions: The Role of the Pseudepigrapha   105
    Yuri Stoyanov

6   The Esoteric Cardinal: Giorgios Gemistos, Bessarion and Theurgy   124
    Ezio Albrile

PART 2
Bridging the Account of the Origins and the Messiah's Advent

7   La création d'Adam à Noravank: Théologie et narrativité   143
      Jean-Pierre Mahé

8   *Translatio corporis Adæ*: Trajectories of a Parabiblical Tradition   153
      Sergey Minov

9   Apostles, Long Dead 'Heretics', and Monks: Noncanonical Traditions on
      Angels and Protoplasts in Two Late Antique Coptic Apocalypses
      (7th–8th Century CE)   179
      Daniele Tripaldi

10 Face as the Image of God in the Jewish Pseudepigrapha   206
      Andrei A. Orlov

11 *On the Perdition of the Higher Intellect and on the Image of Light*: Critical
      Edition, Translation, and Commentary   217
      Maria V. Korogodina and Basil Lourié

12 Bridging the Gaps in the Samaritan Tradition   262
      Abraham Tal

13 'On the Mountains of Ararat': Noah's Ark and the Sacred Topography of
      Armenia   276
      Nazénie Garibian

14 The Historian's Craft and Temporal Bridges in Apocrypha and in Early
      Christian Art: Para-Biblical Sources in the Light of the Work of Marc
      Bloch   296
      Igor Dorfmann-Lazarev

PART 3
Symbols and Figures of the Messianic Expectation

15 Quellen der nichtbiblischen Mose-Überlieferung in der *Kratkaja
      Chronografičeskaja Paleja*   317
      Dieter and Sabine Fahl

CONTENTS

16 Whether Lamb or Lion: Overlapping Metaphors in Jewish and Christian Apocalypticism   340
   Abraham Terian

17 Rescuing John the Baptist   351
   Albert I. Baumgarten

18 The Esoteric Legacy of the Magi of Bethlehem in the Framework of the Iranian Speculations about Jesus, Zoroaster and His Three Posthumous Sons   368
   Antonio Panaino

19 Visual Apocrypha: The Case of Mary and the Magi in Early Christian Rome   383
   Felicity Harley

20 Gnostic and Mithraic Themes in *Sefer Zerubbabel*   411
   Yishai Kiel

PART 4
Angels, Heavenly Journeys and Visions of Paradise

21 1 Enoch 17 in the Geneva Papyrus 187   439
   David Hamidović

22 Enochic Texts and Related Traditions in *Slavia Orthodoxa*   452
   Florentina Badalanova Geller

23 Visions of Paradise in the Life of St Andrew the Fool and the Legacy of the Jewish Pseudepigrapha in Byzantium   521
   Emmanouela Grypeou

24 Eternal Chains and the Mountain of Darkness: The Fallen Angels in the Incantation Bowls   533
   Yakir Paz

25 Iconography of Angels: Roots and Origins in the Earliest Christian Art   559
   Cecilia Proverbio

26   The Gardens of Eden: Compositional, Iconographic and Semantic
      Similarities between the 'Birds Mosaic' of the Armenian Chapel in
      Jerusalem and the Mosaic of the Synagogue at Maʻon (Nirim)   590
          Zaruhi Hakobyan

      Postscript: Border-Crossing Texts   610
          Hartmut Leppin

      Index of Place Names   619
      Index of Modern and Early Modern Authors   621
      Index of Biblical and Mythological Names   623
      Index of Subjects   626
      Index of Ancient and Mediæval Sources   629

Preface

This book has its origin in the international conference 'The Role of Esoteric and Apocryphal Sources in the Development of Christian and Jewish Traditions' which was convened in the Forschungskolleg Humanwissenschaften in Bad Homburg, Germany, in March 2018. The conference was funded by the Leibniz Gemeinschaft in the framework of the research project 'Polyphony of Late Antique Christianity' directed by Professor Hartmut Leppin of Goethe University, Frankfurt am Main. Begun already in Frankfurt, the editorial work on the volume was pursued, between 2019 and 2020, at the Centre for Advanced Studies 'Beyond Canon', University of Regensburg.

I owe a great debt of gratitude to Dr Peter Phillips, SOAS (University of London), for his scholarly and stylistic advice. He has generously revised the entire volume providing valuable comments to each paper. I thank Dr Phillips for his deep and sympathetic understanding of the issues discussed. His critical comments and suggestions have enabled numerous authors to improve the volume enormously. I would like to record the advice and ideas of Professor Ithamar Gruenwald of Tel Aviv University, in the conversations with whom I found a true inspiration. I would like to express my gratitude to other friends and colleagues whose advice and comments have been invaluable in the course of my work: Professor Charles Lock of the University of Copenhagen, Professor Joseph Verheyden of the Katholieke Universiteit Leuven, my teacher Professor Michael E. Stone of Hebrew University of Jerusalem, Professor Alberto Camplani of the Università La Sapienza (Rome), Professor Abraham Terian of St Nersess Armenian Seminary (New York), Professor Tobias Nicklas of the Universität Regensburg and Professor Hartmut Leppin of the Frankfurt University. I am indebted very much to Mrs Charlotte von Schelling from the Centre for Advanced Studies 'Beyond Canon', Universität Regensburg, for providing important technical assistance, especially with the layout of the book. To her and to Mr Marko Jovanović of the same Centre of Studies I am most grateful for their important help in indexing the entire volume. I wish to thank the Editor of the series 'Texts and Studies in Eastern Christianity', Dr Ken Parry of Macquarie University, Sydney, for his keen interest in the present studies, for his kind proposal to publish them here and for the unfailing attention that he paid to the manuscript at different stages of its editing; and Ms Marjolein van Zuylen and Mr Dirk Bakker for seeing the manuscript through the press with utmost care.

Igor Dorfmann-Lazarev
Simignano, December 2020

Figures and Tables

Figures

7.1 The upper tympanum in the gawiṫ of the church of St Stephen, Noravank̇ (north-eastern Armenia), end of the thirteenth–beginning of the fourteenth century. Photo: I. Dorfmann-Lazarev   145

7.2 The upper tympanum in the gawiṫ of the church of St Stephen, Noravank̇ (north-eastern Armenia), end of the thirteenth–beginning of the fourteenth century, schematic representation. A. Alpago Novello, G. Ieni, *Documenti di architettura armena* 14 (Amaghu, Noravank̇), Milan, 1985, p. 40, figure 25   145

11.1 Transmission of PHI within the Slavonic Compilations   219

13.1 The kingdom of Urartu, ninth–seventh centuries BCE, after B. Haruṫyunyan. Courtesy Vardan Mkhitaryan   282

13.2 Historical Armenia according to Anania of Širak (ca. 610–680), after B. Haruṫyunyan. Courtesy Vardan Mkhitaryan   283

13.3 Mount Djudi (Cudi dağı) in the Gordyæan mountains (the Korduk̇ chain). Photo: Timo Roller from Wikipedia. CC BY 3.0   291

13.4 Mount Ararat (Masis): view from the north. Photo: author   293

14.1 The 'Dogmatic sarcophagus' from the basilica of St Paul Outside-the-Walls, Rome, 330–340 CE. Museo Pio Cristiano, Vatican, inv. 31427. Photo: author, with kind permission of the museum   310

14.2 Creation of Eve by the Triune God and Adoration of the Three Magi on the 'Dogmatic sarcophagus'. Photo: author, with kind permission of the Museo Pio Cristiano   312

14.3 Adoration of the Magi, a detail. Photo: author, with kind permission of the Museo Pio Cristiano   313

15.1 Moses in Anton Koberger's Bible (Nuremberg 1483): woodcut after Heinrich Quentell's Cologne Bible (1478/79)   339

19.1 Mural Painting: Adoration of the Magi. Rome, late 3rd or early 4th century CE; Catacomb of Priscilla (Capella Græca). © Scala / Art Resource, NY   384

19.2 'Biographical sarcophagus' (detail: mother and child scene, right short side). Marble, ca. 176–193 CE; 72.39 × 226.06 × 81.28 cm. Los Angeles County Museum of Art (inv. 47.8.9a–c). Photo: LACMA (Image in the public domain)   390

19.3 Sarcophagus lid (detail: Adoration of the Magi). Marble, first third of the fourth century CE; h. 20 cm, l. 40 cm. Rome, Museo Nazionale Romano, Palazzo Altemps (inv. 80717—formerly in the Villa Mattei). Photo: author   393

FIGURES AND TABLES

XIII

19.4 Crater (detail of the neck, Mary and Child enthroned, flanked by six Magi). Marble, second half of the fourth century CE; h. 82 cm × max. diam. 79 cm. Rome, Museo Nazionale Romano, Palazzo Massimo (inv. 67629). Photo: Beat Brenk, with kind permission 393

19.5 Wall painting: Mother and Child, with a Prophet (?), mid-fourth century CE, Catacomb of Priscilla, Rome. Image: watercolour by Carlo Tabanelli over a photograph by Pompeo and Renato Sansaini, 1897–1903. Published by Giuseppe Wilpert, *Roma Sotterranea* (Rome, 1903), plate 22 394

19.6 Child's sarcophagus. Pinkish-white marble, first third of the fourth century (330–350 CE); l. 98 × w. 38 × h. 57 cm (dimensions without lid). Berlin, Staatliche Museen, Sculpture Collection and Museum of Byzantine Art (Inv. No. 17 / 61). Photo: © BPK National Museums, Berlin (Photographer: A. Voigt) 396

19.7 Fragment of a sarcophagus (detail of the Adoration scene, with camel). Marble, second quarter of the fourth century CE; h. 17 cm. Excavated in the Catacomb of Domitilla, Via delle Sette Chiese, Rome. Photo: © DAI, Rome (neg. 61.2539) 398

19.8 Sarcophagus. Marble, early fourth century; h. 105 × l. 205 × b. 109 cm. Arles, Musée de l'Arles Antique (inv. PAP 7400.1–5). Photo: © J.-L. Maby/ L. Roux 400

19.9 Sarcophagus (detail: Adoration of the Magi). Arles, Musée de l'Arles Antique (inv. PAP 7400.1–5). Photo: © M. Lacanaud 403

19.10 Wooden relief: Adoration of the Magi. Cypress wood panel from the doors at the main entrance to the church of Santa Sabina, Rome, ca. 422–432. Photo: © DAI, Rome (neg. 61.2539) 405

19.11 Engraved Gemstone (Mary and Jesus enthroned). Syria (?), jasper or obsidian; 1.9 × 1.5 × 0.2 cm, inscription ιϲ—χϲ, for Ἰ(ησοῦ)ς Χ(ριστό)ς. Ann Arbor, University of Michigan, Special Collections Library. Photo: © Christopher A. Faraone, used with kind permission 407

21.1 Verso of the Geneva Papyrus 187. Courtesy of the Public Library of Geneva 440

22.1 Witch milking the Moon; fresco from the open gallery of the church of the Holy Archangel Michael near the village of Leshko, South-Western Bulgaria; painted in 1889 by the icon-painter Mikhalko Golev [Михалко Голев]. Photo: author 460

22.2 The Devil holding a mirror in front of a maiden putting on make-up; fresco from the open gallery of the church of the Holy Archangel Michael near the village of Leshko, South-Western Bulgaria, painted in 1889 by the icon-painter Mikhalko Golev [Михалко Голев]. Photo: author 483

22.3a The Devil holding a mirror in front of a maiden putting on her face make-up; fresco from the women's section of the monastery of Saint George near the

	villages of Gega, Churilovo and Kukuriakhtsevo; Petrich county, South-Western Bulgaria, painted in 1858. Photo: author 485
22.3b	The Devil holding a mirror in front of a maiden putting on her face make-up, detail. Photo: author 486
22.4	The Devil defecating into the vessel containing cosmetics. Fresco from the open gallery of the church of St Nicholas in the village of Cherven Breg, Dupnitsa county, South-Western Bulgaria; painted in 1882. Photo: author 487
22.5	The Devil defecating into the vessel containing cosmetics. Fresco from the women's section of the church of St George in the village of Zlatolist (formerly Sushitsa), Sandanski county, Melnik district, South-Western Bulgaria, painted by Teofil Minov [Теофил Минов] and/or his elder brother Marko Minov [Марко Минов] (perhaps under the supervision of their uncle Milosh Iakovlev [Милош Яковлев]), most probably in 1876. Photo: author 488
24.1	Detail of IM 50327. After Teixidor, 'Syriac Incantation Bowls,' plate 4, number 7 538
25.1	Ravenna, church of San Vitale, lunette of the presbytery with detail of the three guests of Abraham and the sacrifice of Isaac, first half of the 6th century. Photo: author 563
25.2	Rome, church of Santa Pudenziana: apse mosaic with the *collegium apostolicum*: Peter and Paul jointly beside Christ, first half of the 5th century. Photo: author 565
25.3	Naples, Baptistery of Saint John *In Fonte*: detail of the ceiling with the representation of the *traditio legis*, late 4th–early 5th century. Photo: author 566
25.4	Aquileia, Palæo-Christian Museum of the monastery: slab engraved with busts of Peter and Paul embracing, end of the 4th–beginning of the 5th century. Photo: author 567
25.5	Venice, basilica of Saint Mark: group of the Tetrarchs carved from porphyry; Constantinople, beginning of the 4th century. Photo: author 569
25.6	Rome, catacomb of the Giordani: Tobias with the archangel Raphael (Tob. 6), 4th century. Watercolour from Wilpert 1903 571
25.7	Rome, Capitoline Museum: lid of the sarcophagus of *Publia Florentia* with the three youths in the fiery furnace, first quarter of the 4th century. From Proverbio 2007 572
25.8	Rome, church of Santa Maria Maggiore: detail of the mosaic in the main nave with the meeting between Joshua and the angel (Jos. 5), 432–440 CE. Wilpert's watercolour from Nestori & Bisconti 2000 573
25.9	Istanbul, Archæological Museum: the sarcophagus from Sarıgüzel (Istanbul)

FIGURES AND TABLES

with winged angels holding a Christogram, last third of the 4th century. From Proverbio 2007   579

25.10   Ravenna, Quadrarco di Braccioforte: detail of the right side of the Pignatta sarcophagus with the Annunciation, first quarter of the 5th century. Photo: author   580

25.11   Rome, church of Santa Sabina, detail of the wooden door with the scene of the ascension of Isaiah, first half of the 5th century. Photo: author   582

25.12   Rome, lunette of the tomb of Vibia: introduction of the deceased to the eschatological banquet, second half of the 4th century. From Wilpert 1903   584

25.13   Scheme of the decoration on the *arcosolium* of Paul in the catacomb of Ex Vigna Chiaraviglio (St Sebastian, Rome), late 4th–beginning of the 5th century. Elaboration: author   585

25.14   Rome, church of Santa Maria Maggiore: detail of the scene of the Annunciation on the triumphal arch (originally, the apsidal arch): angels' faces, hands and feet are coloured with red, 432–440 CE. Wilpert's watercolour from Nestori & Bisconti 2000   586

25.15   Ravenna, church of Sant' Apollinare Nuovo: detail of the mosaic illustrating the division of sheep and goats according to the Gospel of Mt. 25,31–33. Photo: author   587

25.16   Rome, church of Santa Maria Maggiore: detail of the mosaic in the main nave representing the meeting between Abraham and the angels at Mamre (Gen. 18), 432–440 CE. Wilpert's watercolour from Nestori & Bisconti 2000   589

26.1   The 'Birds Mosaic' (western detail) in the Armenian chapel on the Mount of Olives, Jerusalem, second half of the sixth century. Photo: Claudia Venhorst   591

26.2   The 'Birds Mosaic', Armenian chapel, Mount of Olives, Jerusalem, second half of the sixth century. From: R. Hachlili, *Ancient Mosaic Pavements: Themes, Issues and Trends* (Leiden, 2009), fig. VI-7   592

26.3   The pavement in the synagogue at Ma'on (near Nirim), Negev, first half of the 6th century. From: R. Hachlili, *Ancient Mosaic Pavements: Themes, Issues and Trends* (Leiden, 2009), fig. VI-5   593

26.4   The 'Birds Mosaic,' Armenian chapel, Mount of Olives, Jerusalem. Photo: Claudia Venhorst   595

26.5   The 'Birds Mosaic': central section. Photo: Claudia Venhorst   597

26.6   The 'Birds Mosaic': eastern fragment with an Armenian inscription. Photo: Claudia Venhorst   598

26.7   Fragment of the pavement in the Ma'on synagogue. Courtesy of the Bornblum Eretz Israel Synagogues. Website: http://synagogues.kinneret.ac.il/synagogues/maon-nirim/   600

26.8	Fragment of the pavement in the Maʿon synagogue. Courtesy of the Bornblum Eretz Israel Synagogues. Website: http://synagogues.kinneret.ac.il/synagogues/maon-nirim/ 601
26.9	Decorative frieze of the church of the Vigilant Heavenly Powers (Zuartnoċ) near Ējmiacin (Armenia), 652 CE (detail). Reconstruction by L. Gasparyan. From: T. Toromanyan, *Materials for the Study of Armenian Architecture* (in Armenian), (Yerevan 1948), vol. 2, fig. 33 608
26.10	The wine frieze engirdling the Church of the Holy Cross, the island of Ałtamar, Lake Van, 915–921 CE, detail. Photo: author 608

Tables

11.1	Repetitions in the Slavonic text of *On the Perdition of the Higher Intellect and on the Image of Light* (PHI) 222
11.2	Passages from Nemesius of Emesa paraphrased in PHI 227
11.3	The Liturgical calendar underlying the Old Testament typology in PHI 230

Notes on Contributors

Ezio Albrile
Independent Scholar, Turin

Florentina Badalanova Geller
University College London

Albert I. Baumgarten
Bar-Ilan University, Ramat Gan

Jan N. Bremmer
The University of Groningen

Igor Dorfmann-Lazarev
Aix-Marseille Université, Aix-en-Provence

Dieter Fahl
University of Greifswald

Sabine Fahl
University of Greifswald

Nazénie Garibian
The Mesrop Mashtots Institute of Ancient Manuscripts (Matenadaran), Yerevan

Ithamar Gruenwald
Tel Aviv University

Emmanouela Grypeou
Stockholm University

Zaruhi Hakobyan
Yerevan State University

David Hamidović
University of Lausanne

Felicity Harley
Yale University, New Haven

Yishai Kiel
Hebrew University of Jerusalem

Maria V. Korogodina
University of Saint Petersburg

Hartmut Leppin
Goethe University, Frankfurt am Main

Basil Lourié
Russian Academy of Sciences, St Petersburg

Jean-Pierre Mahé
Institut de France (Académie des Inscriptions et Belles Lettres), Paris

Sergey Minov
HSE University, Moscow

Tobias Nicklas
Universität Regensburg

Andrei A. Orlov
Marquette University, Milwaukee

Antonio Panaino
University of Bologna

Yakir Paz
Hebrew University of Jerusalem

Cecilia Proverbio
Pontifical Gregorian University, Rome

Yuri Stoyanov
School of Oriental and African Studies (SOAS), University of London

NOTES ON CONTRIBUTORS

Abraham Tal
Tel Aviv University

Abraham Terian
St Nersess Armenian Seminary, New York

Daniele Tripaldi
University of Bologna

Joseph Verheyden
Katholieke Universiteit Leuven

Introduction

> Their impieties [...] required the whole element of water to wash them away, and overwhelmed their memories with themselves; and so shut up the first windows of time, leaving no histories of those longevous generations, when men might have been properly historians, when Adam might have read long lectures unto Methuselah, and Methuselah unto Noah. For had we been happy in just historical accounts of that unparallel'd world, we might have been acquainted with wonders ...
>
> THOMAS BROWNE, *Christian Morals* (1716), III. I

∴

Over recent decades our acquaintance with apocryphal and para-Biblical literature has deepened considerably and this has allowed us to see the Scriptural, exegetical, liturgical and artistic sources of early Christianity in a new light. We are now better able to discern, in numerous elements of Christian traditions, both Eastern and Western, an indebtedness to texts of Jewish or Gnostic origins. Scholars have demonstrated how the literature written during the last centuries of the Second Temple (ca 200 BCE–70 CE) provided inspiration for Christian authors and artists of diverse linguistic, regional and national traditions. Furthermore, this was the case even when the 'explicit meaning' of such documents seemed to contradict New Testament writings. Apocryphal texts have continued to influence Christendom throughout its history.

Apocryphal writings represent a precious historical source, still largely neglected, for the exploration of both the communities from which they arose and those by whom they were adopted during Late Antiquity and the Middle Ages. A number of such writings were intended to explain the emergence of local Churches, to demonstrate their antiquity, to justify their autonomous structures and to defend the validity of their traditions. However, most of the texts that came to be considered 'apocryphal' were transmitted not out of an institutional need, nor with institutional support, but because they attracted the interest of both clerics and lay people—an interest spontaneous and unregulated. Their proliferation should, therefore, be regarded as a response to those existential and cosmological questions which had been raised by an acquaintance with the Hebrew Bible and by Christianity, yet could not be answered

© IGOR DORFMANN-LAZAREV, 2021 | DOI:10.1163/9789004445925_002 exhaustively by the texts officially sanctioned by the Churches: the Scripture, Patristic exegesis, liturgy, the official corpus of hagiography, homiletic literature, or the definitions of the Councils. Precisely to such apocryphal and para-Biblical texts is drawn our main attention.

Seldom verified or authorized, and often rejected by ecclesiastical bodies, numerous apocryphal texts had their own process of development, undergoing significant transformations, often to become a medium of literary and artistic elaboration and mythological creativity. Activities involving the transmission of apocryphal texts were a response to a variety of concerns and took place in diverse and often dissimilar settings. Some may be understood as participating in an attempt to investigate the human past and to open 'the first windows of time' (Thomas Browne). Others reflect attempts to predict the future or to peer into the heavenly realm. Both sometimes undertake an etymological quest for a key to particular Biblical words.

Apocryphal texts played a part, often unacknowledged, in religious controversies; they influenced iconography; their presence can be detected not only in liturgies, but also in spells and in magical rites. By means of apocryphal legends Biblical ideas and images also spilt over into man's secular life: such legends underlay the shaping and accreting of narratives, the development of oral traditions and folklore and much else. As for Christian iconography, it was not only governed by texts, but was sometimes directly influenced by traditions transmitted orally, without any mediation of a written source, so that one may even claim, as is done in this volume, the existence of 'visual apocrypha' (Felicity Harley).

Different nuances of retelling, different interpretations and expansions of early sources can lay bare the interests of the narrators and their intended auditors and readers. Through the centuries the elaboration by scribes in copying apocryphal texts can provide a wealth of information, whether about the broader culture or a scribe's specific context. Consequently, apocryphal literature can give us access to the self-understanding of the communities in the midst of which narrators, writers and copyists lived, as well as to their communities' world pictures. This is not provided through their Churches' normative or canonical writings.

In the transmission of apocrypha one aspect should be especially stressed here: the phenomenon of revising Biblical stories and of expanding them in texts, rituals, figurative arts and oral accounts in diverse cultural and ethnic settings. The evidence of apocrypha indicates that copyists, authors, artists and narrators often conceived of themselves living not in a post-Biblical era, but in direct continuity with the Biblical patriarchs and against the background of their vicissitudes. In iconography, the boundaries between the canonical and the apocryphal are so faint that the apocryphal sources even of popular scenes were forgotten or were left unacknowledged. Even the Protestant Reformers overlooked apocryphal elements, not always perhaps unwittingly.

Certain themes, motifs and images deriving from Second Temple Judaism, which are not present in the canonical Scriptures of Jews and Christians, were inherited by both, and often transmitted without polemical purposes. Each tradition, however, elaborated such themes in its own way, so that the place occupied by them in Christianity is not analogous to their place in Judaism. Nevertheless, the investigation of these two religious worlds may be undertaken as a comparative enterprise, and their divergent voices may sound in polyphony (Hartmut Leppin).

To this scope also contribute the essays that focus not on the dominant traditions within Judaism and Christianity, but on those which developed outside their respective boundaries: the Samaritans, the followers of John the Baptist and the mediæval dualists of Christian origin. In order to achieve a stereoscopic picture of the legacy of apocryphal and para-Biblical literatures, the volume also examines the way in which late antique authors perceived the emerging Christianity against the background of coeval mystery cults and the way Christianity was seen in the Iranian world; it looks at Jewish interactions with Manichæan, Mandæan and Mithraic traditions, as well as at Christian contacts with Mazdeism and the Chaldæan oracles. No synthesis of such complex and divergent phenomena can be attempted in the compass of these introductory pages. Instead, we limit ourselves here to charting some of the avenues explored in the following essays.

The present volume pays special attention to the Christian East and to texts preserved in Coptic, Ethiopian, Syriac, Persian, Armenian and Slavonic. In the East the boundaries of the Biblical canon have never been as clear-cut as in the Latin West; Biblical codices often include texts which in the West were rejected and forgotten. The flexible nature of the Oriental canons of the Scripture, the porosity of their boundaries, allowed numerous apocryphal texts to become integral parts of a living religious culture. This created a complex and unpredictable interplay of diverse and even conflicting elements. The tension between the Church's normative writings and what it deemed apocryphal prevented Christian traditions from being identified with rigid and self-contained systems. The symbiosis between 'canonical' and 'apocryphal', as reflected in literature, liturgy, the figurative arts of Eastern Christianities, and even in their folklore, has not been sufficiently acknowledged. Standard works on the history of the Church have much invested in the maintaining of norms and standards. One of the explanations for the survival of distinctive Oriental Christianities after the Islamic conquests—and up to the present—is to be located within this tension which, following Yurij Lotman, can be defined as the 'dual' character of numerous Christian cultures.

Although *apocrypha* originally meant 'things hidden' or 'concealed', only a limited number of the documents that we now call 'apocryphal' actually claim to contain esoteric knowledge; still fewer can echo secret transmission of religious ideas within distinct and self-delimited groups. Nevertheless, texts which were written between the third century BCE and the second century CE, and which remained outside the canons of either Jewish or Christian Scripture, invited mystical speculation, dramatically or subtly changing the outlook on the Hebrew Bible and on the mysteries and riddles present within the Biblical text. Indeed, they also underlie the New Testament writings. A number of contributions to this volume allow us to catch a glimpse of some of—in Gershom Scholem's terms—the 'religious possibilities' inherent in ancient Judaism and in its Scripture.

During the Christian Middle Ages, the very term 'apocryphal' was sometimes construed as synonymous with the hiddenness of God, of the divine Trinity and of the 'mysteries', i.e. the sacraments celebrated by the Church. The existence of books 'concealed', or 'secret', sprang, as it were, from the very essence of the Christian religion. There are, besides, apocryphal books which inspired distinctly esoteric currents within both Judaism and Christianity and changed the course of the history of each. Such an esoteric element shared by both religions is the focus of Part One.

In recent decades, scholars have paid attention to the role that apocalyptic literature, and in particular the *Revelation of John*, played in mediæval culture and in the mediæval interpretation of the past. Strikingly, the analogous role of the accounts of beginnings, which gave time and history a soteriological value, has seldom been accorded such attention. Yet we may recall that a mere recitation of 'narratives of the beginning', whether in Babylonian antiquity or in the European Middle Ages, could be endowed with performative or magical qualities. One of the central themes that this volume seeks to explore is the perceptions of the origins of the human race—as presented in exegetical, liturgical and iconographic sources.

By defining the nature of the human and the relation between human beings and their Creator, the accounts of the origins in *Genesis* marked an inescapable 'vanishing point' within every interpretation of a vision, every reflection on a heavenly journey, every mystical teaching and every icon. This is already apparent within the Bible itself: 'Who hath ascended up into heaven, or descended? who hath gathered the wind in his fists? who hath bound the waters in a garment? who hath established all the ends of the earth? what is his name, and what is his son's name, if thou canst tell?' (Prov. 30. 4; and henceforth: *Baruch* 3. 26–36; *II Baruch* 48. 2,5,7,8; *passim*). The interpretation of Creation in *Genesis* was one of the main preoccupations of mediæval Jewish mystics. The accounts of the beginnings in the opening pages of the Bible, whose diverse retellings are often possessed of a pronounced esoteric dimension, are also present as a watermark in all Christian thinking, rituals and arts. Through apocryphal texts, their revisions and interpretations, and through the figurative arts inspired by them, we can disclose the extent to which the first human beings occupied the Christian mind.

Various sources tell of the eschatological expectations which the first human beings transmitted to their posterity. The forestalling of the process of history and the anticipation of the last age are, according to Charles A.A. Bennett (1923), inherent in mystical experience. Mystical knowledge was even regarded as a recovery of that once possessed by Adam. Indeed, some sources speak of a secret knowledge passed on by Adam to his progeny. Transmission of divine revelation through Adam and the patriarchs would add substance to the bond between creatures and the Creator, between earth and heaven. The first chapters of *Genesis* were, therefore, not only perceived as the story of the origins of the Universe—a sequence of single and distinct events that had taken place in a remote past—but were also endowed with timeless and enduring validity for human nature and destiny; they foreshadowed the very structure of the cosmos and, in Michael E. Stone's words, its 'redemptive dynamic'.

Such a conception of the human past asked one to attain a disposition whereby one constantly projects one's life beyond the temporal horizons of the surrounding physical world: backwards, to a time before even one's remotest ancestors, and forwards, to the '*new* heavens' and the '*new* earth' (Is. 65. 17; Rev. 21. 1,5; 2 Pet. 3. 13). Christianisation promised the discovery of a new history: the new religion situated the present between, at one extremity, the origins (including the expulsion of Adam and Eve from the Garden of Eden, the Flood and Noah's ark, which would explain the human condition as it is today) and, at the other, the End Times and the Last Adam. This transcendent horizon of human life conditioned the understanding of time and chronology and played a crucial role in the formation of both biographical and historiographical representations across East and West, imprinting on Christian civilisation a peculiar relation between spirituality and the description of the past.

Marc Bloch (1886–1944) maintained that by placing human destiny between the Fall and the Judgement, the Christian religion presents it as a long adventure. Bloch also suggested that this dimension of European civilisation would only be fully apprehended when historiography adopts comparative approaches which would enable historians to identify common cultural factors active within different societies across political and institutional boundaries. Such factors—notably, the shared apocryphal traditions and, in Bloch's words, 'tales of theological origin'—remain overlooked by a historiographical practice that focuses exclusively on the development of institutions. The application of comparative methods to the history of Christianity enables us to relativize the role of institutions—secular or religious—as the dominant actors of historical narrative. By bringing together scholars who investigate the apocryphal legacy in diverse linguistic, regional, religious and national traditions, the present volume makes a step in the direction indicated by Bloch.

Narratives of origins also trace a direct line between Adam and the Messiah. Following Victor Aptowitzer, Joachim Jeremias, Benjamin Murmelstein, Sigmund Mowinckel and Gershom Scholem, numerous scholars since the 1920s have stressed the bond uniting the two. The advent of the Saviour is often accompanied by references to the vicissitudes of the first human beings (in particular, Adam, Eve, Abel, Seth, Enoch, Noah and Shem). Adam is shaped in the anticipation and in the likeness of the future Saviour; in a vision he is shown the total course of the history of the world, including the messianic end; Jesus's Nativity is depicted as the fulfilment of the promises received by Adam, Eve and other antediluvian patriarchs; the new-born child is even visited by Eve who, suddenly reappearing in the world, recognises in him her Saviour. The Magi coming from a foreign country to Bethlehem are revealed as inheritors of a secret writing transmitted to their ancestors from the beginnings of the world through a chain of Biblical patriarchs; the visions that they are granted enable them to perceive in the infant Jesus an actor from the days of Creation.

Melchizedek, a mysterious figure who in *Genesis* 14 disappears as suddenly as he had appeared in the text, is identified as either Noah's son or grandson. He is said to bury Adam's body in the middle of the earth, the place where the creation of the earth was completed, where God also created Adam and where Adam's and his children's salvation shall be realised. There Melchizedek remains as a hidden priest ministering at the burial of the first human being until the appearance in the world of the eschatological saviour. By drawing out invisibly until that event the exercise of primæval priesthood, Melchizedek personifies both the expectation and the *typos* of the priestly Messiah. When he enters the cave of the Nativity, he confers on the new-born Jesus the priesthood which he had received at the dawn of the human history.

Chains of patriarchs linking Adam with the Messiah are also known in the Jewish tradition. Thus, from the seventh-century Book of Zerubbabel we hear of a sceptre given to the Messiah's mother by God, which had earlier been given to Adam, Moses, Aaron, Joshua and David. With this sceptre she fights the eschatological foes and later transmits it to her son. The link between protology and eschatology, and between the first human being and the Messiah, is the focus of Part Two.

INTRODUCTION

The recognition of the Messiah by his contemporaries had to rely on ancient revelations and prophecies; that recognition, which only a few could achieve, was the precondition for the beginning of the Messiah's earthly ministry. Part Three is dedicated to the enigmatic signs prefiguring the Messiah's sudden advent and the figures who foretold and anticipated it, such as Elijah who in the Christian tradition was recognised as a type of John the Baptist. Several papers in this volume analyse pictorial representations of those figures to whom is ascribed special knowledge derived from an otherworldly source. These and other essays also explore the figures of the elect to whom, or through whom, were granted the revelations of the heavenly world, of various kinds of secret knowledge, of the end times and of the Son of Man. Foremost of these is the patriarch Enoch, as seen through the literature associated with his name. Visions, revelations of the angelic world and heavenly journeys are considered in Part Four.

Esotericism has been defined in diverse ways by authors who applied the term to phenomena of different periods and divergent religious traditions. Our focus here is not so much on secrecy or the occult as on the claim advanced by certain figures, groups, movements and texts to decipher 'the latent, inner sense of the Scripture' (Ithamar Gruenwald). To a large extent, such claims of esoteric knowledge shaped the religious and cultural history of the post-Biblical era. The definition of esotericism formulated by Antoine Faivre may be adopted to encompass the phenomena analysed in the present volume:

> [L]a *disciplina arcani* signifie surtout ceci: les mystères de la religion, la nature ultime de la réalité, les forces cachées de l'ordre cosmique, les hiéroglyphes du monde visible ne peuvent pas se prêter à une compréhension littérale, ni à une explication didactique ou univoque, mais doivent faire l'objet d'une pénétration progressive, à plusieurs niveaux, par chaque homme en quête de connaissance.[1]

Part 1. The volume opens with **Ithamar Gruenwald**'s paper 'The Exoteric Appearances of Jewish Esotericism'. In order to approach the theme of esoteric writings in the world of Biblical religions, the author focuses on the phenomenon of re-writing accounts relating to the Bible, both within the corpus of texts recognised as canonical and outside it. To what extent are the textual variants in the synoptic Gospels, for example, due to different sources? And to what

---

1 A. Faivre, *Accès de l'ésotérisme occidental* vol. I, Paris, 1996 (revised edition), pp. 31–32; quoted and discussed in M.E. Stone, *Secret Groups in Ancient Judaism*, Oxford, 2018, p. 15.

extent do they result from a competition between the authors of writings that pretended to a normative status in a community and that were intended to shape a new religious identity? Some re-written accounts, Gruenwald explains, pretend to disclose esoteric content of an earlier text. The ambition to propose a new meaning of a known text implies the belief that a hidden, or secret, message is intrinsic to the Biblical text itself. The different content is usually warranted by an angelic revelation; the novel text, allegedly inspired by God, suggests itself as the ultimate version of truth.

This picture, however, is complicated by the fact that the Hebrew Bible itself contains alternate versions of the same story, which, *ipso facto*, opens a door to further re-writings. Consequently, numerous alternate versions of Scriptural texts outside the Bible may also be regarded as an expansion of this inner Biblical phenomenon. Such a re-writing, however, stands in a dialectical tension with the injunction of *Deuteronomy* (itself being a re-written text) 4. 2, which enjoins: 'Ye shall not add unto the word which I command you, neither shall ye diminish ought from it.'

Gruenwald argues that a new version is not always the result of a hermeneutic enterprise, proposing to distinguish between the re-writing of an account and its interpretation: the latter always remains a note in the margin of a text, existing at its service, whereas re-writing pretends to produce an original document which can be juxtaposed with the former or even supersede it. Such cases are to be found in the Book of Jubilees which in many respects proposes a thorough revision of the stories from *Genesis* and *Exodus*. Although the Book of Jubilees does not present itself as a secret revelation, it wells out of the Scriptural story as its hidden content and in many respects aspires to replace it. According to Gruenwald, it is this ambition, discernible in the Book of Jubilees, which can clearly be regarded as esoteric. The provenance and the role of such esoteric features within the global architecture of this book, however, cannot always be identified.

In the midst of various Christian communities, the spread of writings considered 'hidden' or 'concealed' was dependent on their self-understanding and on the way they conceived of their relations with the outer world. Did Jesus's command 'to go into all the world, and to preach the gospel to every creature' (Mk. 16. 15) allow for the existence of secret rites and secret doctrines within Christian communities? An instance of re-writing, or re-narrating, a story in Christian tradition is discussed by **Tobias Nicklas** in his paper 'The *Gospel of Peter* between the Synoptics, Second Century, and Late Antique "Apostolic Memoirs"'. Nicklas focuses on the passages about the Lord's passion and resurrection, which are preserved in a sixth–seventh century codex from Akhmîm in Upper Egypt. The lines speaking of the Lord 'being silent *as if* he felt no

INTRODUCTION

pain' have sometimes provoked a rather unjustified suspicion of the docetic tendency of this text: did Christ's humanity express the Saviour's true identity or did it rather hide it? Since their discovery in 1886–1887, these passages have often been considered to belong to the Gospel of Peter mentioned by ancient Christian authors. Indeed, their storyline resembles the Gospels that would later be recognised as canonical. Nicklas's analysis has led him to posit that the fragments derive from a Jewish Christian circle of second-century Syria and that the original account, which could have been revised during the subsequent centuries, had represented a 're-enactment' of memories about Jesus. In its form, this text had to be a bridge between the genre of gospels and the late antique genre of 'Apostolic Memoirs' which is especially attested in Egypt.

The author of the Akhmîm document treated the text of the New Testament Gospels so freely that one cannot decide whether he used it as a *Vorlage* or only retained in his mind its main storyline (especially, including important and impressive motifs). He sets forth his own story which, whilst relying on texts that were included in the New Testament, does not always remain true to the details of its account. Nicklas explains this feature by the fact that in the second century the texts of the four Gospels were not available in all the Christian communities. Consequently, the author's lack of precision could be overlooked by his auditors or his readers who had memorized the main stories, but had no chance to read the Gospel text in detail.

In order to discuss the ways in which secret doctrines were perceived in Christianity, **Joseph Verheyden**, in his paper 'All Mysteries Revealed? On the Interplay between Hiding and Revealing and the Dangers of Heavenly Journeys according to the Ascension of Isaiah', proposes to focus on the *Ascension of Isaiah*, a Christian apocalyptic book written, admittedly, in the middle of the second century. The book is put together from material of different genres, and the history of its composition still remains a puzzle. It is even unclear whether the author was aware of Jewish authorship of the sources used by him. The *Ascension of Isaiah* tells the story of the brutal execution of the prophet Isaiah at the order of the evil king Manasseh because of Isaiah's reproaches addressed to the king and of the prophet's claim to have been granted a spiritual experience that had led him to travel through heavenly spheres and even to have seen God. In heaven the prophet beholds the story of Jesus's life, from his birth to his violent death. He watches, notably, Christ's passing through the heavenly spheres, which explains how the incarnation and the ascension will occur. One of the points on which different versions of the book disagree is whether or not, in the course of the revelation granted to him, the prophet beheld God's glory.

Verheyden outlines the decisive elements by which the revelation of hidden knowledge is characterised in the *Ascension of Isaiah*: it presupposes that the divine message may not be disclosed unrestrictedly, yet it is its intrinsic quality that triggers the divulgation of this message; the divine author himself urges his messenger to reveal it. Whilst the message concerns the cosmic battle between God and Satan, its divulgation evinces and even sharpens the conflict between good and evil on earth. Its first victim, or rather martyr, becomes the messenger himself. According to Verheyden, one of the author's primary purposes is to show the dangers with which the disclosure of secret knowledge is fraught. In that sense the *Ascension of Isaiah* is as much a report of a heavenly journey and the revelation of heavenly mysteries, as a call and a warning to those faithful who wished to follow in the steps of the prophet and who claimed to have experienced similar visions.

The claim to keep hidden knowledge, or to have access to the hidden meaning of a text, is related to the stance of various Christian communities on mystery cults. Christian Fathers often used the vocabulary of the mystery religions, which they could have inherited from Philo. **Jan N. Bremmer**, in his paper 'Early Christianity and the Pagan Mysteries: Esoteric Knowledge?', discusses the way in which Christianity articulated its beliefs and its rites between the end of the second and the middle of the third century, precisely during the decades that preceded the important growth of the Christian religion. Celsus was one of the most heedful external observers of emerging Christianity. He was also acquainted with various Mystery cults, and his attitude to them was rather unequal. Whilst he displays an ambiguous attitude towards the Mithraic Mysteries and those of Sabazios, for example, he is much more positive about the Orphic, Samothracian and Eleusinian Mysteries, which he clearly considered as providing a certain kind of wisdom. Moreover, when comparing the Mysteries with Christianity, he takes them all together, without differentiating between them. He clearly regards Christianity as a 'secret doctrine', thus assimilating it to Mystery cults, and he understands Christians' avoidance of making statues and erecting temples as a token of that inner nature of the Christian doctrine. Celsus also mocks the Christians for celebrating their rites not in beautiful sanctuaries but in base places and amidst socially inferior people.

Celsus's opponent Origen seems to have been less informed about the pagan Mysteries, but as an Egyptian he certainly was knowledgeable regarding the Mysteries of Antinoos. Arguing against Celsus, Origen does admit that the Christians kept certain doctrines secret from those who were not baptised, in particular those regarding God, the Logos, the resurrection, the angels and the demons. He indirectly admits the validity of the language of mystery cults for the description of Christianity. Although these examples do not allow us to make global conclusions concerning the nature of Christianity during that period, they show nevertheless that, in some intellectual circles, external and

INTRODUCTION

internal, a similarity between it and mystery cults was admitted. Yet to what extent such views were representative of early Christianity has—Bremmer suggests—to remain a mystery.

Yuri Stoyanov's paper, 'The Medieval Dualist *Nachleben* of Early Jewish and Christian Esoteric Traditions: The Role of the Pseudepigrapha', contextualises some esoteric narratives amongst medieval dualist communities, focusing on Bogomilism and their subsequent reception in Catharism. The corpus of inner doctrines of the Bogomils in Macedonia and Bulgaria was largely indebted to earlier para-Biblical works, and notably *2 Enoch*, *3 Baruch*, *The Apocalypse of Abraham*, *The Vision of Isaiah* and *The Life of Adam and Eve*, as well as compilatory compositions such as the *Palæa Historica* and *Palæa Interpretata*. These and other works imparted to Bogomilism a number of foundational notions in diverse spheres such as cosmogony, cosmology, diabology, angelology, Christology, sacred history and eschatology. Mediæval reports and exposés of Bogomil doctrines display fragments of narratives which clearly represent elaborations of the stories of creation and flood from the book of *Genesis*. These narratives find immediate parallels in the miscellaneous pseudepigraphic works translated and circulated during the formative stages of Slavo-Byzantine learning and theology, which were particularly favourable for the reception of heterodox traditions and the emergence of doctrinal deviances. Amongst the central themes were the downfall of the angels and their corruption of humanity, the identity of the ringleader of the angelic apostasy and the fall of Adam and Eve.

The reports describing the initiation of the elite Bogomil class of the *teleoi* ('perfect') maintain that it evolved in stages. The believers were originally instructed in conventional Christian beliefs and ethics, a process which was followed by a progressive introduction to increasingly heretical precepts, until the overall system of the dualist teachings, safeguarded as the inner dualist doctrines, was presented to the neophyte. Those who attained the stage of the 'perfect' were regarded as protectors and repositories of Christ's genuine teaching which was disclosed—in the light of Mk. 4. 11—secretly to his chosen apostles and maintained and passed on in concealment. These doctrines drew especially on the newly translated apocryphal writings from late antiquity, which were largely spread in the medieval Slavic world, both amongst the mainstream Orthodox and the dissenting groups. Some dualist-leaning and Gnostic tendencies in these texts were interpolated and radicalised during their earlier transmission and adoption in sectarian or heterodox milieux. As a result, some of these traditions acquired a more pronounced esoteric dimension in Bogomil and Cathar circles, amongst which the absorbed pseudepigraphic accounts of heavenly rapture also influenced the reported practices of visionary mysticism and heavenly ascent pursued by their theological elites.

Ezio Albrile takes us to later times: his paper, 'The Esoteric Cardinal: Giorgios Gemistos, Bessarion and Theurgy', examines the career of the Chaldæan Oracles between Byzantium, Florence and Rome in the first half of the fifteenth century. These Oracles are a Middle Platonic writing datable, admittedly, to the end of the second–beginning of the third century CE, which were, in most cases, identified as god's speeches. According to *Souda*, an eleventh-century Byzantine lexicon, its authors were Julian the Chaldæan (the spiritual master of a Mystery circle) and his son Julian the Theurgist, Marcus Aurelius's contemporaries.

The decisive figure in communicating the wisdom of the Chaldæan oracles to the Renaissance world was the Byzantine erudite Giorgios Gemistos Plethon (ca 1360–1452) for whom it was one of the reference texts in his design of a radical religious reform. He also inspired the Florentine Platonic Academy that was conceived by Cosimo de' Medici (the Elder). Giorgios Gemistos must have learnt of the Chaldæan Oracles from one Elisha, the translator and commentator of Averroes into Hebrew and an expert in Kabbala. From indirect references we learn that Elisha attributed the Chaldæan Oracles to Zoroaster, reconnecting them with the traditions of the Iranian Magi who, according to Herodotus, had been experts in sacred things and in religious rituality. Giorgios Gemistos's disciple was Cardinal Bessarion who aspired to shape a new rituality within the Roman Catholic Church, drawing on both the Neoplatonists and the Chaldæan Oracles rather than on Biblical writings.

Part 2. As we have seen, in the *Ascension of Isaiah* the prophet's vision builds a bridge to the messianic times. Some texts discern signs of the future advent of the saviour already in the events of primæval history. Moreover, a number of 'apocryphal' texts speak not only of the expectation by primæval beings and patriarchs of a future redemption: conversely, the eschatological accomplishment can become the moment when the most remote past of the human race is recollected and its principal figures are revived. **Jean-Pierre Mahé**'s paper 'La création d' Adam à Noravank. Théologie et narrativité' examines the enigmatic iconography, datable to the end of the thirteenth or the beginning of the fourteenth century, in the monastery Noravank in northern Armenia. This iconography is tightly linked to the exegesis of the text from *Genesis* about the creation of the first human being. In the scene to which Mahé draws our attention, the creation of Adam by the Ancient of Days is interlaced with the representation of Christ's crucifixion. The author shows that this scene reflects the *Catechesis of St Gregory* transmitted in Agatangełos's *History*, which was edited between 428 and 451. The author of the *Catechesis* supposes that, since in the Scripture man is God's image, the Creator himself, in order to create man, must first have assumed human resemblance. This idea allows the artist of Noravank to repre-

INTRODUCTION   13

sent the invisible God in a visible form in the act of creation in Genesis, even though Armenian art usually prefers purely symbolic representations to the portrayal of divine persons.

We thus see a mysterious encounter of two figures who, in principle, are separated by an infinite time: on one side is the Creator who in the accompanying inscription is described as the 'Ancient of Days': his age implies his eternal existence and is also indicative of the age of the world at the moment of the Messiah's revelation (cf. 2 *Baruch* 56. 3; 85. 10); on the other side is the Son of Man appearing in a given moment in the history of the world. This temporal distance is accentuated by the difference of size between the two. The scene suggests that whilst animating the newly moulded Adam, God envisages making him similar to the Son of Man. The appearance of the Prophet Daniel in the composition accentuates the eschatological dimension of the vision of the Ancient of Days in Noravank. The resemblance of man to God, announced in the first account of creation in Genesis, is only completely realised in the passion of the new Adam whom we behold at the right hand of the Creator.

Sergey Minov's paper, '*Translatio corporis Adæ*: Trajectories of a Para-Biblical Tradition', discusses the traditions relating to Adam's burial in Jerusalem. The author explains that this motif emerged at the intersection of two themes: Jesus's crucifixion on Golgotha and the typological connection between Adam and Christ. Numerous explanations of the arrival of Adam's body at Golgotha, which have been transmitted in diverse linguistic and cultural areas, developed from this motif. According to a Syriac tradition, preserved in an anthology of the eighth or the early ninth century, Noah took the remains of the forefather into the ark and after the flood divided them between his sons. It was Shem who brought them to Jerusalem. This, like analogous traditions transmitted in Armenia, elaborates on the Syriac *Cave of Treasures* (third–sixth centuries). Coptic texts claim, on the other hand, that it was the waters of the flood that brought Adam's relics to Jerusalem. A Greek chronicle ascribed to Peter of Alexandria, composed most likely at the end of the ninth–beginning of the tenth century, relates that after his expulsion from Paradise Adam dwelt on an island in front of Eden. After his death angels took his remains thence to Golgotha.

Various versions of this tradition also reached the Slavic world. One explanation claims the appearance of Adam's remains in Jerusalem in the reign of King Solomon. The demons, asked by the king about the appropriate tree for the building of the temple, brought him a tree from Eden where it had been planted by Seth on his father's grave. When the demons pull the tree out, Adam's skull remains entangled in its roots and thus reaches Jerusalem. Examining further parallels to this story Minov hypothesises that the origins of para-Biblical material related to Adam's skull should be sought in the multi-confessional milieu of Palestine during the eleventh–twelfth centuries, characterised as it was by exchanges between diverse Christians of East and West, whereas other traditions could have developed already on Slavonic soil. Minov's study demonstrates the importance of Slavonic literature as a repository of lost Greek para-Biblical traditions. Reflecting on the genesis and development of these legends, Minov speaks of a 'chain reaction', whereby a para-Biblical tradition of Adam's body on Golgotha, which had emerged already during the second–third centuries, triggered further the proliferation of para-Biblical material in remote lands of the north.

The link between the first and the second Adam is also explored by **Daniele Tripaldi** in his paper 'Apostles, Long Dead "Heretics", and Monks: Noncanonical Traditions on Angels and Protoplasts in Two Late Antique Coptic Apocalypses (7th–8th Century CE)'. Tripaldi takes into examination two Coptic texts dating, admittedly, to the seventh–eighth centuries, the *Investiture of Abbaton* and the *Mysteries of John*, which elaborate apocryphal Adam traditions. These works were mainly used in a liturgical context and were intended to explain the origin and the meaning of the chief liturgical celebrations. The *Investiture of Abbaton* speaks of the virgin soil, from which Adam would be created. In anticipation of all the crimes that man would commit, the pure clay resists the angels sent by God to fetch it. The Son of God then acts as the warrant for Adam, promising the Father to descend to earth and to restore Adam to his prelapsarian condition of the ruler of the created world. In the *Mysteries of John* Christ fashions his flesh into a grain of wheat. This grain Adam will sow, reap and, finally, eat. Both texts tend in different ways to conceive of the links between protology and eschatology. Thus, the *Investiture of Abbaton* underlines that the Son's incarnation is the *apokatastasis* of the world. The *Mysteries of John*, on the other hand, implicitly identifies the very first grain of wheat given to Adam as Christ's flesh, whilst presenting the Eucharistic bread as the first bread in human history, the same which after the fall saved Adam from starving.

The resemblance between the first and the second Adam was also present in Jewish thought of late antiquity. This idea is explored by **Andrei A. Orlov** who, in his paper 'Face as the Image of God in the Jewish Pseudepigrapha', examines the Jewish text of the middle of the first century CE, which is preserved in Old Slavonic and is known to us as *2 Enoch*. In chapter 44, we hear of the first human being created not merely after God's image, as in *Genesis* 1, but precisely 'in the likeness of God's face'. Nowhere is the Slavonic 'face' used in translating the Biblical account of man's creation. In order to explain the genesis of this motif, Orlov observes the replacement of the term *ṣelem* (image) with that of *panim* (countenance) in a series of Jewish texts regarding the Ladder of Jacob. Another first-century Jewish text only surviving in Slavonic, *The*

INTRODUCTION

Ladder of Jacob, speaks of the ladder bridging earth and heaven, which was revealed to Jacob in a dream. According to the Slavonic apocryphon, the ladder had at its top the face of a man, upon which face God himself stood. Orlov observes that when God calls from that last step of the ladder to Jacob, who lies on the earth beneath, the face upon which God stands must appear from earth below as a distinct divine manifestation. Orlov also evokes various Rabbinic sources which, referring to Jacob's vision, speak of the patriarch's heavenly portrait depicted on the throne of glory. Moreover, in some texts this image is even understood as God's anthropomorphic glory.

In *2 Enoch* 22 the protagonist is brought before God's face, where his metamorphosis occurs, whereby the seventh patriarch regains the protoplast's prelapsarian luminosity, thus becoming the 'second Adam'. The new creation of Enoch thus signifies a return of humankind to the initial condition of the first created human being who had been modelled, according to *2 Enoch* 44, after the face of God. This description of Enoch's 'new creation' can explain why the first Adam was created not merely after the image but precisely after the *face* of God: the creation of the first man anticipates Enoch's metamorphosis. Orlov shows that in the author's view the motif of creation after the face of God constitutes a pivotal link between the first Adam, who lost his glorious condition in the Garden of Eden, and Enoch, the 'second Adam'.

Maria V. Korogodina and **Basil Lourié**, in their study '*On the Perdition of the Higher Intellect and on the Image of Light*: Critical Edition, Translation, and Commentary', examine a rare case of a bridge built between Abel and Christ. They provide a critical edition and a detailed analysis of a textual fragment which is only known in Old Slavonic and which was, in all likelihood, translated from Greek. The surviving text expounds peculiar Christology and refers to an Old Testament typology which is not reflected in the mainstream Byzantine exegesis. The authors detect in it features of Origenist theology, whereas in its Biblical typology they recognise ancient Jewish Christian characteristics, including some liturgical (calendrical) patterns, which are attested in the Jerusalem area until the late fifth century. The lost Greek original of the Slavonic text, however, must have been translated from Syriac.

In an apparent disagreement with *Romans* 5.12—the authors contend—as well as with the prevailing Byzantine exegetical tradition, death enters into the world not with Adam but with Abel; in Abel the text identifies the firstborn of the dead and in Christ the firstborn of the living. This typological pairing represents, apparently, an echo of the great Syriac writer Jacob of Sarug (ca 450–521). The history of the fall and salvation outlined in the fragment is a version of the Origenist myth of destruction and restoration of the divine Henad, which bears resemblances with Evagrius's theology. The text is written in a deliberately obscure manner, and even the Biblical figures most often remain unnamed but are recognisable thanks to quotations and allusions. The author certainly considered his doctrine as esoteric, probably because he lived in a milieu hostile to Origenism. Most probably, the text was shaped no earlier than the late sixth century, but hardly later than the early eighth century, by Syriac-speaking Origenists.

Abraham Tal, in his paper 'Bridging the Gaps in the Samaritan Tradition', explores the interpretation of the figures of Biblical patriarchs amongst the Samaritans. He focuses on the book known as *Asāṭīr*, whose name was once thought to relate to the Hebrew/Aramaic root *sṭr* ('to hide', 'to conceal' or 'to shelter') and, thus, to indicate its esoteric character. The name derives, in fact, from an Arabic term meaning merely 'tales', or 'legends'. *Asāṭīr* represents a chronicle written in the form of a midrash in which many no longer extant traditions are embedded. The small number of the surviving manuscripts can be taken as a proof of its being, during a long period, not secret but rather largely neglected, or forgotten, by the members of the community. It was only during the twentieth century that the book was brought to the attention of the scholarly world.

Unlike other Samaritan chronicles, *Asāṭīr* does not continue the Pentateuch's account in time. Its primary focus is on the four 'pillars' of the world: Adam, Noah, Abraham and Moses. Its main concern is to bridge the 'gaps' discovered by its author in the text of the Torah, such as the existence of the wives of Cain and Abel, the reason for God's unequal approach to the brothers' offerings, etc. Some of the traditions transmitted in *Asāṭīr* are very old, because their traces are attested in pre-Christian non-Samaritan sources, whilst other traditions bear traces of Bedouin customs. Since no ancient Samaritan text regarding books other than the Pentateuch has survived centuries of persecution, there is little chance of ascertaining the internal Samaritan sources of this book.

The book attempts to mitigate Adam's responsibility for the fall, hinting that Eve bears the guilt. In spite of the fall, Adam remains the first 'pillar' of the world, whose term shall be closed with the reappearance of Moses, the fourth 'pillar'. *Asāṭīr*, as well as another Samaritan Chronicle, *The Ark of Mårqe*, also speak of the 'Book of Signs', a writing of divine origin, which contained predictions and which was given to Adam who transmitted it to his offspring. Before passing it on further, Enoch thus could learn from it about the future, whereas Noah, in studying it, could perceive in Adam's story anticipatory signs regarding the ark.

According to a consolidated scholarly opinion, in the transmission to the Biblical chroniclers of ancient Mesopotamian accounts relating to the antediluvian world and the Flood an important role was played by an intermediary

INTRODUCTION

from the north. It has also been suggested that this northern intermediary was none other than the Hurrians who, besides, entertained close contacts with the Hebrews. Of Hurrian origin is claimed to be, for example, the name of one of Shem's sons, Arpachshad (Gen. 10. 22; 11. 10; Lk. 3. 36).

Until the early first millennium BCE, Hurrians occupied the area of Harran, Abraham's ancestral land according to *Genesis*, and the highlands rising north of Mesopotamia. Consequently, the topography of *Genesis* can bear traces of the highlands which had once been inhabited by Hurrians and kindred peoples and which would later be known as the Armenian plateau. Departing from Harran and travelling due north, through the defiles of the Gordyæan chain, within a two-days' journey, or even sooner, one could reach a land which from the beginning of the sixth century BCE (or even earlier) had been inhabited by Armenians.

The Armenian plateau is elevated many hundred metres above any other mountainous region surrounding Mesopotamia and Canaan. Consequently, various attempts were made by Jews, Christians and other communities acquainted with the Bible to locate 'the mountains of Ararat' (Gen. 8. 4), upon which Noah's ark had rested, in Armenia. **Nazénie Garibian**'s paper, '"On the Mountains of Ararat": Noah's Ark and the Sacred Topography of Armenia', takes a closer look at the figure of Noah and his particular role in Armenian culture. At least two different traditions regarding Ararat existed in Armenia, one locating it in the Gordyæan chain and the other identifying it with the extinguished volcano which is situated further north and which has borne this name up to the present day. As suggested above, the two localisations may arise from pre-Biblical traditions; however, it may not be excluded that they reflect two successive stages in the gradual integration of the Armenian plateau by late antique readers of the Bible within their sacred topography. At an early date, this tradition would be transmitted to the Armenians.

The perception, infused in the Armenians by the Bible, of inheriting the land upon which postdiluvian humanity had made its first steps, deeply influenced their culture. According to apocryphal texts preserved in Armenian, Noah was the inheritor of a document announcing the future salvation, which God had written with his finger and had given to Adam. Other texts spoke of the bones of Adam and Eve, which Noah transported in the Ark in order to bequeath them to postdiluvian humankind.[2] Adam and his memory of

---

2   M.E. Stone, 'The bones of Adam and Eve', in R.A. Argall et al. (eds), *For a Later Generation: The Transformation of Tradition in Israel, Early Judaism and Early Christianity*, Harrisburg, 2000, p. 244; I. Dorfmann-Lazarev, 'Eve, Melchizedek and the Magi in the Cave of the Nativity According the Armenian Corpus of Homilies Attributed to Epiphanius of Salamis', in J.N. Bremmer et al. (eds) *The Protevangelium of James* (Studies on Early Christian Apocrypha 16), Leuven, 2019, pp. 264–311.

promised redemption were regarded as the foundation stone of the new world, and of the new kingdoms.

Garibian explains that Noah's landing in Armenia even affected popular etymology and modified the toponymy of the country. Thus the city which in the ancient texts is called Ēriwan (deriving its name from the Urartian Erebuni), later became Erewan, i.e. a place 'seen': it was construed in Armenian as the site perceived by Noah and his family from Ararat. The ancient name of another city, Naxčawan, shifted to Naxiĵewan (today Naxçıvan in Azeri), literally 'the place of the first descent' of Noah. A village called Arnoyt also existed where Noah—*Noy* in Armenian—was supposed to have dwelt.

The temporal 'bridges' that various para-Biblical textual and figurative sources built to the origins of humankind exercised a decisive influence on our perception of historical time and even on historical writing. **Igor Dorfmann-Lazarev**'s paper, 'The Historian's Craft and Temporal Bridges in Apocrypha and in Early Christian Art. Para-Biblical Sources in the Light of the Work of Marc Bloch', analyses the perspectives opened up on the study of apocryphal literature by the mediævalist Marc Bloch. Bloch maintained that by placing humankind's destiny between the Fall and the Judgement, the Christian religion depicts it as a long adventure, whilst the figure of the pilgrim stands out as the main paradigm of the individual human life which unfolds between Sin and Redemption.

A series of texts shaped between the second and the sixth centuries, and preserved in Samaritan, Coptic, Greek, Syriac, Latin and Armenian, speak of a written document that the first created human beings passed on to their descendants. That document related a revelation received by Adam regarding his future destiny and that of all his posterity, as well as the history of its transmission. One could never understand from any ecclesiastical document, of what enduring importance across Christendom was the idea of a secret document transmitted to humankind by the first created human being. According to the Armenian 'Script of the Lord's Infancy', that document was written by God himself, eventually reaching the Magi, i.e. the prototypes of the mediæval pilgrims evoked by Bloch. Surprisingly, on the fourth-century 'Dogmatic sarcophagus' from Rome, the Magi's pilgrimage to Bethlehem is depicted as the moment when the first actors of human history are recollected: the narrative sequence of its lower register commences with the scene of the Adoration of the three Wise Men, whereas the opening scene of its upper register, situated exactly above that scene, depicts the Creation of Eve by the Triune God. The postures and gestures of the protagonists suggest that Adam and Eve are in the Magi's minds and form the background of the event that they have come to celebrate. A sarcophagus in Rome and an apocryphal text transmitted in Arme-

INTRODUCTION

19

nian reveal a kindred semantic structure: both link the Messiah's advent to the beginning of history. The Magi figure in both as the main protagonists of that undertaking, building temporal bridges.

Part 3. The symbols and the figures of messianic expectation, the first witnesses of the Messiah's advent, and the ideas concerning his birth, are explored in the following six contributions. **Dieter** and **Sabine Fahl**'s study, 'Quellen der nichtbiblischen Mose-Überlieferung in der *Kratkaja Chronografičeskaja Paleja*', is devoted to Slavonic apocryphal texts regarding Moses who in various traditions was conceived as a messianic figure. No systematic collection of these texts has been prepared to this day. The messianic character of the figure of Moses in Christian exegesis can explain the development in the Slavic world of such a broad tradition, in terms of genre, chronology and geography. The authors focus on the writings pertaining to the *Kratkaja Chronografičeskaja Paleja (The Shorter Chronographic Palæa)*, a compilation encompassing the time from the Creation of the world to 944, the year of the death of Emperor Romanos Lakapenos.

The sources of the *Palæa* are not always easy to identify, because the compiler, who worked in Northern Russia in the beginning of the fifteenth century, chose only snippets from them—sometimes only a few words—rearranging them according to a chronographic pattern. Links between these snippets are mostly missing, yet in a few cases they do appear at the beginning of a phrase. Although the compiler usually disregarded the exegetic passages present in the main source, the *Tolkovaja Paleja (The Interpreted Palæa)*, exegetical material is preserved in some contexts, which show Moses as a prefiguration of Christ. The compiler's particular interest lay in precise chronological data because he expected the end of the world in the year 7000, i.e. 1492 AD. Counting time, systematising and interpreting history, served for him as a preparation for its end.

Abraham Terian's paper, 'Whether Lamb or Lion: Overlapping Metaphors in Jewish and Christian Apocalypticism', is devoted to two apocalyptic metaphors: the lamb and the lion. It is likely that many of John the Baptist's followers perceived him as the awaited priestly messiah. Consequently, the Gospel of John can attribute to him the words that evoke the Temple sacrifices (1. 29). The evangelist's most direct reference is to *Isaiah* 53. 7, a verse regarded as a prophetic anticipation of the Messiah's redemptive death. One of the evangelist's intentions is to ascribe to Jesus all that in Jewish apocalypticism pertains to the priestly messiah. The *Revelation of John*, by contrast, suggests a metaphoric transition of the lamb into the lion of the tribe of Judah (5. 5). The lamb in the Apocalypse is both a sacrificial Redeemer and 'Lord of lords and King of kings' (17. 14), the sovereign possessing authority over the course of history; he directs its unfolding and prepares the way for the ushering in of the new age marked by the opening of 'the seventh seal' (8. 1; 22. 1–2).

This progression from one metaphor to another can also be observed in the work of the tenth-century Armenian author Gregory of Narek (the monastery of Narek was situated near Lake Van in southern Armenia, today in Turkey, and was destroyed ca 1916, during the Genocide) who, by juxtaposing the two images, depicts the crucified Jesus as the triumphant lion 'roaring' from the cross and 'calling to the depths of the earth'. The depths 'shake beneath his mighty voice', releasing their 'captives'. This reminds us of the encounter between the redemptive event and the beginnings of human history represented in the first part of the *Questions of Bartholomew*, written towards the end of the second century: Jesus disappears from the cross at the moment when darkness envelops the earth, then becomes visible again and converses with Adam whom he has delivered from the realm of death (1.7–22).

The figure of John the Baptist is even more central to **Albert Baumgarten**'s paper, 'Rescuing John the Baptist'. The author takes us back to those esoteric traditions which did not outlive antiquity and which are the focus of the first part of this volume. Whilst in the New Testament John is depicted as the Precursor of Christ, Baumgarten proposes to look at him from a different standpoint. He suggests that this figure has to be set free from heavy layers of theological superstructures with which he has been loaded over the two millennia and through which we still look at him. He argues that a 'rescued' John can offer an important lesson for the study of the varieties of esoteric and apocryphal sources in the development of both Christian and Jewish traditions under discussion in this volume. According to Baumgarten, John was a full-fledged independent actor who occupied a distinctive place amongst the numerous religious movements of his time and who had an eschatological view of his own. This is testified, for example, by the fact that John's baptism was named not after its purpose but after his name (e.g. Mk. 11. 30; Lk. 7. 29): this means—Baumgarten explains—that the ritual introduced by him, although loosely based on existing Jewish practices, was directly equivalent to none of them. John assigned himself a senior role in the drama of the end of time, and also after his death his disciples continued to believe in his status.

One of the peculiar features of John's movement is a distinct relation between the extreme exigencies addressed towards himself and the lenience shown towards his followers. The call that he addressed to his contemporaries and to his followers did not imply an imitation of his own rigorous asceticism. Baumgarten compares John with the neo-Pythagorean philosopher Apollonius of Tyana who rejected excessive rigour and severity as vulgarity or pride. Only distant echoes of John's teachings have reached us, some of which probably sur-

INTRODUCTION

21

vive in the Mandæan tradition. The very paradox perceptible in these echoes attests to the esoteric structure of John's teaching. That forgotten esoteric tradition must have played an important role in the development of both Judaism and Christianity.

Before John the Baptist, the 'Wise Men from the East' were, according to the Gospel of Matthew, the earliest witnesses of the Messiah's advent (Mt. 2. 1–12). To them is devoted **Antonio Panaino**'s paper 'The Esoteric Legacy of the Magi of Bethlehem in the framework of the Iranian Speculations about Jesus, Zoroaster and his three Posthumous Sons'. While the number of the Magi is left unspecified in Matthew, it varies in apocryphal and iconographic sources. Panaino observes that the number three, in particular, has interesting resonances in Iran and in the Iranised lands. Because Zoroastrianism was the state religion of Persia, the Magi who had come to Bethlehem to offer homage to the new-born Christ were regarded as Persian ambassadors: in their persons, the second greatest power in the world recognised Christ's supreme lordship. Some claimed that the absolute primacy of the Magi's witness of Christ's advent accorded them a dignity which was even superior to the Apostle Peter.

The Magi's presence in Bethlehem was associated with the Mazdæan expectation of the last of the three posthumous sons of Zoroaster, the saviour *par excellence*, who shall resurrect all the dead and shall start the final battle against Ahreman. The importance of time speculations in the Zoroastrian tradition, with its special focus on millenarian expectations, finds correspondences in the symbolic interpretation of the group of three Magi. In various apocryphal texts the three Magi see Jesus under different aspects. These aspects evoke not only the different ages of the guest entering the Cave of the Nativity, but also reflect the three ages of the world—past, present and future—and, thus, the power of God as the Lord of the cosmos. If the group of the Magi can be interpreted as a symbol of humankind bowing down before Christ, the new-born child— who appears before them as successively an infant, an adult and an elder—is also the Ancient of Days, the Creator of the world: so he appears before them according to numerous sources. Consequently, in the Iranian world the Magi could be regarded not only as a mirror of the atemporal power of Christ-God, but also as an echo of Zoroaster's three sons who shall announce, with their successive births, one millennium after another, not only three different ages, but also the victory of God against evil.

The Adoration of the Magi is also discussed by **Felicity Harley**, whose paper 'Visual Apocrypha: the case of Mary and the Magi in early Christian Rome' is devoted to the analysis of early Christian representations of this account in Rome. Through this case-study she explores the following question: was the creation and reception of Biblical imagery in early Christian communities necessarily governed by texts? Harley submits that, from the outset, the relationship between text, contemporary visual culture and nascent Christian iconography was dialogical; while many images created by artists for early Christian viewers can be related to the written word, there are a variety of ways in which they might be thought of as elaborating beyond, and so working independently from, the written word in the expression of theological positions or devotional beliefs in the way that apocryphal textual traditions are seen to do. In this way, she proposes, images might be regarded as 'visual apocrypha', being calculated to provoke different responses from different viewers and to create meanings or interpretations which did not derive directly from a text.

To explore this idea, Harley draws upon various representations of Mary surviving from Rome, which were made before the œcumenical council of Ephesus of 431 (the council that endorsed Mary's title as 'God-bearer') and which express nascent devotion to Mary. The popularity of the scene of the Adoration in early Christian Rome elevated Mary to a position of especial prominence in that city. The author compares two elaborate sarcophagi from the beginning of the fourth century: one from Rome, known as the 'Dogmatic sarcophagus', and a second, very similar sarcophagus from Arles. The identical disposition of the figure of Mary on both, where she is directly juxtaposed with the figure of God the Father, demonstrates a deliberate emphasis on her role in the history of salvation. Mary is thus not merely depicted as a personage from the story of three Wise Men from the East but is celebrated for being the mother of the incarnate God, the role which, according to some scholars, even correlates her with the Creator himself.

Yishai Kiel, in his paper 'Gnostic and Mithraic Themes in *Sefer Zerubbabel*', examines the Book of Zerubbabel, a Jewish apocalypse which contains a reaction to the Christian account of Christ's Nativity. Admittedly, it was completed in the aftermath of the Sasanian conquest of Jerusalem in 614. This book reflects some unprecedented ideas in the history of post-Biblical Jewish thought regarding the expectation of the messiah. Unlike other ancient Jewish and Christian sources speaking of a suffering messiah, *Sefer Zerubbabel* uniquely speaks of a messiah imprisoned 'until the time of the end'. Kiel suggests that this account can be illuminated by recourse to the imprisonment of the Living Soul in the Manichæan tradition. He shows that the affinities of *Sefer Zerubbabel* with Sethian, Manichæan and Iranian Mithraic circles are especially perceptible in the birth story and the genealogy of 'Armilos, the Messiah's 'evil twin'. The author argues that the figure of 'Armilos, who is said to have emerged from a union of Beli'al with a rock possessing the shape of a beautiful virgin, can be illuminated by recourse to gnostic, particularly Sethian and

INTRODUCTION

Manichæan, traditions concerning the archons' seduction, or rape, of a virgin and the diabolic offspring which issued therefrom.

Part 4. The last six papers draw our attention to the angelic world, to heavenly journeys and to visions of Paradise. **David Hamidović**'s study, '1 Enoch 17 in the Geneva Papyrus 187', is devoted to a damaged Greek papyrus from Egypt deposited in the Library of Geneva. The author shows that the end of the document contains the description of Enoch's heavenly journey from *1 Enoch* 17. The preserved text reveals affinity to both the Greek fragments from Akhmîm and the known Ethiopic recensions of *1 Enoch*. However, the passage also presents many variants departing from these versions. Hamidović finds indices in the papyrus that allow him to hypothesise that the text which has reached us in the form of the Geneva papyrus originally represented another Greek recension of *1 Enoch* 17, different from the known Greek recension of the book in several nuances. The passage also sheds a new light on the process of translation from the Greek version(s) to the Ethiopian version(s) of the *Book of the Watchers*, i.e. the Vigilant Angels (*1 Enoch* 1–36). Finally, the text is embedded in a larger document which remains unidentified. Compared with the Akhmîm fragments, the Geneva papyrus may bring to us a collection of various autonomous texts intended to prove a religious message, most likely the hope of resurrection. It represents, therefore, another witness of a textual relocation of the *Book of the Watchers*.

Florentina Badalanova Geller, in her extensive article 'Enochic texts and related traditions in *Slavia Orthodoxa*', examines the relation of *2 Enoch* to *1 Enoch* in the Slavonic world. A lexicographical analysis allows her to conclude that the Slavonic scribes of *2 Enoch* knew *1 Enoch*. While in the *Book of the Watchers* the emphasis is put on the concept of illicit transmission of knowledge, especially associated with magic and divination, from heaven to earth, from angels to humans, in the case of *2 Enoch* the opposite concept predominates. Also, in *2 Enoch* the focal point is the disclosure of esoteric knowledge to a mortal man by angelic agency, but this time the revelation is endorsed by the Lord himself. It is not Enoch's decision to become an eyewitness of the mysteries of the universe; on the contrary, he is chosen by the Most High in order to become a recipient of divine wisdom, and to learn the eternal secrets unknown even to the angelic host. Enoch thus becomes the first visionary and recipient of the mystical experience endorsed by God. In contrast to the Watchers, who challenge God's commands and therefore fall, Enoch, thanks to his obedience, is granted angelic status. While Watchers descend from God's Throne to Earth, Enoch ascends from Earth to God's Throne. Not only are the divine secrets disclosed in his ascent, but he also becomes God's scribe.

Jewish apocalyptic themes, such as those of the books of Enoch or the ascent to heaven from the tradition of the *Merkabah*, i.e. 'the Divine chariot', were interiorised in various Christian traditions which sometimes 're-enacted' these themes in a different setting. **Emmanouela Grypeou**, in her paper 'Visions of Paradise in the Life of St Andrew the Fool and the Legacy of the Jewish Pseude-pigrapha in Byzantium', analyses the influence of para-Biblical writings that bear apocalyptic stamp, of both Jewish and Christian origin, on the later Byzantine visionary literature. The specific narrative frames of hagiographic writings, in particular, set the scenery and serve mainly as cultural indicators, yet they rarely ever significantly modify the major apocalyptic elements that they adopt. Grypeou observes that especially the descriptions of heavenly journeys and eschatological visions were often integrated in hagiographical accounts, such as the *Life of Andrew the Fool* which was composed, most likely, in the tenth century. Significantly, Andrew's ascent through the heavens on his way to the divine throne, the description of Paradise and the transformation of the visionary into an angel-like figure evoke specifically motifs from *2 Enoch*. Although we miss safe evidence regarding the textual transmission of this book, an eclectic use of various texts available in monastic libraries of the Byzantine Empire by respective authors cannot be ruled out.

The phenomenon of interiorization of pseudepigraphical literature is one of the reasons explaining the fact that it continued to be copied, translated and expanded, and especially on the Empire's periphery where the ecclesiastical control of the monastic scriptoria was looser. The interest in apocalyptic prophecies grew in Byzantium especially around the tenth century: that was the time preceding the advent of the middle of the seventh millennium since the creation of the world. The re-writing and expansion of apocalyptic material was part of a wider trend attested in the Byzantine literature around the tenth century. The broad use of apocalyptic traditions and their elaborate variations in hagiographical works nearly develops into a new hybrid genre which can be described as 'apocalyptic fiction'. These texts provided detailed and informative responses to popular anxieties, questions regarding heavenly mysteries and, more importantly, the fate of the soul after death.

Also related to the history of transmission of *1 Enoch* is **Yakir Paz**'s paper, 'Eternal Chains and the Mountain of Darkness. The Fallen Angels in the Incantation Bowls', in which he discusses the myth of the fallen angels. Paz takes into examination the bowls bearing Jewish Babylonian Aramaic, Mandaic and Christian Syriac inscriptions as well as magical texts found in Mesopotamia and Khuzestan. He shows that in the Sasanian Empire myths of fallen angels were shared by various religious communities. According to the bowl inscriptions, the sin of these angels consisted in revealing God's mysteries which had a magical character. This idea is close to that reflected in the *Book of the Watchers*, which claims that angels taught incantation to the human beings (*1 Enoch* 7. 1;

INTRODUCTION

9. 6), and in other early accounts of the fallen angels. According to Paz, these magical texts can thus be related to the Aramaic *Vorlage* of the books of Enoch, bringing to us echoes of the mental world in which, in particular, *1 Enoch* was shaped. Yet certain elements encountered, inscribed on the bowls and in kindred magical texts, are not present in the *Book of the Watchers*: thus, for their transgression the angels are punished in the mountain of darkness. The texts analysed by Paz shed light on the way in which ancient traditions concerning the fallen angels were received, re-elaborated and employed by the Aramaic-speaking minorities of the Sasanian Empire: Jews, Manichæans, Mandæans and Christians, supplying us with a missing link between the early Enochic literature and the later mediæval accounts of the fallen angels.

A different view on the angels is offered by **Cecilia Proverbio** whose paper, 'Iconography of Angels: Roots and Origins in the Earliest Christian art', is devoted to the evolution in the representation of angels that occurred in Christian iconography in course of the fourth–beginning of the fifth century. Early Christianity had adopted Jewish angelology, and no specific doctrine of the angels was developed in the Church of the Empire during the earliest centuries, because in Patristic thought the Angel, i.e. God's Messenger *par excellence*, was Christ. The words *mal'ak* in the Hebrew Bible and *angelos* in the Septuagint and the New Testament could simply stress the role of an ambassador or a messenger, which was attributed to various personages, both human and superhuman. The figures of angels, conceived of as God's supernatural emissaries, thus only appear on the margins of the Church Fathers' writings. They are perceived as subsidiary figures, existing only in order to accomplish in human reality the will of God himself.

No distinctive characterisation of the figures of angels can be found in the surviving Christian pictorial representations before the later part of the fourth century, even though the idea of winged angels in Christian thought is much older. Already at the end of the second century this idea was endorsed by Tertullian who suggested that thanks to their wings the angels can be ubiquitous. Nevertheless, in the third-century Christian art a necessity to differentiate the representations of angels and humans was not yet really felt. The appearance of the new iconographic pattern, while dependent on a number of apocryphal texts, has to be linked to the Christological controversies of the late fourth and the fifth century. Most of the surviving depictions of angels pertaining to this period express their alterity with regard to Christ, true God and true human being: their æthereal substance is expressed with the red colour and by means of the wings. According to John Chrysostom, their wings show the sublimity of the angels' nature; it is for this reason that Archangel Gabriel is portrayed winged, and not because angels should possess corporeal wings. The angels' wings indicate to the beholders that they leave the highest regions in order to draw near the human nature. The wings are, thus, the visible sign of the angels' capacity to provide a bridge between God and the material world.

A classic example of a bridge between protology and eschatology can be found in the visions and representations of the garden of Eden. **Zaruhi Hakobyan**, in her paper 'The Gardens of Eden: Compositional, Iconographic and Semantic Similarities between the 'Birds Mosaic' of the Armenian Chapel in Jerusalem and the Mosaic of the Synagogue at Ma'on (Nirim)', compares two sixth-century mosaics covering the pavements, respectively, of an Armenian chapel in Jerusalem and of the synagogue of Ma'on in Negev. These are but two of the series of twenty comparable mosaics that survive in the Holy Land and the adjacent regions; both are considered to belong to the Gaza school of mosaics. Hakobyan reveals surprising affinities between the two. Each contains a composition of vine scroll inhabited by birds and animals, which reflects the representations of the heavenly garden as depicted by both Jews and Christians. These elements have also been inherited by early Islamic art: we find inhabited vine scrolls in the mosaic of the Dome of the Rock, at the end of the seventh century, and in the Great Mosque of Damascus, at the beginning of the eighth century. According to the author, such representations derive from international artistic workshops active in late antique Palestine, which played an important role in the formation of diverse pictorial traditions, both Jewish and Christian, and which would then be introduced into Armenia and the South Caucasus. This implies that the ideas of Paradise inherited by three monotheistic religions in the Middle Ages owed much to the exchange of ideas that had occurred in the interreligious environment of the late antique land of Israel.

In Armenia, the image of an inhabited vine, informed by the Holy Land's artistic schools, is attested on a number of churches built between the end of the fifth and the middle of the seventh century, as well on other mediæval monuments. The most vivid examples can be found in the church of the Vigilant Heavenly Powers (652) built near the ancient Armenian capital of Vałaršapat (Ējmiacin) and in the palatine church of the Holy Cross on the island of Ałtamar (915–921) in Lake Van. These monuments show the enduring character of this iconography. At Ałtamar, the living beings of the vine scroll echo those to whom Adam gives names (Gen. 2. 20). Surrounded by them, Adam represents the thematic centre of the east façade, and probably of the entire church. He holds the memory of the Paradise lost. By turning to the east, whence the Saviour shall come at the end of time (Mal. 3. 20; LXX Zech. 3. 8; 6. 12; Mt. 24. 27; Lk. 1. 78–79), Adam prepares to present him the entire creation which expects his advent.

PART 1

Esoteric Writing and
Esoteric Cults in the Biblical Religions

∵

CHAPTER 1

The Exoteric Appearances of Jewish Esotericism

Ithamar Gruenwald

A

This article deals with the subject of esotericism which is often discussed in its literary, historical, and hermeneutical connections.[1] However, less has been said on the subject in the general context of the sociology and phenomenology of religious texts. Our point of departure in this discussion is the nature of extra-biblical texts that rewrite scripture, whether in an esoteric mode or not, and this in light of the prevalence of alternate versions of scriptural texts that are tolerated, and even held canonical, in Scripture itself. Those familiar with the documentary or source theory in biblical studies are likely to argue that different scriptural texts which relate to the same issue are explained by the use of different sources (whether E, P, J, D, or H) that relate to the same material. To those who are less familiar with the source or documentary theory, these duplicates appear to be rewritten versions with no specific orientation in regard to their source(s) or original nature.

There may be various degrees and purposes of rewriting. As indicated, they have been studied and assessed from various angles, mostly textual, literary, and interpretative. In any event, when rewritten texts appear on the extra-

---

1　This paper is written as an afterthought to M.E. Stone, *Secret Groups in Ancient Judaism*, Oxford, 2018. The book follows a programmatic article by the same author, 'Secret Groups in Ancient Judaism: Some Considerations', *Gazzada Lecture* (2015), pp. 1–29. The writer takes the position that modern scholarship should abandon the use of the adjective 'esoteric' for 'secret'. He argues, 'The adjective "esoteric" and the noun "esotericism" have long and complex histories. My own approach to them differs from that of many scholars, whose focus is on "Western esotericism" as it developed from the Renaissance down to modern times. For clarity's sake I shall first present my understanding of "esoteric" and then discuss the way the words "esoteric" and "esotericism" are used in the current study of Western Esotericism. I employ the adjective "esoteric" to refer to written or oral teaching, knowledge, or practice that is available only to a strictly delimited group in society, or to the group that transmits this special teaching. It is often uncovered or taught in stages to a person in the process of joining the said group. The same adjective "esoteric" may also describe a group in which secret or esoteric knowledge or practice is inculcated.' In the current article I shall outline my use of the terms. In this connection, see also I. Gruenwald, *Apocalyptic and Merkavah Mysticism*, 2nd, revised edn, Leiden, 2014, Chapter Two: 'Two Essential Qualities of Jewish Apocalyptic', pp. 44–67.

© ITHAMAR GRUENWALD, 2021 | DOI:10.1163/9789004445925_003

biblical, or post-biblical scene, they are likely, but not necessarily, considered as secret messages, whether or not linked to groups, and clearly not to the theory of biblical-sources.

A conspicuous example of this process is the way Deuteronomy tells the story of the twelve spies that were sent to explore the land of Canaan. Moses, who is the major speaker in the book, says: 'All of you came to me and said, "Let us send men ahead of us to explore the land for us and bring back a report to us regarding the route by which we should go up and the cities we will come to"' (Deuteronomy 1,22). The text to be compared is the one in Numbers 13,1–2: 'The Lord said to Moses: "Send men to spy out the land of Canaan ...".' Thus, it is not clear who initiated the sending out of the spies. Both versions of the story have canonical authority, though the one in Deuteronomy by literary definition belongs to a text that figures as the 'Mosaic' vision, or better revision, of the history of the Israelites. It can therefore be assumed that this version is the secondary one, and, in this respect, represents a rewritten form. Yet, the possibility still exists that these are two versions of separate 'Documents', D (Deuteronomy) and J (Numbers), and do not reflect a (mutually induced) process of rewriting.

Another and more complex example of what may be rewritten texts is found in the New Testament. It contains at least three texts (the Synoptic Gospels) that relate in their own specific ways and differences to the events that happened and shaped the rise of Christianity. It seems that the synoptic issues have seldom been discussed from the point of view of this dilemma: To what extent do the textual variants in the respective gospels reflect different sources or, as I would like to suggest here, an ongoing and deliberate process of *rewriting* of the relevant materials (i.e. the writings that are included in the Apocrypha and Pseudepigrapha)? One possible answer to this question is that both options are equally valid, though the one that highlights the factor of rewriting has not received the kind of attention it deserves.

In Judaism of post-biblical and pre-rabbinic times (third century BCE to second century CE), a considerable number of writings that relate to the Hebrew Scripture appeared on the religious scene. Many of them contain two parallel, complementary, features: interpretation and rewriting. These features are not necessarily self-exclusive; in fact, they may explore or show similar interests. In fact, both features entail the exposure of materials and layers of meaning that are not immediately accessible to the reader of Scripture. When they are labelled 'esoteric', they allegedly disclose secret information that is placed at a considerable distance from the plain sense of the scriptural text. They are group oriented: that is, allegedly they are addressed to a closed group of initiated people. Arguably, they are created within these groups, though an early version of them may have contributed to the creation of the relevant group.

Although esotericism is usually associated with secrecy, it may not always be connected to it. Essentially, it implies the exposure of layers of meaning and realization that have allegedly evaded the attention and knowledge of those who orient themselves by what in rabbinic hermeneutics is called the 'peshat' (plain sense) of Scripture. In other words, in relation to Scripture esotericism implies an expansionary attitude or dynamic. In its core is the latent sense of scriptural texts, which is exposed and usually warranted by an angelic revelation.

As indicated, the purpose of these writings may vary from interpretation to suggesting substitutes, which are often latently implied, to the scriptural text. They concern both poles of Scripture, historical narrative and Halakhah. A crucial problem that needs to be addressed in this connection is: what legitimized writings that position themselves outside the scriptural text and pertain to impose their content and meaning (and above all, behavioral or ritual stances) on the scriptural text? What gave them the kind of authority and prominence they received? Two matters had to be cleared before this could happen. The first concerns the question: where did the materials and ideas come from? Clearly, at their best, most of them were conceived as arising out of Scripture. The second concerns the question: are there other, non-scriptural, materials that found their way into these writings? Scholars have argued that much of the esoteric material came either from the Greek speaking, Hellenistic, world or from Mesopotamian sources. In the case of interpretation, hermeneutic principles of various kinds had to be worked out and applied. Rewriting also underpins the formation of the oral Halakhah.

However, we shall not deal with these questions here. Instead, we shall deal with another, more inclusive, question: What model did these writings follow, if there was one available? The major argument here is that processes of self-interpretation and rewriting are known from Scripture itself. Their appearance there on various levels of contextual configuration—whether narrative or ritual—prefigures later developments as they are found in post biblical writings.

A question which is still an open one, in this connection, is: what was the initial essence of the writings that today are labelled secret, or esoteric, and that were stimulated by sectarian motivations? 'Initial' in this connection means in the eyes of the authors or the group that was addressed. Another question that will be discussed in this connection is whether these post biblical writings represent secret groups or contribute to their formation. All these questions have been discussed in modern scholarship, and different answers and solutions have been given. In the present article a somewhat different approach will be put on the discussion table, in the hope that it will shed light on a rather tantalizing subject in the study of religions.

B

As indicated, the major argument in the present article is that esotericism is best described as a literary, ideologically framed, phenomenon connected with alternate, rewritten, versions of biblical materials.[2] A basic assumption in the case of esoteric interpretation is that a secret message is embedded in the biblical text under discussion. It is exposed either in a commentary or in a rewritten text. Whether it is configured as the ideology of a group, or simply as secret knowledge or information, what makes it esoteric, in my view, is the recognizable link to a scriptural text.

Furthermore, it is here argued that the beginning of the process of rewriting of scriptural materials is in Scripture itself. With time it evolved as an independent literary genre outside the canon. It is generally assumed that Jewish esoteric writings made their first appearance in what is called the post-biblical period: that is, during the Persian and Hellenistic occupation of the Land of Israel (the last centuries BCE) period. Seen from the inside, esoteric writings incline to justify themselves by imitating various modes of biblical inspiration and expression. Practically speaking, however, they defy essential components of canonicity, though, dialectically speaking, they may enhance the status of canonicity from the outside.

In its broad sense, canonical stands for the ultimate, sacred version of what has been authorized to be relevant to religious, normatively configured, knowledge and practice. In this respect, external additions have to seek ways to achieve canonical authority in quarters other than those in which scriptural canonicity evolves. However, the prevailing mood and tone in these matters are expected to follow the notion expressed in Deuteronomy 4,2: 'Do not add to what I command you and do not subtract from it'. In terms of its contents and meaning, Scripture strives to abide by the notion of closed texts and messages. However, paradoxically speaking, Deuteronomy, from which this saying is taken, is a classic example of a text that departs from earlier biblical texts and messages. Hence, scholars were right in characterizing it as a rewritten text.

To sum up, one may surmise that if Scripture itself tolerates alternate versions of the same story, one of the versions must have the status of a rewriting/rewritten one, whether it comes from another source or a divergent conceptual framework. This, it may be argued, as we do, is the preamble to the

---

2   In rabbinic writings of Talmudic times, secrecy (מסטורין) is sometimes attributed to the Torah itself and, hence, also to the Mishnah. For the Torah, see Bavli Shabbat 88a ('who revealed to my sons the secret applied by the ministering angels?'); for the Mishnah, see Tanchuma on Genesis 18,17.

THE EXOTERIC APPEARANCES OF JEWISH ESOTERICISM

process of rewriting known from post-biblical writings. It follows the relative freedom shown in handling alternate versions in Scripture. In other words, alternate versions of scriptural materials as they crystalize outside of Scripture are an expansion of this phenomenon as it occurs in Scripture. One may argue that alternate versions within Scripture may reflect or be the result of different world views, traditions, or religious groupings. Their presence in scripture expands and changes the textual layout of Scripture. They imbue the Scriptural text with new information, ideas, and rulings. In this respect, they are likely to reflect, project, and even bring into being heterodox views and groups.

C

The process of creating alternate versions is often viewed in the context of a hermeneutic enterprise: that is, it claims to fulfil interpretive purposes. However, the processes of creating such versions of a rewritten scripture need not necessarily fulfil hermeneutical tasks. They may have all kinds of purposes, such as attempting to shape new religious identity or laying out guidelines for heterogeneous forms of religious development and behavior.[3] Since, as indicated above, scriptural texts are sealed by notions of divinely inspired revelation, allegedly only an additional revelation can replace an earlier one. This is particularly true of biblical texts that are revised or rewritten in an external, post-biblical, that is, extra-canonical context and setting. They require a new revelatory setting. In any event, several factors must be taken into consideration before the boundaries around scriptural texts can be relaxed, or even lifted, and they can be prepared to undergo revision and rewriting.

Such revelations, in which angels play a major role, often suggest themselves as conveying a secret message, which allegedly contains the true (or specifically relevant) vision and meaning of the scriptural text. Often, this meaning points to future events not foreseen in the scriptural text. Regarding Scripture, it is open to speculation which is the main and which the alternate text. The alternate text is placed on top of the first one (the one that is rewritten). Whether it aims at totally removing the first one or suggests a literary substitute is an open question. However, in my opinion, the essence of esotericism lies in the fact that a new, allegedly divinely inspired, text suggests itself as the ultimate ve-

---

3 See M.R. Niehoff, 'Commentary Culture in the Land of Israel from an Alexandrian Perspective', *DSD* 19/3 (2012), pp. 442–463.

rsion of the truth. If this claim to truth cannot be taken seriously, what is the point in making it, radical as its contents may be?

One should note, though, that the word 'esoteric' derives from the Greek ἐσωτηρικός, secret or belonging to a secret (Stoic or Pythagorean) group. It should not be confused with the Greek μυστήριον, which Liddell & Scott define in *Greek-English Lexicon* (p. 1156) as 'secret revealed by God, i.e. religious or mystical truth'. In practice, 'mysterion' is a common Greek equivalent of the Hebrew/Aramaic רז (from the Middle Persian *raz*), and serves mainly in a religious context that presupposes certain rites of initiation. Two famous examples in this respect are the Dead Sea Sectarians and mystical groups in medieval Germany and Spain, the Ḥasidei Ashkenaz and the Kabbalists, respectively. In their writings רז and its Hebrew parallel, סוד, indicate a message shared by initiated groups.

A notable occurrence of the term רז is in the Aramaic part of Daniel. Daniel is approached by King Nebuchadnezzar to interpret an enigmatic dream vision that plagued his mind. Among other things he praises Belshazzar/Daniel in that 'no mystery (רז) escapes the expertise of his mind'. The translation of *raz* as 'mystery' derives from the Greek translation of the book. The term 'esoteric' is more commonly used in a philosophical context, and is group oriented. In other words, by definition, it fits writings that are addressed by, or create, texts that shape social and ideological identity, often presupposing, as indicated, an act of ritually consecrated initiation into a group. In this respect, when not used in relation to a scriptural text, the frequently-used term in the Qumran writings, רז, indicates 'mysterion' rather than the more technical 'esoteric'.

In my view, then, what makes the alternate versions of post-scriptural texts possible is the fact that scripture itself contains and tolerates alternate versions of stories and other materials. In spite of the fact that in many cases duplicates and variants in the Pentateuchal text are attributed by biblical scholars to 'sources' and textual schools (P, E, J, D, H), the reader in antiquity could hardly be aware of them. Hence, although the notion of *rewriting* was not prevalent in those days, the impact of these 'parallel' texts and what they implied could not escape particularly the minds of those who saw in them precedents for their own literary activity. It should be noted, though, that the literary duplicates in Scripture, with all the differences and changes that they entail, are not presented as being motivated by an esoteric drive or presented as uncovering a secret version or layer of meaning in the relevant texts. Furthermore, there is no indication whatsoever in these scriptural duplicates which makes them a voice-piece of a secret or esoteric group.

A notable, and often-discussed example of this phenomenon are the two versions of the creation story (Genesis 1 and 2; E/P and J, respectively). Another

THE EXOTERIC APPEARANCES OF JEWISH ESOTERICISM

striking example of two alternate versions of the same story is the story of the Great Flood. In Genesis 6 Elohim tells Noah: 'And of every living thing, of all flesh, you shall bring two of every kind into the ark, to keep them alive with you; they shall be male and female. [20] Of the birds according to their kinds, and of the animals according to their kinds, of every creeping thing of the ground according to its kind, two of every kind shall come in to you, to keep them alive.' In chapter 7 it is Yahweh who says: 'Take with you seven pairs of all clean animals, the male and its mate; and a pair of the animals that are not clean, the male and its mate; [3] and seven pairs of the birds of the air also, male and female, to keep their kind alive on the face of all the earth. [4] For in seven days I will send rain on the earth ...'. The differences between the two passages are clear. They constitute alternate versions of the same story. In a sense, they are a show case for what to outsiders may look like a striking permission to rewrite a Scriptural text. Which of the two texts rewrites the other is not clear, though the final editor of the Genesis text preferred to put that of J second to that of E.

Another example, which is equally relevant to our discussion, are the two versions of the revelation on Mount Sinai, including the two versions of the Decalogue (Exodus 19–20; Deuteronomy 4–6). We shall soon refer to them in greater detail, and this in connection with the Book of Jubilees, which is a classic example of rewriting a text.

Ultimately, these alternate versions create a dynamic that culminates in what may be viewed as a literary style. Typical of this style are versions which claim to substitute for, and even supersede, the scriptural materials to which they relate. They often come in unique, mostly divine or angel-induced, modes of revelation. In other words, it is the experiential setting that enhances the status of the new writings as a re-written Scripture. For reasons that need not be discussed here, these writings were collected in what became known as the Apocrypha and Pseudepigrapha of Scripture, and in Hebrew ספרים חיצונים.

D

As already mentioned, a unique and often discussed example of the rewriting of Scripture, though in a post-biblical setting, is the Book of Jubilees. Jubilees rewrites an interesting selection of the Pentateuch story from the creation of the world until the revelation on Mount Sinai. Notably, to announce its status the book begins with a unique version of what happened when Moses ascended Mount Sinai to receive the Torah from God. Accordingly, the introductory section of the book contains programmatic statements and informative utterances about the remodelled or experienced setting of the Sinai event and defines the purpose and plan of the book, and hence, by implication, of the whole Pentateuch mode of messaging. It does so while changing important details in the information that is included in Scripture, thus presenting a new version of the events.

Unlike rabbinic interpretations of Scripture, which link and stick to specific words, expressions and verses, the Book of Jubilees substantially reshapes and changes the narrative layout and particularly the information concerning Moses on the 'Mountain' (Ex. 19,3; 24,1). The result finds its expression in a complete revision of the relevant biblical stories in the Book of Genesis and Exodus. Thus, the question cannot be avoided, what entitled the writer to change the story, almost provocatively disregarding the textual evidence of Scripture? In my view, to assess the special characteristics of Jubilees a distinction must be maintained between interpretation and rewriting. Obviously, there is an element of rewriting in every interpretation, and every interpretation carries with it potentials of rewriting. However, interpretation pertains to be at the service of the verbal evidence and keeps it in its place, while rewriting shows a strong element of supersession vis-à-vis the scriptural text and its messages. In fact, rewriting entails a deliberate departure from the biblical text. It may pose as following it, but it does so in overwriting it.

Clearly, Jubilees does rewriting and, if it contains significant interpretative elements, they crystallize within the rewritten context of the book. However, as indicated above, the very fact that scriptural materials may have two exchangeable versions brings up the question whether each diverging version signals the presence of an interpretative œuvre, or, by definition, entails a more radical procedure, that of rewriting? In my view, if it does not entail a fully-fledged act of rewriting it does not fall far short of it.

A further question that needs to be addressed in this connection is whether Jubilees belongs to the realm of writings that have a secret, esoteric, message or whether it simply fulfils a literary function: that of rewriting. The answer to the question is not simple, since there is no explicit indication of secrecy in the book. However, if one can rely on the textual reconstruction of the Hebrew fragments of Jubilees which were found in the caves of Qumran, then the answer to the question is likely to be positive. The combination of תורה and תעודה found several times in the opening chapter and other sections of the book may designate an element of secrecy. Admittedly, the word used in Gəʿəz, *kûfâlê*, indicates 'covenant'.[4] The word תעודה is rarely found in Scripture (see particu-

---

4 There are several scholarly discussions, many of them in Hebrew. See, particularly, Michael Segal's discussion of these terms in *Megilot* 5–6 (2008), pp. 323–345.

THE EXOTERIC APPEARANCES OF JEWISH ESOTERICISM 37

larly Isaiah 8,16 and 20), and its context may indicate a notion of sealing and secrecy: צוֹר תְּעוּדָה חֲתוֹם תּוֹרָה בְּלִמֻּדָי (Bind up the testimony, seal the teaching among my disciples). In this sense, Jubilees may be viewed in the context of esoteric writings.

The same problem arises in regard to the adjacent but more radical text of the Temple Scroll. It contains many drastic changes of rulings that concern the priestly worship in the temple, and significantly adds to the ritual calendar that allegedly used to prevail there. However, with all its drastic changes it does not openly profess an esoteric position. In any event, space limits prevent us from a full-scale discussion of the Temple Scroll, this in spite of the fact that the degree of rewriting applied in it is really outstanding and drastic, and is much more group oriented than in Jubilees. Jubilees claims to address the whole nation, while the Temple Scroll concerns what seems to be a fraction of the priestly order.

In any event, the important fact is that the process of rewriting relaxes the tightly closed fence around the verisimilitude of scriptural reports and the normative status of the relevant scriptural materials. Initially, such changes can happen only within a scriptural framework. Thus, for instance, the ascent of Moses is not explicitly mentioned in the version in Deuteronomy, though in 9,12–15 Moses mentions the circumstances that forced him to descend from the Mountain.[5] Deuteronomy briefly mentions that alongside the stone tablets (with its divergent wording of the commandments) Moses at once gave laws and ordinances to the People of Israel (Deuteronomy 4,1; 5,1; 6,1). Exodus, however, repeatedly mentions the ascent in detail and in rewritten forms (Exodus 19, 24, 32–33). The additional laws are mentioned as a separate event (Exodus 21–23). Jubilees seems to build on these differences, but creates a new version of the details fitting its special purposes.

Thus, the opening sections of the Book of Jubilees tell that on Mount Sinai Moses received information about the future of the People of Israel. What is important for our discussion is the fact that, according to Jubilees, after Moses had received the stone tablets, God told him to write the new information in a book form. As indicated above, this is not in line with the information contained in either Exodus or Deuteronomy. Equally noteworthy is the date fixed by Jubilees for that event: the sixteenth of the third month (beginning the monthly count from Nissan, which is typical of calendric calculations in similar writings). To some readers, this procedure may seem to be part of a process

---

5   It is noteworthy that in Deuteronomy 3,27 God tells Moses to ascend to the top of a mountain and to look around and see the land to which he was prevented from entering. The sequence of the story in Deuteronomy is interesting, because the Sinai event follows this one.

of updating the biblical story, making it relevant to the annual calendar of the people to whom Jubilees addressed its messages, and to their ritual lifestyle.[6] As indicated, the general orientation of the information mostly concerns the eschatological future of the People of Israel. Once again the question arises: is all this contained within an interpretive œuvre or does it extend to the domain of rewriting?

Whether the new version of Jubilees was considered 'holy' or 'authorized' and served religious purposes, such as the ritual reading and study of the Torah and, even more importantly, the shaping and practice of its new rulings, remains an open question. Whatever the answer to this question, the book form of the new messages in Jubilees makes a significant difference. Scripture mentions no such 'book' to which the Book of Jubilees could connect. A 'Book of the Covenant' is mentioned, however with no specifications, in Exodus 24,7 (and in Deuteronomy 28,69, but not in direct connection with the Sinai event).[7] Although it is not clear what this 'Book of the Covenant' was or to what it specifically related, it is quite likely that it could give rise to a book like that of Jubilees.

E

Notwithstanding the above, a notable indication in Jubilees, though, may be interpreted as pointing in the direction of a secret message without specifically considering the presence of any specific group. Jubilees 1,1 mentions 'the two tables of stone, the Law (Torah) and the commandments', which God intends to give to Moses. In an ensuing comment Jubilees says that God taught Moses 'the divisions of times concerning the Law and the testimony'. As indicated above, the formulaic reference to 'Law and Testimony' very likely designates the duplicate Torah as incorporated in Jubilees. It constitutes the predestined historical program and several other new messages.[8] According to Jubilees, everything

---

6 This might well be the solar calendar of a year consisting of 364 days.

7 See also Exodus 34,27–28: 'The LORD said to Moses: Write these words; in accordance with these words I have made a covenant with you and with Israel. He was there with the LORD forty days and forty nights; he neither ate bread nor drank water. And he wrote on the tablets the words of the covenant, the Ten Commandments.'

8 With all its vagueness, it is worth examining this historical programme, as outlined by the Angel of the Countenance. Essentially, it is a divinely predestined (I prefer this term to '[(pre) determined']) programme. It stretches 'from the time of the creation, of the law and of the testimony of the weeks of the jubilees, according to the individual years, according to all the number of the jubilees according to the individual years, from the day of the [new] creation when the heavens and the earth shall be renewed and all their creation according to the powers of the heaven, and according to all the creation of the earth, until the sanctuary

THE EXOTERIC APPEARANCES OF JEWISH ESOTERICISM 39

that happens in the history of the world is preordained and written on the Heavenly Tablets.[9] This information lacks the specific designation of secrecy but may imply the notion of esotericism. That is, it is a newly revealed text which relates to a previous scriptural text. In other words, it contains the notion of an alternate text which, and this is the crucial point here, relates to a different scriptural corpus from the one that already had the status of canonicity. Its authority derives from a new divinely inspired revelation, which means that the relevant scriptural text had a normative status and that the new text apparently aimed to challenge its initial exclusiveness.

As indicated, at first God tells Moses to write His words 'in a book'. This book contains the covenant between God and the People.[10] Then God empowers an angel, referred to in apocalyptic and early mystical writings as the Minister of the Countenance (שר הפנים), to give Moses the information concerning the future history of the People of Israel. Angelic revelations are an essential part of writings that rewrite or substitute Scripture, mostly with a vision towards the future. This history is presented retrospectively by the writer of Jubilees from the days of the creation of the world, through the patriarchal period to the Sinai event, and from there into the future, whether the one recorded in Scripture or in a post-biblical provenance.

All this involves a massive rewriting of the biblical story as outlined in Genesis and Exodus. It may be viewed as reflecting the kind of literary style that characterizes Deuteronomy. It changes messages and links them to other spheres of reference, meaning, and existence. In other words, the major factor that shapes the style and content of Jubilees is in several respects similar to that applied in Deuteronomy: namely, the almost uninhibited rewriting of scriptural data. However, the manner in which Jubilees uses this factor places its materials in more radical settings than the rewritten ones found in Scripture. It wells out of the scriptural story, as its hidden content, and in essential respects replaces it.

Jubilees not only qualifies for the domain of esoteric literature but in many respects shapes esotericism (reflected in the existence of alternate versions of scriptural texts, allegedly revealed by angels). This Book is a unique specimen of a writing that rewrites a previous canonical writing. Its author claims to be enti-

---

of the Lord shall be made in Jerusalem on Mount Zion, and all the luminaries be renewed for healing and for peace and for blessing for all the elect of Israel, and that thus it may be from that day and unto all the days of the earth.'

9   For the proliferation of this idea in the Ancient Near East, see S.M. Paul, 'Heavenly Tablets and the Book of Life', *Journal of Near Eastern Studies* 5 (1973), pp. 345–354. See further F.G. Martinez, *Between Philology and Theology: Contributions to the Study of Ancient Jewish Interpretation*, Leiden, 2012, pp. 49–69: 'The Heavenly Tablets in the Book of Jubilees'.

10 Compare Exodus 34,27: 'Then the Lord said to Moses: "Write down these words, for in accordance with these words I have made a covenant with you and Israel"'.

tled to replace the original writing found in Scripture by way of exposing hitherto unknown layers of information, knowledge and meaning. In this connection, it can create a superstructure with eschatological dimensions. Formally speaking, it can be aligned with the tradition of books received by Adam, Seth and other primæval beings, though in matters of narrative and content these books address different issues. In other words, during second temple times and thereafter, a corpus of writings became known in which current events are addressed in a context that supersedes that of Scripture. In any event, these books are identified by their unique self-attribution to various biblical figures.

In a way, rewriting Scripture is tantamount to tampering with the original text written by divine command. As mentioned, angels are reported as playing an active part not only in the process of rewriting but also in the central events described in the rewritten text. Rewriting the scriptural text may involve crucial changes in the text and its layout, whether they seek to establish a special system of calendric calculations, a new system of halakhic rulings, or any other kind of modification, as outlined in Jubilees and particularly in the Temple scroll. Furthermore, a new calendric principle is established and contributes to the shaping of the chronology of the world in units of seven times seven weeks of years (i.e. 49 years) that mark a Jubilee. It calibrates the historical setting of the world in a ritual scheme that elsewhere in Scripture has not received the kind of significant role it has in Jubilees. Other changes, in which the details of the biblical story are retold, endow the Book of Jubilees with its unique characteristics.

In many ways, the new features of the historical paradigm as outlined in Jubilees spread over to a wide range of documents that in one way or another rewrite Scripture. Notable examples are the Books of Enoch, 4 Ezra and the Book of Baruch. A major component in these writings is the way in which they conceive the foreseeable future. The future as foreseen in Scripture is confined to imminent events. In its rewritten format the future is substantially stretched to include eschatological times and events. Furthermore, the rewritten program of the future includes events that are often linked to the coming of a messianic, or saviour, figure. In many respects, this kind of vision of the future is conceived in terms that are labeled 'apocalyptic': that is, catastrophic events that entail the total destruction of the prevailing order in every respect possible, whether political, natural or personal.

Most important in this respect are the Halakhic sections in the book. However, since they have been the subject of several studies, also from the points of view of rewriting and the prevalence of comparative materials, we can skip detailed discussion of them here. It should be remarked, though, that ritual changes which are part of the process of rewriting have a stronger impact on religious behaviour and processes of social grouping than do those that

THE EXOTERIC APPEARANCES OF JEWISH ESOTERICISM 41

develop along interpretive lines. However, in accordance with our view of the subject, we must point to the fact that changes in ritual prescription are also prevalent in Scripture. A notable example is Nehemiah 8, which reports two religious festivals—*Rosh Ha-Shanah* (New Year Day) and *Succoth* (Feast of Tabernacles)—that are completely remodelled during the events connected with the re-institution of the Torah in the days of Ezra the Scribe.

Another aspect of this remodelling shows up in the way Jubilees treats biblical issues which have ritual consequences. Specifically, Jubilees presents rituals connected to annual cultic subjects and religious festivals in the Jewish calendar as part of the life of the patriarchs or events that happened in their life-time. These events and their ritual consequences are pre-dated to pre-Sinai days. These changes led to theories about the socio-religious provenance of the book. Generally, a second temple priestly offshoot is considered the 'home' of the book. However, no sectarian characteristics, such as those reported, for instance in relation to the Dead-Sea *Yaḥad/'Edah*, are found in Jubilees.[11]

In this connection it should be noted that scholars debate the authorship and the provenance of its source material and the literary unity of Jubilees. If it derives its materials from various sources and shows considerable differences in its own presentation of these materials, then Jubilees can hardly reflect the spirit of an organized, albeit secret, group. Only its edited version, in as much as it was known in the days of the Second Temple, could reflect the life-style of a group, whether dissident or sectarian.

F

In summary, with all its literary and conceptual peculiarities, Jubilees does not present itself as a secret revelation. On the contrary, it tells its story in a matter-of-fact manner, without any excuse or explanation of its departure from the scriptural story. It does not assume the mode of secrecy to justify its position over against Scripture. One wonders what the writer expected of his readers. Did he expect them to believe that he had unearthed a new version of the biblical story? Or, and this seems to me to be more likely, did he wish them to follow Samuel Taylor Coleridge (*Biographia Literaria*, 1817, Chapter XIV), centuries later and under different circumstances, who advised his readers 'to procure for these shadows of imagination that willing suspension of disbelief for the

---

11   The first systematic study of the halakhic materials in the book is that of C. Albeck, *Das Buch der Jubiläen und die Halacha*, Berlin, 1930, Hebrew translation: *Jewish Studies (Mada'ey Ha-Yahadut)* 45 (2008), pp. 3–48.

moment'? Admittedly, Jubilees is by no means a 'shadow of the imagination' in any negative sense that the term may invoke. For Coleridge 'imagination' stood for a high and intense degree of creativity, and more so, of being: 'The primary imagination I hold to be the living Power and prime Agent of all human perception, and as a repetition in the finite mind of the eternal act of creation in the infinite I AM.'

In other words, literary productions of this kind do not have to stand the normal test of verisimilitude. They stand by their own, self-declared, creative right and status. Their line of argument qualifies for what is considered the subjective, artistic aspect of religious creativity. However, in the case of religious revelation one expects the information to be objectively valid and true. Thus, the question remains: what status can writings like Jubilees claim for themselves as against a corpus of writings that has gained canonical status?

Since the book was not accepted into the rabbinic canon, it did not reach beyond the outskirts of its confined messages and addressees. Thus, it remained within the limits of an unidentified hosting group, though some indications can now be found in the location in which the Hebrew fragments of the book were found, that is, the caves of the 'Qumran' and the community that lived there. However, there is little in Jubilees that aligns with the rigorist style, divisive ideology and the daily ritual manual of the Qumran community.[12] What does this suggest for the role of Jubilees in Qumran? Its presence in the Community could be due to the fact that it confirms the layout of the kind of calendar which prevailed among the people of that Community.

To wind up our discussion, one may ask: was the choice of the Book of Jubilees justified in the context of the subject matter? Jubilees does not deal with the secrets of the world and its (mostly future) history. However, it juxtaposes an alternate version, hitherto unknown, of scriptural events. In some eyes, this version could figure as a latent version of the biblical text to which Jubilees relates. In its very appearance, the book may signal that it contains the true version of the scriptural story, or its inherent truth. In many instances, like the creation story, the patriarchal stories, and the events on Mount Sinai, Jubilees supersedes Scripture. In the sense that the book pertains to put on record new layers of the revelation that relate to scriptural narrative and information, its essence is esoteric. Of course, there are other forms of esoteric revelations, but in Judaism they all relate to scriptural precedents.

---

12   See C. Werman, *The Book of Jubilees: Introduction, Translation, and Interpretation*, Jerusalem, 2015, who discusses this issue in some detail.

CHAPTER 2

The *Gospel of Peter* between the Synoptics, Second Century, and Late Antique 'Apostolic Memoirs'

Tobias Nicklas

In the years 1892 and 1893, when the first, quickly written, partial editions of the Petrine apocrypha from the so-called Akhmim-Codex were published,[1] it was commonly presupposed that the fragmentary story about Jesus's (or better: the Lord's[2]) passion and resurrection preserved in this codex was part of the *Gospel of Peter* known from a few passages of ancient Christian literature.[3] The reasons for this seemed quite clear. First, the final sentence of the fragment presents itself as a story narrated by the apostle Peter[4] and, second, the overall outlook and storyline resemble the Gospels that we know from the New Testament. This led to the assumption that the newly discovered text could be understood

---

1   See, for example, U. Bouriant, *Fragments grecs du Livre d'Énoch* (MMAF 9.1), Paris, 1892, pp. 93–147; O. von Gebhardt, *Das Evangelium und die Apokalypse des Petrus. Die neuentdeckten Bruchstücke nach einer Photographie der Handschrift zu Gizéh in Lichtdruck herausgegeben*, Leipzig, 1893; A. Harnack, *Bruchstücke des Evangeliums und der Apokalypse des Petrus* (TU 9.2), Leipzig, 1893; A. Lods, *L'Évangile et l'Apocalypse de Pierre avec texte grec du livre d'Henoch. Text publié et facsimilé, par l'héliogravure d'après les photographies du manuscrit de Gizéh* (MMAF IX.3), Paris, 1893; J.A. Robinson and M.R. James, *The Gospel of Peter, and the Revelation of Peter. Two Lectures on the Newly Discovered Fragments Together with the Greek Texts*, London, 1892; H. von Schubert, *Das Petrusevangelium. Synoptische Tabelle nebst Übersetzung und kritischem Apparat*, Berlin, 1893, H.B. Swete, *The Apocryphal Gospel of Peter: The Greek Text of the Newly Discovered Fragment*, London, 1893, and T. Zahn, *Das Evangelium des Petrus: Das kürzlich gefundene Fragment seines Textes*, Erlangen–Leipzig, 1893. For an overview of the early history of research on the Gospel of Peter see P. Foster, 'The Discovery and Initial Reaction to the So-Called Gospel of Peter', in T.J. Kraus and T. Nicklas (eds), *Das Evangelium nach Petrus. Text, Kontexte, Intertexte* (TU 158), Berlin–New York, 2007, pp. 9–30.

2   The text never mentions Jesus by name, but it is clear that it refers to him by calling him 'the Lord'.

3   Several ancient Christian authors mention a *Gospel of Peter*, but never quote it. For an overview see T.J. Kraus and T. Nicklas, *Das Petrusevangelium und die Petrusapokalypse: Die griechischen Fragmente mit deutscher und englischer Übersetzung* (GCS NF 11; Neutestamentliche Apokryphen I), Berlin–New York, 2004, pp. 11–23.

4   See *GosPet* 60, 'But I, Simon Peter, and my brother Andrew took our nets and went to the sea. And there was with us Leueis, the son of Alphaios, whom the Lord ...' English translations of the *GosPet* according to Kraus and Nicklas, *Petrusevangelium und Petrusapokalypse*, pp. 50–53.

© TOBIAS NICKLAS, 2021 | DOI:10.1163/9789004445925_004

as a Petrine Gospel or a *Gospel of Peter*. As ancient Christian authors of the pre-Constantinian period knew of only one *Gospel of Peter*, the text from the Akhmim-Codex was identified as part of that *Gospel of Peter*. This assumption persisted despite the fact that the manuscript was soon dated to a time much later than the witnesses given by the ancient Fathers,[5] and even though the fragment itself does not transmit the title of its text.[6]

This misidentification has been crucial for many important aspects of the later history of research on this writing:

(1) The earliest undisputable witness of a *Gospel of Peter* goes back to Serapion, the late second and early third century bishop of Antioch (190–209 CE), who got to know the *Gospel of Peter* on a journey to the Christian community of Rhossus. When the community asked him whether they were allowed to read this Gospel, he first agreed. Only later, in Antioch, when he learned that this text was used by 'docetists,' he rejected it (see Eusebius, *Historia Ecclesiae* VI 12,1–6).[7] Because Serapion connected the *Gospel of Peter* to docetic teachings, the identification of the Akhmim fragment with Serapion's *Gospel of Peter* led to a broad discussion about the Akhmim fragment's possible docetic character. The results of this, however, are rather meager: the only two passages that could be understood as 'docetic,' at least in a broad sense of the word, can be found in vv. 10b and 19. While v. 10b (αὐτὸς δὲ ἐσίωπα ὡς μηδένα πόνον ἔχων) could be translated as 'he [the Lord] was silent *because* he felt no pain,' a (non-docetic) meaning like 'he was silent *as if* he felt no pain' is much more probable.[8] According to v. 19, the 'Lord' dies with the words 'My power, power, you have forsaken me' (ἡ δύναμίς μου, ἡ δύναμίς μου, κατέλειψάς

---

5   While parts of the secondary literature still offer dates like 8th or 9th century, the Akhmim codex is now palæographically dated to the 6th or early 7th century CE. See Kraus and Nicklas, *Petrusevangelium und Petrusapokalypse*, p. 29: '*Summa summarum* sind damit Früh- wie Spätdatierungen (vom vierten bis zum 12. Jahrhundert) abzuweisen, das vielfach angesetzte achte oder neunte Jahrhundert auf das späte sechste bzw. hinsichtlich der Zusammenstellung zum vorliegenden Codex das frühe siebte Jahrhundert zu korrigieren.'

6   This is a problem of the (otherwise very helpful) edition by D. Lührmann (ed.), *Fragmente apokryph gewordener Evangelien in griechischer und lateinischer Sprache* (Marburger Theologische Studien 59), Marburg, 2000, pp. 72–95, esp. 93, who offers an (alleged) title of the text after his transcription, and, thus, creates the impression that this title is part of the manuscript.

7   For text and discussion see shortly Kraus and Nicklas, *Petrusevangelium und Petrusapokalypse*, pp. 12–16, and, more detailed, É. Junod, 'Eusèbe de Césarée, Sérapion d'Antioche et l'Évangile de Pierre. D'un évangile d'un pseudepigraphe', *RSLR* 24 (1988), pp. 3–16.

8   See also P. Foster, *The Gospel of Peter. Introduction, Critical Edition and Commentary* (TENT 4), Leiden–Boston, 2010, p. 284, who translates, 'he was silent as though having no pain'.

THE GOSPEL OF PETER

με),[9] and afterwards 'is taken up' (ἀνελήφθη).[10] But this does not necessarily mean that a divine power had entered Jesus's human body (or even that a divine power had taken on human appearance) beforehand and was now taken up to heaven again. Instead, even at the moment when his power leaves him, Jesus remains the 'Lord.' And this is not the only argument against the text's alleged docetism. Indeed, the surviving text is very interested in many aspects of Jesus's body. According to v. 21, for example, even the Lord's dead body causes an earthquake when it touches the ground. Furthermore, vv. 39–40 describe Jesus's bodily resurrection much more directly and intensely than any canonical writing. All this led to the assumption that at least the Akhmim text could not be called 'docetic.'[11] On the contrary, the text can be compared to ancient descriptions of martyrdom, and thus describes Jesus like a suffering martyr.[12] Does this mean that Serapion's text differed from the Akhmim fragment (perhaps, even to the extent that it referred to a completely different writing)? Or, does our idea of 'docetism' differ from Serapion's? Or else, did Serapion's 'docetists' use the same or a comparable text, but understand it differently? We cannot, and should not, be too certain about our answers.

---

9   For a good interpretation of the passage see T. Hieke, 'Das Petrusevangelium vom Alten Testament her gelesen. Gewinnbringende Lektüre eines nicht-kanonischen Textes vom christlichen Kanon her', in T.J. Kraus and T. Nicklas (eds), *Das Evangelium nach Petrus. Text, Kontexte, Intertexte* (TU 158), Berlin–New York, 2007, pp. 91–115, esp. 106: 'Der Text hat kein Interesse daran, auch nur den Anschein aufkommen zu lassen, *Gott* hätte den *Kyrios* verlassen. Daher ist die 'Kraft' an dieser Stelle auch nicht ein Äquivalent für Gott, sondern die Kraft des Herrn (Jesus), die Wunderwerke bewirkt, wie sie so oft im Neuen Testament beschrieben werden ... Sie ist es auch, die bewirkt, dass der Herr im EvPetr trotz der Schmerzen schweigen kann—und erst, wenn diese Kraft ihn verlassen hat, kann er sterben.' For a comparable view see also M.G. Mara, *Il Vangelo di Pietro. Introduzione, Versione, Commento* (Scritti delle origini cristiane 30), Bologna, 2003, p. 71.

10   See, again, T. Hieke, 'Petrusevangelium', p. 107: 'Im Moment des Sterbens des Herrn vermeidet das EvPetr einen direkten Ausdruck für Tod oder Sterben und greift auf einen biblischen Terminus bzw. ein biblisches Motiv zurück: die Entrückung des Gerechten.'

11   In the most recent discussion of early Christian docetism, the *Gospel of Peter* plays only a marginal role. See, for example, the few sentences by A.C. Stewart, 'Ignatius' "Docetists": A Survey of Opinions and Some Modest Suggestions', in J. Verheyden et al. (eds), *Docetism in the Early Church: The Quest for an Elusive Phenomenon* (WUNT 402), Tübingen, 2018, pp. 143–174, esp. 157–158.

12   For a detailed argument see T. Nicklas, 'Die Leiblichkeit der Gepeinigten: Das *Evangelium nach Petrus* und frühchristliche Märtyrerakten', in J. Leemans (ed.), *Martyrdom and Persecution in Late Antique Christianity. Festschrift Boudewijn Dehandschutter* (BETL 241), Leuven et al., 2010, pp. 195–219.

(2) A second, perhaps a less spectacular, result of the identification of the Akhmim fragment with Serapion's *Gospel of Peter* was that the Akhmim account was understood as a *Gospel* without any further discussion of what this might concretely mean. At first glance, this may look like a rather unimportant matter, but at least in the case of Léon Vaganay's influential commentary, the identification of the Akhmim fragment as a gospel was an argument (and perhaps the decisive argument) against Montague Rhodes James's idea that the two Petrine fragments in the Akhmim codex could belong together.[13] James's argument is not bad: indeed, the two fragments reveal several striking similarities. For example, in both cases the story is told by Peter, and both stories are interested in bodily resurrection and even share linguistic details.[14] In Vaganay's commentary, however, there is not even a discussion whether, and how far, Akhmim 1 (usually '*Gospel of Peter*') and Akhmim 2 (usually '*Apocalypse of Peter*') might belong together. Yet, Akhmim 2 is only close to what we know elsewhere from the *Apocalypse of Peter* (otherwise known from a few Greek fragments and a full Ethiopic version), but is by no means identical to the latter. Wouldn't it be possible that Akhmim 2, as a revised passage from another version of the *Apocalypse of Peter*, was at a certain stage incorporated into what we call the *Gospel of Peter*? What if the whole combination was never intended to be a *gospel*, as Vaganay would have it, but rather a story relating to Jesus, the Apostles, and their visions of the afterlife, as told by Peter?

(3) The idea that Akhmim 1 presents a *Gospel of Peter*, which because of Serapion's (and perhaps a few other authors') witness cannot be dated later than the second century, opened the question of whether the Akhmim 1 *Gospel of Peter* might be an interesting candidate for the reconstruction of the historical Jesus, or at least an important witness of the earliest development of ancient Christian gospel literature. I do not want to

---

13 See L. Vaganay, *L'Évangile de Pierre* (ÉtB), Paris, 1930, pp. 190–192. For James's argument see M.R. James, 'A New Text of the Apocalypse of Peter', *JTS* 12 (1911), pp. 573–583, esp. 577–582, and id., 'The Rainer Fragment of the Apocalypse of Peter', *JTS* 32 (1931), pp. 270–279, esp. 275–279 (with a response to Vaganay).

14 For details see T. Nicklas, 'Zwei petrinische Apokryphen im Akhmim-Codex oder eines? Kritische Anmerkungen und Gedanken', Apocrypha 16 (2005), pp. 75–96, and id., 'Das apokryphe Petrusevangelium. Stand und Perspektiven der Forschung', in L. Roig Lanzillotta and I. Muñoz Gallarte (eds), *Greeks, Jews, and Christians. Historical, Religious and Philological Studies in Honor of Jesús Peláez del Rosal* (Éstudios de Filología Neotestamentaria 10), Cordoba, 2013, pp. 337–370, esp. 342–349. P. Foster, in his magisterial commentary, *Gospel of Peter*, does not even discuss the matter while he devotes many pages to some of the smallest fragments.

repeat the bold ideas brought forward by authors like Helmut Koester, John Dominic Crossan and others.[15] Although I think that Koester's and Crossan's ideas are wrong,[16] they certainly provoked a renewed interest in the text which had been widely neglected before. However, the idea that Akhmim 1 represents an (at least) second century gospel text induced many scholars (including Paul Foster in his magisterial commentary) to understand Akhmim 1 *first and foremost* in its relation to the canonical gospels.[17] This overlooks the fact that what we *really* have is a manuscript from the 6th/7th century which is *usually* understood as a witness of a 2nd century text. This means that (a) we have to prove anew that Akhmim 1 *really* represents a second century (and not a much later) writing; (b) in the event we are successful, we have to discuss this text not *only* in the context of the canonical gospels, but as a part of second century discourses; and, finally, (c) we should not overlook the question why and how Akhmim 1 (perhaps connected with Akhmim 2) made sense at the time when it was copied again and (allegedly) buried in a monk's grave in Panopolis/Akhmim.[18] While all this may sound rather technical, and per-

---

15   For an overview of the Crossan/Koester discussion with all the necessary secondary literature, including the work of J. Denker, *Die theologiegeschichtliche Stellung des Petrusevangeliums. Ein Beitrag zur Frühgeschichte des Doketismus* (EHS XXIII.36), Bern–Frankfurt/Main, 1975, see J.D. Crossan, 'The *Gospel of Peter* and the Canonical Gospels', in T.J. Kraus and T. Nicklas (eds), *Das Evangelium nach Petrus. Text, Kontexte, Intertexte* (TU 158), Berlin–New York, 2007, pp. 117–134, and the recent work by E. Hernitscheck, *Much Ado About Almost Nothing: Eine forschungsgeschichtliche Meta-Analyse zu apokryphen Evangelienfragmenten als Quellen des antiken Christentums* (unpublished diss.), Leuven, 2018.

16   I have discussed this in several articles. See T. Nicklas, 'Das Petrusevangelium im Rahmen antiker Jesustraditionen', in J. Frey and J. Schröter (eds), *Jesus in apokryphen Evangelienüberlieferungen. Beiträge zu außerkanonischen Jesusüberlieferungen aus verschiedenen Sprach- und Kulturtraditionen* (WUNT 254), Tübingen, 2010, pp. 223–252; id., 'Resurrection in the Gospels of Matthew and Peter. Some Developments', in W. Weren et al. (eds), *Life Beyond Death in Matthew's Gospel: Religious Metaphor or Bodily Reality* (Biblical Tools and Studies 13), Leuven et al., 2011, pp. 27–42, and id., 'Rezeption und Entwicklung johanneischer Motive im Petrusevangelium', in A. Dettwiler and U. Poplutz (eds), *Studien zu Matthäus und Johannes/Études sur Matthieu et Jean. Festschrift für Jean Zumstein zum 65. Geburtstag/Mélanges offerts à Jean Zumstein pour son 65e anniversaire* (AThANT 97), Zürich, 2009, pp. 361–376.

17   This does not mean that Foster, *Gospel of Peter*, neglects other second/third century parallels, but his main dialogue partners are the canonical Gospels. This is clearly different from M.G. Mara, *Évangile de Pierre* (SC 201), Paris, 1973, who shows a broader overview of patristic parallels, some of which are little known.

18   Although the idea that the Akhmim codex was found in a monk's grave is repeated in almost every introduction to the *Gospel of Peter*, this is just a good scholarly guess which cannot be proven as the excavations at Akhmim are not well documented.

haps a bit over-cautious, the recent monograph of Alin Suciu, who identified the (former) *Unknown Berlin Gospel* (now *Berlin-Strasbourg Apocryphon*) as a late antique 'Apostolic Memoir,'[19] makes my basic problem a burning issue. This is even more the case as the *Berlin-Strasbourg Apocryphon* seems literarily related to the Akhmim *Gospel of Peter*.[20] Could our Akhmim *Gospel of Peter* perhaps also be a late antique 'apostolic memoir' text—and not a second century gospel?

In what follows, I would like to take up at least a few of the lines suggested. I will (a) make clear that some arguments supporting the Akhmim *Gospel of Peter's* provenance in the second century are weaker than is usually accepted; (b) try to re-evaluate the arguments presenting it as a second century *Neuinszenierung* ('re-enactment') of Jesus memories; and (c) show that this text could be understood as a bridge between second century gospel developments and the late antique development of 'Apostolic Memoirs' recently discussed by Suciu and others.[21]

1   The Gospel of Peter as a Second Century Text: New Question Marks

The usual thesis that Akhmim 1 (which I will from now on, for the sake of convenience, again call *Gospel of Peter*) represents a second century gospel text

---

19   A. Suciu, *The Berlin-Strasbourg Apocryphon. A Coptic Apostolic Memoir* (WUNT 370), Tübingen, 2017. Perhaps one should mention, additionally, the work of H. Lundhaug, *Images of Rebirth: Cognitive Poetics and Transformational Soteriology in the Gospel of Philip and the Exegesis of the Soul* (NHMS 73), Leiden–Boston, 2010, and id., 'The Nag Hammadi Codices in the Complex World of 4th and 5th Cent. Egypt', in L. Arcari (ed.), *Beyond Conflicts: Cultural and Religious Cohabitations in Alexandria and Egypt between the 1st and the 6th Century CE* (STAC 103), Tübingen, 2017, pp. 339–358, who developed the fascinating idea that we should understand the Nag Hammadi writings first and foremost in the monastic contexts where they were found (and not mainly as 2nd and 3rd century evidence).

20   See the discussion of the main arguments by H.-M. Schenke, 'Das Unbekannte Berliner Evangelium, auch "Evangelium des Erlösers" genannt', in C. Markschies and J. Schröter (eds), *Antike christliche Apokryphen in deutscher Übersetzung I: Evangelien und Verwandtes. Teilband 2*, Tübingen, 2012, pp. 1277–1289, esp. 1279–1280.

21   Besides A. Suciu, one should mention R. van den Broek, *Pseudo-Cyril of Jerusalem. On the Life and the Passion of Christ. A Coptic Apocryphon* (VigChr.S 118), Leiden–Boston, 2013. Many of the texts labelled as 'Apostolic Memoirs' are not properly edited yet, others have never been translated into a modern language. This, of course, hampers the discussion of these texts in broader scholarly circles. For an edition of many of these texts, see A. Campagnano, *Ps-Cirillo di Gerusalemme. Omelie copte sulla Passione, sulla Croce e sulla Vergine* (Testi e documenti per lo studio dell'Antichità 65), Milan, 1980.

THE GOSPEL OF PETER

has to face two challenges: (a) We have neither clear early quotations of the (Akhmim) *Gospel of Peter* in a form comparable to 'the *Gospel of Peter* says,'[22] nor any early fragment of the text that is universally acknowledged as representing the *Gospel of Peter*,[23] and (b) there is a growing awareness that in late antique Egypt a whole bulk of gospel-like stories in the form of 'apostolic records' or 'apostolic memoirs' were produced. According to Alin Suciu, these texts 'claim to be first-hand testimonies of the apostles concerning the deeds and words of Christ. The fact that these Coptic writings include much gospel-like material and logia of Jesus, corroborated with the fragmentary state in which many manuscripts that transmit them have survived, has led scholars to publish fragments of them as apocryphal gospels or apocalypses.'[24] Alin Suciu lists nineteen of such 'apostolic memoirs' included in patristic homilies (usually falsely attributed to a great Father like [quite often] Cyril of Jerusalem, Cyriacus of Behnesa, or even John Chrysostom), and adds nine without a homiletic framework (among these the *History of Joseph the Carpenter* and the *Book of Bartholomew* [CANT 80], formerly called *Gospel of Bartholomew*), and three fragmentary texts (among them the *Berlin Strasbourg Apocryphon*).[25] Of course, it is very difficult to describe the main distinguishing features of an 'apostolic memoir' as against what we would usually call 'gospel literature' in a broad sense of the term,[26] and perhaps many of the 'Apostolic memoirs' could be labelled gospel-related literature in a broad sense. Labelling them as such, however, would not solve our problem: the discovery and the addition of the genre, 'Apostolic Memoirs,' shows that, at least in Egypt, the production of gospel-like writings (or Jesus stories) did not stop with the late second or

---

22 Ancient Fathers who mention a *Gospel of Peter*, but do not quote it, like those listed in Kraus and Nicklas, *Petrusevangelium und Petrusapokalypse*, pp. 11–23, do not count as long as we cannot be sure whether they really point to a text close to what we have in the Akhmim codex.

23 See the very critical remarks by P. Foster, 'Are there any Early Fragments of the so-called Gospel of Peter?', *NTS* 52 (2006), pp. 1–28, and id., *Gospel of Peter*, pp. 57–91, where he is even (very) skeptical regarding P.Oxy. xli 2949, 'Given that P.Oxy. 2949 preserves a shorter and at times significantly different form of the text, it appears more likely that the tradition preserved by the papyrus fragment is earlier and represents an alternative development of a narrative that originated ultimately with the canonical gospels.'

24 A. Suciu, *Berlin-Strasbourg*, p. 73.

25 See A. Suciu, *Berlin-Strasbourg*, pp. 71–73.

26 Of course, we know that it is almost impossible to give a proper definition of the term 'Gospel'. For a recent discussion see, for example, F. Watson and S. Parkhouse, 'Introduction', in *Connecting Gospels: Beyond the Canonical/Noncanonical Divide*, Oxford, 2018, pp. 1–11, esp. 3–6.

third century.[27] The whole problem becomes even more evident if we look into Suciu's list of structural features observed in many 'apostolic memoirs.' These features include: (1) Many accounts have as their geographical setting the Mount of Olives where Jesus meets the apostles; (2) one of the apostles, usually Peter or Thomas, who later can be the protagonist from whose perspective the account is told, asks Jesus Christ questions regarding the main topic of the following memoir; and (3) the apostles are exhorted to proclaim Christ's message to the world.[28] The most important feature, however, is that 'the writing must claim to be an apostolic book written by apostles and, more often than not, be embedded in a sermon pronounced by a church father.'[29]

Although the Petrine Akhmim fragments are not part of such a sermon, at least some of the decisive features of 'Apostolic Memoirs' can be recognised in them. Akhmim 2, the *Apocalypse of Peter*, mentions a revelation granted to the twelve disciples who are gathered on a mountain (vv. 4–5), probably the Mount of Olives.[30] Both Akhmim 1 and 2 are told from the perspective of one of the apostles—in this case Peter—who, according to Akhmim 2, vv. 12 and 14, asks questions leading to the revelation of the place of those damned. In the case of Akhmim 1, the *Gospel of Peter*, only v. 60 reveals that the whole story is told by Peter (but see already vv. 26–27). It was this v. 60 which led to the widely accepted identification of this text with Serapion's *Gospel of Peter*, but if we examine, for example, Pseudo-Cyril of Jerusalem's *On the Life and Passion of Christ*, one of the recently edited 'Apostolic Memoirs,' this identification becomes dramatically less certain:

> 13 And after he [our Lord; TN] had been baptized he passed by and saw me, Peter, and Andrew, my brother (ⲁϥⲛⲁⲩ ⲉⲣⲟⲓ ⲁⲛⲟⲕ ⲡⲉⲧⲣⲟⲥ ⲙⲛ̄ ⲁⲛⲁⲣⲉⲁⲥ ⲡⲁⲥⲟⲛ). He went up to us and said to us: 'Follow me, and I shall make you fishers of men.'[31]

---

27 I am, in addition, quite sure that the phenomenon should not be confined to Egypt alone, and that we should concentrate not only on stories told by the Apostles, but also look into Mariological literature. For an interesting example from Armenia to be compared to the Egyptian Apostolic Memoirs see I. Dorfmann-Lazarev, 'Eve, Melchizedek and the Magi according to the Armenian Corpus of Homilies Attributes to Epiphanius of Salamis', in J.N. Bremmer et al. (eds), *The Protevangelium of James* (Studies on Early Christian Apocrypha 16), Leuven, 2019, pp. 264–311, who points to a series of homilies attributed to Epiphanius of Salamis, which in parts show comparable features.

28 Cf. A. Suciu, *Berlin-Strasbourg*, pp. 7–9.

29 A. Suciu, *Berlin-Strasbourg*, p. 10.

30 This identification comes from a comparison of the Akhmim fragment with the Ethiopic *Apocalypse of Peter*.

31 Coptic text and English translation according to R. van den Broek, *Pseudo-Cyril of Jerusa-*

THE GOSPEL OF PETER

Similarly, but perhaps even more clearly than in the *Gospel of Peter*, the chapters of *On the Life and Passion of Christ* which follow are told from the perspective of Peter! What if we had found only a fragment of this text (without a homily attributed to a fourth century church father, which once framed it)? I am sure, we would understand it as a new witness of the *Gospel of Peter* (or at least a text related to it). Suciu's third structural element (which, however, is not crucial for a work to be identified as an 'apostolic memoir') cannot be found in the extant text(s), but we should be aware that Akhmim 1 breaks up in the middle of a sentence, clearly before another vision of the risen Jesus is to be expected. All this means that both Akhmim 1 and 2, and even more if we consider these fragments in connection, can *at least be read* as an 'Apostolic Memoir' (or as something very close to what Suciu understands as an 'Apostolic Memoir')—in this case, perhaps, even connecting gospel-like and apocalyptic elements.

Does this mean that we should give up our usual dating of the *Gospel of Peter* to the second century (even if its extant text is Greek and not Coptic)? There are at least two arguments that could support such a late date of the extant text. (1) First, the language of the Akhmim *Gospel of Peter* displays several strange features.[32] One of them is the use of absolute hapax legomena[33] for terms relating to Jesus's passion. The most important of these are the verbs σταυρίσκω (instead of σταυρόω) for 'crucify' in v. 3 and σκελοκοπέω ('to break a leg') in v. 14.[34] In both

---

lem On the Life and Passion of Christ. A Coptic Apocryphon (VigChr.S 118), Leiden–Boston, 2013, esp. pp. 130–131. This is not the only passage that is told from an explicitly Petrine perspective; see, for example, § 14 ('and they followed him, as we ourselves had done'), § 15 ('we followed him ... we were twelve brothers ... we ate ... A great peace of God surrounded us on every side, and we were of one mind.'), § 16 ('if we wanted to tell them all, we would ...') and many others. English quotations from van den Broek, *Ps-Cyril*, 131. Interestingly, some passages, like § 20 ('When *they* [instead of "we"], then went out ...'), or § 55 ('Then Peter said to Jesus ...'), leave the perspective of Peter as the storyteller (by accident?). § 99 is even more interesting, as it speaks about 'one of his disciples, who was a hotheaded, grey-haired man', and directly afterwards identifies this figure with Peter (§ 100).

32 For recent discussions of at least a few features of the *Gospel of Peter*'s language see T.J. Kraus, 'Die Sprache des Petrusevangeliums? Methodische Anmerkungen und Vorüberlegungen für eine Analyse von Sprache und Stil', and S.E. Porter, 'The Greek of the Gospel of Peter: Implications for Syntax and Discourse Study', both in T.J. Kraus and T. Nicklas (eds), *Das Evangelium nach Petrus. Text, Kontexte, Intertexte* (TU 158), Berlin–New York, 2007, pp. 61–76 and 77–90.

33 As I want to refer to this issue only briefly, I cannot completely follow the sober methodological lines proposed by T.J. Kraus, 'HAPAX LEGOMENA—Definition eines terminus technicus und Signifikanz für eine pragmatisch orientierte Sprachanalyse' *NTS* 59 (2013), pp. 545–564.

34 See Kraus and Nicklas, *Petrusevangelium und Petrusapokalypse*, pp. 33 and 35.

cases we do not find any other witness in the whole of ancient Greek literature. Is it not strange that a second century Gospel, telling such an important
story as Jesus's suffering and death, should use words that in the whole of
later Greek Christian (and even non-Christian) literature were never employed
again? Wouldn't this observation make much more sense if these words were
simply invented by the text's (perhaps only late antique) author or scribe?

(2) As I have already mentioned in brief, the discussion of *early* witnesses
of the *Gospel of Peter* has provoked a fierce controversy during the last two
decades.[35] I think we should not spill too much ink on fragments like P.Oxy.
lx 4009 and P.Vindob G. 2325 where we only find Peter as storyteller in (more
or less plausible) reconstructions.[36] Instead, I want to concentrate on P.Oxy. xli
2949. This is the *only* early fragment—probably going back to the turn of the
second to the third century[37]—which preserves remnants of a text resembling
what we find in vv. 3–5 of the Akhmim *Gospel of Peter*. While it is not possible to
discuss all the different (some quite recent) attempts to re-edit and to read this
text again,[38] two circumstances become quite clear: First, P.Oxy. xli 2949 seems
not to be a whole gospel manuscript, but perhaps it preserves remnants of an
excerpt.[39] Second, and perhaps even more importantly, the few extant words
on P.Oxy. 2949 show that its text *was certainly not identical* to vv. 3–5 of the
Akhmim *Gospel of Peter*. In fact, the decisive words are on line 5 where the usual
transcriptions (including the one by Thomas Kraus and myself) read φίλος Πει-
λάτου ('friend of Pilate')[40]—a syntagma otherwise only found in *Gospel of Peter*
3. We should, however, be aware that *every remaining trace of a letter of the decisive word 'Pilate' is dubious*. This situation has not changed significantly with
Thomas Wayment's 2009 transcription of the fragment, which was made with
the help of recent multi-spectral images. Even if Wayment is quite confident
with the reading 'friend of Pilate' in line 5,[41] his comparison of P.Oxy. xli 2949

---

35   For an overview, see Foster, *Gospel of Peter*, pp. 57–89, including extensive discussion of
the earlier literature.

36   See the discussion in Kraus and Nicklas, *Petrusevangelium und Petrusapokalypse*, pp. 59–
68; (even more detailed and more up-to-date) Foster, *Gospel of Peter*, pp. 69–90; and (most
recently) E. Hernitscheck, *Much Ado* (unpublished).

37   For the date and palæographical description of P.Oxy. 2949, see, for example, Kraus and
Nicklas, *Petrusevangelium und Petrusapokalypse*, pp. 55–58.

38   For an overview, see Foster, *Gospel of Peter*, pp. 58–68.

39   See also Kraus and Nicklas, *Petrusevangelium und Petrusapokalypse*, p. 58: 'Selbst wenn
man mit Recht zögert, von einem ganzen Evangelium hinter P.Oxy. XLI 2949 zu sprechen,
kann doch ein solcher Bericht wie der vorliegende auch einzeln im Umlauf gewesen sein.'

40   See Kraus and Nicklas, *Petrusevangelium und Petrusapokalypse*, pp. 56–58.

41   T. Wayment, 'A Reexamination of the Text of P.Oxy. 2949', *JBL* 128 (2009), pp. 375–382,
esp. 378, 'The most crucial piece of evidence is found in line 5 where Coles reconstructs

THE GOSPEL OF PETER

53

with the text of the Akhmim codex leads to the following conclusion: 'Both texts seem to be reporting basically the same story, with one containing an expanded version of a potentially early and shorter text ... The textual relationship could then be explained as two separate witnesses to a developing textual tradition that culminated in the Akhmîm codex of the *Gospel of Peter* or in some unknown text prior to the eighth century. Certainly it is possible that *P.Oxy.* 2949 witnesses an earlier stage of the *Gospel of Peter*, one that was considerably more concise, but it also seems plausible that the Oxyrhynchus fragment is a patristic summary of, or a commentary on, the *Gospel of Peter*.'[42]

While it is not necessary to re-open here the discussion on the extent to which Wayment misrepresented Foster's transliteration of the manuscript,[43] one thing (already acknowledged in the transcription given by Thomas Kraus and myself)[44] seems to be clear in any case: despite important parallels, P.Oxy. xli 2949 cannot simply be regarded as a witness of a *Gospel of Peter* in the textual form reflected by the Akhmim codex. Even if we identify both texts as related gospel-like stories told by Peter, P.Oxy. xli 2949 shows that there must have been a certain fluidity in the transmission of the account between the second and the sixth/seventh century when the Akhmim text was pinned down. *Does the early date of the Akhmim* Gospel of Peter *thus depend on a few more or less illegible dots of ink?*

---

the name Pilate, marking two letters as illegible and the remaining letters as questionable. Foster subsequently removed the reference to Pilate in line 5 completely, judging the reconstruction to be too hasty, although he did state, 'While there may be traces of a lambda, the rest of the letters are totally abraded, although the vestiges of a pi may perhaps be made out.' The solution of this problem is fortunately preserved in line 7 of the text, where the name Pilate appears again, although quite visible in this instance and acknowledged in Foster's reconstruction. What Foster does not concede is that the *omicron* is completely preserved and the final *upsilon* of line 5 is nearly complete, and both are visible without the aid of the new images. Additionally, traces of ink remain for each letter of the name Pilate, except for *epsilon* and *tau*. By superimposing the name from line 7 on top of the traces of ink in line 5, it becomes obvious that the word is indeed the personal name Pilate.'

42   T. Wayment, 'Reexamination', pp. 379–380. For a comparable, but less detailed statement, see also L.H. Blumell and T. Wayment, *Christian Oxyrhynchus: Texts, Documents, and Sources*, Waco, Tx., 2015, pp. 217–218.

43   But see P. Foster, 'P.Oxy. 2949—Its Transcription and Significance: A Response to Thomas Wayment', *JBL* 129 (2010), pp. 173–176.

44   Kraus and Nicklas, *Petrusevangelium und Petrusapokalypse*, pp. 55–56.

54 NICKLAS

2 A Second Century *Gospel of Peter*: Positive Evidence

As far as I can see, however, P.Oxy. xli 2949 does not offer the only, and certainly not the decisive, argument that the Akhmim *Gospel of Peter* finds its roots in a second century writing. Although Justin Martyr, despite having once mentioned the ἀπομνημονεύματα of Peter (*dial.* 106,3), seems not to have known a *Gospel of Peter* in the Akhmim form,[45] and although the parallels between the Akhmim *Gospel of Peter* and Melito's *Peri Pascha* are not strong enough to prove literary dependence,[46] at least a few other texts offer better evidence. While many parallels between the *Gospel of Peter* and ancient Christian literature discussed, for example, by Maria Grazia Mara, Jürgen Denker, Martin Meiser, and Paul Foster can be reduced to the use of common or comparable motifs,[47] at least a few cases clearly go beyond this evidence. There are good reasons to see the Jewish Christian source in *Pseudo-Clementine Recognitions* 1,27–71 (preserved in both Latin and Syriac translations)[48] as influenced by a *Gospel of Peter*

---

45 For a detailed discussion of the evidence see K. Greschat, 'Justins 'Denkwürdigkeiten der Apostel' und das Petrusevangelium', in T.J. Kraus and T. Nicklas (eds), *Das Evangelium nach Petrus. Text, Kontexte, Intertexte* (TU 158), Berlin–New York, 2007, pp. 197–214 (with discussion of older literature), who concludes: 'Die hier vorgestellten Beispiele haben eine gewisse Nähe zwischen Justins Denkwürdigkeiten der Apostel und dem Petrusevangelium erkennen lassen, die nicht mit direkter literarischer Abhängigkeit erklärt werden muss. Bei beiden Texten handelt es sich um je verschiedene Erzählungen des Christuserereignisses, denen jedoch gemeinsam ist, dass alles auf die Erfüllung der Schrift durch Christus im Unterschied zu den Juden ankommt.'

46 The thesis that Melito is dependent on the *Gospel of Peter* was developed by O. Perler, 'Évangile de Pierre et Méliton de Sardes', RB 71 (1964), pp. 584–590. But see the detailed criticism by T.R. Karmann, 'Die Paschahomilie des Melito von Sardes und das Petrusevangelium', in T.J. Kraus and T. Nicklas (eds), *Das Evangelium nach Petrus. Text, Kontexte, Intertexte* (TU 158), Berlin–New York, 2007, pp. 215–235.

47 See Denker, *Theologiegeschichtliche Stellung*, pp. 9–30, who discusses Justin, the Syriac *Didascalia*, Alexandrian theologians like Clement, Origen and Dionysios (plus the *Dialogue of Adamantius*), extracanonical Acts of the Apostles, the *Sibylline Oracles*, Ps.-Cyprian, Ps.-Ignatius, Cyril of Jerusalem, the *Ascension of Isaiah*, the *Gospel of the Hebrews*, the *Pseudo-Clementines*, Aphrahat, Ignatius, apocryphal literature relating to the figure of Pilate, variants of the Western text of the Gospels (including possible *Diatessaronic* variants) and Manichæan literature. Many of these possible parallels were already discussed in some of the earliest editions and commentaries. While Foster, *Gospel of Peter*, pp. 97–119, concentrates on just some of these texts, M. Meiser, 'Das Petrusevangelium und die spätere großkirchliche Literatur', in T.J. Kraus and T. Nicklas (eds), *Das Evangelium nach Petrus. Text, Kontexte, Intertexte* (TU 158), Berlin–New York, 2007, pp. 183–196, esp. 183, adds a possible parallel from Cyril of Alexandria, *Zach.* 5 (PG 72; 224B).

48 For an introduction to, and discussion of, this text (which can be understood as a kind of a Jewish Christian counter-story polemizing against Luke's Acts of the Apostles) see

THE GOSPEL OF PETER

text very close to what we find in the Akhmim-Codex;[49] and it seems quite clear that at least some Manichæan circles used an account of Jesus's passion very close to the Akhmim *Gospel of Peter*. Perhaps the clearest example is frg. M 18 of the Manichæan *Hymns on Crucifixion* (but see also M 4525). The first seven lines of this text's recto are almost *completely* parallel to a whole scene of the Akhmim *Gospel of Peter*, and even the remaining lines 7–13 show possible parallels to vv. 50–51.[50]

1	He was truly the Son of God.—And	*GosPet* 45
2	Pilate responded: See, I	
3	am clean from the blood of this Son of	
4	God.—The centurions and the soldiers	*GosPet* 46
5	thus received the order from Pilate:	
6	Keep it secret.—And	*GosPet* 49
7	even the Jews gave a sum of money. ...	

Although it is difficult (or even largely impossible) to re-construct exactly how (and when) the *Gospel of Peter* made its way via Manichæan circles to Turfan, if it is possible that M 18 is a witness to a certain textual fluidity of the *Gospel of Peter*, it seems clear that the text found in Akhmim lies behind the Manichæan fragment.[51]

Perhaps the most striking example of a second century *Gospel of Peter*, however, is the Syriac *Didascalia*, a fourth century translation of a probably third

---

F.S. Jones, *An Ancient Jewish Christian Source on the History of Christianity. Pseudo-Clementine Recognitions 1.27–71* (SBL.TT 37), 3rd edn, Atlanta, 2001, and id., 'An Ancient Jewish Christian Rejoinder to Luke's Acts of the Apostles: Pseudo-Clementine *Recognitions 1.27–71*', in his *Pseudoclementina Elchasaiticaque inter Judæochristiana. Collected Studies* (Orientalia Lovaniensia Analecta 203), Leuven et al., 2012, pp. 207–229.

49   See F.S. Jones, 'The Gospel of Peter in Pseudo-Clementine Recognitions 1,27–71', in T.J. Kraus and T. Nicklas (eds), *Das Evangelium nach Petrus. Text, Kontexte, Intertexte* (TU 158), Berlin–New York, 2007, pp. 237–244, who (after a discussion of quite clear parallels to *Gospel of Peter* 15, 22 and 29) concludes 'that the *Gospel of Peter* provides a possible explanation for the presence of these several motifs in *Recognitions* 1. The shared elements are indeed evidence that the source of *Recognitions* 1 might have known and used the *Gospel of Peter*, and in the absence of an explanation other than sheer narrative coincidence or the postulation of yet another uncertain source, this seems to be the most likely conclusion.'

50   For a more detailed discussion see M. Tardieu, 'Le procès de Jésus vu par les Manichéens', in Apocrypha 8 (1997), pp. 9–27, esp. 21–22.

51   See Tardieu, 'Procés de Jésus', p. 23.

century (Greek) writing.[52] Only recently, Joel Marcus discussed this text's significant parallels to the *Gospel of Peter* and pointed to its importance for the understanding of the *Gospel of Peter*'s (not just simply negative) attitude towards the Jews.[53] *Didasc.* 21 not only mentions Christ's *decensus ad inferos* (*Didasc.* 26; *GosPet* 41), but shows a whole series of parallels to the Akhmim *Gospel of Peter*: Jesus is crucified at the order of Herod who, as in *GosPet* 2, is not explicitly identified with Herod Antipas;[54] the darkness during Jesus's crucifixion is interpreted as a 'night' (*GosPet* 18), and also Jesus's resurrection takes place at night (*GosPet* 35, but see also Matt 28:1).[55] Long passages tell how the disciples were fasting and mourning (and that later the believers should follow these practices); the text even asks the believers to stay awake on the Saturday before Easter (cf. *GosPet* 26–27). The Jewish people are described as blind and being 'surrounded by darkness' (cf. perhaps *GosPet* 15), and another passage calls the Jews' deeds 'fulfilment of misdoing' (*GosPet* 17). In addition, as far as I see, *Didasc.* 21, *GosPet* 60, and the *Gospel of Mary* are the only extant ancient Christian texts that speak about an appearance of the risen Jesus to Levi.[56] This creates such a close cluster of parallels that I cannot but see a literary connection between the *Gospel of Peter* and the *Didascalia*; this also shows that both texts find their origins in a common milieu—probably in circles of Jewish Christian groups in Syria.

---

52   The exact dates are a matter of discussion. See B. Steimer, 'Didascalia', in *Lexikon der antiken christlichen Literatur* (1998), pp. 167–168.

53   J. Marcus, 'The Gospel of Peter as a Jewish Christian Document', *NTS* 64 (2018), pp. 473–494. Contrary to most other treatments of the *Gospel of Peter*'s attitude towards Jews and Judaism, Marcus understands v. 27 as describing the Jewish people (against their leaders) on their way to repentance. His main thesis, that the *Gospel of Peter* combines pro-Jewish and anti-Jewish elements in a way typical of Jewish Christian texts, is a clear step forward if compared to my own older plea that the text should not be labelled as hatefully anti-Jewish too quickly. See T. Nicklas, 'Die "Juden" im Petrusevangelium (PCair. 10759). Ein Testfall', *NTS* 47 (2001), pp. 206–221, and now id., 'Anti-Jewish Polemics? The *Gospel of Peter* Revisited', in G. Bady and D. Cuny (ed.), *Les polémiques religieuses du Ier au IVe siècle de notre ère. Hommage à B. Pouderon* (Théologie historique 128), Paris 2019, pp. 153–176.

54   In addition, only *GosPet* 1–2 and the *Syriac Didascalia* 21 seem to bring Pilate's washing of the hands in close contrast with Herod's judgment.

55   Both aspects are connected with the question of how far a resurrection in the night between Saturday and Sunday could fulfill Matt 12:40, according to which the Son of Man had to stay three days and three nights in the heart of the earth.

56   See also Meiser, 'Petrusevangelium', p. 185 n. 19. Of course, *GosPet* 60 breaks off in this passage. Regarding the impact of Levi for the *Gospel of Mary*, see C.M. Tuckett, *The Gospel of Mary* (Oxford Early Christian Gospel Texts), Oxford, 2007, pp. 21–24.

3   The *Gospel of Peter* and 'Apostolic Memoirs': The Case of Ps.-Cyril's *Life and Passion of Christ*

Besides these points (which at least in parts have been argued elsewhere), I want to formulate a final argument that could also point to the *Gospel of Peter*'s origin in the second century. As far as I see, the *Gospel of Peter* treats both Jesus material and the Scriptures of Israel in a manner different from what we find in an 'Apostolic Memoir,' like the above mentioned *Life and Passion of Christ* embedded in a homily attributed to Cyril of Jerusalem. Of course, it would be necessary to compare the *Gospel of Peter* with more than one Memoir text, but such a task would require a monograph. As Pseudo-Cyril of Jerusalem's *On the Life and Passion of Christ* is one of the few texts that are already well-edited *and* are largely told from the perspective of Peter, I think it is a good example to start with.[57]

Before I go into detail, perhaps a few preliminary notes should be made. In a recent article on second century gospel literature, I described the Akhmim *Gospel of Peter* (among others) as a *Neuinszenierung*, that is a 're-enactment' of Jesus material (drawn mainly from the canonical gospels).[58] By using the term *Neuinszenierung*, I try to take seriously that some extracanonical Jesus stories show clear parallels to passages from the canonical gospels, but that these parallels are not close enough to indicate a redaction of written texts. In other words, I use the term *Neuinszenierung* in cases where it seems probable that a second century (or later) author had knowledge of written Gospels, Jesus stories, or logia, that his story follows the main line of these texts and presents some of their decisive motifs, yet treats them so freely that we cannot decide for sure whether the author used these texts in the form of a written *Vorlage*, or just had the main storyline in mind.[59] The Akhmim *Gospel of Peter* shows a few features that (hopefully) make clear what I want to say. Most striking is the obser-

---

57   All English translations of this text follow (if not stated otherwise) Van den Broek, *Ps-Cyril*.

58   T. Nicklas, 'Zwischen Redaktion und 'Neuinszenierung': Vom Umgang erzählender Evangelien des 2. Jahrhunderts mit ihren Vorlagen', in J. Schröter, T. Nicklas and J. Verheyden (eds), *Gospelsand Gospel Traditions in the Second Century* (BZNW), Berlin–Boston, 2019, pp. 311–330, but see also (with the example of P.Oxy. lxxvi 5072) T. Nicklas, 'Eine neue alte Erzählung im Rahmen antiker Jesustraditionen: Reste eines Exorzismus auf P.Oxy. lxxvi 5072', *Annali di storia dell' esegesi* 29 (2012), pp. 13–27.

59   One of the best examples of such a text is the Unknown Gospel on Papyrus Egerton 2 which, as a whole, seems to be aware of several texts from the canonical Gospels, but which, for example in its version of the Healing of the Leper, tells the story in such a way that literary dependence on any of the synoptic versions of the story cannot be proven for sure. For a detailed discussion, see Nicklas, 'Redaktion und Neuinszenierung'.

vation that several passages offer motifs that we find in the canonical gospels as well, but in such a way that one may suspect that the *Gospel of Peter*'s author did not understand their role in the canonical gospels.[60] *GosPet* 14, for example, tells that 'the Jews' 'commanded that (his)[61] legs should not be broken so that he might die in torment.' This passage recalls John 19:31–33, where Jesus's bones are not broken because Scripture must be fulfilled (John 19:36).[62] While John's intention is very likely to describe Jesus as the real Passover lamb, the *Gospel of Peter* just wants to emphasise the torturer's excessive violence. A bit later, *GosPet* 24 tells about Jesus's burial by Joseph of Arimathæa (whom the *Gospel of Peter* simply calls Joseph). According to the text, 'he brought him into his own tomb called the Garden of Joseph.' Not only does John mention Jesus's burial in a garden close to the place of crucifixion (19.41), but this motif also plays an important role in the following story of Mary Magdalene's encounter with the risen Jesus.[63] At the same time, *Gospel of Peter* 24 mentions the 'Garden of Joseph' without *any* narrative function. The narrator simply wants to show his knowledge of an otherwise insignificant detail. Shall we attribute such developments to a conscious *redaction* of John? How silly must such a redactor have been! Perhaps we should suppose instead that the *Gospel of Peter* goes back to an earlier stage of gospel traditions than the canonical parallels? But why, then, has only John taken up these motifs? Why should an earlier Jesus tradition invent a 'Garden of Joseph' (without any obvious function)? And what shall we do with all the other Johannine motifs in the *Gospel of Peter*, or with its careful connection of Matthean and Marcan Resurrection accounts, etc.?[64] These considerations explain why I think that it makes the best sense to understand the Akhmim *Gospel of Peter* (at least in its main lines) as a text which was written at a time and in a context where the later canonical gospels were already extant, when their stories (including many motifs) were already well-known,

---

60 For a broader discussion of both passages and their relation to the Gospel of John, see Nicklas, 'Rezeption und Entwicklung'.

61 Probably referring to Jesus, the 'Lord'.

62 The question which scriptural passage is quoted in John 19:36 is a matter of debate. J. Zumstein, *Das Johannesevangelium* (KEK 2), Göttingen, 2016, pp. 733–734, discusses Ps 34:20–21; Ex 12:46 and Num 9:12.

63 One could even ponder whether this garden motif is part of a 'paradise story'.

64 See Nicklas, 'Rezeption und Entwicklung', but also id., 'Resurrection in the Gospels of Matthew and Peter. Some Developments', in W. Weren, H. van de Sandt and J. Verheyden (eds), *Life beyond Death in Matthew's Gospel: Religious Metaphor or Bodily Reality?*, Leuven et al., 2011, pp. 27–42, and T.J. Kraus, 'EvPetr 12,50–14,60: Leeres Grab und was dann? Kanonische Traditionen, novelistic development und romanhafte Züge', *Early Christianity* 4 (2013), pp. 335–361.

THE GOSPEL OF PETER

but when not many people had the chance to read these texts closely and to study them in detail. In such a context, the author of the *Gospel of Peter* wanted to write *his* story of Jesus's passion and resurrection and to put it into the mouth of Peter.[65] In writing *his story*, however, he did not want to produce a carefully redacted text dealing with other Gospels as his written *Vorlage*; instead, he simply wanted to write *the story* of Jesus's passion and resurrection.[66] As this story was already known as a virtual story in many of its main lines, he had to take up motifs from this virtual story even if he did not exactly remember their original functions.

As far as I see, at least, Ps.-Cyril's *On the Life and the Passion of Christ* does not show comparable features. The way this and other 'Apostolic Memoirs' treat the canonical gospels is reflected in one of the texts themselves—Pseudo-Evodius of Rome's homily *On the Passion and Resurrection*, the introduction to one of the 'Apostolic Memoir' texts.[67] As an answer to the question whether his text adds to the Word of God or even changes it, Pseudo-Evodius writes (§§ 41–44):[68]

> 41. Even before it is exposed to the proper tinctures in which it will be dyed, the wool that is used for the purple of the emperor is suitable for being manufactured into clothes and to be worn as one likes. Yet when it is processed and dyed in colored tinctures it will become more luminous and make splendid dress, worthy to be worn by the emperor. Thus it is with the Holy Gospels. When he who will be appointed as a shepherd acts according to their words and explains them, they will become more luminous and shine brighter in the hearts of the audience. 42. The emperor, indeed, will blame no one when elaborate embroideries are stitched onto his clothes. Rather, he will pay homage to those who applied them, all the more since everybody will bless the garment because of the embroideries that it bears. Similarly, the Lord Jesus will not blame us for applying embellishments (κόσμησις) of the Holy Gospels. He will rather

---

65   At the same time, the *Gospel of Peter* does not make extensive use of this Peter fiction—a point made by J. Frey, ''Apokryphisierung' im Petrusevangelium: Überlegungen zum Ort des Petrusevangeliums in der Entwicklung der Evangelienüberlieferung', in J. Schröter (ed.), *The Apocryphal Gospels within the Context of Early Christian Theology* (BETL 260), Leuven at al., 2013, pp. 157–196, esp. 171–174.

66   Of course, we do not know exactly how much more our author wanted to write.

67   For a more detailed discussion, see J. van der Vliet, 'The embroidered garment: Egyptian perspectives on "apocryphity" and "orthodoxy"', in T. Nicklas et al. (eds), *The Other Side: Apocryphal Perspectives on Ancient Christian Orthodoxies* (NTOA 117), Göttingen, 2017, pp. 177–192.

68   Also quoted by van der Vliet, 'Embroidered Garment', pp. 186–187.

pay homage to us all the more, and bless those who derive benefit from them. 43. For there are many things that the Gospels have left unmentioned and that have been established by the laws (θεσμός) of the Church. Thus they have not told us the day on which He (i.e. Jesus) was born. Likewise, again, custom determined the celebration of these two catholic feasts. Rightly the beloved of Christ, John, said in the Holy Gospel: 'There are many other signs that Jesus worked before his disciples, which are not written in this book' (John 20:30). 'If these,' he said, 'were written down, the world would not be able to contain the books in which they would be written' (John 21:25). 44. Just as gold when it is combined with topaz becomes more luminous so that in the place where it is deposited it will not become dark at all, similarly when the embellishment (κόσμησις) of the words of the Holy Spirit through the teachers comes to bedeck the Holy Gospels, these will shine more brightly and start to beam. As for anybody who will rent the garment of a poor man, let alone the purple of an emperor, the latter will be wroth with him. Likewise, as for anybody who will play havoc with the words of the Holy Gospels, God will destroy his soul and his body in the fiery Gehenna. The house whose foundations are not firmly established, even if it is being adorned with all kinds of beauties, is destined to fall down (cf. Matt. 7:24–27 / Luke 6:47–49). Similarly, also every church where the Four Gospels are not present in order to proclaim and preach the unity of the Trinity, even if its people are numerous as the stars in the sky (cf. e.g. Gen. 15:5), is destined to fall down and is endangered.[69]

To put it in other words, Ps.-Evodius and other authors produce 'Apostolic Memoirs,' that is, new Jesus stories, even if they fully acknowledge the canonical authority of the New Testament gospels as holy Scriptures. Ps.-Evodius both points to the fact that Church tradition (for example, about the day of Jesus's birth) is based on 'many things that the Gospels have left unmentioned,' and points out that the Gospels—like John 20:30 and 21:25[70]—tell us that many events in Jesus's life are not narrated in the canonical accounts. Against this background, the 'Apostolic Memoirs' are compared to embroideries of an

---

69 For the Coptic text see P. Chapman, 'Evodius of Rome: On the Passion and the Resurrection of the Lord', in L. Depuydt (ed.), *Homiletica From the Pierpont Morgan Library. Seven Coptic Homilies Attributed to Basil the Great, John Chrysostom, and Euodius of Rome* (CSCO 524–525), Leuven, 1991, pp. 90–91 (English translation according to CSCO 525, pp. 95–96).

70 Both passages are also important for Ps.-Cyril of Jerusalem, *On the Life and Passion of Christ* 16.

THE GOSPEL OF PETER

emperor's garments, and are presented as 'embellishments (κόσμησις) of the Holy Gospels.' My thesis is: If we take a closer look at a text like Ps.-Cyril's *Life and Passion of Christ*, aspects of the hermeneutics exposed above can be seen.[71] On many of these points, the late antique 'Apostolic Memoir' can be distinguished from the Akhmim *Gospel of Peter*.

3.1

Contrary to the *Gospel of Peter* (or another second century *Neuinszenierung* like the 'unknown Gospel' on Papyrus Egerton 2), Ps.-Cyril regularly offers exact quotations of New Testament gospel passages.[72] As far as I see, it is a clear sign that the authority and the status of these texts have changed in the meantime. A fine example can already be found in Ps.-Cyril's § 13 (already quoted above). This passage combines Peter's perspective as a story-teller with a very concrete quotation from the Gospel text, and offers a short non-canonical embellishment.[73] The text goes:

13 ⲁⲩⲱ ⲙⲛ̄ⲛ̄ⲥⲁ ⲉⲧⲣⲉϥϫⲓ ⲃⲁⲡⲧⲓⲥⲙⲁ ⲁϥⲉⲓ ⲉϥⲡⲁⲣⲁⲅⲉ ⲁϥⲛⲁⲩ ⲉⲣⲟⲓ ⲁⲛⲟⲕ ⲡⲉⲧ-
ⲣⲟⲥ ⲙⲛ̄ ⲁⲛⲇⲣⲉⲁⲥ ⲡⲁⲥⲟⲛ. ⲁϥⲙⲟⲟϣⲉ ⲉⲣⲟⲛ ⲡⲉϫⲁϥ ⲛⲁⲛ ϫⲉ ⲟⲩⲉϩⲧⲏⲩⲧⲛ̄
ⲛ̄ⲥⲱⲓ ⲧⲁⲣ̄ⲧⲏⲩⲧⲛ̄ ⲛ̄ⲟⲩⲱϩⲉ ⲛ̄ⲣⲱⲙⲉ. ⲁⲛⲟⲛ ⲇⲉ ⲁⲛⲙⲟⲩϩ ⲛ̄ⲣⲁϣⲉ ⲁⲛⲟⲩⲁϩⲛ̄
ⲛ̄ⲥⲱϥ ...

After he [Jesus] had been baptized he passed by and saw me, Peter, and Andrew, my brother. He went up to us and said to us: 'Follow me, and I shall make you fishers of men' [Matt 4:19 Sah]. We, then, were full of joy, and followed him ...[74]

This is a version of Peter's and Andrew's calling retold from Peter's perspective. The text not only follows Mark 1:16–18 and Matt 4:18–20, but goes as far as to quote the Sahidic version of Matt 4:19 word-by-word. Another *verbatim* citation of a New Testament passage can be found in § 23, where we read: 'When,

---

71   Of course, I cannot do such a comparison for all the extant sources, which could not be embraced even in a single monograph. This is why it is clear that I can only propose a thesis which, besides, could be contradicted in the near future.

72   In addition, it quotes, and alludes to, other New Testament texts as well, e.g. § 15 ('we were of one mind'; cf. 1 Cor 1:10; Acts 5:12); § 17 ('you will preach when the Holy Spirit comes down upon you'; cf. Acts 1:8; 2:14–36).

73   Other examples can be found in § 16 (cf. John 20.30; 21.25; transformed into Peter's perspective); § 34 ('he was a great teacher in the whole of Israel'; cf. John 3.1,10); § 40 (cf. Matt 2.6); § 42–43 (John 3.1–2,5) and many others.

74   Text and translation Van den Broek, *Pseudo-Cyril*, pp. 130 and 131.

then, our Saviour preached, (he said): 'Come to me, every one who is troubled and laden, and I will give you rest. Take my yoke upon you, for my yoke is easy and my load is light.' And thus every one came to him and he healed them all' (see Matt 11:28–29a.30). But this passage is not only interesting because of its use of Gospel material. It is followed by the sentences: 'He raised the daughter of Jairus, the head of the synagogue, and the son of the widow of Nain. He healed the son of the royal servant and the son of the centurion. He gave light to the blind-born man and to the two blind men who sat beside the way. And he healed the paralysed and the withered man ...' (§ 24–25). Even if these sentences do not *quote* the canonical gospels, they only make sense to readers and listeners who *know* the canonical stories alluded to here (§ 24: Mark 5:21–24.35–43 par. / Luke 7:11–17 / John 4:43–54 / Matt 8:5–13 par., etc.). In other words, the text alludes to stories told in the canonical gospels without retelling them; it simply evokes them. Nowhere is this the case in the extant *Gospel of Peter*. Ps.-Cyril even goes as far as to *distinguish* between two closely interrelated stories like John 4:43–54 and Matt 8:5–13 par., perhaps a sign that he refers to *written* Gospels. §§ 43–45, in turn, first offer an almost word-by-word quotation of Jesus's dialogue with Nicodemus (John 3:1–5). According to Ps.-Cyril, however, the open and ambiguous figure of the Johannine Nicodemus[75] ends up as a believer in Jesus: 'And Nicodemus went to his house, he brought all his money and gave it to Jesus so that he should give it to the poor' (§ 45). The text thus fills a gap in the canonical story—it goes on where John ends.[76] In some cases, however, Ps.-Cyril confuses written Gospel material: § 46, just after the Nicodemus episode, tells us that Jesus goes to Jerusalem 'as the Passover of the Jews, the Feast of Tabernacles, was near at hand'[77]—a passage which makes clear that our author knew the Gospel of John *as a written text even with some of its very special expressions* very well, but at the same time was too distant from Judaism in order to realise that Passover and Tabernacles are two distinct feasts.

3.2

Many of the longer non-canonical passages in Ps.-Cyril's text can be seen as little stories on their own, which were inserted into the canonical stories to fill gaps or to remove inconsistencies in the canonical narratives. This can be seen in small embellishments like, for example, the motif that Judas 'will hang

---

75   A very good discussion of the Johannine Nicodemus figure can be found in R.A. Culpepper, 'Nicodemus: The Travail of New Birth', in S.A. Hunt, D.F. Tolmie and R. Zimmermann (eds), *Character Studies in the Fourth Gospel* (WUNT 314), Tübingen, 2013, pp. 249–259.

76   Nicodemus will play an even more pronounced role later in the text.

77   Van den Broek, *Ps-Cyril*, p. 141 and n. 53.

THE GOSPEL OF PETER

himself on a tree, *namely a tamarisk*' (§ 93). Other passages, like § 20, can be understood as an attempt to harmonize different stories. The passage first connects the story about the temple tax (cf. Matt 17:24–27) with the call of Levi (Mark 2:14; Luke 5:27–28). As the Gospel of Matthew tells the same story, but names the tax-collector Matthew (Matt 9:9), this creates a problem. Ps.-Cyril, who recognizes that the different accounts relate to the same event, harmonizes them in the following creative way: 'When they,[78] then, went out, Jesus looked and saw Levi sitting in his custom house. Jesus said to him, 'Follow me!' He rose and followed him. And he (Jesus) changed his name and called him Matthew and 'Precious Pearl'.'[79] Other examples are §§ 47, 56–59, 70 and 87, which introduce Jesus's mother into the story about Jesus's entry into Jerusalem and the scenes before his passion. While this is certainly a sign of late antique devotion to Mary, it also makes it plausible that later she could become part of the group under the cross (see John 19:25–27[80]).

While some of the extra material goes back to non-canonical writings (or related traditions), like the *Protevangelium of James* (see §§ 35–36)[81] or the *Acts of Pilate* (see §§ 33–34),[82] other details are much less known, and are perhaps even invented by the author himself. § 10, for example, offers an overview of the different apostles' (and, partially, their relatives') occupations, which only goes back to Gospel evidence in certain parts:

> Simon Peter, John, Andrew and James were fishers, fish catchers according to the craft of this world. The father of Philip was a charioteer in the races. Thomas ... was a tender of the waterwheel, Bartholomew was a gardener, a grower and seller of greens. Thaddeus was a stonecutter. Matthew was a tax collector. Simon the Canaanite was an inviter to the wedding ....[83]

---

78   For a moment, the text abandons the alleged Petrine perspective!

79   It is very difficult to trace the tradition about Matthew as the 'precious pearl'. Van den Broek, *Ps-Cyril*, p. 133 n. 30, mentions Theodosius of Alexandria, *On John the Baptist* 15,1 (CSCO 268, 42) as a parallel, but I at least, do not have more evidence on this.

80   The passage is not told by Ps.-Cyril, but is certainly presupposed.

81   Regarding the exact relation between §§ 35–36 and the *Protevangelium* see, however, Van den Broek, *Ps-Cyril*, p. 139 n. 46, 'Pseudo-Cyril also includes later embellishments of the story: that Zechariah and Simeon (also a priest and Zechariah's successor!) served together in the temple and that there were more virgins like Mary, is not found in the *Protevangelium* but in later related literature.'

82   See also § 84 ('behold, the dragon has mingled a cup of poison') which Van den Broek, *Ps-Cyril*, p. 155 n. 106, connects to an otherwise unidentified Sahidic fragment of extra-canonical material.

83   Is it possible that the text misunderstands 'Canaanite' as 'coming from Cana in

Another passage (§ 30) introduces Judas's wife (who is even worse than her husband):

> Judas, however, stole what they put into the treasury (ⲕⲁⲥⲟⲫⲩⲗⲁⲕⲓⲟⲛ— γαζοφυλάκιον).[84] The devil put this wicked thought into his wife because she was a money lover. For that reason, she made him deliver up the Lord for 30 silver pieces.

§ 56, according to which Jesus's mother, Mary, asks her son, who wants to go to Jerusalem where he will be crucified, to flee (again) to Egypt 'which loves strangers,'[85] can perhaps be related to a whole bulk of non-canonical developments of the Matthean story about the Holy Family's flight to Egypt and its relationship to this country even *after* Jesus's death and resurrection.[86] This positive attitude towards Egypt is made even more clear in § 149, which says that 'there will be no longer a covenant made with the Hebrews but it will be made with the Egyptians.' Does this already pre-suppose the idea of something like an Egyptian 'national' church?

§§ 63–64, one of the most fascinating passages, comes back to the story of Judas's wife who convinces her husband to betray Jesus:

> She whom the abyss will swallow up said to him whom the abyss will swallow up without delay: Behold, I see that you are wasting time in great sufferings, both in the burning heat of the day and the darkness of the night, and that you do not gain anything, but what you get you get by theft. But if you listen to me, I shall tell you what has entered my mind. Behold, you say, 'See the elders of the people seek to kill Jesus guilefully.' Let them make an arrangement with you about what they will pay you to deliver him to them.

Galilee'? Then the idea that Jesus got to know Simon during the wedding at Cana (John 2:1–11) would make sense.

84 The text seems to connect John 12:6 with aspects from Mark 12:41–43; Luke 21:2 and John 8:1. See also Van den Broek, *Ps-Cyril*, 135 n. 40.

85 The motif that Jesus would have had a chance to flee to other countries which would have been much more hospitable to him than his homeland could be seen as a parallel to the *Abgar Legend* according to which Jesus receives the offer to flee to Edessa.

86 See, for example, the *Vision of Theophilus*, also called the *Book of the Flight of the Holy Family into Egypt*. For an overall view regarding these developments see, for example, F. Bovon, 'L'enfant Jésus durant la fuite en Égypte: Les récits apocryphes de l'enfance comme légendes profitables à l'âme', in J. Schröter (ed.), *The Apocryphal Gospels within the Context of Early Christian Theology* (BETL 260), Leuven et al., 2013, pp. 249–270.

THE GOSPEL OF PETER

Judas even hesitates to betray Jesus (§ 65), but eventually 'listened to his wicked wife' (§ 66) who is, finally, very pleased when Judas comes home with money. After this 'success' she plans even more: Judas has also to deliver Jesus's mother and his disciples for money (§ 76). Instead, however, Jesus prophesies that 'she will not live to eat from my price but ... will get the burning diarrhoea ...' and will die the same day as Judas himself (§ 95).[87]

Passages like this, however, are neither developed from scriptural interpretation, nor do they openly contradict statements from the canonical gospels— they embellish the story, want to close gaps, and describe Gospel characters in a more vivid manner than the canonical texts do. This is even more impressive as the *Gospel of Peter* still seems to participate in the production of new Jesus stories (and/or motifs of stories related to Jesus stories) with the help of narrative interpretation of the Scriptures of Israel. While one could mention the relationship of *GosPet* 5 and 15 with Deut 21:22–23; *GosPet* 6 and Isa 59:7; *GosPet* 9 and Isa 50.6, and many others,[88] perhaps the most fascinating example can be found in v. 18.[89] At first sight, this strange passage sounds like an embellishment, such as we find in Ps.-Cyril:

Περιήρχοντο δὲ πόλλοι μετὰ λύχνων νομίζοντες ὅτι νύξ ἐστιν ἔπεσαν τε

And many went about with lamps, because they thought it was night, and fell down.

A closer look, however, reveals that this passage could have been developed from Isa 59:9–10 LXX, which shares the motifs of 'walking around' (v. 18: περιέρ-χομαι; Isa 59:9 περιπατέω) and falling (Isa 59:10). Other motifs of Isa 59:9–10 are found in the closely related v. 15 which mentions the combination of darkness (σκότος—Isa 59:9) and midday (μεσημβρία—Isa 59:10). All this can be understood as evidence that, differently from the canonical gospels, the *Gospel of Peter* transmits a tradition that connected the motif of darkness during Jesus's crucifixion not with Amos 8:9, but with Isa 59:9–10. I have not found evidence of comparable narrative interpretation of Old Testament writings in Ps.-Cyril's *Life and Passion*.[90]

---

87 Van den Broek, *Ps-Cyril*, p. 157, the following passage is likely to be corrupt.
88 For details see Hieke, 'Petrusevangelium'.
89 See Nicklas, 'Petrusevangelium im Rahmen', pp. 250–251, and Meiser, 'Petrusevangelium', p. 188.
90 A little counter-example, however, could be found in § 106, according to which the high

3.3

Some non-canonical motifs in both the *Gospel of Peter* and the 'Apostolic Memoirs' can be linked to practices of the community addressed by our texts. While the *Gospel of Peter*'s reference to the disciples fasting and mourning on Good Friday (*GosPet* 26–27) is rather vague,[91] Ps.-Cyril offers at least some instances which give clear indication of the text's (late) date. A very good example is § 37 where we read:

ⲁⲥⲱⲱ ⲉⲃⲟⲗ ⲥ̄ⲛ ⲟⲩⲡ̄ⲛⲁ̄ ⲉ ⲩⲁⲁⲃ ⲁⲇⲭ̄ⲡⲟ ⲙ̄ⲡⲭ̄ⲥ̄ ⲛ̄ⲥⲟⲩ ⲭⲟⲩⲧ ⲓ̄ⲥ ⲙ̄ⲡⲉⲃⲟⲧ ⲭⲟⲓⲁ ⲕ ⲥ̄ⲛ ⲧⲡⲟⲗⲓⲥ ⲃⲏⲑⲗⲉⲉⲙ.

She [Mary] conceived from the Holy Spirit and brought forth Christ, *on the 29th of the month of Choiakh*, in the town of Bethlehem.[92]

The 29th of the month of Choiakh, however, is the 25th of December, the date when the late antique Egyptian church of the time celebrated Christmas—a clear sign that this text cannot go back to the earliest times, but must post-date the introduction of the Christmas feast.[93] This is, however, not the only passage in Ps.-Cyril's *Life and Passion of Christ* where motifs from the canonical gospels are connected with a concrete date specification. Jesus's baptism, for example, is dated to the 11th of January, the month of Tobe (§ 12), a date which is especially interesting as Jesus's baptism was usually celebrated together with the feast of the Epiphany (6th January).[94] Is this short passage a sign that the author wanted to distinguish the events of epiphany and Jesus's baptism? We cannot be sure. While R. van den Broek discovers fascinating evidence that Ps.-Cyril presupposes a chronology of the Holy Week close to what can be found in Epiphanius of Salamis and the Syriac *Didascalia*,[95] Jesus's words to Judas in

---

    priest sinned when he tore his clothes because of Jesus's alleged blasphemy—the text seems to refer to Lev 10:6 and 21:10 (see also Van den Broek, *Ps-Cyril*, p. 181 n. 138).

91   We cannot even be sure whether the passage relates to an already established practice, but this would make good sense.

92   Van den Broek, *Ps-Cyril*, pp. 138 and 139.

93   For the development of the feast of Christmas in the ancient Church see, mainly, H. Förster, *Die Anfänge von Weihnachten und Epiphanias* (STAC 46), Tübingen, 2007.

94   Regarding the development of the feast of Epiphany in late antiquity, see the overview by H. Buchinger, 'Die vielleicht älteste erhaltene Predigt auf das Epiphaniefest: Vier syrische Fragmente des Titus von Bostra (CPG 3578)', in D. Atanassova and T. Chronz (eds), *ΣΥΝΑΞΙΣ ΚΑΘΟΛΙΚΗ. Beiträge zu Gottesdienst und Geschichte der fünf altkirchlichen Patriarchate für Heinzgerd Brakmann zum 70. Geburtstag* (Orientalia—Patristica—Oecumenica 6.1), Wien, 2014, pp. 65–86, esp. 65–69 [with extensive secondary literature].

95   See Van den Broek, *Ps-Cyril*, pp. 39–50.

THE GOSPEL OF PETER

§ 97 ('Oh, this kiss (ἀσπασμός) you guilefully gave me! You have made that the peace (εἰρήνη) of the world is taken away from these days each year.') seem to be related to the liturgical practice to avoid the kiss of peace on Good Friday.[96] Even if this practice could go back to the earliest times, its connection with Judas's kiss seems to be extra-ordinary.[97]

Other passages in Ps.-Cyril's text show a certain awareness of the development of Christological questions,[98] but are clearly not very sensitive to the details of post-Constantinopolitan (or even Post-Chalcedonian) discussion.[99] § 12, for example, writes that Jesus was baptised 'as a man, whereas he was actually God in a triune perfection.'[100] At the same time, however, § 73 ('he does not have a single shape but his appearance changes,' but see also §§ 78–79) seems to presuppose a polymorphic Christology, certainly a sign that the text does not come from the highest representatives of late antique 'orthodoxy.'[101]

While § 39, where Joseph of Arimathæa is called 'holy,' and § 101, which speaks about 'Saint Peter,' already seem to presuppose the figures' veneration as 'saints,'[102] paragraphs 111–153 develop a story about Pontius Pilate, considered here to be a 'believer in God' (§ 113). Pilate admires Jesus, who 'looks like a royal son' (§ 114), sends him back to Galilee (to Herod) (§§ 119–126), does everything to set Jesus free, dines with him, is blessed by Jesus, and even wants to 'give them [i.e. the Jews] his only son ... so that they can kill him' instead of

---

96 See also Van den Broek, *Ps-Cyril*, p. 159 n. 125, who refers to Tertullian, *De oratione* 18, as the earliest witness.

97 I am grateful to my colleague Harald Buchinger (oral communication) who was, as always, helpful in this case.

98 Regarding the text's Christology, see also (much more detailed) Van den Broek, *Ps-Cyril*, pp. 50–56.

99 All this is paired with clear signs of a triumphalistic anti-Judaism (see §§ 21, 31–33, et al.) plus an extreme interest in the wickedness of Judas and his wife (see, for example, Jesus's prophecy about their end §§ 92–97).

100 Van den Broek, *Ps-Cyril*, p. 129 and n. 24 (discussion of the translation from Coptic).

101 The text goes on: 'Sometimes he is ruddy, sometimes he is white, sometimes he is red, sometimes he is wheat-coloured, sometimes he is pallid like ascetics, sometimes he is a youth, sometimes an old man, sometimes his hair is straight and black, sometimes it is curled, sometime she is tall, sometimes he is short.' (Van den Broek, *Ps-Cyril*, p. 151). For more information on the background of this idea, which is usually related to 'heterodox' writings, but can even be traced to canonical Gospels (see, for example, the story of Jesus's transfiguration), see P. Foster, 'Polymorphic Christology: Its Origins and Development in Early Christianity', *JTS* 58 (2007), pp. 66–99.

102 Perhaps we could also ask whether a sentence like, 'Is this one better than Abraham and the prophets? And see, their tomb can still be seen' (§ 61; Van den Broek, *Ps-Cyril*, p. 147), which goes clearly further than the canonical parallel (Matt 23:29), already presupposes the practice of pilgrimage to biblical sites in the 'Holy Land.'

Jesus (§ 133). §§ 138–139 and 141–142, finally, tell about dreams dreamed by Pilate and his wife (who is called here Procla)[103], in which they, among others, envision their future death (see also *Paradosis Pilati* 10[104]). All this can be closely related to the veneration of Pilate as a martyr in the Coptic Church. Finally, § 58, according to which Jesus prophesies to his mother that he will appear to her after his resurrection (see also § 155 according to which the Evangelist John witnessed this event), only makes sense in the context of late antique Egyptian (and comparable Syriac) traditions which interpreted John 20:11–18 (or a form of this text) as an appearance of the risen Jesus to his mother.[105] All this places Ps.-Cyril's way of telling Peter's story of Jesus in a very different time and context from the Akhmim *Gospel of Peter*.

If we acknowledge that these observations depend on details, and if we remember that we were able to compare the *Gospel of Peter* with only one of numerous 'Apostolic Memoirs,' we can perhaps better imagine why the *Gospel of Peter* could have been interesting for the 6th/7th century scribe who copied it, the person who ordered it, and even the person in whose 8th-century, or later, grave it was found. Even after the closure of the canon, it seems not to have been a major problem for many Egyptian Christians to read Jesus stories told by great apostolic authorities of the past. And how could it be a problem if some stories like this were transmitted in the mouths of great ecclesiastical authorities like Cyril of Jerusalem? While I think that the person who put the different writings of the Akhmim codex together was interested in questions of bodily suffering, resurrection, and the world to come, at least Akhmim 1 (and, perhaps, Akhmim 2) could also simply be read as an interesting Jesus story— like the many Jesus stories circulating at that very time.

4 Conclusion

Even if my final argument is far from being exhaustive, and although I was not able to give a systematic overview of how the numerous (some even not well-edited) texts labelled as 'Apostolic Memoirs' deal with both oral Jesus memories and the canonical gospels, I hope I could show that the Akhmim *Gospel of Peter* belongs to a different historical stage than, at least, the text I was able to check.

---

103 See also the *Gospel of Nicodemus* where her name is Procula.
104 Mentioned also by Van den Broek, *Ps-Cyril*, p. 177.
105 See Van den Broek, *Ps-Cyril*, p. 145 n. 74; for the Syriac traditions, see S.J. Shoemaker, 'Rethinking the Gnostic Mary: Mary of Nazareth and Mary of Magdala in Early Christian Tradition', in *Journal of Early Christian Studies* 9 (2001), pp. 555–595.

THE GOSPEL OF PETER

Even though we should be aware that the Akhmim *Gospel of Peter* may not exactly represent a second century *Gospel of Peter*, and even if the text was probably changed and rewritten in the course of centuries, I still think we can treat it (with some caution) as a (not too early) second century writing, and discuss it in the context of the second (and probably third) century developments. The growing awareness that, at least in Egypt, the production and rewriting of gospel-like Jesus stories did not stop even after the closure of the New Testament canon can perhaps help us to understand why the strange combination of Akhmim 1 and 2 could survive until the sixth or seventh century (and even longer). Although its owner(s) may have been well aware of its differences from the canonical gospels, they probably understood it as one of the many allegedly old-but-new stories of Jesus, his disciples, and his mother, which still played a role in his church—texts that did not want to replace biblical accounts, but wanted both to connect them to rituals and celebrations (like Christmas, Epiphany, or the celebrations of the Holy Week), and make them present in a world where most people could not read, but were able to retell stories, as long as they remained lively and full of memorable details.

Acknowledgement

I am extremely grateful to Rebecca Draughon, University of Virginia, who corrected my English.

CHAPTER 3

All Mysteries Revealed? On the Interplay between Hiding and Revealing and the Dangers of Heavenly Journeys according to the *Ascension of Isaiah*

Joseph Verheyden

The *Ascension of Isaiah* (AI) is the title given in the Ethiopic version (E) of a work that is preserved in what seems to be a more or less complete form (there are a few gaps) only in that linguistic tradition, but of which various parts and fragments have been transmitted also in two Latin versions that only partially overlap (L1 and L2), in an Old Slavonic one (S) that largely agrees with L2, and in smaller fragments in Greek (a papyrus fragment dated to the 5/6th century), Coptic, and even Provencal. It is commonly thought once to have existed in this more complete form in Greek, though the various versions do not all go back to the same original, but rather seem to derive from two somewhat different versions (L2 and S differ from E L1 and both pairs agree more among each other than with any of the other witnesses). There has also been preserved in Greek a sort of abbreviated form of part of the work, though the relation between the abridged and the complete version remains unclear.[1]

---

1 Critical edition of AI in all its versions by P. Bettiolo et al., *Ascensio Isaiæ. Textus* (CCSA, 7), Turnhout, 1995. Basic literature includes the older commentaries by R.H. Charles, *The Ascension of Isaiah*, London, 1900, and E. Tisserant, *Ascension d'Isaïe*, Paris, 1909, and above all the more recent one by E. Norelli, *Ascensio Isaiæ. Commentarius* (CCSA, 8), Turnhout, 1995. See further also M. Erbetta, *Gli Apocrifi del Nuovo Testamento*, 3, Torino, 1969, pp. 176–208; E. Hammershaimb, 'Das Martyrium Jesajas', in W.G. Kümmel et al. (eds), *Unterweisung in erzählender Form* (Jüdische Schriften aus hellenistisch-römischer Zeit, 2), Gütersloh, 1973, pp. 15–34; M. Pesce (ed.), *Isaia, il Diletto e la Chiesa. Visione ed esegesi profetica christiano-primitiva nell'Ascensione di Isaia*, Brescia, 1983; A. Acerbi, *Serra lignea. Studi sulla fortuna della Ascensione di Isaia*, Roma, 1984, on the reception history of AI in Christian tradition; A. Díez Macho (ed.), *Apócrifos del Antiguo Testamento*, 1, Madrid, 1984, pp. 258–265; M.A. Knibb, 'Martyrdom and Ascension of Isaiah', in J.H. Charlesworth, *The Old Testament Pseudepigrapha*, 2, London, 1985, pp. 143–177; C.D.G. Müller, 'Die Himmelfahrt des Jesaja', in W. Schneemelcher, *Neutestamentliche Apokryphen in deutscher Übersetzung*, 2, Tübingen, 1989, pp. 547–562; E. Norelli, *L'Ascensione di Isaia. Studi su un apocrifo al crocevia dei cristianismi* (Origini, 1), Bologna, 1994, with an extensive survey of the history of research (pp. 11–67); J. Knight, *The Ascension of Isaiah*, Sheffield, 1995; id., *Disciples of the Beloved One. The Christology, Social Setting and Theological Context of the Ascension of Isaiah* (JSP SS, 18), Sheffield, 1996; A.M. Denis, *Introduction*

© JOSEPH VERHEYDEN, 2021 | DOI:10.1163/9789004445925_005

ALL MYSTERIES REVEALED? 71

AI tells the story of the brutal execution of the famous Jewish prophet Isaiah at the order of the evil king Manasseh, he himself ill-inspired by like-minded advisers and diabolical spirits, because of his criticism of the king's politics and morals and of his claim to have been the recipient of a visionary experience that led him to travel the heavenly spheres and even to see God, the perfect excuse for the king to decide on the prophet's fate.[2] The story of this conflict and of Isaiah's persecution and death constitutes the framework into which are inserted an account of that experience as well as a shorter prophecy on the not-so-bright future of the Church.[3] AI has often been said to be a composite work. I agree, if by this is meant that the three parts are so diverse, and so loosely or artificially interconnected, that they give the impression to have originally circulated independently before being integrated into the work as we know it today. This impression is further strengthened by the fact that the account of the heavenly journey is indeed preserved in two traditions as an apparently autonomous text (L2 and S) and that the story of the prophet's death is known also in Jewish and even in Islamic tradition, though not in the same extensive form as in AI.[4] Impressions, however, are often delusive. There is no reason to assume that the journey ever existed as a separate writing, nor that the AI account of the prophet's death represents a mere copy of a Jewish writing about this topic. Hence, I do not agree on the composite character of the work if taken in this more narrow sense.[5]

à la littérature religieuse judéo-hellénistique, 1, Turnhout, 2000, pp. 633–657 (Martyrdom of Isaiah); J. Verheyden, 'The Greek Legend of the *Ascension of Isaiah*', in B. Janssens et al. (eds), *Philomathestatos. Studies in Greek and Byzantine Texts Presented to Jacques Noret for His Sixty-Fifth Birthday*, Leuven, 2004, pp. 671–700; J. Dochhorn, 'Die Ascensio Isaiæ', in G.S. Oegema (ed.), *Unterweisung in erzählender Form* (Jüdische Schriften aus hellenistisch-römischer Zeit, 6.1.2), Gütersloh, 2005, pp. 1–48; F. Corriente Cordoba and L. Vegas Montaner, 'Ascensión de Isaías', in A. Díez Macho and A. Piñero (eds), *Apócrifos del Antiguo Testamento*, 6, Madrid, 2009, pp. 543–627; J. Knight, *The Theology of the Ascension of Isaiah: a First New Synthesis*, Lewiston–Lampeter, 2014; J.N. Bremmer et al. (eds), *The Ascension of Isaiah* (Studies in Early Christian Apocrypha, 11), Leuven, 2016.

2 Good surveys of the contents of AI and its major theological themes in M. Pesce, 'Presupposti per l'utilizzazione storica dell' Ascensione di Isaia. Formazione e tradizione del testo; genere letterario; cosmologia angelica', in id. (ed.), *Isaia*, pp. 13–69; Knight, *Disciples*, pp. 39–70.

3 On the latter, see J. Verheyden, 'Pessimism in All Its Glory: the Ascension of Isaiah on the Church in the Last Days', in Bremmer et al. (eds), *Ascension*, pp. 305–346.

4 Cf. Charles, *Ascension of Isaiah*, pp. xlv–xlix; Norelli, *Commentarius*, pp. 36–52; Knight, *Disciples*, pp. 28–32.

5 For a strong defence of the unity of the work on the basis of the observation that even if on the level of the narrative the outcome is clear (the prophet is killed already in chapter 5) the full explanation of why that happened, including details of what the prophet 'really' saw on his journey follows only later, see Dochhorn, 'Ascensio', pp. 16–19.

Nothing is known about the author of AI, and one can only speculate about the date of composition, though a mid-second century date is not impossible, but some interesting information can be gained, directly and indirectly, about some of its readers from the versions.[6] That the work shows up in Ethiopia, treasure ground for apocryphal texts of all sorts, should not surprise, as it is indicative of the mentality of Ethiopic tradition and its Church to preserve and cherish this kind of 'knowledge'. AI is mentioned by name (and one verse is even cited) in the minutes of the trial against one of the leaders of the Cathars.[7] The trajectory that can be reconstructed from Provence over Lombardy to the Balkans and further into Asia Minor of groups and movements interested in promoting a more pure form of Christian life, including a more dualistic take on 'who is in and who is out', might give a clue about who else took notice of the work and it would fit the existence of a Latin version in Italy and an Old Slavonic one further east, though one would certainly be overstating the evidence when concluding from this that AI was known and promoted only in these circles.

This perhaps rather long preliminary comment serves two purposes. It makes one aware of the fact that AI is put together from material of different genres and also that its composition history still remains something of a puzzle; and it illustrates already in a preliminary way where potential connections with the overall topic of esoteric knowledge should be found. In the following I will concentrate above all on AI itself, rather than on its composition or reception history, but the difficulties these pose should be kept in mind. More particularly, I will review a number of concepts and topics met in the work on the hypothesis that the author is not so much interested in telling the reader where he got them from and why he wishes to promote them as in showing the challenges there are in revealing this kind of information to the broader world. Hence my focus is not primarily on what the author of AI tells us about the contents of 'the mysteries' that are revealed, but on what is at stake in doing this and what the consequences are.[8]

---

6 See Norelli, *Commentarius*, pp. 53–66; Knight, *Disciples*, pp. 33–39.

7 Cf. Norelli, *Studi*, pp. 265–269.

8 Revealing secrets is naturally and logically linked to hiding (others). The dynamics between the two acts are an integral part of the AI account and are addressed in more detail in nn. 15 and 16 below. For a fine collection of essays by various authors and dealing with various religious traditions that all address this question of revealing vs. hiding, see now M. Popovic, L. Roig Lanzillotta, and C. Wilde (eds), *Sharing and Hiding Religious Knowledge in Early Judaism, Christianity, and Islam* (Judaism, Christianity, and Islam—Tension, Transmission, Transformation 10), Berlin–New York, 2018.

ALL MYSTERIES REVEALED? 73

I guess it is not so difficult to come up with a (more or less) appealing definition of what non-mainstream, or apocryphal, or even esoteric sources are. Secondary literature offers some good examples of such definitions. I will not pick one of these, but instead give a survey of core elements related to the act of revealing hidden knowledge that are found in AI and that also characterise other apocryphal and esoteric writings (the two are not fully identical, but may easily overlap). I have listed sixteen such elements, in a perhaps rather random order. The list is probably not complete, but these elements at least can all be met in AI.

1   For the Few, Not for the Many

A good number of apocryphal or esoteric writings are explicitly or implicitly concerned with not divulging their contents to a larger, or rather an unprepared or inappropriate audience. This is clearly also the case with some of the information in AI. It is important to note that this intention does not always agree with the facts as related in the account, but that is part of the procedure, and this as well can be seen happening in AI. At the end of the long account of his heavenly journey, Isaiah urges king Hezekiah and those present at his court to keep this information to themselves. 'And Isaiah made him swear that he would not tell this to the people of Israel, and that he would not allow any man to copy these words' (11,39).[9] The text continues: 'And then they (varia lectio: 'you') shall read them' (11,40). Clearly, something is missing here in E. s tried to ease the tension by adding: 'But as far as you understand what is said by the king in the prophets, understand such things, all of you' (so s, L2 is less complete), which is an emergency solution.[10] It has been said that the prophet's advice should be regarded as a literary motif and serves an etiological purpose, since it would explain why the text remained unknown for so long,[11] but there is more to it. The author really wants to communicate that this message was not meant to be divulged without further ado, an advice he did not apply to himself.[12] This brings me to the next point.

---

9   Citations of AI are from the translation of Knibb, 'Martyrdom and Ascension'.
10   On the addition, see Norelli, *Commentarius*, pp. 593–594, who thinks that something has dropped out by accident.
11   So Knibb, 'Martyrdom and Ascension', p. 176.
12   Norelli, *Commentarius*, p. 593, who makes a distinction between copying the message in a book and spreading it around.

2   On the Dangers of Not Keeping a Secret

The prophet's advice was ignored, and this in two ways and on two levels. On the level of the story, it has most dramatic consequences. The author gives no details, but immediately jumps to the outcome when continuing in v. 41 to state that Isaiah was murdered, 'because of these visions and prophecies'.[13] Clearly, somebody did not keep his mouth shut. The prophet's advice was also ignored in a second way. The account of his journey was put on paper. The outcome of this decision may look less dramatic, but that may only be an impression. The consequences of this latter move are not addressed by the author, nor are the implications for the status of AI. This is a text that actually should never have existed; hence, was this a good or a bad decision? It would seem the answer depends on who is asking. Obviously, the book was not written *not* to be read. History has shown that some at least of those who took notice of its contents suffered from it when they were persecuted as heretics.[14]

3   Explosive Stuff Indeed

As the author sees it, the reason for the prophet's advice is that this account contains dangerous material. But the reader might ask why this is so, and for whom. AI is not the only account of a heavenly journey, and not all of those who were privileged to live such an experience were killed for it.[15] Was it just a matter of bad luck, of running into the wrong people at the wrong moment? That would in part explain things, but it seems that more is in play. AI 11,41 offers a kind of general explanation. 'Because of these visions and prophecies Sammael Satan sawed Isaiah ... in half by the hand of Manasseh'. The same was told, with other characters involved (Beliar), in 5,1.14–15. However, it seems it was not so much the visionary experience as a whole, but one particular point that raised the anger of the prophet's enemy. Or at least that is how Isaiah's

---

13   The precise referent of the phrase remains somewhat unclear. Norelli (*Commentarius*, p. 599), with good reason, thinks it includes all that was said about visionary experiences of the prophet, including AI 3,13 ff. This whole last section (11,41–43) is usually assigned to the final redactor, or more narrowly still, to the author of the Ethiopic translation.

14   The motif of a book that is both a treasure of truth and a danger for its users is not unknown in apocalyptic literature. The two are inevitably interconnected and the appeal of the former is (thought to be) such that it conquers the latter, at least for those devoted to its contents.

15   On the genre as it is given form in AI, see U. Bianchi, 'L'*Ascensione di Isaia*. Tematiche soteriologiche di *descensus/ascensus*', in Pesce, *Isaia*, pp. 155–178 (with discussion 179–183).

opponent Belkira presents things. Two accusations are held against him: the prophet's claim to have seen the Lord and to have survived (AI 3,9)[16] and his contempt of the legitimate, though morally discredited, successor to the king and of his cronies and the threats he allegedly had announced against the state (see AI 3,6–7.10.13).[17] As things are presented, it seems that the theological factor, which is neither argued nor disclaimed, is mentioned because it offers the opponents an opportunity to have their revenge on the prophet. This is clearly expressed in the dramatic encounter between the prophet and Belkira at the moment of the former's execution, when the victim is given a last opportunity to 'repent' and to withdraw his accusations against the prince (AI 5,4.8).[18] The theological argument seems long forgotten. Actually, the accusation will prove to be false. This is not said here yet, but from the prophet's account of the heavenly journey in 9,37–42, it is made clear for the reader that Isaiah was invited to see 'the great glory' (v. 39), that he tried to see but could not 'behold', even though he was in the Spirit, hence well-disposed to receive a vision of extraordinary dimensions (v. 37), and that what he really saw was the Spirit and the Beloved One worshipping God (v. 40). E and SL2 differ amongst each other, with the first seemingly being more open to the possibility that the prophet indeed saw God's glory (so v. 37 and 39), but those arguing for this may have overestimated the weight of the wording, for after all v. 39 is an invitation only and v. 37 looks like a failed attempt at trying to see what man is forbidden to see. SL2 may have sensed that this is all still a bit too ambiguous and therefore rephrased the passage, so as to make sure the prophet is reported not to have seen God's glory. This is in any case more in line with what the prophet himself says immediately afterwards in 10,2 ('and all ... were directed to that Glorious One whose glory I could not see') and again in 11,32 when referring to Christ: 'And then I saw that he sat down at the right hand of that Great Glory, whose glory I told you I could not behold'.[19] The accusation is false, and exposes the accusers' bad faith. Two

---

16 The accusation is met in other Jewish and Christian texts; see the survey in Norelli, *Commentarius*, pp. 156–159. In 5,15 is added an extra when it is said that Isaiah had also received information concerning 'the Beloved'; this refers back to 1,5 and the vision in 3,13 ff.

17 The fact that they utter this criticism 'as prophets' introduces a strong biblical motif and adds to the seriousness of the accusation. See Norelli, *Commentarius*, p. 152.

18 Beliar tries (in vain) to turn Isaiah into a false or unreliable prophet by pushing him to renounce his former views. Cf. Norelli, *Commentarius*, p. 294. Commentators have of course not missed the echo from or parallel with the temptation story in the gospels.

19 On the differences in the various traditions, see Charles, *Ascension*, p. 68; Knibb, 'Martyrdom and Ascension', p. 172; Norelli, *Commentarius*, pp. 494–498. The latter quite strictly distinguishes between E and SL2 (p. 497: 'Secondo il nostro testo, Isaia a visto Dio? Sec-

conclusions can be drawn from this. Spreading esoteric knowledge is by definition potentially dangerous; in this case it is even used against the messenger for merely political and strategic reasons. Once made public, such knowledge (or claims) can and will be used against the one who brought them into the open. Those who bring such messages should duly realise the consequences.

4 That Unstoppable Urge to Spread the News

The dangers and the consequences of spreading this kind of knowledge do not weigh against the urge of the messenger to bring it into the open, even at the risk of getting murdered for it. It is a truly amazing and at the same time a most disturbing feat. If the prophet's flight from Jerusalem, and then also from Bethlehem (which does not fare better) (2,8), might look like an act of cowardice, which it obviously is not,[20] Isaiah's heroic behaviour at the time of his execution greatly makes up for this false impression. Not only does the hero defy his accusers' last attempt to bring him over to their side, he resists the temptation with the assistance of the Spirit, as he dies without uttering a word to his assailants and while speaking with the Spirit (5,14).[21] He had shown this same heroic behaviour before when boldly speaking out against the king's son as his future murderer (1,7–8).[22] The good and great news he has to bring will not be stopped by manipulative opponents, not even in the face of death.

5 Inspired by God and by the Devil

The prophet is the hero of the story and the accounts of his journey through the heavens and of his death are its two climaxes, but the story is not played out on this level only. The hero is steered, just as this is the case with his opponents. They are all tools in a story that plays on a different level. The author of AI is most conscious of this, and does not tire from telling it to the reader. This is the

---

ondo E, si. ... quindi in SL² Isaia *non* vede Dio'), but may have overstated the difference for it would leave E in utter contradiction with itself in 10,2 and 11,32.

20 Norelli (*Commentarius*, p. 123) rightly compares it to the Spirit's withdrawal in the face of iniquity in 3,26.

21 Both motifs are a common feature of the true martyr as Norelli amply illustrates from examples in Christian literature (*Commentarius*, pp. 303–304).

22 The motif of the prophet foretelling his own death is known from the canonical Book of Isaiah and was much appreciated in Christian literature as well; see Norelli, *Commentarius*, pp. 94–95.

account of a battle between the forces of good and of evil. The former takes the obvious face of God and his angels and of the Beloved and the Spirit. The latter also takes various faces, but they clearly are all representatives or perhaps emanations of the same evil entity. They are servants of Satan, whatever their name—be it Belkira or Beliar, Sammael or Matanbukus (2,4), be they human or pseudo-divine.[23] It puts the whole story in a different perspective. This is not merely an account of the struggle between a prophet and the establishment, it is a battle between heaven and earth, and what is at stake largely transgresses the political or societal level.[24] This is about revealing a truth of a wholly different kind, though it definitely also comprises an ethical component (see below).

6   Drawing the Lines between Good and Evil

Isaiah's claim about his vision and the news he brings to the court and his audience is instrumental in drawing the border lines between those who are on his side and those who wish to oppose him. They are divided along the lines of moral categories, and it is their lack of morality that gives the opponents away. It is not so much that the content of his message creates the division, as that it brings about the opportunity his enemies were looking for to act against the prophet. Hidden knowledge revealed also reveals the true spirit of all those involved, including the addressees. Isaiah is shown to be the privileged messenger he claims to be and is allowed to be in the Spirit; the king is driven to act against his own son, but his plan is aborted by the prophet himself (1,13).[25]

---

23   AI has a keen interest in demonology, though its author does not always seem to be much concerned about 'who is who'. See Norelli, *Studi*, pp. 79–92; Jan Dochhorn, 'Beliar als Endtyrann in der Ascensio Isaiæ. Ein Beitrag zur Eschatologie und Satanologie des frühen Christentums sowie zur Erforschung der Apokalypse des Johannes', in J. Frey et al. (eds), *Die Johannesapokalypse: Kontexte—Konzepte—Rezeption* (WUNT, 287), Tübingen, 2012, pp. 293–315.

24   This does of course not mean that the latter is completely absent or thought to be irrelevant for the author of AI. On the political dimension, which goes beyond the faint allusion to the persecution of Christians by Nero and the polemics with representatives of Judaism, see J. Knight, *Disciples*, pp. 190–196 and pp. 205–212; id., 'The Political Issue of the *Ascension of Isaiah*: A Response to Enrico Norelli', in *JSNT* 35 (2013), pp. 355–379. Knight is critical of Norelli's suggestion (in reply to an earlier publication by Knight) that the martyrdom is meant to be symbolic rather than real: see E. Norelli, 'The Political Issue of the *Ascension of Isaiah*: Some Remarks on Jonathan Knight's Thesis, and Some Methodological Problems', in D.H. Warren, A. Graham Brock and D.W. Pao (eds), *Early Christian Voices in Texts, Traditions and Symbols* (BIS 66), Leiden, 2003, pp. 267–279.

25   Isaiah is designated as the heir of Christ; as such his 'fate is to be one of suffering' (Knibb,

Manasseh and those siding with him use the prophet's revelations as an opportunity to show their criminal intentions which actually are but one aspect of their devilish minds as pictured in 2,5.[26] The esoteric is linked to the ethical.

7 Those Who Have Heard—Then and Now

But the effects of coming to know the contents of Isaiah's message are not limited only to the characters in the story. By putting the contents on paper and producing a book on the prophet's visionary explorations, a potentially much larger audience can be reached and given a chance to take a stance (see above on the prohibition in 11,39 to write down the experience of the prophet). Indeed, if on the level of the story the players are few and it is explicitly said that 'the people did not hear' about the heavenly journey (6,17), the book itself can be accessed by such readers who had perhaps not been intended, but who will have to make up their minds and side with or against the prophet and his message. The book continues to draw lines also among its readers. And even if it were never the intention that this sort of knowledge was meant to be 'spread to the masses', the audience at least is enlarged, and so is the number of those who are urged to take sides.[27]

8 Saving and Ruining

But it is not only about provoking (ethical) decisions on the part of the readers. The account of Isaiah's fate and the announcement of that of his main oppo-

---

'Martyrdom and Ascension', p. 157). What will happen to the prophet is part and parcel of that great battle that is to be fought for the salvation of mankind.

26   The list of Manasseh's helpers evokes the long history of the establishment's resistance to prophets; cf. Norelli, *Commentarius*, p. 119.

27   What we know of the reception history of AI in more radically minded circles shows that this aspect did certainly not go unnoticed, even if it is absent in the book itself, apart from the references to those who sided with Isaiah in his exile, and should be taken as role models for how to live an ascetic life (2,9–11). There is no reason to think that this lifestyle had anything to do with aspirations to receive visionary experiences; it is just how good Christians should live in the spirit of the prophet. Cf. Norelli, *Commentarius*, pp. 132–133. AI shows an interest in self-referencing those who side with the prophet or are counted amongst the righteous, which would indicate that a link with later generations of readers (and followers) was probably well intended. See the comments in M. Henning and T. Nicklas, 'Questions of Self-Designation in the *Ascension of Isaiah*', in Bremmer et al. (eds), *Ascension*, pp. 175–198.

ALL MYSTERIES REVEALED? 79

nent, as well as the contents of the message itself bring judgement about those who are confronted with them. Manasseh will be killed, if not by the hands of his father the king, then surely by the will of God. Let there be no misunderstanding about that. It is said in so many words in the very last verse of the work: 'But Manasseh did not remember these things, nor place them in his heart, but he became the servant of Satan and was destroyed' (11,43).[28] Likewise, the prophet may well have suffered a martyr's death (besides the account proper of the murder, see also its announcement by the prophet himself in 1,7.13), but the reader should trust that he will surely be rewarded for this, even if the reward is not mentioned in any detail. Or perhaps his visionary experience was itself already part of this reward? Those who put their trust in the prophet, and through him in God, should know that reward comes with suffering, but suffering will always also be rewarded.[29]

9   Source of Knowledge and Role Model

The previous point already gives an indication of how to conceive of Isaiah's role and status. He is the shaman-like prophet who brought us the knowledge that leads to salvation and shows by his own fate how the latter can be reached. He is both the source of, or perhaps rather the medium through which, that knowledge is communicated and the role model for those who wish to believe in it. The prophet knows about the things he communicates to the king because he was granted that knowledge and the privilege to see it *de visu*. He shows us both the contents and the way to access them. It raises the question of where

---

28   And with all those who had sided with the malicious king: 'chi disprezza e perseguita la profezia va in perdizione. I 'presbiteri e pastori' erano avvisati' (Norelli, *Commentarius*, p. 599). On AI's critical stance towards the Church establishment, see Knight, *Disciples*, pp. 197–205 and my 'Pessimism in All its Glory', in Bremmer et al. (eds), *Ascension*, pp. 305–346.

29   This is somehow demonstrated by the figure of king Hezekiah who suffers the double fate of being told that his beloved prophet will be butchered by his own depraved son. He will be richly rewarded for his righteousness and loyalty; indeed, he is promised robes and thrones and crowns from the seventh heaven (11,40). In 9,25–26, the same reward is promised to those who believe in Christ and his cross; the latter may well be an allusion to this motif of reward through suffering. ESL2 differs considerably at v. 26, but the general idea of believing in Christ (and his words) is present in all. Cf. Norelli, *Commentarius*, 480. The fact that Isaiah is said to have sent away his disciples at the moment of his arrest because he is the one that has 'to drink the cup' (5,13) does not argue against this. His disciples had suffered with the master in exile, and it is not said that they followed up on the command to leave the scene.

he stands and where the reader is supposed to situate him/herself. The latter knows because the former told him/her *and* gave proof of the truth of his message; at the same time the account of the prophet's fate shows the reader what the consequences of this message will be. The prophet shares the fate of the Beloved, and the reader should be prepared to go the same way. This raises the further question of whether the prophet is unique in his role and person, of whether the privilege of seeing the things Isaiah saw was given only once. Going by the account in AI, the latter seems indeed to be the case—he has seen what no one had seen before (11,34),[30] but evidence from the trial of one of the Cathar leaders shows that some of them at least claimed to have been granted similar visionary experiences. It is difficult to say how far this betrays the spirit of AI or rather builds on it. In any case, it shows the need for later generations who become familiar with AI to see the original experience as being somehow repeated or duplicated. The reader should sense that s/he belongs to the circle of Isaiah's companions and to that wider one of his later followers and believers.

10   Knowing and Doing

As the author of AI sees it, Isaiah's message has to do with knowledge, with wisdom, and with praxis. Those who come to know the contents of the message can act upon it wisely or foolishly. Manasseh is a clear example of the latter, Isaiah's companions of the former. The message obviously is not, or not primarily, about informing the reader on matters of cosmology or the structure of heaven.[31] It is about interiorising the effects this information should provoke on those who are exposed to it or are granted the privilege to become familiar with it. There is a strong ethical component involved; it is not about theory, or not only.

---

30   The motif is further developed in SL2 in a way that is attested broadly throughout Christian literature and is inspired by 1 Cor 2,9; cf. Norelli, *Commentarius*, pp. 590–591.

31   On AI's cosmology in general, see Norelli, *Commentarius*, pp. 375–380; L. Roig Lanzillotta, 'The Cosmology of the *Ascension of Isaiah*: Analysis and Re-Assessment of the Text's Cosmological Framework', in Bremmer et al. (eds), *Ascension*, pp. 259–288. R. Bauckham, 'How the Author of the *Ascension of Isaiah* Created its Cosmological Version of the Story of Jesus', in Bremmer et al. (eds), *Ascension*, pp. 23–44, compares it with Paul's cosmology and points out its purpose in explaining Christ's descent and ascent.

ALL MYSTERIES REVEALED? 81

11   Sanctioned by God

The author of AI clearly is convinced that esoteric information is meant to be revealed, even if only to the pure, the elite or the elect. The initiative for it comes from God through the Spirit. The prophet or the one granted the revelation is but the medium, never the one who triggered the process. Those present when Isaiah is granted his vision praise God 'and they ascribed glory to the One who has thus graciously given a door in an alien world, had graciously given it to a man' (6,9).[32] This is a fundamental principle in AI's views on how Isaiah got access to the message. It also both guarantees the truth of the latter and the status of the one who communicates it to the world. AI puts great weight on this. In line with this, it is not surprising that the prophet's enemies can only counter the message with trumped up accusations. When using the message against the messenger, they call him a fraud and a liar and misrepresent the admittedly quite extraordinary claim of the prophet that he had seen Christ and the Spirit worship God (though not the latter Himself), but they do not explicitly deny he ever made the journey experience. Only its climax they refuse to accept, but otherwise their accusations are far more mundane and primarily politically inspired.

12   Sensing the Experience

The author's information to the reader about the technical aspects of Isa-iah's experience is relatively sparse, but that is not uncommon for the genre. Two things seem to retain his attention. First, what happens to the prophet is divinely inspired, it does not involve any kind of human trickery—no drugs, no potions, no concoctions. Second, Isaiah is utterly passive, indeed mentally absent, all through the process. The visionary experience happens while he is speaking to the king and his court, with the latter experiencing the presence of the Spirit (6,6). AI 6,10–12 gives the following slightly repetitious description: 'And while he was speaking with the Holy Spirit in the hearing of them all, he became silent, and his mind was taken up from him, and he did not see the men who were standing before him. His eyes indeed were open, but his mouth

---

32   E and SL2 once again differ considerably, as do scholars in assessing the various options, but Norelli (*Commentarius*, p. 340) is probably right in calling the reading of SL2 secondary because it is the *lectio facilior* (pace Knibb, 'Martyrdom and Ascension', p. 265). The reader is then treated to a description of how the prophet got in trance and starts seeing a vision (see next section).

was silent, and the mind in his body was taken up from him. But his breath was (still) in him, for he was seeing a vision'. The vision is granted to him by an angel from on high. The prophet obviously is not dead, neither asleep, but mentally he is in a different world. Third, those who are standing by and watching get a completely different impression of what has happened. They can see the prophet and 'did (not: so SL2) think that the holy Isaiah had been taken up' (6,14). For them, he is physically present all the time, sitting on a couch (6,2).[33] It does not mean the heavenly journey did not happen; it is only that the prophet travels another world.[34] To this should be added that the author does not relate the experience in the prophet's words, but from the perspective of one who was present when it happened and clearly saw more or better than the others at court what it was that was happening to the prophet. The author acts as the prophet's interpreter, or rather as the one who steers the prophet and the reader alike in getting a sense of the whole process. It puts him in a unique position but obviously, as he sees it, this in no way affects the truth of his account. The reader is privileged to have run into such an author.

13   Pandora's Box

So far I have mainly focused on the effects which the visionary experience had on the prophet and those hearing about it. I now turn to the contents. In AI 1,5, the author gives the following summary of the contents of the prophet's vision: 'what he himself had seen in the house of the king concerning the judgment of the angels, and concerning the destruction of the world, and concerning the robes of the saints and their going out, and concerning their transformation and the persecution and ascension of the Beloved'. AI reveals or informs the reader about all of this, and more, including the prophet's fate, the future of the church, an occasional doctrinal issue, cosmology, and heaven and how to access it. The differences between AI 1,5 and my list are remarkable and not easy to explain. It could be taken as an indication that the author of 1,5 was ignorant

---

33   The experience has often been compared to the visions of Hermas. So Norelli, *Commentarius*, pp. 317–318. See in more detail also, P.C. Bori, 'L'esperienza profetica nell' *Ascensione di Isaia*', in Pesce, *Isaia*, pp. 133–145 (with discussion on pp. 145–154). I. Czachesz, 'Religious Experience behind the Account of Isaiah's Ascent to Heaven: Insights from Cognitive Science', in Bremmer et al. (eds), *Ascension*, pp. 235–257, places the experience as related in AI in a wider perspective.

34   Cf. P. Piovanelli, ''A Door into an Alien World': Reading the *Ascension of Isaiah* as a Jewish Mystical Text', in Bremmer et al. (eds), *Ascension*, pp. 119–144, situating AI in the context of Jewish mystical traditions.

ALL MYSTERIES REVEALED? 83

of the contents of the prophecy on the church in 3,13 ff. The one who combined this section with others to create AI did not care to take a closer look at the whole of the work. But maybe the explanation is just to be sought in the matter itself—in what one considers to be 'hidden knowledge' or relevant knowledge of this kind. In any case, the knowledge Isaiah has to convey is variegated and of different natures, and not all of it is equally positive—hence Pandora in the title.[35]

14 Promoting the Real Truth

Two important features of such 'hidden-to-be-revealed' knowledge are to be mentioned. The first is a quite obvious one. This knowledge is meant to be revealed to a (selected) audience. It is therefore imperative that the necessary conditions and context are created by and in which this is made possible. It may help to give the setting a certain solemnity (the royal court) and to emphasise the prominence of those attending (the king and his closest advisers). All of this may contribute to enhance the quality of the second feature: it is knowledge or information which is accurate and which cannot be disclaimed in any way, because ultimately it is of divinely inspired origin. Ignoring or countering it is extremely dangerous and actually impossible. What is going to be revealed is nothing else but 'the real truth', whatever Manasseh and his counsellors may think of it.

15 Explaining and Obscuring

Quite remarkably, this claim about the truth of the message is often also in a sense nuanced by the very nature of the information that the reader or audience is granted to receive. It is no different with AI. The vision shows and explains things, but it also obscures other things. The latter happens in two ways: by providing a kind of 'non-information' and by cutting off the information stream. The reader is seemingly overwhelmed with information on the seven heavens the prophet has to pass through, but part of this is purely repetitive and does not bring anything new. The scene in the fourth heaven (7,28–31)

---

35   In addition to the lament on the state of the Church, the reference to the death of Christ (the Beloved) is particularly important as it probably serves also to highlight the fate of the prophet himself and those identifying with him, historically (so Norelli, *Commentarius*, p. 90), but then also in the reception of AI by later generations.

looks very much like that in the fifth (7,32–37) and these two hardly differ from the lower ones, but what is the point?[36] One gets no concrete information on how the prophet passed from one heaven to the other. Also, we are told that in the sixth and the seventh heavens there are no longer two groups of angels worshipping the One sitting on the throne in the middle (8,7), but why this is so is not explained. The information that the angels are attracted or directed 'by the power of the seventh heaven' is at best a kind of pseudo-explanation.[37] Perhaps more frustrating still is the observation that even the prophet is not granted the ultimate experience. He too is barred from seeing God, even though such a claim is falsely held against him by the opponents. At most, he is allowed to see how the Beloved sits at the right of 'that Great Glory', but the latter 'I could not behold' (11,32, and see above).[38] As a rule, the reader is informed about the what rather than the why; and in the end s/he is made thoroughly aware of the limits of the knowledge and information that is granted him/her.

16   The New is Old and the Old is New

But perhaps even more frustrating is the fact that some of this hidden knowledge the reader comes to hear about is actually old stuff sold as new, to put it a bit bluntly. Isaiah was not the first nor the only one to have been rapt to the heavens. That the latter consist of seven spheres one can travel and that there is a qualitative difference between each of them was most probably also not unknown to a second-century Christian audience. The information about the throne, robes and crowns (9,24–26), the choirs of angels and the constant worshipping sounds almost trivial.

But fortunately there is also some other material revealed. Here are three examples. First, the prophet 'sees'—how this is to be understood is not made clear—Jesus's life from his birth to his violent death (11,1–21). Nothing is done with this for now, and no mention is made of how the prophet reacts to this disturbing information. But it helps explain why Isaiah can be cited in Christian

---

36 One difference is the type and quality of 'glory' that is met in the higher heaven, but otherwise it all looks very much the same: 'La descrizione del quarto e del quinto cielo corrisponde a quelle dei tre inferiori, con aumento progressive di Gloria e di lode' (Norelli, *Commentarius*, p. 418). One difference is that for the fourth heaven it is specified that its distance from the third one is greater than that between earth and the firmament, if that can at all be measured or imagined; no reason is mentioned for this observation.

37 The problem is enhanced by the textual differences between the versions; cf. Norelli, *Commentarius*, pp. 430–431.

38 On the term 'G/glory' in AI, see Norelli, *Studi*, pp. 249–252.

ALL MYSTERIES REVEALED? 85

texts and tradition to announce the coming of the Lord and even the outcome of his earthly ministry.[39] Second, the repetitious account of Christ's (the Lord's) travel through the heavens in 11,22–33 serves the double purpose of explaining how the ascension that follows the resurrection is to be understood and, more importantly, how the incarnation, framed as a descent through partly inimical spheres, could happen. The latter was a kenotic event that took away the Lord's glory, so that he passed unnoticed; the former is a return in triumph that is duly recognised by all those inhabiting the seven spheres, including Satan himself (11,23).[40] Third, the stress on the miraculous birth of the child Jesus in 11,8 shows the author being pre-occupied above all with preserving Mary's virginity, at the expense of the physical aspect of the process.[41] Mary was on her own in the house, 'looked with her eyes and saw a small infant, and she was astounded'.[42] It is as simple as that. Some of this material seems to offer new information or new knowledge, but in part it is also heavily linked up with commonly known views on cosmology and the structure of heaven.

Finally, AI also contains 'new' information that is not told as such in the account of the prophet's heavenly journey in AI 6–11. Two items should be mentioned. The first is the prophet's vision of the future of the church which is related in AI 3,13–30, but nevertheless is considered to be a part of Isaiah's journey experience by his opponent Beliar (3,13). It is a sad and quite pessimistic perspective that is evoked of a Church in distress and affected by corruption. The passage is composed of elements and phrases from various NT writings. So again, there is not really much new in this, except that this sort of information is now made part of the prophet's vision and message and is transmitted by

---

39   In that sense, the section serves as a kind of explanation why Isaiah is cited in connection with the coming of the Lord in the gospels and other texts.

40   On this aspect of AI's Christology, see M. Simonetti, 'Note sulla cristologia dell' *Ascensione di Isaia*', in Pesce (ed.), *Isaia*, pp. 185–205 (with discussion, pp. 205–209), esp. 195; Norelli, *Commentarius*, pp. 581–585; Knight, *Disciples*, pp. 146–150 and *passim*, who connects it with the angelomorphic Christology the author is promoting.

41   See T. Karmann, 'Die Jungfrauengeburt in der *Ascensio Isaiæ* und in anderen Texten des frühen Christentums', in Bremmer et al. (eds), *Ascension*, pp. 347–385.

42   Norelli (*Commentarius*, pp. 545–550) notes that it is not a coincidence that this kind of information is mediated through a vision in a work 'in cui la visione profetica ha tanta importanza, apparendo come il mezzo privilegiato di conoscenza dell' economia salvifica' (p. 550). The author of AI is not interested in trivia, but in explaining Christian soteriology. Knight (*Disciples*, pp. 89–90) sees in it an expression of 'a naively docetic quality', which is found above all in E. More critical about the assumed docetic tendencies of AI is D.D. Hannah, 'The Ascension of Isaiah and Docetic Christology', in *VigChr* 53 (1999), pp. 165–196.

the one who also gave us access to the account of that prophet's journey.[43] The second item is the information on the violent death of the prophet. Isaiah's fate was known from Heb 11,37 and from Jewish tradition, but AI offers some more details and context and above all, the reason why the prophet suffered this death.[44] This information is not gained through the visionary experience, but is provided by the prophet himself announcing his death in his private dialogue with the king (AI 1,13), and again transmitted to the reader by the omniscient author of AI. For much of the information listed here one can say that it was or may well have been known to the reader, was then in a sense hidden, and was finally revealed through the combined efforts of the prophet and the author who is instrumental in informing the reader about all of this. So old and new go hand in hand, but this at least AI brings to it: this old knowledge is now confirmed by the famous prophet Isaiah and is made part of, or closely linked to, the latter's visionary experience and his reflection on its consequences.

One has the strong impression that it is above all this experience itself that matters, perhaps even more than its contents; and this impression may well be close to the truth. The contents are appealing and may theologically and otherwise be important, but most important, so it seems, is the information that a human being had once been given the privilege and opportunity to reach out for heaven and was able to return and tell fellow humans about it. That experience remains valuable and should be passed on. But maybe behind it is also the hope or conviction that others, the pure or the elect, will once be granted this same privilege, and bring back to earth new knowledge or further confirmation of the old one. The latter is certainly something that has played a role in the reception of AI in such circles and movements that laid much emphasis on receiving this sort of 'hidden knowledge'.

Conclusion

Very briefly. AI tells a story and conveys a message. The story plays on a double level—on earth and in heaven, and the two levels are closely linked to each other. What happened to the prophet in heaven had dramatic consequences for his own life. The message too has two levels, so to speak. The prophet reveals hidden knowledge, or at least confirms such knowledge to be true. The contents

---

43   See my analysis in 'Pessimism in All Its Glory', in Bremmer et al. (ed.), *Ascension*, pp. 303–346; Norelli, *Studi*, pp. 167–173.

44   Cf. Norelli, *Studi*, pp. 229–234; in more detail, Acerbi, *Serra lignea*, pp. 69–102.

of his message consist on the one hand of the information that is revealed as a result of a heavenly journey, and on the other of emphasising the great value there is in being granted such an experience. The medium is *not* the message, but it definitely is part of it.

CHAPTER 4

Early Christianity and the Pagan Mysteries: Esoteric Knowledge?

Jan N. Bremmer

Esotericism is a popular subject in studies of the modern world.[1] It is less clear, though, what we should understand under that term. Is it helpful to use a term for certain themes in early Christianity on which modern scholars have not even reached agreement? Though one may have one's doubts about this, it is clear that esotericism smells of secrecy. It is, therefore, not surprising that several of the papers in these proceedings have the words 'mystery' or 'esoteric' in their title. That is why I, too, will concentrate on the so-called Mystery cults.

One can choose two approaches in this respect, an emic or an etic one. In other words, one can ask if the pagans saw a certain resemblance between emerging Christianity and the Mystery cults or one can ask if the Christians themselves saw something of a Mystery cult in their own emerging religion. I will pay attention to both points of view but within a limited period of time, viz. the period from about AD 180 to 250, that is, the decades before the Christian movement really took off with ever increasing numbers.[2] Now a first observation should be made about the vocabulary at the time. We need not follow the old Nijmegen School with their claim of Christian Greek and Latin in order to see that the early Christians appropriated many words of the current pagan vocabulary and gave them new meanings.[3] However, terms were not only changed by the Christians but, of course, terms also changed due to normal historical circumstances.

A second observation regards the influence of Clement of Alexandria. As is well known, Clement has given us an important part of an Attic handbook

---

1 See, especially, W. Hanegraaff, *Esotericism and the Academy*, Cambridge, 2012.
2 Cf. J.N. Bremmer, *The Rise of Christianity through the Eyes of Gibbon, Harnack and Rodney Stark*, Groningen, 2012.
3 Cf. C.V. Franklin, 'Christine A.E.M. Mohrmann (1903–1988) and the Study of Christian Latin', in J. Chance (ed.), *Women Medievalists and the Academy*, Madison, 2004–2005, pp. 598–612; T. Denecker, 'The Nijmegen School and its 'sociological' approach to the so-called Sondersprache of early Christians: a preliminary historiographical study', *Latomus* 77 (2018), pp. 335–357.

© JAN N. BREMMER, 2021 | DOI:10.1163/9789004445925_006

on the Mysteries in his *Protreptikos*, which proved highly influential in subsequent centuries.[4] So the earlier the sources we investigate, the more chance there is that we are looking at authors independent from Clement. As Clement has been investigated in great detail by Christoph Riedweg, Fabienne Jourdan and Miguel Herrero,[5] I will concentrate on the philosopher Celsus as presented and discussed by Origen: his treatment of the Mysteries has not been the subject of a specific study since the late 1980s, when Michel Fédou dedicated two chapters to this subject in his study of the relationship between Christianity and the pagan religions in the *Contra Celsum*.[6] Fédou still depended on Franz Cumont's views on what he called Mystery religions. Since the 1980s, however, we have had several studies showing that we should speak of Mystery cults rather than religions as well as detailed studies of a number of the Mysteries themselves, partially based on newly discovered papyri and inscriptions.[7] It is therefore opportune to take a fresh look at Celsus and Origen in the context of the theme of this book.

Recently, we have had two important studies of Celsus. First, Peter Van Nuffelen dedicated an important chapter to this Platonist philosopher's views on Christianity in a dense book in which he argues that for Celsus the Christians are like the charlatans of Apuleius's *Metamorphoses*, people who 'use sham mystery cults to exploit the simple, talkative individuals who reveal the secrets of mystery cults'.[8] On the other hand, Johannes Arnold's recent structural analysis of Celsus's *True Discourse* is much more focused on the Mysteries themselves within the whole of Celsus's argument.[9] His detailed discussion not only analyses the various references to the Mysteries in Celsus but also makes a persuasive argument that Celsus's book itself reflects the very initiatory structure of the Mysteries. Yet it seems not unfair to say that Arnold's interest is in Celsus, rather than in the Mysteries or their relationship with the Christians. In my

---

4   F. Massa, 'La notion de "mystères" au IIe siècle de notre ère: regards païens et *Christian turn*', Mètis NS 14 (2016), pp. 109–132.

5   C. Riedweg, *Mysterienterminologie bei Platon, Philon, und Klemens von Alexandrien*, Berlin–New York, 1987; F. Jourdan, *Orphée et les Chrétiens* vol. 1, Paris, 2010, pp. 159–269; M. Herrero de Jáuregui, *Orphism and Christianity in Late Antiquity*, Berlin–New York, 2010, pp. 144–153.

6   M. Fédou, *Christianisme et religions païennes dans le* Contre Celse *d'Origène*, Paris, 1988.

7   W. Burkert, *Ancient Mystery Cults*, Cambridge MA–London, 1987; J.N. Bremmer, *Initiation into the Mysteries of the Ancient World*, Berlin–Boston, 2014.

8   P. Van Nuffelen, *Rethinking the Gods*, Cambridge, 2011, pp. 217–230 at 226. Elsewhere I have discussed various aspects of this stimulating book: J.N. Bremmer, 'Philosophers and the Mysteries', in C. Riedweg (ed.), PHILOSOPHIA *in der Konkurrenz von Schulen, Wissenschaften und Religionen. Zur Pluralisierung des Philosophie-begriffs in Kaiserzeit und Spätantike*, Berlin–Boston, 2017, pp. 99–126 at 101–108.

9   J. Arnold, *Der* Wahre Logos *des Kelsos. Eine Strukturanalyse*, Münster, 2016, pp. 481–519.

contribution I therefore will first look at what Celsus has to say about the Mysteries (§1), continue with his use of the Mysteries in his polemic against Jews and Christians (§2), proceed with Origen's polemic against Celsus regarding the Mysteries (§3), and conclude with what this discussion tells us about the esoteric in the early history of Christianity (§4). My choice of Celsus may surprise, but, with Lucian,[10] he is the most detailed contemporary pagan observer of emerging Christianity that we have and as such deserves more interest than he has received in recent studies.[11]

1   Celsus and the Pagan Mysteries

Unfortunately, the identity of Celsus has remained elusive despite the great efforts of historians and patristic scholars. We cannot say more than that the author will have lived around AD 200, give or take a few decades, and probably worked in Alexandria.[12] His philosophical leanings were (Middle-)Platonising with perhaps some Epicurean accents;[13] in any case, unlike what Richard Gordon, our best and most erudite scholar of Mithras, has repeatedly stated, he was not a neoplatonist.[14] There can be little doubt that Celsus was quite well informed, and he will have had the same knowledge of the Mysteries that we find in earlier and contemporary authors such as Dio, Lucian or Apuleius. So which Mysteries did he know?

The most valuable information from Celsus concerns the Mysteries of Mithras, which he references several times. The first mention comes in 1.9 in a

---

10   J.N. Bremmer, 'Lucian on Peregrinus and Alexander of Abonuteichos: A Sceptical View of Two Religious Entrepeneurs', in *Beyond Priesthood: Religious Entrepreneurs and Innovators in the Roman Empire*, R.L. Gordon et al. (eds), Berlin–Boston, 2017, pp. 47–76.

11   For example, Celsus receives no attention at all in *Christianity in the Second Century*, J. Carleton Paget and J. Lieu (eds), Cambridge, 2017.

12   See B. Puech, 'Celsus (Aulus Cornelius)', in R. Goulet (ed.), *Dictionnaire des philosophes antiques* vol. 2, Paris, 1994, pp. 257–259. An additional argument may be his knowledge of an Alexandrian Jewish writing, cf. M. Niehoff, 'A Jewish Critique of Christianity from Second-Century Alexandria: Revisiting the Jew Mentioned in Contra Celsum', *JECS* 21 (2013), pp. 151–175.

13   See the doxography in Arnold, *Der* Wahre Logos *des Kelsos*, 2 note 7.

14   R. Gordon, '"Den Jungstier auf den goldenen Schultern tragen". Mythos, Ritual und Jenseitsvorstellungen im Mithraskult', in *Burial Rituals, Ideas of Afterlife, and the Individual in the Hellenistic World and the Roman Empire*, K. Waldner et al. (eds), Stuttgart 2016, pp. 207–240 at 210, and 'Persæ in spelæis Solem colunt: Mithra(s) between Persia and Rome', in *Persianism in Antiquity*, R. Strootman and M.J. Versluys (eds), Stuttgart, 2016, pp. 279–315 at 281 (n. 14) and 283.

EARLY CHRISTIANITY AND THE PAGAN MYSTERIES

discussion by Celsus about reason and faith,[15] in which, according to Origen, 'he (Celsus) compares those who believe without reason to Metragyrtæ and diviners, to the priests of Mithras and Sabazios, and to anything else that one may fall in with, and to the phantoms of Hecate, or any other female demon or demons'.[16] According to Origen, 'in order to parade his erudition in his attack on us', Celsus relates that: 'These truths are obscurely represented by the teaching of the Persians and by the Mysteries of Mithras,[17] which are celebrated among them. For in the latter there is a representation of the two orbits in heaven, the one of the fixed stars and the other assigned to the planets, and of the soul's passage through these, etc.' (6.22). Celsus then continues with a detailed explanation of the connection of the planets with metals, which need not concern us here.

Origen makes clear that Celsus had done some homework as he mentions two different musical theories, which he adds to his investigation into 'the theology of the Persians' (6.22.24). This fits the fact that there was a certain amount of literature circulating in Celsus's time that pretended to offer explanations of the various elements of the Mithraic Mysteries. Unfortunately, we only have some names and a few quotations,[18] but one thing is certain: all these earlier authors seem to have written in Greek, which is a surprising phenomenon, as Mithraism probably originated in Rome just before AD 100, has left us mainly Latin inscriptions, and expanded especially in the western provinces of the Roman Empire.[19]

However, Celsus also knew of other Mysteries, as is shown by his enumeration of wise peoples, which ends with 'Odrysians, Samothracians and Eleusinians' (1.14). The Odrysians were the people of Orpheus so that it is clear that

---

15   For this section as a whole, see L. Perrone, 'Proposta per un commento: un'esemplificazione su "Contro Celso" I, 9–13', in id. (ed.), *Discorsi di verità: Paganesimo, giudaismo e cristianesimo a confronto nel "Contro Celso" di Origene*, Rome, 1998, pp. 225–256.

16   Or. *cc* 1.9 Borret (all citations are from this edition): ἐξομοιοῖ τοὺς ἀλόγως πιστεύοντας μητραγύρταις καὶ τερατοσκόποις, Μίθραις τε καὶ Σαβαδίοις, καὶ ὅτῳ τις προσέτυχεν, Ἑκάτης ἢ ἄλλης δαίμονος ἢ δαιμόνων φάσμασιν. I gratefully use the translation of H. Chadwick, *Origen: Contra Celsum*, Cambridge, 1953, albeit sometimes adapted.

17   Gordon, *'Persæ in spelæis Solem colunt'*, p. 283 n. 23 argues that Celsus himself does not mention 'Mysteries'. Admittedly, here Celsus uses the term *teletê*, as in 6.24.3, but elsewhere (6.22.31) he says: Περσῶν τοῦ Μίθρου μυστήρια καὶ τὴν διήγησιν αὐτῶν. The Mithraic rites are actually called Mysteries by quite a few pagan and Christian authors: Burkert, *Ancient Mystery Cults*, p. 138 n. 50; add Psellus, *Or.* 1.153 Dennis and *Oratoria minora* 18.40 Littlewood.

18   See R. Gordon, 'Mithras', in *RAC* 24 (2012) 964–1009.

19   As rightly stressed by Gordon, *'Persæ in spelæis Solem colunt'*, pp. 302–303; Bremmer, *Initiation into the Mysteries*, pp. 125–129.

Celsus lists here the three oldest and most respected Greek Mysteries (see also § 2). It is not by chance that the triad starts with the Orphic Mysteries. Orpheus was supposed to have lived even before Homer and he was considered to be the inventor of the Mysteries.[20] His Mysteries therefore naturally come first in this triad.[21] Orphic Mysteries are probably also mentioned later in Celsus's work, when he speaks about a divine war and says; 'The Mysteries relating to the Titans and Giants also had some such meaning, as well as the Egyptian Mysteries of Typhon, and Horus, and Osiris' (6.42).[22] Now the battle of the Titans and Giants against the other gods for the supremacy of heaven was a theme in Orphic poems that expanded on the original Orphic theogony.[23] Celsus may well have assumed that the battle also was part of the oldest Orphic theogony that was sung during the initiation, as in his time Orphic Mysteries no longer seem to have existed. As for the other two, Celsus must have said something more about the Mysteries of Samothrace, as he mentions their main gods, the Kabeiroi, elsewhere (6.23), but the Eleusinian Mysteries are mentioned nowhere else by him and only once by Origen (6.22). Were they too solemn perhaps to be ridiculed or attacked?

In any case, it is perhaps not surprising that Celsus has a bit more to say about the Dionysiac Mysteries which were enormously popular in his time, whereas it is unlikely that he had obtained oral information regarding the Mithraic Mysteries about whose initiatory contents he indeed has nothing to say. Not that he has much to tell about the Dionysiac Mysteries either, but he does mention an interesting detail. Talking about the eternal punishments, Celsus compares the Christian doctrines to the evocation of phantoms and terrors during the Dionysiac initiations (4.10). In fact, it was very normal in ancient Mysteries to terrify the initiands before they would receive the final revelation and be properly initiated.[24] Celsus also mentions this procedure in connection with the Mysteries of the Corybants, where the initiands were intimidated with the sounds of pipes and drums (3.16).[25]

---

20   C. Riedweg, 'Orphisches bei Empedokles', *A&A* 41 (1995), pp. 34–59 at 37 n. 27.

21   For the Orphic Mysteries, see, most recently, Bremmer, *Initiation into the Mysteries*, pp. 54–80.

22   Or. *CC* 6.42: τούτου δὲ τοῦ βουλήματός φησιν ἔχεσθαι καὶ τὰ περὶ τοὺς Τιτᾶνας καὶ Γίγαντας μυστήρια θεομαχεῖν ἀπαγγελλομένους καὶ τὰ παρ' Αἰγυπτίοις περὶ Τυφῶνος καὶ Ὥρου καὶ Ὀσίριδος. The passage is lacking in the authoritative edition of A. Bernabé, *Poetæ epici Græci II: Orphicorum et Orphicis similium testimonia et fragmenta, fasc. 1, 2*, Munich–Leipzig, 2004–2005.

23   M.L. West, *The Orphic Poems*, Oxford, 1983, pp. 116–139.

24   Bremmer, *Initiation into the Mysteries*, pp. 98, 107.

25   Cf. Bremmer, *Initiation in the Mysteries*, p. 52.

Terror is a theme that Celsus returns to repeatedly in his discussion of the Christian views of hell and eternal punishment. These Christian doctrines must have really struck him as absurd, which is not that surprising as belief in an afterlife was not much developed among the ancient Greeks and Romans.[26] Thus Celsus also mentions the eternal punishments towards the end of his book and states; 'Just as you (Christians) believe in eternal punishments, so do the exegetes of those Mysteries, initiators and mystagogues. What you threaten the others, those do to you' (8.48).

The last Mysteries mentioned by Celsus are Egyptian ones. In the same context of a divine battle as the mention of the Giants and Titans, Celsus also mentioned 'the Mysteries among the Egyptians of Typhon, Horus and Osiris' (6.42).[27] It is an important argument in favour of Celsus's Egyptian background that he becomes more detailed when speaking about these Egyptian rites: 'by whom, when you approach, you can see splendid enclosures, groves, large and beautiful gateways, wonderful temples surrounded by magnificent tents, and rites full of religious feeling and of mystery; but when you have entered and proceeded to the interior, the object of worship is seen to be a cat, or a monkey, or a crocodile, or a goat, or a dog!' (3.17). Despite this anti-climax in Celsus's eyes, he nonetheless proceeds by stating; 'an impression is produced in the minds of those who have learned these things; that they have not been initiated in vain'.[28]

There can be no doubt that Celsus thinks of a Mysteries initiation in the case of the Egyptians, but this association immediately raises an important question. Whereas we have plenty of evidence about all the other Mysteries, this is not the case with Egypt. In fact, the evidence we have for the Mysteries of Isis is scant and late, not before the second century AD, and those for the Mysteries of Typhon, Horus and Osiris almost non-existent.[29] How can we explain, then, these statements by somebody who, in general, is clearly well informed about the Mysteries? The answer probably has to be found in the development of the significance of the term 'Mysteries'. Recent studies have drawn attention to the fact that in the course of the second century AD the Greek term μυστή-

---

26   J.N. Bremmer, *The Rise and Fall of the Afterlife*, London–New York, 2002, pp. 7–8.

27   The passage seems to be overlooked by F. Massa, 'Le mythe fait-il le mystère? Interprétations chrétiennes des mystères égyptiens (IIe–IVe siècles)', *RHR* 235 (2018), pp. 701–722.

28   Or. *CC* 3.18: φησὶ φαντασίαν ἐξαποστέλλειν τοῖς ταῦτα μεμαθηκόσιν, ὅτι μὴ μάτην μεμύηνται.

29   Bremmer, *Initiation in the Mysteries*, pp. 113–114; J. Steinhauer, 'Osiris mystes und Isis orgia—Gab es "Mysterien" der ägyptischen Gottheiten?', in *Entangled Worlds: Religious Confluences between East and West in the Roman Empire. The Cults of Isis, Mithras, and Jupiter Dolichenus* S. Nagel et al. (eds), Tübingen, 2017, pp. 47–78.

ρια developed in a kind of inflationary manner.[30] A considerable number of cults now called themselves Mysteries without us really knowing whether these cults indeed had all the hallmarks of the traditional Mysteries, such as those of Eleusis and Samothrace. Now as Celsus stresses several times,[31] the Egyptians were believed to possess an impressive antiquity and extraordinary wisdom,[32] which, added to the imposing Egyptian temples with their complicated architecture,[33] must have evoked something of the Greek Mysteries. So either the Egyptian priests themselves appropriated the connection with the Mysteries or outsiders used the Mysteries terminology on the basis of some family resemblances. In fact, they might not have been the only Egyptians to have used the language of the Mysteries, as Numenius fr. 53) seems to have referred to the cult of Sarapis as Mysteries, even though this Egyptian god never had any Mysteries at all, except, perhaps, of all places, in Portugal.[34]

2   Celsus, Christians and the Mysteries

With the Egyptians we have come to the end of what Celsus has to say about the ancient Mysteries. What can we conclude from this? Let us first look again at how and why Celsus refers to the Mysteries I have listed and discussed so far. We should start from the fact that quite at the beginning of his work Origen argues that Celsus often calls the Christian doctrine 'secret' (1.7: κρύφιον τὸ δόγμα). We find a comparable suggestion in the later part of his work when he states that the Christians 'avoid setting up altars and images and temples', since, 'he (Celsus) thinks that our trust (i.e. in the avoidance) is a token (σύνθημα) of a secret

---

30   C. Auffarth, 'Mysterien', in *RAC* 25 (2013), pp. 422–471 at 433–434; N. Belayche, 'L'évolution des formes rituelles: hymnes et mystèria', in *Panthée: Religious Transformations in the Græco-Roman Empire*, L. Bricault and C. Bonnet (eds), Leiden, 2013, pp. 17–40; B. Eckhardt and A. Lepke, 'Mystai und Mysteria im kaiserzeitlichen Westkleinasien', in *Transformationen paganer Religion in der Kaiserzeit*, M. Blömer and B. Eckhardt (eds), Berlin–Boston, 2018, pp. 39–79.

31   Or. *CC.* 3.17, 5.21, 6.80.

32   See the references in A. Hilhorst, '"And Moses was Instructed in All the Wisdom of the Egyptians" (Acts 7,22)', in *The Wisdom of Egypt*, id. and G.H. van Kooten (eds), Leiden, 2005, pp. 153–176, to be added to I. Tanaseanu-Döbler, *Theurgy in Late Antiquity. The Invention of a Ritual Tradition*, Göttingen, 2013, pp. 81–82 (additional bibliography).

33   See S. Baumann and H. Kockelmann (eds), *Der ägyptische Tempel als ritueller Raum: Theologie und Kult in ihrer architektonischen und ideellen Dimension*, Wiesbaden, 2017.

34   Cf. L. Bricault, *Les cultes isiaques* (Paris, 2013) p. 431; Steinhauer, 'Osiris *mystes*, Isis *orgia*', pp. 60 f.

EARLY CHRISTIANITY AND THE PAGAN MYSTERIES

and unspeakable (ἀπορρήτου) community'.[35] The Greek terminology undoubtedly suggests Mysteries here, since the terms 'unspeakable', and a 'token' were typical of the Mysteries.[36] This Christian secrecy as well as its eschatological threats (§ 1) seem to have made the Mysteries a running theme in Celsus's work.

On the other hand, there is something ambiguous about Celsus's suggestions of secrecy, as, when it is suitable for him, he also can complain: 'Moreover, we see that those who display their trickery in the market-places and go about begging would never enter a gathering of intelligent men, nor would they dare to reveal their noble beliefs in their presence; but whenever they see adolescent boys and a crowd of slaves and a company of fools they push themselves in and show off' (3.50). Curiously, the secrecy here is especially directed at intelligent men, whereas in Greece it was typical for the Mysteries that anybody was welcome and certainly not tested regarding his or her intelligence. Even slaves could be initiated, provided they had paid their entrance fee. Yet, as we will see (§ 3), Origen did agree with him on this point to a certain extent.

It is also interesting to observe that we can note a certain hierarchy in Celsus. In the beginning of his work, as we have seen, he spoke of the Mithraic Mysteries in a disparaging tone, as he did in regard to the Mysteries of Sabazios, which he mentions nowhere else, but which were often looked down upon in our literature.[37] In fact, his judgment about the Mysteries' priests is pretty severe: 'just as these evil men often exploit the idiocy of the simple to manipulate them in whatever way they like, so does it happen among Christians' (1.9). Moreover, when Celsus reproaches the Christians that they frighten the lower classes, they behave according to him like the initiators of the Corybantic (3.16) or Dionysiac Mysteries (4.10): hardly a compliment. And although he was not that positive about the Mithraic Mysteries, Celsus was interested enough to read about them. If this seems to point to an ambiguous attitude, he is more positive about the oldest and best-established Mysteries. This seems clear from his enumeration of those people who are wiser than the Jews: 'Egyptians, Assyrians, Indians, Persians, Odrysians, Samothracians and Eleusinians' (1.14). As Arnold

---

35   Or. *CC*. 8.17: ὁ Κέλσος φησὶν ἡμᾶς βωμοὺς καὶ ἀγάλματα καὶ νεὼς ἱδρύεσθαι φεύγειν, ἐπεὶ τὸ πιστὸν ἡμῖν ἀφανοῦς καὶ ἀπορρήτου κοινωνίας οἴεται εἶναι σύνθημα. The translation is debated, cf. Arnold, *Der Wahre Logos des Kelsos*, pp. 188–189, pp. 311–312 n. 367, p. 496 n. 383, but seems supported by the similar wording of 8.20: Οὐκ εἰς τὸ πιστὸν οὖν ἀφανοῦς καὶ ἀπορρήτου κοινωνίας καὶ τὸ τοιοῦτο σύνθημα φεύγομεν βωμοὺς καὶ ἀγάλματα καὶ νεὼς ἱδρύεσθαι.

36   Burkert, *Ancient Mystery Cults*, pp. 9 and 46, respectively.

37   For these Mysteries, see F. Delneri, *I culti misterici stranieri nei frammenti della commedia attica antica*, Bologna, 2006, pp. 15–124; K. Rigsby, 'A Religious Association at Sardes', *Ancient Society* 44 (2014), pp. 1–23 at 12.

astutely observed, the last three peoples are not in alphabetical order,[38] and these are clearly the most important by being put at the end of the list. Moreover, although some of the earlier named peoples had Mysteries, others, such as the Assyrians and Indians, did not. So it is important to note that the three wisest peoples are wise because of their Mysteries.[39]

Now it is interesting to note that Celsus, who had a good knowledge of the ancient Mysteries, repeatedly compares emerging Christianity with these pagan Mysteries. He does this not only in the passage about the priests of Mithras and Sabazios, with which we started, but he returns to this theme several times. Having quoted Celsus's lengthy exposition of the Mithraic Mysteries, Origen observes that he continues as follows: 'After the instance taken from the Mithraic Mysteries, Celsus declares that he who would examine the Mysteries of the Christians with the aforesaid Persian ones, will, on comparing the two together, and on unveiling the Mysteries of the Christians, see in this way the difference between them'.[40]

Here the comparison is crystal clear, but the next reference is less explicit. In a long quotation, Celsus makes fun of the Christian congregation, mocking in particular the social composition of the Christians and their meeting in private houses. However, Celsus also uses the ritual of the Mysteries in his description, as he makes the Christians first drop their previous teachers as a kind of purification, a literary approach that we can find in Plato too, since a ritual purification was a standard preliminary action in the Mysteries.[41] The Christians then promise that their followers will be 'blessed' (μακαρίους) and 'their houses happy' (εὐδαίμονα). For the cognoscenti of Plato the combination of these two words must have been illuminating, as we often find them together in depictions of the *Jenseits* but also in connection with the Mysteries.[42] Yet it is only in the company of women and children in shops of female weavers or fullers, lower-class meeting places, that they 'will attain initiation' (3.55: ἵνα τὸ τέλειον λάβωσι). Here, Celsus obviously mocks the Christians for celebrating

---

38   Arnold, *Der Wahre Logos des Kelsos*, p. 483 n. 306. The same three are enumerated by Celsus in 1.16 with the surprising addition of the mythical Hyperboreans.

39   Herrero de Jáuregui, *Orphism and Christianity*, p. 373, argues that Celsus's natural tendency was 'to disdain the Bacchic mysteries and *teletai*' (*CC* 2.55–56, 3.9, 4.10), but this is not borne out by his references.

40   Or. *CC* 6.24: Ἑξῆς δὲ τῷ ἀπὸ τῶν Μιθραϊκῶν ληφθέντι λόγῳ ἐπαγγέλλεται ὁ Κέλσος τελετήν τινα Χριστιανῶν τελετῇ ⟨τῇ⟩ προειρημένῃ Περσῶν τὸν βουλόμενον συνεξετάσαι, ταῦτα ἀλλήλοις παραβαλόντα καὶ γυμνώσαντα καὶ τὰ Χριστιανῶν, οὕτω θεάσεσθαι τὴν διαφορὰν αὐτῶν.

41   Dropping the wrong teachers as purification: Riedweg, *Mysterienterminologie*, pp. 17–20. For ritual purification in Mysteries, see Bremmer, *Initiation into the Mysteries, passim*.

42   Riedweg, *Mysterienterminologie*, pp. 52–53.

'Mysteries' not in beautiful sanctuaries but in unassuming, even unattractive cult places and amidst socially inferior people.

Given this mocking of Christian behaviour against a background of Mystery ritual, it is not surprising that Celsus compares Christian teaching about welcoming sinners unfavourably with the Mysteries, since the latter invited only those who were pure of hands and heart. In that context, Celsus explicitly says: 'those who call to the other Mysteries' (3.59: εἰς τὰς ἄλλας τελετὰς καλοῦντες). Admittedly, he uses the term τελετή, which can mean anything, from a ritual in general to a Mystery cult,[43] but Pausanias, an author more or less contemporaneous with Lucian, uses *teletê* almost exclusively in the case of Mysteries, just as Lucian often uses *teletê* for Mysteries.[44] In this passage, too, τελετή evidently refers to the Mysteries: the invitations mentioned by Celsus are well attested at the beginning of the ancient Mysteries, such as those of Eleusis. Interestingly, he mentions two types: the older one which excluded those with blood on their hands or who could not speak Greek,[45] and a younger one, which also mentioned a purity of heart[46]—a nice illustration that the growing interiorisation of purity in the time of the Roman Empire had not gone unnoticed by some of its inhabitants.[47]

Celsus returns to the comparison between pagan and Christian Mysteries towards the end of his book, where he says: 'Just as you, my excellent fellow

---

43   G. Sfameni Gasparro, *Misteri e teologie. Per la storia dei culti mistici e misterici nel mondo antico*, Cosenza, 2003, pp. 99–117 ('Ancora sul termine ΤΕΛΕΤΗ. Osservazioni storico-religiose'); K. Dunbabin, 'Domestic Dionysus? Telete in Mosaics from Zeugma and the Late Roman Near East', *JRA* 21 (2008), pp. 193–224; F. Schuddeboom, *Greek Religious Terminology—Telete & Orgia*, Leiden, 2009; V. Pirenne-Delforge, 'Teletê peut-elle être déesse? Note épigraphique (SEG 50, 168)', *Mètis* NS 14 (2016), pp. 35–48.

44   Pausanias: V. Pirenne-Delforge, *Retour à la source. Pausanias et la religion grecque*, Liège, 2008, pp. 292–295. Lucian, *Dem.* 11, 34, *Merc.* 1, *Alex.* 38, *Per.* 28, *Salt.* 15, *Pseudol.* 5, *Nav.* 15.

45   Or. *CC* 3.59–60; see also Aristophanes, *Ra.* 369 with scholion ad loc.; Isocrates 4.157; Suetonius, *Nero* 34.4; Theon Smyrn., *De utilitate mathematicæ* p. 14.23–24 Hiller; Pollux 8.90; Libanius, *Decl.* 13.19, 52; *SHA Alex. Sev.* 18.2, *Marc. Aur.* 27.1; Riedweg, *Mysterienterminologie*, pp. 74–85.

46   Celsus *apud* Or. *CC* 3.59; [Eus]. *Contra Hieroclem* 30.3 (anecdote about Apollonius of Tyana); Libanius, *Decl.* 13.19, 52; Julian, *Or.* 7.25; M.W. Dickie, 'Priestly Proclamations and Sacred Laws', *CQ* 54 (2004), pp. 579–591.

47   J.N. Bremmer, 'How Old is the Ideal of Holiness (of Mind) in the Epidaurian Temple Inscription and the Hippocratic Oath?', *ZPE* 142 (2002), pp. 106–108; A. Chaniotis, 'Greek Ritual Purity: from Automatisms to Moral Distinctions', in P. Rösch and U. Simon (eds), *How Purity is Made*, Wiesbaden, 2012, pp. 123–139 and 'Greek Purity in Context: The Long Life of a Ritual Concept, or Defining the Cs of Continuity and Change', in J.-M. Carbon and S. Peels-Matthey (eds), *Purity and Purification in the Ancient Greek World*, Liège, 2018, pp. 35–48.

(βέλτιστε),[48] believe in eternal punishments, so also do the exegetes, those who introduce and initiate into the sacred mysteries. The same punishments with which you threaten others, they threaten you. Now it is possible to consider, which of the two is nearer the truth or more successful; for both parties contend with equal assurance that the truth is on their side. But if we require proofs, the others (i.e. the priests of the pagan gods) point to a lot of distinct evidence, partly from certain miraculous powers, and partly from oracles, and all kinds of divination'.[49]

A last but debatable example is Celsus's use of *choros* for both Christians and Jews, which Arnold interprets as a reference to the Mysteries.[50] When talking about Jesus, he calls him their 'teacher and *chorostatês*, "leader of a chorus"' (5.33), and somewhat later he says about the Jews: 'Let this *choros*, then, take its leave, after paying the penalty of its vaunting, not knowing the great God, but being led away and deceived by the charlatanerie of Moses, having become his pupil to no good end' (5.41). Arnold wants to see in this usage of *choros*, 'chorus', a reference to the dances of the Mysteries. Now it is certainly true that dances were extremely important in the Mysteries and had perhaps become even more important in the second century, when it seems that some people put these dances on public stages.[51] Yet, as Arnold himself observes, Celsus nowhere uses the metaphors of the Mysteries in connection with the Jews. It seems therefore unlikely that *choros* in 5.41 would suddenly be the exception to this rule. In fact, Celsus clearly had a reasonable knowledge about the Jews so that it is not very probable that he would suggest something secretive about them.[52]

What is striking about Celsus's comparisons is that he does not look at a particular Mystery ritual but takes them all together. Apparently, it seems to make no difference to him for his comparison whether he speaks about the Mysteries of Mithras, those of the Egyptians or those of religious entrepreneurs who

---

48 Socrates uses this expression at moments of triumph or when he sees a triumph coming, and that also seems to be the case here, as Celsus clearly feels that he is scoring an important point, cf. E. Dickey, *Greek Forms of Address: from Herodotus to Lucian*, Oxford, 1996, p. 111.

49 Or. *CC* 8.48: μάλιστα μέν, ὦ βέλτιστε, ὥσπερ σὺ κολάσεις αἰωνίους νομίζεις, οὕτως καὶ οἱ τῶν ἱερῶν ἐκείνων ἐξηγηταὶ τελεσταί τε καὶ μυσταγωγοί· ἃς σὺ μὲν τοῖς ἄλλοις ἀπειλεῖς, ἐκεῖνοι δὲ σοί. πότερα γὰρ αὐτῶν ἀληθέστερα ἢ ἐπικρατέστερα, ἔξεστι σκοπεῖν. λόγῳ μὲν γὰρ ἐξ ἴσου περὶ τῶν σφετέρων σφίσιν ἑκάτεροι διαβεβαιοῦνται· τεκμηρίων δὲ εἰ δέοι, πολλὰ ἐκεῖνοι καὶ ἐναργῆ δεικνύουσιν ἔργα τε δαιμονίων τινῶν δυνάμεων καὶ χρηστηρίων καὶ ἐκ παντοδαπῶν μαντείων προκομίζοντες.

50 Arnold, *Der Wahre Logos des Kelsos*, pp. 489–493.

51 Lucian, *Salt.* 15.8–9, cf. Riedweg, *Mysterienterminologie*, p. 58 n. 144.

52 Cf. M. Rizzi, 'Some reflections on Origen, Celsus and Their Views on the Jews', in P. Lanfranchi and J. Verheyden (eds), *Jews and Christians in Antiquity: A Regional Perspective*, Leuven, 2018, pp. 37–59.

EARLY CHRISTIANITY AND THE PAGAN MYSTERIES

perform initiations in private houses. It seems likely that this neglect of the differences between the various rituals has to do with the inflation of the term Mysteries in the second century (§1). Yet there can be no doubt that Celsus knew that some Mysteries were more established and respected than others. We can see the same with Apuleius who has Lucius initiated into what were, so to speak, upstarts among the Mysteries, viz. those of Isis:[53] contemporary intellectuals knew very well which Mysteries were more ancient and therefore more to be respected than others. Nevertheless, it seems clear that Celsus saw Christianity as one kind of Mysteries, however low quality it may have been, in the wide field of contemporary Mysteries.

3   Origen on Celsus on the Mysteries

Now what did Origen think about this comparison? Admittedly, Origen probably lived several decades after Celsus and wrote his work shortly before AD 250, but the rise of Christianity does not seem to have been so steep in his time that Origen would have reacted differently, if he had written it straight away after the publication of Celsus's work. Let us therefore first look at Origen's knowledge of the pagan Mysteries and then zoom in on his reactions to Celsus.

It is not so easy to be sure what Origen knew about the pagan Mysteries. He was already a second-generation Christian, which makes it highly unlikely that he would have been initiated himself. His knowledge must have come from books or, perhaps, oral gossip about the local Mysteries. Still, it is clear that he was reasonably knowledgeable about them. As an Egyptian, it is hardly surprising that he was best informed about the Mysteries of Antinoos, the emperor Hadrian's much younger boyfriend, who drowned in the Nile before the emperor's very eyes in AD 130. In memory of him, several Mystery cults were instituted such as in Antinoopolis, the city Hadrian founded on the site of the accident, in Klaudiopolis, Antinoos's birthplace in Asia Minor, but also in Mantineia on the Greek mainland, presumably in order to gain privileges from the emperor.[54] Apparently, Celsus had compared the cult of Antinoos to that of

---

53   Cf. Bremmer, 'Philosophers and the Mysteries', p. 108.

54   Or. CC 3.36 (Antinoopolis); Inschriften von Klaudiopolis 7, 56, 65; Paus. *8.9.7–8*; IG V.2 312, 281, cf. L. Robert, *A travers l'Asie Mineure*, Paris, 1980, pp. 132–138; Ph. Harland, *Associations, Synagogues, and Congregations*, Minneapolis, 2003, p. 296; C.P. Jones, *New Heroes in Antiquity: from Achilles to Antinoos*, Cambridge MA–London, 2010, p. 80 n. 11; A. Galimberti, 'P.Oxy. 471: Hadrian, Alexandria, and the Antinous Cult', in E. Muñiz Grijalvo et al. (eds), *Empire and Religion: Religious Change in Greek Cities under Roman Rule*, Leiden,

Jesus, a claim Origen returns to several times (3.36–38, 5.63). Origen tells us that Antinoos gave oracles after his death (3.36) and quotes Celsus's innuendo about the immoral behaviour of his worshippers (5.63). He also mentions that Antinoos was worshipped as a god (8.9). Although he does not say as much, one cannot escape the impression that the figure of Antinoos was still very much alive in his lifetime.[55]

In any case, it is certain that Origen refers less to other Mysteries. He knows the Mithraic Mysteries, but clearly has a low opinion of them since he wonders why Celsus preferred to describe those rather than the much older and more respected Eleusinian Mysteries and the ones of Hecate in Ægina or even the Mysteries in Egypt (6.22), although he does not make clear which ones. Did he mean those of Antinoos, Osiris or Isis? Or perhaps those of Sarapis which, elsewhere in his work, he calls 'ineffective Mysteries' (5.38: ἀτελέστων τελετῶν)? It is not clear and it is easily possible that he rather generously applies the, for him, generally negative term of Mysteries to various cults, the more so as he also mentions 'Mysteries and rituals' of Athena (8.67), which are nowhere attested. However, in this case, it may be just a misguided, albeit unnoticed, quotation from the Wisdom of Solomon.[56]

On the other hand, after mentioning the Mysteries of the Egyptians, he continues with several others; 'those of the Cappadocians who worship Artemis at Comana, or those of the Thracians, or even those of the Romans themselves who initiate the noblest members of the Senate' (6.22). The easiest to recognise from this enumeration are the Mysteries of Artemis, which were celebrated at Comana. Her cult, however, which is the Greek interpretation of the local goddess Ma, is not attested before the first century BC, and the interpretation or transformation of her cult into Mysteries probably did not predate the second century.[57] The mention of Thracians probably refers to the Mysteries of Sabazios, which we have already mentioned (§1), but it is unclear what Origen meant with the 'most noble members of the Senate'. Chadwick (ad loc.) thinks of the cult of the Magna Mater, but that is hardly likely. One would rather think

---

2017, pp. 98–111; L. Bricault and V. Gasparini, 'Un obelisco per Antinoo', in C. Bonnet and E. Sanzi (eds), *Roma città aperta. L'impatto dei culti stranieri nella capitale dell'Impero*, Rome, 2018, pp. 313–324.

55   Similarly, T.W. Thompson, 'Antinoos, The New God: Origen on Miracle and Belief in Third-Century Egypt', in T. Nicklas and J. Spittler (eds), *Credible, Incredible. The Miraculous in the Ancient Mediterranean*, Tübingen, 2013, pp. 143–172.

56   Compare Or. *cc* 8.67: παραδόντων τοῖς ὑποχειρίοις μυστήρια καὶ τελετάς with *Sap. Sal* 14.15: παρέδωκεν τοῖς ὑποχειρίοις μυστήρια καὶ τελετάς.

57   Rigsby, 'A Religious Association at Sardes', p. 13.

of the Mysteries of Ceres or something similar.[58] In any case, none of these rituals would have been called Mysteries by the Romans.

Although Origen, then, was familiar with the broad spectrum of Mysteries in the earlier Roman Empire, it is not easy to see what he thought of the Mysteries as such. He refuses to enter into a discussion of the very popular Dionysiac Mysteries (4.10) and, when it fits his argument, he can write of the Persians: 'among them there are Mysteries (the Mithraic ones?) which are explained rationally by the learned men among them, but which are taken in their external significance by rather superficial minds and by the common people among them' (1.12). He even stresses that the Christians did not derive anything from (the Mysteries of) the Persians (6.23).[59]

On the other hand, already right at the beginning of his polemic against Celsus, he protests against Celsus's 'often repeated' idea that the Christian doctrines are secret. He persuasively argues that Jesus's 'virgin birth, crucifixion and resurrection as well as the last judgement are well known to everybody', whereas the secrecy of the famous Mysteries, both Greek and barbarian, never has been breached. Yet he does concede that certain Christian doctrines do not reach the multitude, just as among philosophers certain doctrines could be kept secret, witness the case of the Pythagoreans who shielded certain aspects of their teachings from 'uninitiated and not yet purified ears' (all quotations: 1.7).[60]

Origen makes the same concession later in his work. When Celsus reproaches the Christians for divulging their secrets in the market-places but not to an assembly of intelligent men (§1), he replies in great detail and does admit that the Christians have two classes among their members. There are those who have passed the test of a decent life, but have not yet 'received the *symbolon* of their purification' (3.51). It is highly interesting to observe here the usage of the word *symbolon*, 'password', as it has appeared in one of the more recently discovered Orphic Gold Leaves.[61] It seems that Origen uses a term connected with

---

58   H. Wagenvoort, *Studies in Roman Literature, Culture and Religion*, Leiden, 1956, pp. 150–168 ('Initia Cereris', first published in 1948), to be added to Ph. Borgeaud, 'Les mystères', in C. Bonnet and L. Bricault (eds), *Panthée: Religious Transformations in the Græco-Roman Empire*, Leiden, 2013, pp. 131–144 at 138–140.

59   He seems to mean the Mysteries of the Persians as he combines them with the Kabeiroi, the gods of the Samothracian Mysteries.

60   Or. *cc* 1.7: ἀκοὰς βεβήλους καὶ μηδέπω κεκαθαρμένας. Origen may allude here to the famous beginning of the Orphic Mysteries, cf. J.N. Bremmer, 'The Place of Performance of Orphic Poetry (*OF* 1)', in M. Herrero et al. (eds), *Tracing Orpheus: Studies of Orphic Fragments in Honour of Alberto Bernabé*, Berlin–New York, 2011, pp. 1–6.

61   *Orphicorum Fragmenta* 493 Bernabé = F. Graf and S.I. Johnston, *Ritual Texts for the Afterlife*,

the Mysteries on purpose, as *symbolon* only gradually developed into a term for the Creed which was proclaimed before baptism, that is, the purification of the sins.[62] These decent newcomers have to be instructed, but Origen admits that the Christians 'conceal and are silent about the more profound (truths? Mysteries?), whenever we see that the meeting consists of simple-minded folk who are in need of teachings we figuratively call "milk"' (3.52). To a certain extent, then, Origen agrees with Celsus that the Christians kept certain doctrines secret.

This secrecy Origen also admits in his argument about the resurrection. Here he quotes the apostle Paul: 'Then because he (Paul) is aware that there is something unspeakable and mysterious (ἀπόρρητόν τι καὶ μυστικὸν) about this doctrine, and as it was fitting for one who left behind in writing for posterity the ideas which he had thought out, he goes on to say: 'Behold, I tell you a mystery' (1 Cor 15.51). This word is usually applied to the deeper and more mysterious doctrines which are rightly concealed from the multitude' (5.19). Once again we are struck by the use of Mysteries terminology: Origen evidently has tried here to bring the Pauline μυστήριον as close as possible to the pagan Mysteries because of the latter's eminence.[63]

Returning to the earlier passage, somewhat later Origen tells us which doctrines he means. He admits that some Christians are not that bright, but others have profound arguments which 'a Greek would call esoteric and epoptic' (3.37: ἐσωτερικῶν καὶ ἐποπτικῶν). Chadwick translates with 'esoteric and mysterious', but that misjudges the terminology. 'Esoteric' alludes to the esoteric teachings of Plato, but 'epoptic' suggests the second and highest stage of initiation in the Eleusinian Mysteries.[64] Origen, thus, claims the best of pagan philosophy and religion for his Christian beliefs. Interestingly, Origen here lists the so-to-speak higher Christian truths, which regard God, the Logos, the angels and the demons, but he does not further explicate them. It seems as if Christian secrecy has to be admitted but not publicly discussed.

2nd edn, London–New York, 2013, pp. 38–39 (first published in 1994). For the later development of the term, see A. Merkt, 'Symbolum. Historische Bedeutung und patristische Deutung des Bekenntnisnamens', *Römische Quartalschrift* 96 (2001), pp. 1–36; L. Westra, 'How Did *Symbolum* Come to Mean 'Creed'?', *Studia Patristica* 45 (2010), pp. 85–91 and 'Cyprian, the Mystery Religions and the Apostles' Creed—an Unexpected Link', in H. Bakker et al. (eds), *Cyprian of Carthage*, Leuven, 2010, pp. 115–125; W. Kinzig, *Faith in Formulæ* vol. 1, Oxford, 2017 pp. 3–7.

62 Bremmer, *Initiation into the Mysteries*, p. 151.

63 Fédou, *Christianisme et religions païennes*, p. 351 rightly cites 1.7 where Origen connects the 'mystery of the resurrection' with the Greek and barbarian Mysteries.

64 For this stage, see Bremmer, *Initiation into the Mysteries*, pp. viii, 11–16.

EARLY CHRISTIANITY AND THE PAGAN MYSTERIES

To conclude, Origen was quite well acquainted with the ancient Mysteries and thought the oldest amongst them reputable enough to be reticent in his criticisms of them, but also reputable enough to use their language when defending the Christian faith. He does not deny the critique by Celsus regarding the secrecy of the Christian faith, but tries to parry the critique by representing the secrecy as resembling that of the Mysteries by using Mysteries vocabulary in his exposition. In the end, his work testifies to the high reputation the Mysteries still had in his days.

4   The Christian Congregation as a Mystery Cult

Let us finally ask what our discussion means for the question we started with. What would early Christians and pagan outsiders have thought of the resemblance of the Christian communities to the pagan Mystery cults? Leading New Testament scholars, such as John Kloppenborg, have argued that 'early Christ-groups were *certainly* (my italics) regarded by external observers as varieties of associations'.[65] However, there is no evidence that the early Jesus followers actually saw it this way before Tertullian.[66] On the other hand, Celsus's contemporary Lucian calls Christianity a 'new *teletê*' in his *Life of Peregrinus* (11). Celsus too compared Christianity to 'the other *teletai*' (Or. *cc* 3.59), as we have seen, and even several Christians, orthodox and heterodox, had been struck by the similarity of some elements of the Christian ritual, such as baptism and the Eucharist, to those of the Mysteries.[67] Origen, as noted, also saw similari-

---

65   J.S. Kloppenborg, http://www.oxfordbibliographies.com/view/document/obo-978019539 3361/obo-9780195393361-0064.xml; see also R. Ascough, 'Paul, Synagogues, and Associations: Reframing the Question of Models for Pauline Christ Groups', *JJMJS* 2 (2015), pp. 27–52; 'What Are They Now Saying about Christ Groups and Associations?', *Currents in Biblical Research* 13 (2015), pp. 207–244 and 'Paul and Associations', in J.P. Sampley (ed.), *Paul in the Greco-Roman World: A Handbook* vol. 1, London–New York, 2016², pp. 68–69. Important discussions: B. Eckhardt, 'The Eighteen Associations of Corinth', *GRBS* 56 (2016), pp. 646–662 and 'Who Thought That Early Christians Formed Associations?', *Mnemosyne* IV 71 (2018), pp. 298–314.

66   E.R. Urciuoli, '"Factio Christiana". Nouvel examen du rapport entre les premiers groupes de croyants en Christ et les associations volontaires antiques', *Apocrypha* 22 (2011), pp. 253–264.

67   C. Auffarth, '"Licht vom Osten": Die antiken Mysterienkulte als Vorläufer, Gegenmodell oder katholisches Gift zum Christentum', *Arch. f. Religionsgesch.* 8 (2006), pp. 206–226; M. Casaux, 'Identité chrétienne, altérité et cultes "orientaux"', in L. Bricault and M.J. Versluys (eds), *Egyptian Gods in the Hellenistic and Roman Mediterranean: Image and reality*

ties. We need not conclude from these observations that Christianity resembled the Mysteries in the second century, but we may perhaps suggest that in some intellectual Christian circles the pagan Mysteries were seen, in some respect, as resembling Christianity. To what extent this 'esoteric' Christianity was representative for the Christian movement as a whole still remains a mystery.

between local and global = Mythos, Suppl. 3, Palermo, 2012, pp. 123–138; Bremmer, *Initiation into the Mysteries*, pp. 156–161; Arnold, *Der* Wahre Logos *des Kelsos*, pp. 484–493 (on Celsus and Origen).

CHAPTER 5

The Medieval Dualist *Nachleben* of Early Jewish and Christian Esoteric Traditions: The Role of the Pseudepigrapha

Yuri Stoyanov

The traditions of doctrinal and cultic esotericism in medieval Christian dualism (as represented by Paulicianism, Bogomilism and related trends in the Eastern Christian world, as well as Catharism in Western Christendom) have not so far been the focus of a methodical and comparative scrutiny and have not emerged as yet as a sphere of study of their own. In view of the undeveloped and fragmentary state of research on this specific problematic, the present article does not aspire to advance a systematic analysis of these medieval dualist traditions against the backdrop of the equivalent antecedent notions and narratives in late antique Gnosticism, Manichæism or early Christianity. Its intention will be to present and contextualize some of the characteristic evidence indicating such ideas and narratives among medieval dualist communities and their sectarian elites, highlighting the central problem (which still remains unsolvable in a number of cases) of their theological, historical and literary pedigrees.

The task of ascertaining and exploring such pedigrees has been complicated by the serious problems arising from the widely adopted application of the traditional contact-diffusion model to the rise and spread of medieval Christian dualism and the resultant reconstructions of sectarian theological and historical continuities between late antiquity and the Middle Ages. In the case of Eastern Christian dualism, most of these problems derive from the substantial gaps and obscurities in the existing evidence of the doctrinal foundations and evolution as well as from the historical backgrounds and development of Paulicianism and Bogomilism over a lengthy period which extended from the early Middle Ages to the early Ottoman era in Asia Minor and the Balkans. A different but similarly challenging set of historical problems has been revisited and highlighted in the reignited and ongoing scholarly debates regarding the nature, patterns and chronology of the inter-relations between Eastern and Western Christian medieval dualism.[1] In earlier nineteenth century

---

1   See the contributions discussing the current state of evidence, research and contrasting per-

© YURI STOYANOV, 2021 | DOI:10.1163/9789004445925_007

phases of research, the crucial discoveries and publication of major primary sources for the history and teachings of Paulicianism, Bogomilism, Catharism (and affiliated medieval sectarian groups) largely moved scholarship beyond the centuries-long Catholic-Protestant polemical battle fought over the origins of medieval dissent and dualist heresy. Concurrently with the expansion of such source-based studies, the characteristic trends of nineteenth-century political, intellectual and social thought also led to the conceptualization of Slavophile, socio-economic and ethno-centric interpretative frameworks of medieval Eastern Christian dualism, with their evident narrow and crude agendas. Such monochromatic approaches to medieval dualist heresy understandably remained unconcerned with its increasingly evidenced, rich and multi-layered intertextual relationship with the abundant and heterogeneous pseudepigraphic literature translated and disseminated during the formative stages of Slavo-Byzantine learning, theology and culture from the late ninth century onwards.[2]

The importance and far-reaching repercussions of this relationship became progressively more obvious during the early phases of text-critical investigation of the Old Slavonic pseudepigrapha when the key internal source for both medieval Eastern and Western Christian dualism, the pseudepigraphon *Interrogatio Iohannis*, attained wider availability and visibility in medievalist and heresiological research.[3] With the growth of authentic and credible textual data of Christian dualist appropriations of Slavo-Byzantine pseudepigrapha, the study of this process has become the most promising trend in research along with the continuing search for actual antecedent heterodox or dissenting religious communities impacting on the rise of medieval Christian dualism. Other promising directions of research include Byzantine and Slavonic Orthodox alternative and popular demonologies, as well as near-dualist developments in lay and monastic mysticism in Byzantine and Eastern Christian cultures which interfaced with, or were conducive to, the formation and embellishment of the anti-somatic, anti-cosmic and docetic features of Paulician and Bogomil theological dualism.

---

spectives on this problematic in A. Sennis (ed.), *Cathars in Question*, Woodbridge, 2016, especially, P. Biller, 'Goodbye to Catharism?', pp. 274–314.

2 Analysis of the state of evidence and research on this problematic in Y. Stoyanov, 'Pseudepigraphic and Parabiblical Narratives and Elements in Medieval Eastern Christian Dualism and Their Implications for the Rise and Evolution of Catharism', in A. Sennis (ed.), *Cathars in Question*, Woodbridge, 2016, pp. 151–177, here 154–156.

3 The pseudepigraphon is preserved only in Latin and in two main versions published alongside each other in the most recent critical edition of text, E. Bozóky, *Le Livre secret des cathares*, Paris, 1980, pp. 41–94; for the history of research of the pseudepigraphon, see ibid., pp. 17–22.

THE MEDIEVAL DUALIST NACHLEBEN

In the case of Paulician early teachings and later doctrinal developments, the current state of evidence does not allow as yet a plausible overall appraisal of the potential impact of pseudepigraphical literature in Armenia and Byzantium on their nascent or mature stages. At the same time, medieval reports and exposés of Bogomil doctrines display fragments or elements of narratives which clearly represent parabiblical elaborations of the Old Testament creation and flood stories, apocryphal and dualist satanologies, docetist Christologies, and so on. They find immediate and obvious parallels in the miscellaneous pseudepigraphic works translated and circulated in the extensive period of 'canonical ambiguity' in the written culture of *Slavia Orthodoxa*.[4]

The specific religious and cultural circumstances accompanying the formation of early Slavonic Orthodox theology and literature thus included the influx of parabiblical narratives and motifs through the medium of the newly translated apocryphal writings from late antiquity, some of which comprised borderline Gnostic and dualist concepts and imagery. These cultural and literary processes created a receptive climate which was particularly favourable for the reception of heterodox traditions and the emergence of novel doctrinal deviances. The early and continuing accessibility and transmission of such pseudepigraphic writings (despite their formal bans in the Slavonic Indexes of Forbidden Books[5]) in clerical, monastic and lay learned textual communities made it also possible for such theological deviances and heterodoxies to acquire theological and literary support through the borrowing of narratives and motifs, whether literally or in reworked variants, from the expanding œuvre of translated apocrypha. As highlighted in early reports of Bogomil New Testament exegesis, for example, appropriated elements of such adopted pseudepigraphic narrations and topoi could be integrated into radical inverse and allegorical interpretations of the canonical text.[6]

As such widespread circulation and impact of pseudepigraphic literature did not take place in early to high medieval Western Christian cultures, the interrelations between Slavo-Byzantine (and Eastern Christian in general) pseudepigraphy and dualist heresy attracted scholarly attention and debate much earlier than any analogous developments in medieval Western Chris-

---

4　On this cultural situation of 'canonical ambiguity' which not only characterized the foundational stages of *Slavia Orthodoxa*'s literary culture but endured into the Late Middle Ages, see the up-to-date analysis in A. Kulik and S. Minov, 'Introduction', in id. (eds), *Biblical Pseudepigrapha in Slavonic Tradition*, Oxford, 2016, pp. xxiv–xxvi.

5　Bibliographic references to scholarship on the Slavonic Indexes of Forbidden Books, in Stoyanov, 'Pseudepigraphic and Parabiblical Narratives', p. 157 n. 15.

6　Analysis of these dualist and rhetorical strategies in Stoyanov, 'Pseudepigraphic and Parabiblical Narratives', pp. 167–168.

tian contexts. Indeed the study of these varied interrelations followed closely the publication and text-critical study of the Slavonic recensions of a series of important pseudepigrapha in the second half of the nineteenth century. Some of these Old Church Slavonic pseudepigrapha such as *The Book of the Secrets of Enoch* (2 Enoch),[7] *The Ladder of Jacob* and *The Apocalypse of Abraham*,[8] are extant only in their Slavonic versions; other texts like the Slavonic recensions of *The Vision of Isaiah*[9] and *The Greek Apocalypse of Baruch* (3 Baruch),[10] have pre-

---

7   Recent major advances in the study of the complex textual history of the apocalypse and its historical, cultural and theological provenance include A. Orlov and G. Boccaccini (eds), *New Perspectives on 2 Enoch. No Longer Slavonic Only*, Leiden–Boston, 2012, and G. Macaskill, *The Slavonic Texts of 2 Enoch*, Leiden–Boston, 2013. For a bibliography of the editions, translations and studies of 2 Enoch, see A. Orlov, 'Selected Bibliography on the Transmission of the Jewish Pseudepigrapha in the Slavic Milieux', in id., *Selected Studies in the Slavonic Pseudepigrapha*, Leiden, 2009, pp. 203–435, here 222–243.

8   Recent critical editions of the apocalypse were published separately by B. Philonenko-Sayar and M. Philonenko, *L'Apocalypse d'Abraham, Introduction, text slave, traduction et notes*, Paris, 1981, and by R. Rubinkiewicz, *L'Apocalypse d'Abraham en vieux slave: Introduction, text critique, traduction et commentaire*, Lublin, 1987. The important textual critical investigation of the apocalypse of A. Kulik, *Retroverting Slavonic Pseudepigrapha: toward the Original of the Apocalypse of Abraham*, Atlanta, 2004, includes an English translation of the text (pp. 9–37); the theology, angelology, demonology and eschatology of the pseudepigraphon has been explored in a series of articles of A. Orlov: Orlov, *Selected Studies*, pp. 21–93; id., *Divine Manifestations in the Slavonic Pseudepigrapha*, New Jersey, 2009, pp. 155–177, 203–237; id., *Dark Mirrors: Azazel and Satanael in Early Jewish Demonology*, New York–Albany, 2011, pp. 11–85. For a bibliography of the editions, translations and studies of *The Apocalypse of Abraham*, see Orlov, 'Selected Bibliography', pp. 246–256.

9   Like the Latin *Visio Isaiæ* (the second Latin translation of the work), the Slavonic version of the apocalypse contains only chapters 6–11 of the *Martyrdom and Ascension of Isaiah* (a pseudepigraphon which weaves together important Jewish and early Christian lore about Isaiah), and on the whole shares the same textual tradition with this Latin version, both clearly representing a separate recension of the pseudepigraphon. For an up-to-date commentary and discussion of the manuscripts' family stemma along with a new edition of the Slavonic text, see A.G. Kossova, 'Visio Isaiæ. Versione paleobulgara', in P. Bettiolo et al. (eds), *Ascensio Isaiæ: Textus*, Turnhout, 1995, pp. 235–319. For a bibliography of the editions, translations and studies of the Slavonic version of the *Vision of Isaiah*, see Orlov, 'Selected Bibliography', pp. 276–278.

10   The study of *The Greek Apocalypse of Baruch* (3 Baruch) entered a new phase after the critical editions of its Greek version by J.-C. Picard, 'Apocalypsis Baruchi Græce', in id., *Testamentum Iobi, Apocalypsis Baruchi Græce*, Leiden, 1967, pp. 81–96, as well as its Slavonic version by H.E. Gaylord, *The Slavonic Version of 3 Baruch* (PhD diss.), Hebrew University of Jerusalem, 1983. It was substantially expanded by the subsequent monographs on the apocalypse: D.C. Harlow, *The Greek Apocalypse of Baruch (3 Baruch) in Hellenistic Judaism and Early Christianity*, Leiden, 1996, and A. Kulik, *3 Baruch: Greek-Slavonic Apocalypse of Baruch*, Berlin–New York, 2010, with a very valuable new English translation of, and com-

served important readings and textual traditions which in a number of cases are more authentic and faithful to the lost original protograph than those displayed in other redactions (Greek in the case of 3 Baruch, etc.). Early studies of the Old Slavonic pseudepigrapha shed light on their role in the principal currents and undercurrents of medieval Orthodox Slavonic and Byzantine religious development and fluctuations (especially the strands of heavenly ascent apocalypticism) as well as in the inter- and cross-cultural literary exchanges in the Eastern Christendom. Even at this early stage the endeavours to stratify their various redactional strata and identify the earliest layers were already starting to show and highlight their broader significance for a variety of crucial fields in the investigation of early Judaism and Christianity. More recent and continued research has expanded the scope and understanding of this importance. The research has now extended also to early Jewish and Christian apocalypticism as well as to the complex of overlapping distinct motifs they share with early Jewish mysticism and rabbinic literature (a complex whose preservation specifically in Slavonic has not yet been satisfactorily explained).[11] Moreover, the scholarly quest for the potential channels of transmission of late antique pseudepigraphic literature into the early Slavonic Orthodox written tradition has also recently been broadened with arguments for a non-Byzantine mediation of some of these works and, in certain cases, reconstruction of textual histories on the basis of direct translations from Syriac into Slavonic.[12]

Finally, the range of research on the Old Slavonic pseudepigrapha has broadened to include also earlier and subsequent heterodox and heretical interest in some of these writings. Further close study is certainly needed to explore the

---

mentary on, the apocalyptic work, pp. 89–386. For a bibliography of the editions, translations and studies of 3 Baruch, see Orlov, 'Selected Bibliography', pp. 278–284.

11 Kulik and Minov, 'Introduction', p. xvii and *passim*; for similar recent reappraisals cf. L. DiTommaso and C. Böttrich, 'Old Testament Apocrypha in the Slavonic Tradition', in Eid. (eds), *The Old Testament Apocrypha in the Slavonic Tradition: Continuity and Diversity*, Tübingen, 2011, pp. 1–5; J.H. Charlesworth, 'The Uniqueness and Importance of Slavonic Pseudepigrapha', in L. DiTommaso and C. Böttrich (eds), *The Old Testament Apocrypha*, pp. 5–12.

12 Discussions of the textual data and arguments for such translations in B. Lourié, 'Direct Translations into Slavonic from Syriac: a Preliminary List', in C. Diddi et al. (eds), *ΠΟΛΥΙΣΤΩΡ. Scripta Slavica. Mario Capaldo Dicata*, Moscow–Rome, 2015, pp. 161–169; see also B. Lurje, 'Okolo Solunskoi legendy: iz istorii missionerstva v period monofelitskoi unii', *Slaviane i ikh sosedi*, Vyp. 6, Moscow, 1996, pp. 23–52; id., 'The Syriac Aḥiqar, Its Slavonic Version, and the Relics of the Three Youths in Babylon', *Slověne*, 2 (2013), pp. 64–117; id., 'Pochemu "Slavianskii" Enokh okazalsia v Nubii', in E.H. Elert (ed.), *Arkheograficheskie i istochnikovedcheskie aspekty v izuchenii istorii Rossii*, Novosibirsk, 2016, pp. 35–43.

various borderline dualist and Gnostic tendencies in these texts and whether they belong to their oldest strata or represent subsequent interpolations introduced during their earlier transmission and adoption in sectarian or heterodox milieux. These tendencies allowed, moreover, further radical dualist interpretations and reworking, which were ultimately carried out by Christian dualist scribes and editors in the medieval period of the circulation of these writings. These heretical channels brought miscellaneous pseudepigraphical material, variously adjusted, reshaped and transfigured, into an array of medieval dualist teachings and related or extra-canonical religious lore, particularly in, but also beyond, Eastern Christendom.

The medieval appropriation of late antique pseudepigraphy could also generate the reception, and even revival, of religious attitudes and theological stances developed by the Jewish and Christian circles who composed and edited these writings, including forms and notions of doctrinal and cultic secrecy cultivated in such groups. Indeed a medieval Christian dualist adoption of such notions can be discerned in several important doctrinal spheres. The understanding of the roots and original contexts of these notions has improved with the steady progress of the study of religious secrecy in antiquity and late antiquity, ranging from the esoteric currents and layers in the Græco/Hellenistic-Roman pagan religious spectrum to early Judaism, early Christianity and various currents in Gnosticism.[13] This dependence of medieval Christian dualist theology on the works of early Jewish and Christian pseudepigraphy also requires closer attention on account of certain typological parallels (in view of the lack of any evidence of actual historical continuity)

---

13   Various facets and manifestation of religious secrecy and esotericism in antiquity and late antiquity have been explored in a series of relevant contributions (especially in the case of Mediterranean and Near and Middle Eastern religious history) in the following edited books and authored monographs: K.W. Bolle (ed.), *Secrecy in Religions*, Leiden–New York, 1987; G.G. Stroumsa, *Hidden Wisdom: Esoteric Traditions and the Roots of Christian Mysticism*, 2nd, revised and enlarged edn, Leiden, 2005; H.G. Kippenberg and G.G. Stroumsa (eds), *Secrecy and Concealment: Studies in the History of Mediterranean and Near Eastern Religions*, Leiden–New York, 1995; E.R. Wolfson (ed.), *Rending the Veil: Concealment and Secrecy in the History of Religions: New York University Annual Conference in Comparative Religions*, New York–London, 1999; A. Lenzi, *Secrecy and the Gods: Secret Knowledge in Ancient Mesopotamia and Biblical Israel*, Helsinki, 2008; S.I. Thomas, *The "Mysteries" of Qumran: Mystery, Secrecy, and Esotericism in the Dead Sea Scrolls*, Leiden–Boston, 2009; C.H. Bull, L.I. Lied and J.D. Turner, *Mystery and Secrecy in the Nag Hammadi Collection and Other Ancient Literature: Ideas and Practices. Studies for Einar Thomassen at Sixty*, Leiden–Boston, 2012; E. Mortensen and S. Grove Saxkjær (eds), *Revealing and Concealing in Antiquity: Textual and Archæological Approaches to Secrecy*, Aarhus, 2015; M. Stone, *Secret Groups in Ancient Judaism*, New York, 2017.

between traditions of doctrinal and cultic secrecy developed in some Gnostic trends, on the one hand, and Bogomilism and Catharism on the other.[14]

The current availability of primary internal and external sources regarding doctrinal and initiatory esotericism are much richer in the case of the diverse Gnostic traditions. The cumulative evidence indicates that in many of the Gnostic traditions the attitudes to the transmission and secreting of knowledge (seen as both esoteric and salvific) was informed by the notion of the progressive revelation of *gnosis* which, furthermore, underpins the respective Gnostic ritual and initiatory practices. Gnostic traditions of doctrinal secrecy usually professed descent from apostolic secret teachings disclosed by Jesus Christ to his disciples, as claimed, for example, in the Gnostic *Pistis Sophia*, or by the Carpocratians and the Gnostic theologian, Basilides (respectively reported in Irenæus, *Adversus hæreses* 1.25.5 and Hippolytus, *Elenchos*, 7.20.1). Such traditions, moreover, had evident antecedents in, and stem at least to an extent from, esoteric lore present among early Christian and Jewish Christian circles, deemed to have been imparted in apostolic times both orally and via apocryphal (categorized as 'hidden' and disseminated selectively) writings.

The existence and influence of such traditions in early Christian and Jewish Christian milieux has been receiving increasing scholarly attention, concentrated primarily on the interconnections between esoteric trends in intertestamental Palestinian and Hellenistic Jewish apocalypticism and early Christian apocalyptic notions concerning the descent and ascent of Jesus Christ, the human soul's heavenly journey in afterlife and the heavenly ascent of the apocalyptic seer aspiring to receive revelations of sublime mysteries. Other topics include the early Christian and Jewish Christian contexts of the notion of secret apostolic transmission of Jesus's teaching (Clement of Alexandria, *Stromateis*, 5.10.61.1, 6.7.61.3; Origen, *Contra Celsum*, III.21, VI.6; Basil the Great, *De Spiritu Sancto*, 27.66; paralleled in Nag Hammadi Gnostic tracts such as *The Apocryphon of Tames*, *The Apocryphon of John*, *The Gospel of Thomas* and *The Book of Thomas the Contender*), emphasized also as securing access to a deeper or mystical scriptural exegesis.

Gnostic use and creative exegesis of the biblical text as well as early Jewish pseudepigraphical literature have been attracting increasing scholarly attention focusing on Gnostic doctrinal and narrative syntheses, which adopted,

---

14   On the differences and some parallels between ancient Gnostic traditions and the medieval dualism of Bogomilism and Catharism (both in the spheres of theology and ritual), see R. van den Broek, 'The Cathars: Medieval Gnostics?', in id., *Studies in Alexandrian Christianity and Gnosticism*, Leiden, 1996, pp. 157–178; Y. Stoyanov, *The Other God. Dualist Religions from Antiquity to the Cathar Heresy*, London, 2000, pp. 262–287, *passim*.

re-worked and re-interpreted some of the central topoi of the intertestamental Jewish pseudepigraphic (particularly apocalyptic) literature. These topoi included the downfall of the angels and their corruption of humanity, the identity of the ringleader of the angelic apostasy, the fall of Adam and Eve, etc. Their selective assimilation and remoulding in Gnostic frameworks also often augmented the esoteric dimensions of some of these traditions (reflecting, for instance, the themes of revelations and expositions of sacred history or 'heavenly secrets') expounded implicitly or explicitly in the original early Jewish parabiblical texts. Similarly, the vivid mythological imagery and narratives used to explicate and illustrate Manichæan radical dualism betray a number of themes traceable to Jewish intertestamental literature,[15] particularly Enochic apocalyptic texts with their strong emphasis on the revelation of divine and heavenly secrets and the supernatural origin of evil. Mani himself not only used pseudepigraphy to uphold and enhance his claims for mission and prophecy,[16] but also likely fostered the practice of the apocalyptic and visionary technique of heavenly ascent which was additionally employed for the induction of his followers and disciples, attaining in this way a characteristic initiatory dimension.[17] Likewise, in Gnostic initiatory lore of cultic secrecy, the topoi of ascent and the frequently affiliated themes of investiture, enthronement, glorification and final rapture (repeatedly occurring in ritual settings), appear associated not only with earlier apocalyptic and pseudepigraphic literary traditions but also with actual ecstatic visionary and contemplative practices observed by the respective Gnostic groups and heresiarchs. Gnostic doctrinal and cultic esotericism were thus inextricably linked and accounts of Gnostic rituals, such as baptism, investiture, chrismation and sacred marriage, variously reflect principal Gnostic mythic narratives regarding the fall and tribulations of the soul or the original androgyne.[18] Gnostic initiatory and baptismal proceedings, as presented, for example, in the apocryphal second *Book of Jeu*, could assert deriva-

---

15   Reappraisal of the evidence and primary sources in J.C. Reeves, *Jewish Lore in Manichæan Cosmogony*, Cincinnati, 1992; id., 'Jewish Pseudepigrapha in Manichæan Literature', in id. (ed.), *Tracing the Threads: Studies in the Vitality of Jewish Pseudepigrapha*, Atlanta, 1994, pp. 173–204.

16   See Reeves, 'Jewish Pseudepigrapha', pp. 181–185; J.C. VanderKam and W. Adler (eds), *The Jewish Apocalyptic Heritage in Early Christianity*, Minneapolis, 1995, pp. 11 ff., 17–21; D. Frankfurter, 'Apocalypses Real and Alleged in the Mani Codex', *Numen* 44 (1997), pp. 60–73.

17   Reeves, 'Jewish Pseudepigrapha', pp. 179–180.

18   Discussion of these links between Gnostic narratives and ritual in J.D. Turner, 'Ritual in Gnosticism', in id. and R. Majercik (eds), *Gnosticism and Later Platonism. Themes, Figures, and Texts*, Atlanta, 2000, pp. 83–139, here 85–87.

tion from secret rites which Jesus was believed to have revealed only to his disciples, itself an important theme in Gnostic cultic esotericism. A consistent tradition attested in diverse Gnostic circles devalued ordinary Christian water baptism as inferior, inefficient and even impure in contrast with the higher, salvific and illumination-bringing Gnostic baptism.[19] The reports of baptismal practices followed in Valentinian Gnosticism indicates that ordinary Christian water baptism, while not considered invalid, was not sufficient for the Gnostic 'spiritual aristocracy' of the 'pneumatics', who needed a second baptism, often depicted as a rite of redemption, granting salvific knowledge regarding the afterlife ascent of the soul. (Clement of Alexandria, *Excerpta ex Theodoto*, 22.1).

The current source base for Paulicianism, Bogomilism and Catharism (and for the exploration of comparable patterns of doctrinal and cultic esotericism) is more limited than in the case of late antique Gnosticism, which makes the interrelations between late antique pseudepigraphy (in its medieval Slavo-Byzantine versions) and medieval Christian dualism even more significant. The process through which the Bogomil version of Eastern Christian dualism was originally fomented by the influx and spread of narratives, themes and notions, made accessible via the newly translated (into Old Church Slavonic) Byzantine Greek versions of pseudepigraphic works from Late Antiquity, also had evident implications for the emergence and evolution of traditions of doctrinal and cultic secrecy in Bogomilism and, later, Catharism. The medieval versions of the aforementioned pseudepigraphic writings: *The Book of the Secrets of Enoch* (2 Enoch), 3 Baruch, *The Apocalypse of Abraham, The Vision of Isaiah* as well as other pseudepigrapha, imparted to Bogomilism a number of foundational notions (which were to become later also influential in western Catharism) in diverse spheres such as cosmogony, cosmology, diabology, angelology, Christology, sacred history and eschatology. Significantly, the medieval versions of some of these works, especially the heavenly ascent apocalypses, have also preserved elements of esotericism and visionary mysticism which were also assimilated and reworked, at least partially, in Bogomil and related milieux, contributing to the persistent, if not always manifest, strand of doctrinal and cultic secrecy in the accounts of Bogomil and to some extent Cathar teachings and practices.

This thread is visible, for example, in reports describing the status as well as the initiatory and ritual procedures related to the elite Bogomil class of the

---

19   See, for example, the attitude to traditional Christian baptism in the Nag Hammadi texts, the *Apocalypse of Adam* (84:5, 85:30) and *Zostrianos* (131: 2–5) as well as in teachings of the Gnostic Archontics, as reported by Epiphanius, *Panarion*, 40.2.6–8.

teleoi ('perfect'), such as Euthymius of the Periblepton's *Epistula contra Phundagiagitas sive Bogomilos*[20] and Euthymius Zigabenus's section, *Kata Bogomilon* in his *Panoplia Dogmatica.*[21] Both accounts maintain that initiation into Bogomil teachings evolved in stages, asserting that prior to *teleiosis* (the spiritual baptism by imposition of hands, known also as 'baptism in fire and the Holy Spirit') ordinary believers were not yet introduced to the complex of teachings which were safeguarded as the inner dualist doctrines, accessible only for the heretical elite. According to Euthymius Zigabenus, as a mark of their initiation and stature the *teleoi* were granted the title of the Virgin Mary, *Theotokos* (God-Bearer), as they were regarded as receptacles of the Holy Spirit and as giving birth to the Word. Accordingly, the parable in Matthew 7:6 ('Do not give dogs what is sacred; do not throw your pearls to pigs') was interpreted as articulating the imperative desideratum of doctrinal secrecy, the pearls alluding to the 'mysterious and precious' tenets of Bogomilism, the esoteric domain of the *teleoi.*[22] Euthymius of the Periblepton asserts that in such elite Bogomil milieux, the enigmatic verses of Mark 4:11 ('The secret of the kingdom of God has been given to you. But to those on the outside everything is said in parables') was referred to and employed to uphold their claims to exclusive knowledge of the mystery of the Kingdom of God.[23] The medieval Bogomil *teleoi* (and subsequently the Cathar *perfecti*) were hence regarded by their adherents and sympathizers as protectors and repositories of Christ's genuine teaching secretly disclosed to his chosen apostles and maintained and

---

20   The text of *Epistula contra Phundagiagitas sive Bogomilos*, of Euthymius of the Periblepton is preserved in five manuscripts but only two contain the whole text. The letter is contained in PG vol. 131, cols. 47–58, but is erroneously attributed to the later theologian, Euthymius Zigabenus. Another edition is to be found in G. Ficker (ed.), *Die Phundagiagiten: Ein Beitrag zur Ketzergeschichte des byzantinischen Mittelalters*, Leipzig, 1908, pp. 3–86; English translation in J. Hamilton, B. Hamilton (eds) and Y. Stoyanov (ass. ed.), *Christian Dualist Heresies in the Byzantine World c. 650–c. 1450*, Manchester, 1998, pp. 142–164.

21   Euthymius Zigabenus, *Panoplia Dogmatica*, PG vol. 130; the Bogomil section, *Kata Bogomilon*, comprises cols. 1289–1331; another version of this Bogomil section, *De hæresi Bogomilorum narratio*, is also edited by Ficker in *Die Phundagiagiten*, 89–111. English translation of the relevant section in Hamilton, Hamilton and Stoyanov (eds), *Christian Dualist Heresies*, pp. 180–207. See also the recent study of the transmission history of *Panoplia Dogmatica* (especially focused on its Greek *editio princeps*, published in Tîrgoviște, Walachia, in 1710 and the single Athonite manuscript of the treatise—Iviron 281), N. Miladinova, *The Panoplia Dogmatike by Euthymios Zygadenos, A Study on the First Edition Published in Greek in 1710*, Leiden, 2014.

22   Euthymius Zigabenus, *Kata Bogomilon, Panoplia Dogmatica*, PG vol. 130, col. 1317C; *De hæresi Bogomilorum narratio*, Ficker (ed.), *Die Phundagiagiten*, pp. 100–101.

23   Euthymius of the Periblepton, *Epistula*, Ficker (ed.), *Die Phundagiagiten*, pp. 37.15–16.

THE MEDIEVAL DUALIST NACHLEBEN 115

passed on in concealment, uncontaminated by the distortions and fabrications of the official Church.

The accounts of the Bogomil course of initiation furnished by Euthymius of the Periblepton and Euthymius Zigabenus indicate that the believers were originally instructed in conventional Christian beliefs and ethics, a process which was followed by a progressive introduction to increasingly heretical precepts, until the overall system of the dualist teachings was presented to the neophyte. According to Euthymius of the Periblepton's description of the rite elevating the novice 'listener' to the rank of 'believer', during the procedure the book of the gospels was rested on the novice's head over which his heretical teachers recited verses from the gospels as well as from a certain 'Revelation of St Peter'.[24]

In Euthymius Zigabenus's account, the rite of acceptance (or second baptism) into the Bogomil community sect occurred after a probationary period (involving confession, purification and prayer) following which the novice was re-baptized. During the ceremony the Gospel of John was put on the neophyte's head, while the Holy Spirit was invoked along with a recitation of the 'Lord's Prayer'. Those accepted believers who aspired to be initiated further into the heretical teachings were subjected to another and stricter probationary period of intense instruction, prayer and purification, variously estimated as lasting one to two or three years. Upon its successful completion they were raised to the highest dualist grade of the *teleoi* and received the *teleiosis*; the *teleoi* presiding over the ceremony imposed hands and placed the gospel on the head of the proselyte against the background of hymns of thanksgiving and liturgical chants.[25]

The corresponding Cathar ritual of the *consolamentum* was closely associated with the Bogomil *teleiosis*, but in Catharism the preceding courses of

---

24   Euthymius of the Periblepton, *Epistula*, Ficker (ed.), *Die Phundagiagiten*, pp. 50–57.

25   Euthymius Zigabenus, *Kata Bogomilon, Panoplia Dogmatica*, PG vol. 130, col. 1312 C–D; *De hæresi Bogomilorum narratio*, Ficker (ed.), *Die Phundagiagiten*, 100–101. The texts of the Bogomil rites of the *teleiosis*, described by Euthymius Zigabenus and alluded to by Euthymius of the Periblepton, is not extant but their descriptions display evident textual parallels in the two surviving texts (Latin and Provencal) of the Cathar *Ritual*. The two texts of the Cathar *Ritual* have been published in C. Thouzellier, *Rituel cathare. Introduction, texte critique, traduction et notes*, Paris, 1976. Part of a later Slavonic Bosnian *Ritual* (written by Radoslav the Christian) corresponds closely to the Cathar *Ritual* of Lyons and was almost certainly used by fifteenth-century Christian dualists in Bosnia. The text was originally published by F. Rački, 'Dva nova priloga za poviest bosanskih Patarena', *Starine*, 14 (1882), pp. 21–29. See the English translation of its text: Y. Stoyanov, 'The Ritual of Radoslav the Christian', in Hamilton, Hamilton and Stoyanov (eds), *Christian Dualist Heresies*, pp. 289–292.

instruction and initiation (two probationary periods and two initiatory rites among the Eastern Christian dualists) were somewhat compressed. The first introductory probationary period and rite was considerably shortened or abandoned, as was the preparation for and the implementation of the *consolamentum*. In the area of doctrinal secrecy, the surviving evidence indicates that both in Bogomilism and Catharism (at least during the mature stages of the latter), the elite class of the *teleoi/perfecti* were considered by both their adversaries and followers as thoroughly proficient in a broad complex of advanced theological teachings, including a core of a kind of dualist *arcana*. They were also reported to have been instructed in a system of allegorical interpretation of the scriptures which was methodically and widely used during their missionary journeys and the various internal or more public theological debates pursued in such tours or heretical councils.

The indebtedness of Bogomil (and subsequently Cathar) theological dualism and narratives to earlier parascriptural works thus assumes an extra significance for the partial reconstruction of the corpus of doctrines and exegetical and literary techniques, which were seen as 'advanced' theological learning and were secreted in the elite Christian dualist milieux. The question, to what extent such vital doctrinal areas in medieval Christian dualism (which could also be described in medieval sources as 'secret') show dependence on the adopted and adapted earlier pseudepigraphic writings, needs also to consider the dynamic and fluctuating nature of some of its teachings during its lifespan. For example, since it remained a fundamental and foundational element of Bogomil theological dualism, Bogomil diabology retained its main precepts during the heresy's existence, whereas other Bogomil traditions such as cosmogonic notions and narratives were not stable and fixed. Textual data suggest that some early and late Bogomil (as well as some of the related Cathar) cosmogonic systems were more fluid, variegated traditions, initially intended to enhance and furnish a descriptive cosmological and narrative background to the early moderate dualism of Bogomilism. In later stages they could endure redactions, alterations and embellishments, expansions, drawing upon new dualist reappraisals, assimilation and merging of canonical and extra-canonical cosmogonic traditions. Such transformations and fluctuations could reflect changing theological or historical circumstances, polemics with the church authorities, internal disputes, schisms, theological and literary creativity, etc.

Characteristically, in its moderate dualist elaboration of the tradition of Satan's revolt, early Bogomil satanology made use of both normative Christian diabology and newly translated pseudepigraphical literature. Such intertextuality in this sphere is evident in the case of *Palæa Historica* and *Palæa*

Interpretata, which integrate heterodox and apocryphal motifs, and narratives in their compilatory compositions recount the tradition of Satanael's revolt in heaven; according to *Palæa Historica*, in the wake of his fall he was deprived of his divine light and angelic garments[26]—significantly, a theme which is also shared in the diabological sections of Zigabenus's *Kata Bogomilon* and *The Battle Between Archangel Michael and Satanael*.[27] The account of Satan's rebellion and fall in *Interrogatio Iohannis* intertwines an exegesis of Isaiah 14:13–14, dualist re-interpretation of the New Testament parables of the Unjust Steward (Luke 16:1–8) and the Unforgiving Servant (Matthew 18:23–35) and themes from Revelation. The tenth-century *Sermon against the Heretics* of Cosmas the Presbyter quotes a Bogomil reading of the Parable of the Prodigal Son (Luke 15.11–32) in which Christ represents the elder and the Devil the younger brother.[28] Euthymius Zigabenus's *Kata bogomilon* depicts Satanael (Samael) as the Father's first-born, being second only to the Father, acting as His steward, with the same form and dress and empowered to reside on a throne at His right hand.[29] This version of Bogomil monarchian dualism also develops the tradition of Satanael's loss of the syllable '-el' in the wake of his rebellion, attested in earlier pseudepigraphical and parabiblical texts such as 2 Enoch 31.5, the Slavonic version of 3 Baruch 4.7, *The Questions of Bartholomew* 4.25 and *The Martyrdom of St Paul and St Juliana*.[30]

---

26   See the Greek text of *Palæa Historica*, in A. Vassiliev (ed.), *Anecdota-Græco-Byzantina*, Moscow, 1893, p. 189, and the Slavonic text, in A.N. Popov (ed.), *Kniga bytīa nebesi i zemli (Paleia istoricheskaia) s prilozheniem sokrashchennoi Palei russkoi redaktsii*, Moscow, 1881, p. 2; for the Slavonic text of *Palæa Interpretata*, see *Paleiia Tolkovaiia po spisku sdelannomu v g. Kolomne 1406g. trud uchenikov N.S. Tikhonravova* vol. 1, Moscow, 1892–1896, p. 37.

27   *The Battle Between Archangel Michael and Satanael*, MS Sofia, Church Historico-Archeological Museum No. 1161, fol. 41ʳ.

28   Text in Y. Begunov, *Kozma prezviter v slavianskikh literaturakh*, Sofia, 1973, p. 331.

29   Euthymius Zigabenus, *Kata Bogomilon, Panoplia Dogmatica*, PG vol. 130, col. 1293.

30   See the edition of the Greek text of *The Questions of Bartholomew* in Vassiliev, 'Quæstiones s. Bartholmæi apostoli', *Anecdota græco-byzantina*, pp. 17–21; for the Slavonic manuscripts of the work, see A. de Santos Otero, *Die handschriftliche Überlieferung der altslavischen Apocryphen* vol. 2, Berlin–New York, 1978–1981, pp. 58–59. On the use of the name 'Satanael' instead of 'Satan', 'Samael', 'Lucifer' or the 'Devil' and the theme of Satanael losing his theophoric suffix '-el' following his fall in pre-Bogomil doctrinal and apocryphal traditions, cf. M. Dando, 'Satanael', *Cahiers d'études cathares*, IIᵉ série 85 (1979), pp. 3–21; É. Turdeanu, 'Apocryphes bogomiles et apocryphes pseudo-bogomiles', *Revue d'histoire des religions* 138 (1950), pp. 22–52, 176–218, here 177–181; H.E. Gaylord, 'The Slavonic Version of 3 Baruch', p. xxxii; id., 'How Satanael lost his '-el'', *Journal of Jewish Studies* 33 (1982), pp. 303–309; R. Stichel, 'Der Verführung der Stammeltern durch Satanael nach der Kurzfassung der Slavischen Baruch-Apocalypse', in R. Lauer and P. Schreiner (eds), *Kulturelle*

Satanael's initial status as God's first-born son in Bogomil monarchian dualism[31] reflects a specific diabology which similarly can be traced to *The Questions of Bartholomew* 4.25–29 where Satanael is depicted as the first angel created by God by a handful of fire, although he is not named explicitly the 'firstborn' or the 'eldest son' of God. The depiction of Satanael as a son of God would have been reinforced by the Bogomil dualist interpretation of the Parable of the Prodigal Son in Luke 15.11–32 as well as the one concerning the unrighteous steward in Luke 16.1–9 (as recounted by Cosmas the Presbyter) illustrating the predilection for the use of parables and allegories in Bogomil scriptural exegesis which is well expounded in Zigabenus's heresiological treatise).[32]

A number of primary sources attribute to Bogomilism a plural-heaven cosmogony and cosmology: for example, Euthymius of the Periblepton's epistle,[33] the *Sermon against the Bogomils for the Sunday of All Saints* (attributed to Patriarch John Xiphilinus [1064–1075]),[34] anti-Bogomil anathema added to the *Synodicon of Orthodoxy*,[35] etc. The *Synodicon of Orthodoxy* anathema pointedly ascribes the Bogomil teaching of a supernal trinity residing in the uppermost of the seven heavens to their use of the pseudepigraphon, *The Vision of Isaiah*.[36] The cumulative textual data offer further indications that Bogomil multiheaven cosmology was shaped under the impact of its earlier formulations and variants in apocalypses influential in the Slavo-Byzantine pseudepigraphy such as 2 Enoch, *The Apocalypse of Abraham* and 3 Baruch, and elaborated with

---

     Traditionen in Bulgarien. Bericht über das Kolloquium der Südosteuropa-Kommission, Juni 1987, Göttingen, 1989, pp. 116–128.

31   Cosmas's assertion that in Bogomil diabology Christ was regarded as the elder and the Devil the younger son of God the Father can be best explained as alluding to the later and conclusive stage in the cosmic drama when Christ defeats Satanael, takes the divine syllable '-el' from his name, acquires his right of a first-born son and sits on his throne at the right hand of the Father, as recounted in Zigabenus's *Kata Bogomilon*, col. 1305; cf. H.-C. Puech and A. Vaillant, *Le Traité contre les Bogomiles de Cosmas le prêtre*, Paris, 1945, pp. 190–192. On the 'inverse symmetrical correspondence' between the divine and demonic in early Jewish demonology through which a protagonist appropriates the place of his adversary and attains the attributes of his counterpart, see Orlov, *Dark Mirrors*, pp. 4–5.

32   Euthymius Zigabenus, *Kata Bogomilon. Panoplia Dogmatica*, cols. 1321–1332; cf. M. Loos, 'Satan als erstgeborener Gottes (ein Beitrag zur Analyse des bogomilischen Mythus)', *Byzantinobulgarica* 3 (1970), pp. 23–36, esp. 30–31.

33   Euthymius of the Periblepton, Ficker (ed.), *Epistula*, p. 34.

34   The *Sermon* is published in *Patrologia Græca*, 120, cols. 1289–1292; for the reference to the Bogomil seven-heaven cosmology, see col. 1292.

35   Text edited in J. Gouillard, 'Le Synodicon de l'orthodoxie', *Travaux et mémoires* 2 (1967), pp. 1–316, here 65.

36   Gouillard, 'Le Synodicon', p. 65.

THE MEDIEVAL DUALIST NACHLEBEN

diabological, angelological and Christological traditions also borrowed from pseudepigraphical literature.[37]

In the *Interrogatio Iohannis*, for example, following his rebellion and fall, Satan assumes his new seat in the firmament (Carcassonne version 64), or above the firmament (Vienna version 70), from where he inaugurates the cosmogonic process. The association between Satan and the realm of the firmament is also evident in Zigabenus's *Kata Bogomilon*, where he is credited with creation and adornment of the firmament as his second heaven[38] The link between the firmament and Satan (along with his ministering powers) is paralleled in *The Vision of Isaiah* 7.9–11 and it is very likely that it was adopted from the pseudepigraphon (which its text describes as a domain of perpetual strife among the fallen angelic orders). The motif of the firmament as a space ruled by Satan is highlighted in the Bogomil exegesis of the New Testament narrative of Jesus's temptation by the Devil, reproduced in Zigabenus's *Kata Bogomilon*, in which the high mountain in this episode is interpreted as being the second heaven or firmament created by Satan.[39]

Interrogatio Iohannis's dependence on 2 Enoch is especially pronounced: both textually discernible and as a source for a number of distinct notions such as the unique imagery of Enoch's throne vision, the ideas of the primal restlessness of the creator and the derivation of fire from rock and various angeological notions.[40] Further characteristic angeological, demonological and cosmological themes and elements in *Interrogatio Iohannis* can be securely traced to both canonical (Ephesians, Revelation) and extra-canonical apocryphal works (*The Vision of Isaiah, The Questions of Bartholomew*).[41]

The accounts of Bogomil sacred history and anthropogony and cosmography narrative (such as their dualist versions of the Genesis paradise story and the fall of Adam and Eve in the *Interrogatio Iohannis* and Euthymius

---

37 Another characteristic motif which betrays the indebtedness of *Interrogatio Iohannis* to *The Vision of Isaiah*, for instance, concerns the angelic guardians/guides of the portals of the air and water in heaven, a theme which is also shared in Jewish Merkabah and Gnostic traditions: cf. the Gnostic Ophite teachings in Origen *Contra Celsum* 6:24–38; for parallels in Merkabah literature, see *Hekhalot Rabbati* 17:1–20:3; 3 Enoch 18:3, 48D:5.

38 Euthymius Zigabenus, *Kata Bogomilon, Panoplia Dogmatica*, cols. 1295–1297.

39 Euthymius Zigabenus, *Kata Bogomilon, Panoplia Dogmatica*, cols. 1324–125.

40 Early analyses of these intertextual dependencies in M. Sokolov, 'Materialy i zametki po starinnoi slavianskoi literature. Vypusk 3. VII, Slavianskaia Kniga Enokha Pravednago. Teksty, latinskii perevdo i issledovanie', *Chteniia v Obshchestve Istorii i Drevnostei Rossiiskikh*, 4 (1910), pp. 1–167, esp. 148–151, and I. Ivanov, *Bogomilski knigi i legend*, Sofia, 1925, pp. 188–191; recent discussion in Stoyanov, 'Pseudepigraphic and Parabiblical Narrative', pp. 170–172.

41 Analysis in Stoyanov, 'Pseudepigraphic and Parabiblical Narrative', pp. 169–172.

Zigabenus's *Kata Bogomilon*) similarly display the visible impact of pseude-pigrapha such as 2 Enoch, 3 Baruch, *The Apocalypse of Abraham*, the Slavonic versions of *The Life of Adam and Eve* and *The Legend of the Cross*. This impact is especially evident in the Bogomil developments of relatively widely attested pseudepigraphic themes such as Satan's planting of paradise, Eve's seduction by Satan/Samael, the association between paradise's primal tree (or trees) and human carnality, etc.[42] Clear textual indications demonstrate the interrelations between Bogomil Christology and elements of the distinct Christology of *The Vision of Isaiah*, and also with apocryphal and popular traditions of the struggle between the archangel Michael and Satanael, as elaborated in medieval apocryphal works such as *The Sea of Tiberias* and *The Battle Between Archangel Michael and Satanael*. Finally, most of the themes and imagery in the concluding eschatological section of the *Interrogatio Iohannis* derive not only from canonical New Testament sources but also from earlier apocryphal works such as 4 Esdras 4.35–37 and the Slavonic version of the *Apocryphal Apocalypse of John*.[43]

This summary of the main patterns of Bogomil dualism's significant dependence on parascriptural writings also shows the complex textual web of interrelations between Bogomil (or Bogomil-influenced) scribal traditions and multifarious, broadly accessible and circulated pseudepigraphical literature, a distinct literary process which did not take place in contemporaneous Western Christendom in general and in the case of medieval Western heresy and Catharism in particular. In the early stages of Catharism the assimilation of such pseudepigraphic material into Cathar teachings and narrative traditions essentially took place through the adoption of the traditions of Bogomil parascripturalism, as shown by the reception and impact of *Interrogatio Iohannis* in varied western dualist milieux. The adoption of apocryphal traditions in early and mature Cathar traditions in France, Italy and elsewhere was filtered initially, and to a large degree, through their dualist continuation and re-interpretation in Bogomilism (as demonstrated by the circulation and reception of *Interrogatio Iohannis*). Subsequently, later Cathar approaches to, and uses of, scriptural and parascriptural texts evolved also within their own specific trajectories and need to be evaluated also in their particular Western cultural and literary settings. For example, the Cathar assumption of creative parascripturalism (in relation to Bogomil-transmitted apocryphal traditions)

---

42   See Y. Stoyanov, 'Diabolizing the Garden of Eden: Re-Interpretations of Jewish Pseudepigraphy in Medieval Christian Dualism', in A. Scafi (ed.), *The Cosmography of Paradise: The Other World from Ancient Mesopotamia to Medieval Europe*, London, 2015, pp. 109–126.

43   Early analysis in Ivanov, *Bogomilski knigi*, 91; cf. Bozóky, *Le Livre secret*, pp. 172–173.

is clearly discernible in the re-interpretations of notions deriving from *Interrogatio Iohannis* initiated by the bishop of the Cathar Church of Concorezzo, Nazarius, and the consequent internal theological controversies triggered by his mythologizing innovations and narratives.[44] Such parabiblical material in the sources for Catharism (usually integrated into the complex of notions and narratives described as 'the mythology' or 'mythic' narratives of Western dualist heresy)[45] need a fresh reassessment which would demonstrate whether the exegetical and compilatory techniques applied to it followed, or started to diverge from, their eastern dualist antecedents.

There are also some indications to suggest that such adopted and re-worked pseudepigraphical material formed a substantial part, if not the bulk, of the teachings considered 'esoteric' in medieval Christian dualism and, in Italian Catharism, this process gave impetus to the formation of a further stratification of secrecy within the *perfecti* class: the appearance of an even more theologically exclusivist elites which secreted some of this material as arcane teachings for their privileged knowledge and use.[46] Some of the extant evidence also suggests that the Bogomil *teleoi* pursued and cultivated certain practices of visionary mysticism and heavenly ascent[47] which could also have been adopted in Cathar circles, on the basis of absorbed pseudepigraphic accounts of heavenly rapture.[48]

A related crucial question which will need further close and comparative study is whether the pseudepigraphical cosmological, diabological and Christological notions adopted in medieval Christian dualism were also seen and

---

44   Analysis in Stoyanov, *The Other God*, pp. 270–273.

45   See, for, example, M. Loos, *Dualist Heresy in the Middle Ages*, Prague, 1974, chs 7 and 11; Bozóky, *Le Livre secret*, pp. 186–217; ead., 'La part du mythe dans la diffusion du catharisme', *Heresis* 35 (2001), pp. 45–58; B. Hamilton, 'Wisdom from the East: the Reception by the Cathars of Eastern Dualist Texts', in P. Biller and A. Hudson (eds), *Heresy and Literacy 1000–1530*, Cambridge, 1994, pp. 38–61; L. Paolini, 'Italian Catharism and Written Culture', in Biller and Hudson (eds), *Heresy and Literacy*, pp. 87–103; H. Fichtenau, *Heretics and Scholars in the High Middle Ages*, *1000–1200*, transl. D.A. Kaiser, University Park, 1998, pp. 155–172; M. Lambert, *The Cathars*, Oxford, 1998, pp. 163 ff., 197 ff.; A. Greco, *Mitologia catara: il favoloso mondo delle origini*, Spoleto, 2000; Stoyanov, *The Other God*, pp. 262–287, *passim*; P. Jiménez-Sanchez, *Les catharismes: modèles dissidents du christianisme médiéval (XIIe–XIIIe siècles)*, Rennes, 2008, 215–254, *passim*.

46   Paolini, 'Italian Catharism', p. 94.

47   Euthymius Zigabenus, *Kata Bogomilon, Panoplia Dogmatica*, col. 1312 C–D; *De hæresi Bogomilorum narratio*, Ficker (ed.), *Die Phundagiagiten*, p. 101.

48   See, for example, the report of Cathar ecstatic and visionary practices based on the heavenly ascent narrative in *The Vision of Isaiah* published in J.J.I. von Döllinger, *Beiträge zur Sektengeschichte des Mittelalters* vol. 2, Darmstadt, 1890, 208–210.

selectively transmitted as esoteric in the period of the original composition of the respective pseudepigrapha. This a question which requires a cautious reassessment in view of the pseudo-esoteric literary strategy behind some of the early Jewish apocalyptic pseudepigrapha[49] and the evidence that a number of Gnostic writings and teachings were not actually considered esoteric in late antiquity, whether by the Gnostic circles which generated them or by the patristic heresiologists who polemicized against them.[50]

At the same time, further important questions continue to arise from the simultaneous emergence of dualist and dualist-leaning schemes and narratives in the same or adjacent geographical areas (Languedoc, Provence, Catalonia and Northern Spain) in medieval Christianity (Catharism) and Judaism (several early Kabbalistic currents). Certain evident analogies in the cosmogonic, cosmological, satanological and demonological schemes in Cathar and early Kabbalistic traditions have generated arguments for some kind of interaction between these two religious trends[51] and even for a Cathar impact on some of the early Kabbalistic schools and individual figures.[52] The current state of evidence rather indicates that these analogies represent the outcome of parallel developments, in the case of early Kabbalistic traditions being conditioned by a complex interplay of internal exegetical patterns and external influences on Talmudic and early medieval Judaism.[53] The possibility of shared pseudepi-

---

49 Stone, *Secret Groups*, 33, pp. 116–118.

50 M.A. Williams, 'Secrecy, Revelation, and Late Antique Demiurgical Myths', in Wolfson (ed.), *Rending the Veil*, pp. 31–58.

51 See, for example, L.I. Newman, *Jewish Influence on Christian Reform Movements*, New York, 1925, pp. 138–207.

52 S. Shahar, 'Catharism and the Beginnings of the Kabbalah in Languedoc', *Tarbiz*, 15:4 (1971), pp. 483–507 (in Hebrew); ead., 'Ecrits Cathares et commentaires d'Abraham Abulafia sur le 'Livre de la creation', images et idées communes', *Cahiers de Fanjeaux* 12 (1977), pp. 345–361. For critiques of these arguments, see A. Borst, *Die Katharer*, Stuttgart, 1953, pp. 99, 105, 125; J.M. O'Brien, 'Jews and Cathari in Medieval France', *Comparative Studies in Society and History*, 10:2 (Jan., 1968), pp. 215–220; M. Idel, *Studies in Ecstatic Kabbalah*, Albany, 1989, pp. 33–45; earlier critical discussion of the problematic in Gershom Scholem, *Origins of the Kabbalah*, R.Z.J. Werblowsky (ed.), transl. A. Arkush, Philadelphia–Princeton, 1987, pp. 12–36, 199–365 *passim*.

53 J. Dan, 'Kabbalistic and Gnostic Dualism', in Joseph Dan (ed.), *Binah: Studies in Jewish History, Thought and Culture* vol. III, Westport–London, 1994, pp. 19–33; id., 'Jewish Gnosticism?', *Jewish Studies Quarterly* 2 (1995), pp. 309–328; M. Idel, *Il male primordiale nella Qabbalah*, transl. F. Lelli, Milan, 2016; M. Idel, 'From Iran to Qumran and Beyond On the Evil Thought of God', in Y. Friedmann and E. Kohlberg (eds), *Studies in Honor of Professor Shaul Shaked*, Jerusalem, 2019, pp. 29–59 (Moshe Idel's studies provide pioneering in-depth study of the provenance and development of the notion of primæval evil in a variety of kabbalistic traditions).

graphic sources clearly also needs to be taken into account. The marked symmetric patterns in early Jewish apocalypticism and demonology, ranging from the realms of protology to eschatology,[54] were certainly conducive to generating or impacting novel dualist or dualist-leaning schemas when 're-discovered' and re-employed in medieval religio-cultural settings, whether heretical, heterodox or 'normative'. The ongoing re-appraisal of early Jewish and Christian esoteric (and pseudo-esoteric) traditions in these currently only partially identified shared pseudepigraphic sources will thus make a crucial contribution to the evaluation of their provenance, evolution and afterlife in medieval Judaism and Christianity.

54   Summary of the problematic in Orlov, *Dark Mirrors*, pp. 1–9.

CHAPTER 6

The Esoteric Cardinal: Giorgios Gemistos, Bessarion and Theurgy

Ezio Albrile

The history of culture is often filled with surprises. In reality one should speak of the history of the 'meaning' to be given to existence. Facts, events, circumstances present themselves to us in different forms, in synchrony with the ages. It is not hazardous to state that interpretations of historical facts reflect the moment in which they were formulated. Every time has its own 'cultural fashion' with which historians—perhaps unconsciously—must come to terms.

I

If reality were a stationary condition and not the result of continuous changes, not only would moments not exist, but even time would not find validation, since only the perception of change can make it evident. Reality as a process generates time. In the absence of it there would be no temporal development, while the inverse relationship is not true.[1] In the ancient world such an altered perception of reality can be found in a series of inspired texts,[2] arising from the ecstasies of late Platonic philosophers, the *Chaldæan Oracles*.

The *Chaldæan Oracles* are a series of poetic compositions, poor from a stylistic point of view,[3] which refer to the so-called philosophical tradition of Middle Platonism (2nd century AD); a term introduced in philosophical historiography at the beginning of the twentieth century by the philologist Karl Praechter to indicate the Platonism ranging from the first century BC up to Plotinus.[4] Only

---

1 A. Hofmann, *Percezioni di realtà*, trad. it. cur. R. Fedeli, Roma, 2006, p. 23.
2 G. Muscolino, *Teurgia. Riti magici e divinatori nell'età tarda-antica*, Bussoleno (Turin), 2017, pp. 35–50 (currently the most complete text on the subject and to which reference is made for the entire retrospective bibliography).
3 E. Des Places, *Platonismo e tradizione cristiana*, a cura di P.A. Carozzi, Milano, 1976, p. 145.
4 R. Chiaradonna, *Platonismo*, Bologna, 2017, p. 35.

© EZIO ALBRILE, 2021 | DOI:10.1163/9789004445925_008

THE ESOTERIC CARDINAL

fragments of them remain, published in a first critical text by Wilhelm Kroll in 1894 and later by the Jesuit Édouard des Places in 1971, the edition to which we refer.

The title *Chaldæan Oracles* (*Chaldaika Logia*) we read in the *Commentary on Parmenides* by Proclus (800, 19 c), but it is unusual in antiquity.[5] In most cases, instead of this title, we find the *Oracles* attributed to the speeches of the gods. Theurgists themselves would have collected these presages. According to *Souda*, the well-known Byzantine lexicon of the eleventh century, the authors would be Julian the Chaldæan and his son Julian the Theurgist who lived at the time of Emperor Marcus Aurelius. Julian the Chaldæan would have been a sort of 'spiritual master' of a very exclusive Mystery circle, subsequently the *Oracles* would have been collected and committed to writing by his son Julian, called the Theurgist, to distinguish him from his father. The *Oracles* should therefore date back to the end of the 2nd century or, at the latest, to the beginning of the 3rd century AD. In fact in the Hellenistic mentality the nickname 'Chaldæan' gave authority to the disciplines professed and to those who taught them.[6]

We are in front of a very fragmentary and elusive materials in which one can read of a first God distinct from a Demiurge, a second god of lower rank in the hierarchy of beings. In the same way—disclose the *Oracles*—there would exist an 'igneous' universe, made up of general Ideas and of which the goddess Hekatē would be the visible personification, as opposed to another world, that of particular Ideas, of a lower level. In fact, this visibility of the divine creates the conditions for the existence of an ethereal cosmos, intermediate between the intelligible world and the terrestrial world, between God and the lowest world. We might think of three levels of reality, one totally transcendent and ineffable, one intermediate and invisible, and finally our world, perceptible by the five senses, visible and corporeal. Even if there are not enough fragments to affirm it, the triplicity of the Chaldæan universe can be deduced from a variety of indirect evidences.[7]

---

5 H. Seng, 'Un livre sacré de l'Antiquité tardive: les Oracles chaldaïques', in *Annuaire de l'École Pratique des Hautes Études* (v^e Section—Sciences Religieuses) 118 (2011), p. 117.

6 F. Cumont, *Astrologia e religione presso i Greci e i Romani. Il culto degli astri nel mondo antico*, trad. it. cur. A. Panaino, Milano, 1990 (ed. or. London 1912), p. 77.

7 Seng, 'Un livre sacré de l'Antiquité tardive', p. 122; Muscolino, *Teurgia*, p. 72.

II

The Chaldæan lexicon refers to the astral spaces,[8] calling them *zōnaioi* and *azōnoi*: the first coming up to the *zōnai*, literally 'bands' or 'belts', the trajectories that designate the gods, or celestial bodies that inhabit the *zōnē*, i.e. the Zodiacal circle. Along the *zōnē* the process of revolution of souls is likely to occur.

In contrast, the *azōnoi* were so called because they personify the band of constellations or fixed stars. Finally, in Damascius (*De princ.* 132), we find the word *kosmagoi* contextualized in the Chaldæan milieu, to indicate the forces that rule the cosmos; they are the Archons of the gnostic myths, the planetary powers that subjugate time and man. It should be emphasized that the word 'planet',[9] or more precisely *planēta astra*, 'wandering star', is found for the first time in Democritus around 400 BC. The term seeks to express the 'vagrant' nature of celestial bodies that, although similar to the fixed stars, are distinguished from them because they move with irregular movements (loops and regressions) within the Zodiacal band. The allusion that Theurgists make to these stellar forces, implies a dynamic and conflicting vision of the cosmos, a space in continuous mutation and in constant conflict, within which the astral gods fight a perpetual war for reciprocal supremacy, fully manifesting their psychagogic force also known as the power of souls' guidance.

Under the sphere of the Moon there is our world, the realm of 'primordial matter', *prōtogenēs hylē* or of 'generative matter', *patrogenēs hylē* (fr. 173). A definition that is influenced by the Platonic teachings on matter and the world of ideas, seen respectively as the mother and father of the visible world (*Tim.* 50 c–d).

III

In the Chaldæan discipline there is no univocal teaching about the descent of the soul: on the one hand, it is presented as a momentary event; more often, it is spoken of as a 'descent' or a 'fall'. During the 'descent', the *katabasis*, the soul undergoes a substantial mutation. Crossing the planetary spheres, it draws from each one some element that gradually stratifies it, wrapping it like a

---

8 H. Seng, *ΚΟΣΜΑΓΟΙ, ΑΖΩΝΟΙ, ΖΩΝΑΟΙ. Drei Begriffe chaldæischer Kosmologie und ihr Fortleben*, Heidelberg, 2009.

9 H.G. Gundel, s.v. 'Pianeti', in *Enciclopedia dell'Arte Antica Classica e Orientale*, Supplemento 1970, Roma, 1973, pp. 614a–623b.

THE ESOTERIC CARDINAL   127

shell: it is the genesis of what is called the 'vehicle' (*ochēma*) of the soul, or *pneuma*, the 'spirit' that unites the worlds. This 'vehicle' is not totally bodiless, but neither is it formed of bodily matter. It becomes tangible only after having captured the corresponding dose of materiality from each astral sphere. Each planetary level enriches the soul with a quality, aspect or attitude: the cosmos is an animated being and the planets are part of a complex psycho-corporeal organism.

Chaldæan theology and the Neoplatonists[10] affirm that at birth the soul travels through the Milky Way, furrowing the spheres of the seven planets accompanied by a guide, an *ochēma*, a 'vehicle' or 'astral body'; from every planet the soul absorbs specific qualities and attitudes, vices and virtues necessary for life on earth, which enrich its 'astral body'.

In fact, Theurgy is intimately linked to the Chaldæan tradition. In the word Theurgy, a compound of *theos* 'god' and *ergon* 'work' or *ergazomai* 'to make, produce', the two peculiar meanings of 'fulfilment of divine actions' and that of 'art of creating the gods'[11] converge. It tends to establish a privileged relationship between the agents of the sacred, the Theurgists and the deities, in order to join with them and benefit from their strength.

Theurgy is a technique revealed by the gods to allow a narrow circle of men, Theurgists, to have contact with the divine. Thanks to the benevolent help of these mysterious forces it is possible to enter into communication with the divinity, through an *anabasis*, an 'ascension'.

Of the three forms that according to the ancient 'Chaldæan magicians' characterized theurgical action, i.e. the *telestica*, the mediumistic art and the *apathanatismos* or immortalization, the last is certainly the most evocative: through it, it was considered possible to ensure the transformation of a human soul into an immortal divine being. In fr. 97 the final ascension of the soul is alluded to: 'Hovering in flight, the soul of mortals encloses the god in itself, and without retaining anything mortal is entirely inebriated by the god. It glories in harmony: under it lies the mortal body'.

Immortalization is obtained through the ascent of the soul, and divinization is considered a new existential state of the initiate, coinciding with its identification with the supreme *Nous*, the first intellect; they are the elements that

---

10   H.D. Saffrey, 'Les néoplatoniciens et les Oracles Chaldaïques', in *Revue des Études Augustiniennes* 27 (1981), pp. 209–225; id., 'La Théurgie comme phénomène culturel chez les Néoplatoniciens (IVe—Ve siècles)', in *Κοινωνία* 8 (1984), pp. 161–171.

11   S. Lilla, s.v. 'Teurgia', in *Dizionario Patristico e di Antichità Cristiane*, II, A. Di Berardino (cur.), Casale Monferrato, 1983, coll. 3438 ff., which refers to the work of Dodds and Lewy.

establish Neoplatonic Theurgy, that is, a 'divine' and magical art that uses the expressive elements of Plato's thought. In it, certain acts of worship, including prayer and the use of vocal sequences, allowed, by virtue of an intimate union with the divine, the ascent of the soul.

An important text to grasp the evolution of these traditions is the *De Mysteriis* by Iamblichus, an aggregate of Chaldæan, Egyptian and Platonic elements[12] united to celebrate Theurgy, considered superior to theology and philosophy, as a way of salvation centred on ritual assumptions.[13] In this ritual breviary[14] the Theurgists derive the knowledge of the names and places necessary for their evocations directly from the gods. The Theurgist accesses an oneiric space, an interzone in which he obtains 'illumination' (*ellampsis*), dispensed— according to *De Mysteriis* (1, 12)—from the divine will, which by making the light shine on the Theurgists reveals its own benevolence, allowing the souls to detach themselves from the bodies and to join it. A secret prayer allows practitioners the ritual of freeing their soul from the bonds of the flesh and ascending into the divine light. The gods remain impassive to this approach and contamination, they are not even minimally stained by the contact with human souls, on the contrary, it is communion with the gods which frees men from the sphere of the passions.

IV

Traces and allusions suggest that Plotinus (205–270 AD)[15] knew the *Oracles*, but the first author to contextualize them in his work is one of his disciples, Porphyry (ca. 233–310 AD). Another Neoplatonist, at variance with Porphyry, the cited Iamblichus (about 240–325 AD) copiously used the Chaldæan oracular materials, skilfully mixing Theurgy and Platonism, laying the foundations for a philosophy based on eminently magical values. But it is only about a century later, with Proclus (412–485 AD), that the *Oracles* become a sort of Bible of the

---

12   H. Lewy, *Chaldæan Oracles and Theurgy. Mysticism Magic and Platonism in the Later Roman Empire*, Nouv. éd. par M. Tardieu, 3rd edn, Paris, 1978, p. 463.

13   C. Van Liefferinge, *La Théurgie. Des Oracles Chaldaïques à Proclus* (Kernos Supplément, 9), Liège, 1999, p. 61.

14   G. Girgenti, *Introduzione a Porfirio*, Roma–Bari, 1977, p. 108; M.P. Nilsson had already defined it as a 'compendium of the late ancient religion' in *Geschichte der griechischen Religion* (Handbuch d. Altertumswissenschaft, 5. Abteilung, 2. Teil), 2 vols, 2nd edn, München, 1955–1961, p. 429.

15   Muscolino, *Teurgia*, pp. 59–68.

THE ESOTERIC CARDINAL

last Neoplatonists.[16] He used to repeat: 'If I were the master, among the books of the ancients I would leave only the *Oracles* and the *Timæus* in circulation'.[17]

Proclus was an expert in meteorological magic and in the technique of evocation, he saw luminous phantoms sent by Hekatē, he practiced the Chaldæan purifications, he was initiated into Theurgical art by the daughter of Plutarch, Asclepigeneia, who, in the Egyptian magic tradition, had inherited it from her father.[18] Proclus then attempted to recode the oracular wisdom in an Orphic and Platonic context; the risk lay in going beyond the original interpretation and in flattening out the inspired hexameters through a totally Neoplatonic hermeneutic. A problem that also arose with one of the last exponents of the school, Damascius (ca. 462–532 AD).

In tenth century Byzantium, Symeon the New Theologian taught that Christians could experience the divine through the uncreated light of the Transfiguration, something very close to Theurgical practices.[19] The purpose of this spiritual journey was *theōsis*, participation in the divine life.[20] Symeon aroused bitter controversy, but from his teachings developed a thread that accompanied Byzantine spirituality throughout its history, in strong contrast to the Western concept of original sin, and in true continuity with the teachings of ancient Neoplatonism.

However, it is undoubted that in the Byzantine world the main witness to the oracular wisdom is Michael Psellus, who provides a series of epitomes of the Chaldæan-Neoplatonic system, four to be precise (which contradict one another on some points). The same Psellus collects a series of *Oracles* and comments on them; the work takes the title of *Exēgēsis tōn Chaldaikōn Rhētōn* (= *Commentary on the Chaldæan Oracles*).[21] The philosopher, while interpreting the fragments in the light of Neoplatonic exegesis, is strongly conditioned by his Christian heritage and formation.[22] An aspect that will severely compro-

---

16   Seng, 'Un livre sacré de l' Antiquité tardive', pp. 117–118.

17   Marino, *Vita Procli* 38, pp. 15–17.

18   A.R. Sodano, 'Introduzione', in id. (ed.), *Giamblico. I misteri egiziani. Abammone. Lettera a Porfirio*, Milano, 1984, p. 19.

19   M. Tardieu, 'Pléthon lecteur des oracles', in *Mètis. Anthropologie des mondes grecs anciens* 2 (1987), p. 149.

20   I.-H. Dalmais, s.v. 'Divinisation II. Patristique grecque', in *Dictionnaire de Spiritualité Ascétique et Mystique*, IV, Paris, 1956, col. 1385.

21   *PG* 122, 1115–1122; cf. S. Lanzi (cur.), *Michele Psello. Oracoli caldaici con appendici su Proclo e Michele Italo*, Milano, 2001, pp. 55–98.

22   É. Des Places, 'Le renouveau platonicien du XIe siècle: Michel Psellus et les Oracles chaldaïque', in *Comptes rendus des séances de l'Acadèmie des Inscriptions et Belles Lettres* 110 (1966), pp. 313–324.

mise his interpretation. On the other hand, the attitude of Psellus is warranted by the fact that he was forced to take vows and to withdraw for a certain period to a monastery;[23] all this because of the intransigence shown by the Patriarch Michael Cerularios in 1054.

V

A decisive figure in communicating the wisdom contained in the *Chaldæan Oracles* to the Renaissance world, and therefore down to us, was, however, an erudite Byzantine, Giorgios Gemistos, whose fervour and dedication in wanting to restore the dictates of ancient Platonism, earned him the epithet of Plethon, drawn on that of its most famous and archetypical mentor.

Giorgios Gemistos Plethon[24] was born around 1360 in Constantinople to a family of senior officials of the patriarchal curia. Decisive, and for some inauspicious,[25] was his meeting with the Jew Elisha, perhaps a Kabbalist, translator and commentator on Averroes in Hebrew, and therefore a follower of those writings that will lead to the definition of a 'Hellenistic philosophy of Islam',[26] i.e. of the *Falsafa*; he is the one who acquaints Plethon with the name and figure of Zarathuštra / Zoroaster, mediated perhaps by the encounter with the Persian Neoplatonic Sohrawardī.[27] The existence of an Arabic version of the *Oracles of Plethon* lends credit to the Iranian hypothesis.[28]

We learn all of this from the epistolary of Giorgios Scolarios (ca. 1405–1472),[29] then patriarch of Constantinople with the name of Gennadios II: Elisha is the first to speak of the *Chaldean Oracles*, attributing them to Zoroaster and renaming them *Logia Magika*, not in the usual sense that we give to the word

---

23　A. Cameron, *I bizantini*, trad. L. Santi, cur. G. Ravegnani, Bologna, 2008 (ed. or. Oxford 2006), pp. 192–193.

24　S. Kennedy, 'Bessarion's Date of Birth. A New Assessment of the Evidence', in *Byzantinische Zeitschrift* 111 (2018), pp. 641–658.

25　C.M. Woodhouse, *George Gemistos Plethon. The Last of the Hellenes*, Oxford, 1986, pp. 25–29.

26　L. Gardet, *L'Islam. Religion et communauté*, Paris, 1970, pp. 213–214; cf. M. Shaki, s.v. 'Falsafa. I: Pre-Islamic Philosophy', in E. Yarshater (ed.), *Encyclopædia Iranica*, IX, New York, 1999, pp. 176b–182a.

27　A. Panaino, 'Da Zoroastro a Pletone: la Prisca Sapientia persistenza e sviluppi', in *Sul ritorno di Pletone. Un filosofo a Rimini*, M. Di Bella (cur.), Rimini, 2003, pp. 109–111.

28　M. Tardieu, 'La recension arabe des ΜΑΓΙΚΑ ΛΟΓΙΑ', in *Oracles Chaldaïques. Recension de Georges Gémiste Pléthon* (Corpus Philosophorum Medii Ævi—Philosophi Byzantini, 7), B. Tambrun-Krasker (ed.), Paris–Bruxelles, 1995, pp. 157–173.

29　Tambrun-Krasker, *Oracles Chaldaïques*, pp. 37–47 (commentary).

THE ESOTERIC CARDINAL

'magic', but rather reconnecting with the traditions of the Iranian Magi. A follower of the *Falsafa*, Elisha draws the notions of the Zoroastrian Magi from the Arab commentators on Aristotle. The sojourn with Plethon is long, a sort of initiation; in the end the young philosopher returns to Constantinople. But his stay does not last long; the pressures from the majority of the clergy, irritated by the ideas of Plethon, lead Manuel II Palaiologos to remove him from Constantinople and to exile him to the hills of Mistra, where he will spend the rest of his days.

Plethon reworks the whole of the oracular material[30] transmitted by Psellus, ignoring a series of fragments, six, to be precise, certainly not in harmony with his genuinely Platonic feeling; the intent of Plethon is in fact to re-propose the ancient philosophy in its original form, free from the interpretations of Neo-platonical Christian exegetes.[31]

We note with disapproval that all the editors of the *Oracles*, starting from Kroll, have taken little account of the interpretation of Plethon. The collection of fragments of the *Oracles* assembled by Kroll[32] is basically achieved by looking at their presence in the form of fragmentary citations in Neoplatonic sources of late antiquity, in which the Zoroastrian paternity does not figure. From this perspective, the edition of Plethon, with the Zoroastrian thesis, like its reception in Renaissance culture, may have appeared unreliable and therefore insignificant, being the result of a late and misleading interpretation. This goes beyond the overlapping of textual materials.

The *Chaldæan Oracles*, the *Chaldaika Logia*, are so named by the manuscript codex *Vaticanus Græcus* 1416 dating back to the sixteenth century, and the attribution is undoubtedly due to Giorgios Gemistos Plethon, who in his ambitious dream of religious reform,[33] appealed in his commentary to Zoroastrian authority. From him, this fraudulent attribution passed to the Neoplatonists of the Renaissance such as Marsilio Ficino[34] or Pico della Mirandola. In reality, the ancient writers never speak of *Oracles of Zoroaster*, but generically of *logia*, and rarely also of *Chaldaika Logia*, not even Porphyry does so in the brief review of the apocryphal works that circulated in his time, and that he probably had to hand.[35]

---

30   Tardieu, 'Pléthon lecteur des oracles', pp. 151–155.

31   Woodhouse, *George Gemistos Plethon*, pp. 48–61.

32   Recently, the dissertation of W. Kroll, *De Oraculis Chaldaicis*, Breslau, 1894, has been revived in French translation, ed. by H.D. Saffrey, Paris 2016.

33   G. Faggin, s.v. 'Zoroastro, oracoli di', in *Enciclopedia Cattolica*, XII, Ente per l'Enciclopedia Cattolica e per il libro cattolico-Sansoni, Città del Vaticano, 1954, col. 1820.

34   *Theol. plat.* 4, 2; *De christ. rel.* 22.

35   Porphyr. *Vit. Plot.* 16.

A well-known book by M. Stausberg, *Faszination Zarathustra*, in which Zoroaster's fortune is traced in the West, speaks of Plethon and the *Oracles* attributed to the same Zoroaster in inspired terms. One of the first chapters starts from 1439 and the arrival of Giorgios Gemistos in Florence,[36] then he introduces the figure of the Jew Elisha, master of Plethon, who is therefore considered a pagan and a friend of Jewish esotericists.[37] A few pages later begins a digression on the *Oracles*. On the other hand, according to Tambrun-Krasker the attribution of the *Oracles* to Zoroaster is Plethon's invention and is linked to political-religious motivations: to give a granitic foundation to his program of restoration of paganism, with a character who lived 5000 years before the Trojan war, and to make Plato out as a student of Zoroaster. In fact Plethon refers to Zoroaster in other works:[38] he writes a *Summary of the Doctrines of Zoroaster and Plato*[39] whose autograph was found in a manuscript of Marciana Library in Venice (*Marcianus Græcus* 406),[40] while in his *Objection to Scolarios* he affirms that the philosophy taught by Plato had distant roots, in the Zoroastrian tradition mediated by the Pythagoreans;[41] the same thought can be found in the correspondence with his disciple Cardinal Bessarion.[42]

VI

Between 1438 and 1439, an elderly and admired Gemistos Plethon will participate in the council that was opened in Ferrara and was then moved to Florence.[43] And indeed from Florence Plethon launches the manifesto for the new

---

36 M. Stausberg, *Faszination Zarathustra. Zoroaster und die europäische Religionsgeschichte der frühen Neuzeit* (Religionsgeschichtliche Versuche und Vorarbeiten, 42), I, New York, 1998, p. 35.

37 Stausberg, *Faszination Zarathustra*, p. 37.

38 Tambrun-Krasker, *Oracles Chaldaïques*, p. 37 (commentary).

39 Ed. C. Alexandre, in R. Brague, *Une cité idéale au XVe siècle: l'utopie néo-païenne d'un byzantin. Pléthon. Traité des Lois*, Paris, 1983 (ed. or. Firmin Didot, Paris, 1858), pp. 262–269; Woodhouse, *George Gemistos Plethon*, pp. 319–321.

40 R. and F. Masai, 'L' œuvre de Georges Gémiste Pléthon', in *Bulletin de l'Académie Royale de Belgique, Classes des Lettres*, 1954, pp. 543–545.

41 B. Lagarde, 'George Gémiste Pléthon: Contre les objections de Scholarios en faveur d' Aristote (Replique)', in *Byzantion* 59 (1989), pp. 412–415; 474–477.

42 L. Mohler, *Kardinal Bessarion als Theologe, Humanist und Staatsmann. Funde un Forschungen*, III. *Aus Bessarion Gelehrtenkreis. Abhandlungen, Reden, Briefe* (Quellen und Forschungen aus dem Gebiete der Geschichte, XXIV), Paderborn, 1942 (repr. Scientia-Verlag, Aalen 1967), p. 459, 8–10.

43 Woodhouse, *George Gemistos Plethon*, pp. 136 ff.

THE ESOTERIC CARDINAL

Platonism, the *De Differentia Platonicæ et Aristotelicæ Philosophiæ* (PG 160, 889–932); in the twenty chapters of the treatise some characteristic theses are discussed: of theology (chapt 1–2), of metaphysics (chapters 3–6), of logic (chapters 7–8), of psychology (chapters 9–11), of ethics (chapters 12–13), of cosmology (chapters 14–16), of physics (chapters 17–20). Aware of a consistent Western tradition favourable to the harmonisation of Aristotelianism with Christianity, Plethon clearly shows the weaknesses of Aristotelian theology and psychology, namely the absence of divine providence towards an eternal world, and the negation of the immortality of the human soul. Precisely on these teachings, however, the comprehension on the part of Plato distinguishes itself in the most arcane theological truths: God the creator of all things, his purely spiritual nature, divine pre-conscience of eternal ideal archetypes, the immortal destiny of the human soul.[44]

The enthusiasm raised by Plethon was remarkable:[45] his is the inspiration of the Florentine Platonic Academy, conceived by Cosimo de' Medici (the Elder) and then realized by Lorenzo il Magnifico. The teaching of Giorgios Gemistos Plethon awoke a widespread reaction, prevalently of consent, but also of explicit disagreements. The most violent reaction was that of one of his former adversaries, Giorgios Gennadios, by then already Patriarch of Constantinople.

What Cosimo the Elder had in mind when, in 1439, he listened to the lessons of Gemistos Plethon, is not known.[46] Marsilio Ficino bears witness to most numerous favourable reactions; in the preface-dedication to the first translation of Plotinus (published in 1492), Ficino traces to Plethon the beginning of a new era for culture:

> The great Cosimo, by public decree father of the fatherland, at the time of the Council of Florence between the Greeks and the Latins, under the pontificate of Eugene IV, often listened to the discussions about the Platonic mysteries by a Greek philosopher named Gemistos, called Plethon, almost a second Plato. His fervent word inflamed him and inspired him to such an extent as to make him conceive in his high mind the design of an Academy, to be realized as soon as he had the opportunity. So, in order to implement such a great idea in a definite way, that great Medici assigned such a great work to me, though still a child, the son of Ficino, his hon-

---

44   A. Ghisalberti, '"Via antiqua" e "via moderna" dal tardo Medioevo al Rinascimento', in *Platonismo e aristotelismo nel Mezzogiorno d'Italia (secc. XIV–XVI)* (Biblioteca dell'Officina di Studi Medievali, 1), G. Roccaro (cur.), Palermo, 1998, pp. 32–33.

45   Lanzi, *Michele Psello. Oracoli caldaici*, p. 21 n. 30.

46   E. Garin, *Ermetismo del Rinascimento*, Roma, 1988, pp. 15–16.

oured physician. For this purpose he came to me day by day, instructing and then arranging to acquire all the books in the original Greek, not only of Plato, but also of Plotinus. Then, in 1463, when I was thirty, he charged me with translating first Hermes [Trismegistos] and then Plato. I translated Hermes in a few months, he being animated; so I also started Plato.[47]

Hearing him speak, Cosimo had conceived the plan to revive the Plato's Academy in Florence, assigning this and so much enterprise to the son, still a child, of his personal physician, Marsilio Ficino. In fact, on September 4, 1462 Ficino, writing to Cosimo, spoke of the Academy in Careggi that his protector had arranged for him. The same Ficino makes abundant use of the oracular materials in the drafting of his *Theologia Platonica de Immortalitate Animarum*, a veritable *summa* of Platonism.

The same applies to the erudite Agostino Steuco (1496?–1548), who in his *Philosophia Perennis*, trying to elaborate a new and organic interpretation of reality, uses the *Chaldean Oracles* as an ideological support. A similar reasoning led Francesco Patrizi da Cherso (1529–1597) to try his hand at a *Nova de Universis Philosophia* and to attempt in 1591 a first collection of the Chaldæan fragments of Proclus, Damascius, Simplicius, Olympiodorus and Sinesius, entitled *Zoroaster et eius CCXXX Oracula Chaldaica*.[48]

VII

The palingenesis advocated by Gemistos Plethon was rooted not in the Scripture but in archaic values such as to paradoxically involve the papacy itself, since in the conclave of 1455 Cardinal Bessarion, his direct disciple, narrowly missed out on ascending the papal throne.[49] Cardinal Bessarion had become a participant in the sublime and mysterious wisdom of Neoplatonism, in which the ancient wisdom, theosophical and magical traditions of the East converged, merging with Greek philosophy and with the initiatory teachings of Orphism and the Pythagoreans.[50] The eminent cardinal spoke of the master as 'the great-

---

47 The translation of the Ficiniana dedication is by E. Garin, 'La letteratura degli umanisti', in *Storia della letteratura italiana*, III, Milano, 1966, p. 58.

48 Reprinted by L.H. Gray in appendix to A.V.W. Jackson, *Zoroaster the Prophet of Ancient Iran*, New York–London, 1899, pp. 259–273.

49 A. Pertusi, 'In margine alla questione dell'Umanesimo bizantino: il pensiero politico del cardinale Bessarione e i suoi rapporti con il pensiero di Giorgio Gemisto Pletone', *Rivista di Studi Bizantini e Neoellenici* N.S. 5 (1968), pp. 95–104.

50 M. Zorzi, 'Ermete Trismegisto nelle biblioteche veneziane', in *Magia, alchimia, scienza dal*

est of the Greeks after Plotinus'. Exemplary, again, is the letter of Gemistos Plethon to his disciple (Ep. 19), in which he celebrated Zoroaster, author of magic oracles (*magika logia*), of books through which to fight the tyranny of becoming, of the *Heimarmenē*, the fatal fabric in which destinies were intertwined, subjugated to the flow of transmigrations.[51]

He who was to become one of the central characters in rewriting the Platonic tradition within Christianity[52] was born in Trebizond probably in 1403 (according to others in 1389 or 1395) from a family of humble origins.[53] Given his particular aptitude for study, at a young age he was entrusted to the metropolitan Dositheos,[54] by whom, after his abdication, he was conducted to Constantinople, where he completed his first studies between 1415 and 1422, following the courses of rhetoric by Giorgios Chrisococce and having as a co-disciple the humanist Francesco Filelfo,[55] then secretary of the bailiff, a sort of Venetian diplomatic representative. On January 30, 1423 he took the monastic habit, changing his name from Basilios[56] to Bessarione (Bēsariōn):[57] the onomastic figure was St Bessarion, a desert father of the fourth-fifth century, known for his great humility and asceticism. A few months later, July 20, 1423, will see the bestowal of the definitive tonsure,[58] his confirmation in the monastic life, which the future cardinal in autobiographical documents will describe as the imposition of the *mega kai angelikon skēma*, that is the investiture of the 'great scapular' followed by that of the 'small scapular',[59] the *mikron skēma*, the monk's habit. But the *mega kai angelikon skēma* is literally the 'great and angelic garment',[60] the marvellous garment of light, which very closely resembles the 'vehicle' (*ochēma*) of the soul, the Theurgical *pneuma* bound to the planetary spheres. In fact, the shape of the scapular, a simple tunic with hood, lent itself

---

'*400 al '700. L'influsso di Ermete Trismegisto*, I, C. Gilly and C. Van Heertum (cur.), Firenze–Venezia, 2002, pp. 113–114.

51   Mohler, *Kardinal Bessarion als Theologe*, III, p. 459, 8–12.

52   G.L. Coluccia, *Basilio Bessarione. Lo spirito greco e l'Occidente* (Accademia delle Arti del Disegno/Monografie, 15), Firenze, 2009.

53   E. Monti, *Vita del Cardinale Bessarione* (Miscellanea Marciana vol. VI [1991]), Venezia–Roma, 1993, pp. 16–22.

54   Monti, *Vita del Cardinale Bessarione*, p. 23.

55   R. Loenertz, O.P., 'Pour la biographie du Cardinal Bessarion', in *Orientalia Christiana Periodica*, 10 (1944), pp. 127–128; *PG* 161, IV.

56   Monti, *Vita del Cardinale Bessarione*, p. 21.

57   Loenertz, 'Pour la biographie du Cardinal Bessarion', p. 123.

58   H.D. Saffrey, 'Recherches sur quelques autographes du cardinal Bessarion et leur caractère autobiographique', in Aa.Vv., *Mélanges Eugène Tisserant*, III: *Orient Chrétien*, pt. 2 (Studi e Testi, 233), Città del Vaticano, 1964, p. 272.

59   Loenertz, 'Pour la biographie du Cardinal Bessarion', p. 122.

60   Saffrey, 'Recherches sur quelques autographes', pp. 275–276.

well to replicating the 'psychic' garment, the celestial vehicle of the soul. Even if its heritage can easily be read in a Christian context.

Bessarion was ordained priest on 8 October 1430, but it was in nearby Selimbria (currently Silivri), to where he later relocated, that he received the first philosophical teachings. It was the archbishop of Selimbria, Iohannes (Ignatius) Chortasmenos,[61] who initiated Bessarion in the discipline that would become such a part of the life of the future Cardinal.[62] However, the decisive meeting will take place shortly, when in the Peloponnese, in Mistra (1431–1436), he will follow the lessons of Giorgios Gemistos Plethon.[63] It will indeed be the venerable master who communicates to him his love for ancient philosophy[64] and in particular for those that the Florentine humanists will define as *Platonica mysteria*.

The rediscovery of Platonism and the 'paganizing' approach of the teaching dispensed by Plethon will certainly be at the bottom of all the diatribes with which in the years to come the literary and philosophical work of the disciple will be endowed.[65] This is the sense in which the writing of Bessarion *In Calumniatorem Platonis* (Rome 1469) should be interpreted; originally conceived as an answer to the Aristotelian Giorgios Trapeziuntios, but which in actuality will become a celebration of Plato and his school, in the light of which Neoplatonic and Christian thought has been able to draw from his teachings. By this key, Giorgios Gemistos Plethon's commentary on *Chaldæan Oracles* would come to be interpreted: in the search for a truth that can restore to the soul its original dimension, Plato is considered the forerunner of the Theurgists, if not the first of them, and Theurgy is a divine art of which Platonism is the first teaching.

The comparison between Plato and Aristotle was a theme that preoccupied the humanists of the time, and Giorgios Gemistos Plethon and Giorgios Scolarios polemicized about it, even violently.[66] The *Treatise on Laws*, the last work of Plethon[67] remaining unfinished, was based on the homonymous Platonic treatise and was burned by Scolarios after the death of the master[68] and obviously after the fall of Constantinople; but this happened before the other

---

61 Monti, *Vita del Cardinale Bessarione*, p. 23.

62 Loenertz, 'Pour la biographie du Cardinal Bessarion', pp. 129; PG 161, 105; Mohler, *Kardinal Bessarion als Theologe*, III, p. 406, 32.

63 PG 161, V; Woodhouse, *George Gemistos Plethon*, pp. 233–239; Monti, *Vita del Cardinale Bessarione*, pp. 47–56.

64 A. Bandini, *De Vita et rebus gestis Bessarionis Cardinali Nicæni* Commentarius, excudebat Benedictus Franzesi, Roma, 1777, p. 5, n. 1.

65 Loenertz, 'Pour la biographie du Cardinal Bessarion', pp. 133–134.

66 Woodhouse, *George Gemistos Plethon*, pp. 32–34; 240–266.

67 Id., *George Gemistos Plethon*, pp. 322–356.

68 Loenertz, 'Pour la biographie du Cardinal Bessarion', p. 133.

THE ESOTERIC CARDINAL

137

members of the circle of Scolarios had taken part in the controversy.[69] Bessarion was a Platonist like Giorgios Gemistos but in the dispute with Scolarios, perhaps because of a personal strategy, he assumed a relatively moderate position, avoiding direct darts that could further undermine the already difficult relationships between the disciples.

Since his time in Mistra, Bessarion proved to be a skilled diplomat in smoothing out the discord between the emperor John VIII Palaiologos and his brother, the despot of Morea, Demetrios; and his diplomatic exertion was always sensed in the negotiations with Trebizond for the defence against the common Turkish danger. In 1436 he was appointed abbot (hēgoumenos) of a monastery in Constantinople and, in 1437, made archbishop of Nicæa (hence the designation 'Nicene'). Under this title he participated in the council held in Ferrara and Florence, where he supported the cause of union between the churches of the East and the West. Having returned to Constantinople with the Greek delegation, in the consistory of 18 December 1439 he was proclaimed Cardinal with the title of the Holy Apostles.

Having settled in Rome, he intensified his study of Latin, into which he translated, among other texts, the *Metaphysics* of Aristotle (Venice 1503 and 1516) and several works of his own, and resumed the examination of issues already debated at the council, in a series of treatises, such as the one dedicated to the procession of the Holy Spirit and the one on the formula of liturgical consecration. In the Roman curia Bessarion became one of the most active and influential cardinals. In the conclave that was held from 4 to 8 April 1455, where pope Callistus III was elected, Bessarion by only a little did not ascend to the papal throne. His Roman residence became the point of reference and a haven for the most famous humanists of the time: the subject tabled at the cardinal's *soirées* was philosophy, above all Platonism, in its nostalgic and practical aspects. The expectation of restoring the great Hellenic culture was in fact combined with the return of a renewed sensibility and æsthetics from the ancient era, which resulted in a fascination which was not merely fleeting and momentary. The constant and insistent thought was to restore Christianity to its proper Platonic dimension, the Patristic one of its origins. But not only that, because Christianity apparently should be rebuilt on a new rituality, that of the Neoplatonists and of the *Chaldæan Oracles*.

The mourning of the death of the master Giorgios Gemistos Plethon provided the Cardinal with the occasion to confirm his adherence to the values of Neoplatonism and Theurgy. The letter of sorrow written for the sons of Plethon,

---

69   Cameron, *I bizantini*, p. 189.

Demetrios and Andronicos, was an example of how a funeral eulogy could encode meanings and understandings that went beyond the verbal data.

The first lines[70] celebrate the master whose homeland is the crystalline, pure sky (*ouranon kai ton akraiphnē*); mystically accepted among the Olympian gods, deified as a new Dionysos (*Iakchos*): 'dancing the mystical dance with the Olympian gods'.[71] There is not much Christianity in Bessarion's words that acclaim the *apotheōsis* of a Plethon transformed into the *Liber pater* Dionysos, immortal among the gods; it is the equitable fulfilment of a teaching which from Pythagoras to Plato tells the infinite ascent and descent of souls: even Giorgios Gemistos had to submit to this ineluctable law of becoming, of *Heimarmenē*, the bond of fate that obliges the soul to spend a period of expiation on earth to free itself from the yoke of the passions. But for him the course will be favoured by having internalized Theurgical virtues.

> I am happy—says Bessarion—to have attended such a man. After the famous men of the early times, Greece has not generated any other person more similar to Plato than he, neither by wisdom nor by any other virtue. So if we accept the doctrine of Pythagoras and Plato on the regular periodicity of the ascent and reincarnation of souls, we would not hesitate to affirm that the soul of Plato, obliged to serve the inviolable laws of the Nemesis and after the necessary period, returning to earth would have chosen Gemistos's body and to live in him.[72]

The letter closes with the couplet that Bessarion dedicates to the memory of the master. In itself it is a small compendium of Theurgical doctrine. Abandoning the body to the earthly goddess (*Gaia*), the soul ascends to its own stellar dimension (*psychē[i] d'astra*): 'The earth holds the body of Plethon, the stars his soul'. The philosopher has collected in a confined space the whole wisdom that comes from the Greek *logos*, which is a metaphor for expressing the 'Platonic' and therefore 'Theurgical' doctrine.[73] It is a teaching that makes 'similar to God' (*theoeidēs*): 'Many divine men generated Greece'. An astral deification equated to the events of Phæthon (*Phæthōn*), the god whose name is an invention inspired by the Homeric epithet of the Sun *Hēlios phæthōn* 'shining, brilliant':[74] as Phæthon-Sun shines among the stars, so Gemistos is between

---

70   *PG* 161, 696.

71   Monti, *Vita del Cardinale Bessarione*, p. 168.

72   Id., *Vita del Cardinale Bessarione*, p. 168.

73   *PG* 161, 697.

74   Hom. *Il.* 11, 735.

THE ESOTERIC CARDINAL

both. The teachings of the philosopher represented a *krasis*, a union between art and life, words that did not fall into the void, because they meant the fulfilment of an astral salvation, realized by him and by the faithful disciples.

Son of Hēlios and the nymph Climene,[75] Phæthon tried to drive his father's chariot and died when losing control of the horses. He was mourned by his sisters, the Heliades, who were turned into poplars and scattered tears of amber on the banks of the river Eridanos. The story of Phæthon, maladroit son of Phoebus (Apollo = Sun),[76] is rewritten by Ovid (*Met.* 2, 111–115): yielding to the insistence, Phoebus permits his son to drive his winged chariot across the sky for a day. First, however, he admonishes him about the dangers and snares he would have to face on the heavenly path. Among them there were the 'horns of Taurus', the 'arrows of Capricorn, the mouth of the violent Lion', and, not least, the fierce claws of Scorpio (*Met.* 2.83), asterisms that mark a stellar path. Admonitions that, however, fell into a void. Young and inexperienced, Phæthon was overwhelmed by the fiery horses of the Sun, which escaping from his hand, left the usual path and dragged the chariot so close to the earth as to risk setting it on fire. The Heliades, daughters of Hēlios, rushed to the bank of the river to mourn the death of their brother, were turned into white poplar trees; their tears, dripping from the branches, became drops of amber (*Hēlektron*),[77] that is, the Elektrides islands, placed at the mouth of the river Eridanos.[78]

The myth of the Heliades and their tears is very old. Perhaps Hesiod mentioned it.[79] The legend, very popular among Hellenistic writers, seems to have been reprised in the funeral eulogy of Bessarion, but it is only an allusion. Substantial fragments of Euripides's *Phæthōn* survive, elaborating the traditional history, adding domestic complications. We find allusions to Phæthon and his sisters in Aratus (*Phæn.* 360) and Apollonios Rhodius (4, 597–611; 624–626). Phæthon is used to mean 'Sun' in *Æneid* 5, 105; this usage is not previously attested but occurs in later Latin and Greek poetry; and it is to this tradition that Bessarion wants to return.

---

75   J. Diggle, s.v. 'Fetonte', in *Enciclopedia Virgiliana*, II, Firenze–Roma, 1985, pp. 506b–507b.

76   Nonn. *Dionys.* 38, 142–434; cf. B. Simon (ed.), *Nonnos de Panopolis. Les dionysiaques* tome XIV/Chants XXXVIII–XL, Paris, 1999, pp. 22 ff.

77   Apoll. Rhod. *Argon.* 4, 603; Hom. *Od.* 15, 460; cf. L.V. Sybel, s.v. 'Eridanos', in W.H. Roscher (ed.), *Ausführliches Lexikon der griechischen und römischen Mythologie*, I/1, Leipzig, 1884–1886, col. 1308.

78   E.H. Warmington, s.v. 'Eridano', in *The Oxford Classical Dictionary*, London, 1953, trad. it. a cura di M. Carpitella, Alba (CN)–Roma, 1963, p. 114.

79   Fr. 150, 21–24 (ed. R. Merkelbach and M.L. West, *Fragmenta Hesiodea*, Clarendon Press, Oxford, 1967).

A tradition in which the Theurgical ritual of the *apathanatismos* intends to purify the soul of the master. Theurgy is a divine work and the Theurgist, in possession of the divine symbols and ascended to the very rank of the gods, performs a divine act. Theurgy allows us to rise towards the unchanging, uncreated reality. Thanks to the benevolent divine initiative the Theurgical rite allows the initiate, even after death, to save the body from the persecution of evil demons, by means of a miraculous dissolution of its material elements and to have the soul rise to heaven. We thus find in Bessarion's thought a search for an 'outer' hidden verity, alternative to the Biblical wisdom, which draws not on apocrypha but on ancient sources deriving from the late antique Near East and which possesses elements sharply contrasting with Christianity. This peculiarity of his thought will largely mark the Renaissance humanism.

Acknowledgement

This article was translated from Italian by Peter Janssen.

This work is the synthesis of my most extensive research on Cardinal Bessarion and Theurgy, which I hope will soon appear as a book: *Il cardinale mago: gnosi, ermetismo, teurgia e i misteri di un codice scomparso*; for their help I must thank Prof. Giancarlo Mantovani, and Dr. Salvatore Amato of the National University Library of Turin for the tracing of some rare materials.

PART 2

Bridging the Account of the Origins and the Messiah's Advent

∴

CHAPTER 7

La création d'Adam à Noravank : Théologie et narrativité

Jean-Pierre Mahé

En hommage à Michael E. Stone

⁝

L'épigraphie et la littérature apocryphe tiennent le premier rang parmi les nombreuses contributions du Professeur Michael E. Stone aux études arméniennes. Élargissant sa documentation à toutes les grandes collections mondiales de manuscrits et découvrant beaucoup d'œuvres nouvelles, le dédicataire de la présente note a porté une attention particulière à la figure d'Adam,[1] aux grands cycles narratifs qui lui furent consacrés dans la littérature judéenne du second Temple et à leurs retentissements paléochrétiens.

À la lisière de ces recherches novatrices, nous souhaiterions revenir, après beaucoup d'autres, sur une des sculptures les plus connues de l'art arménien des XIIIᵉ–XIVᵉ siècles : le tympan supérieur du gawit de Noravank, qui commente, par une inscription toujours énigmatique, une iconographie originale, étroitement liée à l'exégèse du texte biblique de la création d'Adam.

Dans son état actuel, le gawit de l'église Surb Stepanos de Noravank pose des problèmes chronologiques qui ne sont pas tous résolus. D'après une inscription en ceinture lisible à l'intérieur,[2] l'édifice fut rehaussé par Smbat Ōrbe-

---

1 M.E. Stone, *The Penitence of Adam*, CSCO 429-430, Louvain, 1981 ; id., *Armenian Apocrypha Relating to the Patriarchs and Prophets*, Jérusalem, 1982 ; id. [éd. trad.], *Armenian Apocrypha Relating to Adam and Eve*, Leyde, 1996a ; id., *Texts and Concordances of the Armenian Adam Literature*, 1.1, Atlanta, Ga, 1996b ; id., *Adam's Contract with Satan. The Legend of the Cheirograph of Adam*, Bloomington–Indianapolis, 2002 ; V. Hillel, 'Bibliography of the works of Michael E. Stone', in L. Ditommaso, M. Henze and W. Adler, *The Embroidered Bible, Studies in Biblical Apocrypha and Pseudepigrapha in Honour of Michael E. Stone*, Studia in Veteris Testamenti Pseudepigrapha 26, Leyde, 2018, p. XIX-XLVI.

2 S.G. Barxudaryan, Vayoc Jor, Ełegnajori ew Azizbekovi šrjanner, *Corpus Inscriptionum Armenicarum* III, Érévan, 1967, p. 218, № 692.

© JEAN-PIERRE MAHÉ, 2021 | DOI:10.1163/9789004445925_009

lean en 1261. Cependant les tympans sculptés qui ornent les deux étages de la façade occidentale ont été refaits ultérieurement. Une mauvaise lecture de l'inscription du tympan inférieur[3] avait laissé croire que l'ensemble datait de 1321. En réalité, le texte correctement établi ne contient aucune date.[4] On ne dispose donc que d'indices stylistiques, qui invitent à situer la sculpture d'en bas dans le dernier tiers du XIIIe siècle, en tout cas après 1270.[5] Probablement dû à un autre artiste,[6] le tympan supérieur semble plus tardif. Toutefois, nous hésiterions, quant à nous, à l'attribuer au «maître de Spitakawor», qui aurait, dans les années 1330, sculpté les deux tympans de l'église Astuacacin construite en 1331-1339 par Burtel Ōrbelean dans l'enceinte du même monastère.[7] Alors que ces deux derniers reliefs reproduisent, sans originalité, des schémas tout à fait classiques – le Christ entre Pierre et Paul et la Mère de Dieu entre les archanges – notre tympan présente une recherche originale, qui n'a aucun parallèle connu dans toute l'iconographie arménienne (voir Planches 7.1 et 7.2).[8]

Avec sa concision et sa perspicacité habituelles, Sirarpie Der Nersessian décrivait la sculpture comme il suit: «Au centre, l'Ancien des jours, identifié par l'inscription, bénit d'une main, de l'autre, il tient la tête d'Adam; la colombe du Saint Esprit est figurée au centre. À gauche, on voit la crucifixion, et au premier plan, le prophète Daniel, couché, identifié aussi par une inscription. Un ange occupe l'angle droit du tympan. L'idée maîtresse de cette représentation peut être déterminée grâce aux commentaires des écritures saintes: elle évoque la création d'Adam, animé par le souffle divin, et le crucifiement rappelle que l'humanité, perdue par le péché du premier homme, sera sauvée

---

3 Ibid. p. 222, N⁰ 705.

4 Cf. S. Avagyan, *Recherches sur le lexique des inscriptions lapidaires*, Érévan, 1978, p. 274-277 (N⁰ 105) [en arménien]; id., *Recherches épigraphiques*, Érévan, 1986, p. 123-132 [en arménien]; K. Matevosyan, *The Epigraphic Inscriptions and Colophons of Noravank Monastery*, Érévan, 2017 [en arménien; résumé anglais p. 226-227], p. 57-58 il confirme cette interprétation.

5 P. Donabédian, «Les particularités stylistiques d'un monument sculpté de Noravank et sa datation», *Revue des études arméniennes* 17 (1983), p. 395-413.

6 Matevosyan (*Inscriptions and Colophons of Noravank*), p. 53, attribue les deux tympans à Momik et maintient (p. 59) la date de 1321 proposée antérieurement, tout en acceptant la correction du texte de l'inscription suggérée par Avagyan (*Recherches épigraphiques*)! Cette position, presque contradictoire dans les termes, nous paraît difficilement soutenable.

7 C'est l'avis de J.-M. Thierry, *L'Arménie au Moyen Âge*, Paris, 2000, p. 224-225; cf. J.-M. Thierry et P. Donabédian, *Les Arts arméniens*, Paris, 1987, p. 205; toutefois dans le même ouvrage, p. 479, Donabédian propose une datation à la fin du XIIIe siècle.

8 La sculpture intérieure de la coupole de Spitakawor (cf. Matevosyan, *Inscriptions and Colophons of Noravank*, p. 62, fig. 24) dérive manifestement du tympan de Noravank, bien que la date et l'auteur soient controversés.

LA CRÉATION D'ADAM À NORAVANK̇ 145

PLANCHE 7.1   Noravank̇. Tympan supérieur du gawit̔ de Surb Step̔anos
PHOTO: I. DORFMANN-LAZAREV

PLANCHE 7.2   Tympan supérieur du gawit̔ de Surb Step̔anos, représentation schématique

grâce au sacrifice du Christ. Mais le sculpteur n'a pas su intégrer les différents éléments de ce thème complexe et unique en son genre dans une composition harmonieuse. L'ensemble, dominé par la grande figure de l'Ancien des jours, produit néanmoins une forte impression ».[9]

Si l'œuvre demeure impressionnante malgré la gaucherie de l'artiste, c'est probablement parce que l'intention conceptuelle et les références théologiques s'imposent avec trop de vigueur aux dépens de l'image proprement dite. À première vue, il semblerait que le sujet central s'inspire du second récit biblique de la création de l'homme :[10] « Et le Seigneur Dieu façonna l'homme, limon (tiré) de la terre, et il souffla sur son visage un souffle vivant, et l'homme devint en une âme vivante ».[11] Dieu tient encore de la main gauche la tête de l'homme, gisant à terre, qu'il vient de modeler. L'âme vivante qu'il lui insuffle est véhiculée par l'Esprit Saint sous forme de colombe,[12] comme dans le baptême du Christ.[13]

Mais, puisque le Christ est « image » de Dieu,[14] le premier récit biblique de la création de l'homme[15] transparaît également dans notre sculpture : « 'Nous ferons un homme à notre image et à (notre) ressemblance, et ils domineront les poissons de la mer et les oiseaux des cieux et les muets (animaux) et toute la terre, et tous les reptiles qui rampent sur la terre'. Et Dieu fit l'homme à son image ; il le fit à l'image de Dieu, mâle et femelle il les fit. Et Dieu les bénit ».[16] La bénédiction de la dextre divine est bien représentée sur la sculpture. La ressem-

---

9   S. Der Nersessian, *L'Art arménien*, Paris, 1977, p. 182 (ainsi que les figures 143-144, p. 191-192). Voir aussi ead., « Deux tympans sculptés arméniens datant de 1321 », *Cahiers archéologiques* 25 (1976), p. 109-122.

10   Gn 2, 7.

11   D'après l'édition critique de A.S. Zeyt'unyan, *Genèse* [éd. critique en arménien], Érévan, 1985, p. 151. Der Nersessian, « Deux tympans », p. 112, cite en parallèle la fresque du tambour de la coupole de l'église Sainte-Croix d'Ałt'amar, qui représente le modelage d'Adam. L'étape suivante, c'est-à-dire son animation, figurait peut-être sur une scène distincte, qui ne nous est pas conservée. Un bon dessin de ces peintures est donné par Thierry, *L'Arménie au Moyen Âge*, p. 139.

12   Comme le souligne Der Nersessian, « Deux tympans », p. 114, l'identification de l'âme d'Adam à l'Esprit divin n'a aucun parallèle iconographique ni en Arménie, ni dans l'art chrétien en général. On remarquera que la colombe de l'Esprit divin, après avoir animé Adam, remonte vers la bouche du Père. On la voit représentée sur la sculpture dans le sens de la remontée, à demi dissimulée dans la barbe divine.

13   Mt 3, 16 ; Mc 1, 10 ; Lc 3, 22, Jn 1, 32.

14   2 Co 3, 18.

15   Gn 1, 26-28.

16   Zeyt'unyan, *Genèse*, p. 149. Der Nersessian, « Deux tympans », p. 112, ne cite que Gn 2, 7 : l'allusion à Gn 1, 26-28 n'a pas été notée.

blance du Créateur et de sa créature est soulignée par la figuration humaine et le visage barbu de l'un comme de l'autre.

Il est donc clair que l'artiste de Noravankʿ juxtapose les deux récits bibliques de la création de l'homme.[17] À la différence de certains auteurs, comme Philon d'Alexandrie, la tradition exégétique dont il s'inspire ne les considère pas comme deux phases anthropogoniques successives, mais comme deux points de vue complémentaires sur un seul processus. Il est donc légitime de les représenter simultanément sur la même image.

Cette exégèse est celle de la catéchèse de saint Grégoire l'Illuminateur transmise dans l'*Histoire* d'Agathange. L'auteur fait un commentaire syncrétique[18] combinant les deux récits bibliques. Certains points coïncident précisément avec la sculpture de notre gawiṫ.

> Comment l'homme, né du limon, pouvait-il venir au monde sur le modèle du Créateur? Et (comment), alors qu'il vient d'être créé, accessible à tous,[19] (pouvait-il) recevoir pour essence d'être à la ressemblance de l'Essence inaccessible? (...) En effet l'Écriture dit: 'À l'image de Dieu, il le fit';[20] et elle dit ailleurs: 'Dieu établit l'homme dans l'incorruptibilité et, à sa propre image de bienfaisance, il le fit'.[21] Et une autre Sagesse familière de Dieu a dit encore: 'L'homme est image de Dieu'[22] (...). Dieu apparut sous la ressemblance d'un homme quand il 'façonna l'homme, limon (tiré) de la terre, et il souffla sur son visage un souffle vivant, et l'homme devint en une âme vivante'.[23] Ayant façonné l'homme de ses mains, il versa en lui la vitalité, quand sa bouche souffla le souffle vivant, porteur de sage intelligence, d'avis et de raison.[24]

Projetant sur la scène du modelage et de l'animation d'Adam le thème de l'image et de la ressemblance, Agathange en vient à supposer que, pour façon-

---

17 Gn 1, 26-28 et Gn 2, 7.

18 Agathange, § 263-276; cf. R.W. Thomson, *The Teaching of Saint Gregory: An Early Armenian Catechism*, Cambridge, Mass., 1970 [nouvelle édition révisée, New Rochelle, N.Y. 2001, p. 60].

19 Toutes les créatures antérieures à Adam, non seulement les anges, mais aussi l'ensemble des animaux pouvaient approcher librement et contempler sans peine l'homme à l'image de Dieu.

20 Gn 1, 27.

21 Sg 2, 23.

22 1 Co 11, 7.

23 Gn 2, 7.

24 Agathange, § 271 (Thomson, *Teaching*, p. 60).

ner l'homme, le Créateur a lui-même pris une apparence humaine. Ainsi, il justifie d'avance l'interprétation du sculpteur de Noravank. Quoique le texte biblique ne le dise pas explicitement, il devient légitime de représenter le Dieu invisible sous une forme visible dans l'acte de la création.

Jusqu'à présent nous nous sommes délibérément limité à examiner l'image centrale sans faire intervenir l'inscription qui la commente, gravée à droite de la scène, « dans un savant désordre ».[25] Le texte se traduit ainsi : « Quand Dieu, l'Ancien des jours, façonna Adam, le ciel et la terre en furent renouvelés, qui bénissent Dieu à jamais ».[26] À gauche, sous la scène de crucifixion, se lisent des noms propres : « Mère de Dieu », « Jean » et « Daniel ». Les deux premiers personnages se tiennent debout au pied de la croix ; entre eux deux et en dessous, le prophète, allongé sur sa couche,[27] étend le bras en direction du tableau.

Sauf dans le livre de Job,[28] où il est question d'un vieillard, l'expression « l'Ancien des jours »[29] est le nom divin qui intervient dans la vision des quatre bêtes. Après l'apparition effrayante des monstres, le prophète Daniel assiste à leur châtiment.[30] « Je regardais jusqu'à ce que des trônes fussent déployés et que l'Ancien des jours s'y assît (...). Je regardais dans la vision de la nuit et voici que, sur les nuées des cieux, venait comme un Fils d'homme et, arrivant jusqu'à l'Ancien des jours, il fut présenté devant lui. Et il lui fut donné puissance, honneur et royauté, et que les nations, les races et les langues le serviraient : sa puissance est une puissance éternelle qui ne passera pas, et sa royauté ne sera pas détruite ».[31]

Le seul point commun entre ce texte et la scène de la création de l'homme figurant sur notre bas-relief consiste dans la rencontre de deux personnages

---

25   Thierry et Donabédian, *Arts arméniens*, p. 479. Nous reproduisons, pour illustrer notre propos, le dessin de la sculpture et de l'inscription, donné par A. Alpago-Novello, Amaghu/Noravank, *Documenti di Architettura Armena* 14, Milan, 1985, p. 38, figures № 23-24.

26   *Hinawurćn Astuac ənd stełciln Adam, norogećaw erkinḱ ew erkir or mišt awrhnen zAstuac.* Malgré une syntaxe chaotique, il nous semble que le texte doit être compris comme une seule phrase. On peut traduire plus littéralement : « Dieu, l'Ancien des jours. Quand Adam fut façonné, le ciel et la terre furent renouvelés, qui bénissent Dieu à jamais ».

27   Dn 7, 1.

28   Jb 15, 10.

29   *Hinawurc'n.*

30   Dn 7, 9.

31   D'après l'édition critique de S.P. Cowe, *The Armenian Version of Daniel*, Atlanta, Ga, 1992, p. 197 ; voir aussi Dn 7, 22. Sur la vogue de Daniel en Cilicie, comme dans l'Arewelḱ, voir le commentaire de Vardan Arewelċi ; cf. M. Arabyan, Nersisean, *Vardan Arewelċi, Commentaire sur la prophétie de Daniel*, Ējmiacin (Saint-Siège) 2007 [le même volume contient aussi le Commentaire de Yovhannēs Corcoreći, et celui, édité par H. Ḱyoseyan, de Ťovma Mecop̌eći].

qui sont en principe séparés par l'infinité des temps : d'un côté, « l'Ancien des jours », dont l'âge est si vénérable qu'il implique une existence éternelle, de l'autre, le « Fils d'homme », qui a une origine, puisqu'il est fils, et qui est nécessairement plus récent que l'humanité dont il est issu. À vrai dire, il appartient même à l'avenir plutôt qu'au présent, comme le prouvent les temps futurs des verbes décrivant la puissance éternelle qui lui a été concédée.

Sur le tympan de Noravanḱ, le titre « Ancien des jours », qui désigne le Créateur, autorise sa représentation humaine, tout en instituant entre lui et sa créature l'intervalle de temps infinis. Cette distance est encore accentuée par la différence de taille entre les deux personnages. Cependant, comme le Fils d'homme arrivant sur les nuées des cieux[32] se prêtait à une interprétation christologique bien attestée dans les évangiles,[33] le corps humain façonné par Dieu peut aussi bien s'identifier à l'ancien Adam qu'au nouveau,[34] qui fut élevé sur la croix, représentée à gauche de la création.

De plus, la vision de Daniel a une signification eschatologique, soulignée dans l'inscription de Noravanḱ. En projetant l'homme nouveau dès l'instant où il façonne le Protoplaste, l'Ancien des jours jette les bases d'un futur renouvellement de la création tout entière, depuis la terre jusqu'aux cieux. Étroitement liée au pouvoir créateur, « qui fait le droit dans les hauteurs et plaça la justice sur terre ; qui fait toute chose et la renouvelle, qui transforme en aurore les ombres de la mort et obscurcit le jour en nuit »,[35] l'action rénovatrice de Dieu touche à la fois aux origines et aux fins dernières. C'est l'esprit primordial[36] qui « renouvelle la face de la terre »[37] et c'est l'avènement final du Fils de l'homme qui provoquera l'apparition de « cieux nouveaux » et d'une « terre nouvelle »,[38] mentionnés dans notre inscription.[39]

Ainsi, d'après notre sculpture et le texte qui l'accompagne, Dieu prévoit d'emblée, au moment d'animer l'Adam qu'il vient de façonner, de le rendre semblable au Fils de l'homme qui sera cloué sur la croix et dévoilera les fins dernières. En d'autres termes, la ressemblance de l'image, annoncée au futur dans le premier récit de la création, n'est pas réalisée d'un coup au moment

---

32   Dn 7, 13.

33   Mt 24, 30 ; 26, 64 ; Mc 14, 62.

34   1 Co 15, 45-49.

35   Am 5, 7-8.

36   Gn 1, 2.

37   Ps 104, 30.

38   Is 65, 17 ; 66, 22 ; 2 P 3, 13 ; Ap 21, 1.

39   Der Nersessian, « Deux tympans », p. 114, cite à ce sujet le Šarakan du 2ème dimanche après Pâques : « Toi qui, par la mort vivante et en mourant sur terre, as de nouveau renouvelé le monde » (*Šaraknoć*, Jérusalem 1936, p. 457).

du modelage, mais elle ne s'accomplira complètement que par la Passion du nouvel Adam et l'avènement des fins dernières. Or, selon l'artiste de Noravank̕, l'agent de cette évolution est l'esprit divin insufflé dès l'origine. C'est ce que montre la représentation de l'âme vivante: soulignons que la colombe, comme porteuse de cette âme, n'apparaît nulle part ailleurs dans les scènes de création.

Il est fort probable que la tradition exégétique qui s'exprime par ce détail remonte à l'influence d'Irénée. Agathange attribue à Adam un «souffle spirituel»,[40] mais il se garde d'affirmer que l'Esprit lui-même (*Hogi*) véhicule l'âme (*ogi*) dont le premier homme a été gratifié. Au contraire cette affirmation est explicite chez Irénée commentant le même texte de la Genèse.[41] «En se mélangeant à l'âme, l'Esprit s'est uni à l'ouvrage modelé; grâce à cette effusion de l'Esprit, se trouve réalisé l'homme spirituel et parfait et c'est celui-là même qui a été fait à l'image et à la ressemblance de Dieu».[42] Puisque Adam possède bien cette image divine, il devient possible de représenter l'Esprit mêlé à l'âme qui lui est insufflée: «Tout comme l'âme est la vie du corps, l'Esprit Saint est, de quelque manière, la vie de l'âme elle-même, et, par elle, de l'être humain tout entier».[43]

Toutefois, pour que l'image et la ressemblance divine se manifestent pleinement, il faut que l'homme, doté de libre arbitre comme son Créateur, accepte de se laisser conduire par l'Esprit qu'il a reçu.[44] C'est pourquoi la parole de Dieu – «Nous ferons un homme à notre image et à (notre) ressemblance»[45] – n'annonce pas une réalisation instantanée, mais un processus déployé d'un bout à l'autre de l'histoire humaine, depuis la genèse jusqu'aux fins dernières. La ressemblance divine ne doit pas être imposée mais choisie. «Tel est l'ordre, tel est le rythme, tel est l'achèvement par lequel l'homme créé et modelé devient à l'image et à la ressemblance du Dieu incréé: le Père décide et commande, le Fils exécute et modèle, l'Esprit nourrit et fait croître, et l'homme progresse peu à peu et s'élève vers la perfection, c'est-à-dire s'approche de

---

40   *Hogewor šunč̕*: Agathange § 264 (Thomson, *Teaching*, p. 60).

41   Gn 2, 7.

42   Irénée, *Contre les hérésies*, v, 6, 1; A. Rousseau, *Irénée de Lyon, Contre les hérésies*, Paris, 1991, p. 583.

43   A. Rousseau, *Irénée de Lyon, Démonstration de la prédication apostolique*, Sources Chrétiennes 406, Paris, 1995, p. 360; cf. Irénée, *Contre les hérésies*, v, 7, 1; *Démonstration* § 5. 97; R.V. Chetanian et J.-P. Mahé 2016 [trad.] = Irénée de Lyon, Démonstration de la prédication apostolique, in B. Pouderon, J.-M. Salamito et V. Zarini, *Premiers écrits chrétiens*, Paris, p. 1092-1140 (spécialement p. 1095) et p. 1449-1462 (spécialement p. 1138).

44   Rousseau, *Démonstration*, p. 368-369, à propos de *Contre les hérésies*, III, 17, l. v, 9, 2.

45   Gn 1, 26.

LA CRÉATION D'ADAM À NORAVANK̇

l'Incréé (...). Il fallait d'abord qu'il grandît (...), qu'il se multipliât (...), et qu'il vît son Seigneur».[46]

Dans cette perspective, il est naturel que la scène de la Passion côtoie celle de la Création et que leur juxtaposition soit expliquée, comme sur le tympan de Noravank̇, par une allusion prophétique aux fins dernières. Parallèlement, l'inscription du tympan inférieur a la même saveur eschatologique. Au-dessus de la Vierge Hodigitria, et en présence d'Isaïe témoin de la conception virginale,[47] se fait entendre la voix du Père: «Celui-ci a reçu mon Nom, béni et redoutable, Dieu, depuis l'extrémité jusqu'à l'extrémité de l'extrémité, sans coupure ni fin».[48]

L'unique manuscrit cilicien[49] du XIIIᵉ siècle qui nous transmet la version arménienne d'Irénée[50] ne nous donne pas le moyen d'évaluer la diffusion de cette œuvre dans les monastères du Siwnik̇ aux XIIIᵉ–XIVᵉ siècles. Néanmoins, la version d'Irénée est également citée dans le *Sceau de la foi*, florilège patristique composé sous Komitas (611-628), puis remanié au début du VIIIᵉ siècle par Step̄anos Siwneċi.[51] Si l'on en croit l'historien Step̄anos Ōrbelean,[52] la mémoire de ce dernier prélat était toujours auréolée du plus grand prestige à la fin du XIIIᵉ siècle, dans le canton du Vayoċ Jor, où se dresse le monastère de Noravank̇. Quant à Agathange, son autorité est constante dans tous les milieux arméniens, du Vᵉ siècle à nos jours. Il est donc assez vraisemblable que le sculpteur du tympan de la création de l'homme a œuvré dans un milieu où ces deux traditions exégétiques demeuraient vivantes.

---

46   Irénée, *Contre les hérésies*, IV, 38, 3 ; cf. Rousseau, *Contre les hérésies*, p. 553.

47   Is 7, 14 : «Elle enfantera un fils et on l'appellera Emmanuel».

48   *Ays ēar̄ im awrhneal ew ahel anunn Astuac I cagaċ minč̣' I cags cagin or oč̣' hat ew oč̣' včar*. Matevosyan (*Inscriptions and Colophons of Noravank*), p. 57-58, lit *Ays ē ar̄ im* ("Celui-ci est auprès de moi"), ce qui est improbable pour le fond comme pour la forme. L'attribution d'un pouvoir sans fin accordé au Fils d'homme est conforme à Dn 7, 13-14, présent dans le tympan supérieur.

49   C'est également de Cilicie que provient la *Racine de la foi*, florilège patristique compilé par Vardan Aygekċi en 1209, qui cite «Eranos Lugdunaċi (Irénée de Lyon), sectateur des Apôtres» ; cf. Y.S. Anasyan, *Vardan Aygekċi à la lumière de ses œuvres nouvellement découvertes* [en arménien, brochure de 48 pages, San Lazzaro 1969, tirée de *Bazmavēp* 1968], spécialement p. 7. 34.

50   Érévan № 3710 ; cf. Rousseau, *Démonstration*, p. 17-19. Le colophon du copiste désigne comme commanditaire Yovhannēs évêque de Tarse, frère du roi Het̄um Iᵉʳ (1226-1269) ; cf. Chetanian et Mahé, *Premiers écrits chrétiens*, p. 1140.

51   J.-P. Mahé, «L'Église arménienne de 611 à 1066», dans A. Vauchez, J.-M. Mayeur and G. Dagron, *Histoire du christianisme*, t. 4, Paris, 1993, p. 457-547, spécialement p. 466 et 481.

52   Step̄anos Ōrbelean, chapitre 31.

En tout cas, la complexité de sa composition, la subtilité des détails et la singularité du sujet sont nécessairement le fruit de savantes spéculations, qui renvoient sans doute à une école monastique dispensant un enseignement théologique de très haut niveau.

CHAPTER 8

Translatio corporis Adæ: Trajectories of a Parabiblical Tradition

Sergey Minov

During Late Antiquity and the Middle Ages Christians produced an astonishingly rich amount of parabiblical traditions dealing with the figure of Adam, the paradigmatic first human being.[1] While many of them are found in what might be properly termed apocryphal and pseudepigraphical literature, a great number of such traditions are scattered through works of other genres, such as theological tractates, biblical commentaries, historiography, homilies, and poetry. This diversity, both in terms of the content of these traditions and in what concerns diverse formal and ideological contexts in which they appear, reflects a wide array of various theological, social, cultural and other factors that were behind this proliferation of parabiblical material.[2]

In this article, I am going to focus on those late antique and mediæval Christian sources that deal with the problem of when and how the body of Adam reached the place of its burial in Jerusalem. Speculations on this subject are attested already during the fourth century, as one can see from the examples of some Greek-speaking Christian writers, analysed below. During the later period, one comes across a number of different explanations of the transmis-

---

1 For an overview, see M.E. Stone, *A History of the Literature of Adam and Eve* (SBL Early Judaism and Its Literature 3), Atlanta, 1992; id., *Adam's Contract with Satan: The Legend of the Cheirograph of Adam*, Bloomington, 2002; id., *Adam and Eve in the Armenian Tradition: Fifth through Seventeenth Centuries* (SBL Early Judaism and its Literature 38), Atlanta, 2013; B. Murdoch, *Adam's Grace: Fall and Redemption in Medieval Literature*, Cambridge, 2000; id., *The Apocryphal Adam and Eve in Medieval Europe: Vernacular Translations and Adaptations of the Vita Adæ et Evæ*, Oxford, 2009; A.L. Miltenova, 'Adamic Tradition in Slavonic Manuscripts (Vita Adæ et Evæ and Apocryphal Cycle about the Holy Tree)', in A.A. Orlov and G. Boccaccini (eds), *New Perspectives on 2 Enoch: No Longer Slavonic Only* (Studia Judæoslavica 4), Leiden, 2012, pp. 325–340; A. Kulik and S. Minov, *Biblical Pseudepigrapha in Slavonic Tradition*, New York, 2016.

2 On the usefulness of the term 'parabiblical' that I apply to these traditions, as well as on its limitations, see M.M. Zahn, 'Talking about Rewritten Texts: Some Reflections on Terminology', in H. von Weissenberg et al. (eds), *Changes in Scripture: Rewriting and Interpreting Authoritative Traditions in the Second Temple Period* (Beihefte zur Zeitschrift für die Alttestamentliche Wissenschaft 419), Berlin, 2011, pp. 93–119.

© SERGEY MINOV, 2021 | DOI:10.1163/9789004445925_010

sion of Adam's body to Golgotha in works written in Syriac, Coptic, Armenian, Slavonic and other languages of the Christian Orient.

Before starting to discuss this rich and variegated material, I shall summarize briefly what might be characterized as the first stage and a necessary prerequisite for the development of all these traditions: that is, the basic understanding that Adam's body was buried on Golgotha. This notion, deeply rooted in soteriological speculations of early Christians, emerged at the intersection of two ideas, both present in the corpus of New Testament writings: the mention of Golgotha as the place of Jesus's crucifixion and death, and the typological connection between Adam and Christ. In what concerns the former, all four canonical Gospels report that the crucifixion of Jesus took place at the location called 'Golgotha' (Γολγοθᾶ), while explaining this Aramaic toponym as 'the Place of a Skull' (Κρανίου Τόπος).[3] As for the typological connection between Christ and Adam, it was developed already by the apostle Paul, who refers to Adam as 'a type (τύπος) of the one who was to come' (i.e. Christ) in Romans 5:12–19, and proclaims that 'as in Adam all die, so in Christ all will be made alive' in 1 Corinthians 15:22.[4]

The early development of the tradition about Adam's burial on Golgotha has been well studied, so that there is no need to go over it in detail.[5] Its earliest

---

3   See Mt 27:33; Mk 15:22; Lk 23:33; Jn 19:17. For a discussion of Golgotha's possible location, see J. Jeremias, *Golgotha* (Angelos: Archiv für neutestamentliche Zeitgeschichte und Kulturkunde 1), Leipzig, 1926; S. Gibson and J.E. Taylor, *Beneath the Church of the Holy Sepulchre, Jerusalem: The Archæology and Early History of Traditional Golgotha* (Palestine Exploration Fund Monograph, Series Maior 1), London, 1994; J.E. Taylor, 'Golgotha: A Reconsideration of the Evidence for the Sites of Jesus's Crucifixion and Burial', *New Testament Studies* 44:2 (1998), pp. 180–203.

4   See C.K. Barrett, *From the First Adam to the Last: A Study in Pauline Theology*, New York, 1962; N.T. Wright, 'Adam in Pauline Christology', in K.H. Richards (ed.), *Society of Biblical Literature: 1983 Seminar Papers*, Chico, California, 1983, pp. 359–389; M. Kister, '"In Adam": 1 Cor 15:21–22; 12:27 in Their Jewish Setting', in A. Hilhorst et al. (eds), *Flores Florentino: Dead Sea Scrolls and Other Early Jewish Studies in Honour of Florentino García Martínez* (Supplements to the Journal for the Study of Judaism 122), Leiden, 2007, pp. 685–690; N.A. Meyer, *Adam's Dust and Adam's Glory in the Hodayot and the Letters of Paul: Rethinking Anthropogony and Theology* (Supplements to Novum Testamentum 168), Leiden, 2016.

5   On development of this tradition, see A. Le Boulluec, 'Regards antiques sur Adam au Golgotha', in M. Loubet and D. Pralon (eds), *Eukarpa: Études sur la Bible et ses exégètes*, Paris, 2011, pp. 355–363; E. Grypeou and H. Spurling, *The Book of Genesis in Late Antiquity: Encounters between Jewish and Christian Exegesis* (Jewish and Christian Perspectives 24), Leiden, 2013, pp. 71–79; N. Lipatov-Chicherin, 'Early Christian Tradition about Adam's Burial on Golgotha and Origen', in B. Bitton-Ashkelony et al. (eds), *Origeniana Duodecima: Origen's Legacy in the Holy Land—A Tale of Three Cities: Jerusalem, Cæsarea and Bethlehem. Proceedings of the 12th International Origen Congress, Jerusalem, 25–29 June, 2017* (Bibliotheca Ephemeridum Theologicarum Lovaniensium 302), Leuven, 2019, pp. 151–178.

attestations come from the works of two third-century Christian writers, Julius Africanus and Origen, both of whom refer to a Jewish tradition, according to which Adam was buried in Jerusalem or, more specifically, on Calvary.[6] By the second half of the fourth century it becomes a widespread tradition, with one significant exception being Jerome, who dismissed Origen's view and proposed, instead, that Adam was buried in Hebron, relying upon a popular Jewish tradition, well attested in Rabbinic sources.[7] Due to the high authority of Jerome as biblical exegete, his opinion exercised a considerable influence throughout the medieval Latin West.[8]

It is noteworthy that both Julius Africanus and Origen, as well as several other Christian writers who mention the tradition of Adam's burial on Golgotha, ascribe it to Jews or Hebrews. However, as far as surviving Jewish works from the Second Temple and early Roman periods allow us to judge, no identification of Jerusalem as a burial site of Adam seems to exist during that time among the Jews. The earliest attestation of this notion in Jewish sources comes from *Pirqe de-Rabbi Eliezer*, a late midrash, whose author reports (ch. 20) that Adam built for himself a mausoleum on Mount Moriah (the Temple Mount), which he identifies with the Cave of Machpelah, traditionally located near Hebron.[9] This midrash, however, cannot be used for reconstruction of Jewish views on the subject during the early centuries of the Common Era, since it betrays Christian influence, including polemic against the Christian tradition of veneration of Adam.[10] At the moment, it seems to be more judicious to consider the notion of Adam's burial in Jerusalem as a result of internal Christian

---

6   For Julius Africanus, see M. Wallraff et al., *Iulius Africanus Chronographiæ: The Extant Fragments* (Die griechischen christlichen Schriftsteller der ersten Jahrhunderte NF 15), Berlin, 2007, pp. 42–43; for Origen, see E. Klostermann and L. Früchtel, *Origenes Matthäuserklärung, III. Fragmente und Indices* (Die griechischen christlichen Schriftsteller der ersten drei Jahrhunderte 41.1, Origenes Werke 12.1), Leipzig, 1941, pp. 225–226.

7   Cf. his *Comm. Matt.* 4.27.3; *Ep.* 108.11. For a discussion of this tradition in Jerome and Rabbinic literature, see P.W. van der Horst, 'The Site of Adam's Tomb', in M.F.J. Baasten and R. Munk (eds), *Studies in Hebrew Literature and Jewish Culture: Presented to Albert van der Heide on the Occasion of his Sixty-Fifth Birthday* (Amsterdam Studies in Jewish Thought 12), Dordrecht, 2007, pp. 251–255.

8   For some examples, see A.M.L. Prangsma-Hajenius, *La légende du Bois de la Croix dans la littérature française médiévale*, Assen, 1995, pp. 142–143.

9   See D. Börner-Klein, *Pirke de-Rabbi Elieser: Nach der Edition Venedig 1544 unter Berücksichtigung der Edition Warschau 1852* (Studia Judaica 26), Berlin, 2004, pp. 219–220. For a discussion, see Grypeou and Spurling, *Book of Genesis*, pp. 50–54.

10   For a discussion of Christian influence on *Pirqe de-Rabbi Eliezer*, see I. Lévi, 'Éléments chrétiens dans le Pirké Rabbi Eliézer', *Revue des études juives* 18 [35] (1889), pp. 83–89; H. Spurling and E. Grypeou, 'Pirke de-Rabbi Eliezer and Eastern Christian Exegesis', *Collectanea Christiana Orientalia* 4 (2007), pp. 217–243.

development, and regard all references to Jewish informants in this connection as fictive, rooted in the image of Jews as the keepers of reliable knowledge about biblical past and landscape, and meant to provide legitimacy for this recently invented parabiblical tradition.[11]

In what follows, I am going to discuss the second stage in the development of this tradition, namely various explanations of how the body of Adam reached Golgotha. Not pretending to provide a comprehensive examination of all relevant material, I aim at offering a survey of the main scenarios of this transfer that emerged in different Christian cultures, giving particular attention to a rather understudied corpus of Slavonic literature. By focusing on them, I intend to explore how these cases might throw additional light on literary mechanisms that are responsible for the genesis of parabiblical traditions among Christians.

1 Adam Lived and Died in Judæa

The earliest and, perhaps, most straightforward explanation of how the body of Adam turned out to be present at Golgotha is the one according to which the forefather after his expulsion from Paradise reached Judæa, where he lived, eventually died, and was buried. This tradition developed within a Greek-speaking Christian milieu within a century after Julius Africanus and Origen, and gained currency by the second half of the fourth century. One of the earliest witnesses to its existence is Jerome (ob. 420). In his letter to Marcella, written in Bethlehem during the year 386, he relates about Jerusalem that, according to what some people say, 'in this city, nay, more, on this very spot, Adam lived and died'.[12] It should be pointed out, though, that later on in his life Jerome changed position on this issue, having adopted a Jewish tradition according to which Adam was buried in Hebron.

Another early testimony to the idea that Adam died in Jerusalem is found in the *Panarion* of Epiphanius of Salamis (ob. 403), in the chapter dealing

---

11   On this function of Jews in Christian works from Late Antiquity, see O. Limor, 'Christian Sacred Space and the Jew', in J. Cohen (ed.), *From Witness to Witchcraft: Jews and Judaism in Medieval Christian Thought* (Wolfenbütteler Mittelalter-Studien 11), Wiesbaden, 1996, pp. 55–77; A.S. Jacobs, *Remains of the Jews: The Holy Land and Christian Empire in Late Antiquity* (Divinations: Rereading Late Ancient Religion), Stanford, 2004.

12   *Ep.* 46.3: *in hac urbe, immo in hoc tunc loco et habitasse dicitur et mortuus esse Adam*; ed. I. Hilberg, *Sancti Eusebii Hieronymi epistulæ. Pars 1: Epistulæ 1–LXX* (Corpus Scriptorum Ecclesiasticorum Latinorum 54), Wien, 1996, pp. 331–332; trans. W.H. Fremantle et al., *The Principal Works of St. Jerome* (A Select Library of Nicene and Post-Nicene Fathers of the Christian Church: Second Series 6), New York, 1893, p. 61.

with Tatian and his followers. As he constructs a counterargument against Tatian's supposed doctrine that Adam cannot be saved, Epiphanius relates that he found 'in the literature' information that Jesus was crucified on Golgotha, where Adam's body was buried.[13] He continues by adding that after his expulsion from Paradise Adam lived opposite it for a long time, but when he grew old, he 'came and died in this place,' that is Jerusalem, and was buried on the site of Golgotha, which took its name that means 'Place of a Skull' after the skull of Adam, and not because the site itself resembles a skull somehow.

A somewhat more developed version of this parabiblical tradition comes from the Greek *Commentary on Isaiah*, transmitted under the name of Basil of Cæsarea.[14] While discussing Isa 5:1, its author refers to an 'unwritten tradition' (ἄγραφον μνήμην), transmitted in the Church, as his source of information about Adam being the 'first inhabitant' (πρῶτον ... οἰκήτορα) of Judæa, where he was settled as a consolation after his expulsion from Paradise.[15] After Adam died, the 'men of that time' deposited his skull in the place that they named 'Place of the Skull,' i.e. Golgotha. The *Commentary*'s author adds that Noah was, probably, aware of this place and passed knowledge of it to his descendants. Basil's explanation of the arrival of Adam's body at Golgotha appears occasionally in the works of later Greek authors. For instance, one finds it integrated into one of the letters transmitted under the name of Nilus of Ancyra (ob. ca. 430), although without mention of Basil's authorship.[16]

It should be mentioned that this explanation acquired a certain currency among Syriac-speaking Christians. There are several witnesses to reception of Basil's *Commentary on Isaiah* in Syriac. Thus, one comes across an excerpt dealing with Adam's skull incorporated into the florilegium of patristic texts in the manuscript British Library, Add. 17193, produced in the year 874 by the West Syrian monk Abraham.[17] The excerpt that appears on fol. 7ᵛ–8ʳ is introduced

---

13   *Panar.* 1.46.5.1–2; ed. K. Holl and J. Dummer, *Epiphanius II: Panarion hær. 34–64* (Die griechischen christlichen Schriftsteller der ersten drei Jahrhunderte 31), 2nd revised edn, Berlin, 1980, pp. 208–209; trans. F. Williams, *The Panarion of Epiphanius of Salamis, Book I (Sects 1–46)* (Nag Hammadi and Manichæan Studies 63), 2nd revised edn, Leiden, 2009, p. 379.

14   For an argument in favour of its Basilian authorship, see N.A. Lipatov, 'The Problem of the Authorship of the Commentary on the Prophet Isaiah Attributed to St Basil the Great', *Studia Patristica* 27 (1993), pp. 42–48.

15   *Comm. Isa.* 5.141; PG 30, col. 348; trans. N.A. Lipatov, *St. Basil the Great. Commentary on the Prophet Isaiah* (Texts and Studies in the History of Theology 7), Mandelbachtal, 2001, p. 162.

16   *Ep.* 1.2; PG 79, col. 84.

17   For a description of this manuscript, see W. Wright, *Catalogue of Syriac Manuscripts in the British Museum, Acquired since the Year 1838* vol. 2, London, 1870–1872, pp. 989–1002.

as belonging to 'the holy Basil, from the Commentary on the prophet Isaiah,' and in its content is very close to the discussion of Adam's burial in the *Commentary on Isaiah* by Basil of Cæsarea.[18] It is unclear, however, whether there ever existed a complete Syriac translation of Basil's *Commentary*, from which the compiler of the florilegium might have excerpted this passage, or whether he relied for it on Greek sources.

Another testimony, from a somewhat earlier period, is an excerpt from the *Commentary on Isaiah* by Cyril of Alexandria, preserved in the composed manuscript Deir al-Surian, Syr. 28, made up of different parts, bound together during restoration.[19] The text that interests us appears on fol. 164ᵛ, which belongs to the manuscript B (fol. 154–164), dated approximately by the eighth century.[20] While it is introduced as 'Of the holy Cyril, from the Commentary on the prophet Isaiah,' this passage is not found in the original Greek text of Cyril's *Commentary on Isaiah*, as it was published in Migne's *Patrologia Græca*.[21] In fact, the content of the excerpt resembles very much the discussion of Adam's burial in Basil's *Commentary*: it starts by referring to the unwritten tradition, preserved in the Church; then it relates how Adam became the 'first inhabitant' of Judæa after he left Paradise; how after his death the people of that time buried Adam's skull at the place they would call after it; and how Noah was aware of this tradition and transmitted it after the flood. We can conclude, then, that the excerpt on Adam's burial from the *Commentary on Isaiah* in ms. Deir al-Surian, Syr. 28, while coming, originally, from the work of Basil of Cæsarea, was at some point reattributed to Cyril of Alexandria. It is unclear, what the reason was for this reattribution, and whether it took place already during the transmission of Basil's *Commentary* in Greek or, later on, in Syriac milieu.

An additional witness to the reception of the tradition about Adam's burial from the *Commentary* of Basil in Syriac, so far unnoticed as such by scholars, appears in another manuscript, dated by approximately the same period,—ms.

---

18   The Syriac text was published, together with a Russian translation, by Н.А. Липатов-Чичерин, 'Предание о погребении Адама на Голгофе в позднеантичной литературе (III–V вв.)', in К.А. Битнер and Н.С. Смелова (eds), *Источниковедение культурных традиций Востока: гебраистика—эллинистика—сирология—славистика. Сборник научных статей* (Труды по иудаике, Серия "Филология и культурология" 4), С.-Петербург, 2016, pp. 144–176, here 167–168.

19   For a detailed description of this manuscript, see S.P. Brock and L. van Rompay, *Catalogue of the Syriac Manuscripts and Fragments in the Library of Deir al-Surian, Wadi al-Natrun (Egypt)* (Orientalia Lovaniensia Analecta 227), Leuven, 2014, pp. 178–211.

20   The Syriac text of the excerpt was published, together with an English translation, by Brock and Van Rompay, *Catalogue*, p. 205.

21   See PG 70, cols. 9–1449.

Sinai Syr. 16, an anthology of Greek philosophical and patristic writings that was produced during the eighth or early ninth century.[22] On fol. 203r–v, it contains a question and answer on the subject of the place of Adam's burial, exchanged between certain John and Jacob. Since this text is still unpublished, I provide here an English translation, as well as the Syriac original:

> John: Did Adam dwell in the place of Jerusalem, and there ended his life, and there was buried? Jacob: It was there that Adam dwelt, and there ended his life, in the land of Judæa, and there he was also buried. Both Athanasius, that apostolic man and tongue of the Spirit, and Saint Cyril teach (that) in their words. As far as I remember, they said on this account that Adam was the first inhabitant of Judæa. And, moreover, they said about him that when he went to many places and dwelt in various lands, at the end of his life he came (and) was buried on the mountain of Jebus. Jebus, then, is known to be Jerusalem. So then, it is known from these, that Adam dwelt in Judæa, although he dwelt also in other places, and that he was buried in the place of Jerusalem. And all patriarchs afterwards also dwelt there, in the land of Judæa, near it and around it. And Noah also dwelt there, and planted cedars and made the ark in the land of Sodom. And when Noah and his sons entered it before the flood, they took from there with them the bones of Adam. And after the flood Noah divided among his sons also the bones of Adam, as well as the whole earth for dwelling. And the head of Adam, as well as that land, in which was the place of Judæa, was given to Shem, his firstborn son. And when the sons of Shem came to the land of their inheritance, they placed that skull, which accrued to them from the bones of Adam, there, in the place of Adam's grave.[23]

---

22 A digital reproduction of the black and white microfilm of this manuscript is available online at https://www.loc.gov/item/00279386292-ms/. For an overview of its content, see S.P. Brock, 'The Genealogy of the Virgin Mary in Sinai Syr. 16', *Scrinium* 2 (2006), pp. 58–71, here pp. 69–71, who also discusses the problem of its dating (p. 65).

23 ܝܘܚܢܢ: ܐܢ ܥܡܪ ܐܕܡ ܒܐܬܪܐ ܕܐܘܪܫܠܡ ܘܬܡܢ ܫܠܡ ܚܝ̈ܘܗܝ ܘܬܡܢ ܐܬܩܒܪ. ܝܥܩܘܒ: ܕܬܡܢ ܥܡܪ ܐܕܡ: ܘܬܡܢ ܫܠܡ ܚܝ̈ܘܗܝ ܒܐܪܥܐ ܕܝܗܘܕ: ܘܬܡܢ ܐܦ ܐܬܩܒܪ. ܐܬܢܣܝܘܣ ܓܒܪܐ ܗܘ ܫܠܝܚܝܐ ܘܠܫܢܐ ܕܪܘܚܐ: ܘܐܦ ܩܕܝܫܐ ܩܘܪܝܠܘܣ ܡ̈ܠܦܝܢ ܒܡ̈ܠܝܗܘܢ. ܐܡܪܘ ܒܗ ܒܡܠܬܐ ܐܝܟܢܐ ܕܥܗܕ ܐܢܐ: ܕܩܕܡܝܐ ܡܬܝܒܢܐ ܗܘܐ ܕܝܗܘܕ ܠܐܕܡ. ܘܬܘܒ ܐܡܪܘ ܥܠܘܗܝ: ܕܟܕ ܠܕ̈ܘܟܝܬܐ ܣ̈ܓܝܐܬܐ ܐܙܠ: ܘܒܐܬܪ̈ܘܬܐ ܡܫ̈ܚܠܦܬܐ ܥܡܪ: ܠܫܘܠܡܐ ܕܝܢ ܕܚܝ̈ܘܗܝ: ܐܬܐ ܐܬܩܒܪ ܒܛܘܪܐ ܕܐܝܒܘܣ. ܐܝܒܘܣ ܕܝܢ ܝܕܝܥܐ ܗܝ ܕܗܝ ܗܝ ܐܘܪܫܠܡ. ܡܕܝܢ ܝܕܝܥܐ ܡܢ ܗܠܝܢ: ܘܕܥܡܪ ܐܕܡ ܒܝܗܘܕ: ܐܦܢ ܥܡܪ ܐܦ ܒܕܘ̈ܟܝܬܐ ܐܚܪ̈ܢܝܬܐ. ܐܦ ܕܐܬܩܒܪ ܒܕܘܟܬܐ ܕܐܘܪܫܠܡ. ܘܬܡܢ ܥܡܪܘ ܒܐܪܥܐ ܕܝܗܘܕ ܘܠܘܬܗ̇ ܘܠܚܕܪܝܗ̇: ܘܐܦ ܟܠܗܘܢ ܪ̈ܫܝ ܐܒܗ̈ܬܐ ܕܒܬܪܟܢ. ܘܐܦ ܢܘܚ ܬܡܢ ܥܡܪ. ܘܒܐܪܥܐ ܕܣܕܘܡ ܢܨܒ ܐܪ̈ܙܐ ܘܥܒܕܗ̇ ܠܩܒܘܬܐ. ܘܟܕ ܥܠ ܢܘܚ ܘܒܢܘ̈ܗܝ ܡܢ ܩܕܡ

As one can see, the author of the responsum holds the opinion that Adam lived and died in Judæa. It is interesting that he complicates this simple scenario by adding that while preparing for the flood Noah dug out the remains of Adam and brought them with him into the ark, that after the flood he divided them among his sons, and that Adam's head was buried on Golgotha by the descendants of Shem, who received it as his portion. This narrative development, I believe, should be recognized as an attempt to harmonize two different parabiblical traditions about arrival of Adam's body at Golgotha, one claiming that Adam lived and died in Judæa, and another, invented by the author of the Syriac *Cave of Treasures*, according to which Adam's remains were taken into the ark by Noah and, after the flood, brought to Jerusalem by Shem.[24]

In his responsum, Jacob refers explicitly to Athanasius of Alexandria and Cyril of Alexandria as his sources of information regarding Adam's residence and burial in Jerusalem. In what concerns the latter, it should be understood, almost certainly, as a reference to the *Commentary* of Basil, reattributed to Cyril, as in the case of ms. Deir al-Surian, Syr. 28. The reference to Athanasius, however, is more difficult to explain, since no genuine work of this theologian seems to contain a mention of Adam residing and/or dying in Judæa.[25] As for the possible author of the responsum, referred in the text only as 'Jacob,' Sebastian Brock identifies him tentatively as Jacob of Edessa (ob. 708), a famous West Syrian theologian and exegete.[26] Given the fact that a considerable part of Jacob's literary output is comprised of letters in the form of questions-and-answers, some of which deal with exegetical issues, this identification seems very plausible.

ܠܛܘܦܢܐ: ܫܩܠܗ ܡܢ ܬܡܢ ܒܢܘܗܝ ܠܓܪ̈ܡܘܗܝ ܕܐܕܡ. ܘܡܢ ܒܬܪ ܛܘܦܢܐ: ܦܠܓ ܢܘܚ
ܠܒܢ̈ܘܗܝ ܐܦ ܠܓܪ̈ܡܘܗܝ ܕܐܕܡ: ܘܐܦ ܠܐܪܥܐ ܟܠܗ̇ ܐܝܟ ܕܠܡܟܬܒܢܘܬܐ. ܘܝܗܒ ܠܫܝܡ
ܒܪܗ ܒܘܟܪܗ: ܐܦ ܪܝܫܗ ܕܐܕܡ. ܐܦ ܐܪܥܐ ܗܕܐ ܕܒܗ̇ ܐܬܬܘܗܝ. ܗܘܐ ܐܬܪܐ
ܕܝܗܘܕ. ܘܒܗ̇ ܐܬܬܘ ܒ̈ܢܝ ܫܝܡ ܠܐܪܥܐ ܕܝܪ̈ܬܘܬܗܘܢ: ܘܩܒܪܘ ܬܡܢ ܒܓܘܠܓܘܠܬܐ ܕܩܒܪܗ ܕܐܕܡ:
ܠܪܘܦܬܐ ܗ̇ ܕܡܛܬ ܠܗܘܢ ܡܢ ܓܪ̈ܡܘܗܝ ܕܐܕܡ.

24 The latter tradition is discussed below, in Section 3.

25 It might well be that he refers to one of Pseudo-Athanasian writings, such as the *Questions to Antiochus the Dux* (cf. the passage on Adam in PG 28, col. 628).

26 Brock, 'Genealogy of the Virgin Mary', p. 70. On Jacob, see R.B. ter Haar Romeny (ed.), *Jacob of Edessa and the Syriac Culture of His Day* (Monographs of the Peshiṭta Institute Leiden 18), Leiden, 2008.

TRANSLATIO CORPORIS ADÆ

2 Adam's Body Brought by the Flood's Waters

Another, relatively simple, explanation of how the body of Adam happened to be buried in Jerusalem, that developed during Late Antiquity, ascribes its transfer to Judæa to the waters of the flood during the time of Noah. This scenario is attested, first of all, in a number of Coptic works, such as the *Homily on the Resurrection and the Apostles* and *Encomium on John the Baptist*, ascribed pseudepigraphically to John Chrysostom.

Thus, the author of the *Encomium on John the Baptist* (ch. 9), relates that 'When the great flood waters washed over the earth in the days of Noah, the surging waters raised the body of Adam; they carried him and placed him in the middle of Jerusalem. Washing over him, the waters of the earth covered him with mud.'[27] A similar brief account is found in the *Homily on the Resurrection and the Apostles* (§ 38), according to which the body of Adam was transferred to Jerusalem, 'the center of the universe,' by the flood waters from 'the land of the south,' where he was originally buried.[28]

A related account of the transfer of Adam's remains to Jerusalem appears in the unknown Coptic work that survives only partially, in two parchment leaves discovered at the Monastery of Saint Macarius in Wadi el-Natrun. According to this text, the waters of the flood rolled the skull of Adam 'until it came to the place wherein his son's blood was poured forth. When the men saw it, they marvelled greatly, saying: 'This is one of the men of old time:' they buried it in that place. They called it The Place of the Skull unto this day, and they built the city in that place.'[29] Described by its publisher, Hugh Evelyn-White, as 'apocryphal fragment on Adam,' it might be a part of a homiletic composition, not unlike the two Pseudo-Chrysostomian homilies discussed above.

Whereas, as it happens with many other pseudepigraphic homilies transmitted in Coptic, it is very difficult to date these compositions with a satisfactory degree of certainty, many of these works are generally thought to be produced during the last centuries of Late Antiquity, that is between the sixth and eighth centuries.

---

27   Trans. by P.L. Tite, in T. Burke and B.C. Landau (eds), *New Testament Apocrypha: More Noncanonical Scriptures* vol. 1, Grand Rapids, 2016, p. 237.

28   Trans. by Z. Pleše in D. Brakke et al., *Homiletica from the Pierpont Morgan Library: Seven Coptic Homilies attributed to Basil the Great, John Chrysostom, and Euodius of Rome* (CSCO 524–525, Copt. 43–44) vol. 2, Louvain, 1991, p. 66.

29   Trans. H.G. Evelyn-White, *The Monasteries of the Wadi 'n Natrûn, Part 1: New Coptic Texts from the Monastery of Saint Macarius* (Publications of the Metropolitan Museum of Art 2), New York, 1926, p. 5.

A similar explanation of the transfer of Adam's body to Golgotha gained popularity in the Irish literary tradition. The mention of the flood waters bringing it to Jerusalem is found in several compositions coming from early medieval Ireland, such as the *Death of Adam*,[30] the *Saltair na Rann* (or the Psalter of Quatrains, written ca. 10th c.),[31] and some redactions of the *Book of the Taking of Ireland* (*Lebor Gabála Érenn*).[32] Whereas limitations of space do not allow us to discuss these sources in detail, it should be pointed out that the only significant difference between the Irish and Coptic versions of the transfer of Adam's body is that, according to the former, it was brought to Jerusalem from Hebron, where it was originally buried. The mention of Hebron as place of Adam's first burial is an example of the influence exercised by Jerome's exegesis in the Latin West. At the same time, the scenario offered by the Irish sources could be understood as an attempt to bring Jerome's opinion into agreement with the notion of Golgotha as the burial place of Adam, that was popular in the Christian East.[33]

3 Adam's Body Brought by Noah and Shem

Another, more sophisticated, tradition that relates the transfer of Adam's body to Jerusalem to the time of the flood emerged among Syriac-speaking Christians, also during the last centuries of Late Antiquity. Its earliest and most developed expression is found in the work known as the *Cave of Treasures*.[34] Ascribed to the famous fourth-century poet and exegete Ephrem the Syrian, this composition was written in Syriac in the Sasanian-controlled part of northern Mesopotamia somewhere during the sixth or beginning of the seventh

---

30   See M. Herbert and M. McNamara, *Irish Biblical Apocrypha: Selected Texts in Translation*, Edinburgh, 1989, p. 16.

31   See D. Greene and F. Kelly, *The Irish Adam and Eve Story from Saltair na Rann. Vol. 1: Text and Translation*, Dublin, 1976, pp. 108–111.

32   See R.A.S. Macalister, *Lebor Gabála Érenn: The Book of the Taking of Ireland. Part I*, Dublin, 1938, pp. 96–97.

33   On later attempts of Western Christians to adopt the Eastern tradition that took place during the Crusades, see A. Keshman Wasserman, 'The Cross and the Tomb: The Crusader Contribution to Crucifixion Iconography', in R. Bartal and H. Vorholt (eds), *Between Jerusalem and Europe: Essays in Honour of Bianca Kühnel* (Visualising the Middle Ages 11), Leiden, 2015, pp. 13–33.

34   For the Syriac text, see S.-M. Ri, *La Caverne des Trésors: les deux recensions syriaques*. 2 vols (CSCO 486–487, Syr. 207–208), Louvain, 1987; for an English translation, see A. Toepel, 'The *Cave of Treasures*: A New Translation and Introduction', in R. Bauckham et al. (eds), *Old Testament Pseudepigrapha: More Noncanonical Scriptures. Volume 1*, Grand Rapids, 2013, pp. 531–584.

century.[35] The work belongs to the loosely defined category of 'rewritten Bible,' as it offers a particular version of Christian sacred history, where the accounts of both the Old and the New Testaments are creatively merged into a new cohesive narrative that starts with the creation of the world and ends with the Pentecost.

While the author of the *Cave of Treasures* makes use of many earlier exegetical and parabiblical traditions, Jewish as well as Christian, he also exhibits a considerable degree of creativity, introducing a number of motifs and images not attested before. One of such exegetical innovations is his presentation of the adventures of Adam's body after the patriarch's death, which takes a considerable narrative space.

According to this composition, while on his deathbed, Adam commands his son Seth that after he dies, his body should be embalmed and deposited in the 'cave of treasures' (ܓܙܐ ܕܒܝܬ), located on the outskirts of the Paradisiacal mountain, and that in the future, when Seth's descendants would eventually leave that mountain, they should take his remains with them and bury them in the 'middle of the earth' (ܒܡܨܥܬܗ ܕܐܪܥܐ), because it is there that 'salvation will be wrought for me and all my offspring' (6.9–13).[36] After the death of Adam, Seth carries out his father's will (6.19–21). The cave, then, serves as a kind of saint's shrine, in which the descendants of Adam would convene regularly to pray over the body of their father, and to receive blessing from it (7.12–14). When the time of the flood arrives, Noah, following the command of his father Methuselah (16.14–21), takes the bodies of Adam and Eve with him, brings them into the ark, together with the three divine gifts of God to Adam, i.e. gold, myrrh and frankincense, converting thus the ark's interior into a sacred church-like space (17.6–18.7). After the death of Noah, his son Shem implements another part of Methuselah's last will, repeated by Noah on his deathbed (16.22–28, 22.3–9), and takes Adam's body out from the ark, to the place of its final interment: accompanied by Melchizedek and guided by God's angel, he brings Adam's body to Golgotha, located in the 'middle of the earth'. After Shem deposits Adam's body there, he installs Melchizedek as 'a priest of the Most High God' to watch over the place and to minister there to God all the days of his life, offering bread and wine (23.1–23).

It should be noted that the *Cave's* author regards this explanation of the transfer of Adam's body to Golgotha to be his own important contribution to

---

35 See S. Minov, *Memory and Identity in the Syriac* Cave of Treasures: *Rewriting the Bible in Sasanian Iran* (Jerusalem Studies in Religion and Culture 26), Leiden, 2021; id., 'Date and Provenance of the Syriac *Cave of Treasures*: A Reappraisal', *Hugoye* 20:1 (2017), pp. 129–229.

36 Ed. Ri, *La Caverne des Trésors*, pp. 50–52; trans. Toepel, '*Cave of Treasures*', p. 545.

the tradition of ecclesiastical knowledge about the biblical past, as he himself makes explicit in chapter 44. After explaining the primary rationale for his work, i.e. providing a proper genealogy of Mary in order to rebuff the Jewish accusation of adultery against her,[37] and commenting upon his unique stand vis-à-vis the earlier Jewish and Christian writers, our author points to the following specific questions, by addressing which he claims to surpass previous ecclesiastical writers who were not able to answer them correctly,—'from where Adam's body was brought up to Golgotha, from where Melchizedek's ancestors came, and (who are) the ancestors of blessed Mary' (44.12).[38]

As for the function of this evolved subplot within the overall narrative scheme of the *Cave of Treasures*, it serves the purpose of embedding the Adam–Christ typology, a major hermeneutic principle of the author's Christian understanding of the Old Testament, more deeply within the correct version of the biblical past offered by him. In addition to that, it reflects the author's polemical agenda aimed at subverting the Jewish character of the Old Testament. This agenda is manifested in a pronounced propensity to Christianize the primeval period of biblical history. A closer look at the pre-Abrahamic figures in this work reveals that its author significantly reworked this period of biblical history, constructing an axis of righteousness comprising such figures as Adam, Seth and his progeny, Noah, and Melchizedek, who are presented as embodiments of Christian values.[39]

It was, apparently, due to the influence of the *Cave of Treasures*, that the explanation of the transfer of Adam's body to Golgotha as a result of the combined efforts of Noah and Shem became wide-spread among Syriac- and Arabic-speaking Christians during the Middle Ages. Thus, we find it in the works of both West and East Syrian writers, such as Isho'dad of Merv (9th c.),[40] Solomon of Basra (13th c.),[41] and Gregory Barhebræus (13th c.).[42] A simplified

---

37 On anti-Jewish apologetic in the *Cave of Treasures*, see Minov, *Memory and Identity*, pp. 60–71.

38 Ed. Ri, *La Caverne des Trésors*, pp. 338–339; trans. Toepel, 'Cave of Treasures', p. 573.

39 For a detailed discussion of this and other aspects of anti-Jewish polemic in the *Cave of Treasures*, see Minov, *Memory and Identity*, pp. 71–141.

40 See *Commentary on Mark* 13; ed. M.D. Gibson, *The Commentaries of Isho'dad of Merv, Bishop of Hadatha (c. 850 A.D.), in Syriac and English* (Horæ Semiticæ 5–7, 10–11) vol. 1, Cambridge, 1911 and 1916, p. 142.

41 See *Book of the Bee* 21; ed. E.A.W. Budge, *The Book of the Bee: The Syriac Text Edited from the Manuscripts in London, Oxford, and Munich with an English Translation* (Anecdota Oxoniensia, Semitic Series 1.2), Oxford, 1886, p. 35.

42 See *Book of Rays* 10.3; ed. N. Séd, *Le Candélabre du Sanctuaire de Grégoire Abou'lfaradj dit Barhebræus. Douzième base: Du Paradis, suivie du Livre des Rayons: traité X* (Patrologia Orientalis 40.3 [184]), Turnhout, 1981, pp. 478–479.

TRANSLATIO CORPORIS ADÆ 165

version of this tradition that does not mention Shem is found in the *History* of Agapius of Mabbug (10th c.), a Melkite historiographer who wrote in Arabic. Referring to some unspecified 'books' (*al-kutub*) as his source, Agapius relates that Adam was buried on Mount Moriah, the place where Abraham wanted to sacrifice Isaac and where Solomon later built the Temple, and that his body was brought there by Noah, who took it inside the ark.[43]

Outside of the Syriac Christian milieu, this tradition gained certain currency among Armenian Christians. For example, it appears in such anonymous parabiblical compositions of uncertain date as the *History of the Repentance of Adam and Eve*, and the *Story Concerning the Tree of Sabek*.[44] In both these works, it is the pair of Shem and Melchizedek who are said to bring the bodies of Adam and Eve to Judæa, burying the former on Golgotha and the latter in Bethlehem. A similar account is found also in the Armenian *Homily on Genesis and the Gospel of Luke*, ascribed to Epiphanius of Salamis.[45] It may be added that the tenth-century historiographer Tovma Arcruni, who incorporates this explanation of the arrival of Adam's body to Golgotha into his retelling of biblical past, ascribes it to Philo of Alexandria, while claiming that it comes from Philo's work entitled 'The Explanation of the Hebrew Names'.[46] Further investigation is necessary in order to trace the origins, transmission and further development of this parabiblical tradition in Armenian milieu, including the question of the role played in this process by the *Cave of Treasures*.

4   Adam's Body Brought by Angels from the Island of Athoulis

Another version of the transfer of Adam's body to Jerusalem that emerged during the early Middle Ages relates that after his expulsion from Paradise Adam

---

43   Ed. A.A. Vasiliev, *Kitab al-ʿUnvan: Histoire universelle écrite par Agapius (Mahboub) de Menbidj* (Patrologia Orientalis 5.4, 7.4, 8.3, 11.1) vol. 1, Paris, 1909–1915, pp. 108–109.

44   For the former, see W.L. Lipscomb, *The Armenian Apocryphal Adam Literature* (University of Pennsylvania Armenian Texts and Studies 8), Chico, 1990, pp. 232–233; for the latter, see M.E. Stone, *Armenian Apocrypha Relating to Abraham* (SBL Early Judaism and its Literature 37), Atlanta, 2012, pp. 97–98. Cf. also a brief text published in M.E. Stone, 'The Bones of Adam and Eve', in R.A. Argall et al. (eds), *For a Later Generation: The Transformation of Tradition in Israel, Early Judaism, and Early Christianity*, Harrisburg, 2000, pp. 241–245.

45   See F.C. Conybeare, 'The Gospel Commentary of Epiphanius', *Zeitschrift für die neutestamentliche Wissenschaft* 7 (1906), pp. 318–332, here 319–320.

46   Trans. R.W. Thomson, *Thomas Artsruni. History of the House of the Artsruniḱ* (Byzantine Texts in Translation), Detroit, 1985, pp. 80–82. On the reception of Philo and his works in Armenian tradition, see О.С. Вардазарян, *Филон Александрийский в восприятии армянского средневековья. К вопросу об истоках традиции*, Ереван, 2006.

dwelt on an island, where he died. It is the angels, who bring Adam's remains from this location to Jerusalem and rebury them on the site of Golgotha.

The earliest attestation of this tradition comes from the Greek *Chronicle*, transmitted under the name of Peter of Alexandria.[47] This chronographic composition covers the time-span from Adam up until Emperor Leo VI (r. 886–912). According to its editor Zinaida Samodurova, this work was composed, most likely, during the end of the ninth or beginning of the tenth century. In the section following the detailed description of the regions inhabited by the descendants of Shem, the *Chronicle*'s author presents a substantial passage entitled the 'Clime of the North' (Κλίματος ἄρκτου), the main focus of which is on the 'island of Athoulis' ('Αθουλις νῆσος).[48] It opens with the following information:

> The first island, called Athoulis, to which the Paradise of God is near; there Adam dwelt, as it is written, opposite the Paradise, when he was expelled because of the transgression. And after him—nine generations, that is until Noah; and when Adam died on the same island Athoulia, he was buried while put to rest by the angels in the very centre of the earth, called Golgotha by the Hebrews, and Calvary by the Greeks.[49]

After a digression that highlights connection between Adam's body, buried on Golgotha, and the cosmic significance of Jesus's cross, the chronicler moves to the time of the flood. It is related that Noah, who lived on the same island, built there his ark, and that in the aftermath of the flood the island became 'partially uninhabited' (ἀοίκητος ... μερικῶς).

Whereas no other late antique or Byzantine author whose works survived seems to be acquainted with this explanation of how Adam's body reached Golgotha, it did gain certain popularity among the Slavs. The earliest witness to this tradition in Slavonic literature comes from the manuscript #74 in the Scaliger collection in Leiden University, the so-called *Scaliger Paterikon* produced during the second half of the thirteenth century in the Galician-

---

47   For general information and the Greek text, see З.Г. Самодурова, 'Хроника Петра Александрийского', *Византийский временник* 18 (1961), pp. 150–197. For a Russian translation, see М.В. Кривов, 'Хроника Петра Александрийского', *Византийский временник* 100 (2016), pp. 227–253.

48   Ed. Самодурова, 'Хроника Петра Александрийского', pp. 185–186.

49   Πρώτη νῆσος Ἀθουλίας λεγομένη, εἰς ἣν καὶ πλησιάζει ὁ παράδεισος τοῦ θεοῦ, ἐν ᾗ κατῴκησεν Ἀδάμ, καθὼς γέγραπται, ἀπέναντι τὸ παραδείσου ὅτε ἐξεβλήθη διὰ τὴν παράβασιν. Καὶ αἱ μεθ' αὐτὸν γενεαὶ δέκα τοῦτ' ἔστιν ἕως τοῦ Νῶε, τοῦ γὰρ Ἀδὰμ τελειωθέντος ἐν τῇ αὐτῇ Ἀθουλιάδι νήσῳ ἐτάφη κηδευθεὶς ὑπὸ ἀγγέλων ἐν τῷ μεσωτάτῳ τόπῳ τῆς γῆς τῷ παρ' Ἑβραίοις μὲν λεγομένῳ Γολγοθᾷ, παρὰ δὲ Ἕλλησι Κρανίον.

TRANSLATIO CORPORIS ADÆ

Volhynian region.[50] The main part of the codex is taken by an early Bulgarian compilation of apophthegms from Greek paterica and other works, which is followed by a collection of miscellaneous texts that includes chronographic, erotapocritic, eschatological, exegetic and other works. It is in this section, on fol. 144ᵛ, that we find the following brief passage, introduced anonymously as 'a partial word':

> The island into which Adam was exiled is called Aphulis; and he was buried by angels in the place called in Hebrew Golgotha, (and) Calvary in Greek. On that island the ark was made.[51]

The mention of the island of Aphulis as the place of Adam's exile and of the building of Noah's ark, as well as of the transfer of Adam's body to Jerusalem by the angels, leaves no doubt regarding a connection between this excerpt and the passage in the *Chronicle* of Peter of Alexandria. The exact nature of this connection, however, is far from clear, since one can imagine more than one scenario of how this tradition could reach the compiler of the *Scaliger Paterikon*.

Later on, one comes across this tradition in a number of Slavonic works, especially those produced during the fifteenth century. Thus, the famous scribe Euphrosyn, a monk of Kirillo-Belozersky monastery who was active during the second half of that century, includes it in one of his compilations.[52] We also find it in such historiographic compositions as *Letopisec Ellinskij i Rimskij* (ca. 15th c.),[53] or some versions of the *Palæa Interpretata*.[54] The compiler of the

---

50 A digital reproduction of this manuscript is available online at http://hdl.handle.net/1887 .1/item:1595495. For a discussion of its dating and milieu, see W.S. Veder, 'The Scaliger Paterikon (Ms. Scal. 74 Bibl. Acad. Lugd. Bat.)', *Tijdschrift voor slavische taal- en letterkunde* 2 (1973), pp. 111–119.

51 слово часное ∴ Ꙗко афꙋлисъ наречетсꙗ островъ. вонь же изгнанъ быстъ адамъ. и погребенъ быстъ ѿ анг҃лъ. на мѣстѣ нарицаюемѣмъ голгофа. по жидовську. по єлиньскоу главноє. въ томь островѣ сдѣлласꙗ ковчего.

52 See М.Д. Каган, Н.В. Понырко, and М.В. Рождественская, 'Описание сборников XV в. книгописца Ефросина', *Труды Отдела Древнерусской Литературы* 35 (1980), pp. 3–300, here 174, 184.

53 Ed. О.В. Творогов, *Летописец Еллинский и Римский. Т. 1: Текст*, С.-Петербург, 1999, p. 4.

54 Cf. (a) Synodalnaja Palæa of 1477; the relevant passage was edited by Н.С. Тихонравовъ, *Памятники отреченной русской литературы* vol. 1, С.-Петербургъ, 1863, p. 18; (b) Rumjantsevskaja Palæa of 1494; the relevant passage was edited by А.Н. Пыпинъ, *Ложныя и отреченныя книги русской старины* (Памятники старинной русской литературы 3), С.-Петербургъ, 1862, p. 10.

Brief Chronographic Palœa (15th c.) likewise incorporates this tradition into his account of Adam's life, saying that after his expulsion from Paradise the patriarch settled on the island 'Aphrurea' and that after his death the angels took his body to Jerusalem.[55] It is possible that this or a similar tradition was known to the fourteenth-century archbishop of Novgorod Basil Kalika (s. 1330–1352), who in his *Letter on Paradise* to the Bishop of Tver' Fedor refers to the transfer of Adam's body from the place of its burial to Jerusalem by the angels.[56]

Until recently, the 'island of Aphoulia' as the place of Adam's exile and death was known only to the students of Slavonic literature. Since in some of these compositions, such as *Letopisec Ellinskij i Rimskij*, this tradition is introduced as an excerpt from the 'Chronography of John,' scholars would debate whether this attribution should be taken as referring to one of two Greek historiographers of Late Antiquity, John Malalas or John of Antioch.[57] While it remains to be demonstrated that this attribution is not a secondary development, but reflects a line of transmission independent of the *Scaliger Paterikon*, the whole discussion is complicated further by the fact that neither the Greek or Slavonic versions of Malalas's *Chronicle* nor the surviving fragments of the *Chronicle* of John of Antioch contain this tradition.

In what concerns a possible etymology and origins of the toponym 'Athoulis / Aphoulia,' no satisfactory solution has been offered so far.[58] The most promising line of inquiry seems to be found in the suggestion made a long time ago by Ivan Porfiryev that it is related somehow to 'Thule' (Θούλη) of the Classical geographical tradition, the semi-legendary island situated at the north-western extremity of the known world.[59] While absent from the Slavonic sources, the

---

55 For the Slavonic text, see Е.Г. Водолазкин, 'Краткая Хронографическая Палея (текст). Выпуск 1', *Труды Отдела древнерусской литературы* 57 (2006), pp. 891–915, here 895–896.

56 As argued by М.И. Соколовъ, *Матеріалы и замѣтки по старинной славянской литературѣ. Выпускъ 1*, Москва, 1888, p. 162. For the Slavonic text and Russian translation of the *Letter*, see Д.С. Лихачев et al. (eds), *Библиотека литературы Древней Руси. Том 6: XIV–середина XV века*, С.-Петербургъ, 1999, pp. 46–47.

57 See C.E. Gleye, 'Zum slavischen Malalas', *Archiv für slavische Philologie* 16 (1894), pp. 578–591, here 588–589; О.В. Творогов, *Древнерусские хронографы*, Ленинград, 1975, pp. 130–132.

58 For some considerations, see H. Trunte, 'Doctrina Christiana: Untersuchungen zu Komposition und Quellen der sogenannten "Rede des Philosophen" in der Altrussischen Chronik', in G. Birkfellner (ed.), *Millennium Russiæ Christianæ: Tausend Jahre Christliches Rußland, 988–1988* (Schriften des Komitees der Bundesrepublik Deutschland zur Förderung der Slawischen Studien 16), Köln, 1993, pp. 355–394, here 380–381.

59 И.Я. Порфирьевъ, *Апокрифическія сказанія о ветхозавѣтныхъ лицахъ и событіяхъ*, Казань, 1872, p. 107, n. 3. On Thule, see V.H. de P. Cassidy, 'The Voyage of an Island', *Speci-*

location of Athoulis in the North in the *Chronicle* of Peter of Alexandria adds more weight to this hypothesis.

While the Greek background of this tradition in Slavonic sources is now beyond doubt, its ultimate origins, however, remain unclear. So far, Peter's *Chronicle* stands out as a unique witness for it in the Byzantine literature. What complicates attempts to reconstruct the genesis of this tradition even more is the fact that the toponym Ἀθουλις itself is not attested in any other Greek source from antiquity or the Middle Ages. It seems rather unlikely, however, that this explanation of the transfer of Adam's body was invented by the author of the *Chronicle* himself. Only a more comprehensive investigation into the sources used by Peter of Alexandria, combined with a fresh look at the tradition of Christian reception of the Greco-Roman mythological notion of islands, such as the island of Thule or the Islands of the Blessed,[60] as a liminal space between this and the other world, could throw additional light on this parabiblical tradition.

5 Adam's Body Brought during the Time of King Solomon

A remarkable explanation of the transfer of Adam's body to Jerusalem, that situates it in the reign of King Solomon, comes from the Slavonic *Tale on the Tree of the Cross*, a composition, transmitted under the name of Gregory the Theologian, the famous Cappadocian Father of the fourth century, that relates the story of the origins and subsequent vicissitudes of the wood of the crosses of Jesus and the two thieves.[61]

The attribution of the *Tale* to Gregory of Nazianzus is without any doubt fictitious. So far, no textual witnesses of the *Tale* in any language other than Slavonic have been discovered. However, some scholars, inspired by the fact that several parabiblical narrative units incorporated into the *Tale* have close parallels in Byzantine sources, regard either the composition as a whole, or some of

---

 lum 38:4 (1963), pp. 595–602; M. Mund-Dopchie, *Ultima Thulé: histoire d'un lieu et genèse d'un mythe* (Histoire des idées et critique littéraire 449), Genève, 2009.

60 On the appropriation of the latter tradition by Christians, see J.-C. Haelewyck, 'Narratio Zosimi de Vita Beatorum (CAVT 166). Une relecture du mythe de l'île des Bienheureux', in C. Cannuyer (ed.), *L'île, regards orientaux: varia orientalia, biblica et antiqua. Hans Hauben in honorem* (Acta Orientalia Belgica 26), Lille, 2013, pp. 135–147.

61 For the Slavonic text, English translation and commentary, see Kulik and Minov, *Biblical Pseudepigrapha*, pp. 104–168. For additional text-critical observations, see A.L. Miltenova, *South Slavonic Apocryphal Collections*, Sofia, 2018, pp. 149–172.

its individual parts, as having been translated into Slavonic from Greek.[62] The *Tale* enjoyed a considerable popularity among the Slavs and is attested in no less than 44 manuscripts, the earliest of which are dated by the second half of the fourteenth century. In light of that and the fact that many parabiblical traditions that are incorporated into this work are not attested earlier than the twelfth century, the time span from the late twelfth to the early fourteenth century seems to be the most probable period of the *Tale*'s composition.

Scholars who researched the manuscript tradition of the *Tale* usually divide all textual witnesses of this work into three main recensions. The narrative of the *Tale* is structured around the history of the three trees from which the three crosses of the canonical Passion account were made, that is the cross of Jesus and those of the two thieves crucified next to him. The whole composition can be divided into two large parts. In the first one, the author offers separate accounts of the origins of each of the three trees, while in the second part he demonstrates how they were brought together in Jerusalem. The work is built from separate narrative blocks, which could have circulated independently of one another. This suggestion is supported by the rather loose connection between these textual units, and by the fact that some of them are introduced with specific (and diverse) titles such as 'testimony', 'question', or 'narration'. The view of the composite origins of the *Tale* has been pursued by several scholars. It should be stressed, however, that, so far, no exact textual prototypes of any of the separate narrative units that comprise the *Tale* have been discovered. While it is certain that the author of the *Tale* relied on earlier parabiblical traditions, it might be that he reworked them in an extensive and idiosyncratic fashion in order to adapt them to his peculiar narrative and theological agendas.

Returning to the main subject of our inquiry, all three recensions of the *Tale* contain an account of the discovery by King Solomon of the tree planted by Seth.[63] After his failure to utilize two other miraculous trees for his project of building the Temple in Jerusalem, the king questions his demon servants whether an appropriate tree could be found anywhere. Having learned from them that such a tree grows in Eden, the king orders the demons to fetch it for him. When they bring the tree to Jerusalem, the king tries to use it for building the Temple but again without much success, because like the two other trees, it changes its size. Consequently, it is discarded and deposited alongside those two trees.

---

62   Cf. Miltenova, *South Slavonic*, p. 151.

63   Ed. Kulik and Minov, *Biblical Pseudepigrapha*, pp. 120–122 [Slav.], 132–135 [trans.].

The story continues by pointing out that when the demons pulled out the tree planted by Seth at his father's grave, the skull of Adam got entangled in its roots; and in this way it, too, was brought to Palestine. There the skull lies unnoticed until one day when Solomon goes out hunting. The king and his retinue are caught in a storm; one of his servants, however, finds a shelter from the bad weather in a cave that is made not of stone, but of bone. When he informs Solomon about his discovery, the king orders that the place be cleaned, and recognizes instantly that this is the skull of Adam. Solomon then brings the skull to Jerusalem, where he displays it for a public act of stoning, on account of the transgression of God's commandment by Adam. The place, where Adam's skull was covered by stones, was subsequently called Lithostrotos.

Considered as a whole, this parabiblical account of the transfer of Adam's skull to Jerusalem is attested only in Slavonic literary tradition and, so far, has no obvious antecedents. In our recent commentary on the *Tale*, Alexander Kulik and I have pointed out parallels to some of the constituent elements of this story.[64] Most significant among them was, perhaps, a passage from the *synaxarion* reading for Good Friday, composed by Nicephoros Kallistos Xanthopoulos (ob. ca. 1335), that was incorporated into the Byzantine Lenten *Triodion*.[65] According to this testimony, the skull of Adam reached Jerusalem after it jumped out of the earth during the flood. Out of respect for the forefather, King Solomon, assisted by his troops, had it covered with 'many stones' (πολλαῖς πέτραις) at the place that would become known as Lithostrotos.[66] Similarity of this tradition to some details of the narrative about Solomon and Adam's skull in the *Tale* enables us to step outside the domain of Slavonic literature and to look for its origins in the Byzantine milieu. Recently, several additional parallels that lend support to this hypothesis have come to my attention.

One of them comes from the so-called *Chronicle of Ernoul and Bernard the Treasurer*, a historiographic work written in Old French around the year 1231, that covers the period from the First Crusade to 1229.[67] In chapter 17, the *Chron-*

---

64   Kulik and Minov, *Biblical Pseudepigrapha*, pp. 161–163.

65   On Nicephoros, see D. Stiernon, 'Nicéphore Kallistos Xanthopoulos', in *Dictionnaire de spiritualité ascétique et mystique. Tome 11*, Paris, 1982, cols. 203–208; on his *Synaxarion*, see also P.E. Yevics, *Lazarus Saturday in the Byzantine Tradition: An Example of Structural Analysis of the Byzantine Triodion* (PhD diss.), Drew University, 1997, pp. 205–208.

66   Ed. Μ. Κιγάλας, *Νικηφόρου Καλλίστου τοῦ Ξαντοπούλλου Συναξάρια εἰς τὰς ἐπισήμους ἑορτὰς τοῦ Τριῳδίου καὶ τοῦ Πεντηκοσταρίου*, Βενετίαις, 1650, p. 57; for a somewhat different version of this *synaxarion*, included into the printed text of *Triodion*, see Ι. Βελούδης and Σ. Βελούδος, *Τριώδιον κατανυκτικόν, περιέχον ἅπασαν την ανήκουσαν αυτώ ακολουθίαν της Αγίας και Μεγάλης Τεσσαρακοστής*, 2nd edn, Ενετίησιν, 1856, p. 381.

67   For the text, see L. de Mas Latrie, *Chronique d'Ernoul et de Bernard le Trésorier publiée pour*

172   MINOV

icle provides an extended description of Jerusalem, including various churches and holy places found in the city. In his description of the Georgian monastery of the Holy Cross, the chronicler offers a following account of the origins of this relic and its journey to Jerusalem:

> It came about that when Adam lay on his death bed he begged one of his sons, for God's sake, to bring him a frond (*rainsiel*) from the tree of whose fruit he had eaten when he sinned. It was brought to him and he took it and put it in his mouth. When he had the frond in his mouth he clenched his teeth and the spirit left him; and because it was not possible to pull the frond from between his teeth, he was buried with it. That frond, so they say, grew and became a fine tree. And when it came about that there was the Flood, the tree was uprooted and the Flood carried it to Mount Lebanon; and from there it was taken to Jerusalem with the timber of which the Temple was built, which was cut on Mount Lebanon. And it came about, so they say, that when Jesus Christ was crucified, the head of Adam was inside the Wood (*li teste Adan estoit dedens le boise*); and when the blood of Jesus Christ flowed from his wounds, the head of Adam came out of the Cross and received the blood. Thus it is still the case that in all the crucifixes made in the land of Jerusalem at the base of the Cross there is a head in memory of that.[68]

According to the *Chronicle*, then, after Adam died, he was buried with the branch from the Tree of Knowledge in his mouth. This branch grew into a tree that enclosed the patriarch's head inside its trunk. During the flood this tree was uprooted and carried to Mount Lebanon. From there it was taken to Jerusalem during the reign of Solomon, to be used for the building of the Temple. Finally, this tree with the head of Adam still enclosed in it was used to make the cross

---

       la première fois, d'après les manuscrits de Bruxelles, de Paris et de Berne, Paris, 1871. On the work itself, see M.R. Morgan, *The Chronicle of Ernoul and the Continuations of William of Tyre* (Oxford Historical Monographs), New York, 1973.

68   Ed. De Mas Latrie, *Chronique d'Ernoul*, pp. 204–205; the English translation is by D. Pringle, *Pilgrimage to Jerusalem and the Holy Land, 1187–1291* (Crusade Texts in Translation), Aldershot, 2012, p. 160. The same description of Jerusalem, including the passage about the wood of the Cross, appears also in the Old French *Continuations of William of Tyre*, another historiographical work from the thirteenth century, whose author used the *Chronicle of Ernoul*; for the text, see H. Michelant and G. Raynaud, *Itinéraires à Jérusalem et descriptions de la Terre Sainte rédigés en français aux XIᵉ, XIIᵉ & XIIIᵉ siècles* (Publications de la Société de l'Orient latin, Série géographique 3), Genève, 1882, pp. 158–159.

of Jesus. During the crucifixion, Adam's head came out of the wood and was baptized by the blood of Christ.

There are several significant points of agreement between the account of the transfer of the head of Adam in the *Chronicle* and in Pseudo-Gregory's *Tale*. Most importantly, at the core of both narratives stands the shared motif of Adam's head being brought to Jerusalem, while enclosed within a tree, during the construction of the Temple by Solomon. There are, however, enough differences between the two accounts that prevent us from claiming any direct literary connection between them. Following these observations, I would suggest tentatively that both these stories must be somehow related to an earlier Greek account of the transfer of Adam's head to Golgotha from Lebanon in a tree, used for the building of the Temple, that was in circulation in Palestine during the time of Crusades, that is during the twelfth century. At this point, it is difficult to say which of the two versions is closer to this apparently lost local parabiblical narrative. I hope that further research into the middle Byzantine writings dealing with the Wood of the Cross will shed more light on this issue.

The hypothesis of the Middle Eastern origins of the account found in Pseudo-Gregory's *Tale* receives additional support from another noteworthy parallel to the episode when Solomon goes to hunt and discovers the cave that turns out to be Adam's skull. It is found in the Arabic *Story of the Skull and the King*, an anonymous didactic novella with a complicated plot that retells and elaborates considerably the biblical story of Susanna.[69] Not much is known about the time and milieu of composition of the *Story*. Fabrizio Pennacchietti, who edited its Arabic text for the first time on the basis of the only manuscript, Gotha A 2756, dates it to the period before the middle of the ninth century, although, as he acknowledges himself, this date is only approximate.[70]

The first part of the *Story*, which culminates in the birth of Susanna, is of particular interest for my argument.[71] It starts with the account of how an unnamed 'king of Israelites' (ملك من ملوك بني اسرآيل), the future grandfather of Susanna, embarks one day on a hunting expedition. At some point, the king splits off from his entourage, pursuing a beautiful white gazelle. The chase leads him to a mountain with a cave. When he enters the cave, the king finds there a 'huge weatherworn skull' (جمجمة عظيمة نخرة). After pondering about the iden-

---

69   Published originally in F.A. Pennacchietti, *Susanna nel deserto: riflessi di un racconto biblico nella cultura arabo-islamica*, Torino, 1998. I rely on the English version of this monograph, F.A. Pennacchietti, *Three Mirrors for Two Biblical Ladies: Susanna and the Queen of Sheba in the Eyes of Jews, Christians, and Muslims*, Piscataway, 2006.

70   Id., *Three Mirrors*, p. 74.

71   Id., *Three Mirrors*, pp. 121–133 [Arab.], 28–33 [trans.].

tity of the owner of the skull, and ending by doubting the power of God to resurrect it in the future, the king takes the skull with him and brings it back to his palace. He entrusts it to the gardener, who buries the skull in the royal garden. To teach the king a lesson, God performs a miracle. After some time, a 'great tree' (شجرة عظيمة) grows up on the spot where the skull was buried. It bears fruits that are not only delicious, but have the power of rejuvenating or healing those men who eat them. The most striking miracle, however, happens when the king's daughter gets miraculously pregnant after eating a fruit from the tree. It is from this pregnancy that Susanna is born in due time. Looking for an explanation for the miraculous power of the tree, the king questions the gardener regarding the whereabouts of the skull. After the gardener digs a hole next to the tree and discovers there the buried skull 'with the roots of the tree adhering to the centre of its crown' (والشجرة في وسط يافوخ الجمجمة), the king realizes what happened and acknowledges God's omnipotence.

There are two narrative elements in the *Story of the Skull* that draw our attention in connection with the account of King Solomon in Pseudo-Gregory's *Tale*. First of all, the hunting episode, during which the Israelite king discovers the cave with a giant skull inside, constitutes a close parallel to the discovery of Adam's skull by Solomon in the *Tale*. In addition to that, the description of the miraculous tree with the skull enclosed in its roots in the *Story* resembles the episode in the *Tale*, where Adam's skull is entangled in the roots of the miraculous tree planted by Seth at his father's grave.

As in the case of Ernoul's *Chronicle*, the differences between the two narratives are significant enough to rule out a possibility of a direct literary dependence of the *Tale*'s compiler upon the Arabic *Story* or vice versa. However, the presence in these two works of the shared motifs cannot be easily ignored, and the channel through which these parabiblical traditions reached the Slavonic *Tale*, or, what is more probable, the Greek original behind it, is in need of explanation. I believe that the solution to the problem of origins of parabiblical material related to Adam's skull in the *Tale* should be sought in the multi-confessional milieu of Palestine during the eleventh–twelfth centuries, which were characterized by cultural exchange and mediation between the local Christians, Greek or Arabic-speaking, their Muslim neighbours, and their Frankish rulers.

TRANSLATIO CORPORIS ADÆ

6 Adam's Body Brought by the Waters of Jordan during the Lifetime of Jesus

Slavonic literature bears witness to another ingenious scenario of the transfer of Adam's body, according to which it was brought to Jerusalem by the waters of Jordan during the lifetime of Jesus. This tradition is found in the *Tale of the Tree of the Cross*,[72] an original Slavonic composition, whose authorship in some manuscripts is ascribed to the Bulgarian priest Jeremiah who was active during the second half of the tenth century.[73] The *Tale* is a compilative work that brings together various exegetical and parabiblical traditions about the origins and transmission of the wood from which the cross of Jesus was made, as well as several extracanonical stories about Jesus himself.[74]

One of the parabiblical accounts included in this compendium, which is of immediate interest to us, appears in chapter 10, according to Sokolov's edition.[75] This chapter, dealing with the subject of Adam's head, opens by narrating that, when Jesus was ten years old, he discovered the head of Adam at the river Jordan, during a walk with his friends. He pronounced it to be his handiwork and inscribed the phrase 'Adam and the head of Adam' on it with his finger. In the following explanation of how Adam's head happened to be at this location, it is related that after his death Adam's body was buried in a tomb in front of Paradise. After his birth, Jesus commanded the river of Jordan to overflow and to carry the body of Adam out to the four corners of the earth in an act of symbolic baptism. It was then that the head of Adam is said to

---

72   Not to be confused with the Pseudo-Gregory's *Tale of the Tree of the Cross*, discussed in the previous section.

73   The oldest textual witnesses of the *Tale*, such as the *Dragolov sbornik*, go back to the thirteenth century. For its Slavonic text, see V. Jagić, 'Prilozi k historiji književnosti naroda hrvatskoga i srbskoga', *Arkiv za povjestnicu jugoslavensku* 9 (1868), pp. 65–151, here 92–104; id., 'Opisi i izvodi iz nekoliko južnoslovinskih rukopisa. VII. Novi prilozi za literaturu biblijskih apokrifa', *Starine* 5 (1873), pp. 69–108, here 83–95; А.Н. Поповъ, *Первое прибавленіе къ описанію рукописей и каталогу книгъ церковной печати библіотеки А.И. Хлудова*, Москва, 1875, pp. 31–44; Соколовъ, *Матеріалы и замѣтки*, pp. 84–107; for an English translation, see K. Petkov, *The Voices of Medieval Bulgaria, Seventh-Fifteenth Century: The Records of a Bygone Culture* (East Central and Eastern Europe in the Middle Ages, 450–1450 5), Leiden, 2008, pp. 118–131. For a summary of scholarship on Jeremiah, see А.А. Турилов, 'Иеремия', in С.Л. Кравец (ed.), *Православная энциклопедия. Том 21*, Москва, 2009, pp. 288–290.

74   Some of these traditions were analyzed in the discussion of the *Tale*'s sources in Соколовъ, *Матеріалы и замѣтки*, pp. 143–211.

75   Ed. Соколовъ, *Матеріалы и замѣтки*, pp. 95–96; English trans. Petkov, *Voices of Medieval Bulgaria*, pp. 124–125.

have been brought to Jerusalem by the waters of Jordan. Described as gigantic, 'as big as a place for thirty[76] men to sit inside,' the head drew the attention of the local population who gathered to see the marvel. Then, it became a cause of a quarrel between two local princes (or kings), 'Mardarius' and 'Touras'.[77] While the former argued that the head should be reburied, the latter wanted to keep it in his house. After he gained an upper hand in the quarrel, Touras brought the head to his house and placed it by the gate, wishing to be buried in it after his death. However, Jesus intervened and ordered for the head to be taken out of the town and buried at the place of Calvary, where it was eventually baptized by his blood during the crucifixion. In a somewhat puzzling chronological remark that follows, it is said that the burial of Adam's head took place after sixty years.

In Sokolov's opinion, there is a discrepancy between the opening claim about the discovery of Adam's head at Jordan by the ten-year old Jesus and the following statement that it was brought by Jordan soon after Jesus was born.[78] According to him, the latter should be regarded as not belonging to the core of the legend and was, probably, added by the compiler of the *Tale*, in order to explain how Adam's head was transferred from the original place of its burial, near Paradise, to the banks of Jordan.

The version of the transfer of Adam's head to Jerusalem presented in Jeremiah's *Tale* stands out as unique. So far, I have not been able to identify any close parallels to this account in Byzantine or any other Christian tradition that might shed light on its original milieu and literary genesis. It may be pointed out that the image of the gigantic skull of Adam appears also in the story about the discovery of Adam's head by King Solomon during his hunting expedition, incorporated into Pseudo-Gregory's *Tale of the Tree of the Cross*. However, since the two parabiblical accounts differ very much in their details, it is hardly possible to speak about any form of direct intertextual connection between them.

It is to be regretted that not much research on Jeremiah's *Tale* has been done since 1888 when Sokolov published his edition of its text, accompanied by what so far constitutes the most comprehensive historical and source-critical discussion of the work.[79] While Sokolov pointed out several instances of the *Tale*'s

---

76   In some manuscripts: 'three hundred'.

77   Their names vary considerably in the manuscripts.

78   Ed. Соколовъ, *Матеріалы и замѣтки*, p. 165.

79   The fundamental monograph on Jeremiah written by Peyo Dimitrov (П. Димитров, *Презвитер Йеремия* [София: Св. Климент Охридски]) that was announced in the nineties by the publishing house of Sofia University seems to be still unpublished. Some of Dimitrov's views are reflected in Д. Димитрова-Маринова, 'Повест за кръстното дърво на презви-

TRANSLATIO CORPORIS ADÆ

compiler's reliance upon Byzantine Greek sources, one should not exclude a possibility that some of the parabiblical traditions used by him might have developed already on Slavonic soil. One hopes that producing a new critical edition of the *Tale*, accompanied by an in-depth and wide-ranging investigation into the sources used by its author, will provide a satisfying answer to the question of the genesis of the parabiblical narrative about Adam's head in the *Tale*, which at the moment poses more questions than can be answered.

Conclusion

By presenting the diverse array of literary sources dealing with the journey of Adam's remains to Golgotha, I hoped to offer an initial overview of this little-studied cluster of parabiblical traditions, as well as to shed light on some channels of intercultural transmission and driving forces that conditioned parabiblical creativity among different Christian cultures during Late Antiquity and the Middle Ages.

Speaking generally, this cluster of traditions can be understood as a result of a 'chain reaction,' when invention of one parabiblical tradition—in our case, one about the burial of Adam's body on Golgotha that emerged during the second or third century—, creates conditions for, and triggers further proliferation of, parabiblical material.

One should also take into consideration that at a certain point more than one explanation of the arrival of Adam's body at Golgotha might be in circulation within a given Christian literary tradition. Some of the discussed sources clearly reflect a situation where Christian authors tried to harmonize such different scenarios. Thus, the case of the Syriac question-and-answer by Jacob (of Edessa), analysed in Section 1, can serve as a good example of a Christian writer trying to reconcile two hardly compatible traditions: an earlier view that Adam lived and died in Judæa, and a later inner-Syriac development according to which it was brought to Jerusalem by Noah and Shem. The same hermeneutical strategy seems to be at work in the Irish sources, mentioned in Section 2, whose authors try to harmonize Jerome's claim that Adam was buried in Hebron with the Eastern Christian tradition of Golgotha as his burial site.

There is, of course, much more to this body of parabiblical narratives. Due to the constraints of the format, I cannot discuss all aspects of these traditions in

---

тер Йеремия в системата на старобългарската апокрифна литература и фолклора', in T. Тотев (ed.), *Медиевистични изследвания в памет на Пейо Димитров. IV младежка медиевистична конференция, Шумен, 1–3 декеври 1994 г.*, Шумен, 1996, 37–43.

detail, limiting myself to pointing out some avenues for future research. Thus, it may be productive to look at the proliferation of this material as a part of the development of a coherent and non-contradictory picture of the history of salvation that would bring together accounts of the Old and New Testaments undertaken by Christian theologians. In connection with that, it is also worthwhile to ponder to what extent, if at all, creation of these traditions was meant to facilitate popularization of complex theological ideas, such as Adam–Christ typology in our case, by making them more comprehensible to the wider circles of Christian believers. One can think about these stories as an attempt to move away from such intellectually demanding ways of conveying the theological message of the unity of the Old and New Testaments as typology and allegory, to more popular and easily digestible modes, involving emplotment and narrativization.

Finally, a more technical but still important point that emerged during our investigation is the importance of Slavonic literature as a repository of lost Greek parabiblical traditions. This significance is well demonstrated by such cases as the account of the transfer of Adam's body from the island of Athoulis in Section 4, and the story of the journey of Adam's skull to Jerusalem during the reign of Solomon in Section 5. The rich corpus of extracanonical and parabiblical writings preserved in Slavonic is, thus, in need of further systematic investigation, especially by scholars well-versed in the literary tradition of Byzantine Christianity.

CHAPTER 9

Apostles, Long Dead 'Heretics', and Monks: Noncanonical Traditions on Angels and Protoplasts in Two Late Antique Coptic Apocalypses (7th–8th Century CE)

Daniele Tripaldi

1   Introduction

By the time the two texts I am going to discuss were composed, Egypt had had a long history and enjoyed an uninterrupted reputation as the quintessential land of *theosebeia*, acquaintance with the divine, and mystery, things and writings *apokrypha* (cf. respectively Herodotus 2,37; Porphyrius, *Abst.* 4,9; Jamblichus, *Myst.* 6,7). This proves to be no less true for Coptic Egypt in some sense: in what follows I intend to put under focus two late Antique Coptic apocalypses dealing in one way or another with piety and godly behavior, knowledge of hidden things, and 'secret' books or traditions: namely *The Mysteries of John, Apostle and Virgin* (= MystJ; *clavis coptica* 0041) and *The Investiture of Abbaton* (= Abbat; *clavis coptica* 0405). As a matter of fact, as we will see, the production of these writings amounted to a massive and sometimes clumsy interweaving of Biblical, early Jewish and early Christian 'apocryphal' or 'heretical' traditions aimed at fitting them into a single narrative to be read, multiplied and divulged for salvation's sake and for more concrete devotional needs.

First I will introduce the texts under scrutiny and search for the literary traces that they themselves as literary artifacts bear of their own production environment. Then, I will make the attempt to highlight the 'apocryphal' traditions on angels and primeval human beings that both writings evidently rework into their own texture. The main questions of the sources and the Christological and soteriological agenda will be addressed. Lastly, I will gather the evidence in its entirety and draw some conclusions on the polemical stances and ideological strategies at stake in the redaction of such writings.

© DANIELE TRIPALDI, 2021 | DOI:10.1163/9789004445925_011

2 The Horizontal Axis: A Quick Look at a Coptic Monastic Library and Its Siblings

Abbat is transmitted only in Sahidic by BL Or. 7025 (981 CE) and attributed to Timothy of Alexandria;[1] MystJ is witnessed in Sahidic by BL Or. 7026 (1006 CE), which also transmits the *Life of Pisenthius*, as well as in Bohairic by a tiny parchment fragment from the Monastery of St Macarius in Wadi el-Natrun (Cairo, Inv. No. 47), corresponding approximately to BL Or. 7026 Fol. 15a–16a.[2] Both codices were copied in Esna and then donated to the Monastery of St Mercurius at Edfu.[3] As to the date of the two works, the former may be dated in its present

---

1 Coptic text and English translation in E.A.W. Wallis Budge, *Coptic Martyrdoms etc. in the Dialect of Upper Egypt* vol. 1, London, 1914, pp. 225–249 (text) and 474–496 (translation). New English translation and elaborated introduction in A. Suciu (with I. Saweros), 'The Investiture of Abbaton, the Angel of Death. A New Translation and Introduction', in T. Burke and B. Landau (eds), *New Testament Apocrypha. More Noncanonical Scriptures* vol. 1, Grand Rapids, 2016, pp. 534–554 (*Appendix: Kitāb al-īḍāḥ* 9 at 546–554). Dutch translation: P. Oussoren and R. Dekker, *Buiten de vesting. Een woord-voor-woord vertaling van alle deuterocanonieke en vele apocriefe bijbelboeken*, Vught, 2008, pp. 461–472. Italian translation: M. Erbetta, *Gli apocrifi del Nuovo Testamento* vol. 3, Turin, 1981, pp. 472–481. L. Moraldi, *Apocrifi del Nuovo Testamento* vol. 3, Turin, 1994, pp. 427–430, offers just a summary of the work. In quoting from this writing and the excerpt from the *Kitāb al-īḍāḥ* criticizing it I follow the numbering system devised by Suciu and Saweros for their English translations. My own English translation of the passage from the *Investiture of Abbaton* referred to in this article (par. 3.1) is to be found in the *Appendix*.

2 Coptic text and translation in E.A.W. Wallis Budge, *Coptic Apocrypha in the Dialect of Upper Egypt*, London, 1913, pp. 59–74 (text) and 241–257 (translation). The Bohairic fragment was published by H.G. Evelyn White, *The Monasteries of the Wadi 'N Natrûn* 1: *New Coptic Texts from the Monastery of Saint Macarius*, New York, 1926, p. 51. Budge's translation was reprinted in J.M. Court, *The Book of Revelation and the Johannine Apocalyptic Tradition*, Sheffield, 2000, pp. 132–163. A. Alcock published online a more recent, original English translation (https:// alinsuciu.com/2013/09/16/guest-post-anthony-alcok-the-mysteries-of-john-the-evangelist/; last access: 08/13/2018), which last year was followed by H. Lundhaug and L. Abercrombie, 'The Mysteries of John. An Introduction and Translation', in T. Burke and B. Landau (eds), *New Testament Apocrypha. More Noncanonical Scriptures*, vol. 2, Grand Rapids, 2020, pp. 481–498. I would like to thank Hugo Lundhaug and Lloyd Abercrombie for sending me a pre-publication copy of their translation. An Italian translation can be found in Erbetta, *Gli apocrifi*, pp. 417–424. Russian translation: E.B. Smagina, 'Мистерии Иоанна, Апостола И Святого Девственника [The Mysteries of John, The Apostle and Holy Virgin]', Вестник ПСТГУ III: Филология 2015. Вып. 5 [St Tikhon's University Review, Series 3, Volume 5] (45), pp. 97–110. In quoting from this work, I follow the numbering system which I myself devised for the publication in AcA III. My own English translations of the passages from the *Mysteries of John* referred to in this article (parr. 3.2 and 3.3) are to be found in the *Appendix*.

3 See B. Layton, *Catalogue of Coptic Literary Manuscripts in the British Library Acquired since the Year 1906*, London, 1987, pp. 135–136 and 190–192 (nos 121 and 160).

form to the 8th century CE, the text itself without its new title possibly being a century earlier; the latter was probably written in the 6th–7th century—even if a date as late as the end of the 7th century or the beginnings of the 8th cannot be ruled out, as Tito Orlandi suggests in the Corpus dei Manoscritti Copti Letterari (CMCL).[4]

The library of the Edfu monastery preserved the following codices at least, all datable between 974 and 1053/56 CE:[5]

– Pierpont Morgan MS M633: *Martyrdom of the Seven Sleepers of Ephesus*; *Life of St. Phif the Anchorite*
– BL Add. 37534: Greek *Life and Miracles of Saints Cosmas and Damianus*; Greek hymn to the archangel Michael
– BL Or. 6781: Theodosius of Alexandria, *On the Archangel Michael*
– BL Or. 6782: *Dormition of John*; title of a lost homily of Gregory of Nazianzus, *On the Archangel Michael*; Epiphanius of Cyprus, *On the Holy Virgin*; Cyril of Alexandria, *On the Holy Virgin*
– BL Or. 6783: *Passion of Eustathius and Theopistus*; *Life of Cyrus the Anchorite*; Flavianus of Antioch, *On Demetrius and Peter of Alexandria*; Ephrem, *Works*; *History of John of the Golden Gospel*
– BL Or. 6784: Cyril of Jerusalem, *On the Holy Virgin*
– BL Or. 6799: Cyril of Jerusalem, *On the Cross*
– BL Or. 6800: Pisenthius of Keft, *Panegyric of Onophrius*
– BL Or. 6801–6802: texts for St Mercurius' Day
– BL Or. 6803: *Apocalypse of John*
– BL Or. 6804: *Apocalypse of Bartholomew*
– BL Or. 6805: old Nubian literary work dealing with the life of Saint Mena
– BL Or. 7021: Theodosius of Alexandria, *On the Archangel Michael*
– BL Or. 7022: texts on St Victor's Day
– BL Or. 7023: John Chrysostom, *On the Archangel Raphael*; *Apocalypse of Paul*

---

4   Unfortunately, we cannot be certain about the chronology of these texts, as they do not have many hints to offer that may help determine their time of composition. As a matter of fact, J.M. Court, *The Book of Revelation*, pp. 132–163, esp. 134–136, goes even so far as to assume an 11th century origin for *The Mysteries of John*; on their part, Lundhaug and Abercrombie, 'The Mysteries of John', point out that any speculation as to its original date of authorship remains tentative. I owe relevant insights into this problem to informal talks with E. Grypeou and J. Dochhorn: my own understanding of the formation of the works under focus has greatly benefited from these conversations.
5   I combine the lists in T. Orlandi, 'Les manuscrits coptes de Dublin, du British Museum et de Vienne', *Le Muséon* 90 (1976), pp. 323–338, esp. 330–331, and Lundhaug and Abercrombie, 'The Mysteries of John', n. 4.

- BL Or. 7024: John Chrysostom, *Encomium of John the Baptist* (also known under the title: *The Glory of the Precursor*); Pachomius, *Catecheses*
- BL Or. 7025: Timothy of Alexandria, *Investiture of Abbaton*
- BL Or. 7026: *The Mysteries of John, Apostle and Virgin*; *The Life of Pisenthius*
- BL Or. 7027: Papnoute, *History of the Monks*; Demetrius of Antioch, *On the Virgin*
- BL Or. 7028 (+ 6780 + Washington Free Gallery MS 2): Celestine of Rome, *Miracles of the Archangel Gabriel*; Theophilus of Alexandria, *On the Holy Virgin*
- BL Or. 7029 (+ f. 21): *History of the Monks of Aswan*; Athanasius of Alexandria, *Catecheses*; Timothy of Alexandria, *On the Archangel Michael*
- BL Or. 7030: Theodore of Antioch, *On the two Theodores*
- BL Or. 7558: different fragments
- BL Or. 7597 (?): *Catechesis of Psote*; homily of Severus of Antioch, *On the Archangel Michael*

How did this and other monastic libraries alike come to burgeon in Islamic Egypt at the threshold of the 2nd millennium (9th–11th century CE)? The pointed words of T. Orlandi on the topic are still probably one of the best introductions to this stage of Coptic literature and book production:

> Almost all this material reflects in the most accurate way the historical period when the use of texts was almost exclusively liturgical [...]. Texts were mostly read during religious gatherings which possibly, but not necessarily climaxed in the Eucharistic ceremony (*synaxeis*); but it should be kept in mind that as we can infer from the evidence at our disposal, such gatherings took the place of any other cultural and perhaps even recreational event for contemporary Christians, inasmuch as— I believe—public events taking place outside the church were increasingly controlled and directed by Islamic authorities. The same authorities however allowed, and in Egypt they even promoted, the great popular feasts in honor of Christian saints. [...] Texts were chosen from the pre-existing material, or redacted as original literary products, so as to integrate each other and form a sort of wide anthology following the liturgical year. At the same time, texts were provided with titles as well as with pertinent beginnings and endings, which could even have nothing to do with the original destination of the work in hand. Texts were then variously grouped and copied on codices, mostly parchment codices, by professional scribes (usually monks), the clients being pious people, who then donated the codices to churches and monasteries. All this information was reported on the last page of the codex in the so-called colophon, together with other annotations or prayers. The codices con-

APOSTLES, LONG DEAD 'HERETICS', AND MONKS

sisted of quires [...] stitched together and bound with at times luxurious covers in worked leather.[6]

2.1   *The Literary Surface*

Let us get back from the libraries to the texts themselves as single works and as a literary genre: both *Investiture of Abbaton* and *Mysteries of John* purport to relate two revelations, or 'apocalypses', received and written down by apostles. With a significant difference: *Investiture of Abbaton* has a homiletic framework, dealing among other things with the 'historical', i.e. legendary, circumstances of the supposed rediscovery in Jerusalem of the hitherto-hidden apostolic document. This document is then quoted in its full length, being a dialogue of the risen Jesus with the twelve. Meanwhile, *Mysteries of John* has no such homiletic equivalent and sets out right from the start as a 3rd–1st person report of John of Zebedee's post-resurrection dialogue with Christ and the heavenly journey and visions following it.

To Alin Suciu and his groundbreaking monograph we owe the actual 'rediscovery' and identification of the apostolic memoir, this literary genre so dear to Coptic authors, be it embedded in a pseudo-patristic sermon or not.[7] Besides

---

6 'Quasi tutto questo materiale rispecchia nel modo più fedele l'epoca in cui l'uso dei testi era quasi totalmente liturgico [...]. Essi erano infatti per lo più letti durante le riunioni religiose culminanti, ma non necessariamente, nella cerimonia eucaristica (*synaxeis*), ma occorre tener conto che queste riunioni, a quanto si può dedurre, tenevano il posto di ogni altra riunione culturale e forse anche ricreativa per i cristiani dell'epoca, anche perché (noi crediamo) le manifestazioni pubbliche che si svolgevano fuori della chiesa erano sempre più controllate e dirette dall'autorità islamica. Essa invece permetteva, ed in Egitto anche favoriva, le grandi feste popolari in onore dei santi cristiani. [...] Perciò i testi vennero scelti dal materiale preesistente, ovvero creati originalmente, in modo da integrarsi l' un l'altro in una specie di grande antologia modellata sullo svolgersi dell'anno liturgico. Contemporaneamente, vennero rivestiti di titoli e di inizi e finali appositi, che potevano anche non aver nulla a che vedere con l'originaria destinazione. I testi venivano trascritti a gruppi di diversa entità su codici, per lo più in pergamena, da scribi di professione (normalmente monaci) a cura di persone pie che ne facevano poi dono a chiese e monasteri: tutto questo veniva segnalato nell'ultima pagina insieme con altre annotazioni o preghiere nel cosiddetto "colofone". I codici erano formati di quaderni [...] cuciti insieme e rilegati con copertine anche lussuose in pelle lavorata' (T. Orlandi, *Omelie Copte*, Turin, 1981, pp. 19–21, esp. 20–21; English translation by me). More on this and the immediately preceding phases of Coptic text and manuscript production— covering approximately the 7th through the 9th century CE—in T. Orlandi, 'The Future of Studies in Coptic Biblical and Ecclesiastical Literature', in R.McL. Wilson (ed.), *The Future of Coptic Studies*, Leiden, 1978, pp. 143–163; id., *Omelie*, 14–17 and 23–24; id., 'Gli apocrifi copti', *Augustinianum* 23 (1983), pp. 57–71, esp. 58–59 and 63–71; P. Buzi, *Titoli e autori nella tradizione copta. Studio storico e tipologico*, Pisa, 2005, pp. 107–126; Ead., *La Chiesa copta. Egitto e Nubia*, Bologna, 2014, pp. 73–79.

7 A. Suciu, *The Berlin-Strasbourg Apocryphon. A Coptic Apostolic Memoir*, Tübingen, 2017,

184   TRIPALDI

the formal and thematic features common to these writings as a genre and acutely studied by Suciu,[8] specific genre 'borders' between apocalypse and homily are frequently crossed and genre 'norms' transgressed by the indiscriminate intermingling of the same rhetorical techniques, literary formulas, and recurring motifs from text to text, be they properly labelled as homilies or apocalypses.

Such redactional devices blur *ipso facto* too-sharp distinctions between these two genres. I offer here a brief sample of passages, just so as to document and highlight their literary and ideological hybridization in Coptic literature.[9]

2.1.1   From Homilies to Apocalypses, from Apocalypses to Homilies

a.   Calling on stage and directly addressing biblical characters: cf. Ps.-Peter of Alexandria, *On Baptism* 4.8–9 (Orlandi, *Omelie*, 30–32); Ps.-Theodosius of Alexandria, *On the Feast of Baptism* 2,1–3.22,1–4 (Orlandi, *Omelie*, 205.230–232); Ps.-Athanasius of Alexandria, *Encomium of the Archangel Michael* 17; Benjamin of Alexandria, *Exegesis on John* 3 (Orlandi, *Omelie*, 269) with *Glory of the Precursor* 13–16;[10]

b.   formulas praising John for being worthy of laying his holy hand(s) on Jesus' head to baptize Him: cf. *Glory of the Precursor* 10,24 and 30 with Ps.-Peter, *On Baptism* 4–6 (Orlandi, *Omelie*, cit., 30–31) and *On the Feast of Baptism* 21,3 (Orlandi, *Omelie*, cit., 230);

c.   reports of ecstatic experiences and revelations occur frequently in homilies: Ps.-Peter of Alexandria, *On Baptism* 27.29–30 (Orlandi, *Omelie*, 269);

---

pp. 5–10, 72, 91–108, 125–127. Similarly, already J.L. Hagen, 'The Diaries of the Apostles: 'Manuscript Find' and 'Manuscript Fiction' in Coptic Homilies and Other Literary Texts', in M. Immerzeel and J. van der Vliet (eds), *Coptic Studies on the Threshold of a New Millennium. Proceedings of the Seventh International Congress of Coptic Studies, Leiden, 27 August–2 September 2000* vol. 1, Leuven, 2004, pp. 349–367.

8   Suciu, *The Berlin-Strasbourg Apocryphon*, pp. 108–120. I still agree with Suciu in including *Mysteries of John* under the label 'apostolic memoirs', as an atypical member of this group (Lundhaug and Abercrombie, 'The Mysteries of John', n. 20).

9   I have collected more examples in the notes to my forthcoming translation.

10   See also *Encomium of John* 1,3 (the homilist comes and stands amidst his public) and *Exegesis on John* 3 (the homilist plays the role of John who has just been called upon and exhorted to come). German translation of the *Glory of the Precursor*: W. Till, 'Johannes der Täufer in der koptischen Literatur', *Mitteilungen des deutschen archäologischen Instituts. Abteilung Kairo* 16 (1958), pp. 310–332, esp. 327–330; French translation: A. Boud'hors, 'Éloge de Jean-Baptiste', in F. Bovon and P. Geoltrain (eds), *Écrits apocryphes chrétiens* vol. 1, Paris, 1997, pp. 1553–1578, esp. 1571–1574; English translation: P.L. Tite, 'An Encomium on John the Baptist. A New Translation and Introduction', in Burke and Landau (eds), *New Testament Apocrypha* vol. 1, pp. 233–246. In quoting from this work I follow the numbering system devised by Tite for his own translation.

Ps.-Athanasius of Alexandria, *On Michael's Day* 33–37 (Orlandi, *Omelie*, 66–67) with par. 37 probably betraying some acquaintance with the *Apocalypse of Paul*; 43–48 (Orlandi, *Omelie*, 60–70);

d. historical surveys, prophecies *ex eventu* and lists of coming woes are embedded in homilies: Ps.-Athanasius of Alexandria, *Exhortations to the Clergy* 31–66 (Orlandi, *Omelie*, 81–91).

2.1.2   Recurring Motifs: The Art of Refrain

a. The Nile flooding, the dew, and the crops: *Mysteries of John* 4.6–7.14; Athanasius of Alexandria, *Exhortations to the Clergy* 58–59.66,153 (Orlandi, *Omelie*, 88. 91); Ps.-Proclus, *On the Twenty-Four Elders* 23,1 (74 Maresca);[11]

b. Michael's prayers and his intercession on behalf of mankind: *Mysteries of John* 4; Ps.-Athanasius of Alexandria, *On the Feast of Michael* 49 (Orlandi, *Omelie*, 70); Ps.-Athanasius of Alexandria, *Exhortations to the Clergy* 66,154 (Orlandi, *Omelie*, 91); Ps.-Proclus, *On the Twenty-Four Elders* 22,7–11 (ibid.);

c. Michael's role in the rise of Nile: *Mysteries of John* ibid.; Ps.-Athanasius of Alexandria, *On the Feast of Michael* 48 (Orlandi, *Omelie*, 70); Ps.-Athanasius of Alexandria, *Exhortations to the Clergy* 66,153 (Orlandi, *Omelie*, 91). Cf. also Ps.-Proclus, *On the Twenty-Four Elders* 23,1 (ibid.);

d. The 'Æons of Light' and their arrangement as object of investigation and vision: *Investiture of Michael* 2 (CSCO 225, 2,10–15); Ps.-Stephen, *Investiture of Gabriel* 2 (CSCO 225, 61,9–2) and *Mysteries of John* 3. Michael as the head and commander of the 'Æons of Light': *Mysteries of John* 3 and Eustathius of Thrace, *Encomium of the Archangel Michael* 2,24 (112 Campagnano);[12]

e. Jesus tearing his own flesh into small pieces as source of the Eucharistic bread: cf. *Mysteries of John* 4,12 with Ps.-Peter of Alexandria, *On Baptism* 21 (Orlandi, *Omelie*, 35);

f. the baptism of John as baptism undergone by the Creator himself: see above 2.1.1. *From Homilies to 'Apocalypses'*, point b;

---

11   Ps.-Proclo di Cizico, *Encomio dei ventiquattro vegliardi*, in A. Campagnano et al. (eds), *Quattro omelie copte. Vita di Giovanni Crisostomo; Encomi dei 24 vegliardi (Ps. Proclo e Anonimo); Encomio di Michele Arcangelo, di Eustazio di Tracia*, Milano, 1978, pp. 45–82.

12   Ps.-Eustazio di Tracia, *Encomio di Michele Arcangelo*, in Campagnano et al. (eds), *Quattro omelie copte*, pp. 105–172.

g. description of the dreadful appearance of Death and his messengers as an appeal to repentance: *Investiture of Abbaton* 4,7 and 9,4–7; Theophilus of Alexandria, *On Repentance* 103–104 (Orlandi, *Omelie*, 70); Benjamin of Alexandria, *Exegesis on John* 44 (Orlandi, *Omelie*, 280).

2.1.3 Switching the Stage: Earth in Heaven, Heaven on Earth

a. Gathering a heavenly and earthly *synaxis*: cf. *Mysteries of John* 1; *Glory of the Precursor* 9,2; 12,1.13–16; 15,1; Ps.-Stephen, *Investiture of Gabriel* 2–3.7.8 (CSCO 225, 61–63; 71,19–24; 77,5–26) with Ps.-Peter of Alexandria, *De Baptismo* 28–29 (Orlandi, *Omelie*, 37); Ps.-Athanasius of Alexandria, *On Michael's Feast* 18 (Orlandi, *Omelie*, 63); Ps.-Athanasius of Alexandria, *Exhortations to the Clergy* 17 (Orlandi, *Omelie*, 77); Eustathius of Thrace, *Encomium of the Archangel Michael* 2,18–24 (112 Campagnano);[13]

b. Dismissing men, angels and their Lord with a peace greeting: cf. *Investiture of Abbaton* 4,1–3[14] and *Glory of the Precursor* 20[15] with Ps.-Athanasius of Alexandria, *Exhortations to the Clergy* 17 (Orlandi, *Omelie*, 77).

2.2 Inside Literature: Exploring the Context

The sample of references sketched here has hopefully shown that Coptic homilies and apocalypses often build on a common patchwork of traditions, formulas, rhetorical techniques and topics, intruding homiletic elements into a purportedly revelatory text or *vice versa* integrating 'apocalyptic' motifs and

---

13 A. Boud'hors ('Éloge', 1572, n. to 138,20–30) has correctly pointed out that literary representations of heavenly gatherings such as we find in the *Glory of the Precursor* must be read against analogous scenes painted in monastic churches, 'où saints et apôtres sont alignés dans un ordre assez strict, de part et d'autre d'un personnage centrale'. On the participation of the whole heavenly world at church gatherings in honor of saints and angels or at eucharistic meals see also Ps.-Eustatius of Thrace, *Encomium of the Archangel Michael* 2–14 and Ps.-Cyril of Alexandria, *Exegesis on the Apocalypse* 10. Both the literary and the pictorial traditions aim to materialize the heavenly liturgy in the middle of earthly cult and to include the monks or the human assembly in the worship service taking place before God as praise-fellows of forefathers and model figures from the past as well as of angelic hosts and *vice versa*: see B. Dümler, 'Bilder in der Wüste: Fragen zu Funktion und Deutungen von *Maiestas*-Darstellungen in ägyptischen Klöstern', in D. Bumazhnov (ed.), *Christliches Ägypten in der spätantiken Zeit*, Tübingen, 2013, pp. 231–259, and D. Frankfurter, *Christianizing Egypt. Syncretism and Local Worlds in Late Antiquity*, Princeton, NJ, 2018, pp. 167–171 and 202–206.

14 This passage results from a combination of Jesus's farewell discourses according to Mk 16,16–18; Mt 28,19–20; Joh 14,12.27; 16,33; 20,19–23.

15 On the peace greeting as Jesus's last words before the disciples set on their mission see EvMar (BG 1) p. 8,11–9,4 and EpAp 51 (AcA I/2 1092,5 Müller). Cf. Ps.-Stephen, *Investiture of Gabriel* 10 and *Encomium of John* 8,4 (words spoken by the archangel Gabriel).

themes into a supposedly patristic homiletic work.[16] We now turn to a brief description of the more or less explicit *Sitz im Leben* of such a complex redactional interplay and literary enterprise.

I have already quoted extensively Tito Orlandi's general assessment of the formation of Coptic libraries in Islamic Egypt. First-hand evidence validating his conclusions specifically as regards the works under scrutiny comes from the texts themselves and their paratexts. On the one hand, we saw that *Glory of the Precursor* and *Investiture of Abbaton* are transmitted by codices copied in Esna and later donated to and stored in the Monastery of St Mercurius in Edfu;[17] on the other hand, both writings do seem to aim among other things at supporting and enhancing the production and dissemination of books to be donated to churches, sanctuaries and monasteries for liturgical use (cf. respectively 16,4 and 2,4; 4,7; 9,8–9).[18] The Coptic colophon of BL Or. 7026 speaks more generically of the manuscript as a donation to the Monastery of St Mercurius, meant for public readings and dedicated to the 'profit' and the 'assurance' of the listeners (BL Or. 7026 Fol. 83a, ll. 2–6). Especially *Mysteries of John* must have proved itself profitable and edifying enough to enjoy some diffusion, since it travelled downstream and was 'translated' into Bohairic as well as being kept in a northern monastery.

---

16 On the form and development of Coptic homilies the reference works are to my knowledge by M. Sheridan: 'A Homily on the Death of the Virgin Mary Attributed to Evodius of Rome', in Immerzel and van der Vliet (eds), *Coptic Studies on the Threshold of a New Millennium* vol. 1, pp. 393–405; 'Rhetorical Structure in Coptic Sermons', in J.E. Goehring and J.A. Timbie (eds), *The World of Early Egyptian Christianity: Language, Literature, and Social Context. Essays in Honor of D.W. Johnson*, Washington, D.C., 2007, pp. 25–48; 'The Encomium in the Coptic Literature of the Late Sixth Century', in P. Buzi and A. Camplani (eds), *Christianity in Egypt: Literary Production and Intellectual Trends. Studies in Honor of T. Orlandi*, Rome, 2011, pp. 443–464.

17 See above and n. 3.

18 See also the Bohairic version of the *History of Joseph the Carpenter* quoted in Suciu, *The Berlin-Strasbourg Apocryphon*, p. 122. For some book donors cf. the colophons of *Investiture of Abbaton* (BL Or. 7025, Fol. 32b), *Mysteries of John* (BL Or. 7026, Fol. 83a), *Investiture of Gabriel*, and *Sermo de cruce et latrone* attributed to Theophilus of Alexandria (M595; *Clavis Coptica* 0395). The Coptic text of this last homily has been edited by A. Suciu, 'Ps.-Theophili Alexandrini *Sermo de Cruce et Latrone* (CPG 2622): Edition of Pierpont Morgan M595 with Parallels and Translation', *Zeitschrift für Antikes Christentum* 16 (2012), pp. 181–225. In Ms. inv. no. provv. 8548, still unpublished and preserved in the Museo Egizio, Turin, a donation by a woman to the *topos* (monastery) of S. John the Baptist in This/Thinis is explicitly mentioned. I owe this reference to Prof. Paola Buzi (La Sapienza—Università di Roma), to whom my sincere thanks go. More generally on private donation to churches and monasteries in Late Antique and Islamic Egypt, see E. Wipszycka, *The Alexandrian Church. People and Institutions*, Warsaw, 2015, pp. 365–376, esp. 370–371.

Furthermore, Suciu collected and discussed more external evidence pointing at the *Sitz im Leben* of the literary genre to which our works belong: the veneration and festival celebration of saints or angels featured in the Coptic apostolic memoirs (e.g. Abbaton; the Four Living Creatures; Pilate) is well attested in Egypt;[19] such cults sometimes ignited polemical debates concerning their legitimacy and the production and use of the related genre as devotional literature in churches and monasteries.[20]

Suciu's inferences draw on his investigation of the available sources and can be summed up here as follows: this growing literary corpus 'was destined to serve liturgical purposes' by tracing 'the origins of some liturgical feasts of the Egyptian church' and catechetical instructions back to apostolic and patristic times, i.e. to the authority of Jesus himself, of His immediate followers and of Church Fathers including revered Alexandrian bishops of the past; as Coptic apostolic memoirs began to be composed (no earlier than the mid-fifth century CE) some church authority must have inspired and coordinated these efforts.[21]

3 The Vertical Axis: A Diachronic Commentary

Having posed and assessed the classical introductory questions (authorship; date and place of composition; literary genre; production and circulation milieu and redactional tendencies), I will now look at which narratives *Investiture of Abbaton* and *Mysteries of John*, as individual texts, deploy: with respect to the first angelic beings and the human protoplasts, and with respect to the secret knowledge Adam and Eve were taught *qua* sacred tradition as an inheritance meant to verse their descendants in such topics as how to make a living after the Fall and the redemption of humanity. I have selected three thematic clusters to investigate in greater detail: the origins of the Angel of Death, also being an etiology of the rule of physical death over all things earthly and human (Text 1 in the Appendix); the creation of Eve as exegetical *vexata quæstio* (Text 2 in the Appendix); the 'invention' of wheat and agriculture as revelation to the starving Adam (Text 3 in the Appendix). Obviously, my selection is arbitrary, as

---

19   Suciu, *The Berlin-Strasbourg Apocryphon*, pp. 126–128.

20   Suciu, *The Berlin-Strasbourg Apocryphon*, pp. 124–125. J. Dochhorn, 'Mythen von der Einsetzung des Erzengels Michael in der koptischen Literatur', in Bumazhnov (ed.), *Christliches Ägypten*, pp. 23–42, focuses more specifically on *Investiture* literature and the debates relating to it.

21   Suciu, *The Berlin-Strasbourg Apocryphon*, pp. 125, 123, 128–138.

APOSTLES, LONG DEAD 'HERETICS', AND MONKS

clusters and test cases relating to traditions on the protoplasts might be multiplied almost at will. Going through each one of them however would exceed the limits of this paper. Therefore, I leave them to the reader's own curiosity and, what is most important, to future scrutiny.

3.1 *The Birth of Death*

Chapters 5,1 to 6,5 in the *Investiture of Abbaton* interweave three narrative threads of primordial events and figures into a coherent plot of the beginnings of the cosmos as we now know it. The three threads are: a) the story of Adam's creation; b) the story of Satan's fall; c) the story of the investiture of Muriel as the angel of Death, Abbaton. Let us unravel the plot and look at each of its constituent threads as a single unit of traditions.

a. *Investiture of Abbaton* 5,3 introduces on stage the prelapsarian Adam as a glorious creature made of virgin, i.e. the purest, earth, which was a common motif in Jewish and Christian literature (e.g. Philo, Op 136–137; Josephus, Ant I 34; Iren., *hær.* III 21,10 and *dem.* 11; Ath. (?), *descr.* BMV; Ephr., *Diatess.* 2,2; Chrys., *hom. 2 mut. nom.* 3 and *nativ.* 2). Such pure clay however refuses to be seized by the first of the angels sent on this mission by God himself and cries out that, by willingly accepting to be formed into a man, it will lend itself to the most abominable crimes and sins which man is going to commit as an earthly being (*Investiture of Abbaton* 5,4–6). Analogous prophecies of impending doom are put on God's lips in *Investiture of Michael* 3 (CSCO 225, 8,9–10 Müller) after the creation of man, but were also well-known in Jewish and Islamic traditions as protest cries on the part of angels or divine hypostases against God's decision to make man: see BerR 8,4–5 (57,10–58,27 Freedman); *Chronicle of Jerahmeel* 6,3–4 (14,30–15,5 Gaster); Al-Tabari, *Chronicæ* 86–87 (I 257,19–258,28 Rosenthal). In *Investiture of Abbaton* they seem to have coalesced with the motif of the earth crying for all the sins committed upon it (cf. Gen 4,10–11; 1 Hen 6,4–6; 8,4; 9,2–3; VisPaul 6; *Corp.Herm.* fr. 23,59–61 [IV, 19,20–20,13 Nock–Festugière]). Similarly, the *Chronicle of Jerahmeel* 6,6 (15,28–31) has the earth refusing to be seized as it foresees the curse placed upon it because of human beings.

Nor is Abbat *traditionsgeschichtlich* isolated in relating that Adam lay inanimate on earth before God's breath was blown into his nostrils (cf. IV Esr 3,4–5; Iren., *hær.* I 24,1; HA NHC II,4 88,4–6). OW 81 NHC II,5 115,10–11 and later Al-Tabari, *Chronicæ* 89–91 even report the same time indication as *Investiture of Abbaton* 5,12: Adam had lain forty days before he was given life. Such timing probably stems from older Jewish *haggadah*: according to Jub 3,9 and VitAd 54 Adam entered Paradise only forty days after he was created. As far as Adam's crowning and enthronement are concerned, it may suffice here to recall the Syriac *Cave of Treasures* 2,17–19. For that matter, rabbinic tradition refers to more than one crown on Adam's head.[22]

Just like the interpolated *Life of Adam and Eve* and *Apocalypse of Moses*, on which it relies, the whole story of Adam's creation, fall and subsequent expulsion from Paradise is interspersed with episodes and details which either have Jesus as main character or allude to Him.[23]

Some of the episodes and the details have exact counterparts in the Christian interpolations in the two aforementioned writings, e.g. the prophecy of Christ's coming, incarnation and passion in the year 5550 since the creation of the world, meant to bring Adam back into Paradise (cf. *Investiture of Abbaton* 8 with VitAd 42–43, where God reveals all this to Seth, who then goes and informs his father living by now outside Eden).[24]

Other interpolated and rewritten sections do not have similar counterparts, and parallels must be sought elsewhere in Coptic literary production: in *Investiture of Abbaton* 5,12–15 Jesus acts as guarantor for Adam and resolves God's doubts and objections about the latter's creation, just as in *Investiture of Michael* 3. This role of His as guarantor is also briefly alluded to in *Mysteries of John* 4,8. The sole pertinent difference between the two texts lies in the fact that *Investiture of Michael* envisages just Adam's conversion leading him to know God, whereas *Investiture of Abbaton* hints at Adam's reintegration into his *archè*, once again following closely, or more probably even reproducing, the text of ApcMos: here in chapter 39 God promises Adam to bring him back to his original prelapsarian condition of rule (*archè*) over the created world by installing him on the throne of the one who had deceived him, that is, Satan / the serpent (on Adam sitting originally on a throne cf. *Investiture of Abbaton* 5,16). The starting point of the 'crisis' forcing Jesus's intervention in both texts—the Father wavers on His decision to make Adam—echoes Jewish traditions about God's hesitations in creating/giving life to man and the resulting debates with angels or divine attributes (see BerR 8,4–5).

---

22 Cf. SEZ 4 (179 Friedmann) and the passage from an unknown *midraš* quoted in L. Ginzberg, *The Legends of the Jews* vol. 5, 8th edn, Philadelphia, 1968, p. 78, n. 21. On the elevation of the newborn Adam, see G.A. Anderson, 'The Exaltation of Adam and the Fall of Satan', in G.A. Anderson et al. (eds), *Literature on Adam and Eve. Collected Essays*, Leiden et al., 2000, pp. 83–110.

23 J. Dochhorn, *Die Apokalypse des Moses*, Tübingen, 2005, pp. 287–288, n. 1. 308–309, n. 5. 310–312, n. 12, has already highlighted the main parallels in detail and outline between the version of the story of Adam's fall transmitted by *Investiture of Abbaton* and ApcMos.

24 See also Syriac *Cave of Treasures* 5,7–9.12–13. M.E. Stone, *The Angelic Predictions in the Primary Adam Books*, in Anderson et al. (eds), *Literature*, pp. 111–131, offers a dense commentary on this pericope in the *Life of Adam and Eve*.

APOSTLES, LONG DEAD 'HERETICS', AND MONKS

In *Investiture of Abbaton* 5,14 God blows thrice into Adam's body. This act should probably be interpreted as a symbolical allusion to Adam's enlivenment by the power of the Holy Trinity. The very same detail is reported in Ps.-Theodosius of Alexandria, *Encomium to John* 4,1–2 and 16,2, whereas *Investiture of Michael* 3 has at least God and Christ breathing into Adam's nostrils (cf. already Iren., *hær.* IV *prol.* 4, IV 20,1 and V 1,3.5,1–6,1.28,4 on the Son and the Spirit as God's hands fashioning man according to Gen 1,26). Notwithstanding the different number of persons of the Holy Trinity involved in the process, this further correspondence between the two *Investitures* should not be ignored or underestimated, as *Investiture of Abbaton* explicitly understands itself as within the *Investiture* genre (cf. 1,4 and 4,7).

b. In its general outline the story of Satan's refusal to worship the newly created Adam and his consequent spoliation and fall to earth matches essentially with the classical versions we have of this myth both in and outside Coptic and Christian tradition. Just to mention a few, VitAd probably being the more or less direct source of the *Investiture*: 4Q381 10–11; VitAd 13–16; ApcSedr 5,1–6; QuæstBarth 4,52–56; *Investiture of Michael* 3; Ps.-Stephen, *Investiture of Gabriel* 9; Syriac *Cave of Treasures* 20,1–23,7; BerRbt 9 (cf. Ramon Martí, *Pugio Fidei* 5,1); Quran 2,34; 7,11–13; 15,26–35; 17,61–63; 18,50; 38,71–78.[25]

Many single details are not without parallels either. Let us briefly review them.

The title *protoplasma* (*Investiture of Abbaton* 6,1) is appended to Satan as early as Tat., *orat.* 7,4–5, and its use is later widespread in Coptic writings (e.g. *Investiture of Michael* 3 and Ps.-Chrysostomus, *Encomium of the Four Living Beings* 7,9).[26] Besides in our text, Satan is also well attested in Coptic tradition as first *archistrategos* of the heavenly army (*Investiture of Michael* 3 and Ps.-Chrysostomus, *Encomium of the Four Living Beings* 7). According to *Investiture of Abbaton* 6,3–4, as a general he holds in his hand a list of the names of the angels under his command: modelled after the enrolment lists in use among human armies,[27] a 'book of the names of the armies' of all saints

---

25 On the history of the myth and tradition of Satan's fall, see J. Dochhorn, 'Der Sturz des Teufels in der Urzeit. Eine traditionsgeschichtliche Skizze zu einem Motiv frühjüdischer und frühchristlicher Theologie mit besonderer Berücksichtigung des Luzifermythos', *Zeitschrift für Theologie und Kirche* 109 (2012), pp. 3–47. More specifically on Ez 28 as 'Biblical source' of this myth in its different versions, see G.A. Anderson, *Ezekiel 28, the Fall of Satan and the Adam Books*, in Anderson et al. (eds), *Literature*, 133–147.

26 Further evidence from Coptic literary tradition in Dochhorn, 'Mythen von der Einsetzung', pp. 36–37.

27 See Josephus, Ant XII 47; Tacitus, Hist II 94,1; Polyæn. 3,3; Gr. Nyss., *v. Mos.* II 147; Lyd., *de magistratibus populi romani* II 11.

and the elect is already mentioned in 1QM XII 2 as being preserved in God's heavenly abode.

In Coptic literature several different angelic beings are held responsible for stripping, bruising and casting Satan the *archistrategos* down to earth.[28] *Investiture of Abbaton* 6,5 has a great Cherub doing the dirty job, as do *Investiture of Michael* 3; Ps.-Stephen, *Investiture of Gabriel* 9; Ps.-Chrysostom, *Encomium to the Four Living Beings* 10,5–6. Yet unparalleled, to my knowledge, is a central detail in the circumstances preceding and leading to the Cherub's intervention: *Investiture of Abbaton* relates that no angel can wrest the enrolment list from Satan's hand as God wanted, so God orders that a sharp knife be brought and the upper and lower part of the document protruding from Satan's fist be cut off (6,2–4). If it is unparalleled in stories of Satan's fall, the motif of wresting written documents from Satan's hand and then tearing them to pieces is still documented in Jewish legends.[29]

c. According to *Investiture of Abbaton* 5,3–12, God sends seven angels to Eden, one after another, to bring Him virgin soil with which to create Adam: all of them fail upon hearing the oath the earth swears in the name of God, foreseeing all the evil and pollution that will come from Adam and his descendants. As cruel and tyrannical as he is, Muriel, the eighth angel, scorns the terrible oath and dares to grab the clay and bring it back to God to fashion and enliven.[30] After Satan's and Adam's fall Muriel will be promoted to ruler over the sons of men and the physical world as the angel of death, and as such, his name will be changed into Abbaton (9,3–6). *Motiv-* and *traditionsgeschichtlich* the story has its counterparts both in Jewish and in Islamic sources: in the former (*Chronicles of Jerahmeel* 6,6) only one angel, Gabriel, dares to make an attempt; in the latter (Al-Tabari, *Chronicæ* 87) three angels, Gabriel, Michael, and the unnamed angel of death are charged one after another with the task to provide God with clay, two of them failing because of fear of the oath, the third succeeding and finally being invested by God as the angel of death.[31] In another Christian text,

---

28 More on this point in J.L. Hagen, ''The Great Cherub' and His Brothers. Adam, Henoch and Michael and the Names, Deeds and Faces of the Creatures in Ps.-Chrysostom, On the Four Creatures', in N. Bosson and A. Boud'hors (eds), *Actes du huitième congrès international d'études coptes, Paris, 28 juin–3 juillet 2004* vol. 2, Leuven, 2007, pp. 467–480.

29 See H. Schwarzbaum, *Studies in Jewish and World Folklore*, Berlin, 1968, esp. pp. 278–279.

30 The tyrannical attitude of (the angel of) Death enabling him to succeed where others have failed can be traced back to TestAbr (L) 15,1.11–15; 16,4; 17,13, where the other who fails is none but Michael. As a whole the anthropogonic myth related in *Encomium of Abbaton* finds a further echo and a re-elaboration in a Coptic and Arabic *Dormitio Mariæ* attributed to Prochorus: see Suciu, 'The Investiture of Abbaton', p. 532.

31 See M. Gaster, *The Chronicles of Jerahmeel*, Prolegomenon by H. Schwarzbaum, New

QuæstBarth 4,53, according to the G version God sends only Michael to get soil for fashioning Adam's body, whereas in C He dispatches all four archangels, thus including, presumably, both Michael and Gabriel. This work however does not mention any angel of death involved in the enterprise, nor refers to any obstacle faced by the angels in their quest. *Investiture of Abbaton* does not mention names except for that of its 'hero', the angel of death, Muriel-Abbaton; this despite the fact that one of its main sources, the *Testament of Abraham*, explicitly compares Michael's failure to Death's success on another mission from God (see *infra*, n. 30). This discrepancy, along with the aforementioned parallel passages and traditions, leads me to suppose that originally the first envoys in the story did bear names, which are probably to be sought among the mightiest angels in service around God's throne (Michael? Gabriel? Gabriel and Michael? the four archangels?). The names were then erased by the author of *Investiture of Abbaton* for reverence's sake. Numbers probably underwent some adjustments as well, thus confirming the secondary character of Abbat's version of the story. Seven angelic failures, as *Investiture of Abbaton* relates (presupposing the number of the *protoktistai*?), do not look 'original': according to *Mysteries of John* 4,17 Adam fasted seven days instead of the traditional forty, in order that the day his fasting ended should coincide with the eighth day of the week, Sunday, when eucharistic bread is broken and distributed (see *infra*, 3.3.); much in the same way, Muriel succeeds after a series of seven failures, i.e. he is the eighth, with all the Christological implications involved in such a ranking even just by contrast.[32]

York, 1971, esp. Prolegomenon pp. 15–19.26–27.109, with nn. 102 and 108, and Introduction pp. lxii–lxiii. The English translation of the passage from the *Chronicles*, which is of relevance here, is printed at pp. 15–16. Cf. also Suciu, 'The Investiture of Abbaton', pp. 530–531 and n. 22 (with further bibliography). Due to the overarching analogies between *Investiture of Abbaton* and Islamic sources it is still an open question whether the former depends on the latter, as Schwarzbaum assumed, or both Coptic and Muslim accounts rely on similar traditions, as Suciu posits: see Suciu, 'The Investiture of Abbaton', ib. On *Investiture of Abbaton* and its relationship to *Teezâza Sanbat*, see J. Dochhorn, 'Menschenschöpfung und urzeitlicher Teufelsfall in Überlieferungen der Falascha. Der erste Teil von Teezâza Sanbat in der von Halevy veröffentlichten Version', in T. Nicklas et al. (eds), *The Other Side: Apocryphal perspectives on Ancient Christian "Orthodoxies"*, Göttingen, 2017, pp. 193–223.

32   This is not however the only possible reconstruction. In a private talk following my presentation, J. Dochhorn suggested that the nameless version of *Investiture of Abbaton* might actually represent the oldest phase we can reach in the transmission of such Angel of Death material: according to his hypothesis, the names of the failing angels were added later in Jewish and Islamic traditions. In my view TestAbr (L) 15,1.11–15; 16,4; 17,13 and the consensus of all sources in naming either directly or indirectly God's angelic envoys

194 TRIPALDI

Last but not least, it is not irrelevant to point out that the description of Abbaton as king, on his fire-throne suspended in the middle in the middle (*Investiture of Abbaton* 9,5), echoes 'Hermetic' depictions of the Great Demon in the middle overseeing and judging the souls of man and the dead (cf. *Asclepius* NHC VI,8 p. 76,22–28 and CH 1,24; fr. 7,1–2; fr. 23,62) as well as 'Gnostic' portrayals of the so-called Demiurge ruling the worldly abyss (s. e.g. *Ap. John* NHC II,1/IV,1 p. 10,9–26 and *Orig. World* NHC II,5 p. 104,23–106,11), and the earlier and later Jewish throne visions that coalesce into them (cf. Ez 1,4–26; 1 En 14,18–19; Dan 7,9; Apc 4,2.5; ApcAbr 18,3.13; TestAbr [L] 12,4–5 and 13,2–4).[33]

3.2 The Hidden Eve: 'Apocryphal' and 'Gnostic' Sources

Taken as a whole, chapters 7–9 in the *Mysteries of John* show a good general acquaintance with 'apocryphal' texts on Adam. Of the very body of the protoplast, *Mysteries of John* has precise measures to offer: Adam was twelve cubits tall, six cubits wide, and three cubits thick (7,20). Philo of Alexandria (Op 136.140) and ApcAb 23,5 had mentioned Adam's enormous size (cf. later BerR 8,1; 21,3; 24,2, and bHag 12a), but they had given no detailed measures. *Mysteries of John* employs the term 'righteousness' in reference to Adam's primitive conditions almost as an equivalent to the more usual 'glory' (cf. 1 QS 3,20 and 4,14–15.22–23; ApcMos 20–21; ApcAd NHC V,5 p. 64,9–10.24–29). The metaphor by which God strips Adam of his former condition, be it named glory or righteousness, is common to ApcMos 20 and *Mysteries of John* 7,18–19; 9,3. In *Mysteries of John* 9,1–5, staring down at the nails of his feet, Adam is overcome by grief and tears as his nails are a sign of his former righteousness: when it left him from head to toe,[34] vanishing righteousness opened the door to suffering

---

      dispatched to get Him some soil with which to fashion Adam still appear to settle the question.

33   On the 'Gnostic'—or pre-'Gnostic'—myth of the Demiurge and its further reverberations in Coptic *Investiture* literature, see Dochhorn, 'Der Sturz des Teufels', pp. 27–28 and 45–46, and id., 'Mythen von der Einsetzung', pp. 28–29 and 41–42. On Ezekiel's throne vision (Ez 1) and its Jewish exegesis as sources for 'Gnostic' demiurgic traditions, see M. Idel, *Qabbalah. Nuove prospettive*, Milan, 2012, pp. 228–237 (or. ed.: *Kabbalah. New Perspectives* [New Haven, 1988]).

34   'To/including the tips of his fingers' is my own proposed correction of 'except for the tips of his fingers' transmitted by the manuscript: the mechanical corruption from ϣⲁⲛϩⲧⲏϥ to ϣⲁⲧⲛϩⲧⲏϥ is quite easy to explain; moreover, if Adam's nails were exempted from God's punishment and thus preserved their former impassability, why would they get cold and hot as the seasons change? As an external parallel, VitAd 34 further corroborates my conjecture. As a matter of fact, E.W. Budge and A. Alcock both seem to read ϣⲁⲛϩⲧⲏϥ instead

APOSTLES, LONG DEAD 'HERETICS', AND MONKS

from cold and heat, afflicting human nails before any other part of the body (cf. 7,21 and 9,2–3). Now, according to VitAd 34 and ApcMos 8 God inflicted seventy plagues on Adam's body after the Fall 'from the top of his head, of his eyes and of his ears down to the nails of his feet'; ApcMos 24 adds that pain caused by cold and heat came to be as a result of Adam's sin; the Syriac *Cave of Treasures* 5,21–23 encapsulates the penalty in the statement that the new garments of skin covering Adam and Eve brought about every sort of bodily pain.[35] That Adam should have looked down at the nails of his feet as a reminder of his primordial state probably presupposes on the part of our author some knowledge of the Jewish tradition in which the newly created Adam was covered by a white, shining skin made of nail-like horn (s. BerR 20,12 and PRE 14 [98,7–10 Friedländer, with n. 6]).

To my knowledge, the comparison of Adam's body with pure alabaster (*Mysteries of John* 7,19–20) is unprecedented, and as such stands out from the many details documented both here and elsewhere: I wonder whether the choice of such a *comparatum* on the part of our author is to be labelled as Egyptian *Lokalkolorit* meant to stress Adam's original flawlessness, or if it should be traced back to the notion of alabaster as the material of God's throne / the mountain of Eden, as dwelling-place of His glory (cf. 1 Hen 18,8 and 24,3–25,6).

The next chapter of *Mysteries of John* (Fol. 12b–13a) handles the exegesis of Gen 1,27 and 2,21–22, and *de facto* addresses the problem of how to harmonize the two different accounts of the creation of man. This chapter is probably to be considered as a redactional, disruptive insertion into the argumentative flow of a pre-existing text. The earlier text would seem to have consisted of the discussion on Adam's primordial righteousness, gigantic stature and alabaster-like skin, and the description of the impact which the Fall had on his body as well as of the traces which his sin has left on human physiology: as a matter of fact, chapter 9 picks up where chapter 7 left off, and the allocution 'Pay attention to the sign (to be found) in the sons of man!' in 9,1 fits better into its literary and logical context if we skip or erase the intervening chapter 8.

As to the possible sources of this addition, both Philo and the rabbis (see respectively Op 134 and BerR 8,1) discussed the interpretation of the two creation narratives in order to solve their apparent inconsistency, so acutely felt

---

of the *textus traditus* ϢⲀⲦⲚϨⲦⲎϤ, as far as one can judge from their translations, but neither of them offers any explanation whatsoever for his choice.

35   On the punishment of Adam in Adamic traditions, see G.A. Anderson, 'The Punishment of Adam and Eve in the Life of Adam and Eve', in Anderson et al. (eds), *Literature*, pp. 57–81, and Dochhorn, *Apokalypse*, pp. 230–249.

when they were compared to each other; as did later Christian exegetes.[36] This
being said, *Mysteries of John* advances the solution that in the end there was
only one simultaneous creation, insofar as Eve was 'hidden' in Adam's side from
the start: God conceived of fashioning Eve as He was already working on Adam
and thereby formed a single human being, only later to be physically and sexually doubled. The explanation seems to be built around a re-elaboration of the
motif of Eve concealed in Adam *qua* divine thought as we read in many 'Gnostic' writings (see *Ap. John* NHC II,1 p. 20,14–21,16; 22,15–23,14; *Hyp. Arch.* 6–8 NHC
II,4 pp. 88,10–89,17; *Apoc. Adam* NHC II,5 p. 64,6–29). But that is probably not
the whole truth, or in other words, the 'Gnostic' motif is just one development
of a tradition that exists even earlier than, and outside of, 'Gnostic' writings:
traces of an analogous equivalence established between 'creating man, male
and female' and 'creating Adam and *showing* him his side, his wife' (italics
mine) may in fact be detected in much older passages such as Jub 2,14 and
3,8; later on, according to Rabbi Levi as quoted by Rabbi Joshua from Siknin in
BerR 18,2, Gen 2,22 says that God 'formed' (*ybn*) Eve from Adam meaning that
He 'meditated' (*htbwnn*) upon what part of Adam's body He should fashion the
woman from.

3.3 Adam, Jesus and the 'Invention' of Wheat

The long narrative put in the mouth of the Cherub in *Mysteries of John* 4 pur-
ports to function as a double-sided etiology: it aims both to unveil the circumstances that led to the 'invention' of wheat, and to explain why oaths on it,
should they be broken, will be severely prosecuted. Both lines of 'argument'
concur to demonstrate that the Son of God is to be equated with water, wheat,
the seed and God's throne. The explanation of the gravity of oaths on said entities is thus one and the same when it comes to sanction transgressions against
any of them.[37]

Introduced by a probable quotation from the Coptic *Vision of Paul*,[38] the etiological legend itself as narrated by the angel follows broadly the narrative we

---

36   See U. Bianchi (ed.), *La 'doppia creazione' dell'uomo negli Alessandrini, nei Cappadoci e
nella gnosi*, Rome, 1978.

37   On Jesus Christ as water in Coptic tradition cf. LibBarth 9,2 and Ps.-Stephen, *Investiture
of Gabriel* 3.7; as the throne of God: Ps.-Theodosius of Alexandria, *Encomium of John the
Baptist* 9,7. Mt 5,34 had forbidden the reader to swear on heaven, 'because it is the throne
of God'. ApcMos 19 has Eve swear an oath to Satan by the throne of God, the Cherubs and
the tree of life.

38   Cf. 4,2 ('Before God created heaven and earth, waters already existed') with BL Or. 7023,
Fol. 20a ('Before God created heaven and earth, nothing existed but waters only'), the only
manuscript available to date of the Coptic *Visio Pauli*, also deriving from the Monastery

APOSTLES, LONG DEAD 'HERETICS', AND MONKS

can read in VitAd 1–2.4.6–8.13–16.22.[39] It should go without saying that variations and additions are to be expected. Among the latter one may count the
mention of Christ's role as guarantor for Adam when God gave life to enliven
the latter (cf. Ps.-Timothy, *The Investiture of Abbaton* 5,12–14 and Ps.-Stephen,
The Investiture of Gabriel 2); the reduction of Adam's penitence to a period of
eight days from the original 40/47 (cf. VitAd 6 and 17 with *Mysteries of John* 4,17),
which is tantamount to saying that Adam quit fasting and ate on Sunday; the
most material and concrete details on the 'production' of wheat as ingredient
of the eucharistic bread (cf. Ps.-Peter of Alexandria, *De Baptismo* 21,2–3).

On this last point, the reader learns that the seed of wheat is nothing else but
a mix of Christ's and God's ground flesh, sealed in the middle with the light-seal
that God had used to seal the 'æons of light'.[40] Coptic eucharistic bread is actually stamped with a cross in the middle, surrounded by the formula 'Holy God,
Holy Mighty One, Holy Immortal' on the round edge of the bread.[41] Our text
probably presupposes some kind of connection between such praxis and the
tetragrammaton or any nominal formation based upon the divine name, such
as the name Jesus itself. In Coptic literary tradition this name can be referred
to as a component of the seal of all creation.[42] Along these lines, in LibBarth
Jao occurs as a name of Jesus (6,1); Jesus is described as a single entity assem-

---

of St Mercurius in Edfu (see *supra*). It bears noting that both the Greek and the Latin versions of the *Vision of Paul* have here different texts to offer. For more possible echoes of
the *Visio Pauli* in *Mysteries of John* cf. MystJ 3,6 and BL Or. 7023, Fol. 19a // VisPaul(gr) 21;
6,3 and VisPaul(gr) 45; 7,5 and VisPaul(gr) 24; 7,11 and 21a–23b.

39   Whereas in ApcMos 29 Adam is granted access to Paradise one last time after the Fall to
gather other plants' seeds to live on. According to Jub 3,15–16 the angels versed Adam in
agriculture while Adam was still in the garden of Eden. On the etiology of agriculture in
VitAd, see J. Dochhorn, 'Adam als Bauer oder: die Ätiologie des Ackerbaus in Vita Adæ 1–21
und die Redaktionsgeschichte der Adamviten', in Anderson et al. (eds), *Literature*, pp. 315–
346.

40   The expression 'æons of light' sounds of Manichæan origin: cf. *Keph.* 2,20,15 and 23,1–10;
Man. Psal. 134,1–33; 136,13–53; 144,1–32.

41   Archbishop Basilios, 'Eucharistic Bread', *The Coptic Encyclopedia* 4 (1991), pp. 1062–1063;
the liturgical use of such formulas may be seen as early as Ps.-Dioscorus of Alexandria,
Encomium of Macarios 56.

42   See *Encomium of John the Baptist* 21,2: as it comes to account for the meaning of the name
'Johannes' as seal of the world, Jota is said to stand for Jesus, Omega for Father, Alpha for
Unity, Nun for both the Spirit and the æons of light, Eta for Emmanuel, Sigma for Savior.
Accordingly, Ps.-Stephen, *The Investiture of Gabriel* 7, defines John 'baptizer of the æons
of Light'. On sealing as a metaphor for baptism, see Clem. *Ecl.* 13,9 and *Exc.* 80,3; 83; 86,2;
Bas. *Eun.* 2,22 (PG 29,620D); [Bas.] *Struct. hom.* 1 (PG 30,33B); [Ath.] *Sabell.* 8 (PG 28,109C);
Chrys. *Hom. 3.7 in 2 Cor* (PG 10,454B).

198   TRIPALDI

bled out of seven æons (9,2); the name of the Father, of the Son and of the Holy
Spirit is inscribed in seven points on Adam's body (14,2).[43]

Be that as it may, by means of the aforementioned redactional interventions
the 'apocryphal' story of Adam's hunger, fasting and feeding undergoes a deep-
ranging, undisputedly Christological and eucharistic turn aimed to legitimize a
contemporary baking practice as rooted in the actions and revelations of God
and Christ Themselves.

4   Intersecting the Axes: Old and New 'Heretics' and the Production of
         Coptic Apostolic Memoirs

Crossing the synchronic and diachronic evidence we have been collecting thus
far, we are now in a better position to make some final inferences about the
production of the texts we have analyzed, the 'apocryphal' hypotexts or pre-
existing traditions involved, and the cultural environment surrounding it. For
the sake of clarity I present such provisional conclusions as bullet points:

A)   Our brief survey of two texts, *The Investiture of Abbaton* and *The Mysteries
      of John*, highlighted that their 'apocryphal' texture in relating episodes of
      primordial history depends on multiple sources, written or not: Adamic
      legends mainly taken from the (Jewish?) *Life of Adam and Eve* and the
      Apocalypse of Moses;[44] angelological traditions of Jewish and Hermetic,
      Gnostic and Manichæan origins as well as specifically Gnostic *mytholo-
      goumena*—whether still known to the authors of the texts as such or not;
      earlier Christian 'apocalypses'.[45] Next to them—and possibly constituting
      a link in the chain of transmission—the literary influence exerted by such
      works as the *Cave of Treasures* (translated into Coptic probably before

---

43   On 'seal of Truth' as a divine name and the sealing of the world in Jewish tradition, see
      M. Idel, *Il figlio nel misticismo ebraico*, Verona, 2013, pp. 44–45 and 118–119 (or. ed.: *Ben:
      Sonship and Jewish Mysticism* [London, 2007]).

44   Dochhorn, *Apokalypse*, p. 288 n. 1, considers 'erst recht' *Investiture of Abbaton* as 'von der
      Apc Mos mittelbar abhängig'. For the Coptic fragments of the *Vita Adæ*, see J.-C. Haele-
      wyck, *Clavis Apocryphorum Veteris Testamenti* (*Corpus Christianorum*), Turnhout, 1998,
      p. 7; A.-M. Denis et collaborateurs, *Introduction à la littérature religieuse judéo-hellénistique*
      vol. 1, Turnhout, 2000, pp. 16–17; S.J. Gathercole, 'The Life of Adam and Eve (Coptic Frag-
      ments)', in R. Bauckham et al. (eds), *Old Testament Pseudepigrapha: More Noncanonical
      Scriptures* vol. 1, Grand Rapids, 2013, pp. 22–27, esp. 24.

45   On Jewish and Christian apocalyptic literature as a source of inspiration for the pro-
      duction of new texts in Late Antique Egypt, see also E. Grypeou, 'Höllenreisen und
      engelgleiches Leben: Die Rezeption von apokalyptischen Traditionen in der koptisch-
      monastischen Literatur', in Bumazhnov (ed.), *Christliches Ägypten*, pp. 43–54.

APOSTLES, LONG DEAD 'HERETICS', AND MONKS

750–760 CE) and the *Visio Pauli* should probably be analysed in greater detail in the near future, where textual evidence allows it of course.[46] As names, expressions, whole passages, ideas and topics in *The Investiture of Abbaton* and *The Mysteries of John* are in fact paralleled in other Coptic texts of about the same period, one may wonder whether they had by then coalesced into a sort of common cluster of themes, literary motifs and formulas, into a shared 'language', let's say, to be drawn upon in Coptic monastic milieus when forging homilies and re-inventing an apostolic *Urtext*.[47]

B) Sources are not simply registered: that is, reused and copied, if written, or committed to writing if oral—as one might in fact easily expect. Rather, they are interpolated and rewritten so as to fill Christological, eschatological and liturgical gaps in official accounts of sacred history. In one case we may even detect the influence of Coptic eucharistic baking practice on the remodelling of the older story of Adam's penitence. As a Coptic text puts it, commenting upon this process in response to a hypothetical objection to additions to the Gospel text:

> The wool provided for the purple cloth of the king, before its mixtures, with which it is dyed, are applied to it, can be made useful by being fabricated into clothing and being worn as one pleases. Yet when it is worked upon and dyed in colourful mixtures, it becomes exceedingly brilliant and becomes radiant clothing, so that the king wears it. Thus,

---

46   As far as the former text is concerned, readers may profit from the works of A. Su-Min Ri and A. Toepel: the former published the text and French translation of the two Syriac recensions of the *Cave of Treasures* (CSCO 486–487, 1987) as well as a rich commentary on this writing (CSCO 581, 2000); the latter dedicated a whole monograph to Adam and Seth legends in the *Cave of Treasures* and their sources (*Die Adam- und Seth-Legenden im syrischen* Buch der Schatzhöhle, Leuven, 2006]). A still later Copto-Arabic text, the *Conflict of Adam and Eve with Satan*, to which Alin Suciu has recently attributed a previously alleged fragment of the *Life of Adam*, 'is largely based on the story of Adam and Eve from the *Cave of Treasures*' (A. Suciu, 'Note on the Alleged Arabic Manuscript of the Life of Adam', *Journal of Theological Studies* 69/1 [2018], pp. 96–100 [quotation: 98]). One more pseudo-patristic homily containing extensive extracts from the *Cave of Treasures* is known to exist in Coptic: see Suciu, *The Berlin-Strasbourg Apocryphon*, pp. 78–79 and n. 23 (with further literature).

47   Hence such newborn clichés and conventions could be moved at will from one text to another as building blocks, and often end up constituting gross and clumsy interpolations into pre-existing works: cf. Ps.-Chrysostomus, *De resurrectione et apostolis* 37–38 with Ps.-Chrisostomus, *Glory of the Precursor* 8,4–9,2 in light of Suciu's remarks on the Sahidic *additum* to the final part of the *Apocalypse of Paul* (Suciu, *The Berlin-Strasbourg Apocryphon*, p. 114).

the holy gospels, when he who will be ordained a shepherd acts according to their words and reveals them, become illuminated exceedingly. And they are very brilliant in the heart of those who listen. Indeed, the king will not find fault if beautifully crafted plaits are added to his garments, but he will commend those who have added them exceedingly, so that everyone might praise the garment because of the plaits which are on it. Thus, the Lord Jesus will not find fault with us if we add a few embellishments to the holy gospels, but he will commend us all the more and bless those who bear fruit through them.[48]

This emic image of remembering and re-narrating 'Bible' material as the making and enrichment of a garment lends itself to a comparison with the modern notion of *Bible in progress* and the shift of theoretical paradigms in the study of 'apocryphal' traditions, as advanced by, among others, P. Piovanelli.[49]

C) As we have just seen, such 'sartorial' work was not a neutral literary enterprise. It was certainly not perceived as such by contemporaries. Legends and stories were collected, retrieved and narrated anew to fit changed historical circumstances and liturgical needs, even to the point of transforming book production into a saving act and indulging in some kind of self-propaganda, as it were. This move did not go uncontested but rather ignited fierce polemics—or conversely it was resorted to as a result of fierce polemics already ignited. As J. Dochhorn demonstrated, the idea that Michael occupied Satan's place after the latter's fall, and the literary works relating the story of how it actually happened along the lines of Adamic legends (esp. VitAd 11–17), were linked in some branches of Coptic monastic tradition with earlier heretics or heresies: among them one

---

48   Ps.-Evodius of Rome, *Homily on the Passion and Resurrection* 40–42. English translation taken from 'Rhetorical Structure', p. 46. This text is quoted *in extenso* also in Suciu, *The Berlin-Strasbourg Apocryphon*, pp. 123–124, as a sign of its importance for understanding the emic conception—as anthropologists would say—of such literature in our sources.

49   P. Piovanelli, *'Rewritten Bible* or *Bible in Progress*? La réécriture des traditions mémorielles bibliques dans les Judaïsme et le Christianisme anciens', in id., *Apocryphités. Études sur les textes et les traditions scripturaires du Judaïsme et su Christianisme anciens*, Turnhout, 2016, pp. 25–42. Cf. also the category 'Books useful for the Soul' proposed and developed by the late F. Bovon, 'Beyond the Canonical and the Apocryphal Books, the Presence of a Third Category: The Books Useful for the Soul', in id., *The Emergence of Christianity: Collected Studies III*, Tübingen, 2013, pp. 147–160. It bears noting that the image used by the Coptic homilist is still productive in modern, scientific research on apocrypha: see right from the title L. DiTommaso et al. (eds), *The Embroidered Bible: Studies in Biblical Apocrypha and Pseudepigrapha in Honour of Michael E. Stone*, Leiden et al., 2017, which unfortunately I have not yet been able to thumb.

APOSTLES, LONG DEAD 'HERETICS', AND MONKS

may count unknown or yet-undeciphered names like Henotes and Sietes, but also notorious bad guys like Isidore, probably Basilides of Alexandria's son, and Mani's followers.[50] More generally the *Kitāb al-īḍāḥ* sees the Devil himself at work in the author of the *Investiture of Abbaton*, with all the people arranging a feast for the angel of death (9,1.25). As a result, one might quite naturally wonder whether naming a revered Father of the Church and an apostle as the respective authors of a homily and of two apparently lost revelatory texts, or pointing instead at (long-dead) heretics as sources for opponents' teachings were not among Coptic literati's (i.e. mainly monks') deliberate choices, *de facto* mirroring each other and aiming to counter pretensions or allegations advanced by the opposite front. In which case not only would (contested) pseudepigraphy turn out to be an attempt 'of the emerging Coptic church to mould an identity for itself' by demonstrating 'that the Egyptian Christians are the real heirs of the orthodox tradition', but it would also prove an integral part of a polemical strategy perfectly at home in the long intra-Coptic debate surrounding the production and diffusion of the apostolic memoirs.[51]

5   Appendix

5.1   *The Birth of Death*

5.1.1   *Investiture of Abbaton* (CC 0405)

(BL Or. 7025) 5.(1) And it happened, as my Father made the heaven and the earth, and all the creatures that are in them, he spoke and they all arose, Angels, Archangels, Cherubs, Seraphs, Thrones, Rulers, Powers, all the Dominions, and the whole heavenly host. He also made the earth and the animals alike, reptiles, cattle, | birds and all the creatures that move on it. In the east he planted   Fol. 9b

---

50   Dochhorn, 'Mythen von der Einsetzung', pp. 32–35. Cf. Ps.-Athanasius, Homily on Luke 35–36, where Carpocratius (= Carpocrates, the 2nd-century Alexandrian 'gnostic' teacher) shows up in Nicæa stating that Jesus was born after a 7-month pregnancy and thus arguing—in the eye of the redactor—against the full humanity of the Incarnation. For more 'heretical' doctrines attributed to Carpocrates in Coptic literature, see A. Le Tiec, 'Remarques à propos des fragments coptes 159–160, 302–304, conservés à l'IFAO du Caire: une homélie copte sur la Vierge Marie attribuée à Cyrille de Jérusalem', in A. Van den Kerchove and L.G. Soares Santoprete (eds), *Gnose et manichéisme. Entre les oasis d'Égypte et la Route de la Soie: Hommage à Jean-Daniel Dubois*, Turnhout, 2016, pp. 683–698, esp. 692–694.

51   Suciu, *The Berlin-Strasbourg Apocryphon*, pp. 75–95, 124–125, 128–129 (quotation: 129).

a garden, (2) but he saw that the whole world was a wasteland, because there was nobody to cultivate it. So my Father said: 'Let us make man like ourselves, according to our image, that he may praise us day and night and they understand that it is the hand of the Lord that created all this. For I am before it was.' (3) Then my Father commanded an angel: 'Go to the land of Eden at my desire and my command, and bring me virgin soil, that I may make man like ourselves

Fol. 10a |, according to our image, and he may incessantly praise us day and night!' The angel went to the land of Eden, obeying to my Father's command, and stood upon the clay. He stretched out his hand to take the clay and bring it to my Father, (4) but immediately the clay cried out and said in a loud voice: 'I swear to you on the one who sent you to me: you shall not take me to him, that he may mold me to become a man and a living soul, and thus great sins may arise from me! (5) Many fornications, blasphemies, envies, hates, and quarrels will come to pass because of him, many murders and bloodsheds will be commit-

Fol. 10b ted by him |: (6) before my time comes, I will be thrown to dogs and pigs, in pits and wells, and in river waters. At last, after all such things, I will be delivered to the punishments and tormented day and night. Therefore, leave me alone lying here at my ease!' (7) As the Angel of the Lord heard these words, he became afraid of my Father's name, turned away, and went back to my Father. The Angel said, 'My Lord, as I heard your frightening name, I was not able anymore to bring you the clay.' (8) Immediately, my Father commanded a second angel and sent him to the clay, and a third afterwards, and so on until the seventh,

Fol. 11a but none of them was able to get close to the clay | because it swore to them great, frightening oaths. (9) When my Father saw that no one had been able to bring him the clay, he sent the angel Muriel to it saying: 'Go to the land of Eden at my command and bring me virgin clay, that I may make a man resembling us, according to our image, and he may incessantly praise us day and night!' (10) As the Angel of the Lord went to the clay, he stood by extremely mighty and confident, empowered by the Lord's command. He stretched out his hand to take it, and immediately the clay cried out in a loud voice: 'I swear on the one

Fol. 11b |, who created heaven and earth and all the beings that are in them: you shall not get close to take me to God!' (11) But Muriel was not afraid of my Father's name as he heard it, and so he did not have any compassion for the clay: he approached and seized it with tyrannical cruelty. (12) Then, he brought it to my Father. My Father rejoiced over it, took the clay from the hands of the angel and created Adam resembling us, according to our image. He left him lying for forty days and forty nights without giving him breath, and each day complain-

Fol. 12a ing: 'Many | sufferings expect man, if I give him breath.' I said to my Father: 'Give him breath, and I will pledge for him!' (13) My Father said to me: 'My beloved Son, if I give him breath, you will have to descend to the world and endure great sufferings for him, in order to save and restore him to his original rule.' I replied: 'Give him breath! I will pledge for him, descend into the world, and carry out your command.' (14) As he decided to give man breath, he took the book and wrote down his descendants who will enter the kingdom of heaven |, as it is   Fol. 12b written: 'These, whose names are written in the book of life from the foundation of the world.' In this way he gave him the breath of life: he blew a living breath three times into his face saying: 'Live, live, live!', according to the model of my divinity. (15) Immediately man came to life and became a living soul, resembling God, according to his image. When Adam arose, he threw himself down before the Father and said: 'My lord and my God, | you made me come to   Fol. 13a being out of nothing!' (16) Thus, God installed him on a great throne, and put a splendid crown and a royal diadem on his head. After these things, my Father commanded every order in heaven to come and worship Adam, whether Angels or Archangels. So the whole heavenly host came, worshiped first God and then Adam, saying: 'Greetings, you, likeness and image of God!' 6.(1) The order of the First Creature showed up as well to worship Adam. My Father said to him: 'Come, you too, and worship my likeness and my image!' |. Blind haughtiness   Fol. 13b and impudence seized him, and he replied: 'It is fitting for him to come and worship me, because I am before he came to being!' (2) When my Father noticed his blind pride and saw that his malice and mischief had reached full measure, he ordered all heavenly hosts saying: 'Come and take the roll from the hand of the proud one, strip off his armor and throw him down to earth, because his time has come!' (3) For he was the greatest of them all and led them: as a king entrusts his army to a general, and the latter leads it, holding in his hand the written names of the soldiers, (4) so it was with this wicked one and the written names of the angels were in his hand. The Angels assembled against him, but they were not able to take the roll from him. So, my Father ordered to bring a sharp knife and cut off the roll this side and that. Nonetheless, what was left in the palm of his hand could not be taken from him. (5) Immediately, my Father commanded a great Cherub, and he struck and threw him down from heaven to earth | because of his pride: the Cherub broke his wings and his rib, and weak-   Fol. 14b ened him. But those that he took down with him became devils together with him.

5.2 *The Hidden Eve: 'Apocryphal' and 'Gnostic' Sources*
5.2.1 *Mysteries of John (CC 0041)*
(BL Or. 7026) 7. (19) I asked him: 'My lord, what was the righteousness clothing him he was stripped of?' 20 He answered: 'When God created Adam, Adam was twelve cubits tall, six cubits wide, and three cubits thick: he was like flawless alabaster. 21 But after he had eaten from the tree, his body became smaller

and thinner, and the righteousness which he had on disappeared and left him, down to the tip of his fingers, his nails: do not they turn cold in winter and hot in summer?' 8. (1) I kept asking the cherub |: 'My Lord, when God created Adam, did he create Eve with him too or not? For I have heard that God created Adam and Eve together from the beginning, (2) but I further hear that God brought a deep sleep over Adam and, as he fell asleep, he took a rib out of him, fashioned it into a woman and filled Adam's side with flesh in its place. (3) Did the Creator then make two bodies as a single body?' (4) He answered to me: 'Listen and I will disclose everything to you! (5) When God created Adam, he created Eve together with him as a single body, for, as the Lord worked on Adam, the idea of Eve was already there with Adam |. (6) That is the reason why two bodies came into being from a single body; God however did not separate them from each other immediately. (7) When God brought the deep sleep over Adam and he lay down and fell asleep, only then did he take Eve out of him, and she became his wife, (8) for she was hidden in his left side since the time God created him. 9. (1) Pay attention to the sign on the sons of men!' I asked him: 'My Lord, which sign is on the sons of men?' (2) The cherub said to me: 'When the frost comes upon the earth, the nails are the first part of the human body that turns cold. (3) For, as God stripped Adam | of the righteousness that clothed him, his nails were the first to turn cold. (4) Adam burst into tears, crying to the Lord: 'Woe to me, my Lord! When I was still keeping the commandments of God, before I ate from the tree, my whole body was white as my nails!' (5) Therefore, whenever Adam would look at his nails, he would weep and mourn.'

Fol. 12b

Fol. 13a

Fol. 13b

5.3 *Adam, Jesus and the 'Invention' of Wheat*

5.3.1 *Mysteries of John* (CC 0041)

(BL Or. 7026) 4. (1) I further said to the Cherub: 'I have heard that God made heaven and earth and also that he made the water in the beginning.' (2) The Cherub replied: 'Listen to me and I will disclose everything to you! Before God created earth and heaven, the waters were already there. No one knows their creation except God alone. (3) That is the reason why neither the one who swears falsely in the name of the water nor the one who commits a perjury by the grain of wheat will be forgiven: one and the same sanction applies to both!' (4) I said to the Cherub: 'My lord, I want you to explain to me such a provision concerning the grain of wheat, disclosing to me where the grain of wheat was found in the beginning, that it may be sown and men may live on it.' (5) The Cherub told me: 'Listen to me and I will disclose everything to you! When God created Adam, he placed him in the garden of delight and commanded him, speaking in this manner |: 'From every tree in the garden you may eat, except for the tree of knowledge of good and evil. From it you shall not eat! The day you

Fol. 4b

APOSTLES, LONG DEAD 'HERETICS', AND MONKS

will eat from it, you will surely die!' (6) But the devil envied him, because he saw the great glory that surrounded him. Even the sun and the moon, the two great stars, would come every day to worship Adam, before rising over the earth. (7) The devil went and led Adam and his wife astray, and so they were driven from Paradise and banished to the land of Eilat. (8) Adam plunged into trouble: after that he became hungry and found no food like that the two of them were used to eat every day in Paradise. | Deeply grieving, he cried out to the Lord, and the Son of Goodness had pity on him, for he had guaranteed for Adam. (9) He spoke with his good Father, the Lord of the angels and the spirits: 'Behold, the man we created according to our likeness and image has become hungry. Father, I have pity on him: if it is your will, do not let him starve!' (10) So the Father of Mercy answered and said to his beloved Son: 'If you have taken pity on the man we have created, who has neglected our order, then go and give him your flesh to eat. For you guaranteed for him.' (11) The Son of Goodness answered and said to his Father: 'Blessed be your word! | I will do what you have told me'. (12) The beloved Son left his Father's presence and took a small piece out of his right side, a piece of his divine flesh, rubbed it down to a round shape and brought it to his Holy Father. (13) His Father asked him: 'What is this?' He answered: 'This is my flesh, like you told me.' Then his Father said to him: 'All right, my Son! Wait for a while and I will give you a piece of my invisible body!' 14 His Father himself took a piece of his own body, and fashioned it into a grain of wheat; then he took the seal of light which he had sealed the æons of light with, and sealed the grain of wheat in its middle. (15) Then he said to his beloved Son: 'Take it and | give it to the Archangel Michael! He will give it to Adam and Adam will sow it, so that he and his children may live on it. Michael will also teach him how to sow and reap.' (16) Jesus called Michael and said to him: 'Take this flesh and give it to Adam, so that he and all his children may live on it!' (17) Michael went to Adam, as he was at the Jordan for the eighth day without eating, just crying out to the Lord. Michael spoke to him and said: 'Peace be with you! The Lord has heard your prayer and sent you the seed for sowing'. (18) When Adam heard this from Michael, his body recovered strength: he came out of the water and threw himself down at Michael's feet. (19) Michael gave him the sealed seed and taught him how to sow and reap |, afterwards he went up to the heavens in glory. (20) Therefore, (be the perjury sworn by) the water, the wheat, the seed, or the throne of the Father, one and the same sanction is foreseen for them, and the four equal the Son of God.' (21) I, John, saw and rejoiced hearing these things.

Fol. 5a

Fol. 5b

Fol. 6a

Fol. 6b

CHAPTER 10

Face as the Image of God in the Jewish Pseudepigrapha

Andrei A. Orlov

1 Introduction

From a Jewish text, known to us as *2 Enoch*,[1] we learn interesting details about Adam's creation. Both recensions of *2 Enoch* 44 tell us 'the Lord with his own two hands created humankind; in a likeness of his own face (в подобии лица своего), both small and great, the Lord created [them].'[2] It is intriguing that *2 Enoch* departs here from the traditional reading attested in Genesis 1:26–27, where Adam was created, not in a likeness of God's face, but after His image (*ṣelem*).[3] In view of this departure, the author of one of the English translations of *2 Enoch*, Francis Andersen, observes that '2 *Enoch*'s idea is remarkable from any point of view ... This is not the original meaning of *ṣelem* ... The text uses *podobie lica* (in the likeness of the face), not *obrazu* or *videnije*, the usual terms for "image." '[4]

To clarify a possible background of such a conceptual paradigm shift in *2 Enoch* we need to direct our attention to the Ladder of Jacob, another Jewish text preserved in Slavonic.

---

1 *2 Enoch* was probably written in the first century C.E. before the destruction of the Second Jerusalem Temple. On the date of *2 Enoch*, see R.H. Charles and W.R. Morfill, *The Book of the Secrets of Enoch*, Oxford, 1896, p. xxvi; R.H. Charles and N. Forbes, 'The Book of the Secrets of Enoch', in R.H. Charles (ed.), *The Apocrypha and Pseudepigrapha of the Old Testament* vol. 2, Oxford, 1913, p. 429; J.T. Milik, *The Books of Enoch*, Oxford, 1976, p. 114; C. Böttrich, *Das slavische Henochbuch* (JSHRZ 5), Gütersloh, 1995, p. 813; A. Orlov, 'The Sacerdotal Traditions of 2 Enoch and the Date of the Text', in A.A. Orlov, G. Boccaccini and J. Zurawski (eds), *New Perspectives on 2 Enoch: No Longer Slavonic Only* (SJS 4), Leiden, 2012, pp. 103–116.

2 F. Andersen, '2 (Slavonic Apocalypse of) Enoch', in J.H. Charlesworth (ed.), *The Old Testament Pseudepigrapha* vol. 1, New York, 1983–1985, p. 170.

3 Gen 1:26–27 reads: 'Then God said, "Let us make humankind in our image, according to our likeness; and let them have dominion over the fish of the sea, and over the birds of the air, and over the cattle, and over all the wild animals of the earth, and over every creeping thing that creeps upon the earth." So God created humankind in his image, in the image of God he created them; male and female he created them.' (NRSV).

4 Andersen, '2 Enoch', p. 1.171, note b.

© ANDREI A. ORLOV, 2021 | DOI:10.1163/9789004445925_012

FACE AS THE IMAGE OF GOD IN THE JEWISH PSEUDEPIGRAPHA

2   The Ladder of Jacob

The bulk of the *Ladder* survives only in Slavonic as part of the so-called *Palea Interpretata*, in which editors of its various versions reworked and rearranged the text.[5] Despite its long life inside the compendium of different materials and a long history of transmission in both Greek and Slavonic milieus, the text preserves several early traditions that can be safely placed within the Jewish environment of the first century CE. The *Ladder* is most likely derived from its Greek variant, which in turn appears to have been translated from Hebrew or Aramaic. This was corroborated by Reimund Leicht who identified Jacob's prayer from the *Ladder* among a collection of prayers in an eleventh-century codex from the Cairo Genizah.[6]

Scholars usually identify three recensions of the text (A, B, and C); the first is the most 'conservative' type of the text, the second was rewritten in some of parts of the narrative and the third is represented by a brief excerpt.[7]

The content of the book is linked to Jacob's biblical dream about the ladder (Gen 28:10–17) and its interpretation. Recensions A and B offer the following portrayal of the ladder:

Recension A (*Ladder* 1:3–8)	Recension B (*Ladder* 1:3–8)
And behold, a ladder was established on the earth, and its top reached to heaven. And the top of the ladder was the face (*лице*) as of a man, carved out of fire. The ladder had twelve steps to the top, and on each step to the top there were two human faces, on the right and on the left, twenty-four faces on the ladder, including their chests. And the face in the middle was higher than all that I saw, the one of fire, including the shoulders and arms, exceedingly terrifying (*излиха страшно*),	And behold, a ladder was established on the earth and its top reached to heaven. And at the top of it there was the face (*лице*) as of a man, carved out of fire. The ladder had twelve steps, and on each step there were two human faces, on the right and on the left; twenty-four faces on the ladder, including their chests. And the face in the middle was higher than all that I saw: the one of fire, including the shoulders and arms, exceedingly terrify-ing (*излиха страшно*), more than those

---

5   A. Kulik and S. Minov, *Biblical Pseudepigrapha in Slavonic Tradition*, Oxford, 2016, p. 277.

6   See R. Leicht, 'Qedushah and Prayer to Helios: A New Hebrew Version of an Apocryphal Prayer of Jacob', *JSQ* 6 (1999), pp. 140–176. For the Hebrew text of the prayer, see P. Schäfer and S. Shaked, *Magische Texte aus der Kairoer Geniza* (TSAJ, 64), Tübingen, 1997, pp. 2.27–78.

7   Kulik and Minov, *Biblical Pseudepigrapha in Slavonic Tradition*, p. 281.

(cont.)

Recension A (*Ladder* 1:3–8)	Recension B (*Ladder* 1:3–8)
more than those twenty-four faces. And while I was still looking (at it), and behold, angels of God were going, ascending and descending on it. And God was established on it and God was standing above the highest face, and he called to me from there, saying, 'Jacob, Jacob!'	twenty-four faces. And while he was still looking (at it), behold, angels of God were going, ascending and descending on it. And God himself was established on it and God was standing above its highest face, and he called to me from there, saying, 'Jacob, Jacob!'[8]

Notably, the text is virtually identical in both recensions. On the ladder Jacob sees twenty-four human faces with their chests, two on each step of the ladder. At the top, he beholds another human visage 'carved out of fire' with its shoulders and arms. Compared to the previous faces, this one looks 'exceedingly terrifying.' God stands above this highest countenance and calls Jacob by name. This leaves the impression that God's voice is hidden behind the frightening face as a distinct divine manifestation, behind which the deity conveys to Jacob his audible revelation.

Scholars have suggested that the higher Face not only embodies God's Glory but also represents Jacob's heavenly identity.[9] But since Jewish traditions about Jacob's heavenly persona in the *Ladder* are garbled by the text's long transmission in multiple ideological and linguistic milieus, scholars seeking to reconstruct these motifs must rely heavily on Jewish testimonies about Jacob contained in Targumic, Talmudic, and Midrashic accounts.

In rabbinic renderings of Jacob's vision of the ladder, the patriarch's heavenly persona is often depicted as his image engraved on the throne of glory. These traditions are present in several Palestinian Targumic accounts, including *Targum Pseudo-Jonathan*, *Targum Neofiti*, and the so-called *Fragmentary Targum*, all of which render the image of Jacob as *iqonin*—the Palestinian Aramaic transliteration of the Greek εἰκών. Dictionaries often translate this term as 'image,' 'picture,' or 'features,' noting its common usage in midrashim to denote royal statues. *Targum Pseudo-Jonathan* on Gen 28:12 offers the following description of the patriarch's celestial identity:

---

8   Kulik and Minov, *Biblical Pseudepigrapha in Slavonic Tradition*, pp. 289–290.

9   J. Fossum, *The Image of the Invisible God: Essays on the Influence of Jewish Mysticism on Early Christology* (NTOA 30), Fribourg–Göttingen, 1995, pp. 135–151, esp. 143.

FACE AS THE IMAGE OF GOD IN THE JEWISH PSEUDEPIGRAPHA 209

> He [Jacob] had a dream, and behold, a ladder was fixed in the earth with its top reaching toward the heavens ... and on that day angels ascended to the heavens on high, and said, 'Come and see Jacob the pious, whose image (*iqonin*) is fixed in the Throne of Glory, and whom you have desired to see.'[10]

Important to note is that Jacob's heavenly counterpart (i.e. his *iqonin*) is engraved on a very special celestial entity: the *Merkavah*. Besides the tradition of engraving on the Throne, some rabbinic materials point to an even more radical identification of Jacob's image with the *Kavod*. It has been previously noted that in some rabbinic accounts about Jacob's heavenly persona, his image is depicted not simply as engraved on the heavenly throne, but as seated upon the throne of glory. According to Jarl Fossum, this tradition is already observable in some versions of the *Fragmentary Targum* which omit the verb 'engraved' or 'fixed'.[11] He also points to *Bavli Hulin* 91b as evidence of the same tradition, arguing that this second tradition is original and is possibly connected to Second Temple mediatorial currents.[12] Similarly, Christopher Rowland claims that Jacob's image is 'identical with the form of God on the Throne of Glory in the first chapter of Ezekiel.'[13]

An understanding of Jacob's image as an anthropomorphic Glory is already present in some targumic accounts. David Halperin, for example, draws attention to a targumic reading of Ezekiel 1:26 which interprets 'the appearance of a human being' as Jacob's image.[14] Fossum offers additional support for the originality of Jacob's enthronement, pointing out that the Hebrew forms of the Greek loan word εἰκών used in the Targums are synonymous with *ṣelem*. He further suggests that *iqonin* can be seen to denote a bodily form of God, that is, the divine Glory.[15]

The symbolism of Jacob's heavenly image associated with the deity's Throne is widely diffused in rabbinic literature. Comparable to the aforementioned Targumic accounts, these materials emphasize a distance between two identities of the patriarch: one heavenly and the other earthly. In relation to this Rachel Neis states that 'rabbinic texts set up a visual symmetry, between an

---

10 *Targum Pseudo-Jonathan: Genesis*, trans. M. Maher, M.S.C.; ArBib, 1B; Collegeville, 1992, pp. 99–100.

11 Fossum, *The Image of the Invisible God*, p. 141.

12 Fossum, *The Image of the Invisible God*, pp. 139–140.

13 C. Rowland, 'John 1.51, Jewish Apocalyptic and Targumic Tradition', *NTS* 30 (1984), p. 504.

14 D. Halperin, *The Faces of the Chariot: Early Jewish Response to Ezekiel's Vision* (TSAJ 16), Tübingen, 1988, p. 121.

15 Fossum, *The Image of the Invisible God*, p. 142.

earthly Jacob and a divine iconic Jacob.'[16] A possibility that Jacob's celestial identity might be envisioned in these materials as an 'icon' warrants closer attention. Thus, from *Lamentations Rabbah* 2:2 we learn the following:

> Similarly spoke the Holy One, blessed be He, to Israel: Do you not provoke me because you take advantage of the likeness of Jacob which is engraved upon My throne? Here, have it, it is thrown in your face! Therefore, He has cast down from heaven unto the earth the beauty of Israel.[17]

It appears that in this rabbinic passage Jacob's image has a sacerdotal significance, which might be understood as an 'icon' of the deity in a manner similar to how the prelapsarian Adam, installed in heaven, is portrayed in the *Primary Adam Books*. In relation to this concept Neis suggests that in *Lamentations Rabbah* 2:2 'God accuses Israel of taking advantage of the presence of this icon and provoking him with their behaviour. He threatens to cast down the icon of Jacob from his throne.'[18]

It appears that Jacob's exalted profile in the form of his image and its association with the *Kavod* posed a great challenge to rabbinic monotheistic sensibilities since some midrashic passages about the heavenly image of the patriarch are overlaid with distinctive polemical overtones. For example, *Genesis Rabbah* 68:12 presents the following debate between two rabbis:

> They disagreed. One maintained: They were ascending and descending the ladder; while the other said: They were ascending and descending on Jacob. The statement that they were ascending and descending the ladder presents no difficulty. The statement that they were ascending and descending on Jacob we must take to mean that some were exalting him and others degrading him, dancing, leaping, and maligning him.[19]

The contestation of the rabbinic authorities involves an interesting point, namely, a suggestion that Jacob himself might represent an anthropomorphic 'ladder' which connects earthly and celestial realms. The polemical thrust of this passage is not confined merely to a contestation between the rabbis, but also involves a rivalry between otherworldly creatures. In this respect, the inter-

---

16   R. Neis, 'Embracing Icons: The Face of Jacob on the Throne of God', *Images: A Journal of Jewish Art and Visual Culture* 1 (2007), pp. 36–54 at 46.

17   H. Freedman and M. Simon, *Midrash Rabbah*, vol. 7, London, 1961, p. 151.

18   Neis, 'Embracing Icons: The Face of Jacob on the Throne of God', p. 45.

19   Freedman and Simon, *Midrash Rabbah*, p. 2.626.

FACE AS THE IMAGE OF GOD IN THE JEWISH PSEUDEPIGRAPHA 211

esting feature of the text is a postulation that some angelic servants oppose Jacob's heavenly image by 'degrading ... and maligning him,' thus revealing a familiar motif of angelic rivalry found also in the Adamic lore, including the *Primary Adam Books*, where Adam's role as the divine image coincides with the theme of angelic veneration and rejection.[20]

Various versions of the *Primary Adam Books*, the narrative elaborations of the protoplast's story, which are deeply rooted in Second Temple Jewish conceptual currents, describe the primordial act of Adam's endowment with the divine image. After this portentous event the prelapsarian Adam becomes envisioned as the deity's 'icon'—a role very similar to the one which Jacob's image will play in later rabbinic accounts.

A story found in the Armenian, Georgian, and Latin versions of the *Primary Adam Books* depicts the archangel Michael bringing the newly created Adam into the divine presence and forcing him to bow down before God.[21] The deity then commands all the angels to bow down to the protoplast.[22] The results of this order are mixed. Some angels agreed to venerate Adam, while others, including Satan, refuse to do obeisance, on the basis that Adam is 'younger' or 'posterior' to them.[23]

---

20   On the angelic veneration, see C. Fletcher-Louis, 'The Worship of Divine Humanity as God's Image and the Worship of Jesus', in C. Newman et al. (eds), *The Jewish Roots of Christological Monotheism. Papers from the St Andrew's Conference on the Historical Origins of the Worship of Jesus* (JSJSS 63), Leiden, 1999, pp. 112–128 at 125–128.

21   The Latin version of the *Primary Adam Books* 13:2 reads: 'When God blew into you the breath of life and your countenance and likeness were made in the image of God, Michael led you and made you worship in the sight of God.' The Armenian version of the *Primary Adam Books* 13:2 reads: 'When God breathed his spirit into you, you received the likeness of his image. Thereupon, Michael came and made you bow down before God.' G. Anderson and M. Stone, *A Synopsis of the Books of Adam and Eve. Second Revised Edition* (EJL 17), Atlanta, 1999, p. 16E.

22   The Latin version of the *Primary Adam Books* 13:2–14:1 reads: 'The Lord God then said: "Behold, Adam, I have made you in our image and likeness." Having gone forth Michael called all the angels saying: "Worship the image of the Lord God, just as the Lord God has commanded."' The Armenian version of the *Primary Adam Books* 13:2–14:1 reads: 'God said to Michael, "Behold I have made Adam in the likeness of my image." Then Michael summoned all the angels, and God said to them, "Come, bow down to god whom I made."' Anderson and Stone, *A Synopsis of the Books of Adam and Eve*, p. 16E.

23   The Latin version of the *Primary Adam Books* 14:2–15:1 reads: 'Michael himself worshipped first then he called me and said: "Worship the image of God Jehovah." I answered: "I do not have it within me to worship Adam." When Michael compelled me to worship, I said to him: "Why do you compel me? I will not worship him who is lower and later than me. I am prior to that creature. Before he was made, I had already been made. He ought to worship me." Hearing this, other angels who were under me were unwilling to worship him.' The Armenian version of the *Primary Adam Books* 14:2–15:1 reads: 'Michael bowed

As we see in the stories of Adam and Jacob, the anthropomorphic 'icons' of both patriarchs provoke very similar reactions from the angelic host. On the one hand—the actions of veneration and loyalty, and on the other—feelings of resentment and rejection. Such complex and multi-dimensional dialogue between the embodied celestial image and the heavenly servants constitutes the conceptual centre of the later Talmudic and Midrashic accounts of Jacob, in which the angels are depicted as constantly interacting with the patriarch's upper self in the form of his *iqonin* and his lower 'sleeping' identity, connecting them with their ladder-like processions. The motif of peculiar angelic interactions, however, does not originate in the Jacob lore, but stems instead from the formative Adamic account similar to those reflected in the *Primary Adam Books*.

This theme of angelic opposition to Jacob is reflected already in some Talmudic materials that constitute the background of these Midrashic passages. Thus, *Bavli Hulin* 91b contains the following tradition:

> A tanna taught: They ascended to look at the image above and descended to look at the image below. They wished to hurt him, when behold, the Lord stood beside him.[24]

Elliot Wolfson notes that in this rabbinic source the motif of the patriarch's heavenly persona 'is placed in the context of another well-known motif regarding the enmity or envy of the angels toward human beings. That is, according to the statements in *Genesis Rabbah* and *Bavli Hullin* the angels, who beheld Jacob's image above, were jealous and sought to harm Jacob below.'[25] He points out that 'the influence of the Talmudic reworking of this motif is apparent in several later Midrashic sources as well.'[26]

The theme of Jacob's transcendental Self engraved on the divine Throne has also been transmitted in later Jewish mysticism. These mystical currents often add some novel symbolic dimensions to already familiar imagery. Thus, in

---

first He called me and said "You too, bow down to Adam." I said, "Go away, Michael! I shall not bow [down] to him who is posterior to me, for I am former. Why is it proper [for me] to bow down to him? The other angels, too, who were with me, heard this, and my words seemed pleasing to them and they did not prostrate themselves to you, Adam." ' Anderson and Stone, *A Synopsis of the Books of Adam and Eve*, p. 16E–17E.

24   I. Epstein, *The Babylonian Talmud. Hullin*, London, 1935–1952, p. 91b.

25   E. Wolfson, 'The Image of Jacob Engraved upon the Throne', in id., *Along the Path: Studies in Kabbalistic Myth, Symbolism, and Hermeneutics*, Albany, 1995, pp. 1–62 at 4.

26   Wolfson, 'The Image of Jacob Engraved upon the Throne', p. 4.

FACE AS THE IMAGE OF GOD IN THE JEWISH PSEUDEPIGRAPHA 213

Hekhalot Rabbati (*Synopse* § 164) the tradition of Jacob's *alter ego* on the throne is overlaid with striking erotic symbolism:

> You see Me what I do to the visage (*qlaster*) of the face of Jacob your father which is engraved for Me upon the throne of My glory. For in the hour that you say before Men 'Holy,' I kneel on it and embrace it and kiss it and hug it and My hands are on its arms three times, corresponding to the three times that you say before Me, 'Holy,' according to the word that is said, Holy, holy, holy (Isa 6:3).[27]

Here the deity embraces and kisses Jacob's heavenly identity engraved on His Throne. When compared to the previously explored accounts, the striking difference here is that now it is not the image or the *iqonin*, but rather Jacob's face (or more precisely a cast [*qlaster*] of the patriarch's face), that is engraved on the Throne. Reflecting on this obscure term, Rachel Neis says that 'the word *qlaster* in rabbinic texts describes the identity's facial features.'[28] It appears that this terminological change is not merely a slip of a *Hekhalot* writer's pen but a deliberate conceptual shift, given its attestation in some other rabbinic sources. Thus, in some *piyyutim*, which are conceptually very close to the developments found in *Hekhalot Rabbati*, Jacob's heavenly identity again appears to be understood as the 'face' on the Throne.[29]

Another rabbinic testimony found in *Pirke de Rabbi Eliezer* also attempts to replace the *șelem* imagery with the symbolism of Jacob's *panim*, by arguing that the angels went to see the face of the patriarch and that his heavenly countenance is reminiscent of a visage of one of the Living Creatures of the divine Throne.[30]

---

27   J.R. Davila, *Hekhalot Literature in Translation: Major Texts of Merkavah Mysticism* (SJJTP 20), Leiden, 2013, p. 86; P. Schäfer, with M. Schlüter and H.G. von Mutius, *Synopse zur Hekhaloth-Literatur* (TSAJ 2), Tübingen, 1981, p. 72.

28   Neis, 'Embracing Icons: The Face of Jacob on the Throne of God', p. 46.

29   Neis, 'Embracing Icons: The Face of Jacob on the Throne of God', p. 46.

30   *Pirke de Rabbi Eliezer* 35 reads: 'Rabbi Levi said: In that night the Holy One, blessed be He, showed him all the signs. He showed him a ladder standing from the earth to the heaven, as it is said, "And he dreamed, and behold a ladder set up on the earth, and the top of it reached to heaven" (Gen 28:12). And the ministering angels were ascending and descending thereon, and they beheld the face of Jacob, and they said: This is the face—like the face of the Chayyah, which is on the Throne of Glory. Such (angels) who were (on earth) below were ascending to see the face of Jacob among the faces of the Chayyah, (for it was) like the face of the Chayyah, which is on the Throne of Glory.' *Pirke de Rabbi Eliezer*, trans. G. Friedlander, New York, 1965, p. 265.

Such peculiar terminological exchanges between *ṣelem* and *panim* are significant for our study, since they evoke imagery of previously mentioned Jewish pseudepigraphical accounts in which the symbolism of the seer's celestial *alter ego* is closely tied to the *panim* imagery.

After our short excursus into the later Jewish traditions it is time to return to the *Ladder of Jacob*. One of the scholars whose studies probably contributed most to a recovery of the Jewish traditions in the *Ladder* is James Kugel. While reflecting on the terminological peculiarities found in the first chapter of the text, he argued that its authors were familiar with the tradition of Jacob's *iqonin* installed in heaven. Kugel drew attention to a comment made by a translator of the text, Horace Lunt, who, while speculating about the original language of the text, noted that the word used in the *Ladder* to designate the great 'bust' on the ladder is somewhat unusual. Lunt commented that 'no other Slavonic text has лице, "face", used to mean "statue" or "bust", and there is no Semitic parallel.'[31] On the other hand, Kugel proposed that such a Semitic parallel might indeed exist. In his opinion the term represents the Greek loan word incorporated into Mishnaic Hebrew—*iqonin*, which in some rabbinic texts does mean 'face.'[32] In view of these connections, Kugel concludes that 'there is little doubt that the *Ladder of Jacob*, in seeking to "translate" the biblical phrase "his/its head reached to Heaven", reworded it in Mishnaic Hebrew as "his [Jacob's] *iqonin* reached Heaven", and this in turn gave rise to the presence of a heavenly bust or portrait of Jacob on the divine throne.'[33]

Another important feature of the text supporting the possibility that the terrifying face might represent Jacob's heavenly image is the presence of the motif of angelic hostility—the theme, which as shown above, often accompanied the *ṣelem* traditions in rabbinic accounts about Jacob. This motif unfolds in chapter 5, in which the *angelus interpres* explains the seer's vision as follows:

---

31   H. Lunt, 'The Ladder of Jacob', in J.H. Charlesworth (ed.), *The Old Testament Pseudepigrapha* vol. 2, New York, 1983–1985, p. 2.403.

32   J. Kugel, *In Potiphar's House: The Interpretive Life of Biblical Texts*, San Francisco, 1990, p. 119.

33   Kugel, *In Potiphar's House*, p. 119. Jarl Fossum also affirms the presence of the *iqonin* tradition in the *Ladder* by arguing that 'in the fiery bust of the terrifying man we are probably correct to see the heavenly "image" of Jacob.' Fossum, *The Image of the Invisible God*, p. 143, n. 30. Christfried Böttrich also recently cautiously supported the existence of the *Doppelgänger* traditions in the *Ladder* by arguing that 'such an approach to the *Ladder of Jacob* via the idea of a heavenly counterpart opens a further door into Rabbinic Judaism.' C. Böttrich, 'Apocalyptic Tradition and Mystical Prayer in the Ladder of Jacob', *JSP* 23 (2014), pp. 290–306 at 297.

FACE AS THE IMAGE OF GOD IN THE JEWISH PSEUDEPIGRAPHA 215

Recension A	Recension B
Thus he said to me: 'The ladder which you saw had twelve steps, each step having two human faces that change their appearance. The ladder is this age, and the twelve steps are the times of this age. And the twenty-four faces are the kings of the lawless nations of this age. In the times of these kings, the children of your children and the kin of your sons will be tormented. These (kings) will arise against the transgressions of your grandsons.'	The ladder which you saw had twelve steps, each step having two human faces that change their appearance. The ladder is this age, and the twelve steps are the times of this age. And the twenty-four faces are the kings of the nations of the lawless age. Under these kings the children of your children and the kin of your sons will be tormented. And these (kings) will rise up against the lawlessness of your grandsons.[34]

Here the twelve steps of the ladder represent the twelve periods of 'this age,' while twenty-four 'minor' faces embody the twenty-four kings of the ungodly nations. Ascending and descending angels on the ladder are envisioned as the guardian angels belonging to the nations hostile to Jacob and his descendants. The angelic locomotion or 'ascents' appear to be interpreted in the passage as the arrogations against Israel.

3   2 Enoch

This brings us full circle to *2 Enoch*. Here, as in the *Ladder*, the main hero of the story, the patriarch Enoch, has his own vision of the divine Face. This encounter is described in chapter 22 and recurs in chapter 39. In chapter 22, the archangel Michael brings Enoch to the front of God's Face, after which the deity tells his angels, sounding them out: 'Let Enoch join in and stand in front of my face forever!' In response to this address, the angels do obeisance to Enoch, saying: 'Let Enoch yield in accordance with your word, O Lord!'[35] Michael Stone has

---

34   Kulik and Minov, *Biblical Pseudepigrapha in Slavonic Tradition*, pp. 291–292.

35   Andersen, '2 Enoch', p. 1.138. The tradition of the angelic veneration of Enoch is attested in both recensions of *2 Enoch*. *2 Enoch* 22:6–7 in Ms. J (longer recension) reads: 'And the Lord said to his servants, sounding them out, "Let Enoch join in and stand in front of my face forever!" And the Lord's glorious ones did obeisance and said, "Let Enoch yield in accordance with your word, O Lord!"' Andersen, '2 Enoch', p. 1.138. *2 Enoch* 22:6–7 in Ms.

suggested that the story found in *2 Enoch* 22 recalls the account of Adam's elevation and his veneration by angels found in the Armenian, Georgian, and Latin versions of the *Primary Adam Books*. Along with the motifs of Adam's elevation and veneration by angels, Stone notes that the author of *2 Enoch* also appears to be aware of the motif of angelic disobedience, i. e. Satan and his angels' refusal to venerate the first human. Stone draws the reader's attention to the phrase 'sounding them out,' (Slav. *и искуси Господь слуги Своя*) found in *2 Enoch* 22:6, which another translator rendered as 'making a trial of them.'[36] Stone suggests that the expression 'sounding them out' or 'making a trial of them' implies that it is the angels' obedience that is here being tested.[37]

Thus we see a peculiar constellation of the details that are not only reminiscent of the story of Adam in the *Primary Adam Books*, but which also recall the story of Jacob in the *Ladder* and the rabbinic sources where the traditions about the image of God are permeated by motifs of angelic veneration and rejection.

Also important are the details of Enoch's luminous metamorphosis and his anointing with shining oil from the Tree of Life (*2 Enoch* 22), which remind us of familiar Adamic motifs. In light of the aforementioned traditions, it is possible that in *2 Enoch*, like in the legends about Jacob, the divine *Panim* might take on the role of the divine *ṣelem*. The divine Face in *2 Enoch* 22 represents the cause and the prototype after which Enoch's new celestial identity was formed. The new creation after God's *Panim* signifies the return to the prelapsarian condition of Adam, who was also modelled—according to a testimony found in *2 Enoch*—after the Face of God. Support for this view can be found in *2 Enoch* 44, whereas one remembers the protoplast was also created after the Visage of God. This creation in the likeness of God's Face represents an important link that connects the first Adam, who lost his luminous image in the Garden of Eden, to the second Adam, the patriarch Enoch, who regained the lost status and the luminosity of the protoplast during his metamorphosis before the Face of God in heaven.

A (shorter recension) reads: 'The Lord said, "Let Enoch come up and stand in front of my face forever!" And the glorious ones did obeisance and said, "Let him come up!"' Andersen, '2 Enoch', p. 1.139.

36   Charles and Morfill, *The Book of the Secrets of Enoch*, p. 28.

37   M.E. Stone, 'The Fall of Satan and Adam's Penance: Three Notes on the Books of Adam and Eve', in G. Anderson, M. Stone and J. Tromp (eds), *Literature on Adam and Eve. Collected Essays* (SVTP 15), Leiden, 2000, pp. 43–56 at 47.

CHAPTER 11

On the Perdition of the Higher Intellect and on the Image of Light: Critical Edition, Translation, and Commentary

Maria V. Korogodina and Basil Lourié

1 Introduction

1.1 *Preface*

We have given the title *On the Perdition of the Higher Intellect and on the Image of Light* (thereafter PHI) to the treatise that is preserved without any title; its beginning and possibly its end are missing. PHI is known in Slavonic only, though it bears evident marks of being a translation from Greek. Many places in the text seem quite obscure, but at least some of them become much clearer when the reader recalls Greek syntax and Greek lexemes. This means that the translation was not of an especially high level.

The text has no self-standing manuscript tradition, even though it is preserved in dozens of manuscripts. It has survived being encapsulated within other larger literary works; all of them, however, share the same Slavonic translation of PHI. The earliest manuscripts are dated to the fifteenth century; the earliest compilations in which PHI is found date to the thirteenth century (see below). The thirteenth century is the *terminus ante quem*; we do not know the exact date and the exact place at which PHI appeared in Slavonic.

In its present condition, the text contains an afterword written in another style and designed to allow PHI to be accommodated in the mainstream Byzantine literature. Without this afterword, however, the text is not in any way an ordinary one. PHI is a treatise that expounds a peculiar Christology and refers to an Old Testament typology that is non-standard for mainstream Byzantine exegesis. We can demonstrate that the Christology of PHI represents a kind of Origenism in the style of Evagrius, whereas its typology is basically a Jewish Christian one, such as was still available in fifth-century Jerusalem (and probably later). There are reasons to suppose that the lost Greek original of PHI, in turn, was translated from Syriac.

© MARIA V. KOROGODINA AND BASIL LOURIÉ, 2021 | DOI:10.1163/9789004445925_013

1.2 *The Manuscript Tradition*

The manuscript tradition of PHI is described in detail by Maria Korogodina (*Кормчие книги XIV—первой половины XVII века*, Moscow–St. Petersburg, 2017, vol. 1, pp. 173–176). It is divided into two branches: within an anti-Latin treatise *The Epistle against the Romans*, and within the so-called *Selected Words* of Gregory of Nazianzus. In the second branch, the text is somewhat shortened at the beginning and the end, but the lost part is not significant.

The first branch, which is related to anti-Latin polemics, is in turn subdivided into two sub-branches, that of the miscellanies (four manuscripts of the fifteenth century) and that of the Nomocanon (*Kormchaya*) (see Figure 11.1); PHI is present in the Chudov recension of the Nomocanon compiled in the fourteenth century and preserved in more than 30 manuscripts of different dates starting from the middle of the fifteenth century.

The second branch is preserved in four fifteenth-century manuscripts of the *Selected Words* of Gregory of Nazianzus. The original form of this compilation from the works of Gregory of Nazianzus is attributed to Kliment (Clement) Smoljatič, the metropolitan of Kiev in 1147–1155. However, Kliment himself did not include PHI in the original compilation; it was added to it only at some later stage. In the *Selected Words*, PHI is a smooth continuation of the commentary of Nicetas of Serres (metropolitan of Heraclea since 1117) on homilies of Gregory of Nazianzus, as if it were part of the latter. However, the commentary by Nicetas of Heraclea (*CPG* 3027), dated to the turn of the eleven-twelfth centuries, is well known in both Greek and Slavonic,[1] and it does not contain PHI. This commentary was translated into Slavonic almost immediately and

---

1 There is no modern edition of this commentary that is known, beside Greek, in Latin, Slavonic, and Georgian. The bibliography in *CPG* 3027 (which appeared in 1974) deals with the published fragments in Greek and Latin and the unpublished Georgian version but omits the Slavonic entirely; there is no addition in the *Supplementum* (1998), whereas for the Greek fragments, R. Constantinescu, *Nicetae Heracleensis commentariorum XVI orationum Gregorii Nazianzeni fragmenta rem litterariam, historiam atque doctrinam antiquitatis spectantia*, Bucharest, 1977, pp. 170–197 has been added. For the Slavonic version, see Н.К. Никольский, *О литературных трудах митрополита Климента Смолятича*, St. Petersburg, 1892, pp. 161–199, where only a part of the published fragments ascribed to Nicetas is genuine. The Slavonic version remains unpublished as a whole, and its origin is under discussion; the manuscript tradition has not been studied. For a possible Russian origin, see, most recently, Н.В. Понырко, 'Был ли Климент Смолятич создателем первого славянского перевода Толкований Никиты Ираклийского на 16 слов Григория Богослова', *ТОДРЛ* 59 (2008), pp. 133–143, and А.А. Пичхадзе, *Переводческая деятельность в домонгольской Руси*, Moscow, 2011, pp. 33–34, but both leave unanswered and even unmentioned the arguments of Francis Thomson for a South Slavic origin (F. Thomson, '"Made in Russia". A Survey of the Translations Allegedly Made in Kievan Russia,' in: *Millennium Russiae Christianae*,

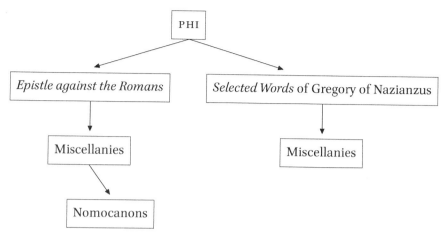

FIGURE 11.1   Transmission of PHI within the Slavonic compilations

was partially included in the *Selected Words* of Gregory of Nazianzus. Thus, the *terminus ante quem* for the Slavonic translation of PHI is the thirteenth century, when it was included in the *Epistle against the Romans*.

1.3   *The Language of the Slavonic Translation*

The language of the Slavonic translation is rather peculiar and certainly deserves to be studied properly, but such an inquiry would be beyond our competence. A surface inspection reveals some archaisms and a number of *hapax legomena*. The archaisms would suggest a date earlier than the thirteenth century (if not much earlier). For instance, единочадыи instead of единородныи as a rendering of μονογενής; the hiatus is preserved in some copies of the text: гортаань, несытааго, подобааше, шбрѣтааше сѧ.

The *hapax legomena* are interesting in another respect. They tell us nothing specific about the *Sitz im Leben* of the translation, but they are sufficient to indicate the translation school—which turns out to be different from all others known to us.

- съчаниє (съчанию мозгомъ) 'imbuing or making sated by sap' ('making sated of the brains') (§ 2). A *hapax legomenon*. The lexeme is known only in this text (*СлРЯ 11–17*, issue 26, 262);
- распловленьє (водоу въ распловленьє брашьноу) 'dissolving' ('dissolving the food') (§ 2). A *hapax legomenon*. The lexeme is known only in this text [(Mik-

---

Cologne, 1993, p. 316, cf. F. Thomson, *The Reception of Byzantine Culture in Mediaeval Russia*, Aldershot—Brookfield, 1999, Addenda, p. 26).

losich 1862–1865, 787), (Срезневский 1893–1912, vol. 3, col. 79); *СлРЯ 11–17*, issue 22, 26];

- соγхостъна (соγхостъна сила) 'dry, solid' ('the power/force of dryness') (§2). In such contexts, this lexeme is known only in this text [(Miklosich 1862–1865, 905), (Срезневский 1893–1912, vol. 3, col. 632)]. Perhaps, the phrase 'the power of dryness' appeared as a result of a Greek scribe's or Slavic translator's mistake: 'power' instead of another word designating food. Indeed, the word соγхостъныи is known in the phrases соγхотъна сънѣдь, соγхотьно ꙗмъı 'dry food' (Miklosich 1862–1865, 905). It would be expected that the meaning of the word соγхостъныи in PHI is the same, because, in the context, it emphasizes that the body needs food first and drink afterwards: 'We thus bring into the body the bread first, then the chalice. Why do we give first the power of dryness to the flesh … then, the water?' The phrase 'the dry food' (соγхостънои сънѣди), and not 'the power of dryness,' would look natural in the contraposition to 'bread' and 'chalice.' The words designating 'food' and 'power' would have been confused already in Greek, by either a Greek scribe or the Slavic translator: compare βρῶμα 'food' and ῥώμη 'strength, force' (Miklosich 1862–1865, 44, 838).

All these phrases are concentrated at the beginning of PHI (§2), almost within a single sentence. All of them deal with the topic of necessity to feed the flesh. The author's attention to the physiological side of human existence is striking and somewhat unexpected in a theological text. It may recall Galen's doctrine on the role of the oppositions, including 'moist' and 'dry,' whose excess or deficiency would lead to illness. A fragmentary Slavonic version of Galen's *De elementis ex Hippocrate* (under the name *Galen's* [sc., *treatise*] *on Hippocrates*) was popular in Russian monastic literature.[2] However, in this monastic literature, there is no wording similar to that of PHI.

There are also lexemes known elsewhere but taking peculiar forms in PHI.

- трешкалннѣ (adverbial form)—'in a thrice-unhappy manner' (§4). The adjective 'thrice-unhappy' (τρισάθλιος) is well known in Slavonic (*СлРЯ 11–17*, issue 30, 122, 160) but the adverb is unknown elsewhere in Slavonic, whereas it does occur, rarely, in Greek (τρισαθλίως).
- тристатною вещню потоплен бы—an apparently meaningless phrase 'with the thing (belonging to) the best officer(s) he was drowned' (§5). One more example of an erroneous translation. The image of the τριστάται '(Pharaoh's) best officers' referring to Exodus 15:4 was quite common in hymnography

---

2 See, for instance, the early fifteenth-century miscellany, Russian National Library (St. Petersburg), collection of the Kirillo-Belozersky monastery, Nr XII, ff. 215ʳ–219ᵛ.

and homiletics, almost exclusively in contexts related to drowning.[3] However, the mention of a 'thing' here looks odd. We provide below (§1.9) a possible explanation of this phenomenon.

Now we have to conclude that the Slavonic translation goes back to a pre-thirteenth-century epoch and belongs to a specific kind of people.

1.4 *The Unity of the Text*

The text contains a postface that is linked to the bulk of the text through a quotation from Gregory of Nazianzus but has nothing in common with its specific contents. It has no common language features described above either. It consists exclusively of liturgical and paraliturgical quotations related to the Nativity of Christ.[4] This text has been compiled from the Slavonic translations known otherwise and, therefore, is not a part of the original text of PHI but an addition inserted in the Slavic version. It looks like a connecting link between PHI and the following long narrative on the twelve apostles, thus filling the gap in the chronological order between the Old Testament and Christian history. We have postponed its analysis to another study and have excluded it from the present edition.

Apart from this afterword, the text of PHI is coherent, being a translation of a unique work which was not a compilation. The following observations would lead to this conclusion.

Throughout the whole text, the author uses the same phrases when he wants to introduce a new idea. For example, in §§1 and 3: прєжє бѣ ... прѣ҇ бо сєго нє бѣ ('earlier was ... earlier it was not').

The long digression about the origin of 'corruption' in the human genus at the beginning of the treatise elaborates on the same key notions, partly borrowed from Nemesius of Emesa: тлѣнномоу тлѣньноє 'the corruptible (thing) the corruptible one' (§1); гадєньє и питьє. тлѣньноє по wсоуждєнии 'eating and drinking (would become) corruptible after the condemnation' (ibid.); нє тлѣннємь тѣлєсє wбновлєнъ. нє гакожє родо҇ нєтлѣнєнъ но блгодатию. ащє бо нєтлѣбєнъ родомь бы бы҇. то нє бы wсоужєнъ бы҇ смр҇тию. ащє ли бы тлѣнєнъ. то нє бы пакы имѣлъ надєжі воскр҇ниіа. то како бы и wсоужєнъ тлѣю. єстьствомь тлѣбєнъ соущь '(he) was not renewed through the incorruptibil-

---

3 Cf. *СлРЯ 11–17*, issue 30, p. 164, s.v. тристатъ.

4 In the following order: a short quotation from the commentary of Nicetas of Heraclea on Gregory of Nazianzus's *Oratio* 38 Εἰς τὰ ἅγια φῶτα, sc., the Nativity, two troparia of the Nativity canon by Kosmas of Maiouma, and relatively long fragments from the anaphora of Basil the Great which is also to be celebrated at the Nativity.

ity of the body, as (he) is incorruptible not by genus but by grace, (as) the renewal through the incorruptibility of the body. It is not that he is incorruptible by genus but by grace. Were he incorruptible by genus, he would not be condemned to death; were he corruptible, he would not have the expectation of resurrection either; and how would he be condemned to corruption, were he corruptible by nature' (§ 3, quotation from Nemesius of Emesa); вси ѡсоуженн бывше в ꙁемлю и тлѣнне 'all having been condemned to the earth and the corruption' (§ 4).

Throughout the text, the translator repeatedly uses the same lexemes, including those that are rare in Slavonic. This feature of PHI in Slavonic reveals repetition of the respective terms in the Greek original. Let us compare several cases of repetition of peculiar wording in different parts of PHI (Table 11.1).

TABLE 11.1   Repetitions in the Slavonic text of *On the Perdition of the Higher Intellect and on the Image of Light* (PHI)

First occurrence	Repetition
въ частыꙗ недоугы и въ великыꙗ болѣꙁни въпадають. толъстостню бо плоти. ѿ таковыꙗ высоты. болѣꙁньнѣ ѿпадше ѡсоужени бывше (§ 2) 'they fall into frequent ailments and great illnesses,—because, with the thickness of the flesh, they were fallen painfully from such a height, when they were condemned'	прѣѹдолѣ бо толстость тонкости. ꙁемьнаꙗ бо ꙁемьныи. а нбнаꙗ нбнымь (§ 10) 'the thickness overcame the thinness— because the earthly (things) are to the earthly (things), the heavenly ones to the heavenly'
перьваго стрти въторaго бестрастнемь гоньꙁнеть (§ 8) (the second lamb) will rescue from the passions of the first with the impassibility of the second	прѣѹдолѣ бо емоу жиꙁни гонꙁненнꙗ (§ 8) 'thus overcame his life rescuing'
ꙗденне и питне не хлѣбно бѣаше. но породно бѣаше и дховно (§ 1) 'eating and drinking was not from bread but it was paradisiac and spiritual'	ндн на перьвоую породоу (§ 12) 'go to the former Paradise'

ON THE PERDITION OF THE HIGHER INTELLECT

TABLE 11.1   Repetitions in the Slavonic text *(cont.)*

First occurrence	Repetition
Ѿ таковыа высоты. болѣзньнѣ Ѿпадше (§2) 'they were fallen painfully from such a height'	Ѿ высоты въ пренсподьнии мракъ сведенъ бы̑ (§4) 'He was brought down from the height to the underworld darkness'
въ прекращенье хитрости. познавъ хитрьца (§12) 'until he will recognise the artist at (the time when) the art is stopped'	сн҃ъ оума и сн҃ъ хитрости (§13) 'the son of the intellect and the son of art'
не въстаноуть бо нижьна҄ къ выспренимь (§10) 'the (things) below will not arise to the (things) above'	на не выспрь высоцѣ. но на краннѣ҄и части (§15) 'not above on the height but on an extreme part'
гыбель перьваго высокаго оума (§4) 'the perdition of the first higher intellect'	в размѣшение оу҄ма прѣвысокаго (§11) 'with the confusion having the highest of the intellect'

This comparison makes it evident that the whole text was penned by a single author.

1.5   *The Two Previous and the Present Editions*

The text has been published previously twice. The *editio princeps* was produced by Andrey Nikolaevič Popov (1841–1881) in 1875, within the *Epistle against the Romans*, according to a fifteenth-century manuscript of his own collection, which now seems to be lost (А.Н. Попов, *Историко-литературный обзор древнерусских полемических сочинений против латинян: XI–XV вв.*, Moscow, 1875, pp. 191–194). Another edition, within the *Selected Words* of Gregory of Nazianzus, was published by Nikolai Konstantinovič Nikol'skij (1863–1936) in 1892 according to a unique fifteenth-century manuscript (Н.К. Никольский, *О литературных трудах митрополита Климента Смолятича*, St. Petersburg, 1892, pp. 174–176). Nikol'skij was not aware of Popov's edition. Oddly enough, nobody so far has realised that the two publications share the same text.

The printed recensions of the Slavonic Nomocanon do not include the Chudov recension, the only one that contains PHI. The present critical edition is based on twelve manuscripts: all four miscellany manuscripts, all four manuscripts of the *Selected Words* of Gregory of Nazianzus, and four fifteenth- and sixteenth-century manuscripts of the Chudov recension of the Nomocanon.

The present edition is not a Lachmannian reconstruction but it follows the best (though not ideal) fifteenth-century manuscript with the variant readings according to eleven other manuscripts. The edition is based on the manuscripts containing the largest fragment of PHI in combination with the *Epistle against the Romans*. The variant readings of the Nomocanons and the *Selected Words* of Gregory of Nazianzus are mostly secondary in comparison with those of the miscellanies containing the *Epistle against the Romans*.[5]

Our main manuscript was written by Martinian of the White Lake († 1483), a famous figure among the ascetics of the Russian 'Northern Thebaid.' It is the earliest copy among the miscellanies, though it has some secondary readings as well. For example, we find the words проповѣдоу проповѣда ('he preached preaching') in the reasoning on God's foresight (§ 3). It seems to be a tautology which breaks the sense of the passage dedicated to the foresight of Christ's advent, his death on the cross, and the salvation he brought, but not of his preaching. Other manuscripts kept the right reading по провѣдоу проповѣда ('he preached according to the foreknowledge'). The word провѣдъ with the meaning of 'foreknowledge' or 'foresight' is attested in the writings of John the Exarch of Bulgaria (late ninth—early tenth century) and the early Slavonic translation of Gregory of Nazianzus.[6] The mistake first appeared not in Martinian's codex but much earlier, because it affected the *Selected Words* of Gregory of Nazianzus, which contains the contaminated phrase по проповѣдоу проповѣда.

Another mistake in the oldest manuscript is the reading да едина та смр҃ть 'in order that the unique death *you*,' the last word being a direct object in the accusative case (§ 8) instead of the reading едина та смр҃ть ('in order that the unique *that* death') in the other miscellanies and the Nomocanons. The *Selected Words* of Gregory, however, contains the erroneous reading, thus making us consider Martinian's manuscript to be close to the protograph used by the editor of the *Selected Words* responsible for including PHI.

---

5 For the examples, see М.В. Корогодина, *Кормчие книги*, Moscow–St. Petersburg, 2017, vol. 1, pp. 175–178.

6 Cf. И.И. Срезневский, *Материалы для словаря древне-русского языка*, St. Petersburg, 1893–1912, vol. 2, col. 1516.

1.6   *Patristic Background*

It is rather easy to see that the theology of PHI is somewhat at odds with the Middle Byzantine sources. It is therefore important to 'factor out' the patristic background shared by PHI with mainstream Byzantine theology. It belongs to the period preceding the parting of the ways and can serve us as a *terminus post quem* for the original of PHI. The list of such 'classical' patristic authors turns out to be short, unless we consider the exegetical part of PHI: Gregory of Nazianzus, who died in 390, and Nemesius of Emesa, who wrote his *De natura hominis* between 390 and 400.

Nemesius is paraphrased in § 3; cf. his *De natura hominis*, I, 5 (46).[7] The two passages from Nemesius paraphrased in PHI originally follow each other in reverse sequence (s. Table 11.2).

The presence of Nemesius blurs the picture. Indeed, Nemesius himself was acquainted with Gregory of Nazianzus personally, and his work was written in the line of the *De hominis opificio* by Gregory of Nyssa. Nevertheless, it is only in the mid-seventh century that Nemesius's work became extremely popular (sometimes ascribed to Gregory of Nyssa or quoted anonymously) after having appeared as if *ex nihilo*. We know practically nothing about the earlier career of Nemesius's work.[8] In Byzantium, this phenomenon is certainly related to the monothelete controversy and especially to Maximus the Confessor's recourse to Nemesius, which kindled interest in Nemesius in various anti-Maximite milieux.[9]

Short passages of Nemesius became available in Slavonic in the earliest Slavonic patristic florilegium translated by order of Tsar Simeon of Bulgaria between 914 and 927 (the Greek original called Σωτήριος dates from before 900).[10] The text is overlapping with the quotation in PHI[11] but the translation is

---

7   Text: M. Morani, Nemesio Emeseni *De natura hominis*, Leipzig, 1987, p. 6; transl. R.W. Sharples, P.J. van der Eijk, Nemesius, *On the Nature of Man*, Liverpool, 1988, p. 41.

8   For the manuscript tradition of Nemesius's in various versions, see especially the literature summarised by Moreno Morani in id., Nemesio Emeseni *De natura hominis*, 1987, pp. v–xv with addition of S.Kh. Samir, 'Les versions arabes de Némésius de Ḥoms,' in: *L'eredità classica nelle lingue orientali*, Rome, 1986, pp. 99–151, and M. Zonta, 'Nemesiana syriaca: New Fragments from the Missing Syriac Version of the *De natura hominis*,' *Journal of Semitic Studies* 36 (1991), pp. 223–258.

9   Cf. Samir, 'Les versions arabes', 100.

10   Often called, after the earliest preserved manuscript, '*Izbornik* ["Miscellany"] of [the Great Prince of Kiev] Svjatoslav of 1073.' On this collection, see especially D.Tj. Sieswerda, 'The Σωτήριος, the original of the Izbornik of 1073,' *Sacris Erudiri* 40 (2001), pp. 293–327, and M. De Groote, 'The Soterios Project revisited: status quaestionis and the future edition,' *Byzantinische Zeitschrift* 108 (2015), pp. 63–78.

11   Nemesius's passage: П. Динеков, *Симеонов сборник (по Светославовия препис от 1073*

different.[12] It is to be concluded that Nemesius was quoted already in the Greek original of PHI and thus was translated into Slavonic without recourse to any previously existing translation.

PHI paraphrases Nemesius without an explicit reference to the author and as if sharing some very common knowledge. It looks as if his work were already classical. Therefore, we can cautiously suppose that this manner of quotation is a later feature, to be dated to the mid-seventh century at the earliest. Nevertheless, this is far from sure. The only safe *terminus post quem* provided to us by Nemesius is AD 390/400 (the date of the composition of his work).

Looking at the 'typological' part of PHI, we could add more patristic evidences, including Basil the Great and even Jacob of Sarug (451–521). The latter is especially interesting, because his understanding of Abel as the firstborn of the dead, while Christ is the firstborn of the living, is in apparent disagreement with Rom. 5:12 and the entire Byzantine exegesis, where the first who brought death was Adam. PHI follows Jacob of Sarug's exegesis, which is not attested in Greek at all: 'He (God) found the one who is caused to become the beginning of death, whose blood the entire earth embraced' (§ 8).

Since we will argue that PHI in Greek was, in turn, a translation from Syriac, a direct influence of Jacob of Sarug cannot be excluded. However, Jacob himself certainly followed an earlier Christian tradition. Because PHI is, in its exegetical part, very archaic, its author could have had an independent access to the same tradition as Jacob of Sarug.

One can add that the imagery of 'miraculously transferred from the darkness to the light' (§ 14) sounds as if it were borrowed from the late fourth-century *Corpus Macarianum*, written in Greek but by a Syrian and in Syria. However, from the fifth century its popularity became overwhelming and, therefore, this source is of little use for identifying the *Sitz im Leben* of PHI.

1.7 *Theological Contents*

The basic theological scheme of PHI is easily recognisable against the background of Evagrian Origenism, but some details remain either unclear or unexplained against this particular background. We are dealing, in PHI, with some unknown or almost unknown form of Origenism.

г.). Т. 1, Sofia, 1991, pp. 458–462 = ff. 132 в 16–134 г 6; for the overlapping fragment, see, ibid., p. 458 = ff. 132 в 20–134 г 22.

12   Cf. comparison between the two translations in Корогодина, *Кормчие книги*, Moscow–St. Petersburg, 2017, vol. 1, p. 174.

ON THE PERDITION OF THE HIGHER INTELLECT

TABLE 11.2 Passages from Nemesius of Emesa paraphrased in PHI

PHI	Nemesius, ed. (Morani 1987)	Translation of Nemesius
Were he incorruptible by genus, he would not be condemned to death; were he corruptible (φθαρτός), he would not have the expectation of resurrection (ἡ ἐλπὶς τῆς ἀναστάσεως) either; and how he would be condemned to corruption [φθορά], were he corruptible by nature [τῇ φύσει)?	εἰ γὰρ ἐξ ἀρχῆς αὐτὸν θνητὸν ἐποίησεν ὁ θεός, οὐκ ἂν ἁμαρτόντα θανάτῳ κατεδίκασε· τοῦ γὰρ θνητοῦ θνητότητα οὐδεὶς καταδικάζει· εἰ δ' αὖ πάλιν ἀθάνατον, οὐδ' ἂν τροφῆς αὐτὸν ἐνδεᾶ κατεσκεύασεν οὐδὲν γὰρ τῶν ἀθανάτων τροφῆς σωματικῆς δεῖται ...	For if God had made him mortal from the beginning He would not have condemned him to death when he had sinned: for nobody condemns the mortal to mortality. If, however, He had rather made him immortal, He would not have made him in need of food, since nothing immortal needs bodily food ...
... he (God) will put him at the borderline of the two natures, the mortal and the immortal.	Ἑβραῖοι δὲ τὸν ἄνθρωπον ἐξ ἀρχῆς οὔτε θνητὸν ὁμολογουμένως οὔτε ἀθάνατον γεγενῆσθαί φασιν, ἀλλ' ἐν μεθορίοις [PHI follows the variant reading ἐν μεθορίῳ, p. 6, apparatus ad l. 7] ἑκατέρας φύσεως, ἵνα, ἂν μὲν τοῖς σωματικοῖς ἀκολουθήσῃ πάθεσι, περιπέσῃ καὶ ταῖς σωματικαῖς μεταβολαῖς, ἂν δὲ τὰ τῆς ψυχῆς προτιμήσῃ καλά, τῆς ἀθανασίας ἀξιωθῇ.	The Hebrews ⟨Philo is meant⟩ say that man came into existence in the beginning as neither mortal nor immortal, but at the boundary of each nature, so that, if he should pursue bodily affections, he would be subjected also to bodily changes, while, if he should estimate more highly the goods of the soul, he might be thought worthy of immortality.

The Evagrian scheme, as it is preserved especially in his works surviving in Syriac, the *Gnostic Chapters* and the *Great Epistle to Melania*, presupposes the following stages:[13]

1. After the Fall of the intellects: the intellects, previously imageless, acquired an image, and
2. God created for them 'practical bodies' bearing this image and aspiring to reach the likeness of God. Then,
3. Christ-Logos, the only unfallen intellect, accepts such a body voluntarily in order to change it into the likeness of his own glorious body—but this is only the first stage of the two-stage process of salvation that has to take place within this aeon; then,
4. beyond this aeon, at the second stage of the two-stage salvation process, the intellects acquire the Son's image, and therefore the essential knowledge of the Trinity.

In PHI, § 6 describes the acquisition of images by the fallen intellects (point 1 above) and their re-creation 'for practice' (на дѣнство), in order to acquire the likeness of God. This is point 2 above and the common Origenistic idea (going back to Origen himself) that the bodily creation is 'according to the image of God' (but not according to the likeness), whereas the very purpose of this creation is to reach the likeness of God. In PHI, God 're-creates' 'them' (intellects), aiming at the achievement by them of his likeness.

The two-stage salvation through the Logos (points 3 and 4 above) is described in §14, where the imagery of the mould seems to be original. When accepting the body, the Logos, in PHI, makes from the material of this body a new form, and what is poured into this form (that is, unified with the Logos) acquires the likeness of the divine light. This act and even the wording correspond to the first stage of the two-stage salvation process in Evagrius: compare *Gnostic Chapters*, 6:14: 'During the aeons God *will change the body of our humiliation into the likeness of the glorious body* (Phil 3:21) of the Lord. Then, after all aeons, he will also make us *in the likeness of his Son's image* (Rom 8:29), if it is the case that the Son's image is the essential knowledge of God the Father.'[14] At the first of the two stages, the bodies of the intellects become identical to the glorious body of the Logos. Then, this Christological part goes on to the topics

---

13 Cf. especially I.L.E. Ramelli, Evagrius, *Kephalaia gnostika*, Atlanta, GA, 2015, A. Guillaumont, *Les 'Képhalaia gnostica' d'Évagre le Pontique et l'histoire de l'origénisme chez les Grecs et les Syriens*, Paris, 1962, and Guillaumont, *Un philosophe au désert. Évagre le Pontique*, Paris, 2004.

14 Ramelli, Evagrius, p. 323, cf. Guillaumont, *Les six centuries des "Kephalaia gnostica" d'Évagre le Pontique*, Turnhout, 1958/1985, p. 223.

ON THE PERDITION OF THE HIGHER INTELLECT

of the Second Coming and the Judgment, whereas the final goal of salvation has already been pointed out in § 6 (giving God's likeness to his image).

What seems to be most problematic is the relationship between the Higher Intellect and other, presumably, intellects referred to in the plural. PHI, especially in §§ 14 to 16, often switches from plural to singular, and we can never be sure of the original meaning. In the Evagrian and the earlier forms of Origenism, there was no such personage as the Higher Intellect at all. The 'intellects' were always in the plural. In PHI, however, there was also a certain Higher Intellect, as well as some other, presumably, intellects, such as the Logos and the fallen beings referred to in the plural. One can suppose, moreover, that these beings are, in some way, the posterity of the Higher Intellect. Here we have no ambition to resolve these problems. It is obvious that the theology of PHI needs to be properly investigated, taking into account, among other matters, our scanty data on the Palestinian *protoktistoi* Origenists.[15]

1.8   *Old Testament Typology*

The rich Old Testament typology of PHI deserves a separate study as well. Now we will sketch only an outline. The sequence of the 'types' follows a liturgical calendar known from several Second Temple Jewish and early Christian texts (see Table 11.3). What is especially important to note is that it roughly corresponds to the liturgical structure described by John II of Jerusalem in his homily on the dedication of the Sion basilica in 394 (preserved in Armenian only).[16] The liturgy is a necessary link between the typological meaning of the Old Testament and the history of salvation.

1.8.1   Some Comments[17]

– 2 Enoch is referred to with the words 'having sent': Enoch's ascension is mediated by angelic figures in 2 Enoch but not in Genesis or 1 Enoch. In 2 Enoch, the main liturgical time is Pentecost.
– Noah at the Summer Solstice: this goes against the chronologies of the Flood but is in conformity with the confusion between the Ark of Noah and the Ark

---

15   Cf. M. van Esbroeck, 'L'homélie de Pierre de Jérusalem et la fin de l'origénisme palestinien en 551,' *Orientalia Christiana Periodica* 51 (1985), pp. 33–59.

16   On the liturgical calendar implied in this homily, see B. Lourié, 'John II of Jerusalem's Homily on the Encaenia of St. Sion and Its Calendrical Background,' in: *Armenia between Byzantium and the Orient: Celebrating the Memory of Karen Yuzbashian (1927–2009)*, Leiden, 2019, pp. 152–196.

17   For bibliography, see the commentary to the translation below and Lourié, 'John II of Jerusalem's Homily'.

TABLE 11.3 The liturgical calendar underlying the Old Testament typology in PHI

Typological scene or figure in PHI	Liturgical meaning	The main source for this liturgical meaning
Abel	Passover/Easter	Abel as the Lamb; the mainstream exegesis
Enoch	Pentecost	2 Enoch
Noah	Summer Solstice	John 11 of Jerusalem
Tower of Babel	Second Pentecost/New Wine	No parallel (normally Tower of Babel at the first Pentecost: cf. 3 Baruch and the mainstream Christian exegesis)
Abraham	Third Pentecost	John 11 of Jerusalem
Isaac and Melchizedek	*Yom Kippur*	3 Baruch

of the Covenant. The latter has had its feast near the Summer Solstice in different Second Temple Jewish calendars (e.g., 3 Baruch, *Joseph and Aseneth et al.*)—as attested in the homily of John 11 of Jerusalem and confirmed in the later Jerusalem liturgical calendar.

- The Tower of Babel at the second Pentecost instead of the first: I do not know of any parallels, but an assimilation between the first two Pentecosts was a common Early Christian phenomenon, in the way that even the Pentecost described in the Book of Acts is now identified by some scholars with the second Pentecost (New Wine festival) and not with the first.[18]
- Abraham at the third Pentecost: attested by John 11 of Jerusalem and confirmed by the later Jerusalem liturgical calendar.
- Isaac and Melchizedek are both prototypes of Christ in mainstream exegesis. The divine High Priest at the Yom Kippur, though not identified with Melchizedek, is described in 3 Baruch. In PHI, however, Melchizedek is certainly a divine figure. It is difficult, however, to identify the precise kind of 'Melchizedekianism' of PHI within the set of the known doctrines where Melchizedek was divine and not human: their number is great but still not exhaustively established. It is worth noting, however, that we do not find any Melchizedekianism in Evagrius.

---

18   Cf. É. Nodet, 'De Josué à Jésus, *via* Qumrân et le "pain quotidien"', *Revue biblique* 114 (2007), pp. 208–236, at p. 216.

1.9 *Syriac behind Greek*

Slavonic PHI is certainly translated from Greek and does not share any features of other (rare) Slavonic texts that were translated directly from Syriac.[19] Nevertheless, the Greek of its lost original seems to be often irregular. Below several examples are outlined:

§ 6. The most difficult place in the Slavonic: свѣтнаіа си тма and, in the next sentence, до промысла свѣтнаго. The literal translation of свѣтнаіа theoretically could be either 'worldly' or 'of light' (but there are no such cases in the known texts in Slavonic[20]), and си тма could be translated as 'his/her/its darkness' (there is also the variant reading сиіа тма 'this darkness'). Some manuscripts have, in both places, the readings свѣтлаіа 'luminous/of light', which are certainly secondary; we follow instead the *lectiones difficiliores*. The same problem arises in the second sentence, where the difficult phrase could theoretically be translated as either 'to the worldly providence' or 'to the providence of light'. Recourse to the possible Greek original turned out to be of no help (no combinations with the relevant roots are attested). However, this conundrum can be resolved with the help of Syriac with its homonymy of the meanings αἰών and κόσμος in the unique ܥܠܡܐ. Incidentally, the Slavonic свѣтъ

---

19 For their non-exhaustive list, see B. Lourié, 'Direct Translations into Slavonic from Syriac: a Preliminary List,' in: *ΠΟΛΥΙΣΤΩΡ. Scripta slavica Mario Capaldo dicata*, Moscow–Rome, pp. 161–168, and *idem*, 'Slavonic Pseudepigrapha, Nubia, and the Syrians,' in: *The Other Side: Apocryphal Perspectives on Ancient Christian "Orthodoxies"*, Göttingen, 2017, pp. 225–250.

20 No lemma свѣтный in F. Miklosich, *Lexicon Palaeoslovenico-Graeco-Latinum*, Vienna, 1862–1865, Срезневский, *Материалы для словаря древне-русского языка*, St. Petersburg, 1893–1912, and *LLP. СлРЯ 11–17*, issue 23, p. 143, s.v. свѣтный refers to the entry совѣтный, (*СлРЯ 11–17*, issue 26, pp. 43–44) which describes свѣтный as a spelling variant for совѣтный and съвѣтный—a frequent word whose main meanings are related to either σύμφωνος 'accordant' or βουλή, συμβουλή 'council', 'to be aware' etc.; cf. (Срезневский, *Материалы для словаря древне-русского языка*, St. Petersburg, 1893–1912, vol. 3, cols. 682–683) and *LLP*, vol. 4, p. 245, s.v. съвѣтьнъ. However, the example with the spelling свѣтный in *СлРЯ 11–17* is the only one among many occurrences of the word, which suggests that this spelling was rare; indeed, otherwise it would not have created difficulty for the scribes of PHI: и бѣ же Двдъ свѣтенъ о всемъ со Анафаномъ сномъ Саулемь 'and David *reported* everything to Jonathan son of Saul' (from a *Palaea interpretata*, 1406; *СлРЯ 11–17*, issue 26, p. 44). In PHI, свѣтный occurs in two sentences following each other, applied in the first sentence to 'darkness' and, in the second, to 'providence.' It is extremely unlikely that the same Slavonic word would render two different words in Greek. However, no Greek word that could be rendered with съвѣтный, to the best of our knowledge, could be *consistently* applied to both 'darkness' and 'providence.' We are grateful to Anna Pichkhadze for her discussion of the theoretical possibility of the meaning 'of light/luminous' (which in fact has been 'restored' here by some scribes).

is also homonymic: either κόσμος or φῶς. The translator has followed, in both cases, the κόσμος-meaning, whereas the αἰών-meaning was the right one in both cases (this does not mean that the Slavonic is translated from Syriac directly: the same error might be committed by the translator into Greek; the sequence between Greek and Syriac is here irrelevant). The translation 'eternal darkness' fits perfectly with the context. It is rather standard in Greek, but see especially Job 10:22 LXX: after having said 'before I go whence I will not return, to the land of darkness and the shadow of death' (10:21), Job continued (10:22 LXX): εἰς γῆν σκότους αἰωνίου 'to the land of darkness eternal.' The pronoun сн 'his/her/its' in PHI could be a remnant of some Syriac construction, e.g., with ܡܠܗ.

§ 5. The phrase тристатною вещию in the sense 'in the same manner as the best officers (τριστάτοι)' seems to be almost impossible in Greek. The word τριστάτης, according to the data of *TLG*, is never used in genitivus possessivus, nor a possessive adjective derived from it is attested. Moreover, the normal Greek equivalents of the Slavonic вещь (especially πρᾶγμα) are not compatible with τριστάτης as a predicate. However, in Syriac, the word with the meaning 'in the same manner as,' ܐܟܘܬܐ, looks similar to the word ܐܝܬܘܬܐ, 'being, reality.'

§ 4. The literal translation of the Slavonic отдано быстъ ко изволъшемꙋ и покоршемꙋсѧ къ воли would be 'It was given to the one who wished and subdued himself to the will.' However, if we consider, at each occurrence of Slavonic ко/къ ('to') the Syriac preposition *l-*, we obtain, in the first instance, the mark of the agent of the passive verb ('it was given by the one who has voluntarily chosen'), and, in the second instance the mark of the Dative: cf. ܠܨܒܝܢܐ = θελήματι (1 Pet 4:2).

1.9.1 Other Possible Hallmarks of a Syriac *Vorlage*?

In the present condition of the Slavonic text, its own syntax is not clear enough to allow us to look for syntactical Semitisms. Nevertheless, in at least one place we can suppose a mistranslation of a typically Syriac phrase:

§ 8: 'the destroyer of the cause' (instead of the expected 'the cause of destruction'): this is possibly a mistranslation of a Syriac phrase with the *status constructus*.

1.10 *Conclusions*

PHI represents a so far unrecognisable branch of Origenism, similar but not identical to the Evagrian one. A date earlier than the middle of the sixth century (when there occurred the major schism within Origenism and other events resulting in its ramification and propagation, often in new guises[21]) is hardly possible, but the most likely date is the mid-seventh century or later. For a later date, we have two mutually enforcing reasons: the way of quoting Nemesius of Emesa and the esoteric style of PHI, which would have been a safety measure in an epoch when Origenism had become not especially welcome.

Several features of the text could be explained on the supposition of a Syriac *Vorlage* behind the lost Greek text. The *Sitze im Leben* of the Slavonic version of PHI, its lost Greek original, and the hypothetical Syriac *Vorlage* of the latter remain so far unknown.

2 On the Perdition of the Higher Intellect and on the Image of Light: Edition

2.1 *Manuscripts*

The edition is based on the earliest of the miscellanies: National Library of Russia (St. Petersburg), collection of the Kirillo-Belozersky monastery, No. 19/1096 (СбМ), ff. 323ʳ–328ʳ. Miscellany of St. Martinian Belozersky; first quarter of the 15th century. Cf. (Н.К. Никольский, *Описание рукописей Кирилло-Белозерского монастыря, составленное в конце XV в.*, St. Petersburg, 1897, 263–271), (Шибаев 2013, 86–90).

The sigla of the manuscripts used for the variant readings indicate their affiliation to different types of books.

Сб   *sbornik* (miscellany),
К   *Kormčaja* (Nomocanon),
Сл   *Slovesa izbrannyja* (*Selected Words*) of Gregory of Nazianzus.

The manuscripts used for the variant readings are listed below.

2.2.1 Miscellanies

СбЕ   National Library of Russia (St. Petersburg), collection of the Kirillo-Belozersky monastery, No. 53/1130, ff. 494ʳ–497ᵛ. Miscellany of Efrosin (Euphrosynos) of White Lake (Belozersky), 1460s. Cf. (Каган, Понырко, Рождественская 1980 [see note 52 on p. 167], 196–215), (Шибаев 2013, 222–226).

---

21   Cf., especially for the later modifications of Origenism, V. Baranov and B. Lourié, 'The Role of Christ's Soul-Mediator in the Iconoclastic Christology,' in: *Origeniana Nona*, Leuven, 2009, pp. 403–411.

СбП1   Russian State Library (Moscow), fund 236, collection of A.N. Popov, No. 147, ff. 54^v–60^r. Miscellany; third quarter of 15th century.[22]

СбП2   the lost miscellany belonged to A.N. Popov, 15th century. Cf. (Попов 1875, 191–195).

2.1.2   Nomocanons

КФ   Perm State Humanitarian-Pedagogical University (Perm), Manuscript collection, No. 1, ff. 276^r–278^v. Nomocanon, Chudov recension; third quarter of the 15th century. The manuscript has been given by Prokhor (Prochoros), the bishop of Sarai and the Don (1471–1491), to the Ferapontov monastery as a contribution for commemoration. Cf. (Н.С. Демкова, С.А. Якунина, 'Кормчая xv б. из собрания Пермского педагогического института', *тодрл*, 43 [1990], pp. 330–337), (Р.Г. Пихоя, 'Пермская Кормчая 1. Описание', *Исторический архив*, 1 [2001], pp. 187–210), (И.В. Поздеева, *Кириллические рукописи xv–xvii веков в хранилищах Пермского края*: Каталог, Perm, 2014, 29–46), and (Корогодина 2017, vol. 2, 117–118).

КО   Russian State Library (Moscow), fund 209, collection of P.A. Ovtchinnikov, No. 150, ff. 357^v–360^r. Nomocanon, Chudov recension; 1480s. Cf. (Корогодина 2017, vol. 2, 122).

КБ   Russian Academy of Sciences Library (St. Petersburg), Main collection of manuscripts, No. 21.5.4, ff. 385^v–389^r. Nomocanon, Chudov recension; early 16th century. Cf. (Корогодина 2017, vol. 2, 113–114).

КТ2   Russian State Library (Moscow), fund 304, collection of the Holy Trinity St. Sergius Laura, No. 205, ff. 351^v–354^v. Nomocanon, Chudov recension; late 15th century. A contribution to the Holy Trinity St. Sergius monastery by monk Arsenij Odinets (late 15th or early 16th century). Cf. (Иларій, Арсеній, *Описание славянских рукописей библиотеки Свято-Троицкой Сергиевой Лавры*, Parts 1–3, Moscow, 1878–1879, part 1, 332–339), (Корогодина 2017, vol. 2, 122–123), (О.Л. Новикова,

---

22   Watermarks: 1) Grapes, variant: (Шварц), Nr 291 (1460); 2) Bull, variant: (Briquet), Nr 2815 (1462); 3) Letter P, unidentified; 4) Vine, slightly similar: (Шварц), Nr 313 (1470); 5) Crown with trefoil, two forms, variant: (Лихачев), Nos 1035–1036 (1460–1461); 6) Bull's head, slightly similar: (Briquet), Nr 15094 (1435); 7) Cross, unidentified; 8) Bull's head, two forms, variant: (Briquet), Nos 14324–14325 (1461, 1465); 9) Gothic letter Z (?), slightly similar: (Briquet), Nr 9209 (1448); 10) Bull's head without eyes, unidentified; 11) Anchor, unidentified; 12) Three mounts, variant: (Piccard), Findb. 16, Nr 2224 (1461–1463); 13) Bull's head, variant: (Лихачев), Nr 1045 (1462); 14) Bull's head, variant: (Лихачев), Nos 1107–1108 (1466); 15) Bull, variant: (Лихачев), Nr 1021 (1455/56); 16) Bull's head, similar: (Лихачев), Nr 1116 (1466/67); 17) Bull, variant: (Лихачев), Nr 2593 (1440–1450); 18) Bull's head, variant: (Лихачев), Nr 1042 (1460/61); 19) Bull's head, two forms, variant: (Лихачев), Nos 1260–1261 (1470).

ON THE PERDITION OF THE HIGHER INTELLECT 235

'К биографии великокняжеского дьяка Андрея Одинца,' *Вестник «Альянс-Архео»*, 27 [2019], 8–9).

2.1.3 The *Selected Words* of Gregory of Nazianzus

СлТ1 Russian State Library (Moscow), fund 304, collection of the Holy Trinity St. Sergius Laura, No. 122, ff. 168^v–172^r. Apocalypse with commentaries by Andrew of Caesarea; last quarter of the 15th century.[23] Belonged to the Metropolitan of Moscow Zosima (1490–1494). Cf. (Иларій, Арсеній 1878–1879, part 1, 89–90).

СлС National Library of Russia (St. Petersburg), collection of the monastery of the Solovki Islands, No. 807/917, ff. 417^r–419^v. Miscellany with commentaries; 1470s–1480s.[24]

СлТих The State Public Scientific Technological Library of the Siberian Branch of the Russian Academy of Sciences (Novosibirsk), collection of M.N. Tikhomirov, No. 397, ff. 120^r–123^r. Miscellany with commentaries; middle of the 15th century. Cf. (В.В. Иткин, 'Постатейное описание рукописного сборника ГПНТБ СО РАН, собр. М.Н. Тихомирова, № 397, сер. 15 века', https://nsu.ru/classics/dionysius/itkin_4sb.htm, accessed on 9 February 2021.).

СлЧ State Historical Museum (Moscow), collection of Chudovo monastery, No. 320, ff. 358^v–361^v. St. Gregory the Great's homilies on the Gospels; second quarter of the 15th century. A contribution to the Pafnutij (Paphnutios) of Borovsk monastery by archimandrite of the Novospassky monastery German (1467–1482). Cf. (Т.Н. Протасьева, *Описание рукописей Чудовского собрания*, Novosibirsk, 1980, 187–188).

---

23 Watermarks: 1) Bull's head with a crown, similar: (Piccard), Findb. 2, Abt. xv, Nr 211 (1479/80); 2) Bull's head with three rays, slightly similar: (Лихачев), Nr 3870 (1476); 3) Three mounts, a fragment of a watermark, unidentified; 4) ligature, unidentified; 5) Bull's head with a cross under the nose, species: (М.А. Шибаев, *Рукописи Кирилло-Белозерского монастыря xv века. Историко-кодикологическое исследование*, Moscow–St. Petersburg, 2013), Nos 129–130 (1480); 6) Bull's head with a cross on the top, variant: (Лихачев), Nos 4081–4082 (last quarter of the 15th century.

24 Watermarks: 1) Bull's head with a crown, variant: (Piccard), Findb. 2, Abt. xv, Nr 233 (1478–1482); 2) Three mounts, similar: (Лихачев), Nr 2623 (1460–1470); 3) Letter P with a flower, species: (Piccard), Findb. 4, Abt. x, Nos 27–62 (1473–1485); 4) Letter Y with a cross, variant: (Лихачев), Nos 2519–2521 (1465–1466); 5) Letter P with a flower, variant: (Piccard), Findb. 4, Abt. ix, Nos 741–744 (1476–1479); 6) Dog with a flower over the back, variant: (Briquet), Nos 3623, 3624 (1475–1482); 7) Bull's head with a cross and a snake, variant: (Лихачев), Nos 3899–3903 (1490), (Briquet), Nr 15364 (1489).

2.2 *Principles of This Edition*

The text from the main manuscript (National Library of Russia, collection of Kirillo-Belozersky monastery, No. 19/1096) is copied as it is, with all Old Slavonic letters and punctuation symbols. The diacritical marks are not reproduced except the mark over the letter ї. The text is divided into paragraphs with titles (in English) for the reader's convenience.

Among the variant readings, on all occasions the meaningful variants are given, such as the lexical changes, omissions and additions of words, morphological differences representing different grammatical forms (including the interchange of the full and short forms). The slips of the pen are taken into account only if they either affect the meaning of the text or are repeated in several manuscripts. Not taken into account are: the orthographical variants, including those caused by historical development of the language, the contraction, the inflexion of the demonstrative pronouns, the gemination of the last vowels, the gemination of the suffix -н-, the variants of inflexions and prefixes (e.g., прѣ-/пре-/при-; соу-/съ-, and others), the numerals denoted by Cyrillic numbers instead of being written out, the Russicisms (such as себѣ/собѣ), and omissions or additions of the particle же and the conjunction и. Not taken into account also are sporadic scribal corrections of some letters in the main manuscript, which do not affect the word inflection and are not corroborated by other manuscripts.

Slavonic Text

Part 1: The Fall and the Second Creation
1. The Pre-fall Condition: Nourished by the Spirit

Преже бѣ[25] в раи. гадение и питие не[26] хлѣбно бѣаше. но породно бѣаше и дховно. лѣпо бѣаше дховномоу дховное.[27] таче послѣди. тлѣнномоу тлѣнъное.[28] трѣбѣ вѣдѣти[29] ны. гако земное наше тѣло ѿ землѧ създано есть. а не гакоже нѣции мнать. нѣ ѿ которыга силы и зѣло прельстишасѧ. легко бѣ гаденье. легко бѣ и тѣло. да оубо гаденье и питье. тлѣньное по ᷍соуженни.

---

25   во *СбП₁, СбП₂, КФ, КО, КБ, КТ2.*

26   нет *СбЕ.*

27   дховное дховномоу (*вм.* дховномоу дховное) *КФ, КО, КБ, КТ2.*

28   тлѣнное тлѣнномоу (*вм.* тлѣнномоу тлѣнъное) *КФ, КО, КБ, КТ2.*

29   видѣти *СбП₁, СбП₂, СбЕ, КТ2.*

2. The Post-fall Condition: Food and Health

Бы̑ꙗкоже рече свѣдѣтельствоуꙗ павелъ. нѣ̑ цр̑твие[30] бж̑ие. пища и питие. а григории б̑гословець[31] ре̑ч. не боудѣмъ ащи се есмы.[32] но боудѣмъ ꙗкоже прѣже бѣхо̑м. нынѣ бо ны жажа оудроучаеть.[33] алчьба томнть. ꙗдъше бо пити хощемь. преже бо хлѣбъ // (л. 323 об.) въносимъ въ тѣло. таже чашю. почто преже соухостъноую силоу дамы плоти. подпоръ жиламъ и оутверьженье костемь. таже водоу[34] въ распловленье брашьноу. и ко исполненню крови. и к наполненню. и съсочаннн[35] мозгомъ. и влагоу тѣлоу.[36] таче расходитьсꙗ во[37] всꙗ съ̑ставы. съмѣсивъшесꙗ съ брашьномь. аще ѡбое и въ мѣроу воспрннмоуть. то съдравие велико. аще ли коего не въ мѣроу прннметь.[38] то вь частыꙗ недоугы и въ великыꙗ болѣзни въпадають. толъстостию бо плоти. ѿ таковыꙗ высоты. болѣзньнѣ ѿпадше ѡсоужени бывше.[39]

3. Nature: Neither Corruptible nor Incorruptible

Пре̑ж бо сего[40] не бѣ сего требѣ. имьже дх̑овьнаꙗ блгдть бѣ. не тлѣннемь телесе ѡбновленъ.[41] не ꙗкоже родо̑м нетлѣненъ но бл̑годатию.

Аще[42] бо нетлѣненъ родомь бы[43] бы̑. то не бы ѡсоуженъ бы̑[44] смртию. аще ли[45] бы тлѣненъ. то не бы[46] пакы имѣлъ надежї // (л. 324) воскр̑ннꙗ. то како[47] бы и ѡсоуженъ тлею.[48] естьствомь тлѣненъ соущь. и преже ꙗкоже ре̑ бъ.[49] въ болѣзнехъ[50] родиши чада своꙗ. ꙗвьлꙗꙗ емоу ѡ воскр̑ннн надежю.[51]

---

30 цр̑кви *СбЕ*; цр̑тво *КТ2*.

31 б̑гословъ *КФ*.

32 ксмъ *СбП1, СбП2, КФ, КО, КБ, КТ2*.

33 оудрꙋ̑чают *КБ*.

34 водою *СбП2*.

35 съчанню *СбП1, СбП2*, сочанню *КФ, КБ*.

36 тѣлом *КФ, КО, КБ, КТ2*.

37 нет *СбП1, СбП2*.

38 въсъприметъ *КФ, КБ*, въсприимоуть *КО, КТ2*.

39 Слова ѡсоужени бывше написаны писцовым почерком на нижнем поле со знаком вставки *СбМ*.

40 всего *КТ2*.

41 ѡбновление *КФ, КО, КБ*, ѡбновленїꙗ *КТ2*.

42 Отсюда начинается общий фрагмент со "Словесами избранными", известный по спискам *СлС, СлТ1, СлТих, СлЧ*.

43 бы̑ *СлТих*.

44 нет *КФ, КО, КБ, КТ2, СлС, СлТ1, СлТих, СлЧ*.

45 нет *СбЕ*.

46 Далее стерто слово пакы, повторенное писцом дважды *СбМ*.

47 пакы *СлС, СлТ1, СлТих, СлЧ*.

48 тлѣнию *СлС, СлТ1, СлТих, СлЧ*.

49 г̑ь *СбЕ*.

50 болѣзни *СбЕ*.

51 надежа *СбЕ*.

проповѣдоу[52] проповѣда. ꙗко не до коньца забьвенъ боудеть ѿ раꙁроушении. да тѣмъ смотраше в немь. ѡ единочадѣмь[53] сн҃ѣ въстаниꙗ. да тѣмь[54] постави и на прѣдѣлѣ. ѡбою естьствоу. см҃ртьна и бесм҃ртьна.[55]

4. The Fall of the First Higher Intellect

Не бо бꙗше на польꙁꙋ см҃ртоноснаго въкоуса въкоусивъши. вси ѿсоужени бывше[56] в ꙁемлю и[57] тлѣние. дш҃а же соупротивьникомъ ѿдана бы. гнѣвоу паче ѡдолѣвающꙋ[58] бж҃ественѣи ꙗрости. ѿдано бы҃ ко иꙁвольшемоу.[59] и покорьше- моуса к[60] воли. Ѿ высоты въ преисподьнии[61] мракъ сведенъ бы. что бы гыбель перьваго высокаго оума. послѣдьнею нищетою. смѣренъ бывъ трешканнѣ[62] ∴

5. The Fall: Exodus Imagery

Тристатною[63] вещию потопленъ бы҃. цр҃ьствова над нимъ тма съ ꙁолию. пагꙋбы и льсти исполнь.[64] съ вихромъ[65] въскакаꙗ.[66]

6. The Second Creation and the Way of Restoration

Ꙗко творимаꙗ[67] // (л. 324 об.) ими на дѣиство.[68] претвараꙗ свое҃ подобиꙗ. и Ѿ беꙁъѡбраꙁнаго[69] въ ѡбраꙁное. прѣврати своимъ лꙋкавьствомъ. тѣми паче наполънꙗꙗ гортаань несытааго[70] ада.[71] тѣми паче въѡбражашеть.[72] даꙗти

---

52 по провѣдоу *СбП1, СбП2, КФ, КО, КБ, КТ2, СлС*; по проповѣдоу *СлТ1, СлТих, СлЧ*.

53 единочадомь исправлено на едино҃ чадѣмъ *СбЕ*.

54 Далее зачеркнуто смотраше в не҃ *СбЕ*.

55 бесм҃ртнаа *СбЕ*. Далее да тѣмь постави и *СлС, СлТ1, СлТих, СлЧ*.

56 Нет слов вси ѿсоужени бывше *СлС, СлТ1, СлТих, СлЧ*.

57 и въ *КФ, КО, КТ2*.

58 Буква а исправлена из буквы о *СбМ*; ѡдолѣвающи *КФ, КБ, КО, КТ2*; ѡдолѣвающоу. и *СлТ1, СлТих, СлЧ*; ѡдоволѣвающоу. и *СлС*.

59 иꙁволшемꙋса *КФ, КО, КБ, КТ2*.

60 въ *КФ, КО, КБ, КТ2*.

61 Далее си *КФ, КО, КБ, КТ2*.

62 прешкаллнѣ *СбЕ*; преоканнѣ *СлТих*.

63 Трисъставною же *КФ, КО, КБ, КТ2*. Фраза Тристатною ... въскакаꙗ написана на нижнем поле писцовым почерком со знаком вставки *СбМ*.

64 исполненъ *КБ*.

65 Нет слов съ вихромъ *СлС, СлТ1, СлТих, СлЧ*.

66 всаческаа *СлТ1, СлЧ*.

67 творима *КТ2*.

68 дѣиствꙋ. и *КБ*.

69 беꙁъѡбраꙁнаа *КФ, КО, КБ, КТ2*.

70 несына҃ *СлТих*.

71 гада *СбЕ*.

72 вовбражаеть *СлТ1, СлТих, СлЧ*.

ON THE PERDITION OF THE HIGHER INTELLECT

ѡбразоу подобига имъ[73] егоже сѣмене наполниса свѣтънага[74] си[75] тма. црь-
ствова[76] до промысла[77] свѣтнаго.[78] донь д̄ е̄ же помѧноу. возвратънаго[79] си
оума. и жалостьнаго забытига. ѿ невѣдомаго[80] и ѿ разоумьнаго. въ скотне то
страстьное[81] чювьственое:[82]

Part II: Key Points of the History of Salvation
7. Looking for the Righteous: The First Failed Attempt

Смотрѧ[83] едва въспѧть пойдеть. ѿ первыга прельсти. возводѧ оумъ ѿ глоу-
бокы нощи.[84] и не ѡбрѣте никого же. растьлиша бо сѧ и ѡмразишасѧ[85] въ начинании.

8. Abel

Ѡбрѣте въ начало смр̄ти повиньнаго. егоже кровь всга землѧ ѡбигать. началь-
ный[86] начатокъ. ѡбрѣте агньцемь. послоужиша // (л. 325) да ч̄т̄ъ агнець
гавитьсѧ.[87] багро м̄ и червленицею покрытъ. чистостию[88] свѣта ѡблигань. да
едина тѧ[89] смр̄ть. всемоу чл̄вчьскомоу родоу[90] бы с̄ :·

Подобаше бо второмоу агньцю. первыимъ воображеноу быти. да перьваго
стр̄ти вътораго бестрастиемь[91] гоньзнеть.[92] сличьный[93] бо[94] ѡбразъ.[95] пос-

---

73 й х̄ *СбП1, СбП2, КФ, КО, КБ, КТ2, СлС, СлТ1, СлТих, СлЧ.*

74 свѣтлаѧ *КБ, СлТ1, СлТих, СлЧ.*

75 сига *СбЕ;* нет *КФ, КО, КБ, КТ2.*

76 цр̄тво *КБ.*

77 добро мысла *(вм.* до промысла*) СлТ1, СлТих, СлЧ.*

78 свѣтлаго *СбЕ.*

79 възвратнаго *СбП2;* възратнаго *КФ, КО;* воздрастнаго *СлС,* възрастнаго *СлТ, СлТих, СлЧ, КБ.*

80 невидимаго *КО, КТ2.*

81 скотостр̄тьное *(вм.* скотне то страстьное*) СлС, СлТ1, СлТих, СлЧ.*

82 чювьствие *СбЕ.*

83 Смотрѧга *СлТ1, СлЧ.*

84 нощіа *СлС,* вещи *СлТ1,* вещіа *СлЧ,* вощіа *СлТих.*

85 ѡбразишасѧ *КО, КТ2, СлТ1, СлЧ,* буква б исправлена из буквы м *СлТих.*

86 начатын *СлТ1, СлТих, СлЧ.*

87 гавлаетьсѧ *СлТ1,* гавѧтсѧ где буквы вѧ написаны на поле со знаком вставки *СлЧ.*

88 ч̄тотою *СлТ1.*

89 та *СбП1, СбП2, КФ, КО, КБ, КТ2;* нет слов едина тѧ *СлТ1, СлС, СлТих, СлЧ.*

90 родоу чл̄вчьскомоу *(вм.* чл̄вчьскомоу родоу*) СлТ1, СлТих, СлЧ.*

91 бестр̄тие *СлТ1, СлТих, СлЧ.*

92 гонзеть *СбП1, СбП2.*

93 сличны *СлТ1.*

94 нет *КБ.*

95 ѡбразы *СлТ1, СлЧ.*

тави хлѣбоу агнець. ѿ единого сѣмене. ѡбѣ ѿрасли. и не возможе перьваіа ѿрасль оуньшемоу ѹдолѣти. имьже не сверьшенъ принесе плодъ. да тѣмь іараса[96] гнѣвашеса на оуньшаго. прешдолѣ бо[97] емоу жизни гонзненіа. разроушьникъ винѣ бывъ. нанесеною же емоу казнью. въ правъдоу[98] мещенье[99] приіатъ. како бо емоу не приіати[100] казни. имьже ѡнъ створи. ѡбразъ подобиіа си разроуши. соупротивьникъ бы͡ самодержьцю твари лоукавьствіемь того сѣменемъ возрастоша. прешдолѣни злобою и лоука // (л. 325 об.) вьствомь. въспитѣни[101] бывьше. да іавить͡[102] со͡у͡д въ правьдоу. соудащемоу всѣ͡х. Іако самовластіемь ѹдерьжими. да не[103] на повиньнаго виноу вьскладають.

9. Enoch

Вжада бо спсеніа и не ѡбрѣте даюшаго емоу. но ѡбрѣтъ нѣкоего въ добродѣтели.[104] и посла изатъ и[105] ѿ временьныіа жизни. и писано не ѡбрѣташеса[106] іако престави и б͡ъ.

10. Noah

Таче избра втораго родоу начальника.[107] к немоу же положи[108] мѣрило правды. тажько͡е бо погроузиса. легкое же[109] возвысиса. прешдолѣ бо толстость тонкости. земьнаіа бо земьный.͡м а нб͡наіа нб͡ныимь. не въстаноуть бо нижьна͡а къ[110] выспренимь. іако расыпашаса кости и͡х при адѣ.

---

96 іараше͡с *СбЕ, СлТих.*

97 нет *СлС, СлТ1, СлТих, СлЧ.*

98 право *КФ, КО, КБ, КТ2.*

99 Ѿмьщеніе *КТ2.*

100 не пріаті ем̀у (вм. емоу не приіати) *СлС, СлТ1, СлТих, СлЧ.*

101 в̀спѣтѣни *СбП1, СбП2;* въспитани *СлС, СлТ1, СлТих, СлЧ.*

102 іаватса *КТ2.*

103 Повторено дважды *КФ, КО, КБ.*

104 добродѣтели͡х *СбЕ.*

105 Написано над строкой писцовым почерком *СбМ.*

106 ѡбрѣташеса *КФ.*

107 началникоу *СбП1, КТ2.*

108 приложи *КО, КТ2.*

109 бо *СбЕ.*

110 Далее стерто три (?) буквы *СбМ.*

11. The Tower of Babel

Сего ради тоуне ѡста прелестьнаꙗ тьма безъ искоуса. доньдеже возвышеноую[111] гордость[112] показа. юже[113] расыпа самъ. дх҃омь оустъ его.[114] в размѣшение[115] оу᷉ма[116] прѣвысокаго // (л. 326) пресѣкъ.

12. Abraham

И превратное. в непревратное претворь. да ѡбрꙗщеть плодъ. ѡбращенниꙗ изъ-ѡбрѣте. бо егоже въжелѣ. не ноужею сътвори. дондеже въ прекращенье[117] хит-рости. познавъ[118] хитрьца. к немоу же и заветъ показа. въстани ре᷉ ѡ ѡбычаꙗ перьвыꙗ прѣльсти. и иди на перьвоую породоу. да боудеши чадомъ ѡц҃ь. иже вос-приимоуть землю перваго бытиꙗ. и родиши[119] сн҃ъ радости.[120] вѣрова ре᷉ бв҃и[121] и въмѣнисꙗ емоу въ правьдоу. и роди сн҃а[122] въ старости[123] маститѣ.

13. Isaac and Melchizedek Prefiguring the Two Natures of Christ (but Not the Logos as an Intellect)

Изъѡбражаеть бо[124] ѿселѣ ѡбразъ послѣдьнꙗꙗ стр᷉ти. сѣнию[125] страсти. соугоубѣ[126] двѣ естьствѣ. ба҃ и чл҃вка. по божествоу. мельхиседекъ. а[127] по чело-вѣчьствоу[128] сн҃ъ радости. а по оутѣшению сн҃ъ оума и сн҃ъ хитрости. ѿ него же возрасте. в҃і. племене.

---

111 възвышеноу *СбП2, СлТ1, СлТих, СлЧ.*

112 Перед словом гордость зачеркнуто слово прелесть *СбЕ.*

113 ꙗже *СбП2.*

114 нет *СлТ1.*

115 размѣшенїи *СбЕ.*

117 превращенїе *СлТ1, СлЧ,* прев᷉крашеѐ *СлТих.*

118 позна *СлС, СлТ1, СлТих, СлЧ.*

119 роди *СлС, СлТ1, СлТих, СлЧ.*

120 вь радости *СлС, СлТ1, СлТих, СлЧ.*

121 авраа᷉ бв҃и *СлТих.*

122 нет *КФ, КО, КБ, КТ2;* сн҃ъ *СлТ1, СлТих, СлЧ.*

123 радости *СбЕ.*

124 нет *КФ, КО, КБ, КТ2.*

125 сѣни *КФ, КО, КБ, КТ2.*

126 Буква ѣ исправлена из буквы ъ *СбМ.*

127 и *СлТ1, СлЧ.*

128 влч᷉твоу *СбП1, СбП2.*

Part III: Christology

14. The Two-Stage Salvation

Люта искоушенїа непреклонныа.[129] ѡкамє // (л. 326 об.) ньнаꙗ срдца. воѡбражаеть ѡпокоу. поставлꙗꙗ[130] ѡбразъ свѣта. доньдеже льꙗное во ѡбразъ боудеть. воѡбражьшагосѧ подобиꙗ[131] чюднѣ преводѧ ѿ тмы на свѣтъ. да[132] свѣдѣтельство ѡного[133] свѣта. великъ свѣтъ боудеть.[134] видимын же син свѣтъ тма боудеть.

15. The Overnight Journey to the First Image Stamping

Ꙗкоже[135] не смѣхомъ нарещи слн̃ца имьже лоуна есть. хотѧщю же восиꙗти слн̃цю. абие разбиваꙗ[136] нощь. свѣтлостию[137] ѕвѣзды. и проведе ꙗ[138] чресъ поучиноу стр̃ти.[139] воѡбраженаго стр̃тию. воѡбраженаго[140] сѣнью. постави н[141] на ѡбѣтованїи[142] перьваго воѡбраженїа.[143] на не[144] выспрь высоцѣ. но на краинѣ̈ части. не возможе бо превести. ѿ глоубокыа нощи.[145] имьже свѣдѣтельства не бꙗше. водѧщю[146] бо рабопокореныа игоу.

16. The Second Coming

В работѣ[147] соущю[148] несвободна тварь. не возъможе наслѣдити свободы. донь // (л. 327) деже въѡбраженый ѡнъ[149] ими. нижьнꙗꙗ ѿрасли сн̃а цр̃ꙗ вышьнꙗго.

---

129 нет *СлС, СлТ1, СлТих, СлЧ.*

130 поставлꙗ҇́ *КБ.*

131 подобию *СлТ1,* въ подобию где въ зачеркнуто *СлЧ.*

132 на *СбЕ.*

133 ѡно бо *СлТ1, СлЧ,* ѡно *СлТих.*

134 бꙋде҇́ свѣ҇́ (*вм.* свѣтъ боудеть) *СлТих.*

135 ꙗко *КФ, КО, КБ, КТ2, СлТ1, СлТих, СлЧ.*

136 разбиꙗ *СбЕ;* разбивашесѧ *СлТ1, СлЧ.*

137 свѣтлостьꙗ *СлС, СлТих, СлТ1, СлЧ.*

138 нет *СлТ1.*

139 стр̃тен *СлТ1, СлТих, СлЧ.*

140 нет *вм.* и *КФ, КО, КБ, КТ2.*

141 нет *СлТих.*

142 ѡбѣтованїа *КБ.*

143 ѡбраженїа *СбЕ;* въѡбраженїи *СлТ1, СлЧ.*

144 не на (*вм.* на не) *СбП1, СбП2, КФ, КО, КБ, КТ2, СлС, СлТ1, СлТих, СлЧ.*

145 нощїи *КБ.*

146 водѧще *КФ, КО, КБ, КТ2, СлТих, СлС.*

147 рабѣ *КФ, КО, КБ, КТ2.*

148 соущи *СбП1, СбП2, КФ, КО, КБ, КТ2, СлС, СлТ1, СлТих, СлЧ.*

149 нет *КФ, КО, КБ, КТ2.*

ON THE PERDITION OF THE HIGHER INTELLECT

мⷣрть. сн҃ъ и наслѣдникъ вышнаго цр҃а. ѡблеченъ[150] въ месть. и ѡдѣ҇ⷩ въ соуⷣ. таино съшествие[151] его. но пакы[152] ꙗръ прихоⷣ его.

A Tentative Translation[153]

The task of translation of the Slavonic text would require understanding the Greek words and syntactical constructions rendered in Slavonic. Therefore, the present translation normally does not represent the whole range of meanings that could be read into the Slavonic text by a reader who has no idea of the Greek original, but refers to a specific restoration of the Greek key words, which are often inserted into the translation in [square brackets]. Also in [brackets] are some additions to the text of the translation intended to provide an interpretation of obscure passages. The words in (ordinary parentheses) are added to make the translation smoother, even though this remains very technical and far from any attempt to render the literary style of the lost Greek original. We hope that, at least, the translation is not too close to the extremely obscure literary style of the Slavonic text either, in order to be a little clearer. The biblical references are given in (parentheses) as well.

Part 1: The Fall and the Second Creation

1. The Pre-fall Condition: Nourished by the Spirit

Formerly, in Paradise, food and drink [βρῶμα καὶ πῶμα/πόσις] were not (earthly) bread but paradisal [**породно** = τοῦ παραδείσου] and spiritual [πνευματική]. The spiritual (nourishment) was such as befitted the spiritual (person), just as the corruptible (food befitted) the corruptible (body). There is a need to know[154] that our earthly body is created out of the earth and not out of some power [τινὸς δυνάμεως], as some, who greatly deceive themselves, think. The food was light [ἐλαφρόν], and the body was light [ἐλαφρόν]—in the way that [**да оубо** =

---

150 воблече҇ⷩ причем буква б исправлена из буквы п *КБ*; ѡбоⷧченъ *СлС, СлТⁱ, СлТих, СлЧ.*

151 шествⁱе *СлС, СлТих,* прⁱшествⁱе *СлТⁱ, СлЧ.*

152 испр., в *СбМ* папакы.

153 The authors are especially grateful to Prof. James O'Leary for his help with this translation, but the responsibility for the possible mistakes and shortcomings should be attributed solely to the authors.

154 *Variant reading*: to see; вѣдѣти 'to know' and видѣти 'to see' are often interchangeable due to the transition *ě > i* in the northern (e.g., Novgorodian) as well as in Ukrainian dialects; cf. (Р.М. Цейтлин, Р. Вечерка, М. Благова, *Старославянский словарь (по рукописям X–XI веков)*. Moscow, 1994, p. 164).

ἵνα γὰρ] eating and drinking (would become)[155] corruptible after the condemnation.

2. The Post-fall Condition: Food and Health

It came about as Paul attests: *the kingdom of God is not eating and drinking* [οὐ ... ἐστιν ἡ βασιλεία τοῦ θεοῦ βρῶσις καὶ πόσις] (Rom 14:17), while Gregory the Theologian says: *Let us not remain what we are, but let us become what we once were* [Μὴ μείνωμεν ὅπερ ἐσμέν, ἀλλ᾽ ὅπερ ἦμεν γενώμεθα].[156] Because now thirst torments us, hunger makes us suffer, so that after having eaten, we wish to drink. Thus we bring into the body the bread first, then the chalice. Why [**почто** = διὰ τί etc.] do we first give the power of dryness to the flesh?—The support for the sinews and the base for the bones; then, the water to dissolve the food and enrich the blood, and also to fill and make sated [(**съ**)**сочанню**[157]] the brains, and (provide) moisture for the body. Then it [*sc.*, water] reaches all the members (after) having been mixed with the food. If they accept both of them (eating and drinking) and according to a measure, then (the result is) great health, but if they accept[158] some (of the two) not according to a measure, then they fall into frequent ailments and great illnesses,—because, with the thickness of the flesh, they have fallen painfully from such a height, when they were condemned.

3. The Nature: Neither Corruptible nor Incorruptible

However, there was no need of this to those who had spiritual grace [χάρις]. He was[159] not renewed through the incorruptibility [ἀφθαρσία] of the body, as he is incorruptible [ἄφθαρτος] not by genus [τῷ γένει] but by grace [τῇ χάρει].[160]

---

155 Missing verb?

156 Gregory of Nazianzus, *Oratio* 39, 2; (C. Moreschini, P. Gallay, Grégoire de Nazianze, *Discours 38–41*, Paris, 1990, p. 152) = PG 36, 336.25–26. The Slavonic allows as well the following translation: *We will not remain what we are, but we will become what we once were*.

157 A *hapax legomenon*. Compare СлРЯ *11–17* (issue 26, p. 262, *s.v.* СОЧАНИЕ) "наполнение живительными соками" 'full of vivifying juices,' with the unique reference to PHI. Cf. (Срезневский, *Материалы для словаря древне-русского языка*, St. Petersburg, 1893–1912/2003, vol. 3, col. 471): СОЧЬНЫИ "касающийся ѣды" 'pertaining to eating.'

158 We follow the variant readings with the plural.

159 Shift from the plural to the singular masculine in the original.

160 The line of thought is that of Theophilos of Antioch, *Ad Autolycum* ii, 27 (G. Bardy, Théophile d'Antioche, *Trois livres à Autolycus*, Paris, 1948, pp. 164, 166), but in a form closer to Nemesius of Emesa (see below). In Theophilos and Nemesius, unlike their predecessors Philo [*De opificio mundi*, 46, p. 134 (L. Cohn, P. Wendland, Philonis Alexandrini *Opera quae supersunt*. Vol. 1, Berlin, 1896, pp. 46–47)] and Origen [*Homilia in Genesim*, 1, 13 (W.A. Baehrens, *Origenes Werke*. Bd. 6, Leipzig, 1920, pp. 15–16), cf. (P. Habermehl, Origenes. *Werke mit deutscher Übersetzung*, hrsg. Alfons Fürst und Christoph Markschies. Bd.

ON THE PERDITION OF THE HIGHER INTELLECT 245

Were[161] he incorruptible by genus, he would not be condemned to death; were he corruptible [φθαρτός], he would not have the expectation of resurrection [ἡ ἐλπὶς τῆς ἀναστάσεως] either; and how would he be condemned to corruption [φθορά], if he was corruptible by nature [τῇ φύσει]? [162]

And formerly God said: *In pain you shall bring forth* your[163] *children* [ἐν λύπαις τέξῃ τέκνα] (Gen 3:16). When making appear the expectation of resurrection [τὴν ἐλπίδα τῆς ἀναστάσεως], he (God) announced according to foreknowledge[164] [κατὰ τὸ προγνώρισμα] that *not for ever* would he[165] be *forgotten*[166] in destruction, in order that he (God) should dispense [смотрѧше = *some form of* οἰκονομέω] to him [в немь = εἰς αὐτόν] the rising [*sc.*, resurrection][167] through the only-begotten Son in order that, in this way, he (God) will put him at the borderline of the two natures, the mortal and the immortal.[168]

      1/2, Berlin, 2011, ss. 50–53)], the ambiguity of human nature lies not in the dualism of the immortal soul and the mortal body but the result of free choice. Placing the human on the borderline between the immortal and the mortal due to the dualism of the soul and the body is, after Philo, a patristic commonplace. However, a reinterpretation of this idea in the vein of Theophilos of Antioch, making from this dualism a dualism of free choice (between the carnal drives and the spiritual intentions) is proper to Nemesius. It is the latter who is followed by our anonymous author.

161   Here the common text of the two sources begins.

162   Cf. Nemesius of Emesa, *De natura hominis* I, 5 (46): εἰ γὰρ ἐξ ἀρχῆς αὐτὸν θνητὸν ἐποίησεν ὁ θεός, οὐκ ἂν ἁμαρτόντα θανάτῳ κατεδίκασε· τοῦ γὰρ θνητοῦ θνητότητα οὐδεὶς καταδικάζει· εἰ δ' αὖ πάλιν ἀθάνατον, οὐδ' ἂν τροφῆς αὐτὸν ἐνδεᾶ κατεσκεύασεν οὐδὲν γὰρ ἀθανάτων τροφῆς σωματικῆς δεῖται ... (Morani, Nemesio Emeseni *De natura hominis*, Leipzig, 1987, pp. 6.10–13); 'For if God had made him mortal from the beginning He would not have condemned him to death when he had sinned: for nobody condemns the mortal to mortality. If, however, He had rather made him immortal, He would not have made him in need of food, since nothing immortal needs bodily food' (Sharples, van der Eijk, Nemesius, *On the Nature of Man*, Liverpool, 1988, p. 41).

163   This 'your' is an authorial addition rather than a variant of a biblical manuscript (no such addition is found in the Göttingen edition of the Greek text, the available Hebrew, the Targums, and the Syriac).

164   For the reading translated here, see Introduction, section 'The Two Previous and the Present Editions.'

165   The subject of the clause—evidently, the human BEING—is not made explicit.

166   Cf. Ps. 73 [MT 74]:19: μὴ ἐπιλάθῃ εἰς τέλος.

167   In the Slavonic: смотрѧше в немь. ѡ єдиночадѣмь сн҃ѣ въстании. In our translation, the syntagmata are смотрѧше ... въстании and (въстании) ѡ єдиночадѣмь сн҃ѣ. Another syntagmatic subdivision is syntactically possible but apparently meaningless: '... was dispensing in him in/for the only-begotten son of rising'.

168   Compare in Nemesius: Ἑβραῖοι δὲ τὸν ἄνθρωπον ἐξ ἄνθρωπον ἐξ ἀρχῆς οὔτε θνητὸν ὁμολογουμένως οὔτε ἀθάνατον γεγενῆσθαί φασιν, ἀλλ' ἐν μεθορίοις [our text follows the variant reading ἐν μεθορίῳ (Morani, Nemesio Emeseni *De natura hominis*, Leipzig, 1987, p. 6, apparatus ad l. 7)] ἑκατέρας φύσεως, ἵνα ἂν μὲν τοῖς σωματικοῖς ἀκολουθήσῃ πάθεσι, περιπέσῃ καὶ ταῖς σωμα-

4. The Fall of the First Higher Intellect

Because it was not helpful for those who had eaten the death-bearing food [*Alternative tr. supposing a lacuna*: Because it was not helpful ⟨...⟩. After having eaten the death-bearing food], all having been condemned to the earth and corruption, while the soul was given to the adversaries—while[169] the wrath [*or* brunt] of the divine anger increasingly prevailed. It was given[170] to the one who has voluntarily chosen and obeyed voluntarily.[171] He was brought down from the height to the underworld darkness. What was the perdition of the first higher intellect [τοῦ πρώτου ὑψηλοτέρου νοῦ]?[172]—You have been humiliated by extreme poverty [τῇ ἐσχάτῃ πτωχείᾳ] in a thrice-unhappy (manner) [τρισαθλίως?]![173]

τικαῖς μεταβολαῖς, ἂν δὲ τὰ τῆς ψυχῆς προτιμήσῃ καλά, τῆς ἀθανασίας ἀξιωθῇ (ibid., p. 6); translation: 'The Hebrews ⟨Philo is meant⟩ say that man came into existence in the beginning as neither mortal nor immortal, but at the boundary of each nature, so that, if he should pursue bodily affections, he would be subjected also to bodily changes, while, if he should estimate more highly the goods of the soul, he might be thought worthy of immortality' [(Sharples, van der Eijk, Nemesius, *On the Nature of Man*, Liverpool, 1988, p. 41), with a little change]. This passage precedes immediately the passage quoted before. Given that our author follows Nemesius, we have to conclude that the corresponding passages (which we have marked with a subtitle) are finished here.

169   We introduce: here a conjunction and a subordinate clause to render the Slavonic phrase with dativus absolutus (a standard rendering, in Slavonic, of the Greek genitivus absolutus).

170   The Slavonic phrase is in the neutral gender whereas 'soul' (which is meant) is feminine in both Slavonic and Greek.

171   This translation is made according to the meaning which is rather obvious from the context and, what is even more important, to be restored in presumption that the Slavonic follows a Semitic clause with two occurrences of the preposition *l-*. Namely, the literal translation of the Slavonic ѿдано бы̏ ко нꙁвольшемоу. и покорьшемоуса к воли would be 'It was given to the one who wished and obeyed himself to the will'. However, if we consider, at each instance of Slavonic ко/къ ('to') the Syriac preposition *l-*, we should obtain, at the first instance, the mark of the agent of the passive verb ('it was given by the one who has voluntarily chosen'), and, at the second instance, as the mark of dative: cf. ܠܨܒܝܢܐ = θελήματι (1 Pet 4:2).

172   The context does not allow understanding this sentence as applied to the Satan. This is a clear mark of the Origenistic myth of the fall of the intellects.

173   Some manuscript variants (трєшканнѣ etc.) allow a translation that keeps in mind the adverb τρισαθλίως, which would result in the translation 'He has been brought down to extreme poverty in a thrice-unhappy manner'; however, this adverb is very rare, whereas the substantivated adjective τρισάθλιος is quite frequent, especially in the vocative. In some manuscript readings, the final word is not vocative but nominative. If we accept this reading, we need to change the beginning of the sentence to 'He has been humiliated ...'

ON THE PERDITION OF THE HIGHER INTELLECT 247

5. The Fall: Exodus Imagery[174]

Similarly to the [Pharaoh's] best officers [τριστάτοι] he was drowned (Exod. 15:4).[175] Darkness reigned over him (Exod. 10:21–23) with the ashes (Exod. 9:8–12), full of perdition and lies; he was tossed about by the whirlwind (cf. Exod. 14:21).

6. The Second Creation and the Way of Restoration

Because having created [ποιήσας] for them [αὐτοῖς][176] [a body] for practice,[177] he (God) re-created [μετεποίησε] them according to his likeness [ὁμοίω-σις],[178] and he transformed (them) with their wickedness from the formless

---

174   The following phrase must continue the preceding one, and, therefore, the preceding marker of the end of a long passage should be ignored. Anyway, this is said about the higher intellect.

175   The term τριστάτης, discernible through the Slavonic, refers to Exodus. The phrase тристатною вещию in the sense 'in the same manner as the best officers (τριστάτοι)' seems to be impossible in Greek. The word τριστάτης, according to the data of TLG, is never used in genitivus possessivus, nor is a possessive adjective derived from it attested. Moreover, the normal Greek equivalents of the Slavonic вещь (especially πρᾶγμα) are not compatible with τριστάτης as a predicate. However, in Syriac, the word with the meaning 'in the same manner as,' ܐܟܘܬܐ, looks similar to the word ܐܝܬܘܬܐ, 'being, reality,' which could have occasioned an error of either the Syriac scribe or the Greek translator.

176   The text has the instrumental case ими 'by them.' This error could easily occur in the process of translation, because the underlying Greek construction would have had αὐτοῖς without the preposition. In the Slavonic translation, such misunderstanding of what the Greek case meant resulted in a radical mistranslation of the whole sentence, making the subject of the actions the fallen intellects instead of God and mentioning them not only in the plural (which is, in this sentence, correct) but also in the singular (because the real subject was singular—God). The most literal translation of the present Slavonic sentence would be the following: 'Because re-creating what they are creating into practice of his/their likeness, and from the formless to the having a form, he transformed them with his/their wickedness.'

177   The so-called 'practical bodies' are meant, the result of the second creation after the fall of the intellects. Cf. Evagrius Ponticus (under the name of Origen), *Selecta in Psalmos*, PG 12, 1097 D: Κρίσις ἐστὶ δικαίων μὲν ἡ ἀπὸ πρακτικοῦ σώματος ἐπὶ ἀγγελικὰ μετάβασις· ἀσεβῶν δὲ ἀπὸ πρακτικοῦ σώματος ἐπὶ σκοτεινὰ καὶ ζοφερὰ μετάθεσις σώματα ('The judgment is, for the righteous, transition from the practical body to the angelic (bodies), whereas for the impious, transposition from the practical body to the dark and gloomy bodies').

178   The main Origenistic idea of creation according to the image of God but re-creation according to his likeness, which has had to pass through the stage of the practical body. Cf. Origen's commentary to Num 24:8 (LXX, not in the Hebrew bible): Καὶ τὰ πάχη αὐτῶν ἐκμυελιεῖ (Peter W. Flint translates either 'And de-marrow their [sc. of the enemies of Israel] stoutness' or 'And suck out their marrow'; in A. Pietersma and B.G. Wright, *A New English Translation of the Septuagint and the Other Greek Translations Traditionally Included under That Title*, New York–Oxford, 2007, p. 131); Origen's commentary: Τότε, φησίν, ὅταν τὴν

[ἀνείδεος] to one having a form [εἶδος].[179] The more[180] the throat of insatiable Hades [τοῦ Ἅιδης ἀκορέστου] filled, the more he (God) was image-making [*some form of* εἰκονίζω[181] *or* ἐντυπόω] so as to give to the image [εἰκών] the likeness [ὁμοίωμα] to him [= the Higher Intellect], with whose seed [σπέρματος][182] the eternal darkness [ἡ σκοτία αἰωνία][183] is filled. He (God) reigned through the eternal providence[184] until he recalled the intellect that could return to

---

σαρκικὴν κατάστασιν εἰς πνευματικὴν διὰ τῆς πραγματικῆς μεταποιῇ 'Then, he [the prophet Balaam] said, when the fleshly state will be re-created into a spiritual one through the practical one' (Origen, *Selecta in Numeros*, PG 12, 584.11–13).

179 The pre-fallen intellects were formless, but they acquired forms (εἴδη) due to the fall. For these forms, the practical bodies were created, thus in conformity with the Aristotelian dichotomy of the matter—(ὕλη = σῶμα in the Origenistic language, where it is applied to the angels too, since they are to a greater or lesser degree fallen as well)—and the form (εἶδος). However, in the unity with the Logos of God (who is the only non-fallen intellect), they will become again formless and reach the likeness of God. For all this, see especially the detailed commentaries by Ilaria L.E. Ramelli (Ramelli, Evagrius, Kephalaia gnostika, Atlanta, GA, 2015). Cf. Evagrius, *Kephalaia gnostika* (*The Gnostic Chapters*), 1:46, 3:31, 5:62 (Guillaumont, *Les six centuries des "Kephalaia gnostica" d'Évagre le Pontique*, Turnhout, 1958/1985, pp. 39, 111, 203, 205) etc.

180 We tentatively translate the construction ⲧⲉⲙⲏ ⲡⲁⲩⲉ ... ⲧⲉⲙⲏ ⲡⲁⲩⲉ ... as 'the more ... the more ...'.

181 This verb does not require as a complement εἶδος but is no less compatible with ὁμοίωσις; cf. John Damascene, *Orationes de imaginibus tres* I, 8: εἰκονίσεις τὸ τοῦ ὁραθέντος ὁμοίωμα (B. Kotter, *Die Schriften des Johannes von Damaskos*. III, Berlin–New York, 1975, p. 82).

182 The 'practical bodies' of the fallen intellects are meant. On the mortal body as a seed, see, in Origenism, e.g., Evagrius, *Gnostic Chapters* 2:25: 'Just as this body is called the seed of the future ear, so will also this aeon be called seed of the one that will come after it'; cf. ibid., 1:24 (Ramelli, Evagrius, p. 105 et *passim*), with the appropriate references to the predecessors, esp. to 1 Cor 15, Philo, Gregory of Nyssa etc.; cf. Guillaumont, *Les six centuries des "Kephalaia gnostica" d'Évagre le Pontique*, pp. 71, 27. These bodies of the intellects are called their seeds in respect to their resurrected state (when these intellects will become 'ears').

183 Here we have 'improved' the Greek original of the Slavonic text by restoring the right Greek translation from Syriac. The Slavonic translation implies that the Greek text has had 'the darkness of the world' (ἡ σκοτία τοῦ κόσμου or κοσμική) instead of ἡ σκοτία αἰωνία. See, for the details, Introduction, section 'Syriac behind Greek.'

184 Cf. above on the understanding of ⲡⲣⲟⲙⲏⲥⲗⲁ ⲥⲃⲉⲧⲏⲁⲅⲟ. In this context, the preposition ⲇⲟ looks as a calque of the Syriac -ܠ, here in the meaning of an instrumental mark (the providence is a tool for reigning). The temporal meaning of this ⲇⲟ would be, moreover, out of place (despite the temporal preposition ⲇⲟⲛⲏⲇⲉⲕⲉ in the next phrase), due to the fact that the providence is not limited temporarily; cf. Ἐπείπερ ἡ μεγαλωσύνη τοῦ Θεοῦ ἐν τῷ Χριστῷ καὶ ἐν τοῖς κτίσμασιν οὖσα θεωρεῖται, καὶ οὐκ ἔστι πέρας τῆς μεγαλωσύνης αὐτοῦ, μήποτε ἡ ἐξ ἀπείρου ἐπ' ἄπειρον καὶ ἐντεῦθεν παρίσταται τοῦ Θεοῦ εἰς τὰ ὄντα ὑπ' αὐτοῦ γενόμενα πρόνοια 'Since indeed the majesty of God is conceivable in Christ and in the creatures, and there is

ON THE PERDITION OF THE HIGHER INTELLECT 249

him[185]—and (this intellects's) lamentable falling off, from the incomprehensible [τὸ ἀνόητον] and reasonable [τὸ λογικόν][186] into the animal [τὸ ζωοτικόν] passionate [παθητικόν] (and?) sensual [αἰσθητικόν].

Part ii: Key Points of the History of Salvation
7. Looking for the Righteous: The First Failed Attempt

[He (God) was] looking for[187] whether[188] somebody would go back[189] from the first lie, raising the intellect from the deep night,[190] and did not find anybody: because *they caused corruption and were abominable in their practices* (Ps 13:1 LXX).[191]

---

no limit/end of his majesty, the providence of God about the things/beings that were generated by him is not to be disposed/limited from the infinity to the infinity and in between' [Pseudo(?)-Origen, *Selecta in Psalmos* (*fragmenta e catenis*), PG 12, 1673 A].

185   The topic of this 'return' (ἀποκατάστασις, ἐπάνοδος etc.) is the central one in the whole Origenistic soteriology. The phrase **возвратънаго си оума** could mean, in Slavonic, 'of his intellect that can return'; it is clear, however, that the subject of action here is God, whereas the intellect belongs to the object of action.

186   The intellect is rational but incomprehensible; Gregory of Nyssa, *De hominis opificio*, 11; PG 44, 153 D: Τίς ἔγνω νοῦν Κυρίου;' φησὶν ὁ Ἀπόστολος. Ἐγὼ δὲ παρὰ τοῦτό φημι, Τίς τὸν ἴδιον νοῦν κατενόησεν; ('*Who hath known the intellect of the Lord?*, said the Apostle [Rom 11:34]. But I rather would say: who has known his own intellect?').

187   The sentence uses adverbial participles (here and later) without any verb. Considered within the framework of Slavonic or Greek syntax, this sentence is incomplete; therefore, we have to either suppose a lacuna or disregard the previous mark of the end of a long passage and add this sentence to the previous one as a continuation of the latter. However, within the framework of Syriac syntax, the participles are suitable for expressing the predicates, and our sentence looks correct. This reading seems to us the one that fits best.

188   To read **еда** instead of **елва**.

189   The terminology of the *apokatastasis* theory (see above).

190   A paraphrase of Ps 13 [MT 14].2: κύριος ἐκ τοῦ οὐρανοῦ διέκυψεν ἐπὶ τοὺς υἱοὺς τῶν ἀνθρώπων τοῦ ἰδεῖν εἰ ἔστιν συνίων ἢ ἐκζητῶν τὸν θεόν. However, the imagery of an intellect within the night is properly Evagrian; cf. his Gnostical Chapters 4:29: 'Just as, if the earth were destroyed, then the night would no more exist on the face of the firmament, likewise, once evilness is removed, then ignorance will no longer exist among rational creatures. For ignorance is the shadow of evilness: those who walk in it, as in the night, are illuminated by the (lamp) oil of Christ and see the stars, in accord with the knowledge that they are worthy of receiving from him. And they too, the stars, will "fall" for them, unless they immediately turn toward the "Sun of Justice"' Ramelli, Evagrius, p. 212, cf. Guillaumont, *Les six centuries des "Kephalaia gnostica" d'Évagre le Pontique*, pp. 147, 149, etc.

191   Albert Pietersma's tr. in Pietersma and Wright, *A New English Translation of the Septuagint and the Other Greek Translations Traditionally Included under That Title*. New York–Oxford, 2007, p. 552; in Greek: διέφθειραν καὶ ἐβδελύχθησαν ἐν ἐπιτηδεύμασιν. Our text has a difference from the Greek in the last word: **начинании** (singular) instead of **начина-**

250   KOROGODINA AND LOURIÉ

8. Abel

He [God] found the one who was caused to become the beginning of death,[192] whose blood the entire earth embraced.[193] He [God] found the premise of the premises [начальныи начатокъ = ἀπαρχὴ τῶν ἀπαρχῶν[194]]. With the lamb [*here identified with Abel himself*],[195] they [*sc.*, Cain and Abel] offered sacrifices[196] in order to [ἵνα] make appear the pure lamb [ἀμνὸς καθαρός[197]] as covered/dressed [*some form of* ἐνδιδύσκω, cf. Lk 16:19] with *purple and* [*red*] *fine linen* [Lk 16:19,[198] *but referring to* Is. 63:1–2], poured out the purity of light [καθαρότης τοῦ

нни^х (plural)—rather because of having lost the letter χ written above the line (as usual) than as a result of an alternative translation of the uncountable singular עֲלִילָה in the Hebrew (cf. the same, עִילָא, in the Aramaic Targum, but plural in the Syriac).

192   An unusual exegesis: the beginning of death is not in Adam (as it is according to Rom 5:12 and almost all patristic exegesis) but in Abel. This idea is attested in Jacob of Sarug (ca 451–521): Abel was the firstborn of the dead, Christ the firstborn of the living (2nd *memra* on Cain and Abel; cf. J.B. Glenthøj, *Cain and Abel in Syriac and Greek Writers* (4th–6th centuries), Leuven, 1997, p. 61). The parallel between Abel and Christ is, on the contrary, the common ground of Christian exegesis.

193   An elaboration on Gen 4:11: Abel's blood is received not by the earth (without further qualification) but by the *entire* earth. The exegesis implying the guilt of the whole earth, which required the punishment by the flood, is preserved by Basil of Caesarea, *Letter* 260, 5: 'the punishment for the entire earth [the flood] because of the flow of sin became great (πάσῃ τῇ γῇ τιμωρία διὰ τὸ πολλὴν γένεσθαι χύσιν τῆς ἁμαρτίας)', the deluge, was necessary to stop the propagation of Cain's sin down the generations. Y. Courtonne, Saint Basile, *Lettres*, t. 3, Paris, 1966, p. 112.

194   There is no adjective from ἀπαρχή 'premise / first fruit'; the expression ἀπαρχὴ τῶν ἀπαρχῶν is very rare: the only case we know is in Origen's *Commentarius in Evangelium Iohannis*, I, 2, 12; C. Blanc, Origène, *Commentaire sur Saint Jean*, t. I, Paris, 1966, p. 64: ἀπαρχὴ τῶν πολλῶν ἀπαρχῶν, where the context is that the Gospels and the study thereof are the premises for all other Scriptures and studies of them, while the latter are, in turn, premises of everything.

195   Cf. Gen 4:4: καὶ Αβελ ἤνεγκεν καὶ αὐτὸς ἀπὸ τῶν πρωτοτόκων τῶν προβάτων αὐτοῦ.

196   The verb послоужиша is to be understood here in the meaning 'to offer sacrifices' (λειτουργέω etc.).

197   This expression is unbiblical and, therefore, relatively rare. Cf., in Cyril of Alexandria, *Glaphyra in Pentateuchum*: Καὶ ὁ μὲν ἀμνὸς ὡς καθαρόν τε καὶ ἄμωμον θῦμα κατὰ νόμον νοεῖται 'And the lamb is to be understood, according to the Law, as a sacrifice pure as well as without blemish' (PG 69, 425 D); only the latter synonym, 'without blemish', is a standard biblical one.

198   The wording багрѣ᷄ и червленицею покрытъ is certainly that of Lk 16:19: ἐνεδιδύσκετο πορφύραν καὶ βύσσον; cf. *LLP*, vol. 4, p. 885. Nevertheless, the meaning is obviously that of the famous prophecy on Christ in Is 63:1–6, esp. vv. 1–2: τίς οὗτος ὁ παραγινόμενος ἐξ Εδωμ ἐρύθημα ἱματίων ἐκ Βοσορ [= 'flesh' in the common Patristic exegesis] ... διὰ τί σου ἐρυθρὰ τὰ ἱμάτια καὶ τὰ ἐνδύματά σου ὡς ἀπὸ πατητοῦ ληνοῦ.

ON THE PERDITION OF THE HIGHER INTELLECT 251

φωτός], so that [ἵνα] that[199] death would be the unique one [*some derivate from once* (ἐφάπαξ)?] for the whole human genus (cf. Heb 7:27).[200]

The second lamb [*sc.*, Christ] ought to be prefigured [воображеноу быти: *some form of* ἐντυπόω] by the first [*sc.*, Abel], so that [ἵνα] the second (lamb) will bring rescue from the passions [παθήματα] of the first by the impassibility [ἀπάθεια] of the second. Thus, he [*sc.*, Abel] added a similar figure [τύπος?] to the bread, a lamb. The two offsprings [*sc.*, of Cain and Abel] were from the unique seed, and the first offspring [*sc.*, Cain's] failed to overcome the junior one [*sc.*, Abel's], in that he brought an imperfect fruit. Therefore, he, being furious, was angry with the junior, thus overcame his life rescuing [*sc.*, and so brought his life to an end], being the cause of destruction,[201] but, with the plague applied to him [*sc.*, to Cain], he received the rightful *vengeance* (cf. Gen. 4:15). How, therefore, could he not receive a plague for what he had done, having destroyed the image of his [*sc.*, God's] similitude [шбразъ подобига си = τὸν εἰκόνα/τύπον τοῦ ὁμοιώματος αὐτοῦ]?[202]

He was an adversary to the autocrator/emperor of the creature[203] by a lie/craftiness. They grew up by his seed,[204] being overtaken with the evilness and were nourished with the lie/craftiness, for [ἵνα] will appear the judgment *with righteousness* [ἐν δικαιοσύνῃ] (cf. Ps 95 [MT 96]:13) of the one who is judging all,[205] because they are controlled [κρατούμενοι] by free will (αὐτεξουσία), so that blame will not fall on the innocent.

---

199   We follow the reading та ('that') and not та ('you' in acc. sg.).

200   This allusion to Heb 7:27 (ἐφάπαξ ἑαυτὸν ἀνενέγκας) is a clear reference to the typology in which Abel is a prefiguration of Christ.

201   The text has 'destroyer of the cause,' which seems to be a mistake for 'the cause of destruction.' Such mistakes could be easily made as a misinterpretation of the Syriac *status constructus*.

202   This phraseology is understandable in an Origenistic framework: the likeness to God is to be reached only in the final salvation (*apokatastasis*), but it has never been lost by the unique intellect of Christ, the Logos; Abel is an image of Christ, while the latter is, in turn, the likeness of God; Abel, being 'an image of the likeness', was destroyed by Cain.

203   This epithet of God, αὐτοκράτωρ τοῦ κτίσματος, seems to be unknown outside this text.

204   In the Slavonic, того съменемъ (instrumental case).

205   Possibly the flood is meant, often considered as the punishment for the Cainites.

9. Enoch

He [God?[206]], therefore, craved for the salvation [σωτηρία, *sc.*, of humans] and did not find any who would render/compensate to him [ἀποδιδόμενος].[207] He found, however, somebody of virtue and sent (2 Enoch 1:8)[208] to take him off from the temporary life. And it is written: *and he was not found, because God transferred him*[209] [καὶ οὐχ ηὑρίσκετο ὅτι μετέθηκεν αὐτὸν ὁ θεός] (Gen 5:24).

10. Noah

Then, he [God] chose the second chief/beginning of the genus [γενεάρχης] and applied to him the right balance [ζυγὸς δίκαιος]:[210] thus, what (was) heavy was drowned, what (was) light rose up, because the thickness overcame the thinness—because the earthly (things) are to the earthly (things), the heavenly ones to the heavenly,[211] so that the (things) below will not rise to the (things) above, because their *bones were strewn beside Hades* [διεσκορπίσθη τὰ ὀστᾶ ⟨... (ἡμῶν *is substituted with* αὐτῶν)⟩ παρὰ τὸν ᾅδην (Ps 140:7[212])].

---

206   The syntax allows reading of this sentence from the point of view of a human (who was seeking for salvation), but, in this case, there would be a rupture in the meaning before the next phrase of this sentence and would preclude our resolution for an obscure reading there (дающаго емоу).

207   In the Slavonic, дающаго емоу. It seems that the meaning is that of the verb ἀποδίδωμι rather than δίδωμι. Cf. Numb 5:8: ὥστε ἀποδοῦναι αὐτῷ τὸ πλημμέλημα πρὸς αὐτόν ... τὸ πλημμέλημα τὸ ἀποδιδόμενον κυρῷ '... to compensate him for the error to him, the error compensated to the Lord ...' [Peter W. Flint's tr. (Pietersma and Wright, *A New English Translation of the Septuagint and the Other Greek Translations Traditionally Included under That Title*. New York–Oxford, 2007, p. 115)].

208   No sending is mentioned in Gen 5:24. In 2 Enoch 1, Enoch is taken to the heaven with 'two huge men' (1:4) appearing before him, who said, among others (1:8): 'The eternal God [*longer rec.*; Lord *in shorter rec.*] has sent us to you' Francis Andersen's tr.: J. Charlesworth, *The Old Testament Pseudepigrapha*. Vol. 1, London, 1983, pp. 106–109.

209   Translation by Robert J.V. Hiebert in: Pietersma and Wright, *A New English Translation of the Septuagint and the Other Greek Translations Traditionally Included under That Title*. New York–Oxford, 2007, p. 9.

210   The right balance is possibly implied to be already given to Enoch, the great-grandfather of Noah, who said to his children (according to the recension in the *Měrilo pravednoe*): '... and the just balance I measured' Andersen's tr. (Charlesworth, *The Old Testament Pseudepigrapha*. Vol. 1, London, 1983, p. 217); cf. the same motive in 1 Enoch 43:2 but applied to 'the stars of heaven' only.

211   On the heavenly (angelic) features of Noah, see especially the description of his birth in 1 Enoch 106–107 and the Qumranic Aramaic *Genesis Apocryphon* (1QapGen, cols. i–ii, v); D. Machiela, *The Dead Sea Genesis Apocryphon*, Leiden, 2009, pp. 33–35, 40–42.

212   Translation by Albert Pietersma in: Pietersma and Wright, *A New English Translation of the Septuagint and the Other Greek Translations Traditionally Included under That Title*. New York–Oxford, 2007, p. 616.

ON THE PERDITION OF THE HIGHER INTELLECT 253

11. The Tower of Babel

Therefore, the darkness of deceit [ἡ σκοτία τῆς πλάνης?[213]] remained[214] in vain [ТОУНЄ = δωρεάν] without attestation—until it revealed the higher pride/insolence (cf. Is 10:33),[215] which he (God) himself *scattered* [διέσπειρεν] (Gen 11:8, 9) *with the spirit of his mouth* [τῷ πνεύματι τοῦ στόματος αὐτοῦ] (Ps 32:6), for the *confusion* [σύγχυσις] (Gen 11:9) he hewed down the highest of the intellects (cf. Is 10:33).[216]

12. Abraham

And he (God) transformed the changeable into the unchangeable[217] to obtain the fruit of conversion/return.[218] Thus, he found what he desired, not created with necessity [ἀνάγκη],[219] until he (this man) recognised the artist [τεχνί-της][220] when the art [τέχνη] stopped [κατάπαυσις *or a similar word*],[221] and he

---

213 Not a frequent phrase in Greek; normally, the main word in the phrase is πλάνη, and the dependent word is some derivate of σκοτία [e.g., διὰ τὸ τῆς πλάνης ἐσκοτισμένον 'because of being darkened with deceit'; John Chrysostom, *In Isaiam* 11, 9 (J. Dumortier, *Jean Chrysostome. Commentaire sur Isaïe*, Paris, 1983, p. 144); ἐφώτισε τὰ ἐσκοτισμένα τῇ πλάνῃ ἔθνη (the Law) 'enlighten the gentiles darkened by deceit'; (Pseudo-)Gregory of Nyssa, Θεογνωσία, fragmenta apud Euthymium Zigabenum, *Panoplia dogmatica*, PG 130, 273 C]. One can suppose, if the main word and the dependent word have switched places, that an intermediary having a Syriac *status constructus* phrase intervened.

214 In the Slavonic, ОСТА (active voice) which we consider to be a mistranslation of a Greek mediopassive verb that would require the translation ОСТАСА. The respective Greek verb must have been a derivate of λείπω, such as καταλείπω (or with another prefix), having the aorist third-person singular forms for active and mediopassive voices such as κατέλιπε and κατελίπετο respectively.

215 Is 10:33: καὶ οἱ ὑψηλοὶ τῇ ὕβρει συντριβήσονται 'and those who are high with pride/insolence will be hewn down.'

216 Cf. in Evagrius, *Gnostic Chapters* 4:53: 'Knowledge is diminished and descends among those who build up the tower with evilness and with false doctrines. Ignorance and confusion of ideas occur to them, just as also to those who were building the tower' Ramelli, Evagrius, p. 228, cf. Guillaumont, *Les six centuries des "Kephalaia gnostica" d'Évagre le Pontique*, p. 159.

217 As becomes clear from the next sentence, here the free will is meant, which is changeable but eventually must become unchangeable.

218 The sentences are divided not according to the punctuation of the manuscripts but so as to keep the particle ВО (γάρ) in second place in the second sentence.

219 Abraham was chosen in God's response to his own will but not created according to God's desire and, therefore, without participation of Abraham's own will.

220 God as the Artist/Constructor (τεχνίτης) of the Universe is a commonplace of Christian exegesis, including the Origenistic one. However, we do not claim to interpret all the peculiarities of the use of the term τέχνη and its derivatives in our text (cf. esp. §13, endnote 83).

221 God did not create, with his art, anything new in Abraham but simply waited to be recognised by him. This is in conformity with the *Apocalypse of Abraham* (8:3), where the

(God) revealed the Covenant [διαθήκη] to the same (man). 'Rise up, he said, from the custom of the first/former deceit [προτέρα πλάνη][222] and go to the first/former Paradise,[223] so as [ἵνα] to become the father of the children who will receive back the earth of the first/former being[224] (cf. Gen 12:1–2),[225] and you will beget the son of joy (Gen 21:6)'.[226] [Abraham], it is said [ρε͡ = φησίν], *believed God, and it was reckoned to him as righteousness*[227] [ἐπίστευσεν ⟨...⟩ τῷ

Mighty One said: 'You are searching for the God of gods, the Creator, in the mind/intellect (въ оумѣ) of your heart. I am he' [translation by Ryszard Rubinkiewicz (Charlesworth, *The Old Testament Pseudepigrapha*. Vol. 1, London, 1983, p. 693)].

222   A common term for idolatry since, at the latest, the fourth century.

223   Abraham begins the *apokatastasis*—the return from deceit to Paradise.

224   'The land of the first/former being' must be Paradise.

225   A symbolic interpretation of Abraham's story in the sense of the Origenistic *apokatastasis*.

226   That is, the name Isaac is etymologised not as 'laughter' (as in the Greek Bible, the Slavonic one, MT, and Vulgate) but as 'joy' (as in the Syriac Christian Bible and the Aramaic Jewish targums). The present text of the Septuagint is in the middle between the Syriac/Aramaic and the Hebrew. In the Septuagint: εἶπεν δὲ Σαρρα γέλωτά μοι ἐποίησεν κύριος ὃς γὰρ ἂν ἀκούσῃ συγχαρεῖταί μοι ('And Sarra said, "The Lord has made laughter for me, for anyone who hears will rejoice with me"'); in Syriac: ܘܐܡܪܬ ܣܪܐ ܚܕܘܬܐ ܪܒܬܐ ܥܒܕ ܠܝ ܐܠܗܐ ܝܘܡܢܐ. ܟܠ ܕܢܫܡܥ ܢܚܕܐ ܠܝ (Institutum Peshittonianum Leidense, *Vetus Testamentum syriace juxta simplicem syrorum versionem*. Pars I, fasc. i, Leiden, 1977, p. 38); 'And Sarra said: God has made a great joy for me today; everyone who hears will rejoice with me'; in some mss, the words 'great' and 'today' are omitted; in Hebrew: וַתֹּאמֶר שָׂרָה, צְחֹק עָשָׂה לִי אֱלֹהִים; כָּל־הַשֹּׁמֵעַ יִצְחַק־לִי ('And Sarah said: God has made me laughter, and all who hear will laugh with me'). The Greek/Slavonic has 'laughter' in the first part of the verse and 'rejoicing' in the second, the Syriac/Aramaic has 'rejoicing' in both parts, whereas the Hebrew has 'laughter' in both. However, the translation of the name of Isaac as 'rejoicing' (χαρά or ἀγαλλίαμα) occurs repeatedly in Philo, and Byzantine exegetes knew it quite well. The peculiarity of our text consists in the identification of this 'rejoicing' with Christ according to the flesh. The only instance known to us is an anonymous ninth- or tenth-century anti-Jewish text: ... ἑρμηνεύεται γὰρ Ἰσαὰκ ἀγαλλίασις καὶ χαρά. Τίς δ' ἄλλός ἐστιν ἀληθῶς καὶ κυρίως ἀγαλλίασις καὶ χαρά, ἀλλ' ἢ μόνος Χριστὸς ὁ τῆς ἐνθέου καὶ ὄντως ἀγαλλιάσεως καὶ χαρᾶς τοῖς πᾶσιν αἴτιος καὶ πρόξενος γεγονὼς ἅτε δὴ καὶ κατ' οὐσίαν ὑπάρχων Θεός, ὁ καὶ κατὰ δύναμιν θείας ἐπαγγελίας ᾗ πέφυκεν ἄνθρωπος ἐπ' ἐσχάτων ἐκ τῆς Ἀβραμιαίας φυλῆς γεννηθεὶς ὡς ὁ σωματικὸς Ἰσαάκ ... (ch. 11 [M. Hostens, *Anonymi auctoris* Theognosiae (*saec. IX/X*) *dissertatio contra Iudaeos*, Turnhout, 1986, pp. 237–238]; translation: '... because 'Isaac' is interpreted as "rejoicing" and "delight." Indeed, who else is truly and in the proper sense joy and delight than the unique Christ, who became responsible and distributor to all of the divine and real joy and delight, who, while being God by essence, in the latter [days], was born from the Abrahamic tribe like the carnal Isaac, by the power of the divine annunciation'). The anti-Jewish context could be a mark of an early Christian origin of the argument used; at least, this anonymous author made intensive use of earlier anti-Jewish works.

227   Translation by Robert J.V. Hiebert (Pietersma and Wright, *A New English Translation of the*

ON THE PERDITION OF THE HIGHER INTELLECT   255

θεῷ καὶ ἐλογίσθη αὐτῷ εἰς δικαιοσύνην] (Gen 15:6; quoted in Rom 4:3, Gal 3:6, James 2:23), and he gave birth to a son in prosperous old age[228] [ἐν γήρει πίονι] (Ps 91:15).

13. Isaac and Melchizedek Prefiguring the Two Natures of Christ (but Not the Logos as an Intellect)

Thus, [God] traces [*some form of* ἐκτυπόω, ἐντυπόω etc.] here[229] the image [τύπος?] of the extreme passion, as a shadow of the passion [*sc.*, of Christ], the two natures [δύο φύσεις], (those of) God and the human, in two ways [διττῶς/δισσῶς]:[230] according to the divinity [κατὰ τὴν θεότην], Melchizedek,[231] but, according to the humanity [κατὰ τὴν ἀνθρωπότητας] the son of rejoicing,[232] but, according to the comforting [κατὰ τὴν παράκλησιν[233]], the son of Intellect[234] and the son of art [τέχνης],[235] from whom the twelve tribes grew.

     Septuagint and the Other Greek Translations Traditionally Included under That Title. New York–Oxford, 2007, p. 14).

228   Translation by Albert Pietersma (Pietersma and Wright, *A New English Translation of the Septuagint and the Other Greek Translations Traditionally Included under That Title*. New York–Oxford, 2007, p. 594). The relevant part of the verse reads 'In prosperous old age they [the righteous] will still increase' (in the Hebrew, where this verse is Ps 92:14 'they shall still bring forth fruit'). This verse is referred to in our text as having been fulfilled in Abraham.

229   'Here' for ѿсель, which means literally 'from this [point, place etc.]'.

230   This sharp Christological formulation puts our author into the camp of the post-451 Chalcedonians. In Old Russian, соугоугъть could have an adverbial meaning (*СлРЯ 11–17*, issue 28, p. 239).

231   The divinity of Melchizedek is a Second Temple Jewish doctrine preserved with some monastic milieux in no necessary connexion with the Origenism. Its condemnation is already witnessed in Epiphanius of Salamine (ca 377) and the *Apophthegmata Patrum*. However, we have no witness on either divinity or humanity of Melchizedek in the preserved corpus of Evagrius. Origen himself (and, if we trust Jerome's testimony, Didymus) considered Melchizedek as some angelic/heavenly power. Such a doctrine is condemned also by Cyril of Alexandria (together with the opinion of those who consider Melchizedek to be the Holy Spirit). See, for the details, F.L. Horton Jr., *The Melchizedek Tradition*, Cambridge, 1976; cf. P.J. Kobelski, *Melchizedek and Melchireša*ʿ, Washington, DC, 1981. Our text is compatible with both 'super-human' interpretations of Melchizedek, as either divine or some heavenly 'power' (δύναμις).

232   Isaac as a prefiguration of Christ is a common topic of Christian exegesis, especially due to the *Aqeda*.

233   The Slavonic has оутѣшенне 'comforting' (παράκλησις), which we consider as connected to 'Comforter' (Παράκλητος), that is, the Holy Spirit.

234   In Origenism, the Logos, being the only non-fallen intellect, is distinct from God, even though acquiring some kind of identity with him. Christ is the incarnate Logos. Therefore, to mark Christ's relations to his two natures, divine and human, would not be enough to specify who Christ is in fact: there is a need to specify him as an intellect.

235   Cf. above on the term 'art.' We must confess that its usage in the present text is not identifiable with any known tradition.

Part III: Christology

14. The Two-Stage Salvation[236]

(O) severe temptations, (O) inflexible, hardened [*lit.* petrified] hearts [πεπωρω-μέναι αἱ καρδίαι, cf. Mk 6:52, 8:17]! He [God] forms[237] a mould [τὸ ἐκμαγεῖον?] By putting/stamping an image of light [εἰκών/εἶδος φωτός][238]—until what will be poured into the image (in the mould) of the formed[239] similitude [ὁμοίωμα—*here in the sense of archetype*], thus miraculously transferred from darkness to light (cf. Eph 1:12–13[240]),[241]—in order that [ἵνα] the witness of [*correct to* that

---

236 The following text will be more easily comprehensible when taking in mind the following chapter of the *Gnostic Chapters* (6:34) by Evagrius: 'During the aeons God *will change the body of our humiliation into the likeness of the glorious body* (Phil 3:21) of the Lord. Then, after all aeons, he will also make us *in the likeness of his Son's image* (Rom 8:29), if it is the case that the Son's image is the essential knowledge of God the Father' Ramelli, Evagrius, p. 335, cf. Guillaumont, *Les six centuries des "Kephalaia gnostica" d'Évagre le Pontique*, p. 231; see also commentary Ramelli, Evagrius, pp. 335–336. The *apokatastasis* implies a two-stage process: (1) during the aeons: the incarnation, that is, when God accepted our body and transformed it into the glory of resurrection; (2) after all aeons, finally: the definitive unity of all reasonable creatures with the Trinity (more on this s. in Evagrius's *Great Letter to Melania*). According to this scheme, the unity with Christ is still not the highest, decisive, and absolute degree of divinisation. For the alternative attitude of the Byzantine Orthodoxy, as it was expressed especially against Origenism, see J.-C. Larchet, *La divinisation de l'homme selon saint Maxime le Confesseur*, Paris, 1996.

237 There is a fitting Scholastic term *informatio* corresponding to such Greek terms as ἐντύπω-σις, some derivates of μορφόω etc.; in Slavonic, as in Latin, there was no such variability of synonyms.

238 The right Greek term here seems to be rather εἰκών than εἶδος, although these words would have been used as synonyms. The expression εἶδος φωτός is not frequent [it is known, however, from *Joseph and Aseneth*, 20, 6 (C. Burchard, Joseph und Aseneth *kritisch herausgegeben*, Leiden, 2003, p. 252)], whereas phrases with derivates of εἰκών and φῶς are common, and here our 'image' (εἰκών) will be put in connexion with the 'similitude' (ὁμοίωμα). Cf., e.g., in Gregory of Nyssa (*In Canticum Canticorum*, 11): the human nature must become a reflection (image produced as a reproduction) of the true Light (John 1:9)—ἡ ἀνθρωπίνη φύσις τοῦ ἀληθινοῦ φωτὸς ἀπεικόνισμα (H. Langerbeck, Gregorii Nysseni *In Canticum Canticorum*, Leiden, 1960, p. 51).

239 In Greek, one would suppose a term such as τυποθείς.

240 This is an elaboration on Eph 1:12–13: εὐχαριστοῦντες τῷ πατρὶ τῷ ἱκανώσαντι ὑμᾶς εἰς τὴν μερίδα τοῦ κλήρου τῶν ἁγίων ἐν τῷ φωτί ὃς ἐρρύσατο ἡμᾶς ἐκ τῆς ἐξουσίας τοῦ σκότους καὶ μετέστησεν εἰς τὴν βασιλείαν τοῦ υἱοῦ τῆς ἀγάπης αὐτοῦ. However, our text follows rather some tradition of paraphrasing. Especially close is a sentence in the *Corpus Macarianum* (type III, homily 16, 3), where the idea of 'transferring' from the darkness to the light is connected with the topic of the 'image' (εἰκών): Δόξα τῷ οὕτως ἀγαπήσαντι τὴν ψυχὴν τὴν κατ' εἰκόνα αὐτοῦ κτισθεῖσαν, τῷ λυτρωσαμένῳ αὐτὴν ἐκ τῆς βασιλείας τοῦ σκότους καὶ μεταστήσαντι αὐτὴν εἰς τὴν βασιλείαν τοῦ φωτὸς τῆς ζωῆς (E. Klostermann and H. Bezold, *Neue Homilien des Makarius/Symeon. I. Aus Typus III*, Berlin, 1961, p. 83); translation: 'Glory to him who so much loved the soul that was created according to his image (εἰκών), who freed it from the kingdom of darkness and transferred it to the kingdom of the light of life.'

241 For the whole inspiration of this passage, cf. Gregory of Nyssa, *On the Beatitudes*, VI, 4:

ON THE PERDITION OF THE HIGHER INTELLECT

257

which is witnessed by[242]] that light should become a great light,[243] whereas this visible light will become darkness.[244]

15. The Overnight Journey[245] to the First Image-Stamping
Because we did not dare to name the sun, when we were with the moon, and when the sun was about to shine forth, the night has been instantly crushed

---

τὸ γάρ σοι χωρητὸν τῆς τοῦ Θεοῦ κατανοήσεως μέτρον ἐν σοί ἐστιν, οὕτω τοῦ πλάσαντός σε τὸ τοιοῦτον ἀγαθὸν εὐθὺς τῇ φύσει κατουσιώσαντος. τῶν γὰρ τῆς ἰδίας φύσεως ἀγαθῶν ὁ θεὸς ἐνετύπωσε τῇ σῇ κατασκευῇ τὰ μιμήματα, οἷόν τινα κηρὸν σχήματι γλυφῆς προτυπώσας. ἀλλ' ἡ κακία τῷ θεοειδεῖ χαρακτῆρι περιχυθεῖσα ἄχρηστον ἐποίησέ σοι τὸ ἀγαθὸν ποκεκρυμμένον τοῖς αἰσχροῖς προκαλύμμασιν. εἰ οὖν ἀποκλύσειας πάλιν δι' ἐπιμελείας βίου τὸν ἐπιπλασθέντα τῇ καρδίᾳ σου ῥύπον, ἀναλάμψει σοι τὸ θεοειδὲς κάλλος (J.F. Callahan, Gregorii Nysseni De oratione dominica. De Beatitudinibus, Leiden, 1992, p. 143). Translation by Stuart George Hall in (H.R. Drobner and A. Viciano, Gregory of Nyssa: Homilies on the Beatitudes. An English Version with the Commentary and Supporting Studies, Leiden, 2000, p. 70): 'The measure of what is accessible to you is in you, for thus your Maker from the start invested your essential nature with such good. God has imprinted upon your constitution replicas of the good things in his own nature, as through stamping wax with the shape of a design. Vice however, overlaying the God-like pattern, has made the good useless to you, hidden under curtains of shame. If you were to wash away once more by scrupulous living the filth that has accumulated upon your heart, the God-like beauty would again light up for you.'

242 The witness must be of somebody or something else, and, therefore, such a correction is tempting. Indeed, the corresponding words are not easily confused in Greek and Slavonic, but, in Syriac, the situation is different. The words for 'witness', such as ܪܕܗܘܬܡܣܐ and ܪܕܗܘܬܡܣܕܐ, looks very similar to ܪܣܡܕܐ 'that of which evidence is given' (TS, col. 2537).

243 This phrase about the witness alludes to John 1:7–9, where the true Light was Christ, whereas John the Baptist was not the Light but sent as a witness of the Light. Here, however, some lesser light is a witness of a greater one. The lesser light is the incarnate Logos, Christ. The great light is the Trinity at the apokatastasis.

244 A mark of the end of the visible world at the apokatastasis, which is to take place 'after all aeons.'

245 For better understanding of the following part, the reader could bear in mind a chapter from the Gnostic Chapters by Evagrius (4:29): 'Just as, if the earth were destroyed, then the night would no more exist on the face of the firmament, likewise, once evilness is removed, then ignorance will no longer exist among rational creatures. For ignorance is the shadow of evilness: those who walk in it, as in the night, are illuminated by the (lamp) oil of Christ and see the stars, in accord with the knowledge that they are worthy of receiving from him. And they too, the stars, will "fall" for them, unless they immediately turn toward the "Sun of Justice"', Ramelli, Evagrius, pp. 212–213, cf. Guillaumont, Les six centuries des "Kephalaia gnostica" d'Évagre le Pontique, pp. 147, 149. To sum up the details we have to keep in mind: the night is produced by the shadow of evilness, which is ignorance; those who are in the night are guided by Christ using stars. From other chapters, we know that these stars are not necessarily the material luminaries (whereas they also serve to help humankind: 6:88) but principally refer to the 'intelligible stars': 'Intelligible stars are rational natures who have been entrusted with illuminating those who are

[ра҃зъбивашесѧ, *not* ра҃зъбиваіа] by the brilliancy [λαμπρότης] of a star, and it [*sc.*, star; *or* he, *sc.* God] led them through the abyss of the passion [ἄβυσσος τοῦ πάθους].[246]

He who was stamped with the image of passion [πάθος], who was stamped with the image of the shadow [*sc.*, the shadow of evil = ignorance], him he [God] made to stand on the promise [ἐπαγγελία/ἐπάγγελμα] of the first image-stamping [*sc.*, that dealt with above]—not[247] above on the height but on an extreme part. Because he failed to convey from the deep night those to whom there was no witness [*sc.*, Christ], because he was guiding those who were slavishly submitted[248] to the yoke.[249]

16. The Second Coming

Being in servitude [δουλεία], the non-free creature [κτίσις] could not inherit [cf. 1 Cor 15:50: κληρονομῆσαι οὐ δύναται][250] liberty [ἐλευθερία] (cf. Rom 8:21)[251] until his [Christ's/Logos's] image is stamped in them,[252] who are the lower

---

in darkness' (3:62; Ramelli, Evagrius, p. 177, cf. Guillaumont, *Les six centuries des "Kephalaia gnostica" d'Évagre le Pontique*, p. 123); almost the same wording in 3:84 (Ramelli, Evagrius, p. 192), cf. Guillaumont, *Les six centuries des "Kephalaia gnostica" d'Évagre le Pontique*, p. 133. In the following description of an overnight journey the author, of course, alludes—once more—to the Exodus, where passing through the abyss took place at night as well.

246 We are grateful to Dmitry Afinogenov for his help in clarifying this difficult passage.

247 We follow the reading не на and not the erroneous на не.

248 In the Slavonic, this is a *hapax legomenon* composite word рабопокоренымъ (never occurring in the lexica of Slavonic and Greek), whereas it is easily imaginable in Greek after the pattern of δουλοκρατούμενοι: e.g., *δουλοταττούμενοι. Such a *compositum* would hardly pass through Syriac. Therefore, this is a piece of linguistic evidence in favour of Greek as the language of the immediate original of the Slavonic.

249 An apparent discrepancy with the Exodus, where those guided were already free from the servitude in Egypt.

250 Inheritance is mentioned here in connection with Rom 8:21 'because the creation itself also will be delivered from the servitude of corruption into the glorious liberty of the children of God' (cf. Greek quote below). Our author means that the creature failed to acquire what is due to the children of God, namely, the liberty from corruption. The allusion to 1 Cor 15:50 (τοῦτο δέ φημι ἀδελφοί ὅτι σὰρξ καὶ αἷμα βασιλείαν θεοῦ κληρονομῆσαι οὐ δύναται οὐδὲ ἡ φθορὰ τὴν ἀφθαρσίαν κληρονομεῖ 'Now this I say, brethren, that flesh and blood cannot inherit the kingdom of God; nor does corruption inherit incorruption') serves to insist that the bodies ('flesh and blood') will not participate in the resurrection; see below on the incarnation in the 'inner man' and not the 'outer' one.

251 The wording of this passage is that of Rom 8:21: ὅτι καὶ αὐτὴ ἡ κτίσις ἐλευθερωθήσεται ἀπὸ τῆς δουλείας τῆς φθορᾶς εἰς τὴν ἐλευθερίαν τῆς δόξης τῶν τέκνων τοῦ θεοῦ.

252 In the Slavonic, имъ (instrumental case). The incarnation of the Logos gives the liberty from corruption or (see Rom 8:20, which is also underlying this passage), from vanity/futility (ματαιότης). This vanity is, according to Origen, the bodies: *Ego quidem arbitror non*

ON THE PERDITION OF THE HIGHER INTELLECT

branches [κλήματα; cf. John 15:5]²⁵³ of the son of the most high [υἱὸς ὑψίστου] (cf. Ps 81:6 LXX) king [βασιλέως²⁵⁴].²⁵⁵ The *wisdom* [σοφία] (1 Cor 1:24), the son and the *heir* [ὁ κληρονόμος; Mk 12:7]²⁵⁶ of the most high king [τοῦ ὑψίστου βασιλέως] is clothed with revenge [ἐνδύον ἐν ἄμυναν] and dressed [περιβάλλον] with judgment [ἐν κρίσιν/ἐκδίκησιν]²⁵⁷ (cf. Is 59:17; Wis 5:17–18).²⁵⁸ His descent [κατά-

aliam esse vanitatem quam corpora 'I therefore consider the vanity to be nothing other than the bodies'; cf. the whole of this commentary on Rom 8:19–21 in Origen, *De principiis*, I, 7, 5; P. Koetschau, *Origenes Werke*, Bd. 5, Leipzig, 1913, pp. 91–94, quoted p. 92, cf. also the parallel places in Origen referred to in the apparatus. The body, however, according to both Origen and Evagrius, is an outer and less important part of the man, whereas the incarnation of the Logos is aiming at the interior one. Thus, according to an Evagrian definition (*Gnostic Chapters*, 6:39), 'The birth of Christ is the birth of our inner human being, which is from the beginning, that which Christ, like a good builder, has founded and built upon the head stone of the building of his body' (Ramelli, Evagrius, p. 338), cf. Guillaumont, *Les six centuries des "Kephalaia gnostica" d'Évagre le Pontique*, p. 233. In these terms, one can reformulate the main idea of this sentence that Logos's image-stamping, which is the incarnation, affected the inner man and not the outer one, thus becoming the main prerequisite for the future deliberation from the corruption and the body (because, in Origenism, where is a body, there is corruption).

253 Here, in the context of liberation from the death and corruption (when the latter is equated with the body itself), the topic of the branches of the Christ as the true vine was actualised in the Origenistic exegesis: 'Indeed, every plant, after its winter death, awaits its spring resurrection. Therefore, if we too have been planted together with Christ in his death, it is necessary that the Father, as a farmer, purifies us like branches of the true vine, that we may bring very much fruit, as Christ himself says in the Gospels: *I am the true vine, you are the branches, and my Father is the Farmer* (John 15:1)' (*Omnis etenim planta post hiemis mortem resurrectionem ueris expectat. Si ergo et nos in Christi morte complantati sumus ei, necesse est ut Pater agricola purget nos tamquam palmites uitis uerae ut fructum plurimum afferamus, sicut et ipse in euangeliis dicit: ego sum uitis uera, uos palmites, pater meus Agricola*); Origen, *Commentarius ad Romanos* 5.9.65–72; see also 1.15.54–66; quoted according to Ramelli, Evagrius, p. 45.

254 'Most high king': this expression is obtained with contraction of Ps 46:3 LXX (ὅτι κύριος ὕψιστος φοβερός βασιλεὺς μέγας ἐπὶ πᾶσαν τὴν γῆν). It is not very frequent, although not unique, e.g. Pseudo-Chrysostom, *De augusta porta et in orationem dominicam*, 1; PG 51, 41, line 7.

255 The reference to Ps 81:6 puts the Logos among a congregation of faithful, but the context is 'singularised', especially with the opposition between the 'most high (king)' and the 'lower (vine branches)'; the latter evokes in imagination vine shoots hanging downward.

256 That is the one who did not fail to inherit what the creature failed.

257 The motive of covering/dressing in something immaterial and divine is juxtaposed to the previous motive of the corruptible body. The reader should have in mind the famous clothing with the *tunics of skin* (Gen 3:21) in patristic and especially Origenist exegesis (in the latter, 'tunics of skin' are the material bodies).

258 The wording is that of Is 59:17 (καὶ ἐνεδύσατο δικαιοσύνην ὡς θώρακα καὶ περιέθετο περικεφαλαίαν σωτηρίου ἐπὶ τῆς κεφαλῆς καὶ περιεβάλετο ἱμάτιον ἐκδικήσεως καὶ τὸ περιβόλαιον) and Wis 5:17–18 (καὶ ὁπλοποιήσει τὴν κτίσιν εἰς ἄμυναν ἐχθρῶν ἐνδύσεται θώρακα δικαιοσύνην καὶ περιθήσεται κόρυθα κρίσιν ἀνυπόκριτον).

βασις] is mysterious [μυστική?],[259] but also [ἀλλὰ πάλιν] relentless [**tаръ** = ἀπό-τομος?][260] is *his coming* [παρουσία αὐτοῦ; 1 Cor 15:23].

Abbreviations

Briquet   Ch.M. Briquet, *Les Filigranes. Dictionnaire historique des marques du papier dès leur apparition vers 1282 jusqu'en 1600. A facsimile of the 1907 edition with supplementary material contributed by a number of scholars*, ed. A. Stevenson, Amsterdam: The Paper Publications Society, 1968.

CPG   M. Geerard, *Clavis Patrum Graecorum*, 4 vols (Corpus Christianorum), Turnhout: Brepols, 1974–1983; M. Geerard, J. Noret, *Clavis Patrum Graecorum. Supplementum* (Corpus Christianorum), Turnhout: Brepols, 1998.

LLP   *Slovník Jazyka Staroslověnského | Lexicon Linguae Palaeoslavenicae*, Hlavní redaktor: J. Kurz [succeded by] Z. Hauptová, 4 vols, Prague: Academia Euroslavica, 1958–1997.

Piccard   G. Piccard, *Die Wasserzeichenkartei Piccard im Hauptstaatsarchiv Stuttgart* (Veröffentlichungen der Staatlichen Archivverwaltung Baden-Württemberg. Sonderreihe), 17 Bde, Stuttgart: W. Kohlhammer, 1961–1997.

TLG   *Thesaurus Linguae Graecae.*

TS   R. Payne Smith, *Thesaurus Syriacus*, Oxford: Clarendon Press, 1879–1901.

TU   Texte und Untersuchungen zur Geschichte der altchristlichen Literatur.

Лихачев   Лихачев, Н.П. *Палеографическое значение бумажных водяных*

---

259   This phraseology refers to a mystical and/or sacramental understanding, rather common in Christian exegesis. Cf. in Origen: τὸ μυστήριον τῆς τοῦ υἱοῦ τοῦ θεοῦ ἐνσωματώσεως καὶ καταβάσεως (*Commentarius in Evangelium Iohannis*, VI, 5, 29; Blanc, Origène, *Commentaire sur Saint Jean*, t. II, Paris, 1970, p. 150).

260   This epithet is problematic, because Slavonic **tарь** refers not to the standard Greek epithet of παρουσία—φοβερά (страшное 'fearful'). Срезневский, *Материалы для словаря древне-русского языка*, St. Petersburg, 1893–1912, col. 1664 provides a case where **tарь** renders ἀπότομος (in the translation of Gregory of Nazianzus!), even though the standard Greek equivalent is θυμώδης. Nevertheless, according to the data of *TLG*, only the adverb ἀποτόμως occurs (rarely!) in the context of the second coming, and there is no instance of the adjective ἀπότομος being applied to the noun παρουσία.

знаков. Части 1–3. (Общество любителей древней письменности, 116). St. Petersburg: Типография "В.С. Балашев и Ко", 1899.

СлРЯ 11–17   Институт русского языка им. В.В. Виноградова [Российской] Академии Наук [СССР]. *Словарь русского языка XI–XVII вв.* Выпуски [issues] 1–31–. Moscow: Наука, 1975–2019–.

ТОДРЛ   *Труды отдела древнерусской литературы Института русской литературы [Российской] Академии Наук [СССР] (Пушкинского дома)*. Тома [volumes] 1–66–. St. Petersburg: Наука, 1934–2019–.

Шварц   Шварц, Е.М. *Новгородские рукописи XV века: кодикологическое исследование рукописей Софийско-Новгородского собрания Государственной Публичной Библиотеки им. М.Е. Салтыкова-Щедрина*. Moscow—Leningrad: Издательство Государственной Публичной Библиотеки им. М.Е. Салтыкова-Щедрина, 1989.

Acknowledgements

This research was carried out by one of the co-authors, Basil Lourié, with a financial support of the Russian Foundation for Fundamental Research, project 18-011-01243 'Formation of the conceptual categorical apparatus of Eastern Christian philosophical and theological thought of the third and the fourth centuries'; and by the other co-author, Maria Korogodina, Saint-Petersburg University, with a financial support of the Russian Science Foundation, project 20-18-00171 'Moscovia & Ruthenia in the 15th–17th centuries: mutual influences of written traditions in liturgy, canon law, the educational systems, and theology'. Both authors express their deepest gratitude to Prof. Joseph O'Leary for improving their English. They are also grateful to all those who helped them at different stages of their work, especially to Dmitry Afinogenov, Andrey Borodikhin, Anissava Miltenova, Anna Pichkhadze, Alexander Simonov, Sergius Temčinas, and Constantine Vershinin.

CHAPTER 12

Bridging the Gaps in the Samaritan Tradition

Abraham Tal

Extra-canonical sources do exist within the body of Samaritan literature, and they may have contributed to the formation of the Samaritan community's traditions. As for esoteric sources, I am not so sure. In fact, a very prominent figure among the illustrious persons who populated the list of researchers of the past century, Moses Gaster, was convinced that a short composition published by him for the first time, namely 'Asāṭīr,' indeed belongs to the genre of literature that we may call 'esoteric,' in the sense that it contains material intended for a restricted number of initiated persons who possess some secret knowledge hidden from the masses. Indeed, Gaster's publication bears the subtitle *The Samaritan Book of the "Secrets of Moses."*[1] It was in the forties of the past century that Z. Ben-Ḥayyīm demonstrated that the real name of the book, الاساطير, is the Arabic term for 'tales,' 'legends,' and has nothing to do with 'secrets.'[2] In other words, Gaster wrongly associated الاساطير to the Hebrew root סתר, while in fact the Samaritans never confused ט with ת. So, having no 'secrets,' Asāṭīr is less 'esoteric' than Gaster would admit.

Be it as it may, as a Midrashic chronicle, Asāṭīr does have an apocryphal character. This is why I proposed one aspect of its contents as the subject of my talk, namely, the way Asāṭīr bridges the gaps left in the Torah.

In contrast to the other Samaritan chronicles, Asāṭīr does not *continue* the Pentateuchal narration. Its first eleven chapters rather re-tell the Biblical story from the Creation to Moses's death in a very detailed way. The story is mostly a collection of traditions, some of them very old, perhaps remnants of compositions no longer in existence, or tales orally transmitted from generation to generation, or both. Since nothing from the Samaritan ancient extra-Pentateuchal literature has survived centuries of persecution, there is little chance of ascertaining the *internal* Samaritan sources of Asāṭīr.[3]

---

1 M. Gaster, *The ASATIR, The Samaritan Book of the "Secret of Moses" Together with the Pitron, or Samaritan Commentary, etc.*, London, 1927.

2 Z. Ben-Ḥayyīm, '(עם תרגום ופירוש) ספר אסטיר' ['The Book of Asāṭīr (with Translation and Commentary)'], *Tarbiẓ* 14, 1943, pp. 107–190.

3 In a recent article, Jean-Marie Duchemin asserted that at least in the parts of *Asāṭīr* concerning the antediluvian times, their main sources are the Torah and its Targum: J.-M. Duchemin,

BRIDGING THE GAPS IN THE SAMARITAN TRADITION

In particular, *Asāṭīr* expands the Biblical narrative focusing on four central figures, Adam, Noah, Abraham and Moses. As such, *Asāṭīr* is faced with a sacred text which is far from generous when facts, events and even ideas are related. What I intend to say is in fact a commonplace, since everyone of us has been exposed to the laconic character of Biblical phraseology with its abundance of omissions, if I may say so. As a parallel chronicler, *Asāṭīr* examines gaps in the narrative and tries to fill them, so that its flow may look natural.[4]

Let us take for example the fourth chapter of Genesis, which tells that, after the eviction from the Garden of Eden, with the discontinuation of Divine Creation, the duty of פרו ורבו, 'be fruitful and multiply' (Gen. 1:28), fell upon humankind's shoulders (Gen. 3:16). This resulted in the birth of the two brothers, Cain and Abel (Gen. 4:1–2). So far so good. The problem arises when these two have to reproduce. Otherwise no פרו ורבו. Nothing is mentioned in the Pentateuch regarding Cain's woman (אשתו) with whom he coupled (וידע) and who conceived and bore Enoch (Gen. 4:17). Killed by his brother, Abel has no progeny, therefore no lineage is mentioned. *Asāṭīr* needs to fill in the gaps. This is how it begins:

ישתבח אלה דעבד עלמה ואקים אדם ארש. ובניו קין והבל כמהו. ויהב לקין מערבה.
ויהב להבל צפונה וימה. ויהב אלעלה תלימת קין להבל לאתה. ויהב מקדה תלימת הבל
לקין לאתה. ושרא קין במיססת מדי מתקריה ניכל: ופלג ארעה לה ולבניו בירח אב.

Praised be God who created the world and set Adam as a foundation, and his sons, Cain and Abel, like him. And he gave to Cain the West, and he gave to Abel the North and the Sea.[5] And he gave El'ale, Cain's (twin) sister, to Abel as wife, and Maqeda, Abel's (twin) sister, to Cain as wife. And Cain started to build a place which is called Nikal. And he divided the earth between himself and his sons in the month of Av.

'La question des sources de l' Asātir: l' example des récits antédiluviens', in J. Frey et al. (eds), *Die Samaritaner Und Die Bibel / The Samaritans and the Bible*, Berlin–Boston, 2012, pp. 323–328.

4   In an illuminating article, Stadel has recently demonstrated that historical events appear in Asāṭīr under the guise of re-telling biblical stories: C. Stadel, 'The Story of the Tower of Babel in the Samaritan Book Asāṭīr as a Historical Midrash on the Samaritan Revolts of the 6th Century C.E.', *JAOS* 135 (2015), pp. 189–207.

5   ימה, 'the sea'. This is perplexing, as ימה, is the common biblical designation of the West (HALOT, s.v.), which according to this introductory sequel, has been given to Cain: מערבה! Therefore the 17th century Arabic commentary of Asāṭīr made by Meshallama ad-Danafi puts الجنوب, 'the south', for ימה. Apparently arbitrarily.

The chronicler does not follow the course of the Biblical story of the Creation. He mentions אלה דעבד עלמה, just *en passant*, reserving larger space to Adam and his deeds. Even the episode that provoked Adam's expulsion from Eden is only briefly referred to in connection with the act of reproduction: ואשתחה אדם וחוה בגנתה ח יומים דלא ידע חוה. וזנת מדעין במלתה דנחשה. 'Adam and Eve sojourned in the Garden eight days [during which Adam] did not know Eve. And (then) their minds strayed through the word of the serpent.' This is referred to some lines earlier in connection with Abel's murder: ודחל אדם דחלה רבה הך יומה דהלקטו פריה. 'Adam was in great fear, as on the day when the fruits were picked.' Obviously, the forbidden fruit is meant here. One gets the impression that Adam's sin is blurred: notice the passive הלקטו ('were picked'), which denotes an impersonal subject!

For the rest, *Asāṭīr* endeavours to adjust the story to the way the reproduction of humankind takes place: by sexual intercourse, since divine creation has stopped. Two women emerge as wives, sisters of Cain and Abel. There is no other solution to the problem of reproduction. After all, incest was forbidden much later. The Talmud was equally concerned with the coupling that contradicts the rules of Leviticus, which forbid incest. In principle, both Talmudim condemn such couplings, but admit a divine exception. So says the Babylonian Talmud (Sanhedrin f. 58ᵛ): מפני מה לא נשא אדם את בתו, כדי שישא קין את אחותו, שנאמר 'כי אמרתי עולם חסד יבנה'. הא לא הכי אסירא. כיון דאשתרי אשתרי. 'Why did not Adam marry his daughter? So that Cain should marry his sister, as it is written, 'For I said, the world shall be built up by grace' (Psalms 89:3). But otherwise, she would have been forbidden [to Cain]. However, once it had been permitted, it remained so.' In other words: in His grace, God admitted this uncommon incest in order to build the world.

The Jerusalem Talmud is a little more explicit with regard to Cain's 'marriage': אמר ר' אבין. שלא תאמר קין נשא את אחותו, הבל נשא את אחותו. חסד הוא. חסד עשיתי עם הראשונים שייבנה העולם מהן. 'אמרתי עולם חסד יבנה' 'R. Abin [said]: lest you say "Cain married his sister, Abel married his sister". It is disgraceful (Lev 20:17). [In this case, by exception] I showed grace to the ancients, so that the world should be built of them: "For I said: the world will be built by grace" (Psalm 89:3).' Obviously, this is an ingenious word-play: חסד in Leviticus means 'disgrace' (so in Proverbs 14:34), elsewhere חסד always meaning 'grace.' The Talmudic saying explains the temporary acceptance of disgraceful incest by the necessity to build the world.

In order to obscure, or at least to mitigate the harshness of the incestuous coupling, *Asāṭīr* mates Abel's (twin) sister to Cain and vice versa, Cain's (twin) sister to Abel: ויהב אלעלה תלימת קין להבל לאתה: ויהב מקדה תלימת הבל לקין לאתה,

'(Adam) gave Elʿale, Cain's (twin) sister, to Abel as wife, and Maqeda, Abel's (twin) sister, to Cain as wife.'[6]

This recalls Haggadic Jewish sources, such as Genesis Rabba sect. 22 which states that twin sisters were born with Cain and Abel: קין ותאומתו, הבל ושתי תאומותיו, 'Cain and his twin sister, Abel and his two twin sisters'. So does also Pseudo-Jonathan Targum to Gen 4:1–2. The latter avoids any suspicion of incest, stating that Eve conceived Cain with the angel Samael, but Abel and his twin sister with 'her husband': ואדם ידע ית חוה אתתיה דהיא מתעברא מן סמאל מלאכה דייי ואוסיפת למילד מן בעלה אדם ית תיומתיה וית הבל, 'And Adam knew his wife Eve who had conceived [Cain] from Samael the angel of the Lord, and she gave birth from her husband Adam to his (Cain's?) twin sister and Abel.' Not all the manuscripts of Pseudo-Jonathan contain this fascinating detail,[7] but some of them at least tend to admit that Cain and his anonymous twin sister stemmed from different fathers, which makes their marriage 'semi-Kosher'. In other words, the verb יָדַע is not taken here in the 'Biblical sense'.

פרקי דרבי אליעזר, an eighth-century midrash, connects this abominable angel with the serpent which tempted Eve in the garden: קרב אליה [סמאל] רוכב נחש ועיברה את קין. ואחר כך בא עליה אדם ועיברה את הבל. שנאמר 'והאדם ידע את חוה אשתו'. מה הוא ידע? ידע שהיתה מעוברת וראה דמותו שלא היה מן התחתונים אלא מן העליונים. '[Samael] approached her riding the serpent, and she conceived Cain. Afterwards Adam approached her, and she conceived Abel. As it is said "And Adam knew his wife Eve" (Gen. 4:1). What did he know? He knew that she was pregnant and he saw his (Samael's) image, that it is not from among the lower ones (= humans), but from among the upper ones (= angels).'[8] Maimonides specifies: 'Samael is Satan. Therefore, it is Satan who fathered Cain' (*Guide of the Perplexed*, book 2, chapter 30).

---

6 A daughter of Adam and Eve, named Awan, is mentioned in Jubilees 4:1, 9 as Cain's wife. The name Awan seems to refer to Cain's replica גדול עוני מנשא (see J. VanderKam, *The Book of Jubilees*, Louvain, 1989, pp. 23–24). For a discussion of the names of Adam's and Eve's daughters in ancient sources, see A. Marmorstein, 'Die Namen der Schwestern Kains und Abels in midraschischen und der apocryphen Literatur', *ZAW* 25 (1905), pp. 141–144. A full account of the targumic treatment of Eve's progeny is in F. García Martínez, 'Eve's Children in the Targumim', in G.P. Luttikhuizen (ed.), *Eve's Children: the Biblical Stories Retold and Interpreted in Jewish and Christian Traditions*, Leiden–Boston, 2003, pp. 27–46. See also C. Werman, *The Book of Jubilees, Introduction, Translation and Interpretation*, Jerusalem, 2015 (in Hebrew), pp. 198–199.

7 M. Ginsburger, *Pseudo-Jonathan (Thargum Jonathan ben Usiël zum Pentateuch). Nach der Londoner Handschrift (Brit. Mus. add. 27031)*, Berlin, 1903, p. 6.

8 As quoted by the 13th century commentator Menaham Recanati in his ביאור על התורה, Venice printing, 1523, p. 31.

The diverse paternity of Eve's sons is also suggested in a much more ancient source, 'Vita Adæ et Evæ.' On the eighteenth day of separation from Adam, Eve was approached by Satan disguised as an angel. He convinced her that he would provide her with the paradisiac food to which she was accustomed. After a long discussion with Adam, she left for the West. There she built a booth where she finally bore a child, Cain. Though Satan's paternity is not explicit, it is clear that Adam is not Cain's father. Later, Adam 'knew' Eve and she bore Abel.[9]

The sons' marriages are also described in the Ethiopian epic account (*Kebra Nagast*, כבוד המלכים, § 3),[10] which also mentions twin sisters. The same source tells us that Maqeda was the queen of Sheba (ibid., ch. 26). Do these names represent allusions to the division of the land between Adam's sons, as in *Asāṭīr*? It is hard to ascertain. The text locates 'the south' in the possession of Abel, which may correspond to the location of מקדה. On the other hand, אלעלה is in Moab, on the eastern bank of the Jordan, and may be considered as the West only if the story were told in a remote East, i.e. in Mesopotamia or Ethiopia.

Before tackling the subject of reproduction, *Asāṭīr* informs us that Adam gave to Cain and Abel estates remote from each other (see above): ויהב לקין מערבה ויהב להבל צפונה וימה, 'And he gave to Cain the West, and he gave to Abel the North and the Sea.' Clearly, Adam tries to separate the sons from each other, following a presentiment of calamity. It is again 'Vita Adæ et Evæ' which tells us that the attempt to separate the two sons followed Eve's dream about Abel's blood being shed.[11]

And now the actual plot begins: the two brothers bring offerings, as told in Gen. 4:3–5: וַיְהִי מִקֵּץ יָמִים וַיָּבֵא קַיִן מִפְּרִי הָאֲדָמָה מִנְחָה לַיהוָה: וְהֶבֶל הֵבִיא גַם־הוּא מִבְּכֹרוֹת צֹאנוֹ וּמֵחֶלְבֵהֶן וַיִּשַׁע יְהוָה אֶל־הֶבֶל וְאֶל־מִנְחָתוֹ: וְאֶל־קַיִן וְאֶל־מִנְחָתוֹ לֹא שָׁעָה וַיִּחַר לְקַיִן מְאֹד וַיִּפְּלוּ פָּנָיו:, 'In the course of time Cain brought to the Lord of the fruit of the ground an offering; and Abel, for his part brought from the firstlings of his flock their fat portions. And the Lord had regard for Abel and his offering. But for Cain and his offering he had no regard. And Cain was very angry and his countenance fell.' This is how Genesis calls both gifts: מנחה, unaware of the priestly terminology which discerns between מנחה, 'cereal offering' (Lev 2–23—Num 4–29), and קרבן, 'animal offering' (Lev 1:2 etc.). But *Asāṭīr* is aware of this distinction, hence its description distinguishes between Cain's מנחה, the produce of a tiller of the ground, and the קרבן of Abel who was a keeper of sheep: והוה

---

9   Ch. IX–XX. See the Latin edition of W. Meyer, *Vita Adæ et Evæ, Abhandlungen der philos.-philol. Cl. der königl. Akademie der Wiss.* 14/iii. Munich 1878/79, pp. 222–228.

10   *Kebra Nagast*, כבוד מלכים, trans. from Gəʿəz, annotated and introduced by R. HaCohen. Tel-Aviv, 2009 (in Hebrew).

11   See W. Meyer's edition (above, note 9), p. 228.

מסכום יומים איתי קין מנחה והבל איתי קרבן, 'It was at the end of (some) days, that Cain brought an offering and Abel brought a sacrifice.'

Moreover, the offerings brought by the brothers have an indispensable accessory omitted in the Pentateuch: *an altar*. This detail does not escape the attention of our chronicler who does not miss the opportunity to draw attention to the location of the first altar (ראשית מדבחה, in his stammering language): וראשית מדבחה הוה בשפול מקדשה. בין לוזה והר גריזים, 'And the first altar was on the slopes (בשפול) of the holy place between Luza and Mount Gerizim.'

One can hardly ignore such an assertion regarding the central position of Mount Gerizim in Samaritan tradition, opposed as it is to Jerusalem and to Mount Moriyyah in Judaism: this was a major point of rivalry between Jews and Samaritans. According to the Samaritans, every important event took place precisely on Gerizim. In chapter III of *Asāṭīr*, we meet a person named Ahidan, a descendant (in fourth generation) of Lamekh (who is not sympathized in *Asāṭīr*): Ahidan built ציון דמתקריה גפנה והיא בית מכתש, 'Zion called Gafna, which is a house of plague.' Obviously, גפנה refers to Judah in Jacob's vision in Gen 49:11, since the masoretic אֹסְרִי לַגֶּפֶן עִירֹה, 'binding his foal to the vine', corresponds in the Samaritan Pentateuch to אסורי לגפן עירו, interpreted by the Samaritans as 'he is tied up to Gafen, his city.'[12] Furthermore, *Asāṭīr* plays on the alliteration of מקדש, 'temple,' and מכתש, 'plague', in order to attain a derogatory imprint on the Jerusalem temple. In ch. XI, 26–29, *Asāṭīr* states that verse 7 of Moses's song in Deut. 33, שמע יהוה קול יהודה, 'O Lord, give heed to Judah,' is an oracle that predicts the building of the Jerusalem temple: מגדל גפנה יבני, 'he (the apostate) will build the tower of Gafna' (= of 'shame', or 'plague'). The Samaritan Midrash known as *Tibåt Mårqe* puts in Moses's mouth the following complain about the villains: ולגפנה עמרו ולביתי חרבו, 'they built Gafna, and destroyed My house' (Book IV, § 99).[13]

In the first chapter of *Asāṭīr* we find an essential detail explaining that Cain first learnt of his inferior status by comparing himself to his father whose offerings were accepted: וכד לא עמה קין מנחתה מתקבלה הך הוה אלוף עמי מנחתה דאבוה ידע דו פסיל, 'And when Cain did not see his offering accepted, as he was accustomed to see the offerings of his father, he learnt that he had been rejected.' And this is how precisely he was informed: והדקרב אתעכר עלמה ורוחה, 'when he (Cain) offered [his sacrifice], the world became disturbed and so did his spirit.' We are told that Cain *saw* that his offering was rejected: דרוה בשעתה קמאיתה

---

12   The reading *asūri*, a passive participle of אסר, 'to tie up', is occasionally rendered by some manuscripts of ST as יסטי לגפנה קרתה, 'he strays to Gifna, his city'.

13   Z. Ben-Ḥayyīm, *Tibat Marqe, a Collection of Samaritan Midrashim*, Jerusalem, 1988 (in Hebrew), p. 297.

ולושה לא אתצטר, 'For he saw at the first hour (that to) his offering he (God) did not pay heed.'[14] Cain was impatient to see whether his offering would be accepted, but he did not wait for three hours like Abel: הקרב הבל וג שען אתרחי יהוה להבל ולמנחתה, 'Abel offered and after three hours God accepted Abel and his offering.' This is clearly a further proof of Cain's bad temper! After waiting merely for an hour, he left in anger: ויחר לקין ועזר לארעה וכתר ד: שנין דלא עמי לאדם ולא הבל, 'Cain was in anger and went back to his land and stayed there four years without seeing neither Adam nor Abel.' So he secluded himself for four years.

At this point, *Asāṭīr* opens a very intriguing parenthesis, in which it discloses the divergence in the parental attitude towards the two sons: Eve loves Cain, whereas Adam loves Abel (v. 15): והות חוה רחמה לקין ואדם רחם להבל, 'Eve was loving Cain, but Adam loved Abel.'

Is that a 'chauvinistic' allusion to the inferiority of the mother who loved the rejected son? After all, Eve was traditionally considered to be the one who succumbed to the Serpent's temptation and who seduced Adam to eat the forbidden fruit.[15] In any case, this is an interesting case of inverted analogy compared to Gen 25:28 where we read: וַיֶּאֱהַב יִצְחָק אֶת־עֵשָׂו ... וְרִבְקָה אֹהֶבֶת אֶת־יַעֲקֹב, 'Isaac loved Esau ... whereas Rebeka loved Jacob.'[16]

At this point *Asāṭīr* is not entirely clear: וכד שחו קין דלא אתי נסבת חוה מלך מן אדם ואזלת לידה והבל עמה ואשקחתה עקיר לאתר מדו מתקריה אחריה ערפאת, 'And when Cain tarried, and was not coming, Eve took permission from Adam and went to him (to Cain?), and Abel (was) with her, and she found him displaced to a place later named 'Arafat.' This would mean that Eve went to see Cain while taking Abel with her: והבל עמה. Then *Asāṭīr* proceeds: מלתה דאמירה לקין ולידך עזרותה וכל דבתרה נהד לברה ודמן תקפד אדמה דהבל אשתפך. וכד השפך אדמה דהבל התעכרת רוחה והות ארעה בקנאה וימיה עכירין ושמשה אשנתה וזרה בניושה. 'The word

---

14   Ben-Ḥayyīm, *Asāṭīr*, p. 115. Notice that דרוה is very uncommon in contemporary Aramaic (which regularly uses חמה, 'to see'). Its filiation goes back to the root ראה common in Hebrew. Its cognate noun רו occurs in Daniel רוה דחיל, 'his appearance is frightening' (Dan 2:31). בשעתה קמאיתה is a collocation meaning 'at once'. As for ולושה, it is a midrashic use of Abraham's words when he urged Sarah (Gen 18:6): מהרי ... לושי ועשי עוגות, 'Quickly ... knead and make cakes', an offering to the messengers of God. לושה is therefore an epithet for מנחה 'offering'.

15   Adam's repulsion for Cain and his predilection for Abel are related in the Ethiopian epos too. *Kebra Nagast*, § 4.

16   Jewish tradition has an explanation for these preferences. Jacob is the righteous son: איש תם יושב אהלים, 'a quiet man living in tents'. The midrash connects the plural אהלים with אהלי שם, 'the tents of Shem' (Gen. 9:27), and concludes that Jacob was learning תורה in the tents of Shem (Yalqut Shim'oni, §110), in contrast with Esau who is linked with אדום (Gen. 36:8), hence the enemy. Jewish post-biblical literature identifies Edom with Rome, the wicked kingdom (e.g., Jerusalem Talmud, tract. Avoda Zara, ch. 1, § 2; Ta'anit ch. 4, § 8).

BRIDGING THE GAPS IN THE SAMARITAN TRADITION 269

said to Cain "to you is his desire" and everything that follows: "let us go to the field",[17] and "by your anger Abel's blood was shed": and when Abel's blood had been shed, his (Cain's) spirit was troubled, and the earth was in ire, and the seas became turbid, and the sun was eclipsed, and the moon in weakness.'

Needless to stress, such treatments of Biblical 'omissions' abound in *Asāṭīr*. The programme of this volume obliges me to skip some captivating episodes, contenting myself with one more case which eloquently exemplifies the ways *Asāṭīr* treats the Pentateuchal text: a confused description of Nimrod, about whom Genesis says some flattering words (10:7–10). First we are informed that Cush begat five sons, while one of them begat two: וּבְנֵי כוּשׁ סְבָא וַחֲוִילָה וְסַבְתָּה וְרַעְמָה וְסַבְתְּכָא וּבְנֵי רַעְמָה שְׁבָא וּדְדָן:, 'The sons of Cush were Seva and Havila and Savta and Raama and Savtecha. And the sons of Raama were Sheva and Dedan.' So far the list of Cush is complete, including the next generation: the sons of Cush's son Raama. Suddenly, the filiation of Cush is repeated and another of his sons appears, Nimrod, to whom Genesis assigns special qualities: וְכוּשׁ יָלַד אֶת־נִמְרֹד הוּא הֵחֵל לִהְיוֹת גִּבֹּר בָּאָרֶץ: הוּא־הָיָה גִבֹּר־צַיִד לִפְנֵי יְהוָה עַל־כֵּן יֵאָמַר כְּנִמְרֹד גִּבֹּר צַיִד לִפְנֵי יְהוָה: וַתְּהִי רֵאשִׁית מַמְלַכְתּוֹ בָּבֶל וְאֶרֶךְ וְאַכַּד וְכַלְנֶה בְּאֶרֶץ שִׁנְעָר:, 'Cush became the father of Nimrod; he was the first on earth to be a mighty man. He was a mighty hunter before the Lord; therefore, it is said, "Like Nimrod a mighty hunter before the Lord".' That is all. And nevertheless: Nimrod's name being homiletically derived from the root *MRD*, meaning 'rebellion,' *Asāṭīr* asserts that his qualities of 'a mighty man' and 'a mighty hunter' made him an arrogant man (as they say: 'the power corrupts'). So, chapter IV relates that 'Nimrod was a king over all the children of Ham, and they gathered themselves together to build Babylon' under his command: ושוי מלך נמרוד על כל בני דחם ובנו בבל רבתה ... ושרי נמרוד למהך גבר בארעה, 'Arpachshad dwelt in Ur Chasdim ... and soon Nimrod reigned over all the sons of Ham, and they built Babylon the great ... and Nimrod began to act as a hero on the earth.'

Also Josephus associates Nimrod with the erection of the tower of Babylon (Antiq. 1:115), and so does the Jewish Midrash פרקי דר' אליעזר, ch. 24 which attributes to the rebellious Nimrod the initiative to build the tower. Apparently, this is what the vicinity of Genesis 11 produced: אמר נמרוד לעמו באו נבנה לנו עיר גדולה ונשב שם בתוכה פן נפוץ על פני כל הארץ בראשונים ונבנה מגדל גדול בתוכה ונעלה לשמים ... ונקנה לנו שם גדול בארץ, 'Nimrod said to his people, come, let us build a great city for ourselves, and let us dwell therein, lest we disperse all over the

---

17 נהך לברה is the Samaritan Targum rendering of the Samaritan Pentateuch נלכה השדה, absent from the masoretic text (Gen 4:8). It is shared by ancient translations, such as the Septuagint, Vulgate, Peshitta and some Jewish Targumim. See *Genesis, Biblia Hebraica Quinta*, fasc. 1. Stuttgart, Deutsche Bibelgesellschaft, 2015, ad loc.

earth, like the ancients, and let us build a great tower in its midst, and ascend to heaven ... and let us acquire a great name on the earth.'

Asāṭīr ch. V reveals Nimrod's hostile encounter with Abraham. After many battles against various coalitions, Nimrod settled in Assyria, where he collided with Arpachshad's descendants on account of his idolatry. ועזר נמרוד לאשור ומלך וכד מלך עבד קרב עם נחור ועבד נמרוד לארפכשד הך דעבד פרעה לעבראי דעמו בספר האותות דעתיד קעם מן ארפכשד גבר מחי כל סגדיה ומבתר כל צלמיה, 'Nimrod returned to Assyria and reigned there, and while he was reigning, he battled against Nahor. And Nimrod did to Arpachshad what Pharaoh did to the Hebrews. For he saw in the Book of Signs that a man of Arpachshad's stock shall arise and smite all the idols and strike all the icons.' The passage suggests that Nimrod was in the possession of a book of predictions named ספר האותות, 'the Book of Signs.' This book is mentioned in ch. II as a book from which already Enoch received his instruction. It had previously been given to Adam: אלף חנוך בספר האותות דהתיהב לאדם, 'Enoch learnt from the Book of Signs [which had been] given to Adam.' Obviously, 'given to Adam' means that the Book of Signs has a divine origin. It then reached Noah's hands (ch. III) as a member of the trilogy of the 'Books of the Creation.'[18] The other two are ספר נגמות, 'the Book of Stars,' and ספר מלחמות 'the Book of Wars',[19] all three revealing the future. Thus in ch. IV we are told that Noah consulted the Book of Signs: וקעם נח בדמי[ס]ספר האותות ועמה טמירת אדם וסכה די לתיבותה, 'Noah perceived the mysteries of the Book of Signs and seeing Adam's hidden [thoughts] he understood that they concern the ark'. In ch. VI we are told about a sorcerer by the name of Tortas, who was instructed from the ספר האותות, and in ch. VII the same Tortas was advising Amraphel and Kedar Laomer with the aid of ספר האותות. It is also 'the Book of Signs' from where Nimrod foresaw the menace of Abraham's birth.

In order to prevent the birth of Abraham, Nimrod ordered the men to be separated from the women: ופקד נמרוד דלא ישתבקון בני ארפכשד גבריה עם נשיה מ: יום ושוי אתעבשו גבריה באתר ונשיה באתר, 'Nimrod ordered that none of the males of Arpachshad's sons may be permitted to approach women for forty days, and immediately they were isolated in different places', הך דעבד פרעה לעבראי 'as Pharaoh did to the Hebrews.'[20] Nimrod's stratagem failed however: Terah did

---

18   Reminiscent of 'The Book of the Heavenly Luminaries' of Enoch, i.e. the 3rd section of the Pseudo-epigraphic 1 Enoch.

19   Whose name may be associated with ספר מלחמות יהוה, of Num. 21:14.

20   The story of Pharaoh is related below in chapter VIII. It is rooted in a tradition reported by Josephus in Antiq. II:205, about an astrologer who predicted the birth of Moses. Such separation, although initiated by Amram, is related by the Babylonian Talmud, tract. Sotah, 12a: עמרם גדול הדור היה כיון שראה שאמר פרעה הרשע כל הבן הילוד היאורה תשליכוהו

BRIDGING THE GAPS IN THE SAMARITAN TRADITION

approach his wife, and Abraham was born. In order to save the idols, Nimrod's resort was radical: ונסבה נמרוד ורמתה לנורה: ובדיל דאמר דלעלמה אלה, 'Nimrod took him and threw him (Abram) into the fire because he (Abram) said that God is everlasting.'

The account of Nimrod throwing Abraham into the fire is also present in the Jewish Midrash.[21] For example Genesis Rabba sect. 38:13, contains the account of a debate between Nimrod and Abraham relating to the right worship. Nimrod makes great efforts to persuade Abraham to worship the natural elements: fire, water, clouds, light, whereas Abraham rules them out one by one. The debate is stopped by the king who throws Abraham into a fiery furnace: הריני משליכך בו ויבוא אלהיך שאתה משתחוה לו ויצילך, 'I cast you in it (fire), and let your god whom you worship come and rescue you.'[22]

Here *Asāṭīr* inserts a very interesting note about the fate of Haran. This was Terah's son, i.e. the brother of Abraham and Nahor and the father of Lot (Gen 11:26–28). He died while his father was alive: וַיְחִי־תֶרַח שִׁבְעִים שָׁנָה וַיּוֹלֶד אֶת־אַבְרָם אֶת־נָחוֹר וְאֶת־הָרָן: וְאֵלֶּה תּוֹלְדֹת תֶּרַח תֶּרַח הוֹלִיד אֶת־אַבְרָם אֶת־נָחוֹר וְאֶת־הָרָן וְהָרָן הוֹלִיד אֶת־לוֹט: וַיָּמָת הָרָן עַל־פְּנֵי תֶּרַח אָבִיו בְּאֶרֶץ מוֹלַדְתּוֹ בְּאוּר כַּשְׂדִּים, 'Terah had lived seventy years, when he became the father of Abram, Nahor, and Haran. Now these are the descendants of Terah. Terah was the father of Abram, Nahor, and Haran; and Haran was the father of Lot. And Haran died before his father Terah in the land of his birth, in Ur of the Chaldeans.' One may wonder about the cause of Haran's untimely death. *Asāṭīr* contains an answer: וכד עצף הרן על אברהם במימר דו חרש נפקת אשתה ואכלתה ומית הרן על פני תרח אביו באור כשדים, 'and when Haran was acting insolently toward Abraham, saying that he was a wizard, the fire came out and consumed him in the presence of his father Terah in Ur Chasdim.' This provides us with the missing justification of his sudden death: Haran was hostile to Abraham, accusing him of sorcery. Also a Jewish midrash sought for a solution. Genesis Rabba § 38:13 narrates Haran's presence at the burning of Abraham, saying: אם נצח אברם אנא אמר מן דאברם אנא. אם נצח נמרוד אמר אנא

אמר לשוא אנו עמלים. עמד וגירש את אשתו. עמדו כולן וגירשו את נשותיהן, 'Amram was the greatest man of his generation; when he saw that the wicked Pharaoh had decreed: 'Every son that is born you shall cast into the river', he said: 'In vain do we labour'. He arose and divorced his wife. All [the Israelites] thereupon arose and divorced their wives'.

21   It seems that the first to tell in detail the story of Abram being cast in the fiery furnace and rescued by God is Pseudo-Philo in *Liber Antiquitatum Biblicarum*, Ch. VI, §§ 15–18.

22   The Babylonian Talmud, tract. Pesahim fol. 118, has a similar story and so have many other sources. The same story is told in various ways in Jubilees, Ephrem the Syrian, etc. (a long list is given in Gaster's notes). See my essay 'Nimrod, 'a Man of Might'—How Many of Them?', in Jan Dušek (ed.), *The Samaritans in Historical, Cultural and Linguistic Perspectives*, Berlin–Boston, 2018, pp. 91–102.

מנמרוד אנא. כיוון דירד אברם לכבשן האש ונוצל ... אמר מן דאברם. נטלוהו והשליכוהו באש
ומת ..., 'If Abraham triumphs, I take his side; if Nimrod triumphs, I take his side.
When Abraham was saved from the furnace ... he took his side. Then Nimrod's
people threw him into the furnace ... and he died.'

This poses a problem: How come Nimrod, the son of Kush (Gen 10:8–10)—
the third generation after Noah—reappears seven generations later to oppress
Abraham, the tenth generation after Noah? *Asāṭīr* solves the anachronistic
appearance of Nimrod explicitly: there were two Nimrods (ch. VI, 1–3): ובו עקב
מלכות חם. מן נמרוד שריאת ועל נמרוד חסלת, 'with him came the kingdom of Ham
to an end; with Nimrod it began and with Nimrod it came to an end.' This statement is followed by: ומן נמרוד א אל נמרוד ב אלף וכ שנה, 'and from Nimrod A to
Nimrod B one thousand and twenty years [elapsed].'

Sometimes *Asāṭīr* tries to dispel an irreverent image of an otherwise respected figure in the Torah. Such is Sarah, Abraham's wife, about whom Gen
12:15 tells, while accounting of Abram's entry into Egypt to keep away from
hunger: וַיְהִי כְּבוֹא אַבְרָם מִצְרָיְמָה וַיִּרְאוּ הַמִּצְרִים אֶת־הָאִשָּׁה כִּי־יָפָה הִוא מְאֹד: וַיִּרְאוּ אֹתָהּ
שָׂרֵי פַרְעֹה וַיְהַלְלוּ אֹתָהּ אֶל־פַּרְעֹה וַתֻּקַּח הָאִשָּׁה בֵּית פַּרְעֹה:, 'When Abram entered Egypt
the Egyptians saw that the woman was very beautiful. When the officials of
Pharaoh saw her, they praised her to Pharaoh. And the woman was taken into
Pharaoh's house.' This is hardly acceptable for a conservative society living,
as the Samaritans did, in a rigorous Muslim environment of the middle ages,
in which no male eyes were allowed to get a glimpse of a married woman's
face. Accordingly, *Asāṭīr* has some details: ותמן חזו שרה ושבחתה נשייה לגבריין
וגבריה לפרעה ואתנסבת אתתה לבית פרעה, 'Then the women saw Sarah and praised
her to their husbands, and the men to Pharaoh, and the woman was taken
into Pharaoh's house.' The chronicler left no doubt about Sarah's decency. She
exposed her face before women alone, whereas men witnessed her beauty only
indirectly. The story apparently reflects a Bedouin custom.

After taking Abraham's wife, Pharaoh could not escape punishment. God
afflicted him and his house with great plagues. Genesis 12:17 tells that Pharaoh
realized that Sarah's abduction is the cause of the affliction, but one wonders
how he could arrive at this insight. It is *Asāṭīr* that provides the missing link
(ch. VI), resorting to the advice of Tortas the sorcerer who was initiated in 'the
Book of Signs'. It was Tortas who revealed the sense of the dream, and the danger of keeping Sarah, saying in an oracular style: סגודיה דאלהה דכלה באהן אתרה
וכל הדה עקתה בגללה הות, 'the worshiper of the God of All is here, and all this
plague is because of him.'[23]

---

23   The story is beautifully told by *Asāṭīr*. It resembles in many respects the Qumranic Gen-

BRIDGING THE GAPS IN THE SAMARITAN TRADITION

To be sure, *Asāṭīr* was not the first Samaritan treatise to bridge gaps in the text of the Pentateuch. Already centuries before it, at the time when the Samaritan version of the Pentateuch was being crystallized—i.e. ca. the second century BCE—one can detect minute additions introduced in order to smooth the flow of the Biblical account. Here is only one example. In MT of Genesis 3:2–3, Eve relates to the serpent a confusing command in the following terms: וַתֹּאמֶר הָאִשָּׁה אֶל־הַנָּחָשׁ מִפְּרִי עֵץ־הַגָּן נֹאכֵל׃ וּמִפְּרִי הָעֵץ אֲשֶׁר בְּתוֹךְ־הַגָּן אָמַר אֱלֹהִים לֹא תֹאכְלוּ מִמֶּנּוּ וְלֹא תִגְּעוּ בּוֹ פֶּן־תְּמֻתוּן, 'The woman said to the serpent, "We may eat of the fruit of the trees of the garden; but God said, 'You shall not eat of the fruit of the tree that is inside the garden, nor shall you touch it, or you shall die.'"' The discrimination is not clear enough: the fruits of the trees of the garden are permitted, while the fruits of the tree that is *within* the garden is prohibited?[24] The Samaritan Pentateuch inserts a word: אשר בתוך הגן ומפרי העץ הזה, 'and from the fruit of *this* tree, which is inside the garden.' Now everything becomes clear: Eve and the serpent are discussing the threat in the presence of the forbidden tree.

A much more elaborate composition, developed from the story of Israel's deliverance from slavery in Egypt, continuing until the death of Moses, is the renowned *Tībåt Mårqe*. Like *Asāṭīr*, it has a pronounced historiographic character and embeds abundant midrashic material. The text of Book I, stemming from the fourth century CE, like *Asāṭīr*, is faced with a sacred text which is far from generous when facts, events and even ideas are related. Such is the appearance of שרח, an obscure personage, who occurs as an appendix in the list of Asher's sons in Genesis 46:17: וּבְנֵי אָשֵׁר יִמְנָה וְיִשְׁוָה וְיִשְׁוִי וּבְרִיעָה וְשֶׂרַח אֲחֹתָם וּבְנֵי בְרִיעָה חֶבֶר וּמַלְכִּיאֵל, 'The children of Asher: Imnah, Ishvah, Ishvi, Beriah, and their sister Serah. The children of Beriah: Heber and Malchiel.' Furthermore, Numbers 26:44–47 has a list of the families descending from Asher's sons: בְּנֵי אָשֵׁר לְמִשְׁפְּחֹתָם לְיִמְנָה מִשְׁפַּחַת הַיִּמְנָה לְיִשְׁוִי מִשְׁפַּחַת הַיִּשְׁוִי לִבְרִיעָה מִשְׁפַּחַת הַבְּרִיעִי׃ לִבְנֵי בְרִיעָה לְחֶבֶר מִשְׁפַּחַת הַחֶבְרִי לְמַלְכִּיאֵל מִשְׁפַּחַת הַמַּלְכִּיאֵלִי׃ וְשֵׁם בַּת־אָשֵׁר שָׂרַח׃ אֵלֶּה מִשְׁפְּחֹת בְּנֵי־אָשֵׁר לִפְקֻדֵיהֶם שְׁלֹשָׁה וַחֲמִשִּׁים אֶלֶף וְאַרְבַּע מֵאוֹת, 'The descendants of Asher by their families: of Imnah, the clan of the Imnites; of Ishvi, the clan of the Ishvites; of Beriah, the clan of the Beriites. Of the descendants of Beriah: of Heber, the clan of the Heberites; of Malchiel, the clan of the Malchielites. *And the name of the daughter of Asher was Serah.* These are the clans of the Asherites: the number of those enrolled was fifty-three thousand four hundred.'

---

esis Apocryphon. See J.A. Fitzmyer, *The Genesis Apocryphon of Qumran Cave 1 (1Q20)*, 3rd edn, Rome, 2004, col. 19–20.

24   Seeking for an instrument of differentiation some English translations render בתוך הגן as 'in the middle of the garden', which not necessarily represents the literal meaning of the verse.

Amidst the detailed descriptions of the families, a laconic note mentions the existence of a sister: וְשֵׁם בַּת־אָשֵׁר שָׂרַח. Neither her family, nor the number of its members are specified; just the name, apparently out of context. What makes her so important? *Tibåt Mårqe* offers the answer, connecting her with the beginning of the Exodus from Egypt. Gen 50:25 relates about Joseph, who on his sickbed made his brothers swear an oath: וַיַּשְׁבַּע יוֹסֵף אֶת־בְּנֵי יִשְׂרָאֵל לֵאמֹר פָּקֹד יִפְקֹד אֱלֹהִים אֶתְכֶם וְהַעֲלִתֶם אֶת־עַצְמֹתַי מִזֶּה, 'Joseph made the Israelites swear, saying: when God delivers you from Egypt, you shall carry up my bones from here.' Indeed, Moses fulfils Joseph's will, though not immediately. The great migration leaves Rameses driven out by the Egyptians, and first arrives at Sukkot (Exod 12:33–39), then avoids the short way through the land of the Philistines and marches through the wilderness of the Sea of Reeds. At this point, on the way to Canaan, Moses exhumes Joseph's bones (Exod 13:19).

One may wonder why Moses tarried in fulfilling Joseph's desire. *Tibåt Mårqe* I 73–76 explains: קעם עמוד ברעמסס דבחו ולסכותה נטלו ואתו בעין מפק מנה ולא יכלו. קעם עמוד עננה ואשתה קמיון דלא יפקון מתחומה דסכות. ומשה ואהרן עמין ודחלין וכל קהלה מבלדין מהו אהן רזה אמר משה לאהרן דחכים דבקהלה עביד אסכלה ... הפסקו חכימיה ביני קהלה ושרו שאלין כל שבט ושבט. וכד אתרמי קלה לגו שבט אשר נפקת שרח לידון מזרזה ואמרת לית לכון כלום ביש. האנה מפרסיה לוכן מהו אהן רזה ... ישר לון אהלין דאנהרו לעביבי ואתון נשיכונה. אלולי קעמו עמוד עננה ועמוד אשתה הויכון נפקין והוא שביק במצרים. נהירה אנה ליומה דמית בגוה והוא משבע לכל עמה יסקון גרמיו ... הלכת שרח וכל שבט אפרים פעלאתה ומשה ואהרן בתרון הלכין עד אתת לאתרה דהוא טמיר לגוה וקעמת תמן וגלו על ארונה וסבלותה ... שעתה דאסתבל הלך עננה ואשתה קמיון וטלו מסכות ושרו באתם, 'In Rameses they offered a sacrifice and journeyed to Sukkot and sought to leave it, but were unable. The Pillar of Cloud and of Fire had stopped in front of them, such that they could not exit the territory of Sukkot. Moses and Aaron were watching afraid, and all the congregation were frightened. "What is this mystery?" said Moses to Aaron, for it was clear that a foolish deed had been done within the congregation [...] the Elders started an inquiry among the tribes, and when they reached the tribe of Asher, Sherah[25] came out to them in haste and said: "There is nothing wrong with you. I shall reveal to you what this mystery is [...] Praise be to those who remember my uncle's bones, which you have forgotten! Had not the Pillar of Cloud and the Pillar of Fire stopped, you would have gone forth, while he would have been left behind in Egypt. I remember the day when he died and took an oath from the whole people to carry his bones with them" [....] Sherah was walking and all the tribe of Ephraim around her, and

---

25   The spelling Sherah represents Samaritan pronunciation which takes every Masoretic שׁ as a שׂ.

BRIDGING THE GAPS IN THE SAMARITAN TRADITION

Moses and Aaron followed them until she arrived at the place where Joseph was buried and she stopped there.[26] They uncovered the coffin and lifted it up [...] When Joseph was carried [...] the Cloud and the Fire went before them. *And they moved on from Sukkot, and encamped at Etham'* (Exod 13:20).[27]

Asāṭīr and *Mårqe* resort to books of divine origin, like 'The Book of Signs,' and to personages with unnatural powers, such as Serah, a woman of extraordinary longevity and remarkable memory,[28] as well as sorcerers and soothsayers such as Tortas mentioned above, in order to solve textual problems. In doing so, they follow the exegetical principles already employed in the Samaritan Pentateuch which attempts, in a relatively discreet way, to settle textual difficulties of the Torah.

26　Serah's role in revealing Joseph's coffin is narrated in the Jewish Midrash too. E.g. Mekhilta de R. Ishmaʻel, sect. Beshallah I says: וכי מנין היה משה יודע היכן יוסף קבור. שנאמר ושם בת אשר סרח. אמרו. סרח בת אשר נשתיירה מאותו הדור והיא הראת למשה היכן יוסף קבור, 'How did Moses know where Joseph is buried? Since it is said "the name of Asher's daughter is Serah". They said: "Serah the daughter of Asher remained from that generation and she showed to Moses where is Joseph buried"'.

27　Quoted from Ben-Ḥayyīm, *Tibåt Mårqe*, pp. 99–101; see my Tibåt Mårqe, *the Ark of* Mårqe. *Edition, Translation, Commentary*, Berlin, 2019, pp. 122–129.

28　She was probably born in Canaan, being the grand-daughter of Jacob (Gen 46:17). Her appearance on the stage occurs much later, after the 430 years of Israel's bondage in Egypt (Gen 15:13; Exod 12:40–41).

CHAPTER 13

'On the Mountains of Ararat': Noah's Ark and the Sacred Topography of Armenia

Nazénie Garibian

With the conversion of the kingdom of Armenia to Christianity at the beginning of the fourth century, a new religious and historical tradition, that of the Bible, was progressively superimposed on the local pagan culture of the country. The transition from paganism to Christianity made the Armenians gradually aware of their new national identity. Described in ancient sources as a 'transition from darkness to light', 'from barbarism to civilization',[1] this process, which lasted for centuries, was accompanied by the abandonment of traditional memory based on ancestral fables and mythical gods who were replaced by figures and episodes of the History of Salvation, from Adam and Eve to Christ and the Apostles.[2]

The urge to destroy the ancient landmarks of identification became all the more justified as the new Christian identity was perceived by the Armenians as that of a new chosen people whose history, after the conversion, had been integrated into the History of Providence as its heir and its continuation.[3] So, the translation of the Bible gave the Armenians access to the true knowledge about the origins of humanity and, thus, about their own origins and history. This enabled them to find their true spiritual fathers who were no longer the heroes of epic songs but the Biblical patriarchs and the prophets, the apostles and Church fathers.[4]

The adoption of the Biblical tradition and the Christianization of the culture also changed the anthropological and religious landscape of Armenia. A new sacred topography was formed, which absorbed important pilgrimage sites of

---

1 See J-P. Mahé, 'Entre Moïse et Mahomet: réflexions sur l'historiographie arménienne', *Revue des Etudes Arméniennes* 23 (1992), pp. 121–153.

2 Ibid.

3 Ibid., See also V. Calzolari, 'La citation du Ps 78 (77), 5–8 dans l'épilogue de l'Histoire de l'Arménie d'Agathange', *Revue des Etudes Arméniennes* 29 (2003–2004), pp. 9–27; N. Garibian, 'La Jérusalem du IVᵉ s. et le récit de la conversion de l'Arménie', in A. Mardirossian et al. (eds), *Mélanges Jean-Pierre Mahé*, Travaux et mémoires 18, Paris, 2014, pp. 353–368.

4 Mahé, 'Entre Moïse et Mahomet'.

the pre-Christian culture and other pagan sanctuaries. Many of these sanctuaries changed their names, receiving new countenances and new biographies; others were erased forever.

Yet we know that among the Christian traditions flourishing on the Armenian soil are many deriving not from the canonical books of the Bible but from the apocryphal and extra-Biblical writings and traditions. The story of Noah and the landing of his ark provides a revealing example of this phenomenon. The story of the Flood became particularly precious to the Armenians because it localized a Biblical event on the soil of their own country, thus confirming, as it were, the Biblical truth about their forgotten origins.

Genesis 8.3–4 reports that at the end of a hundred and fifty days, 'in the seventh month, on the seventeenth day of the month, the ark rested on the mountains of Ararat'.[5] The identification of these 'mountains', as well as the country where they are situated, has a long history in the Hebrew tradition, later inherited by the Christian and Muslim civilizations. It is manifested through different versions and translations of the Bible, and references preserved in extra-Biblical Jewish, Christian and pagan sources.

The analysis of the available documents enables us to define three problems, which are at the root of various attempts of identification of the 'Mountains of Ararat'. The first concerns the interpretation of the name indicated in the Biblical verse, the second regards the identification of the geographical reality designated by this name and the third, ensuing from these two, examines the confusion between the country and the mountains designated by the same name. By juxtaposing the ancient witnesses from this perspective, we can distinguish three streams of underlying textual traditions: the Syriac-Babylonian, the Greek-Roman or Hellenistic and the eclectic tradition combining both.

The earliest direct evidence of this verse in *Genesis* comes from the Greek translation of the *Pentateuch*, the *Septuagint*, which dates from the third century BC. It states that the ark landed 'on the mountains of Ararat' or, more precisely, 'on the mountains, those of Ararat'.[6] 'Ararat' is how the Greek transliterates the Hebrew characters of the name *'RRṬ*.

---

5   J.R. Kohlenberger (ed.), *The NIV Interlinear Hebrew/Greek English Bible*, III, Grand Rapids (Michigan), 1987, p. 17.

6   J.W. Wevers (ed.), *Genesis. Septuaginta: Vetus Testamentum Græce. I*, Göttingen, 1974, p. 121. For this English version, see M.E. Stone, 'Mount Ararat and the Ark', in M.E. Stone, A. Amihay and V. Hillel (eds), *Noah and His Book(s)*, Atlanta, 2010, pp. 307–316.

At the turn of the eras, Philo of Alexandria did not mention any name in his commentary on the verse about the landing of the ark. He only said that it stopped 'on the tops of the mountains'.[7]

The Aramaic Biblical translations, as reflected in the Babylonian Targumic tradition, cite the names 'Qardo', 'Qardu' or 'Kardu' instead of 'Ararat'. In the second century of the Christian era, the *Targum Onqelos* brings down the Ark 'upon the mountains of Kardu'.[8] The same name, this time spelled 'Kardun', appears in the *Targum Neofiti* belonging to the western Aramaic tradition and dating admittedly back to the Amoraic times[9] (third–sixth centuries CE): 'the ark came to rest on the mountains of Kardun'.[10] The *Targum of Pseudo-Jonathan*, also of the western Aramaic tradition, has the form of 'Kardun' as well.[11] The name of the mountains is cited as 'Kardi' in some Hexaplaric witnesses from Greek fragments, which had been translated from a text, or texts,

---

7   *Philon d'Alexandrie, Quæstiones et solutiones in Genesim*, livres I–II, version arménienne, introd. trad. et notes par Ch. Mercier, Paris, 1979, p. 245.

8   J.W. Etheridge, *The Targums of Onkelos and Jonathan Ben Uzziel: with the fragments of the Jerusalem Targum from the Chaldee* vol. 2, New York, 1968, p. 50; See also *The Aramaic Bible*. vol. 6, *The Targum Onkelos to Genesis*, trans., critical introduction, notes by B. Grossfeld, Edinburgh, 1988, p. 56. The Aramaic of this Targum presents a mixture of the Western and Eastern features which has given rise to several opinions about its place of origin. According to Edward M. Cook (see his 'A New Perspective on the Language of Onqelos and Jonathan', in D.R.G. Beattie and M.J. McNamara (eds), *The Aramaic Bible. Targums in their Historical Context*, Journal for the Study of the Old Testament, Supplement Series 166, Sheffield, 1994, pp. 142–157), the language of the *Targum Onqelos* derives from a 'Central Aramaic' dialect tradition, which developed in the Northern Mesopotamia and Syria. However, Bernard Grossfeld states, that it received its final form in Babylon (see *The Aramaic Bible*, Introduction, pp. 10–11 and 32–35); it is attested that in matters of the Flood, the *Targum Onqelos* reflects the Babylonian tradition (see Stone 'Mount Ararat and the Ark').

9   On the dating of this source, see *Targum Neofiti 1, Genesis. The Aramaic Bible* vol. 1A, translated with apparatus and notes by M. McNamara, Edinburgh, 1992, p. 45, but also S.A. Kaufman, 'Dating the Language of the Palestinian Targums and Their Use in the Study of First Century CE Texts' and G. Boccaccini, 'Targum Neofiti as a Proto-Rabbinic Document: A Systematic Analysis', in *The Aramaic Bible. Targums in their Historical Context*, Sheffield, 1994, pp. 118–141 and 254–263 respectively.

10   See *Targum Neofiti 1*, p. 77. There are also renderings 'Qardo' (see Stone, 'Mount Ararat and the Ark') and 'Kurdum', see A. Diez Macho (ed.), *Biblia Polyglota Matritensia*, Madrid, 1988, p. 52.

11   M. Maher (ed.), *Targum Pseudo-Jonathan*: Genesis. *The Aramaic Bible* vol. 1B, Translation, Introduction and Notes, Edinburgh, 1992, p. 42. The Venetian *Editio princeps* of 1598 reads 'Kadrun'. For the language of the text, see Kaufman, 'Dating' and Cook, 'A New Perspective'.

written in Hebrew or Syriac.[12] The common Syriac Bible, the *Peshiṭta*, inherited this tradition and has this name in the form of 'Qardu'.[13]

On the other hand, we have attestations of another Hellenistic tradition of *Genesis*, which developed probably before the Common Era and which replaces the name 'Ararat' by 'Armenia'. It is witnessed, for example, by the Hexaplaric tradition preserved in *reliqui*, namely those of Aquila,[14] where one reads 'on the mountains of Armenia'.[15] This version was inherited by the early Latin translations and in Jerome's *Vulgate*.[16]

Thus, a comparison of witnesses of ancient textual traditions of *Genesis* reveals three different names for the mountains upon which Noah's ark landed: 'Ararat', 'Qardo' (Kardon, Qardu, Kardi) and 'Armenia'. It is worth noting that these names appear as equivalents, designating the same geographical entity, i.e. 'mountains', and not *a* 'mountain'. The equivalence of 'Ararat', 'Qardo' and 'Armenia' can also be evinced from other Biblical passages. In the *Book of Isaiah* (37:38) the Hebrew Bible and its Christian translations cite 'Ararat': 'they went in flight into the land of Ararat'.[17] In the same verse, the LXX has 'Armenia', while the Vulgate has 'Ararat' and the *Targum Isaiah* reads: 'they escaped into the land of Qardu'.[18]

In *2 Kings* 19:37, which reports the same episode, the *Hebrew Bible* and LXX both read 'the land of Ararat', while the *Vulgate* cites the 'land of Armenia' and

---

12 Wevers, *Genesis. Septuaginta*, p. 121; we also find the variants *'oros tetrimménon'* (shaved mountain) and *'oros tetilménon'* (scraped mountain). On the Syriac versions, see A. Vööbus, *The Hexapla and the Syro-Hexapla*, Stockholm, 1971. On the translations from Hebrew and Syriac, see J. Norton and C. Hardin (eds), *Frederic Field's prolegomena to Origenis hexaplarum quæ supersunt, sive veterum interpretum græcorum in totum vetus testamentum fragmenta*, Paris, 2005, pp. 135–153.

13 R.B. Ter Haar Romeny and W.Th. Van Peursen (eds), *The Old Testament in Syriac according to the Peshiṭta Version*, Part I Fasc. 1. (Based on material collected and studied by T. Jansma), Peshiṭta Institute, Leiden, 1977, p. 14.

14 Dating back to the second century CE (Norton & Hardin, *Frederic Field's prolegomena*, pp. 39–41).

15 F. Field (ed.), *Origenis Hexaplorum Quæ Supersunt*, Oxford, 1875, p. 26, n. 8; Stone, 'Mount Ararat and the Ark'.

16 Jerome translated from Hebrew into Latin, in Palestine, in the second half of the 4th century, and he had access to Palestinian Jewish traditions.

17 Kohlenberger, *The NIV Interlinear Bible*, III, p. 76.

18 C.W.H. Pauli (trans.), *The Chaldee Paraphrase on the Prophet Isaiah*, London, 1871. In the Clark edition of the *Aramaic Bible* (edited by B.D. Chilton, *The Aramaic Bible* vol. 11. *The Targum Isaiah*, Introduction, Translation and Notes, Edinburgh, 1987, p. 75) the toponym is transformed into 'Curdistan' which is an anachronism for the period when the *Targum Isaiah* was shaped (between Tannaitic and Amoraic periods, see ibid., xx–xxv).

the *Targum Jonathan of the Former Prophets* has 'the land of Kardu'.[19] Again, in Jeremiah 51:27, the *Hebrew Bible* and *Vulgate* both mention 'the kingdoms of Ararat, Minni and Ashkenaz', while the *Targum Pseudo-Jonathan* reads: 'Oh, the kingdom of the land of Kardu (Qardo); Oh, the troops of Hormine (Hurmini) and Adiabene!'.[20] The *LXX* transliterates only the first and the third names, by 'Ararat' and 'Askenazians' respectively.[21] We may observe that in these cases 'Ararat', 'Qardo' and 'Armenia' clearly indicate countries, or kingdoms, rather than mountains. It is also worth noting that in the Hebrew Bible and the Targum Onqelos Ararat appears as a country distinct from Hormine/Hurmini which is Armenia in Aramaic.[22]

Then the question arises: how did these countries come to be identified and how could they become associated with each other, both historically and geographically? It is generally accepted that the name 'Ararat' is connected with the name 'Urartu' known from Assyrian inscriptions. That the Biblical 'Ararat' implies Urartu can also be confirmed by the variant *hwrrṭ*—Hūrarat that occurs in the Isaiah scrolls from Qumran (1QIsa^a).[23] This name designates the kingdom or rather the empire that, between the ninth and seventh centuries BC, stretched over the Armenian plateau, from the region of Lake Urmia to those of Lake Sevan (see Figure 13.1). However, before the time of its expansion, the land of Urartu, which is mentioned under the name of Uruatri in the sources of the Middle-Assyrian period (between the thirteenth and the eleventh centuries BC), had more modest boundaries, including the territories south of Lake Van and west of Lake Urmia.[24] According to the geographical origins of the main Urartian deities, the original homeland of the ruling class of Urartu must have

---

19   D.J. Harrington and A.J. Saldarini (eds), *The Aramaic Bible*. vol. 10, *The Targum Jonathan of the Former Prophets*, Introduction, Translation and Notes, Edinburgh, 1987, p. 304.

20   R. Hayward (ed.), *The Targum of Jeremiah, The Aramaic Bible* vol. 12, Translation, Critical Introduction and Notes, Edinburgh, 1987, 186.

21   Stone, 'Mount Ararat and the Ark'.

22   Hayward, *The Targum of Jeremiah*, n. 19 on p. 187.

23   See the discussion in N.G. Garsoïan, *The Epic Histories Attributed to Pʻawstos Buzand (Buzandaran Patmutʻiwnkʻ)*, Harvard Armenian Texts and Studies, 8, Cambridge MA, Harvard, 1989, pp. 252–253.

24   Г.А. Меликишвили, *Древневосточные материалы по истории народов Закавказья I. Наири-Урарту* [G.A. Melikishvili, *Ancient Eastern Materials on the History of the People of Transcaucasia. I. Nairi-Urartu*], Tbilissi, 1954, pp. 106, 150–155; E. Grekyan, 'The Will of Menua and the Gods of Urartu', *Aramazd. Armenian Journal of Near Eastern Studies*, 1 (2006), pp. 150–195; id., *Biaynili-Urartu: State and Society* (PhD diss., in Arm.), Yerevan, 2016, p. 88 (http://etd.asj-oa.am/3319, last visit: 20.10.2018). Conversely, in the same period, the most of the plain of Ayrarat was called 'Uaza' or 'Waza' (see R. Biscione and D. Dan, 'Dimensional and Geographical Distribution of the Urartian Fortifications in the Republic

'ON THE MOUNTAINS OF ARARAT'

been located in the territories adjacent to the present-day Mount Djudi, in the land called Kumme or Kumenuni on the left bank of the Upper Tigris, south of Lake Van. This region remained a religious centre of Urartu also during the first imperial period.[25] It is identifiable with that known from Armenian sources as Korduk, a mountainous district approaching the southern borders of Greater Armenia (see Figure 13.2). It was part of the province of Korčayk, the Gordyene of Greco-Roman sources, which was actually larger than Korduk: it more or less covered the territory of Urartu after the political alliance formed between the Nairi tribes during the first half of the ninth century.[26] However, the Korčayk province is often called Korduk by Armenian authors, and appears invariably under the name of Gordyene in the Greek-Roman sources;[27] it is this occurrence that has given rise to the confusion of the two names in contemporary studies.

The name Korduk, or Gordyene, is easily identifiable with the Qardo/Qardu/Kardu/Kardi of the Biblical texts. One can, therefore, suggest that the Biblical references to the land of Urartu/Ararat, and in particular the story of the Flood, of Mesopotamian origin, which makes the ark land on the mountains of that country, could have been crystallized at a time when the region of Gordyene was known as Uruatri and was thereafter considered to lie on the territory of the kingdom of Urartu/Ararat (between the thirteenth and the eighth century). After the fall of the Urartian state and with the appearance of the name Korduk/Korčayk/Gordyene, probably already during the Hellenistic period, the Jewish tradition recorded the new name of the same geographical reality, as the Targumic sources mentioned above suggest.

We can assume an analogous process for the transfer of the name 'Ararat' to 'Armenia', which after the fall of Urartu denoted all the provinces on the Armenian plateau. From the Hellenistic era and until early Christian times, the district of Korduk, which was a border region in the south of Greater Armenia, was a part of it during certain periods, namely in the first century BC and between the third and the fourth century AD. Meanwhile, the name 'Ararat' had ceased to refer to the kingdom of Urartu within its former borders and began to

---

of Armenia', *Aramazd: Armenian Journal of Near Eastern Studies*, VI/2 (2011), pp. 104–120; Grekyan, *Biaynili-Urartu*, p. 87).

25   Grekyan, 'The Will of Menua'; id., *Biaynili-Urartu*, pp. 82–83. At the end of the 8th and the beginning of the 7th century, the region passed under the rule of Assyria.

26   For this political alliance, see Grekyan, *Biaynili-Urartu*, 88.

27   See J. Markwart, *Südarmenien Und Die Tigrisquellen Nach Griechischen Und Arabischen Geographen*, Studien zur armenischen Geschichte 4, Vienna, 1930.

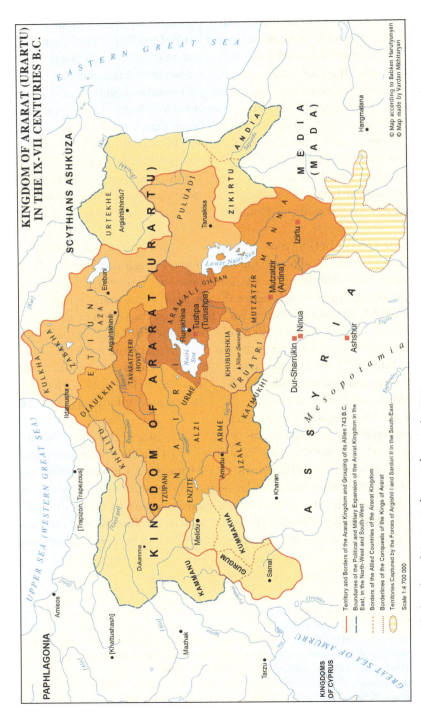

FIGURE 13.1 The kingdom of Urartu, ninth–seventh centuries BCE
COURTESY VARDAN MKHITARYAN

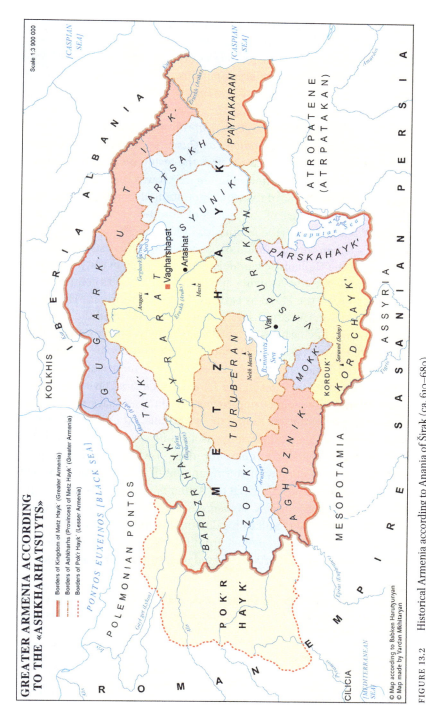

FIGURE 13.2   Historical Armenia according to Anania of Širak (ca. 610–680)
COURTESY VARDAN MKHITARYAN

designate, in the form 'Ayrarat', the heart of Greater Armenia, the royal province situated in the centre of the country.

And so, we can see that these three names are identifiable with the same geographical entity but during different periods. What connects the name 'Ararat/Urartu' with 'Korduḱ' and with 'Armenia' is rather a country, or a kingdom, than a mountain or even mountains. *Could we then understand the phrase 'on the mountains of Ararat' in* Genesis *to indicate the mountains that are located in the land of Ararat, a land otherwise known as 'Qardu' and 'Armenia'?* The question is all the more appropriate because, first, the terminology in the Hebrew text of *Genesis* clearly refers to a mountain range.[28] It was thus translated into other languages by plural forms of the word 'mountain'; Secondly, in Armenian sources the mountainous range of the district of Korduḱ bears the same name as the country: *Korduaċ leṙner* (the mountains of Korduḱ).[29]

It seems that such an interpretation of the verse from *Genesis* had already been circulating in the Hellenistic world, and even more so in the Jewish Hellenistic environment, because 'Armenia' apparently designated a country in the retellings of the story of the Flood as early as the first century BC. The pagan writer Apollonius Molon (1st c. BC) says: 'the man who survived the flood left *Armenia* with his sons, having been expelled from his native place by the inhabitants of the land. Having traversed the Intermediate country, he came to the mountainous part of Syria, which is desolate.'[30] Here 'Armenia' appears without geographical specification. Yet in the *Jewish Antiquities* Flavius Josephus, reporting several traditions concerning the history of the ark, says as following: 'The ark then stops on the top of a mountain *in* Armenia' (AJ 1.90).[31] There is no doubt that Josephus understood Armenia as a country. We may furthermore notice that he speaks of a single mountain, though without mentioning its name, nor making a connection with 'the mountains of Ararat'. Later in the text (1.92), however, he reports the name that the Armenians gave to the spot where Noah had descended from the ark, *'Apobaterion'*, that is the 'Landing-place', or 'Alighting place', and where still to his day the inhabitants showed visitors the remains of the Ark. One can deduce from this, as Josephus probably did, that the place called *'Apobaterion'* was located on a summit or next to the top

---

28   *Genesis* (E.A. Speiser (ed.), *The Anchor Bible*, Introduction, Translation and Notes, New York, 1964, p. 53). It is *harei* < *harim* which could mean both 'mountains' and 'mountain range' in Biblical Hebrew.

29   There are several other examples in Armenia, as *Gugaraċ leṙner* [mountains of Gugarḱ], *Siwneaċ leṙner* [mountains of Siwniḱ] etc.

30   M. Stern, *Greek and Latin Authors on Jews and Judaism* vol. 1, Jerusalem, 1974, p. 150.

31   H. St. J. Thackeray (trans.), M.A., *Flavius Josephus, Jewish Antiquities* vol. 1, London–Cambridge, 1967, pp. 42–44.

'ON THE MOUNTAINS OF ARARAT'

of a mountain. This could be juxtaposed with the denomination '*Oros tetrim-ménon*' (shaved mountain) or '*Oros tetilménon*' (scraped mountain) given to the mountain of the Ark in some Hexaplaric witnesses[32] probably because of the flattened area near its top, which was believed to have been left by the Ark.

The juxtaposition of all these sources thus allows us to conclude that from the Hellenistic period onwards, since 'the land of Ararat' had no longer existed, attempts were made, in the Jewish tradition, to identify and to localize the mountain of the ark among the mountains of a country which was at that time known as Armenia. Our hypothesis can find an additional support in the following paragraphs of the *Jewish Antiquities*, in which Josephus quotes the witness of Berossus (1.93), a Chaldean priest of the third century BCE from Babylon, and that of Nicolaus of Damascus (1.95), a Greek historian born in Damascus, who wrote in the first century BCE. The quotation from Berossus, probably drawn from his historical work, *Babyloniaca*,[33] bears an additional indication regarding the localization of the mountain of the Ark in Armenia: 'It is said, moreover, that a portion of the vessel still survives *in Armenia*, on the mountain of the *Cordyæans*; and that persons carry off pieces of the bitumen, which they take away and use as talismans'.[34]

Thus, for the first time in the extant sources, two out of the three names recorded in the different versions of the verse of *Genesis* are put here into direct and subordinate relationship: there is *the* mountain *of the* Cordyæans, which is *in* Armenia. The name 'Cordyæans' is identifiable with Qardo/Gordyene, that is Korduk̇ or Korčayk̇ in Armenian. It seems even to be a literal translation from Armenian of the plural form of the province's name.[35] At the same time, however, we have seen that also the mountainous range in Korduk̇ was called so.

It is possible that this attempt at geographical precision was achieved by juxtaposing two textual traditions, the Græco-Roman and the Babylonian, which associated respectively the names 'Armenia' and 'Gordyene' with the 'mountains of Ararat', as we have seen above. This eclectic tradition is witnessed again in the *Chronicle* of Eusebius of Cæsarea written at the beginning of the fourth century AD, but quoting Alexander Polyhistor, a Roman historian of the first century BC: 'And from the ark that went and stayed in Armenia, still today there is a part remaining as a relic on the mountain of the Cordeans in the country

---

32   Wevers, *Genesis. Septuaginta*, p. 121.

33   See S.M. Burstein (trans.), Berosius, *Babyloniaca* (vers 280 av. J.-C.), Malibu, 1978.

34   Thackeray, *Phlavius Josephus*, p. 45.

35   *Korduk̇* in Armenian can be understood as both the name of the country and its inhabitants as a whole.

of Armenia'.[36] We may observe that in these two sources Armenia is clearly designated as a country, though Cordeans of the second source cannot be an individual name of the mountain where the inhabitants found the remains of the ark since the text speaks of 'the mountain *of the* Cordeans'. Moreover, the Armenian text of Eusebius has *korduaćuoć lerinn*, that is to say 'on the mountain of the inhabitants of Kordukʿ' (i.e. of the Cordeans).

The name of this single mountain is recorded unequivocally in the other quotation of Josephus (*AJ* 1.95), that of Nicolaus of Damascus, but the name recorded there is not Ararat: 'There is a great mountain in Armenia, above the country of Minyas,[37] called *Baris*, upon which it is reported that many who fled at the time of the Flood were saved; and that one who was carried in an ark came on shore upon the top of it; and that the remains of the timber were a great while preserved'.

With a little effort we could probably relate this name to that recorded in another important source, the *Book of Jubilees*, dating from the first third of the second century BCE. It reads: 'And the ark went and rested on the top of *Lûbâr*, one of the *mountains of Ararat*'.[38] We notice that in this text the name 'Ararat' returns in the classic expression of *Genesis*, 'mountains of Ararat', and that *Lûbâr* is supposed to represent one of the peaks of these mountains.

The name *Lûbâr* in the same relation to the mountains of Ararat reappears in the following verses of the *Book of Jubilees*, where it comes to the tradition of Noah planting vineyard on this mountain (7.1),[39] then being buried on it (10.15),[40] as well as of his sons building three cities around the mountain (7.14–17).[41] It is worth noting that in the second quotation, Mount Lûbâr is said to be in the country of Ararat. We find the name again in the extract from *Jubilees* inserted in *The Book of Asaf the Physician (Sefer Asaf Harofe)*[42] as well as in

---

36   U. Ունգերեանց (Հրատ.), *Եւսեբի Պամփիլեայ Կեսարացւոյ ժամանակականք երկմասնեայ, հայերէն-յունարէն-լատիներէն* [M. Awgereants/Aucher (ed.), *Eusebii Pamphili Chronicon Bipartitum*, Græco-Armeno-Latinum], Venice, 1818, pp. 36–37 (the English translation of the quotation is ours).

37   Thackeray identifies this country with Minni of the Old Testament, which is Armenia (see *Phlavius Josephus*, n. c on p. 47).

38   *The Book of Jubilees* 5.28 (see the critical edition by J.C. VanderKam, *The Book of Jubilees*, CSCO 510, Scriptores Æthiopici 87, Louvain, 1989).

39   'And in the seventh week in the first year thereof, in this jubilee, Noah planted vines on the mountain on which the ark had rested, named *Lûbâr*, one of the Ararat mountains'.

40   'And Noah slept with his fathers, and was buried on Mount Lûbâr in the land of Ararat'.

41   'And behold these three cities are near Mount Lûbâr; Sedeqetlebab fronting the mountain on its east; and Neʾelatamaʾuk on the south; and Adataneses towards the west'.

42   'This is the book of remedies that the ancient sages copied from the book of Shem son of

'ON THE MOUNTAINS OF ARARAT'

some Qumran Scrolls, such as *Genesis Apocryphon* (1Q20, 13)[43] or *4QPseudo-Daniel* (4Q244, frag. 3).[44]

The name 'Lubar' (or *Lûbâr*) is also retained in the text of a fourth-century Christian author, Epiphanius of Salamis, who, in addition, reflects the successive stage in the evolution of these intersecting traditions. In his treatise *Against the Heresies*, he asserts that the ark stopped 'in the highlands of Ararat, between Armenia and Cardyæi, on the mountain called Lubar.'[45] He goes on to say that Noah's descendants left 'mount Lubar and the mountains of Armenia that is Ararat' and that they arrived in Assyria on the plain of Senaar.

In this source, all the three names we have been discussing appear for the first time in the same passage: Ararat, Armenia, Kardyene (which is Qardo). One could observe the author's effort to identify the geographical location indicated in the expression 'mountains of Ararat' by placing it between Armenia and Gordyene and specifying that by this geographical designation the mountains of Armenia should be understood. Epiphanius's localization of the mountains of Ararat can reflect either the political situation of the given period, i.e. when Korduk̇ was no longer part of Armenia, or a more exact knowledge obtained by him of the geography of the region. Be it as it may, it is almost certain that his identification takes into account the existence of a local tradition of the Ark, which is associated with a single mountain known by the name *Lubar*. Finally, we notice in this text a trace of Apollonius Molon who had described the itinerary of the descendants of Noah: they left Armenia, crossed Mesopotamia (the 'intermediary country') and arrived in Syria.

Attempts to identify the mountain of the Ark brought about another result in the *Targum Pseudo-Jonathan* which contains very early traditions.[46] Thus, after stating that the ark rested 'on the mountains of Kardun', the text continues:

Noah. It was transmitted to Noah on Mount Lubar of the mountains of Ararat after the flood'. However, this source is much later (see Stone, 'Mount Ararat and the Ark').

43   N. Avigad and Y. Yadin (eds), *A Genesis Apocryphon*, Jerusalem, 1956, p. 20. It is assumed that the *Genesis Apocryphon* could have served as source for the *Book of Jubilees* (see E. Eshel, 'The Noah Cycle in the Genesis Apocryphon', in *Noah and His Book(s)*, pp. 77–95).

44   F. Garcia Martinez, *The Dead Sea Scrolls Translated. The Qumran Texts in English*, Leiden, 1994, p. 288.

45   F. Williams (trans.), *The Panarion of Epiphanius of Salamis*, Book I, Leiden, 1987, p. 15. According to Michael Stone (oral communication), Epiphanius can go back to *Jubilees*, perhaps via a chronographic tradition.

46   See M. Maher, 'Targum Pseudo-Jonathan of Deuteronomy 1.1–8', in *The Aramaic Bible. Targums in their Historical Context*, pp. 264–290; L.D. Merino, 'Targum Manuscripts and Critical Editions', ibid., pp. 51–91.

'The name of one mountain is Cordyene and the name of the other mountain is Armenia. There the city of Armenia was built, in the land of the East'.[47]

In this quotation we observe several new elements. First, *Kardun* appears as a name distinct from Cordyene and designating a single mountain. Then, two mountains are detected instead of one, probably in attempt at justifying the plural form of 'mountains' in the Biblical text: they are called Armenia and Cordyene. The fact that the names 'Kardun', 'Cordyene' and 'Armenia' are put together without that of 'Ararat' may indicate that the latter was replaced by the name 'Kardun'. In that case, the separate mention of two mountains would be an interpretation of the textual tradition recorded by Epiphanius, according to which rather than two countries, Armenia and Cordyene were understood as a part of the mountains of Ararat/Qardo.

This suggestion is worth noting because it could lead to the idea that the localization of the country of Ararat had been shifted northwards in order to match the province of Ayrarat; secondly, it could imply that Qardiniya and Arminiya designated the two peaks of the mountain Masis, or Masik, situated in the heart of this province.[48] In this respect we will quote Saint Jerome asserting that Ararat is a plain in Armenia.[49]

Finally, the third new element that we find in this quotation is the mention of the building of a city 'there' (i.e. on the very place of the landing of the Ark?), which bears the same name as one of the two separate mountains: 'Armenia'. Josephus speaks of a 'place' called *Apobaterion*, not of a city. The *Book of Jubilees* mentions the planting of vineyards by Noah (7.1), as well as the sacrifice he offered as soon as he had left the ark. Further on, the text specifies that God shall 'enlarge Japhet' and 'shall dwell in the dwelling place of Shem', which could perhaps have been interpreted as a town (7.12). Besides, we are told that the sons of Noah built three cities around Mount Lubar, calling them after the names of their respective wives (7.14–17).[50] The Syriac Christian sources followed by the Armenian sources report the construction of a city[51] but these

---

47 Maher, *Targum Pseudo-Jonathan: Genesis*, p. 42.

48 For the identification with the two peaks of Masis, see Stone, 'Mount Ararat and the Ark'.

49 'Ararat autem regio in Armenia campestris est', see P.P. Peeters, 'La Légende de saint Jacques de Nisibe', *Analecta Bollandiana* 38 (1920), pp. 285–373, n. 5 on p. 330 for the quotation.

50 See above, note 41 for the names of these three cities.

51 See D.A. Machiela, 'Some Jewish Noah Traditions in Syriac Christian Sources' in *Noah and His Book(s)*, pp. 237–252; Peeters, 'La Légende de saint Jacques'. A village by the name of 'For-the-Eight-Souls' founded by Noah and his sons after the Flood is mentioned in *Cavern of Treasures*, XX,8 (see J-P. Mahé (trad.), *La Caverne des Trésors. Version géorgienne*, Louvain, 1992, pp. VI and 37).

sources do not specify its name. What could be the city to which the *Targum Pseudo-Jonathan* refers as Armenia? It is hard to identify it at this stage. A few cities are known both in the district of Kordukʿ, in areas traditionally related to the story of the Flood, and around Mount Masis in the province of Ayrarat, which later inherited the honour of being recognised as the mountain of the Ark.

It is only in an Armenian source dating from the end of the fifth century that the name 'Ararat'—in the deformed form of 'Sararad'—is for the first time applied to a *single* mountain. This is the *Buzandaran patmutʿiwnkʿ, The Epic Histories* attributed to Pʿawstos Buzand.[52] The text in question seems to make a general montage of all known traditions, since it also contains all the names and expressions that we have found in various versions and retellings of the verse of *Genesis*. Yet, the Biblical story of the landing of the ark, as well as the traditions that developed around it, are Christianized by their insertion into the *vita* of St Jacob, one of the first bishops of Nisibis. It is also the first known source that attributes to Saint Jacob the discovery of the remains of the Ark,[53] the very remains that according to more ancient sources ca. three centuries earlier had customarily been shown to visitors by the local inhabitants.

Here is the abbreviated quotation of the *Buzandaran*: 'At about that time the great bishop of Mcbin (Nisibis) departed (...) and was chosen by God to come from his city to the mountains of Armenia, to Mount Sararad in the district of Kordukʿ on the border of the land of Ayrarat. (...) He came with great desire and longing, and fervently prayed God to see the redeeming ark built by Noah that had come to rest on that mountain after the flood ...'.[54]

Here we thus have 'the mountains of Armenia', 'the district of Kordukʿ/Qardo', and the 'land of Ayrarat'.[55] Since this source originated in the southern regions of Armenia, where the Syriac current of Christianity had been predominant and where the ancient Mesopotamian and Hebrew traditions must have been well known, hardly a doubt persists regarding the location of the land which had been chosen for hosting the ark: it must have been situated in the district of Kordukʿ. However, its status is not clear because the phrase '*i sahmans Ayraratean tēruteann*' can be interpreted as either 'on the fringes of the province/land/country of Ayrarat' or 'within the borders of the province/land/

---

52 See Garsoyan, *Buzandaran Patmutʿiwnkʿ*, for the English translation and the study of the text.

53 Peeters, 'La Légende de saint Jacques'.

54 *Buzandaran Patmutʿiwnkʿ*, III, x (Garsoyan, 1989, p. 77).

55 The Armenian word *tērutʿiwn*, used in the quotation, may refer to a family estate, but also to a land, a province, a principality or a kingdom.

country of Ayrarat'. The form 'Sararad', which is repeated a few lines below as *'sararatean lerinn'* (i.e. 'of the Sararatian mountain'), is of course corrupted. According to some opinions, however, this corruption predates the original text of the *Epic Stories*.[56] Indeed, it seems odd to find this corrupted form 'Sararad', while the right one follows in the same sentence immediately after and designates no longer the mountain but the land (*sic!*). Most probably the author of *Buzandaran* (or his predecessor) had joined together diverse traditions within the same passage, while copying 'Sararad' from one source and the 'land of Ayrarat' from another.

This assumption is confirmed by another Armenian source datable to the ninth century, *History of Hripsimē's Saintly Fellows* attributed to Movsēs Xorenači.[57] It states clearly that the Syrians call the mountain of the Ark 'Sararad', while in Armenia it is called 'Sołop'. This early medieval Armenian tradition thus claims that the name of the *mountain* (in singular) of the Ark was not 'Ararat' but 'Sołop'.[58] Furthermore, in some versions of the *Targum Onkelos*[59] we find the name 'Sarnedib', which could represent another form of the names 'Sararad' or 'Sołop'.

As for the location of this mountain, it has been identified with the present-day Djudi Dagh which indeed lay within the territory of the historical district of Korduk (see Figure 13.3). Yet the name 'Djudi' can be relatively late, for it identifies it with the mountain of the Ark according to the Koran (11.46), which Mahomet had allegedly believed to be in Arabia.[60] It must have been identified with this mountain of Korduk at the time of the Arab domination in the region (seventh–ninth centuries),[61] undoubtedly under the influence of the pre-existing local traditions, both Jewish and Christian, in which the previous name of Sararad seems to have been already known. On the other hand, until the nineteenth century another mountain was known close to Mt Djudi, which shared the honour of being associated with the story of the Flood. It bore the

---

56   Stone, 'Mount Ararat and the Ark'.

57   B. Outier and M. Thierry, 'Histoire des saintes Hripsimiennes, Traduction et commentaires', *Syria* 67 (1990), pp. 697–733. Also Peeters mentions this source ('La Légende de saint Jacques', p. 322).

58   Today, the name *Sołop*, in the form of *Silopi*, designates the capital of a caza in the vilayet of Mardin in Turkey (see Outier & Thierry, 'Histoire des saintes Hripsimiennes', p. 716). As the authors of this article note, it is likely that this mountain was known by Assyro-Mesopotamian sources under the names of *Nisir* or *Nibour*.

59   Etheridge, *The Targums of Onkelos*, p. 50, n. 6 reads: (*Sam. Vers.*) *Al teborah Sarnedib* ('Upon the mountains Sarnedib').

60   Peeters, 'La Légende de saint Jacques', n. 3 on p. 120.

61   Suggested by Peeters (ibid.).

FIGURE 13.3 Mount Djudi (Cudi dağı) in the Gordyæan mountains (the Korduk chain)
PHOTO: TIMO ROLLER

name of Barathken. We will not fail to notice that it recalls the names 'Baris' and 'Lubar' already mentioned, which takes us back to the Hebrew-Babylonian tradition. In the late tenth century, another Armenian historian, Tovma Arcruni, who originated from a southern district of Armenia lying close to Gordyene, still recorded the local tradition relating to the 'mountains of Korduk'.[62]

From early antiquity to the Middle Ages, the topography of the holy places memorialising the Flood and the traditions relating to its story was developed around the two mountains of Sararad/Djudi and Barathken. We know of the Monastery of the Ark where the relics of wood or bitumen of the Ark were kept,[63] a mosque built of this wood,[64] the tomb of Noah at Dair Abbun or the

---

62 Tovma Arcruni, I,1. See Մ.Հ. Դարբինյան-Մելիքյան (Հրատ.), Թովմա Արծրունի եւ Անանուն, Պատմութիւն տանն Արծրունեաց [M.H. Darbinyan-Melikyan (ed.), Tovma Arcruni and Anonyme, The History of the Arcruni House], Yerevan, 2006, p. 25.

63 See above, n. 31 for the quotation of Josephus; Peeters 'La Légende de saint Jacques', p. 319 and n. 5.

64 According to the Travels of Rabbi Benjamin of Tudela (trad. B. Gerrans, London, 1784, p. 92) quoted in Peeters, 'La Légende de saint Jacques', n. 3 on p. 320.

village Hassana,[65] the city called Thāmānon founded by him or by his sons,[66] the wonderworking spring of Jacob of Nisibis which gushed on his way while he was searching the ark[67] etc. To these can be added the traditions of apocryphal or extra-Biblical origin, such as the sites of the vineyards planted by Noah, of the sacrifice offered by him on his quitting the Ark, of the Descent from the Ark and other.

The question of these Noachic holy places requires a thorough study, of course. Unfortunately, it is not possible to examine them more closely within the compass of this paper. We will only note the possibility that some of the numerous Urartian (and pre-Urartian) ruins in the region could contain sanctuaries on which were such Noachic traditions could be grafted. We can quote, for example, the Urartian city of Tumurru on the top of mount Nibur (Akkad. Nippur, Sumer. Nibru).[68] This was for the Urartians the sacred mountain *par excellence*, and is identified as Sararad/Djudi. Near the top of this mountain were found large stelæ with bas-reliefs and cuneiform inscriptions.[69] One then can assume that it could represent the real geographical reference for the names 'Lubar', 'Baris' and 'Barathken'. Similarly, it would be tempting to identify the city of Tumurru with the one called Thāmānon, which according to a legend was built by Noah,[70] and also with Temnis of the Armenian tradition preserved in the *History of Hřip̌simē's Saintly Fellows*.[71]

Thus, at the present stage of our knowledge of the Bible and para-Biblical Noachic traditions we are able to posit that before the Christian era *no singular mountain named Ararat existed in the region associated by the tradition with the story of the Flood*. 'Mountains of Ararat', however, did exist, and they were identified with the 'country of Ararat', the oldest mention of which, under the

---

65   Ibid., n. 6 on p. 320.

66   A.E. Wallis Budge (ed.), *Salomon de Bassorah, The Book of the Bee*, Oxford, 1886 (Anecdota Oxoniensa, Semitic series, t. I, i), p. 33. The name Thāmānon recalls that of Ne'elatama'uk built by one of the sons of Noah.

67   According to the legend preserved in *Buzandaran Patmutiwnk̔* (Garsoyan, 1989, p. 77).

68   See Н.В. Арутюнян, *Биайнили (Урарту)*, [N.V. Harutyunyan, Biainili—Urartu], Yerevan, 1970, pp. 71, 364; А. Петросян, 'Два Арарата: гора Кордуены и Масис', *Арменоведческие исследования*, ['Two Ararats: the mountains of Korduena and Massis', in *Armenological Studies*], Yerevan, 2014, pp. 5–20; id., 'Biblical Mt. Ararat: Two Identifications', Comparative Mythology vol. 2/1 (2016), pp. 68–80.

69   Outier & Thierry, 'Histoire des saintes Hripsimiennes', n. 60 on p. 716.

70   Peeters, 'La Légende de saint Jacques', p. 319 and n. 1 on p. 320.

71   Outier & Thierry, 'Histoire des saintes Hripsimiennes'. According to the Armenian text, the etymology of the name *Temnis* is related to the legend of Noah and means: 'Eight people came out of the Ark'.

FIGURE 13.4   Mount Ararat (Masis): view from the north
PHOTO: AUTHOR

form of 'Arardi', reaches us from Middle-Assyrian inscriptions.[72] The idea of attributing the name 'Ararat', or 'Sararad', to one of the mountains of the district of Korduk is thus dependent on an early Christian tradition which, before reaching Armenia, had first developed in Aramaic/Syriac environment.

Secondly, we do not know of a mountain called Ararat in the province of Ayrarat where the tradition of the Flood finally migrated together with the sacred topography woven around the place of the Descent, nor elsewhere in Armenia (see Figure 13.4). The highest mountain in this province, which has double peaks dominating the Ayrarat valley, has been called by the inhabitants Masik, or (in the accusative case) Masis, from distant past until today. Etymologically, this name should mean 'double, twin' in Akkadian, then in Assyrian.[73] The mountain was linked to the legend of Artawazd, the historicized mythical hero enchained by demons in a deep cave situated within the mountain. Its slopes, formerly covered with forests, as well as its surroundings, were known as hunting reserve of the royal family, as evidenced by ancient Armenian sources and by the ancient form 'Naxčawan' of the city of Naxijewan situated opposite the south-eastern slope of the mountain. Admittedly, it derives from *Naxčirawan*, the word 'naxčir' meaning in Parthian 'game, slaughter, hunt' and the 'wan', or 'awan', meaning 'town or settlement'. In the Middle Ages, under the influence of the tradition of the Flood that had migrated to Mount Ararat, Naxčawan began to be transliterated as Naxijewan. The name of the city was thus

---

72   See Арутюнян, *Биайнили (Урарту)*, p. 70.
73   Petrossyan, 'Biblical Mt. Ararat'.

reinterpreted as the site of the 'First Descent' (Nax-Iǰewan). This is doubtlessly related to the ancient *Apobaterion* tradition as already recorded by Josephus.

When did the name 'Ararat' migrate to Mount Masis and its surroundings? It is hard to establish. It is possible that in the Jewish tradition the transfer already occurred during the early Christian era[74] and that it was a result of a search for the geographical localization of the land of Ararat: as we have seen, St Jerome defines Ararat as a plain in Armenia. But in the Christian and especially Armenian tradition, this was not evident before the Middle Ages, and the mountain remained associated with the legend of Jacob of Nisibis and the *Inventio* of the relics of the Ark.

Besides, according to later witnesses,[75] such as the texts of Vincent de Beauvais[76] and Guillaume de Ruysbroeck,[77] the honour seems to be disputed between Mount Masis which has two peaks and Mount Aragats having four peaks. However, these two mountains remained known under their original names to the local inhabitants and to some European travellers who, however, localized Noah's mountain 'in the land of Ararat in Armenia', i.e. in the province of Ayrarat.

So, amongst the sites belonging to the new sacred topography that developed around Mount Masis the following were shown to the travellers: the spring of Saint Jacob,[78] later called *Anhatakan* ('Inexhaustible'), on which once stood a chapel dedicated to Saint Jacob. It then migrated to a monastery built ca. half kilometre away;[79] a site named *Arnoyt* where Noah was supposed to have dwelt after leaving the ark; and the village of *Akoṙi* where Noah had planted a vineyard. The city of *Thamanon* on Mount Djudi was transported to the plain of Araxes, while the tomb of Noah was shown in Naxiǰevan. Even Yerevan was claimed to be built by Noah.[80] The fact that this northerly migration took place long before Mount Masis would be re-baptized Ararat could provide an additional argument for our hypothesis that, apart from some Syriac and Armenian milieux, *the mountain of the Ark was never called Ararat in*

---

74   See M.E. Stone, 'The Book(s) attributed to Noah', in *Noah and his book(s)*, pp. 7–25.

75   For the references, see Stone, 'Mount Ararat and the Ark' and Peeters, 'La Légende de saint Jacques'.

76   *Speculum Historiale*, XXXI, ch. 97, quoted in Peeters, 'La Légende de saint Jacques'.

77   *Itinerarium Willelmi de Rubruk. Recueil de voyages et de mémoires de la Société de géographie*, t. I, Paris, 1839, pp. 213–396.

78   See Վարք սրբոց հարանց [*Life of Saint Fathers*], Venice, 1855, t. II, p. 455.

79   Ղ. Ալիշան, Այրարատ [L. Alishan, *Ayrarat*], Venice, 1890, p. 470.

80   J.-B. Chardin, *Voyage en Perse*, t. I–III, Paris, 1829, pp. 213–214; L. Ինճիճեան, Ստորագրութիւն Հին Հայաստանեայց [L. Injijian, *Description of Ancient Armenia*], Venice, 1822, pp. 454–455.

the attempts to localize the Biblical syntagm 'the mountains of Ararat'. On the other hand, the names Lubar, Baris and, admittedly, also Barathken, recorded in various traditions, seem to have kept a distant link with the sacred Urartian mountain of Nibur, which in its origins had probably been related to the ancient Mesopotamian story of the Flood.

Acknowledgements

I express my sincere gratitude to Michael E. Stone, Yakir Paz, Vahe Torosyan and Jean-Claude Haelewyck for their precious advice and assistance.

CHAPTER 14

The Historian's Craft and Temporal Bridges in Apocrypha and in Early Christian Art: Para-Biblical Sources in the Light of the Work of Marc Bloch

Igor Dorfmann-Lazarev

In memory of Évelyne Patlagean

∴

The present volume possesses two thematic poles: the protagonists of the beginnings of the human race according to the book of Genesis, and the figures related to the advent of the Messiah. The temporal 'bridges' that various para-Biblical textual and figurative sources built between the origins of humankind and the Messiah's advent have exercised a decisive influence on our perception of history and, consequently, on the shaping of historiographical discipline.

In order to reflect on the idea of such 'bridges', I should like to invoke here the considerations of Marc Bloch (1886–1944). Bloch was not a scholar of religion, but one of the founders of modern methodology in the social and economic history of Europe. Yet some of the questions that occupied him already from an early stage are directly related to our theme: the ways in which mediæval and early modern societies preserved and reconstructed their collective memories, and the role of secret and dissimulated documents in this process; the means through which knowledge was passed down across generations; the place of myths, beliefs, apocryphal legends and 'tales of theological origin'[1] in common imagination;[2] and the conception of time and of the past that such beliefs

---

1   See M. Bloch, 'La vie d'outre-tombe du roi Salomon', in *Revue Belge de Philologie et d'Histoire* 4 (1925), pp. 349–377 ('les fables d'origine théologique': ibid., p. 358).

2   The historical section (directed, *in primis*, by H. Berr and L. Febvre) of the *Centre international de synthèse* (founded by H. Berr in 1925) planned to publish a *Vocabulaire historique des sciences dans leur rapport avec la philosophie*, in which ca 900 technical terms used by the historians would be defined and amply discussed. This project never came to completion.

THE HISTORIAN'S CRAFT AND TEMPORAL BRIDGES

implied, as well as their effect upon social conduct.[3] These interests also nourished Bloch's political thinking, his reflections on historian's role in society and, later on, also his project, interrupted by his violent death, of innovative educational programmes.

The reflections upon which I should like to comment here are to be found in his unfinished book which is known under two provisional titles: *Apology for History* or *The Historian's Craft*. Bloch began writing it in hiding, soon after France's defeat in May 1940, followed by the evacuation of his vanquished army to Britain (31 May) and his immediate return to occupied France (2 June). He pursued his work until the early spring of 1943 when he joined the Resistance movement.[4] The book derives its specific form from the author's impossibility

---

However, the lists composed by H. Berr and P. Masson-Oursel in 1930 and 1931 are telling: the articles that had to be entrusted to Bloch were: 'Témoignage', 'Authenticité' and 'Apocryphe'; see M. Platania, *Le parole di Clio. Polemiche storiografiche in Francia 1925–1945*, Naples, 2001, pp. 25–38; M. Mastrogregori, *Il genio dello storico. Le considerazioni sulla storia di Marc Bloch e Lucien Febvre e la tradizione metodologica francese*, Naples, 1987, pp. 30–33. The role of the Dreyfus affair (which sparked out when Bloch was eight years old, thus marking all his school years) in the formation of Bloch's interests has perceptibly been recognised by two Italian scholars: first by Girolamo Arnaldi, 'Introduzione', in *Apologia della storia o mestiere di storico*, Turin, 1969, p. XIII; and, more recently, by the aforementioned Massimo Mastrogregori, *Il manoscritto interrotto di Marc Bloch. Apologia della storia o Mestiere di storico*, Pisa, 1995, p. 11; see also B.Z. Kedar, 'מארק בלוך—בין חייו למחקרו' [Marc Bloch: Between His Life and His Research], in אפולוגיה על ההיסטוריה או מיקצועו של ההיסטוריון, M. Bloch, Jerusalem, 2002, pp. 13–14.

3   Cf. C. Ginzburg, 'Prefazione', in M. Bloch, *I re taumaturghi*, Turin, 1973, pp. xvi–xviii; Mastrogregori, *Il genio dello storico*, pp. 32–33; id., *Il manoscritto interrotto*, p. 74; A. Gurevich, 'Marc Bloch and Historical Anthropology', in H. Atsma (ed.), *Marc Bloch aujourd'hui: histoire comparée et sciences sociales*, Paris, 1990, pp. 403–405; A. Gurevič, *Исторический синтез и "Школа Анналов"* [Historical Synthesis and the 'School of the Annales'], Moscow, 1993, pp. 72–78, 98–101; M. Mastrogregori, 'Reconsidering Marc Bloch's Interrupted Manuscript: Two Missing Pages of *Apologie pour l'Histoire ou Métier d'Historien*', in *The European Legacy: Toward New Paradigms* 3 (1998), pp. 37–39; F. Pitocco, *Crisi della storia, crisi della civiltà europea. Saggio su Marc Bloch e dintorni*, Milan, 2012, pp. 229–230.

4   The book was written between Rennes, where Bloch had succeeded in evading German detection in June 1940, Clermont-Ferrand, Montpellier, the Creuse region and, finally, Lyons where, between February and March 1943, he joined the Resistance movement *Franc-Tireur*. As its member, Bloch was arrested in spring 1944, was several times tortured and, on 16 June 1944, shot in Saint-Didier-de-Formans near Lyons; see P. Klein, '12. Bloch (Marc)', in *Dictionnaire de Biographie Française* 6, Paris, 1954, coll. 681–682; Mastrogregori, *Il genio dello storico*, pp. 48, 59; C. Fink, *Marc Bloch: A Life in History*, Cambridge, 1989, p. 282; Mastrogregori, *Il manoscritto interrotto*, p. 59. According to M. Mastrogregori, who has closely studied Bloch's manuscripts, the author 'had not reached an advanced stage in the elaboration of his book' before his work was interrupted about 20 June 1943 because of his full engagement in the movement *Franc-Tireur*: id., *Il genio dello storico*, p. 211; id., *Il manoscritto interrotto*, p. 79; id., 'Le manuscrit interrompu: *Métier d'historien* de Marc Bloch', in *Annales. Économies, Sociétés, Civilisations*

to access his library, which had remained in occupied Paris and was later sacked by the invaders.[5] Written in the form of a historian's testament[6]—during one of the most critical moments in Europe's entire history—his thoughts on the link that unites European cultures with historical memory, and with the writing of history, thus assume a singular significance for a scholar of Biblical religions.

On the first two pages of his book Bloch declares that the ability of historians to justify their craft matters for the very existence of what he calls 'Western civilisation'. In order to explain such an outstanding role assigned during those years to the writing of history, he maintains that European civilisation 'has always expected much from its memory. Christianity is a religion of historians'. The sacred books of the Christians are history books—claims Bloch; moreover, their liturgies commemorate not only episodes of the life of the Church and of the saints, but even those of 'the earthly life of a God'. Furthermore, Bloch identifies one peculiar aspect of the Christian religion, which, in his view, relates it to the writing of history in 'an even more profound way': 'Placed between the Fall and the Judgement, humankind's destiny depicts, in its eyes [i.e. in the eyes of the Christian religion], a long adventure; every individual life, every particular 'pilgrimage' [composing it], shows, in its turn, a reflection [of that adventure]. It is in duration, therefore in history, that the great drama of Sin and Redemption—the central axis of all Christian meditation—unfolds.'[7]

---

44 (1989), p. 154. Further details on Bloch's preparatory work for the *Apologie pour l'histoire*, carried out in 1939, ibid., pp. 209–210; see also L. Strauss, 'Marc Bloch résistant', in P. Deyon et al. (eds), *Marc Bloch, l'historien et la cité*, Strasbourg, 1997, p. 186. The book was posthumously published by Lucien Febvre in 1949 on an insufficient manuscript basis (in the series *Cahiers des "Annales"*, 3; Paris, A. Colin); see: Mastrogregori, *Il genio dello storico*, pp. 213–214. On the remote origins of Bloch's plan to write a methodological work, see Mastrogregori, 'Le manuscript interrompu', pp. 148–151; Mastrogregori also suggests that Bloch could have begun collaborating with the incipient forms of clandestine movements as early as the end of the summer 1940, i.e. whilst working on the book: id., 'L'expérience politique de Marc Bloch', in P. Schöttler and H.-J. Rheinberger (eds), *Marc Bloch et les crises du savoir* (les communications du colloque franco-allemand tenu du 4 au 6 octobre 2007 à l'Institut Max Planck d'histoire des sciences à Berlin), (preprint), p. 43.

5   Cf. Arnaldi, 'Introduzione', p. IX.

6   Cf. U. Raulff, *Ein Historiker im 20. Jahrhundert: Marc Bloch*, Frankfurt, 1995, pp. 441–442.

7   'Notre civilisation occidentale toute entière y est intéressée. Car, à la différence d'autres types de culture, elle a toujours beaucoup attendu de sa mémoire. [...] Le christianisme est une religion d'historiens. [...] Pour Livres sacrés, les chrétiens ont des livres d'histoire [...]. Historique, le christianisme l'est encore d'une autre façon, peut-être plus profonde: placée entre la Chute et le Jugement, la destinée de l'humanité figure, à ses yeux, une longue aventure, dont chaque vie individuelle, chaque "pèlerinage" particulier présente, à son tour, le reflet; c'est dans la durée, partant dans l'histoire, que se déroule, axe central de toute méditation chrétienne, le grand drame du Péché et de la Rédemption', in M. Bloch, *Apologie pour*

THE HISTORIAN'S CRAFT AND TEMPORAL BRIDGES

While identifying those aspects of Christianity that determine, from Bloch's perspective, the importance of the historical discipline—and precisely during those critical years—within the civilisation shaped by it, the *Apology for History* also leaves the reader puzzled: are we to conclude that the Christian religion, via its constitutive elements and structural characteristics, itself prompts an interest in history and in historical writing, thus generating a new people of historians? or, rather, that this religion could only be received, and could only endure, within a society already possessed of a pronounced historical consciousness? And thirdly, what can be said of those 'history books' (*livres d'histoire*) which, according to Bloch, represent the sacred literature of Christianity? from where did their authors derive the historical dimension proper to those books? Bloch refers to these questions also in a later chapter, but his book does not offer any easy answer to them. Dispersed manuscripts of the *Apology for History* reveal the extent to which the relation between the historian's craft and Christianity, and the importance of the past for a Christian mind, occupied Bloch at various stages in the drafting of this book.[8] We may notice that

---

l'histoire ou *Métier d'historien*, edn annotated by Étienne Bloch, Paris, 2007, p. 38; Raulff, *Ein Historiker*, pp. 155–156.

8 See the chapter 1.4 ('L'idole des origines'), in Bloch, *Apologie*, pp. 54–55. Apart from the manuscripts used by L. Febvre and those held by É. Bloch (and overlooked by Febvre for his edition of 1949), also other manuscripts of this unfinished book exist; for the first time they were taken into consideration in the edition of 1993. M. Mastrogregori, who discovered them in the *Archives Nationales*, Paris, in 1988, observes that 'some passages had been written in four or five different versions.' He summarises the results of his investigation (published in id., *Il manoscritto interrotto*, esp. pp. 71, 89–95) in this way: 'The drafting of the manuscript must have been continuous, if irregular. Bloch wrote straight off by hand, some pages being typed by his wife or dictated to some other person (probably young) of his entourage. The historian then corrected the typed pages, inserting new handwritten passages, at the same time cutting it into pieces, that were then glued onto new pages and connected to each other with handwritten additions. The typewritten sheets were then retyped and newly corrected by Bloch. The interrupted manuscript's dossier document[s] the different phases of the drafting until halfway through the third chapter.', in id., 'Reconsidering Marc Bloch's Interrupted Manuscript', pp. 33–36. The place of memory in a Christian civilisation had already occupied Bloch long beforehand. One of the earliest traces of his reflections on this subject is to be found in his review of Maurice Halbwachs's *Les cadres sociaux de la mémoire* vol. I, Paris, 1925, written fifteen years before the work on the *Apology for History* commenced. The terms of Bloch's last book are reminiscent of these: 'la piété du fidèle se nourrit à la fois de rites, sans cesse renouvelés, et de souvenirs, particulièrement de ceux qui portent sur la vie du Sauveur; mais la plupart des rites ne seraient que des formes vides s'ils ne commémoraient ou ne symbolisaient la carrière du Dieu ou, accessoirement, celle de ses saints; et par ailleurs le trésor historique ou légendaire du christianisme se transmet de génération en génération surtout par l'intermédiaire des rites. En somme, on pourrait dire, en forçant peut-être un peu la pensée de M. Halbwachs, que selon lui la messe est l'acte social par excellence puisqu'elle

he avoids, probably on purpose, the distinction to which we are now well accustomed, namely the distinction between historical and memorial writing.[9] His proposition may be provisionally summarised in this cautious way: because the religion that animated Europe's life relies on a particular account of past events and expresses itself in their ritual commemoration, the historian's craft is of utmost importance for Europe's destiny *today* (i.e. June 1940–March 1943).

In the light of these brief observations we may turn to the opening words of the *Apology for History*. The book begins with a quotation: 'Papa, explain to me, then, what is the use of history'. The author claims that he heard this question posed by a young boy, with whom he was closely acquainted, to his father, a historian. He declares that his exposition of the historian's craft—that is to say, the whole book—is intended to be an answer to this disarming question.[10] Indeed, claims Bloch, a good writer must be able to address himself to both a learned and a simple reader, even one posing naïve or embarrassing questions. From the preparatory papers to the book[11] we gather that such an introduction had been carefully considered by the author.

In reading these lines one is led to recall the Passover *Haggadah*. At the beginning of the fifth part of the *Haggadah*, called *Maggid* (מגיד)—a word which may be translated simply as 'Account' or, in a stronger sense, as 'Exposition', 'Demonstration' or 'Announcement'—, four different questions are posed: each is attributed to a son with a specific temperament, asking his father about the meaning of the present celebration. Amongst these four are, notably, a 'wise' son (חכם) and an 'ingenuous' one (תם). The chapter instructs the father

---

unit indissolublement le caractère d'une cérémonie commémorative de la Cène avec celui d'un sacrifice actuel et actuellement efficace. [...] La mémoire collective, comme la mémoire individuelle, ne conserve pas précisément le passé; elle le retrouve ou le reconstruit sans cesse, en partant du présent. Toute mémoire est un effort.', in M. Bloch, 'Mémoire collective, tradition et coutume. À propos d'un livre récent', in *Revue de synthèse historique* 12 (1925), pp. 76–77.

9 Cf. Raulff, *Ein Historiker*, pp. 447–448.

10 The exceptional character of this introduction was stressed by U. Raulff: 'Die Frage ist weniger einfach, als es scheint. [...] Merkwürdig wird die Sache indes erst dadurch, daß Marc Bloch diese Frage an den Anfang seines Texts stellt und sie so gleichsam zum Aufhänger des gesamten Buches macht. Die ganze *Apologie der Geschichte* nimmt ihren Ausgang von der Frage eines Kindes nach dem Nutzen der Geschichte. Wobei das Erstaunliche nicht der Umstand ist, daß es ein Gespräch zwischen Vater und Sohn ist, aus dem das Buch sich entwickelt—Marc Bloch war selber Sohn eines Historikers und mochte dieselbe Frage einst an seinen Vater gerichtet haben. Verwunderlich ist vielmehr die Tatsache, daß ausgerechnet *diese* Frage einen so prominenten Platz erhält', in id., *Ein Historiker*, pp. 415–416; cf. also Gurevič, *Historical Synthesis*, pp. 104–105.

11 Dated by the editors to June 1940, in Rennes: 'Reliquat probable des Réflexions sur l'histoire', in A. Becker et al. (eds), *M. Bloch, L'histoire, la guerre, la Résistance*, Paris, 2006, p. 819.

THE HISTORIAN'S CRAFT AND TEMPORAL BRIDGES   301

about the different ways of explaining the Exodus, each appropriate to a different listener. This instruction is followed by the account, starting from the remote ancestors of the Jews and, via the history of the patriarchs, reaching the descent into Egypt, the enslavement and, finally, the Exodus.

The opening pages of the *Apology for History* thus suggest that the understanding of the past and the explanation of the historian's craft cannot at all times be couched in strict terms of historiography, even for a non-religious writer like Bloch.[12] The effect of Christianity on Europe is outlined in his book in terms close to the description of the mediæval *mentalité* given by Bloch in the first volume of his *Feudal Society*. The book was finished before the end of 1938, and its first volume, *La formation des liens de dépendance*, was published in July 1939, only a month before his mobilisation.[13] In that book, however, the mediæval *mentalité* was carefully distinguished from that proper to other periods in history. Here, surprisingly, the world of Biblical religions looms in the background of the writer's undertaking. These lines may suggest that at the moment when the world collapses the historian no longer remains its detached observer; the eschatological horizon proper to the object of his studies suddenly becomes his own.[14] Indeed, we read on the same page of the *Apology for History*: 'Behold, the historian is summoned to give account of himself. He cannot venture into this [task] but with a bit of inner trembling'.[15] Here, therefore, Bloch reminds us of one of those mediæval men and women who in *La société féodale* were described by him as standing in terror before the cosmos.[16]

12   On M. Bloch's lack of interest in philosophy and in abstract methodology of historical sciences, cf. C. Ginzburg, 'A proposito della raccolta dei saggi storici di Marc Bloch', in *Studi Medievali* serie III vol. VI (1965), pp. 338–339; Raulff underlines the combination of various genres in the texture of Bloch's *Étrange défaite* (1940): Raulff, 'Vom Ursprung zur Aktualität. Marc Bloch, die Zeitgeschichte und das Problem der Gegenwart', in P. Schöttler (ed.), *Marc Bloch. Historiker und Widerstandskämpfer*, Frankfurt, 1999, p. 212; B.Z. Kedar hypothesises that precisely Bloch's aloofness from religious experience awakened in him curiosity in the effects exercised by Christian faith on society; in Kedar, 'Marc Bloch', p. 15.

13   M. Bloch, *La société féodale. La formation des liens de dépendance* vol. 1, Paris, 1982, II.III.1 (*Les conditions de vie et l'atmosphère mentale. La mémoire collective. L'historiographie*), pp. 140–141. The first volume was printed on the 6th of July 1939 (as indicated in the printer's colophon), and its publications was announced by the editors on the 21st of July (*Bibliographie de la France* 128, 2ᵉ série N29). Bloch was mobilised between the 23rd and the 25th of August 1939; cf. Fink, *Marc Bloch*, p. 208, n. 112.

14   Cf. Fink, *Marc Bloch*, p. 295, n. 6.

15   'Voilà donc l' historien appelé à rendre ses comptes. Il ne s'y hasardera qu'avec un peu de tremblement intérieur: quel artisan, vieilli dans le métier, s'est jamais demandé, sans un pincement de cœur, s'il a fait de sa vie un sage emploi? Mais le débat dépasse, de beaucoup, les petits scrupules d'une morale corporative. Notre civilisation occidentale tout entière y est intéressée', in Bloch, *Apologie pour l'histoire*, p. 38.

16   Bloch, *La société féodale* I, chapter II ('Façons de sentir et de penser'), pp. 114–135.

The explanation of the historian's craft, in order to achieve the educational and testamentary purpose that Bloch assigns to himself in the present work,[17] possesses a very special form and even a special tone, proceeding, as it were, from the historian's inner self. Indeed, it reveals a certain kinship to his Jewish consciousness to which Marc Bloch only seldom confessed, and only under exceptional circumstances.[18] The commemoration of the deliverance from captivity, insinuated by the child's question on the first line of the book, remains in the background of the rest of Bloch's writing.

We may better appreciate the place occupied by these reflections in Bloch's thought, and the process of their emergence, by turning to his paper 'Pour une histoire comparée des sociétés européennes' read before the Congress of the *International Committee of Historical Sciences* convened in Oslo in 1928, in which he alludes to the awaited reconciliation between European nations after the Great War. He argues that various national historiographic traditions are often conditioned by the peculiarities of technical vocabularies proper to each and even by divergent sets of research questions formulated by the historians of different nations.[19] Analogous social and economic developments, which could give way to the study of intercultural contacts and of shared mental references of the Europeans, remain disregarded; the role of such exchanges in the shaping and the transformations of comparable political and social institutions—as well as in the transmission of myths and apocryphal legends[20]—in various parts of Europe[21] remains overlooked.[22] Instead, the origins of sets of formal rules or prescriptive norms, on the model of biological ancestors, are iden-

---

17   Cf. M. Mastrogregori, 'L'expérience politique d'un historien modèle', in id. (ed.), Marc Bloch, *Carnets inédits (1917–1943)*, Turin, 2016, p. 291.

18   Cf. Raulff, *Ein Historiker*, p. 445; Benjamin Kedar has pointed out that both a series of reviews published by Bloch in *Les Annales* and his discussion of projects for future research in his correspondence with L. Febvre evince his interest in Jewish history, and not only that during the Middle Ages: Kedar, 'Marc Bloch', p. 13.

19   M. Bloch, 'Pour une histoire comparée des sociétés européennes', in *Revue de synthèse historique* 46 (1928), pp. 47–50.

20   Bloch, 'La vie d'outre-tombe du roi Salomon', pp. 373–376.

21   M. Bloch, *Les rois thaumaturges* I.II.3, Paris, 1961, pp. 21, 86; Ginzburg, 'A proposito della raccolta dei saggi storici', p. 342; P.L. Orsi, 'La storia delle mentalità in Bloch e Febvre', in *Rivista di Storia Contemporanea* 12 (1983), pp. 372–373; A. Gurevič, 'М. Блок и "Апология истории"' (M. Bloch and the 'Apology for History'), in *Марк Блок, Апология истории или ремесло историка*, 2nd edn, Moscow, 1986, pp. 196–200; Kedar, 'Marc Bloch', p. 11.

22   Bloch, 'Pour une histoire', pp. 42–45; id., 'Chevalerie européenne ou chevalerie allemande', in *Annales d'histoire économique et sociale* 9/48 (1937), p. 615; Kedar, 'Marc Bloch', pp. 8–9; Mastrogregori, *Il genio dello storico*, p. 152.

THE HISTORIAN'S CRAFT AND TEMPORAL BRIDGES

tified with their causes.[23] The reciprocal incomprehension between different national schools, each riveted to its own 'autochthonous' roots (etymological, societal and legal), results in their isolation, and even in reciprocal hostility.

In his perspicacious reviews of the following twelve years Bloch examined particular cases of such a historiographical provincialism: the State, the law and the Church stand out in such works as indissoluble, primordial bodies, as the dominant, or even the exclusive, actors of historical narrative: it is these bodies that, ever since their most remote origins, are claimed to have forged and governed society, economy, culture, consciousness and religion. As a consequence, those branches of historical science that do not focus on the development of institutions—and in particular those juridical—find themselves relegated to the positions of auxiliary disciplines.[24] Elsewhere Bloch also suggests that an inevitable corollary of such a personification of institutions is the hardening of political frontiers.[25]

For Bloch, comparative approaches to history, in which he was especially inspired by Antoine Meillet's *La méthode comparative en linguistique historique* (published in Oslo in 1925),[26] could enable historians to reveal the kinship of European societies precisely in the variety of their social and political structures.[27] Such approaches also opened up a way to overcome the limitations of

---

23   Bloch, *Apologie*, pp. 54–55; A.I. Baumgarten, 'Reflections on the Groningen Hypothesis', in G. Boccaccini (ed.), *Enoch and Qumran Origins. New Light on a forgotten Connection*, Grand Rapids, 2005, pp. 256–262.

24   Cf. M. Bloch, 'Histoire d'Allemagne. VII. Institutions politiques' (about M.F. Keutgen's *Der deutsche Staat des Mittelalters*), in *Revue historique* 158 (1928), p. 124; id., 'L'histoire locale en Allemagne', *Annales d'histoire économique et sociale* 1/2 (1929), p. 306; id., 'Un tempérament: Georg von Below', ibid., 3/12 (1931), pp. 554–558; id., 'Vassalité, fief, seigneurie', ibid., 7/34 (1935), pp. 407–408. See also Gurevič, 'M. Bloch', p. 209; Raulff, *Ein Historiker*, pp. 255–257; O.G. Oexle, 'Marc Bloch et l'histoire comparée de l'histoire', in *Marc Bloch, l'historien et la cité*, pp. 60–61; M. Borgolte, 'Die Erfindung der europäischen Gesellschaft. Marc Bloch und die deutsche Verfassungsgeschichte seiner Zeit', in *Marc Bloch. Historiker und Widerstandskämpfer*, p. 180.

25   In M. Bloch's letter to Fritz Rörig dated at October 1930; see: P. Schöttler, 'Marc Bloch und Deutschland', in *Marc Bloch. Historiker und Widerstandskämpfer*, p. 50; cf. also M. Bloch, 'Johannes Haller. Tausend Jahre deutch-französischer Beziehungen', in *Revue Historique* 175 (1935), p. 158.

26   By the Institute for Comparative Research in Human Culture (Instituttet for sammenlignende kulturforskning) founded in 1922: A. Meillet, *La méthode comparative en linguistique historique*, Oslo, 1925. M. Bloch, 'Comparaison', in 'Projets d'articles du vocabulaire historique', *Bulletin du Centre International de synthèse. Section de Synthèse historique* 9 (*Revue de Synthèse Historique* XLIX; n.s. XXIII) (1930), pp. 32, 38; Pitocco, *Crisi della storia*, pp. 221–228. On a wider context of Bloch's methodological undertaking, see: Platania, *Le parole di Clio*, pp. 16–19 ff.; on the *Vocabulaire historique*, see n. 2 above.

27   M. Bloch, 'Pour une histoire', pp. 16–20; cf. also id., 'Comparaison', p. 39: 'Peut-être la percep-

national, and nationalistic, historiographical traditions and the ensuing sub-servience of man to the sets of political, juridical and religious rules and social norms.[28] It is this conviction that may explain Bloch's exceptional evaluation, found in the *Apology for History*, of the historians' ability to justify their craft, whereas a review dated 1940 reveals that he saw particularly in the universalism of Latin Christianity the antithesis to the forces that were afflicting Europe.[29] Obviously, between 1928, when a professor of Strasburg University read his paper before an international congress, and 1940, when a soldier of a defeated army commenced his *Apology for History* in hiding, the political implications of Bloch's reflections about Europe and the role of historian therein had dramatically changed.

M. Bloch's legacy has opened before us a different perspective on apocryphal and para-Biblical writings and on the conceptions of time expressed in them. We are now able to look at apocrypha preserved by various Christianities not merely as residues of popular piety or of folklore, but as a source attesting to a much more fundamental cultural phenomenon. So Bloch was writing in 1924:

> [P]our comprendre ce que furent les monarchies d'autrefois, pour rendre compte surtout de leur longue emprise sur l'esprit des hommes, il ne suffit point d'éclairer, dans le dernier détail, le mécanisme de l'organisation

---

tion des différences est-elle, en fin de compte, l'objet le plus important—encore que, trop souvent, le moins recherché—de la méthode comparative. Car, par elle, nous mesurons l'originalité des systèmes sociaux, nous pouvons espérer, un jour, les classer, et pénétrer jusqu'au tréfonds de leur nature'. See also Gurevič, 'M. Bloch', pp. 200–201; id., *Historical Synthesis*, pp. 83–87, 91; Mastrogregori, *Il genio dello storico*, pp. 151–152; Platania, *Le parole di Clio*, pp. 71–72.

28   Raulff, *Ein Historiker*, pp. 247–248; Schöttler, 'Marc Bloch und Deutschland', p. 33.

29   In 1940 Bloch contrasts the 'universalism of Latin Christianity' with Germanic myths, 'jusqu'au bout profondément antithétiques à ce que le christianisme avait de plus pur'; i.e. the myths whose 'resurgence' he observed in his contemporary Germany: 'dans l'étonnante et formidable Allemagne que nous avons vu aujourd'hui se dresser sous nos yeux, se prolongent certains penchants, mythiquement guerriers et mystiquement juvéniles que déjà décelait, dans le même groupe, l'évolution des traditions reçues du plus vieux passé indo-européen. [...] [S]ans doute, s'agit-il bien, en réalité, de la résurgence de sources seulement à demi cachées. Leur courant est sensible durant tout le Moyen Age [...]. Il y aurait une belle et curieuse histoire à écrire; celle de la survie profonde, en Allemagne, je n'oserai dire du paganisme germain, mais, du moins, de *tendances sentimentales et religieuses—sociales aussi d'ailleurs—fort étrangères à l'universalisme de la chrétienté latine*.' M. Bloch, 'Georges Dumézil. Mythes et dieux des Germains', in *Revue Historique* 188/189 (1940), pp. 275–276 (the italics are ours, I.D.-L.). See also M. Mastrogregori (ed.), Marc Bloch, *Carnets inédits (1917–1943)*, p. 100, n. 87.

THE HISTORIAN'S CRAFT AND TEMPORAL BRIDGES   305

administrative, judiciaire, financière, qu'elles imposèrent à leurs sujets; il
ne suffit pas non plus d'analyser dans l'abstrait ou de chercher à dégager
chez quelques grands théoriciens les concepts d'absolutisme ou de droit
divin. *Il faut encore pénétrer les croyances et les fables qui fleurirent autour
des maisons princières. Sur bien des points tout ce folklore nous en dit plus
long que n'importe quel traité doctrinal.*[30]

Many texts that at a certain point in the past had come to be considered 'apocryphal' were transmitted during the Middle Ages not out of an institutional
need, and with institutional support, but because they aroused spontaneous
interest in people from different walks of life in various parts of Christendom.
Their proliferation in numerous languages must be regarded as a direct consequence of those metaphysical questions which had been sown by Christianisation, yet could not be answered exhaustively by the texts officially sanc-
tioned by Churches. Apocrypha are the tangible 'traces' left by those questions,[31] which give us a direct access to the mental and spiritual world of various
Christian societies; to their world pictures which defined their conduct.

A series of para-Biblical sources, both textual and pictorial, allow us today
to consider Bloch's reflections from a new angle and within a much wider horizon. The main protagonists of these sources are pilgrims who retain some keys
to the meaning that the writing of history acquired within Christian civilisation. In the texts to which we shall now turn the idea of a writing, and of a
chronicle, transmitted through generations is at the very core of the narrative.
These texts, shaped between the second and the sixth centuries, are preserved
in Coptic, Greek, Syriac, Latin and Armenian—some of which were discovered
only after the Second World War—and speak of a written document that the
first created human beings passed on to their descendants.[32] That document

---

30   M. Bloch, *Les rois thaumaturges* ['Introduction'], Paris, 1961, p. 19 (the italics are ours, I.D.-
      L.); cf. Gurevič, 'M. Bloch', pp. 206–207. The role played by apocryphal traditions about
      Adam in the development of royal ideology in Armenia is discussed in: I. Dorfmann-
      Lazarev, 'Kingship and Hospitality in the Iconography of the Palatine Church at Aḷtamar',
      in *Rivista di Storia e Letteratura Religiosa* 52 (2016), pp. 479–516; id., 'Concerning Four Kings
      From the Land of "Deep Ravines, Dense Forests and Dark Thickets"', in Ph.M. Forness et
      al. (eds), *The Good Christian Ruler in the First Millennium*, Berlin, 2021, pp. 249–288 (forth-
      coming).

31   'Qu'il s'agisse des ossements murés dans les remparts de la Syrie, d'un mot dont la forme
      ou l'emploi révèle une coutume, du récit écrit par le témoin d'une scène ancienne ou
      récente, qu'entendons-nous en effet par documents, sinon une "trace", c'est-à-dire la mar-
      que, perceptible aux sens, qu'a laissé un phénomène en lui-même impossible à saisir?', in
      Bloch, *Apologie pour l'histoire*, p. 71; cf. Kedar, 'Marc Bloch', p. 22.

32   See 'Apocalypse of Adam', in the *Cologne Mani Codex* 48.16–50.7; 50.8–51.20: L. Koenen

related a revelation received by Adam regarding his future destiny and that of all his posterity. From the extant documentation we learn that a 'writing' transmitted by Adam was known to Christians of various doctrinal trends, to Gnostic and even to Manichæan circles. One could never apprehend from any ecclesiastical document, of what vast and enduring importance the idea of a secret revelation transmitted to his posterity by the first created human being possessed in Christian civilisation.

According to some sources, such as the Syriac Chronicle from the monastery of Zuqnin near Amida (today Diyarbakır in the south-east of Turkey), which was written towards the middle of the eighth century (before 774/775) in a language close to that of the *Haggadah*, that revelation was committed to writing by Seth from Adam's spoken words. It is from Seth that the written memory of the world starts: 'And Adam explicated to Seth [the things regarding] his original dignity, [that which he had possessed] before he transgressed the commandment, and [also those regarding] his departure from Paradise. [...] And it was granted to Seth to set down [these things] in a writing (ܪܕܝܘܬܐ ܟܬܒܐ) and [thus] to make known wisdom [...]. And from him a writing was seen in the world for the first time, [namely, the writing] set down in the name of [God] the Highest. And Seth handed over the writing set down [by him] to his descendants, and it was transmitted until Noah ...'[33]

Three Armenian sources speak, by contrast, of a document which was written by God himself. It is, thus, the Creator who, at the dawn of the human history, stipulates the written word and, therefore, the alphabet.[34] Predicting the coming of a Saviour, the writing that came from the first human beings and from the hands that had shaped them oriented the life of all succeeding generations towards that event: all those who became privy to that writing

---

et al. (eds), *Der Kölner Mani-Kodex: über das Werden seines Leibes*, Opladen, 1988, pp. 30, 32; 'Testament of Adam' 3.1–4: M. Kmosko (ed.), 'Testamentum Adæ', in *Patrologia Syriaca* 2, Paris, 1907, pp. 1339–1342, 1345–1348; 'Apocalypse in which Adam informed his son Seth' (NH V.5) 67.15; 85.10–11: D.M. Parrott (ed.), *Nag Hammadi codices V, 2–5 and VI with Papyrus Berolinensis 8502, 1 and 4*, Leiden, 1979, pp. 155, 193, 195; 'Opus imperfectum in Matthæum. Homilia secunda': PG 56, col. 637; J.-B. Chabot (ed.), 'On the Revelation of the Magi': *Chronicon pseudo-Dionysianum vulgo dictum* 1 (CSCO 91; Syri 43), Louvain, 1927, p. 57 (ll. 4–8), p. 58 (ll. 17–27); and three Armenian documents: 'Script of the Lord's Infancy': I. Dorfmann-Lazarev, 'The Cave of the Nativity Revisited: Memory of the Primæval Beings in the Armenian Lord's Infancy and Cognate Sources', *Travaux et Mémoires* 18 (2014), pp. 326–327, 331–332; 'Document Written with God's Finger': ibid., pp. 332–333; 'Departure of Adam and Eve from Paradise' (Recension 'B'): ibid., p. 333. See also p. 270 above.

33   *Chronicon pseudo-Dionysianum vulgo dictum*, p. 58 (f. 17ʳ), ll. 11–21.

34   On the perception of the alphabet and the written word in Armenia, see J.-P. Mahé, *L'Alphabet arménien dans l'histoire et dans la mémoire*, Paris, 2018, esp. pp. 44–60, 105–108, 113–116.

lived awaiting the accomplishment of its promise. Moreover, according to the Armenian 'Script of the Lord's Infancy' (Գիր տղայութեան Տեառն), as well as the short 'Document Written with God's Finger' (Գիր մատամբն Աստուծոյ գրեալ), both of which must have been shaped before the sixth century, the keepers and the readers of God's writing also kept a record of the genealogical descent of their ancestors, which is also its provenance.[35]

However, various apocryphal texts speak not only of the expectation of a future accomplishment. The event of the accomplishment is depicted in some of them as that very moment when the most remote past of humankind is recollected and its principal figures are revived. It is well known that in the first part of the *Questions of Bartholomew*, written towards the end of the second century and attested in different languages, Jesus disappears from the Cross at the moment when the darkness envelops the earth, then becomes visible again and converses with Adam whom he has delivered from the realm of death (1. 7–22). While the descent into Hades implies an encounter between the eschatological accomplishment and the origins of the world, in a number of sources the memory of the first human beings is evoked at Jesus's *birth* in Bethlehem, i.e. at the moment of the Messiah's entrance into the world.[36]

'The central axis of all Christian meditation'—says Bloch—passes through history, whereas an individual life is a 'pilgrimage' reflecting humankind's common adventure. This begins with Adam and Eve, is recorded in the Christians' sacred books and is celebrated in their liturgies. The 'Wise men from the East' from the Gospel of Matthew (*Mt* 2. 1–12) were the first pilgrims in Christian history (see also Studies 18 and 19 in this volume); their journey is the prototype of the pilgrimage invoked by the scholar of mediæval Europe. Now the journey of the Magi to Bethlehem received a surprising development in a number of Syriac and Armenian sources: strikingly, the memory of the primæval beings forms its background. A remote echo of this conception reaches us even from an Uighur text discovered in the Turfan oasis in the north-west of today's China.

Here we shall limit ourselves to the Armenian 'Script of the Lord's Infancy' known to us in numerous recensions which attest to its popularity amongst Armenians: this text was transmitted to Armenia from the Syriac Church of the East, although that Church and the Armenian Church anathematised each other. Following its account, God's written document is inherited by the Magi who even take it on their journey to Judæa. When they reach Jerusalem, they are interrogated by Herod as to the source of their claim concerning the birth of 'a

---

35   Dorfmann-Lazarev, 'The Cave of the Nativity', pp. 298–302.

36   Dorfmann-Lazarev, 'Eve, Melchizedek and the Magi in the Cave of the Nativity According to the Armenian Corpus of Homilies Attributed to Epiphanius of Salamis', in J.N. Bremmer et al. (eds), *The Protevangelium of James*, Leuven, 2020, pp. 264–265, 270–287.

king's son in the land of Judæa'. Without showing him the scroll, they account to Herod of an ancient 'testimony' that they hold from their forefathers, 'written and kept' carefully. 'For a long time' their forefathers 'remained in expectation' of its accomplishment, charging their offspring to pass down that written document from father to son. When Herod desires to know its provenance, the Magi relate to him the following chronicle: the document was written and sealed by God; via Adam, Seth, Noah, Shem, Abraham and Melchizedek it reached King Cyrus, 'God's anointed' (*Is* 45.1), and from him the Magi's direct ancestors who placed it in a chamber for safe-keeping. The document kept by the Magi is not merely an account of theophany: the Creator himself is its author, sealing it and handing it over to Adam and, thus, inaugurating the chain of its historical transmission.

The 'Script of the Lord's Infancy' thus contains both, God's writing and a short chronicle relating of its provenance and its historical transmission. We are not told whether this chronicle reached the Magi by word of mouth or was taken down by their ancestors. Either way, when the Magi present God's writing to the new-born Christ, its quotation in the 'Script of the Lord's Infancy' begins with a preamble relating the circumstances under which Adam had received it. This implies that, in the author's mind, the more ancient part of that chronicle was indeed registered in writing, whereas its succeeding part could have been preserved orally. It is thanks to both, God's writing and the chronicle of its transmission, that the Magi could recognise, in the new-born child, the 'Prince' expected since Adam and Eve. Hence we reach the following conclusion: the 'Wise men from the East' become the witnesses of the Messiah's advent insofar as they and their ancestors are not only the custodians but also the chroniclers of the promise of salvation received by the first human being.[37] It is thanks to the Magi's witness, which relies on their uninterrupted memory and on the written memory of their ancestors, that the messianic age was inaugurated.[38]

The tradition underlying this story was also known to the Armenian author, or group of authors, of the extensive corpus of homilies attributed to Epiphanius of Salamis (fl. 367–403). Interestingly, in these homilies the Magi's genealogy is intertwined with the mythological genealogy of the Armenians and with that of their kings. In this way the national history of the Armenians is grafted onto the Gospel narrative; their ancestors, living in a country remote from the holy shrines of Christianity, are thus made to participate in the expectation

---

37   Dorfmann-Lazarev, 'The Cave of the Nativity', pp. 325–327, 331–332.

38   S. Mowinckel, *He that Cometh*, Oxford, 1959, p. 305; I. Dorfmann-Lazarev, *Christ in Armenian Tradition: Doctrine, Apocrypha, Art (Sixth–Tenth Centuries)*, Leuven, 2016, p. 352.

THE HISTORIAN'S CRAFT AND TEMPORAL BRIDGES

of the coming Saviour.[39] This document shows how the task of recording the national history preceding the Christianisation of the country could acquire a properly religious meaning.[40]

The Magi's journey is not the only way in which Armenian apocryphal sources build a bridge between the Nativity and human origins. Another figure appearing in the Cave of Bethlehem is Melchizedek, the hidden guardian of the sepulchres of Adam and Eve.[41] Furthermore, in a carefully tailored account found in the 'Script of the Lord's Infancy' Eve herself, who had been expecting the Saviour's Nativity since her expulsion from Eden, reaches Bethlehem in order to visit the new-born Christ. Jesus and his contemporaries in Bethlehem thus encounter a figure from the beginning of historical time.

This temporal conception is not exclusive feature of oriental apocrypha. On one of the most elaborate monuments of early Christian art, which is also discussed in Studies 19 and 25 in this volume—the so-called 'Dogmatic sarcophagus' from the basilica of St Paul Outside-the-Walls, Rome—Christ's Nativity and the Wise men's pilgrimage are depicted as the moment when the first actors of human history are recollected. This sarcophagus—dated to 330–340 CE—was originally located in the most honourable place of the sanctuary: in the immediate vicinity of the altar and of the Apostle's sepulchre: its pictorial programme must, therefore, reflect the doctrine upheld by the Roman Church.[42] The narrative sequence of its lower register commences with the scene of the Adoration of the Magi, whereas the opening scene of its upper register, situated exactly above the scene of the Adoration, depicts the Creation of Eve by the Triune God. This act is concretised in the gesture of God the Son laying his right hand on Eve's head (see Figure 14.1).

---

39   Dorfmann-Lazarev, 'Eve, Melchizedek and the Magi', pp. 267–276, 278–282.

40   In such a way, the spread of apocryphal writings contributed to the regionalisation of Christianity and to the emergence of what Peter Brown has called 'micro-Christendoms.' This phenomenon has been described by Brown primarily for the case of Western Christendom: id., *The Rise of Western Christendom. Triumph and Diversity. AD 200–1000*, Chichester, 2013, pp. 15, 355, 364–365, 430. Cf. also pp. 64, 277–294 in this volume.

41   Dorfmann-Lazarev, 'Eve, Melchizedek and the Magi', pp. 287–292.

42   Now preserved in the *Museo Pio Cristiano*, Vatican (inv. 31427), this sarcophagus was conceived for a privileged burial. During the subsequent centuries it was perceived as the principal funerary monument of this church, adjoining the sepulchre of the Apostle under the triumphal arch; see: U. Utro, 'Per un approccio interdisciplinare ai sarcofagi paleocristiani: la Trinità sul sarcofago "dogmatico" dei Musei Vaticani', in R.M. Bonacasa Carra (ed.), *La cristianizzazione in Italia tra tardoantico ed altomedioevo*, 1, Palermo, 2007, pp. 267–282; id., 'I sarcofagi paleocristiani dal complesso di S. Paolo fuori le mura', in id. (ed.), *San Paolo in Vaticano*, Todi, 2009, pp. 50–52.

FIGURE 14.1 The 'Dogmatic sarcophagus' from the basilica of St Paul Outside-the-Walls, Rome, 330–340 CE
PHOTO: AUTHOR

Primarily, it is the figure of the first wise man, in the group of the three 'pilgrims' approaching the child, who realises the link between the two scenes: with his left hand he extends his gift to the new-born child, with the forefinger of his right hand he points to the upper scene, whereas his head is turned backwards, in the direction of his fellow Wise Man. The eyes of the latter are set upwards, in the direction indicated by the preceding figure's gesture. The reciprocal positions of the two Magi's heads and their eyes insinuate a silent dialogue: the artists suggest that the creation of Eve is in the Magi's minds and forms the background of the event that they have come to celebrate (see Figure 14.2). This dialogue echoes that taking place between the two divine persons creating Eve. The bending of the first wise man's head and his hand extending a gift to the child echo the features of the figure set directly above him, i.e. God the Son who, whilst creating Eve, converses with his Father seated behind him (see Figure 14.3). At the same time, the figure of the bearded Logos laying his hand on the head of Eve, barely half the size of her Creator, is sculpted in a clear parallel to the figure of Mary: she holds the child who, seated with his back upright, stretches his right hand towards the gift proffered by the first wise man.[43]

---

43 The Wise man's index-finger pointing at the remotest past of humankind reminds us of the

THE HISTORIAN'S CRAFT AND TEMPORAL BRIDGES 311

In Rome, thus, during Constantine's times, the Magi could be associated not only with human origins, but specifically with Eve. In the Armenian text that we mentioned earlier—the 'Script of the Lord's Infancy'—the visits of Eve and of the Magi, the inheritors of an ancient secret promise and the chroniclers of its transmission, are integrated within the same narrative framework. Whether or not the tradition of God's writing was also known in Rome, the Roman sarcophagus and the Armenian apocryphal text reveal a kindred semantic structure: both link the Messiah's advent to the beginning of history.[44] Furthermore, the Magi—the prototypes of all the succeeding pilgrims in European history—figure in both as the main protagonists of that undertaking, building temporal bridges.

'secret appointment' (*eine geheime Verabredung*) between generations, of which Bloch's contemporary, Walter Benjamin (1892–1940), spoke in his last, uncompleted, essay: we are referring to his theses 'On the Concept of History'. These theses, which represent a radical questioning of the meaning of history, were written in Paris, in the precariousness and emergency of that same year 1940 when Bloch started to draft his 'Apology for History' in Rennes (the drafting of the theses had begun in the winter 1939/40 and had been stopped in May 1940, i.e. a month before Bloch began his book): 'Die Vergangenheit führt einen heimlichen Index mit, durch den sie auf die Erlösung verwiesen wird. [...] Ist dem so, dann besteht eine geheime Verabredung zwischen den gewesenen Geschlechtern und unserem. Dann sind wir auf der Erde erwartet worden.' See 'Über den Begriff der Geschichte' II, in *W. Benjamin, Gesammelte Schriften* I.1, R. Tiedemann et al. (eds), Frankfurt, 1991, pp. 693–694. On the genesis of the theses and the progress of Benjamin's drafting, see G. Bonola and M. Ranchetti, 'Sulla vicenda delle tesi "sul concetto di storia"', in G. Bonola et al. (eds), *W. Benjamin, Sul concetto di storia*, Turin, 1997, pp. 7–11.

44   Cf. A. Momigliano, 'Indicazioni preliminari su Apocalissi ed Esodo nella tradizione giudaica', in id., *Pagine ebraiche*, S. Berti (ed.), Turin, 1987, p. 104.

FIGURE 14.2 Creation of Eve by the Triune God and Adoration of the Three Magi on the 'Dogmatic sarcophagus'
PHOTO: AUTHOR

FIGURE 14.3   Adoration of the Magi, a detail: the first Wise Man extends his gift to the newborn child and points to the Trinity, whilst his head is turned towards his fellow Wise Man. Notice the three medallions set on the frame separating the two scenes and intended to indicate the three divine persons involved in the Creation. See also Figure 19.9.
PHOTO: AUTHOR

PART 3

Symbols and Figures of the Messianic Expectation

∵

CHAPTER 15

Quellen der nichtbiblischen Mose-Überlieferung in der *Kratkaja Chronografičeskaja Paleja*

Dieter and Sabine Fahl

Die am besten bekannten mit Mose verbundenen Apokryphen und Pseud-epigraphen sind im Kirchenslavischen (im Folgenden: Ksl.) nur zum Teil über-liefert:

- Die *Apokalypse des Mose* (*Vita Adæ et Evæ*), bei welcher Mose nur als Offen-barungsträger im Titel genannt wird, hat in ihrer ksl. Fassung gar keinen Bezug zu Mose.
- Die *Himmelfahrt des Mose* (*Assumptio Mosis / Testament des Mose*), worin Mose dem Josua die künftige Geschichte Israels offenbart, ist ksl. nicht bezeugt.
- Das *Jubiläenbuch*, eine an Genesis und Exodus orientierte Offenbarung an Mose bis in seine Gegenwart, hat über indirekte Überlieferungen Spuren in der ksl. Literatur hinterlassen, wovon noch die Rede sein wird.

Auf ksl. Indices erscheinen vom 11. Jh. an zwei Titel mit dem Namen des Mose:
- *Testament des Mose* und
- *Auszug / Aufstieg / Himmelfahrt des Mose.*

Beide Texte sind nicht sicher identifiziert.[1] Möglicherweise beziehen sich beide Titel auf die o. g. *Assumptio Mosis*, die nicht in ksl. Übersetzung vorliegt: Die frühesten Indices (bzw. auch später die entsprechenden Abschnitte der auf sla-vischem Boden weitergeschriebenen) sind größtenteils aus dem Griech. über-setzt und enthalten daher auch Literatur, die ksl. gar nicht übersetzt war.

Einen der beiden Titel *Testament des Mose* oder *Auszug / Aufstieg / Himmel-fahrt des Mose* trägt aber gelegentlich auch die so genannte *Vita des Mose* in den verschiedenen *Paleja*-Überlieferungen. Es handelt sich dabei um auf die Lebenszeit des Mose bezogene Überlieferungen, in denen, an Ex, Num und Dtn orientiert, kanonische und nichtkanonische Texte kompiliert wurden. Die

---

1 Vgl. I.M. Gritsevskaya, ‚Some Problems of Textology of Indexes of Prohibited Books', in L. diTommaso und C. Böttrich (Hgg.), *The Old Testament Apocrypha in Slavonic Tradition. Con-tinuity and Diversity* (Texts and Studies in Ancient Judaism, 140), Tübingen, 2011, S. 201–223, und die dort angegebene Literatur.

© DIETER AND SABINE FAHL, 2021 | DOI:10.1163/9789004445925_017

nichtbiblischen Mose-Überlieferungen im Ksl. konzentrieren sich vor allem auf diese *Paleja*-Traditionen sowie auf die chronographische Literatur.

Der Begriff *Palæa/Paleja* bezeichnet eine Gruppe von byzantinischen und slavischen Rewritten-Bible-Textcorpora[2], die alttestamentliche Erzählstoffe aufgreifen und erweitern:[3]

Zunächst erscheint in der byzantinischen Literatur des 9. Jh.s die *Palæa Historica*[4], die bereits eine Reihe apokrypher Mose-Narrative enthält. Die bislang einzige Edition des griech. Textes besorgte Afanasij Vasil'ev nach zwei Handschriften.[5] Eine kritische Edition, die mehr als 20 Handschriften berücksichtigt, bereitet William Adler gegenwärtig an der North Carolina State University vor. Er war es auch, der den Text als Kommentar zu dem *Großen Bußkanon* des Andreas von Kreta[6] und weiteren liturgischen Hymnen indentifizierte und damit einen neuen Blick auf das *Palæa/Paleja*-Genre als Ganzes eröffnete.[7]

---

2 Zur Problematik des Begriffs *rewritten Bible* und weiterer Termini zur Bezeichnung jüdischer und christlicher biblische Texte fortschreibender Literatur, die hier nicht diskutiert werden sollen, vgl. C. Böttrich, ,Das literarische Genre „Historienbibel". Konturen und Facetten', in C. Böttrich, D. Fahl und S. Fahl (Hgg.), *Von der Historienbibel zur Weltchronik. Studien zur Paleja-Literatur* (Greifswalder Theologische Forschungen, 31), Leipzig, 2020, S. 11–44, hier: 15–18.

3 Bereits der Name signalisiert eine Verbindung zur *Palaia diathēkē*. Zu den Textgruppen, die in der Handschriftentradition den Namen Paleja im Titel führen, vgl. S. Fahl und C. Böttrich unter Mitarbeit von D. Fahl, *Leiter Jakobs* (Jüdische Schriften aus hellenistisch-römischer Zeit, Neue Folge, 1/6), Gütersloh, 2015, insbesondere S. 12, Anm. 77.

4 Vgl. D. Flusser, ,*Palæa Historica* – An Unknown Source of Biblical Legends', in J. Heinemann and D. Noy (Hgg.), *Studies in Aggadah and Folk-Literature* (Scripta Hierosolymitana, 22), Jerusalem, 1971, S. 48–79.

5 A. Vassiliev (= Vasil'ev), *Anecdota Græco-Byzantina*, 1: *Sbornik pamjatnikov vizantijskoj literatury*, Moskva 1893, darin ,13. Palæa historica', S. xlii–lvi (Einleitung), 188–292 (Text); speziell zum Leben des Mose dort: S. 226–258.

6 PG 97, 1329–1386.

7 Vgl. W. Adler, ,Parabiblical Traditions and Their Use in the *Palæa Historica*', in M. Kister, H.I. Newman, M. Segal und R.A. Clements (Hgg.), *Tradition, Transmission, and Transformation from Second Temple Literature through Judaism and Christianity in Late Antiquity. Proceedings of the Thirteenth International Symposium of the Orion Center for the Study of the Dead Sea Scrolls and Associated Literature, jointly sponsored by the Hebrew University Center for the Study of Christianity, 22–24 February 2011* (Studies on the Texts of the Desert of Judah, 113), Leiden–Boston, 2015, S. 1–39 (https://brill.com/view/serial/STDJ); id. ,Observations on the Textual Transmission of the *Palæa Historica* in Greek', in Böttrich, Fahl, Fahl, *Historienbibel*, S. 64–94; vgl. auch die englische Übersetzung des Textes nach Vasil'ev (Vassiliev, *Anecdota*) bei W. Adler, ,Palæa Historica („The Old Testament History"). A new translation and introduction', in R. Bauckham, J.R. Davila und A. Panayotov (Hgg.), *Old Testament Pseudepigrapha. More Noncanonical Scriptures* vol. 1, Grand Rapids (Michigan)–Cambridge (U.K.), 2013, S. 585–599 (Einleitung), 600–672 (englische Übersetzung), die Mose-Geschichte dort in Abschnitt 68–121 auf S. 626–647.

Die Rolle des Mose in der christlichen Liturgie ist insgesamt nur wenig untersucht, speziell

QUELLEN DER NICHTBIBLISCHEN MOSE-ÜBERLIEFERUNG

Die *Palæa Historica* wurde mehrfach ins Ksl. übersetzt.[8] Die früheste, nicht sicher datierte bulgarische Übersetzung (10./11. Jh.?) war am weitesten verbreitet, v. a. in altrussischen Handschriften. Ihren Text edierte, noch ehe der griechische Text im Druck erschien, Andrej Nikolaevič Popov, der auch den russischen Titel *Istoričeskaja Paleja* für diese Übersetzung prägte.[9] Die zweite, serbische aus dem 14. Jh. publizierte Małgorzata Skowronek kürzlich in einer kommentierten kritischen Edition nach 10 Handschriften.[10] Von einer dritten Übersetzung, die wohl im 15. Jh. in Bulgarien oder auf dem Athos entstand und kaum untersucht wurde, ist nur ein Textzeuge bekannt (nicht ediert).

Eine u. a. von der ersten Übersetzung abhängige bei der Herausgabe durch Popov 1881 so genannte *Gekürzte Paleja russischer Redaktion* enthält eine leicht gekürzte Fassung der gleichen Episodenfolge über das Leben des Mose.[11] Vom Ksl. hängt auch die seit dem 18. Jh. bezeugte rumänische Übersetzung der *Palæa Historica* ab.[12]

---

    zur Oster-Liturgie vgl. L. Cuppo-Csaki, ‚Moses and the Paschal Liturgy', in J. Beal (Hg.), *Illuminating Moses. A History of Reception from Exodus to the Renaissance* (Commentaria. Sacred Texts and Their Commentaries: Jewish, Christian and Islamic, 4), Leiden–Boston, 2013, S. 103–115. Eine Übersicht zur jüdischen Liturgie vgl. bei B. Ego, ‚Mose im Judentum', in C. Böttrich, B. Ego und F. Eißler, *Mose in Judentum, Christentum und Islam*, Göttingen, 2010, S. 11–66, hier S. 60–62, und die dort angegebene Literatur.

8   Vgl. J. Reinhart, ‚Die älteste Bezeugung der Historischen Paläa in slavischer Übersetzung (Cod. slav. vindob. Nr. 158)', in *Prilozi za književnost, jezik, istoriju i folklor* 73 (2007), S. 45–75 (hier auch eine Analyse der verschiedenen ksl. Übersetzungen sowie auf S. 60–61 die bislang umfangreichste Handschriften-Liste) sowie M. Skowronek (Hg.), *Palæa Historica. The Second Slavic Translation, Commentary and Text* (Series Ceranea, 3), Łódź, 2016, hier S. 24–26, und die dort angegebene Literatur.

9   A.N. Popov (Hg.), *Kniga bytija nebesi i zemli (Paleja istoričeskaja s priloženiem Sokraščennoj palei russkoj redakcii)*, (Čtenija v Obščestve istorii i drevnostej rossijskich, 1881.1), Moskva, 1881, Ausgabe nach drei Handschriften, Mose-Geschichte: S. 60–110.

10   Mose-Geschichte: Skowronek, *Palæa Historica*, S. 96–139.

11   Edition bei Popov, *Kniga bytija*, im Anhang S. 38–73, nach Ms 1448 der Bibliothek der Novgoroder Sophienkathedrale (jetzt: Russische Nationalbibliothek St. Petersburg, Sophien-Sammlung) aus dem 16. Jh. Heute wird diese individuelle Paleja-Kompilation meist nach dem darin erwähnten Besitzer (oder Kompilator?) als *Paleja des Gurij Rukinec* bezeichnet – nach E.G. Vodolazkin, ‚Kak sozdavalas' Polnaja Chronografičeskaja Paleja', 1, in *Trudy Otdela drevnerusskoj literatury* 60 (2009), S. 327–353, hier: S. 340–353; id., ‚Iz istorii kirillobelozerskich palej', in N.V. Ponyrko und S.A. Semjačko (Hgg.), *Knižnye centry Drevnej Rusi. Knižniki i rukopisi Kirillo-Belozerskogo monastyrja*, Sankt-Peterburg, 2014, S. 186–309, hier: S. 303.

12   A. Moraru und M. Moraru, *Palia istorică* (Cele mai vechi cărţi populare în literatura română, 4), Bucureşti, 2001, Mose-Geschichte dort: S. 155–200, teils mit übernommenen ksl. Zwischenüberschriften.

Unter dem Einfluss der *Palæa Historica* entsteht später auf slavischem, höchstwahrscheinlich nordrussischem Boden die *Palæa Interpretata* (russisch: *Tolkovaja Paleja = Kommentierte Paleja*, von ksl. тлъкъ – „Erklärung" bzw. „Deutung"), die sich durch eine eigenständige Textauswahl und -anordnung sowie durch typologisch-apologetische Kommentare auszeichnet, strukturiert als Dialog mit einem fiktiven Juden. Als Quellenmaterial dienten ausschließlich bereits ksl. vorhandene Texte der Übersetzungsliteratur weit über die *Palæa Historica* hinaus. Die *Tolkovaja Paleja* liegt ihrerseits in drei verschiedenen Fassungen vor und ist in ksl. Handschriften vom 14. Jh. an überliefert.[13] Da ihre Eigenheiten jeweils auch die Überlieferungen zum Leben des Mose betreffen, seien sie hier in Stichworten vorgestellt:

A. *Tolkovaja Paleja = Kommentierte Paleja* (im Folgenden: TP) ist in der Fachliteratur zugleich der Name für einen der spezifischen Typen:
   - entstanden wohl im 13. Jh., handschriftliche Überlieferung seit dem 14./15. Jh.
   - erzählt wird die alttestamentliche Geschichte von der Schöpfung bis zu König Salomo
   - charakteristisch ist die enge Verzahnung zwischen Text- und Erklärungsteil und die ständige Ansprache des fiktiven jüdischen Gesprächspartners
   - der Kompilator arbeitet frei mit seinen Quellen: zitiert wörtlich, paraphrasiert, stellt um, kommentiert
   - einzige kritische Edition (nur in enger Verbindung mit Handschriftenstudien verwendbar) von 1892/1896[14]

B. *Polnaja Chronografičeskaja Paleja = Vollständige Chronographische Paleja* (im Folgenden: PP)
   - entstanden um 1400, seitdem handschriftliche Überlieferung

---

13   Zu den kontroversen wissenschaftlichen Diskussionen um Entstehungszeit und -ort vgl. Fahl, Böttrich, Fahl, *Leiter Jakobs*, S. 12–18; zu Handschriftenlisten ebd., S. 18, Anm. 107.

14   *Paleja Tolkovaja po spisku sdelannomu v g. Kolomne v 1406 g.*, trud učenikov N.S. Tichonravova, Vyp. 1, Moskva, 1892, Vyp. 2, Moskva, 1896; Mose-Geschichte dort, verwoben mit typologisch-apologetischen Deutungen, in Vyp. 2, S. 238–324.
       Die so genannte integrale Textedition von Kamčatnov, Mil'kov und Poljanskij ist für philologisch-historische Studien nicht verwendbar, da dort Varianten verschiedener Traditionen ohne jeglichen Nachweis vermischt werden: A. Kamčatnov, V. Mil'kov und S. Poljanskij (Hgg.), *Paleja Tolkovaja* (Vstupitel'naja stat'ja V. Kožinov, Podgotovka drevnerusskogo teksta i perevoda na sovremennyj russkij jazyk A. Kamčatnov, Kommentarii V. Mil'kov, S. Poljanskij pri učastii G. Barankovoj, A. Kamčatnova i R. Simonova, Stat'ja V. Mil'kov, S. Poljanskij, Redaktor: Ju. Kamčatnova), Moskva, 2002.

QUELLEN DER NICHTBIBLISCHEN MOSE-ÜBERLIEFERUNG

- der biblisch-exegetische Teil ist um eine umfangreiche chronographische Fortsetzung ergänzt (Zeit: von der Schöpfung bis zu Kaiser Romanos Lakapenos)
- Bestand apokrypher Texte weiter ausgebaut und eine große Menge kanonischen Bibeltextes hinzugefügt
- typologische Kommentare reduziert, Dialogstruktur weitgehend aufgegeben
- Kompilator benutzt die TP und weitere Quellen ausschließlich in wörtlicher Übernahme
- Editionen:
  - keine kritische Edition vorhanden
  - am Ende des 19. Jh.s eine unvollständige Faksimile-Edition von Ms 210 der Moskauer Synodalbibliothek, im Jahre 1477 im nordrussischen Pskov geschrieben (heute: Staatliches Historisches Museum zu Moskau, Synodal-Sammlung, Nr. 210)[15]
  - Teil-Edition der Mose-Geschichte nach der so genannten Rumjancev-Paleja von 1494 (heute: Ms 453, Sammlung des Rumjancev-Museums an der Russischen Staatsbibliothek zu Moskau) mit Varianten nach der separaten Mose-Vita (s. unten) nach Ms Pogodin 947 (heute gleiche Signatur in der Russischen Nationalbibliothek zu St. Petersburg, Ende 15. Jh.)[16]
  - diplomatische Teil-Edition der Mose-Geschichte nach der heute verschollenen Paleja von Krechiv (15./16. Jh.)[17]
  - diplomatische Edition des Anfangs der Mose-Geschichte nach Ms Barsov 619 aus dem Staatlichen Historischen Museum zu Moskau (um 1400)[18]

---

15   P.P. Novickij (Hg.), *Tolkovaja Paleja 1477 goda* Vyp. 1 (Izdanija Obščestva ljubitelej drevnej pis'mennosti, 93.1), St-Peterburg, 1892 (Mose-Geschichte dort: f 189ᵛ–251ᵛ).

16   A.N. Pypin (Hg.), *Ložnye i otrečennye knigi russkoj stariny* (Pamjatniki starinnoj russkoj literatury, izdavaemye grafom G. Kuševelym-Bezborodko, 3), Sanktpeterburg, 1862, S. 39–49.

17   I. Franko (Hg.), *Apokrify i legendy z ukraïns'kich rukopysiv*, Tom 1: *Apokrify starozavitni* (Pamjatky ukraïns'ko-rus'koï movy i literatury, 1 / Monumenta linguæ necnon litterarum Ukraino-Russicarum [Ruthenicarum] a collegia archæographico Societatis Scientiarum Ševčenkianæ edita, 1), L'viv, 1896, S. 225–254.

18   A.A. Alekseev, ‚Apokrify Tolkovoj Palei, perevedennye s evrejskich originalov', in *Trudy Otdela drevnerusskoj literatury* 58 (2007), S. 41–57, hier: S. 56–57.
    Evgenij G. Vodolazkin identifizierte dieses Ms 619 der Sammlung Barsov als Rohfassung der PP, vgl. E.G. Vodolazkin (Übersetzung S. Fahl), ‚Zu einer Rohfassung der Polnaja Chronografičeskaja Paleja und zum Verhältnis zwischen den verschiedenen Paleja-Redaktionen', in diTommaso, Böttrich, *Old Testament Apocrypha*, S. 453–470; Auszüge aus

- diplomatische Teil-Edition der Mose-Geschichte in vereinfachter ksl. Orthographie nach demselben Ms Barsov 619 sowie Übersetzung ins gegenwärtige Russische mit Kommentar[19]

C. *Kratkaja Chronografičeskaja Paleja* = *Kurze Chronographische Paleja* (im Folgenden: KP)
  - entstanden im ersten Drittel des 15. Jh., handschriftliche Überlieferung seit den 40er Jahren des 15. Jh., 6 Handschriften aus dem 15. und 16. Jh. bekannt
  - biblisch-exegetischer Teil gestrafft und um eine umfangreiche chronographische Fortsetzung ergänzt, die recht genau mit derjenigen in der *Polnaja Chronografičeskaja Paleja* übereinstimmt (Zeit: von der Schöpfung bis zu Kaiser Romanos Lakapenos)
  - chronographische Erweiterungen sowie eigene Berechnungen zur absoluten und relativen Chronologie kommen hinzu
  - typologische Kommentare noch stärker reduziert als in der *Polnaja Chronografičeskaja Paleja*, Dialogstruktur eliminiert
  - Kompilator benutzt *Tolkovaja Paleja* und weitere Quellen ausschließlich in wörtlicher Übernahme, die Quellen weichen gelegentlich von denen der *Polnaja Chronografičeskaja Paleja* ab oder werden in anderen Ausschnitten übernommen
  - kritische editio princeps[20] und verbesserte kritische Edition mit deutscher Übersetzung und Kommentar[21]

---

19 dieser Handschrift edierten A. Kulik und S. Minov (nichts zur Mose-Geschichte): A. Kulik und S. Minov, *Biblical Pseudepigrapha in Slavonic Tradition*, Oxford, 2016.

19 M.V. Roždestvenskaja (Podgotovka teksta, perevod i kommentarii), ‚Žitie proroka Moiseja', in *Biblioteka literatury Drevnej Rusi*, Tom 3: *XI–XII veka*, Sankt-Peterburg, 1999, S. 120–149 (Text und russ. Übersetzung), S. 376–378 (Kommentar).

20 E.G. Vodolazkin und (ab Vyp. 5) T.R. Rudi, ‚Kratkaja Chronografičeskaja Paleja (tekst)', Vyp. 1, in *Trudy Otdela drevnerusskoj literatury* 57 (2006), S. 891–915; Vyp. 2, in *Trudy Otdela drevnerusskoj literatury* 58 (2007), S. 534–556; Vyp. 3, in *Trudy Otdela drevnerusskoj literatury* 61 (2010), S. 345–374; Vyp. 4, in *Trudy Otdela drevnerusskoj literatury* 63 (2014), S. 238–261; Vyp. 5, in *Trudy Otdela drevnerusskoj literatury* 65 (2017), S. 181–196; Vyp. 6, in *Trudy Otdela drevnerusskoj literatury* 66 (2019), S. 60–75; Vyp. 7 in *Trudy Otdela drevnerusskoj literatury* 67 [im Druck]. Die Mose-Geschichte umfasst hier den Vyp. 2.

21 C. Böttrich und E.G. Vodolazkin (Hgg.), *Die Kurze Chronographische Paleja*, Bd. 1: S. Fahl und D. Fahl unter Mitarbeit von E. Vodolazkin und R. Rudi, *Die Kurze Chronographische Paleja. Kritische Edition mit deutscher Übersetzung*, Bd. 2: D. Fahl, S. Fahl und C. Böttrich unter Mitarbeit von M. Šibaev und I. Christov, *Die Kurze Chronographische Paleja. Einführung, Kommentar, Indices*, Gütersloh, 2019; Mose-Geschichte dort: Kap. 9–11 in Bd. 1, S. 94–175, sowie die auf diese Kapitel bezogenen Kommentare in Bd. 2, S. 184–230.

QUELLEN DER NICHTBIBLISCHEN MOSE-ÜBERLIEFERUNG 323

In Sammelbänden kursierte darüber hinaus eine selbständige *Vita des Mose*, die große Übereinstimmungen mit der Mose-Erzählung in der PP aufweist und möglicherweise als deren Hauptquelle gedient hat (so Vasilij Michajlovič Istrin im Jahre 1906[22], nicht näher untersucht[23]), was nach den Ergebnissen von Evgenij Germanovič Vodolazkin zur Entstehungsgeschichte der PP[24] sogar recht nahe liegt.

In die *Großen Lesemenäen* des Metropoliten Makarij wurde die *Mose-Vita* im 16. Jh. unter dem 4. September gleich zweimal übernommen: Die früheste Handschrift der *Lesemenäen*, die für die Novgoroder Sophien-Kathedrale angefertigte, enthält die erwähnte selbständige *Vita des Mose*[25], die spätere Zaren-Handschrift die Redaktion aus der PP[26]. Nach den Ausgaben dieser beiden Menäen-Fassungen sowie der PP-Fassung nach Pypins Edition aus dem Jahr 1862[27] gestaltete Gottlieb Nathanael Bonwetsch 1908 seine deutsche Übersetzung einer slavischen „Mosessage", die im Wesentlichen dem Text der PP folgt.[28]

Die ksl. chronographische Literatur bietet über die *Paleja*-Überlieferungen hinaus noch weitere wichtige Quellentexte zum Leben des Mose, die teilweise erst kürzlich in Neueditionen und neuen Untersuchungen erschlossen wurden:

Die ausführlichste, mit Kirchenväterkommentaren versehene Erzählung findet sich hier in der ksl. Übersetzung der *Hamartolos-Chronik*.[29]

---

22 V.M. Istrin, ‚Redakcii Tolkovoj Palei', II., in *Izvestija Otdelenija russkogo jazyka i slovesnosti Imperatorskoj Akademii nauk*, 11.1 (1906), S. 1–43, hier: S. 14–27.

23 Vgl. N.V. Ponyrko, ‚Apokrify o Moisee', in D.S. Lichačev et al. (Hgg.), *Slovar' knižnikov i knižnosti Drevnej Rusi*, Vyp. 1: *XI–pervaja polovina XIV v.*, Leningrad, 1987, S. 63–67, hier: S. 65.66.

24 Vodolazkin, ‚Rohfassung'; id., ‚Kak sozdavalas', 1; id., ‚Kak sozdavalas' Polnaja Chronografičeskaja Paleja', 2, in *Trudy Otdela drevnerusskoj literatury* 62 (2014), S. 175–200.

25 Edition: N.S. Tichonravov (Hg.), *Pamjatniki otrečennoj russkoj literatury*, Tom 1, Moskva, 1863, S. 233–253.

26 Edition: *Velikie minei četii, sobrannye Vserossijskim mitropolitom Makariem. Sentjabr', dni 1–13*, Izd. Archeografičeskoj komissii, Sanktpeterburg, 1868, Sp. 164–253. Zu den beiden Fassungen in den Lesemenäen vgl. Ponyrko, ‚Apokrify o Moisee', S. 66.

27 S. Anm. 16; Pypins Ausgabe enthält einen Auszug aus der PP-Redaktion mit Varianten nach der selbständigen *Mose-Vita*.

28 G.N. Bonwetsch, ‚Die Mosessage in der slavischen kirchlichen Litteratur', in *Nachrichten von der Königlichen Gesellschaft der Wissenschaften zu Göttingen, Philologisch-historische Klasse, aus dem Jahre 1908*, Berlin, 1908, S. 581–607.

29 Kritische Edition: V.M. Istrin (Hg.), *Die Chronik des Georgios Hamartolos in altslavischer Übersetzung*, Bd. 1: Nachdruck von Bd. 1 (1920) der Ausgabe von V.M. Istrin mit einer Einleitung und bibliographischen Hinweisen von F. Scholz, Bd. 2: Nachdruck der Bd.e 2 und 3 (1922/30) der Ausgabe von V.M. Istrin mit einer Einleitung und bibliographischen Hinweisen von F. Scholz (Slavische Propyläen, Texte in Neu- und Nachdrucken, 135.1–2), München, 1972; Mose-Geschichte dort: Bd. 1, S. 93–111. Einen Überblick über die aktuell

Auch der so genannte *slavische Synkellos* – eine kompilierte Weltchronik, für welche Georgios Synkellos nur eine von verschiedenen Quellen bildete –, erzählt Biblisches und Außerbiblisches vom Leben des Mose.[30]

Aber nicht allein diese sehr frühen Übersetzungen griechischer Chronik-texte enthalten Abschnitte zum Leben des Mose, sondern auch die älteste russische Chronik *Povest' vremennych let*[31] und die von ihr abhängigen Lokal-chroniken ebenso wie die späteren slavischen Weltchronik-Kompilationen, die in der slavischen Forschungsliteratur unter dem Namen *Chronografy (Chrono-graphen)* bekannt sind. Diese Kompilationen nehmen neben Chronik-Material auch Fragmente aus anderen Genres, etwa aus der Hagiographie, aus Homilien oder Reiseberichten, auch aus apokryphen Quellen, auf und werden zu enzy-klopädischen Sammelwerken ausgebaut. Ihre Quellen sind nicht vollständig ermittelt. Zu den *Chronographen* gehört der *Letopisec Ellinskij i Rimskij* in bei-den bekannten Redaktionen.[32] Ein weiterer *Chronograph*, der nach der darin enthaltenen Übersetzung von Josephus, *Bellum Judaicum*, *Jüdischer Chrono-graf* genannt wird, ist in zwei Handschriften bekannt, dem *Vilenskij* (16. Jh.,

---

bekannten Handschriften gibt T.V. Anisimova, *Chronika Georgija Amartola v drevneruss-kich spiskach XIV–XVII vv.*, Moskva, 2009.

30 Kommentierte kritische Edition: A.-M. Totomanova, *Slavjanskata versija na Chronikata na Georgi Sinkel* (Izdanie i komentar), Sofija, 2007; Mose-Geschichte dort auf S. 44–54, Kom-mentar dazu S. 415–422.

31 Kritische Edition: L. Müller (Hg.), *Handbuch zur Nestorchronik*, Bd. 1: *Die Nestorchronik. Der altrussische Text der Nestorchronik in der Redaktion des Abtes Sil'vestr aus dem Jahre 1116 und ihrer Fortsetzung bis zum Jahre 1305 in der Handschrift des Mönches Lavrentij aus dem Jahre 1377 sowie die Fortsetzung der Suzdaler Chronik bis zum Jahr 1419 nach der Akade-miehandschrift* (Forum slavicum, 48), München, 1977 (= Nachdruck der zweiten Auflage des ersten Bandes der „Vollständigen Sammlung russischer Chroniken" / Polnoe sobra-nie russkich letopisej, Leningrad 1926–1928); Bd. 2: L. Scheffler, *Textkritischer Apparat zur Nestorchronik* mit einem Vorwort von L. Müller (Forum slavicum, 49), München 1977; Bd. 3: B. Gröber und L. Müller, *Vollständiges Wörterverzeichnis zur Nestorchronik* (Forum sla-vicum, 50), München 1986 (erschienen in vier Lieferungen: 1977, 1979, 1984, 1986); Bd. 4: *Die Nestorchronik. Die altrussische Chronik, zugeschrieben dem Mönch des Kiever Höhlen-klosters Nestor, in der Redaktion des Abtes Sil'vestr aus dem Jahre 1116, rekonstruiert nach den Handschriften Lavrent'evskaja, Radzivilovskaja, Akademičeskaja, Troickaja, Ipat'evskaja und Chlebnikovskaja und ins Deutsche übersetzt von L. Müller* (Forum slavicum, 56), München, 2001; Mose-Geschichte dort: Bd. 1, Sp. 93–96, Apparat dazu: Bd. 2, S. 277–286, deutsche Übersetzung dazu: Bd. 4, S. 113–117, Satz 183–232.

32 Kritische Edition der zweiten Redaktion aus dem 15. Jh.: O.V. Tvorogov (Hg.), *Letopisec Ellinskij i Rimskij*, Tom 1: *Tekst* (Osnovnoj spisok podgotovlen O.V. Tvorogovym i S.A. Davy-dovoj, Vstupitel'naja stat'ja, archeografičeskij obzor i kritičeskij apparat izdanija podgo-tovleny O.V. Tvorogovym), Sankt-Peterburg, 1999; Tom 2: O.V. Tvorogov, *Kommentarij i issledovanie*, Sankt-Peterburg, 2001; Mose-Geschichte darin: Tom 1, S. 13–14, Kommentar dazu: Tom 2, S. 10–11. Eine kritische Edition der ersten Redaktion plant Dimităr Peev.

QUELLEN DER NICHTBIBLISCHEN MOSE-ÜBERLIEFERUNG

nicht vollständig ediert) und dem *Archivskij Chronograf* (15. Jh., kürzlich elektronisch ediert durch das Team von Anna-Marija Totomanova an der Universität Sofia[33]). Dieser *Jüdische Chronograf* ist auch durch seine umfangreichen Auszüge aus der *Chronik des Johannes Malalas* bedeutsam. In die Erzählung über das Leben des Mose sind in diesem *Chronograf* zudem lange Zitate aus Num und Dtn eingebettet. Entstehungszeit und -ort sind umstritten: altbulgarisch, 10./11. Jh. oder altrussisch, 13. Jh.[34]

Weitere chronographische Quellen sind einerseits editorisch weniger gut aufbereitet und bieten andererseits kaum zusätzliches Material, so dass die genannten für eine Übersicht über die nichtbiblischen slavischen Mose-Überlieferungen in dieser Textgattung ausreichen mögen.

Kleinere Texteinheiten zum Leben des Mose sind außerdem in Synaxarien und Azbukovniki[35] überliefert.[36]

Ein *Reisebericht vom Heiligen Land*, den die Handschriften-Tradition einem Kaufmann (oder Beamten?) namens Trifon Korobejnikov zuschreibt, enthält eine besondere Erzählung über Mose und den Durchzug durchs Rote Meer[37], die möglicherweise lokale mündliche Überlieferungen des 16. Jh. aufgenom-

---

33   Mose-Geschichte: http://histdict.uni-sofia.bg/chronograph/cshow/doc_17 und http://hist
      dict.uni-sofia.bg/chronograph/cshow/doc_18, f 89c–169a, Zugriff: 18. 06. 2018.

34   Für die spätere Entstehungszeit sprechen v. a. Zitate aus Niketas von Herakleia (11./12. Jh.).
      Literatur zum Thema sowie weitere gute Gründe für eine Datierung ins 13. Jh. vgl. T. Vilkul,
      ,Perevodčik "Istorii Iudejskoj vojny" Iosifa Flavija – čitatel' "Povesti vremennych let"?', in
      A.A. Turilov et al. (Hgg.), *„Vertograd mnogocvetnyj". Sbornik k 80-letiju B.N. Flori*, Moskva,
      2018, S. 133–143.

35   *Azbukovnik* heißt seit dem 16. Jh. eine alphabetisch (Alphabet = azbuka) geordnete Samm-
      lung von Erklärungen zu Wörtern und Kürzeln, meist aus biblischen Texten. Vom 16. bis
      zum 18. Jh. wurden diese lexikographischen Sammlungen zu kleinen Ezyklopädien erwei-
      tert. Man kennt heute etwa 200 Handschriften, die nicht nur verschiedene Redaktionen,
      sondern drei verschiedene „Wörterbücher" dieser Art repräsentieren.

36   Vgl. die Liste bei A.I. Jacimirskij, *Bibliografičeskij obzor apokrifov v južnoslavjanskoj i russkoj
      pis'mennosti (spiski pamjatnikov)*, Vyp. 1: *Apokrify vetchozavetnye*, Petrograd, 1921, S. 165–
      169. Die Kurzvita des Mose unter dem 4. September in der ältesten kirchenslavischen
      Synaxarien-Redaktion ist zugänglich in einer neuen kritischen Edition bei V.B. Krys'ko
      (Hg.), *Slavjano-russkij Prolog po drevnejšim spiskam. Sinaksar' (žitijnaja čast' Prologa krat-
      koj redakcii) za sentjabr'–fevral'*, Tom 1: L.V. Prokopenko, V. Željazkova, V.B. Krys'ko, O.P.
      Ševčuk, I.M. Ladyženskij (Hgg.), *Tekst i kommentarii*, Moskva, 2010, S. 30–31; auch in der
      diplomatischen Edition des so genannten Prolog von Lesnovo bei R. Pavlova und V. Žel-
      jazkova (Hgg.), *Stanislavov (Lesnovskij) Prolog ot 1330 godina* (R. Pavlova: Uvod i naučno
      razčitane na teksta, V. Željazkova: Naučno razčitane na teksta, Kalendar), Veliko Tărnovo,
      1999, S. 24–25. Bei L.S. Kovtun, *Azbukovniki XVI–XVII vv. Staršaja raznovidnost'*, Leningrad,
      1989, sind die ältesten Azbukovniki ediert.

37   Edition: Pypin, *Ložnye i otrečennye knigi*, S. 49–50, nach einer Handschrift von 1602.

men hat: Im Roten Meer schwimmen Fische mit Menschenköpfen; das sind die untergegangenen Truppen des Pharao.[38]

Wie weit die Figur des Mose auch in slavische mündliche Überlieferungen vorgedrungen ist, zeigt das Beispiel eines bulgarischen Märchens zum Thema Erlösung durch Almosen, in welchem Mose die Hauptrolle spielt (aufgezeichnet in der zweiten Hälfte des 19. Jh. in Prilep, Mazedonien).[39] Eine systematische Sammlung slavischer Sagen, Märchen oder Lieder, in denen Mose vorkommt, gibt es nicht.

In den letzten Jahren haben die Forschungen und Texteditionen rund um die ksl. apokryphe und pseudepigraphische Literatur einen enormen Aufschwung genommen.[40] Speziell den ksl. Überlieferungen zum Leben des Mose gewidmete Studien sind jedoch nach wie vor selten. Von der dünnen Forschungslage zeugt etwa, dass in Julian Petkovs Buch von 2016 (immerhin 495 Seiten stark) gerade einmal eine halbe Seite diesem Thema gewidmet ist[41] und es bei Alexander Kulik und Sergey Minov in *Biblical Pseudepigrapha* aus demselben Jahr gänzlich fehlt.

Die wenigen Spezialarbeiten, die ausschließlich slavischen Überlieferungen zu Mose gewidmet sind, schließen v. a. an eine Beobachtung von Ivan Jakovlevič Porfir'ev aus den 70er Jahren des 19. Jh.s an: Er hatte festgestellt, dass die slavische *Vita des Mose*, die ihm aus den Novgoroder *Lesemenäen* des Metropoliten Makarij und aus der PP bekannt war, viele Züge mit jüdischen Mose-Überlieferungen, v. a. mit dem so genannten *Sefer ha-Jaschar* (*Buch des Aufrech-*

---

38   Vgl. K.-D. Seemann, *Die altrussische Wallfahrtsliteratur. Theorie und Geschichte eines literarischen Genres* (Theorie und Geschichte der Literatur und der schönen Künste, Texte und Abhandlungen, 24), München, 1976, S. 288–297; Ponyrko, ,Apokrify o Moisee', S. 66; O.A. Belobrova, ,Korobejnikov Trifon', in D.S. Lichačev et al. (Hgg.), *Slovar' knižnikov i knižnosti Drevnej Rusi*, Vyp. 2: *Vtoraja polovina XIV–XVI v.*, Čast' 1, Leningrad, 1988, S. 490–491.

39   Vgl. den Text mit russischer Übersetzung und Anmerkungen bei F. Badalanova Geller, *Kniga suščaja v ustach. Fol'klornaja Biblija bessarabskich i tavričeskich bolgar*, Moskva, 2017, S. 466–468.

40   Vgl. etwa die Monographien Skowronek, *Palæa Historica*; Kulik, Minov, *Biblical Pseudepigrapha*; J. Petkov, *Altslavische Eschatologie. Texte und Studien zur apokalyptischen Literatur in kirchenslavischer Überlieferung* (Texte und Arbeiten zum neutestamentlichen Zeitalter, 59), Tübingen, 2016; Fahl, Böttrich, Fahl, *Leiter Jakobs* – auf der Grundlage des kritischen ksl. Textes: S. Fal', D. Fal', ,"Lestvica Iakova" (kritičeskij tekst)', in *Trudy Otdela drevnerusskoj literatury* 65 (2017), S. 197–242 und 808–810; A. Miltenova, *South Slavonic Apocryphal Collections*, Sofia 2018; Böttrich, Vodolazkin, *Die Kurze Chronographische Paleja*; Böttrich, Fahl, Fahl, *Historienbibel*.

41   Vgl. Petkov, *Eschatologie*, S. 63.

QUELLEN DER NICHTBIBLISCHEN MOSE-ÜBERLIEFERUNG 327

ten), gemeinsam hat.[42] Diesen kannte er in einer lateinischen Übersetzung des 17. Jh.s[43] und einer zeitgenössischen französischen[44].

Die Dissertation von Melissa Lee Farrall von 1981 war gänzlich der Untersuchung hebräischer Parallelen zur ksl. *Vita des Mose* gewidmet.[45] Sie ermittelte (fast ausschließlich anhand der ihr zugänglichen Druckausgaben aus dem 19. Jh.) fünf Redaktionen des slavischen Textes und kam zu dem Schluss, dass es sich um eine Übersetzung nach den so genannten *Chroniken des Jerachmeel*[46] direkt aus dem Hebräischen handele, die noch in vormongolischer Zeit in der Kiever Rus' angefertigt worden sei. Mindestens was die Mose-Überlieferungen in der KP betrifft, konnten wir bei unseren Untersuchungen feststellen, dass Farralls Arbeit ohne ausreichende Kenntnis der ksl. Texte entstand und oftmals selbst hinter den Erkenntnissen russischer Gelehrter des späten 19. / frühen 20. Jh.s zurückbleibt. Dennoch bedürfen die Ergebnisse von Farrall noch einer weiteren eingehenden Überprüfung, v.a. in Bezug auf die von ihr ermittelten einzelnen Parallelstellen zwischen ksl. und hebräischem Text.

Die *Chroniken des Jerachmeel*, gegründet auf eine Kompilation des süditalienischen Chronographen Jerachmeel ben Salomon (12. Jh.) und überliefert in der wohl erheblichen Erweiterung des Eleazar ben Ascher ha-Levi als *Sefer ha-Zichronot* (*Buch der Erinnerungen*, beendet 1325 im Rheinland)[47], enthalten u. a. den *Sefer Josippon* (10. Jh.)[48] sowie zahlreiche Überlieferungen, die sich auch

---

42 I.Ja. Porfir'ev, *Istorija russkoj slovesnosti*, Čast' 1: *Drevnij period. Ustnaja narodnaja i knižnaja slovesnost' do Petra Velikogo*, Kazan', 1879, S. 245–248. Vgl. auch id., *Apokrifičeskie skazanija o vetchozavetnych licach i sobytijach po rukopisjam Soloveckoj biblioteki* (Sbornik Otdelenija russkogo jazyka i slovesnosti Imperatorskoj Akademii Nauk, 17.1), Sanktpeterburg, 1877, Reprint: Moskva, 2005, S. 67–68.

43 Von Porfir'ev benutzte Ausgabe: G. Gaulmin (Hg.), ‚De vita et morte Mosis libri tres', in A.F. Gfrörer, *Prophetæ veteres pseudepigraphi partim ex abyssinico vel hebraico sermonibus latine versi*, Stuttgart, 1840, S. 303–362.

44 P.L.B. Drach, ‚Le livre Yaschar traduit pour la première fois du texte hébreu', in J.P. Migne, *Dictionnaire des Apocryphes*, T. 2, Paris, 1858, S. 1070–1310.

45 M.L. Farrall, *A Jewish Translator in Kievan Rus': A Critical Edition and Study of the Earliest Redaction of the Slavonic "Life of Moses"* (Ph.D.-Diss. Brown University), Providence, 1981.

46 Der Titel stammt von dem ersten Herausgeber: M. Gaster, *The Chronicles of Jerahmeel or The Hebrew Bible Historiale*, London, ²1899, Reprint: New York, 1971.

47 Vgl. E. Yassif, *The Book of Memory, that is the Chronicles of Jerahme'el*, Tel Aviv, 2001 (Hebräisch).

48 Textedition: D. Flusser, *The Josippon* (*Josephus Gorionides*), Edited with an Introduction, Commentary and Notes, vol. 1, Jerusalem, 1978; vol. 2, Jerusalem, 1980; auf diese Edition aufbauend, mit deutschem Paralleltext: D. Börner-Klein und B. Zuber, *Josippon. Jüdische Geschichte vom Anfang der Welt bis zum Ende des ersten Aufstands gegen Rom*, Hebräisch-Deutsche Textausgabe, Wiesbaden, 2010; Untersuchung, auch zu anderssprachigen Über-

im *Sefer ha-Jaschar* (wohl 12. Jh.)[49] finden. Zu diesen Texten bzw. Textsammlungen fand schon Émile Turdeanu, auf dessen Arbeit M.L. Farrall aufbaute, Beziehungen in ksl. PP- und TP-Texten über das Leben des Mose.[50] Einzelne Motive aus diesen Erzählungen über Mose kennzeichnete Moshe Taube, die Untersuchungen von Farrall präzisierend und weiterführend, als Parallelen zu den *Chroniken des Jerachmeel*.[51] Weitere Hinweise auf eine oder verschiedene Übersetzungen aus dem Hebräischen direkt ins Ksl., welche in die slavische Mose-Überlieferung einflossen, gaben auch (etwa anhand von Lehnwörtern), Nikita Aleksandrovič Meščerskij[52] und an dessen Untersuchungen anknüpfend Anatolij Alekseevič Alekseev[53]. Was die Zeit der Übersetzung(en) betrifft, so ist sie möglicherweise deutlich später als die noch von Farrall und Meščerskij angenommene Kiever Rus' anzusetzen; vermutet wurde das 15. Jh.[54] – angesichts der umfangreichen Übernahmen in die PP (bezeugt in Ms Barsov 619 um 1400) wiederum etwas zu spät.

---

        lieferungen (nicht zum Ksl.): S. Dönitz, *Überlieferung und Rezeption des Sefer Yosippon* (Texts and Studies in Medieval and Early Modern Judaism, 29), Tübingen, 2013.

49   Textedition: J. Genot-Bismuth, *Sefer Hayasar: Reproduction de l'edition de Venise (1625)* (Université de la Sorbonne Nouvelle, Centre de Recherches sur la Culture Rabbinique), Paris, 1984.

50   É. Turdeanu, ‚La "Chronique de Moïse" en Russe', in *Revue des études slaves* 46 (1967), S. 35–64. Er vermutete einen Einfluss der so genannten Judaisierenden im 15. Jh. auf die Entwicklung und/oder Übersetzung der ksl. Mose-Vita, was aufgrund der deutlich vor den „Judaisierenden" einsetztenden Hss-Überlieferung (um 1400) inzwischen ausgeschlossen werden kann. Dennoch bleibt späterer redaktioneller Einfluss dieser Gruppe zu prüfen. Wie aktiv die nordrussischen Gelehrten, die als „Judaisierende" zu Häretikern gestempelt wurden, etwa den altrussischen Pentateuch anhand jüdischer (oft indirekt aus dem hebräischen Text über Turksprachen vermittelter) Quellen redigierten, wies kürzlich Aleksandr I. Griščenko nach (vgl. A.I. Griščenko, *Pravlenoe slavjano-russkoe Pjatiknižie XV veka. Predvaritel'nye itogi lingvotekstologičeskogo izučenija*, Moskva, 2018).

51   M. Taube, ‚The Slavic Life of Moses and Its Hebrew Sources', in W. Moskovich et al. (Hgg.), *Jews and Slavs*, 1, Jerusalem–St Petersburg, 1993, S. 84–119.

52   N.A. Meščerskij, ‚O sintaksise drevnich slavjanorusskich perevodnych proizvedenij', in id., *Izbrannye stat'i*, Sankt-Peterburg 1995, S. 317–337 (= Nachdruck eines Artikels von 1962), hier S. 331.

53   A.A. Alekseev, ‚Russko-evrejskie literaturnye svjazi do 15 veka', in W. Moskovich et al. (Hgg.), *Jews and Slavs*, 1, Jerusalem–St Petersburg, 1993, S. 44–75; A.A. Alexeev (= id.), ‚Apocrypha Translated from Hebrew within the East Slavic Explanatory Palæa', in W. Moskovich (Hg.), *Jews and Slavs*, 9 (FS Professor Jacob Allerhand: *Judæo-Slavica et Judæo-Germanica*), Jerusalem–Vienna, 2001, S. 147–154; id., ‚Apokrify Tolkovoj Palei, perevedennye s evrejskich originalov', in *Trudy Otdela drevnerusskoj literatury* 58 (2007), S. 41–57.

54   So im Anschluss an Turdeanu, ‚Chronique de Moïse', S. 53–58, etwa H.G. Lunt und M. Taube, ‚Early East Slavic Translations from Hebrew?', in *Russian Linguistics* 12 (1988), S. 147–187, hier: S. 157.

QUELLEN DER NICHTBIBLISCHEN MOSE-ÜBERLIEFERUNG

Ohne Bezüge zum Ksl. wurde die Figur des Mose in außerbiblischen jüdischen Traditionen in jüngster Zeit mehrfach betrachtet,[55] ein systematischer Vergleich der ksl. mit der hebräischen und aramäischen nichtbiblischen Mose-Überlieferung fehlt jedoch bislang, insbesondere eine vergleichende Untersuchung zur rabbinischen Literatur.

Während sich für direkte Übersetzungen aus dem Hebräischen vor allem Anhaltspunkte aus der späteren Phase der Überlieferung fanden, haben griechische Quellen die ksl. Texte zum Leben des Mose nachweislich schon früh stark geprägt. Eine direkte Übersetzung der gesamten *Vita des Mose* aus dem Griech. vermuteten u. a. Aleksej Ivanovič Sobolevskij[56] und Michail Nestorovič Speranskij[57]. (Auch sie gingen davon aus, dass der Text als Ganzer in der vormongolischen Rus' übersetzt wurde.) Seitdem sind Zitate aus *Hamartolos-* und *Malalas-Chronik*, aus der *Chronik des Georgios Kedrenos*, indirekte Überlie-

---

55   Vgl. M. Krupp, *Moses Himmel-, Höllen- und Paradiesfahrt. Midrasch Gedulat Mosche oder Ke-Tapuach be-Atze ha-Jaar* (deutsch-hebräisch), Jerusalem, 2012; zur Einordnung dieses Textes *Gedulat Mosche / Die Größe des Mose* über die Höllen- und Himmelsreise des Mose in eine ganze Gruppe ähnlicher jüdischer Visionserzählungen vgl. H. Spurling, 'Hebrew Visions of Hell and Paradise. A new translation and introduction', in R. Bauckham, J.R. Davila und A. Panayotov (Hgg.), *Old Testament Pseudepigrapha. More Noncanonical Scriptures* vol. 1, Grand Rapids (Michigan)–Cambridge (U.K.), 2013, S. 699–713 (Einleitung), S. 714–753 (englische Übersetzungen); zum gleichen Text in mündlicher Überlieferung aus dem Kaukasus: C. Böttrich, 'Die Himmelsreise des Mose in einer jüdischen Legende aus dem Kaukasus', in *Journal for the Study of Judaism* 23 (1992), S. 173–196. Zu weiteren jüdischen Mose-Traditionen, vgl. S. Paganini, 'Mose im Judentum des Zweiten Tempels. Rezeption, Fortschreibung und Aktualisierung einer alttestamentlichen Gestalt', in *Protokolle zur Bibel* 22.2 (2013), S. 98–112; C. Meretz, 'Späte Midraschim zu Mose. Eine Analyse rabbinischer Exegese des Midrasch Petirat Mosche', Teil 1, in *Freiburger Rundbrief* 23.3 (2016), S. 195–210; G. Stemberger, *Mose in der rabbinischen Tradition*, Freiburg i. Br., 2016; J. Dochhorn, 'Der Tod des Mose in Assumptio Mosis', in E. Eynikel (Hg.), *Mosebilder. Gedanken zur Rezeption einer literarischen Figur im Frühjudentum, frühen Christentum und der römisch-hellenistischen Literatur* (WUNT, 390), Tübingen, 2017, S. 167–185. Die kritische Edition und Untersuchung des *Asfar Aschatir* (10. bis 12. Jh.) durch Christophe Bonnard stellt zusätzliches Vergleichsmaterial aus der späten aramäischen Tradition zur Verfügung: C. Bonnard, *Asfār Asāṭīr (Asfar Asâtîr), the "Book of Legends", an Aramaic rewriting of the Samaritan Pentateuch: presentation, critical edition, translation with philological commentary, interpretative commentary* (Diss. theol.), Strasbourg, 2015.

56   A.I. Sobolevskij, 'Osobennosti russkich perevodov do-mongol'skogo perioda', in *Trudy devjatogo Archeologičeskogo S"ezda v Vil'ne 1893*, II, Moskva, 1897, S. 53–61, insbes. S. 58; id., 'Materialy i issledovanija v oblasti slavjanskoj filologii i archeologii', in *Sbornik Otdelenija russkogo jazyka i slovesnosti Imperatorskoj Akademii Nauk* 88.3 (1910), S. I–IV, 1–286, hier: S. 174.

57   M.N. Speranskij, 'Russkie pamjatniki pis'mennosti v jugoslavjanskich literaturach XIV–XV vv.', in id., *Iz istorii russko-slavjanskich literaturnych svjazej. Sbornik statej*, Moskva, 1960, S. 55–103 (Artikel aus dem Jahr 1938), hier: S. 76–77.

ferungen aus den *Antiquitates* des Josephus und aus dem *Jubiläenbuch* sowie aus den *Quæstiones* zum Pentateuch des Theodoret von Kyrrhos nachgewiesen worden.[58]

Das Zusammenlaufen von Überlieferungen aus jüdischen, hellenistisch-heidnischen und christlichen, aus griechischen und hebräischen Mose-Traditionen rückte nach der Jahrtausendwende verstärkt in den Blickpunkt der Forschung.[59] Ksl. Traditionen haben dabei freilich bislang keine Rolle gespielt, da die Voraussetzungen (wissenschaftlich verwendbare Texteditionen, Übersetzungen in nichtslavische Sprachen, textkritische Untersuchungen) fehlen.

Für den dritten Paleja-Typus, die *Kratkaja Chronografičeskaja Paleja* (KP), hat uns unsere Arbeit der letzten Jahre an der kritischen Edition mit Übersetzung und Kommentar in die Lage versetzt, an die vorgenannten Studien anzuknüpfen und im Folgenden eine Übersicht über die dort benutzten nichtbiblischen Quellen vorzulegen. Dabei fanden sich, um ein Ergebnis vorwegzunehmen, in der KP keine eindeutigen Spuren direkter hebräischer Quellen.

Einige statistische Angaben sollen zunächst die Einordnung der Mose-Geschichte in den KP-Zusammenhang erleichtern:

Die KP umfasst die Zeit von der Schöpfung bis 944 n. Chr. (Tod des Romanos Lakapenos), nach eigener Chronologie des Kompilators sind das 6456 Jahre. Die Mose-Geschichte erstreckt sich nach der KP-Chronologie über 127 Jahre, d. h. über knappe 2 % der Zeit, von welcher berichtet wird.

Der Textumfang der KP beträgt in den bekannten Handschriften[60] ca. 225 folia im Format 4°, davon über Mose ca. 34 folia, d. h. 15,1 % der Textmenge.

---

58 Vgl. den Forschungsbericht bei S.I. Chazanova, ‚Apokrify o Moisee v drevnerusskoj literature‘, in *Rus', Rossija: Srednevekov'e i Novoe vremja*, Vyp. 3: *Tret'i čtenija pamjati akademika RAN L.V. Milova, Materialy k meždunarodnoj naučnoj konferencii, Moskva, 21–23 nojabrja 2013 g.*, Moskva 2013, S. 128–136, sowie die einen noch immer weitgehend aktuellen Überblick vermittelnde Bibliographie bei A.I. Orlov, ‚Selected Bibliography on the Transmission of the Jewish Pseudepigrapha in the Slavic Milieux. Life of Moses‘, in id., *Selected Studies in the Slavonic Pseudepigrapha* (Studia in Veteris Testamenti Pseudepigrapha, 23), Leiden–Boston, 2009, S. 264–267.

59 Vgl. z. B. J. Liermann, *The New Testament Moses. Christian Perceptions of Moses and Israel in the Setting of Jewish Religion* (WUNT, 173), Tübingen, 2004; R. Bloch, ‚Moses and Greek Myth in Hellenistic Judaism‘, in Th. Römer (Hg.), *La Construction de la Figure de Moïse. The Construction of the Figure of Moses* (Supplément N. 13 à Transeuphratène), Paris, 2007, S. 195–208; A. Graupner und M. Wolter (Hgg.), *Moses in Biblical and Extra-Biblical Tradition* (Beihefte zur Zeitschrift für die alttestamentliche Wissenschaft, 372), Berlin, 2007; T.E. Klutz, ‚The Eighth Book of Moses. A new translation and introduction‘, in R. Bauckham, J.R. Davila und A. Panayotov (Hgg.), *Old Testament Pseudepigrapha. More Noncanonical Scriptures* vol. 1, Grand Rapids (Michigan)–Cambridge (U.K.), 2013, S. 189–201 (Einleitung), S. 202–235 (englische Übersetzung).

60 Vgl. E.G. Vodolazkin, ‚Redakcii Kratkoj Chronografičeskoj Palei‘, in *Trudy Otdela drevne-*

QUELLEN DER NICHTBIBLISCHEN MOSE-ÜBERLIEFERUNG 331

Mose als messianische Figur nimmt also deutlich überproportionalen Raum ein, was freilich durch seine überproportionale Rolle im AT-Text schon vorgezeichnet ist. Die Sonderstellung des Mose zeigt sich, wie unten noch ausgeführt wird, auch darin, dass gerade im Zusammenhang mit seiner Person die typologische Exegese der TP an etlichen Stellen bewahrt blieb. (Sonst sind solche Passagen in der Regel nicht in die KP übernommen worden.) Hierbei spielt Mose in erster Linie die Rolle einer typologischen Figur, die auf Christus hinweisend gedeutet wird. Dies folgt einer alten Kirchenväter-Tradition[61], die in ksl. Übersetzungen bekannt und verbreitet war.[62] Doch hat sich nicht allein die christliche Exegese, sondern auch die rabbinische Tradition immer wieder auf Mose als Typos bezogen.[63]

Die Mose-Überlieferung der KP folgt im Wesentlichen der Struktur der TP, diese wiederum chronologisch dem Ablauf der Ereignisse im AT. Hauptquellen bleiben demnach die Bücher Exodus, Numeri und Deuteronomium.

---

russkoj literatury 56 (2004), S. 164–180; zur Handschriftenüberlieferung in D. Fahl, S. Fahl und C. Böttrich, *Kurze Chronographische Paleja*, Bd. 2, S. 85–104; vgl. auch die Handschriftenbeschreibungen bei M.A. Šibaev, ‚Kodikologičeskoe opisanie peterburgskich spiskov Kratkoj Chronografičeskoj Palei‘, in *Trudy Otdela drevnerusskoj literatury* 56 (2014), S. 146–163; id., ‚Beschreibung der Handschriften D und V‘, in Fahl, Fahl, Böttrich, *Kurze Chronographische Paleja*, Bd. 2, Anhang, S. 697–705.

61 Vgl. C.A. Hall, ‚Moses and the Church Fathers‘, in J. Beal (Hg.), *Illuminating Moses. A History of Reception from Exodus to the Renaissance* (Commentaria. Sacred Texts and Their Commentaries: Jewish, Christian and Islamic, 4), Leiden–Boston, 2013, S. 81–101.

62 Beispielsweise findet sich ein ganzes „Nest" typologischer Deutungen der Mose-Geschichte in den *Katechesen* des Kyrill von Jerusalem, deren ksl. Übersetzung kürzlich in einer mustergültigen Edition von Eckhard Weiher nach der ältesten ostslavischen Handschrift (11. Jh.) erschienen ist: E. Weiher unter Mitarbeit von N. Kindermann, A. Minčeva und E. Serebrjakova (Hgg.), *Die altbulgarische Übersetzung der Katechesen Kyrills von Jerusalem*, Mit einer detaillierten paläographischen Beschreibung der ältesten ostslavischen Abschrift (GIM Sin. 478) von E. Uchanova (Monumenta Linguæ Slavicæ Dialecti Veteris, Fontes et Dissertationes, 64), Freiburg i. Br., 2017. Zu Mose als Christus-Typos dort, siehe S. 330–331; vgl. die Stelle in der gleichen ksl. Übersetzung nach den Großen Lesemenäen des Metropoliten Makarij unter dem 18. März: E. Weiher, S.O. Šmidt und A.I. Škurko (Hgg.), *Die Großen Lesemenäen des Metropoliten Makarij, Uspenskij spisok, 12.–25. März* (Monumenta Linguæ Slavicæ Dialecti Veteris, Fontes et Dissertationes, 41), Freiburg i. Br., 1998, f 480b–d; griech. Text in PG 33, Sp. 796–790.

63 Vgl. z. B. die Übersicht über Mose als Präfiguration des Erlösers bei B. Ego, ‚Mose im Judentum‘, in C. Böttrich, B. Ego und F. Eißler, *Mose in Judentum, Christentum und Islam*, Göttingen, 2010, S. 11–66, hier: S. 58–59, oder die Arbeit über Mose als Präfiguration des Ezra: G. Stemberger, ‚Ezra as a New Moses in Rabbinic Tradition‘, in J.N. Bremmer, V. Hirschberger und T. Nicklas (Hgg.), *Figures of Ezra* (Studies on Early Christian Apocrypha, 13), Leuven, 2018, S. 1–12.

Die Mose-Geschichte in der KP wird in insgesamt 675 Sätzen erzählt. Der Großteil nimmt biblische Quellen auf, nämlich 500 Sätze, also etwa 74 %, wobei als biblische Quelle auch die indirekte Überlieferung, hier speziell über die TP, gerechnet wurde. Aus nichtbiblischen Quellen schöpfen 175 Sätze, d. h. etwa 26 %. Unter den nichtbiblischen Quellen ist freilich auch eine, die zwar mit Bezug auf die Zeit des Mose wiedergegeben wird, mit Mose selbst aber nichts zu tun hat: Epiphanios, *Über die Edelsteine auf der Brusttafel des Hohenpriesters* (*De Gemmis*). Ziehen wir die 57 Sätze aus dieser Quelle ab, so bleiben 118 Sätze über die Zeit des Mose aus nichtbiblischen Quellen, das sind ungefähr 17 %, also etwas mehr als ein Sechstel der Mose-Überlieferung in der KP. Mit anderen Worten: was wir hier als Hauptthema behandeln, ist im Kontext schon quantitativ als weniger bedeutend gekennzeichnet. Fast drei Viertel des Textes über Mose und seine Zeit beruhen auf dem Bibeltext.

Wenden wir uns nun den nichtbiblischen Quellen zu.

Ein Teil der nichtbiblischen Überlieferungen in der KP wurde bereits aus der TP übernommen, die generell im Bereich der Überlieferung bis Salomo die Hauptquelle der KP bildete. Dazu gehören in erster Linie die *Quæstiones* des Theodoret von Cyrus zu Exodus, Numeri und Deuteronomium (*Quæstiones in Octateuchum: in Exodum / Numeros / Deuteronomium*). Daraus stammen in der TP Erläuterungen zu Bibelstellen, die zuvor zitiert werden. Die meisten dieser Erläuterungen sind beim Kürzen des Textes für die KP entfallen. Erhalten blieben – in der jeweils kürzesten, gerade noch verständlichen Form – folgende Erläuterungen nach Theodoret, die dem Kompilator der KP offenbar als unentbehrlich galten:

- der brennende Dornbusch (Ex 3,1–6) als Präfiguration der Gottesmutter nach QuæstEx VI (KP 9. 3,19–20)[64]
- Mose mit ausgebreiteten Armen während des Kampfes gegen Amalek (Ex 17,11) als Präfiguration des gekreuzigten Christus nach QuæstEx XXIV (KP 10. 3,5)
- die Erklärung für die Sünde von Mose und Aaron am Haderwasser (Num 20,10–13) nach QuæstNum XXXVII (KP 11. 1,52–53)
- die Erklärung für das Sprechen von Bileams Esel (Num 22,28) nach QuæstNum XLI und XLIV 2,35–36 (KP 11. 2,9–10)

---

64 Zur Angabe von Stellen in der KP benutzen wir hier unser Gliederungssystem nach Kapitel, Abschnitt und Satz, wie wir es in der Edition in Fahl, Fahl, *Kratkaja Chronografičeskaja Paleja*, Bd. 1, und im Kommentar in Fahl, Fahl, Böttrich, *Kratkaja Chronografičeskaja Paleja*, Bd. 2, gebrauchen.

QUELLEN DER NICHTBIBLISCHEN MOSE-ÜBERLIEFERUNG

333

- die Deutung des „Sterns aus Jakob" in Bileams Segen über Israel (Num 24,17) auf Christus nach QuæstNum XLIV 1,17–19 (KP 11. 2,50)
- Moses eigene Erklärung dafür, dass er die Gesetzestafeln zerschlug (Dtn 9,16–17) nach QuæstEx LXVIII (KP 11. 5,3)
- die Erklärung für die Herkunft des Holzes, aus dem die Bundeslade gebaut wurde (Dtn 10,3) nach QuæstEx LXX (KP 11. 5,26)
- die Deutung von Moses Segen über den Stamm Juda auf die Geburt Christi (Dtn 33,7) ähnlich wie in QuæstDeut XLIV 2 (KP 11. 9,6)

Eine weitere Quelle der TP, aus der typologische Deutungen in den KP-Text übernommen wurden, ist die *Erzählung vom Kreuzesholz* des bulgarischen Priesters Jeremija.[65] Erzählt werden danach in der KP zwei Begegnungen von Mose mit einem Engel:

- Ein Engel bringt Mose das Holz, mit dem er das bittere Wasser von Mara versüßen soll (Ex 15,25), zeigt ihm, wie es zu gebrauchen ist, und deutet die drei Holzarten (nach Jes 60,13) auf die Dreieinigkeit. Der Engel sagt das Heranwachsen des Holzes zu einem Weltenbaum voraus. Mose deutet ihn auf das Kreuz Christi.[66] (KP 10. 1,7–16)

---

65 Die *Erzählung vom Kreuzesholz* des bulgarischen Priesters Jeremija gehört zum Kreis der Kreuzesholz-Legenden, wie sie mit Schwerpunkt auf unterschiedlichen Einzeltexten sowie auf den Verbindungen zur Adam-Vita untersucht wurden. Vgl. z.B. W. Meyer, ‚Die Geschichte des Kreuzesholzes vor Christus', in *Abhandlungen der Königlich Bayerischen Akademie der Wissenschaften, philosophisch-philologische Classe*, 16.2 (1882), S. 103–165; M.D. Kagan-Tarkovskaja (Podgotovka teksta, perevod i kommentarii), ‚Slovo o krestnom dreve', in *Biblioteka literatury Drevnej Rusi, Tom 3: XI–XII veka*, Sankt-Peterburg, 1999, S. 284–291 (Text), S. 402–406 (Kommentar); A. de Santos Otero, *Die handschriftliche Überlieferung der altslavischen Apokryphen*, Bd. 2 (Patristische Texte und Studien, 23), Berlin 1981, S. 129–149; Kulik, Minov, *Biblical Pseudepigrapha*, S. 104–168; Petkov, *Eschatologie*, S. 67–68; Miltenova, *Apocryphal Collections*, S. 149–171, und die dort angegebene Literatur. Datiert wird die Erzählung von G. Podskalsky, *Theologische Literatur des Mittelalters in Bulgarien und Serbien 865–1459*, München, 2000, S. 280, mit großer Vorsicht in das 10. Jh., ebenso von Petkov, *Eschatologie*, S. 67, und von Minov in seinem Beitrag zum aktuellen Symposium; von Kulik, Minov, *Biblical Pseudepigrapha*, S. 108, jedoch ohne nähere Begründung ins 13. Jh.

   Wie die KP übernimmt diesen Abschnitt auch die Mose-Vita der PP vollständig aus der TP (vgl. den entsprechenden PP-Abschnitt bei Roždestvenskaja, ‚Žitie proroka Moiseja', S. 146).

66 Das entsprechende Textstück aus der *Legende vom Kreuzesholz* ist beispielsweise im Berlinski Sbornik aus dem frühen 14. Jh. nachzulesen, vgl. H. Miklas, L. Taseva und M. Jovčeva (Hgg.), *Berlinski Sbornik. Ein kirchenslavisches Denkmal mittelbulgarischer Redaktion des beginnenden 14. Jahrhunderts, ergänzt aus weiteren handschriftlichen Quellen* (Bulgarische Akademie der Wissenschaften, Kyrillomethodianisches Forschungszentrum, Österreichische Akademie der Wissenschaften, Philosophisch-Historische Klasse, Schriften der Balkan-Kommsision, 47, Fontes Nr. 3), Sofia–Wien, 2006, S. 231–232, 235–236.

– Ein Engel zeigt Mose, wie er die eherne Schlange (Num 21,9) errichten soll, und deutet sie auf das Kreuz Christi.[67] (KP 11. 1,68–71)

Wir haben gesehen, dass alle genannten aus der TP übernommenen Fragmente nichtbiblischer Texte der Deutung von Bibeltext, v. a. der typologischen Deutung, dienen. Die meisten dieser Deutungen sind den Rezipienten auch aus hymnographischen Kontexten bekannt gewesen; insbesondere liturgische Kanones enthalten fast alle der genannten Parallelen, die hier zwischen AT und NT gezogen werden.[68]

Die Quellen, welche der KP-Kompilator neu heranzieht, sind anderer Natur. Sein besonderes Interesse gilt chronographischen und chronologischen Themen, wohl im Zusammenhang mit den Fragen nach dem erwarteten Weltende im Jahre 7000. Er kompilierte die KP wahrscheinlich in den 40er Jahren des 15. Jh.s, d. h., bis zum byzantinischen Jahr 7000, dem Jahr 1492 n. Chr., blieb kaum noch ein halbes Jahrhundert Zeit. Für die KP erarbeitete ihr Kompilator ein eigenes System absoluter Jahreszählung, das mit keinem anderen bekannten übereinstimmt.[69] Diesem besonderen Interesse entsprechend, wendet sich der Kompilator in allen Fragen, die ihm der Bibeltext nicht beantworten kann, vor allem der Chronographie zu.

Seine Hauptquelle dabei ist die *Synopsis historiōn* des Georgios Kedrenos (11./12. Jh.).[70] In welcher Form und welchem Umfang sie ihm in ksl. Übersetzung vorlag, wissen wir nicht. (An einer Stelle wird in der KP ein „Parömienbuch" als Quelle für ein Kedrenos-Zitat genannt, nämlich in KP 9. 4,12 zu Mose als Heerführer der Ägypter.) Was wir jedoch wissen, ist, dass durch einige von Kedrenos übernommenen Textfragmente ein Teil der im Griechischen verlorenen Überlieferung des *Jubiläenbuches* in der ksl. Chronographie wieder auftaucht, und zwar wohl weitgehend wörtlich. Denn Kedrenos ist für seine präzise Über-

---

67 Vgl. z. B. Miklas, Taseva, Jovčeva, *Berlinski Sbornik*, S. 233–234.

68 Im Kommentar in Fahl, Fahl, Böttrich, *Kratkaja Chronografičeskaja Paleja*, Bd. 2, haben wir uns bemüht, liturgische Parallelen möglichst regelmäßig nachzuweisen.

69 Vgl. E.G. Vodolazkin, *Vsemirnaja istorija v literature Drevnej Rusi (na materiale chronografičeskogo i palejnogo povestvovanija XI–XV vekov)*, München, 2000, S. 138–153; Fahl, Fahl, Böttrich, *Kratkaja Chronografičeskaja Paleja*, Bd. 2, S. 46–85; C. Böttrich, S. Fahl und D. Fahl, ‚Biblische Zeit und christliche Historiographie. Literarische Strategien in der *Kratkaja Chronografičeskaja Paleja (KP)*', in S. Beyerle und M. Goff (Hgg.), *Notions of time in Deuterocanonical and Cognate Literature. Proceedings of the ISDCL conference 2019 in Greifswald* (Deuterocanonical and Cognate Literature Yearbook), Berlin 2021 [im Druck].

70 Vgl. L. Tartaglia (Hg.), *Georgii Cedreni Historiarum compendium. Edizione critica* vol. I–II (Bollettino dei Classici, supplemento, 30), Roma 2016; I. Bekker (Hg.), *Georgius Cedrenus Ioannis Scylitzæ ope*, T. I–II (Corpus scriptorum historiæ Byzantinæ, 32, 34), Bonn, 1838, 1839.

QUELLEN DER NICHTBIBLISCHEN MOSE-ÜBERLIEFERUNG

nahme von Quellen bekannt[71], und ebenso gibt die KP ihre Quellen stets wörtlich, allerdings nur ausschnittsweise, wieder.

Die drei umfangreichsten Kedrenos-Zitate zu Mose[72] in der KP betreffen folgende Themen:

– Einschließlich der Quelle „Leptogenesis", was hier das *Jubiläenbuch* meint, wird berichtet, der Pharao habe die neugeborenen Knaben Israels (Ex 1,22) über 10 Monate hin ermorden lassen und daraufhin seien später für jeden getöteten hebräischen Säugling 10 Ägypter im Schilfmeer ertrunken (Ex 14,28); Mose aber sei in die königliche Familie aufgenommen worden – nach *Synopsis historiōn* 62.1–2[73] (KP 9. 2,18–21).[74]

– Der Engel Gabriel lehrt Mose, während dieser die Schafe seines Schwiegervaters hütet (Ex 3,1), in der Wüste die Geschichte der Welt, Astronomie, Arithmetik, Geometrie und „jegliche Weisheit" und sagt ihm den Empfang des Gesetzes voraus – nach *Synopsis historiōn* 63.1[75] (KP 9. 3,4–5). Kedrenos nennt auch hier die *Leptogenesis* als seine Quelle, was jedoch nicht in die KP übernommen wird.[76]

– Später folgt ein ausführliches Kedrenos-Zitat über Mose als Heerführer der Ägypter gegen die Äthiopier – nach *Synopsis historiōn* 62.3[77] (KP 9. 4,2–12).

71   Vgl. Tartaglia, *Compendium* vol. I, S. 23.

72   Darüber hinaus gibt es etliche kleinere Zitate sowie Anklänge und Parallelen zum Kedrenos-Text, die im Kommentar in Fahl, Fahl, Böttrich, *Kratkaja Chronografičeskaja Paleja*, Bd. 2, vermerkt sind.

73   Vgl. Tartaglia, *Compendium* vol. I, S. 144,1–8 (Bekker, *Georgius Cedrenus*, T. I, S. 85,19–86,2).

74   In keiner der heute bekannten Varianten von Jub ist eine genaue inhaltliche Entsprechung zu finden. Vgl. aber sehr ähnlich Jub 47,3 (sieben Monate nach dem Mordbefehl des Pharao wird Mose geboren und danach drei Monate versteckt); 48,14 (zehn Ägypter ertrinken für einen israelischen Säugling); 47,9 (Mose wird an den ägyptischen Hof gebracht). Zu den Bezügen zu Ex vgl. B. Halpern-Amaru, *The Perspective from Mt. Sinai: The Book of Jubilees and Exodus*, Göttingen, 2015, S. 52–53 und 75–76.

75   Vgl. Tartaglia, *Compendium* vol. I, S. 145,4–146,12 (Bekker, *Georgius Cedrenus*, T. I, S. 87,11–20).

76   Im heute bekannten Jub-Text sind wieder nur Anklänge zu finden: Vgl. sowohl Jub 1,27–2,1 (den Auftrag Gottes an den „Engel des Angesichts", Mose zu belehren) als auch die gesamte Struktur von Jub 2–50 als eine an Mose gerichtete Lehrrede des Engels (der dort freilich nicht – wie bei Kedrenos und der KP – Gabriel heißt). Der Passus enthält teils wörtliche Parallelen zur Rede des Philosophen in der altrussischen Nestorchronik (Müller, *Nestorchronik*, Bd. 1, Sp. 94,25–95,1; vgl. deutsch: Bd. 4, S. 114, Satz 200, dort in FN 7 der Hinweis auf Georgios Kedrenos als Quelle). Die KP zitiert hier allerdings Kedrenos erheblich vollständiger als die Nestorchronik, so dass der KP-Kompilator nicht aus dieser geschöpft haben kann, sondern auf die gleiche oder eine ähnliche Quelle wie der altrussische Chronist zurückgriff.

77   Vgl. Tartaglia, *Compendium* vol. I, S. 144,9–145,28 (Bekker, *Georgius Cedrenus*, T. I, S. 86,4–87,3).

Im Hintergrund stehen hier die *Antiquitates* des Josephus (Ant 11 231. 249–253), ein Werk, das im Ksl. ebenso wie das *Jubiläenbuch* nur durch indirekte Vermittlung bekannt war; eine geschlossene Übersetzung der *Antiquitates* gab es nicht (im Unterschied zum früh fast vollständig übersetzten *Bellum Judaicum*).

Ein anderer KP-Zusatz zum TP-Text ist ebenfalls chronographischer Natur: Nach Theodoret, QuæstNum XLIV 2, wird berichtet, wie Bileam dem König Balak rät, Israel mit Speise, Trank und Hurerei zu verführen (KP 11. 2,51–55). Diese Verbindung zwischen Num 25,1–3 und Num 31,16 geht auch auf die *Antiquitates* des Josephus zurück (Ant IV 126–130).

Eine weitere Chronik, die in späteren Abschnitten der KP noch erheblich mehr herangezogen wird, konnte erst kürzlich identifiziert werden: Die einzige bisher bekannte fast vollständige Handschrift der *Chronik des Ps.-Eustathios von Antiochia* (entstanden zwischen dem 6. und dem 9. Jh.) erkannte Paolo Odorico in dem Pariser Codex græcus Nr. 1336 aus dem 11. Jh.[78] Nach derselben Handschrift identifizierte schon vor 120 Jahren der russische Gelehrte Vasilij Michajlovič Istrin einige Fragmente, die dem KP-Kompilator als Quelle dienten.[79] Aus der *Chronik des Ps.-Eustathios* stammt in dem uns hier beschäfti-

---

78 P. Odorico, ‚Du recueil à l'invention du texte: le cas des Parastaseis Syntomoi Chronikai‘, in *Byzantinische Zeitschrift* 107 (2014), S. 755–784; id., ‚Dans le cahier des chroniqueurs. Le cas d'Eustathe d'Antioche‘, in J. Signes Codoñer und I. Pérez Martín (Hgg.), *Textual Transmission in Byzantium: between Textual Criticism and Quellenforschung* (Lectio. Studies in the transmission of texts and ideas, 2), Turnhout, 2014, S. 373–389; id., ‚Une chronique byzantine inconnue‘, in Böttrich, Fahl, Fahl, *Historienbibel*, S. 188–204. Eine kurze Beschreibung des Pergament-Manuskriptes Codex græcus Nr. 1336 der BnF gab H. Omont, *Inventaire sommaire des manuscrits grecs de la Bibliothèque Nationale*, T. 2, Paris, 1888, S. 16; auf diese Beschreibung geht der Titel „Anonymi historia Veteris Testamenti" für die Chronik des Ps.-Eustathios in der Handschrift zurück. (Dem Text fehlt dort das erste folium, was das Erkennen erschwerte.) Seit November 2015 ist die Handschrift nach einem Mikrofilm digitalisiert zugänglich unter gallica.bnf.fr/ark:/12148/btv1b10722877z.

79 V.M. Istrin, ‚Iz oblasti drevne-russkoj literatury‘, I., in *Žurnal Ministerstva narodnogo prosveščenija*, sed'moe desjatiletie, čast' 348 (1903), S. 381–414, hier: S. 411–412; id., ‚Redakcii‘, II., S. 17–27.

Der bis zu Odoricos Arbeiten einzig bekannte Anfangsteil (von der Erschaffung der Welt bis zu Josua) der in den ca. 30 nachgewiesenen Handschriften dem Eustathios von Antiochia zugeschriebenen Chronik ist unter der eher irreführenden Bezeichnung eines Kommentars zum Hexæmeron durch Leo Allatius ediert worden: L. Allatius (Hg.), *S.P.N. Eustathii archiepiscopi antiocheni, et martyris In Hexahemeron Commentarius (…)*, Lugduni [Lyon], 1629 (https://books.google.de/books?id=m34Dl3YGvRkC&printsec=front cover&hl=de&source=gbs_ge_summary_r&cad=0#v=onepage&q&f=false, letzter Zugriff: 18. 02. 2020); vgl. den Nachdruck dieser bis heute einzigen Edition in PG 18, 703–794. Quellen dieses Chronik-Teils suchte Friedrich Zoepfl äußerst sorgfältig auf: F. Zoepfl, *Der Kommentar des Pseudo-Eustathios zum Hexaëmeron* (Alttestamentliche Abhandlungen,

QUELLEN DER NICHTBIBLISCHEN MOSE-ÜBERLIEFERUNG

genden KP-Abschnitt die Erzählung vom kleinen Mose, der auf der Krone des Pharao herumtrampelt (KP 9. 2,9–17). Diese Geschichte, die gleichfalls auf den *Antiquitates* des Josephus beruht (Ant II 232–237), ist weit verbreitet und auch im Ksl. in etlichen Fassungen bekannt; die Redaktion der KP lässt sich jedoch eindeutig auf die Besonderheiten der Erzählung bei Ps.-Eustathios zurückführen (vgl. PG 18, 780B–781B).

In anderen Redaktionen sind mehrere der erwähnten Zusätze zur biblischen Mose-Geschichte auch in der *Palæa Historica* zu finden, darunter die Erzählung vom kleinen Mose und der Krone des Pharao[80] und direkt daran angeschlossen die Geschichte von Mose als Heerführer der Ägypter[81], welche die KP nach Georgios Kedrenos erzählt (s. o.). Diese beiden fanden sogar Aufnahme in die chronographische Redaktion des ksl. Exodus (unmittelbar nach Ex 2,10).[82]

10.5), Münster i. W., 1927. Die Fortsetzung der *Ps.-Eustathios-Chronik* über die Zeit von Josua bis zu Alexander dem Großen scheint nur in Cod. grec 1336 belegt zu sein, vgl. die bislang ausführlichste Inhaltsangabe bei Istrin, ‚Iz oblasti', I., S. 401–406.

Die genannten Arbeiten von V.M. Istrin zu Cod. grec 1336 weisen nicht nur wörtliche Entsprechungen des griech. Textes zu etlichen KP-Stellen, sondern auch zu weiteren ksl. chronographischen Texten nach, v. a. zum so genannten slavischen Synkellos. Diese Auskünfte Istrins sind in der westeuropäischen Forschung bislang nicht und auch in Russland und Bulgarien, den osteuropäischen Ländern mit der stärksten Altslavistik, kaum rezipiert worden. Bis in die jüngste Zeit werden die beiden Publikationen zwar regelmäßig in Literaturverzeichnisse aufgenommen, aber nicht benutzt, so z. B. bei Totomanova, *Georgi Sinkel*.

Die Ps.-Eustathios-Zitate in der KP bietet als Paralleltext D. Fahl, ‚Fragmente aus der Chronik des Ps.-Eustathius von Antiochia in der *Kurzen Chronographischen Paleja*', in Böttrich, Fahl, Fahl, *Historienbibel*, S. 223–257.

80 Griech. vgl. Vassiliev, *Anecdota*, S. 227–228; die erste ksl. Übersetzung vgl. Popov, *Kniga bytija*, S. 62–63; die zweite (serbische) ksl. Übersetzung vgl. Skowronek, *Palæa Historica*, S. 97–98, Abschnitt 68.

81 Griech. vgl. Vassiliev, *Anecdota*, S. 228–229; die erste ksl. Übersetzung vgl. Popov, *Kniga bytija*, S. 63–64; die zweite (serbische) ksl. Übersetzung vgl. Skowronek, *Palæa Historica*, S. 98–99, Abschnitt 69.

82 Vgl. T.L. Vilkul (Hg.), *Kniga Ischod. Drevneslavjanskij polnyj (četii) tekst po spiskam XIV–XVI vekov*, Moskva, 2015, S. 73, Anm. 147.

Von den für das Leben des Mose entscheidenden biblischen Quellen in ksl. Übersetzung war lange nur Gen als vollständiger Lesetext kritisch ediert: A. Michajlov (Hg.), *Kniga Bytija proroka Moiseja v drevne-slavjanskom perevode*, Vyp. 1–4, Varšava, 1900–1908. Seit kurzem sind Gen, Ex und Jos in neuen kritischen Ausgaben erschlossen: T.L. Vilkul (Hg.), *Knyga Buttja. Davn'oslov''jan'skyj četij tekst za spyskamy XIV–XVI stolit'*, Pokažčyky sliv: S.L. Nikolaev (Kyivan Christianity, 22), L'viv, 2020; ead., *Kniga Ischod*; ead. (Hg.), *Knyga Isusa Navyna. Davn'oslov'jan'skyj četij tekst za spyskamy XIV–XVI stolit'*, L'viv, 2017. Hinzu kommt der AT-Text nach dem Parömienbuch, also nach den gottesdienstlichen Lesungen, der teils andere Übersetzungsstadien spiegelt – R. Brandt, *Grigorovičev parimejnik v sličenii s drugimi parimijnikami* (Čtenija v Obščestve istorii i drevnostej rossi-

Die Textfassung der ersten ksl. Übersetzung der *Palœa Historica*, welche in die chronographische Redaktion des ksl. Exodus einging, weicht jedoch deutlich von der KP-Fassung ab, so dass sie hier als Quelle nicht in Frage kommt.

Sie weist uns aber auf etwas anderes hin: Die Trennung in biblische und nichtbiblische Quellen scheint vom heutigen Standpunkt eines feststehenden Kanons aus oft so eindeutig, wie sie noch zur Entstehungszeit der KP, in der ersten Hälfte des 15. Jh.s, keineswegs gewesen ist. So entnimmt beispielsweise die TP und aus ihr die KP die Episode vom Gold an den Lippen der Verehrer des Goldenen Kalbs (KP 10. 5,60) direkt aus der chronographischen Redaktion des ksl. Buches Exodus (Ex 32,20)[83]. Aus heutiger Sicht handelt es sich klar um ein apokryphes Motiv. (Es ist in *Pirke de Rabbi Elieser* 45 bezeugt.) Der Autor der TP jedoch zitiert hier zweifellos einen ihm vorliegenden Exodus-Text.

Solche Überschneidungen kanonischer und nichtkanonischer Überlieferungen waren natürlich kein Privileg der kirchenslavischen oder der byzantinischen Kultur. Ein schönes ikonographisches Zeugnis aus Westeuropa, das wie die russische KP im 15. Jh. geschaffen wurde, sei hier zum Abschluss mit einer Mose-Illustration aus der Koberger-Bibel angeführt: Auf der rechten Bildseite nimmt der Mose-Knabe eben dem Pharao die Krone vom Kopf ....

---

jskich, 1894.1,3; 1900.2; 1901.2), Moskva, 1894, 1900, 1901; Z. Ribarova und Z. Chauptova (= Hauptová) (Hgg.), *Grigorovičev Parimejnik*, Skopje, 1998; B. Jovanović-Stipčević, *Beogradski parimejnik. Početak XIII veka, Tekst so kritičkim apparatom*, Beograd, 2005; am gründlichsten: A.A. Pičchadze, ‚Kniga "Ischod" v drevneslavjanskom Parimejnike‘, in *Učenye zapiski Rossijskogo pravoslavnogo universiteta ap. Ioanna Bogoslova* 4 (1998), S. 5–60. Was freilich Bezüge zu Dtn, Lev und Num betrifft, so ist man nach wie vor auf die frühen Druckausgaben (die Gennadij-Bibel von 1499, die auf ihrer Grundlage geschaffene Ostroger Bibel von 1580/81 sowie, für Studien zur frühen Überlieferung nur eingeschränkt verwendbar, die Elisabeth-Bibel von 1740) und auf eigene Handschriftenstudien angewiesen.

83 Vgl. Vilkul, *Kniga Ischod*, S. 238, im Editionstext.

ABB. 15.1   Mose in der Bibel des Anton Koberger (Nürnberg 1483). Holzschnitt nach der Kölner Bibel von Heinrich Quentell (1478/79)

CHAPTER 16

Whether Lamb or Lion: Overlapping Metaphors in Jewish and Christian Apocalypticism

Abraham Terian

Since my paper, like some of the other papers in this volume, is laden with metaphors, allow me to begin with a definition of metaphor by Donald Davidson, who has written much on the phenomenology of metaphors. 'Metaphor is the dreamwork of language and, like all dreamwork, its interpretation reflects as much on the interpreter as on the originator .... Understanding a metaphor is as much a creative endeavor as making a metaphor, and as little guided by rules.'[1] While this may be true phenomenologically, it is a problematic definition for those of us who come from the historical-critical side of biblical studies. For one thing, we are not the first interpreters of biblical metaphors; they have come down to us through a long history of interpretation that has to be accounted for. Moreover, most biblical metaphors are many-sided and overlapping, such as the ones my paper deals with: whether lamb or lion; or, by interpretative extension, whether priest or king; or, by further interpretative extension, whether priestly or kingly messiah; or, by *neutestamentliche* interpretation with reference to Jesus, both Lamb and Lion, both priestly and kingly Messiah.[2] I shall briefly trace the history of these metaphors through Scripture and certain extra-canonical Jewish apocalyptic writings, and shall dwell on their convergence as they are made to apply to Jesus especially in Johannine writings. I shall conclude with a tenth-century Armenian example illustrative of the convergence of these metaphors in the Christian Middle Ages.

To make the long biblical story short, I shall begin with the Johannine writings, where the lamb metaphor applied to Jesus is one of the special features in both the Gospel and the Apocalypse—with distinctions, of course, to which I shall refer in passing. 'Lamb' as a primary Christological title is quite significant

---

1 D. Davidson, 'What Metaphors Mean', *Critical Inquiry* 5 (1978), pp. 31–47; reprinted in K. Ludwig and E. Lepore (ed.), *The Essential Davidson*, Oxford, 2006, p. 209.

2 On the problematics in the application of the title *Christos* to Jesus, see M.P. Miller, 'The Problem of the Origins of a Messianic Conception of Jesus', in R. Cameron and M.P. Miller (ed.), *Redescribing Christian Origins* (Symposium Series 28), Atlanta, 2004, pp. 301–335, esp. 317–327.

© ABRAHAM TERIAN, 2021 | DOI:10.1163/9789004445925_018

in the Apocalypse of John, where *arnios* is used twenty-seven times.[3] Similar usage is found twice in the Gospel of John, both on the lips of John the Baptist, and nowhere else in the New Testament—including the Johannine Epistles. In the Gospel 'the Lamb of God' is *amnos* (not *arnios*, as in the Apocalypse), and only with the first mention there is the phrase 'Who takes away the sin of the world' (John 1:29, cf. 36).

The genitive in the phrase ἴδε ὁ ἀμνός τοῦ Θεοῦ seems to hold some ambiguity. It could mean either 'belonging to God' or 'provided by God'; perhaps a better English translation would be 'appertaining to God'. The use of the definite article suggests a reference with which the intratextual hearers seem to be familiar. Moreover, the phrase allows the possibility of referencing at least three distinct depictions of lamb in the Hebrew Bible, especially the paschal lamb of Exodus 12 or the sacrificial lambs in the cultic practices of ancient Israel, as prescribed in Numbers 28–29 for example,[4] besides the Genesis 22 account of the *Akedah*, the binding of Isaac, and the 'suffering servant' of Isaiah 53. In the first place, the identification of Jesus with the 'lamb of God that takes away the sin of the world' (John 1:29) recalls the temple sacrifices, and especially those associated with the Passover ritual and sin offering.[5] We also have the explicit declaration by Paul in 1 Cor 5:7, 'Christ, our Passover, has been sacrificed'. Curiously, in the Epistle to the Hebrews we have the same theology wrapped around the Day of Atonement (chs 8–10). The theme of redemption in the theology of the feasts of Pesach and Yom-Kippur needs no elaboration. It would be tempting to move

---

3 Rev 5:6, 8, 12, 13; 6:1, 16; 7:9, 10, 14, 17; 12:11; 13:8, 11; 14:1, 4, 10; 15:3; 17:14; 19:7, 9; 21:14, 22, 23; 22:1, 3.

4 Cf. Exod 23; Lev 23; Deut 16:1–17. Lambs were offered daily, morning and evening (Num 28:3–8; cf. Exod 29:38–41); two additional lambs were sacrificed every Sabbath (Num 28:9–10). The sacrifice of lambs was quite prominent on feast days: on the first of every month (Num 28:11–14); on each of the seven days of Passover (Num 28:16–19); on the Feast of Weeks or Pentecost (Num 28:26–28); on the Feast of Trumpets or New Year (Num 29:12–16); on the Day of Atonement (Num 29:7–10); and on each of the eight days of the Feast of Tabernacles (Num 29:7–38). Lambs were offered as 'peace' or 'fellowship' offering (Lev 3:1–11), for sin (Lev 4:32–35; 5:6; 9:3), for purification and cleansing (Lev 12:6–7; 14:10–14, 23–25), and for various dedications (Num 6:12–14; 7 *passim*).

5 Exod 12:3–5; Lev 4:32; 5:6; cf. John 1:36 (ἀμαρτία appears 17 times in John: 1:29; 8:21, 24 (× 2), 34 (× 2), 46; 9:34, 41 (× 2); 15:22 (× 2), 24; 16:8, 9; 20:23). See also 1 Cor 15:3b–4, on the saving death of Jesus and his resurrection 'on the third day' κατὰ τὰς γραφάς, which seems to allude to Isa 53:4–5, 12 and Hos 6:2 (the phrase 'on the third day' is found also in the pericope of the Temple cleansing in John 2:13–22, interpreted within the context of the Passover and the Passion—a pericope discussed below); cf. Heb 9:28 and 1 Pet 2:18–25, both alluding to Isa 53. For more, see M.D. Hooker, *Jesus and the Servant: The Influence of the Servant Concept of Deutero-Isaiah in the New Testament*, London, 1959; W.H. Bellinger, Jr. and W.R. Farmer (eds), *Jesus and the Suffering Servant: Isaiah 53 and Christian Origins*, Harrisburg, 1998.

directly to the Hebrew Bible and the Septuagintal terminology for the sacrificial offering of lambs or sheep, bypassing the Jewish apocalyptic writings of the intertestamental period. However, for a better understanding of the metaphor we have to consider the more immediate sources. Conversely, it would be just as tempting to say that in Christian understanding, all these sacrificial 'types' anticipate the presumed antitypical aspect of Christ's death, all the while ignoring the fact that the metaphor of lamb (and I may add, of lion) have undergone substantial messianic interpretation long before being utilized in the Gospel and in the Apocalypse.

Since the middle of the last century, Johannine scholarship on our subject dealt primarily with attempts to distinguish between what the Baptist could have meant and what the Evangelist intended. There were those who saw 'The Lamb of God' not in relation to the Pentateuchal sin offering but as the horned lamb of Jewish Apocalyptic writings, to be raised by God to destroy evil in the world and/or the enemy of his people. However, they did not look beyond the familiar apocryphal and pseudepigraphical sources, which were textually questionable for possible (and in some places obvious) Christian interpolations. There was no consideration of the possibility that the biblical metaphor had been variously interpreted in Second-Temple Judaism—prior to the Christian utilization of both the metaphor and its interpretations.

An important question to ask is: Why are the sayings about the Lamb placed in the mouth of the Baptist? The question is more pertinent than the one that asks: How would the Baptist have known of the suffering/dying Messiah when the disciples of Jesus had no such thoughts and were slow to understand whenever Jesus spoke of his own death?

Given the strong possibility that the followers of the Baptist and some of his contemporaries perceived him as the awaited priestly messiah, it is understandable why the Evangelist would attribute such a statement to him full of priestly connotations. Furthermore, it is one of the Evangelist's intentions to ascribe to Jesus—the assumed kingly Messiah (ch. 6)—all that which in Jewish apocalypticism pertains to the priestly messiah. A good example of this is seen early on in the Gospel of John, in the pericope of the Temple cleansing (2:13–22). Unlike the Synoptics which place it toward the end, the narrative placement of this episode in John has weighty implications for interpretation; it is intended—*inter alia*—to establish Jesus and not the Baptist as the expected priestly messiah of late Second Temple Judaism. The Baptist, vis-à-vis the divine Logos, is but an *anthropos* in the prologue of the Fourth Gospel—albeit sent by God (1:6), a *prophetēs* in the Synoptics, who is made to deny ever being the Messiah.

WHETHER LAMB OR LION

Some focus on the Book of Zechariah is essential for its bearing on both the development of the notion of the 'two messiahs' and the pericope of the Temple cleansing in John.

Zechariah ch. 3 introduces the High Priest Joshua, who is reassured by the prophet that God would soon bring his servant, the Branch, an allusion to Zerubbabel, the would-be-king (v. 8). In the next chapter the two are presented as 'the two anointed ones' (4:14). However, in ch. 6 Joshua stands alone to receive royal honor and have both a throne and a crown (vv. 10–13). There seems to be an authorial redaction at this juncture in Zechariah that obscures an abortive attempt by a Jewish-Babylonian delegation, arriving in Jerusalem with gold and silver, to restore the Davidic Kingship by making Zerubbabel king (vv. 14–15); conceivably, his descent from the line of David may have fuelled messianic hopes in Judah.[6] Zerubbabel was probably whisked away by the Persians, yet the longing for the kingly messiah persists in the subsequent chapters (7–14).[7]

Though it is beyond the limits of this paper to underscore the similarities between the Book of Zechariah and the Gospel of John, some commonalities between the two ought to be mentioned, especially the reverberations of the two oracles at the end of Zechariah (chs 9–11, 12–14) in the Gospel narrative.[8] A recurring figure in these oracles is that of the shepherd-king, evoking not only the beginning of the Davidic dynasty but also the history of failed kingships in ancient Israel. In the first oracle Yahweh is angry at the shepherds who have exploited his flock, his people; he appoints the prophet as 'shepherd of the flock marked for slaughter.' He obeys by enacting the role of Yahweh and

---

6 Zerubbabel was a grandson of the exiled King Jehoiachin (1 Chr 3:16–19).

7 We cannot help but draw a parallel between the merger of the priestly and kingly messiahs in Zechariah and the later Hasmonean dynasty, the priestly descendants of the Maccabees assuming kingship: a likely factor in the apocalyptic dissension at Qumran. We are also mindful of the Testament of Levi with its emphasis on the priestly messiah and the Testament of Judah with its emphasis on the kingly messiah, and the priority given to him in the Testament of Joseph.

8 See A. Kubiś, *The Book of Zechariah in the Gospel of John* (Études bibliques, n.s. 64), Pendé, 2012; also F.F. Bruce, 'The Book of Zechariah and the Passion Narrative', *Bulletin of the John Rylands Library* (1961), pp. 336–353. The second-century Church-father, Irenæus of Lyons, is one of the earliest writers to cite the prophecies of Zechariah when describing the events of Holy Week in his book *On the Apostolic Preaching* (*Epideixis tou apostolikou kērygmatos*) extant only in Armenian; text and French trans. in A. Rousseau (ed. and trans.), *Irénée de Lyon: Demonstration de la prédication apostolique* (Sources chrétiennes 406), Paris, 1995; St Irenæus of Lyons, *On the Apostolic Preaching*, trans. John Behr, Crestwood, 1997; for other translations, see *The Cambridge History of Christianity* vol. I: *Origins to Constantine*, Cambridge, 2006, p. 602.

tending the sheep with his two staffs, named 'Grace' (or 'Favor') and 'Union.' He duly deposes the unfaithful shepherds; but, in his frustration with the flock, he breaks the two staffs, one at a time (11:4–14).

A unique point of contact between Zechariah 11:7 (LXX) and John 2:15 is the naming of the second staff which the shepherd uses, σχοίνισμα, to be compared with Jesus's 'making a whip of chords': ποιήσας φραγέλλιον ἐκ σχοινίων. Moreover, Jesus's words 'do not make my father's house a house of merchandise' in John 2:16 echo the words in Zechariah 14:21, 'And there shall no longer be merchants[9] in the house of the Lord of hosts on that day.' The use of the temple courts as a marketplace is certainly the cause of its defilement, more so when the Septuagint reading of 'Canaanites' is considered in lieu of the Masoretic 'merchants.'[10] Jesus is here presented as having a very negative attitude toward the temple priesthood, not unlike the Qumran community,[11] as we read in the Pesher Habakkuk (1QpHab), interpreting the book in terms of an apocalyptic conflict in which a certain Wicked Priest, in association with the priests of the Jerusalem temple, oppresses the poor and does other repulsive acts which defile the מקדש ('sanctuary') of God (1QpHab 12:7–10; especially line 9).

Moreover, the shepherd appointed in Zechariah 11:4, the prophet himself acting Yahweh's role, becomes an eschatological figure who is smitten as a result of his commitment (13:7). This image of the shepherd is recalled in the Gospel of John, a gospel full of paradoxes, where the Lamb has become a Shepherd who not only leads those who follow his voice but who lays down his life for them (10:11–18; 15:13). Among other unique passages in John is the quotation of Zechariah 12:10, 'they shall look upon him whom they pierced' (19:37, just as John alone mentions the piercing of Jesus's side with the spear, v. 34). One cannot help but recall the divine shepherd in 1 Enoch 89–90, who delivers from the wolves the endangered sheep with whom he identifies himself.[12] The tradition of an eschatological shepherd points to a kingly or Davidic messiah, as

---

9   Or Canaanites; LXX has Χαναναῖος. Cf. Zech 11:7, where the LXX has εἰς τὴν Χαναανῖτιν; the MT has עֲנִיֵּי לַכֵּן instead of לְבַנְעָנֵי. See also the discussion in Kubiś, *The Book of Zechariah in the Gospel of John*, pp. 328, 337 n. 73.

10 Cf. the Synoptic 'den of robbers' from Jer 7:11 (Matt 21:13; Mark 11:17; Luke 19:46).

11 See C.A. Evans, 'Jesus' Action in the Temple: Cleansing or Portent of Destruction', *The Catholic Biblical Quarterly* 51 (1989), pp. 237–270; A.X.M. Wedderburn, 'Jesus' Action in the Temple: A Key or a Puzzle?', *Zeitschrift für die Neutestamentliche Wissenschaft* 97 (2006), pp. 1–22.

12 J.A. Goldstein, 'Biblical Promises and 1 and 2 Maccabees', in J. Neusner, W.S. Green and E.S. Frerichs (ed.), *Judaisms and Their Messiahs at the Turn of the Christian Era*, Cambridge, 1987, pp. 69–96. 'From the fact that 1 Enoch 89:59–90:25 is derived from Ezekiel 34, we can infer that at least one can call this messiah "David"', ibid., p. 73.

suggested by Jeremiah 23:5–7; 33:14–22 and Ezekiel 34:23; 37:24 (cf. Isa 40:9–11). As for the first of the Isaiah *pesharim* among the fragments of the Dead Sea scrolls (4Q161), though it shares certain characteristics with the eschatological shepherd in the Major Prophets and Zechariah 11, including the latter's eschatological destruction of Lebanon (vv. 1–2; cf. Isa 10:33–34), it perpetuates the tradition of the 'two messiahs' (or the two in one); for clearly, the messiah of these fragments is also priestly, since he is vested in priestly garments.[13]

The repeated references to the Passover festival in John[14] add to the priestly concerns of the Gospel. I need not go into the detail of the obvious theological implications of the Passover references there (discounting their chronological validity). In the prayer of John 17, generally referred to as the 'high-priestly' prayer,[15] Jesus assumes a priestly role in consecrating his disciples.[16] This prayer, along with other episodes in John, has led to efforts to show the priestly or high priestly identity of Jesus in the Gospel of John.[17]

The notion that with Jesus as the Lamb of God the Evangelist intended to point to Isaiah 53:7, as a prophetic anticipation of the Messiah's death, could be supported by the fact that earlier (according to the chronology of the Fourth Gospel), indeed the day before—in an immediately preceding context, he had alluded to Isaiah 40:3 (in John 1:23, 'I am the voice of the one calling in the desert, "Make straight the way for the Lord"'; cf. the Synoptic tradition, where the baptism of Jesus, introduced with the Isaianic 'voice crying in the wilderness', is thrust into the 'suffering servant' context).

---

13   See the discussion of the shepherd as high priest in J.P. Heil, 'Jesus as the Unique High Priest in the Gospel of John', *The Catholic Biblical Quarterly* 57 (1995), pp. 729–745, here 733.

14   John 2:13, 23; 6:4; 11:55; 12:1; 13:1; 18:28, 39; 19:14.

15   See H.W. Attridge, 'How Priestly is the 'High Priestly Prayer' of John 17?', *The Catholic Biblical Quarterly* 75 (2013), pp. 1–14.

16   In John 17:17 (cf. v. 19) ἁγίασον is reminiscent of the priestly consecration. The LXX translates קדשׁ with ἁγιάζω in a large number of priestly texts: Exod 28:38, 41; 29:1, 27, 33 (2×), 36, 37 (2×), 43, 44 (2 ×); 30:29, 30 (2×); 31:13; 40:9, 10, 13; Lev 6:11, 20; 8:10, 11, 12, 15, 30; 10:3; 11:4; 16:4, 9; 20:3, 8; 21:8 (2×), 15, 23; 22:2, 3, 9, 16, 32 (2×); 25:10; 27:14, 15, 16, 17, 18, 19, 22; Num 3:13; 5:9, 10; 6:11; 7:1 (2×); 8:17; 17:2, 3; 18:8, 9; 20:12, 13; 27:14 (2×).].

17   See e.g. Heil, who proposes 'that the Johannine Jesus does function as a high priest, not in the systematic and sweeping manner of the Letter to the Hebrews, but in a more subtle and symbolic way as part of the fourth Gospel's well-established dramatic irony', id., 'Jesus as the Unique High Priest', p. 730. Heil qualifies this 'irony' in the following way: 'the high priesthood of the Johannine Jesus is ironic, recognized not by the characters in the narrative but only by the reader …' (ibid.).

While the Gospel of John seems to contemplate both the sacrificial connotations of lambs, especially of the paschal lamb, and the redemptive understanding of Isaiah 53 along with other prophetic passages that have given rise to messianic expectations, the Apocalypse of John clearly contemplates more expansive views of Jewish apocalypticism where the metaphoric transition of the lamb into a lion has been realized—a transition with which the author of the Apocalypse must have been far too familiar.[18]

The distinctly Christological references to the Lamb in the Apocalypse deserve special attention, alongside the distinctly Christological and synonymic reference there to the 'Lion from the Tribe of Judah'—albeit a *hapax* (Rev 5:5).

The image of the Messiah as a lion is owed to Jewish apocalyptic interpretations of familiar Old Testament passages that speak of 'the lion from the tribe of Judah': from Jacob's blessing of Judah in Genesis 49:9, and the description of the princes of Judah as 'lion-cubs' in Ezekiel 19:3–6; and, just as importantly from the description of God 'as a lion' in the Minor Prophets (Hos 5:14; 11:10; 13:7–8; Amos 3:8; Mic 5:8). The latter metaphor recurs in 4 Ezra 11:36–46; 12:1–3, 31–34; and the Apocalypse of Elijah 2:6–8.

Of the many-sided Lamb metaphor in the Apocalypse, an important facet is the Lamb as an authority figure, a leader or ruler; for the Lamb is worthy to open the scroll and to receive worship. When John sees the Lamb 'looking as if it had been slain' he also observes that it has 'seven horns and seven eyes' (5:6a). This is no ordinary Lamb but one which has authority and royal dignity. Horns represent power and rulership[19] and the seven horns symbolize absolute authority. There is none greater than the Lamb. The seven eyes 'are the seven spirits of God sent out into all the earth' (5:6b). This aspect of the Lamb's features represents his divine omniscience, his perfect knowledge and perception, as well as his universal sovereignty (anticipating 17:14).

The Lamb is the One who rules with perfect understanding and with unlimited power. In this way the paradox created by the elder who tells John that the Lion of the tribe of Judah is the One to open the scroll is solved. The Lamb that seemingly bears the marks of death is no weak, pathetic figure. He is the triumphant Ruler of the universe, the One 'as if it had been slain,' but the One who has risen and ascended in glory. Indeed, in exegetical contextuality, the Lamb is the Lion of the tribe of Judah. The authority of the Lamb is demonstrated in his right to open the successive seals of the scroll and bring God's redemptive

---

18   A.M. Farrer, *A Rebirth of Images: The Making of St. John's Apocalypse*, Westminster, 1949.

19   Ps 75:4–7 and Zech 1:18–21. For more, see M.L. Süring, *The Horn Motif in the Hebrew Bible and Related Ancient Near Eastern Literature and Iconography* (Andrews University Seminary Doctoral Dissertation Series 4), Berrien Springs, 1982.

WHETHER LAMB OR LION 347

purposes to their consummation. He not only receives the right but he actually does perform this task in the following chapter.[20] Thus the Lamb is seen as having authority over the course of history; he directs its unfolding and prepares the way for the ushering in of the new age marked by opening 'the seventh seal' (8:1).

The Lamb is enthroned (5:6; 22:1, 3). His exalted position is because of his sacrificial role, as the anthems in Rev 5 and 15 indicate. He is in control of the river of the water of life that flows from the throne and provides the reference point for other heavenly entities (22:2). The Lamb is indeed both sacrificial Redeemer and 'Lord of lords and King of kings' (17:14). He is exalted and enthroned because he has effected a means to reconcile humanity to God and has defeated the bestial power. Worshiping the defeated foe is tantamount to denouncing the Redeemer, an act that provokes the Lamb to exhibit his kingly authority by way of judgement. The Lamb is fearsome for those who direct their worship to the beast. To worship one other than he who alone is worthy is to spurn all that he stands for. He is thus intolerant of those who usurp the rulership and glory that are truly his and bestow them upon another. The Lamb's role as Judge is brought most directly to mind in the expression 'the wrath of the Lamb' (6:16; cf. 14:9–11). In the sixth seal tremendous and frightening events take place and drive people into the mountains and caves. From there they call on the mountains and rocks to fall on them and thereby hide them from the wrath of the Lamb (6:12–17). Here the Lamb assumes the stature of the Lion of the tribe of Judah. He is the avenger and destroyer. The punishment of his enemies takes place in his presence (*enopion*), suggesting a forensic scene (14:10–11). The Lamb executes judgement as a warrior. He defeats ten kings who make war against him (17:14). He does not passively submit as he did in laying down his life as a sacrifice. Now that he reigns as King, he goes out to conquer those who attack him and his people: 'the Lamb will conquer them, for he is Lord of lords and King of kings, and those with him are called and chosen and faithful' (17:14).

His rule is beneficent for those who wash their robes in his blood (7:14; for the Lamb has shed his blood that they may be ransomed, 5:9) and follow him wherever he goes (14:4). There is a reversal here, in that the Lamb has become a shepherd, thus evoking the kingship motif through the shepherd-king analogy. The Lamb has the names of the redeemed in the book of life, those privileged to enter the New Jerusalem (13:8; 21:27). They stand triumphant on Mount Zion with the Lamb, who leads his people as they celebrate the joys of heaven (14:1–

---

20   Rev 6:1, 3, 5, 7, 9, 12; 8:1.

4). There is an intimacy and adoration that characterize the relationship of the heavenly citizens towards the Lamb; they are his bride (19:7–9; 21:9). They are devoted to their leader, to whom they owe all that they now possess. The Twelve Apostles are especially identified as belonging to the Lamb. The twelve foundations of the New Jerusalem are inscribed with the 'names of the twelve apostles of the Lamb' (21:14), thus evoking the Apostles' close association with the historical Jesus in a teacher-disciple relationship. This paradoxical role of the Lamb as shepherd is made explicit in Rev 7:17: 'The Lamb in the midst of the throne will be their shepherd, and he will guide them to springs of living water; and God will wipe away every tear from their eyes.' Just as paradoxically, the One seemingly 'slain' guides to the source of eternal life.

The Christological or messianic interpretation of the 'servant of God' of Isaiah 53, the *ebed Yahweh*, who like a docile lamb was led to the slaughter, is so well known that there is no need to detail the history of its Christian interpretation.[21] There can be no doubt that in both exegetical and historical contexts it is a vivid description of Israel's condition in exilic times; the 'servant' consistently being the personification of Israel in Deutero-Isaiah. Of special significance, however, is the Aramaic Targum to Isaiah 53, which transforms the lamb led to be slaughtered into a defying warrior who slaughters the oppressing Gentiles like sheep.[22]

---

21   See above, n. 5.

22   The chapter is here provided in its entirety: '1 Who has believed *this* our *report*? And to whom has *the strength of the mighty* arm of the LORD been so revealed? 2 And *the righteous shall be exalted* before him, *behold*, like *tufts which sprout*, and like *a tree which sends its roots by streams of waters, so holy generations will increase on the* land *which was needing him; his appearance is* not *a common appearance* and *his fearfulness is* not *an ordinary fearfulness*, and *his brilliance will be holy brilliance*, that *everyone* who looks at him will *consider* him. 3 *Then the glory of all the kingdoms will be for contempt* and *cease; they will be faint and mournful, behold, as* a man of sorrows and ap*pointed for* sicknesses; and as when the face *of the Shekhinah was taken up from us, they are* despised and not esteemed. 4 *Then he will beseech concerning our sins* and our *iniquities for his sake will be forgiven;* yet we *were* esteem*ed wounded*, smitten *before the* LORD and afflicted. 5 And he *will build the sanctuary which was profaned* for our sins, *handed over* for our iniquities; *and by his teaching his peace will increase* upon *us*, and in *that we attach ourselves to his words our sins will be forgiven* us. 6 All we like sheep have *been scattered*; we have *gone into exile*, every one his own way; and *before* the LORD *it was a pleasure* to forgive the *sins* of us all *for his sake*. 7 He *beseeches*, and he *is answered*, and *before* he opens his mouth *he is accepted; the strong ones of the peoples he will hand over* like a lamb to the *sacrifice*, and like a ewe *which* before its shearers is dumb, so *there is* not *before him one who* opens his mouth *or speaks a saying*. 8 From *bonds* and *retribution* he *will bring our exiles near; the wonders which will be done for us in his days*, who *will be able to recount? For he will take away the rule of the Gentiles* from

In this reversal of the 'Suffering Servant' to a triumphant Messiah (cf. 52:13–15), the notion of his suffering is completely done away with. The targumist underscores the benefits the Messiah brings to the 'righteous' who depend on him, at the peril of 'all the kingdoms' (vv. 3a, 7, 11, 12). The enemies are to be put in the position of Israel when the Shekinah departed from the Temple (v. 3b; alluding to Ezek 10:18–19). Israel's sufferings are to be relieved because of the Messiah's intercession (vv. 4, 6, 7, 12); he will even '(re)build the sanctuary' (v. 5a, indicating a period after 70 CE). Israel's prosperity is contingent upon adherence to the Messiah's 'words' (v. 5b), which teach the Law (vv. 10–12).[23] To be sure, certain rabbinic writings of the Tannaitic period do address Christian claims; but not so our passage. The last verse (12) does not seem to allude to the belief in a dying Messiah (that would have been an oddity in Second-temple Judaism; neither is there any attempt to claim the Messiah did not 'hand over his soul to the death'). As Chilton observes, 'the point of the phrase is probably that the Messiah risked his very life for the sake of his ministry; that appears to be the sense in which Isa 53:12 is applied to the hero Phinehas (cf. Num 25:13) in *Sifre* (§ 131). As in the case of the Messiah of the *Psalms of Solomon* ... the Targumic Messiah is a zealous victor, a guardian of the righteous (vv. 8–9).'[24]

It is within such interpretative tradition(s) of Jewish apocalypticism that we find the transformation of the lamb into a lion, albeit a warrior in the Targum to Isaiah, a messiah who neither suffers nor dies. Much as the lamb metaphor persists in Christian tradition, thanks to the Apocalypse, there too is the lion (5:5; cf. 10:1–4) as part of the Christian lore. Illustrative of the latter, I shall conclude

---

the land of *Israel; the sins which* my people *sinned he will cast on to them.* 9 And he *will hand over the* wicked *to Gehenna* and *those* rich *in possessions which they robbed* to the death *of the corruption, lest those who commit sin be established,* and *speak of possessions* with *their* mouth. 10 Yet *before* the LORD *it was a pleasure to refine and* to *cleanse the remnant of his people, in order to purify their soul from sins; they* shall see *the kingdom of their Messiah, they shall increase sons and daughters, they* shall prolong days; *those who perform the law of* the LORD shall prosper in his *pleasure;* 11 *from the slavery of the Gentiles he shall deliver their* soul, *they* shall see *the retribution of their adversaries. They shall* be satisfied *with the plunder of their kings;* by his *wisdom* shall *he* make *innocents* to be accounted *innocent, to subject* many *to the law;* and he shall *beseech concerning* their *sins.* 12 Then I will divide him *the plunder of* many *peoples,* and he shall divide the spoil, *the possessions of* strong *fortresses;* because he *handed over* his soul to the death, and *subjected the rebels to the law;* yet he *will beseech concerning* the *sins* of many, and *to the rebels it shall be forgiven for him.'* (*The Aramaic Bible* vol. 11: *The Isaiah Targum,* trans. B.D. Chilton, Wilmington–Collegeville, 1987, pp. 103–105; Chilton's italics, indicating divergencies from the MT).

23   The actual rebuilding of the Temple was a reward promised to Israel along with the Messiah and the defeat of Rome during the Tannaitic period (cf. Pesaḥim 5a). Cf. K. Koch, *The Rediscovery of Apocalyptic,* London, 1972, pp. 18–35.

24   *The Isaiah Targum,* p. 105.

with an example from a tenth-century Armenian author, Gregory of Narek, his 'Ode for the Holy Cross.'[25]

> I speak of the Lion's roar,
>   crying on the four-winged cross;
> On the four-winged cross crying,
>   calling to the depths of the earth.
> The depths of the earth trembled,
>   they shook beneath his mighty voice.
> This mighty voice I heard
>   loosens the bonds I'm in.
> He longs to loosen my bonds,
>   to reverse the captivity of the captives.
> I say, 'Blessed are the captives
>   whom the Lion raised.'
> Those raised by the Lion
>   expect no further suffering;
> They expect no suffering,
>   they await the wreaths that wither not.
> They receive the braided wreaths
>   from the Lion, the immortal King.
> Let us give glory to the Redeemer
>   who rescued the captives from prison.

The main thought in this ode pivots on the universal implications of the crucifixion and the resurrection, theologically broad concepts reduced to a few lines. In this, Gregory follows an early Christian pictorial understanding of the progression from one metaphor to the other: that though Jesus died as a lamb on the cross, he arose as a lion from the tomb. The author juxtaposes the two images, preferring to see the triumphant lion on the cross who, through his death and resurrection, raises from the dead 'the captives' held hostage in death and crowns them in glory.

---

25   *The Festal Works of St. Gregory of Narek: Annotated Translation of the Odes, Litanies, and Encomia*, trans. A. Terian, Collegeville, 2016, p. 171.

CHAPTER 17

Rescuing John the Baptist

Albert I. Baumgarten

Toute vue des choses qui n'est pas étrange est fausse.
'Every view of things that is not strange
(i.e. bizarre or foreign) is false'.

CAROLYN WALKER BYNUM, Quoting a wall slogan from the Paris student revolution of 1968[1]

•••

Too much sanctity in the air .... It poisons the atmosphere. Holiness is only bearable in mild solutions, like bath salts. The concentrated essence is venom.

ARTHUR KOESTLER, *Thieves in the Night*, 199

•••

i

The image of John the Baptist is one of the most frequent in Christian art. He appears in glorious altarpieces, such as the Grünewald-Issenheim masterpiece now in the Unterlinden Museum in Colmar, in portraits by famous artists, such as El Greco, while Caravaggio painted the horrific last step in the beheading of John in a work now found in the St John's co-cathedral in Malta.[2] From that perspective John would hardly seem to need rescuing of any sort.

---

1   C.W. Bynum, 'Why Paradox? The Contradictions of my Life as a Scholar', *The Catholic Historical Review* vol. 98 (2012), p. 435.
2   For Grünewald's, El Greco's and Caravaggio's pieces, see respectively: P. Béguerie-De Paepe and M. Haas, *Der Isenheimer Altar—Das Meisterwerk im Musée Unterlinden*, Paris, 2016; J. Álvarez Lopera, *El Greco, La Obra esencial*, Madrid, 2014; M. Hilaire, *Caravage, le Sacré et la Vie: 33 tableaux expliqués*, Paris, 1995, pp. 58–59.

© ALBERT I. BAUMGARTEN, 2021 | DOI:10.1163/9789004445925_019

Nevertheless, the nature of our ancient sources on John, combined with aspects of modern theological interpretation of these sources, make it important to rescue John from the misunderstandings in which his mission and work have been situated. This abuse of John and perversion of his message in the service of belief in Jesus are already evident in the works of art mentioned above. Against all chronological sequence, as he was dead by then, John was presented in the Grünewald-Issenheim altarpiece and in many other works as present at the crucifixion, pointing to Jesus and affirming his own inferior status. El Greco, following a pattern familiar from numerous other artists, has John proudly displaying a cross and standing next to the 'lamb of God', thereby confirming his belief in the truth of the mission of Jesus and in its culmination on the cross, again, even though John was not alive when Jesus was put on the cross.

These artists did not invent their Christological portrait of John out of thin air. It had its basis in the gospels and a straight line connects John of the gospels with John of Western Christian art.[3] The mission of rescuing John therefore begins with recognizing the biases in the gospels. John of the gospels was regularly demoted in comparison to Jesus. He was portrayed as a mere forerunner, who gladly proclaimed his perfect joy in his inferior status in comparison to Jesus: 'As he grows greater I must grow less (John 3:30)'.

Some scholars have noted that the gospels seem to be protesting too much in insisting on John's secondary role in the scenario of the end of time and have read passages in the gospels against the grain, in light of the 'competition hypothesis', as evidence of a debate of disciples, in which John was the founder of a real movement that exalted his status as opposed to that of Jesus. This line of analysis goes back, at the very least, to Wilhelm Baldensperger at the end of the 19th century[4] and has been continued by many others, most recently by Joel Marcus.[5]

---

3 In light of the hostile place of John in Cathar theology as the enemy of Jesus and the arch representative of Satan (below, n. 7), I cannot help but wonder whether the consistent portrait of John as a fervent believer in the faith of the crucified Christ in Medieval Christian art was a reaction/response to the Cathars. But this possibility is beyond my ability to pursue.

4 W. Baldensperger, *Der Prolog des vierten Evangeliums: Sein polemisch-apologetischer Zweck*, Tübingen, 1898. Along the same lines as Baldensperger, see M. Goguel, *Au Seuil de l'Évangile: Jean-Baptiste*, Paris, 1928, pp. 75–85.

5 J. Marcus, *John the Baptist in History and Theology*, Columbia, 2018, pp. 11–26. Although, as I have written elsewhere, I wish Marcus had taken the 'competition hypothesis' to its logical conclusion, as I see it. See further A.I. Baumgarten, 'John and Jesus in Josephus: A Prelude to the Parting of the Ways', in L. Baron, M. Thiessen and J. Hicks-Keeton (eds), *The Ways that Often Parted: Essays in Honor of Joel Marcus. SBL Early Christianity and Its Literature Series*, Atlanta, 2018, pp. 41–42, n. 1.

RESCUING JOHN THE BAPTIST

However, unlike other scholars, Marcus included, who are not willing to take the 'competition hypothesis' to its logical conclusion, I would insist that any expression by John or about him in the gospels asserting John's subordination to Jesus is suspect: one must consider reading all these remarks against the grain. John must be understood as someone who assigned himself a senior role in the drama of the end of time and who had disciples who continued to believe in his status. They did not necessarily transfer their allegiance to Jesus, one of John's former followers, who developed a message and reputation as a healer on his own, most likely after John's arrest and death. The explicit voice of believers in John's messianic status may be faint, but it can be heard here and there in the later literature of the Fathers of the Church, most prominently in a few remarks in the Pseudo-Clementines.[6] In light of these circumstances, the rescued John is at the beginning of an esoteric tradition, which did not outlive antiquity,[7] but is worthy of our attention, nevertheless, as I will argue in what follows.

---

6 For an elaboration of my position of how the 'competition hypothesis' should be applied, see A.I. Baumgarten, 'An Ancient Debate of Disciples', in M. Bar-Asher Siegal and M. Thiessen (eds), *Perceiving the Other in Ancient Judaism and Early Christianity*, Tübingen, 2017, pp. 1–6.

7 I agree with virtually all scholars who consider John of the Mandean traditions to have no direct contact with the believers in John's special status in the scenario of redemption reconstructed with the help of the competition hypothesis. This despite the detailed attempt of R. Reitzenstein, *Die Vorgeschichte der christlichen Taufe*, Lepizig–Berlin, 1929, to prove the antiquity of the Mandean baptismal traditions and that they preserve accurately the teachings of John's disciples, ibid., p. 18, as a direct continuation of the debate between the disciples of Jesus and John from the first century CE, ibid., pp. 54–66. Reitzenstein insisted that any attempt to explain (away) Mandean baptism as the result of an artificial and ahistorical attempt to connect practices learned in the Euphrates area with John the Baptist and the Jordan was '*wider alle Methode religionsgeschichtliche Forschung*', ibid., p. 51.

Reitzenstein insisted on a Mandean connection with the medieval Cathars, ibid., pp. 67–102, but he had to concede that in Cathar theology John became the arch-devil and symbol of evil, the highest servant of Satan, the enemy of Jesus, rather than the true teacher, whose doctrines were deformed by Jesus, of the Mandeans, ibid., p. 73. Therefore, whatever the origins of the Cathars may have been, a much debated topic in recent scholarship, any connection with the Mandeans must begin with recognition that the place of John in Cathar theology was diametrically opposite that of the Mandeans.

Re-reading Reitzenstein today it is easy to see why his conclusions are problematic. His proofs come from comparisons so diverse in time, place, and content that they prove little or nothing. They are a case of parallelomania, a generation before Samuel Sandmel warned of its dangers in the scholarship of the 1960s, S. Sandmel, 'Parallelomania', *Journal of Biblical Literature* vol. 81 (1962), pp. 1–13. Against Reitzenstein, in his own times, see e.g. E. Lohmeyer, *Das Urchristentum. 1 Buch. Johannes der Täufer*, Göttingen, 1932, pp. 39–40, n. 7. For a recent evaluation of the material, attempting to extract at least some usable information for the competition hypothesis from the Mandean literature, see Marcus, *John the Baptist*, pp. 19–22. See also e.g. below n. 18.

ii

Rescuing John from the bias of the gospels has one further advantage: it allows the differences between John and Jesus to be seen in greater clarity. As one example, whatever John's baptism meant and whatever it was intended to accomplish for the person he baptized it came to be understood differently by the followers of Jesus, who identified it by means of the obscure formula as a baptism that accomplished or was intended to achieve the forgiveness of sins (Mark 1:4 and parallels).[8] Furthermore, as I will argue in what follows, again stressing the differences between John and Jesus, I see John of the gospels as representative of one pattern of holiness, while Jesus of the gospels ('of the gospels': I make no claim for the historical Jesus) represented another.

Finally, concerning John of the gospels, generations of Christian commentators have understood John's teachings in ways that were exceedingly congenial to the theological perspectives of these commentators.[9] When reading their work one gets the feeling that one needs a degree in theology, preferably from a German seminary, to appreciate John. And all this, despite the fact that the gospels informed us that soldiers, tax collectors and prostitutes were among those most taken with John's message (Matt 21:32).

This characterization of those enthused by John's activity is not surprising. As Heidi Wendt has emphasized, freelance experts of the Roman world promised health, healing, afterlife concerns, care for the dead, character improvement, social mobility, opportunities for patronage, group membership and conviviality, among other blessings. These appealed in particular to women, freed persons and slaves.[10] This fits John's message and audience. However, to the best of my knowledge, the members of John's audience noted above did not have degrees in theology and John needs to be rescued from this heavy layer of theologizing that is clearly anachronistic and inappropriate for his time, place, and followers. If anything, to be meaningful for John's audience as presented in the gospels, John needs to be situated in the context of the

---

8   See further A.I. Baumgarten, 'The Baptism of John in a Second Temple Jewish Context', in J.H. Ellens et al. (eds), 'Wisdom Poured Out Like Water': Essays in Honor of Gabriele Boccaccini, Berlin, 2018, pp. 399–414.

9   Of the scholars whose work I read, J. Daniélou, The Work of John the Baptist, trans. J.A. Horn, Baltimore, 1966, is probably the most extreme in a Christological reading of the gospel accounts of the Baptist. At the same time, Daniélou was an honest and careful reader of the texts, aware of the difficulties they posed, even if he solved these difficulties in a thoroughly pious fashion.

10 H. Wendt, At the Temple Gates: the Religion of Freelance Experts in the Roman Empire, New York, 2016, pp. 183–184.

beliefs and practices that Ed Sanders has identified as 'Common Judaism'[11] and in the framework of the following that a preacher of the imminent eschaton can gather, when promoting a ritual somehow intended as preparation for that world-changing event (see above, n. 8).

The other source from which John must be freed is Josephus. The first thing a reader coming to Josephus's John from the gospels notices is that Josephus did not connect John and Jesus in any way. Furthermore, while Josephus did not believe that Jesus was the messiah, dubbing him the 'so-called' messiah (*Ant.* 20.200),[12] he thought John was a good and honest man, who encouraged Jews to live a life of piety (*Ant.* 18.117). Perhaps the next glaring difference is that the eschatological context of John's activity so central in the gospels—his being a voice (inspired by Isaiah) 'crying aloud in the wilderness 'Prepare a way for the Lord; clear a straight path for him' (Mark 1:2–3)' preaching the imminent eschaton—is entirely missing in Josephus. However, in context of Josephus's work, this is not so surprising. His reluctance to explain in detail the meaning of the vision of the stone in Daniel (*Ant.* 10.207) has usually been taken as evidence of his determination to distance himself from any messianic speculation that might offend his Roman patrons.[13] Omitting the eschatological aspect of John's work would fit well with this tendency. Rescuing John from Josephus would therefore involve, at a minimum, restoring the eschatological content of his message. Once that were accomplished the reason Herod Antipas feared John's influence with the crowds and had him executed as a pre-emptive measure, as Josephus told the story, might be more comprehensible.

---

11   E.P. Sanders, *Judaism: Practice and Belief 63 BCE–66 CE*, London–Philadelphia, 1992, pp. 47–49. Sanders acknowledged his debt to Morton Smith (1915–1991) in his understanding of the three fundamentals of 'Common Judaism' (The Pentateuch, The Temple, and the practice of ordinary Jews who were not members of any sect) and of the sources to be studied in order to recover that 'Common Judaism'.

      For Sanders account of the origin of the phrase 'Common Judaism', see E.P. Sanders, 'Common Judaism Explored', in W.O. McCready and A. Reinhartz (eds), *Common Judaism: Explorations in Second-Temple Judaism*, Minneapolis, 2008, pp. 11–23. For Sanders's debt to Morton Smith, see ibid., pp. 16–17. For an assessment of the significance of Sanders's contribution, see W.O. McCready and A. Reinhartz, 'Common Judaism and Diversity Within Judaism', ibid., pp. 1–5.

12   This understanding of *Ant.* 20.200 is confirmed by Origen, *CCels.* 1.47, who cited this passage as indicating that Josephus 'did not believe in Jesus as Christ'.

13   See A. Momigliano, 'What Flavius Josephus Did Not See', in S. Berti (ed.), *Essays on Ancient and Modern Judaism*, trans. M. Masella-Gayley, Chicago, 1994, pp. 71–75. But see also S. Mason, 'Josephus, Daniel and the Flavian House', in F. Parente and J. Sievers (eds), *Josephus and the History of the Greco-Roman Period: Essays in Memory of Morton Smith*, StPB 41, Leiden, 1994, pp. 172–175.

In addition to these considerations for why John needs to be rescued, I would like to argue that a rescued John can offer an important lesson for the varieties of esoteric and apocryphal sources in the development of Christian and Jewish traditions under discussion at the conference and now in the papers in this volume. John, as I intend to rescue him, is an example of a type of eschatological tradition and a pattern for a path to increase the quotient of holiness in life that may seem paradoxical and which we might therefore otherwise not fully appreciate. Following Carolyn Bynum, as in the epigraph to this article, precisely because the rescued John may strike us as somehow strange, it may point to important esoteric truths.

iii

Rescuing John, as already indicated above, means recognizing him as a full-fledged independent actor in the complex circumstances of the search by ancient Jews for authoritative guidance in difficult and complex times, with eighty or so years of independence under the Maccabees followed by its loss to Rome and the eventual imposition of direct Roman rule. John deserves to be characterized as an unusually successful religious freelancer, who carved out a distinctive place of his own in the crowded field of organized sects and charismatic individuals competing for loyalty and followers (for the moment and for the purposes of this paper I ignore the possibility raised by the introductory chapters of Luke that John may have been more than a 'freelancer', because he was born into a Jerusalem priestly family). John's success can be epitomized in his creation of a baptism of his own, loosely based on existing Jewish practice (otherwise it would have been incomprehensible) but directly equivalent to none, which has caused much trouble to commentators and historians seeking to place his baptism in context. Even Qumran texts, offering a new but contemporary window of insight into John's baptism, have not helped as much as was once expected (see above, n. 8).

This ritual was so unique that it acquired a distinctive name. Unlike other immersions, dubbed by their purpose, such as the different immersions intended to remove impurity or proselyte baptism, John's baptism was called by his name, that of an individual. To the best of my knowledge it was also the only ancient Jewish immersion (or that of any other religious freelancers who offered purifications) called by the personal name of its innovator and practitioner. In founding a ritual specifically associated with his name John rivalled Solomon, who according to Josephus, was taught the art concerning *daimones*, which Solomon then imparted to the Jews, turning them into effec-

RESCUING JOHN THE BAPTIST

tive exorcists. Josephus gave the example of one specific case where a fellow countryman, Elazar, exorcised a demon with a root prescribed by Solomon and then adjured the demon never to return, 'speaking Solomon's name and reciting the incantations he (Solomon) had composed (*Ant.* 8.47)'. This is not to say that personal names of central figures do not appear elsewhere in the narrative of other ancient groups.[14] Nor is the analogy to Solomon perfect, as Solomon was a figure from the Biblical past while John was a contemporary. What I want to argue is that John was special in having a *ritual* he practiced named for him and recognition of this achievement may increase the sense that John created a more significant movement than other freelance experts. He had followers, not just a haphazard collection of people he baptized, who came and went, returning home without any change, to their former lives (for John's instructions to his followers on how they were to live, see further below, after n. 22). All this adds one further reason to allocate him a leading role in the scenario of end-times and to consider with suspicion the persistent attempts in the gospel to subordinate him to Jesus.

iv

I believe I have sufficiently elaborated my position on the subordination of John to Jesus in the gospels. I now want to turn to a comparison of John and Jesus that is independent of the ancient argument whether Jesus was superior to John or vice versa. I take my lead from the analysis of Ernst Lohmeyer, who offered a straightforward and simple comparison of John and Jesus, with little attempt to argue the predominance of one over the other.[15] The impetus for this aspect of my analysis also comes from the concern expressed by J.Z. Smith that the

---

14   One thinks of Paul's fellow apostles/competitors in Corinth, whose followers boasted 'I am for Apollos', or 'I follow Cephas', or earlier of Sadducees named for Sadok or Boethusians named for Boethus and of the houses of Hillel and Shammai in Rabbinic sources. Later in the history of the Church there will be Valentinians and Marcionists. Outside of the ancient Jewish context I note the use by the physician Bacchius of the term the 'house (*oikia*) of Herophilus' to refer to the early Herophileans. See further H. von Staden, '*Haireseis and Heresy: The Case of the* haireseis iatrikai', in B.F. Meyer and E.P. Sanders (eds), *Jewish and Christian Self-Definition, Volume Three, Self-Definition in the Greco-Roman World*, Philadelphia, 1982, p. 93.

15   Lohmeyer, *Das Urchristentum.*, pp. 51–53. As an example of Lohmeyer's analysis which served as an impulse to this paper, he noticed that while John the Baptist was scrupulous in observance, Jesus declared all things clean. Lohmeyer also called attention to the gap between John the Baptist's style of observance and the lesser demands he made of his followers, to be discussed below.

usual sorts of comparison of almost any two figures, intended to show which one will flourish and which diminish, or who was superior to whom, are likely tendentious, and tendentious comparisons are regularly inherently flawed.[16]

John of the gospels was portrayed as a shaggy and unkempt individual. He chose to live in a peripheral region and expressed in his body his independence of the established social norms.[17] He wore skins and not fine robes, He did not live in luxury (Mark 1:6; Matt 11:7–11 / Luke 7:25). It was no accident that he refused to eat bread and drink wine, like any 'normal' person, but chose to eat honey from the hive and locusts. These protests against the conventions earned John a rebuke from the wider community. He was reproached as possessed, that is stark raving mad (Matt 11:18: 'For John came neither eating nor drinking, and they say, "He has a demon"' / Luke 7:33: 'For John the Baptist has come eating no bread and drinking no wine; and you say, "He has a demon"'). Some scholars have suggested that John's lifestyle, diet in particular, was a result of the fact that he was once an Essene (or a member of an Essene-like group) who was expelled, but still felt obliged by his oaths to eat only food prepared under the auspices of the group, to which he no longer had access. His only option was to live on 'grasses' (Josephus, *War* 2.143: 'Those who are convicted of serious crimes they expel from the order; and the ejected individual often comes to a most miserable end. For being bound by their oaths and usages, he is not at liberty to partake of other men's food, and so falls to eating grass and wastes away and dies of starvation'), that is, on food that he could take directly himself, raw from nature.[18]

Charlesworth portrays John as a 'son of dawn',[19] who began the process of membership at Qumran (or, I would add, at a similar group) and accepted its

---

16   On the flawed nature of so many of the comparisons offered when Jesus and his followers were the subject, see J.Z. Smith, *Drudgery Divine: On the Comparison of Early Christianities and the Religions of Late Antiquity*, Chicago, 1990, pp. 27, 143.

17   M. Douglas, *Natural Symbols: Explorations in Cosmology*, 2nd edn, London, 1996, p. 97.

18   This conclusion has been disputed by J. Taylor, *The Immerser: John the Baptist within Second Temple Judaism*, Grand Rapids, 1997, p. 77. See also H. Thyen, 'ΒΑΠΤΙΣΜΑ ΜΕΤΑΝΟΙΑΣ ΕΙΣ ΑΦΕΣΙΝ ΑΜΑΡΤΙΩΝ', in J.L. Robinson (ed.), *The Future of our Religious Past: Essays in Honour of Rudolf Bultmann*, New York, 1971, p. 151, who also dismissed the possible Qumran connections of John as 'romantic constructions ... just as untenable as the view that he was the ancestor of the Mandeans.'

   For a thorough critique of Taylor's conclusions, see J. Charlesworth, 'John the Baptizer and the Dead Sea Scrolls', in id. (ed.), *The Bible and the Dead Sea Scrolls, Volume Three, The Scrolls and Christian Origins*, Waco, 2006, pp. 12–17. For the place of John's diet in arguing against Taylor, see ibid., pp. 25–26.

19   A term Charlesworth invented for John's liminal status in Qumran terms, i.e. on the way to become a 'son of light', but not yet quite there.

limitations for life, but was caught in the middle when he refused to utterly condemn all those who were not members of the community he intended to join: he knew how to avoid the concentrated essence of holiness, which Koestler recognized as venom.[20] However, as Charlesworth correctly insisted, the gospel materials concerning John show that we should not turn him into a soft headed and soft hearted pacifist guru, who loved all humanity without reservation and exception: 'it would be inaccurate to suggest that he was a man of love'.[21] He could be bitter in his denunciation of those Jewish leaders with whom he disagreed ('brood of vipers', as an accusation of the crowd, Luke 3:7–9; as an accusation of the Pharisees and Sadducees, Matt 3:7), and his criticism of the marriage of Herod Antipas and Herodias (Mark 6:17–20 and parallels) contributed to his execution. If the 'competition hypothesis', discussed in section iii is correct, his disciples defended his status in confrontation with those of Jesus. All this is perfectly 'normal' in the context of imminent eschatological expectation, which was the core of John's message, when—as Richard Landes has noted, with irony—there is no such thing as baseless hatred (for which, according to the Rabbis, the Second Temple was destroyed) because all hatred is justified.[22]

Where John differed and where this difference is worth attention is in the demands he made of followers. The pattern of holiness to which John conformed was that a high level of holiness required a high level of personal obligation, restriction and sacrifice of identity. But what about his followers? The gospel evidence suggests that they did not have to live as John did and perhaps that was part of his appeal. The practical advice he gave his followers in Luke 3:10–14 did not require followers to adopt John's diet, clothing, or move to the desert. On the other hand, that advice was banal: the man with two shirts should share them with the man who has none; tax assessors should 'exact no more than the assessment'; and soldiers should not bully or take blackmail. They should make do with their pay.

The modern commentators I consulted recognized that John did not invite the crowd to adopt his way of life.[23] He did not insist on extraordinary penances.[24] His advice to followers was a simple selfless concern for others. By way

---

20 Charlesworth, 'John the Baptizer', p. 32.

21 Ibid.

22 See A.I. Baumgarten, 'Four Stages in the Life of a Millennial Movement', in S. O'Leary and G. McGhee (eds), *War in Heaven/Heaven on Earth: Theories of the Apocalyptic*, London, 2005, p. 73 n. 30.

23 J.A. Fitzmyer, *The Gospel According to Luke 1–9*, AB28, New York, 1981, p. 465.

24 F. Bovon, *Luke 1: A Commentary on the Gospel of Luke 1:1–9:50*, trans. C.M. Thomas, Hermeneia, Minneapolis, 2002, p. 124.

of contrast, Ernst Lohmeyer, one of the early scholars to discuss the career of John, recognized that John's advice to followers was so banal as to be virtually meaningless, hence useless. Who would not offer these pieces of advice or disagree with them? This defect is especially acute when considered from the perspective of the liminal time left before the ultimate redemption of the world that John proclaimed. One might expect a severe demand, some significant sacrifice of identity parallel to that made by John for himself, appropriate to the world changing grand finale that John preached would soon take place and for which he was preparing those he baptized.[25]

It is therefore interesting that John did not insist that his followers make a meaningful sacrifice of identity: Tax collectors remained tax collectors and soldiers were still soldiers (prostitutes still prostitutes?). They were to behave properly, but no more than that. Following John also meant that one fasted and prayed (Mark 2:18: 'Now John's disciples and the Pharisees were fasting; and people came and said to him, "Why do John's disciples and the disciples of the Pharisees fast, but your disciples do not fast?"; Luke 5:33: 'Then they said to him (Jesus): John's disciples are much given to fasting and prayer, and so are the disciples of the Pharisees, but yours eat and drink'), but fasting and praying were not exceptional for John's time and place and were not a severe sacrifice of identity.[26] All this is strange and following Bynum, once more, worthy of attention.[27]

Was this leniency simply a cynical ploy to attract followers? I would argue otherwise, based on a comparison of John with other religious freelancers, Apollonius of Tyana in particular. In that comparative light, John's attitude seems plausible and genuine, perhaps even one consequence of his refusal to condemn all mankind, which was the reason for his disagreement and departure from Qumran or a similar group, as suggested by Charlesworth (see above,

---

25   Lohmeyer, *Das Urchristentum*, pp. 105–110.

26   See J. Muddiman, 'Fast, Fasting', in D.N. Freedman, *Anchor Bible Dictionary* vol. 2, New York, 1991, pp. 773–776, esp. p. 774, col. B. According to Suetonius, *Divus Augustus*, 76.2, Augustus wrote to Tiberius that not even a Jew fasted so scrupulously on his Sabbaths than he had today. Jewish fasting was proverbial and widely known. On this passage, see further M. Stern, *Greek and Latin Authors on Jews and Judaism, Volume Two, From Tacitus to Simplicius*, Jerusalem, 1980, #303, p. 110.

27   The pattern of holiness attributed to Jesus in some places in the gospels is quite different. As priests serving in the Temple broke laws of the Sabbath that applied elsewhere, so Jesus was greater than the Temple. As the Son of Man he was sovereign over the Sabbath, Mark 2:23–28//Matt 12:3–8. Whether this freedom extended down and was enjoyed by all those baptized in the name of Jesus would become a subject of debate by the time of Paul. I intend to explore this point in greater detail elsewhere.

n. 19 ff.). The minimal demands of followers may therefore be less surprising and strange than they seem at first sight: they were not an exception. 'Godly Men' might be distinctive in their level of extreme holiness, as a way of countering the ever-present suspicion that they were charlatans.[28] But they did not necessarily require their followers to adopt that same level of strictness. The strictness and asceticism as marks of holiness of the founder did not necessarily obligate the followers to the same degree. That level of holiness may have been reserved for the founder and served as a marker of the founder's unique status. From that perspective, again strange as it may seem, John's minimal demands of his followers may have been at the same time a mark of his openness to the larger world, of his willingness to accept followers from the lowest social and religious classes 'as they were', and also a way of asserting a very special and holy status for himself alone. It would be almost sacrilegious for his followers to live as he did. To complete the circle of the 'competition hypothesis' with which this article began, perhaps the unique place occupied by John allowed his followers to argue that this stature was not shared by his former disciple, Jesus.

Apollonius of Tyana is a prime example of a Godly Man to be compared to John. Apollonius did not oppose everything done by contemporaries in the name of his own higher standards. He remained loyal to those higher standards personally, while allowing others (at least at times) to continue to worship the gods through animal sacrifice as they had done according to their own traditions, so long as he was not obliged to be present at the animal sacrifice and then allowed to sacrifice incense (only) in his own way. As Apollonius told the King of Babylon who invited him to sacrifice: 'Do you, O King, go on with your sacrifice, in your own way, but permit me to sacrifice in mine. And he took up a handful of incense and said ... (Philostratus, *Life*, I.xxxi)'. Apollonius then left the scene of the blood sacrifice, in order not to be present when blood was shed, but immediately offered the king a service appropriate to Apollonius's status as a sage: 'if you have problems that are difficult and hard to settle I will furnish you with solutions (*Life*, I.xxxii)'. As one example, Apollonius then took steps to reconcile the King of Babylon with the Eritreans, with the king declaring:

---

28   See L. Bieler, ΘΕΙΟΣ ΑΝΗΡ *Das Bild des 'göttlichen Menschen' in Spätantike und Frühchristentum*, Vienna, 1935, pp. 87–94, and especially A.M. Reimer, *Miracle and Magic: A Study in the Acts of the Apostles and the Life of Apollonius of Tyana*, London, 2002, pp. 212–244. Frauds aside, it was also very easy to be distressed by the behavior of Godly men and their implicit critique of others, less godly than they. As a response against these extreme expressions of holiness, see the quotation from Arthur Koestler in the epigraph to this article.

'The Eritreans were, until yesterday, the enemies of myself and my fathers ... but henceforth they shall be written among my friends, and they shall have a satrap, a good man, who will rule their country justly (*Life*, 1.xxxxv)'.[29]

In a similar vein, when the Indian king wanted to follow the same stringent life style as Apollonius, he advised the Indian king to be moderate and indulgent in in his life, as guided by philosophy. To be excessively rigorous (*akribēs*) and severe, Apollonius argued, was to seem to be vulgar and cheap for a king, and might be construed by the envious as due to pride, and therefore inappropriate for a king.[30] A moderate and indulgent philosophy would be the best solution under the royal circumstances, Philostratus, *Life*, II.xxxvii.

Furthermore, although Apollonius was vegetarian, he never reproved those who ate meat or fish, or who wore luxurious clothing made from animal skins, *Life* VIII.vii.4. It was precisely on this matter that Eusebius criticized Apollonius, effectively calling him hypocritical. Although himself a vegetarian, he allowed Damis and his other companions to eat meat, contending that 'abstinence from meat had in no way advanced their moral development'. Eusebius, 'Treatise', xiii, found this unbelievable. How could Apollonius not have demanded that Damis, 'his best friend, and as the only disciple and follower of his life', give up consuming the flesh of living animals? How could Apollonius have excused this inconsistency with his own commitment to vegetarianism, commenting that he saw 'no moral advantage in them (i.e. his disciples) produced by such abstinence'.[31]

---

29   On the role of wise men as peace makers, see A.I. Baumgarten, '"Sages Increase Peace in the World": Reconciliation and Power', in C. Hayes, M. Novick, and M. Bar-Asher Siegal (eds), *The Faces of Torah. Studies in the Texts and Contexts of Ancient Judaism in Honor of Steven Fraade*, JAJS 22, Göttingen, 2017, pp. 221–237.

30   Compare the advice the given to Izates of Adiabene by his mother and Jewish adviser Ananias when he first contemplated conversion to Judaism, Josephus, *Ant.* 20.38–42. Izates should not convert because his people would 'not tolerate the rule of a Jew'. He could continue to worship the God of Hebrew Bible without being circumcised and God would forgive him as he was constrained by necessity and fear of his subjects from performing Jewish rites. It was only later that another Jew, Eleazar from the Galilee, who had a reputation for being extremely strict when it came to ancestral laws, urged him to be circumcized that Izates had his physician perform the rite. This incident well illustrates a point which Wendt, *At the Temple Gates*, pp. 87–99 stressed: different free-lance representatives speaking in the name of the same religious tradition could differ in their presentations of the requirements or beliefs of that tradition. For her discussion of the conversion of Adiabene in that context, see ibid., pp. 102–107.

31   I presume that Eusebius avoided the possibility that, as argued above, an analogous charge could have been made against John the Baptist, who did not demand that his followers adopt the stringent diet by which he lived. By contrast, as Eusebius presumably understood the career of Jesus, his demands of followers for the freedom allowed them was

V

To conclude, I intend this discussion of John to teach us that we must be prepared to admit more flexibility and variety to the types of groups that may arise in imminent expectation of the end.[32] At times like that, we are accustomed to encounter hypernomian movements such as the Qumran community and extreme antinomian tendencies, such as exhibited by Shabbetai Tzvi (Sabbatai Sevi) and some of his followers,[33] the Ranters in seventeenth century England,[34] or the Anabaptists of Münster, who rose against the entire existing social order.[35] We are not surprised by statements like the one attributed to a contemporary follower of R. Eliezer Berland, a convicted Israeli sex offender, for which he served a prison sentence, 'He is allowed, he is God'.[36]

However, the complexities to which I point and against whose background I wish to portray John can also be illustrated from seventeenth century England, whose Ranters were noted above: England of that era included other millenarians, not only Ranters, all up and down the social ladder, whose visions of the grand finale were not nearly as radical as those of the Ranters. Lamont has uncovered men who were no less millenarian than the Ranters, but who did not see why the imminent end of the world should mean the forthcoming end of traditional political allegiances. Their millenarian faith was implicit; there was no reason why it should be made explicit.[37]

The double aspect of these complexities is also evident from the material about Shabbetai Tzvi, consistently understood by Scholem in terms of Luri-

---

consistent with his own. For Eusebius, John the Baptist did not matter nearly as much as the greater one to whom he pointed, and Eusebius's Jesus could not be accused of the same inconsistency as Eusebius accused Apollonius of Tyana.

32   This is one sub-category of the phenomenon noted above, n. 30, that self-appointed freelance experts claiming to speak in the name of the same religion can differ widely in their presentation of the doctrines and requirements of that religion.

33   Shabbetai Tzvi encouraged his followers to reinterpret the traditional blessing, מתיר אסורים, meaning that God freed prisoners, to mean 'permitting the forbidden'. Pronouncing this blessing with this new meaning was followed by eating forbidden animal fat. See G. Scholem, *Sabbatai Sevi: The Mystical Messiah, 1626–1676, with a New Introduction by Yaacob Dweck*, Princeton, 1973, pp. 387–388.

34   As one Ranter formulated it, 'those are most perfect … which do commit the greatest sin with no remorse'.

     C. Hill, *The World Turned Upside Down: Radical Ideas During the English Revolution*, London, 1984, p. 208.

35   Ibid., p. 161.

36   The Jerusalem Post, September 27, 2018.

37   W. Lamont, *Godly Rule: Politics and Religion 1603–1660*, London, 1969, p. 19.

anic Kabbalah and his own preference for anarchic mysticism.[38] Variations on the theme of what was now permitted or forbidden in this esoteric tradition abounded, with a lively conversation and debate taking place both above and below the surface of public events and official proclamation. Some of Shabbetai's followers concluded that, 'the (antinomian) action of the Messiah sets an example and is a duty ... We must *all* (emphasis in the original) descend into the realm of evil in order to vanquish it from within'.[39] These actions followed from Shabbetai Tzvi's declaration that there was no 'division or separation between me and Him', that he was 'the Lord your God'.[40] For all this Shabbetai Tzvi was declared a heretic both before and after his apostasy.[41] It was reported 'that the rabbis of Jerusalem wanted to kill Shabbetai because he had blasphemed God and His Law'.[42]

However, not all his believers, even including Nathan of Gaza, followed Shabbetai Tzvi in the blessing that 'permitted the forbidden', which was followed by eating forbidden fat (see above, n. 33). Some, at least, formulated their position as arguing that what was permitted to Shabbetai Tzvi because of his special status was not permitted to them. They needed to be conventionally observant of the usual Jewish legal commandments. Perhaps he was divine, but they were human. Therefore, if the special divine status of the founder allowed the founder and some followers the privilege of 'permitting the forbidden', then other followers maintained that status was also reserved for the founder alone. The paradox of the new religious life was limited to the person of the messiah.[43] The remark made by Abraham Miguel Cardozo (1627–1706) expressed well that perspective: in the current circumstances, the interim period awaiting

---

38 See Jacob Dweck's concluding sentence to his introduction to the new English version of Scholem's *Sabbatai Ṣevi: The Mystical Messiah, 1626–1676*, p. lxv: 'Nearly every page of this extraordinary book is shot through with Scholem's celebration of anarchic nihilism, his profound antipathy for Maimonides, and his deep-seated ambivalence before the law'.
    I have chosen to focus on Shabbetai Tzvi and on Scholem's analysis of his life as a way of turning the tables on Scholem, who made a number of comparisons between Shabbetai Tzvi and Nathan of Gaza and Paul, using Paul as a source of insight into Shabbetai Tzvi. Thus, Nathan's missionary activity was similar to Paul's, Scholem, *Mystical Messiah*, p. 721. Shabbetai Tzvi's doctrine of faith was analogous to Paul's and both had antinomian aspects, ibid., pp. 796–797. In standing Scholem's analysis on its head I am utilizing his study of the Sabbatean movement to illuminate John the Baptist.

39 G. Scholem, *Major Trends in Jewish Mysticism*, 3rd edn, New York, 1961, p. 315.

40 Scholem, *Mystical Messiah*, pp. 235–236.

41 Ibid., pp. 240–246, 644.

42 Ibid., p. 242.

43 Scholem, *Major Trends*, p. 314. Scholem recognized this aspect of the Sabbatean movement despite his own predilection for anarchic nihilism (above, n. 38).

the return of the Messiah, Shabbetai Tzvi, after his apostasy, from his mission in the realms where Cardozo dared not follow him, in the world of the 'husks', where he gathered up the holy sparks, the freedom for mystical apostasy was reserved only for the Messiah. The tradition retained its validity for all others.[44] These differences in the practical consequences of events continued after Shabbetai's apostasy: he did not demand that his followers do likewise, insisting that no one embrace Islam on his own initiative, even if some followers did.[45] However, as one final complication, Shabbetai Tzvi did sometimes encourage certain followers to become Muslims,[46] at times preaching conversion to Islam to his followers in the synagogue.[47]

Returning to John, when he is rescued from the biases of the ancient sources—the gospels and Josephus—he will be seen as the founder of an independent eschatological movement that does not fit comfortably into the usual extremist categories. He remains paradoxical in light of our expectations. Strict himself, but more lenient with his followers, he reminds us that the line between the hypernomians and antinomians is a spectrum with many intermediate possibilities.

Bryan Wilson's distinction between 'reformist' and 'introversionist' sects is most helpful here and indicates some of those possibilities on the spectrum between hypernomism and antinomism.[48] That is, the former hold hopes of reforming the larger society, and have not given up on it or renounced it totally, still perceiving themselves as members of the whole, while the latter have given up on the larger society. It is past hope. Accordingly, the demands of the reformist group for sacrifice of identity were lower and the walls they built between themselves and the larger society were lower.[49] In Wilson's terms, John may have once been on the introversionist end and observed those allegiances

---

44   See G. Scholem, 'The Crisis of Tradition in Jewish Messianism', *The Messianic Idea in Judaism and other Essays on Jewish Spirituality*, New York, 1971, pp. 72–73. See also Scholem, *Mystical Messiah*, pp. 817–819.

45   Ibid., pp. 727–728, 858–859.

46   Ibid., p. 822.

47   Ibid., pp. 823, 839, 847–848. In fact, at one point Nathan of Gaza wrote to Shabbetai imploring him not to demand that Nathan embrace Islam, as Shabbetai was wont to do of others, ibid., p. 850.

48   As I have shown elsewhere, this distinction applies well to the ancient Jewish groups, with the Sadducees and Pharisees as reformist sects, while the Qumran Covenanters would fit Wilson's category of introversionist. See A.I. Baumgarten, *The Flourishing of Jewish Sects in the Maccabean Era: An Interpretation*, SJSJ 53, Leiden, 1997, pp. 13–15.

49   B. Wilson, *Magic and the Millennium: A Sociological Study of Religious Movements of Protest among Tribal and Third-World Peoples*, New York, 1973, pp. 18–26.

in his personal life, but was closer to the reformist end of the spectrum, at least in his public activity.

The millenarian beliefs of John and his followers did not dominate and eventually died out. They lost in the competition to another millenarian movement.[50] They were esoteric in their own time, as evidenced by the fact that we have few direct testimonies and must read the gospels against the grain to recover them. If they left any mark on the later history of the Western tradition it was through the complex traditions of the Mandeans, whose direct connection to the historical John and his disciples is dubious at best.[51] However, in the larger methodological sense for which I want to argue, John reminds us of the variety of possibilities in esoteric traditions. They can be strange in ways other than those which we might anticipate. In John's case, specifically, the holy behaviour of the founder may be a mark of his uniqueness. We should not take the patterns we observe in the modern world as the rubric into which all examples fit: the movement to the extremes by as many believers as possible is not inevitable or inherent in taking religious obligations seriously or in vivid anticipation of the ultimate redemption. This is where I disagree with an important article by a distinguished colleague, now deceased, Charles Liebman, who considered religious extremism the norm. Liebman argued that in religious life it was always true that: 'the more the better'. For Liebman, since religious extremism was the norm it was not the phenomenon that called for explanation; rather, the instances of moderation were the exceptions which called for the effort of understanding why they deviated from the norm of extremism. Liebman's focus was on hypernomianism, and perhaps he might have continued his argument for antinomian movements as well. There too, 'the more was better'.[52]

My disagreement with Liebman is that historical examples show that this rule of thumb, 'the more the better' does not always apply in a simple way. Leaders and freelancers who preach of the imminent eschaton can offer a varied message. Indeed, a figure who was himself severe but more lenient in demands made on followers, who also founded a ritual of his own to prepare followers for the eschaton, can have immense appeal. He could well claim that all these attributes combined made him unique and that therefore his followers were

---

50   W. Bauer, *Orthodoxy and Heresy in Earliest Christianity*, ed. R.A. Kraft and G. Krodel, Philadelphia, 1971.

51   See above, n. 7.

52   C. Liebman, 'Extremism as a Religious Norm', *Journal for the Scientific Study of Religion* vol. 22 (1983), pp. 75–86. See also A.I. Baumgarten, 'The Nature of Religious Extremism', in M. Litvak and O. Limor (eds), *Religious Extremism*, Jerusalem, 2007, pp. 43–56; in Hebrew.

almost forbidden to follow his life style. This may seem paradoxical at first, but examples exist and I propose John the Baptist as one. As strange as he may seem to us, in the context in which I suggest to place him, it was not strange that the Jews of his time, for whom he was a symbol of unique holiness, but whom he refused to reject and did not insist that they live as he did, considered him a just and holy man.[53]

53 'Just and holy', even in the eyes of Herod Antipas, who eventually had John executed, according to Mark 6:19. Compare the similar assessment of John by Josephus: John was a 'good man' who 'exhorted the Jews to lead righteous lives, to practice justice towards their fellows and piety towards God' (*Ant.* 18.117), as discussed above, n. 12 ff.

CHAPTER 18

The Esoteric Legacy of the Magi of Bethlehem in the Framework of the Iranian Speculations about Jesus, Zoroaster and His Three Posthumous Sons

Antonio Panaino

The cycle of the Evangelic Magi has known a number of intriguing evolutions. Although their number was not explicitly stated in the pericope of Matthew (II, 1–12), the standard figure 'three' progressively gained general consensus because of a comprehensible inference strictly connected with the three gifts, originally brought by *all* the Oriental Wise Men together and presented to Jesus without individual distinctions. This implicit determination, in any case, was not universal and compelling; in fact, in the early framework of Christian iconography we can find two, three, four, eight Magi,[1] and in some of the Eastern Christian traditions their number was extended even to 12.[2] While the

---

1 See already G. Ryckmans (1951) 'De l' or (?), de l' encens et de la myrre', *Revue Biblique* vol. 58, no. 3 (1951), pp. 372–376; A. Panaino, *I Magi e la loro stella. Storia, scienza e teologia di un racconto evangelico* (Parola di Dio; Seconda Serie 67), Cinisello Balsamo–Milano, 2012, pp. 69–72.

2 A. Panaino, 'Considerazioni storico-linguistiche e storico-religiose intorno ai nomi dei Magi evangelici: Prolegomena alla redazione di un *Namenbuch*', *Atti del Sodalizio Glottologico Milanese* voll. 8–9 N.S. (2013–2014), 2016, pp. 41–81, with a detailed discussion in connection with their names. In few cases, there are only two Magi for reasons of artistic symmetry, or four, as it happens, for instance, in the *Codex Laurentianus* (Med. Pal. Orient. 387; Codex Orientalis 32; cf. G. Messina, 'Il *Saušyant-* nella tradizione iranica e la sua attesa', *Orientalia* vol. 1 (Nuova serie) (1933), pp. 149–176, in particular 172–173), containing an apocryphal *Arabic Gospel of Jesus' Childhood*. See H. Stocks, 'Die Magierminiaturen des Cod. Med. Pal. 387, die literarische Überlieferung und der "Orientalische Typus"', *Byzantinisch-Neugriechische Jahrbücher* Band 20 (1921), pp. 329–343, in particular pp. 333–334; J. Lafontaine-Dosogne, 'Le cycle des Mages dans l' Évangile arabe de l' Enfance du Christ à Florence', in A. Destrée (ed.), *Mélanges d'Islamologie dédiés à la mémoire de Armand Abel par ses collègues, ses élèves et ses amis* (Correspondance d'Orient 13 vol. II, Centre pour l' étude des problèmes du monde musulman contemporain), Bruxelles–Leiden, 1975, pp. 287–294, especially pp. 289–292, fig. 2; ead., 'Iconography of the Cycle of the Infancy of Christ', in P.A. Underwood (ed.), *The Kariye Djami* vol. 4, *Studies in the Art of the Kariye Djami and its Intellectual Background*, Princeton, N.J., 1975, pp. 195–241, in particular pp. 202, and 210–211; ead, 'L' illustration du cycle des Mages suivant l' homélie sur la Nativité attribuée à Jean Damascène', *Le Muséon* vol. 100 (1987), pp. 211–224, in particular p. 217; M. Provera, *Il Vangelo arabo dell'infanzia secondo il ms. lau-*

© ANTONIO PANAINO, 2021 | DOI:10.1163/9789004445925_020

THE ESOTERIC LEGACY OF THE MAGI OF BETHLEHEM

last solution seems to be clearly later, and based on a multiplication of the more common figure referring to the three Magi (3×4), generally sub-divided in three further distinguished groups of four travellers, one of whom was the main royal person (the others were simply minor 'princes'),[3] the number three offered in itself a very high conspectus of potential connections and speculative associations. For instance, particularly in the theological context of the Christological debates concerning the determination of the economy of the 'divine persons' in God, the Magi were frequently taken as a symbol of the Trinitarian doctrine.[4] In any case, a large number of other implications were possible. Some of them have been already discussed by Olschki,[5] and strictly concern the intricate elaboration of Irano-Hellenistic traditions in the Eastern Christian context. This is, in fact, the case of the impressive interplay produced by the attribution to each of the (three) Magi of a different age: thus, one of them frequently appears as a young boy, another as an adult, mature person, while the third one is usually portrayed as a venerable old man. The distribution of these three different ages of the human life as a sort of mirror of *die Weltalter*, past, present and future, was not only a symbol of the entire humanity and of the whole universe bowing in front of Christ, but it could be also considered as a mirror of the absolute a-temporal power of the Christ-God. This observation can be supported on the basis of some strong evidence, because it was also Christ who, in his turn, manifested himself to the Magi in adoration in the form of a baby, a mature and, finally, a very old man. This kind of mystical interplay was literally mentioned by various Christian sources: the oldest one seems to be a *Homily about the Nativity of our Lord Jesus Christ* (*Homilia in nativitatem Domini nostri Jesu Christi*), chapter 11, lines 25–30, attributed to

---

renziano orientale (*n. 387*) (Quaderni della Terra Santa), Gerusalemme, 1973. There is also an example with eight Magi (see Panaino, *I Magi e la loro stella*, p. 70).

3   J. Daniélou, 'Les douze Apôtres et le Zodiaque', *Vigiliæ Christianæ* vol. 13 (1959), pp. 14–21. See also the legend of the twelve Babylonian astrologers and Zoroaster, on which see A. Panaino, 'The Twelve Babylonian Astrologers and Zoroaster', *Wiener Zeitschrift für die Kunde des Morgenlandes* Band 97 (2007), pp. 305–309.

4   See T. Avner, 'The Impact of the Liturgy on Style and Content: The Triple-Christ Scene in Taphou 14', in *Akten XVI. Internationaler Byzantinistenkongress, Wien, 4.–9. Oktober 1981.* II. Teil, 5. Teilband, *Kurzbeiträge.* 10. *Die Stilbildende Funktion der byzantinischen Kunst, Jahrbuch der Österreichische Byzantinistik* Band 32 (1982), pp. 459/467, in particular 459–461 with bibliography; Lafontaine-Dosogne, 'L'illustration du cycle des Mages suivant l'homélie sur la Nativité attribuée à Jean Damascène', p. 221.

5   L. Olschki, 'The Wise Men of the East in Oriental Traditions', in W.J. Fischel (ed.), *Semitic and Oriental Studies: A Volume Presented to William Popper, Professor of Semitic Languages, Emeritus, on the Occasion of his seventy-fifth birthday, October 29, 1949* (University of California Publications in Semitic Philology vol. 11), Berkeley–Los Angeles, 1951, pp. 375–395, pp. 381–386.

370   PANAINO

Johannes Damascenus (ca. 676–749), although the identity of its real author remains a matter of question.[6] Many scholars, such as Lafontaine-Dosogne,[7] Favaro[8] and Kreahling McKay,[9] have rightly focused on the fact that in an 11th century Byzantine manuscript of Jerusalem (Taphou 14),[10] the text of this *Homely* presents a miniature clearly referring to this particular event of the cycle of the Magi, so that it can be fittingly connected with Johannes Damascenus's text.[11] The same tradition was also reworked in details in the *Armenian*

---

6   P.B. Kotter, *Die Schriften des Johannes von Damaskos* vol. 5., *Patristische Texte und Studien* 29, Berlin–New York, 1988, p. 342. See also the discussion in Lafontaine-Dosogne, 'L'illustration du cycle des Mages suivant l'homélie sur la Nativité attribuée à Jean Damascène', p. 211, n. 1. Cf. also J. Dölger, 'Johannes "von Euboia"', *Analecta Bollandiana* vol. 68, 1950, pp. 5–26; Avner, 'The Impact of the Liturgy on Style and Content: The Triple-Christ Scene in Taphou 14', p. 462. See already H.-Ch. Puech, 'Histoire de l'ancienne église et patristique', *Annuaire de l'École Pratique des Hautes Études, Section des Sciences Religieuses* (1966–1967) tome 74, pp. 128–138, on particular p. 135; P. Bringel, *Une polémique religieuse à la cour perse: le "de gestis in Perside"; histoire du texte, édition critique et traduction* (Thèse de Doctorat sous la direction de J. Gascou à la Sorbonne), Paris, 2008, pp. 122–123.

7   Lafontaine-Dosogne, 'Le cycle des Mages dans l'Évangile arabe de l'Enfance du Christ à Florence', pp. 287–294; ead., 'Iconography of the Cycle of the Infancy of Christ', pp. 195–241; ead., 'L'illustration du cycle des Mages suivant l'homélie sur la Nativité attribuée à Jean Damascène', pp. 211–224.

8   R. Favaro, 'Un'inconsueta adorazione dei magi in un affresco di San Giorgio a Velo d'Astico', *Studi sull'Oriente Cristiano* vol. 4, n° 2 (*Miscellanea Metreveli*) (2000), pp. 229–266, in particular pp. 240–242.

9   Gr. Kraehling McKay, 'Christ's Polymorphism in Jerusalem, Taphou 14: An Examination of Text and Image', *Apocrypha* vol. 14 (2003), pp. 177–191.

10   Unfortunately, the ms. Esphighmenou 14 of Mount Athos, which also includes the *Nativity Sermon* attributed to John Damascenus and a large number of miniatures does not preserve any representation of Jesus's Polymorphism. See Puech, 'Histoire de l'ancienne église et patristique', p. 136; Kraehling McKay, 'Christ's Polymorphism in Jerusalem, Taphou 14: An Examination of Text and Image', pp. 167–209.

11   A. Terian, *The Armenian Gospel of the Infancy with three early versions of the Protevangelium of James*, Oxford, 2008, pp. 55–57; P. Peeters, *Évangiles apocryphes* tome 2: *L'évangile de l'enfance, rédactions syriaques, arabe et arméniennes traduites et annotées*, Paris, 1914, pp. 142–147; cf. G.R. Cardona in *Milione. Versione toscana del Trecento. Edizione critica a cura di V. Bertolucci Pizzorusso, Indice ragionato di G.R. Cardona*, Milano, 1994, pp. 659–660. For some pertinent reflexes visible in the *Armenian Ēǰmiacin Gospel*, see L.A. Dournovo, *Armenian Miniatures*, Preface by S. Der Nersessian, New York, N.Y., 1961, p. 37; Th.F. Mathews, 'The Early Armenian Iconographic Program of the Ejmiadzin Gospel', in N. Garsoian and Th. Mathews, and R. Thomson (eds), *East of Byzantium: Syria and Armenia in the formative Period. Dumbarton Oaks Symposium May 9–11 1980* (The Dumbarton Oaks Research Library and Collection), Washington, District of Columbia, 1982, pp. 199–215. Cf. also D. Kouymjian, 'The Classical Tradition in Armenian Art', *Revue des Études Arméniennes* N.S. vol. 15 (1981), pp. 263–288, plus 11 plances, in particular pp. 267–268; A. Panaino, 'Jesus' Trimorphisms and Tetramorphisms in the Meeting with the Magi',

THE ESOTERIC LEGACY OF THE MAGI OF BETHLEHEM   371

Gospel of Lord's Infancy, a source which has been finally presented in a superb version with all the pertinent textual variants by Terian,[12] and later (for the most pertinent sections here concerned) by Dorfmann-Lazarev,[13] while Marco Polo himself shortly mentioned the same episode,[14] framed in a patent Persian *milieu*. In its turn, eight different visions were reported by the Magi in the *Chronicle of Zuqnīn*, as already remarked by Dorfmann-Lazarev.[15] Furthermore, this sacred drama offered a theme for a number of extraordinarily explicit artistic representations.

The polymorphic manifestation of Jesus (with strict reference to his apparent different ages) does not belong only to the cycle of the Magi;[16] in reality, it

---

in I. Szántó (ed.), *From Aṣl to Zāʾid: Essays in Honour of Éva M. Jeremiás* (The Avicenna Institute of Middle Eastern Studies, Acta et Studia 13), Piliscsaba, 2015, pp. 167–209; id., 'La pericope dei Magi nel Vangelo di Matteo', in A. Panaino and F. Cardini (eds), *La Luce della Stella. I Re magi fra arte e storia* (Indo-Iranica et Orientalia, Series Lazur 17), Milano, 2017, pp. 19–34.

12 See Terian, *The Armenian Gospel of the Infancy with three early versions of the Protevangelium of James, passim.* I have recently discussed in details this subject in the article just quoted in the previous note, 'Jesus' Trimorphisms and Tetramorphisms in the Meeting with the Magi', 167–209. See also the pertinent remarks offered by I. Dorfmann-Lazarev, 'The Cave of the Nativity revisited: memory of the primæval beings in the Armenian *Lord's Infancy* and cognate sources', in A. Mardirossian, A. Ouzounian and C. Zuckerman (eds), *Mélanges Jean-Pierre Mahé* (Travaux et Mémoires 18), Paris, 2014, pp. 285–334, in particular pp. 305–315.

13 Dorfmann-Lazarev, 'The Cave of the Nativity revisited: memory of the primæval beings in the Armenian *Lord's Infancy* and cognate sources', pp. 320–333 with an edition of the most important chapters from manuscript *Matenadaran* 7574.

14 Mediæval French text (*Divisament dou Monde*, ch. XXXI) according to the edition by G. Ronchi (Marco Polo, *Milione—Le Divisament dou Monde. Il Milione nelle redazioni toscana e franco-italiana*, a cura di G. Ronchi, Introduzione di C. Segre, Milano, 1982 [reprinted 2006, p. 339]; for the early Italian text (*Il Milione*, ch. XXX), see also the edition Bertolucci Pizzorusso, pp. 42–43). Cf. also the above quoted edition by Ronchi (pp. 34–35) and the English translation by H. Yule, *The Book of Ser Marco Polo, the Venetian: concerning the kingdoms and marvels of the East, newly translated and edited, with Notes* vol. I, London, 1871, p. 79. See already W.A.V. Jackson, 'The Magi in Marco Polo and the Cities in Persia from Which They Came to Worship the Infant Christ', *Journal of the American Oriental Society* vol. 26 (1905), pp. 79–83. Cf. also Puech ('Histoire de l'ancienne église et patristique', pp. 131–132), who strongly criticizes the earlier commentaries in which Marco Polo's account about the trimorphism of Jesus was considered unorthodox and sometimes even removed from the text.

15 Dorfmann-Lazarev, 'The Cave of the Nativity revisited: memory of the primæval beings in the Armenian *Lord's Infancy* and cognate sources', p. 307, *passim*; see also Panaino, 'Jesus' Trimorphisms and Tetramorphisms in the Meeting with the Magi', pp. 188–189 and n. 117, 196–197, n. 132.

16 P.J. Lalleman, 'The Polymorphy of Christ', in J. Bremmer (ed.), *The Apocryphal Acts of John,*

was anticipated in the Apocryphal *Acts of Peter* 21 as well as in the *Acts of John* 88.[17] According to these sources of the 2nd century AD, Jesus was seen and then described as manifesting himself in three different visible forms corresponding to the same three ages of life.[18] If this motif probably reflects a Gnostic speculative background,[19] which does not contrast with the cultural orientation of these earlier *Apocrypha*, its transfer into the cycle of the Evangelic Magi deserves close attention,[20] and reasonably confirms the fact that the texts that

---

Kampen, 1995, pp. 99–106, has offered a general discussion of Jesus's polymorphism, which includes also other patterns, and that is attested in other *Apocrypha* as the *Acts of Paul*, the *Acts of Andrew* and the *Acts of Thomas*.

17   See D.R. Cartlidge and J.K. Elliot, *Art and the Christian Apocrypha*, London–New York 2001, p. 894.

18   See F. Lapham, *The Myth, the Man and the Writings: a Study of Early Petrine Text and Tradition* (*Journal for the Study of the New Testament*, Supplement Series 239), London, 2003, pp. 55–56; cf. also E. Peterson, 'Einige Bemerkungen zum Hamburger Papyrus-Fragment der Acta Pauli', *Vigiliæ Christianæ* vol. 3 (1949), pp. 142–162, in particular p. 158 (an Italian translation of this study will appear soon by Daniele Tripaldi). Cf. also H. Garcia, 'La polymorphy du Christ dans le christianisme ancien. Remarques sur quelques définitions et quelques enjeux', *Apocrypha* vol. 10 (1999), pp. 16–55.

19   The present statement does not exclude the possibility that Iranian elements were already present in these sources, as it seems to be the case of the *Secret Book of John*, where a Pharisee who speaks against John is called Arimanios. In this text, ch. 3, 1–8, there are some fitting polymorphic elements such as in particular the one in which Johannes sees a child, who becomes an old man. In the tradition collected around the *Apocrypha* of John, we can find also a magical text transferred under the name of 'Book of Zoroaster'. It is clear that this source does not preserve genuine Iranian material, but the cultural presence of some Iranian resonances cannot be excluded. I thank Dr. Daniele Tripaldi (University of Bologna), who has kindly informed me about these sources, and who has put at my disposal his forthcoming translation and comment about this text. I would like to remark that older assumptions like those suggested by J.E. Ménard ('Transfiguration et polymorphie chez Origène', in J. Fontaine and Ch. Kannengiesser [éds], *Épektasis. Mélanges patristiques offerts au cardinal Jean Daniélou*, Paris, 1972, pp. 367–372) regarding the Mazdean *daēnā-* as a mean of inspiration for Christian polymorphism are unnecessary, but this observation (see P.J. Lalleman, 'The Polymorphy of Christ', in J. Bremmer (ed.), *The Apocryphal Acts of John*, Kampen, 1995, pp. 97–118, in particular p. 101) is not sufficient to exclude the evidences concerning an unbroken intercultural and interreligious dialogue with the Iranian and Iranianized areas. I. Dorfmann-Lazarev ('The Cave of the Nativity revisited: memory of the primæval beings in the Armenian *Lord's Infancy* and cognate sources', in *Mélanges Jean-Pierre Mahé*, pp. 285–334, in particular pp. 307–308) insists on a careful distinction between the tradition concerning the polymorphous apparitions in the Armenian *Lord's Infancy* and those attested in the *Acts of Peter* (ch. 21).

20   Another important subject worth of further investigations concerns Jesus dimorphism *puer-senex*, on which see again Dorfmann-Lazarev, 'The Cave of the Nativity revisited: memory of the primæval beings in the Armenian *Lord's Infancy* and cognate sources',

THE ESOTERIC LEGACY OF THE MAGI OF BETHLEHEM 373

developed the legendary mission of the (three) Wise men, had a strong interest in a more efficacious penetration in those Eastern countries where Zoroastrian and generally Iranian motives were strongly present.

For this reason it is very interesting to carefully observe how the adoption of this symbolic theme in the framework of the adoration of the Magi assumed two forms: the first and most simple was the one in which Jesus firstly presents himself as a baby in front of the young Magus, secondly as a mature man in front of the mature Magus, and finally as an old man in front of the third and oldest Magus. In the second version, much more complex, Jesus does not simply change, one after the other, his external appearances, but, after them, he is seen again by all the Magi together. In this way thanks to his divine grace, he allows any single Magus to admire his own three distinguished manifestations in the course of three following steps. This performance can be explained as further patent evidence of his superb power over Time. The sequence presenting Jesus in these three temporal forms (but also three times, so that in the end they become nine), is fully developed only in the *Armenian Gospel of the Infancy*, but it is probably evoked also in Cappadocian iconography.[21]

Clearly the final and resuming image of the baby, sitting on his mother, after the different visions, has been fittingly connected with the Hellenistic and Iranian speculations concerning the tetramorphic manifestation of Aiōn[22]

---

p. 314. Cf. also the discussion in Panaino, *I Magi e la loro stella*, p. 152; id., 'Jesus' Trimorphisms and Tetramorphisms in the Meeting with the Magi', p. 198.

21 See N. and M. Thierry, *Nouvelle Eglises rupestres de Cappadoce, Région du Hasan Daği* (*New Rock-cut Churches of Cappadocia*), Paris, 1963, pp. 5–52, tables 24–37; Favaro, 'Un'inconsueta adorazione dei magi in un affresco di San Giorgio a Velo d'Astico', p. 241. We must recall that J. Duchesne-Guillemin ('A Vanishing Problem', in J.M. Kitagawa and Ch.H. Long (eds) with the collaboration of J.C. Brauer and M.G.S. Hodgson, *Myths and Symbols. Studies in honor of Mircea Eliade*, Chicago, 1969, pp. 417–433 (reprinted in id., *Opera Minora* vol. III, *Iran-Grèce-Israël* (Publication de l'Université de Téhéran), Téhéran, 1978 pp. 275–277, in particular p. 275); id., 'Jesus' trimorphism and the differentiation of the Magi', in E.J. Sharpe and J.R. Hinnells (eds), *Man and his salvation. Studies in memory of Samuel George Frederick Brandon*, Manchester–Totowa, N.J., 1973, pp. 327–334, in particular p. 331) underlined the importance of the 8th century fresco of Quseyr 'Amra in Jordania, where a white-bearded old man, an adult with black hair, and a red-cheeked blond youth are represented together (see also A. Musil, *Ḳuṣeir 'Amra: Reiseergebnisse*, 2 Bände, Wien, 1907).

22 See Lackeit 1916; M. Zepf, 'Der Gott Αἰών in der hellenistischem Theologie', *Archiv für Religionswissenschaft* Band 25, n° 3/4 (1927), pp. 225–244; Ar. D. Nock, 'A vision of Mandulis Aion', *The Harvard Theological Review* vol. 27, n° 1 (1934), pp. 53–104; D. Levi, 'Aion', *Hesperia: The Journal of the American School of Classical Studies at Athens* vol. 13/4 (1944), pp. 269–314; E. Degani, *Αἰών da Omero ad Aristotele*, Prefazione di C. Diano, G. Schirò e Fr. Sartori, Padova, 1961; H.M. Keizer, *Life Time Entirety. A Study of AION in Greek Literature and Philosophy, the Septuagint and Philo* (Thesis discussed on the 7th September 1999, Fac-

and Zurwān,[23] the most important ancient divinities ruling over the Eternal Time.

In a number of previous studies I have already dealt with this subject, showing that Olschki's working hypothesis was very sound and that early Christianity in late Antiquity during its expansion towards the Eastern territories, mostly during the Parthian and Sasanian periods, adopted and transformed a number of Oriental, even Mazdean, concepts and traditions. In the present contribution I desire to analyse more precisely some aspects of the comparative associations, which were developed in connection with the diffusion of Christian propaganda in Mazdean or simply Iranianized lands. This is, in fact,

---

ulteit der Geesteswetenschappen), University of Amsterdam, e-publication (revised and corrected), 2010.

23 H.S. Nyberg, 'Questions de cosmogonie et de cosmologie mazdéennes', *Journal Asiatique* tome 214 (1929), pp. 193–310; *Journal Asiatique* tome 219 (1929), pp. 1–134 and 193–244 (reprinted in id., *Monumentum H.S. Nyberg* (Acta Iranica 7, Hommages et Opera Minora 4), Leiden–Téhéran–Liège, 1975, pp. 75–192 and 193–378). About Zurwān and Zurvanism, see also Is. Scheftelowitz, 'Neues Material über die manichäische Urseele und die Entstehung des Zarvanismus', *Zeitschrift für Indologie und Iranistik* Band 4 (1926), pp. 317–344; also Id., *Die Zeit als Schicksalsgottheit in der indischen und iranischen Religion (Kāla und Zruvan)*, (Beiträge zur indischen Sprachwissenschaft und Religionsgeschichte, Heft 4), Stuttgart, 1929; H.S. Schaeder, 'Urform und Fortbildungen des manichäischen Systems', in Fr. Saxl (ed.), *Vorträge der Bibliothek Warburg*, 1924–1925 Band 4, Leipzig, 1927, pp. 65–157; id., *Iranische Beiträge*, Halle, 1930; id., 'Der iranische Zeitgott und sein Mythos', *Zeitschrift der Deutschen Morgenländischen Gesellschaft* Band 95 (1941), pp. 268–299; H. Junker, 'Über iranische quellen der hellenistischen Aion-vorstellung', in Fr. Saxl (ed.), *Vorträge der Bibliothek Warburg* Band 1, Leipzig–Berlin, 1923, pp. 125–177; O.G. von Wesendonk, 'The Kālavāda and the Zervanite System', *Journal of the Royal Asiatic Society of Great Britain and Ireland* (January, 1931), pp. 53–109; R.Ch. Zaehner, *Zurvan: a Zoroastrian Dilemma*, with a new introduction by the author, New York, 1972 (first edition: Oxford, 1955); U. Bianchi, *Zamān i Ōhrmazd: lo Zoroastrismo nelle sue origini e nella sua essenza*, Torino, 1958; G. Scarcia, 'Zurvanismo subcaucasico', in *Zurvān e Muhammad—Comunicazioni iranistiche e islamistiche presentate al Primo Simposio Internazionale di Cultura Transcaucasica, Napoli–Bergamo–Venezia, 12–15 giugno 1979* (Quaderni dell'Istituto di Iranistica, Uralo-Altaistica e Caucasologia dell'Università degli Studi di Venezia; Cafoscarina 2), Venezia, 1979, pp. 15–21; K. Rezania, *Die zoroastrische Zeitvorstellung. Eine Untersuchung über Zeit- und Ewigkeitskonzepte und die Frage des Zurvanismus* (Göttinger Orientforschungen, III. Reihe: Iranica, N.F. 7), Göttingen, 2010; A. de Jong, sub voce 'Zurwan', and 'Zurwanism', in *Encyclopædia Iranica* on line (January 2000), http://www.iranicaonline.org/articles/zurvan-deity and http://www.iranicaonline.org/articles/zurvanism; A. Panaino, 'Short Remarks about Ohrmazd between Limited and Unlimited Time', in A. van Tongerloo (ed.), *Iranica Selecta, Studies in honour of Professor Wojciech Skalmowski on the occasion of his seventieth birthday* (Silk Road Studies, 8), Turnhout, 2003, pp. 195–200; id., 'Light, Time, Motion and Impulse in the Zoroastrian Pahlavi Texts', *Iran and the Caucasus* 24 (2020), pp. 243–286 (with a large bibliographical survey on the subject).

THE ESOTERIC LEGACY OF THE MAGI OF BETHLEHEM

a phenomenon well studied, and already focused on, for instance, by Messina more than one century ago.[24] There is no reason to doubt that the coming of the Magi to Bethlehem was presented in the East as an event prophesied by Zoroaster himself, and that the expectation of the three posthumous sons of the Mazdean prophet,[25] in particular that of the third one, the Saošiiaṇt *par excellence*, was extremely fitting for a presentation of Christ himself as the true 'saviour', whom Zoroastrian people were longing for since many centuries.[26] This assumption is based not only on a theory, but on different textual evidences, such as, for instance, the one still preserved in the *Arabic Infancy Gospel* (*Codex Laurentianus*), which starts with a prophecy by Zoroaster concerning Jesus's coming.[27] Other sources state that some Iranian Magi were looking for a sign connected with the birth of a 'saviour', who corresponds to Jesus.[28] This happens in Syriac Literature,[29] but in particular occurs in the *Disputatio de*

---

24 Messina, 'Il *Saušyant*- nella tradizione iranica e la sua attesa', pp. 149–176; id., *I Magi a Betlemme ed una predizione di Zoroastro, passim*; Panaino, *I Magi e la loro stella*, pp. 88–89, 109–113, 164.

25 We should recall that Zaraθuštra had during his life three sons: *Isaṭ.vāstra*-, 'Who desires pastures', the oldest one, who, in the framework of Pahlavi literature, was considered the chief of the priests; the other ones, born by another wife, were *Uruuataṭ.nara*-, 'Commander of men' and *Huuarə.ciθra*-, 'Sun-faced'; they respectively became the chief of the warriors and of the farmers. In particular, *Isaṭ.vāstra*- played an enormously important role in the eschatological framework of the last days of the world.

26 This doctrine was, in fact, already known in the later Avestan sources.

27 L. Moraldi, *Tutti gli Apocrifi del Nuovo Testamento*, Casale Monferrato, 2007 (6th edition), pp. 315, in the note, 318–319; id., *I Vangeli sconosciuti del Natale*, Casale Monferrato, 1977, pp. 123–124; Provera, *Il Vangelo arabo dell'infanzia secondo il ms. laurenziano orientale* (*n. 387*), *passim*; S.J. Voicu, *Vangelo arabo dell'infanzia di Gesù*, Roma, 2002, pp. 17–18, 21–22; A. di Nola, *Vangeli apocrifi. Natività e infanzia*, Parma, 1993, pp. 159–162; J. Bidez and Fr. Cumont, *Les mages hellénisés: Zoroastre, Ostanès et Hystaspe d'après la tradition grecque* tome 2, Paris, 1938, pp. 117–135; U. Monneret de Villard, *Le Leggende Orientali sui Magi Evangelici* (Studi e Testi 163), Città del Vaticano, 1952, pp. 129, *passim*; Cf. Panaino, *I Magi e la loro stella, passim*. It is also to be underlined that in the *Codex Laurentianus* (fol. 1ᵛ) there is an interesting image, which can be interpreted as representing Zoroaster with the Magi (see Lafontaine-Dosogne, 'Le cycle des Mages dans l' Évangile arabe de l' Enfance du Christ à Florence', pp. 288–289).

28 Monneret de Villard, *Le Leggende Orientali sui Magi Evangelici*, pp. 6–13, 96–98, and *passim*; cf. Br.Chr. Landau, *The Sages and the Star-Child: An Introduction to the* Revelation of the Magi, *An Ancient Christian Apocryphon*. (A dissertation presented by Br.Chr. Landau to The Faculty of Harvard Divinity School in partial fulfillment of the requirements for the degree of Doctor of Theology in the Subject of New Testament and Early Christianity, Harvard University), Cambridge, Massachusetts, 2008; id., 'The Revelation of the Magi in the Chronicle of Zuqnin: The Magi form the East in the Ancient Christian Imagination', *Apocrypha* vol. 19 (2008), pp. 182–201; id., *Revelation of the Magi*, New York, NY., 2010.

29 See Messina, *I Magi a Betlemme ed una predizione di Zoroastro*, pp. 62–85.

Christo in Persia, a very intriguing Byzantine source, which already introduces the association, apparently un-historical,[30] between Cyrus the Great and Jesus. Cyrus, who, in fact (as stated by Isaiah), was a Messiah, according to this text received an astral sign announcing the future birth of Jesus, so that it was he himself who was to order his Magi to go to Bethlehem.[31] This story was not isolated but it was known also in Arabic sources.[32] Its meaning is simple: we have to do with a *Translatio Imperii*, in which the most powerful human king sends the priests who had anointed him to anoint the new king of the universe.

In the framework of this very complex net of relations, where the expectation of the 'Saviour' was shared by Christians and Mazdeans alike, our interest for a reconsideration of the role attributed to the three posthumous sons of Zoroaster (Av. *Uxšaiiaṯ.ərəta-*[33] 'the one who increases righteousness', Pahl. Ošēdar; Av. *Uxšaiiaṯ.nəmah-*,[34] 'the one who increases honour', Pahl. Ošēdar-

---

30 See Panaino, 'I Magi e la stella nei *Sermoni* di San Pier Crisologo. Qualche riflessione critica a proposito di scienza, fede e metodo storico', in *Ravenna da capitale imperiale a capitale esarcale. Atti del XVII Congresso internazionale di studio sull'alto medioevo. Ravenna, 6–12 giugno 2004*, Spoleto, 2005, pp. 559–592; id., 'Ciro, i Magi Evangelici e la Disputatio de Christo in Persia', *Studi Romagnoli* vol. 52, 2011 (2012), pp. 57–73; id., 'The three Magi, the Stone of Christ and the Christian Origin of the Mazdean Fire Cult', in M. Knüppel and L. Cirillo (eds), *Gnostica et Manichaica. Festschrift für Aloïs van Tongerloo. Anläßlich des 60. Geburtstages überreicht von Kollegen, Freunden und Schülern* (Studies in Oriental Religions 65), Wiesbaden, 2012, pp. 153–164; id., 'I Magi evangelici, Ciro il Grande e il Messia', in M. Milani and M. Zappella (eds), "Ricercare la Sapienza di tutti gli antichi" (Sir. 39.1), *Miscellanea in onore di Gian Luigi Prato* (Supplemento alla *Rivista Biblica* 56), Bologna, 2013, pp. 425–432; id., 'Il βασιλεύς stella dei Magi ed altre *nugæ* bizantino-iraniche', in G. Vespignani (ed.), *Polidoro. Studi offerti ad Antonio Carile*. Vol. II, Spoleto, 2013, pp. 651–664; all these articles contain a large bibliography on the subject that cannot be listed here *in extenso*.

31 See Ed. Bratke, *Das sogenannte Religionsgespräch am Hof der Sasaniden*, Texte und Untersuchungen zur Geschichte der altchristlichen Literatur, 18. Band, Heft 3, Leipzig, 1899; Puech, 'Histoire de l'ancienne église et patristique', *Annuaire de l'École Pratique des Hautes Études* tome 74, p. 136; Bringel, *Une polémique religieuse à la cour perse: le "de gestis in Perside"; histoire du texte, édition critique et traduction*, Paris, 2008; K. Heyden, *Die "Erzählung des Aphroditian": Thema und Variationen einer Legende im Spannungsfeld von Christentum und Heidentum*, Studien zur Antike und Christentum 53, Tübingen, 2009; Panaino, 'Ciro, i Magi Evangelici e la Disputatio de Christo in Persia', pp. 57–73; id., 'Iranica nella *Disputatio de Christo in Persia*', *Electrum* vol. 24, pp. 237–252.

32 As, for instance, in Mas'ūdī and in Ṭabari; cf. Panaino, *I Magi e la loro stella*, p. 104, notes 8 and 9.

33 Cf. M. Mayrhofer, *Die Altiranischen Namen*. Band 1. *Iranisches Personennamenbuch* (Österreichische Akademie der Wissenschaften, Philosophisch-historische Klasse, Sonderpublikation der Iranischen Kommission), Wien 1979, I/87, No. 335.

34 Cf. Mayrhofer, *Die Altiranischen Namen*, I/87, No. 336.

māh; Av. *Astuuaṭ.ərəta-*[35] 'the one who embodies righteousness'; in Pahl. simply referred to as *Sōšāns*) in the framework of the intercultural relations with the Christian tradition, and in particular with the cycle of the three Magi, becomes extremely pertinent. A more fitting relation between the Magi, Jesus and these three Mazdean God's 'apostles' and 'envoys' (we will see more precisely the legitimacy of these titles) is visible, for instance, in some events to which the three Iranian actors were later connected in Mazdean apocalyptic literature, such as the occurrence of a series of very peculiar celestial phenomena connected with the stationary position of the Sun respectively for ten, twenty or thirty days, when each of the three 'apostles' will be aged thirty years. Another interesting fact concerns the birth of the hero Kay Wahrām, who was strongly linked to the first of the Mazdean envoys, i.e. Ošēdar. According to the *Zand ī Wahman Yasn* 7,6,[36] a sign will come to the earth, in the night when that prince will be born: a star will fall from the sky, so that this star will show a sign. It is to be remarked that the manifestation of unknown and unpredictable stars or astral bodies, in particular that of meteors, comets or shooting stars, was never considered as a positive *omen* in Iranian folklore, while a consistent tradition in the Mazdean sources considers the presence of these irregular celestial objects as a demoniac and dangerous manifestation.[37] Contrariwise, the introduction of miraculous (and clearly positive) events like these can only be explained by assuming the presence of a Christian motif, later borrowed in Iran, and probably introduced through the cycle of the Magi at Bethlehem.[38] This conclusion can be suggested in the light of some other Western influences on the Iranian apocalyptic literature,[39] which have strongly elaborated Judæo-

---

35   Cf. Mayrhofer, *Die Altiranischen Namen*, I/22–23, No. 36.

36   C.G. Cereti, *The Zand ī Wahman Yasn. A Zoroastrian Apocalypse* (SOR LXXV), Roma, 1995, pp. 114, 142, 162.

37   See Panaino, 'Astral Omens and their Ambiguity: The Case of Mithridate's Comets', *Iran and the Caucasus* vol. 22, n° 3 (2018), pp. 232–256, *passim*.

38   On the subject of the star of Bethlehem, see Panaino, 'Pre-Islamic Iranian Astral Mythology, Astrology, and the Star of Bethlehem', in G.H. Kooten and P. Barthel (eds), *The Star of Bethlehem and the Magi. Interdisciplinary Perspectives from Experts on the Ancient Near East, the Greco-Roman World, and Modern Astronomy* (Biblical Studies, Ancient Near East and Early Christianity 19), Leiden, 2015, pp. 231–268.

39   Ph. Gignoux, 'L'apocalyptique iranienne est-elle vraiment la source d'autres apocalypses?', *Acta Antiqua Academiæ Scientiarum Hungaricæ* vol. 31 (1985–1988), pp. 67–78; id., 'Nouveaux regards sur l'apocalyptique iranienne', *Comptes-rendus des Séances de l'Académie des Inscriptions et Belles-lettres*, Paris, 1986, pp. 334–346; id., 'L'apocalyptique iranienne est-elle vraiment ancienne?', *RHR* vol. 216, n° 2 (1999), pp. 213–227; C.G. Cereti, *The Zand ī Wahman Yasn*, pp. 11–27; id., '*Padīriftan ī dēn* and the Turn of the Millennium', *East and West* vol. 45, n° 1/4 (1995), pp. 321–327; C. id., 'La figura del redentore futuro nei testi iranici

Christian material, while there is no need to postulate, at least in that case, the persistence of an earlier Iranian tradition, in its turn, transmitted to Matthew's *Gospel* and the Christian *milieu*.

We should also consider that a trend to increase the manifestation of celestial phenomena is well documented also in the Islamic esoteric tradition, in particular where the Mazdean background results more sound;[40] actually, the advent of the Mahdī will be announced by a number of extraordinary events, as summarized by Poonawala:[41]

1) the rise of the Western sun;
2) solar and lunar eclipses taking place respectively at the middle and the end of the month of Ramażān;
3) a lunar eclipse in the East and the West;
4) the stationary position of the Sun in the middle of the day;
5) followed by the most important miracle for our discussion, i.e. the eastern rising of an extraordinary shining star, beaming like the Moon.

It is probable that the motifs of the bright star and that of the stationary position of the Sun were inspired from Zoroastrian sources, although the rising of a miraculous star basically reflects an earlier Christian tradition, which, in its turn, had a Mediterranean and Hellenistic background.[42]

Another interesting matter of discussion, on which I wish to focus in the present contribution, concerns the fact that the representation of three Magi in the mirroring interplay with Jesus as *kosmokrátor*, which determines what

---

zoroastriani; aspetti dell'evoluzione di un mito', *AION* vol. 55, n° 1 (1995c), pp. 33–81; id., 'Again on Wahrām ī warzāwand', in *La Persia e l'Asia Centrale da Alessandro al X secolo* (Atti dei Convegni Lincei 127), Roma, 1996, pp. 629–639; id., *La Letteratura pahlavi. Introduzione ai testi con riferimento alla storia degli studi e alla tradizione manoscritta*, Milano, 2001, pp. 119–138; id., 'Zoroastrian Apocalyptics in the Šāhnāma', *Classical Bulletin* vol. 83, n° 2, 2007, pp. 183–202. G. Widengren, A. Hultgård and M. Philonenko, *Apocalyptique iranienne et dualisme qoumrânien* (Recherches intertestamentaires 2), Paris, 1995, have suggested an opposite point of view.

40   Very useful in this framework are the reflections proposed by H. Corbin, 'Épiphanie Divine et Naissance Spirituelle dans la Gnose Ismaélienne', *Eranos Jahrbuch* Band 23, *Mensch und Wandlung*, Zürich, 1954, pp. 141–249 (translated by R. Manheim, 'Divine Epiphany and Spiritual Rebirth in Ismailian Gnosis', in E. Benz and R. Manheim (eds), *Man and Transformation, Papers from the Eranos Yearbooks* 5, London, 1965, pp. 69–160); H. Corbin, 'Face de Dieu et face de l'Homme', *Eranos Jahrbuch* Band 36 (1967), *Polarität des Lebens*, Zürich, 1968, pp. 167–2291968.

41   I.K. Poonawala, 'Apocalyptic. ii. Muslim Iran', in E. Yarshater (ed.), *Encyclopædia Iranica* vol. II, Fasc. 2, New York, 1986, pp. 154–116.

42   See Panaino, 'The "Trepidation" of the Sun, the 57 years of the Resurrection and the Late Mazdean Speculations on the Apocalypse', *Studia Iranica* vol. 47, n° 1 (2018), pp. 7–50.

THE ESOTERIC LEGACY OF THE MAGI OF BETHLEHEM

has been defined as Christ's 'tetramorphism', offers not only a direct comparison with the similar tetramorphic aspects of Aiōn and Zurwān, frequently described in many pertinent studies,[43] but also with Zoroaster and his three posthumous sons. All together, they actually form a group of four 'messengers' or 'apostles' of Ahura Mazdā. As Widengren has remarked,[44] if the Iranian god Nairiiō.saṇha was already considered as an *ašta-*, i.e. a 'messenger' (*Vd.* 19,34), also the third and last of Zoroaster's posthumous sons, the Saošiiaṇt *par excellence*, Astuuaṭ.ərəta, was literally presented as *aštō mazdå ahurahe*, 'the messenger of Ahura Mazdā' (*Yt.* 19,22). According to the *Dādestān ī Dēnīg* 1,8,[45] Zoroaster, Ošēdar and Ošēdarmāh are all together *frēstagān* 'apostles', and a reference to 'the four apostles of the good-religion' (*čahār hudēnwar frēstagān*), literally 'the sent ones' (*frēstag*), the 'envoys' from Ohrmazd, is again formulated in a very sharp way in the same Mazdean source (48,30):[46] here, Zoroaster, Ošēdar, Ošēdarmāh and Sōšāns (i.e. the Avestan Astuuaṭ.ərəta) are meant without any doubt all together.[47] Thus, if Jesus indeed offered a tetramorphic image, and constituted with the three Magi a group of four, where the universal power of Time might be finally mirrored, Zoroaster himself with his three posthumous sons, who will come at a millennium of distance one after the other, formed another tetradic group, which again interplayed with the four aspects of Zurwān/Aiōn. This kind of comparison was suggested by Widengren,[48] but, to my knowledge, has not been developed further. This suggestion actually results still relevant, although the suggested correspondence does not result *prima facie*

---

43   See again my discussion in A. Panaino, 'Jesus' Trimorphisms and Tetramorphisms in the Meeting with the Magi', *passim*. Cf. J. Duchesne-Guillemin, 'Die Drei Weisen aus dem Morgenlande und die Anbetung der Zeit', *Antaios* Band 7, n° 3 (1965), pp. 234–252, in particular 247–250; id., 'Espace et temps dans l'Iran ancien', *Revue de Synthèse*, Série générale 90, Troisième Série 55–56 (1969), pp. 259–280; id., 'A Vanishing Problem', pp. 275–277; id., 'Jesus' trimorphism and the differentiation of the Magi', pp. 327–334. These articles by Duchesne-Guillemin have been reprinted in Id., *Opera Minora* vol. III, *Iran-Grèce-Israël*, Téhéran, 1978.

44   G. Widengren, *The Great Vohu Manah and the Apostle of God. Studies in Iranian and Manichæan Religion* (Uppsala Universitets Årsskrift 1945: 5), Uppsala–Leipzig, 1945, pp. 61–62.

45   Cf. M. Jaafari-Dehaghi, *Dādestān ī Dēnīg*, Part I: *Transcription, Translation and Commentary* (Studia Iranica, Cahier 20), Paris, 1998, pp. 40–41.

46   Widengren, *The Great Vohu Manah and the Apostle of God*, p. 64.

47   Widengren ('Salvation in Iranian religion', pp. 315–326, in particular p. 317, note 8) assumed that also in *Dēnkard* VIII, 8, the 'Four ones' there mentioned should be understood as a reference to Zoroaster and the three 'apostles'; contrariwise, they can be the four Zoroastrian *dastūr*s, as suggested by M. Molé, *La legende de Zoroastre, selon les testes Pehlevis* (Travaux de l'Institut d'Études Iraniennes de l'Université de Paris 3), Paris, 1967, pp. 70–73.

48   G. Widengren, 'Salvation in Iranian religion', p. 317, n. 8.

striking because these three posthumous sons of Zoroaster are projected into the future history of the world, while the three Magi are contemporary to the advent of Jesus.

Zoroaster, Ošēdar, Ošēdarmāh and Sōšāns, with their births and the following religious manifestations, cover a period of three millennia, albeit they were placed at a distance of 1000 years one after the other. This happens because Zoroaster marked the end of the ninth millennium and the beginning of the tenth one, while his three posthumous sons were chronologically placed as follows:

> the first in the cæsura between the tenth and the eleventh millennium (Ošēdar, will be born in the year 9970);
> the second between the eleventh and the twelfth (Ošēdarmāh, will be born in the year 10970), and before the final apocatastasis;[49]
> the third at the end of the twelfth millennium (Sōšāns, will be, in fact, born in the year 11943, while in 11973 he will start the resurrection of all the dead).[50]

All of them are messengers (apostles), given the power of salvation, but this is particularly true for the last one, who will resurrect the whole humanity in a period of 57 years (*Bundahišn* 33,42).[51] While Zoroaster is explicitly their father (and all of them are sons of a virgin girl like Maria),[52] the last one appears as the

---

49   On the doctrine of the apocatastasis in the Iranian Zoroastrian framework, see Panaino, 'La "misericordia" di Ohrmazd ed il perdono dei dannati secondo la trattatistica zoroastriana tardo-antica e medievale', *Bizantinistica* vol. 17, pp. 27–45; id., 'Mazdeans and Christians Facing the End of the World. Circulations and Exchanges of Concepts', *Entangled Religions* vol. 11, n° 2, 2019 (https://doi.org/10.13154/er.11.2020.8441), with additional bibliography.

50   See F. Pakzad, *Bundahišn. Zoroastrische Kosmogonie und Kosmologie*. Band 1. *Kritische Edition* (Ancient Iranian Studies Series 2, Centre for the Great Islamic Encyclopædia), Tehran, 2005, pp. 370–373; cf. Messina, *I Magi a Betlemme ed una predizione di Zoroastro*, pp. 43–55. On the millennialism in Iran, see id., 'Vecchie e nuove considerazioni sul Millenarismo iranico-mesopotamico ed il Chiliasmo giudaico-cristiano', in A. Panaino, A. Piras and P. Ognibene (eds), *Studi Iranici Ravennati II* (Indo-Iranica et Orientalia, Series Lazur 2), Milano, 2017, pp. 183–229.

51   See Pakzad, *Bundahišn*, p. 372; cf. Messina, *I Magi a Betlemme ed una predizione di Zoroastro*, p. 45. On this subject, see now Panaino, 'The "Trepidation" of the Sun, the 57 years of the Resurrection and the Late Mazdean Speculations on the Apocalypse', *Studia Iranica* vol. 47, n° 1 (2018), pp. 7–50.

52   The names of their mothers are in Avestan: *Srūtaṯ.fəδrī-*, 'She who has a famous father'; *Vaŋhu.fəδrī-*, 'She who has a good father'; * Īrədaṯ.fəδrī-*, 'She who brings fulfillment to the father'; about these names, see U. Remmer, *Frauennamen im Rigveda um im Avesta. Stu-*

youngest one, while the first (Ošēdar) would be the oldest, so that the second, being in the middle, will necessarily represent the intermediate one. In this way, the three apostles, who (in the divine dimension and in its different universal Time) stay all together with their father, Zoroaster, in front of Ohrmazd, can be associated with the different ages of life and of the human world waiting for the final liberation from the darkness. In this respect, if their identity results partly differently from that attested in the Zurwānic tetrad, their image appears, *mutatis mutandis*, as another synthesis of the human journey towards freedom and light, from the earliest moments to the last one, all compressed in the final period of three millennia. It is for this reason that we can develop the implications deriving from this net of associations and observe that the three Magi, as a *speculum temporis et ætatis*, surely offered many occasions for further speculations and assimilations within the Mazdean-Christian ambiance of Eastern Late Antiquity.[53] The Armenian Lord's Infancy is again supportive of our reflection on some striking resonances emerging from Christian and Mazdean millenarian traditions. The ms. *Matenadaran* 7574 (fol. 61^v–62^v)[54] actually shows that the 'Covenant' presented by the Magi to Jesus starts reciting that 'In the year six thousand I shall send my only-begotten Son, God the Word, who shall come, etc. [...].' If we just think that the apocalyptic performance of the Sōšāns will find its full triumph at the end of the sixth millennium of the *gētīg* ('living', but also historical) creation, the link between these traditions is impressive, although it cannot be framed in terms of crude dependence but of mutual and dialectic intercultural influence.

Analysing this particular cultural framework, we can deduce some further developments: in fact, Christ became or was presented as the supreme Saviour (= Sōšāns); he was worshipped by his Magi (i.e. the ones of Jesus, but also those of Zoroaster, and of Cyrus as well) as a resumptive image of divine Time (= the

---

       dien zur Onomastik des ältesten Indischen und Iranischen (Österreichische Akademie der Wissenschaften, Philosophisch-historische Klasse, Sitzungsberichte, 745. Band. Iranische Onomastik No. 3), Wien, 2006, pp. 200–205.

53   In this respect there are some fitting correspondences in the chiliadic doctrines; see Panaino, '6666 or the Figure of Ahreman's Invasion. A Note about Wizīdagīhā by Zādspram 28,2', *Studia Iranica* vol. 45, n° 2 (2018), pp. 165–196.

54   See in particular Dorfmann-Lazarev, 'The Cave of the Nativity revisited: memory of the primæval beings in the Armenian *Lord's Infancy* and cognate sources', pp. 285–334, especially pp. 316–317; cf. also pp. 332–333. Cf. Terian, *The Armenian Gospel of the Infancy with three early versions of the Protevangelium of James*, p. 58, and n. 231. About the very many problems concerning the relations between Iranian millennialism and Jewish-Christian chiliasm, see again Panaino, '6666 or the Figure of Ahreman's Invasion. A Note about Wizīdagīhā by Zādspram 28,2', pp. 165–196.

tetramorphous Zurwān and Aiōn). But if Jesus was announced by Zoroaster, as happens in some Apocryphal Oriental sources, the latter, with his three posthumous sons and God's envoys, was not only Jesus's prophet, but also a sort of father, in the measure in which Jesus was wished not only as the new Messiah (so corresponding again to Cyrus the Great), but as the incarnation of the Sōšāns, in particular of the last one, who will come, born by a virgin, to resurrect the dead and destroy darkness and evil.

We must finally consider another striking fact; as Jesus was connected to God 'the father', not only because of a relation of paternity, but also in force of their innermost primordial consubstantiality, as stated by the Trinitarian doctrine, Ohrmazd, in his turn, will establish himself in the spirit (*warom*) of the third Sōšāns,[55] when this one, leading a superb priestly college,[56] will start to sing the liturgy of the *Yasna*. Thus, all the seven priests, acting the final renovation (*fraškirg-kardārān*) of the world, will be divinely possessed by a corresponding divinity, so that everyone will be as a god in the framework of a universal transfiguration.[57]

In spite of the various differences, it is clear that the eschatological role played by all these saviours might inspire comparisons and associations, through the common expectation of the resurrection in God. The presence of similar traditions, although theologically based on very different premises, might arouse fear, but also hope; probably, the people who developed the cycles of the Magi, and those who later enforced the increasing mass of legends about Jesus's polymorphism, Mary, the Magi, Cyrus the Great, the Mazdean fire, etc., were looking for a possible dialogue, in which the Magi, the Sōšāns, the ages of the world and of the highest divinity mirrored each other, although *inter tela volantia*.

---

55 Ph. Gignoux and A. Tafazzoli, *Anthologie de Zādspram*. Édition critique du texte pehlevi traduit et commentée, Studia Iranica, Cahier 13, Paris, 1993, pp. 130–132.

56 On the Avestan priestly college and its installation, see Panaino, 'Studies on the Recursive Patterns in the Mazdean Ritualism: the 'Installation' and the So-Called 'Disinstallation' of the High Priestly College', *Estudios Iranios y Turanios* vol. 3 (2017), pp. 129–143; id., 'The Avestan Priestly College and its Installation', in T. Daryaee (ed.), *Hanns-Peter Schmidt (1930–2017) Gedenkschrift (Dabir* vol. 6), Irvine, California, 2018, pp. 86–100.

57 On the idea of 'transfiguration' in the Mazdean sources, see Sh. Shaked, 'Eschatology and the Goal of the Religious Life in Sasanian Zoroastrianism', in R.J.Z. Werblowsky and C.J. Bleeker (eds), *Types of Redemption*, Leiden, 1970, pp. 223–230.

CHAPTER 19

Visual Apocrypha: The Case of Mary and the Magi in Early Christian Rome

Felicity Harley

Across the Mediterranean during the third and fourth centuries CE, artists began to develop a distinctive iconography to express Christian religious beliefs. According to the material evidence, the bulk of which survives from funerary contexts, artists focused on a small group of stories from scripture that included instances of salvation and divine revelation, along with cases of Jesus performing acts of healing and restoring life to the dead.[1] The archæological record attests that in Rome by the early fourth century, the adoration of the new-born Jesus by wise men from the East (Matthew 2:1–14) was among the most popular stories within this repertoire; and a largely unacknowledged outcome of this popularity was that in that city at that date, Mary the mother of Jesus was the single most frequently appearing female figure in Christian art.[2]

Among the earliest surviving depictions of the Adoration in Rome is a mural in the Catacomb of Priscilla.[3] Painted sometime perhaps in the third or in the early fourth century, it is prominently positioned on a structural arch dividing the cubiculum known as the *cappella greca* (see Figure 19.1).[4] In that

---

1 The repertoire, first developed in the Roman catacombs in the first half of the third century and on sarcophagi a generation later, included over twenty biblical stories: N. Zimmerman, 'The healing Christ in early Christian funeral art: the example of the frescoes at Domitilla catacomb Rome', in S. Alkier and A. Weissenrieder (eds), *Miracles Revisited. New Testament Miracle Stories and their Concepts of Reality*, Berlin–Boston, 2013, pp. 251–274, provides a clear overview.

2 The observation is S.M. Salvadori's *Per Feminam Mors, Per Feminam Vita: Images of Women in the Early Christian Funerary Art of Rome* (PhD diss.), New York University, 2002, 270.

3 F. Tolotti, *Il cimitero di Priscilla. Studio di topografia e architettura* (Società Amici delle catacombe presso Pontificio istituto di archeologia cristiana), Vatican City, 1970, 258–275. L. Debruyne, 'La Cappella greca di Priscilla', *Rivista di Archeologia Cristiana* 46 (1970), pp. 291–330.

4 The date of the murals is contested. D. Cascianelli, 'Le pitture della parete d'ingresso della cappella greca di Priscilla: ipotesi e nuove riflessioni. Il libro di Daniele affrescato sulle pareti della cappella greca di Priscilla', *Rivista di Archeologia Cristiana* 86 (2010), pp. 265–296, discusses the literature and proposed dates at 289 (supporting a mid-third century date himself). The subject of its formulation needs further attention; and here I subscribe to the view that Adoration iconography emerged in Rome only at the beginning of the fourth century, under

---

© FELICITY HARLEY, 2021 | DOI:10.1163/9789004445925_021

FIGURE 19.1   Mural painting: Adoration of the Magi. Rome, late 3rd or early 4th century CE; Catacomb of Priscilla, Rome
© SCALA / ART RESOURCE, NY

spatial context, the visual potential of depicting the story in a narrow, horizontal and curved frame is cleverly apprehended: three Magi process rhythmically in profile from the left side of the arch to their destination on the far right, as if following the curve of the architectural feature to reach Mary, who is seated in profile to face them, and who holds the infant Jesus on her lap.[5] Describing this image, art historian André Grabar remarked, 'There is no doubt that here the artists followed the text.'[6]

---

the influence of imperial art: N. Zimmermann, 'Catacombs and the Beginnings of Christian Tomb Decoration', in B.E. Borg (ed.), *The Blackwell Companion to Roman Art*, Oxford, 2105, pp. 452–470, esp. 462–463; J. Deckers, 'Die Huldigung der Magier in der Kunst der Spätantike', in F.G. Zehnder (ed.), *Die Heiligen Drei Könige—Darstellung und Verehrung*, Köln, 1982, pp. 20–32; and G. Jeremias, *Die Holztür der Basilika S. Sabina in Rom*, Tübingen, 1980, p. 48. For an opposing view, R.M. Jensen, 'Allusions to Imperial Rituals in Fourth-Century Christian Art', in L. Jefferson and R. Jensen (eds), *The Art of Empire*, Minneapolis, 2015, pp. 13–47, here 15–24.

5   Other stories represented in the cubiculum include Noah and the Ark (Genesis 5:32–10:1), the Raising of Lazarus (John, 11:1–44), and Susanna (Daniel 13).

6   A. Grabar, *Christian Iconography: A Study of its Origins*, Princeton, 1968, pp. 44–45.

The view that texts govern the creation of biblical images and even their reception by early Christian viewers is a well-established and still persistent interpretative model, and it is one to which assessments of Marian iconography in early Christian Rome have long been tethered.[7] For although Rome emerged as an important Marian cult centre in the early Medieval period,[8] when an iconography for Mary was both largely standardised and prominently displayed in diverse visual contexts,[9] the development of Marian iconography in the city prior to the fifth century is comparatively slow and visually underwhelming. The Council of Ephesus in 431 is typically interpreted as the watershed, Mary's newly articulated theological importance as *Dei Genetrix* (Mother of God) or *Theotokos* (God Bearer) ending a period of apparent disinterest in her,[10] and initiating a new era for her visual representation.[11] In support of this view, the representation of the Annunciation is a particularly felicitous case in point: images of this episode are exceptionally rare before the sixth century, and the rudi-

---

7   See, for example, the important and influential article by I. Kalavrezou, 'Images of the Mother: When the Virgin Mary Became Meter Theou', *Dumbarton Oaks Papers* 44 (1990), pp. 165–172, in which she refers to images of Mary in the Roman catacombs as straightforward illustrations of biblical text (at p. 165).

8   J. Osborne, 'Images of the Mother of God in Early Medieval Rome', in A. Eastmond and L. James (eds), *Icon and Word: The Power of Images in Byzantium*. Studies presented to Robin Cormack, Aldershot, 2003, pp. 135–156; id., 'The Cult of Maria Regina in Early Medieval Rome', *Acta ad archæologiam et artium historiam pertinentia* 21 (2008), pp. 95–106; M. Lidova, 'The Earliest Images of Maria Regina in Rome and the Byzantine Imperial Iconography', *Niš and Byzantium. The Collection of Scientific Works* VIII (2010), pp. 231–243, with bibliography at note 1.

9   For some of the evidence, see A. Effenberger, 'Maria als Vermittlerin und Fürbitterin. Zum Marienbild in der spätantiken und frühbyzantinischen Kunst Ägyptens', in L.M. Peltomaa and A. Külzer (eds), *Presbeia Theotokou: The Intercessory Role of Mary across Times and Places in Byzantium 4th–9th Century*, Vienna, 2015, pp. 49–106; and M. Lidova, 'Embodied Word. Telling the Story of Mary in Early Christian Art', in T. Arentzen and M. Cunningham (ed.), *The Reception of the Virgin in Byzantium: Marian Narratives in Texts and Images*, Cambridge 2019, pp. 17–43.

10   M. Lawrence, 'Maria Regina', *The Art Bulletin* 7.4 (1925), pp. 150–161; on p. 150: 'The early Christians laid no special emphasis upon the Virgin'.

11   H. Belting, *Likeness and Presence: A History of the Image before the Era of Art*, Chicago, 1994, pp. 30–41, 47–59. For the position that a Marian cult grew from the fifth century onwards: A.M. Cameron, 'The Cult of the Virgin in Late Antiquity: Religious Development and Myth-Making', in R.N. Swanson (ed.), *The Church and Mary*, Woodbridge, 2004, pp. 1–21; id., 'The Early Cult of the Virgin', in M. Vassilaki (ed.), *Mother of God: representations of the Virgin in Byzantine art*, Milan et al., 2000, pp. 3–15, arguing that the designation of Mary as Theotokos was not motivated by a cult. On the idea that new visual forms were used to stress Mary's 'elevated status' after the Council of Ephesus, see for example J. Herrin, 'The Imperial Feminine in Byzantium', *Past and Present* 169 (2000), pp. 3–35.

mentary iconography of early images (a male figure standing before a seated woman) appears to respond faithfully, if unimaginatively, to the concise Lukan narrative (1:26–38).[12] As Grabar's comment attests, images of the Adoration can be taken to speak equally well to this view. However, in recent decades, the relationship between text and image in antiquity has been shown to have been more interactive than the traditional interpretative paradigms have allowed.[13] For some scholars, this has stimulated a re-examination of nascent Christian iconography in late antiquity, its purposes and relationships with texts; and this paper is a response to that work, and specifically the re-appraisals of early Marian imagery that have formed part of the research process.[14]

---

12 Important here in bringing clarity to the formative stages of the scene's iconographic development is the recent work of M. Lidova, 'ΧΑΙΡΕ ΜΑΡΙΑ: Annunciation Imagery in the Making', *ΙΚΟΝ: Journal of Iconographic Studies* 10 (2017), pp. 45–62. C. Proverbio, *La Figura dell'angelo nella civiltà paleocristiana*, Perugia, 2007, pp. 42–43, tav. 1, supports a mid-third century date for the Annunciation in the Catacomb of Priscilla. On the early iconographic development, and its demonstration of nascent interest in Mary before the Council of Ephesus, see also C.G. Taylor, *Late Antique Images of the Virgin Annunciate Spinning*, Leiden, 2018, for example, at p. 17 n. 10.

13 There are numerous studies, and I cite just three: J. Elsner (ed.), *Art and Text in Roman Culture*, Cambridge, 1996; J.P. Small, *The Parallel Worlds of Classical Art and Text*, Cambridge, 2003; M. Squire, *Image and Text in Græco-Roman Antiquity*, Cambridge, 2009. It must also be noted that the exploration of dynamic relationships between texts and images has been ongoing in the study of Byzantine art, and I think particularly of the work of Henry Maguire—for instance: id., 'The Asymmetry of Text and Image in Byzantium', *Perspectives médiévales* 38 (2017), pp. 1–15.

14 Especially influential for me are: M. Mignozzi, 'Su un tema iconografico: l'Adorazione dei due, quattro, sei Magi', *Vetera Christianorum* 49 (2012), pp. 65–100; and A. Effenberger, 'Maria als Vermittlerin und Fürbitterin. Zum Marienbild in der spätantiken und früh-byzantinischen Kunst Ägyptens', in L.M. Peltomaa and A. Külzer (eds), *Presbeia Theotokou: The Intercessory Role of Mary across Times and Places in Byzantium 4th–9th Century*, Vienna, 2015, pp. 49–106, who at p. 55 cites the case of the Adelphia sarcophagus: 'sind bildliche Darstellungen historische Primarquellen ersten Ranges'. See also: J. Deckers, 'Die Huldigung', at p. 22, concluding from an examination of examples that images of the Adoration do not derive from text alone; B. Brenk, *The Apse, The Image and the Icon: An Historical Perspective of the Apse as a Space for Images*, Wiesbaden, 2010, e.g. at p. 77, arguing that in the West, extant imagery attests to the spread of devotion to the Virgin from the first quarter of the fourth century onwards (and at pp. 61–79 for the Virgin's representation in Adoration scenes); E. Jastrzębowska, 'Boten, Magier und Pilger', *Boreas* 17 (1994), pp. 105–113, discussing iconographic features that have little relationship with the New Testament text (pp. 106–108), and positing (at p. 106) that scenes (such as the two year old Christ seated on the lap of the Virgin) regarded as deriving from apocryphal text Pseudo-Matthew may have in fact influenced text. Other examinations of early Marian iconography include: Slavadori, 'Per Feminam'; Lidova, 'Embodied Word'; U. Utro, 'Maria nell'iconografia Cristiana dei primi secoli', in E. Dal Covolo and A. Serra (eds), *Storia della*

In the analysis of Marian iconography and its development within the Roman world, several studies have established that prior to the Council of Ephesus, art was being used as a means of recognising Mary's importance as mother of Jesus and that artists were not necessarily bound by a gospel or apocryphal text in the visual expression of that recognition. Scholars have demonstrated the ways that the iconography is embedded within contemporary visual culture, where a complex web of connections exists between other images, texts and even devotional expectations on the part of the viewer. In highlighting the dialogical nature of these connections, Marcello Mignozzi's description of this web as a 'system of mutual exchanges' is particularly helpful.[15] For in considering the capacity of extrabiblical sources to further our understanding of ancient Jewish or Christian concerns, the acknowledgement of a dialogical relationship between art and text underscores the capacity of images to elaborate independently beyond a Gospel text in the way that apocryphal textual traditions are seen to do. In foregrounding, and working towards a better understanding of, the capacity of images to act in this way I suggest here that it might be helpful to think of them as 'visual apocrypha'.[16] In exploring this idea I will take as a case-study the representation of Mary within scenes of the Adoration produced in Rome during the fourth and early fifth centuries—a time during which the popularity of the scene in that city elevates Mary to a position of prominence in the visual record, and yet an account for which remains to be provided.

Several scholars have worked to compile a corpus of evidence for the representation of Mary in Rome before and during the fifth century.[17] The corpus is both disparate (in terms of medium, scale, as well as viewing context), and incomplete (there are inevitable losses, while many images survive in a frag-

---

mariologia vol. I, Rome, 2009, pp. 353–381; G. Parlby, 'The Origins of Marian Art in the Catacombs and Problems of identification', in C. Maunder (ed.), *The Origins of the Cult of the Virgin Mary*, London, 2008, pp. 41–56, and the PhD dissertation from which that article draws, 'What can art tell us about the cult of the Virgin Mary in the early Roman Church? A re-evaluation of the evidence for Marian images in Late Antiquity', University of Roehampton, 2010.

15 Mignozzi, 'Su un tema', the quotation at p. 68: 'sistema di scambi reciproci'.

16 I suggest this term in full recognition of the fact that as a moniker for early Christian extrabiblical literature, the word 'apocrypha' is problematic. On the questions raised about terminology, see S. Shoemaker, 'Early Christian Apocryphal Literature,' in S. Ashbrook Harvey and D.G. Hunter (eds), *The Oxford Handbook of Early Christian Studies*, Oxford, 2008, pp. 521–548, esp. 522–528. The term is of course akin to the idea that images function as 'visual texts'—as used, for example, in the analysis of Mithraic imagery by S. Zwirn, 'The intention of biographical narration on Mithraic cult images', *Word and Image* 5 (1989), pp. 2–18, at 15.

17 See the studies cited in note 14.

mentary, abraded or compromised state—through deterioration, but in certain cases also through conservation interventions).[18] Moreover, in some pictorial contexts the identity of a particular figure as Mary is uncertain.[19] Nonetheless, the corpus provides persuasive evidence for the use of art in Rome by the fourth century, in private and public contexts, not simply to acknowledge but also to explore Mary's importance. Many of these images are related to texts; yet there are a variety of ways that they might be thought of as elaborating beyond and so working independently from text in the expression of theological positions or devotional beliefs. As a natural part of the process whereby a story is told through a visual rather than textual medium, a diverse range of considerations is involved—including iconography (how to clothe Mary?) and compositional strategies (who to place in the scene with her?). For instance, narrative details of small or great importance that are not described or dwelt upon in the textual evidence, be they subtle gestures or explicit actions, can be advanced in visual media where they operate exegetically. Similarly, the practical design choices an individual artist or workshop makes in selecting and grouping stories together, organising a pictorial programme for a specific visual context, generate meaning for the viewer. Throughout this multifaceted creative process, artists may be mindful of but not necessarily controlled by one text or exegetical interpretation. The artist structures and then guides the viewer's per-

---

18   Leaving aside the question of the design of the original apse mosaic in the church of Santa Maria Maggiore (on which see M. Andaloro and S. Romano, 'L'immagine nell'abside', in M. Andaloro et al. (eds), *Arte e iconografia a Roma: da Costantino a Cola di Rienzo*, Milan, 2000, pp. 93–132; Lidova, 'Imperial', p. 65 n. 15), I draw attention to the important study by P. Liverani of the inscription originally located on the counter-façade of that church and the now-lost mosaic that accompanied it: 'The Memory of the Bishop in the Early Christian Basilica', in M. Verhoeven et al. (eds), *Monuments and Memory. Christian Cult Buildings and Constructions of the Past*, Belgium, 2016, pp. 185–197. Working from the inscription, Liverani proposes that an image of Mary with Jesus is easy to imagine, given that her motherhood is celebrated, and her chastity noted, in the text. According to him, a better understanding of the model of epigraphic communication that emerged from the fourth century can help us to think more clearly about the content of lost mosaics; and this argument has significant ramifications for the early history of Marian imagery in Rome.

19   Aside from contested Annunciation scenes, here I think specifically of the fragments of gold glass produced in Rome in the fourth century that preserve representations of female figures in prayer, some of which appear with the name Maria or MARA. The idea that these can be interpreted as unequivocal attestation of private devotion to Mary among wealthy Christians in Rome during the second half of the fourth century is not universally held, but remains compelling for some scholars (see Brenk, *The Apse*, pp. 66–68). For the literature, see E. Rubery, 'From Catacomb to Sanctuary: The Orant Figure and the Cults of the Mother of God and S. Agnes in Early Christian Rome, with Special Reference to Gold Glass', *Studia Patristica* LXXIII (2014), pp. 129–174.

THE CASE OF MARY AND THE MAGI IN EARLY CHRISTIAN ROME 389

ception of a story or set of stories in a certain direction, yet without confining it. In this way, early Christian images can be seen to function as apocrypha, and as such they warrant a place alongside textual evidence for early Christian thought, rather than being regarded as subordinate to it.

The parameters of this paper do not allow for a thorough engagement with the corpus of evidence for the representation of Mary in Rome before and during the fifth century. Nonetheless, in pursuing evidence for visually attested apocryphal traditions, important preparatory steps can be made in the analysis of relief sculpture, since more than sixty images of the Adoration are preserved on carved sarcophagi reliefs or fragments thereof dating from the fourth century.[20] Through a close iconographic analysis of a small selection of examples in this medium, my aim in what follows is not to elicit evidence for a cult of Mary in Rome prior to the Council of Ephesus *per se*, so much as to observe techniques used by artists to imaginatively elaborate beyond text in order to explore Mary's importance as mother of Jesus.

According to the surviving evidence, representations of the Annunciation (Lk 1:31–38), Nativity (Lk 2:1–20; Mt. 1:25), and the Adoration (Mt. 2:11), appeared in Roman funerary art by the late third and early fourth century.[21] Each story is connected to the theme of the birth of Jesus, and Mary is consistently portrayed according to the pictorial conventions already established in Roman funerary art for the representation of a mother (see Figure 19.2): seated (usually in a high-backed chair), dressed as a conventional Roman matron (wearing a tunic and veiled in the *palla*) and shown striking gestures that like her clothing, evoke modesty and restraint.[22] These qualities or attributes, well-known in the Roman cultural context at this period, transferred easily into Christian art for the portrayal of Mary, dovetailing with those highlighted in the earliest

---

20   This number is high in comparison to mural paintings in catacombs, which only number around twenty: N. Zimmerman, 'Catacomb Painting and the Rise of Christian Iconography in Funerary Art', in R.M. Jensen and M.D. Ellison (ed.), *The Routledge Handbook of Early Christian Art*, Routledge, 2018, pp. 21–38, cites eighteen extant murals in catacombs. For examples on fourth century Roman Christian sarcophagi, see Utro, 'Maria', *passim*; and the *catalogue raisonné* of Nativity scenes (with which the Adoration often appears) compiled by D. Milinović, 'L'origine de la scéne de la nativité', *AnTard* 7 (1999), pp. 299–329.

21   On the representation of Mary in early Christian art, see the extensive bibliography compiled by Utro, 'Maria', n. 1.

22   In a rare variant, preserved on a relief from a sarcophagus dated to the second third of the fourth century, now in the Palazzo Doria Pamphili, Mary is shown reclining on a bed with the child on her lap as she receives the Magi: G. Bovini and H. Brandenburg, *Repertorium der christlich-antiken Sarkophage* vol. 1, Rom und Ostia, Wiesbaden, 1967, no. 949.

FIGURE 19.2   'Biographical sarcophagus' (detail: mother and child scene, right short side), ca. 176–193 CE
PHOTO: LACMA (PUBLIC DOMAIN)

Christian accounts in the New Testament, where her virginity and her role in the incarnation as Mother of Jesus are emphasised.[23] Yet this was more than a wholesale re-use of a stock-motif with which artists and viewers in Rome were already familiar. The Roman model was a springboard for exploring Mary's virtues,[24] maternal qualities and other dimensions of her motherhood, about which the gospel texts were silent.[25] And here I turn to the story of the Adoration of the Magi specifically, examining the text before closely analysing early visual responses to it.

The story is told in only one of the four canonical Christian gospels, Matthew (2:9–11):

---

23   Matthew 1:18–20, Luke 1:26–35; Galatians 4:4.
24   As argued recently by Taylor, *Late Antique*.
25   A consideration of visual ideas from traditions originating outside of the Roman world is beyond the scope of this paper, although I acknowledge the importance of these ideas and will explore some in a forthcoming paper concerning the representation of the Magi (at the Oxford Patristics Conference, 2019).

When they had heard the king, they set out; and there, ahead of them, went the star that they had seen at its rising, until it stopped over the place where the child was. When they saw that the star had stopped, they were overwhelmed with joy. On entering the house, they saw the child with Mary his mother; and they knelt down and paid him homage. Then, opening their treasure chests, they offered him gifts of gold, frankincense, and myrrh.

NRSA

This single narrative is sparing in detail. There is no reference to how many Magi are involved; rather the text focuses on their action, and their sight. The Magi see the star in the East, they follow it, and when they see the star again above the child, they rejoice. When they enter the house, they see the child with Mary, fall down and worship before opening their treasures and finally presenting the child with three different gifts. This story about the active seeking of God in his incarnate Son is full of extreme movement, both physical (a long journey, kneeling, presentation of gifts) and emotional (joy, awe). Yet in striking contrast, the mother and child are static. Nothing is said about what they see, or about their response to the arrival of the visitors and the vigorous activities that ensue around them; and yet it is their undocumented response upon which artists focus in order to create a meaning for the viewer.

In Rome, two distinct compositions are found for the representation of the Adoration: a horizontal or 'asymmetric' image, and a centralised or 'symmetric' image.[26] The first (and probably the earliest) composition could contain two but usually three Magi walking vigorously from one side of the composition towards Mary and Jesus seated in profile on the other.[27] As we have already seen in the Catacomb of Priscilla (see Figure 19.1), it was especially suited to long horizontal pictorial frames, hence it is often found on the narrow lid or

---

26   G. Schiller, *Iconography of Christian art*, trans. J. Seligman vol. 1, Greenwich, 1971, p. 100; Mignozzi, 'Su un tema'.

27   Deckers, 'Die Huldigung', describes the composition with the term 'dynamische'; he also notes (p. 23) that in the first centuries, the Magi numbered two and six, but three became quickly became standardised. Scholars routinely suggest that the standardisation was likely helped by the fact that the idea of three Magi was subsequently entertained in patristic exegesis—and for the discussion of these sources, see P.M. Paciorek, 'L'adoration des mages (Mt. 2.1–2) dans la tradition patristique et au Moyen Âge jusqu' au 12e siècle', *Augustiniana* 50 (2000), pp. 85–140. On the variation in the number of Magi as a sign of artistic license, Mignozzi, 'Su un tema'.

on the front of sarcophagi (see Figure 19.3).[28] This composition contrasts with a second model, in which the seated Mary and Jesus are placed at the centre of the scene where they receive greater visual prominence, with two, four or even six Magi[29] arranged in a courtly fashion either side of them (see Figure 19.4).[30] The centralised image is not common before the sixth century; and the use of the horizontal model has been used to argue that in pre-Ephesus Adoration iconography, where the scene is regarded as functioning to visualise the incarnation, Mary functions merely as a support for the real focus of the Magi's adoration: Jesus.[31] In exploring ways that Mary is shown to be integral to the scene, let me return to that Roman-pictorial model upon which artists fashioned representations of Mary.

A second century sarcophagus in Los Angeles (see Figure 19.2), preserves a fine example of the pictorial conventions for the representation of a mother in Roman art. A mother is shown seated on a high-backed chair at the far right of the horizontal composition, watching the bathing of her new-born child. As she takes her right hand to her face and rests her left elbow on the high back of the chair, the artist rotates this mother's upper body towards the viewer. This simple but strategic compositional manœuvre affords the viewer a privileged position not just by drawing us into this very private domestic moment, but by enabling us to share the mother's private moment of contemplation.[32] This pictorial model of the seated mother was flexible in that with minor changes, it could be used to represent other activities, such as the nursing of the baby

---

28 For a description of and bibliography for the fragment illustrated here (formerly in the Mattei Collection), see Bovini and Brandenburg, *Repertorium* vol. 1, no. 799.

29 On the variation in the number of Magi as a sign of artistic license, Mignozzi, 'Su un tema'.

30 The remarkable crater illustrated in Fig. 19.4, which on the other side of the neck features a representation of Christ enthroned and flanked by apostles, was apparently imported to Rome from Constantinople between 380 and 430: H.G. Severin, 'Oströmische Plastik unter Valens und Theodosius I', *Jahrbuch der Berliner Museen* 12 (1970), pp. 211–252. Comparanda, in Berlin and Budapest, are preserved in fragments, making the Rome crater especially important.

31 For example, Schiller, *Iconography*, p. 102. For scholarly rejection of this idea, see further: A. Quacquarelli and F. Bisconti, 'L'iconologia mariana antenicena e i suoi presupposti', in S. Felici (ed.), *La mariologia nella catechesi dei Padri—Età pre-nicena* (Biblioteca di scienze religiose 88), Rome, 1989, pp. 242–256, here 253; Salvadori, 'Per Feminam', pp. 315–316.

32 Roman Biographical Sarcophagus, marble, 72.39 × 226.06 × 81.28 cm, Eastern Mediterranean. Los Angeles County Museum of Art, 47.8.9a–c. E.P. Loeffler, 'A Famous Sarcophagus at the Los Angeles Museum', *The Art Bulletin* 39 (1957), pp. 1–7. Further examples are illustrated in Grabar, *Christian Iconography*, fig. 266. Salvadori, 'Per Feminam', pp. 305–310, observes that these scenes are found on biographical sarcophagi produced for children as well as adults, and are modelled on scenes of the birth of Dionysos (further bibliography at note 82).

FIGURE 19.3   Sarcophagus lid (detail: Adoration of the Magi). Marble, first third of the fourth century CE
PHOTO: AUTHOR

FIGURE 19.4   Crater (detail of the neck, Mary and Child enthroned, flanked by six Magi). Marble, second half of the fourth century CE
PHOTO: BEAT BRENK

FIGURE 19.5
Wall painting: Mother and Child, with a Prophet (?), mid-fourth century CE, Catacomb of Priscilla, Rome

(see Figure 19.5). With the torso again turned to face the viewer, and elbows raised and angled outwards in order to hold and thereby display the baby at the breast, new dimensions of intimacy between mother and child could be explored pictorially, through attention to eye-line, angle of the head, or position of the baby.[33]

The model was well-known and deployed in diverse visual contexts within Roman culture. A prominent example is found in the representation of a veiled female goddess on the southeast corner of the *Ara Pacis Augustæ*, dedicated by the Senate in Rome on 30 January 9 BCE. Identified variously as Peace, Tellus, and Venus, the goddess is seated on a rocky throne in the same pose, with two children in her lap.[34] During the third century in Rome, this model formed the

---

33 For example: the sarcophagus of Marcus Cornelius Statius, ca. 150 CE, Roman, marble, l. 1,49 m., H. 0,47 m., L. 0,23 m: Louvre, Department of Greek, Etruscan, and Roman Antiquities (inv. Ma 659).

34 On the identification of the woman, with a survey of past scholarship, see B.S. Spaeth, 'The Goddess Ceres in the Ara Pacis Augustæ and the Carthage Relief', *American Journal of Archæology*, 98.1 (1994), pp. 65–100 and fig. 1.

basis for representing Mary in various moments, including the Adoration, and possibly for imagining messianic prophecy of the birth of Christ—such as that in Isaiah (60:1–6). For in the much-contested third century representation in the Catacomb of Priscilla of a mother actively suckling her naked child (who in a vivid, impressionistic style, the artist has captured wriggling around to face the viewer), many scholars see an early representation of the prophet subsequently seen in representations of the Adoration—the man standing before Mary and gesturing towards her (see Figure 19.5).[35] I will return to his identity shortly. Here it is worth remarking that regardless of his identity, the very intimate engagement that the artist stages between this mother, child, palliate man and viewer in this lively painting is exactly what we find in subsequent representations of Mary where her motherhood is accentuated and arguably honoured in the attention given to her gestures, eye-line, and touch. The stories are not just scenes from the life of Jesus, they are also episodes in which the viewer is drawn to contemplate Mary.

An extremely tender imagining of a connection between Mary and Jesus as mother and child, not elaborated upon in the gospel text, is found on a child's sarcophagus now in Berlin (see Figure 19.6) dating from the first third of the fourth century.[36] As in the catacomb painting, the artist engages the viewer's senses through a representation of Mary that is sensitive to her touch (note her large right hand on the body of the child, her left hand cradling the head), to her eye contact with Jesus, and to other sensory implications of their physical proximity. In the delicacy with which she handles her child's body, tenderly drawing him close to her face for example, the viewer might simultaneously sense the weight of his form and the warmth of both bodies, including their exchange of breath in this moment. Note that Mary, seated on a wicker chair that is draped and has a footrest, is centrally placed beneath a set of parted curtains, which act as a framing device specifically for her veiled head. That she is

---

35   F. Bisconti, 'La Madonna di Priscilla: Interventi di restauro e ipotesi sulla dinamica decorative', *Rivista di Archeologia Cristiana* 71 (1996), pp. 7–34; and Utro, 'Maria', *passim*. For the view that the painting represents an ordinary mother and her child: Parlby, 'The Origins', pp. 41–56.

36   The so-called 'Theusebios' sarcophagus, Staatliche Museen, Berlin, Inv. No. 17/61. J. Huskinson, 'Early Christian Children's Sarcophagi', *Studia Patristica* 24 (1993), pp. 114–118, here p. 115. On the sarcophagus and its lid, which contains a long dedication to the child Theusebio Neofito, see A. Mastino, P. Ruggeri and R. Zucca, 'Un testo epigrafico sul sacramento del battesimo in Sardinia', in R. Martorelli et al. (eds), *Isole e terraferma nel primo cristianesimo*, Atti XI Congresso Nazionale di Archeologia Cristiana, Cagliari, 2015, pp. 511–520.

FIGURE 19.6   Child's sarcophagus. Pinkish-white marble, first third of the fourth century (330–350 CE)
© BPK NATIONAL MUSEUMS, BERLIN (A. VOIGT)

a key player in the scene is underscored in the tightness with which the baby is swaddled, for with the resultant stiffness and lack of bodily interaction, the baby's dependence on her is intensified.[37] Mary is not simply a prop for the main protagonist, Jesus, she is a protagonist. In this assertion the artist does not follow textual cues but constructs their own to engage the emotions of the viewer and elicit a reverential response—perhaps even to meet the prayerful needs of, and expectations brought by, the viewer.[38] Yet in exposing the human interaction between mother and son, the artist also engages contemporary theological issues—specifically, Christological concerns about the humanity of the Godhead. Without polemic, the artist does this visually with the addition of two Magi: pointing and looking to the star above one corner of the curtain, the

---

37 I am indebted to Eunice Dautermann Maguire for this observation.
38 Relevant here is the point that visual narratives serve different functions. For instance, Henry Maguire has contrasted two types of visual narration in early Byzantine art: 'narratives that engage' and 'narratives that work' (in a paper delivered at the conference *Histoires chrétiennes en images: espace, temps et structure de la narration. Byzance et Moyen Age occidental*, Institut national d'histoire de l'art, Paris, 23rd November, 2017—the proceedings are to be published in the series *Byzantina sorbonensia*). I am grateful to Professor Maguire for sharing his thoughts, and this paper, with me.

pair provide an essential framework in which the theme of the dual natures of Christ can be set and so explored visually.[39]

A similar intensity of reflection on the role of Mary as mother is present in the representation of interaction between Mary, Jesus, the leading Magus, and a camel on a small fragment from a Roman sarcophagus found in the Catacomb of Domitilla (see Figure 19.7).[40] In this strikingly cohesive vignette of interaction, each participant in the scene is integral, the sense of intimacy in the moment of exchange being palpable thanks to the intentional representation of gesture, touch, and eyeline. Each figure is in motion. Jesus leans forward to extend his arms, his left hand taking the gold wreath offered by the Magus, who also leans forward and bows his head in the act. To evoke a frisson of anticipation in the viewer, the artist carefully delineates the child's forefinger grazing the bowl on which the crown sits—tantalizingly close, but not quite touching the Magus's thumb. The placement and representation of the lively camel is crucial in the staging of this interaction: its long neck extends vertically between the Magus and the child, its head thrown backwards in profile such that one large eye is seen to turn quizzically downwards to behold (and so draw our eye attention to) the scene below. Of course, for those schooled in biblical literature, the camel links the story to the prophecy of Isaiah (60:1–6); yet in a more practical sense, the camel references the fact of the Magi's journey, its length, and Eastern origin, details noted in the gospel account. There is also a sense that this camel is an individual: augmenting the sense of anticipation, the animal's mouth appears to curl open in response to what it sees, and tiny locks of hair ripple across its forehead. Artistically, the camel's head movement draws the curve of the rein upwards to extend from the chin of the Magus to the animal's mouth, cleverly creating a further physical connection and tension within the composition between the visitor and the child, who fix their gaze on each other. Mary seems to be motionless, but she is not the static mother of the Gospel text.

Remarkably, even though her veiled head is the only part of her body to survive on this fragment of a larger frieze (the tip of her parted hair-line demurely glimpsed beneath the rim of the veil), it is clear that Mary is no passive support-device for Jesus: she is a fulcrum. She is taller than the Magus (even though she is seated), her round-cheeked face proportionally larger than his, and her

---

39   See the comments of Mignozzi, 'Su un tema', on the ways that additional figures to the Mary-Child nucleus strengthen that iconography, pp. 65–66; and on the diffusion of the two-Magi iconography in the fourth century, see the conclusions at pp. 98–99.

40   Bovini and Brandenburg, *Repertorium* vol. 1, no. 525a.

FIGURE 19.7   Fragment of a sarcophagus (detail of the Adoration scene, with camel). Marble, second quarter of the fourth century CE, Catacomb of Domitilla, Rome
© DAI, ROME

gaze suffusing the scene with energy. Mary makes possible the incarnation of divinity in human form—Jesus now portrayed as a child—and thus ensures the redemption of all believers.[41] She is integral to the scene, and perhaps we can go a step further to surmise that she is understood, by the artist and the patron, as worthy of veneration in her own right. The Domitilla fragment is a

---

41   Grabar, *Christian Iconography*, pp. 12–13, proposed that the adoration scene was important as an 'iconographic sign' of the incarnation, and thus of redemption.

THE CASE OF MARY AND THE MAGI IN EARLY CHRISTIAN ROME 399

particularly fine example of the way that an image has the capacity to elaborate the Gospel text in much the same way as a derivative tradition like the *Protevangelium* often seems to do, introducing new details that vibrantly colour and so interpret the text.

Produced in numerous small workshops in Rome,[42] sarcophagi attest to the diversity with which the Adoration was treated in that city in the handling of small and seemingly inconsequential iconographic details by individual craftsmen—from curtains to camels. No two images of Mary holding Jesus in scenes of the Adoration in this medium are the same.[43] So not only from the frequency of appearance of the subject (noted in the introduction), but also from the variety of treatment and careful attention to minutiæ, it is hard to entertain the notion that the Magi are disinterested in Mary and that the viewer is meant to be.[44] Note again that the examples I have discussed so far predate the Council of Ephesus in 431, and Mary's proclamation as 'God Bearer'. The details upon which I have focused are internal to a scene, drawing the eye to Mary. However, decisions relating to where the Adoration was placed within a pictorial programme, aligned or juxtaposed with other stories, are equally important in considering ways that artists could honour Mary, evoking particular emotional or devotional responses in a viewer, and even conveying particular interpretations or theological ideas that may be related to but are not necessarily rooted or preserved in the textual record.

Let me turn to a comparison of the placement of Adoration scenes on two large and elaborate sarcophagi, the complexity of their pictorial programmes suggesting that their respective buyers were committed to their purchase, and so to the themes explored visually upon them. Fourth century Christians in Rome who chose to be interred in sarcophagi were mostly middle class or sometimes aristocrats, and the medium afforded them an opportunity to display their accomplishments and values as well as their religious convictions.[45] A good example of a large marble sarcophagus of fine workmanship, likely commissioned by a specific patron, is a double-frieze sarcophagus produced in the early fourth century, now in Arles. It features a double portrait medallion of a

---

42 R. Couzin, 'The Christian Sarcophagus Population of Rome', *JRA* 27 (2014), pp. 275–303 at 279.

43 This is most easily apprehended in the examples chosen and illustrated by Utro, 'Maria'.

44 Hence Bisconti's point that she is hardly a mere chair for the deity: 'L'iconologia mariana', p. 253—also emphasized by Salvadori, 'Per Feminam', p. 316 n. 118.

45 The socio-economic context is concisely summarised by P.C. Finney, 'Do you think God is a Magician? (Plato, rep. 380D)', in G. Koch (ed.), *Akten des Symposiums "Frühchristliche Sarkophage"*, Mainz, 2002, pp. 99–108.

FIGURE 19.8   Sarcophagus. Marble, early fourth century
© MUSÉE DE L'ARLES ANTIQUE (J.-L. MABY/L. ROUX)

married couple at the centre of the top register, surrounded by an elaborate and densely packed pictorial programme containing stories from the Old and New Testaments (see Figure 19.8).[46] The sarcophagus also features an interesting pairing. At the far left corner of the bottom register, Mary is seated with Jesus, receiving the three Magi; and in the same position in the register directly above, is a scene that some scholars interpret as the three Persons of the Trinity creating Adam and Eve, with God the Father shown seated, the beardless Christ standing before Him, and the bearded Holy Spirit standing behind the Father's chair.[47] The figures of Mary and the Father are in perfect alignment, as though mirror images of each other: both sit in identical high-backed, wicker

---

46   Musée de l'Arles Antique, inv. PAP 7400.1–5. B. Christern-Briesenick, *Repertorium der christlich-antiken Sarkophage* vol. *III: Frankreich, Algerien, Tunesien*, Mainz, 2003, no. 38 pp. 23–25, with bibliography. See also D. Markow, 'Some Born-Again Christians of the Fourth Century', *The Art Bulletin* 63.4 (1981), pp. 650–655; R.M. Jensen, 'The Economy of the Trinity at the Creation of Adam and Eve', *Journal of Early Christian Studies* 7.4 (1999), pp. 527–546.

47   Markow, 'Some Born-Again', n. 7, cites various scholars who have rejected this interpretation.

THE CASE OF MARY AND THE MAGI IN EARLY CHRISTIAN ROME   401

chairs that are draped in the same way; both also sit in the same position, with shoulders slightly rotated towards the viewer, the right leg taken forward, feet arranged in the same way on the same footrest. Beyond this precise duplication of iconography, the figures are visually linked in the treatment of drapery, which creates a further symmetry and unity of line. Further, each is attended by a male figure, dressed in a pallium who stands behind the chair and places his right hand on the back of it. While the figure in the 'Trinity' has been identified as the Holy Spirit, an identity for the corresponding figure behind Mary is, like the curious male figure in the mother and child painting in the Catacomb of Priscilla (see Figure 19.5), highly contested.

We know that across the fourth and fifth centuries, apocryphal texts furnished a range of pictorial details for artists and their theological interlocutors in representing Mary. In prominent monumental[48] and miniature[49] pictorial cycles produced in Rome and Northern Italy in the fifth century for viewing in liturgical contexts, a relationship between iconography and texts can be demonstrated for the representation of Mary as mother—including the canonical gospels, the *Protevangelium* and the *Gospel of Pseudo-Matthew*. The bearded male figure already noted in the Priscilla painting (see Figure 19.5) and the Arles sarcophagus (see Figure 19.8), and who appears in many depictions of the Adoration surviving in Rome, can also be connected with other early Chris-

---

48   The mosaic cycle dedicated to the Childhood and Second Coming of Christ, on the triumphal (former apsidal) arch at Santa Maria Maggiore, Rome, completed under Pope Sixtus III, 432–440. On the representation of the Virgin in the cycle, see Lidova, *Convivium* 11.2 (2015), pp. 60–80. R.M. Jensen, 'The Apocryphal Mary in Early Christian Art', in A. Gregory and C. Tuckett (eds), *Oxford Handbook of Early Christian Apocrypha*, Oxford, 2015, pp. 289–305, argues (against S. Spain, '"The Promised Blessing": The Iconography of the Mosaics of S. Maria Maggiore', *Art Bulletin* 61 (1979), pp. 518–540) that some details from the *Gospel of Pseudo-Matthew* were established in fourth century art such that the apocryphal text may have been a source for artists working on the infancy cycle mosaics at Santa Maria Maggiore, 299–303.

49   The five-part ivory diptych, preserved in the Treasury of the Milan Cathedral, from the second half of the fifth century: J. Spier (ed.), *Picturing the Bible: The Earliest Christian Art*, New Haven, 2007, pp. 256–258, cat. no. 76, with bibliography. The presence of the symbols of the four evangelists, paired at the top of each leaf, is suggestive of their function as a Gospel book cover. D. Wright, 'Review of Wolfgang Fritz Volbach, Elfenbeinarbeiten der Spätantike und des frühen Mittelalters', *Art Bulletin* 63.4 (1981), pp. 675–677, proposes they may have been intended simply for display, whether on an altar or procession. The question of function is not pursued by Z. Frantová, *Heresy and Loyalty: The Ivory Diptych of Five Parts from the Cathedral Treasury in Milan*, Brno, 2014. For the representation of non-canonical stories about Mary in the medium of ivory more broadly: A. Cutler, 'The Mother of God in Ivory', in M. Vassilaki (ed.), *Mother of God: Representations of the Virgin in Byzantine Art*, Milan, 2000, pp. 167–175.

tian writings. Although on the Arles sarcophagus (see Figure 19.9), the leading Magus points to the star—and simultaneously to the figure of God above, an act further uniting the two seated figures—in some pictorial contexts it is the figure behind the chair that points to the star.[50] He has been variously identified as Joseph,[51] an angel,[52] an attendant;[53] or an Old Testament prophet—possibly Isaiah (60:1–6).[54] However, most scholars identify him as the prophet Balaam (Num. 24:19).[55] One of the earliest attested interpretations of Balaam foretelling the incarnation ('a star shall come forth out of Jacob, and a sceptre shall rise out of Israel', Num. 24:17) is that of Justin Martyr in Rome in the second century, who identified the star with Christ himself (1 *Apol.* 32.12; *Dial.* 126.1);[56] and some writers, including Ambrose and Origen, further suggested that Balaam was an ancestor of the Magi.[57]

There is no doubt that different texts (whether gospel, apocryphal, patristic) are profoundly important in the interpretation of early Christian iconography, informing our understanding of images and their possible meaning for early Christian viewers. Yet anticipated correspondences between text and image

---

50   For example, on the fourth century epitaph of Severa from the catacomb of Priscilla— possibly contemporary with the Adoration scene (Fig. 19.1), from the same catacomb. M. Bagnoli (ed)., *Treasures of Heaven: Saints, Relics and Devotion in Medieval Europe*, London, 2011, p. 33, cat. no. 6 (written by U. Utro), with bibliography.

51   According to extant evidence, Joseph was never depicted in philosopher's attire: P. Testini, 'Alle origini dell'iconografia di Giuseppe di Nazareth', *Rivista di Archeologia Cristiana* 48 (1972), pp. 270–347, surveying the earliest iconography of Joseph. For an interesting example of the consistent identification of the figure in Adoration scenes as Joseph, see the catalogue by E.C. Schenck, 'A Painted Wooden Pyxis in the Museo Cristiano of the Vatican Library', *The Art Bulletin* 16.4 (1934), pp. 341–357, at 357, where all but one of the scenes listed as depicting Joseph in the fourth century are Adoration scenes.

52   E. Jastrzębowska, 'New Testament Angels in Early Christian Art: Origins and Sources', *Światowit* 8 (2009–2010), pp. 153–164, plates 176–185, here 158.

53   On the theory that the iconography of the Adoration derives from Imperial art: e.g. Deckers, 'Die Huldigung'.

54   Salvadori, 'Per feminam', pp. 268 (n. 2 with the bibliography), 287–292.

55   For an exhaustive presentation of the case for identifying the figure as Balaam, see E. Kirschbaum, 'Der Prophet Balaam und die Anbetung der Weisen', *RQ* 49 (1954), pp. 144–164.

56   On the interpretation of the verse in patristic literature, see D. Hannah, 'The Star of the Magi and the Prophecy of Balaam in Earliest Christianity, with special attention to the lost books of Balaam', in P. Barthel and G. van Kooten (eds), *The Star of Bethlehem and the Magi*, Leiden–Boston, 2015, pp. 433–462, here 434, with the bibliography.

57   Ambrose suggests this in his commentary on Luke, but Origen is explicit: T. Hegedus, 'The Magi and the Star of Matthew 2:1–12 in Early Christian Tradition', *Studia Patristica* 39 (2006), pp. 213–214.

FIGURE 19.9   Adoration of the Magi on the Arles sarcophagus
© MUSEE DE L'ARLES ANTIQUE (M. LACANAUD)

can obstruct just as much as assist our understanding of what an image might be communicating to the viewer at first glance.[58] There is no evidence to suggest that early Christian viewers expected to find complex theological commentary embedded within iconography or within pictorial programmes. This is not to say that they are not to be found, but to highlight that what immediately shaped a viewer's engagement with an image, activating their imagination or piety, might be interpretative interventions by the artist not the theologian. Having said this, if we return to the Arles sarcophagus, an educated viewer may immediately grasp a prophetic significance for the figure standing behind Mary, the man foretelling the birth of Christ of a virgin woman. But in this visual context there is another message to grasp, one that is not so much driven textually but artistically—in the alignment of the two scenes, and the subsequent association of God the Father and Mary on the Arles sarcophagus. This association is replicated on a second double-register sarcophagus of slightly later date, buried beneath the Church of S. Paolo fuori le Mura in Rome around 340 CE.[59] On the

---

58   Zimmerman, 'The healing', pp. 251–252, advocates the same approach.
59   Vatican, Museo Pio Cristiano (cat. 31427). Bovini and Brandenburg, *Repertorium* vol. 1, no. 43. P. Liverani and G. Spinola, *The Vatican Necropoles: Rome's City of the Dead*, trans. S. Stevens and V. Noel-Johnson, Turnhout, 2010, fig. 11, 32. This sarcophagus, known as

second sarcophagus, now in the Vatican, only the Father's chair is draped; but the almost identical repetition of the juxtaposition seen on the Arles sarcophagus points to the emergence and circulation among artistic workshops of a visual apocryphal tradition, one that in specific details (the standing male; the Magi) might derive from texts, but simultaneously points to other traditions. It has been argued the identical mirroring (one above the other) of the two figures on two different sarcophagi demonstrates an intentional emphasis on Mary's role in the divine story: as God the Father is celebrated as Creator, forming Adam and Eve, so Mary is celebrated for her agency—assimilated to the divine in her human virginity, and mother of the incarnate God; therefore she too is creator.[60] There is a theologically profound message here, but one that is visually articulated.

Moving beyond sarcophagi and private funerary art I would like to conclude with an example from a monumental public context in Rome that furnishes further evidence to suggest that devotion to Mary could be expressed or even stimulated visually in public spaces: a single relief depicting the Adoration, from the cycle of Old and New Testament scenes carved in relief on the wooden doors of the church of Santa Sabina, Rome (see Figure 19.10). The workshop that fulfilled the commission of relief panels in the early fifth century may have been Roman,[61] with carvers trained in different styles—some represent figures as stocky (reminiscent of the Roman sarcophagi we have been examining) while others achieve a higher relief (associated with sculpture from an Eastern, even Constantinopolitan centre, where figures are more fully modelled in higher relief).[62] For the representation of the Adoration, an artist working

---

'Dogmatic' on account of its highly elaborate theological programme, is also discussed in Studies 14 and 25 in this volume.

60 Salvadori, 'Per Feminam', pp. 320–321 and 322–329, referring to the connection made between Mary and the representation of Eve on the sarcophagus (a connection she discusses more broadly in chapter 2); Salvadori argues, moreover, that the iconography for the Genesis scenes was patterned upon the Adoration itself, p. 323. Jensen, 'The Economy', p. 545, argues that together the scenes 'simultaneously represent the original creation *and* the new creation'.

61 The doors are customarily dated to the time of the construction of the basilica under Popes Celestine (421–431) or Sixtus III (432–440): Jeremias, *Die Holztür*; J.-M. Spieser, 'Le programme iconographique des portes de Sainte-Sabine', *Journal des savants* 21 (1991), pp. 47–81; I. Foletti and M. Gianandrea (eds), *Zone Liminare: il nartece di Santa Sabina a Roma, la sua porta e l'iniziazione Cristiana*, Rome, 2016, with specific discussion of the Adoration panel by Foletti at pp. 158–159 (bibliography pp. 159–160).

62 R. Delbrueck, 'Notes on the Wooden Doors of Santa Sabina', *The Art Bulletin* 34.2 (1952), pp. 139–145. However, on the co-existence of styles on this and other monuments in Rome during the fifth century, see now I. Foletti, 'Le porte lignee di Santa Sabina all' Aventino: tra

FIGURE 19.10 Adoration of the Magi on the main doors of the church of S. Sabina, Rome, ca. 422–432
© DAI, ROME

in the Roman style depicts Mary in three-quarter view, veiled and seated on a folding chair with both arms placed either side of Jesus, who is seated on her lap. For the representation of Jesus, the artist follows a pictorial model that is frequently seen in funerary relief sculpture (see Figure 19.3), where he is not a swaddled baby in her arms but a clothed (wearing the tunic and pallium) and sentient child: leaning backwards against his mother's shoulder to behold the Magi, he raises his right arm towards the visitors as they process forwards, their eyes angled down as they reverently extend their gifts with outstretched arms (the first gift decorated with a large cross).[63] The most notable aspect of this composition is the imaginative insertion of Mary and Jesus atop a series of six steep stairs. From this raised position, the fact that the seated Mary is shown to turn her head, her face in full view looking directly out of the image to engage the viewer, is compelling: appearance suggests that she is an ordinary woman,

liturgia stazionaria e funzione iniziatica', *Hortus Artium Medievalium* 20.2 (2014), pp. 709–719 at 711.

63 Jeremias, *Die Holztür*, pp. 48–50, with detailed photograph at Taf. 41.

clothed in a tunic and *palla*, and yet other visual cues within the composition indicate otherwise.[64]

This composition, with the elevated mother-child, is not found for the representation of the Adoration on any other media in Rome or elsewhere at this period. Schiller proposed it may reflect the development of an autonomous, devotional, image of Mary with the Christ child—perhaps originating in Egypt or Syria and circulating independently at this time—one that is combined here with the conventional horizontal Adoration composition.[65] Certainly, images of Mary with the child were circulating independently on portable objects by the late fifth century (see Figure 19.11);[66] and Jeffrey Spier has suggested that their formulation likely preceded the proclamation of Mary as Mother of God at Ephesus in 431.[67] This theory finds support in the striking representation of Mary in strict frontality, enthroned on a high-backed imperial throne, on the late fourth century San Nazaro reliquary in Milan. The front face of the casket, one of the largest silver reliquaries of the early Christian period, features an image that is frequently identified as a representation of the Adoration. Yet as Gemma Sena Chiesa has convincingly argued, Mary can be understood to be represented in a celestial context where, as Mother of God, she is shown to be

---

64 Jeremias, *Die Holztür*, pp. 49–50, discusses the significance of this elevated, seated iconography, concluding that Mary is clearly given higher honor in this composition—which draws upon but modifies the earlier Roman iconography extant in catacomb and sarcophagus sculpture.

65 Schiller, *Iconography*, p. 102, positing an Egyptian or Syrian origin. Indeed, the representation follows iconographic formats for the presentation of deities on Syrian culture reliefs. Compare the pictorial conventions used for such cult images as the first century CE limestone relief depicting Zeus Kyrios-Baalshamin, excavated at Dura-Europos (Yale University Art Gallery, 1935.45): A. Perkins, *The Art of Dura-Europos*, Oxford, 1973, pp. 72–79, pl. 30. Brenk, *The Apse*, p. 68, takes this iconography as evidence for the veneration of Mary, and specifically (given the unusual combination of her clothing with the podium), as an expression the private devotion of the artist.

66 The upright oval jasper or obsidian (?) gemstone possibly produced in Syria (19×15×2 mm) and now in Ann Arbor is a fine example. It is engraved with a profile view of the Virgin and child seated to the left, accompanied by a Greek cross above her head, and the Greek letters ΙΣ and ΧΣ—Ἰ(ησοῦ)ς Χ(ριστό)ς. The cross marking on the chair's seat is conspicuous, perhaps to indicate wicker? University of Michigan, Special Collections Library (formerly the Campbell Bonner Collection no. 62; Taubman amulet 330). J. Spier, *Late Antique and Early Christian Gems*, Wiesbaden, 2007, no. 596, with discussion of its date and the group of which it is a part, pp. 103–104, and noting its fabric (which has previously been described as glass). I am grateful to Christopher Faraone for giving me permission to use his photograph of the gem in this paper.

67 Spier, *Late Antique*, p. 71, commenting on the finely engraved frontal representation of a nimbed Mary enthroned with the child, on a later fifth century chalcedony gem in the British Museum (M&LA 84,5–9,16), no. 440.

FIGURE 19.11
Mary and Jesus enthroned: engraved gemstone, Syria (?)
PHOTO: © CHRISTOPHER A. FARAONE

honoured by the figures around her.[68] In effect, what the Adoration image on the Santa Sabina doors may document, both in terms of its carefully structured composition and its attention to the representation of Mary (pose, gesture, eyeline), is a conspicuous carrying forward in a public context of the individual creativity of artistic expression seen in funerary art such that the silence of the Matthean text about Mary's response to the Magi, and the lack of detailed commentary about her role or importance, is elaborated upon. In so doing, the image divulges interpretive, and even devotional beliefs about Mary, documenting apocryphal traditions visually.

Let me return to the image with which I began (see Figure 19.1). Notwithstanding the absence of the star, the representation of the Adoration in the Catacomb of Priscilla does align with the bald details of the story as they are presented in the Matthean text, as Grabar observed: Magi come, they see the child, and present three gifts. Yet the horizontal composition is also highly selective, and as such is imaginatively conceived: while visualising textual details, the artist simultaneously exercises independence from the text, making decisions about what to depict, to exclude, and so how to construct the scene. For

---

68 Northern Italy (?), late fourth century, silver with gilding, 20,5×20,5×20,6 cm: Museo Diocesano, Milan (MD 2004.115.001). Gemma Sena Chiesa in J. Spier (ed.), *Picturing*, pp. 259–264, cat. no. 77, with the essential bibliography.

instance, the journey and arrival, which constitute separate moments in the textual narrative, are elided in the image, with the representation of the Magi in motion serving to evoke both in the mind of the viewer. Similarly, in the choice to focus on the moment of Adoration, the performance of *proskynesis* and the unpacking of gifts, actions specifically mentioned in the text, are both deliberately omitted.[69] This single scene thus attests to the variety of ways in which Christian images might be thought of as being developed independently of texts.

Recent scholarship has demonstrated that prior to the Council of Ephesus, art was being used to express devotion to Mary, a development that accords with the emphasis some scholars perceive in textual sources but which deserves to be viewed on its own terms.[70] For my purposes in this paper, the Priscilla Adoration painting (and the decorative scheme of which it is part in the *cappella greca*) serves to highlight that at the earliest stages in the visualisation of Christian stories the relationship between text and image was one of lively dialogue, not dependence. The decision to represent the Magi moving towards the mother and child in that pictorial context canalises the viewers perception of Jesus as both human and divine, yet without confining it to one or other doctrinal position as textual discussions may do at this period. In slightly later images, such as the fragment of an Adoration scene from a sarcophagus (see Figure 19.7), I highlighted the effort artists expended in nuancing the human interaction between the protagonists in order to engage the viewer's emotions in ways that the Gospel does not. In some cases, as on the Arles sarcophagus (see Figure 19.9), we might perceive that the structuring of the Adoration scene itself actively sets the figure of Mary firmly within a Christological frame, conveying specific information about her child. Yet at the same time, its alignment with another scene and subsequent juxtaposition of God

---

69   Noting the absence of proskynesis are: Deckers, 'Die Huldigung', p. 22; Brenk, *Apse*, pp. 62 and 78 (where he notes that it would remind viewers of the cult of the emperor). The choice not to depict the proskynesis is clear when viewing the numerous 'city-gate' sarcophagi, most probably from Roman workshops and dating to the late fourth or early fifth century, which preserve examples of diminutively sized male and female figures (generally interpreted as donors, or the deceased and spouse) kneeling deeply in worship at the feet of Christ in images of the *traditio legis*. On the figures as they appear on these and other sarcophagi, B. Mazzei, 'La pittura e la scultura funerarie: tangenze e divergenze nel processo di formazione del repertorio paleocristiano', *Antiquité Tardive* 19 (2011), pp. 79–94, at 92–93; on city-gate sarcophagi specifically, M. Lawrence, 'City-Gate Sarcophagi', *Art Bulletin* 10.1 (1927), pp. 1–45.

70   Stephen Shoemaker's work is pivotal here, e.g. *Mary in Early Christian Faith and Devotion*, New Haven, 2016.

the Father with Mary, prompts the viewer to consider the mother's pivotal role in the divine story. In other cases, as on the doors at Santa Sabina (see Figure 19.10), the imaginative structuring of the Adoration scene exposes this interest in Mary as a sacred figure in her own right more pointedly. So it is that within the contemporary visual culture of fourth century Rome, artistic choices govern small details (how to clothe Mary but also to depict her eyeline for instance) and compositional structure (who to place in the scene with Mary, where, and how to position them) but extend to the overall organisation of a pictorial programme (what other stories or figures to align with Mary and the Adoration scene of which she is part).

As I hope to have demonstrated in my brief exploration of a handful of examples from relief-sculpture, the importance of Mary for Christians in Rome specifically, and the ways that is expressed in the broader corpus of evidence for her representation in that city before 431, deserve further attention. The very popularity of the Adoration story elevates Mary to a position of prominence in that city. However for the purposes of this paper, the very variety of methods by which artists elaborated upon the gospel text and upon other texts or even liturgical traditions that interpreted the Adoration event (whether observed through small details or larger compositional strategies), is significant and demonstrates two things: Mary's perceived importance as a figure not simply in the Adoration story in relation to the child and the Magi, but in Christian history more broadly; and the capacity of art to give voice not simply to textual traditions, but to theological interpretations as well as devotional beliefs and practices. The examples of artistic elaboration that I have elected to analyse in the case of Mary could be multiplied, but my overarching argument would remain unchanged. Early Christian art was not subordinate to the word and did not function always to simply illustrate one text. The initial creation of an image and its coordinated use or juxtaposition with additional images in new pictorial systems and different visual contexts involved autonomous artistic decisions. These were calculated to communicate different messages and provoke different responses from different viewers, to create meanings or interpretations that were in dialogue with other images but not always dependent on the views articulated in texts. In this independence from text, artistic representations of a story can be seen to contribute their own sets of data in the exploration of early Christian thought: a visual apocryphal tradition.

Acknowledgements

I extend my thanks to Igor Dorfmann-Lazarev for his kindness in inviting me to participate in the conference at Bad Homburg and want to acknowledge his boundless patience as I prepared the written version of my paper. For discussion and comment I thank conference participants, especially Antonio Panaino and Cecilia Proverbio. Jaś Elsner, Maria Lidova, Eunice Dauterman Maguire, Vasileios Marinis and Andrew McGowan read earlier drafts of this written paper, engaging with its argument as well as making corrections, supplying additional references and providing invaluable comments. The text was greatly improved as a result and I express my deep gratitude to them. For help with illustrations I thank Daria Lanzuolo of the German Archæological Institute of Rome and Beat Brenk.

CHAPTER 20

Gnostic and Mithraic Themes in *Sefer Zerubbabel*

Yishai Kiel

1   Introduction

Sefer Zerubbabel[1] is a Jewish apocalypse,[2] probably completed shortly after 628,[3] against the political backdrop of the war that took place between the Sasanian and Byzantine empires and, particularly, the Sasanian conquest of Jerusalem in 614 and defeat in 628.[4] The work reflects an outburst of apoca-

---

1   For critical editions of Sefer Zerubbabel, see Y. Even-Shmuel, *Midrashei Geula: Chapters of Jewish Apocalypse Dating from the Completion of the Babylonian Talmud until the Sixth Millennium*, 3rd edn, Jerusalem, 2017, pp. 71–88 [Hebrew]; I. Lévi, 'L'Apocalypse de Zorobabel et le roi de Perse Siroès', *REJ* 68 (1914), pp. 129–160; 69 (1919), pp. 108–121; 71 (1920), pp. 57–65. For an English translation, see M. Himmelfarb, 'Sefer Zerubbabel', in D. Stern and M. Jay Mirsky (eds), *Rabbinic Fantasies: Imaginative Narratives from Classical Hebrew Literature*, Philadelphia, 1990, pp. 67–90; updated in M. Himmelfarb, *Jewish Messiahs in a Christian Empire: A History of the Book of Zerubbabel*, Cambridge, 2017, pp. 147–157; J.C. Reeves, *Trajectories in Near Eastern Apocalyptic: A Postrabbinic Jewish Apocalypse Reader*, Atlanta, 2005, pp. 51–66. For an overview, see J. Dan, *History of Jewish Mysticism and Esotericism: Ancient Times*, Jerusalem, 2008 vol. 3, pp. 998–1027 [Hebrew].

2   For a theoretical definition of apocalypse, see J.J. Collins, 'What is Apocalyptic Literature?', in id. (ed.), *The Oxford Handbook of Apocalyptic Literature*, Oxford, 2014, pp. 1–16.

3   According to Lévi, 'L'Apocalypse de Zorobabel' (1919), pp. 108–121, the work was composed between 629–636, following the short reign and death of the Sasanian king Kavadh II (MP Kawād; NP: قباد), also known as Shiroe (NP شیرویه), in 628. Even-Shmuel, 'Introduction to Sefer Zerubbabel', in *Midrashei Geula*, pp. 61–63, dates the work to 638. See also Himmelfarb, 'Sefer Zerubbabel', pp. 67–68; Himmelfarb, *Jewish Messiahs*, pp. 31–34. Hillel Newman has recently argued for a sixth-century date of redaction (excepting perhaps the mention of the Sasanian king Shiroe). See H. Neuman, 'Dating Sefer Zerubavel: Dehistoricizing and Rehistoricizing a Jewish Apocalypse of Late Antiquity', *Adamantius* 19 (2013), pp. 324–336; H. Newman, 'Yehuda Even-Shmuel's Midrashei Geula: A Methodological-Historical Critique', in *Midrashei Geula*, pp. lxiii–lxxiv. Israel Knohl has argued in the past that, while Sefer Zerubbabel was likely reworked in the seventh century to fit contemporary events (e.g., the mention of the Sasanian king Shiroe), it was modeled on a first-century apocalypse polemicizing against imperial propaganda that viewed Augustus as the long-awaited Son of God destined to rule over the world. Sefer Zerubbabel, according to this thesis, inverts the imperial agenda by identifying Augustus with 'Armilos, the Antichrist. See I. Knohl, *Be-ʿikvot ha-mashiah*, Jerusalem–Tel Aviv, 2000, pp. 68–80 [Hebrew]. For Knohl's more recent suggestions, see below.

4   For the political background, see Y. Stoyanov, *Defenders and Enemies of the True Cross: The*

© YISHAI KIEL, 2021 | DOI:10.1163/9789004445925_022

lyptic, eschatological and soteriological speculation among late ancient Jews, and represents a revival of the apocalyptic genre known from the Second Temple period (the latest systematic articulations of which are 4 Ezra, 2 Baruch, and the Book of Revelation). Between the late-first and early-seventh centuries, we witness only sporadic, and more limited, Jewish engagement with eschatological, soteriological and messianic speculation, as can be gleaned from traditions preserved in rabbinic literature, *Hekhalot* literature, targumim and piyyutim.[5]

While Sefer Zerubbabel exhibits a degree of thematic continuity with earlier Jewish tradition[6]—e.g., the death and resurrection of the Messiah son of Joseph/Ephraim[7] or the suffering Messiah son of David[8]—it reflects at the

---

Sasanian Conquest of Jerusalem in 614 and Byzantine Ideology of Anti-Persian Warfare, Vienna, 2011; A. Cameron (ed.), *Late Antiquity on the Eve of Islam*, Ashgate, 2013, pp. xiii–xxxvii; G. Avni, 'The Persian Conquest of Jerusalem (614 CE)—An Archæological Assessment', *Bulletin of the American Schools of Oriental Research* 357 (2010), pp. 35–48; G.W. Bowersock, *Empires in Collision in Late Antiquity*, Waltham, 2012, pp. 35–48; P. Wood, *The Chronicle of Seert: Christian Historical Imagination in Late Antique Iraq*, New York, 2013, pp. 211–220. For the extent of Jewish involvement in the Sasanian conquest of Jerusalem, see O. Irshai, "'If you see that kingdoms are provoking each other, you can expect the advent of the Messiah': Chronography and Apocalyptic in Late Antiquity—A Historical Introduction to Midreshei Ge'ulah', in *Midreshei Geula*, pp. xxxvii–xxxix, n. 58.

5 For attempts to explain this gap, see P. Alexander, 'The Rabbis and Messianism', in M. Bockmuehl and J. Carleton Paget (eds), *Redemption and Resistance: The Messianic Hopes of Jews and Christians in Antiquity*, London, 2007, pp. 227–244; M. Mach, 'From Apocalypticism to Early Jewish Mysticism?', in J.J. Collins (ed.), *The Encyclopedia of Apocalypticism* vol. 1: *The Origins of Apocalypticism in Judaism and Christianity*, New York, 2000, pp. 229–264; T. Novick, 'Between First-Century Apocalyptic and Seventh-Century Liturgy: On 4 Ezra, 2 Baruch, and Qilir', *Journal for the Study of Judaism* 44 (2013), pp. 356–378; M. Kister et al. (eds), *Tradition, Transmission, and Transformation from Second Temple Literature through Judaism and Christianity in Late Antiquity*, Leiden, 2015, pp. i–xvi, here at vii–xii.

6 See esp. M. Himmelfarb, 'Revelation and Rabbinization in *Sefer Zerubbabel* and *Sefer Eliyyahu*', in P. Townsend and M. Vidas (eds), *Revelation, Literature and Community in Late Antiquity*, Tübingen, 2011, pp. 217–236; Alexander, 'Rabbis and Messianism', pp. 228–234.

7 J. Heinemann, 'The Messiah of Ephraim and the Premature Exodus of the Tribe of Ephraim', *Harvard Theological Review* 68 (1975), pp. 1–15; D. Berger, 'Three Typological Themes in Early Jewish Messianism: Messiah son of Joseph, Rabbinic Calculations, and the Figure of Armilus', *AJS Review* 10 (1985), pp. 143–148; H. Zellentin, 'Rabbinizing Jesus, Christianizing the Son of David: The Bavli's Approach to the Secondary Messiah Traditions', in R. Ulmer (ed.), *Discussing Cultural Influences: Text, Context and Non-Text in Rabbinic Judaism*, Lanham, 2007, pp. 99–127 at 105–107; I.J. Yuval, *Two Nations in Your Womb: Perceptions of Jews and Christians in Late Antiquity and the Middle Ages*, trans. B. Harshav and J. Chipman, Berkeley, 2008, pp. 35–38; D. Boyarin, *The Jewish Gospels: The Story of the Jewish Christ*, New York, 2012, pp. 188–189 n. 19; D.C. Mitchell, *Messiah ben Joseph*, Newton Mearns, 2016; Himmelfarb, *Jewish Messiahs*, pp. 99–119.

8 See e.g. I. Knohl, *The Messiah Before Jesus: The Suffering Servant of the Dead Sea Scrolls*, Berke-

GNOSTIC AND MITHRAIC THEMES IN SEFER ZERUBBABEL   413

same time novel and unprecedented ideas in the history of Jewish thought, which can be significantly illuminated by recourse to non-Jewish sources. Beyond the need to situate Jewish apocalyptic writing in the broader context of the apocalyptic genre exhibited by Christian and Zoroastrian authors,[9] Sefer Zerubbabel can be further informed by a contextual analysis of its innovative themes and motifs in the broader context of late antique culture.

Scholars have long noted Sefer Zerubbabel's engagement with, and possible response to, Christian themes—whether by way of appropriation, subversion, or polemic. Most notably, Sefer Zerubbabel's account of the suffering Messiah son of David, Menaḥem ben 'Ami'el, and the death and resurrection of the Messiah son of Joseph/Ephraim, Neḥemia b. Ḥushiel, were juxtaposed with the suffering, death and resurrection of Jesus;[10] the figure of Ḥephṣibah, the mother of Menaḥem ben 'Ami'el, was juxtaposed with that of the Virgin Mary;[11] and the figure of 'Armilos was juxtaposed with that of the Christian Antichrist.[12]

Not only the figure of Ḥephṣibah, the mother of the Davidic Messiah, was illuminated by recourse to the Virgin Mary, but also the mother of 'Armilos— a marble statue in the likeness of a beautiful virgin, who is depicted in Sefer Zerubbabel as the consort of Beli'al-Satan—was understood as a Jewish re-

---

     ley, 2000; Boyarin, *The Jewish Gospels*, pp. 129–156; P. Schäfer, *The Jewish Jesus: How Judaism and Christianity Shaped Each Other*, Princeton, 2012, pp. 236–272; Himmelfarb, *Jewish Messiahs*, pp. 60–98.

9   See Irshai, 'Chronography and Apocalyptic in Late Antiquity'; O. Irshai, 'Dating the Eschaton: Jewish and Christian Apocalyptic Calculations in Late Antiquity', in A. Baumgarten (ed.), *Apocalyptic Time*, Leiden, 2000, pp. 113–153.

10   See notes 7 and 8.

11   See e.g. P. Speck, 'The Apocalypse of Zerubbabel and Christian Icons', *Jewish Studies Quarterly* 4 (1997), pp. 183–190; D. Biale, 'Counter-History and Jewish Polemics Against Christianity: The *Sefer toldot yeshu* and the *Sefer zerubavel*', *Jewish Social Studies* 6 (1999), pp. 130–145; G. Hasan Rokem, *Web of Life: Folklore and Midrash in Rabbinic Literature*, Stanford, 2000, pp. 163–172; P. Schäfer, *Mirror of His Beauty: Feminine Images of God from the Bible to the Early Kabbalah*, Princeton, 2002, pp. 212–216; M. Himmelfarb, 'The Mother of the Messiah in the Talmud Yerushalmi and Sefer Zerubbabel', in P. Schäfer (ed.), *The Talmud Yerushalmi and Græco-Roman Culture*, TSAJ 93, Tübingen, 2002 vol. 3, pp. 369–389; Himmelfarb, *Jewish Messiahs*, pp. 35–59; A.M. Sivertsev, *Judaism and Imperial Ideology in Late Antiquity*, Cambridge, 2011, pp. 88–90, 101–104; H. Spurling, 'Discourse of Doubt: The Testing of Apocalyptic Figures in Jewish and Christian traditions of Late Antiquity', *Jewish Culture and History* 16, 3 (2015), pp. 109–126.

12   See e.g. L. Greisiger, 'Armilos—Vorläufer, Entstehung und Fortleben der Antichrist Gestalt im Judentum', in M. Delgado and V. Leppin (eds), *Der Antichrist: Historische und systematische Zugänge*, Stuttgart, 2011; J. Dan, 'Armilus: The Jewish Antichrist and the Origins and Dating of Sefer Zerubbavel', in P. Schäfer and M. Cohen (eds), *Toward the Millennium: Messianic Expectations from the Bible to Waco*, Leiden, 1998, pp. 73–104.

sponse to the Virgin.[13] Indeed, the interpretive possibility that both Ḥephṣibah and the mother of ʾArmilos can be construed as responding to the figure of the Virgin at one and the same time, the one by way of appropriation and emulation and the other by way of mockery, parody and ridicule, reflects the complex and multifaceted nature of Sefer Zerubbabel's engagement with Christian thought.

Without denying the significance of Christianity for understanding the symbolism of Sefer Zerubbabel, in the present article I offer two additional (yet complementary) lenses—the one centered on gnostic thought,[14] especially its Sethian and Manichæan manifestations, and the other on Mithraism[15]—which will further aid us in deciphering Sefer Zerubbabel's symbolism. A gnostic reading of Sefer Zerubbabel would seem in order in light of its emphatic dualistic worldview and, not least, the conflict it depicts between two mother figures—the one diabolic and the other redemptive—both of which are part of a Trinity of Father, Mother, and Son.[16] I posit, moreover, that the genealogy of ʾArmilos, who is said to have emerged from a sexual union (or, rather, seminal emission) between Beliʿal-Satan and a marble statue in the shape of a beautiful virgin, is particularly informed by Sethian and Manichæan reports concerning the 'seduction of the archons,' a sexual orgy of sorts involving the archons/Satan, Matter, and a 'shadow' of a beautiful virgin—a union which can also be seen

---

13 See below in detail.

14 For the problematization of the category 'Gnosticism', see M.A. Williams, *Rethinking 'Gnosticism': An Argument for Dismantling a Dubious Category*, Princeton, 1996; K. King, *What is Gnosticism?*, Cambridge, 2003. In the present context, I refer specifically to Sethian and Manichæan thought. For an overview of Sethian thought, see D. Brakke, *The Gnostics: Myth, Ritual and Diversity in Early Christianity*, Cambridge, 2010. For an overview of Manichæan thought, see I. Gardner and S.N.C. Lieu (eds), *Manichæan Texts from the Roman Empire*, Cambridge, 2004.

15 For an overview, see M. Clauss, *The Roman Cult of Mithras: The God and His Mysteries*, trans. R. Gordon, New York, 2001.

16 Unlike ʾArmilos, who is unambiguously presented as the son of Satan-Beliʿal, Menaḥem is not explicitly acknowledged as son of God. Sefer Zerubbabel refers, on the one hand, to Menaḥem son of ʿAmiʾel and, on the other hand, says that Ḥephṣibah was the wife of Nathan, either Nathan the Prophet or Nathan son of David (see the discussion in Himmelfarb, *Jewish Messiahs*, pp. 50–52). That said, the diametrical opposition between Menaḥem and ʾArmilos and the long-established tradition identifying God's chosen/anointed as his son suggests that Menaḥem is, at least metaphorically, the son of God. It is also possible that the author of Sefer Zerubbabel purposely sought to avoid an explicit assertion to the effect that Menaḥem is the son of God, considering the Christian implications of such a statement.

as an act of seminal emission—which produced diabolic offspring.[17] While the idea that, just like Christ, the Antichrist too was born of a virgin mother, was not unknown to contemporaneous Byzantine Christian authors,[18] I argue that the rather bizarre notion that Beliʿal-Satan impregnated a marble statue in the shape of a beautiful virgin, who in turn gave birth to ʾArmilos, is particularly informed by the nuances of the gnostic myth.

In addition to Sethian and Manichæan mythology, I posit that Sefer Zerubbabel can be illuminated by recourse to visual and literary depictions of Mithras's emergence from a rock (and sexual union with a rock). The presence of Mithraic imagery in Sefer Zerubbabel's depiction of the birth of ʾArmilos is not implausible, considering the ubiquity of the visual remains of the ancient cult of Mithras,[19] and the fact that Mithras was often depicted by patristic authors as a diabolic 'reproduction' of Christ (as part of a broader attempt to subvert the similarities between Christ and Mithras)[20] and, therefore, constituted a 'perfect fit,' as it were, for reconstructing an antichrist figure.

Situating Sefer Zerubbabel at the crossroads of late antique 'religions' and the intersection of the Byzantine and Sasanian cultures, I posit that an integrative and panoramic approach—taking into account earlier Jewish traditions, Christian reports, gnostic mythology, and Mithraic symbolism—can shed light on the unprecedented and rather cryptic account of ʾArmilos's rock-birth, resulting from a sexual union between Beliʿal-Satan and a marble statue in the likeness of a beautiful virgin.

That a Jewish apocalypse composed (or at least redacted) in the seventh-century might be informed by Sethian, Manichæan, and Mithraic thought insofar as its construction of the evil sphere is concerned, is not unlikely, given the

---

17   See, in general, G.G. Stroumsa, *Another Seed: Studies in Gnostic Mythology*, Leiden, 1984, pp. 38–45; Y. Kiel, 'Creation by Emission: Recreating Adam and Eve in the Babylonian Talmud in Light of Zoroastrian and Manichean Literature', *Journal of Jewish Studies* 66, 2 (2015), pp. 295–316.

18   See e.g. Pseudo-Hippolytus, *On the Consummation of the World* 22 ('Since the Savior of the world, with the purpose of saving the race of men, was born of the immaculate and virgin Mary, and in the form of the flesh trod the enemy trader foot, in the exercise of the power of His own proper divinity; in the same manner also will the accuser come forth from an impure woman upon the earth, but shall be born of a virgin spuriously'). I would like to thank Emmanouela Grypeou for this reference and for calling my attention to similar ideas present in the Ephraem Græcus tradition.

19   For the decline of the cult of Mithras in the fourth century, see D. Walsh, *The Cult of Mithras in Late Antiquity: Development, Decline and Demise ca. A.D. 270–430*, Leiden, 2018, pp. 42–66.

20   See below in detail.

rabbinic (implicit) engagement with Sethian,[21] Manichæan[22] and Mithraic[23] themes, preserved in the talmudic corpus.[24] Patristic constructions of 'Gnosticism' and 'Mithraism' as emblematic of Satan's inversion of the 'true religion,' moreover, might have contributed to Sefer Zerubbabel's reconstruction of the evil sphere on the basis of Sethian, Manichæan and Mithraic ideas. Whether or not the authors of Sefer Zerubbabel had unmediated access to such sources (literary or visual), the latter certainly underlie other late ancient discussions of the evil sphere and, therefore, might have had at least an indirect impact on the imagery chosen in Sefer Zerubbabel.

While Sefer Zerubbabel is situated in the political and cultural context of seventh-century Palestine, it exhibits at the same time connections with Babylonian rabbinic culture[25] and, accordingly, should be appreciated not only against the backdrop of Byzantine culture but also against that of Sasanian

---

21   For the gnostic dimensions in the rabbinic refutation of the doctrine of 'Two Powers in Heaven', see e.g. A.F. Segal, *Two Powers in Heaven: Early Rabbinic Reports about Christianity and Gnosticism*, Leiden, 1977, who addresses both the heresy of 'complementary powers in heaven,' which naturally lends itself to a Christian interpretation, as well as that of 'opposing powers in heaven,' which echoes a gnostic worldview. Cf. Schäfer, *The Jewish Jesus*, p. 276 n. 21 (and, in general, pp. 103–149); Dan, *History of Jewish Mysticism* vol. 2, p. 642 (and, in general pp. 641–677); D. Boyarin, 'Beyond Judaisms: Metatron and the Divine Polymorphy of Ancient Judaism', *Journal for the Study of Judaism* 41 (2010), pp. 323–365; M. Kister, 'Metatron, God, and the 'Two Powers': The Dynamics of Tradition, Exegesis, and Polemic', *Tarbiz* 82 (2014), pp. 43–88. For the gnostic context of the Adam and Eve legends contained in rabbinic literature, see e.g. A. Altmann, 'The Gnostic Background of the Rabbinic Adam Legends', *Jewish Quarterly Review* 35:4 (1945), pp. 371–391. Cf. Schäfer, *The Jewish Jesus*, pp. 197–213. For the 'gnostic' dimensions of rabbinic depictions of the *shekhinah*, see Schäfer, *Mirror of His Beauty*, pp. 79–102.

22   For Manichæan thought and the Babylonian Talmud, see e.g. Y. Kiel, 'Reimagining Enoch in Sasanian Babylonia in Light of Zoroastrian and Manichæan Traditions', *AJS Review* 39: 2 (2015), pp. 407–432 (cf. A. Schremer, 'Parvanka: The Mandæan Context of an Anti-Heretical Polemic in the Babylonian Talmud', *Tarbiz* 85:2 [2018], pp. 205–232); Kiel, 'Creation by Emission'; Y. Kiel, 'Study Versus Sustenance: A Rabbinic Dilemma in Its Zoroastrian and Manichæan Context', *AJS Review* 38: 2 (2014), pp. 275–302; G. Herman, 'The Talmud in its Babylonian Context: Rava and Bar-Sheshakh: Mani and Mihrshah', in G. Herman, M. Ben Shahar and A. Oppenheimer (eds), *Between Babylonia and the Land of Israel: Studies in Honor of Isaiah M. Gafni*, Jerusalem, 2016, pp. 79–96 [Hebrew].

23   See recently Y. Kiel, 'First Man, First Bovine: Talmudic Mythology in Context', in J. Rubenstein and G. Herman (eds), *The Aggada of the Babylonian Talmud and its Cultural World*, Providence, 2018, pp. 313–334.

24   Certain aspects of Manichæism were explicitly addressed (albeit inaccurately at times) by Jewish authors in the post-talmudic era. See J. Reeves, *Prolegomena to a History of Islamicate Manichæism*, Sheffield–Oakville, 2011.

25   A case in point is the particular affinity of Zerubbabel's encounter with the suffering Messiah in Rome reported in Sefer Zerubbabel and R. Yehoshua b. Levi's encounter with the

culture.[26] Considering, moreover, the Sasanian presence in Jerusalem between 614–628 and the possible Jewish involvement in this political adventure,[27] it is not implausible that Sasanian culture had a more direct impact on Sefer Zerubbabel. In this context, I will explore the possibility that Iranian Manichæan traditions as well as Iranian traditions pertaining to the deity Mitra/Mithra, the counterpart of Roman Mithras, can shed further light on the symbolism of Sefer Zerubbabel.

2   Messianic and Diabolic Mothers

Sefer Zerubbabel's focus on the Messiah's mother might seem anomalous in the context of late ancient Jewish tradition, although a mother of the Messiah is mentioned in a talmudic story recorded in the Palestinian Talmud (*y. Ber.* 2:4 5a) and Lamentations Rabbah (1:51).[28] Martha Himmelfarb observes that 'there is little in rabbinic literature to prepare a reader for Hephzibah, Sefer Zerubbabel's warrior mother of the Davidic Messiah. The depiction of a woman, especially a mother, as a warrior certainly demands explanation, but even without regard to her activity, attention to the mother of the Messiah is most unusual in a Jewish text ... none of the Messiahs of surviving second temple literature is equipped with a mother.'[29]

While several scholars have convincingly argued that Ḥephṣibah's figure was somehow related to that of the Virgin Mary as a messianic mother,[30] Alexei Sivertsev has demonstrated that Ḥephṣibah's specific role as warrior and protector of Jerusalem is informed by the military exploits of the Virgin Mary and her depiction as protector and patron of Constantinople in the surrounding Byzantine Christian culture.[31] In fact, the very choice of the name Ḥephṣibah

---

suffering Messiah in Rome reported in *b. Sanh.* 98a. For the relationship between the two stories, see below.

26   For the Sasanian context—especially in terms of Zoroastrianism, Iranian Manichæism, and East Syrian Christianity—of Babylonian rabbinic culture, see recently Y. Kiel, *Sexuality in the Babylonian Talmud: Christian and Sasanian Contexts in Late Antiquity*, Cambridge, 2016.

27   See n. 4.

28   On this story, see Hasan Rokem, *Web of Life*, pp. 163–172; Schäfer, *The Jewish Jesus*, pp. 214–235; Himmelfarb, 'Mother of the Messiah,' vol. 3, pp. 369–389; Himmelfarb, *Jewish Messiahs*, pp. 39–43.

29   Himmelfarb, *Jewish Messiahs*, p. 35.

30   See n. 11.

31   Sivertsev, *Judaism and Imperial Ideology*, pp. 88–90, 101–104. In fact, the Virgin seems to have replaced *tykhe* as the patron and protector of Constantinople (Sivertsev, ibid., pp. 90–

418   KIEL

for the Messiah's mother discloses her connection to Jerusalem, as Ḥephṣibah
is recorded in the Bible not only as the wife of Hezekiah (2 Kings 21:1), but also
as an epithet of Jerusalem (Isa. 62:4).[32] Sefer Zerubbabel's association of Ḥephṣibah with the rod of Aaron, moreover—a theme further emphasized in a later
piyyut—is likewise informed by recourse to Byzantine homilies and hymns
identifying the Virgin Mary as the blossoming rod of Aaron.[33]

   The Christian underpinnings of Ḥephṣibah's figure are complicated, however, by Sefer Zerubbabel's depiction of her evil counterpart, the mother of
'Armilos and consort of Beli'al-Satan:

> He clung onto me and they brought me (= Zerubbabel, the recipient of
> the prophecy) to the house of disgrace and scorn. He showed me a mar-
> ble stone in the shape of a virgin, and its appearance and form were most
> lovely and beautiful to behold. And he answered and said to me: This
> stone is the man [wife] of Beli'al. Satan will come and lie with her and
> a son will issue from her, his name is 'Armilos, and he will destroy the
> people,[34] according to the Hebrew language.[35]

---

95). For the contrasting images of Jerusalem and Rome/Constantinople, see R. Boustan, 'The Spoils of the Jerusalem Temple at Rome and Constantinople: Jewish Counter-
Geography in a Christianizing Empire', in G. Gardner and K. Osterloh (eds), *Antiquity in
Antiquity: Jewish and Christian Pasts in the Greco-Roman World*, Tübingen, 2008, pp. 327–
372; Irshai, 'Chronography and Apocalypse in Late Antiquity', pp. xxxiii–xxxvii.

32   לֹא־יֵאָמֵר לָךְ עוֹד עֲזוּבָה, וּלְאַרְצֵךְ לֹא־יֵאָמֵר עוֹד שְׁמָמָה—כִּי לָךְ יִקָּרֵא חֶפְצִי־בָהּ, וּלְאַרְצֵךְ בְּעוּלָה
      כִּי־חָפֵץ יְהוָה בָּךְ, וְאַרְצֵךְ תִּבָּעֵל.
      'You shall no more be termed forsaken, and your land shall no more be termed desolate;
      but you shall be called my-delight-is-in-her, and your land married; for the Lord delights
      in you, and your land shall be married' (NRSV).

33   Sivertsev, *Judaism and Imperial Ideology*, pp. 114–122.

34   Several etymologies have been proposed for the name 'Armilos. Some scholars have sug-
      gested that the name derives from Greek Erēmolaos ('destroyer of a people'), an inter-
      pretation based on the spelling ארמילאוס (rather than ארמילוס) that appears in some
      versions. This suggestion is consistent with the folk etymology of the name Balaam (בלעם)
      as 'destroyer (בלע) of a people (עם)' alluded to in the quoted passage and in *b. Sanh.*
      105a, a fact which might suggest that 'Armilos was further identified with the biblical
      Balaam. See Lévi, 'L'Apocalypse de Zorobabel' (1914), p. 152, n. 6; Reeves, *Trajectories in
      Near Eastern Apocalyptic*, pp. 19–20; Berger, 'Three Typological Themes', pp. 158–162. The
      most likely etymological construction is that 'Armilos stems from Romulus, the mythical
      founder of Rome, as this is the Syriac form of the name. See W. Bousset, *The Antichrist Leg-
      end: A Chapter in Christian and Jewish Folklore*, London, 1896, p. 53; T. Nöldeke, 'Momsen's
      Darstellung der römischen Herrschaft und römischen Politik in Orient', *ZDMG* 39 (1895),
      p. 343; Greisiger, 'Armilos', pp. 218–221. Since Romulus, the mythical founder of Rome, is
      not mentioned in any other Jewish text from antiquity, Joseph Dan has suggested, based
      on the same etymology that 'Armilos should be identified with Romulus Augustus, the

GNOSTIC AND MITHRAIC THEMES IN SEFER ZERUBBABEL 419

Martha Himmelfarb suggested at one point that the marble statue in the shape of a beautiful virgin located in a 'house of disgrace and scorn' should be understood as a Jewish response to visual depictions of the Virgin Mary in Byzantine's 'sculptural environment.'[36] More recently, she argued that the conception of 'Armilos through a sexual union between Satan and a marble statue represents a Jewish parody of the Christian nativity story, according to which 'the mother of the antichrist is a statue of the Virgin, but its child is conceived through sexual relations, and the father of the child is not God but Satan. Perhaps no further explanation for Sefer Zerubbabel's story is necessary.'[37]

While the latter suggestion is compelling, it must be further nuanced in my opinion in light of the fact that the author of Sefer Zerubbabel fostered not one, but two messianic mothers, possibly in response to the Virgin, the one appropriating and imitating her figure and the other parodying, ridiculing and mocking it. As per the first suggestion, the depiction of the Virgin as a marble statue does not fit neatly within the 'sculptural environment' of seventh-century Byzantium. Paul Speck has argued in this context that, in this period, the Virgin and other Christian figures were visually depicted mainly on mosaics

---

last emperor of the Western Roman Empire, who was deposed by Odoacer in 476, or that 'Armilos might represent the cult of Romulus the Roman deity, which was widespread throughout the empire in the third and fourth centuries. See Dan, *History of Jewish Mysticism*, pp. 1002–1005; Himmelfarb, 'Sefer Zerubbabel', p. 69 (following the lead of Lévi and Even Shmuel), identifies Romulus as the Emperor Heraclius, but cf. Speck, 'Christian Icons', p. 189. Israel Knohl has suggested that 'Armilos should be identified with Augustus, based on a close affinity of the latter to the mythical founder of Rome. See Knohl, *Be-ʿikvot ha-mashiah*, pp. 70–73. For Knohl's dating of the work, see n. 3. Another etymology, which was by and large abandoned in scholarship, connects 'Armilos with Ahriman (Av. Aŋra Mainyu), the Evil Spirit and representation of Satan in Zoroastrianism and Iranian Manichæism. See W. Bacher, 'Targum zu den Propheten', *ZDMG* 27 (1873), p. 31 (suggesting that the attested forms ארמלגוס and ארמלגון stem from Armainyus [Areimanios], the Greek form of the name Ahriman). Etymology aside, it is not impossible that 'Armilos (or his father Satan-Beliʿal) were perceived as connected thematically to Ahriman.

35 וידבק בי ויביאוני אל בית התורף הלצות. ויראיני שם אבן אחת שייש בדמות אשה בתולה ומראיה
ותוארה נאה ויפה עד מאד לראות. ויען ויאמר אלי. אבן זאת איש [אשת] בליעל הוא [היא]. ויבא
שטן וישכב עמה ויצא ממנה בן ושמו ארמילוס ויחריב עם ובלשון עברית.

All quotations from Sefer Zerubbabel are from the *Sefer Hazikhronot* manuscript, Oxford MS Heb. d. 11, 248ʳ–251ʳ. The translations are based on Himmelfarb, *Jewish Messiahs*, pp. 147–157, with some modifications. For the present passage, see Himmelfarb, ibid., p. 152.

36 Himmelfarb, 'Sefer Zerubbabel and Popular Religion', in E. Mason (ed.), *A Teacher for All Generations: Essays in Honor of James C. VanderKam*, Leiden, 2012, pp. 621–634 at 630.

37 Himmelfarb, *Jewish Messiahs*, p. 57.

420   KIEL

and reliefs, but not in sculptures and statues, at least not to an extent that would warrant an anti-Christian parody centered on this form of representation.[38]

Without denying the significance of Byzantine Christian depictions of the Virgin—as a messianic mother, a warrior-mother, and city protector—for explaining the emergence of her Jewish counterpart, Ḥephṣibah, I posit that Sefer Zerubbabel's portrayal of another 'virgin,' namely the rock-mother of 'Armilos, is a reflection of broader cultural currents in late antiquity connected in particular with gnostic and Mithraic thought. I shall first discuss the gnostic evidence stemming from Sethian and Manichæan sources, and then I will turn to the Mithraic evidence.

The Sethian and Manichæan articulations of the gnostic myth constitute a rather plausible context for Sefer Zerubbabel's dualistic construction of two opposing mother figures, the one redemptive and the other diabolic. In terms of redemptive mothers, the Manichæan tradition assigns a central role in both the cosmogonic and eschatological narratives[39] to a set of female figures, beginning with the Mother of Life (Syriac *emmā dhayyē*; Latin *mater vitæ*; Middle Persian *mādar ī zīndagān*; Arabic *omm al-eḥyā'*) of the first evocation, who parallels Forethought/Barbēlō in Sethian (and Valentinian) mythology.[40] Both

---

38   Speck, 'Christian Icons', See also Himmelfarb's acknowledgement of this point in her *Jewish Messiahs*, p. 56. Another possibility raised by Sivertsev (*Judaism and Imperial Ideology*, pp. 162–170) is that the anomalous statue is connected with contemporary Christian-Byzantine anxieties regarding pagan statues from the past. To this claim Himmelfarb (*Jewish Messiahs*, p. 57) responds: 'The depiction of the statue in Sefer Zerubbabel, then, is not a subtle manipulation of Byzantine anxieties about once-pagan statues but an assertion of the continuity of Christianity and idolatry, whether in ignorance of Byzantine church decoration or in defiance of it'. In light of the Mithraic evidence I will adduce below, I would argue that the relevance of 'pagan statues from the past' should not be so casually dismissed.

39   For overviews of Manichæan cosmogony, see e.g. J.C. Reeves, *Heralds of the Good Realm: Syro-Mesopotamian Gnosis and Jewish Traditions*, Leiden, 1996, pp. 79–88; Reeves, *Prolegomena*, pp. 13–15 (summary) and throughout; W. Sundermann, 'Cosmogony and Cosmology, iii. In Manicheism', *Encyclopedia Iranica* vol. 6, pp. 310–315; J.P. Asmussen, *Manichæan Literature* (Persian Heritage Series 22), New York, 1975, pp. 127–134; Sroumsa, *Another Seed*, pp. 145–167. For overviews of Manichæan eschatology, see e.g. G.G. Stroumsa, 'Aspects de l'eschatologie manichéenne', *RHR* 198, 2 (1981), pp. 163–181; P.O. Skjærvø, 'Iranian Elements in Manicheism: A Comparative Contrastive Approach: Irano-Manichaica I', in R. Gyselen (ed.), *Au carrefour des religions: Hommages à Philippe Gignoux* (Res Orientales 7), Paris, 1995, pp. 263–284 at 275–281; W. Sundermann, 'Manichæan Eschatology', *Encyclopedia Iranica* vol. 8, pp. 569–575; Reeves, *Prolegomena*, pp. 215–222.

40   For Forethought/Barbēlō, see Brakke, *Gnostics*, p. 54: 'Foremost among the æons is the second principle, "the image of the perfect Invisible Virgin Spirit" (*Ap. John* II, 4:34–35), which is the most immediate emanation from the ultimate God ... called Forethought and, more obscurely, Barbēlō.' For the etymology of Barbēlō (possibly from Egyptian 'the great

GNOSTIC AND MITHRAIC THEMES IN SEFER ZERUBBABEL 421

Forethought/Barbēlō and the Mother of Life are portrayed as the mother in a gnostic-type Trinity consisting of a Father, Mother and Son.[41] According to Werner Sundermann, 'it is not self-evident why a misogynistic religion such as Manicheism admits the existence and redeeming contribution of a number of female deities. Indeed, it is remarkable that in the First and Third Evocations of the Manichean pantheon, the second part in the triple sequence of gods is left to goddesses (Mother of Life [I], Twelve Virgins [III], Virgin of Light [III]).'[42]

As for the diabolic mother, the Sethian and Manichæan sources similarly depict the embodiment and personification of Matter as a hyper-sexual and material feminine principle of evil, who functions as a 'mother of demons.' The role of Matter (Greek Hylē) in Sethian sources as a diabolic 'mother,' who sexually mingles with the demons, is reflected in the following passage from the Secret Book of John:

> The source of the demons that are in the entire body is divided into four: heat, cold, wetness, dryness, and the mother of them all is Matter ... The mother of all these, Onorthochras, stands in the midst of them, for she is

---

emission'), see B. Layton, *The Gnostic Scriptures: A New Translation with Annotations and Introductions*, Garden City, 1987, p. 15.

41   In Manichæism, the Father of Greatness evoked from himself the Mother of Life, who in turn evoked the First Man (Syr. *nāšā qadmāyā*; Lat. *primus homo*; Mid. Pers. *Ohrmizdbay*; Parth. *ʾrdʾwʾn mʾd*; Sogd. *ʾrδʾwʾn mʾt*; Ar. *al-ensān al-qadīm*). On the Mother of Life, see A. van Tongerloo, 'Manichæan Female Deities', in L. Cirillo and A. van Tongerloo (eds), *Atti del Terzo Congresso Internazionale di Studi 'Manicheismo e Oriente Cristiano Antico': Arcavacata di Rende—Amantea 31 agosto–5 settembre 1993*, Turnhout, 1997, pp. 361–364. The Mother of Life, the female principle of the first evocation, is 'succeeded' by the Virgin of Light, the main female figure of the third evocation, much like Forethought/Barbēlō is 'succeeded' by Sophia. The Virgin of Light (Mid. Pers. *knygrwšn*, Parth. *knygrwšn, sdwys*, Sogd. *qnygrwšn, rwxšnʾ βypwryc*) is also the female aspect of the Third Messenger, who plays a crucial role in the redemption of the imprisoned light (see below). Instead of the Virgin of Light, Theodore bar Kōnai mentions the Twelve Virgins (Syr. *trtʿsr̄ btwlt*) whose function is similar to that of the Virgin of Light. Not unlike the Byzantine Christian Virgin and the depiction of Ḥephṣibah in Sefer Zerubbabel, these female figures are portrayed as mother-warriors who seek to redeem their imprisoned son from the forces of evil. The Mother of Life descends along with the Living Spirit to assist her suffering and imprisoned son, the First Man, while the Virgin of Light participates in the redemption of the Suffering Jesus (*Jesus patibilis*) or Living Soul, the light imprisoned in Matter until the final redemption.

42   Sundermann, 'Cosmogony and Cosmology', p. 312. For the Sethian Trinity, see e.g. Brakke, *Gnostics*, p. 55 ('Although it can take different forms, a family of father, mother, and son lies at the center of the gnostic conception of the divine'). See also Williams, *Rethinking Gnosticism*, p. 155.

unlimited and mingles with them all. She is Matter and by her they are nourished.[43]

In the Manichæan tradition, Matter is believed to imprison and entrap the diversified particles of the Living Soul/Suffering Jesus.[44] As a counterpart of Hylē (Greek) and Concupiscentia (Latin) in Western Manichæan thought, Matter is identified in the Iranian Manichæan tradition with the demon Āz,[45] a feminine adaptation of a Zoroastrian male demon known from Avestan and Pahlavi sources. Āz is referred to as the 'mother of all demons'[46] and is often presented as a female consort of Satan/Ahriman, the original (male) principle of evil, as can be gleaned from numerous references to the couple 'Āz and Ahriman.'[47]

43　See *The Secret Book of John* 18.1–19.10, in M. Meyer (ed.), *The Nag Hammadi Scriptures: The International Edition*, New York, 2007, p. 123.

44　The Living Soul (Latin *viva anima*; Middle Persian *gryw zyndg*; Coptic *t.psychē etanh*) is also known through a variety of guises, including the Cross of Light, the Five Elements, the World Soul, the Youth, and the Suffering Jesus. The Manichæan doctrine pertaining to the redemption of the Living Soul imprisoned in Matter can be described as the scarlet thread running through Manichæan thought, comprising the very foundation of the cosmogonic myth; individual and collective eschatology; soteriological speculation associated with Jesus, and the ethical system. For a systematic discussion of this doctrine, see Y. Kiel, 'Playing with Children: A Talmudic Polemic against Manichæan Sexual Ethics', in H. Fox and T. Meacham (eds), *Jewish Law Association Studies* 28: The Jewish Family (2019), pp. 112–136.

45　The name Āz (Av. Āzi masc.) is derived from the verb *āz-* ('to strive for, long after'). See C. Bartholomæ, *Altiranisches Wörterbuch*, Berlin, 1904; rpt., 1961, cols. 342–343. The name has been translated variously as avidity, lust, desire, hunger, craving, covetousness, acquisitiveness, and concupiscence. See H.P. Schmidt, 'Von awestischen Dämon Āzi zur manichäischen Āz, der Mutter aller Dämonen', in R.E. Emmerick, W. Sundermann and P. Zieme (eds), *Studia Manichaica IV: Internationaler Kongress zum Manichäismus, Berlin 14–18 Juli 1997*, Berlin, 2000, pp. 517–527; W. Sundermann, 'The Zoroastrian and the Manichæan Demon Āz', in S. Adhami (ed.), *Paitimāna: Essays in Iranian, Indo-European, and Indian Studies in Honor of Hanns-Peter Schmidt*, Costa Mesta, 2003, pp. 328–338; J.P. Asmussen, 'Āz', *Encyclopedia Iranica* vol. 3, pp. 168–169 (last updated online on August 18, 2011); Y. Kiel, 'The Wizard of Āz and the Evil Inclination: The Babylonian Rabbinic Inclination (*yeṣer*) in Its Zoroastrian and Manichean Context', in J. Aitken, H.M. Patmore and I. Rosen-Zvi (eds), *The Evil Inclination in Early Judaism and Christianity*, Cambridge, 2021, pp. 294–314.

46　See e.g. fragment S 9, in W.B. Henning, *Ein manichäischer kosmogonischer Hymnus*, Berlin, 1932, pp. 214–228; Schmidt, 'Von awestischen Dämon Āzi zur manichäischen Āz', p. 517 n. 1.

47　See e.g. M 49; M 7984.2; M 7981.1; M 7980.2, in M. Hutter (ed.), *Manis kosmogonische Šābuhragān Texte*, Studies in Oriental Religions 21, Wiesbaden, 1992. Several examples can be found in D.N. MacKenzie, 'Mani's Šābuhragān, pt. 1 (text and translation)', *BSOAS* 42, 3 (1979), pp. 500–534. R.C. Zaehner, *Zurvan: A Zoroastrian Dilemma*, Oxford, 1955, p. 167, has

GNOSTIC AND MITHRAIC THEMES IN SEFER ZERUBBABEL 423

Sefer Zerubbabel's dualistic construction of two opposing mother figures, the one redemptive and the other diabolic, both of which are part of a gnostic-type Trinity consisting of Father, Mother and Son, can thus be illuminated by recourse to Sethian and Manichæan accounts of the gnostic myth. As a marble statue, who is also the female consort of Satan-Beli'al and mother of his offspring, 'Armilos's mother seems to play a role similar to that of Matter, which is depicted in the Sethian and Manichæan sources, not simply as an embodiment of materiality, but as the feminine principle of evil, the consort of Satan/Ahriman—the male principle of evil—and the mother of his diabolic offspring.

The sexual union between Satan-Beli'al and 'Armilos's mother can be further informed by recourse to Sethian and Manichæan accounts of the mythical scene known as the 'seduction of the archons.' Sethian (and Valentinian) sources narrate the story of the rape of Eve, either by the demiurge/Yaldabaoth or the archons/Satan, which resulted in the birth of Cain and Abel (identified in some sources as Elohim and YHWH, respectively).[48] In some accounts, to be sure, the 'spiritual' Eve is said to have escaped her material body, leaving only her 'shadow' or 'reflection' to be defiled by the archons:[49]

> The authorities approached their Adam. When they saw his female partner speaking with him, they became aroused and lusted after her. They said to one another: 'Come, let us ejaculate our semen [or 'sow our seed'] in her,' and they chased her. But she laughed at them because of their foolishness and blindness. In their grasp she turned into a tree, and when she left for them a shadow of herself that looked like her, they defiled it sexually.[50]

------

suggested that the relationship between the feminine Āz and the masculine Ahriman in the Iranian Manichæan tradition parallels the relationship between the female Rūhā and the male Ur in the Mandæan scriptures. On the female gender of the Manichæan Āz, in contrast to the male gender of the Avestan Āzi, see Asmussen, 'Āz', pp. 168–169; Sundermann, 'The Zoroastrian and the Manichæan Demon Āz', p. 332.

48 See e.g. *The Secret Book of John* 23.35–25.16; Irenæus, *Against the Heresies*, 1: 30.78; Epiphanius, *Panarion* 40, 5.3. For other gnostic versions of the myth, see Stroumsa, *Another Seed*, pp. 38–42. A related tradition concerning the diabolic origins of Cain was widespread in late antiquity. See the survey of ancient sources in J.L. Kugel, *Traditions of the Bible: A Guide to the Bible As It Was at the Start of the Common Era*, Cambridge, 1998, pp. 147–148.

49 See Stroumsa, *Another Seed*, pp. 42–45; K. King, *The Secret Book of John*, Cambridge, 2006, pp. 105–106.

50 *The Nature of the Rulers* 89:17–90:12 (Meyer [ed.], *Nag Hammadi*, p. 193). See also *The Nature of the Rulers* 92:18–93:13 (a similar failed attempt by the archons and the demiurge to rape Norea). For the question of whether the tree referred to is the tree of knowledge,

They came to Adam, and when they saw Eve speaking with him, they said to each other, 'Who is this enlightened woman? She looks like what appeared to us in the light.' Come, let's seize her and ejaculate our semen into her, so that she may be unclean and unable to ascend to her light, and her children will serve us ... since Eve was a heavenly power, she laughed at what they had in mind. She blinded their eyes and secretly left something that resembled her ... They acted rashly. They came to her, seized her, and ejaculated their semen upon her.[51]

The archons, who managed to defile only Eve's 'shadow,' desired the beautiful image they saw in her, which 'looks like what appeared to us in the light.' This refers to the light that shone forth from Forethought/Barbēlō,[52] as well as the light that poured out from Sophia, which resulted in the creation of Eve.

When Sophia let a drop of light fall, it landed on the water, and at once there appeared an androgynous human being. Sophia first made the drop into the form of a female body, and then she took the body and gave it a shape like the Mother who had appeared. She finished it in twelve months. An androgynous human being was born, whom the Greeks call Hermaphrodite. The Hebrews call the child's mother Eve of life ('Eve of Zoe'),[53] which means the female instructor of life.[54]

The 'seduction of the archons' by the forces of light, evident already in the early gnostic sources,[55] becomes a focal point of reference in the Manichæan account of the myth. Already in the first evocation, the Living Spirit is said to have revealed his forms to the sons of darkness, thus foreshadowing the 'seduc-

---

see Stroumsa, *Another Seed*, p. 42 n. 27; B.A. Pearson, "She Became a Tree'—A Note to CG II, 4:89, 25–26', *Harvard Theological Review* 69 (1976), pp. 413–415; B. Layton, 'The Hypostasis of the Archons or the Reality of the Rulers', *Harvard Theological Review* 69 (1976), pp. 56–57 (31–101).

51   *On the Origin of the World* 116:8–117:15 (Meyer [ed.], *Nag Hammadi*, pp. 214–215).

52   Forethought was unable to contain her desire for the beautiful image of Adam of Light (Adamas) and thus poured out her light upon the earth. See *On the Origin of the World* 108:5–109:1 (Meyer [ed.], *Nag Hammadi*, p. 209). See also Stroumsa, *Another Seed*, pp. 63–64.

53   Cf. the Manichæan Mother of Life.

54   *On the Origin of the World* 113:22–34 (Meyer [ed.], *Nag Hammadi*, p. 212).

55   For the shift from the 'rape' of Eve by the archons to the 'seduction' of the archons, evident already in the early gnostic reports, see Stroumsa, *Another Seed*, pp. 64–65. See especially the quotations from Epiphanius, *Panarion*, 25.2.4.

GNOSTIC AND MITHRAIC THEMES IN SEFER ZERUBBABEL   425

tion of the archons' typically associated with the third evocation.[56] In the third evocation, the archons attempt to recapture the beautiful image of the Third Messenger (Syriac *talāṯ izgaddā*; Latin *tertius legatus*)[57] and that of the Virgin of Light,[58] which were revealed to the archons in order to induce them to release the light they swallowed and entrapped.[59] Beyond the creations formed by their emissions and abortions, the archons then unite again sexually with each other, lusting after the forms revealed to them, and produce diabolic offspring. In the Iranian Manichæan tradition, the sexual union between the male and female archons is orchestrated by Matter/Āz, who clothes herself in the male and female archons. This can be gleaned from the following fragment of Mani's Middle Persian Šābuhragān:

> And just as in the beginning in that dark hell, where it itself scurried about, Āz itself had taught the demons and witches, the wrathful the

---

56 Reeves, *Prolegomena*, p. 149 n. 91. See also Stroumsa, *Another Seed*, p. 155.

57 In some of the Iranian Manichæan sources, the Third Messenger is identified with the Zoroastrian deity Narsē (thus in Syriac; cf. Pahlavi Nēryōsang; Avestan Nairyō.sangha). See P. van Lindt, *The Names of Manichæan Mythological Figures: A Comparative Study on Terminology in the Coptic Sources*, Studies in Oriental Religions 26, Wiesbaden, 1992, pp. 81–89; W. Sundermann, 'Namen von Göttern, Dämonen und Menschen in iranischen Versionen des manichäischen Mythos', *AoF* 6 (1979), pp. 95–134, at 100–102; Y. Kiel, 'Dynamics of Sexual Desire: Babylonian Rabbinic Culture at the Crossroads of Christian and Zoroastrian Ethics', *Journal for the Study of Judaism* 47 (2016), pp. 364–410 at 397–399; A. de Jong, 'Jeh the Primal Whore? Observations on Zoroastrian Misogyny', in R. Kloppenborg and W.J. Hanegraaf (eds), *Female Stereotypes in Religious Traditions*, Numen Book Series 66, Leiden, 1995, pp. 15–41 at 38–40. For other cross-cultural identifications of the Third Messenger in the Iranian Manichæan tradition, see my discussion below concerning Mithra/Mitra.

58 The female aspect of the Third Messenger, who revealed her shape to the male archons, is identified in some versions as the Virgin of Light and is described as exceedingly beautiful. Ephrem, in his *Third Discourse to Hypatius*, writes, for example: 'Can it have been that Virgin of Light about whom they say that she manifested her beauty to the Archons, so that they were ravished to run after her'. See C.W. Mitchell (ed.), *S. Ephraim's Prose Refutations of Mani, Marcion and Bardaisan*, Oxford, 1912 vol. 1, p. lxii.

59 After the initial cosmic attack by the King of Darkness (Iran. Ahrimen; Ar. al-Šayṭān, Eblīs al-Qadīm) on the Realm of Light, and the distressing defeat of the five sons of the First Man, who were devoured by, mixed with and imprisoned within the realm of darkness, the forces of light initiated an elaborate plan aimed at liberating and redeeming the lost light and bringing it back to its origin. For this purpose, an androgynous figure called the Third Messenger was evoked. In order to induce the demons to release the light entrapped in them, the Third Messenger appeared in the middle of the sky, revealing his male form to the female demons and his female form to the male demons. Filled with lust the demons begin to emit the imprisoned light along with their semen/abortions.

426   KIEL

monsters and the Āsarēštārs, male and female, rutting and sexual acts,
thus, afterward too, Āz again began to teach in the same manner rutting
and sexual acts to those other monsters and Āsarēštārs that had fallen
from the sky onto the earth so that they would rut and have sex.[60]

The Āsarēštārs mentioned in this passage represent the male and female
archons in which Āz is said to have clothed herself.[61] In other sources, the
male is called Šaklūn/Šaqlūn (Syriac Ašaqlūn; Greek and Latin Saklas) and
the female Pēsūs (Parthian and Sogdian) or Namrā'ēl/Nebrō'ēl (Syriac), which
recall the names of the early gnostic archons.[62] The sexual acts taught by Mat-
ter/Āz constitute a demonic attempt to recapture the fading images of the
Third Messenger and Virgin of Light in an attempt to further entrap the divine
light.

   Viewed in this light, I would like to suggest that Sefer Zerubbabel's marble
statue in the likeness of a beautiful virgin can be illuminated by the Sethian
and Manichæan sources. Indeed, like the Sethian and Manichæan portrayals
of personified Matter, 'Armilos's mother is depicted as the ultimate feminine
principle of evil, the consort of Satan, and the mother of his offspring, and is
marked by her materiality and hyper-sexuality.[63] Satan's arousal by the likeness
of a beautiful virgin engraved into the marble statue, and his sexual union with
(or, rather, emission onto) the statue which ultimately produces 'Armilos, can
likewise be illuminated by recourse to the Sethian and Manichæan accounts
of the 'seduction of the archons.' In the Sethian sources, the archons/Satan
are aroused by Eve's image, which reminds them of the light that shone from
the Invisible Virgin Spirit/Forethought/Barbēlō (and, later in the myth, from
Sophia), but end up defiling only her material 'shadow,' thus producing diabolic offspring in their own image. In the Manichæan sources, Matter, clothed
in the bodies of the male and female archons, and aided by their lust after the
images of the Third Messenger and Virgin of Light, causes the archons to emit

---

60   Mani's Šābuhragān, M 7984.1 (Hutter [ed.], pp. 83–84): *ud āwōn če'ōn az naxust āz xwad
      andar hān tam dōšox dwārišn ī xwēš dēwān ud parīgān xešmen mazanān ud āsarēštārān
      narān ud māyagān awezmāh ud marzišn hammōxt hēnd: āwōn pasā-z dudīy niwist āz awīn
      āsarēštārān abārīgān narān ud māyagān kē az asmān ō zamīg kaft hēnd awēšān-iz hamg-
      ōnag awezmāh ud marzišn hammōzān kū awezmāhānd ud marzānd.*

61   See P.O. Skjærvø, 'Āsarēštār', *Encyclopedia Iranica* vol. 2, pp. 801–802.

62   See e.g. Reeves, *Heralds of the Good Realm*, at pp. 79–88; Stroumsa, *Another Seed*, pp. 155–
      157.

63   It is possible that the figure of Hephṣibah too is indebted, not only to the Byzantine
      warrior-protector image of the Virgin Mary, but also to the Manichæan imagery of warrior-
      protector female redeemers, such as the Mother of Life and Virgin of Light.

GNOSTIC AND MITHRAIC THEMES IN SEFER ZERUBBABEL   427

their semen/abortions and, ultimately, to unite with each other sexually, thus producing diabolic offspring.

3   The Imprisoned Messiah

Before I turn to the Mithraic sources, I note that the gnostic context of Sefer Zerubbabel can also be seen in its distinctive depiction of the imprisonment of the suffering Messiah:

> Then a spirit/wind lifted me between heaven and earth (Ezek. 8:3) and led me about Nineveh, the great city (Jonah 3:3), which is the city of blood (Ezek. 22:2, 24:6–9, Nah. 3:1) ... Then he said to me, 'Go to the house of disgrace, to the market-place.' I went as he commanded ... I saw a man despised, severely wounded, and in pain (Isa. 53:3). Now that despised man said to me, 'Zerubbabel, what is your business here? Who brought you here?' 'The spirit of the Lord lifted me up,' I answered, 'and deposited me in this place.' 'Fear not,' he said, 'for you have been brought here in order to show you' (Ezek. 40:4). When I heard his words, I took comfort, and my mind was at rest. 'Sir,' I asked, 'what is the name of this place?' 'This is Rome the Great in which I am imprisoned,' he said. 'Sir, who are you,' I asked, 'and what is your name? What are you looking for here? And what are you doing in this place?' 'I am the Lord's anointed, the son of Hezekiah,' he answered, 'and I am jailed until the time of the end.'[64]

The notion of a suffering Messiah, connected with the suffering servant of Isa. 53, has a long history in both Jewish and Christian traditions.[65] The account

---

64   ותשאני רוח בין השמים ובין הארץ, ויוליכני בנינווה עיר הגדולה [הדמים] היא עיר ה(ד)מים ...
ויאמר אלי לך אל בית התורף [ההרה] אל מקום השוק ואלך כאשר ציוני ... וראיתי איש נבזה
ופצוע דכא ומכאוב. ויאמר אלי [אותו] האיש הנבזה זרובבל מה מלאכתך בזה או מי הביאך
הלום. ואען ואומר רוח יי נשאני והשליכני בזה המקום. ויאמר אלי אל תירא, כי למען הראותך
הובאת הנה. וכשומעי דבריו ניחמתי ודעתי ישיב לי. ושאלתי לו אדוני מה שם המקום הזה. ויאמר
אלי זו היא רומי רבתי שאני אסור בה. ואומר לו אדוני מי אתה ומה שמך ומה אתה מבקש הנה
ומה אתה עושה בזה המקום. ויאמר אלי אני משיח יי בן חזקיה, שאני אסור בכלא עד עת קץ.
The translation is based on Himmelfarb, *Jewish Messiahs*, pp. 148–149, with minor adjustments.

65   See e.g. J. Blenkinsopp, *Isaiah 40–55* (Anchor Bible 19a), New York, 2002, pp. 166–174; A. Laato, *Who is the Servant of the Lord? Jewish and Christian Interpretations on Isaiah 53 from Antiquity to the Middle Ages*, Winona Lake, 2013; and multiple essays collected in B. Janowski and P. Stuhlmacher (eds), *The Suffering Servant: Isaiah 53 in Jewish and Christian Source*, trans., D.P. Bailey, Grand Rapids, 2004 [German ed. 1996]; Knohl, *The*

428   KIEL

of the suffering Messiah presented in Sefer Zerubbabel is particularly reminiscent of a talmudic story (*b. Sanh.* 98a) narrating the encounter between
R. Yehoshua b. Levi and the Messiah, which similarly features the suffering Messiah located in Rome.[66] It has correctly been noted, however, that in contrast
to the deterministic portrayal of the events leading up to the eschaton in Sefer
Zerubbabel, the rabbinic account concludes with the assertion that the coming
of the Messiah ultimately depends on Israel's hearkening to God's commandments ['today, if you hearken to his voice'].[67]

In the present context, I note that, unlike the talmudic story and other
ancient Jewish and Christian sources featuring the suffering Messiah, Sefer
Zerubbabel uniquely depicts the suffering Messiah as *imprisoned*, describing,
moreover, a continuous state of incarceration and confinement 'until the time
of the end.' I wish to posit, therefore, that Sefer Zerubbabel's distinctive account
of the imprisonment of the suffering Messiah can be illuminated by the continuous imprisonment of the Suffering Jesus/Living Soul in the Manichæan
tradition.[68]

Scholars have noted the different meanings associated with the terms Jesus,
Christ and Messiah in Manichæan sources.[69] Among these, the Suffering Jesus

---

      Messiah Before Jesus; Boyarin, *The Jewish Gospels*, pp. 129–156; Schäfer, *The Jewish Jesus*,
      pp. 236–272.
66   For the significance of Rome as the locus of the suffering Messiah, see Boustan, 'The Spoils
      of the Jerusalem Temple', pp. 368–369 and Himmelfarb, *Jewish Messiahs*, pp. 75–76 (sug-
      gesting an inversion of the Christian story, in which the suffering Christ begins his career
      in Jerusalem, but paves a new path leading to Rome). Cf. Sivertsev, *Judaism and Imperial
      Ideology*, pp. 126–135.
67   This was pointed out in Newman, 'Yehuda Even-Shmuel's Midrashei Geula', pp. lxxiii–
      lxxiv; Himmelfarb, *Jewish Messiahs*, p. 69.
68   For this doctrine, see n. 44. Certain Manichæans read the doctrine of the imprisoned Liv-
      ing Soul/Suffering Jesus into Paul's assertion regarding 'the groaning of the whole creation'
      (Rom. 8:19–23). On the Manichæan view, this was a clear reference to the sufferings of the
      Living Soul/Suffering Jesus crucified and imprisoned in the world. So, Faustus in *Contra
      Faustum* 20:2 (CSEL 25, 536): 'The vulnerable Jesus, who is the life and salvation of men,
      hanging from every tree'. Augustine, for his part, deliberately downplayed the cosmic signif-
      icance of Christ's suffering. See J. van Oort, 'Manichæan Christians in Augustine's Life and
      Work', *Church History and Religious Culture* 90, 4 (2010), pp. 505–546. While Sefer Zerub-
      babel does not address the cosmic diversification of the suffering Messiah, its portrayal
      of his ongoing imprisonment in Rome—a city also associated with the 'material' statue-
      mother of 'Armilos—can be informed perhaps through the Manichæan symbolism of the
      imprisonment of the Suffering Jesus in Matter.
69   On Jesus in Manichæism, see W. Sundermann, 'Christ in Manichæism', *Encyclopedia Iran-
      ica* 5, pp. 335–339; Asmussen, *Manichæan Literature*, pp. 98–112; M. Franzmann, *Jesus in
      the Manichæan Writings*, London, 2003. According to Sundermann, ibid., p. 336, 'In the
      western Manichean tradition, represented principally by Greek, Latin, and Coptic texts,

GNOSTIC AND MITHRAIC THEMES IN SEFER ZERUBBABEL   429

(Jesus *patibilis*) represents the Living Soul, the inflicted light imprisoned and diversified until the end of days, awaiting its redemption. Employing Christian terminology, the Living Soul/Suffering Jesus is also depicted as *crucified* in the world, but, unlike Christian sources, which typically envision the suffering Christ as a singular moment in human history, the Suffering Jesus in Manichæism is largely perceived in terms of a continuous state of imprisonment and diversification.[70]

John Reeves has called attention to the affinity of the confined Messiah in Sefer Zerubbabel with yet another gnostic account depicting the confinement of the Messiah.[71] This account is found in the teachings of a Syro-Mesopotamian sect known as the Ḥewyāyē,[72] as recorded by the Syriac author Theodore bar Kōnai:

> With regard to Christ, they claim that his father's name was N'wr (ܢܘܪܐ)[73] and that he had a wife named Miriam, and that Christ was born from them. They designate Christ with many names—Abel, Manasseh, Per'ūn, Zerubbabel—and assert that he is associated with an androgyne named Babel. This is why they call him 'Zerubbabel,' for he sows seed in Babel.[74]

---

the Greek name Khristós is used for Jesus ... In the Mesopotamian and eastern tradition of Manicheism, represented principally by Iranian, Turkish, and Chinese texts, the original Aramaic form *mšyḥ'* (Mašīḥā) is preferred'.

70   Some of the other meanings associated with the name Jesus are: 1) Jesus the Splendor (Syr. Išōʿ Zīwānā; Mid. Pers. Xradešahryazd) from the Manichæan cosmogonic account, a deity representing either the son of the Father of Greatness himself, the son of the First Man of the first evocation, or, most commonly, the son of the Third Messenger, the main deity of the third evocation. This aspect of the Manichæan Jesus is consistent with the heavenly Jesus in Christianity, the eternal Son who sits on a throne to the right hand of the Father in heaven. 2) The historical Jesus of Nazareth, who, in Manichæan thought, is believed to be one manifestation and embodiment of the apostle of light in a chain of prophetic succession culminating with Mani. 3) The risen eschatological redeemer who will rule over humanity in the end of days, before the collapse of the material existence and the final release of the light.

71   Reeves, *Trajectories*, p. 46.

72   For the Ḥewyāyē in Theodore's account, see S. Gerö, 'Ophite Gnosticism According to Theodore bar Koni's Liber Scholiorum', in H.J.W. Drijvers et al. (eds), *IV Symposium Syriacum 1984: Literary Genres in Syriac Literature (Groningen-Oosterhesselen 10–12 September)*, OrChrAn 229, Rome, 1987, pp. 265–274.

73   Reeves, *Trajectories*, p. 46, notes that the peculiar name of Christ's father, N'wr (ܢܘܪܐ), exhibits at least an audible similarity to one of the most common designations of Metatron, *na'ar* ('youth'), who functions as the medium of revelation in Sefer Zerubbabel.

74   Compare also *b. Sanh.* 38a: 'Zerubbabel—for he was sown in Babel' (זרובבל שנזרע בבבל). Zerubbabel also appears in Matthew 1:12 and Luke 3:27 as an ancestor of Jesus. The Greek spelling of the name (Ζοροβαβελ) is reminiscent of the name Zoroaster, the Greek form

They also claim there is a church at the end of the earth wherein Christ is, along with his father N'wr (ܢܘܪܐ) and his mother Miriam, and that he will come after the antichrist comes and kills the Jews and all of humankind.[75]

As noted by Reeves, the confinement of Christ in a church situated 'at the end of the earth' is reminiscent of the imprisonment of the Messiah in a house of disgrace and scorn reported in Sefer Zerubbabel.[76] He further notes several motifs in Theodore's account of the Ḥewyāyē, which are reminiscent of Sefer Zerubbabel, including the centrality of the biblical figure Zerubbabel, the significance attached to sowing seed/semen, the murderous activities associated with the antichrist, and the eschatological role of the Messiah's mother.[77]

4   'Armilos and Mithras

The missing piece in the puzzle seems to be the motif of the rock-birth of 'Armilos and the related motif of sexual intercourse with a rock, themes which are not sufficiently explained by the gnostic and Christian evidence we have considered. Lutz Greisiger attempted to trace the rock-birth of 'Armilos to Greco-Roman mythology and specifically to the stories surrounding the Great Mother/Cybele.[78] Cybele was associated with rock and particularly with the mountainous landscape of Anatolia and was said to have had 'a stone for a

---

of Zarathustra. Zoroaster too was commonly associated in the Greek tradition with Babel and even identified with the notorious Babylonian king Nimrod. See e.g. Pseudo-Clement of Rome, *Homilies* 9.4–5; *Recognitiones* 1.30; Epiphanius of Salamis, *Panarion* 1.3, 2–3; *Cave of Treasures* 27. See K. van der Toorn and P.W. van der Horst, 'Nimrod Before and After the Bible', *Harvard Theological Review* 83:1 (1990), pp. 1–29; Y. Kiel, 'Abraham and Nimrod in the Shadow of Zarathustra', *Journal of Religion* 95, 1 (2015), pp. 35–50.

75   Theodore bar Kōnai, *Liber Scholiorum*, A. Scher (ed.) vol. 2, Paris, 1910–1912, p. 336, lines 13–23 (trans. in Reeves, *Trajectories*, p. 46). On this work, see S.H. Griffith, 'Theodore bar Kōnî's Scholion: A Nestorian Summa contra Gentiles from the First Abbasid Century', in N.G. Garsoïan et al. (eds), *East of Byzantium: Syria and Armenia in the Formative Period*, Washington, D.C., 1982, pp. 53–72.

76   Reeves, *Trajectories*, p. 46. Notably, however, unlike Sefer Zerubbabel's suffering Messiah and the Manichæan Suffering Jesus, in the gnostic account reported by Theodore, Christ does not seem to be suffering at all.

77   Notably, though, Hephṣibah is at the forefront of the military resistance, whereas Miriam remains secluded with her son.

78   L. Greisiger, 'Die Geburt des Armilos und die Geburt des 'Sohnes des Verderbens': Zeugnisse jüdisch-christlicher Auseinandersetzung um die Identifikation des Antichristen im 7. Jahrhundert', in W. Brandes and F. Schmieder (eds), *Antichrist: Konstruktionen von Feindbildern*, Berlin, 2010, pp. 28–30.

GNOSTIC AND MITHRAIC THEMES IN SEFER ZERUBBABEL 431

face.' According to another account, a sexual union between Zeus and Cybele resulted in the birth of Agdistis.[79] Other relevant Greco-Roman myths concerning sexual intercourse with a rock include the stories of Pygmalion who falls in love and has sex with a statue of his own making and that of a person who attempted to have sexual intercourse with the statue of Aphrodite in Knidos.[80]

Israel Knohl has recently suggested that the rock birth of 'Armilos, which resulted from a sexual union between Satan and a marble statue, is indebted to the Hurrian myth of Ullikummi. Ullikummi, who himself was depicted as a giant rock, is said to have issued from a sexual union between Kumarbi and a rock situated in the midst of a lake.[81] Albert de Jong further noted that the motif of a hero born of a rock and/or conceived through sexual intercourse with a rock is a recurring topos in a cycle of myths that circulated in the Caucasus, as evident in the Hurrian myth of Ullikummi, the myths surrounding Cybele, the epic of the Ossetes, and the Georgian myth of Amirani.[82]

While I embrace the panoramic perspective offered by de Jong, I would argue that the rock-birth of Mithras, attested in numerous visual and textual sources,[83] is particularly relevant for deciphering Sefer Zerubbabel's account of the nativity of 'Armilos. Although the 'mystery religion' surrounding Mithras's cult was in a state of decline in the fourth century and completely eradicated by the turn of the fifth century,[84] the memory of Mithras remained vivid, not least due to the visual remains as well as the similarities between Mithras and Christ which haunted patristic authors from the second century onwards.[85] Jonathan Z. Smith has argued that, paradoxically, it was Christian authors, rather than

---

79   Greisiger, ibid.

80   Himmelfarb, *Jewish Messiahs*, p. 57.

81   I. Knohl, 'A Hurrian Myth in a Late Jewish Text: Sepher Zerubabel', in G. Bohak, R. Margolin and I. Rozen-Zvi (eds), *Te'uda 26: Myth, Ritual and Mysticism: A Festschrift for Ithamar Gruenwald*, Tel-Aviv, 2014, pp. 73–84 [Hebrew].

82   See A. de Jong, *Traditions of The Magi: Zoroastrianism in Greek And Latin Literature*, Leiden, 1997, p. 291, who also mentions the example of 'Armilos in Sefer Zerubbabel. I would like to thank Yakir Paz for calling my attention to some Armenian parallels as well.

83   For Mithras's cult, see in general F. Cumont, *The Mysteries of Mithras*, trans. T.J. McCormack, New York, 1956; Clauss, *The Roman Cult of Mithras*; D. Ulansey, *The Origins of the Mithraic Mysteries: Cosmology and Salvation in the Ancient World*, Oxford, 1989; R. Beck, *The Religion of the Mithras Cult in the Roman Empire: Mysteries of the Unconquered Sun*, Oxford, 2006.

84   For the most recent discussion of the decline of Mithras's cult, see D. Walsh, *The Cult of Mithras in Late Antiquity: Development, Decline and Demise ca. A.D. 270–430*, Leiden, 2018, pp., 42–66.

85   For an excellent discussion of parallelism between Mithras and Christ, see M. Clauss, 'Mithras und Christus', *Historische Zeitschrift* 243 (1986), pp. 264–287. For an English summary, see Clauss, *Cult of Mithras*, pp. 168–172.

their 'pagan' rivals, who substantiated the parallels between Christianity and the 'mystery religions' of the Roman empire, thus enshrining their memory for posterity. In their apologetic attempt to deny any type of connection between Christianity and the 'mystery religions,' it was in fact the patristic authors who projected their own categories and taxonomies onto those of their rivals, thus perpetuating the very parallels they so rigorously denied.[86]

Mithras famously appears emerging from a rock in numerous rock-reliefs and sculptures found in Mithræums throughout the Roman empire and beyond.[87] In contrast to the scarcity of stone representations of the Virgin Mary and other Christian figures in seventh-century Byzantium, the rock-birth of Mithras was abundantly depicted in statues and sculptures. Mithras is also known from the literary evidence, in which he is designated *theos ek petras* ('the god from the rock') as attested in several inscriptions. In one of these inscriptions it says: 'To the almighty god, the invincible sun, the generative god, born from a rock.'[88]

The attributes of Mithras recorded in this inscription—the invincible sun and generative god—are also represented in visual remains in which Mithras often appears holding a torch and a dagger, the former symbolizing his luminosity and the latter symbolizing the slaughtering of the bull, which brought life and creation in its wake. Mithras's rock-birth is also addressed in patristic writings as early as the second century. According to Justin's *Dialogue*:

> And when those who record the mysteries of Mithras (Μίθρου μυστήρια) say that he was begotten of a rock (ἐκ πέτρας γεγενῆσθαι), and call the place where those who believe in him are initiated a cave, do I not perceive here that the utterance of Daniel, that a stone without hands was cut out of a great mountain, has been imitated by them, and that they have attempted likewise to imitate the whole of Isaiah's words?[89]

Similarly, the fourth-century Latin author Firmicus Maternus, asserts in his *De errore profanis religionis*, 20.1:

---

86 See e.g. J.Z. Smith, *Drudgery Divine: On the Comparison of Early Christianities and the Religions of Late Antiquity*, Chicago, 1990.

87 Clauss, *Cult of Mithras*, pp. 62–71.

88 'D(eo) O(mnipotenti) S(oli) Invi(cto), Deo Genitori, r(upe) n(ato)'. See M.J. Vermaseren, *Corpus Inscriptionum et Monumentorum Religionis Mithriacæ*, 2 vols, The Hague, 1956–1960, no. 2007; Clauss, *Roman Cult of Mithras*, p. 62.

89 Justin, *Dialogue*, 70.1.

GNOSTIC AND MITHRAIC THEMES IN SEFER ZERUBBABEL   433

Another pagan sacrament has the key word 'god from a rock' (θεὸς ἐκ πέτρας). Why do you adulterate the faith and transfer this holy and worshipful mystery to pagan doings?[90]

The literary sources provide us information, not only with regard to Mithras's birth, but also with regard to his conception. Of particular interest is Jerome's account, according to which Mithras was not merely rock-begotten, but conceived by 'raging lust':

Heathen fables relate how Mithras and Erichthonius were begotten of the soil, in stone or earth, by raging lust.[91]

The combination of Mithras's rock-birth and conception by manner of 'raging lust' is somewhat reminiscent of the story of 'Armilos, who was similarly conceived by Satan's lusting after the shape of a beautiful virgin, and ultimately born of a rock. Another story recorded by the anonymous author of *De fluviis*, known as Ps. Plutarch, relates that Mithras was not only rock-begotten, but himself engaged in sexual intercourse with a rock:

Next to it (= the river Araxes, the most important river in Armenia) lies the mountain called Diorphos, after Diorphos the earth-born (or the Titan), concerning whom the following story is told: Mithras, who wanted to have a son, but hated the race of women, ejaculated on a stone. The stone became pregnant, and—after the appropriate time—produced a boy called Diorphos. Having grown into his prime, he challenged Ares to a contest of excellence and was killed. In accordance with the providence of the gods, he was transformed into the mountain bearing his name.[92]

This account is strikingly similar to 'Armilos's rock-birth and his conception through Satan's sexual union with (/ejaculation onto) a rock, a motif which, as

---

90   'Alterius profani sacramenti signum est θεὸς ἐκ πέτρας. Cur hoc sanctum venerandumque secretum ad profanos actus adulterata professione transfertis?' See Firmicus Maternus, *De errore profanis religionis*, 20.1; C.A. Forbes (trans.), *Firmicus Maternus: The Error of the Pagan Religions*, New York, 1970, p. 87.

91   'Narrant et gentilium fabulæ Mithram et Erichthonium, vel in lapide, vel in terra, de solo æstu libidinis esse generatos'. See Jerome, *Adversus Jovinianum* 1.7, in *Nicene and Post-Nicene Fathers of the Christian Church, 2nd Series* vol. 6: *St. Jerome, Letters and Select Works*, trans. W.H. Fremantle, G. Lewis and W.G. Martley, New York, 1893, p. 350.

92   Ps. Plutarch, *De fluviis*, 23.4; de Jong (trans.), *Traditions of the Magi*, p. 291.

we have seen, is related to the Sethian and Manichæan accounts of the 'seduction of the archons.' The themes of rock-birth and rock-conception in Sefer Zerubbabel thus seem to partake in a broader cultural discourse, while exhibiting particular affinity with the stories surrounding Mithras, who was not only rock-born, but also conceived through 'raging lust,' and himself engaged in the seminal impregnation of a rock.

What remains to be explained is what inspired or triggered the incorporation of the rock-birth and rock-conception of Mithras into Sefer Zerubbabel's construction of the antichrist's genealogy. Whereas the construction of the evil sphere on the basis of gnostic mythology is perhaps more intuitive, it is not entirely clear why traditions about Mithras would have influenced a story concerning the birth of the antichrist and son of Satan.

I would like to suggest that, beyond the prosaic fact of the availability of Mithraic visual remains, the integration of traditions relating to Mithras's rock-birth and rock-conception into an otherwise gnostic-inspired construction of the nativity of the antichrist in Sefer Zerubbabel can be informed by the following considerations:

1. First, Christian authors occasionally seem to conflate aspects of the 'Gnostic' and 'Mithraic' mythologies, both of which were similarly perceived as inversions of Christianity. Is it merely by chance, for example, that Jerome mentions the 'raging lust' by which Mithras was conceived in the course of a discourse devoted to the demonization of sexual desire, one which reflects (certainly according to Jerome's critics) the impact of gnostic anti-sexual tendencies?[93] And does not Mithras's alleged misog-

---

93   Despite the prevalence of patristic refutation of the Marcionite, Encratite and Manichæan denigration of sex and reproduction (for which see D.G. Hunter, *Marriage, Celibacy, and Heresy in Ancient Christianity: The Jovinianist Controversy*, Oxford, 2007, pp. 90–129), one cannot deny the impact of gnostic, especially Manichæan, thought regarding matters of sex, on authors such as Jerome and Augustine. For Jerome, see e.g. E. Clark, *Reading Renunciation: Asceticism and Scripture in Early Christianity*, Princeton, 1999, p. 263; Hunter, *Marriage, Celibacy, and Heresy*, pp. 207–242. For Augustine, see J.K. Coyle, 'St. Augustine's Manichæan Legacy', in *Manichæism and Its Legacy*, NHMS 69, Leiden, 2009, pp. 307–328, esp. 325–326; J. van Oort, 'Augustine and Mani on concupiscentia sexualis', in J. den Boeft and J. van Oort (eds), *Augustiniana Traiectina: Communications présentées au colloque international d'Utrecht, 13–14 novembre 1986*, Paris, 1987, pp. 137–152; J. van Oort, 'Augustine on Sexual concupiscence and original sin', *Studia Patristica* 22 (1989), pp. 382–386; E. Clark, 'Vitiated Seeds and Holy Vessels: Augustine's Manichean Past', in K. King (ed.), *Images of the Feminine in Gnosticism*, Studies in Antiquity and Christianity Series, Philadelphia, 1988, pp. 367–401 (and see the response by Paula Fredriksen in the same volume, pp. 402–409); P.R. Eddy, 'Can a Leopard Change its Spots?: Augustine and the Crypto-Manichæism Question', *Scottish Journal of Theology* 62, 3 (2009), pp. 16–346, esp. 333–336; T. Nisula,

GNOSTIC AND MITHRAIC THEMES IN SEFER ZERUBBABEL   435

yny according to Ps. Plutarch, and the ensuing discussion of his ability to engender via seminal emission, smack of gnostic influence?

2. Second, it is unclear whether, and to what extent, there might have been a gnostic dimension to Mithras's cult itself. One possible locus of gnostic presence in Mithraism is the ambiguous lion-headed figure found in several Mithraic cites of worship. While this figure was identified by many scholars as Aion, the god of Time; based on a dedicatory inscription to Arimanius, others have suggested that this figure is none other than Ahriman, representing Satan in both Zoroastrianism and Iranian Manichæism. Still others have gone farther in suggesting that the lion-headed figure should be identified with the gnostic demiurge Yaldabaoth.[94] It is not impossible, therefore, that there was an actual gnostic component to Mithras's cult, beyond the confused syncretism reflected in some ancient accounts.

3. Third, Mitra/Mithra, the Iranian counterpart of Roman Mithras,[95] played a prominent role in Iranian versions of the Manichæan myth. In fact, some Iranian Manichæan sources identify Mithra with the Third Messenger and, by implication, with the Virgin of Light. While Mani's Šābuhragān and other Manichæan sources in Middle Persian generally identify Mithra (Mihr) with the Living Spirit (while the Third Messenger is identified with Narsē/Nēryōsang), Parthian and Sogdian sources typically identify Mithra (Mihr/Mišiwas) with the Third Messenger. Given Mithra's role in the Manichæan myth of the 'seduction of the archons,' it is not entirely surprising that the rock-birth of Mithras and his impregnation of a rock were included in Sefer Zerubbabel's otherwise gnostic-inspired construction of the antichrist's genealogy. It is not impossible to imagine that the Jewish

---

Augustine and the Functions of Concupiscence, Supplements to Vigiliæ Christianæ, Leiden, 2012, pp. 6–8.

94   For discussions of the lion-headed figure, see e.g. J.R. Hinnels, 'Reflections on the Lion-Headed Figure in Mithraism', *Monumentum H.S Nyberg*, Acta Iranica 2.1, Leiden, 1975, pp. 333–369; H.M. Jackson, 'The Meaning and Function of the Leontocephaline in Roman Mithraism', *Numen* 32 (1985), pp. 17–45; cf. Clauss, *Cult of Mithras*, pp. 162–167 (and the sources listed on p. 181).

95   For the question of the Iranian and Indic connections of the Roman cult of Mithras, see the summary of scholarship in R. Beck, 'Mithraism', in *Encyclopedia Iranica* (published online July 20, 2002); H.-P. Schmidt, 'Mithra, i. Mitra in Old Indian and Mithra in Old Iranian', in *Encyclopedia Iranica* (published online on August 15, 2006). For the iconography of Mithra in Iran and central Asia, see F. Grenet, 'Mithra, ii. Iconography in Iran and Central Asia', in *Encyclopedia Iranica* (published online on August 15, 2006); M. Shenkar, *Intangible Spirits and Graven Images: The Iconography of Deities in the Pre-Islamic Iranian World*, Magical and Religious Literature of Late Antiquity 4, Leiden, 2014, pp. 102–114.

involvement in the Sasanian conquest and occupation of Jerusalem in the seventh century, the extent of which is yet to be determined, constituted a channel for such intercultural connections.

Be the relationship between the Sethian, Manichæan and Mithraic components of Sefer Zerubbabel's imagery as it may, in constructing the birth narrative and genealogy of the antichrist, the authors of this unique Jewish apocalypse employed a rhetoric similar to that voiced in patristic sources, which presented the 'Gnostic' and 'Mithraic' mythologies as paradigmatic of Satan's attempt to invert the 'true faith.' Not unlike Irenæus's reconstruction of the gnostic myth as Satan's attempt to invert the 'true' creation story or Justin's reconstruction of Mithras's birth as a diabolic attempt to invert the nativity of Christ, the authors of Sefer Zerubbabel similarly employed Sethian, Manichæan and Mithraic themes—whether consciously or not—in their construction of the birth story and genealogy of the Messiah's 'evil twin.'

Conclusion

In this article, I have argued that Sefer Zerubbabel's unprecedented reconstruction of the birth and genealogy of the antichrist, who is said to have issued from a sexual union between Beliʻal-Satan and a marble-statue in the likeness of a beautiful virgin, can be significantly illuminated and informed, not only by Byzantine Christian imagery, but also by recourse to gnostic and Mithraic lore. The first part of the article centred on Sethian and Manichæan traditions pertaining to the nature of the material feminine principle of evil—the consort of Satan and mother of diabolic offspring—and the mythical scene of the 'seduction of the archons,' in which the archons are said to have lusted after the 'likeness' of a beautiful virgin, but ultimately emitted their semen among themselves, thus producing diabolic offspring in their own image. The second part of the article centred on visual and literary depictions of Mithras's emergence from a rock, his conception by 'raging lust,' and his sexual union with a rock. Against the backdrop of this evidence, I have argued that a panoramic exploration of the Christian, Sethian, Manichæan, and Mithraic traditions can shed new light on the symbolism of Sefer Zerubbabel and particularly the cryptic account of 'Armilos's rock-birth that resulted from a sexual union (/seminal emission) between Beliʻal-Satan and a marble statue in the shape of a beautiful virgin.

PART 4

*Angels, Heavenly Journeys
and Visions of Paradise*

∴

CHAPTER 21

1 Enoch 17 in the Geneva Papyrus 187

David Hamidović

The Greek Papyrus 187, which is currently kept at the Public Library of Geneva in Switzerland, preserves a passage which seems to quote the heavenly journey of Enoch in 1 Enoch 17. Amongst many other papyri, the papyrus 187 was bought either at the end of the nineteenth century or at the beginning of the twentieth century for the Geneva Library. The precise location of the papyrus being unclear before the purchase, the Fayyum region in Middle Egypt appears to be the best candidate—according to the register and the notes of the successive staff in charge of the Geneva papyri collection.

The opistograph papyrus is unfortunately badly preserved. Indeed, only one strip remains. It measures 28.4 cm high for 33 lines on the recto and 36 lines on the verso, and 9.9 cm wide for 28 to 44 letters per line, which implies that only two, three or four words are preserved per line. On the recto, the upper, the lower and the right margins are preserved. As the Greek text is unknown and is still unidentified, it is difficult to estimate the missing words at the left on the recto and at the right on the verso. However, the regular shape of the letters, without space between words or strokes, suggests a palæographical date around the second century CE or the beginning of the third century CE for the copy.

1 P. Gen. 187 14ᵛ–17ᵛ Compared to 1 Enoch 17:1–2

The last part of the papyrus contains words close to 1 Enoch 17. The passage begins with lines 14 and 15 on the verso. The first line preserves the expression παρα[λα]βοντ[ε]ς με, 'they took me'. Despite the fragmentary state of the papyrus, a close formulation can be read on line 32 on the recto: π]αραλαβ[ο]ντες μ[ε] απη[νεγκαν με, 'taking me, they led me'. The first verb, in aorist second form, is not so frequent but it is attested in many Greek texts including the New Testament, Christian works, and the Greek version of 1 Enoch 17:1, where it describes the beginning of the heavenly journey of Enoch, more specifically when the angels take the patriarch Enoch. Unfortunately, in the Geneva papyrus it remains difficult to identify the characters, as the papyrus is badly preserved: the angels and Enoch are regrettably missing. However, the formula

© DAVID HAMIDOVIĆ, 2021 | DOI:10.1163/9789004445925_023

FIGURE 21.1
Verso of the Geneva Papyrus 187

παραλαβόντες με seems to function as an expression separating different parts of the text. Indeed, the expression is read on line 32 on the recto, and it appears that the beginning of the recto shares the same context, although the expression is not preserved. Lines 1 to 7 on the recto appear as a journey above the world but with the verb εἴδω. Lines 3 to 5 may be translated as: 'they showed me all the inhabited world'. And the verb ἀποφέρω on line 7 means 'they led me'. Furthermore, the expression παραλαβόντες με on line 14 on the verso corresponds to the Greek text of 1 Enoch 17:1. Line 15 preserves οι οντες εκει, followed by the beginning of a new word οπο[whose end is missing. The two lines match with the Greek version of 1 Enoch 17:1:

Καὶ παραλαβόντες με εἴς τινα τόπον ἀπήγαγον, ἐν ᾧ οἱ ὄντες ἐκεῖ γίνονται ὡς πῦρ φλέγον καὶ, ὅταν θέλωσιν, φαίνονται ὡσεὶ ἄνθρωποι.

It means: 'And they took me, leading me to a place in which the inhabitants turn into burning fire and when they wish, they appear as men'. The beginning of this text seems to correspond to lines 14 and 15 of the Geneva papyrus *but with some nuances.*

Thus, the beginning of the last word of line 15, οπο[, does not correspond to the following words of 1 Enoch 17:1, and it remains too speculative to propose a reconstruction on the basis of these letters, as many propositions are possible in the Greek lexicon. Nevertheless, if I were to suggest a solution, I would reconstruct the word into οπου, the relative adverb 'where' (also found on line 23), so that it would not change the meaning of 1 Enoch 17:1. Nevertheless, lines 14 and 15 of the papyrus do not exactly correspond to the version of the beginning of 1 Enoch 17:1 according to the Codex Panopolitanus, also known as the Akhmim fragments. This view is confirmed on line 16, as the word preserved does not match that found in the respective phrase of 1 Enoch 17:1. The word παραλαβον[τες, 'they took', or perhaps 'they took me', can be read once again as on line 14. Then, line 17 preserves the famous locution του παραδεισου, the genitive form of 'the paradise', which is absent in 1 Enoch 17.

Thus, lines 14 and 15 set forth the wording, 'they took me, leading me to a place in which ...'. The end of the sentence announces the description of places within the framework of a celestial ascent. In 1 Enoch 17, the journey of Enoch takes place in the heavens with angels, but in the context of the Geneva papyrus it may be the ascent of somebody else, as no name has been found in the papyrus preserved. Two hypotheses seem to shed light on the relationship between the two texts. (1) These words may be a well-known expression which the redactional milieu of the Book of the Watchers and the redactional milieu of the papyrus used independently. (2) According to the date of redaction of the

Book of the Watchers, the milieu of the papyrus deliberately used a formula of 1 Enoch 17 in another context.

2 1 Enoch 17 in the Book of the Watchers

However, the relationship between 1 Enoch 17 and the rest of the Book of the Watchers is complex. Indeed, a scholarly consensus exists regarding the perception of different traditions or even texts that have been collected in the Book of the Watchers. For 1 Enoch 17, Enoch's journey is divided into three parts. Although the first and the third part present a coherent text describing Enoch's journey to the extremity of the earth (1 Enoch 17:1–8; 18:6–19:2), the second part in 1 Enoch 18:1–6 appears as a summary of Enoch's visions of the winds in the cosmos. G.W.E. Nickelsburg speaks about 'a digression'.[1] The expression is ambiguous because the passage is not a textual patchwork: Enoch saw the 'winds of darkness' in 1 Enoch 17:7, and the insertion of a textual development on the topic is understandable. Thus, I agree with Nickelsburg who states that the second part on the winds is an internal development, but we cannot claim that the three parts are not coherent. The redactional milieu provided a coherent text in 1 Enoch 17:1–19:2, although the description is not necessarily linear.

Nevertheless, the end of the text of 1 Enoch 19:2 is disturbing because the description of what Enoch sees becomes illogical. When arriving at the end of his journey in the Northwest, at the end of the earth, after the river Oceanus, Enoch finally perceives the throne-mountain of God (18:6–8), followed by places of punishment for the rebellious angels (18:9–19:2). Yet, in 1 Enoch 18:12–16, the description of erring stars is not located after these passages but before them. The text of this last part of 1 Enoch 18 is clearly to be transposed to the description of the places of the Watchers' punishment according to the analogy between the angels and the stars, and here the analogy between the rebellious angels and the erring stars.

I would like to focus on this passage because, even considered alone, it shows the difficulty of considering 1 Enoch 17–19 to be a fully linear text. The passage about the erring stars in 1 Enoch 18:12–16 presents many lines in parallel with 1 Enoch 18:9b–11+19:1–2.[2] For example, according to the Akhmim fragments, there is on the one hand line 10 that mentions 'there the heavens are completed', and on the other hand lines 12a, 'there was neither firmament of

---

1 G.W.E. Nickelsburg, *1 Enoch 1: A Commentary on the Book of 1 Enoch, Chapters 1–36; 81–108*, Minneapolis, 2001, p. 276.

2 Ibid., pp. 288–289.

1 ENOCH 17 IN THE GENEVA PAPYRUS 187

heaven above, nor firmly founded earth,' and 14a, 'this place (is) the end of heaven and earth'. The comparison of these lines not only suggests a parallel but also, potentially, allows us to hypothesise that lines 12–16 were part of a secondary development. Thus, the passage surmises two different descriptions of the place of punishment at the end of the earth. Indeed, on line 11, Enoch 'saw a great chasm between pillars of heavenly fire' where the Watchers were standing according to 1 Enoch 19:1. On lines 12–13, 'the place was desolate and fearful. There I saw seven stars like great burning mountains.' If we agree that these last lines correspond to a textual addition, we can surmise that the original passage was modified in order to insert the tradition of the seven burning mountains at the end of the earth. Thus, I do not believe in the explanation of A. Dillmann[3] and J.T. Milik[4] who discern two different places, one described after another. Moreover, the close comparison between the Akhmim Greek fragments and some Ethiopic manuscripts also highlights the same difficulty of understanding felt by the Ethiopian translators. For example, outside these inserted lines, on line 10, the Greek text has 'there the heavens are completed', while in some Ethiopic manuscripts (t², u², β) we can read, 'there the waters are completed.' Therefore, the comparison between the Greek text of the Geneva papyrus and the Greek text of 1 Enoch 17 is not so easy to make, and it is crucial to remain cautious before making any conclusion. Objectively, at this stage of the study, I notice two similar expressions within the Akhmim version of 1 Enoch 17:1, but it is not exactly the same text. For the time being, I do not wish to conclude by saying that the text of the Geneva papyrus contains another unknown Greek version of 1 Enoch 17, or that it may be the original version, before an addition was introduced into it, thus modifying its structure, or else that it could be a free quotation of 1 Enoch 17 or even a paraphrase of 1 Enoch 17. A lot of hypotheses remain possible.

3   **P. Gen. 187 18ᵛ–27ᵛ Compared to 1 Enoch 17:2–3: The Relationship between the Geneva Papyrus, the Akhmim Fragments and the Ethiopic Version**

In order to find an answer, we need to take into account the next lines of the Geneva papyrus. The speaker seems now to see or to consider Paradise. The

---

3   A. Dillmann, *Das Buch Henoch übersetzt und erklärt*, Leipzig, 1853, p. 118. P. Grelot, 'La géographie mythique d' Hénoch et ses sources orientales', *RB 65* (1958), p. 40, has a different opinion.

4   J.T. Milik, *The Books of Enoch: Aramaic Fragments of Qumrân Cave 4*, Oxford, 1976, p. 39.

reference to 'the trees', τῶν δενδρων, on line 18, may suggest the trees of Paradise. The last word of line 19 may be αναπαυμα,[5] 'the place of rest', which could indicate that Paradise is a place of rest for some dead people. Their identity may be indicated on the next line: τινα μακαριοις, 'amongst the blessed ones'. It stands for the righteous ones. Thus, the paradise seems to be considered as the place reserved for the righteous dead. Line 22, εισηλθον εκει, 'I came here', suggests that the aim of the speaker's journey was to see the paradise. Lines 23 and 24 preserve the expressions το ορος οπου η and κατειδον τοπου[ς, which respectively mean 'the mountain where' and 'I see places'. The lines may correspond to the end of 1 Enoch 17:2 and the beginning of 1 Enoch 17:3:

καὶ εἰς ὄρος οὗ ἡ κεφαλὴ ἀφικνεῖτο εἰς τὸν οὐρανόν. καὶ εἶδον τόπον τῶν φωστήρων

and to a mountain whose summit attained the heaven. And I saw the place of the luminaries

The Greek text of the papyrus is, again, not exactly the same as in 1 Enoch 17, but the meaning seems to be identical as far as the preserved text allows us to judge. Thus, the same questions persist.

In my opinion, a decisive argument is brought to light by the comparison with the so-called 'Ethiopic version,' if we assume a massive and unique trend of translation in the Ethiopic manuscripts. Indeed, the plural of 'places' on line 24 is also found in the Ethiopic version, unlike the singular form encountered in the Greek version. Therefore, the text of the papyrus is closer to the Ethiopic version. Line 25 continues to speak about the 'places' in the plural: και τους τοπους, while 1 Enoch 17:3 has neither a plural nor a double mention of the term 'place'. Then line 26 has των διατρεχον from the verb διατρέχω which means 'to run through' and figuratively 'to err'. The expression may mean 'those who err': but it could either denote people who err or be a designation of the stars, which err across the cosmos. Unfortunately the expression is not present in 1 Enoch 17:3. However, the expression [κ]α[ι] τους θησαυρου[ς on line 27 is preserved in 1 Enoch 17:3, just after the previous quotation: καὶ τοὺς θησαυροὺς τῶν ἀστέρων, 'and the reservoirs of the stars.' In this context, Enoch sees the place of the luminaries and the sources of the stars. Here the text of the Geneva papyrus has exactly the same wording.

---

5 But the papyrus preserves αναπαομ[. It may be a spelling variant.

1 ENOCH 17 IN THE GENEVA PAPYRUS 187

445

In order to explain the passages with common wording and the differences in wording between the Geneva papyrus and the Greek Book of the Watchers, I avoid speaking about the 'fluidity' of the text, simply because the word is nowadays often used in scholarship as an umbrella, which tends to obviate the characterization of the textual phenomenon. The expression 'textual fluidity' does not allow, in my opinion, a precise description of the relationships between manuscripts, texts and versions. In this case, the comparison with the Ethiopic text may add an argument supporting the use of another Greek text by the Ethiopian translators. If so, it may indicate that the Greek text of the Akhmim fragments is not the only one to have existed in Late Antiquity. The Codex Panopolitanus dates from the fifth or sixth century CE. If I am right, such a conclusion suggests a revision of Charles's conclusion,[6] which is also assumed by Nickelsburg.[7] Both scholars believe that both the Greek text of Akhmim and the Ethiopic version derive from the same archetype. Another argument, to my mind, for such a revision is the comparison between the Akhmim fragments and the Ethiopic version, because some parts are longer while other parts are shorter than the Ethiopic version.[8] A potential explanation could be the misunderstanding of some Greek terms in the Akhmim text by the Ethiopian translators. However, we cannot postulate that the differences between the two versions are scribal errors. Therefore, I believe that some Ethiopian translators have used other Greek version(s) for some passages.

4   P. Gen. 187 28ᵛ–36ᵛ Compared to 1 Enoch 17:3–5: An Impossible Distinction between Versions, Variants, Writing and Rewriting

Line 28 of the Geneva papyrus may appear as another example of such understanding, but it is in reality more complex. I read [τ]οπον αεροβαθη, literally 'a place with deep air'. The last word is only found in the Greek version of 1 Enoch 17:3 according to the Thesaurus Linguæ Græcæ. However, the Greek version of Akhmim does not bear the same wording: καὶ εἰς τὰ ἀεροβαθῆ, 'and until the deep air.' This expression probably refers to the journey or ascent of Enoch to this high place. Relying on the Ethiopic version, A. Caquot translated 'until the

---

6   R.H. Charles, *The Ethiopic Version of the Book of Enoch: Edited from Twenty-Three MSS. together with the Fragmentary Greek and Latin Versions*, Anecdota Oxoniensia, Semitic Series 11, Oxford, 1906, xiii–xvi.

7   G.W.E. Nickelsburg, *op. cit., 1 Enoch 1*, p. 12.

8   See 1 Enoch 1:8b; 3:1–5:1.8.

depths of the atmosphere'.[9] R.H. Charles emended the text and read εἰς τὰ ἄκρα βάθη, 'until the outermost depths'[10] relying on the corrected Ethiopic version, *westa 'aṣnăfa 'emaq*. The wording in the papyrus, [τ]οπον αεροβαθη, might indicate a place characterized by the 'deep air' or a place named αεροβαθη, which the redactional milieu does not clearly identify. This would explain why τοπος has been added just before it. As noted by K. Coblentz Bautch,[11] the passage seems to have been reworked in passing from the Greek to the Ethiopic versions. Recently, Florentina Badalanova mentioned a possible parallel with the Slavonic version of 2 Enoch (oral communication). In any case, the Geneva papyrus presents a different text. In my view, to imagine the difficulty of the copyist trying to render the term αεροβαθη in its context is the best hypothesis for us to explain this passage. The Akhmim fragments and the Ethiopic version witness the same difficulty, probably because the word creates an image of depth in describing Enoch's ascent. The redactional milieu of the papyrus seems to have solved this difficulty by associating αεροβαθη and τοπος to create a place name. Thus, the translators of the different versions have faced the same problem of understanding. The choice made in the Geneva papyrus appears to me to be the clearest solution in comparison to the Akhmim and the Ethiopic versions. Nevertheless, all the versions seem to have lost the original meaning of the Aramaic text.

In order to evaluate more precisely the text of the Geneva papyrus, which is in some parts so similar to 1 Enoch 17 and in others so different, we need to study the rest of the preserved text. Line 29, for instance, preserves τα βελη του πυρ[ος, 'the arrows of fire.' The expression is attested in 1 Enoch 17:3, but in two different and consecutive expressions in the Greek version of Akhmim as well as in the Ethiopic version, just after the mention concerning αεροβαθη: ὅπου τόξον πυρὸς καὶ τὰ βέλη, 'where (are) the bow of fire and the arrows'. The text of the Geneva papyrus seems to fuse both expressions related to the weaponry of God in the Hebrew Bible. However, the reverse opinion is possible: the expression may have been dismantled by a scribe. Anyway, these two expressions in 1 Enoch 17:3 and the single expression in the papyrus seem to designate the same phenomenon: a lightning and, more precisely, the place of the lightning's

---

9   A. Caquot, 'Hénoch', in A. Dupont-Sommer et al. (eds), *La Bible. Écrits intertestamentaires*, Paris, 1987, p. 490.

10   R.H. Charles, *The Book of Enoch, or 1 Enoch: Translated from the Editor's Ethiopic Text, and edited with the introduction notes and indexes of the first edition wholly recast enlarged and rewritten; together with a reprint from the editor's text of the Greek fragments*, Oxford, 1912, p. 38.

11   K. Coblentz Bautch, *A Study of the Geography of 1 Enoch 17–19 'No One Has Seen What I Have Seen'* (JSJSup, 81), Leiden, 2003, pp. 66–68.

origin. For this example, the Akhmin and the Ethiopic versions have the same meaning. Thus, it is not so easy to assume the presence of another Greek version, i.e. the Geneva papyrus, as the textual basis of the Ethiopic version. Did the Ethiopian translators have different Greek manuscripts containing different versions in their hands? Did they select the most relevant version for them, and if so, according to which criteria? Or did they mix the versions to obtain the best one, according to them? Many questions are raising another range of questions about the process of translation of the Book of the Watchers into Classical Ethiopic.

Again, line 30, reporting ειδον την ρομφαια[ν, 'I see the sword,' shows the difficulty of having a clear view of the phenomenon. This text only appears in the Ethiopic version of 1 Enoch 17:3, after the mention of 'arrows and their quivers', but is absent from the Greek version of Akhmim. The precise expression in the Ethiopic version turns out to be 'a sword of fire.' However, the comparison with the Ethiopic version again leads one to conclude that the text of the Geneva papyrus is rather different. The literary context of both versions is also different, because the mention of the sword is introduced by the observation of the speaker's vision in the Geneva papyrus. K. Coblentz Bautch rightly wrote that this motif in Ethiopic seems strange in a context describing meteorological phenomena.[12] Therefore, she gave her preference, as M. Black[13] before her, to the omission in the Akhmim version. But the discovery of this passage in the Geneva papyrus pushes further the comparison of the versions. Indeed, the Geneva papyrus may preserve another Greek version of the passage. It could explain the mention found in the Ethiopic version as based on this Greek text. A first conclusion is to say that the Ethiopic variant is not a free invention of the Ethiopian translators. They may have used a Greek text close to the one found in the Geneva papyrus for their translation. Nevertheless, in my opinion, the remark of K. Coblentz Bautch remains valid, although it may be explained by the redactional rewriting of 1 Enoch 17:3 in the Greek texts rather than by a rewriting by Ethiopian translators. Although the context remains very fragmentary, the introduction of the 'sword' in the Geneva papyrus with the verbal form εἶδον, could refer to the beginning of a description of something new, according to the use of this formula elsewhere in the text. The Ethiopic version could have used this Greek tradition for the passage in aggregating the motif of the sword with the celestial phenomena. Thus, this passage is a new argument suggesting the need for reconsideration of the Greek source of the Ethiopic version.

---

12   K. Coblentz Bautch, op. cit., *A Study of the Geography of 1 Enoch 17–19*, p. 66.

13   M. Black, *The Book of Enoch or 1 Enoch: A New English Edition with Commentary and Textual Notes in Consultation with James C. VanderKam*, SVTP 7, Leiden, 1985, p. 156.

The last lines of the Geneva papyrus attest the same textual phenomenon. Indeed, many expressions are also present in the Akhmim fragments, in the Ethiopic version, or in both versions. Nevertheless, a new wording, unknown in the Akhmim and the Ethiopic versions, is also attested in the last part of the Geneva papyrus. The end of line 30 and the beginning of line 31 allow us to read αστρα]πας, the 'lightning'. The word also appears at the end of 1 Enoch 17:3. Then I read απη[νεγ]καν μ[ε, 'they led me.' Again, after lines 7 and 32, the speaker seems to be driven by a group. The verb may again indicate the beginning of a new textual part in the Geneva papyrus. This view corresponds to the shift between the celestial phenomena in 1 Enoch 17:1–3 and the geographical description from 1 Enoch 17:4. In the Akhmim version there is a synonym expressing the same idea: Καὶ ἀπήγαγόν με.

Line 32 may preserve ε]λαλουν to say: 'they spoke.' The group leading the speaker seems to speak, but unfortunately the following text is lost after the article το. The expression is close to the Ethiopic version of 1 Enoch 17:4 which says: 'it is called,' but again without correspondence in the Akhmim fragments. Lines 33 and 34 preserve the same wording as 1 Enoch 17:4 in the Akhmim and Ethiopic versions: μεχρι πυρος δυσεω[ς, 'until the fire of the west,' describing the sunset, and τας δυσεις του ηλιου, 'the setting of the sun.' Line 35 seems to have the same text as the Akhmim version with a lacuna of 24 missing letters. Then I read πυ]ρος εν ω τρεχει πυρο[ς, 'fire where the fire runs'. 1 Enoch 17:5 has the same wording except for the verbal variant with κατατρέχει, which emphasizes the speed of the fire's running. Indeed, the context of this passage is the journey to a river of fire in which the fire flows like water. Line 36, the last line, confirms the reference to 1 Enoch 17:5 with the same wording: [θ]αλασσα δυσ[ε]ως μεγαλη, 'the great sea of the west'. The expression reminds us of the Greek *okéanos*, i.e. the Ocean around the disc of the earth.[14]

Attempts at Conclusion

Many types of conclusion are possible. First, let us attempt a conclusion concerning the meaning of the end of the Geneva papyrus, which is close to 1 Enoch 17. The geography at the end of the papyrus corresponding to 1 Enoch 17:2–5 is difficult to link to the previous part of the papyrus, which has not been studied in this paper.[15] In the previous part, the residence of the dead is Paradise. How-

---

14 G.W.E. Nickelsburg, *op. cit., 1 Enoch 1*, p. 283, is thinking about the Mediterranean Sea.

15 Despite the superficial analysis, see M. Bagnoud, 'P.Gen. inv. 187: un texte apocalyptique apocryphe inédit', *Museum Helveticum* 73 (2016), pp. 129–153.

ever, the reference to the inhabitants with human appearance compared to the fire in 1 Enoch 17:1, and the mention of 'a mountain with the top reaching to heaven' in 1 Enoch 17:2, lead us to think of the status of the dead and the mountain of God with living waters, cited in the Ethiopic version of 1 Enoch 17:4. In this perspective, it would be reminiscent of the paradise where the righteous dead can live. The references to 1 Enoch 17:2–5, through the mentions of the sunset and 'the great sea of the west', may be understood as an interpretation of 1 Enoch with the aim of confirming the hope of resurrection. I do not know if the piece of papyrus is part of a more developed work, but if it is, the potential use of 1 Enoch 17:6 with the continuation of the geographical description would confirm this re-contextualization. Indeed, the reference to 'the great darkness (…) where all flesh walks' seems to designate Sheol or Hades. It would logically be a reference to the dead and their fate. Moreover, we have mentioned the problem of the place of punishment in the passage.

Another conclusion concerns the status of the Greek text of the Geneva papyrus, relating to the text of the Akhmim fragments and the Ethiopic version (or the texts corresponding to the available Ethiopic manuscripts). Clearly, the Geneva papyrus presents a text close to the Akhmim text but without being a copy of the same Greek version. The Geneva papyrus text looks like another version of the same passage, but the absence of textual references, close or remote, to 1 Enoch before line 14 of the verso, indicates that 1 Enoch 17 is embedded in another writing which still has to be identified. Such a view is not a determining factor which would enable us to discredit the existence of another Greek version in the Geneva papyrus. Indeed, we need to keep in mind that the Akhmim fragments, discovered in 1886/7 in a grave of the Coptic cemetery of Akhmim, correspond to a codex. This codex preserves the Gospel of Peter, the Apocalypse of Peter, then 1 Enoch 19:3–21:9 and, without separation or empty spaces, 1 Enoch 1:1–32:6. This means that the combination of different autonomous writings in one document was common in Egypt. The Geneva papyrus may derive from the same kind of combination, probably springing from an identified common interest in the different writings compiled by a milieu.

Moreover, close examination of the Greek text of the Geneva papyrus and the Ethiopic version or texts of 1 Enoch 17, leads one to conclude that the presence of 1 Enoch 17:1–5 in the Geneva papyrus is not simply a rewriting of the Akhmim version. Indeed, the presence of expressions only attested in the Ethiopic version and the text of the Geneva papyrus, although absent in the Akhmim text, suggests the circulation in Egypt of at least another Greek text during the first centuries CE. Likewise, the complex redactional process of 1 Enoch 17–19 should not lead us to dismiss the possible existence of another

Greek version of 1 Enoch 17:1–5. Finally, the discussion taken as a whole, concerning the links between the text of the papyrus, the Akhmim text and the translation(s) into Classical Ethiopic, relates to our modern understanding of what a text was in Late Antiquity. The available manuscripts cannot testify to the existence of an Ur-text of 1 Enoch 17:2–5, and the differences between these texts do not allow us to reconstruct an 'original' text according to a stemmatic perspective. The pretention to design such a textual reconstruction is a modern view considering the texts as fixed, because we are able to get the manuscripts in hand. Indeed, the close analysis of each text for itself, and the comparison between the Greek and the Ethiopic texts, prove that the texts do not have a fixed form although textual sedimentation is at work, i.e. the variants become increasingly rare over time. This explains the proximity between the Akhmim and the Geneva papyrus texts. This sedimentation is also visible in the texts of the Ethiopic manuscripts. Nevertheless, such a conclusion does not reconstruct the relationship between these texts, since the texts are not isolated. The examination of the Greek and Ethiopic texts for 1 Enoch 17:2–5 makes us aware of different texts or textual traditions. The different scribes have selected or deselected the words, expressions and motifs according to their editorial projects in order to proclaim the message desired. Thus, the text of the Geneva papyrus highlights the writing and rewriting of the textual traditions of 1 Enoch 17:2–5 in a dynamic perspective. A close study of the rest of the papyrus could allow us to go further in the characterization of the Geneva papyrus's text and its raison d'être.

Annexe: P. Gen. 187 14ᵛ–36ᵛ

Upper margin

```
14  παρα[λα]βοντ[ε]ς με[
15  οι οντες εκει οπο[
16  .....παραλαβον[τες
17  του παραδεισου .[
18  των δενδρων αυ[
19  φαιας μη αναπαομ[
20  π.ν τινα μακαριοις[
21  με εις τοπον εν ω τ[
22  εισηλθον εκει ε.ς .[
23  ... το ορος οπου η κ.[
24  ..... κατειδον τοπου[ς
```

1 ENOCH 17 IN THE GENEVA PAPYRUS 187

L   25   και τους τοπους του[
e   26   ους των διατρεχον .[
f   27   [κ]α[ι] τους θησαυρου[ς
t   28   . [τ]οπον αεροβαθη .[
       29   ..ν τα βελη του πυρ[ος
m   30   ειδον την ρομφαια[ν (...) αστρα
a   31   πας . απη[νεγ]καν μ[ε (...) ε
r   32   λαλουν .ο... ελυ.[
g   33   μεχρι πυρος δυσεω[ς
i   34   τας δυσεις του ηλιου[(...) πυ
n   35   ρος εν ω τρεχει πυρο[ς
       36   [θ]αλασσα δυσ[ε]ως μεγαλη[

Lower margin

CHAPTER 22

Enochic Texts and Related Traditions in *Slavia Orthodoxa*

Florentina Badalanova Geller

На майка и татко—за Великден,
който така и не можахме да празнуваме заедно тази година

∵

1 Frame of Reference

When examining the transmission history of the Enochic corpus in the Byzantine Commonwealth,[1] and especially its domestication within the realm of *Slavia Orthodoxa*, one conventionally assumes that the discussion will focus exclusively on *2 Enoch*[2] (also known among specialists as *The Slavonic Apoca-*

---

1 The term Byzantine Commonwealth (= Gr. οἰκουμένη) was coined by D. Obolensky; it is conventionally employed to designate the Eastern Orthodox *Pax Slavia Christiana* as a specific intellectual landscape impacted by Byzantine confessional, cultural and socio-political models; see D. Obolensky, *The Byzantine Commonwealth: Eastern Europe, 500–1453*, New York, 1971. See also the discussion in H. Birnbaum, 'The Balkan Slavic Component of Medieval Russian Culture', in H. Birnbaum and M.S. Flier (eds), *Medieval Russian Culture*, Berkeley–Los Angeles–London, 1984, pp. 3–30.

2 Among scholars whose intellectual blueprint is detectable in the current discussion on *2 Enoch* (regardless of whether the author agrees with their interpretations of the studied data or not) are A. Popov, 'Bibliograficheskie Materialy, Sobrannye Andreem Popovym (iv): Iuzhnorusskiĭ Sbornik 1679 goda', *Chteniia v Imperatorskomъ Obshchestvě Istorii i Drevnosteĭ Rossiĭskikh pri Moskovskomъ Universitetě* vol. 3 (1880), pp. 66–139; M. Sokolov, '*Materialy i Zametki po Starinnoĭ Slavianskoĭ Literature*. Vyp. Tretiĭ (vii/2): *Slavianskaia Kniga Enokha*. Tekst s latinskim perevodom', *ChIOIDR* vol. 4 (1899); id., 'Feniks v Apokrifakh ob Enokhe i Varukhe', *Novyĭ Sbornik Stateĭ po Slavianovedeniiu, Sostavlennyĭ i Izdannyĭ Uchenikami V.I. Lamanskago pri Uchastii ikh Uchenikov po sluchaiu 50-letiia ego Ucheno-Literaturnoĭ Deiatel'nosti*, Sankt Peterburg, 1905, pp. 395–405; id., 'Slavianskaia Kniga Enokha Pravednago. Teksty, latinskiĭ perevod i issledovanie (Posmertnyĭ trud avtora prigotovil k izdaniiu M. Speranskiĭ)', *ChIOIDR* vol. 4/235

© FLORENTINA BADALANOVA GELLER, 2021 | DOI:10.1163/9789004445925_024

lypse of Enoch, or *The Book of the Holy Secrets of Enoch the Just*);[3] this is not the case with the present article. In what follows, I shall explore some particular clusters of compositions extant in Old Church Slavonic (i.e. *Florilegia, Chrono-*

(1910); Ĭord. Ivanov, *Bogomilski Knigi i Legendi*, Sofia, 1925, pp. 165–191; G.N. Bonwetsch, *Das slavische Henochbuch* [= *Abhandlungen der königlischen Gesellschaft der Wissenschaften zu Göttingen, Philologisch-historische Klasse*, N.F. Bd. 1, № 3], Berlin, 1896; id., *Die Bücher der Geheimnisse Henochs: Das sogenannte slavische Henochbuch. Texte und Untersuchungen zur Geschichte der altchristlishen Literatur*, 44 Band Heft 2, Leipzig, 1922; N. Meshcherskiĭ, 'Sledy pamiatnikov Kumrana v staroslavianskoĭ i drevnerusskoĭ literature. (K izucheniiu slavianskikh versiĭ Knigi Enokha)', in L.A. Dmitriev and D.S. Likhachev (eds), *TODRL* vol. 19: *Russkaia Literatura XI–XVII Vekov Sredi Slavianskikh Literatur*, Moscow–Leningrad, 1963, pp. 130–147; id., 'K istorii teksta slavianskoĭ knigi Enokha (Sledy Pamiatnikov Kumrana v Vizantiĭskoĭ i Staroslavianskoĭ Literature)', *VV* vol. 24 (1964), pp. 91–108; id., 'Problemy izucheniia slaviano-russkoĭ perevodnoĭ literatury XI–XV vv.', in D.S. Likhachev (ed.), *TODRL* vol. 20: *Aktual'nye zadachi izucheniia russkoĭ literatury XI–XVII vekov*, Moscow–Leningrad, 1964, pp. 180–231; id., 'K voprosu ob istochnikakh slavianskoi Knigi Enokha', *KSINAA* vol. 86 (1965), pp. 72–78; Ém. Turdeanu, 'Apocryphes bogomiles et apocryphes pseudobogomiles', *RHR* vol. 138, issue 1 (1950), pp. 22–52, and vol. 138, issue 2 (1950), pp. 176–218; id., 'Notule I. Une curiosité de l'Hénoch slave: les phénix du sixième ciel', *RÉS* vol. 47, issue 1–4 (1968) [= *Communications de la délégation française au VIe Congrès international des slavistes* (Prague, 1968)], pp. 53–54; A. Vaillant, *Le livre des secrets d'Hénoch. Texte slave et traduction française*, Paris, 1952; S. Pines, 'Eschatology and the Concept of Time in the *Slavonic Book of Enoch*', in R.J. Zwi Werblowsky and C. Jouco Bleeker (eds), *Types of Redemption: Contributions to the Theme of the Study-Conference Held at Jerusalem 14th to 19th July 1968* [= Numen Book Series: *Studies in the History of Religion* vol. 18], Leiden, 1970, pp. 72–87; J. Milik, *The Books of Enoch. Aramaic Fragments of Qumrân Cave 4*, Oxford, 1976; J.C. Greenfield and M.E. Stone, 'The Enochic Pentateuch and the Date of the *Similitudes*', *HTR* vol. 70, issue 1/2 (1977), pp. 51–65; id., 'The Books of Enoch and the Traditions of Enoch', *Numen* vol. 26, issue 1 (1979), pp. 89–103; M. Scopello, 'The Apocalypse of Zostrianos (Nag Hammadi VIII.1) and *The Book of the Secrets of Enoch*', *VC* vol. 34, issue 4 (1980), pp. 376–385; id. 'The Angels in Ancient Gnosis: Some Cases', in L. Brisson, S. O'Neill and A. Timotin (eds), *Neoplatonic Demons and Angels: Studies in Platonism, Neoplatonism, and the Platonic Tradition* vol. 20, Leiden–Boston, 2018, pp. 19–45; F. Andersen, '2 (*Slavonic Apocalypse*) *of Enoch*. A New Translation and Introduction', in J.H. Charlesworth (ed.), *The Old Testament Pseudepigrapha* vol. 1: *Apocalyptic Literature and Testaments*, Garden City, N.Y., 1983, pp. 91–221; M. Himmelfarb, *Tours of Hell. An Apocalyptic Form in Jewish and Christian Literature*, Philadelphia, 1983; id., *Ascent to Heaven in Jewish and Christian Apocalypses*, New York–Oxford, 1993; id., *An Apocalypse: A Brief History*, Chichester, 2010; W. Adler, 'Berossus, Manetho, and *1 Enoch* in the World Chronicle of Panodorus', *HTR* vol. 76 (1983), pp. 419–442; id., *Time Immemorial: Archaic History and Its Sources in Christian Chronography from Julius Africanus to George Syncellus* [Dumbarton Oaks Studies 26], Washington, D.C., 1989; id., 'The Survival and "Christianization" of Older Jewish Apocalypses', in J.C. VanderKam and W. Adler (eds), *The Jewish Apocalyptic Heritage in Early Christianity* [*Compendia Rerum Iudaicarum Ad Novum Testamentum*, Section III: *Jewish Traditions in Early Christian Literature* vol. 4], Van Gorcum, 1996, pp. 25–129; A. Yarbro Collins, *Cosmology and Eschatology in Jewish and Christian Apocalypticism*, Leiden–Boston–

grapha, Hexameral compilations) that circulated concurrently with 2 *Enoch*, thus clarifying the trajectories of its transmission against the background of the scribal culture of the medieval *Orbis Orthodoxus*. Of particular importance for our investigation will be the indigenous taxonomy coined by the

---

Köln, 2000; J. Collins, 'The Genre Apocalypse in Hellenistic Judaism', in D. Hellholm (ed.), *Apocalypticism in the Mediterranean World and the Near East*, Tübingen, 1983, pp. 531–548; id., *The Apocalyptic Imagination: An Introduction to Jewish Apocalyptic Literature*, Grand Rapids, MI–Cambridge, UK, 1998; id., *Seers, Sibyls and Sages in Hellenistic-Roman Judaism*, Boston–Leiden, 2001; id., *Apocalypse, Prophesy, and Pseudepigraphy: On Jewish Apocalyptic Literature*, Grand Rapids, MI–Cambridge, UK, 2015; Ch. Böttrich, 'Recent Studies in the Slavonic *Book of Enoch*', *JSP* vol. 9 (1991), pp. 35–42; id., *Weltweisheit Menschheitsethik Urkult: Studien zum slavischen Henochbuch* [Wissenschaftliche Untersuchungen zum Neuen Testament: Reihe 2; Bd. 50], Tübingen, 1992; id., *Adam als Mikrokosmos: eine Untersuchung zum slavischen Henochbuch*, Frankfurt et al., 1995; id., *Das slavische Henochbuch* [Jüdische Schriften aus hellenistisch-römischer Zeit. Bd. 5, Apokalypsen, Lfg. 7], Gütersloh, 1996; id., 'Astrologie in der Henochtradition', *ZAW* vol. 109 (1997), pp. 222–245; id., 'The Melchizedek Story of 2 (*Slavonic*) *Enoch*: A Reaction to A. Orlov', *JSJ* vol. 32, issue 4 (2001), pp. 445–470; id., 'Frühjüdische Weisheitstraditionen im slavischen Henochbuch und in Qumran', in C. Hempel, A. Lange and H. Lichtenberger (eds), *The Wisdom Texts from Qumran and the Development of Sapiential Thought* [*BETL* 159], Leuven, 2002, pp. 297–321; id., 'Die vergessene Geburtsgeschichte. Mt 1–2 / Lk 1–2 und die wunderbare Geburt des Melchisedek in slHen 71–72', in H. Lichtenberger and G.S. Oegema (eds), *Jüdische Schriften in ihrem antik-jüdischen und urchristlichen Kontext* [JSHRZ-St 1], Gütersloh, 2002, pp. 222–249; id., 'Biblische Figuren im slavischen Henoch-Buch', in H. Lichtenberger und U. Mittmann-Richert (eds), *Biblical Figures in Deuterocanonical and Cognate Literature* [*Deuterocanonical and Cognate Literature; Yearbook 2008*], Berlin–New York, 2009, pp. 303–335; id., *Geschichte Melchisedeks* [JSHRZ.NF 2:1], Gütersloh, 2010; id., 'The *Book of the Secrets of Enoch* (2 *En*): Between Jewish Origin and Christian Transmission. An Overview', in A. Orlov and G. Boccaccini (eds), *New Perspectives on 2 Enoch: No Longer Slavonic Only* [Studia Judæoslavica 4], Leiden–Boston, 2012, pp. 37–67; id., 'The Angel of Tartarus and the Supposed Coptic Fragments of 2 Enoch', *EChr* vol. 4 (2013), 509–521; P. Schäfer, 'In Heaven as It Is in Hell', in R.S. Boustan and A.Y. Reed (eds), *Heavenly Realms and Earthly Realities in Late Antique Religions*, Cambridge, 2004, pp. 233–274; id., *The Origins of Jewish Mysticism*, Tübingen, 2009.

3   For a survey of variations of the original Old Church Slavonic titles/headings in different Mss., see in Sokolov, *Slavianskaia Kniga Enokha*, p. 1 (note 2); id., *Slavianskaia Kniga Enokha* (Part 1), pp. 111, 133, 145, 155; (Part 2), pp. 1, 10, 32, 33, 47, 69, 72, 76, 84, 92, 94; A. Iatsimirskiĭ, *Bibliograficheskiĭ Obzor Apokrifov v Iuzhnoslavianskoĭ i Russkoĭ Pis'mennosti* (*Spiski Pamiatnikov: Apokrify Vetkhozavetnye*), Vyp. 1, Petrograd, 1921, pp. 81–88; G.N. Bonwetsch, *Die Bücher der Geheimnisse Henochs: Das sogenannte slavische Henochbuch*, p. 3 (note 1); A. Vaillant, *Le livre des secrets d'Hénoch*, p. 4 (note 1); F. Andersen, '2 (*Slavonic Apocalypse*) *of Enoch*', p. 102 (notes 1a, 1b); A. de Santos Otero, 'Libro de los secretos de Henoc (Henoc eslavo)', in A.D. Macho et al. (eds), *Apocrifos del Antiguo Testamento*, Tomo 4: *Ciclo de Henoc*, Madrid, 1984, p. 161; Ch. Böttrich, *Weltweisheit Menschheitsethik Urkult: Studien zum slavischen Henochbuch*, pp. 130–131; G. Macaskill, *The Slavonic Texts of* 2 Enoch, Leiden–Boston, 2013, p. 38 (note 1), p. 39 (note 28).

ENOCHIC TEXTS AND RELATED TRADITIONS IN SLAVIA ORTHODOXA   455

local scribes to identify parabiblical writings penned in the name of Enoch (as listed in the earliest Slavonic renditions of the Byzantine Greek *Indices of Prohibited Books*), as well as some fashionable for the period para-Hexameral compilations containing cosmogonic and anthropogonic, cosmological and cosmographic, chronographic and historiographic accounts. By the time *2 Enoch* caught the attention of the local literati, these types of compositions must have amalgamated into a flexible hyper-narrative, thus creating the scribal culture that welcomed *2 Enoch* in its new homeland.

As promptly noted by W. Adler in his comments on *2 Enoch*, this 'mysterious work' may be considered 'especially illustrative of the difficulties of establishing meaningful criteria for authorship and origin,' since 'almost nothing certain can be said about its provenance, date or original language.' In fact, '*2 Enoch* exemplifies the difficulties that often arise in identifying an apocalypse's Jewish or Christian provenance on the basis of inconclusive internal evidence.'[4] Despite decades of research, no scholarly consensus regarding the intellectual homeland of the antecedent textual corpus of *2 Enoch* (conventionally designated by Nikita Meshcherskiĭ as *Proto-Enoch 2* [*Протоенох 2*])[5] has been achieved. Its hypothetical locations are sought either in Ancient Mesopotamia, or Palestine, or Hellenistic Alexandria, or Byzantium, or even Medieval Bulgaria, while the chronological framework of the assemblage of its earliest edition stretches from the 3rd–1st centuries BCE to the 9th–10th centuries CE.[6] Besides, there is no certainty as regards the original language of the underlying Ur-text of the *Proto-Enoch 2*, with opinions supporting either the Semitic (e.g. Hebrew, Aramaic), or Indo-European (e.g. Greek) linguistic environment. Nor does a coherent set of ideas concerning its transmission history exist, since there are virtually no traces of scribal traditions outside the Slavonic intellectual landscape.[7] It is safe to surmise, therefore, that the epistemological

---

4   See W. Adler, 'The Survival and "Christianization" of Older Jewish Apocalypses', pp. 27–28.

5   Cf. N. Meshcherskiĭ, 'Sledy pamiatnikov Kumrana v staroslavianskoĭ i drevnerusskoĭ literature', p. 143.

6   This astonishing variety of epistemological templates in the studies on *2 Enoch* is discussed by J. Greenfield and M. Stone, 'The Books of Enoch and the Traditions of Enoch', pp. 98–99; F. Andersen, '2 (*Slavonic Apocalypse*) *of Enoch*', pp. 94–97; A. Pennington, '*2 Enoch*', in H.F. Davis Sparks (ed.), *The Apocryphal Old Testament*, Oxford, 1984, pp. 323–326; M. Himmelfarb, *Ascent to Heaven in Jewish and Christian Apocalypses*, pp. 37–44; J. Collins, *The Apocalyptic Imagination: An Introduction to Jewish Apocalyptic Literature*, p. 34; id., *Apocalypse, Prophesy, and Pseudepigraphy*, p. 211, and others.

7   It has been announced that fragments of *2 Enoch* (chapters 36–42) were discovered in 1972 in Coptic manuscripts from Qasr Ibrim in Egyptian Nubia. They were studied by J. Hagen,

framework of Enochic traditions in the *Orbis Orthodoxus* is still being negotiated between Slavonic specialists representing different, occasionally conflicting, scholarly discourses.[8]

'No Longer 'Slavonic' Only: *2 Enoch* Attested in Coptic from Nubia', in A. Orlov and G. Boccaccini (eds), *New Perspectives on 2 Enoch: No Longer Slavonic Only* [Studia Judæoslavica 4], Leiden–Boston, 2012, pp. 7–34. Regrettably, no *editio princeps* of these data has been produced as yet; hence it would be somewhat precipitous to include the Coptic material in the list of the text witnesses of *2 Enoch* (although some scholars are inclined to do so). See also the discussion in Ch. Böttrich ('The Angel of Tartarus and the Supposed Coptic Fragments of 2 Enoch', pp. 509–521), with whom the present author is in total agreement.

8 See in this connection the discussion in A. Popov, 'Bibliograficheskie Materialy, Sobrannye Andreem Popovym (iv): Iuzhnorusskiĭ Sbornik 1679 goda', *ChIOIDR* vol. 3 (1880), pp. 66–139; Sokolov, *Slavianskaia Kniga Enokha*; id., 'Feniks v Apokrifakh ob Enokhe i Varukhe', pp. 395–405; id., *Slavianskaia Kniga Enokha Pravednago*; G.N. Bonwetsch, *Das slavische Henochbuch*; id., *Die Bücher der Geheimnisse Henochs: Das sogenannte slavische Henochbuch*; W.R. Morfill and R.H. Charles, *The Book of the Secrets of Enoch*. Translated from the Slavonic by W.R. Morfill and edited, with introduction, notes and indices by R.H. Charles, Oxford, 1896; A.S.D. Maunder, 'The Date and the Place of Writing of the *Slavonic Book of Enoch*', *The Observatory* vol. 41 (1918), pp. 309–316; J.K. Fotheringham, 'The Date and Place of Writing of the *Slavonic Enoch*', *JThSt* vol. 20 (1919), p. 252; id., 'The Easter Calendar of the *Slavonic Enoch*', *JThSt* vol. 23 (1922), pp. 49–56; R.H. Charles, 'The Date and Place of Writing of the *Slavonic Enoch*', *JThSt* vol. 22, issue 1 (1921), pp. 161–163; N. Schmidt, 'The Two Recensions of *Slavonic Enoch*', *JAOS* vol. 41 (1921), pp. 307–312; K. Lake, 'The Date of the *Slavonic Enoch*', *HTR* vol. 16, issue 4 (1923), pp. 397–398; A. Rubinstein, 'Observations on the *Slavonic Book of Enoch*', *JJS* vol. 13 (1962), pp. 1–21; J. Milik, *The Books of Enoch. Aramaic Fragments of Qumrân Cave 4*, pp. 107–116; N.A. Meshcherskiĭ, 'Sledy pamiatnikov Kumrana v staroslavianskoĭ i drevnerusskoĭ literature', pp. 130–147; id., 'K istorii teksta slavianskoĭ knigi Enokha', pp. 91–108; id., 'Problemy izucheniia slaviano-russkoĭ perevodnoĭ literatury xi–xv vv.', pp. 180–231; id., 'K voprosu ob istochnikakh slavianskoi Knigi Enokha', pp. 72–78; F. Repp, 'Textkritische Untersuchungen zum Henoch-Apokryph des cod. slav. 125 der Österreichischen Nationalbibliothek', *WSJ* vol. 10 (1963), pp. 58–68; M. Philonenko, 'La cosmogonie du Livre des secrets d'Hénoch', in Ph. Derchain (ed.), *Religions en Egypte hellénistique et romaine*, Paris, 1969, pp. 109–116; S. Pines, 'Eschatology and the Concept of Time in the *Slavonic Book of Enoch*', pp. 72–87; F. Andersen, '2 (*Slavonic Apocalypse*) *of Enoch*', pp. 91–100; M. Himmelfarb, *Ascent to Heaven in Jewish and Christian Apocalypses*, pp. 37–44, 83–87; P. Schäfer, *The Origins of Jewish Mysticism*, pp. 77–85; J. Collins, *The Apocalyptic Imagination*, pp. 243–247; W. Adler, 'The Survival and "Christianization" of Older Jewish Apocalypses', pp. 25–129; Ph. Alexander, 'From Son of Adam to Second God: Transformations of Biblical Enoch', in M. Stone and T. Bergen (eds), *Biblical Figures Outside the Bible*, Harrisburg, PA, 1998, pp. 87–122; T. Jovanović, 'Apokrif o Enohu prema Srpskom Prepisu is Narodne Biblioteke u Beču', *Arheografski Prilozi* vol. 25 (2003), pp. 209–223; B. Lourié, 'Metatron i prometaia—vtoraia kniga Enokha na perekrestke problem', in Basil Lourié (ed.), *Scrinium 2: Universum Hagiographicum Mémorial R.P. Michel van Esbroeck, s.J.* [1934–2003], Saint Petersburg, 2006, pp. 371–407; id., 'After-

ENOCHIC TEXTS AND RELATED TRADITIONS IN SLAVIA ORTHODOXA   457

As for the research lemmata implemented by the present author, they can be outlined as follows: the text of what we now designate as *2 Enoch* was translated into Old Bulgarian/Old Church Slavonic from a (no longer extant) Greek protograph[9] which, in turn, was a derivative from a (now lost) Aramaic (or less likely Hebrew) *Vorlage*. The translation of the Semitic text into Greek may

---

life of the *2 Enoch* Calendar: Major Christian Feasts on the Sixth Day', *Henoch* vol. 33, issue 1 (2011), pp. 102–107; id., 'One *hapax legomenon* and the date of *2 Enoch*', *Henoch* vol. 33, issue 1 (2011), pp. 94–96; id., 'Calendrical Elements in *2 Enoch*', in A. Orlov and G. Boccaccini (eds), *New Perspectives on 2 Enoch: No Longer Slavonic Only* [Studia Judæoslavica 4], Leiden–Boston, 2012, pp. 191–219; id., 'Pochemu 'Slavianskiĭ Enokh' okazalsia v Nubii?', in A.Kh. Èlert (ed.), *Arkheograficheskie i Istochnikovedcheskie Aspekty v Izuchenii Istorii Rossii. Sbornik Nauchnykh Trudov. Arkheografiia i Istochnikovedenie Sibiri*, Novosibirsk, 2016, pp. 35–42; G. Macaskill, '*2 Enoch*: Manuscripts, Recensions, and Original Language', in A. Orlov and G. Boccaccini (eds), *New Perspectives on 2 Enoch: No Longer Slavonic Only* [Studia Judæoslavica 4], Leiden–Boston, 2012, pp. 83–101; id., *The Slavonic Texts of* 2 Enoch; L. Navtanovich, 'Ѡдьанїе ею и пьнїю раздаанїю v slavianskom perevode Knigi Enokha', in O.V. Tvorogov (ed.), *TODRL* vol. 53, Saint Petersburg, 2003, pp. 3–11; id., 'The Provenance of *2 Enoch*: a Philological Perspective. A Response to Christfried Böttrich's Paper "*The Book of the Secrets of Enoch*: Between Jewish Origin and Christian Transmission. An Overview"', in A. Orlov and G. Boccaccini (eds), *New Perspectives on 2 Enoch: No Longer Slavonic Only* [Studia Judæoslavica 4], Leiden–Boston, 2012, pp. 69–82; A. Orlov, 'Celestial Choirmaster: the Liturgical Role of Enoch-Metatron in *2 Enoch* and the Merkabah Tradition' *JSP* vol. 14, issue 1 (2004), pp. 3–29; id., *The Enoch-Metatron Tradition* [TSAJ, 107], Tübingen, 2005; id., *From Apocalypticism to Merkabah Mysticism: Studies in Slavonic Pseudepigrapha* [JSJSup 114], Leiden–Boston, 2007; id., *Selected Studies in Slavonic Pseudepigrapha*, Leiden–Boston, 2009; id., 'The Sacerdotal Traditions of *2 Enoch* and the Date of the Text', in A. Orlov and G. Boccaccini (eds), *New Perspectives on 2 Enoch: No Longer Slavonic Only*, Leiden–Boston, 2012, pp. 103–116; id., 'The Watchers of Satanail: the Fallen Angels Traditions in *2 Enoch*', in A. Orlov and G. Boccaccini (eds), *New Perspectives on 2 Enoch: No Longer Slavonic Only*, Leiden–Boston, 2012, pp. 149–180; L. Schiffman, '*2 Enoch* and Halakhah', in A. Orlov and G. Boccaccini (eds), *New Perspectives on 2 Enoch: No Longer Slavonic Only* [Studia Judæoslavica 4], Leiden–Boston, 2012, pp. 221–228; D. Stökl Ben Ezra, 'Halakha, Calendars, and the Provenance of *2 Enoch*', in A. Orlov and G. Boccaccini (eds), *New Perspectives on 2 Enoch: No Longer Slavonic Only* [Studia Judæoslavica 4], Leiden–Boston, 2012, pp. 229–242; C.H.T. Fletcher–Louis, '*2 Enoch* and the New Perspective on Apocalyptic', in A. Orlov and G. Boccaccini (eds), *New Perspectives on 2 Enoch: No Longer Slavonic Only* [Studia Judæoslavica 4], Leiden–Boston, 2012, pp. 127–148; A. Stoĭkova, 'Ot Mesopotamiia do Etropole. Transformatsii na mita za gigantskata kosmicheska ptitsa', *SL* vol. 49–50 (2014), pp. 126–168; E. Syrtsova, 'Apokrificheskaia kontseptsiia tvoreniia v Knige Enokha (II)', *VSK* vol. 2 (2014), pp. 49–61.

9   In contrast to some scholars who argue that the translation was made directly from a Hebrew protograph in Kievan Rus'; see N. Meshcherskiĭ, 'Sledy pamiatnikov Kumrana v staroslavianskoĭ i drevnerusskoĭ literature', p. 147; id., 'Problemy izucheniia slaviano-russkoĭ perevodnoĭ literatury XI–XV vv.', p. 191. The present author is in agreement with the argument put forward in H.G. Lunt and M. Taube, 'Early East Slavic Translations from Hebrew', *RL* vol. 12 (1988), p. 181.

well have occurred in Alexandria, and was accomplished most probably by a Hellenised Jew, approximately in the 1st century CE, prior to (or concurrently with) the commencement of the Gnostic movement.[10] Although there is no surviving evidence for the circulation in Byzantium of any manuscripts containing Greek editions of what we now designate as 2 *Enoch*, it would be logical to assume that such types of 'maverick' sources did exist. Having remained steadily under the radar of mainstream scribal convention for centuries, they surfaced once again in the new intellectual landscape of *Slavia Orthodoxa*, the homeland of the final phase in the transmission history of 2 *Enoch*.

The translation of its Greek protograph into Old Bulgarian/Old Church Slavonic, which was originally produced in Glagolitic script, was accomplished no later than the beginning of the 11th century, most probably in one of the monastic scriptoria in the vicinities of Preslav, the then capital of the First Bulgarian Kingdom. The composition circulated in shorter and longer recensions.[11]

---

10   As shown by some scholars, there are close textual parallels between 2 *Enoch* and *The Apocalypse of Zostrianos* (Nag Hammadi VIII.1); see M. Scopello, 'The Apocalypse of Zostrianos (Nag Hammadi VIII.1) and The Book of the Secrets of Enoch', pp. 376–385; id., 'The Angels in Ancient Gnosis: Some Cases', p. 39.

11   Various editions of a number of Church Slavonic text witnesses (both to the longer and shorter recensions of 2 *Enoch*, as well as their abbreviated redactions), along with segments from the composition, were published by A. Popov, *Obzor Khronografov Russkoĭ Redaktsii*, Vyp. 2, Moscow, 1869, pp. 162–169; id., 'Bibliograficheskie Materialy, Sobrannye Andreem Popovym (iv): Iuzhnorusskiĭ Sbornik 1679 goda', p. 67, pp. 75–83, pp. 89–139; S. Novaković, 'Apokrif o Enohu', *Starine* vol. 17 (1884), pp. 70–81; Sokolov, *Slavianskaia Kniga Enokha*, pp. 1–80; id., *Slavianskaia Kniga Enokha Pravednago* (Part 1, pp. 109–161); Ĭord. Ivanov, *Bogomilski Knigi i Legendi*, pp. 165–191; St. Ivšić, 'Hrvatski Glagoljski Apokrif o Melhisedekovu Rođenju i Spasenju Za Općega Potopa', *Nastavni Vjesnik* (Zagreb, Matica Hrvatska), Knjiga 15 (1931/1932), pp. 101–108; A. Vaillant, *Le livre des secrets d'Hénoch*; L. Navtanovich, 'Kniga Enokha', in D.S. Likhachev (ed.), *Biblioteka Literatury Drevneĭ Rusi* vol. 3: *XI–XII veka*, Sankt Peterburg, 2004, pp. 204–241; T. Jovanović, 'Apokrif o Enohu prema Srpskom Prepisu is Narodne Biblioteke u Beču', pp. 224–237; J. Reinhart, 'A Croatian Glagolitic Excerpt of the Slavonic Enoch (2 *Enoch*)', *Fundamenta Europæa* vol. 4 (2007), pp. 31–46; V. Mil'kov and S. Polianskiĭ, *Kosmologicheskie Proizvedeniia v Knizhnosti Drevneĭ Rusi* vol. 2: *Teksty Ploskostno-Komarnoĭ i Drugikh Kosmologicheskikh Traditsiĭ*, Sankt Peterburg, 2009, pp. 459–493; G. Macaskill, *The Slavonic Texts of 2 Enoch*, pp. 38–268. (This list is not complete; for a survey of published text witnesses see the Appendix). For English, German, and French translations of the apocryphon (with commentaries), see W. Morfill, R. Charles, *The Book of the Secrets of Enoch*; G.N. Bonwetsch, *Das slavische Henochbuch*; id., *Die Bücher der Geheimnisse Henochs: Das sogenannte slavische Henochbuch*; A. Vaillant, *Le livre des secrets d'Hénoch. Texte slave et traduction française*; F. Andersen, '2 (*Slavonic Apocalypse*) *of Enoch*. A New Translation and Introduction', pp. 102–221; A. Pennington,

The debate as to whether the longer recension represents an expanded edition of the shorter, or that the shorter is an abridged edition of the longer, is far from over; there is still no consensus among scholars as to whether the longer recension represents the pristine version of the earliest Old Church Slavonic translation of 2 Enoch from Greek (thus preceding the shorter one), or the other way around. The earliest surviving text witnesses are dated to the 14th century.[12]

The main goal of the current discussion is therefore to examine the concept of hermetic knowledge, as interpreted in parabiblical narratives circulating in the Byzantine Commonwealth, and identify the sources facilitating the conversion, transfer and diffusion of certain mythographic templates (the earliest

---

'2 Enoch', pp. 321–362; Ch. Böttrich, *Das slavische Henochbuch*; F. Badalanova Geller, *Second (Slavonic Apocalypse of) Enoch: Text and Context*, Berlin (Preprint 410), 2010; G. Macaskill, *The Slavonic Texts of 2 Enoch*, pp. 269–322. (See further the Appendix.)

12   See also the discussion in N. Schmidt, 'The Two Recensions of *Slavonic Enoch*', pp. 307–312; N. Meshcherskiĭ, 'Sledy pamiatnikov Kumrana v staroslavianskoĭ i drevnerusskoĭ literature (K izucheniiu slavianskikh versiĭ Knigi Enokha)', pp. 130–147; id., 'K istorii teksta slavianskoĭ knigi Enokha', pp. 91–108; Ph. Alexander, 'From Son of Adam to Second God: Transformations of Biblical Enoch', pp. 101–108, pp. 116–117; Ch. Böttrich, 'Recent Studies in the Slavonic *Book of Enoch*', pp. 35–42; id., *Adam als Mikrokosmos: eine Untersuchung zum slavischen Henochbuch*; id., 'Astrologie in der Henochtradition', pp. 222–245; id., 'The Book of the Secrets of Enoch (2 En): Between Jewish Origin and Christian Transmission (An Overview)', pp. 37–67; A. Orlov, 'Celestial Choirmaster: the Liturgical Role of Enoch-Metatron in 2 Enoch and the Merkabah Tradition', pp. 3–29; B. Khristova, *Kniga na Enokh*, Sofia, 2008; F. Badalanova Geller, 'Heavenly Writings: Celestial Cosmography in *The Book of the Secrets of Enoch*', SL vol. 45–46 (2012), pp. 197–244; id., 'Poetics of Errors', in K. Geus and M. Geller, *Productive Errors: Scientific Concepts in Antiquity* [TOPOI—Dahlem Seminar for the History of Ancient Sciences: Max Planck Preprint 430], Berlin, 2012, pp. 207–218; id., 'Geography of Heavens in the Byzantine Commonwealth: the Enochic Chronotope', in K. Geus and M. Thiering (eds), *Common Sense Geography and Mental Modeling* [Max Planck Preprint 426], Berlin, 2012, pp. 74–100; id., 'Recasting the Bible, Recapturing Eden (Parascriptural Cosmologies in the Byzantine Commonwealth)', in E.J.C. Tigchelaar (ed.), *Old Testament Pseudepigrapha and the Scriptures* [BETL 270], Leuven, 2014, pp. 479–482; id., 'Creation Encrypted: Ontology Through Metaphor (*The Books of the Holy Secrets of Enoch the Just*)', in M. Witte and S. Behnke (eds), *The Metaphorical Use of Language in Deuterocanonical and Cognate Literature* [Deuterocanonical and Cognate Literature Yearbook 2014/2015], Berlin–Boston, 2014–2015, pp. 381–409; id., 'Astronomical Knowledge in *The Slavonic Apocalypse of Enoch*: Traces of Ancient Scientific Models', in J. Renn and M. Schemmel (eds), *Culture and Cognition: Essays in Honor of Peter Damerow*, Berlin, 2019, pp. 103–119. Several essays gathered in the collective monograph *New Perspectives on 2 Enoch* (published in 2012 under the editorship of A. Orlov and G. Boccaccini), are valuable and pertinent to the study of Enochic traditions in the Slavonic realm of the Byzantine Commonwealth.

FIGURE 22.1   Witch milking the Moon; fresco from the church of Archangel Michael, Leshko, South-Western Bulgaria. Painted in 1889. The inscription reads: 'А се магесница щото лаже людето ке свале месецо да го мазе въ место месецо дяволо мазе' ('And this is a witch who lies to people, that she takes down the Moon to milk it, but milks [in fact] the Devil').
PHOTO: AUTHOR

attestations of which occur in ancient Enochic literature)[13] through the last *lingua sacra* of Europe, Old Church Slavonic (see Figure 22.1).[14]

---

13 A synoptic overview of Enochic motifs in early Christian literature is produced by J. VanderKam, '1 *Enoch*, Enochic Motifs, and Enoch in Early Christian Literature', in J.C. VanderKam and W. Adler (eds), *The Jewish Apocalyptic Heritage in Early Christianity: Compendia Rerum Iudaicarum Ad Novum Testamentum*, Section III: Jewish Traditions in Early Christian Literature vol. 4, Van Gorcum, 1996, pp. 33–101. For a comparative analysis of passages from and/or references to writings attributed to Enoch in post-biblical Jewish, Christian and Muslim traditions, see J.C. Reeves and A. Yoshiko Reed, *Enoch from Antiquity to the Middle Ages* vol. 1: *Sources From Judaism, Christianity and Islam*, Oxford, 2018.

14 It is most intriguing that there are some parallel mythologemes (e.g. the idolatrous use of heavenly bodies) that occur both in *3 Enoch* 5:7–9, and in vernacular Slavonic witchcraft narratives (e.g. demonological fabulæ of cosmologically-oriented sorceries enabling witches to bring the moon down to earth to serve their will, etc.); these types of parallel mythologemes related to magical aspects in the *3 Enoch* tradition on the one hand, and Slavonic (and Greek) folklore and iconography on the other, are analysed in F. Badalanova Geller, 'Mythographies of the Demonic (Notes on Slavonic and Balkan Ethnohermeneutics)', in J.M. Hartley and D.J.B. Show (eds), *Magic, Texts and Travel. Homage to a Scholar,*

2 Enochic Traditions in *Slavia Orthodoxa*: Tracing Primary Scribal Evidence

2.1 *The Book(s) of Enoch in Old Church Slavonic Indices of Hermetic/Secret Books: The Case of The Symeonic Florilegium*

The first reference to the Enochic apocryphal corpus in *Slavia Orthodoxa* appears in the *Symeonic Florilegium*,[15] the earliest edition of which was com-

---

Will Ryan, London, 2021, pp. 118–123, 126–127. Further on the attestations of the 'Bringing Down the Moon' demonologeme in modern Balkan oral traditions and iconography (without any reference to the Enochic traditions, however), see the discussion in L. Mikov, 'Luna/Krava, Lamia/Viatŭr: Metamorfoza i Tŭzhdestvo', *IIMK* vol. 4, issue 1 (1992), pp. 153–159 and O. Chokha, 'Novogrŭtski i bŭlgarski razkazi za mag'osnitsi, koito svaliat mesechinata', *BF* vol. 3 (2017), pp. 287–299; see also Figure 22.1 above.

15   Its earliest extant copy, the *Sviatoslav's Miscellany* (written in Cyrillic), is dated to 1073. The prevailing scholarly opinion holds that it was made in Kiev for Prince Sviatoslav the Second (hence its conventional designation), on the basis of an earlier—now nonexistant—Bulgarian protograph. The manuscript containing the original Bulgarian edition was most probably taken as booty by his grandfather, Sviatoslav the First (945–972), during his military campaign against the First Bulgarian Kingdom, resulting in the devastation of the capital Preslav in 969; see K. Kuev, 'Poiava i razprostranenie na Simeonoviia sbornik', in P. Dinekov et al. (eds), *Simeonov Sbornik* (*Po Svetoslavoviia Prepis ot 1073*) vol. 1, Sofia, 1991, p. 35. The optico-photographic analysis of the palimpsest of the *Sviatoslav's Miscellany* conducted by palæographers shows that the name of the Kievan Prince Sviatoslav was written over the scratched name of the Bulgarian Tzar Symeon; see I. Levochkin, 'Izbornik Sviatoslava i ego slavianskiĭ protograf', *SL* vol. 8 (1980), pp. 46–49; id., 'Izbornik Sviatoslava 1073—pamiatnik drevnerusskoĭ kul'tury', in L.P. Zhukovskaia (ed.), *Izbornik Sviatoslava 1073* vol. 2: *Nauchnyĭ apparat faksimil'nogo izdaniia*, Moscow, 1983, p. 10. See also the discussion in J. Vrooland and W. Veder, 'O rukopisnoĭ traditsii *Simeonova Sbornika*', *Polata к"nigopis'naia* vol. 35 (2006), p. 70. The codex of the *Sviatoslav's Miscellany* is now part of the Synodal Collection [Синодальное собрание] of the State Historical Museum [Государственный исторический музей] in Moscow, Catalogue № 1043 (f. 80370). Fragments from the Ms. were published for the first time by K. Kalaĭdovich in his monograph *Ioann, Ekzarkh Bolgarskiĭ: Issledovanie, ob'iasniaiushchee istoriiu slovenskogo iazyka i literatury IX i X stoletiĭ*, Moskva, 1824, pp. 102–104, 133–136; a phototype edition of the codex was produced half a century later in Saint Petersburg, with an introduction by Gennadiĭ Karpov; see *Izbornik Velikogo Kniazia Sviatoslava Iaroslavicha 1073 goda*, Peterburg, 1880. In 1883, the first half of the corpus (with Greek parallels and Latin translation) was published in the academic series *ChIOIDR*, кн. 4 [Октябрь-Декабрь 1882], pp. 1–184, under the editorship of the late O. Bodianskiĭ, with an introduction by E. Barsov (ibid., pp. i–xxv), and with commentaries by A. Diuvernua (ibid., pp. 1–32). A century later a facsimile edition of the codex was produced under the editorship of L. Zhukovskaia; see *Izbornik Sviatoslava 1073*, Kn. 1: *Faksimil'noe Izdanie*; Kn. 2: *Nauchnyĭ Apparat Faksimil'nogo Izdaniia*, Moscow, 1983. The present study refers to the Old Church Slavonic edition of the text of the *Symeonic Florilegium / Sviatoslav's Miscellany* (1073) prepared under the editorship of P. Dinekov

piled[16] during the reign of Tzar Symeon (893–927) by scribes belonging to the Preslav Literary School,[17] on the basis of a Greek (Byzantine) *Vorlage*.[18] The editorial work on this encyclopædic compendium was most probably carried

> et al., *Simeonov Sbornik*. Taken into consideration is also the second, updated edition by P. Ianeva et al., *Simeonov Sbornik (Po Svetoslavoviia Prepis ot 1073)* vol. 3: *Grŭtski Izvori*, Sofia, 2015, pp. 119–1221, in which the Old Church Slavonic text is presented together with the parallel Byzantine Greek sources (see also notes 16, 17 and 18 below). For a concise bibliographic survey of editions of the original Church Slavonic Mss. containing the *Symeonic Florilegium*, along with relevant secondary literature, see O. Tvorogov, 'Izbornik 1073', in D.S. Likhachev (ed.), *Slovar' Knizhnikov i Knizhnosti Drevneĭ Rusi*, Vyp. 1: XI—pervaia polovina XIV veka, Leningrad, 1987, pp. 194–196; P. Ianeva et al. (eds); see *Simeonov Sbornik* vol. 3: *Grŭtski Izvori*, pp. 102–108, 1223–1239; M. Dimitrova, 'Bulgarian Studies on the Reception of Byzantine Literature in Medieval Bulgaria', in E. Bakalova, M. Dimitrova and M.A. Johnson (eds), *Medieval Bulgarian Art and Letters in a Byzantine Context*, Sofia, 2017, pp. 323–324. See also http://catalog.shm.ru/entity/OBJECT/178472?fund=21&index=11.

16   As pointed out by scholars, the corpus of the *Florilegium* is extant in Greek (Σωτή-ριος), including the final list of emperors, and the Slavonic version is a translation-by-compilation using extant translations; see the discussion in W. Veder, 'Shest tsitata ot *Lestvitsata*', in V. Panaĭotov et al. (eds), *ΤΡΙΑΝΤΑΦΥΛΛΟ: In Honorem Hristo Trendafilov* [Iubileen sbornik v chest na 60-godishninata na Khristo Trendafilov], Shumen, 2013, pp. 283–294; id., 'Michael Syncellus' *Libellus de recta fide*: Translation and Revision', *RS* 15 (2017), pp. 359–383. For a second translation, see F.J. Thomson, 'A Comparison of the Contents of the Two Translations of the *Symeonic Florilegium* on the Basis of the Greek Original Texts', *KMS* vol. 17 (2007), pp. 721–758. (Courtesy William R. Veder).

17   Further on the *Symeonic Florilegium*, see the discussion in I. Ševčenko, 'Remarks on the Diffusion of Byzantine Scientific and Pseudo-Scientific Literature among the Orthodox Slavs', *SEER* vol. 59, issue 3 (1981), pp. 330–334; H. Lunt, 'On the *Izbornik* of 1073', *HUS* vol. 7 (1983) [= *Okeanos: Essays presented to Ihor Ševčenko on his Sixtieth Birthday by his Colleagues and Students*], pp. 359–376; F. Thomson, 'The *Symeonic Florilegium*: Problems of Its Origin, Content, Textology and Edition (Together with an English Translation of the *Eulogy* of Tzar Symeon)', *Palæobulgarica* vol. 17, issue 1 (1993), pp. 37–53; id., 'A Contribution to the Textology of the *Symeonic Florilegium* (Together with the 'Editio Princeps' of the Part of Anastasian Question 20 Missing in the Codex of 1073)', *Harvard Ukrainian Studies* vol. 28, issues 1–4 (2006) [= *Rus' Writ Large: Languages, Histories, Cultures. Essays Presented in Honor of Michael S. Flier on His Sixty-Fifth Birthday*], pp. 307–327; I. Duĭchev, 'Kŭm izuchavaneto na Izbornika ot 1973', *SL* vol. 5 (1979), pp. 115–122; P. Dinekov, 'Simeonoviiat (Svetoslavoviiat) *Izbornik* 1073 v razvitieto na bŭlgarskata literatura', *SL* vol. 5 (1979), pp. 3–9; id., 'Kulturno-Istoricheskoto Znachenie na Simeonoviia Sbornik', in P. Dinekov et al. (eds), *Simeonov Sbornik*, pp. 9–17; K. Ivanova, 'Simeonoviiat Sbornik Kato Literaturen Pametnik', in *Simeonov Sbornik* pp. 18–33; K. Kuev, 'Arkheografski belezhki za razprostranenieto na Simeonoviia (Svetoslavoviia) sbornik v starite slavianski literaturi', *SL* vol. 5 (1979), pp. 38–56; id., 'Poiava i razprostranenie na Simeonoviia sbornik', pp. 34–98; N. Rozov, 'Stareĭshiĭ bolgarskiĭ *Izbornik* i ego russkaia rukopisnaia traditsiia', *IANSSSR/SLIA* vol. 28, issue 1 (1969), pp. 75–79; I. Levochkin, 'Izbornik Sviatoslava i ego slavianskiĭ protograf', 46–49; id., 'Izbornik Sviatoslava (Simeona) v russkoĭ dorevoliutsion-

ENOCHIC TEXTS AND RELATED TRADITIONS IN SLAVIA ORTHODOXA 463

out in the royal scriptorium, where medieval Bulgarian literati also translated a cluster of other landmarks of Byzantine Greek intellectual thought and scientific culture (e.g. *The Hexæmeron*,[19] *The Exact Exposition of the Orthodox*

noĭ i sovetskoĭ nauke (1817–1982)', *SL* vol. 16 (1984), pp. 33–40; id., 'Izbornik Sviatoslava i russkie sborniki XV–XVII vekov', in D.S. Likhachev (ed.), *TODRL* vol. 40, Leningrad, 1985, pp. 373–378; G. Barankova et al., 'Izbornik Sviatoslava 1073 goda. Nekotorye drevnerusskie i iuzhnoslavianskie cherty rukopisi', in N.I. Tolstoĭ (ed.), *Slavianskoe Iazykoznanie: X Mezhdunarodnyi S"ezd Slavistov (Sofiia 1988). Doklady Sovetskoĭ Delegatsii*, Moscow, 1988, pp. 3–17; A. Iurchenko, 'Izbornik 1073 goda: interpretatsiia osnovnykh drevnerusskikh filosofskikh terminov', *VoprIazyk* vol. 2 (1988), pp. 75–90; D. Likhachev, 'Sud'ba rukopisi *Izbornika* 1073g. v XIV v.', in D.S. Likhachev, A.A. Alekseev and M.A. Salmina (eds), *TODRL* vol. 49, Saint Petersburg, 1996, pp. 297–299; P. Ianeva et al. (eds), *Simeonov Sbornik* vol. 3: *Grŭtski Izvori*, pp. 11–118; J. Vrooland and W. Veder, 'O rukopisnoĭ traditsii *Simeonova Sbornika*', pp. 68–80; A. Angusheva-Tikhanova et al., 'Knizhovnostta po vremeto na Tsar Simeon', in V. Giuzelev, Il. Iliev and K. Nenov (eds), *Bŭlgarskiiat Zlaten Vek. Sbornik V Chest Na Simeon Veliki* (893–927), Plovdiv, 2015, pp. 228–230; S. Temcinas (= Temchin), 'Novyĭ vostochnoslavianskiĭ spisok Izbornika bolgarskogo tsaria Simeona iz Velikogo kniazhestva Litovskogo', *Knygotyra* (Vilnius) vol. 65 (2015), pp. 254–268.

18   See the discussion in M. Bibikov, *Vizantiĭskiĭ Prototip Drevneĭsheĭ Slavianskoĭ Knigi: Izbornik Svyatoslava 1073 g*, Moscow, 1996; P. Ianeva, 'Notions of fate, happiness and unhappiness in Byzantine and Old Bulgarian Cultural Environment (based on material from Tzar Symeon's *Florilegium* and its corresponding Greek anthologies)', in V. Giuzelev and A. Miltenova (eds), *Srednovekovna Khristianska Evropa: Iztok i Zapad*, Sofia, 2002, pp. 586–593; P. Ianeva, S. Ivanov and M. Slavova, *Spasitelna Kniga: Grŭtskiiat Original na Simeonoviia Sbornik: Kniga, Proizkhozhdashta i Sŭstavena ot Razlichni Rechi i Dushepolezni Razkazi, Narechena Spasitelna* [Transl. from Greek, with Introduction and Commentaries by Petia Ianeva and Sergeĭ Ivanov; ed. by Mirena Slavova], Sofia, 2008; P. Ianeva and S. Ivanov, 'Dubliranite pasazhi v *Izbornika* ot 1073', *Godishnik na Sofiĭskiia Universitet "Sv. Kliment Okhridksi" (Tsentŭr za Slaviano-Vizantiĭski prouchvaniia "Ivan Duĭchev")* vol. 96/15 (2009), pp. 173–180; F. Thomson, 'A Comparison of the Contents of the Two Translations of the Symeonic Florilegium on the Basis of the Greek Original Texts', *KMS* vol. 17 (2007), pp. 721–758; id., 'The Symeonic Florilegium: An Analysis of Its Relation to the Greek Textological Tradition and Its Association with Tsar Symeon, Together with an Excursus on the Old Believers and the Codex of 1073', *KMS* vol. 18 (2009), pp. 248–308. The recent collective monograph by P. Ianeva et al. (eds), *Simeonov Sbornik* vol. 3: *Grŭtski Izvori*, offers concise textological analysis of the Greek Byzantine counterparts of the *Symeonic Florilegium* (i.e. *Coislinianus græcus* 120, *Coislinianus græcus* 258, *Vaticanus grækus* 423, *Ambrosianus græcus* 489, olim L 88 sup, along with *Athous Lauræ G* 115).

19   Assembled by John the Exarch, one of the most prominent scholars of the Preslav Literary School, the compilation offers the earliest Old Bulgarian/Old Church Slavonic edition of translated fragments from the *Homiliæ in Hexæmeron* of Basil of Cæsarea (ca. 329–379) and *In Cosmogoniam homiliæ* of Severian of Gabala (ca. 380–ca. 408/425). The authorship of the selected excerpts from Severian's *Homilies*, however, is ascribed to John Chrysostom. As pointed out by scholars, the Greek protograph used by John the Exarch must have followed the contemporary Byzantine scribal tradition of pseudepigraphic

Faith of John Damascene,[20] several collections of excerpts from the *Homilies* of John Chrysostom (*Chryssorrhoas*),[21] along with *The Chronography of*

---

attribution of the authorship of Severian's *Homilies* to John Chrysostom; see V. Mil'kov and S. Polianskiĭ, *Kosmologicheskie Proizvedeniia v Knizhnosti Drevneĭ Rusi* vol. 2: *Teksty Ploskostno-Komarnoĭ i Drugikh Kosmologicheskikh Traditsiĭ*, p. 94. Included in the content of John the Exarch's *Hexœmeron* are also selected excerpts from the Byzantine redaction of Aristotle's *History of Animals*, along with some other compositions. For text editions of John the Exarch's *Hexœmeron*, see R. Aitzetmüller, *Das Hexœmeron des Exarchen Johannes. Editiones monumentorum slavicorum veteris dialecti*. Bd. 1–6, Graz, 1958–1975. For other editions of the Old Church Slavonic text (with translation into modern Russian and commentary apparatus), see G. Barankova and V. Mil'kov, *Shestodnev Ioanna Ekzarkha Bolgarskogo*, Sankt Petersburg, 2001; V. Mil'kov and S. Polianskiĭ, *Kosmologicheskie Proizvedeniia v Knizhnosti Drevneĭ Rusi* vol. 1: *Teksty Geotsentricheskoĭ Traditsiĭ*, Sankt Peterburg, 2008, pp. 125–209; vol. 2: *Teksty Ploskostno-Komarnoĭ i Drugikh Kosmologicheskikh Traditsiĭ*, pp. 120–157. See also the discussion in Ts. Cholova, *Estestvenonauchnite znaniia v Srednovekovna Bŭlgariia*, Sofia, 1988, pp. 16–22, 35–36; V. Mil'kov and S. Polianskiĭ, *Kosmologicheskie Proizvedeniia v Knizhnosti Drevneĭ Rusi* vol. 1: *Teksty Geotsentricheskoĭ Traditsiĭ*, pp. 21–24, 110–124; vol. 2: *Teksty Ploskostno-Komarnoĭ i Drugikh Kosmologicheskikh Traditsiĭ*, pp. 9–10, 87–91, 117–119; L. Sels and S. Van Pee, 'Scholia from Severian of Gabala's *In Cosmogoniam homiliœ* in the 14th-century Slavonic *Hexœmeron* Collection', in A. Angusheva, M. Dimitrova et al. (eds), *Vis et Sapientia: Studia in honorem Anisavœ Miltenova*, Sofia, 2016, pp. 89–110; Kh. Trendafilov, *Tsar i Vek: Vremeto na Simeona (Chetiri Instalatsii)*, Shumen, 2017, pp. 231, 445–446. For a concise bibliographical survey of publications on John the Exarch's *Hexœmeron*, see G. Prokhorov, 'Shestodnevy', in D.S. Likhachev (ed.), *Slovar' Knizhnikov i Knizhnosti Drevneĭ Rusi*, Vyp. 1: *XI—Pervaia Polovina XIV Veka*, Leningrad, 1987, pp. 481–483; V. Mil'kov and S. Polianskiĭ, *Kosmologicheskie Proizvedeniia v Knizhnosti Drevneĭ Rusi* vol. 2: *Teksty Ploskostno-Komarnoĭ i Drugikh Kosmologicheskikh Traditsiĭ*, pp. 91–94; M. Dimitrova, 'Bulgarian Studies on the Reception of Byzantine Literature in Medieval Bulgaria', pp. 319–321. See also the discussion below (§2.4).

20   The Slavonic designation of John of Damascus's Ἔκθησις ἀκριβὴς τῆς ὀρθοδόξου πίστεως (= *De Fide Orthodoxa*) is rendered either as *Богословие* [*Theology*], or *Небеса* [*Heavens*]. The translation into Old Bulgarian/Old Church Slavonic was made by John the Exarch. For editions of the text, see L. Sadnik, *Des Hl. Johannes von Damaskus* Ἔκθησις ἀκριβὴς τῆς ὀρθοδόξου πίστεως *in der Übersetzung des Exarchen Johannes* vol. 1: *Monumenta Linguœ Slavicœ Dialecti Veteris* 5, Wiesbaden: Harrassowitz, 1967; vol. 2: *Monumenta Linguœ Slavicœ Dialecti Veteris* 14; vol. 3: *Monumenta Linguœ Slavicœ Dialecti Veteris* 16; vol. 4: *Monumenta Linguœ Slavicœ Dialecti Veteris* 17, Freiburg, 1981–1984. Fragments from the Old Bulgarian/Old Church Slavonic corpus (with translation into modern Russian and commentaries) are published by V. Mil'kov and S. Polianskiĭ, *Kosmologicheskie Proizvedeniia v Knizhnosti Drevneĭ Rusi* vol. 1: *Teksty Geotsentricheskoĭ Traditsiĭ*, pp. 51–109. See also the discussion in F. Thomson, 'John the Exarch's theological education and proficiency in Greek as revealed by his abridged translation of John of Damascus's *De Fide Orthodoxa*', *Palœobulgarica* vol. 15, issue 1 (1991), pp. 35–58; Kh. Trendafilov, '*Nebesa* Ioanna Ekzarkha kak porozhdaiushchaia model' (obzor spiskov i struktura teksta)', in T. Totev (ed.), *1100*

ENOCHIC TEXTS AND RELATED TRADITIONS IN SLAVIA ORTHODOXA   465

John Malalas,[22] *The Chronography of George Hamartolos,*[23] *The Chronography of George Synkellos* (containing abridged edited fragments from *The Chroni-*

Godini Veliki Preslav vol. 2, Shumen, 1995, pp. 60–90; id., 'Perevody *Bogosloviia* Ioanna Damaskina v russkoĭ i slavianskoĭ filologii', in A.A. Alekseev et al. (eds), TODRL vol. 50, Sankt Peterburg, 1996, pp. 658–667; id., '*Bogoslovie* Ioanna Damaskina v perevode Ioanna Ekzarkha Bolgarskogo (*Nebesa*) i original'nye proizvedeniia drevnerusskoĭ literatury XI–XVI vv.', *PrKnSh* vol. 3, Shumen, 1998, pp. 85–118; id., 'Ioann Ekzarkh i stanovlenie slavianskogo teologicheskogo monologizma', in A. Angusheva and A. Miltenova (eds), *Medievistika i Kulturna Antropologiia. Sbornik v chest na 40-godishnata tvorcheska deĭsnost na Prof. Donka Petkanova*, Sofia, 1998, pp. 154–161; id., 'Predislovie Ioanna Ekzarkha Bolgarskogo k perevodu *Bogosloviia* (*Nebesa*) Ioanna Damaskina v drevnerusskoĭ rukopisnoĭ traditsii', in V.M. Zagrebin (ed.), *Rus' i Iuzhnye Slaviane. Sbornik Stateĭ k 100-letiiu so Dnia Rozhdeniia V.A. Moshina (1894–1994)*, Sankt Peterburg, 1998, pp. 305–313; id., *Ioann Ekzarkh Bŭlgarski*, Sofia, 2001; id., '*Nebesa* Ioanna Ekzarkha Bolgarskogo v drevnerusskoĭ rukopisnoĭ traditsii', in *Glubini Knizhnie* vol. 2, Shumen, 2004, pp. 9–73; id., *Tsar i Vek: Vremeto na Simeona*, p. 242; V. Mil'kov and S. Polianskiĭ, *Kosmologicheskie Proizvedeniia v Knizhnosti Drevneĭ Rusi* vol. 1: *Teksty Geotsentricheskoĭ Traditsii*, pp. 43–50; T. Ilieva, *Terminologichnata Leksika v Ioan–Ekzarkhoviia Prevod na "De Fide Orthodoxa"* Sofia, 2013.

21   See F. Thomson, 'The Nature of the Reception of Christian Byzantine Culture in Russia in the Tenth to Thirteenth Centuries and Its Implications for Russian Culture', *Slavia Gandensia* vol. 5 (1978), pp. 109–110; Kh. Trendafilov, *Tsar i Vek: Vremeto na Simeona*, pp. 227–228; M. Dimitrova, 'Bulgarian Studies on the Reception of Byzantine Literature in Medieval Bulgaria', pp. 327–328.

22   Cf. V.M. Istrin, 'Pervaia Kniga Khroniki Ioanna Malaly', *Zapiski Imperatorskoĭ Akademii Nauk*, Seriia 8: *Istoriko-Filologicheskoe Otdelenie* vol. 1: 3 (1897), pp. 1–29; M. Chernysheva (ed.), *Khronika Ioanna Malaly v slavianskom perevode*. Reprintnoe izdanie V.M. Istrina. Podgotovka izdaniia, vstupitel'naia stat'ia i prilozheniia M.I. Chernyshevoĭ, Moscow, 1994. Malalas's corpus is the earliest extant representative of the Byzantine chronographic genre. Scholars suggest that the author makes use of some earlier sources (e.g. the *Ecclesiastical History* of Eusebius of Cæsarea, the *Chronological Epitome* of Eustathius of Epiphania, etc.). Apart from the 'classic' annals from Creation until the reign of Justinian I (482–565), this historical synopsis contains an idiosyncratic mythographic account devoted to the Hellenistic pantheon (with an elaborate list of deities functioning as heroes-demiurges). Woven into the fabric of the *Chronography* is also a picturesque tale describing the events of the Trojan War (thus further transmitting Homeric tradition). It has been suggested that this particular portion of Malalas's corpus most probably recycles a number of sources, the purported authorship of which may be attributed either to one of the legendary contemporaries of Idomeneus (one of Helen's suitors), Dictys of Crete (*Dictys Cretensis Ephemeris belli Trojani*), or to the no less mysterious Dares Phrygius (*Daretis Phrygii de excidio Trojæ historia*), or to some other writers working in the Mediterranean world in Late Antiquity. In any case, Malalas's rendition of the history of the Trojan War became one of the 'bestsellers' among the elite circles of medieval Bulgaria, and in particular in Symeon's court; see Ĭ. Moskova, '*Troianskiiat Tsikŭl* v traktovkata na Ĭoan Malala', *PrKnSh* vol. 9 (2006), pp. 257–269. Furthermore, according to the domesticated editions of Malalas's tale of the Trojan War, the ethnicity of 'the Bulgarians' is identical to that of 'the Myrmidons', the warriors of Achilles; see ibid., pp. 267–268. Further on *The Chronogra-*

cle of Julius Africanus),[24] together with works like *The Christian Topography of Cosmas Indicopleustes*,[25] etc.). This remarkable undertaking was certainly con-

phy of John Malalas in *Slavia Orthodoxa*, see O. Tvorogov, 'Antichnye mify v drevnerusskoĭ literature XI–XIV vekov', in D.S. Likhachev (ed.), *TODRL* vol. 33 (1977), pp. 6–20; D. Bulanin, *Antichnye Traditsii v Drevnerusskoĭ Literature XI–XVI vv.* [Slavistische Beiträge, Band 278], München, 1991, pp. 30–34, 41–44, 53; Ĭord. Moskova, 'Mitologichni motivi v Khronikata na Ĭoan Malala za proizkhoda na tsarskata institutsiia i na vladetelskite insignia', *PrKnSh* vol. 12 (2012), pp. 210–221; id., 'Geroite ot antichnata mitologiia spored Khronikata na Ĭoan Malala', in Tz. Ianakieva et al. (eds), *Quadrivium: In Honorem Veselin Panaĭotov*, Shumen, 2016, pp. 237–257; id., 'Simvolikata na khipodruma v Svetovnata Khronika na Ĭoan Malala', *PrKnSh* vol. 18 (2018), pp. 211–216; D. Peev, 'Portretni opisaniia i lichnostni kharakteristiki v Khronikata na Ĭoan Malala', *PrKnSh* vol. 9 (2006), pp. 270–293. For a brief survey of primary and secondary sources, see O. Tvorogov, 'Khronika Ioanna Malaly', in D.S. Likhachev (ed.), *Slovar' Knizhnikov i Knizhnosti Drevneĭ Rusi*, Vyp. 1: XI—pervaia polovina XIV veka, Leningrad, 1987, pp. 471–474.

23   *The Chronography of George Hamartolos* was translated in Bulgaria during the reign of Tsar Symeon by unnamed scribe(s)/scholar(s) of the Preslav literary school; see the discussion in R. Stankov, 'Drevnebolgarskiĭ perevod Khroniki Georgiia Amartola v drevnerusskoĭ pis'mennoĭ traditsii', *SL* vol. 39–40 (2008), pp. 45–103; id., 'Drevnebolgarskiĭ perevod Khroniki Georgiia Amartola i Khronograf po Velikomu Izlozheniiu', *PrKnSh* vol. 12 (2012), pp. 191–209; id.,'Iz nabliudeniĭ nad leksikoĭ drevnebolgarskogo perevoda Khroniki Georgiia Amartola', in V. Panaĭotov et al. (eds), *ΤΡΙΑΝΤΑΦΥΛΛΟ: In Honorem Hristo Trendafilov*, Shumen, 2013, pp. 327–332; V. Zheliazkova, 'Edin paralel mezhdu Kniga Izkhod, Simeonoviia Sbornik i Khronikata na Georgi Amartol', *PrKnSh* vol. 10 (2008), pp. 266–280; Kh. Trendafilov, *Tsar i Vek: Vremeto na Simeona*, p. 229; D. Bulanin, *Antichnye Traditsii v Drevnerusskoĭ Literature XI–XVI vv.*, pp. 37, 43–44; M. Dimitrova, 'Bulgarian Studies on the Reception of Byzantine Literature in Medieval Bulgaria', pp. 361 (note 235). Among the first to publish Russian redactions of *The Chronography of George Hamartolos* was V.M. Istrin, *Knigy Vremennyia i obraznyia Georgiia Mnikha: Khronika Georgiia Amartola v drevnem slaviano-russkom perevode* (Tekst, izsledovanie i slovar'), Tom 1, Petrograd, 1920; see also the edition provided by T. Anisimova, *Khronika Georgiia Amartola v drevnerusskikh spiskakh XIV–XV vv.*, Москва, 2009.

24   See Kh. Trendafilov, 'Nabliudeniia vŭrkhu Slavianskiia Prevod na Khronikata na Georgi Sinkel', *Palæobulgarica* vol. 14, issue 4 (1990), pp. 100–110; id., *Tsar i Vek: Vremeto na Simeona*, p. 228; A. Totomanova, *Slavianskata Versiia na Khronikata na Georgi Sinkel: Izdanie i Komentar*, Sofia, 2008; id., 'A Lost Byzantine Chronicle in Slavic Translation', *SC* vol. 1 (2011), pp. 191–204; id., 'The Chronicle of Julius Africanus in Slavic Translation', Scripta & e-Scripta vol. 19–11 (2012), pp. 237–246; id., 'Nazvaniiata na bibleĭskite knigi v slavianski ekstserpt ot Khronikata na Iulii Afrikan', *Palæobulgarica* vol. 38, issue 1 (2014), pp. 45–53. See also the discussion below (§ 2.3). Because of significant divergences between the original Greek edition of *The Chronography of George Synkellos* [Ἐκλογὴ Χρονογραφίας] and its heavily redrafted Slavonic version, we prefer to designate the latter compilation as *The Slavonic Derivative of the Chronicle of George Synkellos*.

25   Translated in the Preslav Literary Centre most probably in the 10th century; see Kh. Trendafilov, *Tsar i Vek: Vremeto na Simeona*, pp. 227–228. For a survey of extant Slavonic Mss. and critical text-edition of one of the witnesses, with commentaries, see V.V. Mil'kov and S.M. Polianskiĭ, *Kosmologicheskie Proizvedeniia v Knizhnosti Drevneĭ Rusi* vol. 2: *Teksty*

sidered by the ambitious Bulgarian ruler to be of highest priority and utmost importance for his reputation as an erudite sovereign of a mighty kingdom, the intellectual standing of which was to challenge that of glorious Byzantium. Indeed, at that time the *Florilegia* were rather fashionable among the men of letters of the 'upper-crust' *Orbis Orthodoxus*. Since Symeon himself had spent his formative years in the famous School of Magnaura, which was conventionally attended by the prosperous youth of the imperial nobility, it was no doubt his ultimate ambition to acquire for his library all the mandatory items of contemporary literature which his Byzantine counterparts had in their possession. It was a matter of prestige; and, of course, prestige has always been the precious commodity bolstering the reputation of statesmen. The library of the Bulgarian Tzar Symeon—praised as a 'new Ptolemy' in the solemn *Eulogy*[26] included in the *Florilegium* (which, needless to say, was commissioned by him)—was supposed to attest not only to his erudition, but also to his impeccable image as a key player in the socio-political games shaping the *mappa mundi* of contemporary *Pax Christiana*.[27] Although he was regarded by his Greek contemporaries as an endless source of trouble,—an adversary as dangerous as he was unpredictable,—Symeon was first and foremost a sophisticated, learned offspring of Byzantium, whose intellectual pedigree stemmed straight from the heart of elitist Constantinople.[28] In fact, his tutor was none other than the most prolific theologian of his time, the eminent Patriarch Photios (ca. 810–ca. 893),

---

    Ploskostno-Komarnoĭ i Drugikh Kosmologicheskikh Traditsiĭ, pp. 22–86. See also the general discussion in W. Wolska-Conus, *La topographie chrétienne de Cosmas Indicopleustes: théologie et sciences au Vɪe siècle* vol. 3, Bibliothèque Byzantine, Paris, 1962.

26   Cf. F. Thomson, '*The Symeonic Florilegium*: Problems of Its Origin, Content, Textology and Edition (Together with an English Translation of the *Eulogy* of Tzar Symeon)', pp. 37–53.

27   The royal library of Symeon was most probably a repository of different types of Mss. written in either Old Bulgarian/Old Church Slavonic, or in Greek. The books gathered in the Greek collection must have been imported, of course, from Byzantium. As for the items in Slavonic—they were either translations from Greek, or compilations made on the basis of domesticated editions of such translations, or original Slavonic compositions written by intellectuals belonging to the local Preslav Literary School. On the hypothetical reconstruction of the list of titles that the royal library of Symeon may have contained, see Kh. Trendafilov, *Tsar i Vek*: *Vremeto na Simeona*, pp. 418–420, 430–447.

28   See in this connection the recent discussion in P. Angelov, 'Obrazŭt na Tsar Simeon vŭv vizantiĭskata knizhnina', in V. Giuzelev, Il. Iliev and K. Nenov (eds), *Bŭlgarskiiat Zlaten Vek. Sbornik V Chest Na Simeon Veliki* [893–927], Plovdiv, 2015, pp. 331–346; A. Angusheva-Tikhanova et al., 'Knizhovnostta po vremeto na Tsar Simeon', pp. 213–276; Kh. Trendafilov, *Mladosttta na Tsar Simeon*, Sofia, 2010; id., *Tsar i Vek*: *Vremeto na Simeona*; M. Kaĭmakamova, 'Svetovnata istoriia v propagandnata politika na Tsar Simeon Veliki i razvitieto na bŭlgarskata khronografiia', in V. Giuzelev, Il. Iliev and K. Nenov (eds), *Bŭlgarskiiat Zlaten Vek. Sbornik V Chest Na Simeon Veliki* [893–927], Plovdiv, 2015, pp. 301–330.

whose authority profoundly influenced not only the Bulgarian Tzar, but also the production of the Preslav Literary School. Furthermore, the current research shows that some works featuring in the content of the *Symeonic Florilegium* were analogous to those included in Photios's *Bibliotheca* (*Myriobiblon*).[29]

To sum up, the *Symeonic Florilegium* was meant to be part of the royal celebrated library in Preslav reflecting the Byzantine imperial model; it was designed as an anthology containing diverse articles dealing with various spheres of knowledge. An emblematic representative of its genre, it was assembled as an exegetical compendium of erotapocritical[30] and gnomological, homiletic and apophthegmatic texts discussing matters related to Christian theology and ethics, doctrinal education, grammar and rhetoric,[31] philosophy[32] and science (including astronomy[33] and calendrical data,[34] mineralogy[35] and

29   See P. Ianeva, 'Bibliotekata na Patriarkh Fotiĭ i *Simeonoviia Sbornik*', in E. Gergova (ed.), *Medievistichni Rakursi: Topos i enigma v kulturata na pravoslavnite slaviani*, Sofia, 1993, pp. 28–32; Kh. Trendafilov, *Mladostta na Tsar Simeon*, pp. 23–32; A. Totomanova, 'A Lost Byzantine Chronicle in Slavic Translation', pp. 202–203.

30   E.g. Pseudo–Anastasian's *Quæstiones et responsiones*; see K. Ivanova, 'Simeonoviiat Sbornik Kato Literaturen Pametnik', pp. 19–21, 23–24, 27; F. Thomson, 'A Contribution to the Textology of the *Symeonic Florilegium* Together with the 'Editio Princeps' of the Part of Anastasian Question 20 Missing in the Codex of 1073', pp. 307–327.

31   E.g. George Choiroboskos's treatise *On Poetic Figures* (Περὶ τρόπων). In the *Symeonic Florilegium*, the title is rendered as Геѡрьгнꙗ Хоуровьска о ѡбраꙁѣхъ. The text is copied on fols 237–240 of *Sviatoslav's Miscellany*; see P. Ianeva et al. (eds), *Simeonov Sbornik* vol. 3: *Grŭtski Izvori*, pp. 1100–1113. Among the first to prepare an edition of the original Old Church Slavonic text of Choiroboskos's treatise (on the basis of *Sviatoslav's Miscellany*) was the Bulgarian scholar B. St. Angelov, who published it together with the original Greek text (Γεωργίου Χοιροβοσκοῦ περὶ τρόπων) in his study 'Georgi Khirovosk: *Za poeticheskite figuri*'; see ibid., *Iz starata bŭlgarska, ruska i srŭbska literatura*, Kn. 2, Sofia, 1967, pp. 89–105. See also the discussion in E. Velkovska, 'Traktatŭt na Georgi Khirovosk *Za tropite*, negoviiat slavianski prevod i vizantiĭskata ritoricheska traditsiia', *SL* vol. 19 (1986), pp. 75–83; K. Ivanova, 'Simeonoviiat Sbornik Kato Literaturen Pametnik', pp. 27–28. For the translation of the text into modern Russian (with commentaries), see K. Maksimovich, 'O Tropakh ili Ob Oborotakh Rechi: Traktat Georgiia Khirovoska v *Izbornike* Sviatoslava 1073. (Perevod i kommentariĭ)', in *Istoriko-Kul'turnyĭ Aspekt Leksikologicheskogo Opisaniia Russkogo Iazyka* vol. 1, Moscow, 1991, pp. 112–119.

32   On philosophical terminology attested in the *Symeonic Florilegium*, see A. Iurchenko, 'Izbornik 1073 goda: interpretatsiia osnovnykh drevnerusskikh filosofskikh terminov', pp. 75–90.

33   See W. Ryan, *The Bathhouse at Midnight. An Historical Survey of Magic and Divination in Russia*, Phoenix Mill–Thrupp–Stroud, 1999, p. 376, pp. 384–385; Iv. Dobrev, 'Redŭt na Zodiakalnite Znatsi v *Izbornika* ot 1073', *SL* vol. 5 (1979), pp. 101–106; El. Musakova, 'Redŭt na zodiakalnite znatsi v Simeonoviia sbornik (Svetoslavov prepis ot 1073): opit za rekonstruktsiia', *Palæobulgarica* vol. 16, issue 2 (1992), pp. 123–132.

34   See W. Ryan, *The Bathhouse at Midnight*, p. 381.

35   E.g. the treatise *On the Twelve Stones* (Περὶ τῶν δώδεκα λίθων, *De duodecim gemmis*) of

medicine,[36] dietary prescriptions and proscriptions,[37] etc.), along with dogmatic patristic writings.[38]

It is in one of the concluding chapters of the *Symeonic Florilegium* where the earliest reference to the Enochic traditions in *Slavia Orthodoxa* is found, in the fragment entitled 'These [books] are [considered] hermetic / secret / esoteric'[39] [ѩлнкоже съкровьнъıнхъ],[40] the authorship of which is attributed to Isidore (of Pelusium?) (d. ca. 450). In fact, *Enoch* is listed at the very top of the *Index*, coming in second position after the *Vita Adæ*:

ѩлнкоже съкровьнъıнхъ · адамъ ·Ḃ· ѩнохъ ·Г̇· малехъ ·Д̇· патрьарсн ·Е̇· молнтва носнфова ·Ѕ̇· ѩлдад ·Ż· ҁавѣтъ мооусннъ ·Н̇· въсходъ мооуснн

Epiphanius of Salamis; on the reception history of this text in *Slavia Orthodoxa*, see I. Trifonova, 'Za dvanadesette kamŭka (*De duodecim gemmis*) na Epfaniĭ Kipŭrski v sŭstava na iuzhnoslavianskata tŭlkovna redaktsiia na Apokalipsisa', *Palæobulgarica* vol. 42, issue 4 (2018), pp. 73–90.

36   See also the discussion in I.A. Gerasimova, V.V. Mil'kov and R.A. Simonov, *Sokrovennye Znaniia Drevneĭ Rusi*, Moscow, 2015, pp. 166–167.

37   On the explication of temporal characteristics of dietology (in relation to months) in the *Symeonic Florilegium*, see Ts. Cholova, *Estestvenonauchnite znaniia v Srednovekovna Bŭlgariia*, pp. 288–290; W. Ryan, *The Bathhouse at Midnight*, p. 381; I.A. Gerasimova, V.V. Mil'kov and R.A. Simonov, *Sokrovennye Znaniia Drevneĭ Rusi*, pp. 356–364.

38   Included in the *Symeonic Florilegium* are fragments from works of Justin Martyr, Irenæus of Lyons, Clement of Alexandria, Athanasius of Alexandria, Cyril of Alexandria, Basil of Cæsarea (Basil the Great), Gregory of Nazianzus (Gregory the Theologian), John Chrysostom, etc.; see K. Ivanova, 'Simeonoviiat Sbornik Kato Literaturen Pametnik', p. 21.

39   Var. 'Those of [books] which are [considered] hidden / apocryphal'; in Western scholarship designated as *The Index of Prohibited / Proscribed Books* [Lat. *Index Librorum Prohibitorum*] (see also the discussion below). For a general survey of various redactions (and Mss. copies) of these types of *Indices* in *Slavia Orthodoxa*, see A. Iatsimirskiĭ, *Bibliograficheskiĭ Obzor Apokrifov v Iuzhnoslavianskoĭ i Russkoĭ Pis'mennosti*, pp. 1–75; B. Angelov, 'Spisŭkŭt na zabranenite knigi v starobŭlgarskata literatura', *IIBL* vol. 1 (1952), pp. 107–159; B. Semenovker, 'Grecheskie spiski istinnykh i lozhnykh knig i ikh retseptsii na Rusi', in D.S. Likhachev (ed.), *TODRL* vol. 40, Leningrad, 1985, pp. 206–228; I. Gritsevskaia, *Indeksy Istinnykh Knig*, Saint Petersburg, 2003; id., 'Indeksy istinnykh i lozhnykh knig v Volokolamskom monastyre', in N.V. Ponyrko (ed.), *TODRL* vol. 58, Saint Petersburg, 2008, pp. 494–504; I. Gritsevskaya, 'Some Problems of Textology of Indexes of Prohibited Books', in L. DiTommaso and Ch. Böttrich (eds), *The Old Testament Apocrypha in the Slavonic Tradition: Continuity and Diversity*, Tübingen, 2011, pp. 201–223; I.A. Gerasimova, V.V. Mil'kov and R.A. Simonov, *Sokrovennye Znaniia Drevneĭ Rusi*, pp. 253–257. See also F. Thomson, 'The Nature of the Reception of Christian Byzantine Culture in Russia in the Tenth to Thirteenth Centuries and Its Implications for Russian Culture', p. 123 (note 21).

40   *The Index of Hermetic/Secret/Esoteric Books* is copied on Fol. 254 of the *1073 Sviatoslav's Miscellany* codex from the Synodal Collection of the State Historical Museum in Moscow (Catalogue № 1043, f. 8037); see also note 15 above.

·Ѳ· ѱалмосн соломонн ·Ĩ· нлнннo oбавленнιє ·Ĩа· нсаннно вндѣннιє ·Ĩв· софонннно oбавленнιє ·Ĩг· ҁахарннно ιавленнιє ·Д̃і· нιаковла повѣсть ·Ĩĕ· петрово oбавленнιє ·Ĩѕ· oбьходн н oуұеннιа аплска ·Н̃і· варнавлe посыла-ннιε ·Ĩѳ· дѣιаннιε пауле ·К̃· паулово oбавленнιε ·К̃а· oуұеннιε клментово ·К̃в· нгнатово oуұеннιε ·К̃г· полоукарпово oуұеннιε ·К̃д· еуаггелнιε oтъ варнавъ ·К̃ĕ· еуаггелнιε oтъ матѳеа.[41]

These [books] are [considered] hermetic/secret:[42] [first,] *Adam* ⟨*Adamъ*⟩;[43] second, [*The Book(s) of*] *Enoch* ⟨*Ienokhъ*⟩; third, *Malech* ⟨*Ma-lekhъ* (*Lamech?*)⟩;[44] fourth, [*The Testaments of the Twelve*] *Patriarchs*

---

41   Cf. Dinekov et al. (eds), *Simeonov Sbornik* vol. 1, p. 701; see also P. Ianeva et al. (eds), *Simeonov Sbornik* vol. 3: *Grŭtski Izvori*, pp. 1166–1167.

42   Var. 'esoteric'/'treasured'/'hidden'/'apocryphal'; see the discussion below.

43   Unclear; it either refers to *The Life of Adam and Eve* (which in Greek tradition is conventionally designated as *The Apocalypse of Moses*), or to another apocryphal composition, such as *The Book About the Daughters of Adam*: *Leptogenesis* (i.e. *The Book of Jubilees*), *The Book Which is Called the Penitence of Adam*, *The Apocalypse of Adam*, etc. (as listed in the so-called *Decretum Gelasianum*, for instance); see W. Schneemelcher (ed.), *New Testament Apocrypha* vol. 1: *Gospels and Related Writings* [Revised edition ed. by Wilhelm Schneemelcher; English translation edited by R. McL. Wilson], Cambridge, 1990, p. 39. See further M.D. Johnson, 'Life of Adam and Eve', in J.H. Charlesworth (ed.), *The Old Testament Pseudepigrapha* vol. 2: *Expansions of the 'Old Testament' and Legends, Wisdom and Philosophical Literature, Prayers, Psalms, and Odes, Fragments of Lost Judeo–Hellenistic Works*, Garden City, N.Y., 1985, pp. 249–295; G.A. Anderson and M. Stone (eds), *A Synopsis of the Books of Adam and Eve* (Second Revised Edition) [Society of Biblical Literature. Early Judaism and Its Literature, № 17], Atlanta, Ga., 1994; G.A. Anderson, M. Stone and J. Tromp (eds), *Literature on Adam and Eve*, Leiden–Boston–Köln, 2000; B. Murdoch, *The Apocryphal Adam and Eve in Medieval Europe: Vernacular Translations and Adaptations of the Vita Adæ et Evæ*, Oxford Press, 2009. For Slavonic redactions of *The Life of Adam and Eve*, see N.S. Tikhonravov, *Pamiatniki Otrechennoĭ Russkoĭ Literatury* vol. 1, Sankt Petersburg, 1863, pp. 1–18, 298–304; Ĭ. Ivanov, *Bogomilski Knigi i Legendi*, pp. 207–227. See also the discussion in F. Badalanova Geller, 'The Sea of Tiberias: Between Apocryphal Literature and Oral Tradition', in L. DiTommaso and Ch. Böttrich (eds), *The Old Testament Apocrypha in the Slavonic Tradition: Continuity and Diversity*, Tübingen, 2011, p. 14 (note 9).

44   In some redactions of the *Index* the name *Malekh* is replaced (due to metathesis) by that of *Lamekh*. On the other hand, it can be suggested that the term *Malekh* is a hypochoriston referring to the apocryphal *Legend about Melchisedek*, the purported authorship of which is attributed to Saint Athanasius of Alexandria [*О том же Мелхиседеке сказание святого Афанасия Александрийского*]; see N. Tikhonravov, *Pamiatniki Otrechennoĭ Russkoĭ Literatury* vol. 1, Sankt Petersburg, 1863, pp. 26–31; I. Porfir'ev, 'Apokrificheskie Skazaniia o Vetkhozavetnykh Litsakh i Sobytiiakh po Rukopisiam Solovetskoĭ Biblioteki', *SbORIS* vol. 17, issue 1 (1877), pp. 53–55, 131–135, 222–225, 256–259; Iv. Franko, *Apokrifi i Legendi z Ukraïnskikh Rukopisiv* (*Codex Apocryphus e manuscriptis ukraino-russicis collectus*

ENOCHIC TEXTS AND RELATED TRADITIONS IN SLAVIA ORTHODOXA

⟨*Patriarsi*⟩;[45] fifth, *Joseph's Prayer* ⟨*Molitva Iosifova*⟩;[46] sixth, *Eldad* [*and Modad*] ⟨*Ieldad*⟩;[47] seventh, *The Testament of Moses* ⟨*Zavětъ Mousinъ*⟩;[48] eighth, *The Assumption of Moses*[49] ⟨*Vъskhodъ Mousiin*⟩;[50] ninth, *The Psalms* [*and Odes*] *of Solomon* ⟨*Psalmosi Solomoni*⟩;[51] tenth, *The Revelation of Elijah*[52] ⟨*Iliino Obavleniie*⟩;[53] eleventh, *Isaiah's Vision*[54] ⟨*Isaino*

---

opera Dr. Joannis Franko) vol. 1, L'viv, 1896, pp. 92–101. Its position immediately after *Enoch* (in the *Symeonic Florilegium*'s version of the *Index*) supports this identification. In other redactions of the *Index*, both Byzantine and Slavonic, the term *Malekh* is systematically replaced by *Lamekh*; see A. Iatsimirskiĭ, *Bibliograficheskiĭ Obzor Apokrifov v Iuzhnoslavianskoĭ i Russkoĭ Pis'mennosti*, pp. 2–3.

45   Cf. H.C. Kee, 'Testaments of the Twelve Patriarchs', in J.H. Charlesworth (ed.), *The Old Testament Pseudepigrapha* vol. 1, pp. 775–828; M. de Jonge, 'The Testaments of the Twelve Patriarchs', in *The Apocryphal Old Testament*, pp. 505–600. For the Slavonic redactions of *The Testaments of the Twelve Patriarchs*, see N.S. Tikhonravov, *Pamiatniki Otrechennoĭ Russkoĭ Literatury* vol. 1, pp. 96–232. See also the discussion in Ém. Turdeanu, 'Les Testaments Des Douze Patriarches en Slave', *JSJ* vol. 1, issue 2 (1970), pp. 148–186; F.J. Thomson, 'The Slavonic Translation of the Old Testament', in J. Krašovec (ed.), *The Interpretation of the Bible* [= *JSOTSS* 289], Ljubljana–Sheffield, 1998, p. 870 (note 1259); M. Dimitrova, 'Bulgarian Studies on the Reception of Byzantine Literature in Medieval Bulgaria', pp. 356 (note 208).

46   Cf. J.Z. Smith, 'Prayer of Joseph', in J.H. Charlesworth (ed.), *The Old Testament Pseudepigrapha* vol. 2, pp. 699–714; see also G.T. Zervos, 'History of Joseph', in J.H. Charlesworth (ed.), *The Old Testament Pseudepigrapha* vol. 2, pp. 467–475.

47   Cf. E.G. Martin, 'Eldad and Moldad', in J.H. Charlesworth (ed.), *The Old Testament Pseudepigrapha* vol. 2, pp. 463–465.

48   Followed here is the same pattern of cataloguing the apocryphal writings, as the one presented in the Byzantine *Index of the Sixty Books* (or *Catalogue of the Sixty Canonical Books*) and the *Stichometry of Nicephorus*, where the compositions *The Testament of Moses* and *The Assumption of Moses* are listed as separate items; consult further J. Priest, 'Testaments of Moses', in J.H. Charlesworth (ed.), *The Old Testament Pseudepigrapha* vol. 1, pp. 919–934. See also the discussion below.

49   Lit. *The Ascension of Moses*.

50   Cf. J. Tromp, *The Assumption of Moses: A Critical Edition With Commentary*, Leiden, 1997.

51   See R.B. Wright, 'Psalms of Solomon', in J.H. Charlesworth (ed.), *The Old Testament Pseudepigrapha* vol. 2, pp. 639–670; see also J.H. Charlesworth, 'Odes of Solomon', in id. (ed.), *The Old Testament Pseudepigrapha* vol. 2, pp. 725–771. According to the *Stichometry of Nicephorus*, the composition *Psalms and Odes of Solomon* (described as containing 2100 lines) is included in the catalogue of the *antilegomena* (i.e. disputed/heretical writings) of the Old Testament (together with *Maccabees, The Wisdom of Solomon*, etc.).

52   Var.: *The Apocalypse of Elijah*.

53   See O.S. Wintermute, 'Apocalypse of Elijah', in J.H. Charlesworth (ed.), *The Old Testament Pseudepigrapha* vol. 1, pp. 721–753; K.H. Kuhn, '*The Apocalypse of Elijah*', in *The Apocryphal Old Testament*, pp. 753–773.

54   Var. *The Ascension of Isaiah*.

Viděniie);[55] twelfth, *The Revelation of Sofonia*[56] ⟨*Sofoniino Obavlenie*⟩;[57] thirteenth, *The Revelation of Zechariah*[58] ⟨*Zakhariino Iavleniie*⟩; fourteenth, *The Protogospel of Jacob*[59] ⟨*Iakovle Povĕstъ*⟩;[60] fifteenth, *The Revelation of Peter*[61] ⟨*Petrovo Obavlenie*⟩;[62] sixteenth [and seventeenth], *The*

---

55   Cf. R.H. Charles, *The Ascension of Isaiah: Translated from the Ethiopic Version, Which, Together with the New Greek Fragment, the Latin Versions and the Latin Translation of the Slavonic, is here Published in Full*, London, 1900; Ĭ. Ivanov, *Bogomilski Knigi i Legendi*, pp. 131–164; R.H. Charles and J.M.T. Barton, 'The Ascension of Isaiah (The translation of R.H. Charles revised by J.M.T. Barton)', in *The Apocryphal Old Testament*, pp. 775–812; M.A. Knibb, 'Martyrdom and Ascension of Isaiah', in J.H. Charlesworth (ed.), *The Old Testament Pseudepigrapha* vol. 2, pp. 143–176; C.D.G. Müller, 'The Ascension of Isaiah', in Schneemelcher, *New Testament Apocrypha* vol. 2: *Writings Relating to the Apostles; Apocalypses and Related Subjects*; English translation edited by E. McL. Wilson], Cambridge, 1992, pp. 603–620; A. Giambelluca Kossova et al., *Ascensio Isaiæ: Textus* [CCSA 7], Turnhout, 1995; V. Mil'kov, *Drevnerusskie apokryfy* [Pamiatniki Drevnerusskoĭ mysli: issledovaniia i Teksty, Vyp. 1], Sankt Peterburg, 1999, pp. 499–527; V. Mil'kov and S. Polianskiĭ, *Kosmologicheskie Proizvedeniia v Knizhnosti Drevneĭ Rusi* vol. 2: *Teksty Ploskostno-Komarnoĭ i Drugikh Kosmologicheskikh Traditsiĭ*, pp. 552–582. See also the discussion in R. Bauckham, *The Fate of the Dead: Studies on the Jewish and Christian Apocalypses* [Novum Testamentum Supplements, 93], Leiden–Boston–Köln, 1998, pp. 363–390. For studies dedicated exclusively to Slavonic tradition, see A.V. Rystenko, *K literaturnoĭ istorii apokrifa "Voskhozhdenie Isai"*, Odessa, 1912. See also the discussion in A. Vaillant, 'Un apocryphe pseudobogomile: *La vision d'Isaïe*', RÉS T. 42, fasc. 1–4, 1963, pp. 109–121; A. Giambelluca Kossova, 'Nabliudeniia vŭrkhu starobŭlgarskata traditsiia na *Videnie Isaĭevo*: Sŭotvetstviia i razlichiia s tekstovata traditsiia na *Vŭzneseniie Isaievo*', *Palæobulgarica* vol. 7, issue 2 (1983), pp. 66–79; id., 'Edin prenebregnat rŭkopis na *Videnie Isaĭevo*: Iatsimirski prepis 19', *Palæobulgarica* vol. 12, issue 4 (1988), pp. 13–25.

56   That is, *The Apocalypse of Sophonias* (i.e. *The Apocalypse of Zephaniah*).

57   Sophonias is the Greek name for Zephaniah; see also O.S. Wintermute, 'Apocalypse of Zephaniah', in J.H. Charlesworth (ed.), *The Old Testament Pseudepigrapha* vol. 1, pp. 497–515; K.H. Kuhn, 'The Apocalypse of Zephaniah and An Anonymous Apocalypse', in *The Apocryphal Old Testament*, pp. 915–925.

58   That is, *The Apocalypse of Zechariah*.

59   That is, *Protevangelium of James*.

60   Cf. O. Cullmann, 'Infancy Gospels', in Schneemelcher, *New Testament Apocrypha* vol. 1: *Gospels and Related Writings*, pp. 421–439. For the Slavonic tradition, see B. Khristova, *Protoevangelieto na Iakov v starata bŭlgarska knizhnina*, Sofia, 1992. See also the discussion in M. Dimitrova, 'Bulgarian Studies on the Reception of Byzantine Literature in Medieval Bulgaria', pp. 356 (note 209).

61   That is, *The Apocalypse of Peter*.

62   Cf. C.D.G. Müller, 'The Apocalypse of Peter', in Schneemelcher, *New Testament Apocrypha* vol. 2: *Writings Relating to the Apostles; Apocalypses and Related Subjects*, pp. 620–638. See also the essays gathered in the collective monograph *The Apocalypse of Peter*, Leuven, 2003, published under the editorship of J.N. Bremmer and I. Czachesz. On a hypothetical interplay between concepts of hellscape attested in *1 Enoch* and *The Apoc-*

ENOCHIC TEXTS AND RELATED TRADITIONS IN SLAVIA ORTHODOXA 473

Tours [*of the Apostles*] *and Teachings of the Apostles* ⟨*Obkhody i Ucheniia Apostolska*⟩; eighteenth, *The Epistle of Barnabas* ⟨*Varnavle Posylaniie*⟩;[63] nineteenth, *The Deeds of Paul* ⟨*Dĕianiie Paule*⟩; twentieth, *Paul's Revelation*[64] ⟨*Paulovo Obavleniie*⟩;[65] twenty-first, *Clement's Teaching* ⟨*Ucheniie Klimentovo*⟩; twenty-second, *Ignatius's Teaching* ⟨*Ignatovo Ucheniie*⟩; twenty-third, *Polycarp's Teaching* ⟨*Polukarpovo Ucheniie*⟩; twenty-fourth, *The Gospel According to Barnabas* ⟨*Evangelie otъ Varnava*⟩;[66] twenty-fifth, *The Gospel According to Matthias* ⟨*Evangelie otъ Matfea*⟩.[67]

---

alypse of Peter, see the discussion in J.N. Bremmer, 'Descents to the Underworld from Gilgamesh to Christian Late Antiquity', *Studia Religiologica* vol. 50, issue 4 (2017), pp. 302–305.

63   In the *Stichometry of Nicephorus* the composition entitled *The Epistle of Barnabas* (containing 1360 lines) is classified as a 'disputed' work (together with *The Revelation of John*, *The Revelation of Peter* and *The Gospel of the Hebrews*); see Schneemelcher, *New Testament Apocrypha* vol. 1: *Gospels and Related Writings*, p. 41.

64   That is, *The Apocalypse of Paul*.

65   Various Slavonic redactions of this apocryphal composition were edited and published (starting from the second half of the 19th century onwards) by a number of scholars; the list provided below is far from exhaustive. Among the most frequently quoted ones are the following: Al.N. Pypin, *Lozhnyia i otrechennyia knigi russkoĭ stariny: Pamiatniki starinnoĭ russkoĭ literatury, Izdavaemye Grafom Grigoriem Kushelevym-Bezborodko*, Vyp. 3, Sankt Petersburg, 1862, pp. 129–133; N.S. Tikhonravov, *Pamiatniki Otrechennoĭ Russkoĭ Literatury* vol. 2, Moscow, 1863, pp. 40–58; V. Mil'kov, *Drevnerusskie apokryfy*, pp. 528–582; L. Jiroušková, *Die Visio Pauli: Wege und Wandlungen einer orientalischen Apokryphe im lateinischen Mittelalter unter Einschluß der alttschechischen und deutschsprachigen Textzeugen* [Mittellateinische Studien und Texte, 34], Leiden, 2006; N.H. Trunte, *Reiseführer durch das Jenseits: die Apokalypse des Paulus in der Slavia Orthodoxa* [Slavistische Beiträge 490], München–Berlin–Washington, D.C., 2013. See also the discussion in É. Turdeanu, 'La 'Vision de Saint Paul' dans la tradition littéraire des Slaves orthodoxes', *WSL* 1 (1956), pp. 401–430; J. Stradomski, 'Neskol'ko zamechaniĭ o neobychnoĭ slavianskoĭ redaktsii *Videniia Apostola Pavla* iz rukopisnykh sobraniĭ v Pol'she', *SC* vol. 4 (2014), pp. 193–207. For a general overview of scholarly discourses on *the Apocalypse of Paul*, see Th. Silverstein and A. Hilhorst (eds), *Apocalypse of Paul. A New Critical Edition of Three Long Latin Versions*, Geneva, 1997; J.N. Bremmer and I. Czachesz (eds), *The Visio Pauli and the Gnostic Apocalypse of Paul* [Studies on Early Christian Apocrypha, 9], Leuven, 2007. On Enoch's 'grand cosmic tours' and the 'hellscape' template employed in *The Apocalypse of Paul*, see the discussion in J.N. Bremmer, 'Descents to the Underworld from Gilgamesh to Christian Late Antiquity', pp. 305–306.

66   In the so-called *Decretum Gelasianum*, it is listed as an apocryphal work; see Schneemelcher, *New Testament Apocrypha* vol. 1, p. 38.

67   On the heterodox *Gospel According to Matthias* (or *Traditions of Matthias*), composed most probably in Alexandria before the beginning of the 3rd century, see Schneemelcher, *New Testament Apocrypha* vol. 1, pp. 382–386.

It should be pointed out that the scheme of the hermetic / secret / esoteric / apocryphal writings, as attested in the *Symeonic Florilegium*, is almost identical with that presented in the 7th century Byzantine *Index of the Sixty Books* (or *Catalogue of the Sixty Canonical Books*), and more precisely, to its addendum, the rubric devoted to the writings 'outside the sixty.' Thus, having listed the thirty-four Old Testament and twenty-six New Testament sanctified books (in accordance with the view held at that time in the Greek Byzantine Church, that the canonical biblical corpus consists of sixty books), its compiler proceeds to the rubric of the writings 'outside the sixty,' and attaches the section devoted to 'the apocryphal' writings. Included in this category are: 1. *Adam*; 2. *Enoch*; 3. *Lamech*; 4. *The Patriarchs*; 5. *The Prayer of Joseph*; 6. *Eldad and Modad*; 7. *The Testament of Moses*; 8. *The Assumption of Moses*; 9. *The Psalms of Solomon*; 10. *The Revelation of Elias*; 11. *The Vision of Isaiah*; 12. *The Revelation of Zephaniah*; 13. *The Revelation of Zechariah*; 14. *The Revelation of Ezra*; 15. *The History of James* (i.e. *The Protogospel of James*); 16. *The Revelation of Peter*; 17. *The Circuits and Teachings of the Apostles*; 18. *The Epistle of Barnabas*; 19. *The Acts of Paul*; 20. *The Revelation of Paul*; 21. *The Teaching of Clement*; 22. *The Teaching of Ignatius*; 23. *The Teaching of Polycarp*; 24. *The Gospel According to Barnabas*; 25. *The Gospel According to Matthias*.[68]

A similar list is attested in the *Stichometry of Nicephorus* (9th century), in which the Old Testament apocryphal writings are presented (with further information concerning the exact number of the lines contained in each composition) in the following order: 1. *Enoch* (4800 lines); 2. [*The Testaments of the Twelve*] *Patriarchs* (5100 lines); 3. *The Prayer of Joseph* (300 lines); 4. *The Testament of Moses* (1100 lines); 5. *The Assumption of Moses* (1400 lines); 6. *Abraham* (300 lines); 7. *Eldad and Modad* (400 lines); 8. [*Book of the*] *Prophet Elias* (316 lines); 9. [*Book of the*] *Prophet Zephaniah* (600 lines); 10. [*Book of*] *Zacharias, the Father of John* (500 lines); 11. *Pseudepigraphica of Baruch, Habakkuk, Ezekiel, and Daniel*.[69]

In the same source (i.e. *Stichometry of Nicephorus*), the Apocrypha of the New Testament are presented as follows: 1. *The Circuit of Paul, or The Acts of Paul* (3600 lines); 2. *The Circuit of Peter* (2750 lines); 3. *The Circuit of John* (2500 lines); 4. *The Circuit of Thomas* (1600 lines); 5. *The Gospel of Thomas* (1300 lines); 6. *The Teaching* [*Didache*] *of the Apostles* (200 lines); 7. *The Thirty-Two* [*Books*] *of Clement* (2600 lines); 8. [*Writings*] *of Ignatius* [*of Antioch*], *Polycarp* [*of Smyrna*], *and of the Shepherd of Hermas*.[70]

---

68   See Schneemelcher, *New Testament Apocrypha* vol. 1, pp. 42–43.
69   Cf. Schneemelcher, *New Testament Apocrypha* vol. 1, p. 41.
70   Cf. Schneemelcher, *New Testament Apocrypha* vol. 1, p. 42.

ENOCHIC TEXTS AND RELATED TRADITIONS IN SLAVIA ORTHODOXA   475

However, the standard English designation *Index of Prohibited / Proscribed Books* (conventionally used to render Gr. *Κατάλογος Ἀπαγορευμένων Βιβλίων* and / or Lat. *Index Librorum Prohibitorum*), does not adequately convey the Old Church Slavonic taxonomy (that is, ѥлнкоже съкровьнъынхъ), as found in the *Symeonic Florilegium*. The semantic web of the adjective съкръвенъ/съкровьнъ, also rendered as скровенный/сокровенный, or съкрьвень/съкрьвеньнь (= Gr. κρυπτός, κρύφιος, ἀπόκρυφος, ἀποκεκρυμμένος, etc.),[71] which is in fact a past passive participle form of the verb съкръ̈вати/скръ̈вати/сокръ̈вати, съкръ̈ти/скръ̈ти/сокръ̈ти (= Gr. κρύπτειν),[72] covers a set of synonyms (e.g. 'cryptic'/'hermetic'/'apocryphal'/'secret'/'esoteric', etc.), the lexicographic definitions of which appear to have been originally free of negative axiological connotations (such as 'prohibited'/'proscribed'/'banned').[73] Furthermore the survey of related linguistic data shows that the compound Old Church Slavonic adjective сокровеннотайнъый[74] (съкръвенъ/съкровьнъ + тайнъый/ таннъ) is used as an epithet applied to the (Holy) Trinity [Трⷪ҇ца] to convey the meaning of κρυφιομυστικός (the closest English equivalent 'sacrosanctly-mystic,' or 'sacramentally-mystic'). To the same semantic cluster belongs the noun тайна,[75] denoting both 'secret' (τὸ κρυπτον, as in Matth 6:4; τὸ κρυφαῖον, as in Matth 6:18; τὸ ἀπόκρυφον, as in Ps 9:30) and 'mystery' (τὰ μυστήρια, as in Lk 8:10; Rev 10:7; 1 Cor. 13:2; or μυστήριον, as in the *Corpus Areopagiticum slavicum*).[76] Most importantly, the adjective сокровеннотайнъый may also denote the mysterious dimensions of the Eucharist.[77]

As pointed out by A.I. Iatsimirskiĭ, only in the later redactions of the *Index* do the compilers/copyists emphasise, with reference to the writings of Saint Athanasius of Alexandria (ca. 296/298–373), that the 'hermetic' / 'esoteric'/ 'secret' books (or scriptures) listed in it are actually 'heretical' [еретнческа],

---

71   Consult G. Bogatova et al., *Slovar' Russkogo Iazyka XI–XVII vv.*, Vyp. 25, Moscow, 2000, pp. 24–28; A. Bonchev, *Rechnik na Tsŭrkovnoslavanskiia Ezik* vol. 2, Sofia, 2012, p. 161, p. 182; S. Fahl, J. Harney and D. Fahl, *Das Corpus des Dionysios Areopagites in der slavischen Übersetzung von Starec Isaija (14. Jahrhundert)* [Monumenta linguæ slavicæ dialecti veteris. Fontes et dissertationes, t. LIV], Bd. 4.2: *Indices*, Weilburg–Freiburg i. Br., 2012, pp. 1375–1378.

72   Cf. G. Bogatova et al., *Slovar' Russkogo Iazyka XI–XVII vv.*, Vyp. 25, pp. 30–33.

73   Consult S. Fahl, J. Harney and D. Fahl, *Das Corpus des Dionysios Areopagites in der slavischen Übersetzung von Starec Isaija (14. Jahrhundert)*, Bd. 4.3: *Indices*, p. 1737.

74   Consult A. Bonchev, *Rechnik na Tsŭrkovnoslavanskiia Ezik* vol. 2, p. 182.

75   See the survey of related linguistic data in V. Krysko et al. (eds), *Slovar' Russkogo Iazyka XI–XVII vv.*, Vyp. 29, Moscow, 2011, pp. 176–196.

76   Consult S. Fahl, J. Harney and D. Fahl, *Das Corpus des Dionysios Areopagites in der slavischen Übersetzung von Starec Isaija (14. Jahrhundert)*, Bd. 4:2, p. 1434.

77   Consult A. Bonchev, *Rechnik na Tsŭrkovnoslavanskiia Ezik* vol. 2, p. 182.

and hence prohibited.[78] This is clearly not the case, however, with the semantic coverage of the adjective съкровьнъ (= κρυπτός, κρύφιος, ἀπόκρυφος, ἀποκε-κρυμμένος, etc.), as employed in the designation of the *Index* in the *Symeonic Florilegium*. In the latter case, the adjective съкровьнъ may designate the concept of 'hermetic' (var. 'secret' / 'concealed' / 'mystic' / 'esoteric' / 'treasured' / 'hidden' / 'apocryphal'), but by no means that of 'proscribed' (var. 'forbidden'/ 'banned').[79]

On the other hand, the reference to a composition entitled *Enoch* (as attested in the *Index* in the *Symeonic Florilegium*) does not either support or refute the conjecture that the actual apocryphon—be it *First* or *Second Enoch*— was in circulation in *Slavia Orthodoxa* at the time when the *Florilegium* was compiled, since the Slavonic scribes may have simply reproduced the original template of the *Index*, as encountered by them in the Greek *Vorlage*.[80] The occurrence of the designation *Enoch* in the *Index* in the *Symeonic Florilegium* proves indisputably only the assumption that, among men of letters working in the royal scriptorium of the First Bulgarian Kingdom, there was awareness of the existence of apocryphal book(s), the authorship of which was attributed to Enoch.

Missing from the *Index* in the *Symeonic Florilegium*, however, are some apocryphal works emblematic for *Slavia Orthodoxa* (and indeed for the Byzantine Commonwealth), such as *The Apocalypse of Abraham*,[81] *The Testament of Abra-*

---

78   Among the most frequently attested versions of the Church Slavonic designations of the *Index* are the following: *Concerning the So-Called Cryptic/Esoteric Heretical Books* [О глаголемыхъ скровныхъ кннгахъ еретнческа], or *A Discourse / Tale Concerning the So-Called Cryptic/Esoteric/ Secret Books, Which are Heretical Writings* [О глаголемыхъ съкровенныхъ/тайныхъ кннгахъ сказаніе/повѣданіе, іако еретнческа суть спнсанііа], etc.; see A. Iatsimirskiĭ, *Bibliograficheskiĭ Obzor Apokrifov v Iuzhnoslavianskoĭ i Russkoĭ Pis'mennosti*, pp. 3–4.

79   Significant in this connection is the fact that, some apocryphal compositions (such as *The Protogospel of James*), which were never considered as 'prohibited' in *Slavia Orthodoxa* (since they were part of Church services), were also enumerated in the Symeonic *Index*.

80   Cf. Ĭ. Ivanov, *Bogomilski Knigi i Legendi*, p. 166.

81   Cf. N. Tikhonravov, *Pamiatniki Otrechennoĭ Russkoĭ Literatury*, pp. 32–78; see further the discussion in G.N. Bonwetsch, *Die Apocalypse Abrahams: Das Testament des vierzig Märtyrer* [Studien zur Geschichte der Theologie und der Kirche, Bd. 1. Hft 1], Leipzig, 1897; A. Rubinstein, 'Hebraisms in the Slavonic *Apocalypse of Abraham*', *JJS* vol. 4, issue 3 (1953), pp. 108–115; id., 'Hebraisms in the Slavonic *Apocalypse of Abraham*', *JJS* vol. 5, issue 3 (1954), pp. 132–135; É. Turdeanu, 'L'Apocalypse D'Abraham En Slave', *JSJ* vol. 3, issue 2 (1972), pp. 153–180; B. Philonenko-Sayar and M. Philonenko, *L'Apocalypse d'Abraham* [Semitica vol. 31], Paris, 1981; R. Rubinkiewicz, 'Les Semitismes dans l'Apocalypse d'Abraham', *Folia Orientalia* T. 21 (1980), pp. 141–148; id., 'Apocalypse of Abraham (First to second century AD). A new translation and introduction by R. Rubinkiewicz', in J.H. Charlesworth (ed.),

ham,[82] *The Ladder of Jacob*,[83] *The Apocalypse of Baruch* (*3 Baruch*),[84] *The Apocalypse of the Virgin Mary*, etc.[85] These omissions suggest that the version presented by the Slavonic scribe reproduced an earlier Greek scheme, similar to—yet not identical with—that attested in the seventh-century Byzantine *Index of the Sixty Books* (or *Catalogue of the Sixty Canonical Books*) and the ninth-century *Stichometry of Nicephorus*.

2.2 *The Book(s) of Enoch and Their Scribal Escort in Slavia Orthodoxa: The Usual Suspects*

It should be noted that some of the ascent apocalypses, which were omitted from the *Index* in the *Symeonic Florilegium* (e.g. *3 Baruch*), appear to have been habitually copied in various miscellanies alongside *2 Enoch*, thus becoming part of its literary convoy;[86] attested in them are also some common cosmo-

---

    The Old Testament Pseudepigrapha vol. 1, pp. 681–688; R. Rubinkiewicz and H.G. Lunt, 'The Apocalypse of Abraham (transl. by R. Rubinkiewicz; revised and notes added by H.G. Lunt)', in J.H. Charlesworth (ed.), *The Old Testament Pseudepigrapha* vol. 1, pp. 689–705; R. Rubinkiewicz, *L'Apocalypse d'Abraham en vieux slave: Introduction, texte critique, traduction et commentaire* [Źródła i monografie, 129], Lublin, 1987; A. Pennington, 'The Apocalypse of Abraham', in *The Apocryphal Old Testament*, pp. 363–391; H.G. Lunt, 'On the language of the *Slavonic Apocalypse of Abraham*', *SH* vol. 7 (1985), pp. 55–62; J.C. Poirier, 'The ouranology of the *Apocalypse of Abraham*', *Journal for the Study of Judaism in the Persian, Hellenistic and Roman Period* vol. 35, issue 4 (2004), pp. 391–408; A. Kulik, *Retroverting Slavonic Pseudepigrapha: Toward the Original of the Apocalypse of Abraham* [Society of Biblical literature. Text-Critical Studies vol. 3], Leiden, 2005; A. Orlov, 'Praxis of the Voice: The Divine Name traditions in the *Apocalypse of Abraham*', in id. *Selected Studies in the Slavonic Pseudepigrapha* [Studia in Veteris Testamenti Pseudepigrapha vol. 23], Leiden, 2009, pp. 21–40; id., *Heavenly Priesthood in the Apocalypse of Abraham*, Cambridge, 2013; B. Uspenskiĭ, 'Filologicheskie nabliudeniia nad tekstom *Otkroveniia Avraama*', *VoprIazyk* vol. 5 (2015), pp. 49–86.

82   Cf. N. Tikhonravov, *Pamiatniki Otrechennoĭ Russkoĭ Literatury*, pp. 79–90. Consult also N. Turner, 'The Testament of Abraham', in *The Apocryphal Old Testament*, pp. 393–421.

83   Cf. A. Pypin, *Lozhnyia i otrechennyia knigi russkoĭ stariny*, pp. 27–32; N. Tikhonravov, *Pamiatniki Otrechennoĭ Russkoĭ Literatury*, pp. 91–95; A. Pennington, 'The Ladder of Jacob', in *The Apocryphal Old Testament*, pp. 453–463; J. Kugel, 'The Ladder of Jacob', *HTR* vol. 88 (1995), pp. 209–227; Ch. Böttrich, 'A New Approach to the Apocryphal Ladder of Jacob', *Journal for the Study of the Pseudepigrapha* vol. 28 (2019), pp. 171–181. (The amount of scholarly contributions on this topic is significant, and the survey provided here is by no means exhaustive).

84   See the discussion in A. Kulik, *3 Baruch: Greek Slavonic Apocalypse of Baruch*, Berlin, 2010.

85   Consult also J. Baun, *Tales from Another Byzantium. Celestial Journey and Local Community in the Medieval Greek Apocrypha*, Cambridge, 2007.

86   See Sokolov, *Slavianskaia Kniga Enokha Pravednago* (Part 2) pp. 70–71.

logical motifs (e.g. the heavenly gates through which the two great luminaries, the Sun and the Moon, enter and exit, the celestial escort accompanying them, etc.).[87]

Of particular importance for the current discussion is the apocryphal cycle of compositions relating to the Patriarch Abraham,[88] in the narrative clusters of which cosmological and angelological concepts (similar to those attested in *2 Enoch*) are profoundly and intensely woven.[89] One such case is *The Testament of Abraham*, in which special reference is made to the 'forefather Enoch' as 'the scribe of righteousness'[90] [Slav. кънигъуна праведнꙑиѫ; кннгѵ́й правднв].[91] Maintained in this text is that Enoch, together with Abel, encounters the souls of the newly departed in the Beyond, and writes into the 'scriptures of retention' [Slav. пнсанниѧ памꙗтнаѧ; съпнсана памѧтн] their earthly deeds, whilst the primordial Adam directs them to the respective celestial gates (depending on their conducts—left for sinners, or right for the righteous).

The picture gets even more interesting, should we consider the fact that some Slavonic versions of the sub-plot about the judgement of the souls in the Beyond contain motifs that are not attested in any of the extant Greek witnesses to *The Testament of Abraham*.[92] One such apocryphal tale (entitled *A Discourse About the Death and Life of Abraham* [*Слово ꙍ сьмртн н ꙍ жнт Аврамове*]), copied in the 16th century Tikveshki Miscellany, was discovered and published by the Bulgarian scholar N. Nachov.[93] According to this version of the text, when God opened 'the eyes of the heart' (cf. Eph 1.18) of Abraham [ꙍврьꙁетъ аврамоу срдеѵннн ꙍѵн] and the Archangel Michael [Арх̅гль Мнханль] took him to the Fourth Heaven [на ѵетврьтомь н̅б̅ѣ], the Patriarch noticed first the primordial Adam [пръвоꙁ᷉ѹ̑аннꙑ Адамь] and then—the elderly Enoch [Енохь] who, together with the youth Abel [Авель], was monitoring the judgement of the souls. He was also the one recording the sins of recently departed

---

87   Cf. Sokolov, 'Feniks v Apokrifakh ob Enokhe i Varukhe', pp. 395–405; A. Stoĭkova, 'Ot Mesopotamiia do Etropole. Transformatsii na mita za gigantskata kosmicheska ptitsa', pp. 126–168.

88   See F. Badalanova and A. Miltenova, 'Apokrifniiat tsikŭl za Avraam vŭv folklora i srednovekovnite balkanski literaturi', in R. Popov and S. Grebenarova (eds), *Etnografski problemi na narodnata kultura* vol. 4, Sofia, 1996, pp. 204–208, 228–236, 250.

89   See the discussion in Sokolov, *Slavianskaia Kniga Enokha Pravednago* (Part 2), pp. 128–136.

90   On the designation of Enoch as 'the scribe of righteousness' (or 'scribe of truth'), see G. Nickelsburg, *A Commentary on the Book of 1 Enoch (Chapters 1–36; 81–108)*, Minneapolis, 2001, pp. 65–67, pp. 72–77.

91   Cf. Sokolov, *Slavianskaia Kniga Enokha Pravednago* (Part 2), pp. 130.

92   Cf. Sokolov, *Slavianskaia Kniga Enokha Pravednago* (Part 2), pp. 130–131.

93   Cf. N. Nachov, 'Tikveshki rŭkopis', *Sbornik za Narodni Umotvorenia* vol. 8 (1892), pp. 411–413.

ENOCHIC TEXTS AND RELATED TRADITIONS IN SLAVIA ORTHODOXA   479

people [расписȢетъ всакомȢ ѧ́лкȢ грѣхы], while Abel was escorting the souls
to the gates through which they were supposed to enter [проважмаеть дш̃Ȣ
коꙗждⷷе вь своꙗ сн], according to their status. At this point follows an enigmatic statement on behalf of the Archangel Michael, the meaning of which is
hard to comprehend:

того рамн рⷡе г҃ь. ма не ѡзываеть се енохова цр҃ковь н крⷭть на землн.

This is why God pronounced that the *Church of Enoch* and the [Holy]
Cross may not be implored on Earth.[94]

A somewhat different wording of this statement is found in the 15th century
Slavonic Ms. № 109 from the Library of the Monastery of St Paul on Mount
Athos, containing yet another version of *The Testament of Abraham*; the text is
entitled *Concerning the Death of Abraham, How the Archangel Michael Came to
Abraham; Father, Bless Us* [*О смⷬтн Аврамовѣ како прнїде Арх҃гль Мнханл къ
Аврааму Бл̃свн Оѱⷷе*]. When Abraham asks the Archangel Michael, who is the
man handling the issues of the sins of men in the Beyond [кто ѥс нже сьдрь-
жет грѣхы ѧ́лѱе], he answers:

То ес Ѥнох с теломь соудныꙗ ѧ́лком. Томоу бо рⷡе г҃ь: Да не озовет се
Енохова цр҃ькъвь на землн, н ннкто же не прнзоветь нме его.[95]

This is Enoch [who was taken] bodily [to the Beyond] to be the Judge of
mankind. This is why God pronounced that the *Church of Enoch* is not to
be invoked on earth, and nobody may call his name.[96]

Notwithstanding the vagueness of the texts quoted above, one thing is indis-
putable: in the theological thesaurus of *Slavia Orthodoxa* there appears to have
circulated a special term denoting 'the Church of Enoch.' Before conducting the
necessary survey of empirical data, however, it is not possible to state with certainty what was the nature of the phenomenon designated by this enigmatic
expression.[97]

---

94   Author's translation.
95   See F. Badalanova and A. Miltenova, 'Apokrifniiat tsikŭl za Avraam vŭv folklora i sred-
      novekovnite balkanski literaturi', p. 236.
96   Author's translation.
97   This detail will be discussed elsewhere.

As for the ascent apocalypses mentioned in the *Index* in the *Symeonic Florilegium* together with *Enoch* (e.g. *Isaiah's Vision, The Apocalypse of Paul*, etc.), scholars have already pointed out that the narratives of heavenly journeys and tours of otherworldly realms presented in them systematically parallel some celestial descriptions found in *2 Enoch*.[98] It will be safe to say that this remains one of the unexplored dimensions of apocalyptic intertextuality in *Slavia Orthodoxa*.

The same can be said about the traces of Enochic traditions in the extant Slavonic recensions of *The Testaments of the Twelve Patriarchs*.[99] Arguably translated in the same period when the *Florilegium* was compiled, these types of texts were subsequently integrated into the corpus of the *Interpretative Palæa*. Of particular importance for our discussion is the celebrated fragment from *The Testament of Reuben, About Ideas* 5: 1–7,[100] in which the first-born son of Jacob forewarns his offspring about the danger of women's charms, including the traps of their cosmetic wiles. Our analysis is based on one of the Russian redactions of *The Testaments of the Twelve Patriarchs* (copied in 1477), published by N. Tikhonravov in his *Monuments of Proscribed Russian Literature*. The Slavonic title of the chapter in question is given as *The Testament of Ruvim Concerning Prudence* [Ӡавѣтъ Рувнмовъ ѡ блгоумнн]. Although the text does not mention explicitly 'the writings of Enoch' as its source, its discourse as a counter-narrative to the *Book of Watchers* is clear. Furthermore, it is in this particular chapter where the translation into Church Slavonic of the Greek term denoting the Fallen Angels occurs. In contrast to *2 Enoch*, where the form *Gregoroi* [Γρήγοροι, Ἐγρήγοροι] is transliterated (see below § 3), in *The Testament of Ruvim* it is translated. The lexeme used for this purpose is бодрыіа / бодры, which is the plural masculine form of the Old Church Slavonic adjective бъдръ/бъдрый (lit. 'the Wakeful [one]'). Below follows the fragment concerned:

лоукавъı соут женъı ѱада моа. ꙗко не нмѣющіе власти нн снлъı на моужех лстат крашеннемь како ꙗ к собѣ прнвадꙗт. егже снлоюю не могоут прнноуднт. того лестью прнноужають. нбо ѡ тех мн реѱ агглъ бїн наоуѱн ма. ꙗко женъı ѕѣло распалаютса на блоуд. паѱе мѫжа н

---

98 See Sokolov, *Slavianskaia Kniga Enokha Pravednago* (Part 2), pp. 123–127; W. Morfill and R. Charles, *The Book of the Secrets of Enoch*, p. xix.

99 W. Morfill and R. Charles were among the first to analyse Enochic quotations occuring in *The Testaments of the Twelve Patriarchs* (see Morfill, Charles, *The Book of the Secrets of Enoch*, pp. xxiii–xxiv), but this detail escaped their attention.

100 Cf. M. de Jonge, 'The Testaments of the Twelve Patriarchs', pp. 519–520 (Chapter 5).

в срдци ражжнѕают на моужа. и крашеннемь прелщают их. первое мыслью и взорѡм ꙗдъ всѣвают. и потом дѣломь плѣнают. не бо может жена мⷹжа приноудити. бѣганте оубо блоуженїꙗ ѵад моꙗ. и заповѣданте женамь вашимь и дщерем да не красат главъ своихъ и лиць на прелесть оумⷹ. ꙗко всꙗка жена красащисе ѡ том в мⷹкоу вѣѵною соблюдетса. так бо провабиша бодрыꙗ прежде потопа. ѡни бо съ прилежаннемь зраще на на быша. в помыслех дроугъ дргⷹ. и заѵаша в помисле дѣло и прешѡбразовахоуса въ мⷹжа. и в соблажненїи моужь своих ꙗвлꙗхоуса имь. ѡни же помышлающе на оумѣ образы их. ражахоу гигатни. ꙗвлꙗхоу бо имь бодры до нбⷭн досазающе. храниреса оубо ѵада ѿ блоуженїа.[101]

For women are cunning, my children: as they have no power or strength [to stand up] to men, they seduce them by adornments [var. use of cosmetics, or jewellery], so that they may come to them; and a man whom a woman cannot subdue by strength, she subdues by a stratagem. For the angel of God told me about them and taught me that women are prone to fornication [var. promiscuity] much more than a man; and their hearts blaze [with desire] for men. In the way they adorn themselves, they first lead men's minds astray, and by a look they instil the poison, and then in the act itself they take them captive; for a woman cannot coerce a man [by force]. So shun fornication, my children, and command your wives and daughters not to adorn their heads [var. dye their hair][102] and [not to put cosmetics on] their faces to seduce the mind; for every woman who adorns herself [by hair dye and cosmetics] has been reserved for eternal punishment. This is how the 'Wakeful ones' were [conducting themselves] initially, before the Flood. As a result of seeing them [women] continually, they lusted after each other in their thoughts, and they conceived the act in their minds, and [the 'Wakeful ones'] changed themselves into the shape of [human] men and appeared to the women when they were having intercourse with their husbands. And the women, lusting in their minds after the phantom images [var. creatures], gave birth to giants, for the 'Wakeful ones' seemed to them tall enough to touch the sky.[103]

---

101   Cf. N. Tikhonravov, *Pamiatniki Otrechennoĭ Russkoĭ Literatury*, pp. 149–150.

102   With henna?

103   Author's translation; taken into consideration is also the translation of the same paragraph by M. de Jonge, 'The Testaments of the Twelve Patriarchs', pp. 519–520.

Based on the redrafted framework of Genesis 6:1–4, *The Testament of Ruvim Concerning Prudence* 5: 1–7 unfolds as a cosmogonic narrative, with its story-line implementing the ancient magical trope of the *incubus*, the evil spirit who adopts a male form in order to have sexual encounter with female human victims in their sleep, with the aim being to reproduce demonic progeny. This nocturnal set-up explains how 'the Wakeful ones' happened to impregnate the beautiful daughters of men, who then gave birth to a race of giants of mixed human and demonic lineage. But, equally important, *The Testament of Ruvim* conveys in a rather subtle manner the sub-plot of the illicit origins of cosmetics, as formulated in *The Book of Watchers*. Charged with fierce condemnation of the wicked lusty women, whose use of adornments is branded as embodiment of evil, the story provides the necessary grounds for opening an ideological war on the sinful ethos of seductive female conduct. The impact of this discourse is also palpably visualised in religious art. The motif of eternal condemnation of sinful wives and daughters who dare put cosmetics on their faces is depicted in a number of churches and monasteries in the Balkans.

One of the most popular iconographic schemes interpreting the idea of diabolical origin of cosmetics involves the portrayal of a young woman putting on make-up, with the Devil holding a mirror in front of her face; and if the onlookers hesitate how to interpret the scene, the inscriptions accompanying the frescoes duly informs them that: 'should a woman dare putting make-up on her face, it would be the Devil who would hold the mirror for her.' (See Figures 22.2 and 22.3.)

There exist even more drastic types of frescoes interpreting the thorny matter of cosmetics; depicted on them are women holding containers with colouring matter which they are smearing on their faces; painted above the containers, however, are devils who defecate in them. In this—rather extreme, but unequivocal matter—the cosmetics are defined as demonic excrements (see Figures 22.4 and 22.5). As a rule, these types of scenes are situated either in the open gallery, or in the women's section of the church. Judging from the abundance of sites sheltering these images—whose painters were most probably influenced by the home-grown exegesis of polemical treatises and didactic tractates[104] thematically akin to (albeit not directly stemming from) *The Testa-*

---

104   One such case is the 18th century compilation entitled *Homily on Womenfolk and Maidens* [*Поучение към жените и момите*], composed by the Bulgarian monk Joseph the Bearded [Йосиф Брадати], one of the translators of the celebrated *Thesauros* (Θησαυρός) of the Greek ecclesiastic Damaskinos Stouditis (Δαμασκηνός ὁ Στουδίτης); see D. Dimitrova-Marinova, 'Pouchenieto kŭm zhenite i momite v rŭkopisnata traditsiia ot vtorata polov-

FIGURE 22.2   The Devil holding a mirror in front of a maiden putting on make-up; fresco from church of Archangel Michael (Leshko), painted in 1889. The inscription reads: 'Който се бѣлатъ и царват даволо имъ даржи огледалото' ('Those who put on [their faces] white and red [colouring matter] have the Devil holding the mirror before them').
PHOTO: AUTHOR

ment of Ruvim—one may estimate the level of the indirect impact of *The Book of Watchers* upon visual propaganda in *Slavia Orthodoxa*.

Indicative in this connection is the very thesaurus of the Slavonic recensions of *The Testaments of the Twelve Patriarchs*.[105] The stock phrase 'the Books of Enoch' has multiple attestations in them.[106] However, apart from the repeti-

---

ina na 18 vek', SL 33–34 (2005), pp. 380–393; V. Dimitrov, 'Khramŭt 'Sveti Georgi' pri selo Igumenets', PI 43: 3 (2010), pp. 42–49; A. Angusheva-Tikhanova and M. Dimitrova, 'Samokov i borbata na Tsŭrkvata sreshtu baeneto i gadaeneto', *Godishnik na Asotsiatsiia "Ongŭl"* 12 (2013): *Etnologiia na Obshtuvaneto*, p. 129.

105   Cf. N. Tikhonravov, *Pamiatniki Otrechennoĭ Russkoĭ Literatury*, pp. 96–232.
106   Thus in Chapter 5: 5–6 of *The Testament of Simeon* [Завѣт Семоновъ], the following statement is made: 'I have come to know from the account of the books of Enoch that your sons, together with you, will be corrupted by fornication' [вндѣхъ оубо въ сказаньн кннгъ ıеноховъ ıако снве вашн с вамн въ бълуженьн нстлѣютъ] (see N. Tikhonravov, *Pamiatniki Otrechennoĭ Russkoĭ Literatury*, p. 100; I. Porfir'ev, 'Apokrificheskie Skazaniia o Vetkhozavetnykh Litsakh i Sobytiiakh po Rukopisiam Solovetskoĭ Biblioteki', p. 161). Similar quotations can be found in *The Testament of Levi* [Завѣт Левгнн]: 'as it stands

tive references to Enoch the Just, who is portrayed as the ultimate antediluvian authority, *The Testaments* discuss notions that are parallel to cosmogonic concepts attested exclusively in the longer recension of *2 Enoch* (e.g. the idea of 'seven traits,' or 'seven spirits' which were given to man at Creation).[107] This, in turn, indicates that the earliest Slavonic editions of these two apocryphal compositions (e.g. *2 Enoch* and *The Testaments of the Twelve Patriarchs*) can be traced back to a common intellectual landscape—that of the First Bulgarian Kingdom.[108] These types of cosmogonic parallels bring forth once again the

---

written in the book(s) of the righteous Enoch' [во рече въ кннгахъ ієноха праведнаго]; 'I understand from the writing(s)/testimony of Enoch' [разоумехъ ѿ пнсменн Енохова]; 'I understand from the book(s) of Enoch' [оуведахъ в кннгахъ Еноховахъ]; see N. Tikhonravov, *Pamiatniki Otrechennoĭ Russkoĭ Literatury*, pp. 110–111, as well as I. Porfir'ev, 'Apokrificheskie Skazaniia o Vetkhozavetnykh Litsakh i Sobytiiakh po Rukopisiam Solovetskoĭ Biblioteki', p. 169. Related phraseology is attested in *The Testament of Judah* [Завѣт Нюдннъ]: 'And I have come to know from the books of the righteous Enoch about the evils you will commit in the last days' [оувндѣхъ оубо реʸ в кннгахъ ієнохо- вахъ ієлнко зла створнте в послѣднаꙗ дни; var. оувндѣхъ во рече въ кннгахъ Енохо- вахъ елнко зло сотворнте в послѣднꙗꙗ дни]; see N. Tikhonravov, *Pamiatniki Otrechennoĭ Russkoĭ Literatury*, p. 115 and I. Porfir'ev, 'Apokrificheskie Skazaniia o Vetkhozavetnykh Litsakh i Sobytiiakh po Rukopisiam Solovetskoĭ Biblioteki', p. 172. Parallel excerpts feature in *The Testament of Dan* [Завѣт Ланов]: 'I have understood from the books of the righteous Enoch' [разумѣхъ во во кннгахъ ієноха праведнаго; var. разоумехъ во во кнн- гахъ Еноха Праведнаго]; see N. Tikhonravov, *Pamiatniki Otrechennoĭ Russkoĭ Literatury*, p. 126 and I. Porfir'ev, 'Apokrificheskie Skazaniia o Vetkhozavetnykh Litsakh i Sobyti- iakh po Rukopisiam Solovetskoĭ Biblioteki', p. 181. Somewhat redrafted statements containing alleged Enochic discourse occur in *The Testament of Benjamin* [Завѣт Веныꙗмн- новъ]: 'I gather from the words of the righteous Enoch that you must not give yourselves up to Sodomite fornication' [разумѣхомъ же о словесн ієноха праведнаго съвлюднте- жеса ꙋада моꙗ влоуженыꙗ содомьска; var. разоумехомъ же во словесн Еноха правед- наго соблюдетежесꙗ ꙋада моꙗ влоуженнꙗ содомска]; see I. Porfir'ev, 'Apokrificheskie Skazaniia o Vetkhozavetnykh Litsakh i Sobytiiakh po Rukopisiam Solovetskoĭ Biblioteki', p. 193; see also N. Tikhonravov, *Pamiatniki Otrechennoĭ Russkoĭ Literatury*, p. 229. However, in some cases, as in *The Testament of Asher* [Завѣтъ Аснровъ], when the Slavonic text gives a reference to 'the books of the righteous Enoch' (see I. Porfir'ev, 'Apokri- ficheskie Skazaniia o Vetkhozavetnykh Litsakh i Sobytiiakh po Rukopisiam Solovetskoĭ Biblioteki', p. 187), this very reference may be missing from the extant Greek versions; the latter case suggests that Slavonic recensions most probably preserve earlier redactions.

107   Cf. *2 Enoch* 30:9.

108   Further on the relationship between *Enoch* and *The Testaments of the Twelve Patriarchs* (which circulated as part of the text of the *Palæa*), see Forbes and Charles, '*2 Enoch*, or *The Book of the Secrets of Enoch*', pp. 428–429; F. Badalanova Geller, *Second (Slavonic Apocalypse of) Enoch: Text and Context*, p. 5. See also the discussion in A.J.B. Higgins, 'Priest and Messiah', *VT*, vol. 3: 4 (1953), pp. 322–324, 326–332]; Nickelsburg, *A Commentary on the Book of 1 Enoch (Chapters 1–36; 81–108)*, p. 96.

FIGURE 22.3A   The Devil holding a mirror in front of a maiden putting on her face make-up; fresco from the Monastery of St George, Petrich county, South-Western Bulgaria. Painted in 1858
PHOTO: AUTHOR

FIGURE 22.3B   The Devil holding a mirror in front of a maiden putting on her face make-up, detail
PHOTO: AUTHOR

thorny matter of the relationship between 'the longer' and 'the shorter recension.' From the same period (concurrent with that of the *Florilegium*) comes yet another compilation, the anthropogonic account of which parallels some ideas featuring in the 'longer recension' of *2 Enoch* 30:13–14. The examination of additional sources contemporary to the *Florilegium* sheds additional light on the matter in question. Let us examine the evidence.

2.3   Enochic Traditions and the Slavonic Redactions of Byzantine Chronographa: Parabiblical Intertextuality (*the Case of The Slavonic Derivative of the Chronicle of George Synkellos*)

As pointed out earlier, concurrently with the *Symeonic Florilegium* there appeared in medieval Bulgaria an historiographic compilation based on redrafted extracts from the chronographies of George Synkellos (d. 810)[109] and Julius

---

109   While referring to extracts from *The Chronography of George Synkellos* ['Ἐκλογὴ Χρονογραφίας], the present author follows the English translation of the text by W. Adler and P. Tuffin, *The Chronography of George Synkellos: A Byzantine Chronicle of Universal History from the Creation*, Oxford, 2002.

FIGURE 22.4 The Devil—depicted above two young women dressed in traditional clothes putting make-up on their faces—shown defecating into the vessel containing cosmetics. Fresco from the church of St Nicholas, Cherven Breg, South-Western Bulgaria. Painted in 1882
PHOTO: AUTHOR

FIGURE 22.5   The Devil—depicted above the heads of three young women dressed in traditional clothes putting make-up on their faces—shown defecating into the vessel containing cosmetics. Fresco from the church of St George, Sandanski county, South-Western Bulgaria. Painted by Teofil and Marko Minov, 1876 (?). The inscription reads: 'Моми който ке царвѣтъ а дявола се сери во паницата' ('Maidens who put on [their faces] white and red [colouring matter] have the Devil defecating into the bowl [containing their cosmetics]').
PHOTO: AUTHOR

Africanus (ca. 160–240).[110] As indicated above,[111] we prefer to designate it as *The Slavonic Derivative of the Chronicle of George Synkellos*[112] (hereafter *Slavonic Derivative of Synkellos*).

110 The extant fragments of the *Chronographiæ* of Julius Africanus are translated by W. Adler and published in collaboration with U. Roberto and K. Pinggéra under the editorship of M. Wallraff, *Iulius Africanus: Chronographiæ. The Extant Fragments* [*Die griechischen christlichen Schriftsteller der ersten Jahrhunderte*, NF 15], Berlin–New York, 2007. Of particular importance for the current discussion is Africanus's description of the antediluvian period (F23 The Circumstances of the Flood); the chronographer argues that 'the sons of God' should be identified with the descendants of Seth, who mingled with the descendants of Cain (i.e. the human seed), thus triggering God's anger:

When humankind became numerous upon the earth, angels of heaven had intercourse with daughters of men. In some manuscripts, I found: 'the sons of God'. In my opinion,

ENOCHIC TEXTS AND RELATED TRADITIONS IN SLAVIA ORTHODOXA 489

It is well known that Synkellos was one of the last Byzantine writers to refer to the writings of Enoch.[113] Included in his *Ekloge chronographias* ['Εκλογὴ Χρονογραφίας] is a long (albeit extensively reworked) excerpt, 'From the first book of Enoch, concerning the Watchers' ['Εκ τοῦ πρώτου βιβλίου 'Ενὼχ περὶ τῶν ἐγρηγόρων] (i.e. *1Enoch* 6.1–9.11).[114]

---

this is to be understood figuratively: ⟨the descendants⟩ of Seth are called 'the sons of God' by the Spirit, since the genealogies of the righteous and the patriarchs up until the Saviour are traced from him. But the descendants of Cain it designates as human seed, as having had nothing divine because of the wickedness of their line and the dissimilarity of their nature, so that when they were mingled together, God grew angry. [Quoted after M. Wallraff et al., *Iulius Africanus: Chronographiæ*, pp. 49–50].

But immediately afterward Africanus reluctantly contemplates the possibility that 'the sons of God' might not be a figurative phrase, but a literal, direct designation, in which case it should be interpreted as the 'angels of heaven' (instead of 'the sons of Seth'):

But let us suppose they refer to 'angels'. Then it was they who transmitted knowledge about magic and sorcery, as well as the numbers of the motion of astronomical phenomena, to their wives, from whom they produced the giants as their children; and when depravity came into being because of them, God resolved to destroy every class of living things in a flood. [Quoted after M. Wallraff et al., *Iulius Africanus: Chronographiæ*, p. 51].

The latter statement indicates that Africanus was certainly acquainted with Enochic traditions; see also the discussion in G. Nickelsburg, *A Commentary on the Book of 1Enoch (Chapters 1–36; 81–108)*, p. 92.

111 See note 24 above.

112 Among the first to discuss this text was V. Istrin, 'Iz oblasti drevne-russkoĭ literatury', *ZhMNP* vol. 8 (Avgust 1903), pp. 381–414; see also the first chapter (entitled 'Khronika Georgiia Sinkela') of his monograph *Issledovaniia v oblasti drevnerusskoĭ literatury*, Sankt Petersburg, 1906, pp. 2–34. A text-critical edition of the *Chronicle* was published by A. Totomanova, with the 15th–16th century Russian redaction from the Undolsky Miscellany from the Palæographic collection of the Russian State Library in Moscow (Ms.1289) as a primary text witness (see id., *Slavianskata Versiia na Khronikata na Georgi Sinkel: Izdanie i Komentar*, Sofia, 2008). A. Totomanova was also the first to point out that the Slavonic version of the *Chronicle* recycles rephrased fragments from Julius Africanus. Our analysis is based on Totomanova's edition of *The Slavonic Version of the Chronicle of Synkellos*.

113 See W. Adler and P. Tuffin, *The Chronography of George Synkellos*, pp. liv–lv; L. Arcari, 'Are Women the *Aition* for the Evil in the World? George Syncellus's Version of *1Enoch* 8:1 in Light of Hesiod's *Theogony* and *Works and Days*', *Henoch* vol. 34, issue 1 (2012), pp. 5–12, 18–20. It has been argued that Synkellos's excerpts represent re-writing of traditions transmitted by the early fifth century Alexandrian monks Panodorus and Annianus; see W. Adler, *Time Immemorial*, pp. 73–74; G. Nickelsburg, *A Commentary on the Book of 1Enoch (Chapters 1–36; 81–108)*, pp. 12–13; A.Y. Reed, 'Enoch in Armenian Apocrypha', in K.B. Bardakjian and S. La Porta (eds), *The Armenian Apocalyptic Tradition: A Comparative Perspective*, Leiden, 2014, p. 165. For Panodorus's use of *1Enoch*, see W. Adler, 'Berossus, Manetho, and *1Enoch* in the World Chronicle of Panodorus', pp. 419–442; id., *Time Immemorial*, p. 81, pp. 86–96, p. 154, p. 177, p. 179.

114 See K.W. Dindorf, *Georgius Syncellus et Nicephorus Cp* vol. 1. Corpus Scriptorum Historiæ

While listing the sins committed by the Watchers[115] who engaged in carnal relationships with 'the beautiful daughters' of men and initiated them into the esoteric illicit lore of potions and spells (thus trespassing both cosmological

---

Byzantinæ, Bonn, 1829, pp. 20–30; W. Adler and P. Tuffin, *The Chronography of George Synkellos*, pp. 16–23. On textual emendation in Synkellos's Enoch excerpts, see W. Adler, *Time Immemorial*, pp. 175–182.

115 The amount of literature on the *Watchers myth* (along with the *Shemihazah myth* and/or the *Asael myth*) is considerable; for a concise survey of scholarly discourse on the topic see the publications of the following authors (in alphabetical order): A. Annus, 'On the Origin of the *Watchers*: A Comparative Study of the Antediluvian Wisdom in Mesopotamian and Jewish Traditions', *JSP* vol. 19, 2010, pp. 277–320; L. Arcari, 'Are Women the *Aition* for the Evil in the World? George Syncellus's Version of *1 Enoch* 8:1 in Light of Hesiod's *Theogony* and *Works and Days*', *Henoch* vol. 34, issue 1 (2012), pp. 5–20; J.S. Bergsma, 'The Relationship between *Jubilees* and the Early Enochic Books (*Astronomical Book* and the *Book of the Watchers*)', in G. Boccaccini and G. Ibba (eds), *Enoch and the Mosaic Torah. The Evidence of Jubilees*, Grand Rapids, MI–Cambridge, UK, 2009, pp. 36–51; S. Bhayro, *The Shemihazah and Asael Narrative of 1 Enoch 6–11: Introduction, Text, Translation and Commentary with Reference to Ancient Near Eastern and Biblical Antecedents*, Münster, 2005; K. Coblentz Bautch, 'What Becomes of the Angels' 'Wives'? A Text Critical Study of *1 En.* 19: 2', *JBL* vol. 125, issue 4 (2006), pp. 766–780; J. Collins, *The Apocalyptic Imagination: An Introduction to Jewish Apocalyptic Literature*, pp. 47–59; id., *Seers, Sibyls and Sages in Hellenistic-Roman Judaism*, pp. 289–298; id., *Apocalypse, Prophesy, and Pseudepigraphy*, pp. 301–307; P. Crone, 'The Book of Watchers in the Qur'ān', in H. Ben-Shammai, S. Shaked and S. Stroumsa (eds), *Exchange and Transmission Across Cultural Boundaries: Philosophy, Mysticism and Science in the Mediterranean*, Jerusalem, 2013, pp. 16–51; M. Himmelfarb, *Ascent to Heaven in Jewish and Christian Apocalypses*, pp. 20–21, 72–74, 77–78; R. Lesses, 'The Most Worthy of Women is a Mistress of Magic': Women as Witches and Ritual Practitioners in *1 Enoch* and Rabbinic Sources', in K.B. Stratton with D.S. Kalleres (eds), *Daughters of Hecate: Women and Magic in the Ancient World*, Oxford, 2014, pp. 74–78; J. Milik, *The Books of Enoch*, pp. 22–41; G. Nickelsburg, *A Commentary on the Book of 1 Enoch (Chapters 1–36; 81–108)*, p. 7, pp. 12–13, pp. 165–201; A.Y. Reed, 'From Asael and Šemiḥazah to Uzzah, Azzah, and Azael: *3 Enoch* 5 (§§ 7–8) and Jewish Reception-History of *1 Enoch*', *Jewish Studies Quarterly* vol. 8 (2001), pp. 106, pp. 114–136; id., 'Heavenly Ascent, Angelic Descent, and the Transmission of Knowledge in *1 Enoch* 6–16', in R. Boustan and A.Y. Reed (eds), *Heavenly Realms and Earthly Realities in Late Antique Religions*, Cambridge, 2004, pp. 47–66; id., *Fallen Angels and the History of Judaism and Christianity. The Reception of Enochic Literature*, New York–Cambridge, 2005; id., 'Gendering Heavenly Secrets? Women, Angels, and the Problem of Misogyny and Magic', in K.B. Stratton with D.S. Kalleres (eds), *Daughters of Hecate: Women and Magic in the Ancient World*, Oxford, 2014, pp. 110–138; P. Sacchi, 'The Book of the Watchers as an Apocalyptic and Apocryphal Text', *Henoch* vol. 30, issue 1 (2008), pp. 9–26; P. Schäfer, *The Origins of Jewish Mysticism*, pp. 53–67; M. Stone, 'Enoch and the Fall of the Angels: Teaching and Status', *DSD* vol. 22, issue 3 (2015), pp. 342–357; L. Stuckenbruck, 'The 'Angels' and 'Giants' of Genesis 6:1–4 in Second and Third Century BCE Jewish Interpretation: Reflections on the Posture of Early Apocalyptic Traditions', *DSD* vol. 7, issue 3 [*Angels and Demons*] (2000), pp. 354–377; id., 'The Origins of Evil in Jew-

and epistemic boundaries),[116] Synkellos provides a long register of the transgressions attributed to different angels.[117] Thus he points out that the chief of the Watchers, Semiazas, disclosed to mankind knowledge about the roots of plants.[118] Azaël (the tenth leader) taught men technologies of extraction of 'the metals of the earth and gold' and the deadly craft of smithing 'swords and armour and every instrument of war.' He also made them acquainted with the art of cosmetics and manufacturing colouring tinctures (i.e. alchemy). The resourcefulness of beautification and enhancement of the countenances of 'the daughters of men' is classified as a subset of war-craft. Flesh is weapon. Erotic is entrapment. Sexual inducement is implicitly defined as warfare. The impact of the 'manmade' carnal beauty is equated to that of deadly armaments.

Last but not least, Azaël taught men how to make gold and silver adornments for their wives. Yet it was not just the specialized craft skills of jewellery-making that he bestowed upon them; the implied subtext is that Azaël instructed men how to produce amulets and talismans, since it was the protective function of metal ornaments as charms that was at stake here, not just their æsthetic properties. At the same time, metalwork was further linked to wealth and social stratification, of which jewellery became the ultimate marker. Thus the knowledge revealed by Azaël is branded as lethal arts causing the destruction of mankind, both physical and moral.

The eleventh Watcher, who revealed 'the uses of potions, spells, lore, and the remedies for spells,'[119] was called Pharmaros [Φαρμαρός]. In this connection Adler points out that the latter appellation was a deliberately altered form

---

ish Apocalyptic Tradition: The Interpretation of Genesis 6:1–4 in the Second and Third Centuries BCE', in Ch. Auffarth and L. Stuckenbruck (eds), *The Fall of the Angels* [Themes in Biblical Narrative: Jewish and Christian Traditions 6], Leiden–Boston, 2004, pp. 99–118; id., '*The Book of Enoch*: Its Reception in Second Temple Judaism and in Christianity', *EChr* vol. 4, issue 1 (2013), pp. 14–15; id., 'The Myth of Rebellious Angels: Ethics and Theological Anthropology', in M. Konradt and E. Schläpfer (eds), *Anthropologie und Ethik im Frühjudentum und im Neuen Testament: wechselseitige Wahrnehmungen*. Internationales Symposium in Verbindung mit dem Projekt Corpus Judæo-Hellenisticum Novi Testamenti (CJHNT) 17.–20. Mai 2012, Heidelberg [Wissenschaftliche Untersuchungen zum Neuen Testament vol. 322], Tübingen, 2014, pp. 163–176; id., *The Myth of the Rebellious Angels. Studies in Second Temple Judaism and New Testament Texts*, Tübingen, 2014, pp. 12–35, p. 43, pp. 47–48. See also the discussion below.

116   See P. Crone, '*The Book of Watchers* in the *Qurʾān*', p. 18.
117   Cf. Adler, Tuffin, *The Chronography of George Synkellos*, pp. 16–17.
118   Cf. Adler, Tuffin, *The Chronography of George Synkellos*, p. 17.
119   Cf. Adler, Tuffin, *The Chronography of George Synkellos*, p. 17.

of the angelonym Harmoni (i.e. 'from Mt. Hermon'); by using it, the author intended to turn the Watcher's name into the eponym of his revelations (i.e. the lore of using potions and remedies).[120] But while the Ethiopic version of *1Enoch* (8:1–17) quotes the names of the chief Watchers responsible for the transmission of different kinds of proscribed knowledge one by one (i.e. Baraqiel, Kokabel, Tamiel, Asradiel), Synkellos's list is somewhat abbreviated. The Byzantine chronographer simply clarifies which types of 'exact' sciences concerning particular terrestrial and celestial matters are illicitly disclosed to the human race by the rebellious angels (whose names he occasionally omits). Unnamed in his Chronicle, for instance, is the third chief of the Watchers, who is portrayed as the demiurge of *geomancy* and/or *seismomancy* (i.e. the skills of prophesying/forecasting by means of 'encoding' calendric characteristics of earthquakes), since he is reported to have taught people 'the signs of the Earth.' The rest of the anonymous Fallen Angels are connected with illicit revelations of esoteric knowledge concerning various aspects of astronomy, with special emphasis on astrology and divination. Thus the ninth chief Watcher is reported to have taught mankind 'the study of the stars'—a rather broad epistemic category, most probably enveloping all kinds of sciences about celestial bodies, including skills for mapping the sky and calculating the trajectories of heavenly luminaries (stars and/or planets, including the positioning of constellations), locating and tracking them within the specific time/seasonal coordinates. This particular Watcher was most probably considered to have likewise taught time-measurement and time-keeping (i.e. calendar as a subset of astronomy). His functions are intertwined with those of the fourth chief Watcher (who instructed the human race about astrology). Similar is the role of the eighth chief Watcher, who trained people in the art of 'divination by observing the heavens' (that is, the skills of interpreting the 'language' of celestial signs and stellar omens). The seventh is portrayed as the demiurge of heliomancy, since he taught mankind 'the signs of the Sun' (i.e. sun-related omens, with reference to solar eclipses?), while the twentieth revealed 'the signs of the Moon' (i.e. *selenomancy*, or moon-related omens). All of them, as summarized by Synkellos, revealed 'mysteries to their wives and offspring.'[121]

Significantly, the famous narrative unit, 'From the First Book of Enoch concerning the Watchers' ('Ἐκ τοῦ πρώτου βιβλίου Ἐνὼχ περὶ τῶν ἐγρηγόρων), as

---

120   Cf. Adler, Tuffin, *The Chronography of George Synkellos*, p. 17 (note 4); W. Adler, *Time Immemorial*, p. 176 (note 61).

121   Cf. Adler, Tuffin, *The Chronography of George Synkellos*, p. 14.

ENOCHIC TEXTS AND RELATED TRADITIONS IN SLAVIA ORTHODOXA 493

attested in the original text of *The Chronography of George Synkellos*, is missing from its rewritten Slavonic descendant. Yet the latter text contains some intriguing details indicating that its compilers were aware of the existence of *1Enoch*. Thus in the opening chapter of *The Slavonic Derivative of Synkellos*[122] one finds a short paragraph[123] making the following important statements:

1) Enoch was 165 years old when he became the father of his firstborn son Methuselah [Енох бъівъ лѣт рⷨе лѣт роди мафоусал8] (Fol. 406ʳ, line 23);[124]

2) he was a pious, reverent man who 'pleased God' [и оугоⷣн Енох Бгоу] (Fol. 406ʳ, line 24);[125]

3) after Enoch's having followed the path of righteousness without deviating from it for two hundred years after Methuselah's birth, another—more grand—life was bestowed upon him [пожъівъ к снмъ лѣт .ⷭ. не соѣрааще са преставлен во въіс в болшую жъіⷥнь] (Fol. 406ʳ, lines 24–25);[126]

4) Enoch, who was seventh from Adam, was presented (to God) [седмъін съі ѿ адама престави са] (Fol. 406ʳ, lines 24–25);[127]

5) the tradition holds that the narrative of 'his prophesy' is preserved 'in five secret /esoteric / hermetic books' [и мнат же и пророуство сего в патерⷯъіхъ кннгах въ таннъіх] (Fol. 406ʳ, lines 26–27).

The concluding phrase of the above quoted fragment from *The Slavonic Derivative of Synkellos* undoubtedly indicates that reference is being made here to *First*, rather than to *Second Enoch*, since only *First Enoch* is known to be a *Pentateuch*.[128]

---

122 Used in the current discussion is A. Totomanova's edition of the text from the aforementioned Ms. № 1289 (the Undolsky Miscellany) from the Palæographic collection of the Russian State Library in Moscow (see note 112 above).

123 See A. Totomanova, *Slavianskata Versiia na Khronikata na Georgi Sinkel*, p. 33.

124 Cf. (LXX) *Gn.* 5:18.

125 Cf. (LXX) *Gn.* 5:22, 24; *The Epistle to Hebrews* 11:5.

126 Cf. (LXX) *Gn.* 5:22, 24.

127 Cf. *The Epistle of Jude* 1:14.

128 On the term *Enochic Pentateuch*, see (the now classical) study of J.C. Greenfield and M.E. Stone 'The Enochic Pentateuch and the Date of the *Similitudes*', pp. 51–65. While J. Milik maintains that a Greek Enochic Pentateuch had developed by the year 400 C.E. and hence functioned as the basis for the Ethiopic version, J. Greenfield and M. Stone, on the other hand, argue that '[i]t is by no means evident that, because five works are combined in the Ethiopic version of Enoch, they were considered by the Greek or Ethiopic compiler to be a Pentateuch. If such a title is to be meaningful, presumably it implies that they were arranged as a Pentateuch based on the model of the Mosaic Pentateuch. Even if

After the laconic statement about Enoch and his 'five secret/esoteric/hermetic books,' *The Slavonic Derivative of Synkellos* gives a concise list of his offspring (with Methuselah being the eighth after Adam) up to the generation of Noah and his three sons Sim [Снмъ], Ham [Хамъ] and Japhet [Афетъ], in the days in which people multiplied greatly on earth [множъству улкь бъıвъшоу на ꙁемли] and the angels of heaven [аг҃ли н҃бнïи] mixed with the daughters of men [къ дщеремъ улуⁿкъıмъ прнмѣснша са] (Fol. 406ᵛ, lines 6–8);[129] there follows a short note that 'in other scriptures' [въ дроугïихⁿ же пнсанïихъ] the divine husbands of earthly women were identified as 'sons of God' [сн҃ве бжïи] (Fol. 406ᵛ, line 8).[130] The offspring of Seth remained righteous, while those of Cain were wicked, and the sins committed aroused the wrath of God, who sent the Flood to wash away the unrighteousness and purify the earth.[131]

But why is the narrative unit about the Watchers missing from *The Slavonic Derivative of Synkellos*? The argument of A. Totomanova that the initial chapters of its corpus followed the account of Julius Africanus (the surviving excerpts of which do not contain fragments from *The Book of Watchers*) rather than that of Synkellos (which does contain such fragments), might just provide a clue to a convincing answer.

On the other hand, the corpus of *The Slavonic Derivative of Synkellos* contains some small, but recognisable quotations from *2 Enoch*; this, in turn, would indicate that the scribe(s) who translated the former were most probably acquainted with the latter. Thus the laconic account about the creation of man in *The Slavonic Derivative of Synkellos*, which is encapsulated in the cosmogonic scenario of the sixth day, redrafts some distinctive formulaic expressions that are likewise attested in *2 Enoch* 30:10–12 (the longer recension). But in contrast to *2 Enoch*, where the anthropogonic story is part of God's testimony and thus

---

this were true for the Ethiopic book, nothing in the evidence adduced by Milik shows that it was true at Qumran' (see id., 'The Enochic Pentateuch and the Date of the *Similitudes*', p. 53).

129 Quoted after A. Totomanova, *Slavianskata Versiia na Khronikata na Georgi Sinkel*, p. 34.

130 Quoted after A. Totomanova, *Slavianskata Versiia na Khronikata na Georgi Sinkel*, p. 34. Cf. Synkellos, *Chron.* 19: 24–26 (from Africanus): Πλήθους ἀνθρώπων γενομένου ἐπὶ τῆς γῆς ἄγγελοι τοῦ οὐρανοῦ θυγατράσιν ἀνθρώπων συνῆλθον. ἐν ἐνίοις ἀντιγράφοις εὗρον· οἱ υἱοὶ τοῦ θεοῦ ['When humankind became numerous upon the earth, angels of heaven had intercourse with daughters of men. In some manuscripts, I found: the "sons of God"']; see F23 (lines 1–2) in *Iulius Africanus Chronographiae*, p. 48. The English translation by W. Adler.

131 The narrative appears to follow a tradition (first attested in Julius Africanus and subsequently adopted by George Synkellos) according to which God was angered by the sinful mixing of the lineages of the righteous Seth and the sinful Cain; see note 110 above.

ENOCHIC TEXTS AND RELATED TRADITIONS IN SLAVIA ORTHODOXA   495

is presented as a first-person narrative, in *The Slavonic Derivative of Synkellos* the statement concerning the creation of man is rendered as a third-person narrative:

> СЕГО БꙊ МꙐСЛНВЪ ХНТРОЕ СЛОВО СКАꙀАТН. Н ЖНВОТЪ ЕДННЪ ѿ ОБОЕГО ѿ ВНᲁНᲂМагᲃО рекоу н невндꙵнмаго естьства. съꙁᲁа ѵлка од вещн же вꙁемъ:. велнкоу. на ꙁемлн постанв. агг҃ла дроугаго. ѵстна велнка славна. ц҃ра ꙁемнꙑмъ. цр҃ство нмоуща ѿ б҃а.¹³²

Thence [He] thought of uttering a wise word, and a sole living creature from both the invisible and visible natures [came into being]; [He] created man, having taken him from the material substance; [He created him] great, and appointed him to be the second angel on earth: honourable, great and glorious, and to be the King [of everything dwelling] on earth. And his kingdom was granted to him by God.¹³³

In *2 Enoch*, on the other hand, the creation of man is described in a much more elaborate fashion,¹³⁴ but the central storyline is based on a template analogous to that attested in the aforementioned anthropogonic narrative of *The Slavonic Derivative of Synkellos*. The fragment in question (that is, *2 Enoch* 30:10–12) runs as follows:¹³⁵

---

132 Cf. A. Totomanova, *Slavianskata Versiia na Khronikata na Georgi Sinkel*, pp. 31–32 (Fol. 405a, lines 21–22 and Fol. 405ᵛ, lines 1–7).

133 Author's translation.

134 Cf. *2 Enoch* 30:8–18; 31:1–3.

135 Unless otherwise mentioned, references to the original Slavonic text of *2 Enoch* in the present article are based on the Bulgarian redaction of *The Books of the Holy Secrets of Enoch* [Кннгн ст҃нх таннь Енохо ᲁ] (that is, Ms. S). The text was copied in a miscellany (Ms. № 321, fols 269ʳ–323ʳ) formerly kept in the palæographic collection of the Serbian National Library in Belgrade. However, there is no consensus concerning the chronological characteristics of this text witness; some scholars (e.g. M. Sokolov and Ĭ. Ivanov) date Ms. S to the 16th–17th centuries, while others (e.g. B. Khristova)—to the 14th century. We follow M. Sokolov's edition (*Slavianskaia Kniga Enokha*, pp. 1–80), the amended version of which was subsequently published by Ĭ. Ivanov in his *Bogomilski Knigi i Legendi*, pp. 167–191 (with parallel readings from other text witnesses); see also F. Badalanova Geller, *Second (Slavonic Apocalypse of) Enoch: Text and Context*. The version preserved in Ms. S represents the longer recension of *2 Enoch*; see Sokolov, *Slavianskaia Kniga Enokha Pravednago* (Part 2, pp. 8–32), as well as Morfill and Charles, *The Book of the Secrets of Enoch*, pp. xiii–xiv; A. Iatsimirskiĭ, *Bibliograficheskiĭ Obzor Apokrifov v Iuzhnoslavianskoĭ i Russkoĭ Pis'mennosti*, p. 83 (список No. 4); A. Vaillant, *Le livre des secrets d'Hénoch*, pp. iii–iv, p. vii, pp. 86–119]. As for Ms. № 321, it was destroyed during the bombardment of Belgrade in

СЕ ПОМЫСЛН˟ ХНТРОЕ СЛОВО. СКАЗАТН ѿ НЕВНДНМАГО ЖЕ Н ВНДНМАГО ЕⷭТВА
СЪЗДА˟ ѹЛка ѿ ОБОЕГО СЬМРⷮЬ Н ЖНВОⷮ. Н сѡБРАЗЬ ВѢСТЬ СЛОВО, ꙗкЪІ НѢКА-
КОУ ТВАРЬ ЙНЖ ВЪ ВЕЛНЦѢ МАЛЖ, Н ПАКЪІ ВЪ МАЛѢ ВЕЛНКЖ. Н НА ЗЕМЛН
ПОСТАВН˟ ЕГО АГ҃ЛА ВТОРАГО ѹСТНА Н ВЕЛНКА Н СЛАВНАА. Н ПОСТАВН˟ ЕГО ЦР҃Ѣ
ЗЕМЛН. ЦРСТВО НМАЦІА МОЕА МЖДРОСТІЖ, Н НЕ БѢ ЕМОУ ПОДБНА НА ЗЕМЛН Н
ѿ СЖЦІН˟ ТВАРН МОН˟.[136]

Thence I thought of uttering [this] wise word: from invisible and visible
natures I created man, from both death and life. The image came to know
the Word and a new small creature [came into being]—small in greatness and great in smallness. And I placed him on earth as a second angel,
honourable, great and glorious. And I put him as the King on earth, having [rule through] My wisdom, and there was no equal to him on earth
among My creatures.[137]

To sum up; the parallel use of matching phraseological units (e.g. 'thence He/I
thought of uttering this wise word,' 'from invisible and visible natures,' 'the second angel (on earth): honourable, great and glorious,' 'the King on earth,' etc.)
in the anthropogonic account of *The Slavonic Derivative of Synkellos* and that of
2 Enoch 30:10–12 (the longer recension) suggests that the scribes who produced
the former were familiar with the latter. This certainly indicates that the longer
recension of this apocryphal composition was already in circulation at the time
when the earliest edition of *The Slavonic Derivative of Synkellos* was made. This,
in turn, may support N. Schmidt's hypothesis, that there were most probably
two Greek recensions that were translated by different Slavonic scribes at different times.[138] Alternatively, it may likewise imply that the longer recension
of *2 Enoch* preceded the shorter one (since *The Slavonic Derivative of Synkellos*
was among the earliest documents to occur concurrently with the *Symeonic
Florilegium*).

Then again, the lack of any, even redrafted, quotations from *The Book of
Watchers* in *The Slavonic Derivative of Synkellos* stands in sharp contrast to the
numerous attestations of the parallel use of identical phraseological expressions employed in both *The Slavonic Derivative of Synkellos* and *2 Enoch* 30:10–

1941; the material absence of the actual codex makes the issue of its dating even more
complicated.

136 Cf. Sokolov, *Slavianskaia Kniga Enokha*, p. 30 (lines 59–63), Ї. Ivanov, *Bogomilski Knigi i
Legendi*, p. 177.

137 Author's translation.

138 Cf. N. Schmidt, 'The Two Recensions of *Slavonic Enoch*', p. 310.

ENOCHIC TEXTS AND RELATED TRADITIONS IN SLAVIA ORTHODOXA 497

12. This may well indicate that the Slavonic scribes most probably treated *2 Enoch* as part of a collection akin to *1 Enoch*; thus the former may have been perceived as a substitute for the latter.

2.4 Shared Mythologemes in Anthropogonic Templates in *2 Enoch* and John the Exarch's *Hexæmeron*: The Name of Adam as Acronym-Tetragram

Apart from *The Slavonic Derivative of Synkellos*, during the reign of Symeon in the literary landscape of the First Bulgarian Kingdom, there also circulated a cluster of other parabiblical works (likewise translated / compiled /edited by the scribes from the Preslav Literary School) that contained cosmogonic and anthropogonic narratives akin to those attested in *2 Enoch* (the longer recension).[139] One such work is John the Exarch's *Hexæmeron*.[140] The account of the creation of man, and especially the micro-narrative about the origin of his name, as presented in the *Homily on the Sixth Day*, renders an anthropogonic scenario similar to that in *2 Enoch* 30:13–14.[141] According to the latter, the biblical anthroponym ADAM is composed of four letters signifying the four cardinal directions of the Universe:

---

139 That is, Ms. S, Ms. J, Ms. P and Ms. SokRum.

140 See § 2.1 above, note 19.

141 Consult also Stith Thompson's *Motif-Index of Folk Literature: A Classification of Narrative Elements in Folktales, Ballads, Myths, Fables, Medieval Romances, Exempla, Fabliaux, Jest-Books and Local Legends* vol. 1, Copenhagen, 1955, entry A1281.6.1: *Adam's name composed of initial letters of four stars from the four quarters of the heaven*. Among earlier sources in which the anthroponym *Adam* is envisaged as an acronym composed of the initial letters of the words denoting the four corners of the Universe (East, West, North and South) are *The Sibylline Oracles* (3: 24–27); cf. J. Collins, 'Sibylline Oracles', in J.H. Charlesworth (ed.), *The Old Testament Pseudepigrapha* vol. 1, p. 362. For an overview of texts and traditions in Medieval Greek and Slavonic sources interpreting the idea of the appellation 'Adam' as an acronym (and thus constructing the name of the primordial man as a verbal icon of the Universe), see W.R. Morfill and R.H. Charles, *The Book of the Secrets of Enoch*, pp. xvi, xxvii; Ch. Böttrich, *Adam als Mikrokosmos*, pp. 17–34, 59–72; A. Orlov, *From Apocalypticism to Merkabah Mysticism*, pp. 158–161; W. Ryan, 'Curious Star Names in Slavonic Literature', *RL* vol. 1 (1974), pp. 139–142; id., 'Astronomy in Church Slavonic: Linguistic Aspects of Cultural Transmission', in G. Stone and D. Worth (eds), *The Formation of Slavonic Literary Languages*, Columbus, OH, 1985, p. 56; F. Badalanova, 'The Bible in the Making: Slavonic Myths of Creation', in M.J. Geller and M. Schipper (eds), *Imagining Creation*, Leiden–Boston, 2008, pp. 233–235; S. Voicu, 'Adamo, acrostico del mondo', *Apocrypha* vol. 18 (2007), pp. 205–230; id., 'Gematria e acrostico di Adamo: nuovi testimoni', *Apocrypha* vol. 25 (2014) pp. 181–193.

н поставн^х ємоу нма ѿ ѵєтырн съставь¹⁴² ѿ въстокь, ѿ ӡапа^а, ѿ сѣвєра, ѿ юга. Н поставн^х ємоу ·д̄· ӡвѣӡды нароунтн, н рєкь нма єго ада^м.¹⁴³

And I assigned to him a name from four elements: from East, from West, from North, and from South.[144] And I assigned to him four special stars; and I called his name 'Adam.'[145]

However, the decipherment of the name of Adam as an acronym-appellation composed from the first letters of the words denoting the four principal corners of the Universe—A for Ἀνατολή (East), D for Δύσις (West), A for Ἄρκτος (North) and M for Μεσαμβρία (South)—was far from transparent for those among the Slavonic readers who were not acquainted with the Greek subtext of this linguistic riddle. In fact, it is exactly this particular fragment to which many scholars refer when arguing for the existence of a Greek protograph of *2 Enoch*, on the basis of which the Slavonic translation/edition was made, rather than directly from a Semitic *Vorlage*.

In a similar way, in John the Exarch's *Hexæmeron*, the 'etymology' of the biblical anthroponym *ADAM* is explicated as a symbolic designation of the Universe; as such, it is identified as a verbal icon of the 'micro-cosmos.' As in *2 Enoch* 30:13–14, in the *Homily on the Sixth Day*, it is emphasized that each letter of Adam's name is bound to the Greek terms denoting the four cardinal directions (Ἀνατολή, Δύσις, Ἄρκτος, Μεσαμβρία).

But while the anthropogonic fragments in *The Slavonic Derivative of Synkellos* and *2 Enoch* 30:10–12 use almost identical phraseological expressions, representing two congenital renditions of one and the same intrinsic narrative (thus showing common origin and similar transmission history), the case with the parallels between *2 Enoch* 30:13–14 and John the Exarch's *Homily on the Sixth Day* is of a totally different nature. Although the content of the two anthropogonic narratives is anchored by one and the same mythologeme—that of

---

142   The Old Bulgarian/Old Church Slavonic lexeme съставь may well be used in other sources to render Gr. στοιχεῖα, φύσις, ὑπόστασις, thus denoting scientific, philosophic and theological concepts such as 'element' / 'component' / 'ingredient' / 'constituent' / 'essence'/ 'hypostasis', but also 'letter' / 'grapheme'. Thus the biblical anthroponym Adam is transformed by Enochic taxonomy into an ontological category.

143   Cf. Sokolov, *Slavianskaia Kniga Enokha*, p. 30 (lines 59–63), Ĭ. Ivanov, *Bogomilski Knigi i Legendi*, p. 177.

144   The same in Ms. J. In Mss. P and SokRum: from East, from West, from South and from North.

145   Author's translation.

ENOCHIC TEXTS AND RELATED TRADITIONS IN SLAVIA ORTHODOXA 499

the name of Adam being an acronym of the four cardinal directions of the Universe,—their modes of explication are totally different.

It should be noted that John the Exarch's edition of the narrative about the creation of man and the origin of Adam's name is based on an excerpt from Severian of Gabala's *In Cosmogoniam homiliæ vi*,[146] which in Greek Byzantine tradition was conventionally appended to Basil of Cæsarea's *Homiliæ ix in Hexæmeron*.[147] In contrast to the Antiochian exegete Severian, the Cappadocian Church Father Basil never mentioned the appellation *ADAM* in his *Hexæmeron*; this is why Severian's anthropogonic account became the primary constituent of John the Exarch's *Homily on the Sixth Day*.[148]

Having adopted Severian's exegetical discourse on the hermeneutics of Adam's name, the medieval Bulgarian scholar John the Exarch constructs his own deliberations as a two-fold nexus. Thus, while redrafting in his *Homily on the Sixth Day* the narrative template akin to that attested in *2 Enoch* 30:13–14, he implicitly refers to the comments of the Antiochian exegete Severian regarding the Greek linguistic ancestry of the acronym-tetragram 'Adam.' John the Exarch embarks, following in the steps of his predecessor, on the decipherment of yet another philological riddle, but this time aiming at proving a new, alternative, Hebrew-based etiology of the name of Adam.

In Severian's *Homily*, this argument is based on wordplay (constructible only in Hebrew) between the appellation for 'man' [איש] and that for 'fire' [אש] (see below). Obviously, on this occasion the Antiochian exegete refers to one of the most fashionable cosmological concepts within his intellectual environment, that of the four primordial elements from which the Universe is constituted: earth, water, air and fire,[149] with fire having a different mode of being in contrast to the other three. By the same token, Severian states: the nature of fire should be considered as comparable to that of man, since the modes of existence of the former shape the ontological paradigm of the latter.

---

146   See also in this connection G. Barankova and V. Mil'kov, *Shestodnev Ioanna Ekzarkha Bolgarskogo*, pp. 955–966; G. Barankova, 'K voprosu o perevodakh *Shestodneva* Severiana Gaval'skogo v drevneslavianskoĭ i drevnerusskoĭ knizhnosti', in *Lingvisticheskoe istochnikovedenie i istoriia russkogo iazyka*: 2001, Moscow, 2002, pp. 7–8; L. Sels and S. Van Pee, 'Scholia from Severian of Gabala's *In Cosmogoniam homiliæ* in the 14th-century Slavonic *Hexæmeron* Collection', p. 94.

147   Basil of Cæsarea's *Ninth Homily*, which is devoted to the creation of terrestrial animals and mankind, offers a general exegetical discourse on *Genesis* 1:26 ('Let us make man in our image'), but lacks a detailed anthropogonic narrative *per se*.

148   In John the Exarch's text the authorship of this fragment is ascribed to John Chrysostom; see the discussion above, note 19.

149   This epistemological model originated in Greek pre-Socratic philosophy, and in particular in Empedocles's theory of the four 'root elements', to be developed later in Plato.

Severian's discourse is enhanced by a rather sophisticated—resembling the style of rabbinical exegesis—elegant linguistic pun which, as already pointed out, can only be constructed in Hebrew, since the word for 'man' (*'ish* [איש]) is a near homonym of that for 'fire' (*'esh* [אש]).[150] Using the rhetoric of paronomasia, Severian designs and formulates an idiosyncratic hermeneutical algorithm for encoding not only the mystery of anthropogenesis, but also the very ontological principle of man's existence.

Unfolded in Severian's (and subsequently, John the Exarch's) discourse, along with the Greek 'etymology' of Adam's name, is thus one further strategy for illuminating its hermetic meaning, referring to man's nature as a manifestation of the superior among the elements of the Universe—fire. Once again the acronym-tetragram is interpreted as an appellation of the Cosmos/Universe itself, but this time the emphasis shifts to Adam's function as a progenitor of mankind, since, as the text states, it is from him, from the primordial human, that the terrestrial realm, up to its four corners (East, West, North and South), is to be inhabited and filled up by people; Adam is likened to a vessel of cosmic fire from which the candles of his progeny are to be set alight. Henceforth the 'archetypal' meaning of the biblical phrase 'Let us make man' (*Genesis* 1:26), Severian argues, is to be read as 'Let us make fire.' Here follows the relevant fragment from Severian's *Homily*, as rendered in John the Exarch's edition:

у͞че нма еврѣнскъ. огнь са сказаеть. вънима" молю та.[151] [...] у͞лкъ еврѣнскож бесѣдож огнь са гл͞ть. се нма не дастьса адамоу праздьно. но четырн соуть вещн въ оутварн сен. пакъ естьствословлю. аще н не хотать земла, вода, въздух', огнь. н нны вещн iакъ же соуть къиаждо. тако же пребъвають. тако же се. аще възмешн гр8доу ѿ земла. тсо прнлсожнтн к' нен не можешн ѿ того дер'жнмаго. но iака же есть. така же пребъваеть. вод8 аще вълѣешн мѣрож нѣкако͡ж. то пребъваеть то же. вода прнбътъка не прнемлеть. въздоуха аще нанмешн мѣхъ мѣра пребъваеть. нного мѣха напол'ннтн ѿ того не м°жешн. а огнь не пребъваеть iакъ же съ. мала свѣ̇ца въж'жет'са. н несъвѣдн ѿ неа въж'жешн доуплатнць. пеꙡьнньцю всю пламъ многъ горꙡь въ своемь оустьн. но елнко же аще прнемлеть древо то множнт'са огнь. ел'ма же н преже вѣдаше б͞ъ. iакоже ѿ еднного тѣлесе у͞луа. нспол'ннт'са

---

150 See also the analysis of this topic in L. Sels and S. Van Pee, 'Scholia from Severian of Gabala's *In Cosmogoniam homiliæ* in the 14th-century Slavonic *Hexæmeron* Collection', p. 94; consult also S. Voicu, 'Adamo, acrostico del mondo', pp. 212–214.

151 Quoted after G. Barankova and V. Mil'kov, *Shestodnev Ioanna Ekzarkha Bolgarskogo*, p. 629 (Fol. 258ᵛ, lines 2–4).

вьселенъіа кран. н едина свєціа толнко въж'жеть свєціъ. н ҙападъ, н
въстокъ. н полоудьнїе. н полоуноцїе. положн нма достонно того дѣла.
сего дѣла н нма то адамово въҙванїе бѣаше оуселенѣн. понеже хотѣахо-
уса, н четырн страны ѿ него нсполнити. положн ада︮м︦. въстокъ ҙападъ
полоуноцⸯ пладьннна. се же по еллньскоу са. іаҙыкоу ключаеть тако
нма. н нма н дѣлеса съвѣдѣтельств︮8︦еть у︮лк︦оу, ему же нсполънити
бѣаше вселеноуж. ҙоветь же са оубо еврѣнскъімъ г︮лас︦омъ огнь.[152] [...]
прїем'лн оубо нма достонн'но вецⸯн. нм' же бо ѿ огна іакоже н въіше
г︮лах︦ъ. ѿ мала велнкъ бъіваеть. н у︮лк︦ъ ѿ мал︮а︦ краа ҙемныіа нспол'нн.
проҙванъ бъість у︮лк︦ъ огнь. сего дѣла сътворнмъ у︮лк︦а еврѣнскож бесѣдож г︮лет'︦са.[153]

The word 'man' in Hebrew designates 'fire.' Please consider [diligently], I
urge you. [...] In Hebrew language, 'man' designates 'fire.' This name was
not given to Adam in vain, because there are four elements in the Universe: earth, water, air, and fire; and here I am talking about the nature
of [matter], although this is not acceptable for many. All the elements
exist and are present in one and the same content / volume. If you take a
clod of earth, you cannot extend its quantity [var. volume, size] to more
than what it already contains. It will remain the way it was [in its original
state]. If you pour a certain quantity of water [into a vessel], it will remain
the same and will not expand its contents. The measure of air, if you fill
a bellows, remains the same and you cannot fill other bellows with the
same air. As for fire, it does not remain the same. You light a small candle and from it you can light countless candelabra, and then a furnace,
engulfed in huge flames, as the wood catches fire, the fire multiplies. This
is how God envisaged that from one single human body, the four corners
of the universe will be filled up. Just like one candle may kindle as many
candles as in the West and East and South and North, He gave a name
which is suitable to the deed. This is why the name of Adam was [designed
as] the appellation of the Universe, because from it the four corners of
the Universe were supposed to be populated; and [hence] God gave him
[i.e. man] the name 'Adam.' This is in Greek that such a name can be
assigned. The name and the deeds attest to man being tasked with filling
the Universe. In Hebrew, 'man' designates 'fire.' [...] Consider a designa-

---

152 Quoted after G. Barankova and V. Mil'kov, *Shestodnev Ioanna Ekzarkha Bolgarskogo*, pp.
629–630 (Fol. 258ᵛ, lines 10–25; Fol. 259ʳ, lines 1–25).

153 Quoted after G. Barankova and V. Mil'kov, *Shestodnev Ioanna Ekzarkha Bolgarskogo*, p. 631
(Fol. 260ʳ, lines 1–8).

tion which substantiates the matter/object. Since fire, as I said previously, from small may become big, so does man, who, being one small [creature], is [assigned] to fill the Universe up to its corners. This is why man is given the appellation 'fire,' while the [phrase] 'Let us make man' means ['Let us make fire'[154]] in Hebrew.[155]

To sum up, Severian builds his argument by narrativization of *ad hoc* etymological constructions, while philological deliberations are transformed into theological discourse. Of particular importance for the current discussion, however, is the fact that the Antiochian scholar recycles the tale about the meaning of the name of the first man (with a glossed reference to its Greek-bound exegesis); it indicates that at the time when Severian composed his *Homily*, this tradition was already in circulation. It is most probably in the same period when the Greek protograph of what we now designate as *2 Enoch* was taking shape; the mythologeme of Adam's name as an acronym-tetragram was just one among many cosmogonic and anthropogonic motifs that was drawn into its fabric.

As for the transmission history of Severian of Gabala's anthropogonic excerpt in *Slavia Orthodoxa*, it continued to be copied in later renditions of various Slavonic *Hexamœral* collections (e.g. *Shestodnevnik*, etc.),[156] but the circle of its transmission remained relatively limited within the scope of this particular genre.[157]

In contrast, the mythologeme attested in *2 Enoch* 30:13–14 enjoyed immense popularity in medieval Slavonic cosmological writings, and especially in erotapocritic compilations. Among the typical representatives of this discursive realm is the fifteenth-century Serbian recension of the *Razumnik* (Разѹмникь) erotapocritic apocryphal text (published by N. Tikhonravov in the second vol-

---

154 Reconstructed on the basis of some other Slavonic witnesses of the text of Severian of Gabala's *Homily* (e.g. *Codex Athous Chilandaricus* 405, dated to s. 1400); see *Scholion Slav5* in L. Sels and S. Van Pee, 'Scholia from Severian of Gabala's *In Cosmogoniam homiliæ* in the 14th-century Slavonic *Hexæmeron* Collection', pp. 100–101. See also G. Barankova and V. Mil'kov, *Shestodnev Ioanna Ekzarkha Bolgarskogo*, p. 957 (note 222).

155 Author's translation.

156 See the discussion in L. Sels and S. Van Pee, 'Scholia from Severian of Gabala's *In Cosmogoniam homiliæ* in the 14th-century Slavonic *Hexæmeron* Collection', pp. 89–110.

157 As pointed out by scholars, the full text of Severian's composition *In Cosmogoniam homiliæ VI* was translated in the 13th–14th centuries in Bulgaria; fragments from it were found in some miscellanies produced during the reign of Tzar Ivan–Alexander, and in later periods; see G. Barankova, 'K voprosu o perevodakh *Shestodneva* Severiana Gaval'skogo v drevneslavianskoĭ i drevnerusskoĭ knizhnosti', p. 5.

ume of his *Monuments of Proscribed Russian Literature*). The micro-narrative about the creation of the primordial man out of eight[158] substances is followed by yet another one about the origin of his name, which is untangled as an abbreviation containing four separate letters gathered from the four corners of the Universe (East, West, South and North) by the Archangels Michael, Gabriel, Raphael and Uriel. Each of the heavenly protagonists was given an assignment by God to bring along a letter, while each of these four letters was supposed to be extracted from the respective name of a designated star. Having thus fetched from the heavenly luminaries the desired four letters, the Archangels delivered them before God who assembled them into one single entity, thus forming the name of the primordial man, *ADAM*. The Archangel Uriel was the first to read it out, hence proclaiming its creation. Then again, the spelling of the archetypal anthroponym *ADAM* is rendered by the Serbian scribe according to the conventions of the Slavonic alphabet, in which every single letter is assigned a unique designation.[159] Thus the name of the letter *A* (A) is 'Азъ' (which is the form for the first person singular pronoun 'I'); the name of the second letter, *Д* (D), is 'Добро' (denoting 'goodness'), while the name of the letter *M* (M) is 'Мыслнте' (which means 'think'). At the same time, these same four Slavonic letters are identified by the scribe as phonetic constituents extracted from the names of the four heavenly luminaries: *Ana-*

---

158   There are other cases (e.g. *The Discussion Between the Three Hierarchs*, *The Legend About the Sea of Tiberias*, etc.), in which the number of substances may be seven (as in the anthropogonic template attested in *2 Enoch* 30:8–9). It should be noted in this connection that the recurring shift between the two numerical icons of divine Creation (i.e. 'seven' and 'eight') is typical for anthropogonic narratives attested in *Slavia Orthodoxa*; see the discussion in V. Mochul'skiĭ, 'Istoriko-literaturnyi analiz *Stikha o Golubinoi Knige*', RFV vol. 17, issue 1 (1887), pp. 174–177; R. Nachtigall, 'Ein Beitrag zu den Forschungen über die sogenannte 'Беседа трехъ святителей' (Gespräch dreier Heiligen)', *Archiv für Slavische Philologie Bd.* 23 (1901), 1–95; *Bd.* 24 (1902), pp. 321–408; F. Badalanova Geller, 'The Sea of *Tiberias*: Between Apocryphal Literature and Oral Tradition', pp. 73–78. For a detail survey of mythological motifs attested in the narrative about the creation of the first man from the element of the cosmos (with a special emphasis on *2 Enoch* and other related compositions, such as the spiritual folk poem *The Book of the Dove*) within the context of other Indo-European traditions, see B. Lincoln, *Myth, Cosmos, Society: Indo-European Themes of Creation and Destruction*, Cambridge, MA–London, UK, 1986, pp. 10–26. See also the discussion in G. Macaskill, 'Adam Octipartite/Septipartite', in R. Bauckham, J.R. Davila and Al. Panayotov (eds), *Old Testament Pseudepigrapha: More Noncanonical Scriptures* vol. 1, Grand Rapids, MI–Cambridge, UK, 2013, pp. 3–21.

159   Cf. R. Mathiesen, 'A new reconstruction of the original Glagolitic alphabet', in M.S. Flier, D.J. Birnbaum and C.M. Vakareliyska (eds), *Philology Broad and Deep: In Memoriam Horace G. Lunt*, Bloomington, IN, 2014, p. 190, p. 206.

toli, Disis, Artos and [*Me*]*sevria*.[160] Intriguingly, but not surprisingly, these four quasi-astronyms represent domesticated Slavonic (occasionally erroneous)[161] transcriptions of the Greek lexemes denoting the four corners of the Universe: East (Ἀνατολή), West (Δύσις), North (Ἄρκτος), and South (Μεσαμβρία); but, most importantly, the somewhat mosaic yet lavishly elaborated narrative about the creation of primordial man and the ætiology of his name, as presented in the erotapocrisis *Razumnik* (Разȣмникъ), redrafts virtually all the basic motifs constituting the anthropogonic storyline in 2 *Enoch* 30:7–14; these include the list of substances involved in the crafting of the primordial man and the astral constituents of the anagram of his name, thus manifesting the association of *ADAM* with 'the four special stars' assigned to him by the Creator. Below follows the fragment in question from the erotapocrisis *Razumnik* (Разȣмникъ):

ѿ ѵто сьтворн Бь Адама?—ѿ.: ѿ Н ѵестн ·а̄· ѵес тело его ѿ землїє ·в̄· ѵес
ѿ морѣ ·г̄· ѵес ѿ каменїа ·д̄· ѵес ѿ вѣтра ·е̄· ѵес ѿ облак ·ѕ̄· ѵес ѿ слнца
н ѿ росы ·з̄· ѵес ѿ помысла ѿ брьзостн агг҃льскыхъ ·н̄· ѵес ѿ ст҃го дх҃а. ѿ
того събра Бь н сътвотн в еднн8 ѵес. н реѵ. аще ιєс семе ѿ ѵл҃ка того ѿ
мѡрѣ то лакѡм, аще ιєс ѿ слнца семе то б8деть м8дрь оумень. ацнелï
ιєс ѿ облака семе то прѣльстнво. аще ѿ вѣтра семе то срьднто. ацнелн
ѿ каменïе семе то б8деть млстнво; аще лн ѿ дх҃а ст҃а семе то смѣрено
н доброволно къ всемь. въпрос. кто обрете нменïн его. ѿвѣт. ·д̄· ангг҃лн
архгг҃ль мхналь нзъıде на въстокь. н внде звѣзд8 нме ен анатолн. н
въземь слово ѿ нιєе азь. н прïнесе прѣд Г҃а. архгг҃ль гаврïнль нзъıдѣ на
запад. н вндѣ звѣзд8 нмѣ ен днснсь н въземь слово ѿ нее добро. н прïнесе прѣд Г҃а. рафаналь нзъıдѣ ѿ пол8днє н внде звѣзд8 нме ен артось. н
въземь слово ѿ нѣе слово азь. н прïнесе прѣд Г҃а. оурналь нзндѣ на пол8-
ноцıь н внде звѣзд8 нмѣ ен. севрïа[162] н въземь слово ѿ нѣе слово мъıс-
лнте. н прïнесе прѣд Г҃а. н реѵь Г҃ь ѵьтн оурнле н реѵ оурналь адамь.[163]

[Question:] From what [substances] did God create Adam? Answer: From eight parts; the first part, the flesh of his body [was] from earth; the second part—from the sea [intended for his blood]; the third part—from stone [intended for his bones]; the fourth part—from the wind [intended

---

160 See also the discussion in W. Ryan, 'Curious Star Names in Slavonic Literature', RL vol. 1 (1974), pp. 141–142.

161 See in this connection notes 162, 166, 167.

162 The quasi-astronym севрïа should be interpreted as abridgement of месеврïа (= Gr. Μεσαμβρία); see note 167 below.

163 Quoted after N. Tikhonravov, *Pamiatniki Otrechennoĭ Russkoĭ Literatury* vol. 2, pp. 443–444.

ENOCHIC TEXTS AND RELATED TRADITIONS IN SLAVIA ORTHODOXA   505

for his breath]; the fifth part—from cloud [intended for his faculties]; the sixth part—from the sun and dew [for his eyes]; the seventh—from angelic alacrity [intended for his thoughts], the eight part—from the Holy Spirit [intended for man's soul]. From all these [elements] God created one entity and said, 'If in the seed [i.e. progeny] which comes from this man supremacy were given to sea, [the offspring] would be greedy; if only to the sun, [the offspring] would be wise and reasonable. If [supremacy were given] only to the cloud, [the offspring] would be prone to temptation; if only to the wind, [the offspring] would be angry. If only to the stone, [the offspring] would be merciful. If only to the Holy Spirit, [the offspring] would be humble and good towards everybody. Question: Who instituted his name? Answer: Four angels. The Archangel Michael went to the East and saw a star whose name was *Anatoli*.[164] From it he took the letter 'Az' [= A] and presented it before God. The Archangel Gabriel went to the West, and saw a star whose name was *Disis*.[165] From it he took the letter 'Dobro' [= D] and presented it before God. Raphail went to the South and saw a star whose name was *Artos*.[166] And he took from it the letter 'Az' [= A] and presented it before God. Uriel went to the North and saw a star whose name was *Sevria*.[167] He took from it the letter 'Myslite' [= M] and presented it before God. And God said: 'Uriel, read [it] out!' And Uriel said: 'Adam.'[168]

In general, the types of vernacular parabiblical compositions, similar to the one quoted above, follow the (somewhat abridged and redrafted) storyline of 2 *Enoch* 30:8–13 (the longer recension); as a rule, the account concerning the origin of appellation *ADAM* is presented in them as the final sequel in a series of flexible text-units tailored in an elaborate, manifold anthropogonic tale. The

---

164   Cf. Greek Ἀνατολή (East).
165   Cf. Greek Δύσις (West).
166   The Slavonic scribe renders the designation of the star from the South as *Artos*, thus erroneously associationg it with the Northern corner of the Universe (Gr. Ἄρκτος); see also the next note.
167   The star fetched from the North appears to be called *Sevria* (from Gr. Μεσαμβρία, denoting South); this would indicate that the scribe copied his text from an earlier Slavonic version which no longer preserved the correct spelling of the Greek terms denoting the corners of the Universe. Furthermore the copyist obviously had rather scarce (if any) knowledge of Greek; hence the confusion in translating Ἄρκτος as South and Μεσαμβρία as North.
168   Author's translation.

17th century Russian version of the apocryphal *Legend About How God Created Adam* [Сказанне, како сотворн Богъ Адама] (published by A. Pypin)[169] exemplifies yet another such a case.

The first of the narrative sequels in its storyline deals with the creation of man out of eight substances (e.g. his body—from earth, his bones—from stones, his blood—from sea, his eyes—from the Sun; his thoughts—from clouds, his brightness—from the primordial light, his breath—from the wind, his warmth—from fire).[170] The second sequel (which has numerous parallel attestations in other dualistic cosmogonic compositions, such as *The Legend About the Sea of Tiberias*, etc.)[171] is about the Devil's attempt to defile the body of the primordial human; the next, third, sequel relates God's countermove against his adversary's harmful actions. It is the fourth sequel that explains the etymology of the appellation *ADAM*; the ensuing subplot is rather similar to that found in the above-mentioned fifteenth-century Serbian recension of the erotapocrisis *Razumnik* (published by N. Tikhonravov). Stated in the text of *The Legend About How God Created Adam*, however, is that the letters of which the name of primordial man consists—A, D and M—are brought, following God's command, from the four corners of the Universe by one single angel (in contrast to the erotapocrisis *Razumnik*, according to which God's celestial envoys are four), with the letter *A* being fetched from the East, *D* from the West, and *M* from both North and South:

Н посла Господь ангела своего, повелѣ взıати азъ на востоцѣ, добро на ꙁападѣ, мыслете на сѣверѣ н на юꙃѣ. Н бысть ѱеловѣкъ въ душу жнву, нареѱе нмıа ему Адамъ.[172]

And the Lord sent his angel, and ordered him to take the letter *A* [= *az'*] from the East, the letter *D* [= *dobro*] from the West, the letter *M* [= *myslete*] from the North and from the South. And the man became living soul, and He assigned him the name of Adam.[173]

---

169 Cf. *Lozhnyia i otrechennyia knigi russkoĭ stariny. Sobrannyia A.N. Pypinym. Pamiatniki starinnoĭ russkoĭ literatury, Izdavæmye Grafom Grigoriem Kushelevym-Bezborodko*, Vyp. 3, Sankt Petersburg, 1862, pp. 12–14.

170 See note 158 above.

171 Cf. F. Badalanova Geller, 'The Sea of Tiberias: Between Apocryphal Literature and Oral Tradition', pp. 78–80.

172 Quoted after A.N. Pypin, *Lozhnyia i otrechennyia knigi russkoĭ stariny*, p. 13.

173 Author's translation.

ENOCHIC TEXTS AND RELATED TRADITIONS IN SLAVIA ORTHODOXA   507

Missing from this abrupt anthropogonic narrative, however, is the motif of the 'four special stars' assigned to the primordial man by God (as in *2 Enoch* 30:14). Significantly, these types of omissions became emblematic for the cosmogonic accounts copied in the later period, perhaps due to the increased interest (on behalf of both the scribal community and the reading audience) towards the indigenous, home-spun exegesis of their content. The substitution of the list of the 'four special stars' by the narrativized spelling of the appellation-acronym *ADAM*, according to the conventions of the Slavonic alphabet, becomes their hallmark. *The Legend About How God Created Adam* is among the typical representatives of these types of para-Enochic anthropogonic narratives.

In contrast, the sub-plot about the creation of the first man from the elements of the cosmos (as in *2 Enoch* 30:8–9) became one of the most popular *topoi* featuring profoundly and intensely in the orally transmitted verses of folk spiritual chants, originally composed by the itinerant singers of tales ['калики перехожие'] in *Slavia Orthodoxa*. The survey of anthologies published at the end of the 19th and the beginning of the 20th centuries in Russia and elsewhere shows that these types of vernacular religious stanzas circulated under the general title *The Rhyme of the Book of the Dove* ['Стих о Голубиной книге'].[174] In fact, these songs—which may be labelled as oral best-sellers of the Middle Ages—are still being performed in remote parts of Russia; as such, *The Rhyme of the Book of the Dove* religious chants can be regarded as surviving witnesses to ancient Enochic traditions.

One further point; as already emphasised, the micro-narrative about the 'etymology' of the biblical anthroponym *ADAM* as a verbal icon of the 'microcosmos' (with each letter being bound to the Greek lexemes denoting the four cardinal directions—Ἀνατολή, Δύσις, Ἄρκτος, Μεσαμβρία) features concurrently in both John the Exarch's *Homily on the Sixth Day*, and in the longer recension of *2 Enoch* 30:13–14. If we were to consider the hypothesis that the translation of *2 Enoch* into Old Church Slavonic occurred concurrently with the compilation/translation of John the Exarch's *Hexæmeron*, then we ought to confirm once again the conjecture that the longer recension most probably represents an earlier stage in the transmission history of *2 Enoch* in *Slavia Orthodoxa*.[175]

---

174   Cf. *Kaleki Perekhozhie: Sbornik stikhov i issledovanie P. Bezsonova*, Chast 1, Vypusk 2, Moskva, 1861, pp. 269–275 (text 76), pp. 299–305 (text 82), pp. 316–323 (text 86).

175   See the discussion above (§ 2.4).

508   BADALANOVA GELLER

3   *Slavia Orthodoxa* Domesticating Enochic Vocabulary

Although the chapter Ἐκ τοῦ πρώτου βιβλίου Ἐνὼχ περὶ τῶν ἐγρηγόρων (i.e.
1 Enoch 6.1–9.11) was omitted from *The Slavonic Derivative of Synkellos* (see § 2.3
above), the term originally used by the Byzantine Greek chronographer to designate the Watchers, *Gregoroi* [Γρήγοροι, Ἐγρήγοροι],[176] survived in *Slavia Orthodoxa* as a *hapax* attested exclusively in the lexicon of *2 Enoch*. As in Synkellos'
extract, 'From the First Book of Enoch concerning the Watchers,' this same
term (the transliterated versions of which appear in various orthographies,
e.g. *Grigore* [Грнгоре],[177] *Grigorě* [Грнгорѣ],[178] *Grigori* [Грнгорн],[179] *Grigorie*
[Грнгорїе],[180] *Grigorii* [Грнгорїн/Грнгорнн],[181] *Grigor'i* [Грнгорьн],[182] *Grig-
ory* [Грнгоры],[183] *Egrigorъ, Egrigori, Egrigorii* [Егрнгорь, Егрнгорн, Егрнго-

---

176   See also the discussion in N. Forbes and R. Charles, '2 *Enoch*, or *The Book of the Secrets
       of Enoch*', in R. Charles (ed.), *Apocrypha and Pseudepigrapha of the Old Testament* vol. 2:
       Pseudepigrapha, Oxford, 1913, pp. 439–440 (note XVIII.3); F. Andersen, '2 (*Slavonic Apoc-
       alypse) of Enoch*', p. 130 (note 18a); G. Nickelsburg, *A Commentary on the Book of 1 Enoch*
       (*Chapters 1–36; 81–108*), p. 80. See further the linguistic data presented by H.G. Liddell and
       R. Scott in their *Greek-English Lexicon*, Oxford, 1963. The authors provide exhaustive anal-
       ysis of the semantic coverage of the verb γρηγορέω (formed from ἐγρήγορα, *to be* or *become
       fully awake, watch*), and some of its cognates (e.g. γρηγόρησις, *wakefulness*; γρηγορικός,
       wakeful, watchful); see ibid., p. 360. Taken into consideration are also related forms, such
       as ἐγρηγορικός (*waking*); ἐγρήγορος (*wakeful*); ἐγρήγορσις (*waking, wakefulness*); ἐγρηγορ-
       τέον (*one must keep awake*); ἐγρήγορσις (*waking, wakefulness*); ἐγρηγορτί (*awake, watching*);
       see ibid., p. 475. Significantly, the term Ἐγρήγοροι was also used by Mani; see W.B. Hen-
       ning, 'The Book of the Giants', *BSOAS* vol. 11, issue 1 (1943), p. 53; E. Morano, 'Some New
       Sogdian Fragments Related to Mani's *Book of Giants* and the Problem of the Influence
       of Jewish Enochic Literature', in M. Goff, L.T. Stuckenbruck and E. Morano (eds), *Ancient
       Tales of Giants from Qumran and Turfan. Contexts, Traditions, and Influences*, Tübingen,
       2016, p. 187.

177   Cf. Ms. S: Na .Е҃-ж нбо҃. н внде҃ˣ тоу мнѡгыж вое ненꙁѵьтеннїе рекомїн *грнгоре*.

178   Cf. Ms. U: н восл8жнша *грнгорѣ*, ꙗко еднне҃ᴹ гла҃мь вꙁн҃ᴬ гла҃с н҃ˣ в лнце гн҃е.

179   Cf. Ms. P: Вꙁаша ма м8жїе на е҃ нбо҃, н поставнша ма, н внде҃хъ т8 вон мнѡгн н ненсѵет-
       ны, рекомїа *Грнгорн*; Ms. S: Сн сжт *грнгорн*, нже ѿврьгошжс҃ ѿ га҃ .с҃. тьмж съ кнаꙁем
       свонм сатананлем; Ms. S: въспѣшж *грнгорн* еднноглас҃но. н въꙁыде гла҃с н҃ˣ прѣᴬ лнце҃ᴹ
       гн҃а.

180   Cf. Ms. J: н рекоша къ мнѣ мжжїе ѡны сн сж҃т *грнгорїе* нже ѿврьгоша҃с ѿ га҃. ст҃ъᴹ съ
       кnase҃ᴹ свон҃ᴹ сатананле҃ᴹ.

181   Cf. Ms J: Н въꙁаше ма на крнлѣˣ свон҃ˣ мжжїе ѡны, н поставнста ма на пѣтое нбо҃, н
       внде҃ˣ тоу мнѡгы вон ненсѵетенн, рекомыа *грнгорїн*; Ms U: сн соу҃т *грнгорнн* н҃ж ѿтор-
       гоу ѿ себе с҃ кн҃ꙁь с҃ ходацн҃ˣ во слѣᴬ.

182   Cf. Ms U: н воꙁнесоста ма на патое нево. н внде҃ˣ тоу мнѡга вса. н *грнгорьн* внде҃ хї ꙗко
       внде҃ннꙗ ѵлвѵ҃ско велнѵьство҃ж нхъ ваꙃце ѵюдѡв҃ велнкы҃ˣ.

183   Cf. Ms. P: Н рекоша ко мнѣ. сїн с8тъ *Грнгоры*, нже ѿвергошаса Га҃ ст҃а со кнаꙁе҃ᴹ свон҃мъ
       Сатананлом҃ъ.

ENOCHIC TEXTS AND RELATED TRADITIONS IN SLAVIA ORTHODOXA 509

рнн],[184] *Igrigory* [Игригори], *Gory* [Горы],[185] *Govory* [*Говоры*],[186] etc.) are likewise used by the Slavonic scribe(s) to designate the Fallen Angels. In fact, the domesticated (Slavicised) versions of the Greek angelonym *Gregoroi* [Γρή-γοροι, Ἐγρήγοροι] occurs *only* in Enoch's testimony about the Fifth Heaven (that is, *2 Enoch* 18:1–9), described by the visionary as a celestial dungeon, where the condemned brotherhood of the Watchers is sentenced. Their appearance was like that of humans [видѣнїе н͓ ꙗко видѣнїе члвѹе], yet their immensity was even bigger than the vastness of huge/great giants [велнѹьство нхь веще цѣждовь велнкъ͓]. Their faces were morose [лнца н͓ драхла] and their mouths are constantly silent [млѹане оусть н͓ въсегда]. Enoch finds it important to emphasise that in the Fifth Heaven there was no divine service [не бѣ слѹженїа на е͂-мь нѣсн]. The latter detail indicates that the celestial realm is imagined as a temple in which the heavenly liturgy is held; the only exception is the place where Watchers were sentenced.[187]

Enoch is even explicitly informed about their exact number since, as he himself admits when he first encountered them, they seemed to him as a great assembly of countless warriors [многыж вое ненѹьтенїе]. The shorter recension of *2 Enoch*[188] agrees with *1 Enoch* 6:6, that the number of Watchers 'who came down' on 'the summit of Mount Hermon' is two hundred, while in the longer recension (*2 Enoch* 18:3), it is maintained that it was 'two hundred myriads' of *Gregori* that 'parted from God with their prince Satanail' [нже ѿврьгошж ѿ Га͆ с͆ тьмж съ кнаѕе᷃ свон᷃ Сатананле᷃]. Yet in both *1 Enoch* and *2 Enoch*, the summit of Mount Hermon is imagined as the standard topos of wickedness. According to *1 Enoch* 6:6, this is the spot where the Watchers came down and swore their oath. In *2 Enoch*, however, the narrative is more elaborate: the crest of Mount Hermon [на рамѣ горы Ермонскые; на мѣсто Ермона][189] is described as the place where *Gregori* descended from the Throne of the Lord [нже сьндошж на ѕемла ѿ прѣстола гн͂ѣ] (a detail missing from *1 Enoch*) and broke their covenant with Him [прѣтрьгоша соьѣщанїе],[190] thus polluting the Earth with their deeds [соскврьнн са ѕемла дѣламн н͓]. The longer and the

---

184 Attested in Ms. Bars/Sok.
185 Cf. Ms. N: Н вьѕнесоста ме мѹжа на петое небо, н вндѣхь тѹ многые вое, н *горы* вндѣнїе нхь ꙗко вндѣнїе члобѹче н велнѹьство же нхь паѹе ѹюдесь велнкынхь.
186 Attested in Ms. Bars1/Sok.
187 See Sokolov, *Slavianskaia Kniga Enokha*, pp. 15–17. See also in this connection the discussion in M. Himmelfarb, *An Apocalypse: A Brief History*, pp. 76–78.
188 For Ms. U, see A. Pennington, '2 *Enoch*' (§ 7: 4), p. 335; see also F. Andersen, '2 (*Slavonic Apocalypse*) *of Enoch*', (§ 18: 3), p. 131.
189 See F. Andersen, '2 (*Slavonic Apocalypse*) *of Enoch*', p. 132 (note 18e).
190 See Sokolov, *Slavianskaia Kniga Enokha*, p. 16. Cf. *1 Enoch* 6:7.

shorter recensions of 2 *Enoch* diverge at this point. In the longer recension it is emphasised that the daughters of men sinned greatly [вєлнко ѕло творⷶ] during all times of that epoch [въ вса врѣмєна вѣка сєго], by lawlessly committing the mixing of species [бєзаконоуѫщіє творѧщє смѣшєнїа], giving birth to giants [раждаѫт сѧ нсполн] and enormous colossi [цѫждовє вєлнцн], thus bringing about great malevolence [вєлнка нєпрїазнь];[191] because of this, God condemned those who seduced them to 'the Great Tribunal' [ѡсѫдн нⷯ бѣ вєлнкоⷨ сѫдѡⷨ]. The shorter recension lacks the details about the birth of the giants [нсполн, цѫждовє] and simply states that the *Gregori* were condemned by God because they defiled themselves with human women.

Encouraged by Enoch to serve God, so that they do not anger him further, the *Gregori* listened to the visionary's advice [послоушашє накѕанїа]; having lined up in four ranks in their heavenly prison [сташѫ на чєтнрн чннн нбⷭн сєⷨ], they began singing in one voice [въспѣшѫ грнгорн єⷣнногласно], and their chant ascended to God's face [възъыдє глаⷭ нⷯ прѣ лнцєⷨ гнⷶ]. Thus Enoch's mystical encounter with the angelic prisoners sentenced on the Fifth Heaven is rendered (in both shorter and longer recensions of 2 *Enoch*) as a narrative about their atonement, with the visionary acting as their human solicitor and intercessor, advising them to commence their repentance before the Lord. In a similar way, in *The Book of Watchers* 'Enoch the scribe' communicates with the Fallen Angels and mediates between their petitions for forgiveness and God's declaration of judgment (*1 Enoch* 12–16).[192]

Then again, in *The Book of Watchers* Enoch is instructed in 'a vision of wrath' (*1 Enoch* 13:8–9),—given to him 'by the waters of Dan in Dan, which is southwest of Hermon' (i.e. on earth, but not during a celestial journey)!—that he 'should speak to the sons of heaven and reprove them,' and tell them 'with the tongue of flesh' (14:2), that their petition will not be granted 'for all the days of eternity, and complete judgement has been decreed' against them (14:8). The events in the Slavonic text follow a somewhat different, 'open-end' scenario. In 2 *Enoch* the fate of *Gregori* is not sealed; there is no oracle of judgement—the matter remains open. The visionary is not informed about God's rejection of the Watchers' petition; there is no final sentence pronounced, apart from the general statement concerning their condemnation to 'the Great Tribunal' (see above). This vagueness about the *Gregori*-destiny is one of the most peculiar

---

191   Cf. *1 Enoch* 7:1–3, 9:8–10; see Sokolov, 'Materialy i zametki po starinnoĭ slavianskoĭ literature. Vyp. Tretiĭ (vii/2): Slavianskaia Kniga Enokha. Tekst s latinskim perevodom', p. 16.

192   See also the discussion in L. Stuckenbruck, 'The 'Angels' and 'Giants' of *Genesis* 6:1–4 in Second and Third Century BCE Jewish Interpretation: Reflections on the Posture of Early Apocalyptic Traditions', p. 367.

features of *2 Enoch*, especially in the light of the visionary's intervention into their silent existence, when he persuades them to resume their former services, 'in the Lord's name,' and they begin to do so by singing with a single voice.

The domesticated Slavonic versions of the Greek appellation *Gregoroi* [Γρή-γοροι, Ἐγρήγοροι], as attested in *2 Enoch*, are absent from the main lexicographic sources of Old Church Slavonic, such as the *Lexicon Linguæ Palæoslovenicæ*,[193] the *Palæoslavonic Dictionary*,[194] the *Dictionary of Old Church Slavonic Language*,[195] etc. Yet the use of this distinctive term in both *The Chronography of George Synkellos* and *2 Enoch* is one of the strongest arguments indicating that the Slavonic protograph of this apocalyptic work must have originated from an earlier Greek translation of the apocryphon, rather than directly from its Hebrew or Aramaic *Vorlage*;[196] it further suggests that in the Byzantine Commonwealth there existed a certain common Enochic thesaurus which was attested in both Greek and Slavonic versions of the pseudepigraphic corpus, as well as in chronographic tradition.[197] Shared terminology is likely to suggest a common intellectual and ideological background, and this particular methodology of linguistic archæology has so far remained unexplored in the studies of Enochic heritage in the Byzantine Commonwealth.

4 Demarcating Magic and Mysticism: The Enochic Epistemology in *Slavia Orthodoxa*

While in *The Book of Watchers* (i.e. *1 Enoch*) the emphasis is put on the concept of the illicit transmission of knowledge from heaven to earth, from angels to humans, in the case of *2 Enoch* the opposite concept predominates. Once more the focal point of the narrative is the disclosure of esoteric knowledge to a mortal man by angelic agency, but this time the revelation is endorsed by the Lord himself. Furthermore it is not Enoch's decision to become an eyewitness to the mysteries of the universe; on the contrary, he is the one chosen by the Most High to become a recipient of divine wisdom, and to learn the eter-

---

193   Cf. A. Dostál et al. (eds), *SJS/LLP* vol. 8, Praha, 1964.

194   Cf. R. Tseĭtlin et al. (eds), *Staroslavianskiĭ Slovar'* (*Po Rukopisiam X–XI vekov*), Moscow, 1994.

195   Cf. A. Bonchev, *Rechnik na Tsŭrkovnoslavanskiia Ezik* vol. 1.

196   One of the strongest advocates of an opposing hypothesis was N. Meshcherskiĭ, 'K istorii teksta slavianskoĭ knigi Enokha', pp. 93–102.

197   To the same cluster of witnesses to *1 Enoch* in the Byzantine Greek historiographical tradition belongs *The Chronicle of* (*Skylitzes-)Kedrenos*; see Ĭ. Ivanov, *Bogomilski Knigi i Legendi*, p. 186.

nal secrets unknown even to the angelic host. In contrast to the Watchers, who challenge God's commands and therefore fall, Enoch is granted angelic status, since he obeys the Lord's will unconditionally. While Watchers descend from God's Throne to Earth, Enoch ascends from Earth to God's Throne. In the case of the Watchers, the practices of esoteric knowledge—magic and divination—are revealed to women (and hence illicit). At the same time, Enoch becomes the first visionary and recipient of the mystical experience endorsed by God.

To sum up, the Watchers are markers of magic, Enoch—of mysticism. Enoch is 'the anti-Watcher.' Not only are the divine secrets disclosed in his ascent, but he also becomes God's scribe, his heavenly amanuensis. *Slavonic Enoch* focuses on the specific particulars of his mystical mission.

Concluding Remarks

The various strands of scribal production circulating in the Slavonic domain of the Byzantine Commonwealth in the second half of the 9th and the beginning of the 10th centuries appear to point in the same direction: that the first translation of the Greek *Vorlage* of the work we now designate as *2 Enoch* into Old Church Slavonic must have occurred in Preslav, the then capital of the First Bulgarian Kingdom. It is unclear whether the scribe who accomplished the original translation worked in the royal scriptorium or in one of the adjacent monastic centres, but there is no doubt that he belonged to the local community of intellectuals engaged in theology and science, astronomy and calendar, grammar and philosophy, historiography and geography. Most probably, he was a contemporary of John the Exarch—the scholar who was responsible for the translation into Old Church Slavonic of fragments from the *Homiliæ in Hexæmeron* of Basil of Cæsarea and *In Cosmogoniam homiliæ* of Severian of Gabala, along with *The Exact Exposition of the Orthodox Faith* of John Damascene. The survey of questions discussed in John the Exarch's compositions—relating to cosmogonic and anthropogonic, astronomic and calendrical matters—shows close connection with themes presented in *2 Enoch*. Circulating during the same period were also important historiographical works, such as *The Chronography of John Malalas*, *The Chronography of George Hamartolos*, *The Chronography of George Synkellos* (containing, in fact, a cluster of abridged edited fragments from *The Chronicle of Julius Africanus*). The linguistic analysis of their glossaries indicates further connections with Enochic texts and traditions which so far remain understudied. As for the narrative about carnal encounters between the Fallen Angels and the beautiful daughters of men, it also survived as a demonological tale incapsulated in the various domesticated recensions

ENOCHIC TEXTS AND RELATED TRADITIONS IN SLAVIA ORTHODOXA   513

of *The Testament of the Twelve Patriarchs*, while the motif of cosmetics as a devilish matter (a hallmark of the *Watchers myth*) had a significant impact on vernacular iconography.

Acknowledgements

This article has benefited from the comments and insightful suggestions of William R. Veder and William Adler.

Appendix
Second (Slavonic Apocalypse of) Enoch: Survey of Published Text Witnesses[198]

Sigla and Abbreviations

ANL   The Austrian National Library, Vienna [Österreichische Nationalbibliothek, Wien]; formerly (until 1920) The Imperial Court Library [Kaiserliche Hofbibliothek]

BAN   The Library of the Russian Academy of Sciences (Biblioteka Rossiĭskoĭ Akademii Nauk [Библиотека Российской Академии Наук]), Saint Petersburg; formerly (until 1992) The Library of the Academy of Sciences of USSR (Biblioteka Akademii Nauk SSSR [Библиотека Академии Наук СССР])

---

198   The current survey is based on earlier research carried out by various scholars; see Sokolov, *Slavianskaia Kniga Enokha*; id., *Slavianskaia Kniga Enokha Pravednago* (Part 2), pp. 1–105; A. Iatsimirskiĭ, *Bibliograficheskiĭ Obzor Apokrifov v Iuzhnoslavianskoĭ i Russkoĭ Pis'mennosti* (*Spiski Pamiatnikov: Apokrify Vetkhozavetnye*), pp. 81–88; G.N. Bonwetsch, *Die Bücher der Geheimnisse Henochs: Das sogenannte slavische Henochbuch*, pp. v–x; Ĭ. Ivanov, *Bogomilski Knigi i Legendi*, pp. 165–167; A. Vaillant, *Le livre des secrets d'Hénoch*, pp. iii–viii; N. Meshcherskiĭ, 'Sledy pamiatnikov Kumrana v staroslavianskoĭ i drevnerusskoĭ literature (K izucheniiu slavianskikh versiĭ Knigi Enokha)', pp. 135–139; id., 'K istorii teksta slavianskoĭ knigi Enokha', pp. 93–95; P. Dinekov, K. Kuev and D. Petkanova (eds), *Khristomatiia po starobŭlgarska literatura*, Sofia, 1967, pp. 146–147; F. Andersen, '2 (*Slavonic Apocalypse*) of Enoch', pp. 92–93; A. Pennington, '2 *Enoch*', pp. 321–323, pp. 326–327; A. de Santos Otero, 'Libro de los secretos de Henoc (Henoc eslavo)', pp. 147–157, 160; Ch. Böttrich, '*The Book of the Secrets of Enoch* (2 *En*): Between Jewish Origin and Christian Transmission (An Overview)', pp. 39–44; V. Mil'kov and S. Polianskiĭ, *Kosmologicheskie Proizvedeniia v Knizhnosti Drevneĭ Rusi* vol. 2: *Teksty Ploskostno-Komarnoĭ i Drugikh Kosmologicheskikh Traditsiĭ*, pp. 451–453; F. Badalanova Geller, 'Heavenly Writings: Celestial Cosmography in *The Book of the Secrets of Enoch*', pp. 199–203; G. Macaskill, '2 *Enoch*: Manuscripts, Recensions, and Original Language', pp. 84–87; id., *The Slavonic Texts of* 2 Enoch, pp. 9–19.

BIHP   The Institute of History and Philology of Count Bezborodko (Istoriko-Filologicheskiĭ Institut Kniazia A.A. Bezborodko [Историко-филологический Институт Князя А.А. Безбородко]), Nezhin; in 1919–1920 transformed into The Nezhyn Institute of People's Education [Нежинский Институт народного образования]; in 1939—into N. Gogol' State Pedagogical Institute in Nezhin [Нежинский государственный педагогический институт имени Николая Гоголя]; since 2004—Mykola Gogol' State University in Nizhyn [Ніжинський державний університет ім. Миколи Гоголя], Ukraine

GIM   The State Historical Museum (Gosudarstvennyĭ Istoricheskiĭ Muzeĭ [Государственный исторический музей]), Moscow

RNB   The M. Saltykov-Shchedrin National Library of Russia (Rossiĭskaia Natsional'naia Biblioteka imeni M. Saltykova-Shchedrina [Российская национальная библиотека имени М. Салтыкова-Щедрина]); between 1917 and 1925—The Russian Public Library (Rossiĭskaia Publichnaia Biblioteka [Российская публичная библиотека]); before 1917—The Imperial Public Library (Imperatorskaia Publichnaia Biblioteka [Императорская публичная библиотека]), Saint Petersburg

NLS   The National Library of Serbia (Narodna Biblioteka Srbije [Народна библиотека Србије]), Belgrade, Serbia

RGB   The Russian State Library (Rossiĭskaia Gosudarstvennaia Biblioteka [Российская государственная библиотека]); between 1925 and 1992—V.I. Lenin State Library of the USSR [Государственная библиотека СССР им. В.И. Ленина]; between 1862 and 1924—The Library of the Moscow Public Museum and the Rumiantsev Museum (or The Rumiantsev Library) [Библиотека Румянцевского музея], Moscow.

SANU   The Serbian Academy of Sciences and Arts (Srpska akademija nauka i umetnosti [Српска академија наука и уметности]), Belgrade, Serbia

The Longer Recension

S   Ms. № 321 (fols 269ʳ–323ʳ), NLS; Bulgarian redaction (between the 14th–16th centuries).
Designated by Sokolov as **A**; by Bonwetsch—as **S**; by Morfill and Charles—as **Sok**; by Schmidt—as ***Codex Belgradensis***; by Vaillant, Andersen, Pennington, Böttrich, Orlov, and Macaskill—as **R**.

J   Ms. № 13.3.25 (fols 93ʳ–125ʳ), BAN; Bulgarian redaction (15th–16th centuries).
Designated by Sokolov as **Я** [= **Ja**]; by Bonwetsch, Vaiilant, Andersen, Böttrich, Orlov, Macaskill—as **J**.

P   Ms. Khlud D. 69 [Хлуд. Д. 69] (fols. 58–82), *The Addendum to the Khludov Collection* [Хлудовское Дополнительное Собрание], GIM; Ruthenian redaction (copied from an earlier Bulgarian protograph in 1679 in *The Orthodox Monastery of the Exaltation of the Cross* in the city of Poltava).

Designated by Sokolov as П (= P); by Morfill and Charles—as A; by Schmidt—as *Codex Chludovianus*; by Bonwetsch, Andersen, Böttrich, Orlov, Macaskill—as P.

The Shorter and Abbreviated Recensions

U Ms. № 3/18 (fols 626ʳ–638ᵛ), *The Uvarov Collection*, GIM; Russian redaction (15th century, based on an earlier Bulgarian protograph), the shorter recension.

Designated by Sokolov as У [= U]; by Bonwetsch, Vaillant, Andersen, Pennington, Böttrich, Orlov, Macaskill—as U.

Srezn/Navt Ms. № 45.13.4 (fols 357ʳ–366ᵛ), BAN; Russian redaction (16thcentury), the shorter recension.

Designated by Vaillant, Andersen, Böttrich, Orlov and Macaskill as A.

N Ms. № 151/443 (fols 1ʳ–10ʳ), NLS; Serbian redaction (16th century, copied from an earlier Russian text); the abbreviated redaction.

Designated by Sokolov as H [= N]; by Charles (and Morfill)—as B; by Schmidt—as *Codex Belgradensis Serbius*; by Bonwetsch—as Vᴺ; by Vaillant, Andersen, Böttrich, Orlov, Macaskill—as N.

VL/Jov Ms. *Slave* № 125 (fols 308ᵛ–330ᵛ), ANL; Serbian redaction (copied in the 16th–17th centuries from an earlier Russian text); the abbreviated redaction.

Designated by Sokolov as B [= V]; by Bonwetsch—as Vᵛ; by Schmidt—as *Codex Vindobonensis Slavonicus* 125; by Vaillant, Andersen, Böttrich, Orlov, Macaskill—as V.

MPU Ms. № 1828 (fols 522ʳ–544ʳ), *The Uvarov Collection*, GIM; Russian redaction (17th century), the shorter recension.

Bars/Sok Ms. 2729 (fols 9ʳ–34ᵛ), *The Barsovian Collection*, GIM; Russian redaction (17th century); the shorter recension.

Designated by Sokolov as Б [= B]; by Schmidt—as *Codex Moscovitanus Barsovii*; by Bonwetsch, Vaillant, Andersen, Böttrich, Orlov and Macaskill—as B.

Bars1/Sok Ms. № 2730 (fols 87ʳ–98ᵛ), GIM; Russian redaction (copied in 1701); the abbreviated redaction.

Designated by Sokolov as Б¹ [= B¹]; by Bonwetsch—as B¹; by Vaillant, Andersen, Böttrich, Orlov, Macaskill—as B².

Fragments (*in Chronological Order*)

MPr Ms. № 15/2026 (fols 36ʳ–38ᵛ), *The Collection of the Trinity Lavra of Saint Sergius* (Troitse-Sergieva Lavra), RGB; part of the 14th century *Měrilo Pravednoe* [*Мѣрило праведное*] (*The Just Balance*)

	Designated by Bonwetsch as **M**; by Vaillant—as **Mpr**; by Andersen, Böttrich, Orlov, Macaskill—as **MPr**.
Gennadius	Ms. № 730 [1855] (fols 246ʳ–253ᵛ), from *The Collection of the Trinity Lavra of Saint Sergius* (Troitse-Sergieva Lavra), RGB; the fragment is inserted in *The Epistle of the Archbishop Gennadius of Novgorod to Archbishop Joasaph of Rostov* [*Посланіе Новгород. Архиеп. Генна-дія къ Архиеп. Ростовск. Іоасафу*] from 1489; the copy is dated to the 16th century.

Designated by Bonwetsch as **Genn**; by Böttrich—as **G 38**; by Andersen, Orlov and Macaskill—as **G**.

GMR Makariĭ	*The Great Menaion Reader* [Великие Четьи-Минеи], compiled in the 1530s–1540s; the Uspenskiĭ's edition [Успенский список] (№ 177, fols 688–689).
SokRum578/Pisk143	Ms. № 143 (fols 164ᵛ–168ᵛ) from *The Piskarëv Collection* [Собра-ние Д. В. Пискарёва], formerly Ms. № 578 from *The Rimiantsev Museum*, currently RGB; dated to the 16th century

Designated by Vaillant, Andersen, Böttrich, Orlov and Macaskill as **Rum**.

Tikh/TSL	Ms. № 793 [1639] (fols 401ʳ–402ᵛ) from *The Collection of the Trinity Lavra of Saint Sergius* (Troitse-Sergieva Lavra), RGB; dated to the end of the 16th and the beginning of the 17th century.

Designated by Vaillant, Andersen, Böttrich, Orlov and Macaskill as **Tr**.

Pyp/Rum	Ms. № 238 (fols 727ᵛ–729), RGB; copied in 1620.
SokHSL	Ms. № 253 (fols 543ʳ–545ᵛ), GIM; dated to ca. 1622.

Designated by Andersen as **TSS 253**.

SokNezhin/IHP 39	Ms. № 39 (fols 16ᵛ–17ᵛ; fol. 20ʳ; fol. 20ᵛ; fol. 36ʳ; fols 50ᵛ–53ʳ), BIHP (Nezhin/ Nizhyn); dated to the 17th century.

Designated by Bonwetsch as **C**; by Vaillant, Andersen, Böttrich, Orlov and Macaskill—as **Chr**.

Tikh/KBM	Ms. № 27/1104, *The Collection of the Kirillo-Belozersky Monastery* (fols 232ᵛ–238ᵛ), currently kept in the RNB; dated to the 17th century.

Designated by Orlov as **K**.

SokRum	Ms. № 3058 (fols 391ʳ–393ʳ), formerly kept in the collection of *The Rumiantsev Museum*, now *The Muzeĭnoe Collection* [Музейное со-брание], RGB; the MS is dated to the 1730s.

Designated by Vaillant, Andersen, Böttrich, Orlov and Macaskill as **P²**.

Vrbnik	Ms. Vrbnik № 15 (fols 72–73); fragment in Glagolitic; copied between 1633–1652.

Designated by Orlov as **I**; by Macaskill—as **Vrbnik** [Ivšic].

SokRum590/Pisk155   Ms. F. 228 № 155 (fols 134ᵛ–136ʳ) of *The Piskarëv Collection*,
formerly Ms. F. 178 № 590 from the collection of *The Rumiantsev Museum*, now RGB; the MS is dated to the 17th–18th centuries.
Designated by Bonwetsch as C; by Vaillant, Andersen, Böttrich, Orlov and Macaskill—as **Chr²**.

Pop/Khron [1]   Ms. № 1449, *The Pogodin's Collection*; RNB.

Pop/Khron [2]   Ms. № 168, previously part of *The Collection of Count Tolstov* from *The Imperial Public Library*, now RNB.

Pop/Khron [3]   Ms. № 108, previously part of *The Collection of Count Tolstov* from *The Imperial Public Library*, now RNB.

Pop/Khron [4]   Ms. from Popov's private collection; to the best of my knowledge, there is no information about its current location.

Editions

Dolgov 1912. S.I. Dolgov (ed.). *Velikie Minei Chetii Sobrannye Vserossiĭskim Mitropolitom Makariem* (*Dekabr': Dni 25–31*). *Izdanie Archeografcheskoĭ Komissii* Moscow: Sinodal'naia Tipografiia, 1912, pp. 2496–2499. (Ms. GMR **Makariĭ**)

Franko 1896–1910. Ivan Franko. *Apokrifi i Legendi z Ukraïnskikh Rukopisiv. Zibrav, uporiadkuvav i poiasniv Dr. Ivan Franko.* Tom 1: *Apokrifi Starozavitni* (Codex Apocryphus e manuscriptis *ukraino-russicis collectus opera Dr. Joannis Franko*). L'viv: Nakladom Naukovogo Tovaristva Imeni Shevchenka, Vols 1–5, 1896–1910, pp. 39–64. (Ms. **P**)

Ivanov 1925. Ĭordan Ivanov. *Bogomilski Knigi i Legendi.* Sofia: Pridvorna Pechatnitsa (Izdava se ot Fonda D.P. Kudoglu), 1925, pp. 167–180. (Ms. **S**)

Ivšić 1931/1932. Stjepan Ivšić. 'Hrvatski Glagoljski Apokrif o Melhisedekovu Rođenju i Spasenju Za Općega Potopa.'—*Nastavni Vjesnik* (Zagreb, Matica Hrvatska), Knjiga 15 (1931/1932), pp. 101–108. (Ms. **Vrbnik**)

Jovanović 2003. Tomislav Jovanović. 'Apokrif o Enohu prema Srpskom Prepisu is Narodne Biblioteke u Beču.'—*AP* 25 (2003), pp. 209–238. (Ms. **VL/Jov**)

Kagan-Tarkovskaia, Tarkovskiĭ 2000. M.D. Kagan-Tarkovskaia, R.B. Tarkovskiĭ. 'Skazanie o Melkhisedeke.' In: Dmitriĭ Sergeevich Likhachev (ed.). *BLDR*, Vol. 3: *XI–XII veka.* Saint Petersburg: Nauka, 2000, pp. 115–119, 374–376. http://lib.pushkinskijdom.ru/ Default.aspx?tabid=4916 (Fragment from Ms. **Srezn/Navt**)

Lur'e 1999. Ia. S. Lur'e. 'Poslanie Gennadiia Ioasafu.' In: Dmitriĭ Sergeevich Likhachev, L.A. Dmitriev, A.A. Alekseev, N.V. Ponyrko (eds). *BLDR*, Vol. 7: *Vtoraia Polovina XV veka.* Saint Petersburg: Nauka, 1999, pp. 540–553. http://lib.pushkinskijdom.ru/Defa ult.aspx?tabid=5073 (Ms. **Gennadius**)

Macaskill 2013. Grant Macaskill. *The Slavonic Texts of 2 Enoch.* Leiden/Boston: Brill, 2013. (Ms. J; Ms. **Srezn/Navt**; Ms. **Gennadius**; Ms. **MPr**)

Mil'kov, Polianskiĭ 2009. Vladimir Vladimirovich Mil'kov, Sergeĭ Mikhailovich Polianskiĭ. *Kosmologicheskie proizvedeniia v knizhnosti Drevneĭ Rusi*, Vol. 2: *Teksty ploskost-no-komarnoĭ i drugikh kosmologicheskikh traditsiĭ*. Sankt Peterburg: Izdatel'skiĭ Dom 'Miгъ', 2009, pp. 459–493. (Ms. **MPU**)

Navtanovich 2000. Liudmila Navtanovich. 'Kniga Enokha.' In: Dmitriĭ Sergeevich Likhachev (ed.). *BLDR*, Vol. 3: *XI–XII veka*. Sankt Peterburg: Nauka, pp. 204–241, 387–392. http://lib.pushkinskijdom.ru/Default.aspx?tabid=4921 (Ms. **Srezn/Navt**)

Novaković 1884. Stojan Novaković. 'Apokrif o Enohu.'—*Starine* (Zagreb, Jugoslavenska akademija znanosti i umjetnosti), Knjiga XVI (1884), pp. 67–81 (70–81). (Ms. **N**)

Popov 1869. Andreĭ Popov. *Obzor Khronographov Russkoĭ Redaktsii*, Vyp. 2. Moscow: A.I. Mamontov, 1869, pp. 162–169. (Mss. **Pop/Khron [1–4]**)

Popov 1880. Andreĭ Popov. 'Bibliograficheskie Materialy, Sobrannye Andreem Popovym (iv): Iuzhnorusskiĭ Sbornik 1679 goda.'—*ChIOIDR* 3 (1880), pp. 89–139; 142–154. (Ms. **P**; Ms. **Gennadius**)

Pypin 1862. Aleksandr Nikolaevich Pypin. *Lozhnyia i otrechennyia knigi russkoĭ stariny. Sobrannyia A.N. Pypinym. Pamiatniki starinnoĭ russkoĭ literatury, Izdavaemye Grafom Grigoriem Kushelevym-Bezborodko*, Vyp. 3. Sankt Petersburg: Tip. Kulisha, 1862, pp. 15–16. (Ms. **Pyp/Rum**)

Reinhart 2007. Johannes Reinhart. 'A Croatian Glagolitic Excerpt of the *Slavonic Enoch* (2 Enoch).'—*FE* 4 (2007), pp. 31–46. (Ms. **Vrbnik**)

Schneider 1986. Rudolf Schneider. *Die Moralisch-Belehrenden Artikel im altrussischen Sammelband* (*Monumenta Linguæ Slavicæ Dialecti Veteris, Fontes et Dissertationes*, Vol. 23, eds R. Aitzetmüller, L. Sadnik, E. Weiher). Freiburg i. Br.: U.W. Weiher, 1986, pp. 93–99. (Ms. **MPr**)

Sokolov 1899. Matveĭ Sokolov. *Materialy i Zametki po Starinnoĭ Slavianskoĭ Literature*. Vyp. Tretiĭ (vii/ii): *Slavianskaia Kniga Enokha. Tekstъ s latinskimъ perevodomъ* [*Матеріалы и замѣтки по старинной славянской литературѣ*, Вып. 3 (7/2): *Славянская книга Эноха. Текстъ с латинскимъ переводомъ*].—*ChIOIDR* 4 (1899). Moscow: Universitetskaia Tipografiia, 1899. (Ms. **S**; Ms. **Bars/Sok**)

Sokolov 1910. M. Sokolov. *Slavianskaia Kniga Enokha Pravednago. Teksty, latinskiĭ perevod i issledovanie. Posmertnyĭ trud avtora. Prigotovil k izdaniiu M. Speranskiĭ*. Izdanie Imperatorskago Obshchestva Istorii i Drevnosteĭ Rossiĭskikh pri Moskovskom Universitetě.—*ChIOIDR* 4/235 (1910). Moscow: Sinodal'naia Tipografiia, 1910. (Ms. **U**; Ms. **Bars1/Sok**; Ms. **SokRum**; Ms. **SokRum590/Pisk155**; Ms. **SokNezhin/IHP 39**; Ms. **SokRum578/Pisk143**; Ms. **SokHSL**; Ms. **Tikh/TSL**)

Sreznevskiĭ 1903. Vsevolod Izmailovich Sreznevskiĭ. 'Otchet Otdeleniiu Russkogo Iazyka i Slovesnosti Imperatorskoĭ Akademii Nauk o Poezdke v Olonetskuiu, Vologodskuiu i Permskuiu Gubernii (Iun' 1902). Perechen' priobretennykh rukopiseĭ.'—*IORISIAN* 8: 4 (1903), pp. 109–111, 122–123. (Ms. **Srezn/Navt**)

Tikhomirov 1961. Mikhail Nikolaevich Tikhomirov. *Merilo Pravednoe po Rukopisi 14 veka*. Moscow: Izdatel'stvo Akademii Nauk SSSR, 1961, pp. 71–76. (Ms. **MPr**)

Tikhonravov 1863. Nikolaĭ Savvich Tikhonravov. *Pamiatniki Otrechennoĭ Russkoĭ Literatury*, Vol. 1, Sankt Petersburg, pp. 19–23 (Ms. MPr; Ms. Tikh/TSL).

Vaillant 1952. André Vaillant. *Le livre des secrets d'Hénoch. Texte slave et traduction française*. Paris: Institut d'études slaves, 1952. (Ms. U; and fragments from Ms. S)

Bibliographic Abbreviations

AP	*Arheografski Prilozi*
BETL	*Bibliotheca Ephemeridum Theologicarum Lovaniensium*
BF	*Bŭlgarski Folklor* [Български фолклор]
BLDR	*Biblioteka Literatury Drevneĭ Rusi* [Библиотека Литературы Древней Руси]
BSOAS	*Bulletin of the School of Oriental and African Studies*
CCSA	*Corpus Christianorum Series Apocryphorum*
ChIOIDR	*Chteniia vъ Imperatorskomъ Obshchestvě Istorii i Drevnosteĭ Rossiĭskikh pri Moskovskomъ Universitetě* [Чтенія въ Императорскомъ Обществѣ Исторіи и Древностей Россійскихъ при Московскомъ Университетѣ]
DSD	*Dead Sea Discoveries*
EChr	*Early Christianity*
FE	*Fundamenta Europæa*
HTR	*The Harvard Theological Review*
HUS	*Harvard Ukrainian Studies*
IANSSSR/SLIA	*Izvestiia Akademii Nauk SSSR. Seriia Literatury i Iazyka* [Известия Академии наук СССР. Серия литературы и языка].
IIBL	*Izvestiia na Instituta za Bŭlgarska Literatura* [Известия на Института за българска литература]
IIMK	*Izvestiia na Istoricheski Muzeĭ Kiustendil* [Известия на Исторически музей Кюстендил]
IORISIAN	*Izvestiia Otdeleniia Russkogo Iazyka i Slovesnosti Imperatorskoĭ Akademii Nauk* [Известия Отделения Русского Языка и Словесности Императорской Академии Наук]
JAOS	*Journal of the American Oriental Society*
JBL	*Journal of Biblical Literature*
JJS	*Journal of Jewish Studies*
JSJ	*Journal for the Study of Judaism*
JSP	*Journal for the Study of Pseudepigrapha*
JSQ	*Jewish Studies Quarterly*
JSOTSS	*Journal for the Study of the Old Testament Supplement Series*
JThSt	*The Journal of Theological Studies*
KMS	*Kirilo-Metodievski studii* (Kirilo-Metodievski Nauchen Tsentŭr, Bŭlgarska Akademiia na Naukite) [Кирило-Методиевски студии (Кирило-Методиевски Научен Център, Българска Академия на науките)]

KSINAA	*Kratkie Soobshcheniia Instituta Narodov Azii i Afriki* [Краткие Сообщения Института народов Азии и Африки]
PI	*Problemi na Izkustvoto* [Проблеми на изкуството]
PrKnSh	*Preslavska Knizhovna Shkola* [Преславска Книжовна Школа]
RÉS	*Revue des études slaves*
RFV	*Russkiĭ Filologicheskiĭ Vestnik*
RHR	*Revue de l'histoire des religions*
RL	*Russian Linguistics*
RS	*Ricerche slavistiche*
SbORIS	*Sbornik Otdeleniia Russkogo Iazyka i Slovesnosti Imperatorskoĭ Akademii Nauk* [Сборник Отделения русского языка и словесности Императорской Академии наук]
SEER	*Slavonic and East European Review*
SH	*Slavica Hierosolymitana*
SJS/LLP	*Slovník Jazyka Staroslověnského. Lexicon Linguæ Palæoslovenicæ.*
SC	*Studia Ceranea*
SL	*Starobŭlgarska Literatura* [Старобългарска литература]
TODRL	*Trudy Otdela Drevnerusskoĭ Literatury* [Труды Отдела Древнерусской Литературы]
VC	*Vigiliæ Christianæ*
VoprIazyk	*Voprosy Iazykoznaniia* [Вопросы языкознания]
VSK	*Vestnik Slavianskikh Kul'tur* [Вестник славянских культур]
VT	*Vetus Testamentum*
VV	*Vizantiĭskiĭ Vremennik* [Византийский Временник]
WSJ	*Wiener Slavistisches Jahrbuch*
WSL	*Die Welt der Slaven*
ZAW	*Zeitschrift für alttestamentliche Wissenschaft*
ZhMNP	*Zhurnal Ministerstva Narodnogo Prosveshcheniia* [Журнал Министерства Народного Просвещения]

CHAPTER 23

Visions of Paradise in the Life of St Andrew the Fool and the Legacy of the Jewish Pseudepigrapha in Byzantium

Emmanouela Grypeou

Greek Byzantine apocalyptic literature has long been a largely unexplored and understudied field. Byzantine eschatological ideas used to be mainly investigated on the basis of theological writings, or liturgical texts, such as hymnography.[1] The popular ideas relating to the afterlife that circulated through writings of an apocalyptic or visionary character remain neglected by modern scholarship.[2]

Significantly, one of the main questions which has hardly been investigated with regard to this body of literature is how far and in which ways those texts form part of a long Jewish and Christian apocalyptic-eschatological tradition. Notably, Alexander Golitzin observed certain common themes between the Byzantine visionary literature and the Jewish Merkabah tradition as well as the *Hekhalot* literature. He stressed the 'interiorization of the ascent to heaven and other motifs from Second Temple and early Christian apocalypses'.[3]

The official theology of the Byzantine Empire has naturally influenced the formation of eschatological beliefs. As is well-known, however, even if the production and dissemination of esoteric literature was frowned upon by the

---

1   Cf. D. Olster, 'Byzantine Apocalypses', in B. McGinn (ed.), *The Encyclopedia of Apocalypticism* vol. 2, New York, 2000, pp. 48–73; E. Patlagean, 'Byzance et son autre monde: observations sur quelques récits', in A. Vauchez (ed.), *Faire Croire: modalités de la diffusion et de la reception des messages religieux du XXe au XVe siècle*, Rome, 1981, pp. 201–221.

2   Following statement by Lennard Rydén reflects the common view of Byzantine scholars of the genre: 'Byzantine apocalypses tend to be fairly simple-minded documents. True, they are made up to a large extent of *topoi* deriving from the eschatological tradition, yet each one of them reflects the fears and aspirations of the time of its composition' (id., *The Life of St. Andrew the Fool: Introduction, testimonies and Nachleben, indices*, Uppsala, 1995, p. 305). Notably, Rydén was one of the few scholars who edited and studied extensively some of the texts in view.

3   A. Golitzin, ' 'Earthly Angels and Heavenly Men': The Old Testament Pseudepigrapha, Niketas Stethatos and the Tradition of 'Interiorized Apocalyptic' in Eastern Christian Ascetical and Mystical Literature', in *Dumbarton Oaks Papers* 55 (2002), p. 147.

© EMMANOUELA GRYPEOU, 2021 | DOI:10.1163/9789004445925_025

Church authorities, pseudepigraphical literature continued to be copied, translated and expanded upon in monastic scriptoria and most notably in those in the periphery of the Empire.[4]

According to a widespread scholarly opinion, the Byzantine times are characterised by a relative lack of interest in writings relating to the afterlife and heavenly journeys. Indeed, although political apocalyptic texts, which were based mainly on the Book of Daniel, and dealt with the political fate of the Empire, circulated in multiple copies and versions, texts that were concerned with the fate of the souls after death seem to have existed rather marginally. Therefore, these writings are few in number and possibly also of a relatively limited popularity.

Notably, descriptions of eschatological visions are often integrated into hagiographical literature of the time, as part of out-of-body or after-death experiences of holy men and women, monks or nuns and their novices, and righteous people in general. The hell and paradise tours often also include a vision of the divine throne.

The descriptions of afterlife, which were included in the hagiographical literature, marked a shift with respect to the attribution of authority of the visionaries. The traditional revelatory figures of the earlier Jewish and Christian apocalyptic tradition, such as biblical patriarchs, become obsolete and even New Testament and apostolic authorities are viewed as distant figures of the past. The centre of attention is occupied almost exclusively by the figure of the Holy Man or Holy Woman. This shift becomes the norm for the Byzantine literature that seeks to transmit theoretical but also practical otherworldly knowledge to its clerical or non-clerical audience.

Furthermore, these writings demonstrate typical features of the literature of the time and reflect contemporary Byzantine popular views on life after death. In this regard, they represent valuable witnesses of their period and culture. However, it is important to note that a homogeneous tradition of eschatological views and motifs cannot be claimed in the context of Byzantine literature.

Significantly, the bodies of texts which deal with afterlife visions and narratives demonstrate a disproportionate interest in visions of hell punishments. The interest in ideas about paradise is relatively limited. It appears that the horrifying, hair-raising descriptions of hell punishments were considered to be more interesting and urgent because of their moralising intentionality for the broad public compared to the positive and at least superficially optimistic ideas of rewards promised in the afterlife for the very few righteous.

---

4 See M. Himmelfarb, *Ascent to Heaven*, Oxford–New York, 1993, p. 99.

VISIONS OF PARADISE IN THE LIFE OF ST ANDREW THE FOOL 523

Descriptions of paradise can be found in a number of Byzantine texts that recount visionary experiences. A short description of paradise is included, for example, in one version of the Apocalypse of the Virgin Mary.[5] A longer description can be found in a tenth century text known as the Apocalypse of Anastasia.[6] It is important to note that these texts rely heavily on older apocalyptic texts and most notably on the Apocalypse of Paul. In certain aspects, texts such as the Apocalypse of the Virgin Mary and the Apocalypse of Anastasia can be regarded as medieval 're-writings' or expansions of this most popular Christian apocalyptic text of Late Antiquity.

Detailed narratives on paradise are integrated into hagiographical texts, such as the Life of Andrew the Fool and the Life of St Basil the Younger.[7] Lennart Rydén commented that the Lives of Basil and Andrew are 'fascinated by apocalypses to such an extent' that they 'almost appear to be pretexts for writing apocalyptic fiction' and for lengthy, complicated eschatological digressions.[8]

The mentioned texts are approximately dated to the tenth century. This dating confirms a newly discovered interest in apocalyptic prophecies around the tenth century in Byzantium. Ideas about the coming of the end of the world, the Last Judgment, Heaven and Hell seem to have been particularly popular around that period. It is an era when the Byzantine world appears to discover anew apocalypticism and eschatology.

According to Paul Magdalino: 'the very existence of these texts is important as confirmation that speculation about the afterlife was intense during the tenth century, when apocalyptic expectations ran high with the advent of the middle of the seventh millennium since the creation of the world'.[9]

In the following I am going to discuss the paradise visions narrated in the Life of Andrew the Fool. As I would like to demonstrate, complicated—and at times rambling—Byzantine hagiographical texts, such as the Life of Andrew,

---

5 See R. Bauckham: '... in most manuscripts, the Greek Apocalypse of the Virgin, consists only of a tour of hell, though in some a brief visit to Paradise is appended' ('The Four Apocalypses of the Virgin Mary', in id., *The Fate of the Dead*, Leiden, 1998, p. 336). There is an impressive number of manuscripts and recensions of this text. However, a critical edition is still lacking.

6 See R. Homburg (ed.), *Apocalypsis Anastasiæ*, Leipzig, 1903. For an exhaustive analysis of this text, see J. Baun, *Tales from Another Byzantium. Celestial Journey and Local Community in the Medieval Greek Apocrypha*, Cambridge, 2007.

7 L. Rydén, 'The Life of St. Basil the Younger and the Date of the Life of St. Andreas Salos', in C. Mango and C. Pritsak, *Okeanos*, Cambridge, 1983, pp. 568–586. P. Magdalino, ''What we heard in the Lives of the saints we have seen with our own eyes': the holy man as literary text in tenth-century Constantinople', in J. Howard-Johnston and P.A. Hayward, *The Cult of Saints in Late Antiquity and the Early Middle Ages*, Oxford, 1999, pp. 83–112.

8 *The Life of St. Andrew the Fool* vol. 1, p. 53.

9 Magdalino, 'What we heard in the Lives of the saints we have seen with our own eyes', p. 99.

preserve, recycle and transmit various established apocalyptic motifs already documented in the early Jewish apocalyptic tradition. Thus, these texts bear evidence to the longevity, popularity and preservation of this vivid tradition through various trajectories, languages and cultural contexts. Furthermore, they suggest that the apocalyptic tradition as preserved, developed and documented in later writings, demonstrates a deeply conservative character regarding the choice of main structural elements and motifs integrated in the respective narratives. The particular narrative frames set the scenery and serve mainly as cultural indicators but they rarely ever significantly modify the major apocalyptic elements used.

1   The Life of Andrew the Fool

The Life of Andrew, a fool of God, was composed by his disciple Nikephoros and takes place in a fictive context in Constantinople of the sixth century. However, the text stems most probably from the tenth century.[10] The Life presents a very complex and comprehensive work of an almost encyclopedic character.[11]

The text narrates two visions of paradise. The first vision (490–735) refers to Andrew's visit to paradise, when he was seriously ill and went through a near-death experience during a terrible winter storm in Constantinople. Shortly before Andrew freezes to death, he sees a handsome young man coming over to him, whose face shines like the sun. He greets Andrew with a bunch of golden flowers. A voice orders that Andrew should be transferred to a quiet place

---

10   On the dating of the Life between 950–1000, see L. Rydén, *The Life of St. Andrew the Fool* vol. 1, pp. 41–56; and also id., 'The Date of the Life of Andreas Salos', *Dumbarton Oaks Papers* 32 (1978), pp. 127–156; J. Wortley, 'The Political Significance of the Andreas-Salos Apocalypse', *Byzantion* 43 (1973), pp. 248–263; cf. C. Mango, 'The Life of Saint Andrew the Fool Reconsidered', *Rivista di studi bizantini e slavi* 2 (1982), pp. 297–313, who argued for a late-seventh-century date of the text; this early dating, however, has been commonly rejected.

11   The Life of Andreas Salos (Andrew the Fool) is witnessed in over 100 Greek mss from the eleventh–nineteenth centuries; cf. S. Efthymiadis: 'a text with a remarkably wide circulation as it survives in whole or in part, in some 90 codices: popularity extended to the Slav world' (id., *The Ashgate Companion to Byzantine Hagiography* vol. 1, Farnham, 2011, p. 126); cf. C. Ludwig, *Sonderformen byzantinischer Hagiographie und ihr literarisches Vorbild, Untersuchungen zu den Viten des Äsop, des Philaretus, des Symeon Salos und des Andreas Salos*, Frankfurt, 1997, pp. 220–290; S. Ivanov, *Holy Fools in Byzantium and Beyond*, Oxford, 2006, pp. 139–173; see also A. Kazhdan, *A History of Byzantine Literature* (850–1000), ed. C. Angelidi, Athens, 2006, pp. 185–200.

for two weeks. Immediately, Andrew finds himself in a wonderful garden. He realises that he is transferred to this garden without his body. However, even if he does not have a material body, he is dressed with a dazzling garment, white as snow, set with precious stones and a marvellously red girdle. He also has a golden flower wreath and sandals on. Thus, he is properly dressed for his visit to heaven.

In the garden Andrew marvels at the beautiful, ever-green trees dripping honey that appear like the crystal of heaven. Wonderful birds with wings like gold or snow sit on these trees. A mighty river flows through the garden and irrigates it. A grape vine full with heavy grapes and golden leaves leans over the river like a lamp. This lamp is identified with Christ, the cornerstone. Four winds blow in paradise and spread beautiful odours and colours. Andrew falls in ecstasy and finds himself on the firmament, where he meets again the handsome young man who now becomes his guide in heaven. Andrew starts a heavenly journey to the throne of God, passing through three firmaments.

On the first firmament of heaven, they see a cross and four shining curtains and innumerable magnificent looking singers. Their eyes shine like fire, as they sing a hymn in honour of the Crucified One. The second firmament appears like snow and there are two crosses there in a fiery surrounding. The third firmament looks like a golden leaf and has three crosses, also surrounded by fire. Innumerable heavenly hosts praise God. Andrew and his guide pass through splendid curtains until they reach the throne of God that hangs in the air without support. Andrew sees there the Son of Man, Jesus Christ clad in shining purple and linen.

Andrew descends from the heavens and finds himself again in a wonderful, fragrant flower garden with a well wherefrom milk and honey spring. He encounters there a dazzling man, dressed in a garment like a shining cloud who holds a cross and explains why Andrew, the fool of God, was worthy of a vision of God and a vision of paradise. This man is presumably the Good Thief.

Andrew's vision of paradise as a lavish, marvellous garden reveals the future reward of the righteous in a spiritual way. However, the garden is still empty. The heavenly journey of Andrew borrows a number of common eschatological motifs, but also demonstrates certain original elements such as the presence of the crosses on the various heavens and their veneration by Andrew and his guide. The presence of the good thief as a revelatory figure is an additional original trait of the apocalypse. His presence in this context emphasises even more strongly the importance of the crucifixion motif for the text.

The vision of the throne of the Son of Man is described in its full imperial glory. It is assumed that such representations in visionary Byzantine literature were inspired by the symbolism and ritualism of the Byzantine imperial court.[12] Jane Baun even suggests that the Byzantine representations of the heavenly world were transformed in order to match the model of the Byzantine imperial court. As Baun further remarks: 'The transformation is most striking in Andrew the Fool's otherworld vision, which reads like a celestial De Cere-moniis, and in fact mirrors Liutprand of Cremona's famous audience before Constantine VII Porphyrogennetos. Andrew progresses through the various gardens (filled with marvellous birds, real-life versions of the palace automata) and forecourts of the heavens like a highly favoured diplomat through the imperial palace. He witnesses theatrical display of treasures and wonders, and singers shouting holy acclamations. (...) All the wonders, including Jesus Christ himself, are located behind huge curtains of fine linen and purple.'[13] However, it should be noted that there is a long tradition of descriptions of the divine throne, in which the limits between heavenly and earthly reality are often fluid. Heaven and the divine throne were often envisioned in terms of a royal court in general.[14]

The second heavenly vision in the Life of Andrew (1690–1775) is attributed to his disciple Epiphanius. Epiphanius wishes to receive a vision of Andrew in heaven. He sees in a dream how an old man visits him. The man holds a gospel and a papyrus scroll and leads Epiphanius to paradise.[15] Together they reach

---

12 See, for example, P. Magdalino, 'The Year 1000 in Byzantium', in id. (ed.), *Byzantium in the Year 1000*, Leiden, 2003, pp. 151–154.

13 Baun, *Tales from Another Byzantium*, p. 229.

14 See P. Magdalino, 'The assimilation of the earthly empire to the Kingdom of Heaven. The idea that the Roman empire was a pale imitation of heaven, and that the heavenly order could be described in terms of imperial court procedure, was not new in the sixth century. It has been adumbrated in the 330s by Eusebius of Cæsarea in his writings in praise of Constantine, and had been elaborated by later writers, notably St. John Chrysostom' (id., 'The history of the future and its uses: prophecy, policy and propaganda', in R. Beaton and C. Roueché (eds), *The Making of Byzantine history: studies dedicated to Donald M. Nicol*, London, 1993, p. 14); Cf. J.E. Wright, *The Early History of Heaven*, Oxford, 1999, pp. 76–78; on heaven as a 'parallel universe' in Jewish apocalyptic literature, see P. Alexander, who also stresses that: 'there is no ontological discontinuity between earth and heaven: both belong, so to speak, to the same space-time continuum' (id., 'The Dualism of Heaven and Earth in Early Jewish Literature and its Implications', in A. Lange et al. (eds), *Light Against Darkness: Dualism in Ancient Mediterranean Religion and the Contemporary World*, Göttingen, 2011, pp. 169–185, here 170).

15 According to iconographic and legendary traditions, the old man might represent John the Evangelist, who was also identified with John of Revelation and who was the only person among the Evangelists to reach an old age; see *Lexikon der christlichen Ikonographie* vol. 7, col. 112. Notably, Epiphanius does not receive a youthful person as a guide and in that sense, he does not have an angelic escort but an older man reflecting thus perhaps in this way his own status as a novice.

a court full of light, in which there is a palace, 'built of a solar breeze'. They further walk through a hall full of strange and incredible mysteries and fiery thrones. On one of the thrones, which rises to an immense height, he sees an awe-inspiring and ineffable king shining like the sun, while balls of fire proceed from his face, so that the ether itself is illuminated by an abundance of glory and brilliance. Around him there are innumerable legions and armies of cherubim, seraphim and powers. The king allows Epiphanius to enter the kingdom of heaven reserved for the saints, a chamber full of light. In this chamber, there sits Andrew in full glory. Epiphanius wakes up and realises that he has seen a vision of Jesus Christ as the king.

This short vision clearly demonstrates basic differences to Andrew's vision. Epiphanius is directly translated to the divine throne. The divine residence is described quite precisely like a royal palace. In spite of his awesome appearance Jesus Christ appears approachable and merciful. Epiphanius is allowed to see the Saints in the kingdom of heavens, which is described like a chamber of light.

As observed, Andrew experiences paradise as a luscious garden. Separate elements in the description of the garden of paradise recall motifs that are already evidenced in older apocalyptic texts. Andrew stresses in the text repeatedly the fragrances of Paradise, a motif that corresponds to a well-known motif in apocalyptic texts.[16] Springs of milk and honey in paradise are also mentioned and quite similarly described in 2 Enoch 8:5, Moreover, they also relate to the rivers of honey and milk in the Apocalypse of Paul 22 (cf. Apocalypse of Paul 45). Luscious trees in the garden also present a very common apocalyptic image.[17]

Andrew needs to ascend through the heavens, before he can reach the throne. The paradise is located on the third heaven, as in 2 Enoch 8:1. The motif of the golden third heaven also recalls the Apocalypse of Paul 19, in which the third heaven is described as a golden gate with golden columns.

Each firmament has a different appearance and represents a gradual ascent, since in the first heaven there is one cross, in the second heaven two crosses and in the third heaven three crosses. Already before the first cross there are wonderful curtains and angel choirs which highlight the holiness of the place. These curtains in front of the crosses possibly represent the arrangement and design of Byzantine church altars, with which the author must have been familiar through his everyday liturgical experience. The third curtain which hides

---

16   Cf. 1En 31; 2En 8. Similar descriptions of fragrant winds in the garden of God can be found in 3 Enoch 23:18 based on the Song of Songs 4:16.

17   Cf. 1En 17 f.; 23–25; Apocalypse of Peter (Greek, achm. 15 ff.) Apocalypse of Paul 45.

the throne of the Son of Man looks purple and linen, similar to the curtain of the Temple.[18] Jesus is also clad in the priestly-imperial garments of purple and linen (cf. Ex 28:5). The three crosses that represent a forecourt to the throne court are surrounded by fire in accordance with common apocalyptic images. The idea of the fiery throne of the Son of Man is a topos in apocalyptic literature.[19]

Similarly, the fiery palaces in the vision of Epiphanius recall 1 Enoch 14:8 ff., in which Enoch passes through fiery marble houses, until he reaches a fiery throne. 2 Enoch 22 (and Vita Adæ 25:3) also mention, similarly to Epiphanius, the 'burning face of God emitting sparks'. The description of God's throne as 'flashing fire' bears strong similarities to Andrew's fiery heaven.[20]

The paradise garden is totally empty in the Life of Andrew. Similarly, the paradise is not inhabited, for example, in 1 Enoch 32 and in 2 Enoch 8f. It is also interesting to note that Andrew receives a vision of paradise, while he is still alive. In certain terms, the paradise that awaits him is shown to him in advance. The golden bunch of flowers in the beginning of the paradise story of the Life of Andrew the Fool most possibly represents the good deeds of Andrew and could be understood as a symbol of his righteousness.[21] However, Andrew does not meet the souls of the righteous in paradise. Even if he is considered one of the righteous, he does not yet belong there, since he is not yet dead.

Furthermore, the transformation of Andrew corresponds to a typical motif of the rapture of the visionary in apocalyptic literature. Enoch in 2 Enoch 22:8 ff. is clad with the garments of 'divine glory' and is transformed accordingly into an angel-like figure.[22] Andrew is also transformed in an ideal way, shortly before his upcoming trip to the heavens and only then is he ready to enter the garden of God.

The author recycles common angelic imagery which would have easily been recognisable by his audience, even if they were not familiar with apocalyptic literature and ideas. The description of the garments of Andrew refers to iconographic depictions of angels from the Byzantine time that might have been inspired by the Book of Daniel or other canonical books. Similar images can further be found in texts such as 2 Enoch 1:6 that describe 'gigantic men' with faces like 'shining suns, eyes like burning lamps' and hands white as snow.

---

18   Cf. Exod. 26.1.31.36; see Josephus, Bell. 5.212; Ant. 8.75.
19   See Daniel 7:9–10; ApocAbraham 18:3; 2En 22:1.
20   See 1En 14:8–25.
21   In the Psalms of Solomon 14:2 and in the Odes of Solomon 11:18.20 f. the trees of paradise are the righteous themselves.
22   Cf. 3En 15:1–12.

VISIONS OF PARADISE IN THE LIFE OF ST ANDREW THE FOOL 529

A special emphasis is put on the description of the angels, although they are rarely called angels but rather handsome young men, who are distinguished through their glorious garments and magnificent appearance.[23] The stereotypical depiction of the angels as guides and assistants during the heavenly tours follows standard apocalyptic motifs. However, their precise physical description seems to have been inspired by Byzantine culture and art and, more specifically, Byzantine iconography. Angelic garments were commonly coloured white in Byzantine icons, as a symbol of spiritual purity and transcendence. Furthermore, a number of scholars have argued that the angels imagined as gloriously dressed youths bring to mind court eunuchs.[24] As Ringrose in her study of Byzantine eunuchs maintains, the correspondence refers to 'the imagined parallels of divine and imperial courts and the use of white robes; it is not hard to see why eunuchs were mistaken for angels. In the Vita of St Symeon the Stylite the Younger, for example, Symeon has a vision that includes 'a corps of angel-like men who were eunuchs, whose clothing was white as snow''.[25] However, especially after the sixth century, it was also common for the angels and archangels to be depicted in imperial dress and in the colours red, violet or blue and purple, colours that were especially assigned for the imperial court officers.

In contrast to Andrew's at least partly bucolic vision, Epiphanius' otherworldly vision bears almost urbane features. His out-of-body experience takes place exclusively in closed spaces. The throne vision is located in a palace, where Epiphanius proceeds through fiery halls. The heavenly kingdom is depicted like a chamber of light. The symbol of fire as a medium to describe a theophanic experience is prominent in both visions. It is striking, however, that Epiphanius does not have a vision of the garden of paradise.

The difference in the experiences and in the description probably depends on a distinction of a spiritual character between the two protagonists. Epiphanius, as a novice of Andrew, is granted only a brief audience before the throne in the palace of the king so that his wish to see Andrew's transcendent persona in heaven would be fulfilled.

---

23 Angels with hair like snow and in purple red garments can be found again in the Apocalypse of Abraham 11.

24 See C. Mango: 'The angels, being sexless and acting as God's attendants, had their closest earthly analogy in the eunuchs of the imperial palace' (id., 'The Invisible World of Good and Evil in Byzantium', in id., *Byzantium. The Empire of New Rome*, New York–London, 1980, p. 155).

25 K.M. Ringrose, *The Perfect Servant. Eunuchs and the Social Construction of Heaven in Byzantium*, Chicago–London, 2003, p. 80.

It is possible that the author stressed the difference between the two visions in order to demonstrate the spiritual difference between the master and the novice. Andrew experiences a more esoteric vision due to his spiritual maturity and superiority. He witnesses a genuine heavenly ascent and partakes in the divine secrets. Epiphanius' vision has the sole intention of showing a glimpse of Andrew's glory. Only in this context does Epiphanius also receive a brief insight into the mercy of Jesus Christ, who grants him a transcendent vision of Andrew. In both versions, the visions can only take place after spoken permissions that are understood as special gifts of the divine grace.

The double paradise narrative with their different characteristics is a unique feature of these hagiographic texts. The paradise vision of the novice clearly stresses the blessed elevated status of the master and indirectly confirms his visionary authority. Thus, it provides a very helpful literary device that transforms the hagiographic text into an apocalyptic narrative.

Similarly, the roughly contemporary hagiographic text, Life of Saint Basil the Younger, contains two visions of paradise as well.[26] The first vision refers to the journey of blessed Theodora, the former housekeeper of Basil, who has recently died and has been received into paradise after a short audience in front of the divine throne. In the second vision, Gregory, Basil's disciple, wanders through a paradisiacal garden, that represents the life of his spiritual father, St Basil. Thus, also in this text the novice is granted a brief insight into the blessed state of his masters in heaven. As Paul Magdalino notes about the two Lives: 'The visions and their edifying messages occupy so much space that the Lives can easily be seen as frame stories of set pieces of apocalyptic exegesis, in which the saints themselves are of secondary importance.'[27]

Accordingly, we observe that heavenly ascents and audiences in front of the throne of God (commonly located on the third heaven) become part of hagiographic literature. The monks and nuns or fools of God in our texts all visit the throne of God—evidence of their closeness to God in this life. The description of Paradise is influenced by a number of older motifs and traditions. The paradise is described as a wonderful garden in numerous pseudepigraphical texts.[28] However, as Jane Baun also notes: 'Paradise as a walled garden of

---

26   On this text see D.F. Sullivan, A.-M. Talbot and S. McGrath (eds and trans.), *The Life of Saint Basil the Younger, Critical Edition and Annotated Translation of the Moscow Version*, D.O. Studies 45, Cambridge, 2015.

27   Magdalino, 'What we heard in the Lives of the saints we have seen with our own eyes', p. 89.

28   Most importantly, similar descriptions can be found in 2 Enoch 8, in 1 Enoch 23–25; in the

VISIONS OF PARADISE IN THE LIFE OF ST ANDREW THE FOOL   531

indescribable fertility and beauty is common in dreams, visions, edifying tales, and Byzantine Last Judgment iconography.'[29]

Main motifs are also shared with other contemporaneous texts that describe paradise. The motifs of the paradise as a beautiful, walled garden, of Abraham's bosom and of the banquet for the merciful are also attested in the Apocalypse of Anastasia. Similar descriptions of Paradise as a fantastic garden can also be found in works such as the Life of Philaretos the Merciful by Nicetas[30] and in the funerary oration by Michael Psellos to his daughter Styliane.[31] Both texts describe Paradise as a garden that surpasses all imagination.

The tenth century vision of the Monk Kosmas, a former imperial chamberlain, is the only other extensive Middle Byzantine near-death narrative. Kosmas' 'relaxed, alfresco heaven'[32] includes Abraham in the world of the Blessed, the heavenly city and the banquet of the righteous. According to Christina Angelidi, Kosmas recognised everything he saw in the Other World, either because it was so similar to the imperial palace, or because it looked 'just like an icon'.[33]

These texts can be regarded as more or less elaborate variations of major apocalyptic themes. However, the apocalyptic elements were integrated into hagiographical literature and, as such, achieved a more 'mainstream status' that facilitated their broader acceptance and circulation. Moreover, these texts were also deeply rooted in the canonical church tradition. The eschatological narratives integrated various elements, which were familiar from the Byzantine liturgy and iconography. Thus they merged various traditions both from their contemporary religious culture and older pseudepigraphical literary traditions. The Byzantine visionary literature indicates that non-canonical texts were further copied, read and discussed and even served as inspiration sources for the production of new original literature in Byzantium.

As Evelyne Patlagean has noted, these works constitute narrative justifications of representations of the afterlife according to the normative theo-

---

       Apocalypse of Peter 15 ff. (Greek achmimic) and in the Apocalypse of Paul 45. The trees provide fruit for the pleasure of the righteous (1En 32; 2En 84).

29   Baun, *Tales from another Byzantium*, p. 124.

30   L. Rydén, *The Life of St. Philaretos the merciful, written by his grandson Niketa*, Studia Byzantina Upsaliensa 8, Uppsala, 2002.

31   See A. Kaldellis, *Mothers and Sons, Fathers and Daughters: the Byzantine Family of Michael Pselllos*, Notre Dame, 2006, pp. 111–138.

32   See Magdalino, 'What we heard in the Lives of the saints we have seen with our own eyes', p. 100.

33   C. Angelidi, 'La version longue de la Vision du Moine Cosmas', *Analecta Bollandiana* 101 (1903), pp. 73–99, 84, 125–128.

logical system. The descriptions of the afterlife provide answers to questions about Byzantine eschatological beliefs of the time. These variations on a theme emerge during a cultural period that follows the iconoclastic crisis in the middle of the ninth century and lasts until the decline of the ruling Macedonian (also known as the Armenian) dynasty, that is, in 1025.[34] The historical context is thus related to the aftermath of the iconoclastic crisis that triggered an important cultural innovation in all the fields of literary and scholarly production in Byzantium through new editions of ancient works, compilations of encyclopædias, and a renewal of the imperial legislation.

In other words, the Greek Byzantine literature of the tenth century appears to reflect the evolution of the apocalyptic genre and its accommodation with the broader culture and with its specific cultural, religious and literary needs. Apocalyptic ideas become re-adapted and integrated into the Byzantine world and also reflect specific developments in the Byzantine history.

Pseudepigrapha and apocalyptic literature are often viewed as marginal literary genres that led an obscure life in dark corners of the libraries of remote monasteries. However, these texts survived not only due to the efforts of a few curious librarians and monks. They obviously also survived because they filled a vacuum regarding popular questions about death and the afterlife.[35] Furthermore, this textual legacy in the garb of hagiography would appeal to both learned religious specialists and the largely illiterate common believers.

Greek Byzantine apocalyptic literature reflects a stage in the history of apocalyptic literature, in which motifs, which can be more or less easily traced back to famous Jewish and Christians apocalyptic texts, were interiorised and also became integrated into other literary genres. Thus, it is no longer possible to claim a direct textual dependence, even if we can imagine that the authors might have made eclectic use of various texts available in monastic libraries. Finally, even if largely neglected by modern scholarship, accounts of heavenly journeys from tenth century Constantinople are important witnesses for the development of apocalyptic and eschatological literature in Greek language as well as for the development of Byzantine popular religious literature.

---

34   Patlagean, *Byzance et son autre monde*, pp. 201 ff.

35   Cf. M.E. Stone, *Ancient Judaism: New Visions and Views*, Grand Rapids, 2011, pp. 29–30.

CHAPTER 24

Eternal Chains and the Mountain of Darkness: The Fallen Angels in the Incantation Bowls

Yakir Paz

The ongoing publication of the incantation bowls—dated to the 5th–7th century CE, written in Jewish Babylonian Aramaic, Mandaic and Syriac and found mainly in modern-day Iraq and Khuzestan—has significantly increased our understanding of ancient magic, Aramaic dialects and the society of the Sasanian Empire. Yet, although the bowls also contain many allusions to Early Jewish literature in general, and Enochic literature in particular, these traditions have not yet received due attention.[1] In this paper, through a close reading of sections from three bowls, I hope to demonstrate how the bowls can contribute to our knowledge of the myth of the fallen angels, its transmission and reception.[2]

---

1 The notable exception is J.T. Milik, *The Books of Enoch: Aramaic Fragments of Qumran Cave 4*, Oxford, 1976, pp. 125–135, 335–339. See also J. Greenfield, 'Notes on Aramaic and Mandaic Magic Bowls', *Journal of Ancient Near Eastern Society* vol. 5, 1973, pp. 150–154; A.Y. Reed, *Fallen Angels and the History of Judaism and Christianity: The Reception of Enochic Literature*, New York, 2005, pp. 252–254. For other examples of the reception of Mesopotamian and Early Jewish traditions in the incantation bowls, see S. Bhayro, 'The Reception of Mesopotamian and Early Jewish Traditions in the Aramaic Incantation Bowls', *Aramaic Studies* vol. 11, 2013, pp. 187–196; id., 'On Early Jewish Literature and the Aramaic Magic Bowls', *Aramaic Studies* vol. 13, 2015, pp. 54–68. Further on the importance of the bowls and other magical texts for the study of early Jewish literature, see also P.T. Lanfer, 'Why Biblical Scholars Should Study Aramaic Bowl Spells', *Aramaic Studies* vol. 13, 2015, pp. 9–23, and G. Bohak, 'From Qumran to Cairo: The Lives and Times of a Jewish Exorcistic Formula' (with an Appendix by Sh. Shaked)', in I. Csepregi et al. (eds), *Ritual Healing: Magic, Ritual and Medical Therapy from Antiquity until the Early Modern Period*, Florence, 2012, pp. 31–52.

2 Other possible allusions to the fallen angels, not discussed in this article, include the mentioning of the oath on Mount Hermon (חירמון טורא; see C.D. Isbell, *Corpus of the Aramaic Incantation Bowls*, Missoula, 1975, p. 19 [2:6]; ibid., p. 31 [7:9]; J.A. Montgomery, *Aramaic Incantation Bowls from Nippur*, Philadelphia, 1913), p. 212 [27:9] and of Shamhiza (ܫܡܚܝܙܐ; M. Moriggi, *A Corpus of Syriac Incantation Bowls: Syriac Magical Texts from Late-Antique Mesopotamia*, Leiden, 2014, p. 23 [1:8], cf. below note 9). See also D. Levene, *A Corpus of Magic Bowls: Incantation Texts in Jewish Aramaic from Late Antiquity*, London, 2003, p. 136, and below note 38. For general surveys on the reception of the myth of the fallen angels in Late Antiquity, see e.g. J.C. VanderKam, '1 Enoch, Enochic Motifs, and Enoch in Early Christian Literature', in id. et al. (eds), *The Jewish Apocalyptic Heritage in Early Christianity*, Minneapolis, 1996, pp. 33–101;

© YAKIR PAZ, 2021 | DOI:10.1163/9789004445925_026

1 Eternal Chains

In 1962 Javier Teixidor published a Syriac incantation bowl written in Estrangela script, which, according to him, came from Tell Ramadi (near Najaf).[3] Yet he was able to transcribe only a part of the first four lines, as was also Victor Hamilton in his later edition, although in his comments he added some readings to lines 8, 9 and 11.[4] Recently, Marco Moriggi was able to read a part of all 11 lines relying on the photograph supplied by Teixidor. This new edition helps us to realize the importance of this bowl for the reception of the myth of the fallen angels, which has yet to be fully appreciated by scholars.[5] I cite here the first seven lines:[6]

ܥܒܕ (end of photograph) ܟܠ ܚܠܦܝ, ܘܕ ܘܕܝ ܚܠܦ, ܕܝ ܡܚܪܘܗܘܢ
ܟܬ̈ܒ ܕܥܒܪ ܚܒܬ (end of photograph) [...] ܚܒܬ, ܘܟܬ ܠܟܐ ܠܗܘܢ (6)
(1) Prepared is this amulet for the pressing and for the binding of all (2) evil sorcery and of the hateful magical acts and of the men or women who performed them (3) to the limbs, to the body [...] to ʾymʾ daughter mḥdṭ

Reed, *Fallen Angels*; Crone, 'The Book of the Watchers in the Quran', in H. Ben-Shammai et al. (eds), *Exchange and Transmission across Cultural Boundaries: Philosophy, Mysticism, and Science in the Mediterranean World*, Jerusalem, 2013, pp. 16–51.

3   J. Teixidor, 'The Syriac Incantation Bowls in the Iraq Museum', *Sumer* vol. 18, 1962, pp. 51–62, plates 1–4.

4   V.P. Hamilton, *Syriac Incantation Bowls*, Ann Arbor, 1971, p. 150.

5   A couple of scholars, based on the four-line transliteration provided by Teixidor, noted a connection to the myth of fallen angels but did not analyse it. See Levene, *Corpus*, p. 136; Crone, 'Book of Watchers', p. 191.

6   Moriggi, *Corpus*, pp. 71–73; text and translation (both slightly modified) after Moriggi, ibid., pp. 71–72.

7   Cf. 4QEnᵃ 1 1:3: ‏ומן מלי [עירין] וקדישין‎.

8   Moriggi (following Teixidor and Hamilton) reads here: ܬܘܠܟ which he does not translate. See the discussion below.

9   Moriggi suggests reading [ܡܗ]ܒܚܒ ('by the signet'). Cf. Moriggi, *Corpus*, p. 23 [1:8] which mentions 'the signet ring of Šamḥiza, the Lord Bagdana' (ܚܬܡܬܗ ܕܫܡܚܝܙܐ ܒܓܕܢܐ ܡܪܐ).

10   I wish to thank Ohad Abudraham for suggesting this reading. Moriggi (ibid., p. 72) reads ‏ܕ(ܠ)ܐܬܝ‎.

ETERNAL CHAINS AND THE MOUNTAIN OF DARKNESS 535

evil (4) sorcery. In the name of […] and pressed are all sorcery that they performed to her, that they perform to her, to *'ym'* (5) daughter of *m'ḥdṭ* […]

They listened[11] to [*end of photograph*] the words of the angels who revealed the mysteries (*rzy*) of their Lord,[12] by an eternal (6) chain they suspended (them), by a […] [*end of photograph*] performed to their God, until the Day of Judgment comes he will not take vengeance (7) from them […]

The short historiola of the fallen angels is presented as part of the 'protection from sorcery and sorcerers operating against the client'.[13] It would seem that it is used as a precedent for a punishment directed against revealers of magic. Below I shall mainly focus on the sin and the punishment of the angels and examine their relation to other versions of this myth.

1.1   *The Sin*

The sin of the angels according to the bowl consists in revealing the mysteries (*raza*) of the Lord. What exactly these mysteries are is not stated. However, it is clear that the *raza* here refers to some kind of magical knowledge. First, this is suggested from the anti-sorcery context of the bowl. More importantly, in the vocabulary of the bowls the term *raza* is intimately connected with magical practices and knowledge and at times could be actually rendered as 'spell'.[14] It appears many times at the beginning of an incantation in both Syriac and Jew-ish Aramaic bowls, as in the following example: רזא רזא דנן לשתוקי ולסכורי פומה דכל בני אינשה בישי ותקיפי דקמין לקובליה דבריך יהביה בר ממא (Mystery [*raza*]. This mystery [*raza*] is for silencing and shutting the mouth of all evil and violent people who stand against Berik-Yehabya son of Mama).[15] In addition, expres-sions such as רזי חרשי (mysteries of sorcery) and ܪ̈ܙܐ ܕܣܕ̈ (spells of mysteries) appear several times inscribed on the bowls.[16]

---

11   ܐܨܝܬܘ: another possibility is to read this as an imperative: 'Listen!'.

12   ܕܡܪܗܘܢ: Moriggi translates: 'their Lords'.

13   Moriggi, *Corpus*, p. 71.

14   See M. Sokoloff, *A Dictionary of Jewish Babylonian Aramaic of the Talmudic and Geonic Periods*, Ramat-Gan, 2020², p. 1044, s.v. רזא.

15   Text and translation: J. Naveh and Sh. Shaked, *Amulets and Magic Bowls: Aramaic Incan-tations of Late Antiquity*, Jerusalem, 1998³, pp. 164–165 (B6:1–3). Cf. e.g. eid., *Magic Spells and Formulæ: Aramaic Incantations of Late Antiquity*, Jerusalem, 1993, p. 124 (B19:1); ibid., p. 127 (B21:1); Moriggi, *Corpus*, p. 28 (2:4); ibid., p. 75 (13:1); ibid., p. 85 (15:1).

16   See e.g. Montgomery, *Aramaic Incantation Texts*, p. 146 (7:13); Naveh and Shaked, *Magic Spells*, p. 124 (B19:6); Moriggi, *Corpus*, p. 110 (22:6); ibid., p. 116 (23:7).

The idea that the sin of the angels had to do with the revelation of secrets, and in particular magical secrets, goes back to the *Book of Watchers*. In 1 Enoch 7:1 the angels are said to have taught their human wives sorcery and incantations (ולאלפה אנין חרשה ו[כשפה]).[17] This is also stated in the plea to God by the angels Michael, Gabriel, Suriel and Uriel (1 Enoch 9:6):[18] 'You see what Asael has done, who has taught all iniquity upon the earth, and has revealed the eternal mysteries that are in heaven.'

Moreover, the Aramaic *Vorlage* of the *Book of Watchers* used the very same vocabulary for the revealing of mysteries, which is found inscribed on the bowl (גלון רזי), as can be seen in a combination of two Aramaic fragments (possibly of 1 Enoch 7:3 or 8:3):[19] וכולהון שריו לגליה רזין לנשיהן ('and they all began to reveal mysteries to their wives').[20] This tradition is found later also in the Manichæan *Kephalaia*:[21]

The watchers of heaven, who came down to the earth in his watch-district, they did all the deeds of treachery. They have revealed crafts in the world and have unveiled to people the mysteries [of] heaven (ⲁⲩϭⲱⲗⲡ ⲁ ⲛ̄ⲣⲱⲙⲉ ⲛ̄ⲙⲙⲩⲥⲧⲏⲣⲓⲟⲛ [ⲛ] ⲧⲡⲉ).

An almost exact parallel to the phrasing in the bowl is found in a similar incantation in the magical compilation known as *Havdala d'Rabbi Akiva* (hereafter:

---

17   4QEnᵃ 1 2:15 (ולאלפה אנין חרשה ו]) + 4QEnᵇ 1 2:19 (שתא ולכש[). On these fragments, see G.W.E. Nickelsberg, *1 Enoch 1: A Commentary on the Book of 1 Enoch, Chapters 1–36; 81–10*, Minneapolis, 2001, pp. 197–198. Cf. 1 Enoch 65:6.

18   Cf. 1 Enoch 16:3. Translation of 1 Enoch throughout the paper follows Nickelsberg, *1 Enoch*.

19   4QEnᵃ 1 4:5 (ה רזין לנשיהן]) + 4QEnᵇ 1 3:5 ([וכולהון שריו לגליה). See Nickelsberg, *1 Enoch*, 189; M.A. Knibb, *The Ethiopic Book of Enoch: A New Edition in the Light of the Aramaic Dead Sea Fragments* vol. 2, Oxford, 1978, p. 83; Milik, *Books of Enoch*, 170; S. Bhayro, *The Shemihazah and Asael Narrative of 1 Enoch 6–11: Introduction, Text, Translation and Commentary with reference to Ancient Near Eastern and Biblical Antecedents*, Münster, 2005, p. 152.

20   For the revealing of mysteries in Mandaic literature, see e.g. *The Mandaic Book of John* (ed. M. Lidzbarski, *Das Johannesbuch der Mandäer*, Giessen, 1915, p. 7): ܝܘܫܡܝܢ ܓܠܐ ܪܙܐ; *iušamin gla raza drbia utigra bnhura rma.* ('Yushamin revealed the mystery of the Great One and cast strife in the Light'). See also G. Scholem, 'Havdalah de-Rabbi 'Aqiva—A Source for the Tradition of Jewish Magic During the Geonic Period', *Tarbiẓ* vol. 50, 1981, pp. 243–281 [Hebrew], 274, note 112; *Ginza Rabba*, Yamina (J.H. Petermann, *Thesaurus sive Liber Magnus, vulgo 'Liber Adami' apellatus opus Mandæorum summi ponderis*, Leipzig, 1867), p. 153:14–20.

21   Text: H.-J. Polotsky et al. (eds), *Kephalaia*, Stuttgart, 1940, p. 92:28–31; trans. I. Gardner, *The Kephalaia of the Teacher: The Edited Coptic Manichæan Texts in Translation with Commentary*, Leiden, 2016, p. 97.

ETERNAL CHAINS AND THE MOUNTAIN OF DARKNESS

Havdala), written mainly in Jewish Babylonian Aramaic and most probably compiled during the Geonic period:[22]

עוזא ועוזיאל רזאי רזא דמריהון גלון ונקוב יתהון מן נחיריהון[23] ותלי יתהון בטורי קבל,
שמשא לא חזיין ורוחא נשבא על אפיהון כל זמן וכל שעה. מאן דתבר עצתיה דעוזא
ועוזיאל הוא יתבר עצתיה דכל זרע אדם וחוה די קיימין לקבלן ויתבר תפתרה דימיניהון
דכל חרשיא וחרשייתא כמילת זקן במאמר פיהו.

'Uza and 'Uziel revealed the mystery of their Lord, and he pierced them from their nostrils and hung them in the mountains of darkness,[24] they did not see the sun and a wind blew ceaselessly on their face. He who broke the scheme of 'Uza and 'Uziel, shall break the scheme of all the off-spring of Adam and Eve who stand against us and shall break the record book (?)[25] of the right hand of all male and female sorcerers, as the word of the elder in his statement.[26]

The two texts reveal several similarities, such as the use of the account of fallen angels as a historiola to counter sorcery and the punishment of the angels by suspension or hanging (discussed below). For our purposes it is important to note that both texts use the same formula:[27]

Havdala d'R. Akiva	Bowl IM 50327
רזא דמריהון גלון	ܕܓܠܘ ܪܙ ܕܡܪܝܗܘܢ
They revealed the mystery of their Lord	Who revealed the mysteries of their Lord

---

22 Scholem, 'Havdalah', pp. 274–275.

23 Scholem (ibid., p. 274 note 113) notes that he has not found a parallel to the motif of the piercing of the nostrils. For a Biblical precedent, see Job 40:26; 37:29.

24 Another possible translation here and in the following sources: '*on* the mountains of dark-ness'. However, in the light of the Manichæan text to be discussed below it would seem preferable to assume that the angels were bound inside the mountains of darkness.

25 Following Scholem's suggestion to read דפתרא instead of תפתרה (Scholem, 'Havdalah', p. 275 note 118).

26 The meaning of the last words in Hebrew is unclear, and this might be, as Scholem suggests hesitantly, an obscure citation (ibid., p. 25 note 119).

27 A similar phrasing in found in an unpublished bowl from the Schøyen collection (MS 2053/

This script, like others in *Havdala*, is 'written in a conservative type of Aramaic similar to the bowl texts'.[28] This, together with the parallel with the Syriac bowl, would indicate that the incantation pre-dates the Geonic period and provides further proof of the circulation of the myth of the fallen angels among Jews in the Sasanian period.[29]

1.2   The Punishment

In lines 5–6 Moriggi, following Teixidor and Hamilton, read ܟܪܣܐ ܥܠܡܐ ܙܠܘܡ (*b'sr 'lm' zlwm*). However, they all bracket the unknown word ܙܠܘܡ (ZLWM), without translating it. An examination of the photograph[30] with the assistance of Moriggi's script chart of this bowl would suggest that one should read the word as ܬܠܘܢ (TLWN), 'they hung, suspended', as could be seen in the image below:[31]

FIGURE 24.1
Detail of IM 50327

The verbal form ܬܠܘܢ (TLWN, a 3rd p. masc. pl. perfect with the ending ܢ-) accords well with ܓܠܘܢ (GLWN) earlier in the line. Furthermore, the motif of suspension of the fallen angels is attested in several sources, mainly Jewish and Muslim. The earliest attestation is probably in the long version of 2 Enoch 7:1:[32]

---

68), which includes a fragmentary account of the fallen angels: רזא דמריהון גלו. I wish to thank James Nathan Ford for sharing with me his preliminary edition of the bowl.

28   H. Juusola, 'Notes on the Aramaic Sections of Havdalah de-Rabbi Aqiba', *Studia Orientalia* vol. 99, 2004, pp. 106–119, 113, see also ibid., pp. 115–116 for discussion on the 3rd p. masc. pl. perfect ܢ-.

29   The bowl also has further connections with Jewish Babylonian Aramaic formulæ. See Moriggi's note on line 9 of the bowl (*Corpus*, p. 72): '[*b*]*šwm 'l dytyb 'l sysy sb'wt* "in the name of the god who sits upon the brightness of Ṣebaot".' The sentence recalls an analogous sequence in the Jewish Babylonian Aramaic bowl no. Wolfe 10: 5 (private collection to be published by Ford), where it is read: *bšmy' d'l ḥy dq'ym wytyb 'l sysy sb'wt* 'in the name of the living God who stands and sits upon the brightness of Ṣebaot.' Further on Jewish magic and Jewish Babylonian Aramaic formulæ in the Syriac Bowls, see H. Juusola, 'Who Wrote the Syriac Incantation Bowls?', *Studia Orientalia* vol. 85 (1999), pp. 75–92 with further bibliography.

30   Moriggi, *Corpus*, 73.

31   Detail of IM 50327, in Teixidor, 'Syriac Incantation Bowls', pl. 4 N°7.

32   Text: G. Macaskill, *The Slavonic Texts of 2 Enoch*, Leiden, 2013, p. 54; trans. F.I. Andersen, '2 (Slavonic Apocalypse of) Enoch', in J.H. Charlesworth (ed.), *The Old Testament Pseudepigrapha* vol. 1, New York, 1983, p. 112. Cf. F. Badalanova Geller, *2 (Slavonic Apocalypse of) Enoch: Text and Context*, Berlin, 2010, p. 44. For a discussion on the translation of the

ETERNAL CHAINS AND THE MOUNTAIN OF DARKNESS

'And there I perceived prisoners under guard, hanging up (высаще; *visjaše*), waiting for the measureless judgment.'

Precisely the same verb as in the bowl (תלי) is used several times in Jewish sources to describe the punishment of the fallen angels. Our earliest example is to be found in the text of *Havdala* cited above (ותלי יתהון בטורי קבל). This motif also appears in an addition to the medieval *Aggadat Bereshit*:[33]

עוזא ועזאל המה הגבורים אשר מעולם אנשי השם. מתחילה היו אנשי שם, ועכשיו היכן
הם? אמר רבי אליעזר ברבי יוסף: **תלויים** היו בשלשלת של ברזל **ותלויין** בהרי החושך.

Uzza and Azael 'were the heroes of old, the men of renown' (Gen. 6:4). At the beginning they were men of renown, and now where are they? R. Eliezer so of R. Yosef said: They were *suspended* by iron chains and *suspended* in the mountains of darkness.

Another example can be found in an addition to *Deuteronomy Rabba* where the soul of Moses cries out:[34]

רבונו של עולם מאצל שכינתך ממרום ירדו שני מלאכים עזא ועזאל וחמדו בנות ארצות
והשחיתו דרכם על הארץ עד **שתלית** אותם בין הארץ לשמים.

Master of the World, from your Divine Presence on high two angels, 'Aza and 'Azael, descended and they lusted for the daughters of the lands and they corrupted their way upon the earth until *you suspended* them between earth and heaven.

According to the 11th century *Bereshit Rabbati*, after Shemhazai repents he suspends himself upside-down between heaven and earth (ותלה עצמו בין שמים וארץ וראשו למטה ורגליו למעלה).[35] Furthermore, in many Muslim accounts of the 'Tale of Hārūt and Mārūt' the angels are punished by suspension. So, for example, Mujāhid's account, cited by Ṭabarī in his *Jāmiʿ al-bayān ʿan taʾwil āy al-Qurʾān*,

---

Slavonic verb here, see ibid., p. 113 note e. See also C. Böttrich, *Das slavische Henochbuch*, Gütersloh, 1995, p. 844 note f. I wish to thank Sergey Minov for his help with the Slavonic.

33   *Aggadat Bereshit* (ed. S. Buber, Krakow, 1902), p. 39.

34   *Deuteronomy Rabba* (Vilna) *ve-Zot ha-Bracha* 11:10; cf. Cf. *Sefer Pitron Torah* (ed. E.E. Urbach, Jerusalem, 1978), p. 307.

35   *Bereshit Rabbati* (ed. H. Albeck, Jerusalem, 1983), p. 31. Cf. *Sefer Pitron Torah* (ed. Urbach), p. 67 (מה עשה עזה חזר בתשובה ותלה את עצמו בין שמים וארץ ראשו למטה ורגליו למעלה); *Sefer ha-Zikhronot* (ed. E. Yassif, Tel Aviv, 2001), p. 117; *Yalqut Shimoni* (ed. Shiloni vol. 1, Jerusalem 1993), 155.

ends with the following punishment of Hārūt and Mārūt: 'It is said that they are *suspended* in iron (chains), inverted (and) flapping their wings (معلقان في الحديد مطويان يصفقان باجنحتهما).'[36]

Thus, if the reading ܬܠܐ ('suspended') in the bowl is accepted, it will attest to the existence of the suspension motif already in Sasanian Babylonia, bridging the transmission gap between earlier accounts, such as 2 Enoch, and the later Jewish and Muslim versions. Finally, it is important to note that in the bowl and in most of the other sources the punishment by suspension is directly related to the angels awaiting the Day of Judgement. This would indicate that the punishment by suspension is a concretisation of the angels' 'suspended' judicial status, because the verb תלי (TLY) is used in Hebrew and Aramaic to designate both hanging and suspension of judgement.[37] The motifs of binding and awaiting the Day of Judgement, which appear in the bowl, go back to the *Book of Watchers*.[38] In 1 Enoch 10:6 God commands Raphael to bind Azazyel and to cast him into the darkness: 'And on the day of the great judgment, he will be led away to the burning conflagration'. Similarly, Michael is commanded concerning Shemhazya (1 Enoch 10:12–13; cf. 1 En. 19:1; Jub. 5:10.):

---

36   Ṭabarī, *Jāmiʿ al-bayān ʿan taʾwil āy al-Qurʾān (Tafsīr al-Ṭabarī)* vol. 1, Beirut, 2002, p. 602 (#1692); trans. J.C. Reeves and A.Y. Reed, *Enoch from Antiquity to the Middle Ages* vol. I, Oxford, 2018, pp. 181–182. Similarly, al-Maqdisī (10th c.) writes in his *Book of Creation and History (Kitāb al-badʾ waʾl-taʾrīkh*, C. Huart [ed.] vol. 3, Paris, 1899–1919, p. 14; trans. Reeves, 'Resurgent Myth'): 'He gave the angels a choice between punishment in this world or final (punishment), and they chose punishment in this world, which consisted of their being suspended by their hair (معلقان بشعورهما) inside a pit in Babylon'. For a comprehensive survey of the Muslim sources, see Reeves, 'Some Parascriptural Dimensions of the Tale of Hārūt wa-Mārūt', *JAOS* vol. 135 (2015), pp. 817–842, especially the table on p. 824; Reed and Reeves, *Enoch*, pp. 181–184.

37   For the use of תלי in a judicial context, in the sense of a punishment 'suspended' until the Day of Atonement, see e.g. m. *Yoma* 8:8.

38   The motif of binding until the day of Judgement is found also in another bowl where, however, it refers to the fixed position of the heavenly bodies: אסרנא לכון באיסורא בישא ומרירא תוב אסרנא [לכון בא]יסורא דאתסרו ביה שבעה ככבין ותרין עשר מלויי^א^שין מלויאשין עד יומא רבא דדינא ועד שעתא רבתי דפרקנא. (I will bind you with the bond with which the seven planets and the twelve sign of the zodiac have been bound unto the great day of judgement and unto the great hour of redemption.) See Montgomery, *Aramaic Incantation Texts*, p. 133 (4:4–5) and a parallel bowl in Isbell, *Corpus*, p. 31 (7:15), whose translation I have used. For a discussion, see Montgomery, ibid., pp. 135–137 and Milik, *Books of Enoch*, pp. 336–339, who connects this myth also with 1 En. 18:13–16; 21:3–6. Further on the Day of Judgement in the incantation bowls, see A. Manekin-Bamberger, 'Intersections between Law and Magic in Ancient Jewish Texts', PhD Thesis, Tel Aviv University, 2018, pp. 92–98 [in Hebrew].

ETERNAL CHAINS AND THE MOUNTAIN OF DARKNESS 541

And when their sons perish and they see the destruction of their beloved ones, bind them for seventy generations in the valleys of the earth, until the day of their judgment and consummation,[39] until the eternal judgment is consummated.

This binding of the angels until the Day of Judgment is also found in 2 Peter 2:4 and the Epistle of Jude 6. The latter is of a special interest in the context of the bowl: ἀγγέλους τε τοὺς μὴ τηρήσαντας τὴν ἑαυτῶν ἀρχὴν ἀλλὰ ἀπολιπόντας τὸ ἴδιον οἰκητήριον εἰς κρίσιν μεγάλης ἡμέρας δεσμοῖς ἀϊδίοις ὑπὸ ζόφον τετήρηκεν· (And the angels who did not keep their positions of authority but abandoned their proper dwelling—these he has kept in darkness, bound with eternal chains for judgment on the great Day. [NIV, slightly modified]).

Both the authors of Jude and the bowl mention the Day of Judgement and refer to rebellious angels simply as 'angels' without naming them. More importantly, both texts make use of the very same idiom 'by eternal chain(s)' (ܐܣܘ̈ܪܐ ܥܠܡܐ; δεσμοῖς ἀϊδίοις) to designate the binding of the angels. This similarity is all the more striking since, as far as I know, it is only in these two texts that 'eternal chains' are mentioned in the context of the fallen angels. Yet despite these similarities, it would seem that the description in the bowl is not dependent on that of Jude, since there are some important differences between the two accounts, especially concerning the description of the angels' sin (in Jude they had abandoned the proper dwellings, whereas in the bowl they revealed the mysteries of their Lord).[40] It would seem more likely that the texts are separately dependent on an earlier tradition, which in all likelihood contained the idiom 'eternal chains'. Furthermore, it is quite possible that the bowl preserves the original Aramaic formulation which was later to be translated into Greek, as it appears in Jude.[41] This Syriac bowl thus contains several motifs that can be traced back to early accounts of the fallen angels, and possibly also preserves some of the original Aramaic formulæ. Yet no text of those that have come down to us contains all these motifs. The historiola might therefore represent a lost ancient account or a later combination of discrete motifs and formulæ by magic practitioners.

---

39   4QEn[b] 1 4:10–11: שבעין ד]רין [.... ארעא עד יומא רבא.

40   The Syriac rendering of δεσμοῖς ἀϊδίοις in Jude is ܕܠܐ ܒܐܣܘ̈ܪܐ ('in unknown chains'), which is unrelated to the formulation used in the bowl.

41   In a future study I shall discuss the implications of these parallels for the understanding of the Enochic literature used by the author of the Epistle of Jude.

542   PAZ

As the bowl contains several motifs attested mainly in Jewish texts, it is likely that this historiola was originally composed and used by Jewish scribes. Nonetheless, the fact that it appears in Syriac is of importance, since our knowledge of the reception by Syriac authors of the myth of the fallen angels in particular and of Enochic literature in general, is very limited.[42] Thus this bowl can shed some light on the transmission and reception of this myth among Syriac Christians.

2   The Mountain of Darkness

The incantation bowl M163, published by Dan Levene, is a Jewish Aramaic curse bowl.[43] It has received some scholarly attention owing to its surprising use of the formula 'in the name of Jesus'. However, this bowl also preserves references to various mythical accounts (some of which have yet to be identified in a satisfactory manner) which are used as precedents with the purpose of incantation. One of these accounts is that of the fallen angels:[44]

---

42   On the Enochic books in Syriac tradition, see S. Brock, 'Fragment of Enoch in Syriac', *JTS* vol. 19 (1968), pp. 626–631; S. Minov, 'Early Jewish Texts and Traditions in Syriac Transmission', in A. Kulik et al. (eds), *A Guide to Early Jewish Texts and Traditions in Christian Transmission*, Oxford, 2019, pp. 129–130 with comprehensive bibliography. The earliest citation from the book of Enoch in Syriac is from the 12th century. However, already Jacob of Edessa (died 708 CE) defends the use of 'The Secret Book of Enoch'. See W. Adler, 'Jacob of Edessa and the Jewish Pseudepigrapha in Syriac Chronography', in J.C. Reeves (ed.), *Tracing the Threads: Studies in the Vitality of Jewish Pseudepigrapha*, Atlanta, 1994, pp. 144–146; J.C. Reeves, 'Jacob of Edessa and the Manichæan Book of Giants?', in M. Goff et al. (eds), *Ancient Tales of Giants from Qumran and Turfan: Contexts, Traditions, and Influences*, Tübingen, 2016, pp. 199–211. For allusions to the fallen angels in Syriac literature, see 2 Baruch 56:7–15; *Acts of Thomas* (ed. W. Wright, *Apocryphal Acts of the Apostles* vol. 1, London, 1871), p. 158 (trans. A.F.J. Klijn, *The Acts of Thomas: Introduction, Text, and Commentary*, Leiden, 2003, p. 93); H.J.W. Drijvers, *The Book of the Laws of Countries: Dialogue on Fate of Bardaiṣan of Edessa*, Piscataway, 2006², pp. 14–15. On the last two sources, see VanderKam, '1 Enoch', pp. 67, 72–73. See also the Syriac version of Zosimos of Panopolis in M.P.E. Berthelot, *Histoire des sciences: La chimie au moyen âge* vol. 2, Paris, 1893, p. 238 (I wish to thank Sergey Minov for this reference). For further possible allusions, see N.A. Pedersen, 'Observations on the Book of Giants from Coptic and Syriac Sources', in S.N.C. Lieu (ed.), *Manichæism East and West*, Turnhout, 2017, pp. 192–193.

43   See D. Levene, '"… and by the name of Jesus …" An Unpublished Magic Bowl in Jewish Aramaic', *JSQ* vol. 6 (1999), pp. 283–308; id., *Corpus*, pp. 120–138; id., *Jewish Aramaic Curse Texts from Late-Antique Mesopotamia: "May These Curses Go Out and Flee"*, Leiden, 2013, p. 110. It has also received a thorough analysis by Sh. Shaked, 'Jesus in the Magic Bowls. Apropos Dan Levene's "… and by the Name of Jesus …"', *JSQ* vol. 6 (1999), pp. 309–319.

44   Text and translation, in Levene, *Corpus*, pp. 123, 125–126 (slightly modified).

ETERNAL CHAINS AND THE MOUNTAIN OF DARKNESS

(17) (...) היכדין דאיתכבישו הנון (18) דעל פוקדן ^ד^מריהון עברו עזאל ועזאל ועזזיאל
ואישתלחו מלאכי עליהון מן קדם אלהא וכבשינון על טור]א דקביל^[45 ואהדרו אפיהון
לאפי דחשוכא (...) הכדין ניתכבש (19) הדין אישה בר הורמיז וניתכבשן מיליה סניתא
ומחשבתיה סניתא וכוכביה ומזליה וגדיה וחומריה.

(17) (...) Just as (18) those who transgressed the command of their Lord,
'Azael and 'Azael and 'Azaziel, were pressed, and angels were sent against
them from the presence of God and pressed them upon the mountain
[of darkness] and their faces were turned towards the face of darkness.
(...)—just so (19) may this Isha son of Ifra Hurmiz be pressed. And may
his hateful words and hateful thoughts and stars and star signs and lot and
magic be pressed.

This bowl, like the Syriac bowl and the incantation from *Havdala*, uses the historiola of the fallen angels as a historiola, as part of an incantation to counter
sorcery (both this bowl and the Syriac bowl even use the same terminology of
כבש, to press). Moreover, in both this bowl and the *Havdala* incantation the historiola is directly connected with the desired outcome by repeating the same
formula:[46]

Bowl M163	*Havdala d'R. Akiva*
הכדין דאיתכבשו [...] עזאל ועזאל ועזזיאל	מאן דתבר עיצתיה דעוזא ועוזיאל הוא יתבר
[...] הכדין ניתכבש הדין אישה בר הורמיז	עיצתיה דכל זרע אדם וחוה
Just as [...] 'Azael and 'Azael and 'Azaziel *were pressed* [...]—just so may this Isha son of Ifra Hurmiz *be pressed*.	He who *broke the scheme* of 'Uza and 'Uziel, *shall break* the scheme of all the offspring of Adam and Eve

Each scribe adapted the wording of historiola so as to suit the specific goals
of the incantation. This bowl has received a detailed and thorough commen-

---

45   Levene reconstructs: [א דחשוכא]טור. See the discussion below.
46   A similar structure is also found in bowl MS 2053/68 (see above note 27): [...]א]ית[פ]רע מן
עזא עוזא ועזאל קאים ומתפרע מינכון ([...] took vengeance on 'Aza, 'Uza and 'Azael, he shall
take vengeance on you).

tary by Dan Levene, and in the following I shall build upon his findings, while adducing additional sources and arguments and focusing mainly on the sin of the angels, their punishment and their names.

2.1   *The Sin*

Unlike some of the sources discussed above, the sin of the angels in this bowl is not that of revealing the Lord's secrets, but rather of transgressing their Lord's command. It is unclear what exactly the command was. Yet in the light of the magical context of the bowl it would seem that also here it is related to magic. A similar motif of transgressing the Lord's command has been identified by Levene in another bowl: אשבעית עליכין כל מיני לילתא בש[ום] זרעיתכין דילדין דילדין שידי ולילתא לבני נירא סטין וימרדין ועברין [על] גזירתא דמריהון (I adjure you all species of liliths in respect to your posterity, which is begotten by demons and liliths to the children of light who go astray and rebel *and transgress against the proscription of their Lord*.)[47] Yet it is unclear whether this bowl actually refers to the fallen angels. Another interesting parallel can be found in 1 Enoch 18:15–16 where the angel describes the sin of the stars:[48]

> The stars that are rolling over in the fire, these are they that *transgressed the command of the Lord* in the beginning of their rising, for they did not come out in their appointed times. And he was angry with them and bound them until the time of the consummation of their sins—ten thousand years.

An even more direct parallel is found in 1 Enoch 106:13–14 (Birth of Noah):

> For in the generation of Jared my father, *they transgressed the word of the Lord from the covenant of heaven* (παρέβησαν τὸν λόγον κυρίου ἀπὸ τῆς διαθήκης τοῦ οὐρανοῦ). And behold, they are sinning and *transgressing the custom* (παραβαίνουσιν τὸ ἔθος), and getting together with women and sin with them and have married (some) from them, and they are giving birth to those who are not like spirits, but to those who are of the flesh.[49]

Yet it should be noted that the transgression of the angels here consists of their sexual union with women, and it is not directly linked to sorcery. Another use

---

47   Text: Isbell, *Corpus*, p. 17 (1:8–9); trans. Levene, *Corpus*, pp. 135–136.

48   Cf. 1 Enoch 21:6: 'These are (some) of the stars which transgressed the command of the Lord Most High, and they have been bound here until ten thousand ages are complete'.

49   Trans. L. Stuckenbruck, *1Enoch 91–108*, Berlin, 2007, p. 655.

ETERNAL CHAINS AND THE MOUNTAIN OF DARKNESS 545

of a similar formula is found in the Damascus Document's concise retelling of the myth of the fallen angels: בלכתם בשרירות לבם נפלו עירי השמים. בה נאחזו אשר **לא שמרו מצות אל.** (For having walked in the stubbornness of their hearts the Watchers of the heavens fell; on account of this they were caught, for they *did not heed the precepts of God.*)[50] The expression לא שמרו מצות אל ('they did not heed the precepts of God'), a recurrent one in the historical narrative of the Damascus Document,[51] is very similar to the Aramaic formula in the bowl: דעל פוקדן מריהון עברו ('transgressed the command of their Lord'). Although the formula in the bowl has magical connotations lacking in the Damascus Document and in 1 Enoch 106:13, they all seem to be based on a shared tradition: that the sin of the angels consisted in their transgression of God's commandment.

2.2 *The Punishment*

According to the bowl, as a punishment 'angels were sent against them from the presence of God and pressed them upon the mountain [of darkness] and their faces were turned towards the face of darkness'. Levene has brilliantly reconstructed the place of punishment as [טור[א דחשוכא (mountain [of darkness]). This is now further corroborated by an unpublished bowl[52] in the light of which one should slightly modify Levene's suggestion to the semantically equivalent collocation: [טור[א דקביל (mountain [of darkness]), also documented in *Havdala*. As noted by Levene, the motif of the Mountain of Darkness as the place of punishment of the fallen angels appears in later Jewish sources.[53] Thus, as we have seen above, in *Havdala* the fallen angels are said to be suspended in the Mountain of Darkness (טורא דקבל) where they cannot see the sun (שמשא לא חזיין). Similarly, in *Aggadat Bereshit*, also cited above, we are told that 'Aza and 'Azael were suspended in the Mountain of Darkness (ותלויין בהר החושך). This motif also appears later in Aramaic, in the *Zohar*, where God is said to have bound 'Aza and 'Azael with iron chains in the Mountain of Darkness (קשר לון בשלשלאי דפרזלא בטורא דחשוכא). In addition, according to the *Zohar*, God throws darkness onto the face of 'Aza (וזריק חשוכא באנפוי), similarly to the description found on the bowl.[54]

---

50 CDᵃ 2:17–18. trans. F.G. Martínez et al. (eds), *The Dead Sea Scrolls Study Edition*, Leiden, 1999, p. 553.

51 See Y. Paz, 'Prior to Sinai: The Patriarchs and the Mosaic Law in Rabbinic Literature in View of Second Temple and Christian Literature', MA Thesis, Hebrew University of Jerusalem, 2009, pp. 15–18 [Hebrew].

52 MS 2053/68 (see above note 27), which mentions in l. 9: טורא דיקביל אתר בית חשוכא (mountain of darkness, a place of darkness).

53 Levene, *Corpus*, p. 135.

54 *Zohar*, Balak, 3:208a. See Scholem, 'Havdalah', p. 275 note 14; Levene, *Corpus*, p. 135.

Furthermore, as Levene notes, following Torgny Säve-Söderbergh,[55] in Mandæan literature the Dark Mountain (*ṭura ḏhašuka*) appears dozens of times as a
place where the sinners are bound. So, for example, in the first book of the right
side of the *Ginza Rabba*: ܐܬܟܠܬ ܥܪܟܣܪܪ ܘ ܟܠ ܠܬܩܥܘܪ ܘܥܚܪܕܠܥ
ܐܪܩܥܬ ܟܠ (*ḏmanzia nišmuṭ ʿlh nisirunh bṭura ṭur haška*: Whoever shall
tear out his hair over it (i.e. over the dead) will be bound in the mountain, the
dark mountain.)[56] Similarly, in the second book: ܐܪܩܥܬ ܟܠܕ ܐܪܕܠܬܟܕ ܬܟܕܠܬܪܪ
ܐܪܕܟܠܬܪܩܘܥ ܘܥܥܩܥ ܐܥܩܠܡ ܬܟܠܘܚ ܬܟܪܟ ܬܟܕ ܠܬܕܠܟ ܘܠܠ (*ubalalun
ṭura haška alma liuma ium dina ualma lšita šaiia ḏpurqana*: And the Mountain
of Darkness shall swallow them until the day [which is the] Day of Judgement
and until the hour [which is] the Hour of Redemption.)[57]

While in the Mandæan texts the Mountain of Darkness is not directly associated with the fallen angels, in the Manichæan Psalms of Thomas, which are
likely translated from Aramaic and contain striking parallels to Mandaic literature,[58] the Dark Mountain is mentioned explicitly in the context of the
rebelling gods as, for example, in Psalm v:[59]

> The Adamas armed himself and sped down; [...]
> he put fetters on the feet of the demons; he put iron on the hands of the
>   goddesses;
> the stinking and foul devils,

---

55   Ibid.; T. Säve-Söderbergh, *Studies in the Coptic Manichæan Psalm-Book: Prosody and Man-
      dæan Parallels*, Uppsala, 1949, pp. 127–128.

56   Petermann, *Thesaurus*, p. 19, following the transliteration in the *Comprehensive Aramaic
      Lexicon* (http://cal.huc.edu/).

57   Ibid., p. 66. Cf. ibid., p. 302: ܬܟܕܠܟ ܬܟܟܟܥ ܥܥܪܪ ܥܘ ܠܟܪܕܠܟܥ ܘ ܥܟܪܕܥܟܘܕ ܠܟܘܪܕܠܥ ܘ ܥܪܪܥ ܥܟܕܠ ܠܬܪ
      ܥܟܕܟܬܥ ܘ ܪܥܕܟܠܟܥ ܘܕ ܘܣܥܩܘ ܥܥ (*kul ḏabid ginia lʿkuria upatikria bṭura ḏhšuka naqmunh*: Who-
      ever sacrifices to temple-demons and idols will be placed in the Mountain of Darkness).

58   Säve-Söderbergh (*Studies*) has argued that the author of the Manichæan Psalms of
      Thomas was influenced by Mandaic literature. For a re-evaluation, see now K. van Bladel,
      From Sasanian Mandæans to Sābians of the Marshes, Leiden, 2017, pp. 86–88, who sug-
      gests an Elchasite origin: 'It is possible that the Mandæan funeral verses, found in both
      published Mandaic prayerbooks as well as the Left Ginzā, and the almost identical verses
      found among the Manichæan Psalms of Thomas, in a Coptic translation from Aramaic,
      attest to a funeral prayer used by Elchasaites.' (ibid., p. 88).

59   C.R.C. Allbery (ed.), *A Manichæan Psalm-Book. Part* II, Stuttgart, 1938, p. 210:5–10 (cf.
      p. 210:1 and Psalm VI, p. 210:21). This also has been noted by Levene, *Corpus*, p. 135. A dark
      mountain (ⲡⲧⲁⲩ ⲛ̄ⲕⲙⲏⲙⲉ) is also mentioned in *Kephalaia* (ed. Polotsky-Böhlig), p. 112:5
      (trans. Gardner, *Kephalaia*, p. 117). However, this appears in the context of a mythical
      geography. On the mountains of darkness as designating the ends of earth in Ancient
      Near Eastern literature, see D.M. Goldenberg, *The Curse of Ham: Race and Slavery in Early
      Judaism, Christianity, and Islam*, Princeton, 2003, pp. 61–64.

ETERNAL CHAINS AND THE MOUNTAIN OF DARKNESS

—he made their neck break beneath the collar;
the false gods also that rebelled
he bound beneath the dark mountain (ϩⲁⲡⲧⲁⲩ ⲛ̄ⲕⲙⲏⲙⲉ).

Several of the motifs concerning the punishment of the angels in the bowl seem to go back to the *Book of Watchers* (1 Enoch 10:4–5; 11–12):

> To Raphael he said, 'Go, Raphael, and *bind Asael hand and foot*, and cast him into the *darkness*; And make an opening in the wilderness that is in Doudael. There cast him, and lay beneath him sharp and jagged stones. And *cover him with darkness*, and let him dwell there forever. *Cover up his face, and let him not see the light.'* [...]
> And to Michael he said, 'Go, Michael, *bind* Shemihazah and the others with him, who have mated with the daughters of men, so that they were defiled by them in their uncleanness. And when their sons perish and they see the destruction of their beloved ones, *bind* them for seventy generations in the valleys[60] of the earth'.

In this passage, as in the bowl, the punishment of the rebellious angels is to be meted out by angels sent by God (unlike most later Jewish sources, in which God himself punishes the fallen angels). In addition, Azazyel, similarly to the angels on the bowl, is to be bound and cast into a place of darkness, and his face is to be covered with darkness so that he should not see the light.[61]

In the light of this, Levene has argued that the punishment of the angels by pressing them in (or on) the mountain of darkness, while their faces are turned towards the darkness, is found in 1 Enoch 10.[62] Yet his statement can be qualified. While some of the themes indeed go back to *The Book of Watchers*, the Mountain of Darkness as the place of the punishment is not mentioned there.[63] This motif seems only to be attested in Manichæan, Mandæan and

---

60   In the Greek version (Gr[Pan Sync b]): εἰς τὰς νάπας (in the valleys). In the Ethiopic version: 'beneath the hills (አውጋር; *'awgar*)'. See Knibb, *Ethiopic Book* vol. 1, p. 35. Knibb (ibid. vol. 2, p. 89) notes that '(t)here is no obvious explanation of the variant'. Cf. M. Black, *The Book of Enoch or 1 Enoch: A New English Edition*, Leiden, 1985, p. 137; Nickelsberg, *1 Enoch*, p. 218.

61   Cf. also 2 En. 7; 18:3–7 where the angels are said to be imprisoned in great darkness. Cf. A. Orlov, 'The Watchers of Satanail: The Fallen Angels Traditions in "2 (Slavonic) Enoch"', in id., *Selected Studies in the Slavonic Pseudepigrapha*, Leiden, 2009, pp. 133–164. See also Jub. 10:5.

62   Levene, *Corpus*, p. 135.

63   In the Ethiopic version of 1 Enoch 17:7, Enoch sees: 'the mountains of the darkness of winter' (አድባረ : ቆባራት : እለ : ክረምት; *'adbār ḳobārāt 'alla kramt*). However, the Greek version

548 PAZ

Jewish Babylonian texts, which suggests its ancient Mesopotamian provenance and its independence from the *Book of Watchers*. Our hypothesis could be reinforced by traditions prevalent in ancient Mesopotamian geography. It knows of mountains located at the extremities of the earth, which are known as the 'Dark and Shining Mountains'.[64] These mountains are also regarded as the abode of demons. For example, in the bilingual Sumerian-Akkadian series of incantations against evil demons known as *Udug.hul* (Akkadian: *Utukkū Lemnūtu*) the seven demons are said to be born on 'The Dark Mountain' ($hur.sag gi_6.ga$) in the Sumerian version, which in the Akkadian is rendered as 'The Mountain of Sunset' (*šad ereb šamši*).[65] Furthermore, also the idea of placing evil powers under a mountain is found in Mesopotamian magic, as in an incantation from *Maqlû*, a magical text against witchcraft: 'May the mountain cover you (*šadû liktumkunūši*). [...] May a strong mountain fall upon you (*šadû dannu elikunu limqut*)'.[66] Thus the motif of the Dark Mountain as a place of punishment reserved for demons (or fallen angels) may have its roots in a shared Mesopotamian tradition.

2.3   *Three Fallen Angels*

The bowl explicitly names three fallen angels: עזאל ועזאל ועזזיאל ('Azael and 'Azael and 'Azaziel). The appearance of two apparently identical names—עזאל ועזאל—might seem at first to be a dittography since in almost all other Jewish sources regarding the fallen angels there are only two named angels:[67] usu-

---

(Gr^Pan) has 'the winds' (τοὺς ἀνέμους) instead of 'the mountains'. Moreover, this expression does not appear in the context of fallen angels but in the survey of mythical geography (see above note 59). See Knibb, *Book of Enoch* vol. 1, p. 66; vol. 2, p. 104; Nickelsberg, *1 Enoch*, p. 284.

64   W. Horowitz, *Mesopotamian Cosmic Geography*, Winona Lake, 1998, pp. 331–332. Further on the 'Mountains of Darkness' as designating the ends of the earth in ancient Near Eastern literature, see D.M. Goldenberg, *The Curse of Ham: Race and Slavery in Early Judaism, Christianity, and Islam*, Princeton, 2003, pp. 61–64.

65   Tablet IV.46–47 (cf. ll. 53–54). Text and trans. M. Geller, *Healing Magic and Evil Demons: Canonical Udug-hul Incantations*, Boston, 2016, pp. 447–448. Cf. Horowitz, *Cosmic Geography*, p. 332; W. Hempel, 'The Sun at Night and the Doors of Heaven in Babylonian Texts', *Journal of Cuneiform Studies* vol. 38, 1986, p. 145; A.R. George, *The Babylonian Gilgamesh Epic: Introduction, Critical Edition and Cuneiform Texts* vol. 1, Oxford, 2003, p. 493, no. 169.

66   Tablet v.149–157, text and trans.: Tz. Abusch, *The Magical Ceremony Maqlû: A Critical Edition*, Leiden, 2015, p. 337. A similar description of punishment of demons appears in a Jewish Babylonian Aramaic incantation bowl (Naveh and Shaked, *Amulets and Magic Bowls*, pp. 200–201 [B13, l. 13]): כבשונכו ואחיתונכו תחות טורא רב(ה) דפרזלא (They suppressed you, they brought you underneath the big mountain of iron).

67   See, however, the list of angels in 1 En. 69:2, where two angels named Azazel are mentioned.

ETERNAL CHAINS AND THE MOUNTAIN OF DARKNESS

ally 'Uza and 'Azael (עוזא ועזאל), as in b. Yoma 67b and in *Havdala*,[68] or, at times, Shemhazai and 'Azazyel, following the tradition of the *Book of Watchers*.[69] However, three fallen angels are also documented in another fragmentary bowl where they are named 'Aza, 'Uza and 'Azael (עזא עוזא ועזאל).[70] Moreover, in 3 Enoch 5 the three angels are said to have taught sorcery to mankind:[71]

ומה היו בני דורו עושין. היו הולכים מסוף העולם ועד סופו ומביאין כל אחד ואחד מהן
כסף וזהב ואבנים טובות ומרגליות בהרים הרים וגבעות גבעות ועושין אותן עבודה־זרות
בארבע רוחות העולם. והיו מעמידין אותן בכל רוח ורוח שבעולם. ע'ז כשיעור אלף
פרסה. ומורידין חמה ולבנה וכוכבים ומזלות ומעמידין לפניהם מימינם ומשמאלם לשמש
בהן כדרך שהיו משמשין להב'ה.[...] והיאך היה בהם כח שיהו מורידין אותן. אלא עזא
עזא ועזאל היו מלמדים להם כשפים שיהו מורידין אותם ומשתמשין בהם. שאלמלא כן
לא היו יכולין להורידן.

What did the men (of Enosh's generation) do? They roam the world from end to end, and each of them amassed silver, gold, precious stones, and pearls in mountainous heaps and piles. In the four quarters of the world they fashioned them into idols, and in each quarter they set up idols about 1000 parasangs in height. They brought down the sun, the moon, the stars and the constellations and stationed them before the idols, to their right

---

68   Besides the sources cited above, see also e.g. *Pesikta Rabbati* 34 (159a); *Kalla Rabbati* 3:6. For further references, see R. Margolioth, *Mal'akey 'elyon*, Jerusalem, 1945, pp. 274–280.

69   See e.g. Ps.-Jonathan to Gen. 6:4; *Midrash of Shemhazai and Azael*, in A. Jellinek (ed.), *Bet ha-Midrash* vol. 4, Leipzig, 1853–1877, pp. 127–128; *Yalqut Shimoni* (ed. Shiloni) vol. 1, pp. 154–155; *Sefer ha-Zikhronot* (ed. Yassif), pp. 115–117. For further references, see J.C. Reeves, *Jewish Lore in Manichæan Cosmogony: Studies in the Book of Giants Traditions*, Cincinnati, 1992, p. 113; Reed, *Fallen Angels*, p. 258.

70   MS 2053/68 ll. 7, 12 (see note 27 above). Cf. *Seder Eliahu Zuta* § 25 (עזה ועוזי ועזאל). Three descending angels appear also in 2 Enoch 18:4 (long recension), but unnamed. See also J.C. Reeves, 'Resurgent Myth: On the Vitality of the Watchers Traditions in the Near East in Late Antiquity', in K. Harkins et al. (eds), *The Fallen Angels Traditions: Second Temple Developments and Reception History*, Washington D.C., 2014, note 51. On Muslim traditions of three fallen angels see below note 85. For three demons in Zoroastrian accounts see D. Shapira, 'Hārūt wa-Mārūt, Again', *Scrinium* vol. 2 (2006), pp. 418–432.

71   P. Schäfer (ed.), *Synopse zur Hekhalot-Literatur*, Tübingen, 1981, § 8 (cited according to *Ma'agarim The Historical Dictionary Project* [http://maagarim.hebrew-academy.org.il/Pages/PMain.aspx], without the editorial signs; trans. P.S. Alexander, '3 (Hebrew Apocalypse of) Enoch', in J.H. Charlesworth (ed.), *The Old Testament Pseudepigrapha* vol. 1, New York, 1983, p. 260. The three angels also appear in 3 Enoch 4, on which see the discussion below. This similarity between the bowl and 3 Enoch has been briefly noted by Levene, *Corpus*, pp. 134–135.

and to their left, to serve in the way they serve the Holy One, blessed be He. [...] How was it that they had the strength to bring them down? It was only because 'Uza, 'Aza and 'Azael[72] taught them sorceries that they brought them down and employed them, for otherwise they would not have been able to bring them down.

Annette Reed has argued in a detailed article, and later in her book on the fallen angels, that this account of the fallen angels in 3 Enoch is a distinct case of 'back-borrowing'.[73] That is, 'portions of 1 Enoch may have influenced 3 Enoch (§§ 7–8), not due to the independent transmission of early Enochic traditions by subterranean channels on the margins of rabbinic Judaism, but due to a later re-introduction of BW's (i.e. *Book of Watchers* Y.P.) myth of angelic descent into certain Jewish circles from the Christian chronographic tradition.'[74] One of the main arguments she puts forth is that in rabbinic literature the angel Asael 'is never associated with improper teaching', unlike in the *Book of Watchers*.[75] More specifically, Reed argues that the unit of 3 Enoch 5 reflects dependence mainly on excerpts of the *Book of Watchers* preserved by the 8th–9th century Byzantine chronographer George Syncellus.[76] This would mean that the account of the fallen angels 'represents a later addition to the Enoch-Metatron material in 3 Enoch', which took place in the Byzantine period, after an earlier Babylonian redaction in 5th–6th century.[77]

According to Reed, the 'most notable' similarity between the excerpt from the *Book of Watchers* preserved/adapted by Syncellus and the account in 3 Enoch is that in both there is a 'total lack of reference to Enoch'.[78] In addi-

---

72   On the slight variations of the names in the manuscripts, see P. Schäfer and K. Herrmann, *Übersetzung der Hekhalot-Literatur* vol. 1, Tübingen, 1995, p. 14 note 19; A.Y. Reed, 'From Asael and Semihazah to Uzzah, Azzah, and Azael: 3 Enoch 5 (§§ 7–8) and the Jewish Reception-History of 1 Enoch', *JSQ* vol. 8 (2001), p. 22 note 64.

73   Ibid.; ead., *Fallen Angels*, pp. 256–258.

74   ead., 'From Asael', p. 129. For the ramifications of her model of 'back-borrowing', see Reed, *Fallen Angels*, pp. 269–272. The model in and of itself is quite plausible.

75   ead., 'From Asael', p. 122.

76   ead., *Fallen Angels*, pp. 256–257. cf. ead., 'From Asael', p. 135: 'in the light of the particular affinities both in scope and content, between 3 Enoch 5 (§§ 7–8) and excerpts of BW preserved by Syncellus, this raises the possibility that this unit may reflect knowledge of 1 Enoch derived from anthologies compiled by Byzantine chronographers, possibly in Hebrew translations.'

77   Reed, *Fallen Angels*, pp. 239, 249. For a critique of this dating, see Y. Paz, 'Metatron is not Enoch: Reevaluating the Evolution of an Archangel', *JSJ* vol. 50 (2019), pp. 1–49.

78   Reed, *Fallen Angels*, p. 257 (cf. eadem, 'From Asael', pp. 126–127). See also ibid., p. 129: 'Interestingly, Syncellus includes the bulk of 1 Enoch 6–11 (i.e. 1 Enoch 6–10:15), but omits the

ETERNAL CHAINS AND THE MOUNTAIN OF DARKNESS

tion, she points to several rather superficial similarities between the version in 3 Enoch and Syncellus.[79] None of them accounts for most of the distinct features in the version in 3 Enoch—such as the bringing down of the luminaries to serve,[80] the sin of idolatry[81] and the appearance of three named angels (Syncellus mentions only Asael). Reed was apparently unaware of the incantation bowl[82] and the account in *Havdala*, although she does stress the importance of

---

subsequent description of Enoch's role in punishing the Watchers, as described in 1 Enoch 12–16'.

79   Reed also argues that the parallels to the list 'silver, gold, precious stones and pearls' (כסף וזהב ואבנים טובות ומרגליות) used in 3 Enoch 'are most evident in the version preserved by George Syncellus' of 1 En. 8:1, who departs from the Ethiopic version and Greek version in Codex Panopolitanus (the variations in Gr^{syn} are italicized): 'And he showed them the metals *of the earth and gold* and the working of them [...]. *And he showed them silver* and stibium and eyepaint and *precious stones* and dyes' (Reed, 'From Asael', p. 120). Thus it would seem that only in the version of Gr^{syn} are gold and silver mentioned. However, Reed fails to note that silver (כספא) appears already in an Aramaic fragment of 1 Enoch (4QEn^b 1 2:27; see Knibb, *Book of Enoch* vol. 2, p. 80; Nickelsberg, *1 Enoch*, p. 188; Bhayro, *Shemihazah and Asael*, p. 146). In addition, in 1 Enoch the precious materials are used for ornamentation of the women, whereas in 3 Enoch 'they fashioned them into idols'. Furthermore, Reed does not account for the fact that none of these versions of 1 Enoch mentions pearls (מרגליות), which appear in 3 Enoch. There is no need, however, to assume that the author of 3 Enoch was acquainted with Syncellus's version. This exact list of precious materials— כסף וזהב ואבנים טובות ומרגליות—is in fact simply a stock phrase which is very common in rabbinic sources. See e.g. *Mekh. R. Yishmael*, Beshalah §1 (ed. Horovitz-Rabin, repr. ed. Jerusalem, 1998, p. 88); §5 (p. 108); §6 (p. 113); Shira §2 (p. 122); §7 (pp. 139–140); *Mekh. R. Shimon* 14:5 (ed. Epstein-Melamed, Jerusalem, 1956, p. 50); 14:6 (p. 51); 14:25 (p. 65); 15:9 (p. 89); *Sifre Deut.* §354 (ed. Finkelstein, repr. ed. New York, 1969, p. 416); t.Sot. 3:12; y. San. 29b. Reed (*Fallen Angels*, p. 257) presents another problematic argument: 'Syncellus' version of 1 En. 8:1–2 also suggests that Asael descended to earth first, only later followed by the other Watchers, and this may help to account for this unit's location of the activity of Uzzah, Azzah, and Azael in the Generation of Enosh, rather than the Generation of the Flood'. However, there is nothing in 1 Enoch (even in Syncellus's version) to suggest that Asael descended during the generation of Enosh. Rather, as Reed herself notes, the generation of Enosh was considered by the rabbis to be a generation corrupted by idolatry.

80   Cf. b.AZ 43b: לא תעשון כדמות שמשי המשמשין לפני במרום כגון חמה ולבנה כוכבים ומזלות. A similar (though not identical) motif is found in Jub. 8:3: 'He (Kainan) found an inscription which the ancients had incised in a rock. He read what was in it, copied it, and sinned on the basis of what was in it, since in it was the Watchers' teaching by which they used to observe the omens of the sun, moon and stars and every heavenly sign.' (trans. J.C. VanderKam, *Jubilees 1–21*, Minneapolis, 2018, p. 358; cf. 1 Enoch 69:16–17). See Reed, 'From Asael', p. 106 note 4; p. 121 note 60.

81   As Reed concedes (ibid., p. 120): 'Admittedly, there is no mention of idolatry within BW's narrative account of the angels' descent in 1 Enoch 6–11'. See ibid., pp. 120–121 for proposed solutions to this problem. Idolatry is associated with the fallen angels outside of 1 Enoch 6–11. See e.g. 1 En. 19:1; Tertullian, *On Idolatry* 4:2–3.

82   See Reed, *Fallen Angels*, p. 264 note 116, where she notes that, to her knowledge, the only

552   PAZ

the magical tradition for the transmission of early Enochic traditions.[83] Both
texts clearly attest to a written Jewish Babylonian tradition according to which
the sin of the fallen angels consisted in revealing magical secrets to humans.
In addition, none of these texts mentions Enoch, who, in fact, does not appear
in any of the incantation bowls published to date.[84] Finally, the bowl under
discussion clearly demonstrates that the tradition concerning 'Aza, 'Uza and
'Azael as the three fallen angels was already established in Babylonia by the
6th–7th century.[85]

In the light of the Syriac and Jewish Aramaic bowls studied here, as well
as the text from *Havdala*, it would seem plausible that an Aramaic account
containing all these elements circulated in Babylonia and was adapted and
abridged by magic practitioners for their purposes. It is likely that in this specific case the author of 3 Enoch—who, as I have recently proposed, could be
active in Palestine in the 7th–8th centuries, where he could make recourse
to diverse sources, both Babylonian and Palestinian[86]—combined such an

---

       exception to the consistent focus on two fallen angels in Jewish traditions is found in
       3 Enoch.

83   Ibid., p. 254: '[T]he magical tradition offers a plausible setting in which some early Enochic
       traditions about the Watchers could have been transmitted and developed apart from the
       interpretation of Gen 6:1–4'.

84   See Paz, 'Metatron', p. 21 note 92.

85   At an early stage, the version of three fallen angels seems to have influenced several
       Muslim accounts, even though it is difficult to harmonise it with the traditional Mus-
       lim account of the two fallen angels, Hārūt and Mārūt. According to al-Maqdisī, 'After He
       had created Adam and his descendants had become corrupted by wickedness, the angels
       said, "O Lord! How horrible are those whom You have appointed as caliphs on the earth!"
       So God commanded them to select three of their most worthy representatives (يختاروا
       من أفاضلهم ثلاثة) to descend to earth so as to convey to humanity information about
       a proper behaviour.' (text: Maqdisī, *Kitāb al-bad'*, vol. 3, p. 14; trans. Reeves, 'Resurgent
       Myth'). While al-Maqdisī does not name these angels, in an account of the 8th-century
       scholar al-Kalbī, as reported by al-Tha'labī (11th c.), the angels are named and an effort
       is also made to harmonise the two traditions: 'According to al-Kalbī, God said: "Choose
       three among you (اختروا ثلاثة منكم)", and they chose 'Azā, who is Hārūt (فاختاروا عزا وهو
       هاروت), and 'Azābiyā, who is Mārūt (وعزابيا وهو ماروت), and 'Azriyā'īl (وعزريائيل), but He
       changed the names of two of them when they sinned, just as God changed the name of
       Iblīs, whose name had been 'Azāzīl.' (text: Tha'labī, *Kitāb Qiṣaṣ al-anbiyā' al-musammā bi-
       l-'arā'is*, Cairo, 1880, p. 48; trans. W.M. Brinner, *'Arā'is al-majālis fī qiṣaṣ al-anbiyā' or "Lives
       of the Prophets"*, Leiden, 2002, p. 87). See also Crone, 'The Book of Watchers', p. 30; Reeves,
       'Resurgent Myth', no. 51; idem, 'Parascriptural Dimensions', p. 825 and no. 23 (who notes
       some similarities with Jewish traditions). I address the relation between the Jewish and
       Muslim traditions regarding the three angels in a future study.

86   Paz, 'Metatron'.

ETERNAL CHAINS AND THE MOUNTAIN OF DARKNESS 553

account with rabbinic traditions concerning the idolatrous generation of Enosh, without any need of Christian mediation.[87]

3 Metatron and the Fallen Angels?

The final bowl to be discussed here contains a reference which would seem at first to deal with the fallen angels 'Aza and 'Azael. Yet a closer examination will reveal that these angels are in fact non-fallen, ministering angels. Nonetheless, this tradition most probably impacted later accounts concerning the fallen angels, especially in 3 Enoch. In this bowl, first published by Gordon and later by Isbell, we find the following formula:[88]

כולהון שביתין ובטילין מן מימריה דאל קנא ונוקים הוא דשלח עזא ועזאל ומיטטרון
איסרא רבא דכורסיה אינון ייתון וינטרון דירתיה ואיסקופתיה דפרוכדד בר זבינתא
ודקמוי בת זארק

---

87 Reed adduces in this context another example for 'back-borrowing', arguing that the coherent legend known as 'Midrash on Šemhazai and Azael', as it appears in *Yalqut Shimoni* and *Sefer ha-Zichronot*, 'is the result of redactional efforts by a later tradent [...] who constructed a smooth narrative out of a group of discrete midrashim' admittedly based on non-canonical texts and Jewish texts transmitted by Christians (Reed, *Fallen Angels*, p. 260). The earlier stage could supposedly be detected in *Bereshit Rabbati*, where there are three distinct units, since, as Reed notes, 'R. Moshe ha-Darshan attributes only part of the material concerning Šemhazai and 'Azael to R. Joseph, and this material is interspersed with two additional traditions, attributed to Rabbi and R. Zadok' (ibid., pp. 259–260). However, as noted already by Albeck (*Bereshit Rabbati*, p. 3, no. 4), followed by Reeves ('Parascriptural Dimensions', p. 829), these two additional traditions are in fact a clear interpolation taken from *Pirqe d'R. Eliezer* 22 (the similarity is indeed noted by Reed, *Fallen Angels*, p. 260). Furthermore, R. Moshe ha-Darshan indicates that he himself has inserted an interpolation as he attributes the continuation of the legend to R. Joseph—the same sage to whom he also attributes the beginning of the legend. Finally, Reed seems to have overlooked the fact that an almost *verbatim* parallel to the coherent legend appears also in a midrashic compilation known as *Pitron Torah* (ed. Urbach, p. 67) which was most probably composed in a Judeo-Persian milieu around the 10th c. (ibid., p. xxxii), and thus pre-dates the 11th-century R. Moshe ha-Drashan (the only significant difference is that in *Pitron Torah* the two angels are named 'Uza and 'Azael rather than Šemhazai and 'Azael as in the other versions of the legend). For a similar critique, see M. Idel, 'Hārūt and Mārūt: Jewish Sources for the Interpretation of the two Angels in Islam', in M.A. Amir-Moezzi (ed.), *L'Ésotérisme shi'ite, ses racines et ses prolongements*, Turnhout, 2016, p. 133.

88 Isbell, *Corpus*, pp. 112–113 (49:10–11); C.H. Gordon, 'Aramaic Magical Bowls in the Istanbul and Baghdad Museums', *Archiv Orientální* vol. 6 (1934), p. 328.

They are all cancelled and annulled by the command of 'the jealous and avenging God' (Nah. 1:2), the one who sent 'Aza, 'Azael and Metatron, the great prince of His throne. They will come and guard the dwelling and threshold of Parrukdad the son of Zebinta and of Qamoi daughter of Zarak.

As we have seen, 'Aza and 'Azael appear in rabbinic and magic sources as the two fallen angels, which could indicate that this is also the case in this bowl.[89] Furthermore, in 3 Enoch, Enoch-Metatron recounts that after he had been taken up to heaven during the generation of the flood, 'Uza, 'Aza and 'Azael were defaming him before God:[90]

באותה שעה באו שלשה מלאכים ממלאכי השרת עוזה עזה ועזאל והיו מסטינין עלי בשמי מרום ואמרו לפני הב׳ה. לא יפה אמרו ראשונים לפניך. לא תברא אדם.

Then three of the ministering angels, 'Uza, 'Aza, and 'Azael came and laid charges against me in the heavenly height. They said before the Holy One, blessed be He, 'Did not the primeval ones give you good advice when they said, "Do not create man!"?'[91]

'Uza, 'Aza and 'Azael are described here as ministering angels. However, in the following chapter in 3 Enoch, as we have seen above, they are depicted as fallen angels. This has led some scholars to assume that Metatron is associated with the fallen angels already in the incantation bowls, and hence Metatron was also identified with Enoch.[92] However, there is a crucial difference between

---

89   See Levene, *Corpus*, 135.

90   Schäfer, *Synopse*, §§ 5–6; trans. Alexander, '3 Enoch', pp. 258–259. For the chronological problem of placing Enoch in the generation of the flood, even though he was supposedly translated 600 years earlier, see P.S. Alexander, '3 Enoch and the Talmud', *JSJ* vol. 18 (1987), p. 52.

91   cf. b.San 38b. On the way the author of 3 Enoch used this Talmudic source, see Alexander, '3 Enoch and the Talmud', pp. 45–54.

92   For such a reading, see e.g. Reed and Reeves, *Enoch*, p. 180: 'While the reference to these three angelic names may be an allusion to their 'testing' after their condemnation of human sinfulness, or perhaps their opposition to the elevation of Enoch-Metatron, this however fails to explain why the name 'Metatron' appears here as an agent who was dispatched by God. It seems more likely that this magic bowl's reference to God's dispatch of Metatron is based on the latter figure's role as a messenger and mediator between the denizens of heaven and earth such as is visible in *1 Enoch*, the apocryphal *Book of Giants*, and *Bereshit Rabbati*.' See also Greenfield, 'Notes', 152; Schäfer and Herrmann, *Übersetzung* vol. 1, p. 14 note 1; Levene, *Corpus*, p. 135.

ETERNAL CHAINS AND THE MOUNTAIN OF DARKNESS

the bowl and 3 Enoch. While on the bowl Metatron seems to be a companion of ʿAza and ʿAzael, in 3 Enoch the angels are antagonistic towards Enoch-Metatron.[93] In the light of this, several scholars have argued that ʿAza and ʿAzael in this bowl are in fact not fallen angels. Indeed, in several magical texts ʿAza and ʿAzael are presented as positive archangels who are part of the retinue of the most holy angels, which include Michael and Raphael.[94] So, for example, in an incantation bowl we find the following formula: בשום גבריאל ומיכאל ורפיאל ובשום עסאל עסיאל מלאכה ואירמיס מ[ריה רבה] (In the name of Gabriel and Michael and Rafael and in the name of ʾAsael ʾAsiel, the angel, and Hermes the g[reat lord].)[95] This pair of angels is depicted as part of the retinue of the holy angels also in the Greek magical papyri (Μιχαήλ, Ῥαφαήλ [...] Ἀζαήλ, Ἀζιήλ).[96] Yet is this indeed the case also in the bowl under discussion? And why would ʿAza and ʿAzael be associated with Metatron, 'the great prince of His throne'? I believe that we can answer these questions by reading this bowl alongside a silver amulet found at Ağabeyli in Turkey, near the Syrian border:[97]

---

93   Ibid.

94   See e.g. Milik, *Books of Enoch*, p. 131 (with references in note 3): 'We know that ʿAzaʾel [...] plays an ambivalent role in theological and magical ideas. He is at one time one of the two chiefs of the fallen angels and the main instructor in wicked arts and sciences, at another time one of the good archangels of God.' See also Reed, *Fallen Angels*, p. 253: 'Here, Azza and Azael seem to be heavenly angels invoked to protect Parrukukdad and Qamoi from sorcery—although the reference to 'sending' allows for the possibility that they have already descended to earth, whether because of sin or adjuration.' Crone, 'Book of Watchers', pp. 42–43; Crone, 'Book of Watchers', pp. 42–43; G. Scholem, *Jewish Gnosticism, Merkavah Mysticism and Talmudic Tradition*, New York, 1960, p. 87 (without reference to this bowl).

95   Montgomery, *Aramaic Incantation Bowls*, p. 146 (7:8). Cf. a Jewish Aramaic amulet published by Roy Kotansky ('Two Inscribed Jewish Aramaic Amulets from Syria', *Israel Exploration Journal* vol. 41, 1991, p. 275) which invokes a list of Holy Angels (מלאכיה קדישיה) including עזזאל (ʿAzazel, l. 7) and עזיאל (ʿAziel, l. 8).

96   See K. Preisendanz (ed.), *Papyri Græcæ Magicæ: Die griechischen Zauberpapyri* vol. 2, Stuttgart, 1974, p. 168 (XXXVI:170–174). For references only to one of these angels, see e.g. ibid., 180 (XLV:7—Ἀζαήλ); vol. 1, p. 138 (IV:2142—Ἀζιήλ); Testament of Solomon 7:7. For further references, see Milik, *Books of Enoch*, p. 131 note 3; Reed, *Fallen Angels*, p. 253; H. Odeberg, *3 Enoch: or, The Hebrew Book of Enoch*, Cambridge, 1928, p. 12.

97   Text and translation (slightly modified) Naveh and Shaked, *Amulets and Magic Bowls*, pp. 68–69 (A7). The amulet was first published by A. Dupont-Sommer, 'Deux lamelles d'argent à inscription hébréo-araméenne trouvée à Ağabeyli (Turquie)', *Jahrbuch für Kleinasiatische Forschung* vol. 1 (1950–1951), pp. 201–217 and also received a detailed study by Scholem, *Jewish Gnosticism*, pp. 84–93. See also Milik, *Books of Enoch*, pp. 128–131.

Amulet (A7)	Bowl (M163)

(2) בשם מיכאל רפאל

(3) עזאל עזריאל

אריאל

(4) רבה סררי

אתון מלאכיה קדשיה דקימי[ז]

(5) קדם כרסיה דאלה רבה

עזא ועזאל

ומיטטרון

איסרא רבא

דכורסיה

In the name of Michael, Raphael

'Azzael, 'Azriel,

'Ari'el

The Great Princes

You, the holy angels who stand in front

of the throne of the Great God

'Aza' and 'Azael

and Metatron

The Great Prince

of His throne

The two formulæ share a similar structure. In the amulet 'Azael and 'Azriel are holy angels,[98] which would strongly support the assumption that this is also the case in the bowl. In addition, the parallel also clearly shows that Metatron replaces one (or more) of the holy angels who stands before God's throne. Furthermore, this comparison could help solving a crux in the amulet. In lines 3–4 Shaked and Naveh transcribe ס(רר)ו רבה and translate it with hesitation as 'the great dominion (?)' (probably deriving this from שררה).[99] However, it would seem more likely, both from the context and the parallel to the bowl, to read סררי רבה as 'the great princes'.[100] Another possibility is to read this as סרה רבה, 'The Great Prince'. This designation would then refer only to Ariel, similarly to the ascription of the title איסרא רבא, 'The Great Prince', to Metatron in the bowl.[101]

From this comparison it is difficult to conclude which angel is replaced by Metatron. If we regard the amulet as a parallel, then it is possible that Meta-

---

98 For positive references in Aramaic amulets to one of these angels, see e.g. Naveh and Shaked, *Amulets and Magic Bowls*, p. 41 (A1:1 עוזיאל); Naveh and Shaked, *Magic Spells*, p. 62 (A19:23 עוזאל).

99 Similarly, Scholem, *Jewish Gnosticism*, pp. 87–88 and Dupont-Sommer, 'Deux lamelles'.

100 The double *resh* might represent a reduplication in order to form the plural. רבה should in this case be read as *rabbe*. On the other hand, the reduplication could also be a scribal error.

101 I wish to thank Ohad Abudraham for this suggestion.

tron replaces Ariel. However, a more plausible solution could be suggested if we compare the bowl with the opening of a list of angels in a Greek-Aramaic silver amulet found in Egypt:[102]

Amulet (l. 19)	Bowl M163
עזיא אזיאל מיכאל	עזא ועזאל ומיטטרון
'Azia, 'Aziel, Michael	'Aza and 'Azael and Metatron

In the light of this comparison it is possible that Metatron in the bowl takes the place of Michael, as he does also in other sources. In any case, it is unlikely that Metatron was already identified with Enoch in the incantation bowl.

Thus, by juxtaposing Metatron, a distinctly Babylonian angel, to other holy angels and by allocating to him the title of The Prince of the Throne,[103] the author of the bowl (or his source) adapted a pre-existing formula (probably, of Palestinian provenance) to his Babylonian context. Some form of this Babylonian formula, which associated Metatron with 'Aza and 'Azael, was likely known to the author of 3 Enoch.[104] It would seem, therefore, that the accounts concerning 'Aza, 'Uza and 'Azael in 3 Enoch fuse together two trajectories concerning these angels—as ministering angels and as fallen angels—thus creating a unique tradition of the confrontation between Enoch-Metatron and the three angels.[105]

---

102   R. Kotansky, J. Naveh and Sh. Shaked, 'A Greek-Aramaic Silver Amulet from Egypt in the Ashmolean Museum', *Le Muséon* vol. 105 (1992), p. 9. I wish to thank Rivka Elitzur-Leiman for drawing my attention to this parallel.

103   For further instances where Metatron replaces Michael and on Metatron's Babylonian provenance, see Paz, 'Metatron'.

104   The association of Metatron with the angels 'Aza and 'Azael coupled with the tradition that Enoch was a mediator between the fallen angels and God (see e.g. 1 Enoch 15–16) could have facilitated a later identification of Enoch and Metatron rather than reflecting a pre-existing one (on this, see Paz, 'Metatron'). The combination of these traditions could be seen in the later *Midrash of Shemhazai and Azael* (Jellinek, *Bet ha-Midrash* vol. 4, pp. 127–128 = *Yalqut Shimoni*, [ed. Shiloni] vol. 1, p. 155): שגר הקדוש ברוך למטטרון שליח לשמחזאי ('the Holy One sent Metatron as a messenger to Shemhazai').

105   In the light of the discrepancies between chapters 4 and 5 in 3 Enoch, Reed ('From Asael') has argued that they represent two distinct stages of redaction. However, it would seem more likely that the author of 3 Enoch used two different sources, which he did not completely harmonize.

The three incantation bowls studied in this paper contribute to our knowledge of the myth of the fallen angels, and of Enochic literature more generally, in several ways: first, they may preserve earlier material such as motifs and precious Aramaic formulæ which could go back to the Aramaic *Vorlage* of the books of Enoch and other early accounts of the fallen angels. In addition, these bowls shed light on the way in which these ancient traditions were received and creatively adapted, supplemented and employed by the Aramaic speaking minorities in the Sasanian Empire. Finally, the traditions preserved in such bowls supply us with a missing link between the early Enochic literature and the later medieval accounts of the fallen angels and help us to reassess the various channels of transmission of Enochic traditions. It is to be hoped that as the corpus of published incantation bowls grows, they will arise more interest amongst the scholars of Jewish pseudepigrapha and the traditions developed therefrom.

Acknowledgements

I wish to thank my friends and colleagues—Avigail Manekin-Bamberger, Rivka Elitzur-Leiman, Shlomi Efrati, Sergey Minov, Gideon Bohak, Ohad Abudraham, Moshe Idel and Menachem Kister—for their helpful comments and critiques. I would also like to thank the Azrieli Foundation for their generous support for this research.

CHAPTER 25

Iconography of Angels: Roots and Origins in the Earliest Christian Art

Cecilia Proverbio

It is understood that the second half of the fourth century was the period when the Roman Church was becoming aware of its growing role, religious and political, and images began to proliferate in the Roman sphere of influence as instruments of propaganda; against this specific background something new was invented in art, and something was forever changed. Starting from the birth and the early developments of Christian images, the author will explore the origins of the iconography of angels and especially the representation of winged angels, a tradition that emerged by the end of the fourth century.

1 The Origins of the Earliest Christian Art

Although many points regarding the origins of Christian art remain debatable, especially the question of aniconism amongst Christians during the first two centuries,[1] scholars now agree that a distinct Christian art had been born by the first half of the third century, both in the East and in the West of the Roman Empire.[2] The first examples of scriptural episodes depicted in the Christian cat-

---

[1] The reason why the Christians had not had any explicitly visual (iconic) culture of their own during the first centuries is still under discussion; traditionally this absence was attributed to the clear prohibition, followed by Christians, on making images in the Torah, but recently other hypotheses have been proposed. These take into consideration the restricted number of believers in the first and second centuries and their social position, which (with some exceptions) was generally modest. On the different explanations of this phenomenon P.C. Finney, *The Invisible God. The Earliest Christians on Art*, New York, 1994, pp. 99–135; C. Bordino, *I padri della Chiesa e le immagini*, Università della Tuscia, 2010, pp. 1–11; G. Cantino Wataghin, 'I primi cristiani tra *imagines, historiæ* e *pictura*. Spunti di riflessione', in *Antiquité Tardive*, vol. 19 (2011), pp. 17–21; M. Dulaey, 'L'image et les Pères de l'Église. À propos du cubiculum F de la catacombe de la Via Latina', in *Antiquité Tardive* vol. 19 (2011), pp. 47–51; J.M. Spieser, *Le décor figuré des édifices ecclésiaux*, in *Antiquité Tardive* vol. 19 (2011), pp. 99–100.

[2] About the beginnings and the development of the early Christian art, see: A. Grabar, *Le premier art chrétien (200–395)*, Paris, 1966; A. Grabar, *Christian Iconography. A study of its Origins*,

---

© CECILIA PROVERBIO, 2021 | DOI:10.1163/9789004445925_027

acombs of Rome and Naples[3] and in the *domus ecclesiæ* at Dura Europos[4] show us simple pictorial schemes, in which the idea of Salvation is expressed through a few essential elements. The role of these pictorial elements was to bring the theological narrative alive.

According to written sources and archæological finds, by the beginning of the third century at the latest it is possible to identify specific collective Christian cemeteries in various areas of the Mediterranean region. In Rome we can observe the beginnings and the development of burial spaces in the subterranean catacombs,[5] either founded by the institutional Church—such as the cemetery of Callixtus—or created by owners as private tombs which were available to the 'brothers' in faith. Also those belonging to the latter group, such as the tombs of Priscilla, Domitilla and Pretextatus, quite soon began to be administered by Catholic hierarchy. In these specific contexts, the images directly linked to Christian stories are, in any case, exceptional: inhumations were either anonymous or were only characterised by symbols or essential inscriptions with the names of the deceased and some succinct information

---

New York, 1968; K. Weitzmann (ed.), *Age of Spirituality. Late Antique and Early Christian Art, Third to Seventh Century*, New York, 1979; P. Prigent, *L'arte dei primi cristiani. L'eredità culturale e la nuova fede*, Roma, 1997; M. Dulaey, *I simboli cristiani. Catechesi e Bibbia (I–VI)*, Cinisello Balsamo, 2004; J. Spier (ed.), *Picturing the Bible. The Early Christian Art*, New Haven–Fort Worth, 2007; V. Fiocchi Nicolai, F. Bisconti and D. Mazzoleni, *The Christian Catacombs of Rome: History, Decoration, Inscriptions*, Regensburg, 2009; J. Dresken-Weiland, 'Bilder im Grab und ihre Bedeutung im Kontext der Christianiserung der frühchristlichen Welt', in *Antiquité Tardive* 19 (2011), pp. 63–78; J. Dresken-Weiland, *Immagine e parola. Alle origini dell'iconografia cristiana*, Città del Vaticano, 2012.

3   About Rome, see: Fiocchi Nicolai, Bisconti, Mazzoleni, *The Christian Catacombs of Rome*; about Naples, see: U.M. Fasola, *Le catacombe di San Gennaro a Capodimonte*, Roma, 1975; D. Korol, 'Le celebri pitture del Vecchio e del Nuovo Testamento eseguite nella seconda metà del III ed all'inizio del V secolo a Cimitile/Nola', in *Die berühmten alt- und neutestamentlichen Bilder aus der zweiten Hälfte des 3. und dem beginnenden 5. Jh. in Cimitile/Nola*, in M. de Matteis, A. Trinchese (eds), *Cimitile di Nola. Inizi dell'arte cristiana e tradizioni locali. Cimitile bei Nola. Anfänge der christlichen Kunst und lokale Überlieferungen*, Oberhausen, 2004, pp. 147–208.

4   C. Kraeling, *The Excavation at Dura-Europos. Final Report VIII, Part II. The Christian Building*, New Haven–Dura Europos, 1967; E. Adams, *The Earliest Christian Meeting Places. Almost exclusively Houses?*, London–New York, 2013, pp. 89–95; D. Korol, 'Neues zu den alt- und neutestamentlichen Darstellungen im Baptisterium von Dura Europos', in D. Hellhom et al. (eds), *Ablution, Initiation and Baptism. Late Antiquity, Early Judaism and Early Christianity*, Berlin, 2011, pp. 1611–1672.

5   The word is now commonly used for indicating any underground cemetery, although a distinction should be observed between a *catacomb*, managed by Christian or Jewish communities, and a *hypogeum*, also dug under the ground but belonging to private owners such as families or other restricted groups.

about their age and crucial points about their life and death.[6] Only a restricted number of believers were able to purchase or to create larger funerary spaces, such as *cubicula* or *arcosolia*,[7] suitable for decoration with motifs from the Holy Scriptures: in the *Sacramenti*, in Lucine's Crypts in Callixtus, in the *Coronatio* cubiculum in Pretextatus, in the Annunciation cubiculum and in the niche decorated with a depiction of Virgin Mary in the tomb of Priscilla.[8]

Sometimes, in the themes appearing in these early Christian paintings we can recognise the starting points of long series of analogous depictions frequently reproduced during the following centuries; some of the visual solutions adopted there endured, giving life to stable patterns, such as the illustration of the story of prophet Jonah, which would only seldom change. From the time of its first appearance in the earliest surviving catacombs, this scene was divided into numerous sketches frequently repeated as popular subjects in early and medieval Christian art.[9] One of the most favourite motifs was Jonah's repose after his ejection by the sea monster. Usually, Jonah is depicted lying on his side under the trellis which has miraculously sprouted, with one of his arms bent behind his head. The same position can also be observed on former pagan sarcophagi with the representation of myths of the sleeping Arianna or Endymion.

In other cases, however, the way in which specific scenes and motifs were represented was modified over time, in an attempt at finding a better expression of Christian faith and the idea of Salvation. A clear instance of such a

---

6 C. Carletti, '"Epigrafia cristiana" "epigrafia dei cristiani": alle origini della terza età dell'epigrafia', in A. Donati (ed.), *La terza età dell'epigrafia. Colloquio AIEGL—Borghesi '86*, Faenza, 1988, pp. 115–135; D. Mazzoleni, 'Origini e sviluppo dell'epigrafia cristiana', in F. Bisconti and O. Brandt (eds), *Lezioni di archeologia cristiana*, Città del Vaticano, 2014, pp. 445–499.

7 A burial chamber in a catacomb or in a private *hypogeum* which is reserved for a restricted group of people is normally termed a *cubiculum*. The word *arcosolium* indicates a specific kind of tomb, larger and more complex than an ordinary grave. Its upper part has the form of an arch and its lower area, normally rectangular in plan, is reserved for the proper inhumations.

8 F. Bisconti, 'La Madonna di Priscilla: interventi di restauro ed ipotesi sulla dinamica decorativa', in *Rivista di Archeologia Cristiana* vol. 72 (1996), pp. 7–34; id., 'La *coronatio* di Pretestato. Storia delle manomissioni del passato e riflessioni sui recenti restauri', in *Rivista di Archeologia Cristiana* vol. 73 (1997), pp. 7–49; B. Mazzei, 'Il cubicolo dell'Annunciazione nelle catacombe di Priscilla. Nuove osservazioni alla luce dei recenti restauri', in *Rivista di Archeologia Cristiana* vol. 75 (1999), pp. 233–280; F. Bisconti, 'L1–L2, A1–A6, x-y, C–E. Relitti iconografici e nuovi tracciati figurativi alle origini della pittura catacombale romana', in *Rivista di Archeologia Cristiana* vol. 85 (2009), pp. 7–54; R. Giuliani and B. Mazzei, *Le catacombe di Priscilla*, Città del Vaticano, 2016; F. Bisconti (ed.), *Catacombe di Domitilla. Restauri nel tempo*, Todi, 2017.

9 On the representation of Jonah in early Christian art: D. Mazzoleni, s.v. 'Giona', in F. Bisconti (ed.), *Temi di iconografia paleocristiana*, Città del Vaticano, 2000, pp. 191–193; Dulaey, *I simboli cristiani*; Dresken-Weiland, *Immagine e parola*, pp. 93–98.

562   PROVERBIO

changing pattern is the representation of the sacrifice of Abraham, which first appeared around the 230s, in cubiculum A3 of St Callixtus cemetery. This scene would soon be modified. In its original form, Abraham and Isaac are shown in the posture of prayer beside the tree, while the ram appears as the happy conclusion of the story. This episode was shaped *ad hoc* on the basis of the account from *Genesis* (22,1–18), but the gesture *expansis manibus* was borrowed from figurative pagan representations of the female figure of *Pietas*, i.e. the personification of a political and religious value praised by Romans. The Christians gave a new connotation to this specific gesture of openly stretched arms and hands, and it started to be used in order to express gratitude to and devotion for God's gift of salvation.[10]

These few examples, to which numerous other could be added, show that Christians learnt from pagan art a way to stress individual redemption and God's intervention in human life by representing select episodes from Scripture. The *expansis manibus*, an attitude of prayer of Abraham and Isaac, which was popular in early Christian art, can no longer be found on later monuments. About seventy or eighty years later, the way of representing the sacrifice of Isaac became more dramatic, and as such it would become one of the most popular during the Middle Ages (see Figure 25.1): the son is depicted bound beside the altar, whereas the father is stopped by the Lord who prevents him from inflicting a blow with his sword. Nevertheless, despite the changing iconography, the salvific significance of the scene remained identical.[11]

2   The New Developments of Christian Art in The Fourth Century

Another point on which scholars now agree is that the transformations that occurred in Christian art during the fourth century accompanied institutional changes in the Church. While during the third century the dominant part of Christian images can be related to specific scriptural episodes taken from

---

10   On the *orans* attitude in early Christian art: V. Saxer, '"Il étendit les mains à l'heure de la Passion": le thème de l'orant dans la littérature chrétienne du IIe et du IIIe siècle', in *Augustinianum* vol. 20 (1980), pp. 35–39; L. De Maria, s.v. 'Battesimo', in F. Bisconti, *Temi di iconografia paleocristiana*, Roma, 2000, pp. 136–137; A. Donati and G. Gentili, *Deomene. L'immagine dell'orante fra Oriente e Occidente*, Milano, 2001.

11   I. Speyart Van Woerden, 'The Iconography of the Sacrifice of Abraham', in *Vetera Christianorum* vol. 15 (1961), pp. 214–255; B. Mazzei, s.v. 'Abramo', in F. Bisconti (ed.), *Temi di iconografia paleocristiana*, Città del Vaticano, 2000, pp. 92–95; Dulaey, *I simboli cristiani*, pp. 116–127; Dresken-Weiland, *Immagine e parola*, pp. 228–234, bibliography at note 1144, pp. 287–288.

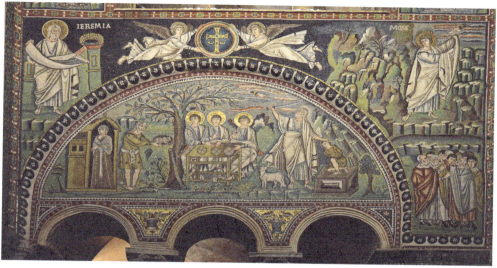

FIGURE 25.1   Ravenna, church of San Vitale, lunette of the presbytery with detail of the three guests of Abraham and the sacrifice of Isaac, first half of the 6th century
PHOTO: AUTHOR

the Old and New Testaments, following the Peace achieved in 313 the Church adopted new aims, also developing new iconography.[12] Thus, in the fourth century a new emphasis was given to the figures of Peter and Paul, who became the symbols of the primacy of the Roman Church founded by them. In the first half of the century this process can be observed in the individualisation of the facial features of Peter and Paul, especially in the representations of their martyrdoms on sarcophagi.[13]

---

12   About the Edict of Milan and the conversion of Roman society in the fourth century: P. Biscottini and G. Sena Chiesa, *Costantino 313 d.C. L'editto di Milano e il tempo della tolleranza*, Milano, 2012.

13   The production of sarcophagi with Christian images began after 259, when the hard persecution against Christians had ended and the new long peaceful period of about 50 years allowed members of the Christian Church to develop their institutions and to grow in number, also involving members of upper social classes, who were able to buy very important carved products. Up to the beginning of the fourth century the images portrayed on marble sarcophagi can be considered 'neutral'. When specifically Christian images began to appear on the sarcophagi, they were similar to those already developed in pictorial funerary art. This situation, however, changed drastically with Constantine, as a result of the legalization of Christianity all around the Mediterranean Sea and beyond. On the production of early Christian sarcophagi in the third and fourth centuries: G. Koch, *Frühchristliche Sarkophage*, München, 2000; F. Bisconti and H. Brandenburg (eds), *Sarcofagi tardoantichi, paleocristiani e altomedievali, Atti della giornata tematica dei Seminari*

Their elaborate physiognomies were widely accepted around Christendom. They were translated into more complex funerary imagery, particularly in course of the second half of the century. During that time, Peter and Paul were increasingly depicted jointly in paintings and mosaics, on sarcophagi and other objects, and often side by side with Jesus. This composition declared their theological significance without providing specific scriptural references.[14] Good examples of the new tendency are the scenes in which both Apostles appear with Christ (although Paul never personally met Him) in the *collegium apostolicum* (see Figure 25.2)[15] or the compositions called *maiestas Domini* and *traditio legis* (see Figure 25.3),[16] where Peter and Paul can be clearly told apart.

---

di *Archeologia Cristiana (École Française de Rome—8 maggio 2002*), Città del Vaticano, 2004; J. Engemann, *Segni dell'imperializzazione del cristianesimo nell'età di Costantino e dei suoi figli nella decorazione dei sarcofagi romani*, in *Costantino e i costantinidi. L'innovazione costantiniana, le sue radici e i suoi sviluppi*, Acta XVI Congressus Internationalis *Archæologiæ Christianæ, Romæ 22–28.9.2013* vol. I, pp. 901–914. About the representation of Peter and Paul on Christian sarcophagi by the first half of the fourth century: U. Utro, 'Radici e sviluppi della produzione urbana dei sarcofagi costantiniani fra committenza e officine', in *Costantino e i costantinidi. L'innovazione costantiniana, le sue radici e i suoi sviluppi*, Acta XVI Congressus Internationalis *Archæologiæ Christianæ, Romæ 22–28.9.2013*, Città del Vaticano, 2016 vol. I, pp. 935–956.

14   On the emphasis given to the iconography of Peter and Paul in the fourth century: P. Testini, 'L'iconografia degli apostoli Pietro e Paolo nelle cosiddette "arti minori"', in B.M. Apollonj Ghetti et al. (eds), *Sæcularia Petri et Pauli*, Città del Vaticano, 1969, pp. 241–323; J.M. Huskinson, Concordia apostolorum. *Christian Propaganda at Rome in the Fourth and Fifth Centuries. A Study in Early Christian Iconography and Iconology*, Oxford, 1982, pp. 51–59; A. Donati (ed.), *Pietro e Paolo. La storia, il culto, la memoria nei primi secoli, Catalogo della mostra, Roma, 30 giugno 10 dicembre 2000*, Milano, 2000; U. Utro, *Raffigurazioni agiografiche sui vetri dorati paleocristiani*, in *Atti della Pontificia Accademia Romana di Archeologia. Serie III. Rendiconti* vol. 74 (2002), pp. 196–197, p. 211; S. Patitucci Uggeri, *San Paolo nell'arte paleocristiana*, Città del Vaticano, 2010, pp. 61–68; J. Janssens, 'Gli apostoli Pietro e Paolo nei monumenti paleocristiani di Roma', in O. Bucarelli and M.M. Morales (eds), Paulo apostolo martyr. *L'apostolo Paolo nella storia, nell'arte e nell'archeologia*, Roma, 2011, pp. 163–181; U. Utro, 'Alle origini dell'iconografia paolina', ibid., pp. 31–32.

15   P. Testini, 'Osservazioni sull'iconografia di Cristo in trono tra gli apostoli', in *Rivista dell'Istituto Nazionale di Archeologia e Storia dell'Arte* vol. 11–12 (1963), pp. 230–300.

16   The *traditio legis* is considered to be one of the most complex subjects ever represented in early Christian art by the second half of the fourth century, and its true meaning is still debated among scholars. The different hypotheses formulated by the end of the nineteenth century include scriptural and symbolic interpretations, although they raise different problems. Within the vast bibliography on the subject, the following recent essays offer a comprehensive overview of new hypotheses advanced: M. Bøgh Rasmussen, '*Traditio legis?*', in *Cahiers archéologiques* vol. 47 (1999), pp. 5–37; M. Bøgh Rasmussen, '*Traditio legis—Bedeutung und Kontext*', in J. Fleischer et al. (eds), *Late Antiquity. Art in Context*, Copenhagen, 2001, pp. 21–52; J.M. Spieser, *Autour de la "Traditio Legis"*, Thessaloniki, 2004;

FIGURE 25.2   Rome, church of Saint Pudenziana: apse mosaic with the *collegium apostolicum*: Peter (on the right) and Paul (on the left) jointly beside Christ, first half of the 5th century
PHOTO: AUTHOR

The new symbolic language that can primarily be attested in private funerary monuments was not born in cemeteries or in reserved burial spaces, but most likely developed under the influence of monumental or official images intended for religious buildings. The foundation of numerous churches in the second half of the fourth century[17] had probably been an inspiration for

J.M. Spieser, *Images du Christ. Des catacombes aux lendemains de l'iconoclasme*, Genève, 2015; I. Foletti and I. Quadri, 'Roma, l'Oriente e il mito della Traditio Legis', in *Opuscula Historiæ Artium* vol. 62 (2013), *Supplementum*, pp. 16–37; R. Couzin, *The Traditio legis: Anatomy of an image*, Oxford, 2015; G. Noga Banai, '*Dominus legem dat*: Von der Tempelbeute zur römischen Bildinvention', in *Römische Quartalschrift* vol. 110 (2015), pp. 157–174; A.F. Bergmeier, 'The *Traditio Legis* in Late Antiquity and Its Afterlives in the Middle Ages', in *Gesta* vol. 56/1 (2017), pp. 27–52.

17   Ch. Pietri, *Roma Christiana. Recherches sur l'église de Rome, son organisation, sa politique, son idéologie de Miltiade à Sixte III*, Rome, 1976, pp. 561–573; F. Guidobaldi, 'L'organizzazione dei tituli nello spazio urbano', in Christiana loca *lo spazio cristiano nella Roma del primo millennio*, Roma, 2000, pp. 123–129; V. Fiocchi Nicolai, *Strutture funerarie ed edifici di culto paleocristiani di Roma dal IV al VI secolo*, Città del Vaticano, 2001, pp. 93–105; M. Cecchelli, 'Le strutture murarie di Roma tra IV e VII secolo', in *Materiali e tecniche dell'edilizia paleocristiana a Roma*, Roma, 2001, pp. 11–101; L. Spera, 'Il vescovo di Roma e la città: regioni ecclesiastiche, tituli e cimiteri. Ridefinizione di un problema amministrativo e territoriale', in O. Brandt et al. (eds), *Episcopus, civitas, territorium, Atti del XV Congresso Internazionale*

FIGURE 25.3   Naples, Baptistery of St John *In Fonte*: detail of the ceiling with the representation of the *traditio legis*, late 4th–early 5th century
PHOTO: AUTHOR

the Roman Church, which could thus convey theological and pastoral messages through images and share them with the entire religious community of the city and even the entire Christendom.

We can hypothesise that the relatively well-known depictions of Peter and Paul embracing—on frescoes, marble slabs (see Figure 25.4), ivory plaques

---

di Archeologia Cristiana, Toledo 8–12 settembre 2008, Città del Vaticano, 2013, pp. 163–186; L. Spera, 'La cristianizzazione di Roma: forme e tempi', in F. Bisconti and O. Brandt (eds), *Lezioni di archeologia cristiana*, Città del Vaticano, 2014, pp. 221–225.

FIGURE 25.4 Aquileia, Palæo-Christian Museum of the monastery: slab engraved with busts of Peter and Paul embracing, end of 4th–beginning of the 5th century
PHOTO: AUTHOR

and other media dating to the decades between the late fourth and the early fifth century—represented reduced copies of official decorations in religious assemblies. As is witnessed by the Church Fathers, the two apostles were seen to represent the two parts of the universal Church, *ex circumcisione* and *ex gentibus*, meeting in Rome, embracing and crying, as in the apocryphal Acts of Peter and Paul.[18] This illustration of the *concordia apostolorum* was probably conceived by ecclesiastical hierarchy to be an image of brotherhood and unity, so vital in the late fourth century because of new challenges facing the Roman Church.[19] The images of Peter and Paul embracing, which

18 'Acta Petri et Pauli', in R.A. Lipsius (ed.), *Acta Petri, Acta Pauli, Acta Petri et Pauli, Acta Pauli et Theclæ, Acta Thaddæi*, Leipzig, 1891, cap. 24, p. 189.

19 Ch. Pietri, '*Concordia apostolorum* et *renovatio Urbis* (culte des martyrs et propagande pontificale)', in *Mélanges d'Archeologie et d'Historie de l'École française de Rome* vol. 73 (1961), pp. 275–322; V. Saxer, 'Le culte des apotres Pierre et Paul dans les plus vieux formulaires romains de la messe du 29 juin', in B.M. Apollonj Ghetti et al. (eds), *Sæcularia Petri et Pauli*, Città del Vaticano, 1969, pp. 199–240; Huskinson, *Concordia apostolorum*; F. Bisconti, 'Il finarello dell'ex Vigna Chiaraviglio', in *La conservazione delle pitture nelle*

were produced between the fourth and the fifth centuries, have their roots in the specific iconography of imperial power, delivering the political message of cohesion among the tetrarchs; indeed, the famous porphyry sculptures today preserved in Venice (see Figure 25.5)[20] and the Vatican Apostolic Library show the *fraternitas principum* through an embrace.

It is hardly a coincidence that important innovations in Christian art in Rome occurred during the second half of the fourth century. The invention of new pictorial patterns and the semantic enrichment of traditional visual language must reflect urgent concerns—cohesion, construction of ecclesiastical structures based on the imperial administration, concord—that characterised the period as one of profound transformation. Owing to the Church's growing awareness of its new political, administrative and religious role in the Empire, the traditional biblical images could not respond exhaustively to the new tasks standing before it.

3 The Iconography and the Understanding of Angels

Before the late fourth century, angels were not characterised with any specific traits, as can be evinced from paintings and other ancient archæological remains.[21] The first location where an angel's image has been recognised is probably the ceiling of the 'cubiculum of Annunciation' in the Priscilla cata-

---

catacombe romane: acquisizioni e prospettive. Roma, 3 marzo 2000, Città del Vaticano, 2000, n. 15; id., 'Nuovi affreschi dal cimitero della ex Vigna Chiaraviglio', in *Atti della Pontificia Accademia Romana di Archeologia. Serie III. Rendiconti* vol. 73, 2000–2001 (2002), pp. 3–42; M. Guj, 'La *concordia Apostolorum* nell'antica decorazione di San Paolo fuori le mura', in F. Guidobaldi and A. Guiglia Guidobaldi (eds), *Ecclesiæ Urbis, Atti del congresso internazionale di studi sulle chiese di Roma (IV–X secolo)*, Roma, 4–10 settembre 2000, Città del Vaticano, 2002, pp. 1874–1892; C. Proverbio, 'I dipinti della catacomba di San Sebastiano, ex Vigna Chiaraviglio', in M. Andaloro (ed.), *La pittura medievale a Roma. 312–1431. Corpus, I, L'orizzonte tardoantico e le nuove immagini, 312–468*, Milano, 2006, pp. 194–205.

20   L. Rebaudo, 'Il gruppo dei Tetrarchi: una lettura del reimpiego', in G. Cuscito (ed.), *Riuso di monumenti e reimpiego di materiali antichi in età postclassica: il caso della Venetia*, Trieste, 2012, pp. 147–158, with bibliography.

21   U.M. Fasola, 'Gli angeli nelle catacombe', in *Studia Miscellanea* vol. 6 (1985), pp. 5–16; D.E. Estivill, *La imagen del angel en la Roma del siglo IV: estudio de iconologia*, Roma, 1994; D.E. Estivill, 'Un contributo per lo studio dell'iconografia degli angeli nel secolo IV', in *Arte Cristiana* vol. 85, 778 (1997), pp. 3–10; R. Giuliani, s.v. 'Angelo', in F. Bisconti (ed.), *Temi di iconografia paleocristiana*, Città del Vaticano, 2000, pp. 106–109; C. Proverbio, *La figura dell'angelo nella civiltà paleocristiana*, Todi, 2007.

FIGURE 25.5　Venice, Basilica of St Mark: group of the Tetrarchs carved from porphyry from Constantinople, beginning of the 4th century
PHOTO: AUTHOR

570   PROVERBIO

comb, dating to the first half of the third century.[22] Mary appears seated in front
of a male figure who can be identified as the archangel Gabriel thanks to comparison with similar, later depictions, namely that on the ceiling of cubiculum
17 in the catacomb of Saint Peter and Marcellinus and that in cubiculum A in
the via Latina *hypogeum*.[23]

   This plain way of representing angels is to be regarded as typical,[24] especially
during the fourth century, as is attested by numerous examples of funerary
imagery. During that time, the number of Christian images that have reached
us rises steeply, reflecting an analogous increase of conversions. On a sarcophagus of the first quarter of the fourth century, left uncompleted for unknown
reasons and now conserved in the church of St Sebastian on the via Appia—
the ancient *basilica Apostolorum*—two different scenes involving angels were
carved.[25] In the first, Balaam on his donkey is stopped by an angel (Nm 22,21)
who is depicted as a bearded man wearing a short tunic similar to that of a
soldier. Similar pictorial representations of this story can be found in cubicula B and F in a private cemetery on the Via Latina, where such scenes were
depicted in a later part of the fourth century.[26] In the latter, located on the
right of the sarcophagus, Tobias, wearing characteristic fisherman clothes, is
facing the angel who is pointing at Tobias's eyes. The same episode, following
a similar iconographic pattern, was depicted around the middle of the fourth
century in the catacomb of the Giordani (see Figure 25.6): near Daniel who is
portrayed praying we see Tobias dressed in a loincloth and carrying a fishing

---

22   G.G. Bottari, *Sculture e pitture sagre estratte dai cemiterj di Roma, pubblicate già dagli
      autori della Roma Sotterranea ed ora nuovamente date alla luce colle spiegazioni* vol. III,
      Roma, 1754, p. 141; R. Garrucci, *Storia dell'arte cristiana nei primi otto secoli della chiesa*
      vol. II, Prato, 1873–1881, pp. 81–82; J. Wilpert, *Le pitture delle catacombe romane*, Roma,
      1903, pp. 187–188; Mazzei, *Il cubicolo dell'Annunciazione nelle catacombe di Priscilla*; Giu-
      liani, s.v. 'Angelo'; Proverbio, *La figura dell'angelo nella civiltà paleocristiana*, pp. 42–43,
      tav. 1; R. Giuliani, B. Mazzei, *Le catacombe di Priscilla*, pp. 31–33. Against this interpre-
      tation, see: P.A. Février, 'Les peintures de la catacombe de Priscille. Deux scènes rela-
      tives a la vie intellectuelle', in *Mélanges d'Archéologie et d'Histoire* vol. 71 (1959), pp. 301–
      319.
23   J.G. Deckers, H.R. Seeliger and G. Mietzke, *Die Katakombe "Santi Marcellino e Pietro". Reper-
      torium der Malereien*, Città del Vaticano–Münster, 1987, pp. 223–226; A. Ferrua, *Catacombe
      sconosciute. Una pinacoteca del IV secolo sotto la via Latina*, Firenze, 1990; Bisconti, *Il
      restauro dell'ipogeo di via Dino Compagni. Nuove idee per la lettura del programma deco-
      rativo del cubicolo "A"*, Vatican, 2003, pp. 83–87.
24   Proverbio, *La figura dell'angelo nella civiltà paleocristiana*, pp. 44–65.
25   G. Bovini, H. Brandenburg, *Repertorium der christlich-antiken Sarkophage. I. Rom und
      Ostia*, Wiesbaden, 1967, n. 176.
26   Ferrua, *Catacombe sconosciute*, pp. 59, 83–87; Dulaey, *L'image et les Pères de l'Église*, pp. 47–
      62.

FIGURE 25.6   Rome, catacomb of the Giordani: Tobias with the archangel Raphael, 4th century

pole on his shoulder. He brings the fish to the archangel Raphael who is represented in oratory attitude.[27]

The examples mentioned so far show that until the late fourth century no distinctive iconography had been devised for angels in Christian art and that angels were mostly represented as ordinary men. It has been noted that sometimes angels were portrayed with beards, as in the depictions in the via Latina catacomb cited above, and, indeed, the same attribute can also be observed in numerous other cases. Thus, on the lid of the sarcophagus of *Publia Florentia* dating to the first quarter of fourth century, the bearded angel appears side by side with the three youths in the fiery furnace (see Figure 25.7).[28] Another example is to be found on the famous sarcophagus from the basilica of St Paul Outside-the-Walls—the so called 'Dogmatic' sarcophagus[29]—which

---

27 No. 1993, p. 14, n. 6; M. Perraymond, s.v. 'Tobia', in F. Bisconti (ed.), *Temi di iconografia paleocristiana*, Città del Vaticano, 2000, pp. 287–288.

28 Bovini, Brandenburg, *Repertorium der christlich-antiken Sarkophage. I. Rom und Ostia*, n. 834, p. 68; C. Carletti, *I tre giovani ebrei di Babilonia nell'arte cristiana antica*, Brescia, 1975; J. Engemann, 'Zur Interpretation der Darstellungen der drei Jünglingen in Babylon in der frühchristlichen Kunst', in K. Koch (ed.), *Akten des Symposiums "Frühchristliche Sarkophage", Atti del convegno, Marburg 30 giugno–4 luglio 1999*, Mainz, 2002, pp. 81–91.

29 Bovini, Brandenburg, *Repertorium der christlich-antiken Sarkophage. I. Rom und Ostia*, n. 43; E. Russo, *Il sarcofago 104 "dogmatico" del Museo Pio Cristiano*, in *Rivista di Archeologia Cristiana* vol. 54 (1978), pp. 159–164; U. Utro (ed.), *S. Paolo in Vaticano. La figura e la parola dell'Apostolo delle Genti nelle raccolte pontificie*, Todi, 2009, pp. 50–54, 118–120; U. Utro,

FIGURE 25.7　Rome, Capitoline Museum: lid of the sarcophagus of *Publia Florentia* with the three youths in the fiery furnace, first quarter of the 4th century

shows two bearded angels in the story of Daniel: the first bearded angel is beside the praying Daniel (on the left), following the account in Dn 6,22, whilst the second one is portrayed, following Dn 14,35–38, carrying the prophet Habakkuk to the lions' den.

Angels were usually depicted clad in a way similar to the biblical male figures in the iconography preceding the early third century. The dalmatic was a common tunic with long sleeves, widely used, and increasingly so in Rome in the second century;[30] it was frequently decorated with parallel purple stripes, the so-called *clavi*, running from the shoulders to the bottom hem. Originally possessed of a political and high social significance, it was endowed with new moral and religious meaning by Christians.[31] Very important for its symbolic value was the *pallium*[32] which replaced the traditional Roman *toga*. According to Tertullian, this coarse woollen garment was a typical attribute of philosophers, chosen for its simplicity and humility and particularly suited to Christians: *gaude, pallium, et exsulta! Melior iam te philosophia dignata est, ex quo Christianum uestire coepisti.*[33] Only a few visible exceptions to this pattern in

---

'Programmi iconografici e impianti dottrinali nell'arte cristiana a Roma nella piena età costantiniana. L'esempio del "sarcofago Dogmatico"', in O. Brandt et al. (eds), *Episcopus, civitas, territorium, Atti del XV Congresso Internazionale di Archeologia Cristiana, Toledo 8–12 settembre 2008*, Città del Vaticano, 2013, pp. 1029–1038. The iconography of this sarcophagus is also examined in Studies 14 and 19 in this volume.

30　M. Bussagli, *Storia degli angeli: racconto di immagini e di idee*, Milano, 1991, pp. 50–51; M. Minasi, s.v. 'Vestiario', in F. Bisconti (ed.), *Temi di iconografia paleocristiana*, Città del Vaticano, 2000, pp. 296–300.

31　L. Heuzei, s.v. 'Clavus latus, angustus', in Ch. Daremberg, E. Saglio (eds), *Dictionnaire des Antiquités grecques et romaines* vol. I, 2, Paris, 1887, pp. 1242–1253.

32　G. Leroux, s.v. 'Pallium', in Ch. Daremberg, E. Saglio (eds), *Dictionnaire des Antiquités grecques et romaines* vol. IV, 1, Paris, 1907, pp. 285–293; Minasi, s.v. 'Vestiario'.

33　*Pall.*, 6,2, Corpus Christianorum Series Latina vol. 2,6; 'Joy, *pallium*, and exult! A better philosophy has now deigned to honour thee, ever since thou hast begun to be a Christian's vesture!'

FIGURE 25.8   Rome, church of Santa Maria Maggiore: detail of the mosaic in the main nave with the meeting between Joshua and the angel, 432–440 CE

the iconography of angels are attested: one is to be found on the sarcophagus, already mentioned, in the church of St Sebastian; another example represents the meeting between Joshua and the angel in the mosaic of the main nave of the church of S. Maria Maggiore in Rome (see Figure 25.8).[34] These exceptions were surely conditioned by the military character of the story.[35]

It should be stressed that the only way the figures of angels can be identified between the third and the fourth centuries is through the context and their associations with other pictorial elements. Deprived of the complete background scene, we should not be able to distinguish angels from ordinary men. The absence of any specific characterisation of angels in the earliest Christian art was not at all surprising if we consider the understanding of angels in the canonical writings of the Scripture. In the Hebrew Bible, in fact, the name 'angel' can be applied to any figure of human or otherworldly nature linking two distinct and conceptually distant realities. The original term *mal'āk*, which is usually used, is actually a noun which Hebrew shares with the Phœnician language, meaning literally 'messenger' or 'herald', the one who delivers messages

---

34   M.R. Menna, 'I mosaici della basilica di Santa Maria Maggiore. Storie dei patriarchi della navata centrale', in M. Andaloro (ed.), *La pittura medievale a Roma. 312–1431. Corpus, I, L'orizzonte tardoantico e le nuove immagini, 312–468*, Milano, 2006, pp. 305–330, including an extensive bibliography.

35   Proverbio, *La figura dell'angelo nella civiltà paleocristiana*, pp. 47–49, 89–90.

574   PROVERBIO

among men[36] or from God to men.[37] Therefore, whether the angel is a human or a celestial being, it is his function of mediator which is emphasised, as happens also in the case of heralds and ambassadors. Only the context can allow us to understand whom a *mal'āk* denotes in a given case, yet, tellingly, the Biblical writers often find it unnecessary to specify his nature. Following the Scriptures, it becomes clear, however, that the angels sent by God are thought of as supernatural creatures, who can be named in different ways but who are conceived of not very differently from the intermediate demi-divine figures of the Near East.[38]

Before the sixth century BC, owing to the new role assumed by the Jews in the land of Canaan, the idea of angels began to include the image of a heavenly fighting host: thus, the divine favour could be manifested through the support for the conquest of the promised land. Moreover, angels also assumed the role of militia in defence of the Chosen People. In the Age of the Kings this aspect saw the most noticeable proliferation, with the development of Israel's military power.[39] The military commitment is precisely expressed in several episodes, such as the siege of Jericho, when Joshua is joined by the angel described as the 'captain of the host of the Lord' (Josh. 5.14), or the extermination of Sennacherib's soldiers by an angel.[40] At the same time when this innovative con-

---

36   With this acceptation the word *mal'āk* is referred: to prophets in Hag 1,13 and Is 44,26; to priests in Ml 2,7; to other men in Sam 29,9.

37   E.g. Judg. 13,18; Nm 22,24 and Dn 6,22; *passim*.

38   In fact, other names, especially in the Old Testament, denote beings that act as intermediaries between man and divinity: the *mal'ākim* are called, for example, 'sons of God' in Gn 6,2; Gb 1,6; 2.1; 38.7; Sal 29.1; 89.7, but this term is not literally translated by the LXX; 'Saints' in Gb 5.1; 15,15; Sal 89.6.8; 'Power' in Sal 103,20 (see R. Lavatori, *Gli angeli. Storia e pensiero*, Genova, 1991, pp. 21 ss.). Very peculiar is the syntagm *mal'āk Jhwh*, sometimes hinting at God Himself, as it does in Gn 16,13; Gn 18 and 19,1–9; Gn 22,11–17; Gn 32,23–33; Hos 12,5 and Judg. 6,11–24. Diverse interpretations are offered by: M.J. Lagrange, *Etudes sur le religions sémitiques*, Paris, 1903, pp. 212–225; J. Rybinski, *Der Mal'ak Jahwe*, Paderborn, 1930; F. Stier, *Gott und sein Engel im Alten Testament*, in *Alttestamentliche Abhandlungen* 12/2, Münster, 1934; G. von Rad, *Teologia dell'Antico Testamento*, Brescia, 1972, pp. 327–329; M. Simonetti, *Angeli pagani giudei cristiani*, in C. Carletti and G. Otranto (eds), *Culto e insediamenti micaelici nell'Italia meridionale fra Tarda Antichità e Medioevo, Atti del Convegno, Monte Sant'Angelo 18–21 novembre 1992*, Bari, 1994, pp. 305–322.

39   Traces remain, for example in Psalms 103,20–21, where we read: 'Bless the Lord, ye his angels, that excel in strength, that do his commandments, hearkening unto the voice of his word. Bless ye the Lord, all ye his hosts; ye ministers of his, that do his pleasure', and in Ps. 148,2, where, while exhorting to praise God, the psalmist exclaims: 'Praise ye him, all his angels: praise ye him, all his hosts'.

40   2 Kings 19,35–37, Is 37,36 and 2 Chron 32,21.

cept was diffused, the new epithets 'God of hosts' and '*Jhwh* of the armies' were supposedly shaped.[41]

Israel's interaction with different polytheistic nations influenced the Biblical ideas about angels. The complex system of minor Egyptian and Assyrian-Babylonian divinities left a mark on the Israelites' monotheism, so that in later Jewish religiosity some heavenly figures were assimilated to angelic categories, including the Cherubim and the Seraphim.[42] In the Hebrew Bible, the Cherubim had the function of guardians in venerated sites in which the divine presence was recognised, while the Seraphim were related to visions. The Seraphim's role was to glorify the Lord through praise and to purify the prophets' lips. Originally, both the Cherubim and the Seraphim—the only heavenly creatures described as possessing wings in the Bible—are, however, not called *mal'ākim*; nor do they play the role of messengers as the angels. The very fact that they are mentioned in the Scriptures by collective names borrowed from a non-Jewish mythological world indicates, admittedly, their special sacral function. This is expressed in theophanies in which God, exceptionally, Himself speaks to humans. In the course of such visions, reserved to

---

41   Hos 12,5, Am 3,13; 1 Sam 1,3.11, Ps 24,10, Is 1,9 e 6,3, Jer 7,3 and 9,15.

42   The name *kerubim* derives from the Akkadian *keribû* or *karibû* whose root meaning is 'to pray/to bless', so that these heavenly beings are almost always described as God's heavenly court. In the Assyrian-Babylonian religious world, from which the Cherubim of the Hebrew tradition surely derive, they are semi-divine figures depicted on door jambs or on entrances as guardians of a house, or more often of a temple. They also represent symbols of both fertility and power. They are represented with the body of an animal (often a bull), wide wings on their back and the face (and often also the torso and the arms) of a human. In these representations the divine attribute of the crown is also found with a certain frequency. The term *seraphim* derives from the root *serap* indicating either a being 'burning' or, more likely, a serpentine being (as is suggested by the use of the word in Nm 21,6.8, in Is 14,29 and 30,6), with links to Egyptian tradition (in particular, to figures of sphinxes). See: J. Michl, s.v. 'Angelo', in H. Firies (ed.), *Dizionario Teologico* vol. 1, Brescia, 1968, p. 94; R. van der Hart, *Teologia degli angeli e dei demoni*, Catania, 1971, p. 53; M. Seeman, *Gli angeli*, in *Mysterium Salutis* vol. IV, Brescia, 1972, pp. 745–746; Lavatori, *Gli angeli*, pp. 24–25; Bussagli, *Storia degli angeli*; G. Ravasi, 'Gli angeli nella Bibbia', in E. Bruno and E. Alberione (eds), *Angeli*, Milano, 1993, pp. 24–25.

      The Cherubim guard the access to the Tree of Life after the expulsion of Adam and Eve from Eden (Gn 3,24), and their depictions are affixed to the cover of the Ark of the Covenant (Ex 25,18–20.22; 1 Kings 8,6) and before the entrance to the temple of Jerusalem (1 Kings 6,23–28). They are also represented as bearers of the throne of God (1 Sam 4, 4, 2 Sam 6,2, Ps 80, 2, Ps 9, 1), especially during the theophanies (2 Sam 22,11, Ps 18,11) and the visions of the prophet Ezekiel (Ezek 1, 10). The Seraphim are mentioned in the book of the prophet Isaiah (Is 6), who describes them as possessing six wings: two wings cover their face, two cover their body and with two wings they fly.

prophets, Cherubim and Seraphim form a heavenly procession with the precise purpose of revealing, through their presence, the power and majesty of *Jhwh*.

Another external influence on the traditional Jewish conception of angels came from the Zoroastrian religious tradition of Persia. In its certain formulations, Zoroastrianism represented a monotheistic system, regarding *Ahura Mazdā* as the one positive divine entity, on which six intermediate figures, the *Ameša Spenta*, directly depended and whose tasks were akin to those played by the *mal'ākim* in the Bible.[43] This divine court was also accompanied by the *Fravaši*, entities believed to be part of human souls and existing eternally as a heavenly copy of every single human being. The complexity of the Iranian religious system must have inspired the increase in number and functions of heavenly messengers in Judaism, especially when the concept of the divine itself evolved. The transcendent characteristics of God and the necessity of intermediaries between humanity and the divine sphere were stressed in this process.[44] This idea of a necessary mediation was also inherited by Christianity.

The innovation which had greater consequences for later speculations, however, is the precise identification of some of the divine messengers, to whom, at least in three cases attested in the canonical texts of the Bible, individual names are attributed.[45] It is not surprising that this identification took place after the Babylonian exile. Under new influences, the understanding of angels as individualised beings reaches its peak and continues to prosper later in Jewish apocalyptic literature. Also the intervention of angels now took place in an individual way, while angels began to act as figures clearly distinct from *Jhwh*. Nevertheless, their interventions were always directly related to the divine will. In later apocryphal literature, the appellations of the angels were particularly diversified.[46]

---

43   Bussagli, *Storia degli angeli*; A. Piras, 'I progenitori degli angeli. Gli angeli nella religione zoroastriana', in M. Bussagli and M. D'Onofrio (eds), *Le ali di Dio: messaggeri e guerrieri alati tra Oriente e Occidente*, Cinisello Balsamo, 2000, pp. 13–16.

44   At the same time, when the emphasis was put on the unintelligibility and ineffability of God, the new concept of *angelus interpres*, an intermediary between God and the prophet, was introduced. See: Seeman, *Gli Angeli*, coll. 748–749; Lavatori, *Gli angeli*, p. 26; P. Teyssedre, *Angeli, astri e cieli: figure del destino e della salvezza*, Genova, 1991, pp. 110–112.

45   The subordination to God is clearly expressed in the construction of angels' names, which imply the derivation from God and dependence on him: Raphael (Tb 12), Michael (Dn 10,13; 10,21 and 12,1) and Gabriel (Dn 8,15–24; 9,20–27; Lk 1,11; 20, 26–38) embody the three roles, stratified and well defined, of a personal guide, a fighting angel and a direct intermediary.

46   H.B. Kuhn, 'The Angelology of the Non-Canonical Jewish Apocalypses', in *Journal of Biblical Literature* vol. 67 (1948), pp. 217–232.

The encounter between the Jewish tradition and the Greek and Hellenistic cultures implied numerous points of contact between the semi-divine figures of the classical and post-classical imagination and the angels. The Greek religious system was populated by hosts of figures possessing divine characters, while also operating as intermediaries on behalf of the gods, like Iris, the favourite spokesperson in the Iliad,[47] and Hermes, who in the Odyssey[48] is indicated as a messenger of Zeus himself. The collective term that identifies them must also refer to the fundamental connecting role played by them, i.e. that of messengers, ἄγγελοι in Greek—hence the word now in use, although its meaning had to change semantically before it came to identify exclusively a divine envoy.

Originally, the word ἄγγελος was used in social contexts, indicating a herald or an ambassador who was often the only link between two distinct or conflicting realities. This term displays a range of similarities to the Hebrew word mal'āk, being applied to both human and divine emissaries. Any figure who performed the role of a messenger could be surrounded, merely on account of its task, by sacred aura. Consequently, starting from the Septuagint the word ἄγγελος was chosen in order to translate, almost literally, the Hebrew mal'āk. During the time when the Septuagint was edited, as well as during the period when the New Testament writings were edited, the term 'angel' gradually became reserved to a particular category of beings.[49] Philo, who discussed the substance of demons and angels,[50] recognised them as intermediate beings between the human and the divine spheres. The angels thus acquired a distinct nature denoted as ὑποκείμενον or substantia. Consequently, in the New Testament and early Fathers, ἄγγελος is in most cases perceived as a celestial creature,[51] an intermediary between God and man.[52]

---

47   Il. II, 786, III, 121, VIII, 398 and 409.

48   Od. V,29.

49   R. Ficker, s.v. 'Mal'āk', in E. Jenni, C. Westermann (eds), Dizionario Teologico dell'Antico Testamento vol. I, Torino, 1978, col. 782.

50   Filone, De gigantibus "ψυχὰς οὖν καὶ δαίμονας καὶ ἀγγέλους ὀνόματα μὲν διαφέροντα, ἐν δὲ καὶ ταὐτόν ὑποκείμενον διανοηθείς", in Les Œuvres de Philon d'Alexandrie publiées sous la direction de R. Arnoldez, C. Mondésert, J. Pouilloux 8, Paris, 1939, 16.

51   For example, Lk 7,24 and 9,52; Mt 11,10 and Mk 1,2.

52   The Latinized name angelus can first be found within the Vetus Latina of Tertullian and, later, in the Vulgata of Jerome. Jerome stresses the difference between human and divine messengers, calling them respectively nuntius and angel; see Seeman, Gli angeli, p. 739.

578   PROVERBIO

4   Angels between Tradition and Innovation

With the birth of Christianity, the perspective on angels gradually changed
because Christ embodied in Himself both the human and the divine aspects,
presenting Himself as the only true intercessor before the Father and thus making the communicative work of divine messengers almost superfluous. Compared to the later books of the Hebrew Bible, in the New Testament writings
angels play a relatively limited role, especially during Jesus's earthly life.[53] They
seem, however, to reacquire their importance as agents connecting heaven and
earth precisely after the disappearance of the Messiah. Subsequently they start
acting as defenders of the *Ecclesia*.[54]

By considering the Church Fathers' views on angels it is important to bear in
mind that they were familiar with the early iconography. It would be impossible to find a systematic doctrine concerning the angels in the Fathers for whom
the Trinitarian and the Christological doctrines were of primary importance.
Angels attracted the Fathers' attention when they were considered in relation
to God or to Christ. Although no consistency concerning the angels can be
found in early Christian writings, the common feature of Christian thought
between the third and the fifth century is that the angelic nature is different
from both the Trinity and humanity: the angels are not completely devoid of a
body, complete incorporeity being only distinctive of the Trinity. The common
tendency in the Patristic literature is to attribute a certain immaterial body
to the angels, which would distinguish them from both the humans and the
divine Persons. The angelic body was thought to be composed of 'light' elements, such as air and fire, suspended between the material and the spiritual
spheres, between earth and heaven.[55]

---

53   In the Gospels, the appearance of angels marks two fundamental stages in Jesus's life, the
     incarnation and the resurrection; indeed, each of the four Synoptics narrates the appear-
     ance of heavenly creatures near the tomb of Jesus: Mk 16,5–7; Mt 28,2–7; Lk 24,4–7; Jn
     20,12–13.

54   On the understanding of angels in the apocryphal writings of the Old Testament, see:
     Kuhn, *The Angelology of the Non-Canonical Jewish Apocalypses*, especially pp. 220–221 on
     the influence exercised by them on natural elements. In Rev 7,1; 14,18 and 16,5, angels are
     related to natural celestial bodies; in Rev 14,6 and 18,1–22, an angel announces the judg-
     ment or the fall of Babylon; in Rev 3,5; 5,11 and 7,11, angels represent the celestial court of
     God's throne; in Rev 8,2–11 and 15,1–16,17, angels are material executors of the punishment
     sent by God.

55   According to Irenæus, the Son's superiority over angels is warranted by his incarnation.
     Angels are the only creatures endowed with a spiritual semblance, and do not possess
     a real body ('Adversus hæreses', in *Sources Chrétiennes* vol. 210–211, cap. 3,20,4). Clement

FIGURE 25.9   Istanbul, Archæological Museum: the sarcophagus from Sarıgüzel (Istanbul) with winged angels holding a Christogram, last third of the 4th century

Already at the end of the second century, in his *Apologeticus* Tertullian equated angels with spirits, affirming that, like spirits, heavenly messengers are endowed with wings. The wings are directly linked to the angels' speed and to their ubiquity, qualities transcending human limits and underlining their otherworldly dimension:

> Omnis spiritus ales est: hoc et angeli et dæmones. Igitur momento ubique sunt. Totus orbis illis locus unus est; quid ubi geratur tam facile sciunt quam annuntiant. Velocitas divinitas creditur, quia substantia ignoratur.[56]

Despite Tertullian's affirmation, the earliest representations of winged angels can only be found between the end of the fourth and the beginning of the fifth century. One of the earliest examples is the Theodosian sarcophagus—the so-called 'sarcophagus of a Prince'—found in the Istanbul suburb of Sarıgüzel (see Figure 25.9).[57] Other representations of winged angels datable to the later

---

of Alexandria compares the substance of which the angels' bodies are composed to that of the stars, made of fire and air ('Excerpta ex theodoto', in *Sources Chrétiennes* vol. 23, cap. 11,4 and 12,2). According to Origen, the fundamental difference between the nature of angels and that of men is physical, since angels—unlike men—are endowed with an ethereal and subtle body ('De oratione', in PG vol. 11, 416–452, cap. 7), whilst only the Trinity is incorporeal ('De principiis', in *Sources Chrétiennes* vol. 253, II, cap. 1,6,4; 1,7,1; 12,2,2; *Sources Chrétiennes* vol. 269, II, cap. 4,3,15).

56   'Apologeticum', in *Corpus Scriptorum Ecclesiasticorum Latinorum* vol. 69, cap. 22,8.
57   The discovery (A. Mutif, *Ein Prinzesarkophag aus Istanbul*, Istanbul, 1934) occurred in 1933 in the Istanbul suburb of Sarıgüzel; for the dating, relying on stylistic considerations, see: A. Grabar, *Sculptures byzantines de Costantinople (IVe–Xe siècle)*, Paris, 1963, p. 30;

FIGURE 25.10   Ravenna, Quadrarco di Braccioforte: detail of the right side of the Pignatta sarcophagus with the Annunciation, first quarter of the 5th century
PHOTO: AUTHOR

fourth–early fifth century are known: on clay lamps imported from Africa, on which an angel in the fiery furnace is portrayed;[58] in the Annunciation of Mary working the purple yarn for the temple, as depicted on the 'Pignatta' sarcophagus from Ravenna (see Figure 25.10);[59] on the wooden doors of the church of

---

A. Pasinli, *Istanbul Archæological Museums*, Istanbul, 1989, n. 76, p. 72; N. Firatli, *La sculpture byzantine figurée au Musée Archéologique d'Istanbul*, Paris, 1990, n. 81; B. Kiilerich, 'The Sarigüzel sarcophagus and triumphal themes in theodosian art', in *Akten des Symposiums "Frühchristliche Sarkophage"*, pp. 137–144.

58   Now conserved at the Bibliotheca Apostolica Vaticana. Type Dressel 31/Hayes II B, cm 14,9×8,6; A. Ennabli, *Lampes chretienne de Tunisie, Musée du Bardo et de Carthage*, Paris, 1976, pp. 27, 44, nn. 25–26; C. Spantigati and G. Romano (eds), *Il museo e la pinacoteca di Alessandria*, Alessandria, 1986, pp. 79–84, nn. 25–26; Bussagli, D'Onofrio, *Le ali di Dio*, p. 180, n. 39; F. Bejaoui, 'Iconografia delle lucerne a olio dell'Africa cristiana (IV secolo-inizio V secolo)', in P. Pasini (ed.), *387 d.C. Ambrogio e Agostino. Le sorgenti dell'Europa*, Milano, 2003, p. 27, cat. 60.

59   G. De Francovich, 'Studi sulla scultura ravennate, I.I sarcofagi', in *Felix Ravenna* vol. 26–27 (1958), pp. 51, 79; G. Valenti Zucchini, 'Il sarcofago di Eliseo profeta', in G. Valenti Zucchini and M. Bucci (eds), *"Corpus" della scultura paleocristiana, bizantina ed altomedievale di*

ROOTS AND ORIGINS IN THE EARLIEST CHRISTIAN ART

S. Sabina in Rome (first half of the fifth century), where all the angelic figures are winged[60] (see Figure 25.11); and on the triumphal arch in S. Maria Maggiore. These examples demonstrate the success of the new iconographical pattern.[61]

5   Old and New Hypotheses

Some scholars have spoken of similarities between the angels holding a Christogram on the Sarıgüzel sarcophagus and the Victories supporting a shield on second–third century sarcophagi. It has furthermore been claimed that wings were transferred from the Victories to angels because the latter symbolised the triumph of Christianity over the pagan religions.[62] According to G. Stuhlfauth,[63] however, several elements counter these formal analogies. Indeed, the representations of angels had from the outset been associated with Biblical stories, independently from the iconography of the Victories. Some

---

        Ravenna vol. II, *I sarcofagi a figure a carattere simbolico*, Roma, 1968, n. 11, pp. 30 ff.; J. Kollwitz and H. Herdejürgen, *Die Sarkophage der westlichen Gebiete des Imperium Romanum. Die ravennatischen Sarkophage*, Berlin, 1979, B1, pp. 105–106, taf. 24; J. Dresken-Weiland, *Repertorium der Christlich-antiken Sarkophage. II. Italien mit einem Nachtrag Rom und Ostia, Dalmatien, Museen der Welt*, Mainz, 1998, n. 376, p. 118, taf. 108,3. The detail of purple yarn appears in the Gospels of James (11,2) and of Pseudo-Mathew (9,2).

60   Weitzmann (ed.), *Age of Spirituality*, pp. 486–488; G. Jeremias, *Die Holztür der Basilica S. Sabina in Rom*, Tübingen, 1980; M. Cecchelli, 'Le più antiche porte cristiane: S. Ambrogio a Milano, S. Barbara al Vecchio Cairo, S. Sabina a Roma', in S. Salomi, *Le porte di bronzo dall'antichità al XIII secolo*, Roma, 1990, pp. 66–69.

61   M.R. Menna, 'I mosaici della basilica di Santa Maria Maggiore. Storie dell'infanzia di Cristo sull'arco trionfale', in M. Andaloro (ed.), *La pittura medievale a Roma. 312–1431. Corpus, I, L'orizzonte tardoantico e le nuove immagini, 312–468*, Milano, 2006, pp. 331–346.

62   J. Strzygowski, *Orient oder Rom. Beitrage zur Geschichte der spätantiken und frühchristlichen Kunst*, Leipzig, 1901, pp. 25 ss.; O. Wulff, *Altchristlichen und byzantinische Kunst*, in *Handbuch der Kunstwissenschaft* 2, München, 1914, p. 136; C.L.M. Beck, *Genien und Niken als Engel in altchristlichen Kunst*, Giessen, 1936; L. Réau, s.v. 'Anges', in *Iconographie de l'art chrétienne* vol. II, 2, Paris, 1956, pp. 30–55; E. Panofsky, *Tomb sculpture: its changing aspects from ancient Egypt to Bernini*, London, 1964, p. 43. On the contrary, H. Leclercq, s.v. 'Anges', in F. Cabrol-H. Leclercq (eds), *Dictionnaire d'Archéologie Chrétienne et de Liturgie* vol. I, 2, Paris, 1909, coll. 2080–2161; K. Felis, *Die Niken in altchristlichen Kunst*, in *Römische Quartalschrift für christlichen Altertumskunde und Kirchengeschichte* vol. 26 (1912), pp. 3–25 and G. Berefelt, *A study on the winged angel: the origin of a motif*, Stockholm, 1968, stressed the similarities between Victories and angels in formal aspects but they did not claim the angels' direct derivation from Victories.

63   The author highlights the male characteristics of angels and the feminine characteristics of Victories, indicating diverse clothing styles and hairstyle (G. Stuhlfauth, *Die Engel in der altchristlichen Kunst*, Freiburg i. B. 1897).

FIGURE 25.11   Rome, church of Santa Sabina, detail of the wooden door with the scene of the ascension of Isaiah, first half of the 5th century
PHOTO: AUTHOR

ROOTS AND ORIGINS IN THE EARLIEST CHRISTIAN ART

aspects in the representation of angels did not undergo any modification, and the traditional pictorial pattern of the angels with masculine traits both in their dress (dalmatic and pallium) and in their hair endured through centuries. Another recent theory suggests that the reason for the innovation in the representation of angels can be recognised in the iconography of the Winds, indeed similar but very rarely attested in this form.[64] However, compositions comparable to the Sarıgüzel sarcophagus can also be found in connection to various winged figures on pre-Christian Roman monuments. No analogy represents a sufficient ground for recognising the prototype for the depiction of winged angels specifically in the Victories or in the Winds.

Since the idea of winged angels—as we learn from Tertullian—is more ancient than their representation, the origin of the visual change must have had different grounds. As we have stressed, in the late fourth century a need was felt to distinguish angels from humans in a visible way. For John Chrysostom, artists depicted the angels winged in order to express their sublimity:

> They show the sublimity of a nature; for this reason Gabriel is portrayed winged, not because angels do really have wings, but because you shall know that they leave the highest regions and the supreme residence to approach the human nature; so, the wings attributed to these forces do not have any other meaning than to indicate the sublimity of their nature.[65]

The question, therefore, is not so much 'why in Christian art were angels portrayed with wings?' as rather 'why did winged angels appear only in the late fourth century?' Two points should here be made: in the representation of angels, something had already started to change before the appearance of wings; the revolution in the iconography of angels reflected both the invention of a new symbolic language and a more specific definition of the angels' nature by the Fathers.

All the images examined above are related to Biblical episodes, and no distinct extra-textual attribute can be identified in their depictions. And so, if

---

64 Bussagli, *Storia degli angeli*, pp. 63–71.

65 "'Ώσπερ γὰρ ἄγγελος λέγεται, ἐπειδὴ τὰ τοῦ Θεοῦ τοῖς ἀνθρόποις ἀναγγέλλει καὶ ἀρχάγγελος λέγεται ἐπειδὴ τῶν ἀγγέλων ἄρχει, οὕτω καὶ αὗται προσηγορίας ἔχουσι τὴν σοφίαν αὐτῶν καὶ καθαρότητα αὐτῶν ἡμῖν δηλοῦσας καὶ ὥσπερ δι πτέρυγες τὸ ὕψος ἐμφαίνουσι τῆς φύσεος -καὶ γὰρ ὁ Γάβριηλ πετόμενος φαίνεται, οὐκ ἐπειδὴ πτηρὰ περὶ τόν ἄγγελον, ἀλλ'ἵνα μαθῆς ὅτι ἐκ τόν ὑψηλοτάτων χωρίων καὶ τῶν ἄνω διατριβῶν πρός τὴν ἀνθρωπίνην ἀφίκται φύσιν- οὕτω δὴ καὶ ἐπὶ τούτων οὐδέν ἄλλο δῆλοι τὰ πτερὰ ἤ τὸ τῆς φύσεως ὕψος", 'Homily 3', in *Sources Chrétiennes* vol. 28 bis, 317–323.

FIGURE 25.12   Rome, lunette of the tomb of Vibia: introduction of the deceased to the eschatological banquet, second half of the fourth century

angels were not recognised in their pictorial contexts or in inscriptions, they could not be distinguished from humans. In the late fourth century, we observe the appearance of angels who were not intended to illustrate any specific Biblical episode. In order to enable the spectators to identify them, they were accompanied by inscriptions. Thus, the inscription *angelus bonus* (probably a type of guardian angel) was set above the young man bringing Vibia to the afterlife banquet in the decoration of Vibia's tomb datable to the second half of the fourth century (see Figure 25.12).[66] The same solution was adopted in a very badly preserved frescoed tomb in the St Sebastian catacomb, where two figures are defined as angels in an inscription set above their heads (see Figure 25.13).

Red brush strokes around the outline, on the face and the hand of the upper figure are indicative of the artist's intention to define the 'nature' of the angelic body, made of red-hot air according to the Fathers. In the following century the identical feature can be observed in the mosaic of the triumphal arch in S. Maria Maggiore, where angels have their faces, hands and feet coloured with red (see Figure 25.14); in S. Apollinare Nuovo in Ravenna red and blue colours are used to express the opposite natures of the goats and the sheep (see

---

66   C. Cecchelli, *Monumenti cristiano-eretici di Roma*, Roma, 1944, pp. 167–180; F. Cumont, *Lux Perpetua*, Paris, 1949, pp. 256–257; A. Ferrua, *La catacomba di Vibia*, in *Rivista di Archeologia Cristiana* vol. 47 (1971), pp. 5–62; A. Ferrua, *La catacomba di Vibia*, in *Rivista di Archeologia Cristiana* vol. 49 (1973), pp. 131–161; F. Bisconti, *Altre note di iconografia paradisiaca*, in *Bessarione* vol. 9 (1992), pp. 101–109; Estivill, *La imagen del angel en la Roma del siglo IV*, pp. 201–208.

FIGURE 25.13   Scheme of the decoration on the *arcosolium* of Paul in the catacomb of Ex Vigna Chiaraviglio (St Sebastian, Rome), late 4th–beginning of the 5th century
ELABORATION: AUTHOR

Figure 25.15) according to Matthew 25:31–33, as well as the opposite natures of two angels.[67]

In all these cases, the colour expresses the understanding of the angels, directing the beholder's attention to their body as a visual manifestation of their 'nature'. This subject was important in the late fourth-century Church on account of Christological debates, and the Fathers of that period stressed the superiority of Jesus Christ to all the angels.[68] Since a truly human body was only

---

67 *When the Son of man shall come in his glory, and all the holy angels with him, then shall he sit upon the throne of his glory: And before him shall be gathered all nations: and he shall separate them one from another, as a shepherd divides this sheep from the goats: And he shall set the sheep on his right hand, but the goats on the left.* See on this topic E. Kirschbaum, 'L'angelo rosso e l'angelo turchino', in *Rivista di Archeologia Cristiana* vol. 17 (1940), pp. 209–227.

68 When applied to Christ, the word ἄγγελος was not originally intended to define a specific nature. The role of angelomorphic doctrines within orthodox Christian thought is evident, for example, in Justin: the Son is associated with the *mal'āk Jhwh* of the Hebrew Bible, who represents his manifestation before his incarnation, in anticipation of the Trinitarian

FIGURE 25.14   Rome, church of Santa Maria Maggiore: detail of the scene of the Annunciation on the triumphal arch (originally, the apsidal arch): angels' faces, hands and feet are coloured with red, 432–440 CE

admitted for Christ, the depiction of the angels had to distinguish them.[69] A number of apocryphal sources[70] enabled the artists to distinguish Jesus's body from that of the angels, which was defined as composed of an airy substance, either fire or cold air.[71] These texts offered an explanation of the way in which angels appearing in the Scriptures could be perceived by human beings. At the same time, the unique character of God's incarnation in Christ could be reasserted.

The importance of this distinction is also suggested by the resistance of the official Church to the veneration of angels, about which very few details can

---

revelation ('1 Apologia', in *Sources Chrétiennes* vol. 507, cap. 63,2). Justin introduces a distinction between the Son of God, who participates in the divine nature, and the heavenly ministers, pure creatures, and therefore composed of different substance (*Dialogus cum Tryphone Iudæo*, M. Marcovich (ed.), 'Iustini Martyris Dialogus cum Tryphone', in *Patristische Texte und Studien*, Berlin–New York, 1997, cap. 128,1–4).

69   See: Kuhn, *The Angelology of the Non-Canonical Jewish Apocalypses*.

70   The angels' bodies are perceived as composed of fire or similar substances, for example, in: Enoch 67,8; 2 Enoch 20,1–21,1; 29,1–3; 2 Baruch 21,6 and 59,11. The substance of spirits is also discussed in classical literature; see: Kirschbaum, 'L'angelo rosso e l'angelo turchino'.

71   Numerous Fathers suggest that since the heavenly messengers cannot be either totally immaterial or completely corporeal, their essence ought to be 'spiritual', similar to fire or steam; see: Gregory of Nazianzus, 'Epistulæ Theologicæ', in *PG* vol. 37, 21–388, cap. 2,31; Basil of Cæsarea, 'De Spiritu Sancto', in *Sources Chrétiennes* vol. 17 bis, cap. 16,38; Ambrogio, 'De Spiritu Sancto', in *Corpus Scriptorum Ecclesiasticorum Latinorum* vol. 79, cap. 1, 5.75; Augustin, 'De Genesi ad litteram', in *Corpus Scriptorum Ecclesiasticorum Latinorum* vol. 28, I, cap. 3, 10; id., 'De civitate Dei', in *Corpus Christianorum Series Latina* vol. 48, cap. 21, 10; id., 'De Trinitate', in *Corpus Christianorum Series Latina* vol. 50, cap. 3, 1.4–5.

FIGURE 25.15　Ravenna, church of Sant' Apollinare Nuovo: detail of the mosaic illustrating the division of sheep and goats according to Mt. 25,31–33
PHOTO: AUTHOR

be gleaned before the fifth century. From Josephus Flavius[72] we know that the Essenes kept the names of angels, derived from diverse apocalyptic sources, as a secret of their sect. Such a devotion could also be transmitted to Jewish Christian groups. Already rejected in the Epistle to the Colossians,[73] the veneration of angels persisted amongst Christians,[74] and centuries later was formally condemned in canon 35 of the council of Laodicea, held admittedly between the 340s and the Second Œcumenical council of Constantinople (381), and quoted by Theodoret of Cyrus.[75] In this canon, a clear intention to resist unofficial veneration of angels can be perceived.

In the second half of the fourth century, marked as its was by debates regarding the body and the soul of Christ, angels began to be visually distinguished from humans, as well as from Jesus, acquiring pictorial attributes never used

---

72　*Bellum Iudaicum* 2, 142.
73　Col. 2,18: 'Let no man beguile you of your reward in a voluntary humility and worshipping of angels, intruding into those things which he hath not seen, vainly puffed up by his fleshly mind'.
74　In the Gospel of Bartholomew (4, 25–47) the head of the rebel angels, Beliar, describes to the apostle the creation of angels, specifying their names and functions.
75　'Commentarii in epistula ad Colossæseos', in *PG* vol. 82, 613–620, cap. 2,18 and 3,17. Already in the second century Justin had admitted the veneration of angels but had stressed that it should be subordinated to that of the Trinity ('1 Apologia', in *Sources Chrétiennes* vol. 507, cap. 6,2).

before in their representation: for example, the red colour symbolised their fiery body, while the wings expressed their heavenly nature. These representations contrast not only the Victories, but also the winged seasonal genii and putti.

Although by the fifth century the representation of winged angels becomes preponderant, some exceptions can be found in specific contexts and in particular scenes, for example, in the mosaics of the nave of S. Maria Maggiore (even though wings characterise the angels on the mosaic of the triumphal arch in the same church): in the episode of Joshua meeting the angel and in the vision of Abraham at Mamre (see Figure 25.16). In the former, the superhuman nature of the angel is stressed by the halo around his head. As for the latter, the three angels meeting Abraham are without wings but have red skin, while the central figure's head is surrounded by a halo. It seems that this is not an isolated case but reflects a wider tendency, as the presbyterial area of the church of S. Vitale in Ravenna in the sixth century shows (see Figure 25.1). In this case the biblical passage was interpreted as a revelation of the Trinity, following Augustine,[76] while the central figure represented in the act of speaking was seen as the Logos, i.e. the Son before His incarnation. While Abraham's three guests could still be occasionally interpreted as mere angels also during later centuries, the understanding of this scene as a revelation of the Trinity gradually prevailed.

Towards the end of the fourth century, and especially during the fifth and the sixth centuries, angels were constantly portrayed with wings. They also acquired new roles, sometimes representing a kind of a guard of Jesus or Mary, or a divine cortege, attracting the beholders' attention. Angels began to populate sacred representations as a celestial court which mirrored in heaven the earthly symbols of power. Later, two different ways of perceiving sacred art developed in the Latin West and in the Byzantine East, but the winged angels remained firmly accepted everywhere. Once invented, this iconographic pattern has persisted even until modern times.

Acknowledgements

My gratitude goes to Edith Yeung Quinto, Igor Dorfmann-Lazarev, Peter Philips and Felicity Harley for the English text revision and for stylistic advice.

---

76   'Abraham tres vidit et unum adoravit': Contra Maximinum Arianorum episcopum, cap. 2, 25, M. Schanz, Geschichte der römischen Literatur, IV,2, München, 1920.

ROOTS AND ORIGINS IN THE EARLIEST CHRISTIAN ART 589

FIGURE 25.16   Rome, church of Santa Maria Maggiore: detail of the mosaic in the main nave representing the meeting between Abraham and the angels at Mamre (Gen. 18), 432–440 CE

CHAPTER 26

The Gardens of Eden: Compositional, Iconographic and Semantic Similarities between the 'Birds Mosaic' of the Armenian Chapel in Jerusalem and the Mosaic of the Synagogue at Ma'on (Nirim)

Zaruhi Hakobyan

One of the original and particularly interesting aspects of Near-Eastern visual art are the floor mosaics, the pictorial programmes of which are closely related to both the coeval religious context and the Holy Scripture on which the symbolic perception of the images was based. During the first centuries of the Christian era, an unprecedented and rich cultural environment was created in Palestine, being conditioned by the historical, political and cultural circumstances as well as by the multi-ethnic and multi-confessional population of the region. The extant artistic monuments of the Holy Land belong to diverse communities. While possessing individual features, they also display important similarities, since they were based on, and had absorbed, the rich cultural heritage of the region. From this viewpoint, especially fruitful was the period from the fifth to the sixth century, i.e. the period when the art of floor mosaic was flourishing in various parts of the Near East, but particularly in Palestine. During this period both synagogues and churches of different creeds were decorated with such pavements, whose compositions demonstrate remarkably similar, not to say identical, features.

Our purpose here is to compare two floor mosaics of the era, in terms of their pictorial, iconographic and symbolic programmes: the pavement of the Armenian chapel in Jerusalem (see Figures 26.1 and 26.2) and that of the synagogue at Ma'on (Nirim) in Negev (see Figure 26.3). Although these pavements were commissioned and made by two diverse religious communities, the compositions of the mosaics as well as their iconographic programmes and principles of artistic approaches have much in common, as M. Avi-Yonah, S. Der Nersessian and B. Narkiss previously observed.[1] Our choice is conditioned by the following five considerations: a) both were made in the sixth century; b) both belong

---

1 M. Avi-Yonah, 'Mosaic Pavements in Palestine', *Quarterly of the Department of Antiquities in Palestine* (*QDAP*) II, Jerusalem, 1932, No. 132, pp. 163–181; S. Der Nersessian, *L'art armé-*

FIGURE 26.1 The 'Birds Mosaic' (western detail) in the Armenian chapel on the Mount of Olives, Jerusalem second half of the sixth century
PHOTO: CLAUDIA VENHORST

to group II of pavements, according to Michael Avi-Yonah's classification,[2] and are ascribed to the so-called Gaza school of mosaic; c) the two mosaics have the analogous composition of a vine scroll 'inhabited' by birds, animals and other symbolic figures; d) the details present in each (namely, the inscriptions and cultic iconography) show that they belong to two distinct ethno-religious communities; and e) the quality of workmanship of the pavements is very high, their artistic style approaching that of Hellenistic monuments.

1   The Armenian Chapel

The presence of Armenians in the Holy Land and their engagement in early Palestinian monasticism—both in Armenian and international monasteries—is attested since early Christian times by various textual sources[3] and by archæ-

---

nien, Paris, 1977, pp. 69–71, fig. 44, 45; B. Narkiss, 'Mosaic Pavements', in B. Narkiss, M. Stone and A. Sanjian (eds), *Armenian Art Treasures of Jerusalem*, Jerusalem, 1979, p. 24, fig. 39, 40; D. Amit and S. Wolff, 'An Armenian Monastic Complex at Morasha, Jerusalem', in H. Geva (ed.), *Ancient Jerusalem Revealed*, 2nd edn, Jerusalem, 2000, pp. 293–298.

2 M. Avi-Yonah, 'Une école de mosaïque à Gaza au sixième siècle', in id. (ed.), *Art in Ancient Palestine. Selected Studies*, Jerusalem, 1981, pp. 389–395; id., 'The Mosaic Floor of the Ma'on Synagogue', in *Eretz Israel* 6 (1960), pp. 86–93.

3 Cyril of Scythopolis, *Lives of the Monks of Palestine*, trans. R.M. Price, Kalamazoo, 1991, pp. 126–127, 220–242; J. Patrich, *Sabas, Leader of Palestinian Monasticism*, Washington, 1995, pp. 46–47, 250–251; L. Alishan, 'Anastas d'Arménie (VIIe siècle). Les LXX couvents arméniens de

FIGURE 26.2
The 'Birds Mosaic', Armenian chapel, Mount of Olives, Jerusalem, second half of the sixth century

ological evidence[4] (architectural remains, pavements, building and dedicatory inscriptions, epitaphs and pilgrims' graffiti).[5] Furthermore, according to the

---

Jérusalem', in *Archives de l'Orient Latin* vol. 2 (1884), pp. 395–399; Л.Х. Тер-Мкртичян, *Армянские источники о Палестине, V–XVIII вв.* [L.X. Ter-Mkrtichian, *Armenian Sources on Palestine, V–XVIII cc.*], Москва, 1991.

4 Evidence for the cultural presence of Armenians in the Holy Land is known in Jerusalem (on the Mount of Olives and on Mount Scopus), in Wadi el-Qilt, in Hammat Gadar, in Nazareth, in Negev and in Sinai. See the next note.

5 Մ.Աղավնունի, *Հայկական Հին վանքեր եւ եկեղեցիներ Սուրբ Երկրին մէջ. Ուսումնասիրութիւններ* [M.Aghavnuni, *Old Armenian Monasteries and Churches in the Holy Land*], Jerusalem, 1931; M.E. Stone, 'Holy Land Pilgrimage of Armenians before the Arab Conquest', *Revue Biblique* (RB) 93 (1986), pp. 93–110; A. Lindner, 'Christian Communities in Jerusalem', in J. Prawer (ed.), *The History of Jerusalem: Early Islamic Period (638–1099)*, Jerusalem, 1987, pp. 97–132 (in Hebrew); M.E. Stone, 'Armenian Inscriptions of the Fifth Century from Nazareth', *REArm* 22 (1990–1991), pp. 315–322; M.E. Stone, T. van Lint and J. Nazarian, 'Further Armenian Inscriptions from Nazareth', *REArm* 26 (1996–1997), pp. 321–337; M.E. Stone,

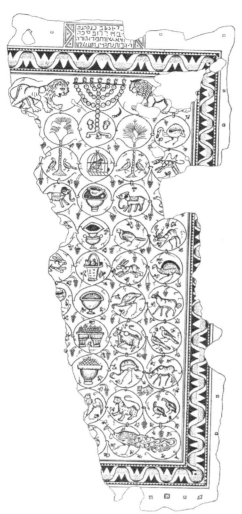

FIGURE 26.3
The pavement in the synagogue at Ma'on (near Nirim), Negev, first half of the 6th century

R. Ervine and N. Stone (ed.), *Armenians in Jerusalem and the Holy Land*, Louvain, 2002; M.E. Stone, 'Armenian Pilgrimage of the Mountain of Transfiguration and the Galilee', *St. Nersess Theological Review* 9 (2004), pp. 79–89, 268; M.E. Stone et al., 'New Armenian Inscription from a Byzantine Monastery on Mt. Scopus, Jerusalem', *Israel Exploration Journal* (*IEJ*) 61/2 (2011), pp. 230–235; M.E. Stone, D. Ben Ami and Y. Tchekhanovets, 'New Armenian Inscription from the City of David, Jerusalem', *Journal of the Society for Armenian Studies* (JSAS) 23 (2014), pp. 145–148; M.E. Stone, *Uncovering Ancient Footprints: Armenian Inscriptions and the Pilgrimage Routes of the Sinai*, Atlanta, 2017; Y. Tchekhanovets, *The Caucasian Archæology of the Holy Land: Armenian, Georgian and Albanian Communities between the Fourth and Eleventh Centuries CE*, Leiden–Boston, 2018, pp. 41–136.

famous list attributed to Anastas Vardapet (an Armenian archimandrite also known as Anastasios of Hierapolis), seventy Armenian monasteries existed in and around Jerusalem during the early Middle Ages.[6] Witnessing to this presence, and to the highly important Armenian heritage of the Holy Land, are the floor mosaics with Armenian inscriptions that surfaced in course of archæological excavations. The finest amongst them is the so-called 'Great Mosaic', or the 'Birds Mosaic', which was discovered in 1894 during construction works in the quarter of Musrara near the Damascus Gate, outside the walls of the Old City[7] (see Figure 26.4). According to the palæographical data and the formal analysis of the representation, the mosaic dates to the second half of the sixth century.[8] For a long time it was considered as the site of the monastery of St Polyeuctos, which is mentioned in Anastas *Vardapet's* List of the Armenian monasteries of Jerusalem (N8),[9] but this hypothesis is no longer accepted. In particular, after recent archæological discoveries it has become clear that a large monastery or a pilgrimage hospice stood on the territory of the quarter of Musrara. It could even be the largest monastic compound in Jerusalem, while an Arme-

---

6 A. Sanjian, 'Anastas Vardapet's List of Armenian Monasteries in Seventh-Century Jerusalem: A Critical Examination', *Le Muséon* 82 (1969), pp. 284–287; Պ.Չոբանյան, 'Անաստաս վարդապետի կազմած Երուսաղեմի հայկական վանքերի ցուցակի ժամանակի հարցի շուրջ' [P. Chobanyan, 'On the Date of the List of Armenian Monasteries in Jerusalem Compiled by Archimandrite Anastasius',], *Պատմաբանասիրական Հանդես* [Historical-Philological Journal], v. 1 (2011), pp. 27–46; Մատենագիրք Հայոց (Է դար), Ե [Armenian Classical Authors (7th century), v], Antelias, 2005, pp. 1273–1279; N. Garsoïan, 'Le témoignage d' Anastas *vardapet* sur les monastères arméniens de Jérusalem a la fin du VIᵉ siècle', in *Travaux et Memoirs* (Mélanges Gilbert Dagron), Paris, 2002, pp. 257–267; A. Terian, 'Rereading the Sixth-century List of Jerusalem Monasteries by Anastas Vardapet', in M.D. Findikyan, D. Galadza and A. Lossky (eds), *Sion, Mère des Eglises. Mélanges liturgiques offerts au Père Charles Athanase Renoux, Semaines d'Etudes Liturgiques Saint-Serge, S1*, Münster, 2016, pp. 267–282.

7 C. Clermont-Ganneau, *Archæological Researches in Palestine during the Years 1873–1874* vol. 1, London, 1899 (repr. Jerusalem, 1971); K. Owsepian, 'Mosaik mit armenischer Inschrift im Norden Jerusalems', *Zeitschrift des Deutschen Palästina-Vereins* 18 (1895), pp. 88–90; A.S. Murray, 'The Mosaic with Armenian Inscription from Near Damascus Gate, Jerusalem', *Palestine Exploration Fund Quarterly* (*PEFQ*), (1898), pp. 126–127; Narkiss, Stone and Sanjian, *Armenian Art Treasures*, p. 28. For an extensive bibliography, see: N. Stone, 'Birds from Heaven in Heavenly Jerusalem', in id., *Studies in Armenian Art: Collected Papers. Armenian Texts and Studies*, Leiden–Boston, pp. 236–246.

8 M.E. Stone, 'A Reassessment of the Bird and the Eustathius Mosaics', in M.E. Stone, R. Ervine and N. Stone (eds), *Armenians in Jerusalem and the Holy Land*, Louvain, 2002, p. 215; Avi-Yonah, 'Une école de mosaïque à Gaza au sixième siècle', p. 379; E. Kitzinger, *Byzantine Art in the Making*, London, 1977, p. 89.

9 K. Hintilian, *History of the Armenians in the Holy Land*, Jerusalem, 1976, p. 13; B. Narkiss, 'Mosaic Pavements', in B. Narkiss, M. Stone and A. Sanjian (eds), *Armenian Art Treasures of Jerusalem*, Jerusalem, 1979, p. 28.

FIGURE 26.4   The 'Birds Mosaic', Armenian chapel, Mount of Olives, Jerusalem
PHOTO: CLAUDIA VENHORST

nian chapel could be part of it.[10] Furthermore, in 1991 another fragment of floor mosaic, known as the 'Eustathius Mosaic'—also this one with an Armenian inscription—was found not far from the 'Birds Mosaic'. Originally it was located in the main compound.[11] The evidence of a multi-ethnic monastery on the territory of Musrara has been supported by further finds—namely, other Armenian burial and Greek dedicatory inscriptions at the same place.[12] These finds point to coexistence of Greek and Armenian monks in a single monastery.[13]

The 'Birds Mosaic'—the best-preserved example amongst the Armenian pavements of the Holy Land—has been allotted attention in various studies of Armenian and Early Christian Art,[14] yet its numerous aspects still require

---

10   Stone, 'A Reassessment', pp. 225–226; K. Britt, 'Identity Crisis? Armenian Monasticism in Early Byzantine Jerusalem', *Aramazd: Armenian Journal of Near Eastern Studies* (AJNES) VI /1 (2011), pp. 128–153; Tchekhanovets, *The Caucasian Archæology of the Holy Land*, pp. 76–93.
11   Stone, 'A Reassessment', pp. 203–219; Y. Tchekhanovets, *The Caucasian Archæology*, p. 93.
12   Մ.Սթոուն, 'Երուսաղեմի նորագյուտ հայերէն արձանագրությունները' [M.E. Stone, 'The New Armenian Inscriptions from Jerusalem'], *Պատմաբանասիրական հանդես* [*Historical-Philological Journal*], Հ. 1–2 (1993), pp. 15–24; M.E. Stone, 'The New Armenian Inscriptions from Jerusalem', in N. Awde (ed.), *Armenian Perspectives. 10th Anniversary Conference of the Association Internationale des Etudes Arméniennes* (AIEA), Surrey, 1997, pp. 263–268; Stone, 'A Reassessment', p. 209, fig. 8; D. Amit and S. Wolff, 'An Armenian Monastic Complex at Morasha, Jerusalem', in H. Geva (ed.), *Ancient Jerusalem Revealed*, 2nd edn, Jerusalem, 2000, p. 296; Tchekhanovets, *The Caucasian* Archæology, pp. 84–93.
13   Tchekhanovets, *The Caucasian Archæology*, p. 93.
14   Owsepian, 'Mosaik mit armenischer Inschrift', pp. 88–90; Avi-Yonah, 'Mosaic Pavements', pp. 69–71; З. Բյուրտեան, 'Խճանկարը (Mosaique) հայոց մոտ (կանխագույն շրջանին),

a multifaceted examination. Among such aspects are the questions of mutual influence and of collaboration between different ethnic and religious communities and workshops in early Christian Palestine.

The dimensions of the 'Birds Mosaic', dated to the second half of the sixth century, are ca. 6.30 m by 3.90 m. It bears the following inscription: 'ՎԱՍՆ ՅԻՇԱՏԱԿԻ ԵՒ ՓՐԿՈՒԹԵԱՆ ԱՄԵՆԱՅՆ ՀԱՅՈՑ ՋՈՐԱՑ ԱՆՈՒԱՆՍ ՏԵՐ ԳԻՏԷ'[15] / 'For the memory and salvation of all Armenians whose names the Lord knows'[16] (see Figure 26.6). Ch. Clermont-Ganneau and M.E. Stone stress that it is not unique.[17] Inscriptions with analogous formulæ in Hebrew, Aramaic and Greek are known from various floor mosaics of the time and are analogous to other inscriptions from the Holy Land, dated to the sixth century and to later periods.[18] Because of its Armenian inscription, most scholars considered the 'Birds Mosaic' to be a work of Armenian craftsmen, and only Nira Stone attributed it to the local, Palestinian school, both in its artistic style and iconography, regardless of the donor's origin.[19]

The mosaic is composed of a carpet-like rectangular field edged with a wide interlaced ornamental frame. Semantically, it starts from the bottom in the western part, where the vine scroll emerges out of an amphora with acanthus. Branching and coiling, the scroll forms forty-three circles evenly covering the

---

Երուսաղէմի խճանկարները. անոնց զիւտр' [Y. K'urtean, 'The Armenian Mosaics (Early period), the Jerusalem Mosaic'], *Բազմավէպ* [*Pazmaveb*] (1934), pp. 60, 193–199; Б.Н. Аракелян, Армянская мозаика IV–VII вв. [B.N. Arakelyan, 'Armenian mosaic in the IV–VII centuries'], *Вестник общественных наук* [*Herald of the Social Sciences*], 3 (1971), pp. 17– 25; Der Nersessian, *L'art armenien*, pp. 68–69; Narkiss, Stone and Sanjian, *Armenian Art Treasures*, p. 28; H. Evance, 'Nonclassical Sources for the Armenian Mosaic near the Damascus Gate in Jerusalem', in N. Garsoïan, R. Thomson and T. Mathews (eds), *East of Byzantium: Syria and Armenia in the Formative Period*, Washington, 1982, pp. 217–222; R. Hachlili, *Ancient Mosaic Pavements: Themes, Issues and Trends*, Leiden–Boston, 2009; R. Talgam, *Mosaics of Faith, Floors of Pagans, Jews, Samaritans, Christians and Muslims in the Holy Land*, Jerusalem–Pennsylvania, 2014; Tchekhanovets, *The Caucasian Archæology*, pp. 76– 84.

15   Stone, 'A Reassessment', p. 212.

16   *Corpus Inscriptionum Iudææ/Palestinæ* (*CIIP*) 1/2, fig. 812.1; Narkiss, Stone and Sanjian, *Armenian Art Treasures*, p. 147; Stone, 'A Reassessment', p. 208.

17   Clermont-Ganneau, *Archæological Researches*, p. 326; Stone, 'A Reassessment', p. 208. See also: C. Foss, 'Two Inscriptions Attributed to the Seventh Century AD', *Zeitschrift für Papyrologie und Epigraphik* 25 (1977), p. 283 n. 4.

18   While the inscription has been interpreted as 'in memory of unknown soldiers', according to Michael Stone it supposes a group of pilgrim donors or individuals who did not want their names to be written directly. See M. Stone, 'A Reassessment', p. 212.

19   N. Stone, 'Birds from Heaven in Heavenly Jerusalem', in M. Stone and A. Bereznyak (eds), *Studies in Armenian Art. Collected Papers*, Leiden, 2019, pp. 236–246.

FIGURE 26.5 The 'Birds Mosaic': central section
PHOTO: CLAUDIA VENHORST

surface of the composition, divided into five columns and nine rows. On both sides of the amphora and inside the vine scrolls various birds are depicted, such as a peacock, a cock, a pheasant, a duck, a pelican, a flamingo and an eagle (see Figure 26.5). All the 'inhabitants' of the vine are presented in heraldic order facing the central axis. Here we may recall that the other 'Birds Mosaic' with an Armenian inscription known in Jerusalem—in the so-called Chapel of Yakob—has a slightly different composition with the birds represented not within a vine scroll but inside ornamental medallions.[20]

Above the *tabula ansata*, which encloses the inscription on the Musrara mosaic, is a representation of a bowl surrounded by four birds and framed by a meander border (see Figure 26.6). Inside the main central vertical column are additional depictions: two fruit-filled baskets, a kantharos and a caged bird. All these images possess a very plastic and dynamic shape, being inspired by Hellenistic traditions (see Figure 26.2).

---

20 Narkiss, Stone and Sanjian, *Armenian Art Treasures*, pp. 24–25, fig. 36–38.

FIGURE 26.6 The 'Birds Mosaic': eastern fragment with an Armenian inscription
PHOTO: CLAUDIA VENHORST

2 The Synagogue at Ma'on (Nirim)

The Ma'on synagogue is situated in Negev, twenty km off Gaza (Kibeo el-Main). Its mosaic was discovered in 1957–1958.[21] Unfortunately, its left part is damaged (see Figure 26.3). The erection of the synagogue is dated to the second half of the fifth or to the early sixth century, while its decorative floor is dated to the first half of the sixth century (Avi-Yonah dated it to 538),[22] i.e. slightly earlier than the Armenian 'Birds Mosaic' from Musrara. The size of the pavement is ca. 8.9 m by 4.95 m. The pavement composition, unlike the Armenian one, is oriented from south to north, as the Torah niche is on the northern wall facing Jerusalem. The following Aramaic inscription appears inside the *tabula ansata*:[23]

---

21 S. Levi, 'The Ancient Synagogue at Ma'on (Nirim)', *Louis M. Rabinowitz Fund Bulletin* III, pp. 6–13: M. Avi-Yonah, 'The Mosaic Pavement of Ma'on (Nirim)', *Louis M. Rabinowitz Fund Bulletin* III, pp. 25–35; D. Barag, 'Ma'on Nirim', in E. Stern (ed.), *The New Encyclopedia of Archeological Excavations in the Holy Land*, Jerusalem, 1993, pp. 944–946.

22 O. Yogev, 'The Synagogue at Ma'on—New Discoveries', *Eretz Israel* 19 (1987), pp. 208–215 (in Hebrew); R. Hachlili, *Ancient Synagogues—Archæology and Art: New Discoveries and Current Research*, Leiden–Boston, 2013, p. 600.

23 The inscription on the Ma'on pavement was probably made by a mosaicist who did not master Aramaic perfectly. It is surmised, therefore, that he was not a Jew. See: Hachlili,

THE GARDENS OF EDEN

599

1. ‏[ד][כ]'ר]רין לטב כל קהלה‏ / [Reme]mbered for good be the whole congregation—

2. ‏[די]עבדו הדן פספה‏ / [those who ha]ve laboured on this mosaic,

3. ‏[ו]כן דאיש]'ן ותמה [ו]'יהודה‏ / and [so also] Daisin and Thoma [and] Judah

4. ‏דיהבו תג תרי דינרין‏ / who have donated the sum of two denarii.[24]

The mosaic carpet of the synagogue is engirdled with twisting acanthus. As in the Armenian mosaic, also here the composition starts at the bottom segment where two large peacocks are flanking a crater in the middle, which is partly damaged (see Figure 26.8). Also here a vine scroll flows out of an amphora and spreads to form fifty-five medallions distributed across five vertical and eleven horizontal rows.[25] If birds are dominant in the Armenian mosaic, in the Maʿon synagogue both birds and animals are represented in equal quantity. The birds are nearly all of the same kind, and among the animals are a bull, a deer, a tiger, a rabbit and an elephant. In the middle row, as in the Armenian mosaic, are depicted three baskets and three bowls as well as a caged bird.[26] The Maʿon artist followed Hellenistic prototypes very closely and all of the animals represented there appear in movement.

The most important segment of the synagogue mosaic, which also indicates its religious context, are the Menorah with a *lulav* (the frond of a date palm tree), a *shofar* (ritual horn) and *etrogs* (fragrant citrus fruit) surrounding it, as well as the images of two lions and two palm-trees[27] (see Figures 26.7 and 26.8).

3   Symbolism of the Mosaics

The comparison of these mosaics raises questions regarding the meaning of the compositions and the grounds for their similarity. It should be mentioned that not all the scholars accept the existence of symbolic meaning of the pavement compositions. Thus, C. Dauphin, R. Hachlili, K. Dunbabin and R. Talgam uphold the decorative function of the compositions, noting that the iconogra-

---

Ancient Mosaic Pavements, p. 233; Л. Чаковская, Воплощённая память о храме: художественный мир синагог Святой Земли III–VI вв. н.э. [L. Chakovskaya, The Memory of the Temple Embodied: the Artistic Realm in the Synagogues of Holy Land in the Third-Fourth Centuries A.D.], Moscow, 2011, p. 206.

24   S. Yevin, 'Maon Inscription', *Louis M. Rabinowitz Fund Bulletin III*, p. 36; J. Naveh, *On Stone and Mosaic: inscriptions from Ancient Synagogues*, Jerusalem, 1978, pp. 92–93 (in Hebrew).

25   Hachlili, *Ancient Mosaic Pavements*, pp. 116–122.

26   Ibid.

27   Avi-Yonah, 'The Mosaic Pavement of Maʿon (Nirim)', pp. 26–27; Hachlili, *Ancient Mosaic Pavements*, pp. 116–122.

FIGURE 26.7　Fragment of the pavement in the Ma'on synagogue

phy of the vine scroll derives from Hellenistic and Roman arts and has been used in different secular buildings as well.[28]

Indeed, the motif and the iconography of vine scroll had a long prehistory. But the question that remains unanswered is why there was a need to return to this motif in a radically new political context and, what is more, to fill it with figures saturated with new religious associations. Indeed, close to the beginning of the period under examination is the date of the imperial decree against painting human figures and the cross on pavements: 427 AD. Once that prohibition had been lifted, a new period of the art of floor mosaic could commence.

28　C. Dauphin, 'Symbolic or Decorative? The Inhabited Scroll as a Means of Studying Some Early Byzantine Mentalities', *Byzantion* 48 (1979), pp. 10–34; K. Dunbabin, *The Mosaics of Roman North Africa, Studies in Iconography and Patronage*, Oxford, 1978, pp. 230–233; R. Talgam, 'Similarity and Differences between Synagogues and Churches Mosaics in Palestine during the Byzantine and Umayyad Periods', in L.I. Levine and Z. Weiss (eds), *From Dura to Sepphoris: Studies in Jewish Art and Society in Late Antiquity*, Rhode Island, 2000, pp. 95–98; Hachlili, *Ancient Synagogues*, pp. 256–273.

FIGURE 26.8   Fragment of the pavement in the Ma'on synagogue

This period of flourishing was only to be interrupted in the late seventh century, after the Umayyad conquests.

One of the most important forms of early Christian art, the floor mosaics mark the beginning of a new cultural era by developing a new symbolic language of visual arts. Many scholars, such as the aforementioned Avi-Yonah, as well as S.J. Saller, B. Bagatti, E. Goodenough, A. Grabar, E. Kitzinger and H. Maguire,[29] accept the symbolic character of the floor mosaic compositions. On the evidence of Psalms (80:9–16), the books of the prophets, such as Isaiah (5:1–17) and Hosea (10:1), the Gospel of Matthew (21:33–43), apocrypha and Talmud, where the faithful are described as the vineyard of the Lord, they interpret these compositions as the Garden of Eden, both in the Jewish and the Christian cases. At the same time, the grape itself becomes the symbol of Israel and

---

29   S.J. Saller and B. Bagatti, 'The Town of Nebo (Kirbet el-Mekhayyat)', *Publications of the Studium Biblicum Franciscanum* 7, Jerusalem, 1949, pp. 94–98; E. Goodenough, *Jewish Symbols in the Greco-Roman Period*, abridged edition, Ed. J. Neusner, Princeton, 1988; A. Grabar, *Christian Iconography, a Study of its Origins*, New York, 1968, pp. 33–34; E. Kitzinger, *Mosaïques byzantines israéliennes*, Paris, 1965, pp. 5–24; H. Maguire, *Earth and Ocean. The Terrestrial World in Early Byzantine Art*, London, 1987, pp. 9–10, 21–24.

of the Kingdom of God. A specifically Christian context may furthermore be found in the Gospel of John (John, 15:1–7) where Christ is described as the true vine.

The symbolic representation of the Garden of Eden is supplemented by a palm tree, as in the Ma'on mosaic (see Figure 26.7). For both the Jews and the Christians, the palm was the symbol of the Promised, or the Holy land, as well as of the trees of the heavenly Garden. It was also considered to be the symbol of saints (Ps. 91:13).

In both mosaics the vine scroll is complemented by birds, animals and other figures. The birds are generally endowed with spiritual meaning in Judaism and Christianity. Christian authors interpreted them as the souls of the believers. Furthermore, the birds and the animals are seen as the 'inhabitants' of the Heavenly Garden, while according to the *Physiologus* certain kinds of birds, such as the peacock and the eagle, symbolize immortality and resurrection.[30]

The semantic emphasis in the central vertical row, where baskets, bowls, an eagle and a bird in cage[31] are presented, is characteristic of the above-mentioned group II of mosaics [Schs. 1 and 2]. All of these images possess symbolic meanings based on Biblical and philosophical texts. Thus, according to Grabar and Maguire, the motif of the birdcage is based on the Neoplatonic idea of the soul (in our case, of a holy man or the donor) enclosed in a body, like bird in cage.[32]

The basket full of ripe fruits, as well as the ripe clusters of grapes, also belong to the imagery of the Garden of Eden, as an ideal garden is usually represented in the season when the fruits are ripe.[33] Additionally, in Deuteronomy 26:2–4 we find a requirement to grant the first fruits to the priest, while the Mishnah (*Sukkah* 1:3; 3:8) describes the placement of seven species of fruits in woven bas-

---

30 Aurelius Augustinus, *De civitate Dei*, lib. XXI, cap. 4; Goodenough, *Jewish Symbols* vol. VIII, pp. 52–58; Maguire, *Earth and Ocean*, p. 65; G. Muradyan, *Physiologus: The Greek and Armenian Versions with a study of Translation Technique*, Leuven–Dudley, 2005, pp. 85–140, 163.

31 The 'bird-in-cage' is one of the common motifs in the mosaics of the Groups I and II to which the Ma'on mosaic and the Armenian 'Birds Mosaic' belong.

32 A. Grabar, 'Un thème de l'iconographie chrétienne: l'oiseau dans la cage', *Cahiers Archéologiques* XVI (1966), pp. 9–16; Ø. Hjort, 'L'oiseau dans la cage: exemples médiévaux a Rome', *Cahiers Archéologiques*, XVIII (1968), pp. 21–31; Maguire, *Earth and Ocean*, p. 65.

33 H. Petrosyan, 'Symbols of Armenian Identity: The World as a Garden', in L. Abrahamyan and N. Sweez (eds), *Armenian Folk Arts, Culture and Identity*, Bloomington–Indianapolis, 2001, pp. 25–32: Հ. Պետրոսյան, 'Հայ միջնադարյան պատկերացումներն իդեալական կենսատարածքի եւ կենսընթացի մասին. Աշխարհը որպես այգի' [H. Petrosyan, 'The Medieval Armenian Perceptions of the Ideal World and Space: World as a Garden'], *Հանդէս Ամսօրեայ [Handes Amsorya]* (2002), pp. 411–440.

THE GARDENS OF EDEN

603

kets.[34] The symbolic meaning ascribed to bowls and other vessels (amphora, kantharos) is connected with the idea of the source of faith and life, being also associated with the rite of Baptism in Christianity.[35]

The depiction of the Heavenly Garden, both in Jewish and Christian contexts, also possesses an eschatological significance. This is expressed on the synagogue floors by the image of a lion—or a lion and a bull together, as in the Ma'on mosaic—since these animals are among the symbols of Paradise (see Figure 26.8).[36] Moreover, they symbolize the two Messiahs—one from the tribe of Efraim and the other from the tribe of Judah, about which the Qumran Scrolls (second century BC) and the Babylonian Talmud (sixth century AD) speak. Already in the Bible the lion symbolizes the tribe of Judah (Gen. 49:9–12), especially the Judah who will dwell in the grapevine (Gen. 49:11), whereas in 3 Ezra (3Ez. 12:31–32), the lion is identified with the Messiah. These associations exercised a strong influence on the formation of Christian symbolic language, and particularly iconography, as the images of lions and bulls on medieval monuments, including Armenian sculptures, attest.[37] So, on the floor mosaics of the fifth–sixth centuries, the imagery of the Garden of Eden and of the Messianic peace possess common features, both in their semantics and their iconography.

One can thus state that during the fifth and the sixth century, the symbolic language of visual arts was employed in order to communicate the ideas of the other-worldly, which directly or indirectly had been expressed in religious texts. This allowed Sergei Averintsev to assert that an image can express as much as a text,[38] the most spectacular manifestation of which can be found in the iconographic programmes of the floor mosaics in the Holy Land.

---

34   Z. Weiss, 'The Sepphoris Synagogue Mosaic and the Role of Talmud Literature in Its Iconographical Study', in L.I. Levine and Z. Weiss (eds), *From Dura to Sepphoris: Studies in Jewish Art and Society in Late Antiquity*, Rhode Island, 2000, p. 24.

35   Ժ.-Պ. Մահէ, 'Սիրամարգն ու սկահակը հայկական ավետարանների խորանում' [J.-P. Mahé, 'The Peacock and the Goblet in the Concordances of Armenian Gospels'], *Պատմաբանասիրական հանդես* [*Historical-Philological Journal*] 1 (1986), pp. 106–112.

36   M. Piccirillo, *The Mosaics of Jordan*, Amman, 1993, p. 128.

37   We may recall numerous reliefs on medieval Armenian churches and the corresponding images in the illuminated Armenian manuscripts. It is telling that for the Bagratid princely family (ruling from the 9th to the 11th century), who considered themselves offspring of the Biblical king David and during whose rule eschatological expectations were vivid, the main symbolic image was a lion. This image was particularly popular in the coeval Armenian reliefs.

38   С.С.Аверинцев, 'Судьбы европейской культурной традиции в эпоху перехода от Античности к Средневековью' [S.S. Averintsev, 'The Fate of the European Cultural Tradition in the Era of the Transition from Antiquity to the Middle Ages'], in В. Карпушин (ред.), *Из истории культуры Средних веков и Возрождения* [in V. Karpushin

There is no doubt that both written and oral sources played a significant role in the formation of Jewish and Christian iconographic languages, especially in the former. At the same time, Jewish visual art, along with Hellenistic arts, played an important role in the shaping of Christian iconography. First Goodenough, then Weitzmann and Grabar, observed that by the second and the third century Jews had already developed a pictorial art, which had originated in and around the land of Israel and elsewhere in the Near East, especially in Hellenised Jewish communities.[39] This was first demonstrated by the discovery of frescoes in the synagogue of Dura-Europos and of the pavements in Sepphoris (Zippori). Initially, this opinion was not supported widely. Later, K. Weitzmann discussed Jewish illustrated manuscripts, paying attention to the fact that not only texts but also Jewish miniatures became important sources for the development of Christian iconography.[40] This can be demonstrated by the fact that some Christian miniatures contain scenes that are not described in the Christian Canon of the Bible but are present in Midrashim and in Aggadah, e.g. the Ashburnham Pentateuch (Ms. Lat. 2334, BN, Paris, 6th–7th cc.), the Cotton Genesis (Ms. Cotton Otho B VI, 5th–6th cc.) and the Vienna Genesis (cod. Theol. Gr. 31, Vienna, 6th c.). As a consequence, Jewish and Christian artistic traditions shared common features in the process of their formation, almost becoming, during a short period at the beginning of the Christian era, an organic cultural phenomenon.

4 The Artists and the Craftsmen

The next important issue concerning the monuments under discussion is that of the artists and the craftsmen who worked in the Holy Land. We know of about twenty mosaics possessing features similar to those of the Armenian

---

(ed.), *From the History of the Culture of the Middle Ages and the Renaissance*], Москва, 1976, pp. 17–64.

39   Goodenough, *Jewish Symbols* vol. XII, pp. 3–21; A. Grabar, 'Recherches sur les sources juives de l' art paléochrétien, II', *Cahiers Archéologiques* vol. 12 (1962), pp. 115–152; K. Weitzman, 'The Question of the Influence of Jewish Pictorial Sources on Old Testament Illustration', in id., *Studies in Classical and Byzantine Manuscript Illumination*, Chicago, 1970, pp. 76–110; K. Weitzman (ed.), *Age of Spirituality: Late antique and early Christian art*, New York, 1979, pp. 412–417; K. Weitzmann and H.L. Kessler, *The Frescoes of the Dura Synagogue and Christian Art*, Washington, 1990.

40   K. Weitzman, 'The Question of the Influence of Jewish Pictorial Sources on Old Testament Illustration', in id., *Studies in Classical and Byzantine Manuscript Illumination*, Chicago, 1970, pp. 76–110.

THE GARDENS OF EDEN   605

'Birds Mosaic' and the Maʿon mosaic. The iconographic, stylistic and technical similarities have allowed scholars to classify these as a single group (the
so-called group II, according to Avi-Yonah). Among the works belonging to
this group are the pavements in the synagogue at Gaza (508–509) and in the
churches at Shellal (561–562), Beʾer Shemʿa (St Stephan's church, mid 6th c.)
and Beth Sheʾan (late 6th c.).

In relation to the 'Birds Mosaic' we should first observe that, apart from the
Armenian inscription, no other feature indicates that it is a work of Armenian
craftsmen. Helen Evans's attempts to explain the images of birds by means
of Armenian theological heritage and the possible identification of Armenian
fauna species[41] were rightly refuted by Nira and Michael Stone.[42] It should be
borne in mind that various 'Birds Mosaics' extant in the Holy Land are certainly not Armenian, such as those preserved in the churches in Ein Karem,
in Beit Guvrin, in Kyria Maria and in the synagogues in Ein Gedi and in Khirbet
Susiya, all dating to the same century. Therefore, the motif of birds cannot be
taken for evidence of the mosaic's Armenian origin. As for the synagogue pavements, despite the Jewish religious objects in the synagogue at Maʿon (Nirim),
the examination of the Aramaic inscription provided scholars with every reason to surmise the artists' non-Jewish origin.[43]

The scholars agree that mosaic workshops in the Holy Land employed craftsmen and artists of different origins—Arameans, Jews, Syrians, Greeks[44] and,
admittedly, also the Armenians who lived there from early Christian times.
Armenians could be members of the same workshops, could be inspired by
the same sacred texts and could use the same pattern books[45] for designing
the mosaic compositions. They could work within multi-ethnic workshops of
Palestine (we also know of itinerant groups of artists active there) at the commission of diverse religious communities. The result of this co-operation were
the three main international centres of mosaic workshops in Palestine, two of
which—in Jerusalem and in Gaza—were located along the same main route
Jerusalem–Eleutheropolis–Gaza, which also acted as a pilgrimage route and
along which the monuments under examination stood. These workshops contributed to the formation of a new iconographical canon in the visual arts.

---

41   Evans, 'Nonclassical Sources', p. 220.
42   Stone, 'A Reassessment', p. 212, n. 21.
43   Hachlili, *Ancient Synagogues*, p. 518.
44   Ibid., p. 508.
45   C.M. Dauphin, 'Byzantine Pattern Books and 'Inhabited Scroll' Mosaics', *Art History* vol. 4
      (1978), pp. 401–413; R. Hachlili, *Ancient Jewish Art and Archæology in the Land of Israel*,
      Leiden, 1988, p. 395.

This syncretistic artistic milieu left a significant mark on the coeval culture, whose echoes can also be perceived in the artistic traditions of later centuries. Thus, the universal image of the Garden of Eden, with its multi-layered symbolism, is reflected in the art of various cultures. Its vivid example can be found in the depiction of grapevine on the plates and vessels of the sixth and seventh centuries in the Sasanian and post-Sasanian art.[46] Such imagery might have been conveyed to diverse cultures precisely via Palestine, where the image of the Heavenly Garden had taken roots; Palestinian models must also have been inherited in early Islamic art. We may especially think of the famous mosaics in the Dome of Rock in Jerusalem (end of the seventh century) and in the Great Mosque of Damascus (beginning of the eighth century), made by the same mixed workshop of artists and preserving the distinctive iconographic traditions of the region.[47] Numerous depictions of inhabited vine scrolls are also to be found in the decoration of Canon Tables in early Christian manuscripts, especially in Byzantine and Armenian Gospels. Because earlier examples of illuminated manuscripts have seldom survived, such as those from the sixth–seventh centuries, the floor mosaics have a particularly important value for the study of manuscript illumination.

5   From the Holy Land to Armenia

The active engagement of Armenians in the cultural life of the Holy Land made a significant contribution to the development of Armenian arts, and particularly iconography, in their historical homeland. The inhabited vine scroll, owing to its highly evocative nature and its underlying symbolism, became one of the beloved and the widely spread motifs in Medieval Armenian art, visible especially in sculpture decorations. Such decorations have been preserved better than the book illuminations or the wall paintings of the early Christian times. The following early examples can be cited: the church in Kasax (fifth–sixth centuries), the church in Tekor (480s, destroyed), the Ciranawor

---

46   P. Harper, *The Royal Hunter. Art of the Sasanian Empire*, New York, 1978, pp. 71–73, 117, fig. 241; Л.Микаелян, 'Тема сбора винограда в изобразительной традиции поздней античности, раннего христианства и в искусстве Сасанидского Ирана' [L. Mikaelyan, 'The Theme of Vintage in the Pictorial Traditions of Late Antiquity, Early Christianity, and the Art of Sasanian Iran'], *Actual Problems of Theory and History of Art* vol. VI, St Petersburg, 2016, pp. 124–132.

47   R. Ettinghausen, O. Grabar and M. Jenkins-Madina, *Islamic Art and Architecture 650–1250*, New Haven, 2001, pp. 207–209; F.B. Flood, *The Great Mosque of Damascus. Studies on the Making of an Ummayyad Visual Culture*, Leiden–Boston–Köln, 2001, pp. 15–30.

THE GARDENS OF EDEN   607

church in Aštarak (fifth–sixth centuries) and the fragment of a lintel from the
church in Duin.[48] But the most vivid expression of this motif can be found in
the church of the Vigilant Heavenly Powers (Zuartnoć; 652 AD) near Ējmiacin
and the church of the Holy Cross of Ałtamar (915–921). In the church of Zuartnoć the idea of Heavenly Jerusalem is expressed firstly in its architectural
conception—the multi-storied, tower-like structure.[49] It is supplemented with
the sculptural belt indicating the Heavenly Garden, above the arches of the first
storey, with the depictions of vine scrolls and pomegranate trees inhabited by
animal (notably, a bear—only one such image has survived in Armenia, but
more must have existed) and human figures (only eleven figures have survived
from presumably thirty-two).[50] (see Figure 26.9.)

     As for the church of the Holy Cross on the island of Ałtamar, with its glori-
ous belt of a vine scroll inhabited by various animals, birds and human figures
(see Figure 26.10),[51] it reveals a direct quotation of the iconographical programme of the Palestinian floor mosaics. Noteworthy is the fact that various
images on the 'heavenly' belt of the church of Ałtamar have their direct parallels, or prototypes, in floor mosaics of the Near East, and in particular: the
scene of vintage representing people carrying baskets with ripe fruits, on its
north façade (cf. the monastery of Lady Mary, Beth She'an, 567–569, Jerusalem;
the church of Sts Lot and Procopius, Mukhayyat, Mt. Nebo, ca. 557, Jordan); the
treading of grapes, on the south façade (cf. the El-Hammam funerary chapel
at Beth She'an, 6th c., Israel; the church of Sts Lot and Procopius, Mukhayyat,
Mt. Nebo, ca. 557, Jordan); the hunter spearing and fighting a bear, on the north
and south façades (cf. the church of St Elijah at Kissufim, 576, Jerusalem; the
Old Diakonikon, Mt. Nebo, 530), the hare eating grapes, on the north façade

---

48   J.-M. Thierry and P. Donabédian, *Les arts arméniens*, Paris, 1987, fig. 197, 198, 213; M. Асра-
      тян, *Армянская архитектура раннего христианства* [M. Hasratyan, *Early Christian
      Architecture of Armenia*], Москва, 2000, pp. 22–23, fig. 4a, 4б, 5a, 5б.

49   A. Kazaryan, *Church architecture of the 7th century in Transcaucasian countries. Formation
      and development of the tradition* vol. II, Moscow, 2012, pp. 492–506, fig. 1017–1018, 1021, 1101–
      1103 (in Russian); N. Garibian de Vartavan, *La Jérusalem Nouvelle et les premiers sanctuaries
      chrétiens de l'Arménie*, Yerevan, 2009; C. Maranci, *Vigilant Powers: Three Churches of Early
      Medieval Armenia*, Turnhout, 2015, pp. 113–200.

50   Թ. Թորամանյան, *Նյութեր Հայկական ճարտարապետության պատմության* [T. Toro-
      manyan, *Materials for the Study of Armenian Architecture*], Հ. 1, Երեւան, 1942, fig. 33;
      Զ. Հակոբյան, 'Զվարթնոցի խորհրդաբանական կերպարը (Պատկերաբանդակների
      մեկնաբանման Հարցի շուրջ)' [Z. Hakobyan, 'The Symbolic Image of Zvartnots (To the
      question of interpretation)'], *Էջմիածին* [*Ējmiacin*] 6 (2006), pp. 76–85.

51   S. Der Nersessian, *Aght'amar. Church of the Holy Cross*, Harvard University Press 1965,
      fig. 13–17, 23, 31, 37–41, 53–55.

FIGURE 26.9   Decorative frieze of the church of the Vigilant Heavenly Powers (Zuartnoć) near Ējmiacin, 652 CE (detail)

FIGURE 26.10   The wine frieze engirdling the Church of the Holy Cross, the island of Ałtamar, Lake Van, 915–921 CE, detail
PHOTO: AUTHOR

(cf. the Petra church chapel, 550, Israel; the El-Hammam funerary chapel at Beth She'an, 6th c., Israel[52]).[53]

As for the Jewish visual arts, under new political circumstances, following the Umayyad conquests in the first half of the seventh century, when the uni-

---

52 Cf. И.А. Орбели, 'Памятники армянского искусства на острове Ахтамар' [I.A. Orbeli, 'The Monuments of Armenian Art on Aghtamar Island'], in id., *Избранные труды* [id., *Selected Papers*] Москва, 1963, таб. XX, XXXVI, XLIII, рис. 1; Piccirillo, *The Mosaics of Jordan*, fig. 36, 37, 204, 205; R. Cohen, 'The Marvelous Mosaics of Kissufim', *Biblical Archæology Review*, VI-1 (1980), pp. 16–23.

53 As the iconographic compositions mentioned are numerous, their examination could become a topic of its own.

THE GARDENS OF EDEN

fied cultural environment of the Mediterranean and the Near East had been broken, Jewish arts lost their role as a point of departure and as a mediator of ancient pictorial motifs for Christian culture. Nevertheless, their mark on Christian visual arts has endured.

Postscript: Border-Crossing Texts

Hartmut Leppin

1 The Allure of the Hidden

The success of Dan Brown's *Da Vinci Code* (and other thrillers of its kind) points to a particular tendency in modern perceptions of ancient Christianity: there is a strong interest in apocryphal texts. More specifically, the idea that dark forces, namely church authorities, concealed important facts of early Christian history is exceedingly popular. These accounts usually feature powerful women silenced by dominant men, sacred books of truth hidden away by influential functionaries and generous doctrines eliminated by oppressive bishops. The idea that well-kept secrets are being purposefully concealed by the institutions of the church is pervasive: if they were unveiled, a much more friendly, humane, female and equitable form of Christianity would come into light. Of course, most of these narrations are mere phantasies that serve commercial interests—texts that have the aura of uncovering secrets sell.

Despite their misinterpretation in popular culture, however, apocryphal texts are also of great interest to scholars from various disciplines. In fact, the idea that important, so far hidden concepts have survived in non-canonical Christian texts fascinated many specialists in the field of the history of Christianity. There is no doubt that apocryphal texts preserve ideas, concepts and narratives that were—at a certain point in time—as important as the texts we now consider Scripture. Therefore, not only theologians, but also historians, linguists, scholars of Judaism and art historians have dealt with these texts, to name but a few disciplines represented at the Bad Homburg conference. From the historian's perspective, apocryphal texts are just as valuable as canonical ones, even if theologians may disagree vehemently as to their relevance.

No serious scholar, however—theologian or otherwise—would argue anymore that the history of Christianity was always destined to develop into the church organisations we see today. This awareness is one of the reasons why there is a growing interest in Christian texts outside the canon, which in turn leads to an ever-increasing body of research devoted to the subject.

Nonetheless, the concept of apocryphal texts is a contentious one in itself. There is no such thing as an inherently apocryphal text. All writings discussed in this volume were certainly regarded as sacred and important by their readerships, groups which can in some cases be defined as textual communities. Typically, the audiences believed that apostles or other holy people had authored

© HARTMUT LEPPIN, 2021 | DOI:10.1163/9789004445925_029

POSTSCRIPT: BORDER-CROSSING TEXTS   611

these texts; they would not have found an audience had they been considered recent inventions. In spite of this, influential authorities regarded them as non-canonical, some bishops or councils even condemned certain writings. Other authorities, however, would accept the very same texts. Still other texts were neither officially recognised nor suppressed and this grey area facilitated their continued use in religious practice. The borders between canonical and non-canonical texts could be blurred (Sabine and Dieter Fahl). On that account, German scholars often prefer terms such as *apokryph gewordene Evangelien* (gospels that have become apocryphal).[1]

This goes to show that apocryphal texts are not mere folklore or residue. Rather, they are a testament to the plurality of Christianities as well as to the historical and metaphysical issues raised by the process of Christianization (Igor Dorfmann-Lazarev). Apocryphal texts gave answers to pertinent theological questions or filled gaps in the narratives on important persons from the earliest generations of Christians and including Jesus himself, whose childhood was of great interest to these communities. More often than not, it was the theological and narrative questions of certain communities, rather than official ecclesiastical support, which was the driving force in the preservation of apocryphal texts.

Several apocryphal texts were extremely popular and easy to understand. But a large group of them, the so-called esoteric texts, were not intended for a broad audience. The label 'esoteric' can either refer to the claim that only few people were able to understand these writings properly or to the fact that they were exclusive to certain groups. Oftentimes, the readers were anxious not to divulge their exclusive knowledge of these texts. Yet, over the course of history, many did become known to the general public to a lesser or higher degree. Secrecy was obviously not kept consistently in this world. Accordingly, the concept of esoteric texts remains fluid.

Generally speaking, various types of apocryphal texts continued to be rewritten and adapted, thus assuming the character of living texts (David Hamidović). This means that when we study texts in the forms in which they have been transmitted and are edited nowadays, their different layers of tradition cannot be distinguished easily. But precisely this work is what makes it possible for us to retrace a complex history of Christian practices and concepts, which are often not attested elsewhere. Several apocryphal texts have a Jewish layer more or less adapted to Christian needs. Therefore, apocryphal texts provide insights into the partings and the crossings of the ways of Christians and Jews.

---

1   E.g. D. Lührmann, *Fragmente apokryph gewordener Evangelien: in griechischer und lateinischer Sprache*, Marburg, 2000.

In addition to this, apocryphal texts tended to get translated quite frequently. Texts discussed in Bad Homburg were written in Hebrew, Greek, Latin, Syriac, Coptic, Ethiopian, Persian, Armenian, Georgian, Arabic, and Old Slavonic to name just a few. Thus, the polyphony of ancient Christianities can be heard in many languages that are connected by the common reference to traditions that were traced back to Jesus Christ—their great differences notwithstanding.

Finally, apocryphal texts had a great impact on visual arts. The *Protevangelium Iacobi* found a large audience and was the main source of medieval depictions of the nativity in spite of its absence from the biblical canon. Generally speaking, early Christian images were in mutual exchange with texts and do not simply illustrate them. Thus, they might even be called 'visual apocrypha' (Felicity Harley). Even the decoration of the Church of Nativity in Bethlehem from the time of the crusaders refers back to esoteric texts, which allowed the builders to address a wide range of Christian groups. Besides, motives such as vine scrolls appealed to both Jewish and Christian recipients (Zaruhi Hakobyan).

As these examples show, the study of apocryphal texts is a genuinely transcultural and transdisciplinary field. But it is also a field of basic research: in many cases the relation between the sources is unclear, the dates and the origins remaining open to discussion and thus controversial. Maria V. Korogodina and Basil Lourié remind us that even for important works modern editions are still missing.

Given the nature of the apocryphal texts, it is not easy to break them down to a common denominator. In this postscript, I would like to highlight two aspects that connect the seemingly diverse group papers found in this volume: the tension between universalism and secrecy in esoteric texts, and the bordercrossing character of apocryphal writings. Therefore I will not give an abstract of every single contribution—which can be found in the introduction—but emphasize certain points from them, even if they fall outside the text's main argument. Finally, I will discuss questions which remain open.

2   Between Universalism and Secrecy

From early on, Christians claimed that Jesus had exhorted his disciples to *teach all nations* (Mt 28.19). In that sense Christianity was understood as a universal religion, explicitly opposed to esoteric knowledge. Christians who took this admonishment literally, felt the obligation to share what they perceived as their good message with everybody everywhere. Baptism, which indicated the entrance into the Christian community was—in principle at least—open to

POSTSCRIPT: BORDER-CROSSING TEXTS

everybody: *There is neither Jew nor Greek, there is neither bond nor free, there is neither male nor female: for ye are all one in Christ Jesus* (Gal 3.28). But baptism also limited the universality of Christian practice: non-baptized people were excluded from crucial practices such as receiving the Eucharist. Thus, a certain degree of secrecy was inherent to Christianity early on, even if the religion was, in principle, open to everyone.

Despite this supposed openness, Christians must have seemed elusive to many contemporaries: in contrast to most classical cults, Christian religious service was not performed before altars under open sky, but under a roof, usually in private houses. In addition, the political pressure exerted on Christians by local and imperial authorities certainly made it more difficult for Christians to become visible. There were times (and places) when Christians had to meet covertly, although they also saw decades of peaceful coexistence.

It should therefore not be surprising that observers such as the Alexandrian philosopher Celsus perceived Christians as secretive (Orig., C. Cels. 1.7). Additionally, gnostic groups, many of whom used Christian semantics, established an esoteric hierarchy, distinguishing various groups according to their knowledge, which was imparted only to people who had proven themselves worthy of it (Yishai Kiel).

As Origen himself underlines in the passage quoted above, secret cults were by no means foreign to the ancient world: although most rituals did take place in public and were thus very visible, numerous mystery cults existed at the same time, which admitted only the initiated who had taken vows of secrecy. Some Christians and non-Christians alike saw similarities between Christian practices and the practices of other mystery cults, as Jan Bremmer und Yishai Kiel make clear.

All of this is to say that, even in cases where it was perceived as an esoteric cult, this aspect did by no means make it unique in the context of ancient circum-Mediterranean cultures. Yet, the tension between the claim of universality and secrecy remained an issue in Christian history for Christians and non-Christians alike. While a high number of esoteric texts began to be circulated among Christians, defining certain textual communities, most Christians still expected their teaching to be accessible to everybody of good will.

To talk of 'studying the secret Christian texts of antiquity' today may sound paradoxical. After all, the groups that used them pretended to keep them strictly among themselves. But if this esotericism had prevailed consistently, these texts would not have been preserved. While some texts, however, such as the group from Nag Hammadi, were hidden away by their readers, to be detected only centuries later, nonetheless many seemingly esoteric texts survived precisely because they became known to an ever-wider audience, even being transmitted between linguistic communities and generations. Still, it was likely their secret character that heightened their reputation in the eyes of certain groups.

Thus, the relationship between esoteric writings and publicity is dialectical: Jewish esotericism had exoteric settings (Ithamar Gruenwald). The same is true for Christian esoteric texts. But we should keep in mind that there might have been esoteric texts, even a high number of esoteric texts, that have remained esoteric and therefore are unknown to us. Yet, writing down religious knowledge made it easier to divulge it, as Joseph Verheyden remarks. Typically, books are written to be read.

3 Connecting the World in Time and Space

Many Christians were driven by an insatiable appetite to know in every detail and authentically what had happened in the times of Jesus and the apostles. Apocryphal texts sometimes rewrite Scripture to give alternative versions or fill gaps in the canonical tradition: they inform about Jesus's childhood; they connect figures of the Old Testament with later narratives. A *Neuinszenierung* (a re-enactment), as Tobias Nicklas calls it, of Jesus memoirs took place as early as the second century CE, in a time before the canon itself was established. These efforts are a testament to early Christians' desire to learn more about Jesus as a real-life person. The second century *Protevangelium Iacobi* provides detailed accounts of Mary's life and displays a complex Mariology, which anticipated cultic practices of the fifth century—a significant example of the impact of authoritative texts, which are taken as scripts by some users. In other texts, John the Baptist appears as a man who is more than just Jesus's Precursor (Albert Baumgarten).

Furthermore, apocryphal texts aided in bridging a wide time-span in the history of the world. Adam appears as a core figure because he represented the origins of the human race. Problems started with his creation, which the Book of Genesis narrates in two versions, and still more versions were disseminated later on. Unsurprisingly, in Jewish apocryphal writings Adam was of central importance, which is mirrored in the second, Slavonic book of Enoch (Andrei Orlov). Samaritan writings also expanded the narratives on Adam and other figures (Abraham Tal). Perhaps most importantly, Adam linked the beginning of the world with Jesus by a typological relationship, the details of which were spelled out in various ways (Sergey Minov and Daniele Tripaldi). It is also one of the reasons why the relationship between Adam and Jesus was a popular motive in Christian art, especially in medieval Armenia where the theology of

Gregory the Illuminator was the basis for the interpretation of Christian texts (Jean-Pierre Mahé). This makes clear again how important it is to set these writings in a wider historical and not only a religious context.

Another Biblical figure brought into a typological connection with Jesus was Moses. He was prominent in both canonical and non-canonical texts and appears among the figures who received special revelations (Dieter and Sabine Fahl). Important figures of speech attributed to Hebrew prophets appeared in biblical and in extra-canonical texts, shaping the semantics of Messianic hope in Christian contexts (Abraham Terian).

Various other figures of the Christian Old Testament show up in apocryphal narrations as well: Eastern Christian authors constructed a bridge between Abel und Jesus (Maria V. Korogodina / Basil Lourié). The antediluvian patriarch Enoch, who was taken by God and disappeared from earth, relates to the ascension and connects heaven and earth. He is a significant figure in apocryphal texts, which include writings called Books of Enoch (Florentina Badalanova Geller; David Hamidović). For Armenians, the story of Noah was crucial since his ark is thought to have landed at the mountain Ararat (located in what is now Turkey), which became the focal point of a sacred landscape, shaped by apocryphal texts (Nazénie Garibian).

But apocryphal texts do not only restructure Christian time, they remap Christian space as well. The Magi, the first pilgrims, connected East and West. Narrations about them had a significant impact on Iranian writings. According to Persian sources, Zoroaster prophesized their coming to Bethlehem (Antonio Panaino)—they thus affect not only Christian spatiality, but also Christian temporality. The Magi were popular in the West as well and appear in Christian art from early on. While this iconography was based on biblical and non-biblical texts, it did not depend on them completely (Igor Dorfmann-Lazarev; Felicity Harley).

Furthermore, apocryphal texts connected heaven and earth. The connection is well established by the Son of God, Jesus, and by his mother. In addition, the visions narrated in many texts created links between earthly individuals and heaven. Holy people experienced visions in which not only heaven, but also the throne of God and hell were revealed to them, providing themes and images that would become popular in Byzantine literature (Emmanouela Grypeou). Another case is the ascension of Isaiah who beheld Jesus's life during his stay in heaven (Joseph Verheyden). Other prophets and holy men came to know what would happen at the end of the world, often in the guise of apocalyptic events (Daniele Tripaldi). Quite often protology and eschatology went hand in hand.

Angels, the messengers of God, served various functions in Jewish writings. Although they are not as prominent in the New Testament as they are in the

Old, they were quite prominent in early Christian texts. Especially Christians with a strong Jewish background were inclined to liken Christ to angels, as a being between human and God. But the majority distinguished Christ sharply from the angels as creatures who could sin. In spite of this commonly ascribed quality, angels were ambivalent figures in the Jewish world already (Andrei Orlov). Therefore, fallen angels, which appear for example in Enochic literature, were an important issue for Jewish authors and were invoked in the context of magical practices (Yakir Paz). Despite their importance in literature, angels were not significant figures in the earliest stages of the emerging Christian iconography. But from the late fourth century onwards they begin to appear quite frequently, often as winged and thus recognizably as super-human beings between heaven and earth. And while the images that depicted them relate to the Bible, many represent non-canonical traditions (Cecilia Proverbio).

4 Consequences and New Questions: Connecting (Not Only) Christianities

The history of apocryphal texts is a history of entangled Christianities. This becomes apparent in the remarkably high number of translations, but also in the transcultural impact of their visual representation. The study of these connections helps to define relations between various Christian cultures in more precise and complex ways. To give some more examples from the Bad Homburg Conference: The Armenian 'Script of the Lord's Infancy' goes back to a text from the Church of the East anathematized by the Armenians (Igor Dorfmann-Lazarev). Christian Gnostic ideas along with Mithraic concepts influenced Jewish authors as late as during the seventh century CE (Yishai Kiel).

Another important question is the influence of ancient esoteric writings on medieval theological ideas, especially in the East where their circulation seems to have been much more widely spread than in the Latin West (Yuri Stoyanov). Christians adopted the so-called Chaldæan Oracles, which claimed to have Babylonian roots and certainly had a Jewish background. Nonetheless, they preserved their appeal for people in non-Christian circles, as became visible in the Italian Renaissance epoch again (Ezio Albrile). In this way, esoteric texts (or at least ideas contained in esoteric texts) even crossed borders between religions. This begs the question as to whether seeming continuities in belief systems were continuities of people or continuities of texts, transmitted, and perhaps ignored for a while, but exercising influence at specific points in time.

POSTSCRIPT: BORDER-CROSSING TEXTS

More often than not, however, crucial questions have been left unanswered by modern research so far. How can the relationships between various Christian cultures be described more precisely? How were the contacts between languages, visual traditions, confessions and religions realised in practice? How did semantics interrelate and develop in such widely diverging contexts?

With all these difficulties, the study of apocryphal texts opens new perspectives on the circum-Mediterranean cultures of late antiquity. The Christian worlds of Late Antiquity and the early Middle Ages can be defined on the basis of divisions caused by political borders, personal allegiances, confessional conflicts, and so on. But all these disputes presuppose at least some degree of commonality in interests, texts or memories shared among the conflicting parties. Considering this crucial fact, apocryphal texts allow us to paint a more detailed picture of the entanglements of various groups. The Christian worlds considered through this lens are defined by a common heritage, appropriated in different ways.

Certain heroes of the Jewish-Christian world such as Abraham and Moses, who commanded respect among non-Christians, can be considered connective figures in a transcultural and trans-religious outlook. In this respect, they resemble heroes from the world of wars and politics such as Cyrus the Great, Alexander the Great or Cæsar who feature prominently in the historical narratives of many cultures in the Euro-Mediterranean world (and beyond). The same holds true for a wide range of non-Christian texts. Extremely varied works such as Aristotle's *Organon*, Menander's *Sentences*, the *Physiologus*, writings of Galen, or Porphyrius's *Eisagoge*, were translated in multiple languages. Not only Jewish-Christian texts connected the Eurasian world.

But no ancient text (apart perhaps from the Qur'an) could compare with the Bible in respect to dissemination, authority and the sheer size of the audience. The contours of the Biblical canon, however, varied between confessions and languages. The apocryphal texts that were less controlled by authorities, and therefore more adaptable, give a still better idea of the plurality of Christianities. It will be a fascinating task to look deeper into the ways in which connective texts and figures continued to cross religious and cultural borders. The Bad Homburg conference organized by Igor Dorfmann-Lazarev has made important steps in this direction.

Acknowledgement

Thanks are addressed to Felicity Harley for her stylistic advice.

Index of Place Names

Ağabeyli (Maraš) 555, 555n97
Ałtamar 26, 146n11, 607–608
Akhmîm 8–9, 23, 43–44, 44n5, 45–47,
 47n18, 48–49, 49n22, 50, 50n30, 51–
 58, 61, 68–69, 441–443, 445–450
Alexandria 90, 455, 458, 474n67, 490n113,
 613
Amida (Diyarbakır) 306
Aphoulia see Athoulis
Aquileia 567
ʿArafat, Mt 268
Ararat 17–18, 276–281, 284–286, 286nn39–
 40, 287, 287n42, 288, 288nn48–49,
 289–290, 292–295, 615. See also
 Urartu
Arles 22, 399–400, 400n46, 401–404, 408
Athoulis 165–166, 168–169, 178
Ayrarat, plain 280n24, 284, 283, 288, 289–
 290, 293–294

Babel 230, 241, 253, 429, 429–430n74
Balkans 72, 105, 461n14, 482
Bethlehem 6, 18, 21, 66, 76, 156, 165, 307,
 309, 368, 375–377, 377n38, 612, 615
Bulgaria (South-Western) 460, 483, 485,
 487, 488
Bulgarians 167, 175, 457, 458, 461n15, 463,
 463n19, 464n20, 465n22, 467, 467n27,
 468, 468n31, 476, 478, 482n104, 484,
 495n135, 497, 498n142, 499, 512

Constantinople 130–131, 133, 135–137,
 392n30, 417, 417n31, 418n31, 467, 524,
 532, 569, 579, 579n57, 587
Cudi, Mt see Djudi, Mt

Djudi, Mt 281, 290–292, 294
Dura Europos 406n65, 560, 604

Edfu 180–181, 187, 197n38
Ējmiacin see Vałaršapat
Esna 180, 187
Ethiopia 72, 266

Fayyum 439
Florence 12, 132–134, 136, 137

Gaza 26, 364, 364n38, 365n47, 591, 598, 605
Gerizim, Mt 267
Golgotha 13–14, 154, 15n3, 155–157, 160, 162–
 167, 173, 176–177
Gordyæan mountains see Gordyene
Gordyene 17, 278–279, 281, 284–285, 287, 291

Harran 17
Hebron 155–156, 162, 177
Hermon, Mt 492, 509–510, 533n2

Istanbul see Constantinople

Jerusalem 13, 15, 22, 26, 39n8, 62–64, 76,
 153, 155–157, 159–162, 165–172, 172n68,
 173, 175–178, 183, 206n1, 217, 230, 264,
 267, 268n16, 307, 343–344, 347–348,
 356, 364, 370, 411, 412n4, 417–418,
 418n31, 428n66, 436, 575n42, 590–
 592, 592n4, 594–595, 597–598, 605–
 607
Jordan 175–176, 205, 266, 353n7, 607

Kiev and Kievan Rus' 218, 218n1, 225n10,
 327–328, 461n15
Kirillo-Belozersky Monastery 167, 220n2,
 233, 235, 516

Maʿon (Negev) 26, 590, 593, 598–602,
 602n31, 603, 605
Mesopotamia 16–17, 24, 31, 162, 266, 270,
 278n8, 281, 285, 287, 289, 290n58, 293,
 295, 361, 416, 429, 429n69, 455, 533n1,
 540, 549, 552, 575, 575n42
Milan 401n49, 406, 563n12
Moriah, Mt 155, 165
Mount Lebanon 172

Naples 560, 560n3, 566
Naxčawan see Naxiĵewan
Naxiĵewan 18, 293
Noravank 12–13, 143, 144n8, 145, 147–151
Novgorod 168, 243n154, 323, 326

Olives, Mt of 50, 591, 592, 592nn4–5, 595

Preslav   458, 461n15, 462, 463n19, 466n23,
    466n25, 467n27, 468, 497, 512
Pskov   321

Qardu   *see* Gordyene

Ravenna   563, 580, 584, 587–588
Rome   12, 18, 21–22, 91, 136–137, 182, 268n16,
    309–311, 349n23, 356, 383, 383n4, 384–
    385, 387–388, 388nn18–19, 389–391,
    392n30, 394, 398–399, 401, 401n48,
    402–404, 404n62, 405–406, 409–410,
    416–417n25, 418n31, 418–419n34, 427–
    428, 428n66, 428n68, 560, 560n3, 565,
    567–568, 570–573, 581–582, 584–586, 589

Sarıgüzel (Istanbul)   579, 579–580n57, 581, 583

Selimbria   136
Silivri   *see* Selimbria
Sinai, Mt   35, 37, 37n5, 38–39, 41–42

Tell Ramadi   534
Turfan   55, 307

Urartu   18, 280–282, 284, 292, 295
Ur Chasdim   269, 271

Vałaršapat   26, 607–608
Venice   132, 137, 265n8, 568–569

Wadi el-Natrun   158n19, 161, 180

Zion, Mt   39n8, 229, 267, 347

Index of Modern and Early Modern Authors

Adler, William 318, 455, 492
Andersen, Francis 206
Arnold, Johannes 89, 95, 98
Avi-Yonah, Michael 590–591, 598, 601, 605

Benjamin, Walter 311n43
Bennett, Charles A.A. 5
Bisconti, Fabrizio 399n44
Bloch, Marc 5–6, 18, 296–305, 307, 311n44
Browne, Thomas 1, 2
Bynum, Carolyn Walker 351, 356, 360

Charles, Robert H. 75n19, 206n1, 445, 446, 480n99, 484n108, 508n176
Charlesworth, James H. 358, 358n19, 359–360
Coblentz Bautch, Kelley 446–447

Dan, Joseph 122, 418–419n34, 419n34
Davidson, Donald 340
de Jong, Albert 431
Der Nersessian, Sirarpie 144, 590
Dochhorn, Jan 181n4, 193n32, 200

Faivre, Antoine 7
Febvre, Lucien 2, 297–298n4, 299n8, 302n18
Fossum, Jarl 209, 214n33
Foster, Paul 44n8, 46n14, 47, 47n17, 49n23, 52n36, 53, 53n41, 54, 54n47, 67n101

Gaster, Moses 189, 262, 271n22
Grabar, André 384, 386, 407, 601–602, 604

Halbwachs, Maurice 299–300n8
Himmelfarb, Martha 417, 419, 420n38

Idel, Moshe 122n53, 194n33, 198n43, 553n87
Istrin, Vasiij M. 323, 336, 336–337n79

James, Montague Rhodes 46
Jeremias, Joachim 6

Kraus, Thomas J. 43n4, 44nn5, 7, 51nn32–33, 52, 52n36, 39, 53
Kroll, Wilhelm 125, 131, 131n32
Kugel, James 214

Levene, Dan 542–547, 543n45, 546n59, 549n71
Liebman, Charles 366
Lohmeyer, Ernst 357, 357n15, 360
Lotman, Yurij M. 3
Lührmann, Dieter 44n6, 611

Magdalino, Paul 523, 530
Mastrogregori, Massimo 297–298n4, 299n8
Meillet, Antoine 303
Moriggi, Marco 534, 534nn6&8–10, 535n12, 538, 538n29

Neis, Rachel 209–210, 213
Nickelsburg, George W.E. 442, 445
Nijmegen School 88
Norelli, Enrico 73nn10&12, 74n13, 76nn20–21, 77n24, 79n28, 81n32, 82n33, 83n35, 84n36, 85n42

Olschki, Leonardo S. 369, 374
Orlandi, Tito 181–182, 184–187

Popov, Andrej N. 223, 319, 456n8
Porfir'ev, Ivan Ja. 168, 326, 327n43

Raulff, Ulrich 300n10, 301n12
Reed, Annette Yoshiko 550–551, 551n72, 552, 552n74, 553n80, 557n99
Reeves, John 429–430, 553n80

Sanders, Ed P. 355, 355n11
Scholem, Gershom 4, 6, 363, 364n38, 364n43, 537nn23&25–26, 555n97
Sivertsev, Alexei 417, 417n31, 420n38
Smith, Jonathan Z. 357, 431
Sokolov, Matvej I. 119n40, 175–176, 454n3, 495n135, 513n198
Stone, Michael E. 5, 143, 215–216, 287n45, 494n128, 596, 596n18, 605
Suciu, Alin 48, 48n21, 49–51, 180n1, 183–184, 184n8, 188, 193n31, 199nn46–47

Teixidor, Javier 534, 534nn5&8, 538
Totomanova, Anna-Maria 325, 337n79, 489n112, 494

Vaganay, Léon   46

Wendt, Heidi   354
Widengren, Geo   378–379
Wilson, Bryan   365, 365n48

Index of Biblical and Mythological Names

Aaron 6, 274–275, 332, 418
Abbaton 188–189, 192–194
Abel 6, 15–16, 226, 230, 239, 250, 250nn192–
    193, 250–251, 251n200&202, 263–268,
    268n15, 168, 423, 429, 478–479, 615
Abraham 16–17, 67n102, 157, 164–165,
    230, 241, 253–254, 253n219&221,
    254nn223&225–226, 255n228, 263,
    268n14, 270–272, 308, 474, 478–479,
    531, 562–563, 588–589, 617
Adam 1, 5–6, 11–18, 20, 26, 40, 112, 119,
    143–144, 146nn11–12, 147, 147n19, 148,
    148n26, 149–150, 153–160, 160n25, 161–
    169, 171–178, 188–190, 190nn22–23,
    191–194, 194n32, 194n34, 195, 195n35,
    196–197, 197n39, 198–199, 199n46, 202–
    206, 210–211, 211nn22–23, 212, 212n23,
    216, 226, 250n192, 263–265, 265n6, 266,
    268, 268n15, 270, 276, 306–309, 333n65,
    400, 404, 416n21, 423–424, 424n52, 470,
    474, 478, 493–494, 497, 497n141, 498,
    498n142, 499–507, 537, 544, 575n42, 614
Ahidan 267
ʾArmilos 22, 411n3, 413–414, 414n16, 415,
    418, 418n34, 419, 419n34, 420, 423, 426,
    428n68, 430–431, 431n82, 433, 436
Arpachshad 17, 269–270

Balaam 248n178, 332–333, 336, 402, 402n55,
    418n34, 570

Cain 16, 250, 250nn192–193, 250–251,
    251n202, 263, 263n5, 264–265, 265n6,
    266–268, 268n15, 269, 423, 423n48,
    489n110, 494, 494n131
Cherubim 192, 196, 201, 203, 204, 527, 575,
    575n42, 576
Christ 9, 11–15, 19–22, 25, 49–50, 54n45,
    56, 60, 66, 75, 77n25, 79n29, 80n31,
    81, 83n35, 85, 111, 114, 117, 118n31,
    144, 146, 154, 172–173, 183, 190–191,
    196n37, 197–198, 221, 224, 226, 228,
    230, 241, 248–249n184, 249n190,
    250n192, 250n198, 251, 251n200&202,
    254n226, 255, 255n232&234, 256n236,
    257nn243&245, 257, 259nn252–253,

    276, 308–309, 331, 331n62, 332–334,
    341–342, 352n3, 355n12, 369, 375, 379,
    381, 381n1, 386n14, 392n30, 395, 397,
    400, 401n48, 402–403, 406, 408n69,
    415, 428, 428n66, 428n68, 429, 429n73,
    430, 430n76, 431, 431n85, 436, 525–527,
    530, 564–565, 578, 585, 585n68, 586–
    587, 602, 612–613, 616
Crucifixion 12–13, 20, 51–52, 56, 58, 64–
    65, 101, 144, 148, 154, 157, 172–173, 176,
    350, 352, 429, 525
Epiphany 66, 66n94
Incarnation 9, 14, 85, 190, 201n50,
    256n236, 258n250, 258–259n252, 382,
    390, 392, 398, 398n41, 402, 578n53,
    578n55, 585n68, 586, 588
Nativity 6, 21–22, 221, 221n4, 309, 369,
    370n10, 389, 389n20, 419, 436, 612
Passion 8, 13, 43, 50–51, 55, 57, 59, 61, 63,
    65–66, 150–151, 170, 190, 255, 258, 341n5
Polymorphous apparitions 67, 67n101,
    369, 370n10, 371, 372n16, 372n19, 372–
    373, 379, 382
Resurrection 8, 10, 23, 43, 45–46, 56,
    56n55, 58–59, 64, 68, 85, 101–102,
    102n63, 341n5, 350, 412–413, 578n53
Cush see Kush

Daniel 13, 34, 144, 148, 148n31, 149, 268n14,
    355, 384n5, 432, 475, 522, 528, 528n19,
    570, 572
David 6, 231n20, 343–344, 344n12, 412–413,
    414n16, 417, 603n37

Elʿale 263, 265
Enoch 6–7, 15–16, 23, 25, 40, 108, 119, 215,
    215–216n35, 216, 229–230, 240, 252,
    252n210, 263, 270, 270n18, 439, 441–
    446, 453, 455, 460n13, 461, 469–470,
    471n44, 474n65, 476–478, 478n90,
    479–481, 484, 484n106, 486, 486n108,
    489–490, 490n114, 493–494, 494n128,
    508–512, 528, 542n42, 548n60, 550, 551,
    551n78, 552, 554, 554n90&92, 554n85,
    555, 557, 557n104, 558, 586n70, 614–615
Enosh 549, 551n79, 553

INDEX OF BIBLICAL AND MYTHOLOGICAL NAMES

Eve   5–6, 11, 16–18, 112, 119–120, 163, 165, 188, 190, 194–196, 196n37, 198, 199n46, 203–204, 264–265, 265n6, 266, 268, 273, 276, 307–312, 400, 404, 404n60, 416n21, 423–424, 424n55, 426, 470n43, 537, 544, 575n42

Gabriel, archangel   25, 182, 185–186, 186n15, 191–193, 197, 335, 335n76, 503, 505, 536, 555, 570, 576n45, 583

Habakkuk   344, 475, 572
Ham   269, 272, 494
Haran   271
Ḥephṣibah   413–414, 414n16, 417–418, 420, 421n41, 426n63, 430n77
Herod   56, 56n54, 67, 307–308, 355, 359, 367n53
Hezekiah   73, 79n29, 418, 427

Isaac   165, 230, 241, 254n226, 255, 268, 341, 562–563
Isaiah   9–12, 19, 37, 54n47, 70–71, 73–75, 75n16, 75n18, 76, 76n22, 77, 77n25, 78, 78n27, 79, 79n29, 80–85, 85n39, 86, 108, 108n9, 113, 117–119, 119n37, 120, 121n48, 157–158, 279, 279n18, 280, 341, 345–346, 348–349, 355, 376, 395, 397, 402, 432, 472, 472n54, 474, 480, 575n42, 582, 601, 615

Jacob   14–15, 108, 159–160, 160n26, 177, 206–213, 213n30, 214, 214n33, 215–216, 226, 250n192, 267–268, 268n16, 275n28, 289, 292, 294, 333, 346, 402, 473, 477, 480
Japhet   288, 494
Jesus   see Christ
John, the Apostle   58, 58n60, 58n62, 60, 63, 68, 148, 526n15
John the Baptist   3, 7, 19–21, 161, 182, 184–185, 197n42, 205, 257n243, 341, 351–352, 352n3, 353, 353n7, 354–357, 357n15, 358, 358nn18–19, 359–361, 362n31, 363, 363n31, 364n38, 365–367, 367n53, 566, 614
Jonah   427, 561, 561n9
Joseph (Jacob's son)   274–275, 412–413
Joshua   6, 317, 336–337n79, 343, 573–574, 588

Judah (Jacob's son)   19, 267, 343, 343n7, 346–347, 484n106, 599, 603
Judas   62, 64–67, 67n99

Kush   269, 272

Lamech   470, 474

Magi   6, 12, 18–19, 21, 23, 131, 307–313, 368, 368n2, 369, 369n2, 370–373, 375, 375n27, 376–384, 389n22, 390, 390n25, 391, 391n27, 392, 392n29, 393, 396–397, 397n39, 399–400, 402–405, 407–409, 615
Manasseh   9, 71, 74, 78, 78n26, 79–80, 83, 429
Maqeda   263, 265–266
Mary   see Theotokos
Melchizedek   6, 163–165, 230, 241, 255, 255n231, 308–309
Methuselah   1, 163, 493–494
Michael, archangel   117, 117n27, 120, 181–182, 184–186, 189–192, 192n30, 193, 200, 205, 211, 211nn21–23, 212n23, 215, 460, 479, 483, 503, 505, 536, 540, 547, 555–557, 557n96, 576n45
Moses   6, 16, 19, 30, 35–37, 37n5, 38, 38n7, 39, 39n10, 94n32, 98, 262–263, 267, 270n20, 273–275, 275n26, 317–339, 333, 539, 615, 617
Muriel   189, 192–193, 202

Nahor   270–271
Nimrod   269–272, 430n74
Noah   1, 5–6, 13, 16–18, 35, 157–167, 177, 229–230, 240, 252, 252nn210–211, 263, 270, 272, 276–277, 279, 284, 286, 286nn39–40, 287, 287n42, 288–289, 291–292, 292n66, 292n71, 294, 306, 308, 384n5, 494–495, 615

Paul   80, 102, 117, 144, 154, 244, 341, 357n14, 360n27, 364n38, 428n68, 473–475, 563–564, 564n13–14, 565–567, 585
Peter   21, 43, 46, 50–51, 51n31, 52, 54, 57, 59, 59n65, 61, 61n73, 63, 67–68, 115, 473, 473n63, 474–475, 541, 563–564, 564nn13–14, 565–567, 570

INDEX OF BIBLICAL AND MYTHOLOGICAL NAMES

Raphael, archangel   503, 540, 547, 555, 556, 571, 576n45

Samael   117, 117n30, 120, 265
Sarah   254n226, 268n14, 272
Satanael   117, 117n30, 118, 118n31, 120
Serah   273, 275, 275n26
Seraphim   201, 527, 575, 575n42, 576
Seth   6, 13, 40, 163–164, 170–171, 174, 190, 199n46, 306, 308, 489n110, 494, 494n131
Shem   6, 13, 17, 159–160, 162–166, 177, 268n16, 286n42, 288, 308, 494, 605
Solomon   13, 100, 164–165, 169–174, 176, 178, 320, 332, 349, 356–357, 471, 472n51, 474, 528n21, 555n89
Susanna   173, 174, 384n5

Terah   270–271
Theotokos   21–22, 63n81, 63, 63n81, 64, 66, 85, 114, 144, 148, 151, 164, 310, 332, 380, 382–385, 385n7, 385nn10–11, 386n12, 386n14, 387–388, 388nn18–

19, 389, 389nn21–22, 390–393, 395–397, 397n39, 398–401, 401n48–49, 403–404, 404n60, 405–406, 406nn64–67, 407–409, 413–414, 415n18, 417, 417n31, 418–420, 426n63, 429–430, 430n77, 432, 478, 523, 561, 570, 580, 588, 614
Tortas   270, 272, 275

Uriel   503, 505, 536

Vigilant heavenly powers   *see* Watchers

Watchers   23, 26, 442, 443, 480–482, 490–492, 494, 508, 508n176, 509–513, 537, 545, 551nn71–72, 552nn73&76, 607, 608. See also *Book of Watchers*

Zerubbabel   343, 418, 427, 429, 430. *See also Sefer Zerubbabel* (Index of Ancient and Mediæval Sources)
Zuartunk̒   *see* Watchers

Index of Subjects

afterlife 24, 46, 93, 111, 113, 123, 138, 140, 354, 448–449, 521–523, 531–532, 584

Akkadian 292, 293, 548, 575n42

akribeia 20, 42, 362

amulets 285, 491, 534, 555, 555n97, 556, 556n98, 557

Ancient of Days 12–13, 21, 144, 146, 148, 148n26, 149

anthropogony 119, 147, 192n30, 455, 486, 494–500, 502, 503n158, 504, 505, 507, 512

anticipation of the Messiah 6, 12, 19, 21–23, 26, 306–309, 342–343, 345–346, 359, 363–365, 375–376, 378, 382, 412n3, 449, 603n37, 615

antinomism 363–366

apokatastasis 14, 249n189, 251n202, 254nn223&225, 256n236, 257nn243–244, 380, 380n49

Apostolic Memoirs 8–9, 43, 48, 48n21, 49–50, 50n27, 57, 59–60, 66, 68, 184n8, 188, 198, 201

arcane teaching see hidden knowledge

archons 23, 113n19, 126, 414, 423, 423n50, 424, 424n55, 425, 425n58, 426, 434–436

Armenians 13, 17, 18, 20, 26, 50n27, 107, 143–144, 146n12, 151–152, 154, 165, 211, 211nn21–23, 216, 229, 276–277, 279–294, 305–311, 340, 343n8, 350, 370–371, 372n19, 373, 381, 431n82, 433, 532, 590–592, 594–599, 602n30, 603–607, 614–616

Bedouins 16, 272

Bogomils 11, 105–107, 111, 113–121

Bosnians 115n25

Calendar 15, 19, 24, 37, 38, 40, 41, 42, 62, 66, 163, 190, 229, 230, 330, 334, 341n4, 456–457n8, 468, 492, 512, 523

Canon 3–4, 32, 42, 68–69, 221n4, 587, 604–606, 610, 612, 614, 617

Cathars 11, 72, 80, 105–106, 111, 113–116, 120–122, 352n3, 353n7

Christology 11, 15, 25, 67, 107, 113, 119, 120, 121, 149, 179, 180, 193, 198, 199, 217, 228, 242, 255n230, 256, 340, 346, 348, 352, 354n9, 369, 396, 408, 578, 585. *See also* Christ (Index of Biblical and Mythological Names)

chronography 5, 19, 40, 153, 165–168, 171, 262–264, 273, 287n45, 296, 305, 308, 311, 318, 321–325, 327, 334, 336–338, 455, 464–466, 486, 492, 511, 512, 550

corruption 11, 112, 147, 221, 222, 227, 237, 243–246, 249, 258nn250&252, 259nn252–253&257, 349n22, 483n106, 539

Council of Ephesus (431) 22, 385, 385n11, 386n12, 387, 389, 399, 406, 408

Council of Florence (1438–1445) 132–133, 137

Creation of the world iv, 4–6, 11–15, 18–19, 21, 22, 24, 26, 34, 35, 38n8, 39, 42, 107, 119, 133, 143–152, 163, 178, 188–190, 195–197, 204, 206, 216, 228, 247–248n178, 262–264, 306, 308–313, 404, 424–425, 436, 486, 494, 495, 497, 499, 503–504, 506, 507, 523

Creator see Creation of the world

curses 189, 542

Cyrus the Great 308, 376, 381–382, 617

Davidic Messiah 343, 344, 413, 417

Demiurge 125, 194, 194n33, 423, 423n50, 435, 465n22, 492–493

disclosure of secrets see divulgation of secrets

divination 23, 98, 492, 512

divine chariot 23, 119n37, 521

divine throne see heavenly throne

divulgation of secrets 10–11, 23, 30, 73–74, 76, 101, 111, 114, 179, 204, 491–492, 511–512, 541, 611, 614

docetism 9, 44, 45, 45n11, 68, 85n42, 106, 107

dreams 15, 34, 68, 82, 128, 204, 207, 209, 212, 213n30, 266, 272, 340, 482, 526, 531, 561

dualism 3, 11, 72, 105–107, 110–123, 245n160, 414, 420, 423, 506

Eden 5, 13, 15, 23–24, 26, 58n63, 119–120, 156–158, 163, 165–166, 168, 170, 175–176,

189–190, 192, 195, 197n39, 202, 204–
205, 216, 222, 243, 254, 254n223–224,
263–266, 273, 273n24, 306, 309, 441,
443–444, 448–449, 521–523, 523n5,
524–528, 528n21, 529–531, 575n42, 590,
601–603, 606–607

eschatology   5, 6, 11–14, 20, 24, 26, 38, 40,
95, 108n8, 113, 120, 123, 149, 151, 167, 199,
301, 307, 344, 345, 355, 356, 359, 365,
375n25, 382, 412, 420, 422n44, 429n70,
430, 521–523, 525, 531, 532, 584, 603, 615

esotericism   4–5, 7–8, 11, 16, 20, 21, 23, 29–
37, 39, 42, 72–73, 76, 78, 81, 88, 90, 102,
104, 105, 110–115, 121–123, 124, 132, 233,
262, 353–356, 364, 366, 378, 469, 475–
476, 491–494, 511–512, 521, 530, 610–614,
616

Eucharist   14, 103, 182, 185, 186n13, 193, 197–
199, 475, 613

Fallen angels   11, 23–25, 112, 119, 442, 480,
492, 509, 510, 512, 533–535, 533n2,
534n5, 537–539, 538n27, 541–550,
542n42, 548n63, 549n70, 551n81, 552–
555, 552nn82&85, 553n87, 555n94, 557,
557n124, 558, 616

firmament   84n36, 119, 257n245, 442, 525,
527

Flood   1, 5–6, 11, 13, 16–18, 35, 107, 157–167,
171–172, 177, 229–230, 240, 250n193,
251n205, 252, 252n210–211, 263, 270,
272, 276–277, 278n8, 279, 281, 284, 286,
286n39–40, 287, 287n42, 288, 288n51,
289–292, 292n66, 292n71, 293–295,
306, 308, 384n5, 482, 489n110, 494, 545,
551n72, 554, 554n83, 615. *See also* Noah
(Index of Biblical and Mythological
Names)

Garden   *see* Eden
Georgians   172, 211, 216, 218n1, 431, 612
glory   9, 15, 75, 81, 84, 84n36, 84n38, 85, 194–
195, 205, 208–210, 213, 213n30, 256n236,
256n240, 346–347, 348n22, 350, 525,
527–528, 530, 585n67

Gnosticism   1, 11, 22, 105, 107, 110–113, 119n37,
122, 126, 194, 196, 198, 228, 306, 372,
414–416, 420–421, 423–424, 427, 429,
430, 434–436, 458, 613, 616

heavenly throne   15, 23, 24, 79n29, 84, 112,
117, 118n31, 119, 189, 190, 193–196, 201,
205, 208–210, 212–214, 343, 347–348,
429n70, 442, 509, 512, 522, 525–530,
554–557, 575n42, 578n54, 585n67, 615

Hermetism   134, 198, 555
hidden knowledge   4–11, 16, 18, 23, 29n1, 30–
34, 36–39, 41–42, 55, 72n8, 73, 74, 77,
83–84, 86, 88–89, 94–95, 98, 101–103,
110–116, 121, 128, 133, 179, 188, 196, 262,
296, 306, 310n43, 311, 424, 433, 433n90,
461, 469–470, 474–476, 493–494, 512,
530, 535–536, 544, 552, 587, 610–614

Hurrians   17, 431

image of God   12, 14–15, 146–147, 147n19,
148, 150, 202–203, 205–206, 206n3, 211,
211nn21–23, 216, 228–229, 247n178, 251,
251n202

imprisonment of the Messiah   427–428,
428n68, 429–430

incantation   24, 357, 533, 533n1, 534–536,
538, 540n38, 542–543, 548, 551–552,
554–555, 557–558

incorruptibility   *see* corruption
Islam   3, 26, 71, 130, 173n69, 174, 182, 183n6,
187, 189, 192, 193nn31–32, 272, 277, 365,
365n47, 378, 460n13, 538–540, 540n36,
549n70, 552n85, 606

Kavod   *see* glory

magic   2, 4, 24–25, 127–129, 131, 134–135,
372n19, 460n14, 482, 489n110, 511–512,
533–536, 538n29, 541, 543–545, 548,
552, 554–555, 554n92, 555n94, 616

Mandæans   3, 21, 24, 25, 423n47, 353nn6–
7, 358n18, 366, 423n47, 533, 536n20,
546–547, 546n58, 549

Manichæans   3, 22–23, 25, 54n47, 55, 105,
112, 197n40, 198, 306, 414, 414n14, 415–
416, 416n22, 417, 420, 420n39, 421–422,
422n44, 423, 423n47, 424, 424n53, 425,
425n57, 426, 426n63, 428, 428n68,
429n70, 430n76, 434, 434n93, 435–436,
536, 537n25, 547, 547n55, 549

Mazdeism   3, 21, 372n19, 374–382, 576
memory of the primæval beings   17–18, 26,
159, 172, 291, 306–308

INDEX OF SUBJECTS

Messianic hope   *see* anticipation of the
    Messiah
Metatron   429n73, 550, 553–557, 554n92,
    557nn103–104
micro-Christendoms   64, 274–295, 309n40
Mithraism   3, 10, 22, 90–92, 95–96, 98, 100,
    101, 387n16, 414–417, 420, 430–436,
    616
Moon   iv, 126, 205, 257, 269, 378, 444, 460,
    460–461n14, 478, 492, 549, 551n80
mystery cults   3, 10–11, 88–89, 97, 99, 103, 613

oral traditions   2, 29n1, 460n14, 68, 111, 157–
    158, 262, 308, 460n14, 507, 604. *See also*
    tales
Origenism   15, 16, 217, 226, 228, 229,
    232–233, 233n21, 246n172, 247n177,
    249n185, 251n202, 253n220, 254n225,
    255nn231&234, 256n236, 258–
    259nn252–253. *See also* Origen
    (Index of Ancient and Mediæval
    Sources)

Paradise   *see* Eden
Paulicians   105–107, 113
pilgrimage   18, 67n102, 276, 298, 305, 307,
    309–311, 592, 594, 596n18, 605, 615

redemption   *see* soteriology
re-enactment of Gospel stories   9, 48, 57,
    614
re-telling of the Scripture   2, 5, 62, 165, 284,
    289, 545
re-writing of the Scripture   2, 5, 7–8, 24, 29,
    30–40, 62, 69, 163, 165, 190, 199, 262,
    263n4, 284, 289, 318, 318n2, 445, 447,
    449–450, 493, 523, 611, 614
Romanos Lakapenos   19, 321–322, 330
Russians   19, 218n1, 220, 224, 255n230, 319,
    320, 324, 325, 327, 328n50, 335n76,
    466n23, 480, 489n112, 506, 507

Sabbatai Sevi   *see* Shabbetai Tzvi
sacred topography   17, 276, 291, 293–294
salvation   *see* soteriology
Samaritans   3, 16, 18, 262, 267, 269n17, 272–
    273, 274n25, 275, 614

Sasanians   22, 24, 25, 162, 374, 411, 411–412n4,
    415–417, 417n26, 436, 533, 538, 540, 558,
    606
secrecy   *see* hidden knowledge
Serbians   319, 502, 503, 506
Sethians   22, 414, 414n14, 415–416, 420–421,
    421n42, 423, 426, 434, 436
Shabbetai Tzvi   363, 363n33, 364, 364n38,
    365
Son of Man   7, 13, 56n55, 360, 525, 528,
    585n67
sorcery   270–272, 275, 425, 460, 460n14,
    489n110, 534–537, 543–544, 548–550,
    555n94
soteriology   4–6, 12, 17–20, 22, 79, 85n42,
    113, 154, 163, 178–179, 188, 228–229, 239,
    241, 249, 249n185, 252, 256, 298, 308,
    341, 346, 354n7, 360, 366, 398, 398n41,
    412, 414, 420, 421n41, 422n44, 423, 429,
    540n36, 547, 560–562
spells   2, 490, 491, 535
Symeon, tzar   225, 461n15, 462, 466nn22–23,
    467, 467n27, 497

tales   5, 16, 192, 262, 293, 296, 296n1, 305,
    326, 465n22, 478, 497n141, 502, 507, 531.
    See also oral traditions
tailismans   *see* amulets
theurgy   12, 124–129, 135–138, 140
Trinity   4, 60, 67, 118, 191, 228, 234, 255n236,
    257n243, 312–313, 333, 369, 389, 400–
    401, 414, 421, 421n42, 423, 475, 515–516,
    578, 579n55, 587n75, 588
typological exegesis   6, 13, 15, 110, 154, 164,
    178, 217, 226, 229–230, 251n200, 320–
    322, 331, 331n62, 333–334, 614–615

Valentinians   113, 357n14, 420, 423
visual apocrypha   2, 21–22, 383, 387, 404,
    409, 612

witchcraft   *see* sorcery

Zoroastrianism   12, 21, 130–132, 134–135, 368,
    369n3, 372n19, 373, 375–376, 378–382,
    413, 417n26, 419n34, 422, 429–430n74,
    435, 552n78, 576, 615

Index of Ancient and Mediæval Sources

Acts of John 372
Acts of Peter 372, 372n19
Acts of Peter and Paul 567
Agapius of Mabbug 165
Agatangełos 12, 147, 147n18, 147n24, 150, 150n40, 151
Aggadat Bereshit 539, 545
Anastas Vardapet 594
Apocalypse in which Adam informed his son Seth (NH V.5) 305n32
Apocalypse of Abraham 11, 108, 108n8, 113, 118, 120, 253–254n221, 476, 529n23
Apocalypse of Adam (CMC) 113n19, 305n32, 470n43
Apocalypse of Elijah 346, 472n52
Apocalypse of Moses *see* Life of Adam and Eve
Apocalypse of Paul 181, 185, 199n47, 473n64, 473–474n65, 480, 523, 527, 527n17, 531n28
Apollonius Molon 284, 287
Apollonius of Tyana 20, 97n46, 360–361, 363n31
Asāṭīr 16, 262, 262–263n3, 263, 263n4–5, 264, 266–272, 272n23, 273, 275
Ascension of Isaiah 9–10, 12, 54n47, 70, 108n9, 472n54, 582, 615
Ascension of Moses 317, 471n49
Assumption of Moses 470–471, 471n48, 474, 317
Athanasius of Alexandria 159–160, 182, 185, 469n38, 470n44, 475

Baruch 4, 40, 108, 108n10, 475, 477
2 Baruch 4, 13, 412, 542n42, 586n70
3 Baruch 11, 108, 108–109n10, 109, 113, 117–118, 120, 230, 477
Basil of Cæsarea 111, 157–158, 221n4, 226, 250n193, 463n19, 469n38, 499, 499n147, 512, 586n71
Basil Kalika 168
Bereshit Rabbati 539, 553n80, 554n85
Bessarion 12, 124, 132, 134–140
Book of Signs 16, 270, 272, 275

Book of Watchers 23–25, 441–442, 445, 447, 480–482, 484, 489, 490n115, 494, 496, 510–511, 536, 540, 548–551
Buzandaran 289, 289n54, 290

Cave of Treasures 13, 160, 162–164, 164n37, 164n39, 165, 190, 190n24, 191, 195, 198, 199n46, 430n74
Celsus 10, 89–90, 90n11, 91, 91n17, 92–96, 96nn38–39, 97, 97n46, 98, 98n48, 99–103, 104n67, 613
Chaldæan Oracles 12, 124–125, 129–131, 134, 136–137, 616
Chronicle of Ernoul and Bernard the Treasurer 171, 172n68, 174
Chronicles of Yerahmeel 189, 192, 327–328
Clement of Alexandria 54n47, 88–89, 111, 113, 469n38, 578–579n55
Cosimo de' Medici 12, 133–134
Cyril of Alexandria 54n47, 158, 160, 181, 250n197, 25n231, 469n38
Cyril of Jerusalem 49, 54n47, 57, 68, 181, 331n62

Damascus Document 545–546
Departure of Adam and Eve from Paradise 306, 306n32
Document Written with God's Finger 17, 306n32, 307

Elisha (translator of Averroes) 12, 130–132
1 Enoch 23–25, 229, 252n208, 252nn210–211, 270n18, 344, 344n12, 439, 441–445, 445n8, 446–450, 473n62, 475–476, 490, 490n113, 492–493, 497, 508–509, 509n190, 510, 510n191, 511, 511n197, 528, 530n28, 536, 536nn18–19, 540, 544–545, 544n48, 546, 547, 547n63, 548n60, 550, 551nn76–79&81, 552nn73–74, 554n92, 557n98
2 Enoch 11, 14–15, 23–24, 108, 108n7, 113, 117–120, 206, 206n1, 215, 215n35, 216, 229–230, 252, 252n208, 446, 452, 452n2, 454–455, 455n6, 455–456n7, 457–458, 458nn10–11, 459, 474, 476–478, 480–481, 484, 486, 486n107, 493–495,

2 Enoch (*cont.*)   495n134–135, 496–499,
    502, 503n158, 504–505, 507–513,
    527–528, 530n28, 538, 540, 552n78,
    586n70
3 Enoch   119n37, 460n14, 527n16, 549,
    549n70&71, 550, 550n76, 551, 551n79,
    552n82, 552–555, 554n84, 557,
    557n104
Epiphanius of Salamis   50n27, 66, 113n19,
    156–157, 181, 255n231, 287–288, 308,
    332, 430n74, 469n35
Eusebius   44, 285–286, 362, 362–363n31,
    465n22, 526n14
Euthymius of the Periblepton   114, 114n20,
    114n23, 115, 115n24–25, 118, 118n33
Euthymius Zigabenus   114, 114nn20–22, 115,
    115n25, 117, 117n29, 118, 118nn31–32, 119,
    119nn38–39, 120, 121n47
Evagrius   15, 217, 228, 230, 247n177,
    248n179&182, 253n216, 255n231,
    256n236, 257n245, 259n252
4 Ezra   40, 346, 412

Georgios Gemistos Plethon   130–134, 136–
    137
Georgios Kedrenos   329, 334–335, 335n72,
    335n76, 337
Georgios Synkellos   324, 337n79, 465,
    466n24, 486, 488, 488n109, 489,
    489n112, 490nn113–114, 491–498,
    494n131, 508, 511–512, 550–551,
    550nn76&78, 551n79
Ginza Rabba   546, 546n58
Gospel of Peter   9, 43, 43n1, 43n3, 44, 45n11,
    46, 47nn17–18, 48–49, 49n22, 50–51,
    51n32, 52–54, 54n46, 55, 55n49, 56,
    56n53, 57–59, 59n65, 61–62, 65–66,
    68–69, 449
Gospel of Pseudo-Matthew   401, 401n48
Great Menaion   323, 323n26, 326, 331,
    331n62, 516
Gregory of Narek   20, 350
Gregory of Nazianzus   169, 181, 218–219, 221,
    224–225, 233–234, 236, 244, 244n156,
    260n260

Haggadah of Passover   189, 300, 306
Havdala d'Rabbi Akiva   536–539, 543, 545,
    549, 551–552

Hekhalot literature   119n37, 213, 412, 521
History of the Repentance of Adam and Eve
    165
Homily about the Nativity of our Lord Jesus
    Christ   369
Hypostasis of the Archons   *see* Nature of
    the Rulers

Infancy accounts and iconography   6, 18, 21,
    85, 307–313, 369, 371, 372nn19–20, 373,
    375, 381, 383, 389n22, 390–398, 401n48,
    405–409, 611, 614, 616
Interrogatio Iohannis   106, 117, 119, 119n37,
    120–121
Investiture of Abbaton   14, 179, 180n1, 182–
    183, 186–187, 187n18, 188–190, 190n23,
    191–193, 193nn31–32, 194, 197–198,
    198n44, 199, 201
Irenæus of Lyon   151n49, 343n8, 469n38

Jacob of Edessa   160, 177, 542n42
Jacob of Nisibis   289, 292, 294
Jacob of Sarug   15, 226, 250n192
Jerome   155, 155n7, 156, 162, 177, 255n231,
    279, 279n16, 288, 294, 433, 433n91, 434,
    434n93, 577n52
John Chrysostom   25, 49, 161, 181–182,
    253n213, 464, 464n19, 469n38, 499n148,
    526n14, 583
John Malalas   168, 325, 329, 465, 465–
    466n22, 512
Josephus Flavius   324, 330, 336–337, 587
Jubilees   8, 35–38, 38n8, 39, 39n9, 40–
    42, 265n6, 271n22, 286, 286n38,
    287n43&45, 317, 330, 334–336, 389,
    470n43
Julian the Chaldæan   12, 125
Julian the Theurgist   12, 125
Julius Africanus   155, 155n6, 156, 466, 486–
    488, 488–489n110, 489n112, 494,
    494n131, 512
Justin Martyr   54, 54n47, 402, 432, 436,
    469n38, 585n68, 586n68, 587n75

Kebra Nagast   266, 266n10, 268n15
Kephalaia (Manichæan)   536, 564n59
King Solomon's Life Beyond the Grave
    296n1, 302n20
Koran   *see* Qur'an

INDEX OF ANCIENT AND MEDIÆVAL SOURCES

Kosmas the Monk 531
Kosmas the Presbyter 117–118, 118n31

Ladder of Jacob 14–15, 108, 206–207, 214,
 214n33, 477
Legend About How God Created Adam
 506–507
Letopisec Ellinskij i Rimskij 167–168, 324
Life of Adam and Eve 190, 198, 317, 266,
 333n65, 469, 470n43, 528
Life of Andrew the Fool 24, 523–524,
 524n11, 528
Life of Moses 317–335, 337–339
Life of St Andrew the Fool 24, 521, 523n8
Life of St Basil the Younger 530

Maimonides 265, 364n38
Marco Polo 371, 371n14
Martinian Belozerskij 224, 233
Merkabah literature *see* divine chariot
 (Index of Subjects)
Michael Psellos 531
Midrash Rabbah 210, 212, 265, 271, 417, 539
Mishnah 32n2, 602
Moshe ha-Darshan 553n87
Mysteries of John 14, 179, 180n2, 181n4, 182–
 183, 184n8, 185–187, 187n18, 188, 190,
 193–197, 197n38, 198–199, 203–204

Nag Hammadi codices 48n19, 111, 113n19, 613
Nature of the Rulers (NH II.4) 423
Nicephoros Kallistos Xanthopoulos 171

On the Origin of the World (NH II.5) 424
Opus imperfectum in Matthæum 306n32
Origen 10, 54n47, 89–92, 94–96, 99–101,
 101n60, 102, 102n63, 103, 104n67, 111,
 119n37, 155, 155n6, 156, 228, 244n160,
 247n177, 247–248n178, 249n184,
 250n194, 255n231, 258–259n252,
 259n253, 260n259, 355n12, 402,
 402n57, 579n55, 613. *See also* Origenism (Index of Subjects)
Oxyrhynchus papyri 49n23, 52, 52nn37&39,
 53, 54, 57n58

Palæa literature 11, 19, 116–117, 117n26, 167,
 167n54, 168, 231n20, 317–323, 330, 337–
 338, 480, 486n108

Ṗawstos Buzand *see Buzandaran*
Pesher Habakkuk 344
Peter of Alexandria 13, 166–167, 169, 181,
 184–186, 197
Philo 10, 147, 165, 165n46, 189, 194–195, 227,
 278n7, 244n160, 245–246n168, 248n182,
 254n226, 278, 278n7, 577
Photios 467–468
Pirqe de-Rabbi Eliezer 155, 155n10, 213,
 213n30, 338, 553n80
Povest' vremennykh let (Tale of the Bygone
 Years) 324, 335n76
Proclus 125, 128–129, 134
Protevangelium of James 63, 63n81, 399,
 401, 473n59, 474, 612, 614
Psalms of Thomas 546, 546n58
Pseudo-Cyril 50, 57, 59, 60n70, 61–63,
 63nn80–81, 65–68
Pseudo-Epiphanius of Salamis 50n27, 165,
 308
Pseudo-Eustathius of Antioch 336–337,
 336–337nn78–79

Questions of Bartholomew 20, 117, 117n30,
 118–119, 307
Qumran documents 34, 36, 42, 252n211,
 273n23, 280, 287, 356, 603
Qur'an 191, 290, 617

The Rhyme of the Book of the Dove
 503n158, 507

Šābuhragān 425–426
Scaliger Paterikon 166–168
Script of the Lord's Infancy 18, 306n32,
 307–309, 311, 370–371, 372n19, 372n20,
 373, 381, 381n54, 616
Seal of Faith 151
Secret Book of John 372n19, 421–422,
 422n43, 423n48
Sefer ha-Yashar 326, 328
Sefer ha-Zikhronot 327, 419n35, 540n34,
 549n63, 553n80
Sefer Yosippon 327
Sefer Zerubbabel 22, 411, 411n1, 411n3, 412–
 414, 414n16, 415–416, 416n25, 417–419,
 419n35, 420, 420n38, 421n41, 423, 426–
 428, 428n68, 429, 429n73, 430, 430n76,
 431, 431n82, 434–436

Sifre   349, 551n72
Severian of Gabala   464n19, 499–500, 502,
   502n154, 512
Souda   12, 125
Stichometry of Nicephorus   471nn48&51,
   473n63, 474, 477
Story Concerning the Tree of Sabek   165
Story of the Skull and the King   173–174

Ṭabarī   189, 192, 376n32, 539–540, 540n36
Tale of the Bygone Years   *see Povest' vremen-*
   nykh let
Tale on the Tree of the Cross   169, 175,
   175n72, 175n74, 176, 333, 333nn65–66
Talmud   264, 268n16, 270n20, 271n22,
   416n22, 417, 601, 603
Targum *Fragmentary*   208–209
Targum *Neofiti*   208, 278, 278nn9–10
Targum of Onqelos   278, 278n8, 280, 290
Targum to Isaiah   348, 349, 348–349n22
Targum of Pseudo-Jonathan   208, 209n10,
   265, 278, 280, 287, 289

Temple Scroll   37, 40
Tertullian   25, 67n96, 103, 572, 577n52, 579,
   583
Testament of Abraham   193, 476–479
Testament of Adam   305n32
Testament of Ruvim Concerning Prudence
   480–483
Testaments of the Twelve Patriarchs   470–
   471, 471n45, 474, 480, 480n99, 483, 484,
   486, 486n108, 513
Theodore bar Kōnai   421n41, 429–430,
   429n72
Theodoret of Cyrus   330, 332–333, 336, 587
Thomas Arcruni   *see* Ṭovma Arcruni
Tibåt Mårqe   267, 273–274
Ṭovma Arcruni   165, 291

Vision of Isaiah   11, 108, 108n9, 113, 118–119,
   119n37, 120, 121n48, 471–472, 474, 480

Zohar   545
Zuqnin, Chronicle of   371

Acknowledgments

I thank full-heartedly my brother Ilya Dorfman (Yerevan) without whose competences the updating of the Indices through the successive versions of the manuscript would have been impossible; and my son Suren for his patient help in checking the proofs.